DIGITAL NETS AND SEQUENCES

Indispensable for students, invaluable for researchers, this comprehensive treatment of contemporary quasi–Monte Carlo methods, digital nets and sequences, and discrepancy theory starts from scratch with detailed explanations of the basic concepts and then advances to current methods used in research. As deterministic versions of the Monte Carlo method, quasi–Monte Carlo rules have increased in popularity, with many fruitful applications in mathematical practice. These rules require nodes with good uniform distribution properties, and digital nets and sequences in the sense of Niederreiter are known to be excellent candidates. Besides the classical theory, the book contains chapters on reproducing kernel Hilbert spaces and weighted integration, duality theory for digital nets, polynomial lattice rules, the newest constructions by Niederreiter and Xing and many more. The authors present an accessible introduction to the subject based mainly on material taught in undergraduate courses with numerous examples, exercises and illustrations.

DIGITAL NETS AND SEQUENCES

Discrepancy Theory and Quasi–Monte Carlo Integration

JOSEF DICK
University of New South Wales, Sydney

FRIEDRICH PILLICHSHAMMER
Johannes Kepler Universität Linz

CAMBRIDGE
UNIVERSITY PRESS

CAMBRIDGE
UNIVERSITY PRESS

University Printing House, Cambridge CB2 8BS, United Kingdom

One Liberty Plaza, 20th Floor, New York, NY 10006, USA

477 Williamstown Road, Port Melbourne, VIC 3207, Australia

314-321, 3rd Floor, Plot 3, Splendor Forum, Jasola District Centre, New Delhi - 110025, India

79 Anson Road, #06-04/06, Singapore 079906

Cambridge University Press is part of the University of Cambridge.

It furthers the University's mission by disseminating knowledge in the pursuit of education, learning and research at the highest international levels of excellence.

www.cambridge.org
Information on this title: www.cambridge.org/9780521191593

First published 2010

A catalogue record for this publication is available from the British Library

ISBN 978-0-521-19159-3 Hardback

To Jingli and Gisi

Contents

	Preface	*page* xi
	Notation	xv
1	**Introduction**	**1**
	1.1 The one-dimensional case	1
	1.2 The general case	4
	Exercises	13
2	**Quasi–Monte Carlo integration, discrepancy and reproducing kernel Hilbert spaces**	**16**
	2.1 Quasi–Monte Carlo rules	16
	2.2 Numerical integration in one dimension	17
	2.3 Reproducing kernel Hilbert spaces	20
	2.4 Connections to classical discrepancy theory	29
	2.5 Numerical integration in weighted spaces	34
	Exercises	42
3	**Geometric discrepancy**	**46**
	3.1 Uniform distribution modulo one	46
	3.2 Discrepancy	55
	3.3 General bounds for the discrepancy	67
	3.4 Discrepancy of special point sets and sequences	72
	3.5 Tractability of discrepancy	88
	3.6 Weighted discrepancy	94
	Exercises	103
4	**Nets and sequences**	**108**
	4.1 Motivation, fair intervals	108
	4.2 (t, m, s)-nets and their basic properties	117
	4.3 $(\mathbf{T}, s)$- and (t, s)-sequences and their basic properties	130

4.4 Digital (t, m, s)-nets and digital $(\mathbf{T}, s)$- and (t, s)-sequences 145
Exercises 177
5 Discrepancy estimates and average type results 180
5.1 Discrepancy estimates for (t, m, s)-nets and $(\mathbf{T}, s)$-sequences 181
5.2 Some discussion about the discrepancy estimates 197
5.3 Discrepancy estimates for digital (t, m, s)-nets and digital $(\mathbf{T}, s)$-sequences 199
5.4 Average type and metrical results 210
Exercises 231
6 Connections to other discrete objects 234
6.1 Nets and orthogonal squares 234
6.2 Nets and (ordered) orthogonal arrays 239
Exercises 242
7 Duality theory 244
7.1 $\mathbb{F}_b$-linear subspaces 244
7.2 Duality theory for digital nets 248
7.3 Digital nets and linear codes 252
7.4 Duality theory for digital sequences 256
Exercises 261
8 Special constructions of digital nets and sequences 263
8.1 Sobol′, Faure and Niederreiter sequences 263
8.2 Niederreiter–Özbudak nets 268
8.3 Niederreiter–Xing sequence 275
8.4 Xing–Niederreiter sequence 278
Exercises 283
9 Propagation rules for digital nets 285
9.1 The $(u, u + v)$-construction 286
9.2 The matrix-product construction 288
9.3 A double m construction 290
9.4 A base change propagation rule 292
9.5 A dual space base change propagation rule 294
9.6 A base change propagation rule for projective spaces 295
Exercises 296
10 Polynomial lattice point sets 298
10.1 Polynomial lattice point sets and digital nets 298
10.2 Discrepancy of polynomial lattice point sets 309
10.3 Fast CBC-construction of polynomial lattice point sets 322
10.4 Extensible polynomial lattice point sets 329
Exercises 342

11 Cyclic digital nets and hyperplane nets **344**
11.1 Cyclic nets, hyperplane nets and their generating matrices 344
11.2 The quality parameter of hyperplane nets 352
11.3 Discrepancy of hyperplane nets 355
Exercises 360
12 Multivariate integration in weighted Sobolev spaces **363**
12.1 Digital shift invariant kernels 363
12.2 Weighted Sobolev spaces 368
12.3 A formula for the mean square worst-case error and existence results for good nets 376
12.4 Constructions of polynomial lattices 383
Exercises 390
13 Randomisation of digital nets **395**
13.1 Randomisation algorithms 396
13.2 Crossed and nested ANOVA decomposition 401
13.3 Variance of the integral estimator using scrambled nets 403
13.4 Mean square worst-case error in the Sobolev spaces $\mathscr{H}_{\mathrm{sob},s,\gamma}$ 412
13.5 Improved rate of convergence for smooth functions 424
Exercises 432
14 The decay of the Walsh coefficients of smooth functions **434**
14.1 Motivation 434
14.2 A formula by Fine 437
14.3 On the Walsh coefficients of polynomials and power series 440
14.4 On the Walsh coefficients of functions in $C^{\alpha}([0, 1])$ 445
14.5 On the Walsh coefficients of Bernoulli polynomials 450
14.6 On the Walsh coefficients of functions in Sobolev spaces 458
Exercises 463
15 Arbitrarily high order of convergence of the worst-case error **465**
15.1 Motivation for the definition of higher order digital nets and sequences 465
15.2 Construction of higher order digital nets and sequences 471
15.3 Geometrical properties of higher order digital nets 477
15.4 Squared worst-case error in $\mathscr{H}_{s,\alpha,\gamma}$ 481
15.5 A bound on the Walsh coefficients 484
15.6 A bound on the worst-case error 486
15.7 Higher order polynomial lattice point sets 493
Exercises 507
16 Explicit constructions of point sets with the best possible order of L_2-discrepancy **509**
16.1 Point sets with the best possible order of L_2-discrepancy 510

16.2 Further results from duality theory 513
16.3 The proof of Theorem 16.3 520
16.4 Explicit constructions 531
16.5 Mean square weighted L_2-discrepancy of digitally shifted digital nets 536
16.6 Asymptotics 550
Exercises 556
Appendix A Walsh functions 559
Appendix B Algebraic function fields 572
References 583
Index 597

Preface

The theory of digital nets and sequences has its roots in uniform distribution modulo one and in numerical integration using quasi–Monte Carlo (QMC) rules. The subject can be traced back to several influential works: the notion of uniform distribution to a classical paper by Weyl [265]; the Koksma–Hlawka inequality, which forms the starting point for analysing QMC methods for numerical integration, to Koksma [121] in the one-dimensional case and to Hlawka [111] in arbitrary dimension. Explicit constructions of digital sequences were first introduced by Sobol′ [253], followed by Faure [68] and Niederreiter [173]. A general principle of these constructions was introduced by Niederreiter in [172], which now forms one of the essential pillars of QMC integration and of this book. These early results are well summarised in references [61, 114, 130, 171 and 177], where much more information on the history and on earlier discoveries can be found.

Since then, numerical integration based on QMC has been developed into a comprehensive theory with many new facets. The introduction of reproducing kernel Hilbert spaces by Hickernell [101] furnished many Koksma–Hlawka-type inequalities. The worst-case integration error can be expressed directly in terms of a reproducing kernel, a function which, together with a uniquely defined inner product, describes a Hilbert space of functions.

Contrary to earlier suppositions, QMC methods are now used for the numerical integration of functions in hundreds or even thousands of dimensions. The success of this approach has been described by Sloan and Woźniakowski in [249], where the concept of weighted spaces was introduced. These weighted spaces nowadays permeate the literature on high-dimensional numerical integration. The result was a weighted Koksma–Hlawka inequality which yields weighted quality measures (called discrepancies) of the quadrature points and the need for the construction of point sets which are of high quality with respect to this new criterion. This led to computer search algorithms for suitable quadrature points which were first developed for lattice rules [246, 247] and subsequently extended to polynomial lattice rules [45].

The construction of low-discrepancy point sets and sequences has also undergone dramatic improvements. The constructions of Sobol′ [253], Faure [68] and Niederreiter [173] have been developed into the prevailing notion of (digital) (t, m, s)-nets and (t, s)-sequences. The problem of asymptotically optimal constructions in the context of this theory (i.e. which minimise the quality parameter t) have been developed by Niederreiter and Xing in [191, 267], with several subsequent extensions. From a theoretical perspective, the development of a duality theory for digital nets is interesting, see [189], which gives a general framework for the theory of digital nets.

Another development has been a partial merging of Monte Carlo (MC) methods, where the quadrature points are chosen purely at random, with QMC. The aim here is to introduce a random element into the construction of low-discrepancy points that, on the one hand, preserves the distribution properties and is, at the same time, sufficiently random to yield an unbiased estimator (and which also has further useful properties). Such a method, called scrambling, has been introduced by Owen [206], and was first analysed in [207, 209]. As a bonus, one can obtain an improved rate of convergence of $O(N^{-3/2}(\log N)^c)$ (for some $c > 0$) using this randomisation.

The topic of improved rates of convergence was further developed first in [104] for lattice rules, and then in [27] for polynomial lattice rules, using a random shift and the tent transformation. This method achieves convergence rates of $O(N^{-2}(\log N)^c)$ (for some $c > 0$). The quadrature points which can be used in this method can be found by computer search.

A general theory of higher order digital nets and sequences has been developed in [35] for periodic functions, and in [36] for the general case. There, the convergence rate is of $O(N^{-\alpha}(\log N)^c)$ (for some $c > 0$), with $\alpha > 1$ arbitrarily large for sufficiently smooth functions.

A breakthrough concerning the classical problem of finding an explicit construction of point sets which achieve the optimal rate of convergence of the L_2-discrepancy came from Chen and Skriganov [22]. This problem goes back to the lower bound on the L_2-discrepancy by Roth [228].

The aim of this work is to describe these achievements in the areas of QMC methods and uniform distribution. The choice and presentation of the topics is naturally biased towards our, the authors, interests and expertise. Another consideration for such choice of topics concerns the monographs already available, many of which are cited throughout the book.

In order to give a consistent and comprehensive treatment of the subject, we use Walsh series analysis throughout the book. In a broader context this has already featured in [130, 170] and in the context of analysing digital nets in [133, 148].

Some authors, especially those concerned with the analysis of the mean-square worst-case error of scrambled nets, prefer to use Haar wavelets, which were also used, for instance, by Sobol′ [252, 253].

In the analysis of scrambled nets, no disadvantage seems to arise from replacing Haar functions with Walsh functions. The locality of Haar functions is offset by the locality of the Walsh–Dirichlet kernel. As illustration, Owen's description of a nested Analysis of Variance (ANOVA) decomposition [207] can also be neatly described using the Walsh–Dirichlet kernel; see Section 13.2. For where Walsh functions are seen to be of considerable advantage, see Chapter 14. The Walsh coefficients of smooth functions exhibit a certain decay which is an essential ingredient in the theory of higher order digital nets and sequences. This property is not shared in the same way by Haar coefficients of smooth functions. Furthermore, the construction of point sets with optimal L_2 discrepancy has its origin in the Walsh series expansion of the characteristic function $\chi_{[0,x)}$. This makes Walsh functions more suited to our endeavour than Haar functions. However, this does not mean that this is always the case; in future work, researchers should consider such a choice on a case-by-case basis.

The aim of this book is to provide an introduction to the topics described above as well as to some others. Parts of a theory which has already appeared elsewhere are repeated here in order to make the monograph as self-contained as possible. This is complemented by two appendices, one on Walsh functions and one on algebraic function fields. The latter is the underlying basis for the constructions of digital nets and sequences by Niederreiter, Xing and Özbudak described in Chapter 8.

The text is aimed at undergraduate students in mathematics. The exercises at the end of each chapter make it suitable for an undergraduate or graduate course on the topic of this book or parts thereof. Such a course may be useful for students of science, engineering or finance, where QMC methods find their applications. We hope that it may prove useful for our colleagues as a reference book and an inspiration for future work. We also hope for an advancement in the area in the next few decades akin to that which we have seen in the past.

Acknowledgements

The germ of this book goes back many years now to a handwritten manuscript by Gerhard Larcher that was the basis for the first author's master's thesis under Gerhard's supervision and which now forms the main part of Chapters 4 and 5. This manuscript was in fact the first comprehensive introduction to the topic for the authors. For this and other contributions, we are immensely grateful. Thank you, Gerhard!

The text has also greatly benefited from valuable comments and suggestions by several colleagues which we would like to mention here: Jan Baldeaux, Johann Brauchart, Henri Faure, Michael Gnewuch, Stefan Heinrich, Peter Hellekalek, Roswitha Hofer, Stephen Joe, Peter Kritzer, Gerhard Larcher, Gunther Leobacher, Harald Niederreiter, Erich Novak, Art Owen, Gottlieb Pirsic, Wolfgang Ch. Schmid, Ian Sloan, and Henryk Woźniakowski.

It is a pleasure to thank the staff at Cambridge University Press for their professionalism in the production of the book, in particular Clare Dennison, Cheryl Gibson, Diana Gillooly, Abigail Jones and David Tranah.

Finally, we are greatly indebted to our families without whom this book would not exist.

Josef Dick
Friedrich Pillichshammer

Notation

Note: In the following, we list only symbols that are used in a global context.

Some specific sets and numbers

$\mathbb{C}$	Complex numbers.
$\mathbb{F}_b$	Finite field with b elements for a prime power b (if b is a prime, then we identify $\mathbb{F}_b$ with $\mathbb{Z}_b$). The elements of $\mathbb{F}_b$ (for b not a prime) are sometimes denoted by $\overline{0}, \overline{1}, \ldots, \overline{b-1}$.
$\mathbb{F}_b[x]$, $\mathbb{Z}_b[x]$	Set of polynomials over $\mathbb{F}_b$ or $\mathbb{Z}_b$.
$\mathbb{F}_b((x^{-1}))$, $\mathbb{Z}_b((x^{-1}))$	Field of formal Laurent series over $\mathbb{F}_b$ or $\mathbb{Z}_b$.
$G_{b,m}$	$G_{b,m} = \{q \in \mathbb{F}_b[x] : \deg(q) < m\}$.
i	$\mathrm{i} = \sqrt{-1}$.
$\mathcal{I}_s$	Index set $\{1, \ldots, s\}$.
$\mathbb{N}$	Positive integers.
$\mathbb{N}_0$	Non-negative integers.
$\mathcal{P}$	Finite point set in $[0, 1)^s$ (interpreted in the sense of the combinatorial notion of 'multiset', i.e. a set in which the multiplicity of elements matters).
$\mathcal{P}_{\mathfrak{u}}$	Point set in $[0, 1)^{\lvert\mathfrak{u}\rvert}$ consisting of the points from $\mathcal{P}$ projected to the components given by $\mathfrak{u} \subseteq \mathcal{I}_s$.
$\mathbb{R}$	Real numbers.
$\mathcal{S}$	Infinite sequence in $[0, 1)^s$.
$\mathfrak{u}, \mathfrak{v}, \ldots$	Subsets of $\mathcal{I}_s$.
ω_b	$\omega_b = \mathrm{e}^{2\pi \mathrm{i}/b}$.
$\lvert X\rvert$	Cardinality of a set X.
X^m	The m-fold Cartesian product of a set X.

$(X^m)^\top$	The set of m-dimensional column vectors over X.
$\mathbb{Z}$	Integers.
$\mathbb{Z}_b$	Residue class ring modulo b (we identify $\mathbb{Z}_b$ with $\{0, \ldots, b-1\}$ with addition and multiplication modulo b).
$\boldsymbol{\gamma}$	Set of non-negative weights, i.e. $\boldsymbol{\gamma} = \{\gamma_{\mathfrak{u}} : \mathfrak{u} \subseteq \mathcal{I}_s\}$. In the case of product weights, $\boldsymbol{\gamma} = (\gamma_i)_{i \ge 1}$ is understood as the sequence of one-dimensional weights. In this case we set $\gamma_{\mathfrak{u}} = \prod_{i \in \mathfrak{u}} \gamma_i$.

Vectors and matrices

$\mathbf{a}, \mathbf{b}, \mathbf{c}, \ldots, \mathbf{x}, \mathbf{y}, \mathbf{z}$	Row vectors over $\mathbb{F}_b$ or $\mathbb{Z}_b$.
$\boldsymbol{a}, \boldsymbol{b}, \boldsymbol{c}, \ldots, \boldsymbol{x}, \boldsymbol{y}, \boldsymbol{z}$	Row vectors over $\mathbb{N}$, $\mathbb{N}_0$, $\mathbb{Z}$ or $\mathbb{R}$.
$\mathbf{a}^\top, \mathbf{b}^\top, \ldots$	Transpose of a vector $\mathbf{a}, \mathbf{b}, \ldots$ in $\mathbb{F}_b$ or $\mathbb{Z}_b$.
$A, B, C, D, \ldots$	$m \times m$ or $\mathbb{N} \times \mathbb{N}$ matrices over $\mathbb{F}_b$.
$A^\top$	Transpose of the matrix A.
$C^{(m)}$	Left upper $m \times m$ sub-matrix of a matrix C.
$C^{(m \times n)}$	Left upper $m \times n$ sub-matrix of a matrix C.
$\boldsymbol{x}_{\mathfrak{u}}$	For an s-dimensional vector $\boldsymbol{x} = (x_1, \ldots, x_s)$ and for $\mathfrak{u} \subseteq \mathcal{I}_s$ the $\lvert\mathfrak{u}\rvert$-dimensional vector consisting of the components of $\boldsymbol{x}$ whose index belongs to $\mathfrak{u}$, i.e. $\boldsymbol{x}_{\mathfrak{u}} = (x_i)_{i \in \mathfrak{u}}$. For example, for $\boldsymbol{x} = (\frac{1}{10}, \frac{1}{3}, \frac{1}{5}, \frac{1}{4}, \frac{1}{8}) \in [0,1)^5$ and $\mathfrak{u} = \{2, 3, 5\}$, we have $\boldsymbol{x}_{\mathfrak{u}} = (\frac{1}{3}, \frac{1}{5}, \frac{1}{8})$.
$(\boldsymbol{x}_{\mathfrak{u}}, \boldsymbol{w})$	For $\boldsymbol{w} = (w_1, \ldots, w_s)$, the vector whose ith component is x_i if $i \in \mathfrak{u}$ and w_i if $i \notin \mathfrak{u}$.
$\boldsymbol{x} \cdot \boldsymbol{y}$ (or $\mathbf{x} \cdot \mathbf{y}$)	Usual inner product of the two vectors $\boldsymbol{x}$ and $\boldsymbol{y}$ (or $\mathbf{x}$ and $\mathbf{y}$, respectively).
$(\boldsymbol{x}_{\mathfrak{u}}, \mathbf{0})$	For an s-dimensional vector $\boldsymbol{x} = (x_1, \ldots, x_s)$ and for $\mathfrak{u} \subseteq \mathcal{I}_s$ the s-dimensional vector whose ith component is x_i if $i \in \mathfrak{u}$ and 0 if $i \notin \mathfrak{u}$. For example, for $\boldsymbol{x}$ and $\mathfrak{u}$ as above, we have $(\boldsymbol{x}_{\mathfrak{u}}, \mathbf{0}) = (0, \frac{1}{3}, \frac{1}{5}, 0, \frac{1}{8})$.
$(\boldsymbol{x}_{\mathfrak{u}}, \mathbf{1})$	Like $(\boldsymbol{x}_{\mathfrak{u}}, \mathbf{0})$ with zero replaced by one.

Some specific functions

$\overline{a}$	Complex conjugate of a complex number a.
$A(J, N, \mathcal{P})$	For a $\mathcal{P} = \{\boldsymbol{x}_0, \ldots, \boldsymbol{x}_{N-1}\}$, the number of indices n, $0 \le n < N$, for which the point $\boldsymbol{x}_n$ belongs to J.
$A(J, N, \mathcal{S})$	For $\mathcal{S} = (\boldsymbol{x}_n)_{n \ge 0}$, the number of indices n, $0 \le n < N$, for which the point $\boldsymbol{x}_n$ belongs to J.

${}_b\mathrm{wal}_k$	kth b-adic Walsh function (see Definition A.1).
B_k	kth Bernoulli polynomial.
$d \mid n$, $d \nmid n$	d divides n (d does not divide n).
D_N	Extreme discrepancy (see Definition 3.13).
D_N^*	Star discrepancy (see Definitions 2.2 and 2.14).
$D_{N,\gamma}^*$	Weighted star discrepancy (see Definition 3.59).
$\mathbb{E}$	Expectation.
$I(f)$	Integral of the function f over the s-dimensional unit-cube with respect to the s-dimensional Lebesgue measure, i.e. $I(f) = \int_{[0,1]^s} f(\boldsymbol{x})\,\mathrm{d}\boldsymbol{x}$.
$\log x$	Natural logarithm of x.
$\log_b x$	Base b logarithm of x.
$L_{q,N}$	L_q-discrepancy (see Definition 3.19).
$L_{q,N,\gamma}$	Weighted L_q-discrepancy (see Definition 3.59).
$O(f(x))$	For $f, g : \mathbb{R} \to \mathbb{R}$, $f \ge 0$, $g(x) = O(f(x))$ for $x \to a$ if there exist $C, \delta > 0$ such that $\lvert g(x)\rvert \le Cf(x)$ for all x with $\lvert x - a\rvert < \delta$ (or $x > \delta$ if $a = \infty$).
Prob	Probability.
$Q_N(f)$	Quasi–Monte Carlo (QMC) rule for f and an N-element point set $\mathcal{P} = \{\boldsymbol{x}_0, \ldots, \boldsymbol{x}_{N-1}\}$, i.e. $Q_N(f) = \frac{1}{N}\sum_{n=0}^{N-1} f(\boldsymbol{x}_n)$.
$\mathrm{tr}_m(\mathbf{k})$	$\mathrm{tr}_m(\mathbf{k}) = (\kappa_0, \ldots, \kappa_{m-1})^\top$ for $k \in \mathbb{N}_0$ with b-adic expansion $k = \sum_{j\ge0} \kappa_j b^j$.
$\mathrm{tr}_m(k)$	$\mathrm{tr}_m(k) = \kappa_0 + \kappa_1 b + \cdots + \kappa_{m-1} b^{m-1}$ for $k \in \mathbb{N}_0$ with b-adic expansion $k = \sum_{j\ge0} \kappa_j b^j$.
Var	Variance.
$\{x\}$	Fractional part of a real number x.
$\lfloor x\rfloor$	Integer part of a non-negative real number x, i.e. $\lfloor x\rfloor = x - \{x\}$.
$\lceil x\rceil$	The smallest integer larger than or equal to x.
$(x)_+$	$x_+ = \max(x, 0)$.
$\lvert\boldsymbol{x}\rvert_1$	L_1-norm; $\lvert\boldsymbol{x}\rvert_1 = \lvert x_1\rvert + \cdots + \lvert x_s\rvert$ if $\boldsymbol{x} = (x_1, \ldots, x_s)$.
$\lvert\boldsymbol{x}\rvert_\infty$	Maximum norm; $\lvert\boldsymbol{x}\rvert_\infty = \max_{1\le i\le s} \lvert x_i\rvert$ if $\boldsymbol{x} = (x_1, \ldots, x_s)$.
λ_s	s-dimensional Lebesgue measure (for $s = 1$ simply λ).
$\pi_m(\mathbf{c})$	Projection of $\mathbf{c} \in \mathbb{F}_b^{\mathbb{N}} = \{(c_1, c_2, \ldots) : c_1, c_2, \ldots \in \mathbb{F}_b\}$ onto its first m components.
φ	Bijection from $\{0, \ldots, b-1\} \to \mathbb{F}_b$.
φ_b	b-adic radical inverse function (see Definition 3.10).
φ^{-1}	Inverse of the bijection $\varphi : \{0, \ldots, b-1\} \to \mathbb{F}_b$.
$\chi_J(x)$	Characteristic function of a set J, i.e. $\chi_J(x) = 1$ if $x \in J$ and $\chi_J(x) = 0$ if $x \notin J$.

1
Introduction

In this introductory chapter we review some current methods of numerical integration in order to put subsequent chapters into a wider context. This serves as motivation for later investigations.

The problem of numerical integration occurs in applications from physics, chemistry, finance, biology, computer graphics, and others, where one has to compute some integral (for instance, an expectation value) which cannot be done analytically. Hence, one has to resort to numerical methods in this case. We shall, in the following, consider only the standardised problem of approximating an integral of the form

$$\int_{[0,1]^s} f(\boldsymbol{x})\,\mathrm{d}\boldsymbol{x}.$$

The books of Fox [81], Tezuka [256], Glasserman [85] and Lemieux [154], and the surveys of Keller [120] and L'Ecuyer [151] deal more directly with questions arising from applications.

1.1 The one-dimensional case

Let us consider the case $s = 1$ first. Let $f : [0, 1] \to \mathbb{R}$ be a Riemann integrable function. We proceed now as follows. Take a sample of N points $x_0, \ldots, x_{N-1}$ in the interval $[0, 1)$ and calculate the average function value at those points, i.e.

$$\frac{1}{N}\sum_{n=0}^{N-1} f(x_n).$$

As approximation to the integral, we use the value

length of the interval $\times$ average function value,

that is, we approximate the integral of f by

$$\int_0^1 f(x)\,\mathrm{d}x \approx \frac{1}{N}\sum_{n=0}^{N-1} f(x_n).$$

The question arises as to how large the approximation error is using this method, i.e. how large is the value

$$\left|\int_0^1 f(x)\,\mathrm{d}x - \frac{1}{N}\sum_{n=0}^{N-1} f(x_n)\right| ?$$

Intuitively, we expect the integration error to depend on two quantities, namely,

- on the quadrature points $x_0, \ldots, x_{N-1} \in [0, 1)$, and
- on the function f.

Let us consider these two points in turn. The quadrature points should have no big gaps in between, otherwise large portions of the function are not considered in the approximation. Hence, $\{x_0, \ldots, x_{N-1}\}$ should be well distributed in $[0, 1)$. For instance, assume we want to integrate the function $f : [0, 1] \to \mathbb{R}$ given by

$$f(x) = \begin{cases} 0 & \text{if } x \le \frac{1}{2}, \\ 1 & \text{if } x > \frac{1}{2}. \end{cases}$$

If all the points $x_0, \ldots, x_{N-1}$ are in the interval $[0, 1/2]$, i.e. the points are not well distributed in $[0, 1)$, then we obtain

$$\frac{1}{N}\sum_{n=0}^{N-1} f(x_n) = 0$$

as an approximation to the integral

$$\int_0^1 f(x)\,\mathrm{d}x = \frac{1}{2},$$

see Figure 1.1.

Hence we obtain an integration error

$$\left|\frac{1}{N}\sum_{n=0}^{N-1} f(x_n) - \int_0^1 f(x)\,\mathrm{d}x\right| = \frac{1}{2}.$$

Of course the error also depends strongly on the integrand f itself, and, in particular, on the smoothness and a suitable norm of the integrand f, which in a sense measures how greatly f varies; for instance, constant functions are always

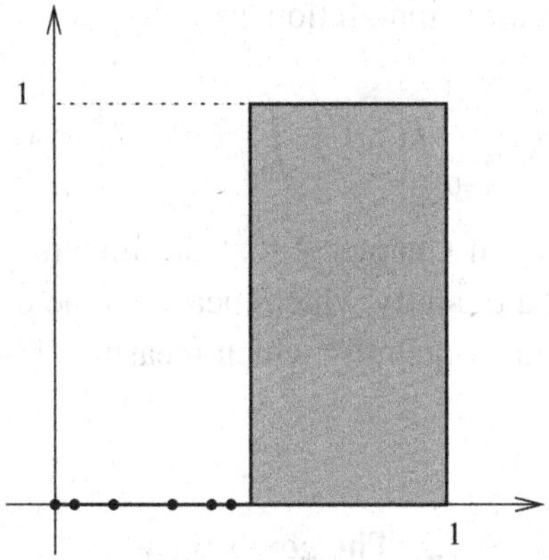

Figure 1.1 Example of badly distributed quadrature points.

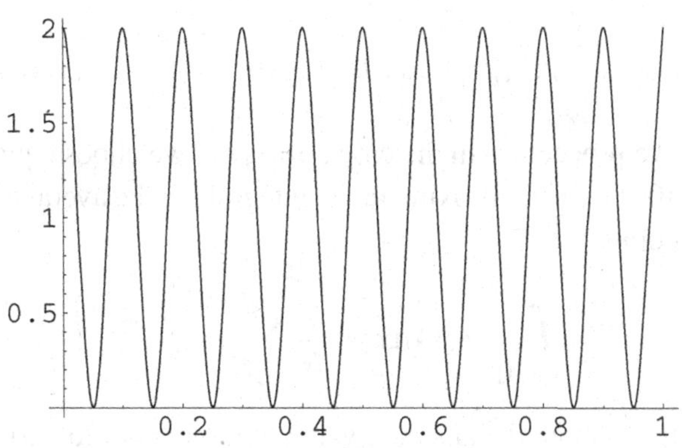

Figure 1.2 Example of the strongly varying function $f(x) = 1 + \cos(2\pi kx)$ with $k = 10$.

integrated exactly, using this method. On the other hand, assume that we have an integrand f which varies strongly, like the function $f(x) = 1 + \cos(2\pi kx)$ in Figure 1.2 for some large value of k. If we choose for $N = k$ the points $x_0, \ldots, x_{N-1}$ as $x_n = (2n + 1)/(2N)$ for $0 \leq n < N$, then they can be said to be 'well' distributed in $[0, 1)$, but we still obtain a large integration error. Indeed, we have

$$\int_0^1 f(x)\,\mathrm{d}x = 1,$$

but

$$\frac{1}{N}\sum_{n=0}^{N-1} f(x_n) = 0.$$

Hence, again we obtain a large integration error

$$\left| \frac{1}{N} \sum_{n=0}^{N-1} f(x_n) - \int_0^1 f(x)\,\mathrm{d}x \right| = 1.$$

Remark 1.1 We see later in Chapter 2 that the integration error can indeed be bounded by a product of a quantity which measures the distribution properties of the points $x_0, \ldots, x_{N-1}$ and a quantity which measures how greatly the integrand f varies.

1.2 The general case

Now let us consider the case where $s \in \mathbb{N}$. Let $f : [0, 1]^s \to \mathbb{R}$ be, say, a Riemann integrable function. We want to approximate the value of the integral

$$\int_0^1 \cdots \int_0^1 f(x_1, \ldots, x_s)\,\mathrm{d}x_1 \cdots \mathrm{d}x_s = \int_{[0,1]^s} f(\boldsymbol{x})\,\mathrm{d}\boldsymbol{x}.$$

For this purpose we proceed as in the case $s = 1$; i.e. we choose quadrature points $\boldsymbol{x}_0, \ldots, \boldsymbol{x}_{N-1} \in [0, 1)^s$ and approximate the integral via the average function value of f at those N points; i.e.

$$\int_{[0,1]^s} f(\boldsymbol{x})\,\mathrm{d}\boldsymbol{x} \approx \frac{1}{N} \sum_{n=0}^{N-1} f(\boldsymbol{x}_n).$$

Again, we want to estimate the absolute value of the integration error

$$\left| \int_{[0,1]^s} f(\boldsymbol{x})\,\mathrm{d}\boldsymbol{x} - \frac{1}{N} \sum_{n=0}^{N-1} f(\boldsymbol{x}_n) \right|.$$

Now the question arises as to how we should choose the quadrature points $\boldsymbol{x}_0, \ldots, \boldsymbol{x}_{N-1}$. Considering the case $s = 1$, a solution which suggests itself for $s > 1$ would be to choose the points on a centred regular lattice. For $s = 1$ we would choose, as above, the points $x_n = (2n + 1)/(2N)$ for $0 \le n < N$. In general, for $m \in \mathbb{N}$, $m \ge 2$, the *centred regular lattice* Γ_m^{c} is given by the points

$$\boldsymbol{x}_{\boldsymbol{k}} = \left(\frac{2k_1 + 1}{2m}, \ldots, \frac{2k_s + 1}{2m} \right) \tag{1.1}$$

for all $\boldsymbol{k} = (k_1, \ldots, k_s) \in \mathbb{N}_0^s$ with $|\boldsymbol{k}|_\infty := \max_{1 \le i \le s} |k_i| < m$ (hence, we have $N = m^s$ points). An example of a centred regular lattice is shown in Figure 1.3.

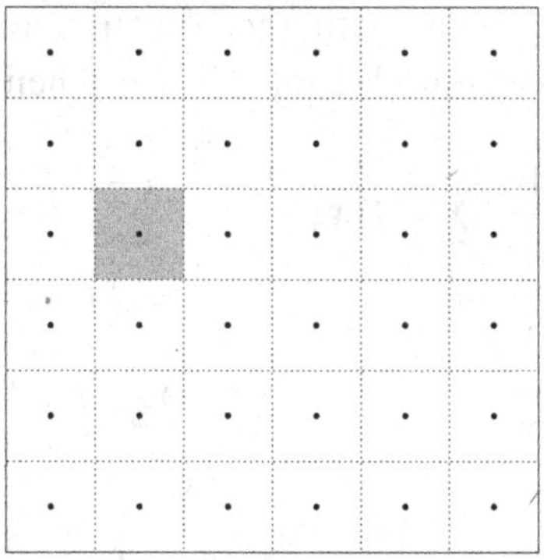

Figure 1.3 Centred regular lattice Γ_6^c in $[0, 1)^2$, i.e. $s = 2$ and $m = 6$.

As mentioned above, we need to make some assumptions on the smoothness of the integrand f. We therefore assume that the integrand f is continuous. In this case we can introduce the following concept as a measure of how much the function f varies.

Definition 1.2 For a continuous function $f : [0, 1]^s \to \mathbb{R}$, the *modulus of continuity* is given by

$$M_f(\delta) := \sup_{\substack{\boldsymbol{x}, \boldsymbol{y} \in [0,1]^s \\ |\boldsymbol{x}-\boldsymbol{y}|_\infty \le \delta}} |f(\boldsymbol{x}) - f(\boldsymbol{y})| \quad \text{for} \quad \delta \ge 0,$$

where $|\cdot|_\infty$ is the maximum norm, i.e. for $\boldsymbol{x} = (x_1, \ldots, x_s)$ we set $|\boldsymbol{x}|_\infty := \max_{1 \le i \le s} |x_i|$.

If we assume that the function f is uniformly continuous on $[0, 1]^s$, then we have $\lim_{\delta \to 0^+} M_f(\delta) = 0$. Note that for any function f, its modulus M_f is non-decreasing and subadditive. Recall that a function f is non-decreasing if $f(x) \le f(y)$ for all $x \le y$, and that a function f is subadditive if $f(x + y) \le f(x) + f(y)$ for all x, y in the domain of f.

Furthermore, for non-constant functions f, the smallest possible order of M_f is $M_f(\delta) = O(\delta)$ as $\delta \to 0^+$. Recall that we say $h(x) = O(g(x))$ as $x \to 0$ if and only if there exist positive real numbers δ and C such that $|h(x)| \le C|g(x)|$ for $|x| < \delta$.

For $\boldsymbol{k} = (k_1, \ldots, k_s) \in \mathbb{N}_0^s$ with $|\boldsymbol{k}|_\infty < m$, let $Q_{\boldsymbol{k}} = \prod_{i=1}^s [k_i/m, (k_i + 1)/m)$. Then each point of the centred regular lattice (1.1) is contained in exactly one interval $Q_{\boldsymbol{k}}$, namely the point $\boldsymbol{x}_{\boldsymbol{k}}$ (see again Figure 1.3).

Now let $f : [0,1]^s \to \mathbb{R}$ be a continuous function and let $\boldsymbol{x_k}$ for $\boldsymbol{k} \in \mathbb{N}_0^s$ with $|\boldsymbol{k}|_\infty < m$ be the points of a centred regular lattice. Then we have

$$\begin{aligned}\left| \int_{[0,1]^s} f(\boldsymbol{x})\,\mathrm{d}\boldsymbol{x} - \frac{1}{m^s} \sum_{\substack{\boldsymbol{k}\in\mathbb{N}_0^s \\ |\boldsymbol{k}|_\infty<m}} f(\boldsymbol{x_k}) \right| &= \left| \sum_{\substack{\boldsymbol{k}\in\mathbb{N}_0^s \\ |\boldsymbol{k}|_\infty<m}} \int_{Q_{\boldsymbol{k}}} f(\boldsymbol{x}) - f(\boldsymbol{x_k})\,\mathrm{d}\boldsymbol{x} \right| \\ &\le \sum_{\substack{\boldsymbol{k}\in\mathbb{N}_0^s \\ |\boldsymbol{k}|_\infty<m}} \int_{Q_{\boldsymbol{k}}} M_f(|\boldsymbol{x} - \boldsymbol{x}_{\boldsymbol{k}}|_\infty)\,\mathrm{d}\boldsymbol{x} \\ &\le m^s \int_{B(\frac{1}{2m})} M_f(|\boldsymbol{x}|_\infty)\,\mathrm{d}\boldsymbol{x}, \qquad (1.2)\end{aligned}$$

where $B(\varepsilon) := \{\boldsymbol{x} \in \mathbb{R}^s : |\boldsymbol{x}|_\infty \le \varepsilon\}$.

Assume that the function f is in addition Lipschitz continuous (for example, it suffices if f has partial derivatives), i.e. there is a real number $C_f > 0$ such that

$$M_f(\delta) \le C_f\delta \quad \text{for all } \delta > 0.$$

Then, using (1.2), we have

$$\begin{aligned}\left| \int_{[0,1]^s} f(\boldsymbol{x})\,\mathrm{d}\boldsymbol{x} - \frac{1}{m^s} \sum_{\substack{\boldsymbol{k}\in\mathbb{N}_0^s \\ |\boldsymbol{k}|_\infty<m}} f(\boldsymbol{x_k}) \right| &\le m^s \int_{B(\frac{1}{2m})} C_f|\boldsymbol{x}|_\infty\,\mathrm{d}\boldsymbol{x} \\ &\le \frac{C_f}{2m} = \frac{C_f}{2N^{1/s}}, \qquad (1.3)\end{aligned}$$

where the last inequality can be obtained by estimating $|\boldsymbol{x}|_\infty \le 1/(2m)$.

This result cannot be improved significantly for uniformly continuous functions. Before we show the corresponding result, let us give some examples. For instance, take $s = 1$ and consider the function $f(x) = c(1 + \cos(2\pi Nx))/(2N)$ for some constant $c > 0$ (see Figure 1.4). Notice that $f'(x) = -c\pi \sin(2\pi Nx)$, hence the Lipschitz constant is $C_f = \sup_{0\le x\le 1} |f'(x)| = c\pi$ and the modulus of continuity satisfies $M_f(\delta) \le c\pi\delta$ for all $\delta > 0$. Thus, unlike the function itself, the Lipschitz constant and the modulus of continuity do not depend on N. If we consider the Lipschitz constant or the modulus of continuity of f as a measure of how strongly f varies, then this measure does not depend on N. Hence, we have a family of functions which all vary equally strongly. Let us now consider the integration errors of these functions.

We have

$$\frac{1}{N}\sum_{n=0}^{N-1} f\left(\frac{2n+1}{2N}\right) = 0 \quad \text{and} \quad \int_0^1 f(x)\,\mathrm{d}x = \frac{c}{2N},$$

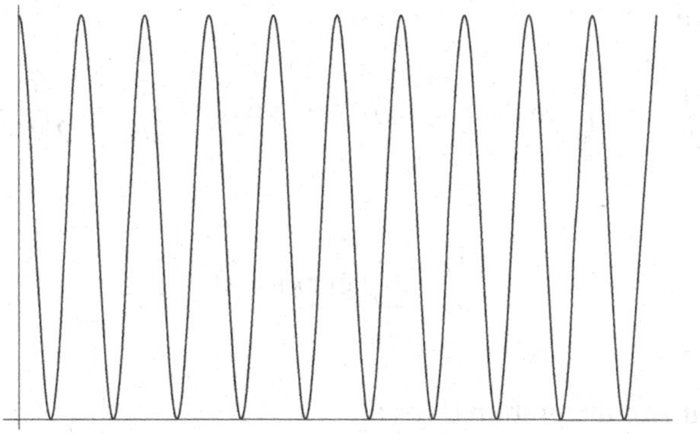

Figure 1.4 The function $f(x) = \frac{c}{2N}(1 + \cos(2\pi Nx))$ for $N = 10$.

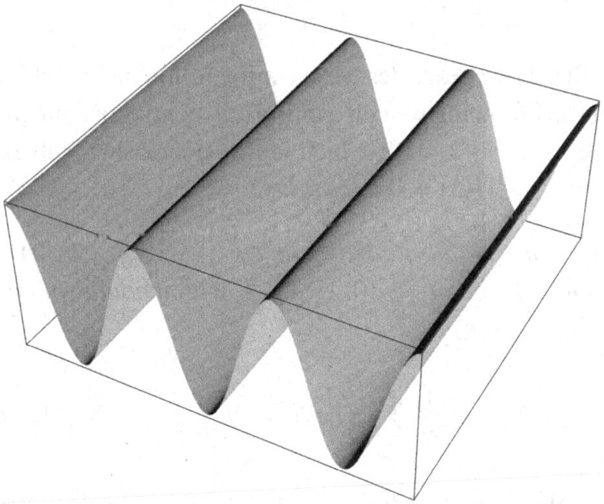

Figure 1.5 The function $g(x_1, x_2) = \frac{c}{2m}(1 + \cos(2\pi mx_1))$ for $m = 3$.

and hence

$$\left| \int_0^1 f(x)\, \mathrm{d}x - \frac{1}{N} \sum_{n=0}^{N-1} f\left(\frac{2n+1}{2N}\right) \right| = \frac{c}{2N}.$$

A convergence of $O(N^{-1})$ is reasonable in many practical applications, which makes the quadrature method a useful tool in dimension $s = 1$.

Consider now the case $s > 1$. Choose a function

$$g(x_1, x_2, \ldots, x_s) = \frac{c}{2m}(1 + \cos(2\pi mx_1));$$

see Figure 1.5. Again, the functions $g = g_m$ vary equally strongly for each m.

Then we have

$$\int_0^1 \cdots \int_0^1 g(x_1, \ldots, x_s)\,\mathrm{d}x_1 \cdots \mathrm{d}x_s = \frac{c}{2m} = \frac{c}{2N^{1/s}}$$

and

$$\frac{1}{m^s} \sum_{\substack{\boldsymbol{k} \in \mathbb{N}_0^s \\ |\boldsymbol{k}|_\infty < m}} g(\boldsymbol{x}_{\boldsymbol{k}}) = 0.$$

Hence, we obtain an integration error of

$$\left| \int_{[0,1]^s} f(\boldsymbol{x})\,\mathrm{d}\boldsymbol{x} - \frac{1}{m^s} \sum_{\substack{\boldsymbol{k} \in \mathbb{N}_0^s \\ |\boldsymbol{k}|_\infty < m}} g(\boldsymbol{x}_{\boldsymbol{k}}) \right| = \frac{c}{2N^{1/s}}.$$

Motivated by the above examples we show the following unpublished result due to G. Larcher. In the following we call a uniformly continuous function $M : \mathbb{R}_0^+ \to \mathbb{R}_0^+$, where $\mathbb{R}_0^+ = \{x \in \mathbb{R} : x \geq 0\}$, which is non-decreasing, subadditive, and for which we have $\lim_{\delta \to 0^+} M(\delta) = 0$ a *modulus*.

Theorem 1.3 *For any modulus M and any $\boldsymbol{x}_0, \ldots, \boldsymbol{x}_{N-1}$ in $[0, 1)^s$, there is a uniformly continuous function $f : [0, 1]^s \to \mathbb{R}$ with modulus of continuity $M_f \leq M$, such that*

$$\left| \int_{[0,1]^s} f(\boldsymbol{x})\,\mathrm{d}\boldsymbol{x} - \frac{1}{N} \sum_{n=0}^{N-1} f(\boldsymbol{x}_n) \right| \geq N \int_{B\left(\frac{1}{2N^{1/s}}\right)} M(|\boldsymbol{x}|_\infty)\,\mathrm{d}\boldsymbol{x}.$$

Proof Consider the Voronoi diagram $\{V_0, \ldots, V_{N-1}\}$ of $\boldsymbol{x}_0, \ldots, \boldsymbol{x}_{N-1}$ with respect to the maximum norm, i.e.

$$V_n = \{\boldsymbol{x} \in [0, 1]^s : |\boldsymbol{x} - \boldsymbol{x}_n|_\infty = \min_{0 \leq j < N} |\boldsymbol{x} - \boldsymbol{x}_j|_\infty\}$$

for $0 \leq n < N$, and define $f : [0, 1]^s \to \mathbb{R}$ by $f(\boldsymbol{x}) := M(|\boldsymbol{x} - \boldsymbol{x}_n|_\infty)$ for $\boldsymbol{x} \in V_n$. Then f is uniformly continuous since M is continuous, $\{V_0, \ldots, V_{N-1}\}$ is a Voronoi diagram, and f is defined on a compact domain.

We show that $M_f \leq M$. Let $\boldsymbol{x}, \boldsymbol{y} \in [0, 1]^s$ and assume that $f(\boldsymbol{x}) > f(\boldsymbol{y})$. If $\boldsymbol{x}, \boldsymbol{y}$ are in the same Voronoi cell, say V_n, then we have

$$\begin{aligned} |f(\boldsymbol{x}) - f(\boldsymbol{y})| &= M(|\boldsymbol{x} - \boldsymbol{x}_n|_\infty) - M(|\boldsymbol{y} - \boldsymbol{x}_n|_\infty) \\ &\leq M(\max(|\boldsymbol{x} - \boldsymbol{x}_n|_\infty - |\boldsymbol{y} - \boldsymbol{x}_n|_\infty, 0)) \\ &\leq M(|\boldsymbol{x} - \boldsymbol{y}|_\infty), \end{aligned}$$

where we used that M is subadditive and non-decreasing. If $\boldsymbol{x}, \boldsymbol{y}$ are not in the same Voronoi cell, say $\boldsymbol{x} \in V_n$ and $\boldsymbol{y} \in V_k$ with $n \neq k$, then we have

$$\begin{aligned}|f(\boldsymbol{x}) - f(\boldsymbol{y})| &= M(|\boldsymbol{x} - \boldsymbol{x}_n|_\infty) - M(|\boldsymbol{y} - \boldsymbol{x}_k|_\infty) \\ &\leq M(|\boldsymbol{x} - \boldsymbol{x}_k|_\infty) - M(|\boldsymbol{y} - \boldsymbol{x}_k|_\infty) \\ &\leq M(\max(|\boldsymbol{x} - \boldsymbol{x}_k|_\infty - |\boldsymbol{y} - \boldsymbol{x}_k|_\infty, 0)) \\ &\leq M(|\boldsymbol{x} - \boldsymbol{y}|_\infty),\end{aligned}$$

where we again used that M is subadditive and non-decreasing. Hence we have $M_f \leq M$.

It remains to show the lower bound on the integration error. We have

$$\left| \int_{[0,1]^s} f(\boldsymbol{x})\,\mathrm{d}\boldsymbol{x} - \frac{1}{N}\sum_{n=0}^{N-1} f(\boldsymbol{x}_n) \right| = \sum_{n=0}^{N-1} \int_{V_n} M(|\boldsymbol{x} - \boldsymbol{x}_n|_\infty)\,\mathrm{d}\boldsymbol{x}. \tag{1.4}$$

Let $W_n := \left\{\boldsymbol{x} \in [0,1]^s : |\boldsymbol{x} - \boldsymbol{x}_n|_\infty \leq 1/(2N^{1/s})\right\}$. Then we have

$$\begin{aligned}&\sum_{n=0}^{N-1} \int_{V_n} M(|\boldsymbol{x} - \boldsymbol{x}_n|_\infty)\,\mathrm{d}\boldsymbol{x} \\ &\quad = \sum_{n=0}^{N-1} \left(\int_{V_n \cap W_n} M(|\boldsymbol{x} - \boldsymbol{x}_n|_\infty)\,\mathrm{d}\boldsymbol{x} + \int_{V_n \setminus W_n} M(|\boldsymbol{x} - \boldsymbol{x}_n|_\infty)\,\mathrm{d}\boldsymbol{x} \right).\end{aligned} \tag{1.5}$$

Let $\boldsymbol{y} \in V_n \setminus W_n$ for some n and let $\boldsymbol{x} \in W_k \setminus V_k$ for some k. Then we have $|\boldsymbol{y} - \boldsymbol{x}_n|_\infty > 1/(2N^{1/s})$ and $|\boldsymbol{x} - \boldsymbol{x}_k|_\infty \leq 1/(2N^{1/s})$. Since M, by definition, is non-decreasing, it follows that $M(|\boldsymbol{y} - \boldsymbol{x}_n|_\infty) \geq M(|\boldsymbol{x} - \boldsymbol{x}_k|_\infty)$.

We also have $\sum_{n=0}^{N-1} \lambda_s(V_n) = 1$ and $\sum_{n=0}^{N-1} \lambda_s(W_n) \leq 1$, where λ_s is the s-dimensional Lebesgue measure. Hence, we have

$$\begin{aligned}0 &\leq \sum_{n=0}^{N-1} \lambda_s(V_n) - \sum_{n=0}^{N-1} \lambda_s(W_n) \\ &= \sum_{n=0}^{N-1} [\lambda_s(V_n \setminus W_n) + \lambda_s(V_n \cap W_n)] - \sum_{n=0}^{N-1} [\lambda_s(W_n \setminus V_n) + \lambda_s(V_n \cap W_n)] \\ &= \sum_{n=0}^{N-1} \lambda_s(V_n \setminus W_n) - \sum_{n=0}^{N-1} \lambda_s(W_n \setminus V_n),\end{aligned}$$

from which it follows that $\sum_{n=0}^{N-1} \lambda_s(W_n \setminus V_n) \le \sum_{n=0}^{N-1} \lambda_s(V_n \setminus W_n)$. From these considerations it follows that

$$\sum_{n=0}^{N-1} \int_{V_n \setminus W_n} M(|\boldsymbol{x} - \boldsymbol{x}_n|_\infty)\,\mathrm{d}\boldsymbol{x} \ge \sum_{n=0}^{N-1} \int_{W_n \setminus V_n} M(|\boldsymbol{x} - \boldsymbol{x}_n|_\infty)\,\mathrm{d}\boldsymbol{x}.$$

Inserting this inequality in (1.5), we obtain

$$\begin{aligned}
&\sum_{n=0}^{N-1} \int_{V_n} M(|\boldsymbol{x} - \boldsymbol{x}_n|_\infty)\,\mathrm{d}\boldsymbol{x} \\
&\quad \ge \sum_{n=0}^{N-1} \left(\int_{V_n \cap W_n} M(|\boldsymbol{x} - \boldsymbol{x}_n|_\infty)\,\mathrm{d}\boldsymbol{x} + \int_{W_n \setminus V_n} M(|\boldsymbol{x} - \boldsymbol{x}_n|_\infty)\,\mathrm{d}\boldsymbol{x} \right) \\
&\quad = \sum_{n=0}^{N-1} \int_{W_n} M(|\boldsymbol{x} - \boldsymbol{x}_n|_\infty)\,\mathrm{d}\boldsymbol{x} \\
&\quad = N \int_{B\left(\frac{1}{2N^{1/s}}\right)} M(|\boldsymbol{x}|_\infty)\,\mathrm{d}\boldsymbol{x}.
\end{aligned}$$

Now the result follows by (1.4). □

Combining Theorem 1.3 with (1.2), we obtain the following result from G. Larcher which states that the centred regular lattice yields the smallest possible integration error for the class of uniformly continuous functions with a given modulus of continuity.

Corollary 1.4 *Let $N = m^s$ and let M be any modulus. Then we have*

$$\inf_{\mathcal{P}} \sup_{f} \left| \int_{[0,1]^s} f(\boldsymbol{x})\,\mathrm{d}\boldsymbol{x} - \frac{1}{N} \sum_{n=0}^{N-1} f(\boldsymbol{x}_n) \right| = N \int_{B\left(\frac{1}{2N^{1/s}}\right)} M(|\boldsymbol{x}|_\infty)\,\mathrm{d}\boldsymbol{x},$$

where the infimum is extended over all point sets $\mathcal{P}$ consisting of N points in $[0, 1)^s$ and the supremum is extended over all uniformly continuous functions $f : [0, 1]^s \to \mathbb{R}$ with modulus of continuity $M_f = M$. Moreover, the infimum is attained by the centred regular lattice.

The problem in the upper bounds (1.2) and (1.3), respectively, is that the integration error depends strongly on the dimension s. For large s the convergence of $N^{-1/s}$ to 0 is very slow as $N \to \infty$. This phenomenon is often called the *curse of dimensionality*. The question arises as to whether one can choose 'better' quadrature points $\boldsymbol{x}_0, \ldots, \boldsymbol{x}_{N-1}$, i.e. for which the integration error depends only weakly (or not at all) on the dimension s. The question can be answered in the affirmative, which can be seen by the following consideration.

Assume that we want to approximate the integral of a function $f : [0, 1]^s \to \mathbb{R}$ by

$$\frac{1}{N} \sum_{n=0}^{N-1} f(\boldsymbol{x}_n),$$

where $\boldsymbol{x}_0, \ldots, \boldsymbol{x}_{N-1} \in [0, 1)^s$. Then one can ask how large the integration error

$$\left| \int_{[0,1]^s} f(\boldsymbol{x}) \, \mathrm{d}\boldsymbol{x} - \frac{1}{N} \sum_{n=0}^{N-1} f(\boldsymbol{x}_n) \right| =: R_{N,f}(\boldsymbol{x}_0, \ldots, \boldsymbol{x}_{N-1})$$

is on average; that is, if one chooses the quadrature points $\boldsymbol{x}_0, \ldots, \boldsymbol{x}_{N-1} \in [0, 1)^s$ uniformly, independent and identically distributed, then how large is $R_{N,f}$ on average, i.e. what is the expectation value of $R_{N,f}$?

Let $f : [0, 1]^s \to \mathbb{R}$ be a square integrable function, i.e. $f \in L_2([0, 1]^s)$. In the following, we calculate the expectation value of $R^2_{N,f}$, i.e. $\mathbb{E}[R^2_{N,f}]$ and then use the inequality

$$\mathbb{E}[R_{N,f}] \leq \sqrt{\mathbb{E}[R^2_{N,f}]}.$$

Let $g(\boldsymbol{x}) := f(\boldsymbol{x}) - \int_{[0,1]^s} f(\boldsymbol{y}) \, \mathrm{d}\boldsymbol{y}$. Then we have

$$\int_{[0,1]^s} g(\boldsymbol{x}) \, \mathrm{d}\boldsymbol{x} = 0. \tag{1.6}$$

Now we have

$$\begin{aligned}\left(\frac{1}{N} \sum_{n=0}^{N-1} f(\boldsymbol{x}_n) - \int_{[0,1]^s} f(\boldsymbol{x}) \, \mathrm{d}\boldsymbol{x} \right)^2 &= \left(\frac{1}{N} \sum_{n=0}^{N-1} g(\boldsymbol{x}_n) \right)^2 \\ &= \frac{1}{N^2} \sum_{n=0}^{N-1} g^2(\boldsymbol{x}_n) + \frac{2}{N^2} \sum_{0 \leq m < n < N} g(\boldsymbol{x}_m) g(\boldsymbol{x}_n).\end{aligned}$$

Hence,

$$\begin{aligned}\mathbb{E}[R^2_{N,f}] = {} & \frac{1}{N^2} \sum_{n=0}^{N-1} \int_{[0,1]^s} \cdots \int_{[0,1]^s} g^2(\boldsymbol{x}_n) \, \mathrm{d}\boldsymbol{x}_0 \cdots \mathrm{d}\boldsymbol{x}_{N-1} \\ & + \frac{2}{N^2} \sum_{0 \leq m < n < N} \int_{[0,1]^s} \cdots \int_{[0,1]^s} g(\boldsymbol{x}_m) g(\boldsymbol{x}_n) \, \mathrm{d}\boldsymbol{x}_0 \cdots \mathrm{d}\boldsymbol{x}_{N-1} \\ =: {} & \Sigma_1 + \Sigma_2.\end{aligned}$$

We consider Σ_2. For any $0 \le m < n < N$, (1.6) implies that

$$\int_{[0,1]^s} \cdots \int_{[0,1]^s} g(\boldsymbol{x}_m) g(\boldsymbol{x}_n) \, \mathrm{d}\boldsymbol{x}_0 \cdots \mathrm{d}\boldsymbol{x}_{N-1} = \int_{[0,1]^s} g(\boldsymbol{x}_m) \, \mathrm{d}\boldsymbol{x}_m \int_{[0,1]^s} g(\boldsymbol{x}_n) \, \mathrm{d}\boldsymbol{x}_n = 0.$$

Hence, $\Sigma_2 = 0$ and therefore $\mathbb{E}[R_{N,f}^2] = \Sigma_1$. Further, for every $0 \le n < N$, we have

$$\int_{[0,1]^s} \cdots \int_{[0,1]^s} g(\boldsymbol{x}_n)^2 \, \mathrm{d}\boldsymbol{x}_0 \cdots \mathrm{d}\boldsymbol{x}_{N-1} = \int_{[0,1]^s} g^2(\boldsymbol{x}) \, \mathrm{d}\boldsymbol{x} = \int_{[0,1]^s} \left(f(\boldsymbol{x}) - \int_{[0,1]^s} f(\boldsymbol{y}) \, \mathrm{d}\boldsymbol{y} \right)^2 \mathrm{d}\boldsymbol{x}.$$

Hence, we have the following theorem.

Theorem 1.5 *Let $f \in L_2([0,1]^s)$. Then for any $N \in \mathbb{N}$ we have*

$$\mathbb{E}[R_{N,f}^2] = \frac{1}{N} \int_{[0,1]^s} \left(f(\boldsymbol{x}) - \int_{[0,1]^s} f(\boldsymbol{y}) \, \mathrm{d}\boldsymbol{y} \right)^2 \mathrm{d}\boldsymbol{x} = \frac{\mathrm{Var}\,(f)}{N},$$

where we set $\mathrm{Var}\,(f) := \int_{[0,1]^s} \left(f(\boldsymbol{x}) - \int_{[0,1]^s} f(\boldsymbol{y}) \, \mathrm{d}\boldsymbol{y} \right)^2 \mathrm{d}\boldsymbol{x}$.

Theorem 1.5 can now be understood in the following way. The absolute value of the integration error is, on average, bounded by $\sigma(f)/\sqrt{N}$, where $\sigma(f) = \sqrt{\mathrm{Var}\,(f)}$ is the standard deviation of f. Note that the convergence rate does not depend on the dimension s (although for some functions $\sigma(f)$ may depend on s). We have $N^{-1/2} < N^{-1/s}$ for $s > 2$. Hence, roughly speaking, for $s > 2$ it is on average better to use random points for the approximation of the integral of f than using the centred regular grid (f does not even have to be continuous if one chooses random samples). This method of using random sample points $\boldsymbol{x}_0, \ldots, \boldsymbol{x}_{N-1}$ is called the *Monte Carlo (MC) method.*

Nevertheless the MC method also has some disadvantages:

1. The error bound is only probabilistic, that is, in any one instance one cannot be sure of the integration error. However, further probabilistic information is obtained from the central limit theorem, which states (see reference [177]) that, if $0 < \sigma(f) < \infty$, then

$$\lim_{N \to \infty} \mathrm{Prob}\left[R_{N,f}(\boldsymbol{x}_0, \ldots, \boldsymbol{x}_{N-1}) \le \frac{c\sigma(f)}{\sqrt{N}} \right] = \sqrt{\frac{2}{\pi}} \int_0^c \mathrm{e}^{-t^2/2} \, \mathrm{d}t,$$

   for any $c > 0$, where $\mathrm{Prob}[\cdot]$ is the infinite-dimensional Lebesgue measure λ_∞ of all sequences $\boldsymbol{x}_0, \boldsymbol{x}_1, \ldots$ of elements of $[0,1)^s$ that have the property indicated between the brackets.

2. A second problem is that the generation of random samples is difficult. This problem is a topic in its own right. For more information on this, see Lemieux [154], Niederreiter [177], or the overview article of L'Ecuyer and Hellekalek [152].
3. The convergence rate of $O(N^{-1/2})$ is too slow for some applications and it does not reflect the regularity of the integrand.

For more information concerning the MC method we refer to Niederreiter [177], Lemieux [154] or Glasserman [85]. The latter deals with the application of MC to financial problems.

The aim is now to find *deterministic* constructions of quadrature points which are at least as good as the average. This method is called the *quasi–Monte Carlo (QMC) method* as opposed to MC, where randomly chosen quadrature points are used. In the deterministic case, we therefore need quadrature points which are in some sense 'well' distributed in $[0, 1)^s$. We consider this problem in the next two chapters, where we specify the space of integrands first, since this also determines what the correct distribution properties of the quadrature points should be. Chapter 3 illustrates what distribution properties the quadrature points should satisfy from a geometrical point of view and presents some classical constructions of 'good' quadrature points.

Exercises

1.1 Define a modulus M by $M(\delta) = \delta$ for all $\delta \geq 0$. Find a function $f : [0, 1] \to \mathbb{R}$ which has modulus of continuity $M_f \leq M$. Verify the lower bound on the integration error of Theorem 1.3 for this function.

1.2 A well-known measure of how strongly a function $f : [0, 1] \to \mathbb{R}$ varies is the so-called *total variation* $V(f)$. For functions whose first derivative f' is continuous, it is known that the total variation can be computed by

$$V(f) = \int_0^1 |f'(x)| \, \mathrm{d}x.$$

(Note that this is a semi-norm of f which should be compared to the norm in the Koksma–Hlawka inequality, presented in Chapter 2 as Proposition 2.18.)

Compute the total variation of the function $f(x) = \frac{c}{2N}(1 + \cos(2\pi N x))$.

Note: Observe that the total variation of this function is independent of N.

1.3 Assume that the function $f : [0, 1]^s \to \mathbb{R}$ satisfies a Hölder condition, that is $|f(\boldsymbol{x}) - f(\boldsymbol{y})| \leq C_f |\boldsymbol{x} - \boldsymbol{y}|_\infty^\lambda$ for some constant $C_f > 0$ which only depends on f and $0 < \lambda \leq 1$. Show, then, that

$$\left| \int_{[0,1]^s} f(\boldsymbol{x}) \, \mathrm{d}\boldsymbol{x} - \frac{1}{m^s} \sum_{\substack{\boldsymbol{k} \in \mathbb{N}_0^s \\ |\boldsymbol{k}|_\infty < m}} f(\boldsymbol{x}_{\boldsymbol{k}}) \right| \leq \frac{C_f}{2^\lambda m^\lambda},$$

where $\boldsymbol{x}_{\boldsymbol{k}}$ with $\boldsymbol{k} \in \mathbb{N}_0^s$ and $|\boldsymbol{k}|_\infty < m$ is a centred regular lattice.

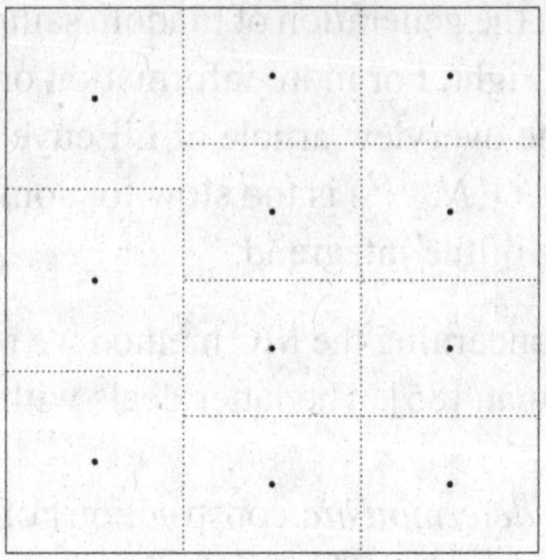

Figure 1.6 Centred quasi-regular lattice in $[0, 1)^2$ with $s = 2$ $N = 11$, $m = 3$, $l = 2$ and $k = 2$.

1.4 Let $m^s < N < (m+1)^s$, and, in particular, $m^l(m+1)^{s-l} \le N < m^{l-1}(m+1)^{s-l+1}$ for some $1 \le l \le s$, say $N = m^l\,(m+1)^{s-l} + k$ with some $0 \le k < m^{l-1}(m+1)^{s-l}$. Consider $m^{l-1}\,(m+1)^{s-l}$ intervals

$$\prod_{i=1}^{l-1}\left[\frac{a_i}{m}, \frac{a_i+1}{m}\right) \times \prod_{i=l}^{s-1}\left[\frac{b_i}{m+1}, \frac{b_i+1}{m+1}\right) \times [0, 1)$$

with integers $0 \le a_i < m$ and $0 \le b_i < m+1$. For $m^{l-1}(m+1)^{s-l} - k$ of these intervals, divide the last coordinate into m equal parts and for the remaining k intervals divide the last coordinate into $m+1$ equal parts. This gives N boxes. Take the N mid points of these boxes. This gives a *centred quasi-regular lattice*. See Figure 1.6 for an example.

Let $f : [0, 1]^s \to \mathbb{R}$ be continuous with modulus of continuity M_f and let $r(f) := \sup_{\boldsymbol{x}\in[0,1]^s} |f(\boldsymbol{x})|$. Show that for a centred quasi-regular lattice $\boldsymbol{x}_0, \ldots, \boldsymbol{x}_{N-1}$ with $m^s < N < (m+1)^s$, we have

$$\left|\int_{[0,1]^s} f(\boldsymbol{x})\,\mathrm{d}\boldsymbol{x} - \frac{1}{N}\sum_{n=0}^{N-1} f(\boldsymbol{x}_n)\right| \le N \int_{B(\frac{1}{2m})} M_f(|\boldsymbol{x}|_\infty)\,\mathrm{d}\boldsymbol{x} + r(f)\frac{1}{N^{1/s}}.$$

1.5 Let $f : [0, 1]^s \to \mathbb{R}$ be Lipschitz continuous. Show that for a quasi-regular lattice $\boldsymbol{x}_0, \ldots, \boldsymbol{x}_{N-1}$ with $m^s < N < (m+1)^s$, we have

$$\left|\int_{[0,1]^s} f(\boldsymbol{x})\,\mathrm{d}\boldsymbol{x} - \frac{1}{N}\sum_{n=0}^{N-1} f(\boldsymbol{x}_n)\right| = O(N^{-1/s}).$$

1.6 For a Borel set $E \subseteq [0, 1]^s$, we say a point set $\mathcal{P} = \{\boldsymbol{x}_0, \ldots, \boldsymbol{x}_{N-1}\}$ in $[0, 1]^s$ is *fair with respect to* E if the proportion of points of $\mathcal{P}$ that belong to E is equal to the volume of E, i.e. if $A(E, N, \mathcal{P}) := \sum_{n=0}^{N-1} \chi_E(\boldsymbol{x}_n) = \lambda_s(E)N$. We say that the point set $\mathcal{P}$ is fair with respect to a non-empty collection $\mathcal{E}$ of Borel sets in $[0, 1]^s$ if $\mathcal{P}$ is fair with respect to every $E \in \mathcal{E}$.

Let $\mathcal{E} = \{E_1, \ldots, E_k\}$ be a partition of $[0, 1]^s$ into non-empty Borel subsets of $[0, 1]^s$. For a Lebesgue integrable function $f : [0, 1]^s \to \mathbb{R}$ and for $1 \le j \le k$, put

$$G_j(f) := \sup_{t \in E_j} f(t) \quad \text{and} \quad g_j(f) := \inf_{t \in E_j} f(t).$$

Show that for any $\mathcal{P} = \{\boldsymbol{x}_0, \ldots, \boldsymbol{x}_{N-1}\}$ which is fair with respect to $\mathcal{E}$, we have

$$\left| \int_{[0,1]^s} f(\boldsymbol{x}) \,\mathrm{d}\boldsymbol{x} - \frac{1}{N} \sum_{n=0}^{N-1} f(\boldsymbol{x}_n) \right| \le \sum_{j=1}^{k} \lambda_s(E_j)(G_j(f) - g_j(f)).$$

Note and Hint: This is a special case of [181, Theorem 2] where there is a proof.

1.7 Let $f : [0, 1]^s \to \mathbb{R}$ be continuous and let $\mathcal{E} = \{E_1, \ldots, E_k\}$ be a partition of $[0, 1]^s$ into non-empty Borel subsets of $[0, 1]^s$. Show that for any $\mathcal{P} = \{\boldsymbol{x}_0, \ldots, \boldsymbol{x}_{N-1}\}$ which is fair with respect to $\mathcal{E}$, we have

$$\left| \int_{[0,1]^s} f(\boldsymbol{x}) \,\mathrm{d}\boldsymbol{x} - \frac{1}{N} \sum_{n=0}^{N-1} f(\boldsymbol{x}_n) \right| \le M_f(\delta(\mathcal{E})),$$

where $\delta(\mathcal{E}) := \max_{1 \le j \le k} \sup_{\boldsymbol{x}, \boldsymbol{y} \in E_j} |\boldsymbol{x} - \boldsymbol{y}|_\infty$.
Hint: Compare with [181, Theorem 3].

1.8 Prove an analogue of Theorem 1.5 for functions $f : D \to \mathbb{R}$ defined on an integration domain $D \subset \mathbb{R}^s$ which has a Lebesgue measure $0 < \lambda_s(D) < \infty$.

1.9 Let $f : [0, 1]^2 \to \mathbb{R}$, $f(x_1, x_2) = 1$ if $x_1^2 + x_2^2 \le 1$ and 0 otherwise. We are interested in $\int_0^1 \int_0^1 f(x_1, x_2) \,\mathrm{d}x_1 \,\mathrm{d}x_2$ (which is $\pi/4$). Write a computer program (for instance with MATHEMATICA) which applies the MC method to this problem. Run some experiments and compare the integration error with $1/\sqrt{N}$, where N is the sample size.

1.10 Let $f : [0, 1] \to \mathbb{R}$ and $g(x) = \frac{1}{2}[f(x) + f(1 - x)]$. Show that $\sigma^2(g) \le \frac{1}{2}\sigma^2(f)$.
Hint: This is [177, Proposition 1.3].

2

Quasi–Monte Carlo integration, discrepancy and reproducing kernel Hilbert spaces

In this chapter we explore the ideas behind concepts such as discrepancy, uniform distribution, quasi–Monte Carlo algorithms and others from the point of view of numerical integration. Most discrepancies considered here can be derived from numerical integration and can therefore be understood as worst-case errors of numerical integration of functions from certain function spaces. Using reproducing kernel Hilbert spaces as function spaces removes many technicalities and gives a nice pathway to the connections between discrepancies and worst-case errors of numerical integration.

2.1 Quasi–Monte Carlo rules

We consider the problem of integrating a high-dimensional Lebesgue integrable function $f : [0, 1]^s \to \mathbb{R}$ where this cannot be done analytically and therefore one has to resort to numerical algorithms. Indeed, we consider the simplest of possible algorithms; namely, we approximate

$$\int_{[0,1]^s} f(\boldsymbol{x}) \,\mathrm{d}\boldsymbol{x} \approx \frac{1}{N} \sum_{n=0}^{N-1} f(\boldsymbol{x}_n), \tag{2.1}$$

where $\boldsymbol{x}_0, \ldots, \boldsymbol{x}_{N-1} \in [0, 1]^s$ are the quadrature points needed. Because the volume of the unit-cube $[0, 1]^s$ is one, the value of the integral is just the average value of the function, which is exactly what the algorithm tries to approximate.

If the quadrature points $\boldsymbol{x}_0, \ldots, \boldsymbol{x}_{N-1} \in [0, 1]^s$ are chosen deterministically, the algorithm $\frac{1}{N} \sum_{n=0}^{N-1} f(\boldsymbol{x}_n)$ is called a *quasi–Monte Carlo (QMC) algorithm* or a *QMC rule*. On the surface the algorithm looks simple, but of course, the difficulty is how to choose the quadrature points. The following two main questions arise from this: how can we assess the quality of some given quadrature points? And, how can we find quadrature points of particularly high quality?

In order to answer these questions, we need to specify which integrands $f : [0, 1]^s \to \mathbb{R}$ we want to consider. Indeed, we want our algorithm to work not just for one specific integrand, but for a whole class of functions. That is, for a set of functions which have certain properties, so that, if we know that the integrand satisfies a certain property, i.e. is 'smooth', then we know that the method we use works well. In other words, the point set is chosen a priori and we apply the QMC algorithm to an arbitrary function belonging to a certain class.

As we know from classical integration rules, in dimension $s = 1$, like Simpson's Rule, the smoother the integrand the faster the error (which for QMC rules is given by $|\int_{[0,1]^s} f(\boldsymbol{x})\,\mathrm{d}\boldsymbol{x} - \frac{1}{N}\sum_{n=0}^{N-1} f(\boldsymbol{x}_n)|$) goes to zero as N increases. The same can of course be observed for QMC rules. We first develop the classical theory on QMC methods which deals with integrands of bounded variation [177]. In order to avoid too many technicalities though, we deal with absolutely continuous functions with partial first derivatives which are square integrable, instead of functions of bounded variation (see [177, p. 19] for an equivalence or [36, Section 3.1] for a discussion of the similarities between those two concepts).

2.2 Numerical integration in one dimension

As a first example, consider a one-dimensional function $f : [0, 1] \to \mathbb{R}$ with continuous first derivative which is bounded on $[0, 1]$. For a subset $J \subseteq [0, 1]$ let $\chi_J(x)$ denote the characteristic function of J, i.e.

$$\chi_J(x) = \begin{cases} 1 & \text{if } x \in J, \\ 0 & \text{if } x \notin J. \end{cases}$$

Considering the integration error of a QMC rule using a point set $\mathcal{P} = \{x_0, \ldots, x_{N-1}\} \subseteq [0, 1]$, we obtain, by substituting $f(1) - \int_x^1 f'(y)\,\mathrm{d}y$ for $f(x)$, that

$$\begin{aligned}
&\int_0^1 f(x)\,\mathrm{d}x - \frac{1}{N}\sum_{n=0}^{N-1} f(x_n) \\
&= \frac{1}{N}\sum_{n=0}^{N-1}\int_{x_n}^1 f'(y)\,\mathrm{d}y - \int_0^1\int_x^1 f'(y)\,\mathrm{d}y\,\mathrm{d}x \\
&= \int_0^1 \frac{1}{N}\sum_{n=0}^{N-1}\chi_{(x_n,1]}(y) f'(y)\,\mathrm{d}y - \int_0^1\int_0^y f'(y)\,\mathrm{d}x\,\mathrm{d}y \\
&= \int_0^1 f'(y)\left[\frac{1}{N}\sum_{n=0}^{N-1}\chi_{(x_n,1]}(y) - y\right]\mathrm{d}y.
\end{aligned}$$

(Note that, alternatively, we could use $\chi_{[x_n,1]}(y)$ instead of $\chi_{(x_n,1]}(y)$, but the latter is used more commonly.) Note that

$$\sum_{n=0}^{N-1} \chi_{(x_n,1]}(y) = \sum_{n=0}^{N-1} \chi_{[0,y)}(x_n) =: A([0, y), N, \mathcal{P}),$$

the number of points of $\mathcal{P}$ which lie in the interval $[0, y)$. The expression between the squared brackets in the above integral leads to the following definition.

Definition 2.1 For a point set $\mathcal{P}$ consisting of N points in $[0, 1)$ the function $\Delta_{\mathcal{P}} : [0, 1] \to \mathbb{R}$,

$$\Delta_{\mathcal{P}}(y) := \frac{A([0, y), N, \mathcal{P})}{N} - y$$

is called the *discrepancy function* of $\mathcal{P}$.

The discrepancy function permits a geometric interpretation. Namely: $A([0, y), N, \mathcal{P})/N$ is the proportion of points of $\mathcal{P}$ which lie in the interval $[0, y)$. The length or Lebesgue measure of the interval $[0, y)$ is of course y and so, for a given $y \in [0, 1]$, the function $\Delta_{\mathcal{P}}(y)$ measures the difference between the proportion of points of $\mathcal{P}$ in the interval $[0, y)$ and the length of the interval $[0, y)$. We see that the discrepancy function is small when the points $x_0, \ldots, x_{N-1}$ are evenly spread over the interval $[0, 1]$. A more detailed discussion of this geometric interpretation is given in Section 3.

Hence, we have

$$\int_0^1 f(x)\,\mathrm{d}x - \frac{1}{N}\sum_{n=0}^{N-1} f(x_n) = \int_0^1 f'(y)\Delta_{\mathcal{P}}(y)\,\mathrm{d}y. \tag{2.2}$$

This equation is a simplified form of Hlawka's identity [112], which is also known as Zaremba's identity [272].

Thus, the criterion for $\mathcal{P}$ should be to choose $\mathcal{P}$ such that $\Delta_{\mathcal{P}}(y)$ is small for all $y \in [0, 1]$. Then (2.2) guarantees that the error committed by $\mathcal{P}$ is also small for the class of functions which have continuous first derivative. To make the statement '$\Delta_{\mathcal{P}}(y)$ small for all $y \in [0, 1]$' more tangible, we can take the absolute value on both sides of (2.2) and apply Hölder's inequality to the right-hand side to obtain

$$\left| \int_0^1 f(x)\,\mathrm{d}x - \frac{1}{N}\sum_{n=0}^{N-1} f(x_n) \right| \tag{2.3}$$

$$\leq \int_0^1 |f'(y)||\Delta_{\mathcal{P}}(y)|\,\mathrm{d}y \leq \left(\int_0^1 |f'(y)|^q\,\mathrm{d}y\right)^{1/q} \left(\int_0^1 |\Delta_{\mathcal{P}}(y)|^p\,\mathrm{d}y\right)^{1/p}$$

for $p, q \geq 1$ and $1/p + 1/q = 1$.

The last inequality, (2.3), now separates the effects of the function and the point set on the integration error. Note that $(\int_0^1 |f'(y)|^q \, dy)^{1/q}$ is a semi-norm on the function space, while $\|f\|_q := (|f(1)|^q + \int_0^1 |f'(y)|^q \, dy)^{1/q}$ is a norm on the function space.

Two choices of p received particular attention, namely, $p = \infty$ and $p = 2$.

Definition 2.2 Let $\mathcal{P} = \{x_0, \ldots, x_{N-1}\}$ be a point set in the unit-interval [0, 1). The *star discrepancy* of $\mathcal{P}$ is defined as

$$D_N^*(\mathcal{P}) := \sup_{y \in [0,1]} |\Delta_{\mathcal{P}}(y)|$$

and the *L_2-discrepancy* of $\mathcal{P}$ is defined as

$$L_{2,N}(\mathcal{P}) := \left(\int_0^1 |\Delta_{\mathcal{P}}(y)|^2 \, dy \right)^{1/2}.$$

From the definition of the discrepancy function, we can now see that the star discrepancy $D_N^*(\mathcal{P})$ and the L_2-discrepancy $L_{2,N}(\mathcal{P})$ of a point set $\mathcal{P}$ are small if the points in $\mathcal{P}$ are evenly spread over the interval [0, 1] (see Exercise 2.1).

We can write (2.3) as

$$\left| \int_0^1 f(x) \, dx - \frac{1}{N} \sum_{n=0}^{N-1} f(x_n) \right| \le \|f\|_1 D_N^*(\mathcal{P}) \tag{2.4}$$

for $p = \infty$ and $q = 1$ and for $p = q = 2$ we can write

$$\left| \int_0^1 f(x) \, dx - \frac{1}{N} \sum_{n=0}^{N-1} f(x_n) \right| \le \|f\|_2 L_{2,N}(\mathcal{P}). \tag{2.5}$$

We remark that (2.4) is a simplified version of Koksma's inequality [121] (see [130, Theorem 5.1] for the original version).

Remark 2.3 Note that (2.4) and (2.5) are slightly weaker than (2.3) because we switched from a semi-norm to a norm. On the other hand, the QMC algorithm integrates all constant functions exactly so that for all $c \in \mathbb{R}$, we have

$$\begin{aligned} \left| \int_0^1 f(x) \, dx - \frac{1}{N} \sum_{n=0}^{N-1} f(x_n) \right| &= \left| \int_0^1 (f(x) - c) \, dx - \frac{1}{N} \sum_{n=0}^{N-1} (f(x_n) - c) \right| \\ &\le \left(|f(1) - c|^q + \int_0^1 |f'(y)|^q \, dy \right)^{1/q} \\ &\quad \times \left(\int_0^1 |\Delta_{\mathcal{P}}(y)|^p \, dy \right)^{1/p}. \end{aligned}$$

By choosing $c = f(1)$, we see from the last expression that in our error analysis we could restrict ourselves to consider only functions for which $f(1) = 0$.

We now aim to develop this theory for arbitrary dimensions $s \geq 1$. The use of reproducing kernel Hilbert spaces makes this generalisation somewhat simpler, hence we introduce them in the following section.

2.3 Reproducing kernel Hilbert spaces

Before we introduce reproducing kernel Hilbert spaces in a general setting, we work out an example which we already used implicitly in the previous section.

2.3.1 A first example

As we have seen from the one-dimensional example, the error analysis hinges on the substitution

$$f(x) = f(1) - \int_x^1 f'(y)\,\mathrm{d}y, \tag{2.6}$$

i.e. the analysis works for all functions which have such an integral representation. For functions f, g permitting such a substitution, and for which $f', g' \in L_2([0, 1])$, we can introduce an inner product by using the value of f, g at one and the derivatives of f, g; that is

$$\langle f, g \rangle := f(1)g(1) + \int_0^1 f'(x)g'(x)\,\mathrm{d}x. \tag{2.7}$$

The corresponding norm $\|f\|_2 := \sqrt{\langle f, f \rangle}$ is exactly the norm used in (2.5). This defines a Hilbert space

$$\mathscr{H} = \{f : [0, 1] \to \mathbb{R} : f \text{ absolutely continuous and } \|f\|_2 < \infty\}$$

of absolutely continuous functions (hence, the fundamental theorem of calculus applies) whose first derivative is square integrable. With this, we can introduce a criterion for how well a given QMC rule $Q_N(f) = \frac{1}{N}\sum_{n=0}^{N-1} f(x_n)$ works by looking at the worst performance of Q_N among all functions in $\mathscr{H}$ with norm at most one.

Definition 2.4 Let $\mathscr{H}$ be a Hilbert space of Lebesgue integrable functions on $[0, 1]$ with norm $\|\cdot\|$ for which function values are well-defined, and let $\mathcal{P}$ be the quadrature points used in the QMC rule Q_N. The *worst-case error* for QMC integration in the Hilbert space $\mathcal{H}$ is then given by

$$e(\mathcal{H}, P) = \sup_{f \in \mathcal{H}, \|f\| \le 1} \left| \int_0^1 f(x)\,\mathrm{d}x - Q_N(f) \right|.$$

A particularly nice theory now develops when we combine Equations (2.6) and (2.7); i.e. for each $y \in [0, 1]$ we want to have a function $g_y : [0, 1] \to \mathbb{R}$ such that $\langle f, g_y \rangle = f(y)$. As we modelled the inner product after (2.6) in the first place (we used $f(1)$ and f' which both appear in (2.6)), it is not hard to see that this can be done. Indeed, $g_y(1) = 1$ for all $y \in [0, 1]$ and $g_y'(x) = \frac{\mathrm{d}g_y}{\mathrm{d}x} = -1$ for all $x \in [y, 1]$ and $g_y'(x) = 0$ for $x \in [0, y)$. This implies that g_y has to be of the form

$$g_y(x) = 2 - \begin{cases} c & \text{for } 0 \le x < y, \\ x & \text{for } y \le x \le 1, \end{cases}$$

for some arbitrary fixed constant $c \in \mathbb{R}$.

We add one more sensible condition on g_y, namely, that $g_y \in \mathcal{H}$ for each $y \in [0, 1]$. Then the condition that g_y is an absolutely continuous function of x completely determines g_y, and we obtain that $c = y$, i.e.

$$g_y(x) = 2 - \begin{cases} y & \text{for } 0 \le x < y, \\ x & \text{for } y \le x \le 1, \end{cases}$$

which we can write as $g_y(x) = 2 - \max(x, y) = 1 + \min(1 - x, 1 - y)$.

To summarise, for each $y \in [0, 1]$ we now have a function $g_y \in \mathcal{H}$ such that $\langle f, g_y \rangle = f(y)$. The function $(x, y) \mapsto g_y(x)$ is called a *reproducing kernel* [4] and has several useful properties. In the following we denote the reproducing kernel by K, so in our case

$$K(x, y) = g_y(x) = 1 + \min(1 - x, 1 - y).$$

Definition 2.5 A Hilbert space $\mathcal{H}$ of functions $f : X \to \mathbb{R}$ on a set X with inner product $\langle \cdot, \cdot \rangle$ is called a *reproducing kernel Hilbert space*, if there exists a function $K : X \times X \to \mathbb{R}$ such that

P1: $K(\cdot, y) \in \mathcal{H}$ for each fixed $y \in X$ and
P2: $\langle f, K(\cdot, y) \rangle = f(y)$ for each fixed $y \in X$ and for all $f \in \mathcal{H}$.

Note that here we consider K as a function of the first variable denoted by $\cdot$ and in $\langle f, K(\cdot, y) \rangle$ the inner product is taken with respect to the first variable of K. Sometimes we indicate this by writing $\langle f(x), K(x, y) \rangle_x$. The last property, i.e. P2, is the *reproducing property*, i.e. the function values of f can be reproduced via the kernel and the inner product.

It follows that a function K with these properties must also be symmetric, unique and positive semi-definite:

P3 (symmetry): this holds as

$$K(x, y) = \langle K(\cdot, y), K(\cdot, x)\rangle = \langle K(\cdot, x), K(\cdot, y)\rangle = K(y, x),$$

P4 (uniqueness): this holds since for any function $\widetilde{K}$ satisfying P1 and P2, we have

$$\widetilde{K}(x, y) = \langle \widetilde{K}(\cdot, y), K(\cdot, x)\rangle = \langle K(\cdot, x), \widetilde{K}(\cdot, y)\rangle = K(y, x) = K(x, y),$$

P5 (positive semi-definiteness): this holds as for all choices of $a_0, \ldots, a_{N-1} \in \mathbb{R}$ and $x_0, \ldots, x_{N-1} \in X$, we have

$$\begin{aligned}\sum_{m,n=0}^{N-1} a_m a_n K(x_m, x_n) &= \sum_{m,n=0}^{N-1} a_m a_n \langle K(\cdot, x_n), K(\cdot, x_m)\rangle \\ &= \left\langle \sum_{n=0}^{N-1} a_n K(x_n, \cdot), \sum_{m=0}^{N-1} a_m K(x_m, \cdot)\right\rangle \\ &= \left\| \sum_{m=0}^{N-1} a_m K(x_m, \cdot)\right\|^2 \geq 0.\end{aligned}$$

As was shown in [4], a function K which satisfies P3 and P5 also uniquely determines a Hilbert space of functions together with an inner product for which P1 and P2 (and hence also P4) hold. Thus, it makes sense to speak of a reproducing kernel without explicitly specifying a Hilbert space of functions.

Remark 2.6 In our example, according to the construction of $K(x, y) = g_y(x)$, the conditions P1 and P2 are satisfied and hence $\mathscr{H} = \{f : [0, 1] \to \mathbb{R} : f$ absolutely continuous and $\|f\|_2 < \infty\}$ is a reproducing kernel Hilbert space. We wrote $K(x, y) = 1 + \min(1 - x, 1 - y)$ rather than $K(x, y) = 2 - \max(x, y)$, as the function $\min(1 - x, 1 - y)$ is a reproducing kernel of the Hilbert space of absolutely continuous functions with square integrable first derivative for which $f(1) = 0$ for all f in this space (see Exercise 2.5).

Remark 2.7 We note that if we include complex functions $f : X \to \mathbb{C}$, then $\langle f, g\rangle = \overline{\langle g, f\rangle}$, $\langle f, ag\rangle = \overline{a}\langle f, g\rangle$ for $a \in \mathbb{C}$. Thus P3 becomes $K(x, y) = \overline{K(y, x)}$ and we call a function positive semi-definite if for all choices of $a_0, \ldots, a_{N-1} \in \mathbb{C}$

and $x_0, \ldots, x_{N-1} \in X$, we have

$$\sum_{m,n=0}^{N-1} \overline{a}_m a_n K(x_m, x_n) \geq 0.$$

Example 2.8 We give another example of a reproducing kernel Hilbert space which was considered in [50]. This reproducing kernel Hilbert space is based on Walsh functions.

We recall some notation from Appendix A. Assume that $x, y \in [0, 1)$ have b-adic expansions $x = \xi_1 b^{-1} + \xi_2 b^{-2} + \cdots$ and $y = \eta_1 b^{-1} + \eta_2 b^{-2} + \cdots$. Further, let $k \in \mathbb{N}_0$ have b-adic expansion $k = \kappa_0 + \kappa_1 b + \cdots + \kappa_{a-1} b^{a-1}$. Further, let $\omega_b = \mathrm{e}^{2\pi \mathrm{i}/b}$. Then, the kth Walsh function in base b is defined by

$${}_b\mathrm{wal}_k(x) = \omega_b^{\kappa_0 \xi_1 + \kappa_1 \xi_2 + \cdots + \kappa_{a-1} \xi_a}.$$

Further, we set

$$x \ominus y = \frac{\zeta_1}{b} + \frac{\zeta_2}{b^2} + \cdots,$$

where $\zeta_j = \xi_j - \eta_j \pmod b$ for all $j \geq 0$ and $\ominus x = 0 \ominus x$. See Appendix A for more information on Walsh functions.

Let $K_{\mathrm{wal}}(x, y) = \sum_{k=0}^{\infty} r_{\mathrm{wal},b,\alpha}(k)\, {}_b\mathrm{wal}_k(x \ominus y)$, where $r_{\mathrm{wal},b,\alpha}(0) = 1$ and for $k > 0$ with base b ($b \geq 2$) representation $k = \kappa_0 + \kappa_1 b + \cdots + \kappa_{a-1} b^{a-1}$ and $\kappa_{a-1} \neq 0$, we define $r_{\mathrm{wal},b,\alpha}(k) = b^{-\alpha a}$, where $\alpha > 1$. The reproducing kernel Hilbert space with kernel K_{wal} is called a *Walsh space* and consists of Walsh series $\sum_{k=0}^{\infty} \widehat{f}(k)\, {}_b\mathrm{wal}_k(x)$, where $\widehat{f}(k) = \int_0^1 f(x) \overline{{}_b\mathrm{wal}_k(x)}\, \mathrm{d}x$. The inner product in this space for two Walsh series $f(x) = \sum_{k=0}^{\infty} \widehat{f}(k)\, {}_b\mathrm{wal}_k(x)$ and $g(x) = \sum_{k=0}^{\infty} \widehat{g}(k)\, {}_b\mathrm{wal}_k(x)$ is given by $\langle f, g \rangle = \sum_{k=0}^{\infty} r_{\mathrm{wal},b,\alpha}(k)^{-1} \widehat{f}(k) \overline{\widehat{g}(k)}$.

The reproducing property can be verified in the following way: the kth Walsh coefficient of $K_{\mathrm{wal}}(\cdot, y)$ (considered as a function of the first variable) is given by $r_{\mathrm{wal},b,\alpha}(k)\, {}_b\mathrm{wal}_k(\ominus y)$ and hence,

$$\langle f, K_{\mathrm{wal}}(\cdot, y) \rangle = \sum_{k=0}^{\infty} \frac{\widehat{f}(k) \overline{r_{\mathrm{wal},b,\alpha}(k)}\; \overline{{}_b\mathrm{wal}_k(\ominus y)}}{r_{\mathrm{wal},b,\alpha}(k)} = \sum_{k=0}^{\infty} \widehat{f}(k)\, {}_b\mathrm{wal}_k(y) = f(y).$$

2.3.2 Numerical integration in one dimension revisited

Using the framework of reproducing kernel Hilbert spaces, we can now revisit Section 2.2. Hence, we define the reproducing kernel K as in Section 2.2 by

$$K(x, y) = 1 + \min(1 - x, 1 - y)$$

and the inner product by $\langle f, g\rangle = f(1)g(1) + \int_0^1 f'(x)g'(x)\,\mathrm{d}x$. We have

$$\int_0^1 f(y)\,\mathrm{d}y = \int_0^1 \langle f, K(\cdot, y)\rangle\,\mathrm{d}y = \left\langle f, \int_0^1 K(\cdot, y)\,\mathrm{d}y\right\rangle,$$

where the second equality is obtained by a change of the order of integration, and

$$Q_N(f) = \frac{1}{N}\sum_{n=0}^{N-1} f(x_n) = \frac{1}{N}\sum_{n=0}^{N-1}\langle f, K(\cdot, x_n)\rangle = \left\langle f, \frac{1}{N}\sum_{n=0}^{N-1} K(\cdot, x_n)\right\rangle,$$

where the inner product is taken with respect to the first variable of K. Thus, using the Cauchy–Schwarz inequality, we have

$$\begin{aligned}\left|\int_0^1 f(y)\,\mathrm{d}y - Q_N(f)\right| &= \left|\left\langle f, \int_0^1 K(\cdot, y)\,\mathrm{d}y - \frac{1}{N}\sum_{n=0}^{N-1} K(\cdot, x_n)\right\rangle\right| \\ &\le \|f\|_2 \left\| \int_0^1 K(\cdot, y)\,\mathrm{d}y - \frac{1}{N}\sum_{n=0}^{N-1} K(\cdot, x_n)\right\|_2. \quad (2.8)\end{aligned}$$

Note that for $x \neq x_0, \ldots, x_{N-1}$ we have $\Delta_{\mathcal{P}}(x) = \frac{\mathrm{d}}{\mathrm{d}x}\left(\int_0^1 K(x, y)\,\mathrm{d}y - \frac{1}{N}\sum_{n=0}^{N-1} K(x, x_n)\right)$ and hence

$$L_{2,N}(\mathcal{P}) = \left\| \int_0^1 K(\cdot, y)\,\mathrm{d}y - \frac{1}{N}\sum_{n=0}^{N-1} K(\cdot, x_n)\right\|_2.$$

Let us now calculate the worst-case error. For short we write now $h(x) = \int_0^1 K(x, y)\,\mathrm{d}y - \frac{1}{N}\sum_{n=0}^{N-1} K(x, x_n)$. Since $K(\cdot, y) \in \mathscr{H}$ and also $\int_0^1 K(\cdot, y)\,\mathrm{d}y \in \mathscr{H}$, it is clear that $h \in \mathscr{H}$. We have equality in (2.8) if $f(x) = h(x)$. Let

$$\begin{aligned} e(f, \mathcal{P}) &:= \int_0^1 f(y)\,\mathrm{d}y - Q_N(f) \\ &= \left\langle f, \int_0^1 K(\cdot, y)\,\mathrm{d}y - \frac{1}{N}\sum_{n=0}^{N-1} K(\cdot, x_n)\right\rangle = \langle f, h\rangle.\end{aligned}$$

Then, for all f with $\|f\|_2 \neq 0$, we have $\frac{e(f,\mathcal{P})}{\|f\|_2} = e(f/\|f\|_2, \mathcal{P}) \le e(h/\|h\|_2, \mathcal{P}) = \frac{e(h,\mathcal{P})}{\|h\|_2}$ by a property of the inner product and hence

$$e(\mathscr{H}, \mathcal{P}) = \frac{e(h, \mathcal{P})}{\|h\|_2} = \frac{\langle h, h\rangle}{\|h\|_2} = \|h\|_2.$$

This means, that for a given point set $\mathcal{P}$, among all functions in the space $\mathscr{H}$, the function $h \in \mathscr{H}$ is the hardest to integrate. For the function h we have equality in (2.8).

2.3.3 The worst-case error for arbitrary reproducing kernel Hilbert spaces

In the following we use the approach of Hickernell [102] and Sloan and Woźniakowski [249]. Let us now consider an arbitrary Hilbert space $\mathscr{H}$ of Lebesgue integrable functions $f : [0, 1]^s \to \mathbb{R}$, $s \geq 1$, with inner product $\langle \cdot, \cdot \rangle$ and norm $\| \cdot \| = \sqrt{\langle \cdot, \cdot \rangle}$. Consider the functional $T_{\boldsymbol{y}}$ which evaluates a function at the point $\boldsymbol{y}$, i.e.

$$T_{\boldsymbol{y}}(f) = f(\boldsymbol{y}) \quad \text{for all } f \in \mathscr{H}.$$

Because we want to approximate the integral $\int_{[0,1]^s} f(\boldsymbol{y}) \, \mathrm{d}\boldsymbol{y}$ by the average of some function values $\frac{1}{N} \sum_{n=0}^{N-1} f(\boldsymbol{x}_n)$, it is reasonable to demand that $|f(\boldsymbol{x}_n)| < \infty$, which is ensured by the condition that the functional $T_{\boldsymbol{y}}$ is bounded, i.e. that there is an $M < \infty$ such that $|T_{\boldsymbol{y}}(f)| \leq M$ for all $f \in \mathscr{H}$ with $\|f\| \leq 1$. Riesz' representation theorem now implies that there exists a unique function $K(\cdot, \boldsymbol{y}) \in \mathscr{H}$ such that $T_{\boldsymbol{y}}(f) = \langle f, K(\cdot, \boldsymbol{y}) \rangle$ for all $f \in \mathscr{H}$. Since K satisfies P1 and P2, it follows that K is the reproducing kernel for the Hilbert space $\mathscr{H}$ (and hence $\mathscr{H}$ is a reproducing kernel Hilbert space).

An essential property which we used in the previous section is the fact that

$$\int_0^1 \langle f, K(\cdot, y) \rangle \, \mathrm{d}y = \left\langle f, \int_0^1 K(\cdot, y) \, \mathrm{d}y \right\rangle$$

holds for the reproducing kernel $K(x, y) = 1 + \min(1 - x, 1 - y)$, as this represents only a change of the order of integration. As changing the order of integration and inner product is essential for our error analysis, we consider in the following those conditions under which this holds for arbitrary reproducing kernels.

Let T now be another bounded linear functional on $\mathscr{H}$ (not necessarily integration); then, again by the Riesz representation theorem, it follows that there exists a unique function $R \in \mathscr{H}$ such that $T(f) = \langle f, R \rangle$ for all $f \in \mathscr{H}$. On the other hand, we have

$$R(\boldsymbol{x}) = \langle R, K(\cdot, \boldsymbol{x}) \rangle = \langle K(\cdot, \boldsymbol{x}), R \rangle = T(K(\cdot, \boldsymbol{x})),$$

where in the first equality we used the reproducing property of K and in the third equality we used R as the representer of the functional T (note that $R \in \mathscr{H}$ and for any given $\boldsymbol{x}$, also $K(\cdot, \boldsymbol{x}) \in \mathscr{H}$). Here, the inner product and the operator T are applied to the first variable of K. Thus, for any bounded linear functional T, we have, by abusing notation,

$$T(\langle f(\boldsymbol{x}), K(\boldsymbol{x}, \boldsymbol{y}) \rangle_{\boldsymbol{x}}) = T(f) = \langle f, R \rangle = \langle f(\boldsymbol{x}), T(K(\boldsymbol{y}, \boldsymbol{x})) \rangle_{\boldsymbol{x}},$$

where the inner product is always with respect to the variable $\boldsymbol{x}$ (which is indicated by writing $\langle \cdot, \cdot \rangle_{\boldsymbol{x}}$ instead of $\langle \cdot, \cdot \rangle$) and the operator T is always applied to a function of the variable $\boldsymbol{y}$.

Example 2.9 Consider the operator $I(f) = \int_{[0,1]^s} f(\boldsymbol{y})\,\mathrm{d}\boldsymbol{y}$. First, we have

$$I(f) = \int_{[0,1]^s} f(\boldsymbol{y})\,\mathrm{d}\boldsymbol{y} = \int_{[0,1]^s} \langle f, K(\cdot, \boldsymbol{y})\rangle\,\mathrm{d}\boldsymbol{y}.$$

By the above, the representer R of the functional I is given by

$$R(\boldsymbol{x}) = I(K(\cdot, \boldsymbol{x})) = \int_{[0,1]^s} K(\boldsymbol{y}, \boldsymbol{x})\,\mathrm{d}\boldsymbol{y} = \int_{[0,1]^s} K(\boldsymbol{x}, \boldsymbol{y})\,\mathrm{d}\boldsymbol{y}.$$

Hence, we obtain

$$\int_{[0,1]^s} \langle f, K(\cdot, \boldsymbol{y})\rangle\,\mathrm{d}\boldsymbol{y} = I(f) = \langle f, R\rangle = \left\langle f, \int_{[0,1]^s} K(\cdot, \boldsymbol{y})\,\mathrm{d}\boldsymbol{y}\right\rangle. \tag{2.9}$$

Hence, integral and inner product in a reproducing kernel Hilbert space can always be interchanged as long as the integration functional I is bounded.

We are especially interested in two operators:

- the integration operator $I(f) := \int_{[0,1]^s} f(\boldsymbol{x})\,\mathrm{d}\boldsymbol{x}$, and
- the QMC rule $Q_N(f) := \frac{1}{N}\sum_{n=0}^{N-1} f(\boldsymbol{x}_n)$ using the quadrature points $\boldsymbol{x}_0, \ldots, \boldsymbol{x}_{N-1} \in [0, 1]^s$.

For an arbitrary f with $\|f\| \neq 0$, we have

$$\begin{aligned} \frac{|f(\boldsymbol{y})|}{\|f\|} &= |\langle f/\|f\|, K(\cdot, \boldsymbol{y})\rangle| \\ &\le \langle K(\cdot, \boldsymbol{y})/\|K(\cdot, \boldsymbol{y})\|, K(\cdot, \boldsymbol{y})\rangle \\ &= \sqrt{\langle K(\cdot, \boldsymbol{y}), K(\cdot, \boldsymbol{y})\rangle} = \sqrt{K(\boldsymbol{y}, \boldsymbol{y})}. \end{aligned}$$

Thus, we have $|T_{\boldsymbol{y}}(f)|/\|f\| \le \sqrt{K(\boldsymbol{y}, \boldsymbol{y})}$ and that

$$|I(f)|/\|f\| \le \int_{[0,1]^s} |f(\boldsymbol{y})|\,\mathrm{d}\boldsymbol{y}/\|f\| \le \int_{[0,1]^s} \sqrt{K(\boldsymbol{y}, \boldsymbol{y})}\,\mathrm{d}\boldsymbol{y}$$

for all $f \in \mathscr{H}$ with $\|f\| \neq 0$.

First note that reproducing kernel Hilbert spaces are defined as Hilbert spaces of functions in which pointwise evaluation is a continuous linear functional, in other words, in which point evaluation is a bounded linear functional as introduced at the beginning of this subsection. As $K(\cdot, \boldsymbol{y}) \in \mathscr{H}$, we have $K(\boldsymbol{y}, \boldsymbol{y}) < \infty$ for all $\boldsymbol{y} \in [0, 1]^s$ by the definition of reproducing kernel Hilbert spaces. Hence, $|f(\boldsymbol{y})| \le \|f\|\sqrt{K(\boldsymbol{y}, \boldsymbol{y})} < \infty$ and the QMC rule is well defined for integrands which lie in some reproducing kernel Hilbert space.

If a reproducing kernel also satisfies

C: $\int_{[0,1]^s} \sqrt{K(\boldsymbol{y}, \boldsymbol{y})}\, \mathrm{d}\boldsymbol{y} < \infty$,

then, by the above, the integration operator and the QMC rule are both bounded linear functionals. In this case, (2.9) always holds.

Like the reproducing kernel from the previous section, the other reproducing kernels considered in this book also satisfy condition C.

Definition 2.10 Let $\mathscr{H}$ be a reproducing kernel Hilbert space for which the integral operator I is a bounded linear functional. Then, the *initial error* is defined as

$$e(\mathscr{H}, 0) = \|I\| = \sup_{f \in \mathscr{H}, \|f\| \le 1} |I(f)|$$

and the *worst-case error* for a QMC rule based on the quadrature points $\mathcal{P} = \{\boldsymbol{x}_0, \ldots, \boldsymbol{x}_{N-1}\} \subseteq [0,1]^s$ is defined as

$$e(\mathscr{H}, \mathcal{P}) = \|I - Q_N\| = \sup_{f \in \mathscr{H}, \|f\| \le 1} |I(f) - Q_N(f)|.$$

The initial error is introduced as a reference. We always assume that the initial error is finite, which is equivalent to saying that the integral operator is bounded.

With this, the same error analysis as in the previous section applies, namely:

$$I(f) = \left\langle f, \int_{[0,1]^s} K(\cdot, \boldsymbol{y})\, \mathrm{d}\boldsymbol{y} \right\rangle,$$

where we used the fact that the representer for the functional I is given by $I(K(\cdot, \boldsymbol{x})) = \int_{[0,1]^s} K(\boldsymbol{x}, \boldsymbol{y})\, \mathrm{d}\boldsymbol{y}$ and

$$Q_N(f) = \left\langle f, \frac{1}{N} \sum_{n=0}^{N-1} K(\cdot, \boldsymbol{x}_n) \right\rangle,$$

where we used that the representer for the functional Q_N is given by $Q_N(K(\cdot, \boldsymbol{x})) = \frac{1}{N} \sum_{n=0}^{N-1} K(\boldsymbol{x}, \boldsymbol{x}_n)$.

The initial error is thus given by

$$\begin{aligned} e(\mathscr{H}, 0) = \|I\| &= \sup_{f \in \mathscr{H}, \|f\| \le 1} |I(f)| \\ &= \sup_{f \in \mathscr{H}, \|f\| \le 1} \left| \left\langle f, \int_{[0,1]^s} K(\cdot, \boldsymbol{y})\, \mathrm{d}\boldsymbol{y} \right\rangle \right| \\ &= \sqrt{\left\langle \int_{[0,1]^s} K(\cdot, \boldsymbol{y})\, \mathrm{d}\boldsymbol{y}, \int_{[0,1]^s} K(\cdot, \boldsymbol{y})\, \mathrm{d}\boldsymbol{y} \right\rangle}, \end{aligned}$$

since the largest value of the supremum occurs for $g/\|g\|$, where $g(\boldsymbol{x}) = \int_{[0,1]^s} K(\boldsymbol{x}, \boldsymbol{y})\, \mathrm{d}\boldsymbol{y} \in \mathscr{H}$ is the representer of the integration functional. Therefore,

we have

$$e^2(\mathcal{H}, 0) = \|I\|^2 = \int_{[0,1]^s} \int_{[0,1]^s} \langle K(\cdot, \boldsymbol{x}), K(\cdot, \boldsymbol{y}) \rangle \,\mathrm{d}\boldsymbol{x}\,\mathrm{d}\boldsymbol{y}$$
$$= \int_{[0,1]^{2s}} K(\boldsymbol{x}, \boldsymbol{y}) \,\mathrm{d}\boldsymbol{x}\,\mathrm{d}\boldsymbol{y}.$$

The integration error is given by

$$I(f) - Q_N(f) = \langle f, h \rangle, \tag{2.10}$$

where the *representer* of the integration error is given by

$$h(\boldsymbol{x}) = \int_{[0,1]^s} K(\boldsymbol{x}, \boldsymbol{y}) \,\mathrm{d}\boldsymbol{y} - \frac{1}{N} \sum_{n=0}^{N-1} K(\boldsymbol{x}, \boldsymbol{x}_n).$$

We can estimate this error using the Cauchy–Schwarz inequality with

$$|I(f) - Q_N(f)| \leq \|f\| \|h\|.$$

From (2.10), it is then clear that the function in the unit ball of $\mathcal{H}$ which is hardest to integrate is $h/\|h\|$ and hence the worst-case error is given by

$$e(\mathcal{H}, \mathcal{P}) = \|h\|.$$

For the square worst-case error, $e^2(\mathcal{H}, \mathcal{P}) = \langle h, h \rangle$.

Proposition 2.11 *Let $\mathcal{H}$ be a reproducing kernel Hilbert space whose reproducing kernel K satisfies condition* C. *Then, the square initial error is given by*

$$e^2(\mathcal{H}, \mathcal{P}) = \int_{[0,1]^{2s}} K(\boldsymbol{x}, \boldsymbol{y}) \,\mathrm{d}\boldsymbol{x}\,\mathrm{d}\boldsymbol{y}$$

and the square worst-case error for QMC integration of functions from $\mathcal{H}$ using the quadrature points $\mathcal{P} = \{\boldsymbol{x}_0, \ldots, \boldsymbol{x}_{N-1}\}$ is given by

$$e^2(\mathcal{H}, \mathcal{P}) = \int_{[0,1]^{2s}} K(\boldsymbol{x}, \boldsymbol{y}) \,\mathrm{d}\boldsymbol{x}\,\mathrm{d}\boldsymbol{y} - \frac{2}{N} \sum_{n=0}^{N-1} \int_{[0,1]^s} K(\boldsymbol{x}_n, \boldsymbol{y}) \,\mathrm{d}\boldsymbol{y}$$
$$+ \frac{1}{N^2} \sum_{n,m=0}^{N-1} K(\boldsymbol{x}_n, \boldsymbol{x}_m).$$

Next we give a modification of a classical result for the star discrepancy (see Proposition 3.16). The following result, called the *triangle inequality for the worst-case error*, which was first proved in [106], gives a bound for the worst-case error in $\mathscr{H}$ of a QMC rule using a point set $\mathcal{P}$ which is a superposition of several smaller point sets.

Lemma 2.12 *Let $\mathscr{H}$ be a reproducing kernel Hilbert space of functions on $[0, 1]^s$. For $1 \leq i \leq k$, let $\mathcal{P}_i$ be point sets consisting of N_i points in $[0, 1)^s$ with worst-case error $e(\mathscr{H}, \mathcal{P}_i)$. Let $\mathcal{P}$ be the point set obtained by listing in some order the terms of $\mathcal{P}_i$, $1 \leq i \leq k$. We set $N = N_1 + \cdots + N_k$, which is the number of points of $\mathcal{P}$. Then, we have*

$$e(\mathscr{H}, \mathcal{P}) \leq \sum_{i=1}^{k} \frac{N_i}{N} e(\mathscr{H}, \mathcal{P}_i).$$

Proof We have

$$\begin{aligned} N e(\mathscr{H}, \mathcal{P}) &= \left\| N \int_{[0,1]^s} K(\boldsymbol{x}, \boldsymbol{y}) \,\mathrm{d}\boldsymbol{y} - \sum_{i=1}^{k} \sum_{\boldsymbol{y} \in \mathcal{P}_i} K(\boldsymbol{x}, \boldsymbol{y}) \right\| \\ &\leq \sum_{i=1}^{k} \left\| N_i \int_{[0,1]^s} K(\boldsymbol{x}, \boldsymbol{y}) \,\mathrm{d}\boldsymbol{y} - \sum_{\boldsymbol{y} \in \mathcal{P}_i} K(\boldsymbol{x}, \boldsymbol{y}) \right\| \\ &= \sum_{i=1}^{k} N_i e(\mathscr{H}, \mathcal{P}_i). \end{aligned}$$

□

The formulae in this section give us a convenient method for finding the worst-case and initial errors of arbitrary reproducing kernel Hilbert spaces. In the following section we obtain some classical results by making use of reproducing kernel Hilbert spaces and the results in this section.

2.4 Connections to classical discrepancy theory

We now turn to classical results on numerical integration in arbitrary dimension $s \geq 1$, which we already considered for dimension $s = 1$ in Section 2.2. Let the quadrature points be given by $\mathcal{P} = \{\boldsymbol{x}_0, \ldots, \boldsymbol{x}_{N-1}\}$, where $\boldsymbol{x}_n = (x_{n,1}, \ldots, x_{n,s})$.

In the previous section we have already analysed the worst-case error for arbitrary reproducing kernel Hilbert spaces. An interesting as well as practical feature of the worst-case error is that we only need to know the reproducing kernel for the space to obtain formulae for the worst-case and initial error. To generalise from the one-dimensional case, considered at the beginning, to arbitrary high dimensions, we consider tensor product spaces of the one-dimensional spaces considered before. From [4, Section 8] we know that the reproducing kernel for this space is simply the product of the one-dimensional reproducing kernels. Hence, for the one-dimensional reproducing kernel $K(x, y) = \min(1 - x, 1 - y)$ considered in Section 2.3 (see, in particular, Remark 2.6), we obtain that the reproducing kernel of the s-fold tensor product is given by

$$K(\boldsymbol{x}, \boldsymbol{y}) = \prod_{i=1}^{s} K(x_i, y_i) = \prod_{i=1}^{s} \min(1 - x_j, 1 - y_j),$$

where $\boldsymbol{x} = (x_1, \ldots, x_s)$, $\boldsymbol{y} = (y_1, \ldots, y_s) \in [0, 1]^s$.

What functions are in this space? The one-dimensional space contains all absolutely continuous functions $f : [0, 1] \to \mathbb{R}$ for which $f(1) = 0$ and the first derivative is square integrable. The inner product in one dimension is given by $\langle f, g\rangle = \int_0^1 f'(x)g'(x)\,\mathrm{d}x$.

For the tensor product space we then have, for example, if $f_1, \ldots, f_s$ are functions in the one-dimensional space, that $f(x_1, \ldots, x_s) = \prod_{i=1}^s f_i(x_i)$ is in the tensor-product space. The inner product of two such functions f and $g(x_1, \ldots, x_s) = \prod_{i=1}^s g_i(x_i)$ is then

$$\langle f, g\rangle = \prod_{i=1}^{s} \langle f_i, g_i\rangle = \prod_{i=1}^{s} \int_0^1 f_i'(x_i) g_i'(x_i)\,\mathrm{d}x_i = \int_{[0,1]^s} \frac{\partial^s f}{\partial \boldsymbol{x}}(\boldsymbol{x}) \frac{\partial^s g}{\partial \boldsymbol{x}}(\boldsymbol{x})\,\mathrm{d}\boldsymbol{x}.$$

The tensor product space contains not only those products, and sums of those products, but also its completion with respect to the norm induced by the inner product

$$\langle f, g\rangle = \int_{[0,1]^s} \frac{\partial^s f}{\partial \boldsymbol{x}}(\boldsymbol{x}) \frac{\partial^s g}{\partial \boldsymbol{x}}(\boldsymbol{x})\,\mathrm{d}\boldsymbol{x},$$

where $\frac{\partial^s f}{\partial \boldsymbol{x}}(\boldsymbol{x}) = \frac{\partial^s f}{\partial x_1 \ldots \partial x_s}(\boldsymbol{x})$.

Note that, as for the one-dimensional space we have $f(1) = 0$, it follows that $\frac{\partial^{|\mathfrak{u}|} f}{\partial \boldsymbol{x}_{\mathfrak{u}}}(\boldsymbol{x}_{\mathfrak{u}}, \boldsymbol{1}) = 0$ for all $\mathfrak{u} \subsetneq \mathcal{I}_s := \{1, \ldots, s\}$, where $(\boldsymbol{x}_{\mathfrak{u}}, \boldsymbol{1})$ is the vector whose ith component is x_i if $i \in \mathfrak{u}$ and 1 otherwise.

We now consider numerical integration in this space. From the previous section, we know that

$$|I(f) - Q_N(f)| \le \|f\|\|h\|,$$

where $e(\mathscr{H}, \mathcal{P}) = \|h\|$ with

$$\begin{aligned} h(\boldsymbol{x}) &= \int_{[0,1]^s} K(\boldsymbol{x}, \boldsymbol{y})\,\mathrm{d}\boldsymbol{y} - \frac{1}{N} \sum_{n=0}^{N-1} K(\boldsymbol{x}, \boldsymbol{x}_n) \\ &= \prod_{i=1}^{s} \frac{1 - x_i^2}{2} - \frac{1}{N} \sum_{n=0}^{N-1} \prod_{i=1}^{s} \min(1 - x_i, 1 - x_{n,i}), \end{aligned}$$

where we used $\int_0^1 K(x_i, y_i)\,\mathrm{d}y_i = \int_0^1 \min(1-x_i, 1-y_i)\,\mathrm{d}y_i = (1-x_i^2)/2$. Then

$$\frac{\partial^s h}{\partial \boldsymbol{x}}(\boldsymbol{x}) = (-1)^s \left(\prod_{i=1}^{s} x_i - \frac{1}{N} \sum_{n=0}^{N-1} \chi_{[\boldsymbol{0},\boldsymbol{x})}(\boldsymbol{x}_n) \right), \tag{2.11}$$

for $\boldsymbol{x} \neq \boldsymbol{x}_0, \ldots, \boldsymbol{x}_{N-1}$, where $[\boldsymbol{0}, \boldsymbol{x})$ denotes the interval $\prod_{i=1}^{s}[0, x_i)$.

Apart from the factor $(-1)^s$, the right-hand side of (2.11) permits some geometrical interpretation. We write $A([\boldsymbol{0}, \boldsymbol{x}), N, \mathcal{P}) := \sum_{n=0}^{N-1} \chi_{[\boldsymbol{0},\boldsymbol{x})}(\boldsymbol{x}_n)$, which is the number of points of $\mathcal{P} = \{\boldsymbol{x}_0, \ldots, \boldsymbol{x}_{N-1}\}$ that belong to the interval $[\boldsymbol{0}, \boldsymbol{x})$.

Definition 2.13 For a point set $\mathcal{P}$ consisting of N points in $[0,1)^s$ the function $\Delta_{\mathcal{P}} : [0,1]^s \to \mathbb{R}$, given by

$$\Delta_{\mathcal{P}}(\boldsymbol{x}) = \frac{A([\boldsymbol{0}, \boldsymbol{x}), N, \mathcal{P})}{N} - \prod_{i=1}^{s} x_i,$$

denotes the s-dimensional *discrepancy function* of $\mathcal{P}$.

It generalises the one-dimensional discrepancy function given in Definition 2.1 in Section 2.2. The geometrical interpretation also generalises from the one-dimensional example, i.e. it measures the difference between the proportion of points in a cube $[\boldsymbol{0}, \boldsymbol{x})$ and the volume of this cube.

Hence,

$$e(\mathscr{H}, \mathcal{P}) = \|h\| = \left(\int_{[0,1]^s} |\Delta_{\mathcal{P}}(\boldsymbol{x})|^2 \,\mathrm{d}\boldsymbol{x} \right)^{1/2},$$

and this is the classical L_2-discrepancy.

Definition 2.14 For a point set $\mathcal{P} = \{\boldsymbol{x}_0, \ldots, \boldsymbol{x}_{N-1}\}$ the *L_2-discrepancy* $L_{2,N}(\mathcal{P})$ is given by

$$L_{2,N}(\mathcal{P}) := \left(\int_{[0,1]^s} |\Delta_{\mathcal{P}}(\boldsymbol{x})|^2 \,\mathrm{d}\boldsymbol{x} \right)^{1/2},$$

and the *star discrepancy* is given by

$$D_N^*(\mathcal{P}) := \sup_{\boldsymbol{x} \in [0,1]^s} |\Delta_{\mathcal{P}}(\boldsymbol{x})|.$$

There is a concise formula for the classical L_2-discrepancy due to Warnock [263], which we derive in the following. We have $\int_0^1 K(x, y)\,\mathrm{d}y = \int_0^1 \min(1-x, 1-y)\,\mathrm{d}y = (1-x^2)/2$ and $\int_0^1 \int_0^1 K(x, y)\,\mathrm{d}x\,\mathrm{d}y = 1/3$. Thus, Proposition 2.11 yields the following formula for the L_2-discrepancy.

Proposition 2.15 *For any point set $\mathcal{P} = \{\boldsymbol{x}_0, \ldots, \boldsymbol{x}_{N-1}\}$ in $[0,1]^s$ we have*

$$(L_{2,N}(\mathcal{P}))^2 = \frac{1}{3^s} - \frac{2}{N}\sum_{n=0}^{N-1}\prod_{i=1}^{s}\frac{1-x_{n,i}^2}{2} + \frac{1}{N^2}\sum_{m,n=0}^{N-1}\prod_{i=1}^{s}\min(1-x_{m,i}, 1-x_{n,i}),$$

where $x_{n,i}$ is the ith component of the point $\boldsymbol{x}_n$.

Remark 2.16 Using the formula in Proposition 2.15, the L_2-discrepancy of a point set consisting of N points in $[0,1)^s$ can be computed in $O(sN^2)$ operations. Based on this formula, Heinrich [92] introduced an asymptotically even faster algorithm using $O(N(\log N)^s)$ operations for fixed s, which has been further improved to $O(N(\log N)^{s-1})$ operations by Frank and Heinrich [82]. Note that there is no concise formula which allows a computation of the star discrepancy (apart from the one-dimensional case; see [130, Chapter 2, Theorem 1.4] or [177, Theorem 2.6]). It was shown by Gnewuch, Srivastav and Winzen [87] that the computation of star discrepancy is an NP-hard problem. For a more detailed discussion of this topic, see [87] and the references therein.

The condition on the integrands is rather stringent. As we can see from the definition of the space, lower dimensional projections are ignored. Hence, one often considers the reproducing kernel Hilbert space with reproducing kernel

$$K(\boldsymbol{x}, \boldsymbol{y}) = \prod_{i=1}^{s}(1 + \min(1-x_i, 1-y_i)).$$

Again, from Section 2.2, we know that the inner product for the one-dimensional space is given by $\langle f, g\rangle = f(1)g(1) + \int_0^1 f'(x)g'(x)\,\mathrm{d}x$. Hence, the inner product in the tensor product space $\mathcal{H}_s$ for functions $f(\boldsymbol{x}) = \prod_{i=1}^s f_i(x_i)$ and $g(\boldsymbol{x}) = \prod_{i=1}^s g_i(x_i)$ is then

$$\begin{aligned}\langle f, g\rangle &= \prod_{i=1}^{s}\langle f_i, g_i\rangle = \prod_{i=1}^{s}\left(f_i(1)g_i(1) + \int_0^1 f_i'(x_i)g_i'(x_i)\,\mathrm{d}x_i\right)\\ &= \sum_{\mathfrak{u}\subseteq\mathcal{I}_s}\int_{[0,1]^{|\mathfrak{u}|}}\prod_{i\in\mathfrak{u}} f_i'(x_i)\prod_{i\in\mathcal{I}_s\setminus\mathfrak{u}} f_i(1)\prod_{i\in\mathfrak{u}} g_i'(x_i)\prod_{i\in\mathcal{I}_s\setminus\mathfrak{u}} g_i(1)\,\mathrm{d}\boldsymbol{x}_{\mathfrak{u}}.\end{aligned}$$

In general, the inner product for arbitrary functions f, g in this space is given by

$$\langle f, g\rangle = \sum_{\mathfrak{u}\subseteq\mathcal{I}_s}\int_{[0,1]^{|\mathfrak{u}|}}\frac{\partial^{|\mathfrak{u}|} f}{\partial\boldsymbol{x}_{\mathfrak{u}}}(\boldsymbol{x}_{\mathfrak{u}}, \boldsymbol{1})\frac{\partial^{|\mathfrak{u}|} g}{\partial\boldsymbol{x}_{\mathfrak{u}}}(\boldsymbol{x}_{\mathfrak{u}}, \boldsymbol{1})\,\mathrm{d}\boldsymbol{x}_{\mathfrak{u}}.$$

From (2.10) we know that $I(f) - Q_N(f) = \langle f, h \rangle$, with

$$h(\boldsymbol{x}) = \int_{[0,1]^s} K(\boldsymbol{x}, \boldsymbol{y}) \, \mathrm{d}\boldsymbol{y} - \frac{1}{N} \sum_{n=0}^{N-1} K(\boldsymbol{x}, \boldsymbol{x}_n)$$

$$= \prod_{i=1}^{s} \frac{3 - x_i^2}{2} - \frac{1}{N} \sum_{n=0}^{N-1} \prod_{i=1}^{s} (1 + \min(1 - x_i, 1 - x_{n,i})).$$

Then, for $\mathfrak{u} \subseteq \mathcal{I}_s$ and $(\boldsymbol{x}_\mathfrak{u}, \boldsymbol{1}) \neq \boldsymbol{x}_0, \ldots, \boldsymbol{x}_{N-1}$ we have

$$\frac{\partial^{|\mathfrak{u}|} h}{\partial \boldsymbol{x}_\mathfrak{u}}(\boldsymbol{x}_\mathfrak{u}, \boldsymbol{1}) = (-1)^{|\mathfrak{u}|} \left(\prod_{i \in \mathfrak{u}} x_i - \frac{1}{N} \sum_{n=0}^{N-1} \chi_{[\boldsymbol{0}_\mathfrak{u}, \boldsymbol{x}_\mathfrak{u})}(\boldsymbol{x}_{n,\mathfrak{u}}) \right),$$

where $[\boldsymbol{0}_\mathfrak{u}, \boldsymbol{x}_\mathfrak{u})$ denotes the interval $\prod_{i \in \mathfrak{u}} [0, x_i)$. Note that $\frac{\partial^{|\mathfrak{u}|} h}{\partial \boldsymbol{x}_\mathfrak{u}}(\boldsymbol{x}_\mathfrak{u}, \boldsymbol{1}) = (-1)^{|\mathfrak{u}|+1} \Delta_\mathcal{P}(\boldsymbol{x}_\mathfrak{u}, \boldsymbol{1})$.

The following formula due to Hlawka [112] is called *Hlawka's identity* (but it is also known as *Zaremba's identity* [272]), and follows from $I(f) - Q_N(f) = \langle f, h \rangle$ by substitution.

Proposition 2.17 *The QMC integration error for any function $f \in \mathcal{H}_s$ is given by*

$$Q_N(f) - I(f) = \sum_{\mathfrak{u} \subseteq \mathcal{I}_s} (-1)^{|\mathfrak{u}|} \int_{[0,1]^{|\mathfrak{u}|}} \frac{\partial^{|\mathfrak{u}|} f}{\partial \boldsymbol{x}_\mathfrak{u}}(\boldsymbol{x}_\mathfrak{u}, \boldsymbol{1}) \Delta_\mathcal{P}(\boldsymbol{x}_\mathfrak{u}, \boldsymbol{1}) \, \mathrm{d}\boldsymbol{x}_\mathfrak{u}.$$

Note that we have $\Delta_\mathcal{P}(\boldsymbol{x}_\emptyset, \boldsymbol{1}) = \Delta_\mathcal{P}(\boldsymbol{1}) = 0$ and hence, the case $\mathfrak{u} = \emptyset$ can be excluded in the above sum.

Applying the estimate $|\Delta_\mathcal{P}(\boldsymbol{x}_\mathfrak{u}, \boldsymbol{1})| \leq \sup_{\boldsymbol{x} \in [0,1]^s} |\Delta_\mathcal{P}(\boldsymbol{x})| = D_N^*(\mathcal{P})$, the star discrepancy of the point set $\mathcal{P}$, to Hlawka's identity, we obtain the classical Koksma–Hlawka inequality.

Proposition 2.18 (Koksma–Hlawka inequality) *Let $\mathcal{P}$ be the quadrature points employed by the QMC rule Q_N and for a function $f : [0,1]^s \to \mathbb{R}$ for which all partial mixed derivatives are continuous on $[0,1]^s$ let $\|f\|_1 = \sum_{\mathfrak{u} \subseteq \mathcal{I}_s} \int_{[0,1]^{|\mathfrak{u}|}} \left| \frac{\partial^{|\mathfrak{u}|} f}{\partial \boldsymbol{x}_\mathfrak{u}}(\boldsymbol{x}_\mathfrak{u}, \boldsymbol{1}) \right| \mathrm{d}\boldsymbol{x}_\mathfrak{u}$. Then the integration error for functions with $\|f\|_1 < \infty$ can be bounded by*

$$|I(f) - Q_N(f)| \leq \|f\|_1 D_N^*(\mathcal{P}).$$

Remark 2.19 Koksma [121] proved the inequality for dimension $s = 1$ and Hlawka [111] generalised it to arbitrary dimension $s \geq 1$. Those inequalities in their original version consider functions of bounded variation in the sense of Hardy and Krause (which is, in the one-dimensional case, the same as the total variation) rather than functions f for which $\|f\|_1 < \infty$. The variation in the sense of

Hardy and Krause and the norm considered here, without the summand $|f(\mathbf{1})|$, coincide whenever all the mixed partial derivatives are continuous on $[0, 1]^s$; see, for example, [177, p. 19] or [36, Section 3.1].

Further information concerning the relationship between integration and discrepancy can be found in the books of Novak and Woźniakowski [200, 202] and of Triebel [258].

2.5 Numerical integration in weighted spaces

We now generalise the function spaces considered above using ideas from Sloan and Woźniakowski [249]. The motivation is at least twofold. One comes from the observation that integrands appearing in applications are often such that they vary more in some coordinates than in others and hence not all variables are of equal importance for the integration problem. The second one comes from the bounds on the various discrepancies. Here we introduce the first motivation; the second motivation is given in Section 3.6. In the following we use toy examples to highlight the features we are after (but which do not directly appear in practice, as it is not obvious there that the integrand varies more in some coordinates than in others).

An extreme example of a function varying more in one coordinate than in another would be $f : [0, 1]^2 \to \mathbb{R}$ given by $f(x_1, x_2) = g(x_1)$, with $g : [0, 1] \to \mathbb{R}$. This function does not depend on the second variable x_2, so although it is defined as a two-dimensional function, it is, as far as numerical integration is concerned, only a one-dimensional function. Or, less extreme, we can have a function $f(x_1, x_2) = f_1(x_1) + f_2(x_2)$, with $f_1, f_2 : [0, 1] \to \mathbb{R}$. In this case we can apply the same rule to the first and second coordinates simultaneously, i.e. $Q_N(f) = \frac{1}{N}\sum_{n=0}^{N-1} f(x_n, x_n) = \frac{1}{N}\sum_{n=0}^{N-1} f_1(x_n) + \frac{1}{N}\sum_{n=0}^{N-1} f_2(x_n)$. Again, as far as numerical integration is concerned, a one-dimensional rule would be sufficient.

More generally, we can have $f(\boldsymbol{x}) = \sum_{\mathfrak{u}\subseteq \mathcal{I}_s} f_{\mathfrak{u}}(\boldsymbol{x}_{\mathfrak{u}})$, where $f_{\mathfrak{u}}$ depends only on x_i for which $i \in \mathfrak{u}$ (this representation is, of course, not unique) and where for some $\mathfrak{u}$ we may have $f_{\mathfrak{u}} = 0$. Therefore $I(f) = \sum_{\mathfrak{u}\subseteq \mathcal{I}_s} I(f_{\mathfrak{u}})$. In general, we might not directly have $f_{\mathfrak{u}} = 0$, but something 'small' (for the purpose of numerical integration). In this case our QMC rule does not need to have 'good' projections onto the coordinates in $\mathfrak{u}$ if the contribution of $f_{\mathfrak{u}}$ to the value of the integral $\int_{[0,1]^s} f(\boldsymbol{x})\,\mathrm{d}\boldsymbol{x}$ is negligible; that is, we do not need to pay much attention to obtain good accuracy in approximating $I(f_{\mathfrak{u}})$ by $Q_N(f_{\mathfrak{u}})$, allowing us to focus on the important projections.

In order to account for that, we want such properties to be reflected in the reproducing kernel Hilbert spaces and thus also in the criterion for assessing the quality of the quadrature points. This leads to weighted reproducing kernel Hilbert spaces originating from [249].

In the following, we introduce a decomposition $f(\boldsymbol{x}) = \sum_{\mathfrak{u} \subseteq \mathcal{I}_s} f_{\mathfrak{u}}(\boldsymbol{x}_{\mathfrak{u}})$, which has some further useful properties. These properties are then used to introduce weighted reproducing kernel Hilbert spaces.

2.5.1 Orthogonal decomposition of a reproducing kernel Hilbert space

As an example, we first consider the Hilbert space $\mathscr{H}$ of absolutely continuous functions $f : [0, 1] \to \mathbb{R}$ whose first derivative is square integrable. The inner product in $\mathscr{H}$ is given by

$$\langle f, g \rangle = \int_0^1 f(y)\,\mathrm{d}y \int_0^1 g(y)\,\mathrm{d}y + \int_0^1 f'(y)g'(y)\,\mathrm{d}y.$$

From the inner product, one can see that constant functions are orthogonal to functions which integrate to 0, i.e. for $f(x) = c$, with $c \in \mathbb{R}$ a constant and hence $f' = 0$, and a function $g \in \mathscr{H}$ with $\int_0^1 g(y)\,\mathrm{d}y = 0$, we always have $\langle f, g \rangle = 0$.

On the other hand, every function $f \in \mathscr{H}$ can be written as $f(x) = c + g(x)$ such that $g \in \mathscr{H}$ with $\int_0^1 g(y)\,\mathrm{d}y = 0$. Thus, if we set $\mathscr{H}_1 = \{f = c : c \in \mathbb{R}\}$, the set of all constant functions in $\mathscr{H}$, and $\mathscr{H}_2 = \{g \in \mathscr{H} : \int_0^1 g(y)\,\mathrm{d}y = 0\}$, we obtain an orthogonal decomposition of $\mathscr{H}$: $\langle f_1, f_2 \rangle = 0$ for all $f_1 \in \mathscr{H}_1$, $f_2 \in \mathscr{H}_2$ and for every $f \in \mathscr{H}$ there are unique functions $f_1 \in \mathscr{H}_1$, $f_2 \in \mathscr{H}_2$ such that $f = f_1 + f_2$. Indeed, for a given $f \in \mathscr{H}$, we set $f_1 := \int_0^1 f(y)\,\mathrm{d}y$ and $f_2 := f - f_1$, then $f_1 \in \mathscr{H}_1$ and $f_2 \in \mathscr{H}$ with $\int_0^1 f_2(y)\,\mathrm{d}y = \int_0^1 f(y)\,\mathrm{d}y - f_1 = 0$, and so $f_2 \in \mathscr{H}_2$.

It can be checked (see Exercise 2.11) that the reproducing kernel for $\mathscr{H}$ is given by

$$K(x, y) = 1 + B_1(x)B_1(y) + \frac{B_2(|x - y|)}{2},$$

where $B_1(t) = t - 1/2$ and $B_2(t) = t^2 - t + 1/6$ (B_1 is the first and B_2 is the second Bernoulli polynomial). Hence, we have

$$\langle f, K(\cdot, y) \rangle = f(y).$$

Remark 2.20 Note that $\int_0^1 B_1(y)\,\mathrm{d}y = \int_0^1 B_2(y)\,\mathrm{d}y = 0$ (see Exercise 2.18). Since $B_2(y) = B_2(1 - y)$, we have $\int_0^1 B_2(|x - y|)\,\mathrm{d}y = \int_0^x B_2(x - y)\,\mathrm{d}y + \int_x^1 B_2(1 - (y - x))\,\mathrm{d}y = \int_0^1 B_2(z)\,\mathrm{d}z = 0$. Altogether, we obtain that $\int_0^1 K(x, y)\,\mathrm{d}y = 1$.

It is not too hard to see that we can obtain $f_1 = \int_0^1 f(y)\,\mathrm{d}y$ using the inner product. Indeed, there is a linear functional which maps f to f_1, and its representer is, as we have seen above, $\int_0^1 K(x, y)\,\mathrm{d}y = 1$. Thus,

$$\langle f, 1\rangle = \int_0^1 f(y)\,\mathrm{d}y \int_0^1 1\,\mathrm{d}y + \int_0^1 f'(y)0\,\mathrm{d}y = \int_0^1 f(y)\,\mathrm{d}y.$$

Therefore, we can also obtain $f_2 = f - f_1$. We have

$$f_2(y) = f(y) - f_1 = \langle f, K(\cdot, y)\rangle - \langle f, 1\rangle = \langle f, K(\cdot, y) - 1\rangle.$$

Hence, we have

$$\mathscr{H}_1 = \{f_1 \in \mathscr{H} : f_1 = \langle f, 1\rangle, \text{ for some } f \in \mathscr{H}\}$$

and

$$\mathscr{H}_2 = \{f_2 \in \mathscr{H} : f_2(y) = \langle f, K(\cdot, y) - 1\rangle \ \forall y \in [0, 1], \text{ for some } f \in \mathscr{H}\}.$$

Further, $\mathscr{H}_1, \mathscr{H}_2$ are reproducing kernel Hilbert spaces themselves with inner products $\langle f, g\rangle_1 = \int_0^1 f(y)\,\mathrm{d}y \int_0^1 g(y)\,\mathrm{d}y$ and $\langle f, g\rangle_2 = \int_0^1 f'(y)g'(y)\,\mathrm{d}y$ and reproducing kernels $K_1(x, y) = 1$ and $K_2(x, y) = B_1(x)B_1(y) + B_2(|x - y|)/2$. Obviously, we have $K = K_1 + K_2$. For a general result, see [4].

Remark 2.21 We call the Hilbert space $\mathscr{H}$ considered in this section the *unanchored Sobolev space*. The Hilbert space with kernel $K(x, y) = 1 + \min(1 - x, 1 - y)$ is called *anchored Sobolev space* (with anchor 1), as the inner product $\langle f, g\rangle = f(1)g(1) + \int_0^1 f'(y)g'(y)\,\mathrm{d}y$ is anchored at the point 1.

In the next section we consider tensor products of the unanchored Sobolev space and obtain orthogonal decompositions in this case.

2.5.2 *Unanchored Sobolev spaces over* $[0, 1]^s$

Again let $K(x, y) = 1 + B_1(x)B_1(y) + B_2(|x - y|)/2$ and let

$$K(\boldsymbol{x}, \boldsymbol{y}) = \prod_{i=1}^{s} K(x_i, y_i)$$

be the reproducing kernel of the s-fold tensor product of the one-dimensional unanchored Sobolev space. We again call the corresponding reproducing kernel Hilbert space $\mathscr{H}_s$ with domain $[0, 1]^s$ *unanchored Sobolev space*. The inner product in this space is given by

$$\langle f, g\rangle = \sum_{\mathfrak{u}\subseteq \mathcal{I}_s} \int_{[0,1]^{|\mathfrak{u}|}} \left(\int_{[0,1]^{s-|\mathfrak{u}|}} \frac{\partial^{|\mathfrak{u}|} f}{\partial \boldsymbol{x}_{\mathfrak{u}}}(\boldsymbol{x})\,\mathrm{d}\boldsymbol{x}_{\mathcal{I}_s\setminus\mathfrak{u}}\right)\left(\int_{[0,1]^{s-|\mathfrak{u}|}} \frac{\partial^{|\mathfrak{u}|} g}{\partial \boldsymbol{x}_{\mathfrak{u}}}(\boldsymbol{x})\,\mathrm{d}\boldsymbol{x}_{\mathcal{I}_s\setminus\mathfrak{u}}\right)\mathrm{d}\boldsymbol{x}_{\mathfrak{u}}. \tag{2.12}$$

Recall that for $f \in \mathcal{H}_s$ we want to have a decomposition of the form

$$f(\boldsymbol{x}) = \sum_{\mathfrak{u} \subseteq \mathcal{I}_s} f_{\mathfrak{u}}(\boldsymbol{x}_{\mathfrak{u}}),$$

where $f_{\mathfrak{u}}$ only depends on the variables x_i for $i \in \mathfrak{u}$. From the previous section we know that we can decompose a one-variable function into a constant part and a variable part. We can now apply this same procedure to each of the s variables of f to decompose it into functions $f_{\mathfrak{u}}$ which depend only on the variables x_i for which $i \in \mathfrak{u}$. For $i \notin \mathfrak{u}$, the function $f_{\mathfrak{u}}$ is constant with respect to x_i, i.e. it does not depend on x_i.

For $\mathfrak{u} \subseteq \mathcal{I}_s$ let

$$K_{\mathfrak{u}}(\boldsymbol{x}_{\mathfrak{u}}, \boldsymbol{y}_{\mathfrak{u}}) = \prod_{i \in \mathfrak{u}} (B_1(x_i)B_1(y_i) + B_2(|x_i - y_i|)/2),$$

where $K_{\emptyset} = 1$. We write $K_{\mathfrak{u}}(\boldsymbol{x}_{\mathfrak{u}}, \boldsymbol{y}_{\mathfrak{u}})$ and $K_{\mathfrak{u}}(\boldsymbol{x}, \boldsymbol{y})$ interchangeably. Then $K(\boldsymbol{x}, \boldsymbol{y}) = \sum_{\mathfrak{u} \subseteq \mathcal{I}_s} K_{\mathfrak{u}}(\boldsymbol{x}_{\mathfrak{u}}, \boldsymbol{y}_{\mathfrak{u}})$.

Now let

$$\mathcal{H}_{\mathfrak{u}} = \{f_{\mathfrak{u}} \in \mathcal{H}_s : f_{\mathfrak{u}}(\boldsymbol{y}) := \langle f, K_{\mathfrak{u}}(\cdot, \boldsymbol{y})\rangle \ \forall \boldsymbol{y} \in [0,1]^s \text{ for some } f \in \mathcal{H}_s\}.$$

Then, for $i \in \mathfrak{u}$ we have

$$\int_0^1 f_{\mathfrak{u}}(\boldsymbol{y})\,\mathrm{d}y_i = \int_0^1 \langle f, K_{\mathfrak{u}}(\cdot, \boldsymbol{y})\rangle\,\mathrm{d}y_i = \left\langle f, \int_0^1 K_{\mathfrak{u}}(\cdot, \boldsymbol{y})\,\mathrm{d}y_i \right\rangle = \langle f, 0\rangle = 0,$$

as $\int_0^1 K(x, y)\,\mathrm{d}y = 1$ according to Remark 2.20. Further, by definition, $f_{\mathfrak{u}}$ does not depend on variables y_i for $i \notin \mathfrak{u}$ and thus $\frac{\partial f_{\mathfrak{u}}}{\partial y_i} = 0$ for $i \notin \mathfrak{u}$. For $f_{\mathfrak{u}} \in \mathcal{H}_{\mathfrak{u}}$ we often write $f_{\mathfrak{u}}(\boldsymbol{y}_{\mathfrak{u}})$ instead of $f_{\mathfrak{u}}(\boldsymbol{y})$, to emphasise that $f_{\mathfrak{u}}$ only depends on y_i for $i \in \mathfrak{u}$.

On the other hand, if $f \in \mathcal{H}_s$ with $\int_0^1 f(\boldsymbol{x})\,\mathrm{d}x_i = 0$ for $i \in \mathfrak{u}$ and $\frac{\partial f}{\partial x_i} = 0$ for $i \notin \mathfrak{u}$ and $g \in \mathcal{H}_s$, then

$$\begin{aligned}
\langle f, g\rangle &= \sum_{\mathfrak{v} \subseteq \mathcal{I}_s} \int_{[0,1]^{|\mathfrak{v}|}} \left(\int_{[0,1]^{s-|\mathfrak{v}|}} \frac{\partial^{|\mathfrak{v}|} f}{\partial \boldsymbol{x}_{\mathfrak{v}}}(\boldsymbol{x})\,\mathrm{d}\boldsymbol{x}_{\mathcal{I}_s \setminus \mathfrak{v}} \right) \left(\int_{[0,1]^{s-|\mathfrak{v}|}} \frac{\partial^{|\mathfrak{v}|} g}{\partial \boldsymbol{x}_{\mathfrak{v}}}(\boldsymbol{x})\,\mathrm{d}\boldsymbol{x}_{\mathcal{I}_s \setminus \mathfrak{v}} \right) \mathrm{d}\boldsymbol{x}_{\mathfrak{v}} \\
&= \int_{[0,1]^{|\mathfrak{u}|}} \left(\int_{[0,1]^{s-|\mathfrak{u}|}} \frac{\partial^{|\mathfrak{u}|} f}{\partial \boldsymbol{x}_{\mathfrak{u}}}(\boldsymbol{x})\,\mathrm{d}\boldsymbol{x}_{\mathcal{I}_s \setminus \mathfrak{u}} \right) \left(\int_{[0,1]^{s-|\mathfrak{u}|}} \frac{\partial^{|\mathfrak{u}|} g}{\partial \boldsymbol{x}_{\mathfrak{u}}}(\boldsymbol{x})\,\mathrm{d}\boldsymbol{x}_{\mathcal{I}_s \setminus \mathfrak{u}} \right) \mathrm{d}\boldsymbol{x}_{\mathfrak{u}} \\
&=: \langle f, g\rangle_{\mathfrak{u}},
\end{aligned}$$

as we have $\int_{[0,1]^{s-|\mathfrak{v}|}} \frac{\partial^{|\mathfrak{v}|} f}{\partial \boldsymbol{x}_{\mathfrak{v}}}(\boldsymbol{x})\,\mathrm{d}\boldsymbol{x}_{\mathcal{I}_s \setminus \mathfrak{v}} = \frac{\partial^{|\mathfrak{v}|}}{\partial \boldsymbol{x}_{\mathfrak{v}}} \int_{[0,1]^{s-|\mathfrak{v}|}} f(\boldsymbol{x})\,\mathrm{d}\boldsymbol{x}_{\mathcal{I}_s \setminus \mathfrak{v}}$ and therefore $\int_0^1 f(\boldsymbol{x})\,\mathrm{d}x_i = 0$ for $i \in \mathfrak{u}$ and $\frac{\partial f}{\partial x_i} = 0$ for $i \notin \mathfrak{u}$ imply that we obtain $\int_{[0,1]^{s-|\mathfrak{v}|}} \frac{\partial^{|\mathfrak{v}|} f}{\partial \boldsymbol{x}_{\mathfrak{v}}}(\boldsymbol{x})\,\mathrm{d}\boldsymbol{x}_{\mathcal{I}_s \setminus \mathfrak{v}} = 0$ for $\mathfrak{v} \neq \mathfrak{u}$. (That the order of integration and differentiation can be interchanged can be seen in the following way: as the order can be changed for the reproducing kernel, it follows that $\langle \cdot, \cdot \rangle'$ given by

$$\langle f, g\rangle' = \sum_{\mathfrak{u} \subseteq \mathcal{I}_s} \int_{[0,1]^{|\mathfrak{u}|}} \frac{\partial^{|\mathfrak{u}|}}{\partial \boldsymbol{x}_{\mathfrak{u}}} \left(\int_{[0,1]^{s-|\mathfrak{u}|}} f(\boldsymbol{x}) \,\mathrm{d}\boldsymbol{x}_{\mathcal{I}_s \setminus \mathfrak{u}} \right)$$

$$\times \frac{\partial^{|\mathfrak{u}|}}{\partial \boldsymbol{x}_{\mathfrak{u}}} \left(\int_{[0,1]^{s-|\mathfrak{u}|}} g(\boldsymbol{x}) \,\mathrm{d}\boldsymbol{x}_{\mathcal{I}_s \setminus \mathfrak{u}} \right) \mathrm{d}\boldsymbol{x}_{\mathfrak{u}},$$

is also an inner product in $\mathscr{H}_s$. From [4] we know that the inner product is unique and hence, $\langle f, g\rangle = \langle f, g\rangle'$ for all $f, g \in \mathscr{H}_s$. Therefore, we can change the order of integration and differentiation.)

For a function $f \in \mathscr{H}_s$ with $\int_0^1 f(\boldsymbol{x}) \,\mathrm{d}x_i = 0$ for $i \in \mathfrak{u}$ and $\frac{\partial f}{\partial x_i} = 0$ for $i \notin \mathfrak{u}$, we then have

$$f(\boldsymbol{y}) = \langle f, K(\cdot, \boldsymbol{y})\rangle = \langle f, K_{\mathfrak{u}}(\cdot, \boldsymbol{y}_{\mathfrak{u}})\rangle = \langle f, K_{\mathfrak{u}}(\cdot, \boldsymbol{y}_{\mathfrak{u}})\rangle_{\mathfrak{u}}.$$

Thus,

$$\mathscr{H}_{\mathfrak{u}} = \left\{ f \in \mathscr{H}_s : \int_0^1 f(\boldsymbol{x}) \,\mathrm{d}x_i = 0 \text{ for } i \in \mathfrak{u} \text{ and } \frac{\partial f}{\partial x_i} = 0 \text{ for } i \notin \mathfrak{u} \right\}$$

and for $f, g \in \mathscr{H}_{\mathfrak{u}}$ we have the inner product

$$\langle f, g\rangle_{\mathfrak{u}} = \int_{[0,1]^{|\mathfrak{u}|}} \left(\int_{[0,1]^{s-|\mathfrak{u}|}} \frac{\partial^{|\mathfrak{u}|} f}{\partial \boldsymbol{x}_{\mathfrak{u}}}(\boldsymbol{x}) \,\mathrm{d}\boldsymbol{x}_{\mathcal{I}_s \setminus \mathfrak{u}} \right) \left(\int_{[0,1]^{s-|\mathfrak{u}|}} \frac{\partial^{|\mathfrak{u}|} g}{\partial \boldsymbol{x}_{\mathfrak{u}}}(\boldsymbol{x}) \,\mathrm{d}\boldsymbol{x}_{\mathcal{I}_s \setminus \mathfrak{u}} \right) \mathrm{d}\boldsymbol{x}_{\mathfrak{u}}. \tag{2.13}$$

As for $f \in \mathscr{H}_{\mathfrak{u}}$ and $g \in \mathscr{H}_s$ we have $\langle f, g\rangle = \langle f, g\rangle_{\mathfrak{u}}$, $K_{\mathfrak{u}}(\cdot, \boldsymbol{y}_{\mathfrak{u}}) \in \mathscr{H}_{\mathfrak{u}}$ and $f(\boldsymbol{y}_{\mathfrak{u}}) = \langle f, K_{\mathfrak{u}}(\cdot, \boldsymbol{y}_{\mathfrak{u}})\rangle_{\mathfrak{u}}$, it follows that $K_{\mathfrak{u}}$ is the reproducing kernel for $\mathscr{H}_{\mathfrak{u}}$ with inner product $\langle \cdot, \cdot \rangle_{\mathfrak{u}}$.

Let $f \in \mathscr{H}_s$ and again let

$$f_{\mathfrak{u}}(\boldsymbol{y}) = \langle f, K_{\mathfrak{u}}(\cdot, \boldsymbol{y})\rangle,$$

then $f_{\mathfrak{u}} \in \mathscr{H}_{\mathfrak{u}}$ and we have

$$\sum_{\mathfrak{u} \subseteq \mathcal{I}_s} f_{\mathfrak{u}}(\boldsymbol{y}_{\mathfrak{u}}) = \sum_{\mathfrak{u} \subseteq \mathcal{I}_s} \langle f, K_{\mathfrak{u}}(\cdot, \boldsymbol{y}_{\mathfrak{u}})\rangle = \left\langle f, \sum_{\mathfrak{u} \subseteq \mathcal{I}_s} K_{\mathfrak{u}}(\cdot, \boldsymbol{y}_{\mathfrak{u}}) \right\rangle = \langle f, K(\cdot, \boldsymbol{y})\rangle = f(\boldsymbol{y}).$$

Further, for $f, g \in \mathscr{H}_s$ we also have

$$\langle f, g\rangle = \sum_{\mathfrak{u} \subseteq \mathcal{I}_s} \langle f, g\rangle_{\mathfrak{u}} = \sum_{\mathfrak{u} \subseteq \mathcal{I}_s} \langle f_{\mathfrak{u}}, g_{\mathfrak{u}}\rangle_{\mathfrak{u}}.$$

The first equality follows from (2.12) and (2.13) and the second equality follows as, for $\mathfrak{v} \neq \mathfrak{u}$ and $f_{\mathfrak{v}} \in \mathscr{H}_{\mathfrak{v}}$, we have $\langle f_{\mathfrak{v}}, g\rangle_{\mathfrak{u}} = 0$ for all $g \in \mathscr{H}_s$. In particular,

we have

$$\|f\|^2 = \sum_{\mathfrak{u} \subseteq \mathcal{I}_s} \|f_{\mathfrak{u}}\|_{\mathfrak{u}}^2. \tag{2.14}$$

2.5.3 ANOVA decomposition

The orthogonal decomposition of $\mathcal{H}_s$ considered in the previous section has some other interesting properties, as shown in [54, Section 6]. The functions $f_{\mathfrak{u}}$ can also be found in an inductive way by using the properties $\int_0^1 f_{\mathfrak{u}}(\boldsymbol{x})\,\mathrm{d}x_i = 0$ for $i \in \mathfrak{u}$ and $\int_0^1 f_{\mathfrak{u}}(\boldsymbol{x})\,\mathrm{d}x_i = f_{\mathfrak{u}}(\boldsymbol{x})$ for $i \notin \mathfrak{u}$ ($f_{\mathfrak{u}}$ does not depend on x_i for $i \notin \mathfrak{u}$). Thus,

$$\int_{[0,1]^{s-|\mathfrak{u}|}} f(\boldsymbol{x})\,\mathrm{d}\boldsymbol{x}_{\mathcal{I}_s\setminus\mathfrak{u}} = \sum_{\mathfrak{v}\subseteq\mathcal{I}_s} \int_{[0,1]^{s-|\mathfrak{u}|}} f_{\mathfrak{v}}(\boldsymbol{x}_{\mathfrak{v}})\,\mathrm{d}\boldsymbol{x}_{\mathcal{I}_s\setminus\mathfrak{u}} = \sum_{\mathfrak{v}\subseteq\mathfrak{u}} f_{\mathfrak{v}}(\boldsymbol{x}_{\mathfrak{v}}).$$

Starting with $\mathfrak{u} = \emptyset$, we can obtain the functions $f_{\mathfrak{u}}$ inductively: $f_\emptyset = \int_{[0,1]^s} f(\boldsymbol{x})\,\mathrm{d}\boldsymbol{x}$ and if $f_{\mathfrak{v}}$ is known for all $\mathfrak{v} \subset \mathfrak{u}$, we obtain

$$f_{\mathfrak{u}}(\boldsymbol{x}_{\mathfrak{u}}) = \int_{[0,1]^{s-|\mathfrak{u}|}} f(\boldsymbol{x})\,\mathrm{d}\boldsymbol{x}_{\mathcal{I}_s\setminus\mathfrak{u}} - \sum_{\mathfrak{v}\subset\mathfrak{u}} f_{\mathfrak{v}}(\boldsymbol{x}_{\mathfrak{v}}).$$

Example 2.22 Let $f(x_1, x_2) = \mathrm{e}^{x_1} - x_2 + x_1 \sin(\pi x_2)$. Then

$$\begin{aligned} f_\emptyset = \int_0^1\int_0^1 f(x_1,x_2)\,\mathrm{d}x_1\,\mathrm{d}x_2 &= \mathrm{e} - 1 - 1/2 + \frac{1}{2\pi}(\cos(0) - \cos(\pi)) \\ &= \mathrm{e} - 3/2 + \frac{1}{\pi}. \end{aligned}$$

Now we can calculate $f_{\{1\}}$ and $f_{\{2\}}$, we have

$$f_{\{1\}}(x_1) = \int_0^1 f(x_1,x_2)\,\mathrm{d}x_2 - f_\emptyset = \mathrm{e}^{x_1} + \frac{2x_1}{\pi} - \mathrm{e} + 1 - \frac{1}{\pi}$$

and

$$f_{\{2\}}(x_2) = \int_0^1 f(x_1,x_2)\,\mathrm{d}x_1 - f_\emptyset = -x_2 + \frac{1}{2}\sin(\pi x_2) + \frac{1}{2} - \frac{1}{\pi}.$$

Finally, we can calculate $f_{\{1,2\}}$, we have

$$\begin{aligned} f_{\{1,2\}}(x_1,x_2) &= f(x_1,x_2) - f_{\{1\}}(x_1) - f_{\{2\}}(x_2) - f_\emptyset \\ &= (x_1 - 1/2)\sin(\pi x_2) + \frac{1-2x_1}{\pi}. \end{aligned}$$

The variance Var of a function f is given by $\mathrm{Var}(f) = \int_{[0,1]^s} f^2(\boldsymbol{x})\,\mathrm{d}\boldsymbol{x} - \left(\int_{[0,1]^s} f(\boldsymbol{x})\,\mathrm{d}\boldsymbol{x}\right)^2$. Using the decomposition of f, we obtain

$$\begin{aligned}\mathrm{Var}(f) &= \int_{[0,1]^s} f^2(\boldsymbol{x})\,\mathrm{d}\boldsymbol{x} - \left(\int_{[0,1]^s} f(\boldsymbol{x})\,\mathrm{d}\boldsymbol{x}\right)^2 \\ &= \sum_{\emptyset \neq \mathfrak{u}, \mathfrak{v} \subseteq \mathcal{I}_s} \int_{[0,1]^s} f_{\mathfrak{u}}(\boldsymbol{x}_{\mathfrak{u}}) f_{\mathfrak{v}}(\boldsymbol{x}_{\mathfrak{v}})\,\mathrm{d}\boldsymbol{x}.\end{aligned}$$

Using the fact that $\int_0^1 f_{\mathfrak{u}}(\boldsymbol{x}_{\mathfrak{u}})\,\mathrm{d}x_i = 0$ for $i \in \mathfrak{u}$, we obtain $\int_{[0,1]^s} f_{\mathfrak{u}}(\boldsymbol{x}_{\mathfrak{u}}) f_{\mathfrak{v}}(\boldsymbol{x}_{\mathfrak{v}})\,\mathrm{d}\boldsymbol{x} = 0$ for $\mathfrak{u} \neq \mathfrak{v}$. Further, $\int_{[0,1]^s} f_{\mathfrak{u}}(\boldsymbol{x}_{\mathfrak{u}}) f_{\mathfrak{u}}(\boldsymbol{x}_{\mathfrak{u}})\,\mathrm{d}\boldsymbol{x} = \int_{[0,1]^{|\mathfrak{u}|}} f_{\mathfrak{u}}^2(\boldsymbol{x}_{\mathfrak{u}})\,\mathrm{d}\boldsymbol{x}_{\mathfrak{u}} = \mathrm{Var}(f_{\mathfrak{u}})$, since $\int_{[0,1]^s} f_{\mathfrak{u}}(\boldsymbol{x}_{\mathfrak{u}})\,\mathrm{d}\boldsymbol{x}_{\mathfrak{u}} = 0$. Therefore and since $\mathrm{Var}(f_\emptyset) = 0$, we obtain

$$\mathrm{Var}(f) = \sum_{\mathfrak{u} \subseteq \mathcal{I}_s} \mathrm{Var}(f_{\mathfrak{u}}). \tag{2.15}$$

ANOVA decomposition stands for *ANalysis Of VAriance*. The decomposition of f as used above can be used to analyse the contributions of lower dimensional projections $f_{\mathfrak{u}}$ to the total variance via the formula $\mathrm{Var}(f) = \sum_{\mathfrak{u} \subseteq \mathcal{I}_s} \mathrm{Var}(f_{\mathfrak{u}})$.

Example 2.23 We calculate the variances of f, $f_{\{1\}}$, $f_{\{2\}}$, $f_{\{1,2\}}$ from Example 2.22. We have

$$\begin{aligned}\mathrm{Var}(f) &= \frac{-4 - 8\,\mathrm{e}\pi + 24\,\pi - 2\,\pi^2\mathrm{e}^2 - 5\,\pi^2 + 8\,\mathrm{e}\pi^2}{4\pi^2}, \\ \mathrm{Var}(f_{\{1\}}) &= \frac{12\,\mathrm{e}\pi^2 + 36\,\pi - 9\,\pi^2 - 3\,\pi^2\mathrm{e}^2 + 2 - 12\,\mathrm{e}\pi}{6\pi^2}, \\ \mathrm{Var}(f_{\{2\}}) &= \frac{-24 + 5\,\pi^2}{24\pi^2}, \\ \mathrm{Var}(f_{\{1,2\}}) &= \frac{-8 + \pi^2}{24\pi^2},\end{aligned}$$

and therefore, $\mathrm{Var}(f) = \mathrm{Var}(f_{\{1\}}) + \mathrm{Var}(f_{\{2\}}) + \mathrm{Var}(f_{\{1,2\}})$.

2.5.4 Weighted reproducing kernel Hilbert spaces

Equation (2.14) now holds the key to weighted reproducing kernel Hilbert spaces. Recall that for the worst-case error, we consider all functions in the unit ball of the space, i.e. all $f \in \mathscr{H}_s$ with $\|f\| \le 1$. Using (2.14), this amounts to $\sum_{\mathfrak{u} \subseteq \mathcal{I}_s} \|f_{\mathfrak{u}}\|_{\mathfrak{u}}^2 \le 1$, where $f(\boldsymbol{x}) = \sum_{\mathfrak{u} \subseteq \mathcal{I}_s} f_{\mathfrak{u}}(\boldsymbol{x}_{\mathfrak{u}})$.

The worst-case error is used as a criterion for choosing the quadrature points. By a small change to the norm, we can change the shape of the unit ball considered in the worst-case error, and thereby also the criterion used for measuring the quality of quadrature points.

It has been observed that many integrands from applications seem to vary more in lower dimensional projections than higher dimensional ones. We model this behaviour now in the following way: we can write $f(\boldsymbol{x}) = \sum_{\mathfrak{u}\subseteq\mathcal{I}_s} f_{\mathfrak{u}}(\boldsymbol{x}_{\mathfrak{u}})$. Some of the $f_{\mathfrak{u}}$ are 'small', which we can now make more precise by saying that $\|f_{\mathfrak{u}}\|_{\mathfrak{u}}$ is small compared with the norm of other projections. In order to change the unit ball such that only functions for which $\|f_{\mathfrak{u}}\|_{\mathfrak{u}}$ is small are contained in it, we multiply $\|f_{\mathfrak{u}}\|_{\mathfrak{u}}$ by a real number $\gamma_{\mathfrak{u}}$. Let $\boldsymbol{\gamma} := \{\gamma_{\mathfrak{u}} : \mathfrak{u} \subseteq \mathcal{I}_s\}$. Then we define a new 'weighted' norm by

$$\|f\|_{\boldsymbol{\gamma}}^2 = \sum_{\mathfrak{u}\subseteq\mathcal{I}_s} \gamma_{\mathfrak{u}}^{-1} \|f_{\mathfrak{u}}\|_{\mathfrak{u}}^2.$$

The condition $\|f\|_{\boldsymbol{\gamma}} \le 1$ in the definition of the worst-case error (Definition 2.10) implies that if $\gamma_{\mathfrak{u}}$ is small, $\|f_{\mathfrak{u}}\|$ also has to be small in order for f to satisfy $\|f\|_{\boldsymbol{\gamma}} \le 1$. The corresponding inner product then has the form

$$\langle f, g\rangle_{\boldsymbol{\gamma}} = \sum_{\mathfrak{u}\subseteq\mathcal{I}_s} \gamma_{\mathfrak{u}}^{-1} \langle f, g\rangle_{\mathfrak{u}}. \tag{2.16}$$

We now work out how this modification affects the theory that we have already established. The Hilbert space $\mathscr{H}_{\boldsymbol{\gamma}}$ with inner product (2.16) is a reproducing kernel Hilbert space with reproducing kernel

$$K_{\boldsymbol{\gamma}}(\boldsymbol{x}, \boldsymbol{y}) = \sum_{\mathfrak{u}\subseteq\mathcal{I}_s} \gamma_{\mathfrak{u}} K_{\mathfrak{u}}(\boldsymbol{x}_{\mathfrak{u}}, \boldsymbol{y}_{\mathfrak{u}}).$$

Indeed, we have $K_{\boldsymbol{\gamma}}(\cdot, \boldsymbol{y}) \in \mathscr{H}_{\boldsymbol{\gamma}}$ and

$$\langle f, K_{\boldsymbol{\gamma}}(\cdot, \boldsymbol{y})\rangle_{\boldsymbol{\gamma}} = \sum_{\mathfrak{u}\subseteq\mathcal{I}_s} \gamma_{\mathfrak{u}}^{-1} \langle f, \gamma_{\mathfrak{u}} K_{\mathfrak{u}}(\cdot, \boldsymbol{y}_{\mathfrak{u}})\rangle_{\mathfrak{u}} = \sum_{\mathfrak{u}\subseteq\mathcal{I}_s} \langle f, K_{\mathfrak{u}}(\cdot, \boldsymbol{y}_{\mathfrak{u}})\rangle_{\mathfrak{u}} = f(\boldsymbol{y}).$$

Using Proposition 2.11, we obtain the weighted square worst-case error

$$\begin{aligned} e^2(\mathscr{H}_{\boldsymbol{\gamma}}, \mathcal{P}) &= \frac{1}{N^2} \sum_{m,n=0}^{N-1} \sum_{\emptyset\ne\mathfrak{u}\subseteq\mathcal{I}_s} \gamma_{\mathfrak{u}} K_{\mathfrak{u}}(\boldsymbol{x}_m, \boldsymbol{x}_n) \\ &= \frac{1}{N^2} \sum_{m,n=0}^{N-1} \sum_{\emptyset\ne\mathfrak{u}\subseteq\mathcal{I}_s} \gamma_{\mathfrak{u}} \prod_{i\in\mathfrak{u}} (B_1(x_{m,i}) B_1(x_{n,i}) + B_2(|x_{m,i} - x_{n,i}|)/2) \\ &= \sum_{\emptyset\ne\mathfrak{u}\subseteq\mathcal{I}_s} \gamma_{\mathfrak{u}} \frac{1}{N^2} \sum_{m,n=0}^{N-1} \prod_{i\in\mathfrak{u}} (B_1(x_{m,i}) B_1(x_{n,i}) + B_2(|x_{m,i} - x_{n,i}|)/2). \end{aligned}$$

The worst-case error is a measure for the quality of the quadrature points. Observe that $\frac{1}{N^2} \sum_{m,n=0}^{N-1} \prod_{i\in\mathfrak{u}} (B_1(x_{m,i}) B_1(x_{n,i}) + B_2(|x_{m,i} - x_{n,i}|)/2)$ is the worst-case error for the reproducing kernel Hilbert space $\mathscr{H}_{\mathfrak{u}}$ and hence measures the quality of the projection of the quadrature points onto the coordinates in $\mathfrak{u}$.

Recall that if for some $\emptyset \neq \mathfrak{u} \subseteq \mathcal{I}_s$ the value of $\gamma_{\mathfrak{u}}$ is small, then $\| f_{\mathfrak{u}} \|_{\mathfrak{u}}$ also has to be small. On the other hand, if $\gamma_{\mathfrak{u}}$ is small (compared to $\gamma_{\mathfrak{v}}$ for $\mathfrak{v} \neq \mathfrak{u}$), then $\gamma_{\mathfrak{u}} \frac{1}{N^2} \sum_{m,n=0}^{N-1} \prod_{i \in \mathfrak{u}} (B_1(x_{m,i}) B_1(x_{n,i}) + B_2(|x_{m,i} - x_{n,i}|)/2)$ is also small, regardless of whether $\frac{1}{N^2} \sum_{m,n=0}^{N-1} \prod_{i \in \mathfrak{u}} (B_1(x_{m,i}) B_1(x_{n,i}) + B_2(|x_{m,i} - x_{n,i}|)/2)$ is large or small. This makes sense, since if $\| f_{\mathfrak{u}} \|$ is small, we do not need to focus on approximating the integral $\int_{[0,1]^{|\mathfrak{u}|}} f_{\mathfrak{u}}(\boldsymbol{x}_{\mathfrak{u}}) \,\mathrm{d}\boldsymbol{x}_{\mathfrak{u}}$ and so the quality of the approximation does not matter much.

In the next chapter, we look more closely at the geometrical properties of the discrepancy.

Exercises

2.1 Calculate the star discrepancy and the L_2-discrepancy of the point sets
- $\mathcal{P}_1 = \{\frac{n}{N} : 0 \le n \le N-1\}$,
- $\mathcal{P}_2 = \{\frac{2n+1}{2N} : 0 \le n \le N-1\}$,
- $\mathcal{P}_3 = \{\frac{n}{2N} : 0 \le n \le N-1\}$.

2.2 Let $P = \{p(x) = a_0 + a_1 x + \cdots + a_r x^r : a_0, \ldots, a_r \in \mathbb{R}\}$ be the space of all polynomials of degree at most r. We define an inner product on this space by: for $p(x) = a_0 + a_1 x + \cdots + a_r x^r$ and $q(x) = b_0 + b_1 x + \cdots + b_r x^r$, let $\langle p, q \rangle = a_0 b_0 + a_1 b_1 + \cdots + a_r b_r$. What is the reproducing kernel for this space? Prove properties P1–P5 for this kernel.

2.3 Let $P = \{f(x) = a_0 + a_1 \mathrm{e}^{2\pi \mathrm{i} x} + \cdots + a_r \mathrm{e}^{2\pi \mathrm{i} r x} : a_0, a_1, \ldots, a_r \in \mathbb{C}\}$ be the space of all trigonometric polynomials of degree at most r. We define an inner product on this space by: for $f(x) = a_0 + a_1 \mathrm{e}^{2\pi \mathrm{i} x} + \cdots + a_r \mathrm{e}^{2\pi \mathrm{i} r x}$ and $g(x) = b_0 + b_1 \mathrm{e}^{2\pi \mathrm{i} x} + \cdots + b_r \mathrm{e}^{2\pi \mathrm{i} r x}$, let $\langle f, g \rangle = a_0 b_0 + a_1 b_1 + \cdots + a_r b_r$. What is the reproducing kernel for this space? Prove properties P1–P5 for this kernel.

2.4 The one-dimensional Korobov space $\mathscr{H}_{\mathrm{kor},\alpha}$ for real $\alpha > 1$ consists of all one-periodic L_1-functions $f : [0,1] \to \mathbb{C}$ with absolute convergent Fourier series representation such that $|\widehat{f}(h)| = O(1/\max(1, |h|^\alpha))$ for integers h. The reproducing kernel for the Korobov space is given by $K(x, y) = 1 + \sum_{h \in \mathbb{Z}, h \neq 0} |h|^{-\alpha} \mathrm{e}^{2\pi \mathrm{i} h (x-y)}$. What is the inner product for this space?

2.5 Verify Remark 2.6, by showing that $K(x, y) := \min(1-x, 1-y)$ satisfies P1–P5 for a suitable inner product.

2.6 Verify that for $y \neq x_0, \ldots, x_{N-1}$ we have $\Delta_{\mathcal{P}}(y) = \frac{\mathrm{d}}{\mathrm{d}y} \Big(\int_0^1 K(x, y) \,\mathrm{d}x - \frac{1}{N} \sum_{n=0}^{N-1} K(x_n, y) \Big)$, where $\Delta_{\mathcal{P}}$ is the discrepancy function and $K(x, y) = 1 + \min(1-x, 1-y)$.

2.7 Let $\mathscr{H}_{\mathrm{wal}}$ be the Walsh space as defined in Example 2.8. Show that the worst-case error for a QMC rule using a point set $\mathcal{P} = \{x_0, \ldots, x_{N-1}\}$ is given by

$$e^2(\mathscr{H}_{\mathrm{wal}}, \mathcal{P}) = \sum_{k=1}^{\infty} r_{\mathrm{wal},b,\alpha}(k) \left| \frac{1}{N} \sum_{n=0}^{N-1} {}_b\mathrm{wal}_k(x_n) \right|^2 .$$

Hint: See Appendix A for more information on Walsh functions; see [50, Sections 2 and 4] for more information on the reproducing kernel Hilbert space generated by K and numerical integration therein.

2.8 Evaluate the integral $\int_{[0,1]^s} |\Delta_{\mathcal{P}}(\boldsymbol{x})|^2 \, \mathrm{d}\boldsymbol{x}$ to obtain Proposition 2.15.

2.9 For $s = 2$, prove Proposition 2.17 directly by evaluating the integrals on the right-hand side of the formula.

2.10 Study the proof of the classical Koksma–Hlawka inequality in [130, pp. 143–153].

2.11 Check that for $K(x, y) = 1 + B_1(x)B_1(y) + B_2(|x - y|)/2$, with $B_1(t) = t - 1/2$ and $B_2(t) = t^2 - t + 1/6$ and an inner product $\langle f, g \rangle = \int_0^1 f(y) \, \mathrm{d}y \int_0^1 g(y) \, \mathrm{d}y + \int_0^1 f'(y)g'(y) \, \mathrm{d}y$, we always have $\langle f, K(\cdot, y) \rangle = f(y)$ and thus conclude that K is the reproducing kernel of the Hilbert space of absolutely continuous functions with square integrable first derivative.

2.12 Obtain a Warnock type formula, Hlawka identity and Koksma–Hlawka inequality for the reproducing kernel

$$K(\boldsymbol{x}, \boldsymbol{y}) = \prod_{i=1}^{s} (1 + B_1(x_i)B_1(y_i) + B_2(|x_i - y_i|)/2),$$

where $B_1(t) = t - 1/2$ and $B_2(t) = t^2 - t + 1/6$ (this is the kernel considered in Section 2.5). The inner product in the associated reproducing kernel Hilbert space is given by

$$\langle f, g \rangle = \sum_{\mathfrak{u} \subseteq \mathcal{I}_s} \int_{[0,1]^{|\mathfrak{u}|}} \left(\int_{[0,1]^{s-|\mathfrak{u}|}} \frac{\partial^{|\mathfrak{u}|} f}{\partial \boldsymbol{x}_{\mathfrak{u}}}(\boldsymbol{x}) \, \mathrm{d}\boldsymbol{x}_{\mathcal{I}_s \setminus \mathfrak{u}} \right) \times \left(\int_{[0,1]^{s-|\mathfrak{u}|}} \frac{\partial^{|\mathfrak{u}|} g}{\partial \boldsymbol{x}_{\mathfrak{u}}}(\boldsymbol{x}) \, \mathrm{d}\boldsymbol{x}_{\mathcal{I}_s \setminus \mathfrak{u}} \right) \mathrm{d}\boldsymbol{x}_{\mathfrak{u}}.$$

Note: The discrepancy function differs from the discrepancy function in Definition 2.13 in this case. See [251] for more information on this space.

2.13 The s-dimensional Korobov space $\mathcal{H}_{\mathrm{kor},s,\alpha}$, $s \in \mathbb{N}$ and $\alpha > 1$ is the reproducing kernel Hilbert space of complex-valued functions of period one which is defined by

$$K_\alpha(\boldsymbol{x}, \boldsymbol{y}) = \sum_{\boldsymbol{h} \in \mathbb{Z}^s} \frac{1}{r_\alpha(\boldsymbol{h})} \mathrm{e}^{2\pi \mathrm{i} \boldsymbol{h} \cdot (\boldsymbol{x} - \boldsymbol{y})},$$

where $r_\alpha(\boldsymbol{h}) = \prod_{i=1}^{s} (\max(1, |h_i|))^\alpha$. The inner-product is given by

$$\langle f, g \rangle_\alpha = \sum_{\boldsymbol{h} \in \mathbb{Z}^s} r_\alpha(\boldsymbol{h}) \widehat{f}(\boldsymbol{h}) \overline{\widehat{g}(\boldsymbol{h})},$$

where $\widehat{f}(\boldsymbol{h}) = \int_{[0,1]^s} f(\boldsymbol{x}) \mathrm{e}^{-2\pi \mathrm{i} \boldsymbol{h} \cdot \boldsymbol{x}} \, \mathrm{d}\boldsymbol{x}$.

Show that the worst-case integration error for a QMC rule in $\mathcal{H}_{\mathrm{kor},s,\alpha}$ using $\mathcal{P} = \{\boldsymbol{x}_0, \ldots, \boldsymbol{x}_{N-1}\}$ is given by

$$e^2(\mathcal{H}_{\mathrm{kor},s,\alpha}, \mathcal{P}) = \sum_{\boldsymbol{h} \in \mathbb{Z}^s \setminus \{\boldsymbol{0}\}} \frac{1}{r_\alpha(\boldsymbol{h})} \left| \frac{1}{N} \sum_{n=0}^{N-1} \mathrm{e}^{2\pi \mathrm{i} \boldsymbol{h} \cdot \boldsymbol{x}_n} \right|^2.$$

2.14 Let $\widetilde{e}^2_{\alpha,N} := \int_{[0,1]^{Ns}} e^2(\mathscr{H}_{\mathrm{kor},s,\alpha}, \{\boldsymbol{x}_0, \ldots, \boldsymbol{x}_{N-1}\})\,\mathrm{d}\boldsymbol{x}_0 \cdots \mathrm{d}\boldsymbol{x}_{N-1}$. Show that for $\alpha > 1$, we have

$$\widetilde{e}^2_{\alpha,N} \le \mathrm{e}^{2\zeta(\alpha)s}/N,$$

where $\zeta(\alpha) = \sum_{j=1}^{\infty} j^{-\alpha}$.

Hint: See [250, Theorem 1] or reference [103].

2.15 Let $s \ge 1$ and $b \ge 2$ be integers, $\alpha > 1$ a real and $\boldsymbol{\gamma} = (\gamma_i)_{i\ge 1}$ be a sequence of non-negative reals. The s-dimensional weighted version of the Walsh space from Example 2.8 is the reproducing kernel Hilbert space $\mathscr{H}_{\mathrm{wal},s,b,\alpha,\boldsymbol{\gamma}}$ of b-adic Walsh series $f(\boldsymbol{x}) = \sum_{\boldsymbol{k}\in\mathbb{N}_0^s} \widehat{f}(\boldsymbol{k})\, {}_b\mathrm{wal}_{\boldsymbol{k}}(\boldsymbol{x})$ with reproducing kernel defined by

$$K_{\mathrm{wal},s,b,\alpha,\boldsymbol{\gamma}}(\boldsymbol{x},\boldsymbol{y}) = \sum_{\boldsymbol{k}\in\mathbb{N}_0^s} r_{\mathrm{wal},b,\alpha}(\boldsymbol{k},\boldsymbol{\gamma})\, {}_b\mathrm{wal}_{\boldsymbol{k}}(\boldsymbol{x}\ominus\boldsymbol{y}),$$

where for $\boldsymbol{k} = (k_1,\ldots,k_s)$, we put $r_{\mathrm{wal},b,\alpha}(\boldsymbol{k},\boldsymbol{\gamma}) = \prod_{i=1}^{s} r_{\mathrm{wal},b,\alpha}(k_i,\gamma_i)$ and for $k \in \mathbb{N}_0$ and $\gamma > 0$, we write

$$r_{\mathrm{wal},b,\alpha}(k,\gamma) = \begin{cases} 1 & \text{if } k = 0, \\ \gamma b^{-\alpha a} & \text{if } k = \kappa_0 + \kappa_1 b + \cdots + \kappa_a b^a \text{ and } \kappa_a \ne 0. \end{cases}$$

The inner product is given by

$$\langle f, g\rangle = \sum_{\boldsymbol{k}\in\mathbb{N}_0^s} r_{\mathrm{wal},b,\alpha}(\boldsymbol{k},\boldsymbol{\gamma})^{-1} \widehat{f}(\boldsymbol{k})\overline{\widehat{g}(\boldsymbol{k})}.$$

Show that the worst-case integration error for a QMC rule in $\mathscr{H}_{\mathrm{wal},s,b,\alpha,\boldsymbol{\gamma}}$ using $\mathcal{P} = \{\boldsymbol{x}_0,\ldots,\boldsymbol{x}_{N-1}\}$ is given by

$$e^2(\mathscr{H}_{\mathrm{wal},s,b,\alpha,\boldsymbol{\gamma}}, \mathcal{P}) = \sum_{\boldsymbol{k}\in\mathbb{N}_0^s\setminus\{\boldsymbol{0}\}} r_{\mathrm{wal},b,\alpha}(\boldsymbol{k},\boldsymbol{\gamma}) \left| \frac{1}{N}\sum_{n=0}^{N-1} {}_b\mathrm{wal}_{\boldsymbol{k}}(\boldsymbol{x}_n)\right|^2.$$

Hint: Compare with Exercise 2.7. See [50, Sections 2 and 4].

2.16 Let $\widetilde{e}^2_{\alpha,\boldsymbol{\gamma},N} := \int_{[0,1]^{Ns}} e^2(\mathscr{H}_{\mathrm{wal},s,b,\alpha,\boldsymbol{\gamma}}, \{\boldsymbol{x}_0,\ldots,\boldsymbol{x}_{N-1}\})\,\mathrm{d}\boldsymbol{x}_0\cdots\mathrm{d}\boldsymbol{x}_{N-1}$. Show that for $\alpha > 1$, we have

$$\widetilde{e}^2_{\alpha,\boldsymbol{\gamma},N} \le \mathrm{e}^{\nu_b(\alpha)\sum_{i=1}^{s}\gamma_i}/N,$$

where $\nu_b(\alpha) = \sum_{k=1}^{\infty} b^{-\alpha a(k)} = \frac{b^\alpha(b-1)}{b^\alpha - b}$ and where $a(k) = a$ whenever $k = \kappa_0 + \kappa_1 b + \cdots + \kappa_a b^a$ with $\kappa_a \ne 0$.

Hint: See [50, Theorem 1].

2.17 Obtain an orthogonal decomposition of the reproducing kernel Hilbert space with reproducing kernel $K(x,y) = 1 + \min(1-x, 1-y)$. What are the spaces $\mathscr{H}_1$, $\mathscr{H}_2$, K_1, K_2 and respective inner products in this case?

2.18 Show that $\int_0^1 B_1(x)\,\mathrm{d}x = 0$ and $\int_0^1 B_2(x)\,\mathrm{d}x = 0$.

2.19 Let $f(x_1,x_2) = \mathrm{e}^{x_1 - x_2} - x_2\cos(\pi(x_1 + x_2^2))$. Calculate the ANOVA decomposition and the variances of $f_{\mathfrak{u}}$ and check that (2.15) holds.

2.20 Using similar arguments as in Sections 2.4 and 2.5, obtain a weighted version of the L_2-discrepancy, Warnock's formula, Hlawka's identity and the Koksma–Hlawka inequality for the reproducing kernel Hilbert space with reproducing kernel $K(\boldsymbol{x}, \boldsymbol{y}) = \prod_{i=1}^{s}(1 + \min(1 - x_i, 1 - y_i))$.
Hint: See [249].

2.21 Calculate the worst-case error for numerical integration in the reproducing kernel Hilbert space $\mathscr{H}_{\mathrm{u}}$ from Section 2.5.

3

Geometric discrepancy

In this chapter we introduce the theory of uniform distribution modulo one, for which the main motivation is the application of equidistributed points for numerical integration with QMC algorithms as we have seen in Chapter 2. The quality of the equidistribution of a point set is measured by the so-called discrepancy. We introduce different notions of discrepancy including the rather new weighted discrepancies now from the perspective of their geometrical properties. Because of their geometric interpretation, these discrepancies are also often called geometric discrepancies. We provide some classical as well as new results for geometric discrepancies. A standard reference for the theory of uniform distribution modulo one is the work of Kuipers and Niederreiter [130] to which we refer for a further, more detailed discussion (mainly from a number-theoretic viewpoint). See, also, the work of Drmota and Tichy [61].

3.1 Uniform distribution modulo one

As discussed in Chapter 2, we are concerned with approximating the integral of a function f over the s-dimensional unit-cube $[0, 1]^s$ with a QMC rule, which gives the average of function values $f(\boldsymbol{x}_n)$, where the points $\boldsymbol{x}_0, \ldots, \boldsymbol{x}_{N-1}$ are deterministically chosen sample points from the unit-cube; see (2.1).

For Riemann integrable functions f, we would, of course, demand that for growing N, the error of this approximation goes to zero, i.e. for a sequence $(\boldsymbol{x}_n)_{n\geq 0}$ in $[0, 1)^s$, we would like to have

$$\lim_{N\to\infty} \frac{1}{N} \sum_{n=0}^{N-1} f(\boldsymbol{x}_n) = \int_{[0,1]^s} f(\boldsymbol{x})\,\mathrm{d}\boldsymbol{x}. \tag{3.1}$$

Hence, the question arises as to how the sequence of sample points has to be chosen such that this is indeed the case. Let us, for a moment, assume that the function f

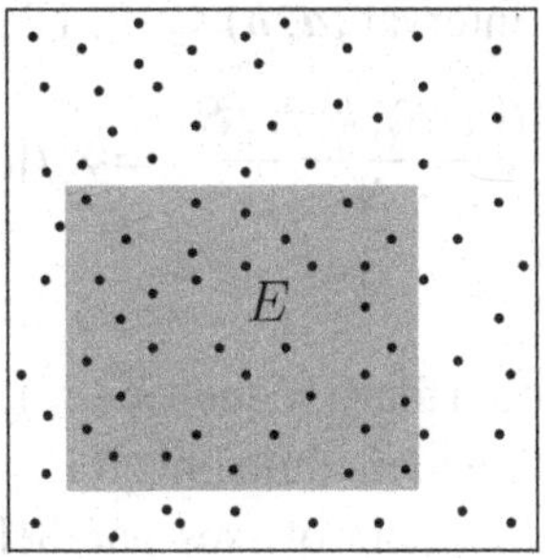

Figure 3.1 The number of points in E should be approximately $N\lambda_s(E)$.

to be integrated comes from the class of finite linear combinations of characteristic functions of axes-parallel rectangles. This is probably one of the simplest subclasses of Riemann-integrable functions. Then our question leads directly to a branch of number theory, namely to the theory of Uniform Distribution Modulo One, which goes back to a fundamental work by Weyl [265] from the year 1916.

Intuitively, one may consider a sequence of points in the unit-cube as uniformly distributed, if each set E from some suitable subclass of measurable sets contains (asymptotically) the right proportion of points, namely $N\lambda_s(E)$, where λ_s is the s-dimensional Lebesgue measure (see Figure 3.1). This leads to the following exact definition of uniform distribution modulo one.

For a sequence $\mathcal{S} = (\boldsymbol{x}_n)_{n\geq 0}$ in the s-dimensional unit-cube $[0, 1)^s$ and a subset E of $[0, 1]^s$, let $A(E, N, \mathcal{S})$ be the number of indices n, $0 \leq n \leq N-1$ for which the point $\boldsymbol{x}_n$ belongs to E; that is, $A(E, N, \mathcal{S}) = \sum_{n=0}^{N-1} \chi_E(\boldsymbol{x}_n)$.

Definition 3.1 A sequence $\mathcal{S} = (\boldsymbol{x}_n)_{n\geq 0}$ in the s-dimensional unit-cube $[0, 1)^s$ is said to be *uniformly distributed modulo one*, if for every interval $[\boldsymbol{a}, \boldsymbol{b}) \subseteq [0, 1]^s$, we have

$$\lim_{N\to\infty} \frac{A([\boldsymbol{a}, \boldsymbol{b}), N, \mathcal{S})}{N} = \lambda_s([\boldsymbol{a}, \boldsymbol{b})), \tag{3.2}$$

or in other words, if (3.1) holds for the characteristic function $\chi_{[\boldsymbol{a},\boldsymbol{b})}$ of any subinterval $[\boldsymbol{a}, \boldsymbol{b}) \subseteq [0, 1]^s$.

We remark that the choice of half-open intervals in the above definition and in the following is of minor importance.

Remark 3.2 There is also the stronger concept of well-distribution modulo one. For a sequence $\mathcal{S} = (\boldsymbol{x}_n)_{n\geq 0}$ in the s-dimensional unit-cube $[0, 1)^s$ and a subset E of $[0, 1]^s$, let $A(E, k, N, \mathcal{S})$ be the number of indices n, $k \leq n \leq k + N - 1$, for which the point $\boldsymbol{x}_n$ belongs to E. Then the sequence $\mathcal{S}$ is said to be *well-distributed* *modulo one*, if, for every sub-interval $[\boldsymbol{a}, \boldsymbol{b}) \subseteq [0,1]^s$, we have

$$\lim_{N\to\infty} \frac{A([\boldsymbol{a}, \boldsymbol{b}), k, N, \mathcal{S})}{N} = \lambda_s([\boldsymbol{a}, \boldsymbol{b})) \tag{3.3}$$

uniformly in $k = 0, 1, 2, \ldots$.

It is obvious from the definition that a sequence $(\boldsymbol{x}_n)_{n\geq 0}$ in the s-dimensional unit-cube $[0,1)^s$ is uniformly distributed modulo one, if (3.1) holds for every finite linear combination of characteristic functions of axes-parallel rectangles $f : [0,1]^s \to \mathbb{R}$.

Now it is well known from analysis that any Riemann integrable function on $[0,1]^s$ can be approximated arbitrary closely in $L_1([0,1]^s)$ by finite linear combinations of characteristic functions of axes-parallel rectangles. From this fact we obtain the following equivalence (see [130, Chapter 1, Corollary 1.1] for a more detailed proof).

Theorem 3.3 *A sequence $\mathcal{S} = (\boldsymbol{x}_n)_{n\geq 0}$ in $[0,1)^s$ is uniformly distributed modulo one, if and only if for every Riemann integrable function $f : [0,1]^s \to \mathbb{R}$ we have*

$$\lim_{N\to\infty} \frac{1}{N} \sum_{n=0}^{N-1} f(\boldsymbol{x}_n) = \int_{[0,1]^s} f(\boldsymbol{x})\, \mathrm{d}\boldsymbol{x}. \tag{3.4}$$

Note that there is no sequence such that (3.4) holds for all Lebesgue integrable functions. For a given sequence $\mathcal{S}$ with support $\overline{\mathcal{S}}$ the characteristic function of $[0,1]^s \setminus \overline{\mathcal{S}}$ is a counterexample. Furthermore, it was shown by de Bruijn and Post [31] that for every function $f \in L_1([0,1])$, which is not Riemann integrable, there exists a sequence which is uniformly distributed modulo one but for which (3.4) does not hold.

One can also show the following theorem whose proof is left as an exercise (see Exercise 3.4).

Theorem 3.4 *A sequence $(\boldsymbol{x}_n)_{n\geq 0}$ in the s-dimensional unit-cube $[0,1)^s$ is uniformly distributed modulo one, if and only if (3.4) holds for every continuous, complex-valued function $f : [0,1]^s \to \mathbb{C}$ with period one.*

For example, let $f : [0,1]^s \to \mathbb{C}$ be given by $f(\boldsymbol{x}) = \mathrm{e}^{2\pi \mathrm{i} \boldsymbol{h}\cdot\boldsymbol{x}}$, where $\boldsymbol{h} \in \mathbb{Z}^s$ is some s-dimensional integer vector. If a sequence $(\boldsymbol{x}_n)_{n\geq 0}$ in the s-dimensional unit-cube is uniformly distributed modulo one, then by Theorem 3.4 we have

$$\lim_{N\to\infty} \frac{1}{N} \sum_{n=0}^{N-1} \mathrm{e}^{2\pi \mathrm{i} \boldsymbol{h}\cdot\boldsymbol{x}_n} = \int_{[0,1]^s} \mathrm{e}^{2\pi \mathrm{i} \boldsymbol{h}\cdot\boldsymbol{x}}\, \mathrm{d}\boldsymbol{x},$$

where the last integral is 0 if $\boldsymbol{h} \in \mathbb{Z}^s \setminus \{\boldsymbol{0}\}$ and 1 if $\boldsymbol{h} = \boldsymbol{0}$. Astonishingly, the opposite is true as well: that is, the relation $\lim_{N\to\infty} \frac{1}{N} \sum_{n=0}^{N-1} \mathrm{e}^{2\pi \mathrm{i} \boldsymbol{h}\cdot\boldsymbol{x}_n} = 0$ for all

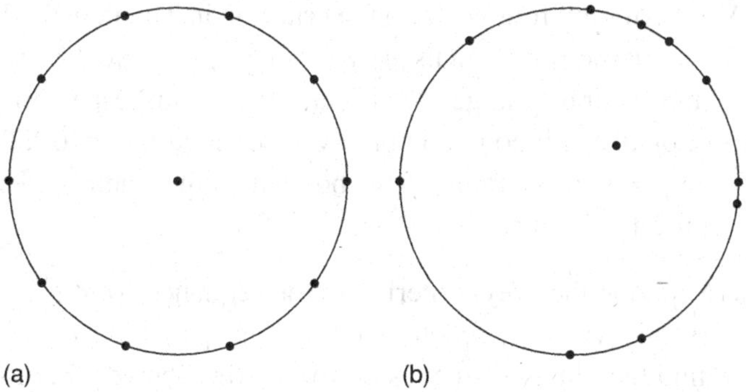

Figure 3.2 Ten points on the unit-circle. (a) The points are perfectly balanced and hence the centroid is exactly the origin. (b) For the points, the centroid is far away from the origin.

$\boldsymbol{h} \in \mathbb{Z}^s \setminus \{\boldsymbol{0}\}$ is also a sufficient condition for the sequence $(\boldsymbol{x}_n)_{n\geq 0}$ to be uniformly distributed modulo one (for $\boldsymbol{h} = \boldsymbol{0}$ we trivially have equality for any sequence). This fact is the famous Weyl criterion for uniform distribution modulo one.

Let us make this assertion a little more plausible. We consider the one-dimensional case and we identify the unit-interval $[0, 1)$ equipped with addition modulo one, i.e. $\mathbb{R}/\mathbb{Z}$, with the one-dimensional torus $(\mathbb{T}, \cdot)$, where $\mathbb{T} = \{z \in \mathbb{C} : |z| = 1\}$, via the group isomorphism $x \mapsto \mathrm{e}^{2\pi \mathrm{i} x}$. Let $(x_n)_{n\geq 0}$ be a sequence in $[0, 1)$. Then $\frac{1}{N}\sum_{n=0}^{N-1} \mathrm{e}^{2\pi \mathrm{i} x_n}$ is nothing other than the centroid of the N points $\mathrm{e}^{2\pi \mathrm{i} x_0}, \ldots, \mathrm{e}^{2\pi \mathrm{i} x_{N-1}} \in \mathbb{T}$. If the centroid is now close to the origin, then the points are evenly balanced on the torus $\mathbb{T}$, whereas this is not the case when the points are badly balanced (see Figure 3.2). However, this need not mean that the sequence $(x_n)_{n\geq 0}$ is uniformly distributed modulo one. For example, consider the case where $x_{2k} = 0$ and $x_{2k+1} = 1/2$ for all $k \in \mathbb{N}_0$. Then $(x_n)_{n\geq 0}$ is obviously not uniformly distributed, but the centroid of the points $\mathrm{e}^{2\pi \mathrm{i} x_0}, \ldots, \mathrm{e}^{2\pi \mathrm{i} x_{N-1}}$ tends to the origin when N grows to infinity. Thus, for uniform distribution one needs more than just the property that the centroid of the points, transformed onto the torus, is close to the origin. The Weyl criterion states that it is enough to demand this property for the sequence $(\{h x_n\})_{n\geq 0}$ for all integers $h \neq 0$.

Theorem 3.5 (Weyl criterion) *A sequence $\mathcal{S} = (\boldsymbol{x}_n)_{n\geq 0}$ in the s-dimensional unit-cube $[0, 1)^s$ is uniformly distributed modulo one, if and only if*

$$\lim_{N\to\infty} \frac{1}{N} \sum_{n=0}^{N-1} \mathrm{e}^{2\pi \mathrm{i} \boldsymbol{h}\cdot \boldsymbol{x}_n} = 0 \tag{3.5}$$

holds for all vectors $\boldsymbol{h} \in \mathbb{Z} \setminus \{\boldsymbol{0}\}$.

Proof The Weyl criterion follows from the criterion in Theorem 3.4 by using the fact that the trigonometric polynomials of the form $\sum_{|\boldsymbol{h}|_\infty \le R} a_{\boldsymbol{h}} \mathrm{e}^{2\pi \mathrm{i} \boldsymbol{h}\cdot \boldsymbol{x}}$ with complex coefficients $a_{\boldsymbol{h}}$ and arbitrarily large $R \in \mathbb{N}_0$ are dense with respect to the uniform norm in the space of all continuous, complex-valued functions on $[0,1]^s$. A detailed proof for the case $s = 1$ can be found in the book of Kuipers and Niederreiter [130, pp. 7, 8, Theorem 2.1]. See also [61]. □

Example 3.6 Applying the Weyl criterion to the sequence $(\{n\boldsymbol{\alpha}\})_{n\ge 0}$, where $\boldsymbol{\alpha} = (\alpha_1, \ldots, \alpha_s) \in \mathbb{R}^s$ and where $\{\cdot\}$ denotes the fractional part applied componentwise to a vector, we find that this sequence is uniformly distributed modulo one, if and only if the numbers $1, \alpha_1, \ldots, \alpha_s$ are linearly independent over $\mathbb{Q}$. Namely, if we assume that this holds true, then for each non-zero integer vector $\boldsymbol{h}$, we have $\boldsymbol{h} \cdot \boldsymbol{\alpha} \notin \mathbb{Z}$. Therefore, using the periodicity of the fractional part and the formula for a geometric sum, we have

$$\left|\sum_{n=0}^{N-1} \mathrm{e}^{2\pi \mathrm{i} \boldsymbol{h}\cdot \boldsymbol{x}_n}\right| = \left|\sum_{n=0}^{N-1} \mathrm{e}^{2\pi \mathrm{i} n \boldsymbol{h}\cdot \boldsymbol{\alpha}}\right| = \left|\frac{\mathrm{e}^{2\pi \mathrm{i} N \boldsymbol{h}\cdot \boldsymbol{\alpha}} - 1}{\mathrm{e}^{2\pi \mathrm{i} \boldsymbol{h}\cdot \boldsymbol{\alpha}} - 1}\right| \le \frac{2}{|\mathrm{e}^{2\pi \mathrm{i} \boldsymbol{h}\cdot \boldsymbol{\alpha}} - 1|}$$

and hence by the Weyl criterion it follows that the sequence $(\{n\boldsymbol{\alpha}\})_{n\ge 0}$ is uniformly distributed modulo one.

If, on the other hand, $\boldsymbol{h}^* \cdot \boldsymbol{\alpha} \in \mathbb{Z}$ for some integer vector $\boldsymbol{h}^* \ne \boldsymbol{0}$, then $\frac{1}{N}\sum_{n=0}^{N-1} \mathrm{e}^{2\pi \mathrm{i} n \boldsymbol{h}^*\cdot \boldsymbol{\alpha}} = \frac{1}{N}\sum_{n=0}^{N-1} 1 = 1$, which implies that the Weyl criterion is not satisfied and the sequence $(\{n\boldsymbol{\alpha}\})_{n\ge 0}$ is not uniformly distributed.

As Walsh functions play a very important part in this book, we also present the Weyl criterion for the Walsh function system in more detail. See Appendix A for the definition and basic properties of Walsh functions.

Before we state the Weyl criterion for the Walsh function system, let us consider an example in dimension $s = 1$ and base $b = 2$. For $k \in \mathbb{N}_0$ with 2-adic expansion $k = \kappa_0 + \kappa_1 2 + \cdots + \kappa_r 2^r$, the 2-adic Walsh function is given by ${}_2\mathrm{wal}_k(x) = (-1)^{\xi_1\kappa_0 + \cdots + \xi_{r+1}\kappa_r}$ for $x \in [0,1)$ with canonical 2-adic expansion $x = \xi_1 2^{-1} + \xi_2 2^{-2} + \cdots$. This is, of course, a step function defined on the unit-interval $[0,1)$; see Figure 3.3 for some examples. Hence, if a sequence $(x_n)_{n\ge 0}$ in $[0,1)$ is uniformly distributed modulo one, then we have $\lim_{N\to\infty} \frac{1}{N}\sum_{n=0}^{N-1} {}_2\mathrm{wal}_k(x_n) = \int_0^1 {}_2\mathrm{wal}_k(x)\,\mathrm{d}x$. This can be seen in the following way: if $k = 0$, then ${}_2\mathrm{wal}_k(x) = 1$ and $\int_0^1 {}_2\mathrm{wal}_k(x)\,\mathrm{d}x = 1$ and the equality holds trivially. If $k > 0$, then the last integral is zero, the Walsh function is 1 on a union of intervals with combined length $1/2$ and -1 on a union of intervals with combined length $1/2$. As $(x_n)_{n\ge 0}$ is uniformly distributed, it follows that the equality also holds for $k > 0$.

On the other hand, assume that for a given sequence $(x_n)_{n\ge 0}$ in $[0,1)$ we have $\lim_{N\to\infty} \frac{1}{N}\sum_{n=0}^{N-1} {}_2\mathrm{wal}_1(x_n) = 0 = \int_0^1 {}_2\mathrm{wal}_1(x)\,\mathrm{d}x$. The first Walsh function

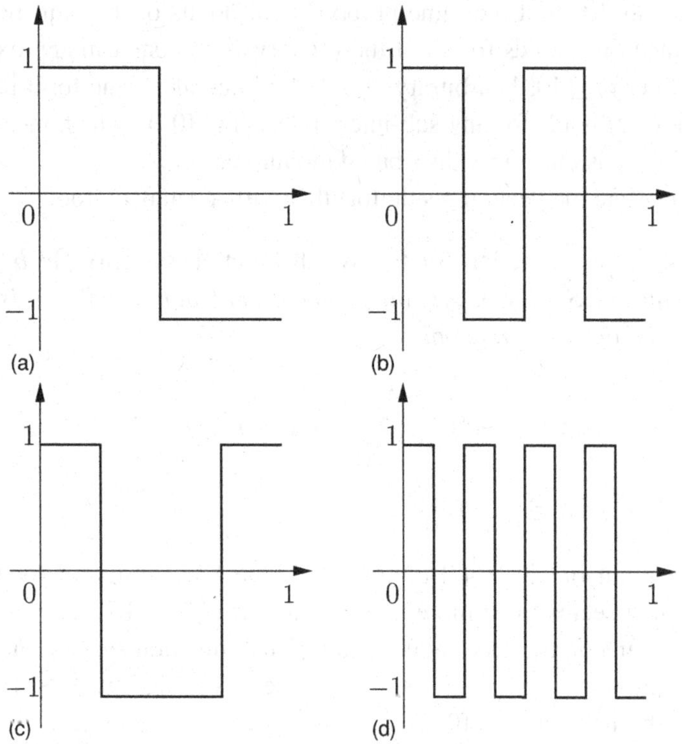

Figure 3.3 The 2-adic Walsh functions (a) ${}_2\mathrm{wal}_1(x)$, (b) ${}_2\mathrm{wal}_2(x)$, (c) ${}_2\mathrm{wal}_3(x)$ and (d) ${}_2\mathrm{wal}_4(x)$.

${}_2\mathrm{wal}_1(x)$ is constant with value 1 on the interval $[0, 1/2)$ and constant with value -1 on the interval $[1/2, 1)$; see Figure 3.3. Hence, asymptotically, in each of these two intervals we must have the same proportion of points of the sequence, namely 1/2. Assume, further, that we also have $\lim_{N\to\infty} \frac{1}{N} \sum_{n=0}^{N-1} {}_2\mathrm{wal}_k(x_n) = 0$ for $k \in \{2, 3\}$. The Walsh functions ${}_2\mathrm{wal}_2(x)$ and ${}_2\mathrm{wal}_3(x)$ are both constant on the intervals $J_1 = [0, 1/4)$, $J_2 = [1/4, 1/2)$, $J_3 = [1/2, 3/4)$ and $J_4 = [3/4, 1)$ of length 1/4; see again Figure 3.3. Let j_l be the proportion of points of the sequence $(x_n)_{n\ge 0}$ that belong to the interval J_l, $l \in \{1, 2, 3, 4\}$. Then we have from the above that $j_1 + j_2 = 1/2$ and $j_3 + j_4 = 1/2$, and from the asymptotic relation for the third and fourth Walsh function, we obtain (see Figure 3.3) that $j_1 - j_2 + j_3 - j_4 = 0$ and $j_1 - j_2 - j_3 + j_4 = 0$. From these four equations we easily find that $j_1 = j_2 = j_3 = j_4 = 1/4$. Hence, each interval J_l, $l \in \{1, 2, 3, 4\}$ contains in the limit the same proportion of points of the sequence $(x_n)_{n\ge 0}$.

If $\lim_{N\to\infty} \frac{1}{N} \sum_{n=0}^{N-1} {}_2\mathrm{wal}_k(x_n) = 0$ for all $0 \le k < 2^r$, then, by an extension of the above argument, one can conjecture (and we see below that this does indeed hold) that each interval of the form $\left[\frac{a}{2^r}, \frac{a+1}{2^r}\right)$, with $a \in \{0, \ldots, 2^r - 1\}$, of length

2^{-r}, contains in the limit the same proportion of points of the sequence, namely 2^{-r}, and hence (3.2) holds for all of these intervals. As one can approximate any sub-interval $[x, y) \subseteq [0, 1)$ arbitrary closely by intervals of the form $\left[\frac{a}{2^r}, \frac{a+1}{2^r}\right)$, it follows that (3.2) holds for any sub-interval $[x, y) \subseteq [0, 1)$ which means that the sequence $(x_n)_{n\geq 0}$ is uniformly distributed modulo one.

Now let us state the general result, together with a detailed proof.

Theorem 3.7 (Weyl criterion for the Walsh function system) *Let $b \geq 2$ be an integer. A sequence $\mathcal{S} = (\boldsymbol{x}_n)_{n\geq 0}$ in the s-dimensional unit-cube $[0, 1)^s$ is uniformly distributed modulo one, if and only if*

$$\lim_{N\to\infty} \frac{1}{N} \sum_{n=0}^{N-1} {}_b\mathrm{wal}_{\boldsymbol{k}}(\boldsymbol{x}_n) = 0 \tag{3.6}$$

holds for all vectors $\boldsymbol{k} \in \mathbb{N}_0^s \setminus \{\boldsymbol{0}\}$.

From the point of view of Definition 3.1, the Weyl criterion for the Walsh function system seems to be more natural than the classical Weyl criterion using trigonometric functions, since by using the Walsh function system one measures directly the proportion of points of a sequence in certain intervals. However, if we identify the unit-interval $[0, 1)$ with the torus, and therefore define uniform distribution on the torus, then the classical Weyl criterion using trigonometric functions becomes more natural.

For the proof of the result, we need some preparation. The following fundamental definition is used throughout the book.

Definition 3.8 Let $b \geq 2$ be an integer. An s-dimensional, b-adic *elementary interval* is an interval of the form

$$\prod_{i=1}^{s} \left[\frac{a_i}{b^{d_i}}, \frac{a_i+1}{b^{d_i}}\right)$$

with integers $0 \leq a_i < b^{d_i}$ and $d_i \geq 0$ for all $1 \leq i \leq s$. If $d_1, \ldots, d_s$ are such that $d_1 + \cdots + d_s = k$, then we say that the elementary interval is of *order k*.

Lemma 3.9 *For $b \geq 2$ consider an s-dimensional, b-adic elementary interval $J = \prod_{i=1}^{s}\left[\frac{a_i}{b^{d_i}}, \frac{a_i+1}{b^{d_i}}\right)$ with integers $0 \leq a_i < b^{d_i}$ and $d_i \in \mathbb{N}_0$ for all $1 \leq i \leq s$. Let, further, $\boldsymbol{k} = (k_1, \ldots, k_s) \in \mathbb{N}_0^s \setminus \{\boldsymbol{0}\}$ be such that $k_i \geq b^{d_i}$ for at least one index $1 \leq i \leq s$. Then, for the $\boldsymbol{k}$th Walsh coefficient of the characteristic function of J, we have*

$$\widehat{\chi}_J(\boldsymbol{k}) = 0.$$

Proof First we show the one-dimensional case. Let $k \geq b^d$ and $0 \leq a < b^d$ be integers with b-adic expansions $k = \kappa_0 + \kappa_1 b + \cdots + \kappa_g b^g$ with $\kappa_g \neq 0$ and $g \geq d$, and $a = \alpha_0 + \alpha_1 b + \cdots + \alpha_{d-1} b^{d-1}$. For $x \in \left[\frac{a}{b^d}, \frac{a+1}{b^d}\right)$, we have that the b-adic expansion of x is of the form

$$x = \frac{\alpha_{d-1}}{b} + \frac{\alpha_{d-2}}{b^2} + \cdots + \frac{\alpha_0}{b^d} + \sum_{j \geq d+1} \frac{\xi_j}{b^j},$$

where $\xi_j \in \{0, \ldots, b-1\}$ are arbitrary b-adic digits for $j \geq d+1$. Therefore, we obtain

$$\begin{aligned}\int_{a/b^d}^{(a+1)/b^d} {}_b\mathrm{wal}_k(x)\,\mathrm{d}x &= \omega_b^{\kappa_0\alpha_{d-1}+\cdots+\kappa_{d-1}\alpha_0} \int_{a/b^d}^{(a+1)/b^d} \omega_b^{\kappa_d\xi_{d+1}+\cdots+\kappa_g\xi_{g+1}}\,\mathrm{d}x \\ &= \omega_b^{\kappa_0\alpha_{d-1}+\cdots+\kappa_{d-1}\alpha_0} \frac{1}{b^{g+1}} \prod_{j=d}^{g} \sum_{\zeta=0}^{b-1} \omega_b^{\kappa_j\zeta} = 0,\end{aligned}$$

as for $\kappa \neq 0$ we have $\sum_{\zeta=0}^{b-1} \omega_b^{\kappa\zeta} = (\omega_b^{\kappa b} - 1)/(\omega_b - 1) = 0$.

Now let $\boldsymbol{k} = (k_1, \ldots, k_s) \in \mathbb{N}_0^s$ with $k_i \geq b^{d_i}$ for at least one index $1 \leq i \leq s$. Then we obtain from the above that for $J = \prod_{i=1}^s \left[\frac{a_i}{b^{d_i}}, \frac{a_i+1}{b^{d_i}}\right)$ we have

$$\begin{aligned}\widehat{\chi_J}(\boldsymbol{k}) &= \int_{[0,1]^s} \chi_J(\boldsymbol{x})\,{}_b\mathrm{wal}_{\boldsymbol{k}}(\boldsymbol{x})\,\mathrm{d}\boldsymbol{x} = \int_J {}_b\mathrm{wal}_{\boldsymbol{k}}(\boldsymbol{x})\,\mathrm{d}\boldsymbol{x} \\ &= \prod_{i=1}^s \int_{a_i/b^{d_i}}^{(a_i+1)/b^{d_i}} {}_b\mathrm{wal}_{k_i}(x)\,\mathrm{d}x = 0.\end{aligned}$$

□

Proof of Theorem 3.7 Assume first that the sequence $\mathcal{S} = (\boldsymbol{x}_n)_{n\geq 0}$ is uniformly distributed modulo one. As the Walsh function ${}_b\mathrm{wal}_{\boldsymbol{k}}$ with $\boldsymbol{k} = (k_1, \ldots, k_s) \in \mathbb{N}_0^s$, $0 \leq k_i < b^{r_i}$ for all $1 \leq i \leq s$, is constant on each interval of the form

$$J = \prod_{i=1}^s \left[\frac{a_i}{b^{r_i}}, \frac{a_i+1}{b^{r_i}}\right),$$

with integers $0 \leq a_i < b^{r_i}$ for all $1 \leq i \leq s$, we can write ${}_b\mathrm{wal}_{\boldsymbol{k}}$ as a step function, i.e.

$${}_b\mathrm{wal}_{\boldsymbol{k}}(\boldsymbol{x}) = \sum_{l\in M} c_l \chi_{J_l}(\boldsymbol{x})$$

with a finite set M, $c_l \in \mathbb{R}$ and pairwise disjoint intervals $J_l \subseteq [0, 1]^s$. Then we obtain

$$\lim_{N\to\infty} \frac{1}{N} \sum_{n=0}^{N-1} {}_b\mathrm{wal}_{\boldsymbol{k}}(\boldsymbol{x}_n) = \sum_{l\in M} c_l \lim_{N\to\infty} \frac{1}{N} \sum_{n=0}^{N-1} \chi_{J_l}(\boldsymbol{x}_n) = \sum_{l\in M} c_l \lambda_s(J_l),$$

as the sequence $(\boldsymbol{x}_n)_{n\geq 0}$ is uniformly distributed modulo one. Since for $\boldsymbol{k} \neq \boldsymbol{0}$ we have

$$0 = \int_{[0,1]^s} {}_b\mathrm{wal}_{\boldsymbol{k}}(\boldsymbol{x})\,\mathrm{d}\boldsymbol{x} = \sum_{l\in M} c_l \lambda_s(J_l),$$

we find that (3.6) holds for all $\boldsymbol{k} \neq \boldsymbol{0}$.

Now we show the other direction. Assume that (3.6) holds for all $\boldsymbol{k} \neq \boldsymbol{0}$. First let J be a b-adic elementary interval with $d_1 = \cdots = d_s = r \in \mathbb{N}_0$, i.e. of the form

$$J = \prod_{i=1}^{s} \left[\frac{a_i}{b^r}, \frac{a_i+1}{b^r}\right), \tag{3.7}$$

with integers $0 \leq a_i < b^r$ for all $1 \leq i \leq s$. Then it follows from Lemma 3.9 that the characteristic function of J has a finite Walsh series representation, i.e.

$$\chi_J(\boldsymbol{x}) = \sum_{\substack{\boldsymbol{k}\in\mathbb{N}_0^s \\ |\boldsymbol{k}|_\infty < b^r}} \widehat{\chi}_J(\boldsymbol{k})\, {}_b\mathrm{wal}_{\boldsymbol{k}}(\boldsymbol{x}),$$

where for $\boldsymbol{k} = (k_1, \ldots, k_s)$ we write $|\boldsymbol{k}|_\infty := \max_{1\leq j\leq s} |k_j|$. Hence,

$$\lim_{N\to\infty} \frac{A(J,N,\mathcal{S})}{N} = \sum_{\substack{\boldsymbol{k}\in\mathbb{N}_0^s \\ |\boldsymbol{k}|_\infty < b^r}} \widehat{\chi}_J(\boldsymbol{k}) \lim_{N\to\infty} \frac{1}{N} \sum_{n=0}^{N-1} {}_b\mathrm{wal}_{\boldsymbol{k}}(\boldsymbol{x}_n) = \widehat{\chi}_J(\boldsymbol{0}) = \lambda_s(J),$$

by our assumption. Now let $[\boldsymbol{x}, \boldsymbol{y}) \subseteq [0,1)^s$ be an arbitrary interval with $\boldsymbol{x} = (x_1, \ldots, x_s)$ and $\boldsymbol{y} = (y_1, \ldots, y_s)$. For $r \in \mathbb{N}_0$ choose $u_i, v_i \in \{0, \ldots, b^r - 1\}$ such that $u_i \leq x_i b^r < u_i + 1$ and $v_i \leq y_i b^r < v_i + 1$ for $1 \leq i \leq s$. Then we have

$$J_1 := \prod_{i=1}^{s} \left[\frac{u_i+1}{b^r}, \frac{v_i}{b^r}\right) \subseteq [\boldsymbol{x}, \boldsymbol{y}) \subseteq \prod_{i=1}^{s} \left[\frac{u_i}{b^r}, \frac{v_i+1}{b^r}\right) =: J_2$$

and $A(J_1, N, \mathcal{S}) \leq A([\boldsymbol{x}, \boldsymbol{y}), N, \mathcal{S}) \leq A(J_2, N, \mathcal{S})$. As both J_1 and J_2 are disjoint, finite unions of b-adic elementary intervals of the form (3.7), we obtain from the above considerations that

$$\prod_{i=1}^{s} \frac{v_i - u_i - 1}{b^r} \leq \lim_{N\to\infty} \frac{A([\boldsymbol{x}, \boldsymbol{y}), N, \mathcal{S})}{N} \leq \prod_{i=1}^{s} \frac{v_i - u_i + 1}{b^r}.$$

But, as for all $1 \leq i \leq s$ we have $\lim_{r\to\infty} \frac{v_i - u_i - 1}{b^r} = \lim_{r\to\infty} \frac{v_i - u_i + 1}{b^r} = y_i - x_i$, it follows that

$$\lim_{N\to\infty} \frac{A([\boldsymbol{x}, \boldsymbol{y}), N, \mathcal{S})}{N} = \lambda_s([\boldsymbol{x}, \boldsymbol{y})),$$

and hence the sequence $\mathcal{S}$ is uniformly distributed modulo one. □

Now we can easily give a further example for a uniformly distributed sequence.

Definition 3.10 Let $b \geq 2$ be an integer. For any $n \in \mathbb{N}_0$ with b-adic expansion $n = n_0 + n_1 b + n_2 b^2 + \cdots$ (this expansion is obviously finite) the (b-adic) *radical inverse function* $\varphi_b : \mathbb{N}_0 \to [0, 1)$ is defined as

$$\varphi_b(n) = \frac{n_0}{b} + \frac{n_1}{b^2} + \cdots.$$

Then the *b-adic van der Corput sequence* is defined as the one-dimensional sequence $\mathcal{S} = (x_n)_{n \geq 0}$ with $x_n = \varphi_b(n)$ for all $n \in \mathbb{N}_0$.

Example 3.11 For $b = 2$ the first elements of the 2-adic van der Corput sequence are $0, \frac{1}{2}, \frac{1}{4}, \frac{3}{4}, \frac{1}{8}, \frac{5}{8}, \frac{3}{8}, \frac{7}{8}, \frac{1}{16}, \ldots$.

Example 3.12 Using Theorem 3.7 we show that the b-adic van der Corput sequence is uniformly distributed modulo one. Let $k \in \mathbb{N}$ with $k = \kappa_0 + \kappa_1 b + \cdots + \kappa_{r-1} b^{r-1}$, where $\kappa_{r-1} \neq 0$. For the b-adic van der Corput sequence the nth element is of the form $x_n = n_0 b^{-1} + n_1 b^{-2} + \cdots$ and hence we have

$$E(N) := \sum_{n=0}^{N-1} {}_b\mathrm{wal}_k(x_n) = \sum_{n=0}^{N-1} \omega_b^{\kappa_0 n_0 + \cdots + \kappa_{r-1} n_{r-1}}.$$

First let $N = b^r$. Then we have $E(b^r) = \prod_{j=0}^{r-1} \sum_{n=0}^{b-1} \omega_b^{\kappa_j n} = 0$ as at least $\kappa_{r-1} \neq 0$ and the same holds for each multiple of b^r, i.e. $E(v b^r) = 0$ for all $v \in \mathbb{N}$. From this we find that $|E(N)| \leq b^r$ for all $N \in \mathbb{N}$ and hence,

$$\lim_{N \to \infty} \frac{1}{N} \sum_{n=0}^{N-1} {}_b\mathrm{wal}_k(x_n) = 0.$$

Now it follows from the Weyl criterion for the Walsh function system that the b-adic van der Corput sequence is uniformly distributed modulo one.

3.2 Discrepancy

In the last section we found that a sequence should be uniformly distributed modulo one to satisfy our purpose of approximating the integral of a Riemann integrable function arbitrarily closely with a QMC algorithm using the first N points of this sequence. In practice, however, we can only use finite sets of sample points (where here and throughout this book by a set of points we always mean a multi-set where the multiplicity of elements matters). However, a finite sequence can never be uniformly distributed modulo one. Nevertheless, Theorem 3.3 and the results from Chapter 2 suggest the use of point sets whose empirical distribution is close to uniform distribution modulo one.

In the following, we introduce several quantitative measures for the deviation of a finite point set from uniform distribution. Some of them have already been introduced and used in Chapter 2. Such measures are usually called discrepancies. The definition of uniform distribution modulo one leads directly to the following definition.

Definition 3.13 Let $\mathcal{P} = \{\boldsymbol{x}_0, \ldots, \boldsymbol{x}_{N-1}\}$ be a finite point set in $[0, 1)^s$. The *extreme discrepancy* D_N of this point set is defined as

$$D_N(\mathcal{P}) := \sup_J \left| \frac{A(J, N, \mathcal{P})}{N} - \lambda_s(J) \right|,$$

where the supremum is extended over all sub-intervals $J \subseteq [0, 1)^s$ of the form $J = [\boldsymbol{a}, \boldsymbol{b})$. For an infinite sequence $\mathcal{S}$, the extreme discrepancy $D_N(\mathcal{S})$ is the extreme discrepancy of the first N elements of the sequence.

It can be shown (see Exercise 3.9) that a sequence $\mathcal{S}$ is uniformly distributed modulo one, if and only if $\lim_{N\to\infty} D_N(\mathcal{S}) = 0$. Hence, for uniformly distributed sequences, the extreme discrepancy goes to zero as N tends to infinity. However, this convergence to zero cannot be arbitrarily fast. Consider, for example, an interval of volume $\varepsilon > 0$ which contains exactly one point of the first N elements of the sequence $\mathcal{S}$. Then, by choosing $\varepsilon > 0$ arbitrarily small, we find $D_N(\mathcal{S}) \geq 1/N$. This gives a first lower bound on the extreme discrepancy.

Very often, one uses a slightly weaker version of the extreme discrepancy which is commonly known as the star discrepancy. Here, the supremum in Definition 3.13 is only extended over all sub-intervals of the unit-cube with one vertex anchored at the origin. The star discrepancy D_N^* of a finite point set $\mathcal{P}$ has been introduced in Definition 2.14 as the supremum-norm of the discrepancy function $\Delta_{\mathcal{P}}(\boldsymbol{x}) := A([\boldsymbol{0}, \boldsymbol{x}), N, \mathcal{P})/N - \lambda_s([\boldsymbol{0}, \boldsymbol{x}))$ (see Definition 2.13), which can be considered as a local measure for the deviation from uniform distribution; that is, for a point set $\mathcal{P} = \{\boldsymbol{x}_0, \ldots, \boldsymbol{x}_{N-1}\}$ in $[0, 1)^s$ the star discrepancy is given by

$$D_N^*(\mathcal{P}) := \sup_{\boldsymbol{x}\in[0,1]^s} |\Delta_{\mathcal{P}}(\boldsymbol{x})|.$$

For an infinite sequence $\mathcal{S}$, the star discrepancy $D_N^*(\mathcal{S})$ is the star discrepancy of the first N elements of the sequence.

From these definitions we immediately obtain the following relation between the extreme discrepancy and the star discrepancy.

Proposition 3.14 *For any point set $\mathcal{P}$ consisting of N points in $[0, 1)^s$, we have*

$$D_N^*(\mathcal{P}) \leq D_N(\mathcal{P}) \leq 2^s D_N^*(\mathcal{P}).$$

Proof The left inequality is obvious. For the right inequality, we mention that any sub-interval of $[0, 1]^s$ can be written as composition of, at most, 2^s sub-intervals of $[0, 1]^s$ with one vertex anchored in the origin. For example, for $s = 2$ and $\boldsymbol{a} = (a_1, a_2)$ and $\boldsymbol{b} = [b_1, b_2)$, we have

$$[\boldsymbol{a}, \boldsymbol{b}) = ([0, b_1) \times [0, b_2) \setminus [0, a_1) \times [0, b_2)) \setminus ([0, b_1) \times [0, a_2) \setminus [0, a_1) \times [0, a_2)) .$$

From this composition the result immediately follows. □

On account of Proposition 3.14 we deal mainly with the simpler star discrepancy instead of the extreme discrepancy in the following. A further motivation for concentrating on the star discrepancy is its appearance in the Koksma–Hlawka inequality (Theorem 2.18). Results for the extreme discrepancy can be obtained from results for the star discrepancy together with Proposition 3.14.

Obviously this also holds in the other direction. From our results for the extreme discrepancy, we find now that a sequence is uniformly distributed modulo one if and only if its star discrepancy tends to zero. Furthermore, we find the (weak) lower bound $D_N^*(\mathcal{S}) \geq 1/(2^s N)$ for the star discrepancy of any sequence $\mathcal{S}$ in $[0, 1)^s$.

In the following we present three important statements on the star discrepancy that are used often (sometimes implicitly) within this book.

Somctimes, it is very useful to know that the star discrepancy is a continuous function on $[0, 1)^{Ns}$. This is more or less the assertion of the following proposition.

Proposition 3.15 *Let $\mathcal{P} = \{\boldsymbol{x}_0, \ldots, \boldsymbol{x}_{N-1}\}$ be a point set in $[0, 1)^s$ with star discrepancy $D_N^*(\mathcal{P})$. Let $\boldsymbol{x}_n := (x_{n,1}, \ldots, x_{n,s})$ for $0 \leq n \leq N-1$, and let $\delta_{n,i}$, $0 \leq n \leq N-1$, $1 \leq i \leq s$, be non-negative reals with $\delta_{n,i} < \varepsilon$, such that $x_{n,i} + \delta_{n,i} < 1$ for all $0 \leq n \leq N-1$ and $1 \leq i \leq s$. Then, for the star discrepancy $D_N^*(\widetilde{\mathcal{P}})$ of the shifted point set $\widetilde{\mathcal{P}} = \{\widetilde{\boldsymbol{x}}_0, \ldots, \widetilde{\boldsymbol{x}}_{N-1}\}$, with $\widetilde{x}_{n,i} := x_{n,i} + \delta_{n,i}$ for all $0 \leq n \leq N-1$ and $1 \leq i \leq s$, we have*

$$|D_N^*(\mathcal{P}) - D_N^*(\widetilde{\mathcal{P}})| \leq \varepsilon s.$$

Proof For an arbitrary interval $B = \prod_{i=1}^s [0, \alpha_i) \subseteq [0, 1)^s$, we define for $j \in \{0, 1\}$ the intervals

$$\widetilde{B}_j := \prod_{i=1}^s [0, \widetilde{\alpha}_i^{(j)})$$

with

$$\widetilde{\alpha}_i^{(j)} := \begin{cases} 0 & \text{if } \alpha_i + (-1)^j \varepsilon < 0, \\ 1 & \text{if } \alpha_i + (-1)^j \varepsilon > 1, \\ \alpha_i + (-1)^j \varepsilon & \text{otherwise.} \end{cases}$$

Then one can prove, by induction on the dimension s, that $|\lambda_s(B) - \lambda_s(\widetilde{B}_j)| \leq \varepsilon s$ holds for $j \in \{0, 1\}$.

Then we have $A(\widetilde{B}_1, N, \mathcal{P}) \leq A(B, N, \widetilde{\mathcal{P}}) \leq A(B, N, \mathcal{P})$ and hence,

$$A(B, N, \widetilde{\mathcal{P}}) - N\lambda_s(B) \leq |A(B, N, \mathcal{P}) - N\lambda_s(B)| \leq D_N^*(\mathcal{P})$$

and

$$\begin{aligned} N\lambda_s(B) - A(B, N, \widetilde{\mathcal{P}}) &\leq N\lambda_s(B) - A(\widetilde{B}_1, N, \mathcal{P}) \\ &= N\lambda_s(\widetilde{B}_1) - A(\widetilde{B}_1, N, \mathcal{P}) + N\lambda_s(B) - N\lambda_s(\widetilde{B}_1) \\ &\leq D_N^*(\mathcal{P}) + N\varepsilon s. \end{aligned}$$

Therefore, we have $|A(B, N, \widetilde{\mathcal{P}}) - N\lambda_s(B)| \leq D_N^*(\mathcal{P}) + N\varepsilon s$. Since B is an arbitrary interval, we obtain from this inequality that $D_N^*(\widetilde{\mathcal{P}}) \leq D_N^*(\mathcal{P}) + \varepsilon s$.

In the same way we can show that $D_N^*(\mathcal{P}) \leq D_N^*(\widetilde{\mathcal{P}}) + \varepsilon s$, which shows the result. □

Sometimes it is possible to split a given point set into smaller point sets with low star discrepancies. In this case the following result, which is often called the *triangle inequality for the discrepancy*, may be very useful to obtain an upper bound on the star discrepancy of the superposition of the small point sets (see [130, p. 115, Theorem 2.6]).

Proposition 3.16 *For $1 \leq i \leq k$, let $\mathcal{P}_i$ be point sets consisting of N_i points in $[0, 1)^s$ with star discrepancy $D_{N_i}^*(\mathcal{P}_i)$. Let $\mathcal{P}$ be the point set obtained by listing in some order the terms of $\mathcal{P}_i$, $1 \leq i \leq k$. We set $N = N_1 + \cdots + N_k$, which is the number of points of $\mathcal{P}$. Then we have*

$$D_N^*(\mathcal{P}) \leq \sum_{i=1}^{k} \frac{N_i}{N} D_{N_i}^*(\mathcal{P}_i),$$

and the same result holds with the star discrepancy replaced by the extreme discrepancy.

The third statement on the star discrepancy gives the error when we replace the supremum in its definition by a maximum over a finite, equidistant grid with given mesh size. For an integer $m \geq 2$, let $\Gamma_m := \frac{1}{m}\mathbb{Z}^s \pmod 1$ be the equidistant grid with mesh size $1/m$.

Proposition 3.17 *Let $\delta > 0$ and define $m = \lceil s/\delta \rceil$. Further, let Γ_m be the equidistant grid on $[0, 1]^s$ with mesh size $1/m$. Then, for any point set $\mathcal{P}$ consisting of N points in $[0, 1)^s$, we have*

$$D_N^*(\mathcal{P}) \leq \max_{y \in \Gamma_m} |\Delta_{\mathcal{P}}(y)| + \delta.$$

For the proof of this result, we need the following lemma.

Lemma 3.18 *Let* $u_i, v_i \in [0, 1]$ *for* $1 \le i \le s$ *and let* $\delta \in [0, 1]$ *be such that* $|u_i - v_i| \le \delta$ *for* $1 \le i \le s$. *Then*

$$\left|\prod_{i=1}^{s} u_i - \prod_{i=1}^{s} v_i\right| \le 1 - (1-\delta)^s \le s\delta.$$

Proof As in [177], we prove the result by induction on s. Trivially, the result holds for $s = 1$. Let $s > 1$. We may assume that $u_s \ge v_s$. Then, by assuming that the result holds true for $s - 1$, we have

$$\begin{aligned}
\left|\prod_{i=1}^{s} u_i - \prod_{i=1}^{s} v_i\right| &= \left|(u_s - v_s)\prod_{i=1}^{s-1} u_i + v_s\left(\prod_{i=1}^{s-1} u_i - \prod_{i=1}^{s-1} v_i\right)\right| \\
&\le |u_s - v_s| + v_s(1 - (1-\delta)^{s-1}) \\
&= u_s - v_s(1-\delta)^{s-1} \\
&= u_s(1 - (1-\delta)^{s-1}) + (u_s - v_s)(1-\delta)^{s-1} \\
&\le 1 - (1-\delta)^{s-1} + \delta(1-\delta)^{s-1} \\
&= 1 - (1-\delta)^s.
\end{aligned}$$

This shows the first inequality. For the second inequality, we consider the real function $x \mapsto x^s$. According to the mean value theorem, for all reals $y > z$ we have $y^s - z^s = s\,\xi^{s-1}(y - z)$ for some $\xi \in (z, y)$. Now we obtain the result by using this insight with the choice $y = 1$ and $z = 1 - \delta$. □

Proof of Proposition 3.17 For $\varepsilon > 0$, we choose $\boldsymbol{y}^* = (y_1^*, \ldots, y_s^*) \in [0, 1)^s$ such that

$$D_N^*(\mathcal{P}) \le \left|\frac{A([\mathbf{0}, \boldsymbol{y}^*), N, \mathcal{P})}{N} - \lambda_s([\mathbf{0}, \boldsymbol{y}^*))\right| + \varepsilon.$$

Now choose $\boldsymbol{x} = (x_1, \ldots, x_s)$ and $\boldsymbol{y} = (y_1, \ldots, y_s)$ in Γ_m with $x_i \le y_i^* < x_i + \frac{1}{m} =: y_i$ for all $1 \le i \le s$. Using Lemma 3.18, we obtain

$$\prod_{i=1}^{s} y_i - \prod_{i=1}^{s} x_i \le 1 - \left(1 - \frac{1}{m}\right)^s \le \frac{s}{m} \le \delta.$$

Hence, we get $-\delta + \prod_{i=1}^{s} y_i \le \prod_{i=1}^{s} y_i^* \le \prod_{i=1}^{s} x_i + \delta$ and therefore, we have

$$\begin{aligned}
\frac{A([\mathbf{0}, \boldsymbol{x}), N, \mathcal{P})}{N} - \lambda_s([\mathbf{0}, \boldsymbol{x})) - \delta &\le \frac{A([\mathbf{0}, \boldsymbol{y}^*), N, \mathcal{P})}{N} - \lambda_s([\mathbf{0}, \boldsymbol{y}^*)) \\
&\le \frac{A([\mathbf{0}, \boldsymbol{y}), N, \mathcal{P})}{N} - \lambda_s([\mathbf{0}, \boldsymbol{y})) + \delta.
\end{aligned}$$

From these inequalities, we get

$$D_N^*(\mathcal{P}) \le \max_{\boldsymbol{y}\in\Gamma_m} \left| \frac{A([\boldsymbol{0},\boldsymbol{y}),N,\mathcal{P})}{N} - \lambda_s([\boldsymbol{0},\boldsymbol{y})) \right| + \delta + \varepsilon.$$

Since $\varepsilon > 0$ can be chosen arbitrarily small, the result follows. □

Similarly, as the star discrepancy is defined as the supremum norm of the discrepancy function, we may now introduce other notions of discrepancies by taking different norms of the discrepancy function. In particular, we take the L_q norm in the following (the special case of L_2-discrepancy has been introduced in Definition 2.14 already).

Definition 3.19 Let $1 \le q < \infty$ be a real number. For a point set $\mathcal{P}$ in $[0,1)^s$ the L_q-discrepancy is defined as the L_q norm of the discrepancy function, i.e.

$$L_{q,N}(\mathcal{P}) := \left(\int_{[0,1]^s} |\Delta_{\mathcal{P}}(\boldsymbol{x})|^q \,\mathrm{d}\boldsymbol{x} \right)^{1/q}.$$

For an infinite sequence $\mathcal{S}$ the L_q-discrepancy $L_{q,N}(\mathcal{S})$ is the L_q-discrepancy of the first N elements of the sequence.

Obviously, for any point set $\mathcal{P}$ and any $1 \le q < \infty$ we have $L_{q,N}(\mathcal{P}) \le D_N^*(\mathcal{P})$. Conversely, it is also possible to give an upper bound for the star discrepancy in terms of the L_q-discrepancy; see, for example, [61, Theorem 1.8]. From this it follows that a sequence is uniformly distributed modulo one if and only if its L_q-discrepancy tends to zero.

We gave already some (trivial) lower bounds for the extreme and the star discrepancy of finite point sets in the unit-cube. While it can be shown that these bounds are the best possible in the order of magnitude in N for one-dimensional point sets (compare with Exercise 2.1) this is by no means true in the higher dimension. The following remarkable result was first proved by Roth [228] in 1954.

Theorem 3.20 (Roth's lower bound on the L_2-discrepancy) *For any dimension $s \in \mathbb{N}$ and for any point set $\mathcal{P}$ consisting of N points in the s-dimensional unit-cube, we have*

$$L_{2,N}(\mathcal{P}) \ge \frac{1}{N}\sqrt{\binom{\lfloor \log_2 N \rfloor + s + 1}{s-1}} \frac{1}{2^{2s+4}} \ge c_s \frac{(\log N)^{(s-1)/2}}{N},$$

where $c_s = \frac{1}{2^{2s+4}(\log 2)^{(s-1)/2}\sqrt{(s-1)!}}$.

Remark 3.21 The inequality in the above theorem also applies to the extreme- and the star discrepancy as $D_N(\mathcal{P}) \ge D_N^*(\mathcal{P}) \ge L_{2,N}(\mathcal{P})$.

The original proof of Roth's result can be found in [228] (this proof is in $s = 2$ dimension only, but can easily be generalised). A detailed proof (in arbitrary dimension) using the orthogonality relation of Rademacher functions can be found in Kuipers and Niederreiter [130]. We also refer to Beck and Chen [11].

The constant in Theorem 3.20 here is better than that in Kuipers and Niederreiter; see [130, p. 104]. This can be obtained by a few slight modifications in the proof as in reference [130], which we describe in the following.

For the proof of Theorem 3.20 we need several lemmas and some notation which we introduce in the following. Henceforth we follow the proofs of [130, Chapter 2, Lemma 2.1–Lemma 2.5].

Let $\mathcal{P} = \{\boldsymbol{x}_0, \ldots, \boldsymbol{x}_{N-1}\}$ with $\boldsymbol{x}_n = (x_{n,1}, \ldots, x_{n,s})$ and let $\psi(x) = -{}_2\mathrm{wal}_1(x) = (-1)^{\xi_1+1}$ for $x \in \mathbb{R}$ with $x = X + \xi_1 2^{-1} + \xi_2 2^{-2} + \cdots$ where $X \in \mathbb{Z}$, $\xi_1, \xi_2, \ldots, \in \{0, 1\}$ and infinitely many of the $\xi_1, \xi_2, \ldots$ are 0. Further, let t be a natural number such that $2^{t-1} > N$, which will be specified below. For a vector $\boldsymbol{r} = (r_1, \ldots, r_s) \in \mathbb{N}_0^s$, we define $|\boldsymbol{r}|_1 = r_1 + \cdots + r_s$.

For a vector $\boldsymbol{r} \in \mathbb{N}_0^s$ with $|\boldsymbol{r}|_1 = t - 1$, we define a function $G_{\boldsymbol{r}}$ on $\mathbb{R}^s$ as follows: if there exists an $0 \le n < N$ such that

$$(\lfloor 2^{r_1} x_{n,1} \rfloor, \ldots, \lfloor 2^{r_s} x_{n,s} \rfloor) = (\lfloor x_1 \rfloor, \ldots, \lfloor x_s \rfloor),$$

then we set $G_{\boldsymbol{r}}(x_1, \ldots, x_s) = 0$. Otherwise, we set

$$G_{\boldsymbol{r}}(x_1, \ldots, x_s) = \psi(x_1) \cdots \psi(x_s).$$

Furthermore, we define

$$F_{\boldsymbol{r}}(x_1, \ldots, x_s) = G_{\boldsymbol{r}}(2^{r_1} x_1, \ldots, 2^{r_s} x_s)$$

and

$$F(x_1, \ldots, x_s) = \sum_{\substack{\boldsymbol{r} \in \mathbb{N}_0^s \\ |\boldsymbol{r}|_1 = t-1}} F_{\boldsymbol{r}}(x_1, \ldots, x_s).$$

Lemma 3.22 *For a given vector $\boldsymbol{r} \in \mathbb{N}_0^s$ with $|\boldsymbol{r}|_1 = t - 1$ and for some i with $1 \le i \le s$, let $a = h 2^{-r_i}$ and $b = m 2^{-r_i}$, where $h, m \in \mathbb{Z}$ and $h < m$. Then, for any fixed $x_1, \ldots, x_{i-1}, x_{i+1}, \ldots, x_s$, we have*

$$\int_a^b F_{\boldsymbol{r}}(x_1, \ldots, x_s) \,\mathrm{d}x_i = 0.$$

Proof Using the substitution $t = 2^{r_i} x_i$ we have

$$\int_a^b F_{\boldsymbol{r}}(x_1, \ldots, x_s)\,\mathrm{d}x_i = \int_a^b G_{\boldsymbol{r}}(2^{r_1}x_1, \ldots, 2^{r_s}x_s)\,\mathrm{d}x_i$$
$$= \frac{1}{2^{r_i}} \int_h^m G_{\boldsymbol{r}}(2^{r_1}x_1, \ldots, t, \ldots, 2^{r_s}x_s)\,\mathrm{d}t.$$

Split up the interval $[h, m]$ into sub-intervals of the form $[c, c+1]$ with integers c. Then the integrand $G_{\boldsymbol{r}}(2^{r_1}x_1, \ldots, t, \ldots, 2^{r_s}x_s)$ is zero on certain sub-intervals of these intervals. On the remaining intervals the integrand is equal to $\psi(2^{r_1}x_1) \cdots \psi(t) \cdots \psi(2^{r_s}x_s)$. But for any c, we have

$$\int_c^{c+1} \psi(t)\,\mathrm{d}t = -\int_0^1 {}_2\mathrm{wal}_1(t)\,\mathrm{d}t = 0$$

and hence the result follows. □

Lemma 3.23 *We have*

$$\int_0^1 \cdots \int_0^1 x_1 \cdots x_s F(x_1, \ldots, x_s)\,\mathrm{d}x_1 \cdots \mathrm{d}x_s \geq \binom{t-1+s-1}{s-1} \frac{2^{t-1} - N}{2^{2(s+t-1)}}.$$

Proof First, we show that for all $\boldsymbol{r} \in \mathbb{N}_0^s$ with $|\boldsymbol{r}|_1 = t-1$, we have

$$\int_0^1 \cdots \int_0^1 x_1 \cdots x_s F_{\boldsymbol{r}}(x_1, \ldots, x_s)\,\mathrm{d}x_1 \cdots \mathrm{d}x_s \geq \frac{2^{t-1} - N}{2^{2(s+t-1)}}.$$

Using the substitution $t_i = 2^{r_i} x_i$ for $1 \leq i \leq s$, we have

$$\int_0^1 \cdots \int_0^1 x_1 \cdots x_s F_{\boldsymbol{r}}(x_1, \ldots, x_s)\,\mathrm{d}x_1 \cdots \mathrm{d}x_s$$
$$= \frac{1}{2^{2|\boldsymbol{r}|_1}} \int_0^{2^{r_1}} \cdots \int_0^{2^{r_s}} t_1 \cdots t_s G_{\boldsymbol{r}}(t_1, \ldots, t_s)\,\mathrm{d}t_1 \cdots \mathrm{d}t_s$$

We have

$$\int_{h_1}^{h_1+1} \cdots \int_{h_s}^{h_s+1} t_1 \cdots t_s G_{\boldsymbol{r}}(t_1, \ldots, t_s)\,\mathrm{d}t_1 \cdots \mathrm{d}t_s = 0$$

whenever $(h_1, \ldots, h_s) \in \mathbb{N}_0^s$ with

$$(h_1, \ldots, h_s) = (\lfloor 2^{r_1} x_{n,1} \rfloor, \ldots, \lfloor 2^{r_s} x_{n,s} \rfloor)$$

for some $0 \le n \le N-1$. Therefore, we have

$$\int_0^1 \cdots \int_0^1 x_1 \cdots x_s F_{\boldsymbol{r}}(x_1, \ldots, x_s)\,\mathrm{d}x_1 \cdots \mathrm{d}x_s$$
$$= \frac{1}{2^{2(t-1)}} \sum_{\boldsymbol{h}}{}^{*} \int_{h_1}^{h_1+1} \cdots \int_{h_s}^{h_s+1} t_1 \cdots t_s G_{\boldsymbol{r}}(t_1, \ldots, t_s)\,\mathrm{d}t_1 \cdots \mathrm{d}t_s, \quad (3.8)$$

where the sum $\sum_{\boldsymbol{h}}^{*}$ is over all lattice points $\boldsymbol{h} = (h_1, \ldots, h_s)$ with $0 \le h_i < 2^{r_i}$ for $1 \le i \le s$ and with $\boldsymbol{h} \ne (\lfloor 2^{r_1} x_{n,1} \rfloor, \ldots, \lfloor 2^{r_s} x_{n,s} \rfloor)$ for all $0 \le n \le N-1$. Hence, this sum is extended over at least $2^{|\boldsymbol{r}|_1} - N = 2^{t-1} - N$ lattice points.

For any integer h, we have

$$\int_h^{h+1} t\psi(t)\,\mathrm{d}t = -\int_h^{h+1/2} t\,\mathrm{d}t + \int_{h+1/2}^{h+1} t\,\mathrm{d}t = \frac{1}{4}$$

and hence

$$\sum_{\boldsymbol{h}}{}^{*} \int_{h_1}^{h_1+1} \cdots \int_{h_s}^{h_s+1} t_1 \cdots t_s G_{\boldsymbol{r}}(t_1, \ldots, t_s)\,\mathrm{d}t_1 \cdots \mathrm{d}t_s \ge \frac{2^{t-1} - N}{4^s}.$$

From this, together with (3.8), it follows that

$$\int_0^1 \cdots \int_0^1 x_1 \cdots x_s F_{\boldsymbol{r}}(x_1, \ldots, x_s)\,\mathrm{d}x_1 \cdots \mathrm{d}x_s \ge \frac{2^{t-1} - N}{2^{2(s+t-1)}}.$$

To obtain the final result, note that the number of vectors $\boldsymbol{r} \in \mathbb{N}_0^s$ with $|\boldsymbol{r}|_1 = t-1$ is given by $\binom{t-1+s-1}{s-1}$. □

Lemma 3.24 *We have*

$$\int_0^1 \cdots \int_0^1 F^2(x_1, \ldots, x_s)\,\mathrm{d}x_1 \cdots \mathrm{d}x_s \le \binom{t-1+s-1}{s-1}.$$

Proof We have

$$\int_0^1 \cdots \int_0^1 F^2(x_1, \ldots, x_s)\,\mathrm{d}x_1 \cdots \mathrm{d}x_s$$
$$= \sum_{\substack{\boldsymbol{r} \in \mathbb{N}_0^s \\ |\boldsymbol{r}|_1 = t-1}} \int_0^1 \cdots \int_0^1 F_{\boldsymbol{r}}^2(x_1, \ldots, x_s)\,\mathrm{d}x_1 \cdots \mathrm{d}x_s$$
$$+ \sum_{\substack{\boldsymbol{r}, \boldsymbol{w} \in \mathbb{N}_0^s \\ \boldsymbol{r} \ne \boldsymbol{w} \\ |\boldsymbol{r}|_1 = |\boldsymbol{w}|_1 = t-1}} \int_0^1 \cdots \int_0^1 F_{\boldsymbol{r}}(x_1, \ldots, x_s) F_{\boldsymbol{w}}(x_1, \ldots, x_s)\,\mathrm{d}x_1 \cdots \mathrm{d}x_s.$$

Now $F_{\boldsymbol{r}}^2(x_1, \ldots, x_s) \leq 1$ and hence the first sum is bounded by $\binom{t-1+s-1}{s-1}$. It remains to show that the second sum is zero.

We show that each term in the second sum is zero. Choose $\boldsymbol{r}, \boldsymbol{w} \in \mathbb{N}_0^s$, $\boldsymbol{r} \neq \boldsymbol{w}$, and $\boldsymbol{r} = (r_1, \ldots, r_s)$ and $\boldsymbol{w} = (w_1, \ldots, w_s)$. Then there exists an index $1 \leq i \leq s$ such that $r_i \neq w_i$. Without loss of generality we may assume that $r_i < w_i$. For fixed $x_1, \ldots, x_{i-1}, x_{i+1}, \ldots, x_s$ we show that

$$\int_0^1 F_{\boldsymbol{r}}(x_1, \ldots, x_s) F_{\boldsymbol{w}}(x_1, \ldots, x_s) \,\mathrm{d}x_i = 0.$$

The result then follows.

Using the substitution $t = 2^{w_i} x_i$ transforms the above integral into

$$\frac{1}{2^{w_i}} \int_0^{2^{w_i}} G_{\boldsymbol{r}}(2^{r_1} x_1, \ldots, 2^{r_i - w_i} t, \ldots, 2^{r_s} x_s) G_{\boldsymbol{w}}(2^{w_1} x_1, \ldots, t, \ldots, 2^{w_s} x_s) \,\mathrm{d}t.$$

Split the interval $[0, 2^{w_i})$ into sub-intervals $[c, c+1)$ with integers c. In such an interval the integrand is either identical to zero or equal to

$$\psi(2^{r_1} x_1) \cdots \psi(2^{r_i - w_i} t) \cdots \psi(2^{r_s} x_s) \psi(2^{w_1} x_1) \cdots \psi(t) \cdots \psi(2^{w_s} x_s).$$

Here, the only dependence on t is in $\psi(2^{r_i - w_i} t)\psi(t)$ and hence it suffices to show that $\int_c^{c+1} \psi(2^{r_i - w_i} t)\psi(t) \,\mathrm{d}t$ is zero. Since $r_i - w_i < 0$, it follows that $\psi(2^{r_i - w_i} t) = -{}_2\mathrm{wal}_1(2^{r_i - w_i} t)$ is constant on the interval $[c, c+1)$ and hence we have

$$\int_c^{c+1} \psi(2^{r_i - w_i} t)\psi(t) \,\mathrm{d}t = {}_2\mathrm{wal}_1(2^{r_i - w_i} c) \int_0^1 {}_2\mathrm{wal}_1(t) \,\mathrm{d}t = 0. \qquad \square$$

Lemma 3.25 *For $0 \leq n < N$, we have*

$$\int_{x_{n,1}}^1 \cdots \int_{x_{n,s}}^1 F(x_1, \ldots, x_s) \,\mathrm{d}x_1 \cdots \mathrm{d}x_s = 0.$$

Proof It suffices to show that

$$\int_{x_{n,1}}^1 \cdots \int_{x_{n,s}}^1 F_{\boldsymbol{r}}(x_1, \ldots, x_s) \,\mathrm{d}x_1 \cdots \mathrm{d}x_s = 0$$

for all $0 \leq n \leq N - 1$ and all $\boldsymbol{r} \in \mathbb{N}_0^s$ with $|\boldsymbol{r}|_1 = t - 1$. For fixed n and for $1 \leq i \leq s$, let a_i be the least integral multiple of 2^{-r_i} that is $\geq x_{n,i}$. Then we have $\int_{x_{n,1}}^1 \cdots \int_{x_{n,s}}^1 = \int_{x_{n,1}}^{a_1} \cdots \int_{x_{n,s}}^{a_s}$ +(sum of integrals in which for at least one variable x_i, we integrate over an interval $[a_i, 1]$). The first integral on the right-hand side is zero, since for all $(x_1, \ldots, x_s)$ in the interval $\prod_{l=1}^s [x_{n,l}, a_l]$, we have

$$(\lfloor 2^{r_1} x_1 \rfloor, \ldots, \lfloor 2^{r_1} x_1 \rfloor) = (\lfloor 2^{r_1} x_{n,1} \rfloor, \ldots, \lfloor 2^{r_1} x_{n,1} \rfloor)$$

and hence by definition $F_{\boldsymbol{r}}(x_1, \ldots, x_s) = G_{\boldsymbol{r}}(2^{r_1} x_1, \ldots, 2^{r_s} x_s) = 0$.

The remaining integrals, however, are zero by Lemma 3.22 and hence the result follows. □

Proof of Theorem 3.20 For $0 \le n \le N-1$, let $J_n := \prod_{i=1}^{s}(x_{n,i}, 1]$ and let $\chi_{J_n}(\boldsymbol{x})$ be the characteristic function of this interval. Then $A([\boldsymbol{0}, \boldsymbol{x}), N, \mathcal{P}) = \sum_{n=0}^{N-1} \chi_{J_n}(\boldsymbol{x})$, where $\boldsymbol{x} = (x_1, \ldots, x_s) \in [0,1]^s$. Therefore,

$$\int_{[0,1]^s} A([\boldsymbol{0}, \boldsymbol{x}), N, \mathcal{P}) F(\boldsymbol{x}) \, \mathrm{d}\boldsymbol{x} = \sum_{n=0}^{N-1} \int_{[0,1]^s} \chi_{J_n}(\boldsymbol{x}) F(\boldsymbol{x}) \, \mathrm{d}\boldsymbol{x}$$
$$= \sum_{n=0}^{N-1} \int_{J_n} F(\boldsymbol{x}) \, \mathrm{d}\boldsymbol{x} = 0$$

by Lemma 3.25. Hence, using Lemma 3.23 we obtain

$$\int_{[0,1]^s} (-N \Delta_{\mathcal{P}}(\boldsymbol{x})) F(\boldsymbol{x}) \, \mathrm{d}\boldsymbol{x} = N \int_0^1 \cdots \int_0^1 x_1 \cdots x_s F(x_1, \ldots, x_s) \, \mathrm{d}x_1 \cdots \mathrm{d}x_s$$
$$\ge N \binom{t-1+s-1}{s-1} \frac{2^{t-1} - N}{2^{2(s+t-1)}}.$$

Then

$$\left(N \binom{t-1+s-1}{s-1} \frac{2^{t-1}-N}{2^{2(s+t-1)}} \right)^2 \le \left(\int_{[0,1]^s} (-N \Delta_{\mathcal{P}}(\boldsymbol{x})) F(\boldsymbol{x}) \, \mathrm{d}\boldsymbol{x} \right)^2$$
$$\le \left(\int_{[0,1]^s} (-N \Delta_{\mathcal{P}}(\boldsymbol{x}))^2 \, \mathrm{d}\boldsymbol{x} \right) \left(\int_{[0,1]^s} F(\boldsymbol{x})^2 \, \mathrm{d}\boldsymbol{x} \right)$$
$$\le \left(\int_{[0,1]^s} (-N \Delta_{\mathcal{P}}(\boldsymbol{x}))^2 \, \mathrm{d}\boldsymbol{x} \right) \binom{t-1+s-1}{s-1}$$

by Cauchy–Schwarz' inequality and by Lemma 3.24. Hence, we obtain

$$\int_{[0,1]^s} (N \Delta_{\mathcal{P}}(\boldsymbol{x}))^2 \, \mathrm{d}\boldsymbol{x} \ge N^2 \binom{t-1+s-1}{s-1} 2^{-4(s+t-1)} (2^{t-1} - N)^2.$$

Let t now be the unique integer for which $2N < 2^{t-1} \le 4N$. Then

$$\int_{[0,1]^s} (N \Delta_{\mathcal{P}}(\boldsymbol{x}))^2 \, \mathrm{d}\boldsymbol{x} \ge N^4 2^{-4(t-1)} \binom{t-1+s-1}{s-1} 2^{-4s}$$
$$\ge \binom{t-1+s-1}{s-1} \frac{1}{2^{4s+8}}.$$

Further, $1 + \log_2 N < t - 1 \le 2 + \log_2 N$, which implies $2 + \lfloor \log_2 N \rfloor = t - 1$ and substituting on the right-hand side above yields

$$\int_{[0,1]^s} (N \Delta_{\mathcal{P}}(\boldsymbol{x}))^2 \,\mathrm{d}\boldsymbol{x} \ge \binom{\lfloor \log_2 N \rfloor + s + 1}{s-1} \frac{1}{2^{4s+8}}$$
$$\ge \frac{(\log N)^{s-1}}{(\log 2)^{s-1} (s-1)!\, 2^{4s+8}},$$

where we used $\binom{\lfloor \log_2 N \rfloor + s + 1}{s-1} \ge \frac{(\lfloor \log_2 N \rfloor + 3)^{s-1}}{(s-1)!} \ge \frac{(\log_2 N)^{s-1}}{(s-1)!}$ and $\log_2 N = \frac{\log N}{\log 2}$ in the last inequality. Thus, the result follows. □

As the L_q norm is monotone increasing in q, it follows that Roth's lower bound holds for all L_q-discrepancies with $q \ge 2$, too. Furthermore, it was shown by Schmidt [238] that the same is true for all $1 < q < 2$. Summing up, for any $1 < q < \infty$ and any dimension s, there exists a $c_{s,q} > 0$ with the following property: for any point set $\mathcal{P}$ consisting of N points in the s-dimensional unit-cube, we have

$$L_{q,N}(\mathcal{P}) \ge c_{s,q} \frac{(\log N)^{(s-1)/2}}{N}.$$

On the other hand, it is known that this bound is the best possible in the order of magnitude in N, as was shown first for the L_2-discrepancy by Davenport [29] for $s = 2$ and by Roth [229, 230] and Frolov [84] for arbitrary dimensions $s \in \mathbb{N}$ and by Chen [21] for the general L_q case. But we know even more. For any $q > 1$, any dimension $s \in \mathbb{N}$ and any integer $N \ge 2$, there is an explicit construction of a point set $\mathcal{P}$ consisting of N points in the s-dimensional unit-cube such that

$$L_{q,N}(\mathcal{P}) \le C_{s,q} \frac{(\log N)^{(s-1)/2}}{N}.$$

Such a construction was first given by Davenport for $q = s = 2$ and by Chen and Skriganov [22] for the case $q = 2$ and arbitrary dimension s. Later, Skriganov [244] generalised this construction to the L_q case with arbitrary $q > 1$. We deal with this topic in Chapter 16.

For the star discrepancy the situation is quite different. For $s = 2$, we have an improvement due to Schmidt [237] (see also [130]) or Béjian [12] who showed that there is a $c > 0$ (for example, $c = 0.06$ as shown in [12]) such that for the star discrepancy of any point set $\mathcal{P}$ consisting of N points in the two-dimensional unit square, we have

$$D_N^*(\mathcal{P}) \ge c \frac{\log N}{N}.$$

In dimension $s = 3$ it was shown by Beck [10] that for any $\varepsilon > 0$ there exists an $\overline{N}(\varepsilon)$ such that for any point set $\mathcal{P}$ consisting of $N \ge \overline{N}(\varepsilon)$ points in the three-dimensional unit-cube, we have

$$D_N^*(\mathcal{P}) \geq \frac{\log N(\log\log N)^{1/8-\varepsilon}}{N}.$$

An improvement on Beck's result in dimension $s = 3$ has been shown by Bilyk and Lacey [15]. They showed that there is a choice of $0 < \eta < 1/2$ such that for any point set $\mathcal{P} \subset [0, 1)^3$ of cardinality N, we have

$$D_N^*(\mathcal{P}) \geq c\frac{(\log N)^{1+\eta}}{N}$$

for some constant $c > 0$. This breakthrough led to the paper of Bilyk *et al.* [16], where it is shown that for any $s \in \mathbb{N}$, $s \geq 2$, there is a $c_s > 0$ and a $0 < \eta_s < 1/2$ with the property that for any point set $\mathcal{P}$ consisting of N points in the s-dimensional unit-cube, we have

$$D_N^*(\mathcal{P}) \geq c_s\frac{(\log N)^{(s-1)/2+\eta_s}}{N}.$$

This is the best result for dimensions $s \geq 3$ currently known.

If we consider infinite sequences, then it follows from Roth's lower bound that there exists a $c_s > 0$ such that for the star discrepancy of any sequence $\mathcal{S}$ in the s-dimensional unit-cube, we have

$$D_N^*(\mathcal{S}) \geq c_s\frac{(\log N)^{s/2}}{N}$$

for infinitely many values of $N \in \mathbb{N}$. For a proof, see, for example, [130, Chapter 2, Theorem 2.2].

However, the exact lower order of the star discrepancy in N is still one of the most famous open problems in the theory of uniform distribution modulo one. It is widely believed that there exists some $c_s > 0$ such that for any point set $\mathcal{P}$ consisting of N points in the s-dimensional unit-cube $[0, 1)^s$, the inequality

$$D_N^*(\mathcal{P}) > c_s\frac{(\log N)^{s-1}}{N}$$

holds true. This lower bound would be the best possible for the star discrepancy D_N^*, as we see later. For infinite sequences, a lower bound for the star discrepancy of order $(\log N)^s/N$ for infinitely many values of $N \in \mathbb{N}$ is conjectured.

3.3 General bounds for the discrepancy

From the Weyl criterion (Theorem 3.5), we know that the behaviour of exponential sums is closely related to uniform distribution modulo one. The following important result, which is usually attributed to Erdős, Turán and Koksma, gives a quantitative version of this insight.

Theorem 3.26 (Erdős–Turán–Koksma inequality) *For the discrepancy of any point set* $\mathcal{P} = \{\boldsymbol{x}_0, \ldots, \boldsymbol{x}_{N-1}\}$ *in* $[0, 1)^s$, *we have*

$$D_N(\mathcal{P}) \leq \left(\frac{3}{2}\right)^s \left(\frac{2}{m+1} + \sum_{\substack{\boldsymbol{h} \in \mathbb{Z}^s \\ 0 < |\boldsymbol{h}|_\infty \leq m}} \frac{1}{r(\boldsymbol{h})} \left| \frac{1}{N} \sum_{n=0}^{N-1} \mathrm{e}^{2\pi \mathrm{i} \boldsymbol{h} \cdot \boldsymbol{x}_n} \right| \right),$$

where m *is an arbitrary positive integer and where* $r(\boldsymbol{h}) = \prod_{i=1}^s \max(1, |h_i|)$ *for* $\boldsymbol{h} = (h_1, \ldots, h_s) \in \mathbb{Z}^s$.

A proof of this bound can be found in [61, Section 1.2.2]. See also [130, Chapter 2, Section 2] for the special case of $s = 1$. The original version of Theorem 3.26 in the one-dimensional case is due to Erdős and Turán [64, 65] and in the higher dimensional case is due to Koksma [122].

In practice, one is mainly concerned with point sets whose elements only have rational components. For such point sets, Niederreiter [177, Theorem 3.10] proved a general upper bound for the discrepancy in terms of exponential sums. To formulate this result, we need some notation.

For an integer $M \geq 2$, let $C(M) = (-M/2, M/2] \cap \mathbb{Z}$ and let $C_s(M)$ be the Cartesian product of s copies of $C(M)$. Furthermore, let $C_s^*(M) = C_s(M) \setminus \{\boldsymbol{0}\}$. For $h \in C(M)$ put

$$r(h, M) = \begin{cases} M \sin(\pi |h|/M) & \text{if } h \neq 0, \\ 1 & \text{if } h = 0. \end{cases}$$

For $\boldsymbol{h} = (h_1, \ldots, h_s) \in C_s(M)$, put $r(\boldsymbol{h}, M) = \prod_{i=1}^s r(h_i, M)$.

Theorem 3.27 *Let* $\mathcal{P} = \{\boldsymbol{x}_0, \ldots, \boldsymbol{x}_{N-1}\}$ *be a point set in the* s*-dimensional unit-cube where* $\boldsymbol{x}_n$ *is of the form* $\boldsymbol{x}_n = \{\boldsymbol{y}_n/M\}$ *with* $\boldsymbol{y}_n \in \mathbb{Z}^s$ *for all* $0 \leq n < N$, *and let* $M \geq 2$ *be an integer. Then we have*

$$D_N(\mathcal{P}) \leq 1 - \left(1 - \frac{1}{M}\right)^s + \sum_{\boldsymbol{h} \in C_s^*(M)} \frac{1}{r(\boldsymbol{h}, M)} \left| \frac{1}{N} \sum_{n=0}^{N-1} \mathrm{e}^{2\pi \mathrm{i} \boldsymbol{h} \cdot \boldsymbol{y}_n / M} \right|.$$

For a proof of this theorem, see [175, Chapter 3].

In the following, we consider point sets for which all coordinates of all points have a finite digit expansion in a fixed base $b \geq 2$. A bound similar to that of Theorem 3.27 on the star discrepancy of such point sets was first given by Niederreiter [170, Satz 2] (see also reference [177, Theorem 3.12]). An approach to this result by means of Walsh functions was described by Hellekalek [96, Theorem 1]. To formulate Hellekalek's result we again need some notation.

Let $b \geq 2$ be an integer. For a vector $\boldsymbol{k} = (k_1, \ldots, k_s) \in \mathbb{N}_0^s$, we put $\rho_b(\boldsymbol{k}) := \prod_{i=1}^s \rho_b(k_i)$ where for $k \in \mathbb{N}_0$, we set

$$\rho_b(k) := \begin{cases} 1 & \text{if } k = 0, \\ \frac{1}{b^{r+1}\sin(\pi\kappa_r/b)} & \text{if } b^r \leq k < b^{r+1} \text{ where } r \in \mathbb{N}_0 \end{cases}$$

and where κ_r is the most significant digit in the b-adic expansion of k.

Theorem 3.28 *Let $\mathcal{P} = \{\boldsymbol{x}_0, \ldots, \boldsymbol{x}_{N-1}\}$ be a point set in the s-dimensional unit-cube where $\boldsymbol{x}_n$ is of the form $\boldsymbol{x}_n = \{\boldsymbol{y}_n/b^m\}$ with $\boldsymbol{y}_n \in \mathbb{Z}^s$, and integers $m \geq 1$ and $b \geq 2$. Then we have*

$$D_N^*(\mathcal{P}) \leq 1 - \left(1 - \frac{1}{b^m}\right)^s + \sum_{\substack{\boldsymbol{k} \in \mathbb{N}_0^s \\ 0 < |\boldsymbol{k}|_\infty < b^m}} \rho_b(\boldsymbol{k}) \left| \frac{1}{N} \sum_{n=0}^{N-1} {}_b\mathrm{wal}_{\boldsymbol{k}}(\boldsymbol{x}_n) \right|.$$

The proof of this result is based on the following idea. We only consider elementary b-adic intervals, since we know from Lemma 3.9 that the characteristic functions of such intervals have a finite Walsh series representation. The remaining Walsh coefficients can be bounded independently of the chosen elementary interval. Then we approximate each interval with one corner anchored in the origin by elementary b-adic intervals and in this way the result will follow.

For the complete proof of Theorem 3.28, we need the following lemma which provides the announced bound on the Walsh coefficients for the characteristic function of an interval.

Lemma 3.29 *Let $J = [0, \beta)$ with $0 < \beta < 1$, and let $b^r \leq k < b^{r+1}$, where $r \in \mathbb{N}_0$. Then, for the kth Walsh coefficient of the characteristic function of J, we have*

$$|\widehat{\chi_J}(k)| \leq \rho_b(k).$$

Proof Let $\beta = \beta_1 b^{-1} + \beta_2 b^{-2} + \cdots$ be the b-adic expansion of β and let $\beta(r) := \beta_1 b^{-1} + \cdots + \beta_r b^{-r}$. Then we can write the interval $[0, \beta(r))$ as a disjoint union of finitely many one-dimensional b-adic elementary intervals $J(a, b^r) = [ab^{-r}, (a+1)b^{-r})$ of order r. As $k \geq b^r$, it follows from Lemma 3.9 that for each of these intervals $J(a, b^r)$, we have $\int_{J(a,b^r)} {}_b\mathrm{wal}_k(x)\,\mathrm{d}x = 0$. Therefore, we obtain

$$\widehat{\chi_J}(k) = \int_{\beta(r)}^{\beta} \overline{{}_b\mathrm{wal}_k(x)}\,\mathrm{d}x.$$

Let $k = \kappa_0 + \kappa_1 b + \cdots + \kappa_r b^r$ with $\kappa_r \neq 0$ and let $k(r) := k - \kappa_r b^r$. Then, the Walsh function ${}_b\mathrm{wal}_{k(r)}$ is constant on the interval $[\beta(r), \beta(r) + b^{-r})$ with value

${}_b\mathrm{wal}_{k(r)}(\beta(r))$. Hence, with $x = \xi_1 b^{-1} + \xi_2 b^{-2} + \cdots$, we obtain

$$\overline{\widehat{\chi_J}(k)} = \int_{\beta(r)}^{\beta} {}_b\mathrm{wal}_k(x)\,\mathrm{d}x = \int_{\beta(r)}^{\beta} \omega_b^{\xi_1\kappa_0+\cdots+\xi_r\kappa_{r-1}+\xi_{r+1}\kappa_r}\,\mathrm{d}x$$

$$= {}_b\mathrm{wal}_{k(r)}(\beta(r)) \int_{\beta(r)}^{\beta} \omega_b^{\xi_{r+1}\kappa_r}\,\mathrm{d}x. \tag{3.9}$$

For the last integral we split up the integration domain in β_{r+1} one-dimensional, b-adic elementary intervals of order $r+1$ and in a rest interval with length of at most $b^{-(r+1)}$. Then, we obtain

$$\int_{\beta(r)}^{\beta} \omega_b^{\xi_{r+1}\kappa_r}\,\mathrm{d}x = \sum_{l=0}^{\beta_{r+1}-1} \int_{\frac{\beta_1}{b}+\cdots+\frac{\beta_r}{b^r}+\frac{l}{b^{r+1}}}^{\frac{\beta_1}{b}+\cdots+\frac{\beta_r}{b^r}+\frac{l+1}{b^{r+1}}} \omega_b^{\xi_{r+1}\kappa_r}\,\mathrm{d}x + \int_{\frac{\beta_1}{b}+\cdots+\frac{\beta_{r+1}}{b^{r+1}}}^{\beta} \omega_b^{\xi_{r+1}\kappa_r}\,\mathrm{d}x$$

$$= \frac{1}{b^{r+1}} \sum_{l=0}^{\beta_{r+1}-1} \omega_b^{l\kappa_r} + \omega_b^{\beta_{r+1}\kappa_r}(\beta - \beta(r+1))$$

$$= \frac{1}{b^{r+1}} \frac{\omega_b^{\beta_{r+1}\kappa_r} - 1}{\omega_b^{\kappa_r} - 1} + \omega_b^{\beta_{r+1}\kappa_r}(\beta - \beta(r+1)). \tag{3.10}$$

From (3.9) and (3.10), we now obtain

$$|\widehat{\chi_J}(k)| = \frac{1}{b^{r+1}} \left| \frac{\omega_b^{\beta_{r+1}\kappa_r} - 1}{\omega_b^{\kappa_r} - 1} + b^{r+1}\omega_b^{\beta_{r+1}\kappa_r}(\beta - \beta(r+1)) \right|$$

$$= \frac{1}{b^{r+1}} \left| \omega_b^{\beta_{r+1}\kappa_r} \left(\frac{1}{\omega_b^{\kappa_r} - 1} + b^{r+1}(\beta - \beta(r+1)) \right) - \frac{1}{\omega_b^{\kappa_r} - 1} \right|$$

$$\le \frac{1}{b^{r+1}} \left(\left| \frac{1}{\omega_b^{\kappa_r} - 1} + b^{r+1}(\beta - \beta(r+1)) \right| + \frac{1}{|\omega_b^{\kappa_r} - 1|} \right).$$

For any $0 \le \gamma \le 1$ and any $z \in \mathbb{C}$, $z \ne 1$, with $|z| = 1$, we have $\left|\frac{1}{z-1} + \gamma\right| \le 1/|z-1|$. Applying this inequality to the term above, we find that

$$|\widehat{\chi_J}(k)| \le \frac{1}{b^{r+1}} \frac{2}{|\omega_b^{\kappa_r} - 1|} = \frac{1}{b^{r+1}} \frac{1}{|\sin(\pi\kappa_r/b)|}.$$

Since $\kappa_r \in \{1, \ldots, b-1\}$, it follows that $0 < \pi\kappa_r/b < \pi$ and hence, we can omit the absolute value for the sine function in the above term and the lemma is proved. □

Remark 3.30 In Lemma 14.8 below, we provide the Walsh series expansion of the function $\widehat{\chi_{[0,x)}}(k)$.

Proof of Theorem 3.28 Let $\boldsymbol{x} = (x_1, \ldots, x_s) \in [0,1]^s$. For $1 \le i \le s$, define $a_i := \min\{a \in \{1, \ldots, b^m\} : x_i \le a \cdot b^{-m}\}$ and set $\boldsymbol{y} := \frac{1}{b^m}\boldsymbol{a}$ with

$\boldsymbol{a} = (a_1, \ldots, a_s)$. Then we have

$$|\Delta_{\mathcal{P}}(\boldsymbol{x})| \le |\Delta_{\mathcal{P}}(\boldsymbol{x}) - \Delta_{\mathcal{P}}(\boldsymbol{y})| + |\Delta_{\mathcal{P}}(\boldsymbol{y})|.$$

As $\mathcal{P} \subseteq \frac{1}{b^m}\mathbb{Z}^s \pmod 1$, it follows that $A([\boldsymbol{0}, \boldsymbol{x}), N, \mathcal{P}) = A([\boldsymbol{0}, \boldsymbol{y}), N, \mathcal{P})$ and hence

$$|\Delta_{\mathcal{P}}(\boldsymbol{x})| \le |x_1 \cdots x_s - y_1 \cdots y_s| + |\Delta_{\mathcal{P}}(\boldsymbol{y})|. \tag{3.11}$$

Since $|x_i - y_i| \le \frac{1}{b^m}$ for all $1 \le i \le s$, we obtain with Lemma 3.18 that

$$|x_1 \cdots x_s - y_1 \cdots y_s| \le 1 - \left(1 - \frac{1}{b^m}\right)^s. \tag{3.12}$$

It remains to estimate $|\Delta_{\mathcal{P}}(\boldsymbol{y})|$. Obviously, the interval $G := [\boldsymbol{0}, \boldsymbol{y})$ can be written as a finite disjoint union of b-adic elementary intervals of the form $\prod_{i=1}^s \left[\frac{c_i}{b^m}, \frac{c_i+1}{b^m}\right)$ with integers $0 \le c_i < b^m$ for all $1 \le i \le s$. Hence, it follows from Lemma 3.9 that $\widehat{\chi}_G(\boldsymbol{k}) = 0$ for all $\boldsymbol{k} \in \mathbb{N}_0^s$ with $|\boldsymbol{k}|_\infty \ge b^m$. Therefore, and by invoking the identity $\widehat{\chi}_G(\boldsymbol{0}) = \lambda_s(G)$, we find

$$\Delta_{\mathcal{P}}(\boldsymbol{y}) = \frac{1}{N}\sum_{n=0}^{N-1} (\chi_G(\boldsymbol{x}_n) - \lambda_s(G)) - \sum_{\substack{\boldsymbol{k} \in \mathbb{N}_0^s \\ 0 < |\boldsymbol{k}|_\infty < b^m}} \widehat{\chi}_G(\boldsymbol{k}) \left(\frac{1}{N}\sum_{n=0}^{N-1} {}_b\mathrm{wal}_{\boldsymbol{k}}(\boldsymbol{x}_n)\right).$$

Using Lemma 3.29, it follows that $|\widehat{\chi}_G(\boldsymbol{k})| \le \rho_b(\boldsymbol{k})$ and hence, we obtain

$$|\Delta_{\mathcal{P}}(\boldsymbol{y})| \le \sum_{\substack{\boldsymbol{k} \in \mathbb{N}_0^s \\ 0 < |\boldsymbol{k}|_\infty < b^m}} \rho_b(\boldsymbol{k}) \left|\frac{1}{N}\sum_{n=0}^{N-1} {}_b\mathrm{wal}_{\boldsymbol{k}}(\boldsymbol{x}_n)\right|. \tag{3.13}$$

From (3.11), (3.12) and (3.13), we now have

$$|\Delta_{\mathcal{P}}(\boldsymbol{x})| \le 1 - \left(1 - \frac{1}{b^m}\right)^s + \sum_{\substack{\boldsymbol{k} \in \mathbb{N}_0^s \\ 0 < |\boldsymbol{k}|_\infty < b^m}} \rho_b(\boldsymbol{k}) \left|\frac{1}{N}\sum_{n=0}^{N-1} {}_b\mathrm{wal}_{\boldsymbol{k}}(\boldsymbol{x}_n)\right|.$$

As this bound holds for any $\boldsymbol{x} \in [0, 1]^s$, it follows that the star discrepancy of $\mathcal{P}$ also satisfies this bound and hence the result is proved. □

Remark 3.31 Note that for the point set $\mathcal{P}$ as considered in Theorem 3.28, we also have

$$D_N^*(\mathcal{P}) \ge 1 - \left(1 - \frac{1}{b^m}\right)^s.$$

This follows easily from the assumption that the components of the points of $\mathcal{P}$ are of the form a/b^m with $a \in \{0, \ldots, b^m - 1\}$ and hence $\mathcal{P} \subseteq [0, 1 - b^{-m}]^s$.

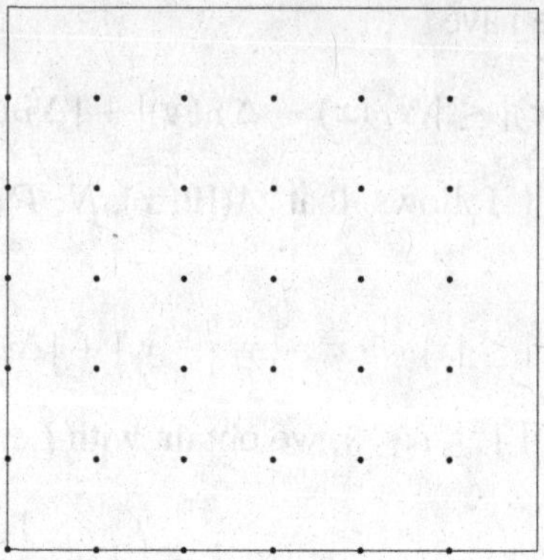

Figure 3.4 Regular lattice Γ_6 in $[0, 1)^2$, i.e. $s = 2$ and $m = 6$.

3.4 Discrepancy of special point sets and sequences

In this section we analyse the discrepancy of some classical constructions of point sets in $[0, 1)^s$.

3.4.1 The regular lattice

If we think of a point set whose points are very uniformly distributed in the unit-cube, we immediately might have a regular lattice (or equidistant grid) in mind see Figure 3.4.

By a *regular lattice* of $N = m^s$ points in the s-dimensional unit-cube, we understand the point set

$$\Gamma_m := \frac{1}{m}\mathbb{Z}^s \pmod 1 = \left\{\left(\frac{n_1}{m}, \ldots, \frac{n_s}{m}\right) : 0 \le n_i < m \text{ for } 1 \le i \le s\right\}. \tag{3.14}$$

However, we show in the next result that, with respect to discrepancy, this is not a good choice.

Proposition 3.32 *Let $m \ge 2$ be an integer. For the star discrepancy of the regular lattice Γ_m consisting of $N = m^s$ points in $[0, 1)^s$, we have*

$$D_N^*(\Gamma_m) = 1 - \left(1 - \frac{1}{m}\right)^s.$$

Remark 3.33 Note that $N^{-1/s} \le 1 - (1 - 1/m)^s \le s/m = sN^{-1/s}$, and hence, for the star discrepancy of the regular lattice (3.14), we have

$$\frac{1}{N^{1/s}} \le D_N^*(\Gamma_m) \le \frac{s}{N^{1/s}}.$$

Proof of Proposition 3.32 As in Remark 3.31, we find that

$$D_N^*(\Gamma_m) \geq 1 - \left(1 - \frac{1}{m}\right)^s.$$

Now consider an arbitrary interval of the form $J = [0, \alpha_1) \times \cdots \times [0, \alpha_s)$. For $1 \leq i \leq s$, let $a_i \in \{0, \ldots, m-1\}$ be such that $a_i/m < \alpha_i \leq (a_i + 1)/m$. Then we have $A(J, N, \Gamma_m) = \prod_{i=1}^s (a_i + 1)$ and

$$0 \leq \frac{A(J, N, \Gamma_m)}{N} - \lambda_s(J) \leq \prod_{i=1}^s \frac{a_i + 1}{m} - \prod_{i=1}^s \frac{a_i}{m}.$$

Therefore, and by invoking Lemma 3.18, we obtain

$$\left|\frac{A(J, N, \Gamma_m)}{N} - \lambda_s(J)\right| \leq \left|\prod_{i=1}^s \frac{a_i + 1}{m} - \prod_{i=1}^s \frac{a_i}{m}\right| \leq 1 - \left(1 - \frac{1}{m}\right)^s.$$

As J was chosen arbitrarily, the result follows. (Alternatively, one may also use Theorem 3.27; see Exercise 3.21.) □

For dimension $s > 1$, the star discrepancy of the regular lattice is very poor. But for dimension $s = 1$, the order of the star discrepancy of the regular lattice is the best possible.

For the centred regular lattice Γ_m^c consisting of $N = m^s$ points defined by (1.1), one can show in the same way as above (see Exercise 3.22) that

$$D_N^*(\Gamma_m^c) = 1 - \left(1 - \frac{1}{2m}\right)^s.$$

Moreover, in dimension $s = 1$, it can be shown that the centred regular lattice $\Gamma_N^c = \{x_n = \frac{2n+1}{2N} : 0 \leq n < N\}$ has star discrepancy $D_N^*(\Gamma_N^c) = \frac{1}{2N}$ (see Exercise 2.1). This is the best possible among all point sets consisting of N points in $[0, 1)$. For a proof, we refer to [130, Chapter 2, Corollary 1.2] or to [177, Theorem 2.6].

3.4.2 The van der Corput–Halton sequence

Now we turn to another construction which is a multi-dimensional generalisation of the van der Corput sequence as introduced in Definition 3.10.

Definition 3.34 Let $b_1, \ldots, b_s \geq 2$ be integers. The *van der Corput–Halton sequence* is the sequence $\mathcal{S} = (\boldsymbol{x}_n)_{n \geq 0}$ with $\boldsymbol{x}_n = (\varphi_{b_1}(n), \ldots, \varphi_{b_s}(n))$ for all $n \in \mathbb{N}_0$. Here, φ_b is the b-adic radical inverse function as defined in Definition 3.10. The integers $b_1, \ldots, b_s$ are often called the *bases* of the van der Corput–Halton sequence.

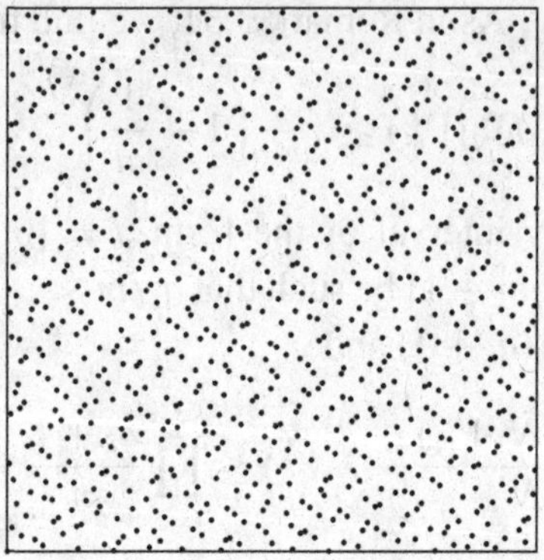

Figure 3.5 The first 1000 points of the two-dimensional van der Corput–Halton sequence in bases $b_1 = 2$ and $b_2 = 3$.

Example 3.35 For dimension $s = 2$ and bases $b_1 = 2$ and $b_2 = 3$. The first points of the van der Corput–Halton sequence are given by $\boldsymbol{x}_0 = (0, 0)$, $\boldsymbol{x}_1 = (1/2, 1/3)$, $\boldsymbol{x}_2 = (1/4, 2/3)$, $\boldsymbol{x}_3 = (3/4, 1/9)$, $\boldsymbol{x}_4 = (1/8, 4/9)$ and so on. The first 1000 points of this sequence are shown in Figure 3.5.

It was known for a long time that, provided that the bases $b_1, \ldots, b_s$ are chosen to be pairwise relatively prime, the star discrepancy of the first N elements of the van der Corput–Halton sequence can be bounded by $c(b_1, \ldots, b_s)(\log N)^s/N + O((\log N)^{s-1}/N)$. For example, this was shown in [66, 89, 114, 163, 177]. Informally, one calls a sequence in the s-dimensional unit-cube a *low-discrepancy sequence* if its star discrepancy is of order $(\log N)^s/N$. While it is widely believed that this order of convergence is the best possible for any infinite sequence in the s-dimensional unit-cube, those results have a disadvantage in practical application. Namely, the constant $c(b_1, \ldots, b_s) > 0$ depends very strongly on the dimension s. The minimal value for this quantity can be obtained if one chooses for $b_1, \ldots, b_s$ the first s prime numbers. But also, in this case, $c(b_1, \ldots, b_s)$ grows very fast to infinity if s increases.

This deficiency was remedied by Atanassov [6], who proved the following result.

Theorem 3.36 *Let $b_1, \ldots, b_s \geq 2$ be pairwise relatively prime integers and let $\mathcal{S}$ be the van der Corput–Halton sequence with bases $b_1, \ldots, b_s$. Then, for any $N \geq 2$, we have*

$$N D_N^*(\mathcal{S}) \leq \frac{1}{s!} \prod_{i=1}^{s} \left(\frac{\lfloor b_i/2 \rfloor \log N}{\log b_i} + s \right) + \sum_{k=0}^{s-1} \frac{b_{k+1}}{k!} \prod_{i=1}^{k} \left(\frac{\lfloor b_i/2 \rfloor \log N}{\log b_i} + k \right).$$

In the following we present the proof of this result of Atanassov [6]. From now on let $b_1, \ldots, b_s \geq 2$ be pairwise relatively prime integers and let $\mathcal{S}$ be the van der Corput–Halton sequence with bases $b_1, \ldots, b_s$.

Lemma 3.37 *Let J be an interval of the form $J = \prod_{i=1}^{s} \left[u_i/b_i^{m_i}, v_i/b_i^{m_i}\right)$ with integers $0 \leq u_i < v_i < b_i^{m_i}$ and $m_i \geq 1$ for all $1 \leq i \leq s$. Then, for the van der Corput–Halton sequence $\mathcal{S}$, the inequality*

$$|A(J, N, \mathcal{S}) - N\lambda_s(J)| \leq \prod_{i=1}^{s}(v_i - u_i)$$

holds for every $N \in \mathbb{N}$. Furthermore, for every $N \leq \prod_{i=1}^{s} b_i^{m_i}$ we have $A(J, N, \mathcal{S}) \leq \prod_{i=1}^{s}(v_i - u_i)$.

Proof For $n \in \mathbb{N}_0$ we denote the b_i-adic expansion by $n = n_0^{(i)} + n_1^{(i)} b_i + \cdots$. Choose $\boldsymbol{l} = (l_1, \ldots, l_s) \in \mathbb{N}_0^s$ with $0 \leq l_i < b_i^{m_i}$ and with b_i-adic expansion $l_i = l_{i,m_i-1} + l_{i,m_i-2} b_i + \cdots + l_{i,0} b_i^{m_i-1}$ for all $1 \leq i \leq s$. We consider the interval

$$J_{\boldsymbol{l}} = \prod_{i=1}^{s} \left[\frac{l_i}{b_i^{m_i}}, \frac{l_i + 1}{b_i^{m_i}}\right).$$

Then the nth element $\boldsymbol{x}_n$ of the van der Corput–Halton sequence is contained in $J_{\boldsymbol{l}}$, if and only if

$$\frac{l_{i,0}}{b_i} + \cdots + \frac{l_{i,m_i-1}}{b_i^{m_i}} \leq \frac{n_0^{(i)}}{b_i} + \frac{n_1^{(i)}}{b_i^2} + \cdots < \frac{l_{i,0}}{b_i} + \cdots + \frac{l_{i,m_i-1}}{b_i^{m_i}} + \frac{1}{b_i^{m_i}}$$

for all $1 \leq i \leq s$. This, however, is equivalent to $n_0^{(i)} = l_{i,0}, \ldots, n_{m_i-1}^{(i)} = l_{i,m_i-1}$, which in turn is equivalent to $n \equiv l_{i,0} + l_{i,1} b_i + \cdots + l_{i,m_i-1} b_i^{m_i-1} \pmod{b_i^{m_i}}$ for all $1 \leq i \leq s$.

As $b_1, \ldots, b_s$ are pairwise relatively prime, we obtain from the Chinese remainder theorem that among every $b_1^{m_1} \cdots b_s^{m_s}$ consecutive elements of the van der Corput–Halton sequence, exactly one element is contained in $J_{\boldsymbol{l}}$ or, in other words, $A(J_{\boldsymbol{l}}, t b_1^{m_1} \cdots b_s^{m_s}, \mathcal{S}) = t$ for all $t \in \mathbb{N}$ and hence,

$$A(J_{\boldsymbol{l}}, t b_1^{m_1} \cdots b_s^{m_s}, \mathcal{S}) - t b_1^{m_1} \cdots b_s^{m_s} \lambda_s(J_{\boldsymbol{l}}) = 0.$$

Therefore, for every $N \in \mathbb{N}$, we obtain

$$|A(J_{\boldsymbol{l}}, N, \mathcal{S}) - N\lambda_s(J_{\boldsymbol{l}})| \leq 1.$$

Now we write the interval J as a disjoint union of intervals of the form $J_{\boldsymbol{l}}$,

$$J = \bigcup_{l_1=u_1}^{v_1-1} \cdots \bigcup_{l_s=u_s}^{v_s-1} J_{\boldsymbol{l}},$$

where $\boldsymbol{l} = (l_1, \ldots, l_s)$. Then we have

$$|A(J, N, \mathcal{S}) - N\lambda_s(J)| \le \sum_{l_1=u_1}^{v_1-1} \cdots \sum_{l_s=u_s}^{v_s-1} |A(J_{\boldsymbol{l}}, N, \mathcal{S}) - N\lambda_s(J_{\boldsymbol{l}})| \le \prod_{i=1}^{s}(v_i - u_i),$$

which proves the first assertion.

For $N \le b_1^{m_1} \cdots b_s^{m_s}$ we have $A(J_{\boldsymbol{l}}, N, \mathcal{S}) \le 1$ for all $\boldsymbol{l} = (l_1, \ldots, l_s) \in \mathbb{N}_0^s$ with $0 \le l_i < b_i^{m_i}$ for $1 \le i \le s$ and hence,

$$A(J, N, \mathcal{S}) = \sum_{l_1=u_1}^{v_1-1} \cdots \sum_{l_s=u_s}^{v_s-1} A(J_{\boldsymbol{l}}, N, \mathcal{S}) \le \prod_{i=1}^{s}(v_i - u_i).$$

This was the second assertion of the lemma. □

Lemma 3.38 *Let $k \in \mathbb{N}$ and let $b_1, \ldots, b_k \ge 2$ be integers. For $N \in \mathbb{N}$, let $d(b_1, \ldots, b_k; N)$ be the number of tuples $(j_1, \ldots, j_k) \in \mathbb{N}^k$ such that $b_1^{j_1} \cdots b_k^{j_k} \le N$. Then we have*

$$d(b_1, \ldots, b_k; N) \le \frac{1}{k!} \prod_{i=1}^{k} \frac{\log N}{\log b_i}.$$

Proof Assume that $\boldsymbol{j} = (j_1, \ldots, j_k) \in \mathbb{N}^k$ satisfies $b_1^{j_1} \cdots b_k^{j_k} \le N$. Then the interval $E_{\boldsymbol{j}} := \prod_{i=1}^{k}[j_i - 1, j_i)$ of volume one is entirely contained in the simplex

$$S := \{(x_1, \ldots, x_k) \in [0, \infty)^k \ : \ x_1 \log b_1 + \cdots + x_k \log b_k \le \log N\}$$

of volume $\frac{1}{k!} \prod_{i=1}^{s} \frac{\log N}{\log b_i}$. Hence,

$$d(b_1, \ldots, b_k; N) = \lambda_k \left(\bigcup_{E_{\boldsymbol{j}} \subseteq S} E_{\boldsymbol{j}} \right) \le \lambda_k(S) = \frac{1}{k!} \prod_{i=1}^{s} \frac{\log N}{\log b_i}.$$ □

Lemma 3.39 *Let $N \in \mathbb{N}$ and let $b_1, \ldots, b_k \ge 2$ be integers. Furthermore, for $1 \le i \le k$, let $c_0^{(i)}, c_1^{(i)}, \ldots \ge 0$ be given such that $c_0^{(i)} \le 1$ and $c_j^{(i)} \le f_i$ for all $j \ge 1$ and all $1 \le i \le k$. Then we have*

$$\sum_{\substack{(j_1, \ldots, j_k) \in \mathbb{N}_0^k \\ b_1^{j_1} \cdots b_k^{j_k} \le N}} \prod_{i=1}^{k} c_{j_i}^{(i)} \le \frac{1}{k!} \prod_{i=1}^{k} \left(f_i \frac{\log N}{\log b_i} + k \right).$$

Proof Let $\mathfrak{u} \subseteq \{1, \ldots, k\}$. Then the number of k-tuples $(j_1, \ldots, j_k)$ with $j_i > 0$ if $i \in \mathfrak{u}$, $j_i = 0$ if $i \notin \mathfrak{u}$ and $\prod_{i \in \mathfrak{u}} b_i^{j_i} \le N$ is by Lemma 3.38 bounded above by $\frac{1}{|\mathfrak{u}|!} \prod_{i \in \mathfrak{u}} \frac{\log N}{\log b_i}$. Furthermore, each of these k-tuples contributes at most $\prod_{i \in \mathfrak{u}} f_i$ to the sum on the left-hand side in the statement of the lemma. From this, and invoking the inequality $\frac{1}{|\mathfrak{u}|!} \leq \frac{k^{k-|\mathfrak{u}|}}{k!}$, we obtain

$$\sum_{\substack{(j_1,\ldots,j_k)\in\mathbb{N}_0^k \\ b_1^{j_1}\cdots b_k^{j_k}\leq N}} \prod_{i=1}^{k} c_{j_i}^{(i)} \leq \sum_{\mathfrak{u}\subseteq\{1,\ldots,k\}} \frac{1}{|\mathfrak{u}|!} \prod_{i\in\mathfrak{u}} f_i \frac{\log N}{\log b_i}$$

$$\leq \frac{1}{k!} \sum_{\mathfrak{u}\subseteq\{1,\ldots,k\}} k^{k-|\mathfrak{u}|} \prod_{i\in\mathfrak{u}} f_i \frac{\log N}{\log b_i} = \frac{1}{k!} \prod_{i=1}^{k} \left(f_i \frac{\log N}{\log b_i} + k \right),$$

and this is the desired result. □

Now we need to introduce some notation: let $J \subseteq \mathbb{R}^s$ be an interval. Then a *signed splitting* of J is a collection of not necessarily disjoint intervals $J_1, \ldots, J_r$ together with signs $\varepsilon_1, \ldots, \varepsilon_r \in \{-1, 1\}$ such that for all $x \in J$, we have

$$\sum_{\substack{i=1 \\ x\in J_i}}^{r} \varepsilon_i = 1.$$

As a consequence, for any additive function ν on the class of intervals in $\mathbb{R}^s$, we have

$$\nu(J) = \sum_{i=1}^{r} \varepsilon_i \nu(J_i).$$

Here, as usual, a function ν on the class of intervals in $\mathbb{R}^s$ is said to be additive if, whenever A and B are disjoint intervals, then $\nu(A \cup B) = \nu(A) + \nu(B)$.

Lemma 3.40 *Let $J = \prod_{i=1}^{s} [0, z_i)$ be an s-dimensional interval and let for each $1 \leq i \leq s$ be given a finite sequence $(z_{j,i})_{j=1,\ldots,n_i}$ of numbers in $[0, 1]$. Define, further, $z_{0,i} := 0$ and $z_{n_i+1,i} := z_i$ for all $1 \leq i \leq s$. Then the collection of intervals*

$$\prod_{i=1}^{s} \left[\min\left(z_{j_i,i}, z_{j_i+1,i}\right), \max\left(z_{j_i,i}, z_{j_i+1,i}\right)\right)$$

together with the signs $\varepsilon_{j_1,\ldots,j_s} = \prod_{i=1}^{s} \operatorname{sgn}(z_{j_i+1,i} - z_{j_i,i})$ for $0 \leq j_i \leq n_i$ and $1 \leq i \leq s$ defines a signed splitting of the interval J.

Proof First, we show the result for $s = 1$. For simplicity we omit the index i for the dimension. Let $J = [0, z)$ and let $z_0, \ldots, z_{n+1} \in [0, 1)$ with $z_0 = 0$ and $z_{n+1} = z$. Assume that we are given a point $x \in [0, z)$. If $z_j \leq x$ for all $j = 0, \ldots, n+1$, then it follows that $x \notin J$. Now we define finite sequences $\underline{j}_k, k = 0, \ldots, K$ and $\overline{j}_k$, $k = 0, \ldots, K-1$ in the following way: let $\overline{j}_0 > 0$ be minimal, such that $z_{\overline{j}_0} > x$

and let $\underline{j}_0 > \overline{j}_0$ be minimal such that $z_{\underline{j}_0} \leq x$, let $\overline{j}_1 > \underline{j}_0$ be minimal, such that $z_{\overline{j}_1} > x$ and let $\underline{j}_1 > \overline{j}_1$ be minimal such that $z_{\underline{j}_1} \leq x$. We repeat this procedure and finally we choose $\overline{j}_K > \underline{j}_{K-1}$ to be minimal, such that $z_{\overline{j}_K} > x$ and $z_j > x$ for all $j \geq \overline{j}_K$. Since $z_{n+1} = z > x$, we always end in such a case.

With this definition, we have $z_{\overline{j}_k - 1} \leq x < z_{\overline{j}_k}$ for $k = 0, \ldots, K$ and $z_{\underline{j}_k} \leq x < z_{\underline{j}_k - 1}$ for $k = 0, \ldots, K-1$.

For $J_j := \left[\min(z_j, z_{j+1}), \max(z_j, z_{j+1})\right)$ and $\varepsilon_j := \operatorname{sgn}(z_{j+1} - z_j)$, we then have $x \in J_{\overline{j}_k - 1}$ with $\varepsilon_{\overline{j}_k - 1} = +1$ and $x \in J_{\underline{j}_k - 1}$ with $\varepsilon_{\underline{j}_k - 1} = -1$ and $x \notin J_j$ for $j \neq \underline{j}_k - 1$ or $j \neq \overline{j}_k - 1$. Hence,

$$\sum_{\substack{j=0 \\ x \in J_j}}^{n} \varepsilon_j = \sum_{\substack{j=0 \\ z_j \leq x < z_{j+1}}}^{n} 1 - \sum_{\substack{j=0 \\ z_{j+1} \leq x < z_j}}^{n} 1 = \sum_{k=0}^{K} 1 - \sum_{k=0}^{K-1} 1 = 1,$$

and thus we have a signed splitting of the interval $J = [0, z)$.

Now we turn to the multi-dimensional case: assume that we are given a point $\boldsymbol{x} = (x_1, \ldots, x_s) \in J$. Then we have

$$\boldsymbol{x} \in J_{j_1,\ldots,j_s} = \prod_{i=1}^{s} J_{j_i,i} := \prod_{i=1}^{s} \left[\min\left(z_{j_i,i}, z_{j_i+1,i}\right), \max\left(z_{j_i,i}, z_{j_i+1,i}\right)\right),$$

if and only if $x_i \in J_{j_i,i}$ for all $1 \leq i \leq s$. Then we have

$$\underbrace{\sum_{j_1=0}^{n_1} \cdots \sum_{j_s=0}^{n_s}}_{\boldsymbol{x} \in J_{j_1,\ldots,j_s}} \varepsilon_{j_1,\ldots,j_s} = \prod_{i=1}^{s} \sum_{\substack{j_i=0 \\ x_i \in J_{j_i,i}}}^{n_i} \operatorname{sgn}(z_{j_i+1,i} - z_{j_i,i}) = 1,$$

where the last equality follows from the fact that for each $1 \leq i \leq s$ the collection of intervals $J_{j_i,i}$ together with the signs $\varepsilon_{j_i} = \operatorname{sgn}(z_{j_i+1,i} - z_{j_i,i})$ for $0 \leq j_i \leq n_i$, defines a signed splitting of the interval $[0, z_i)$ as shown above. □

For the proof of Theorem 3.36, we need a digit expansion of reals $z \in [0, 1)$ in an integer base $b \geq 2$ which uses signed digits. The next lemma shows that such an expansion exists.

Lemma 3.41 *Let $b \geq 2$ be an integer. Then every $z \in [0, 1)$ can be written in the form*

$$z = a_0 + \frac{a_1}{b} + \frac{a_2}{b^2} + \cdots$$

with integer digits $a_0, a_1, a_2, \ldots$ such that $-\left\lfloor \frac{b-1}{2} \right\rfloor \leq a_j \leq \left\lfloor \frac{b}{2} \right\rfloor$ for all $j \in \mathbb{N}_0$. This expansion is called the signed b-adic digit expansion of z.

Proof For $b = 2$, we may use the usual b-adic digit expansion. For $b \geq 3$, let $c = \lfloor \frac{b-1}{2} \rfloor$ and $x = cb^{-1} + cb^{-2} + cb^{-3} + \cdots \in [0, 1)$. For $z \in [0, 1)$, we have $z + x \in [0, 2)$ with b-adic expansion $z + x = u_0 + u_1 b^{-1} + u_2 b^{-2} + \cdots$, where $u_0 \in \{0, 1\}$ and $u_1, u_2, \ldots \in \{0, \ldots, b-1\}$. Hence,

$$z = u_0 + \frac{u_1 - c}{b} + \frac{u_2 - c}{b^2} + \cdots$$

with $-\lfloor \frac{b-1}{2} \rfloor \leq 0 \leq u_0 \leq 1 \leq \lfloor \frac{b}{2} \rfloor$ and $-\lfloor \frac{b-1}{2} \rfloor \leq u_j - c \leq b - 1 - \lfloor \frac{b-1}{2} \rfloor = \lfloor \frac{b}{2} \rfloor$ for $j \in \mathbb{N}$. □

Proof of Theorem 3.36 Let $J = [\mathbf{0}, \boldsymbol{z}) \subseteq [0, 1)^s$ with $\boldsymbol{z} = (z_1, \ldots, z_s)$. According to Lemma 3.41, for all $1 \leq i \leq s$ we consider the signed b_i-adic digit expansion of z_i of the form $z_i = a_{i,0} + a_{i,1} b_i^{-1} + a_{i,2} b_i^{-2} + a_{i,3} b_i^{-3} + \cdots$ with $-\lfloor (b_i - 1)/2 \rfloor \leq a_{i,j} \leq \lfloor b_i/2 \rfloor$.

For all $1 \leq i \leq s$ let $n_i := \lfloor \log N / \log b_i \rfloor$ and for $1 \leq l \leq n_i$ define the truncations of the expansions $z_{l,i} = \sum_{j=0}^{l-1} a_{i,j} b_i^{-j}$ and let $z_{0,i} = 0$ and $z_{n_i+1,i} = z_i$.

According to Lemma 3.40 the collection of intervals

$$J_{\boldsymbol{j}} = \prod_{i=1}^{s} \left[\min\left(z_{j_i,i}, z_{j_i+1,i}\right), \max\left(z_{j_i,i}, z_{j_i+1,i}\right)\right)$$

together with the signs $\varepsilon_{\boldsymbol{j}} = \prod_{i=1}^{s} \operatorname{sgn}(z_{j_i+1,i} - z_{j_i,i})$ for $\boldsymbol{j} = (j_1, \ldots, j_s)$ and $0 \leq j_i \leq n_i$, $1 \leq i \leq s$ define a signed splitting of the interval $J = [\mathbf{0}, \boldsymbol{z})$.

Since both λ_s and $A(\cdot, N, \mathcal{S})$ are additive functions on the set of intervals, we obtain

$$A(J, N, \mathcal{S}) - N\lambda_s(J) = \sum_{j_1=0}^{n_1} \cdots \sum_{j_s=0}^{n_s} \varepsilon_{\boldsymbol{j}} (A(J_{\boldsymbol{j}}, N, \mathcal{S}) - N\lambda_s(J_{\boldsymbol{j}})) =: \Sigma_1 + \Sigma_2,$$

where Σ_1 denotes the sum over all $\boldsymbol{j} = (j_1, \ldots, j_s)$ such that $b_1^{j_1} \cdots b_s^{j_s} \leq N$ and Σ_2 denotes the remaining part of the above sum.

First, we deal with the sum Σ_1. For any $1 \leq i \leq s$ the length of the interval $\left[\min\left(z_{j_i,i}, z_{j_i+1,i}\right), \max\left(z_{j_i,i}, z_{j_i+1,i}\right)\right)$ is $|a_{i,j_i} b_i^{-j_i}|$ and also the limit points of this interval are rationals with denominator $b_i^{j_i}$. Hence, the intervals $J_{\boldsymbol{j}}$ are of the form as considered in Lemma 3.37 from which we now obtain

$$|A(J_{\boldsymbol{j}}, N, \mathcal{S}) - N\lambda_s(J_{\boldsymbol{j}})| \leq \prod_{i=1}^{s} \left|a_{i,j_i}\right|.$$

We have $|a_{i,j_i}| \leq \lfloor b_i/2 \rfloor =: f_i$. An application of Lemma 3.39 then yields

$$\Sigma_1 \leq \frac{1}{s!} \prod_{i=1}^{s} \left(\frac{\lfloor b_i/2 \rfloor \log N}{\log b_i} + s \right).$$

It remains to estimate Σ_2. To this end we split the set of s-tuples $\boldsymbol{j} = (j_1, \ldots, j_s)$ for which $b_1^{j_1} \cdots b_s^{j_s} > N$ into disjoint sets $B_0, \ldots, B_{s-1}$, where, for $1 \le k \le s-1$, we set

$$B_k = \{\boldsymbol{j} \in \mathbb{N}_0^s : b_1^{j_1} \cdots b_k^{j_k} \le N \text{ and } b_1^{j_1} \cdots b_k^{j_k} b_{k+1}^{j_{k+1}} > N\}$$

and $B_0 = \{\boldsymbol{j} \in \mathbb{N}_0^s : b_1^{j_1} > N\}$.

For a fixed $0 \le k \le s-1$ and a fixed k-tuple $(j_1, \ldots, j_k)$ with $b_1^{j_1} \cdots b_k^{j_k} \le N$, define r to be the largest integer such that $b_1^{j_1} \cdots b_k^{j_k} b_{k+1}^{r-1} \le N$. Then the tuple $(j_1, \ldots, j_k, j_{k+1}, \ldots, j_s)$ is contained in B_k if and only if $j_{k+1} \ge r$ (and $j_{k+2}, \ldots, j_s$ can be chosen arbitrarily).

Therefore, for any $k \ge 0$ and fixed $j_1, \ldots, j_k \in \mathbb{N}_0$ such that $b_1^{j_1} \cdots b_k^{j_k} \le N$, we have

$$\sum_{\substack{j_{k+1}, \ldots, j_s \in \mathbb{N} \\ \boldsymbol{j} \in B_k}} \varepsilon_{\boldsymbol{j}}(A(J_{\boldsymbol{j}}, N, \mathcal{S}) - N\lambda_s(J_{\boldsymbol{j}})) = \pm(A(K, N, \mathcal{S}) - N\lambda_s(K)),$$

where

$$K = \prod_{i=1}^{k} \left[\min\left(z_{j_i,i}, z_{j_{i+1},i}\right), \max\left(z_{j_i,i}, z_{j_{i+1},i}\right)\right)$$
$$\times \left[\min\left(z_{r,k+1}, z_{k+1}\right), \max\left(z_{r,k+1}, z_{k+1}\right)\right) \times \prod_{i=k+2}^{s} [0, z_i)\,.$$

Let $\boldsymbol{j} \in B_k$. As

$$\left|z_{k+1} - z_{r,k+1}\right| \le \left\lfloor \frac{b_{k+1}}{2} \right\rfloor \frac{1}{b_{k+1}^r} \frac{b_{k+1}}{b_{k+1} - 1} \le \frac{1}{b_{k+1}^{r-1}}$$

it follows that the interval $\left[\min\left(z_{r,k+1}, z_{k+1}\right), \max\left(z_{r,k+1}, z_{k+1}\right)\right)$ is contained in some interval $\left[m_1/b_{k+1}^r, m_2/b_{k+1}^r\right)$ for $m_1, m_2 \in \mathbb{N}_0$ and with $m_2 - m_1 \le b_{k+1}$ and hence K is contained in the interval

$$K' = \prod_{i=1}^{k} \left[\min\left(z_{j_i,i}, z_{j_{i+1},i}\right), \max\left(z_{j_i,i}, z_{j_{i+1},i}\right)\right) \times \left[\frac{m_1}{b_{k+1}^r}, \frac{m_2}{b_{k+1}^r}\right) \times [0, 1)^{s-k-1}.$$

Note that $\boldsymbol{j} \in B_k$ and hence $N < b_1^{j_1} \cdots b_k^{j_k} b_{k+1}^r$. Thus, an application of Lemma 3.37 yields

$$A(K, N, \mathcal{S}) \le A(K', N, \mathcal{S}) \le b_{k+1} \prod_{i=1}^{k} \left|a_{i,j_i}\right|.$$

But on the other hand we also have $N\lambda_s(K) \leq b_{k+1} \prod_{i=1}^{k} |a_{i,j_i}|$ and hence,

$$|A(K, N, \mathcal{S}) - N\lambda_s(K)| \leq b_{k+1} \prod_{i=1}^{k} |a_{i,j_i}| \leq b_{k+1} \prod_{i=1}^{k} c_{i,j_i},$$

where $c_{i,j_i} = 1$ if $j_i = 0$ and $c_{i,j_i} = \lfloor b_i/2 \rfloor$ otherwise.

Summing up, we obtain

$$|\Sigma_2| \leq \sum_{k=0}^{s-1} \sum_{\substack{j_1,\ldots,j_k \in \mathbb{N}_0 \\ b_1^{j_1}\cdots b_k^{j_k} \leq N}} \left| \sum_{j \in B_k} \varepsilon_j (A(J_j, N, \mathcal{S}) - N\lambda_s(J_j)) \right|$$

$$\leq \sum_{k=0}^{s-1} \sum_{\substack{j_1,\ldots,j_k \in \mathbb{N}_0 \\ b_1^{j_1}\cdots b_k^{j_k} \leq N}} b_{k+1} \prod_{i=1}^{k} c_{i,j_i} \leq \sum_{k=0}^{s-1} \frac{b_{k+1}}{k!} \prod_{i=1}^{k} \left(\frac{\lfloor b_i/2 \rfloor \log N}{\log b_i} + k \right),$$

where we used Lemma 3.39 again. Hence, the result follows. □

Corollary 3.42 *Let $b_1, \ldots, b_s \geq 2$ be pairwise relatively prime integers and let $\mathcal{S}$ be the van der Corput–Halton sequence with bases $b_1, \ldots, b_s$. Then, for any $N \geq 2$, we have*

$$D_N^*(\mathcal{S}) \leq c(b_1, \ldots, b_s) \frac{(\log N)^s}{N} + O\left(\frac{(\log N)^{s-1}}{N} \right),$$

with

$$c(b_1, \ldots, b_s) = \frac{1}{s!} \prod_{i=1}^{s} \frac{\lfloor b_i/2 \rfloor}{\log b_i}.$$

Furthermore, if $b_1, \ldots, b_s$ are the first s primes, then $c(b_1, \ldots, b_s) \leq \frac{7}{2^s s}$.

Proof The first part of the corollary follows immediately from Theorem 3.36. Hence, let us assume that $b_1, \ldots, b_s$ are the first s prime numbers in increasing order. Then $b_2, \ldots, b_s$ are odd and hence $\lfloor b_i/2 \rfloor = (b_i - 1)/2$ for $2 \leq i \leq s$. Let $\pi(x)$ denote the prime counting function, i.e. $\pi(x)$ counts all prime numbers less than or equal to x. For any $x \geq 11$ we have $\pi(x) > x/\log x$; see [231, Chapter VII]. Therefore, we find that for $i \geq 6$ we have $i - 1 = \pi(b_i - 1) > \frac{b_i - 1}{\log(b_i - 1)} > \frac{b_i - 1}{\log b_i}$. Consequently, for $i \geq 6$, we have $\frac{b_i - 1}{i \log b_i} < \frac{i-1}{i}$ and hence, for $s \geq 6$ we have

$$c(b_1, \ldots, b_s) \leq \frac{2^5 A}{2^s} \prod_{i=6}^{s} \frac{i-1}{i}$$

where $A = \frac{2\cdot3\cdot5}{5!\log 2\cdot\log 3\cdot\log 5\cdot\log 7\cdot\log 11}$. Since $2^5 A \prod_{i=6}^{s} \frac{i-1}{i} = 2^5 A \frac{5}{s} < \frac{7}{s}$, it follows that

$$c(b_1, \ldots, b_s) \leq \frac{7}{2^s s}$$

for all $s \geq 6$. The bound $c(b_1, \ldots, b_s) \leq \frac{7}{2^s s}$ for $1 \leq s \leq 5$ can be shown numerically. □

Remark 3.43 For $s = 1$ let $\mathcal{S}$ be the one-dimensional van der Corput sequence as introduced in Definition 3.10. In this case, Faure [67] proved that

$$\limsup_{N\to\infty} \frac{N D_N^*(\mathcal{S})}{\log N} = \begin{cases} \frac{b-1}{4\log b} & \text{if } b \text{ is odd,} \\ \frac{b^2}{4(b+1)\log b} & \text{if } b \text{ is even.} \end{cases}$$

For more exact results when $b = 2$, see [13]. A Central Limit Theorem for the star discrepancy of the van der Corput sequence in base 2 can be found in [60, Theorem 2]. Concerning results on the star discrepancy of generalisations of the one-dimensional van der Corput sequence, see, for example, [67, 70, 71, 72, 73, 127].

Based on the (infinite) $(s-1)$-dimensional van der Corput Halton sequence, one can introduce a finite s-dimensional point set which is known as a Hammersley point set.

Definition 3.44 For dimensions $s \geq 2$ the *Hammersley point set* with integer bases $b_1, \ldots, b_{s-1} \geq 2$ consisting of $N \in \mathbb{N}$ points in the s-dimensional unit-cube is the point set $\mathcal{P} = \{\boldsymbol{x}_0, \ldots, \boldsymbol{x}_{N-1}\}$ where the nth element is given by $\boldsymbol{x}_n = \left(n/N, \varphi_{b_1}(n), \ldots, \varphi_{b_{s-1}}(n)\right)$ for $0 \leq n \leq N-1$.

We deduce a discrepancy bound for the Hammersley point set with the help of Theorem 3.36 in combination with the following general result that goes back to Roth [228] (see also [177, Lemma 3.7]).

Lemma 3.45 *For $s \geq 2$ let $\mathcal{S} = (\boldsymbol{y}_n)_{n\geq 0}$, where $\boldsymbol{y}_n = (y_{n,1}, \ldots, y_{n,s-1})$ for $n \geq 0$, be an arbitrary sequence in the $(s-1)$-dimensional unit-cube with star discrepancy $D_N^*(\mathcal{S})$. For $N \in \mathbb{N}$ consider the point set $\mathcal{P} = \{\boldsymbol{x}_0, \ldots, \boldsymbol{x}_{N-1}\}$ in the s-dimensional unit-cube given by $\boldsymbol{x}_n = (n/N, y_{n,1}, \ldots, y_{n,s-1})$ for $0 \leq n \leq N-1$ with star discrepancy $D_N^*(\mathcal{P})$. Then we have*

$$D_N^*(\mathcal{P}) \leq \frac{1}{N}\left(\max_{1\leq m\leq N} m D_m^*(\mathcal{S}) + 1\right).$$

Proof Consider a sub-interval of the s-dimensional unit-cube of the form $E = \prod_{i=1}^{s}[0, u_i)$. Then a point $\boldsymbol{x}_n$, $0 \leq n \leq N-1$, belongs to E if and only if $0 \le n < Nu_1$ and $\boldsymbol{y}_n \in \prod_{i=2}^{s}[0, u_i)$. Denoting $E' = \prod_{i=2}^{s}[0, u_i)$ we have $A(E, N, \mathcal{P}) = A(E', m, \mathcal{S})$ with $m := \lceil Nu_1 \rceil$ and therefore,

$$|A(E, N, \mathcal{P}) - N\lambda_s(E)| \le |A(E', m, \mathcal{S}) - m\lambda_{s-1}(E')| + |m\lambda_{s-1}(E') - N\lambda_s(E)|.$$

We have $|m\lambda_{s-1}(E') - N\lambda_s(E)| \le \left|(\lceil Nu_1 \rceil - Nu_1)\prod_{i=2}^{s} u_i\right| \le 1$ and hence,

$$|A(E, N, \mathcal{P}) - N\lambda_s(E)| \le mD_m^*(\mathcal{S}) + 1$$

and the result follows. □

Now we can give an estimate for the star discrepancy of the Hammersley point set. The proof of the subsequent result follows directly from Theorem 3.36 and Lemma 3.45.

Theorem 3.46 *Let $b_1, \ldots, b_{s-1} \ge 2$ be pairwise relatively prime integers and let $N \in \mathbb{N}$. Then the star discrepancy of the Hammersley point set $\mathcal{P}$ with bases $b_1, \ldots, b_{s-1}$ consisting of N points in the s-dimensional unit-cube is bounded by*

$$ND_N^*(\mathcal{P}) \le \frac{1}{(s-1)!}\prod_{i-1}^{s-1}\left(\frac{\lfloor b_i/2 \rfloor \log N}{\log b_i} + s - 1\right)$$
$$+ \sum_{k=0}^{s-2} \frac{b_{k+1}}{k!} \prod_{i=1}^{k}\left(\frac{\lfloor b_i/2 \rfloor \log N}{\log b_i} + k\right) + 1.$$

It follows from Theorem 3.46 that for the star discrepancy of the s-dimensional Hammersley point set $\mathcal{P}$ in pairwise relatively prime bases $b_1, \ldots, b_{s-1}$ consisting of N points, we have

$$D_N^*(\mathcal{P}) \le c(b_1, \ldots, b_{s-1})\frac{(\log N)^{s-1}}{N} + O\left(\frac{(\log N)^{s-2}}{N}\right),$$

where $c(b_1, \ldots, b_{s-1}) = \frac{1}{(s-1)!}\prod_{i=1}^{s-1}\frac{\lfloor b_i/2 \rfloor}{\log b_i}$. Where $b_1, \ldots, b_{s-1}$ are the first $s-1$ prime numbers, we have $c(b_1, \ldots, b_{s-1}) \le \frac{7}{2^{s-1}(s-1)}$.

An exact formula for the star discrepancy of the two-dimensional Hammersley point set can be found in [32]; see also [90, 144] for the base 2 case, [69, Theorem 1] for a bound and [74] for exact results on the star discrepancy of generalised versions of the two-dimensional Hammersley point set.

Informally, one calls a point set consisting of N points in the s-dimensional unit-cube a *low-discrepancy point set* if its star discrepancy is of order $(\log N)^{s-1}/N$. In this sense the Hammersley point set in pairwise relatively prime bases is a low-discrepancy point set. Recall that it is widely believed that this order is the best possible for the star discrepancy of a finite point set.

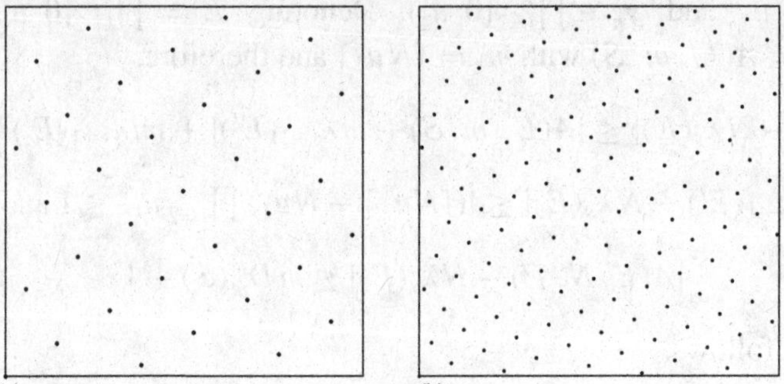

(a) (b)

Figure 3.6 Two-dimensional lattice point sets with (a) $N = 34$ and $\boldsymbol{g} = (1, 21)$, and with (b) $N = 144$ and $\boldsymbol{g} = (1, 89)$.

3.4.3 Lattice point sets

Now we turn to a further construction of finite point sets with low star discrepancy that is often called the method of good lattice points. Those point sets originated independently from Hlawka [113] and Korobov [123].

Definition 3.47 Let $\boldsymbol{g} \in \mathbb{N}^s$ and let $N \in \mathbb{N}$. A point set $\mathcal{P} = \{\boldsymbol{x}_0, \ldots, \boldsymbol{x}_{N-1}\}$ in the s-dimensional unit-cube with $\boldsymbol{x}_n = \{n\boldsymbol{g}/N\}$ for all $0 \le n \le N-1$ is called a *lattice point set* and $\boldsymbol{g}$ is called the *generating vector* of the lattice point set. A QMC rule that uses a lattice point set as underlying quadrature points is often called a *lattice rule*.

Example 3.48 For example, if we choose $N = 34$ and $\boldsymbol{g} = (1, 21)$, then we obtain the point set shown in Figure 3.6(a). For $N = 144$ and $\boldsymbol{g} = (1, 89)$ we obtain the point set shown in Figure 3.6(b).

For a lattice point set $\mathcal{P} = \{\boldsymbol{x}_0, \ldots, \boldsymbol{x}_{N-1}\}$ consisting of N points and with generating vector $\boldsymbol{g} \in \mathbb{N}^s$, we have that each point $\boldsymbol{x}_n$ is of the form $\boldsymbol{x}_n = \{\boldsymbol{y}_n/N\}$ with $\boldsymbol{y}_n = n\boldsymbol{g} \in \mathbb{Z}^s$. Hence, we can apply Theorem 3.27, from which we obtain

$$D_N(\mathcal{P}) \le 1 - \left(1 - \frac{1}{N}\right)^s + \sum_{\boldsymbol{h} \in C_s^*(N)} \frac{1}{r(\boldsymbol{h}, N)} \left| \frac{1}{N} \sum_{n=0}^{N-1} \mathrm{e}^{2\pi i n \boldsymbol{h} \cdot \boldsymbol{g}/N} \right|.$$

Using the formula for a geometric sum, we obtain

$$\sum_{n=0}^{N-1} \mathrm{e}^{2\pi i n \boldsymbol{h} \cdot \boldsymbol{g}/N} = \begin{cases} N & \text{if } \boldsymbol{h} \cdot \boldsymbol{g} \equiv 0 \pmod{N}, \\ 0 & \text{if } \boldsymbol{h} \cdot \boldsymbol{g} \not\equiv 0 \pmod{N}. \end{cases} \tag{3.15}$$

Furthermore, for $\boldsymbol{h} \in C_s^*(N)$ we have $r(\boldsymbol{h}, N) \ge 2r(\boldsymbol{h})$ where $r(\boldsymbol{h}) = \prod_{i=1}^s r(h_i)$ for $\boldsymbol{h} = (h_1, \ldots, h_s)$ and $r(h) = \max(1, |h|)$. This follows from the fact that

$\sin(\pi t) \geq 2t$ for $0 \leq t \leq 1/2$. Altogether, we obtain the following bound on the extreme discrepancy of a lattice point set.

Proposition 3.49 *For the extreme discrepancy of a lattice point set $\mathcal{P}$ consisting of N points and with generating vector $\boldsymbol{g} \in \mathbb{N}^s$, we have*

$$D_N(\mathcal{P}) \leq \frac{s}{N} + \frac{1}{2} \sum_{\substack{\boldsymbol{h} \in C_s^*(N) \\ \boldsymbol{h}\cdot\boldsymbol{g} \equiv 0 \pmod{N}}} \frac{1}{r(\boldsymbol{h})}.$$

Starting from this bound, one can show (see, for example, [177, Section 5]), by using an average argument that for every dimension s and every $N \in \mathbb{N}$, that there exist generating vectors $\boldsymbol{g} = (g_1, \ldots, g_s)$ with $0 \leq g_i < N$ and $\gcd(g_i, N) = 1$ for all $1 \leq i \leq s$ such that the corresponding lattice point set has extreme discrepancy of order $(\log N)^s/N$. Such a vector is often called a *good lattice point*. However, this result is by no means constructive, i.e. it is not known how a general construction principle for a good lattice point can be deduced from it. For a long time one had to rely on time-consuming computer searches for good lattice points. A considerably faster search algorithm was introduced by Sloan and Reztsov [248] that allows one to find good lattice points in reasonably high dimension with a reasonably large number of points. This method is nowadays known as *component-by-component construction* or short *CBC-construction*. Here, the basic idea is to start with a good one-dimensional lattice point and then to append step by step a further dimension to the already constructed good lattice point such that the new lattice point is also a good one. Joe [115] was the first to use this approach to search for lattice point sets with low discrepancy.

First, we mention that by using (3.15), the sum which appeared in Proposition 3.49 can be written as

$$R_N(\boldsymbol{g}) := \sum_{\substack{\boldsymbol{h} \in C_s^*(N) \\ \boldsymbol{h}\cdot\boldsymbol{g} \equiv 0 \pmod{N}}} \frac{1}{r(\boldsymbol{h})}$$

$$= -1 + \frac{1}{N} \sum_{n=0}^{N-1} \prod_{i=1}^{s} \left(1 + \sum_{\substack{-N/2 < h \leq N/2 \\ h \neq 0}} \frac{\mathrm{e}^{2\pi \mathrm{i} h n g_i/N}}{|h|} \right). \tag{3.16}$$

Therefore, for given dimension s, the calculation of $R_N(\boldsymbol{g})$ would require $O(N^2 s)$ operations, which can be reduced to $O(Ns)$ operations by using an asymptotic expansion due to Joe and Sloan [118].

Now we use the following component-by-component algorithm for the construction of a good lattice point.

Algorithm 3.50 *Let $N \in \mathbb{N}$ and let $G_N = \{1, \ldots, N-1\}$.*

1. *Choose $g_1 = 1$.*
2. *For $d > 1$, assume that we have already constructed $g_1, \ldots, g_{d-1}$. Then find $g_d \in G_N$ which minimises $R_N((g_1, \ldots, g_{d-1}, g_d))$ as a function of g_d.*

If N is a prime number, then one can show that Algorithm 3.50 provides a good lattice point. (For results concerning composite N, see [242].)

Theorem 3.51 *Let N be a prime number and suppose that $\boldsymbol{g} = (g_1, \ldots, g_s)$ is constructed according to Algorithm 3.50. Then, for all $1 \leq d \leq s$, we have*

$$R_N((g_1, \ldots, g_d)) \leq \frac{1}{N-1}(1 + S_N)^d,$$

where $S_N = \sum_{h \in C_1^*(N)} |h|^{-1}$.

Proof Since N is a prime number, it follows that $R_N(g_1) = 0$ for all $g_1 \in G_N$. Let $d \geq 1$ and assume that we have

$$R_N(\boldsymbol{g}) \leq \frac{1}{N-1}(1 + S_N)^d,$$

where $\boldsymbol{g} = (g_1, \ldots, g_d)$. Now we consider $(\boldsymbol{g}, g_{d+1}) := (g_1, \ldots, g_d, g_{d+1})$. As g_{d+1} minimises $R_N((\boldsymbol{g}, \cdot))$ over G_N, we obtain

$$\begin{aligned} R_N((\boldsymbol{g}, g_{d+1})) &\leq \frac{1}{N-1} \sum_{g_{d+1}=1}^{N-1} \sum_{\substack{(\boldsymbol{h}, h_{d+1}) \in C_{d+1}^*(N) \\ \boldsymbol{h}\cdot\boldsymbol{g} + h_{d+1} g_{d+1} \equiv 0 \pmod{N}}} \frac{1}{r(\boldsymbol{h})} \frac{1}{r(h_{d+1})} \\ &= \sum_{(\boldsymbol{h}, h_{d+1}) \in C_{d+1}^*(N)} \frac{1}{r(\boldsymbol{h})} \frac{1}{r(h_{d+1})} \frac{1}{N-1} \sum_{\substack{g_{d+1} \in G_N \\ \boldsymbol{h}\cdot\boldsymbol{g} + h_{d+1} g_{d+1} \equiv 0 \pmod{N}}} 1, \end{aligned}$$

where we just changed the order of summation. Separating out the term where $h_{d+1} = 0$, we obtain

$$\begin{aligned} &R_N((\boldsymbol{g}, g_{d+1})) \\ &\quad \leq R_N(\boldsymbol{g}) + \sum_{\boldsymbol{h} \in C_d(N)} \frac{1}{r(\boldsymbol{h})} \sum_{h_{d+1} \in C_1^*(N)} \frac{1}{r(h_{d+1})} \frac{1}{N-1} \sum_{\substack{g_{d+1} \in G_N \\ h_{d+1} g_{d+1} \equiv -\boldsymbol{h}\cdot\boldsymbol{g} \pmod{N}}} 1. \end{aligned}$$

Since N is a prime, the congruence $h_{d+1} g_{d+1} \equiv -\boldsymbol{h} \cdot \boldsymbol{g} \pmod{N}$ has exactly one solution $g_{d+1} \in G_N$ if $\boldsymbol{h} \cdot \boldsymbol{g} \not\equiv 0 \pmod{N}$ and no solution in G_N if $\boldsymbol{h} \cdot \boldsymbol{g} \equiv 0$

(mod N). From this insight it follows that

$$\begin{aligned}
R_N((\boldsymbol{g}, g_{d+1})) &\le R_N(\boldsymbol{g}) + \frac{1}{N-1} \sum_{\boldsymbol{h} \in C_d(N)} \frac{1}{r(\boldsymbol{h})} \sum_{h_{d+1} \in C_1^*(N)} \frac{1}{r(h_{d+1})} \\
&= R_N(\boldsymbol{g}) + \frac{S_N}{N-1} \sum_{\boldsymbol{h} \in C_d(N)} \frac{1}{r(\boldsymbol{h})} \\
&= R_N(\boldsymbol{g}) + \frac{S_N}{N-1}(1+S_N)^d \\
&\le \frac{1}{N-1}(1+S_N)^d + \frac{S_N}{N-1}(1+S_N)^d \\
&= \frac{1}{N-1}(1+S_N)^{d+1},
\end{aligned}$$

where we used the induction hypotheses to bound $R_N(\boldsymbol{g})$. This completes the proof of Theorem 3.51. □

It can be shown that $S_N \le 2 \log N + 2\gamma - \log 4 + 4N^{-2}$, where $\gamma = 0.577\ldots$ is the Euler constant (for a proof of this fact, see [168, Lemmas 1 and 2]). Therefore, from Proposition 3.49 and Theorem 3.51 we obtain the following bound on the extreme discrepancy of the lattice point set whose generating vector is constructed with Algorithm 3.50.

Corollary 3.52 *Let N be a prime number and suppose that $\boldsymbol{g} = (g_1, \ldots, g_s)$ is constructed according to Algorithm 3.50. For $1 \le d \le s$ let $\mathcal{P}_d$ to denote the lattice point set generated by the lattice point $(g_1, \ldots, g_d)$. Then we have*

$$D_N(\mathcal{P}_d) \le \frac{d}{N} + \frac{1}{N}\left(2 \log N + 2\gamma + 1 - \log 4 + \frac{4}{N^2}\right)^d.$$

Hence, with Algorithm 3.50, one can construct a lattice point set in the s-dimensional unit-cube whose extreme discrepancy is of order $(\log N)^s/N$. This is not quite as good as it can be. For example, for the Hammersley point set we had an order of $(\log N)^{s-1}/N$. Nevertheless, the bound on $R_N(\boldsymbol{g})$ is the best possible in the order of magnitude in N. This follows from a general lower bound due to Larcher [132], which states that for every $s \ge 2$ there exists a $c_s > 0$ such that for all $N \in \mathbb{N}$ and all lattice points $\boldsymbol{g}$ we have $R_N(\boldsymbol{g}) \ge c_s (\log N)^s/N$. For dimensions $s > 3$ it is still an open problem whether there are lattice point sets with discrepancy of order $(\log N)^{s-1}/N$. For dimension $s = 2$, such an order can be obtained with so-called Fibonacci lattice rules; see [177, Section 5].

Lattice point sets can have small extreme- and star discrepancy. However, one should mention that the full power of lattice point sets lies in QMC integration of

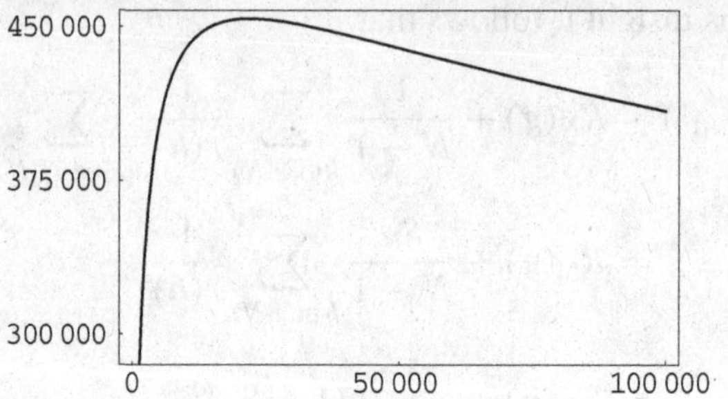

Figure 3.7 The function $N \mapsto (\log N)^s/N$ for $s = 10$.

smooth, one-periodic functions. For a detailed treatment of this topic, see [177, Section 5] or [245].

3.5 Tractability of discrepancy

In many applications the dimension s can be rather large. But in this case, the asymptotically very good bounds on the discrepancy from the previous section are not useful already for modest cardinality N of a point set. For example, assume that for every $s, N \in \mathbb{N}$ we have a point set $\mathcal{P}_{s,N}$ in the s-dimensional unit-cube of cardinality N with star discrepancy of at most

$$D_N^*(\mathcal{P}_{s,N}) \le c_s \frac{(\log N)^s}{N},$$

for some $c_s > 0$. Hence, for any $\varepsilon > 0$ the star discrepancy behaves asymptotically like $N^{-1+\varepsilon}$, which is, of course, excellent. However, the function $N \to (\log N)^s/N$ does not decrease to zero until $N \ge \mathrm{e}^s$. For $N \le \mathrm{e}^s$ this function is increasing, which means that for cardinality N in this range, our discrepancy bounds are useless. But already, for moderately large dimension s, the value of e^s is huge, so huge that point sets with cardinality $N \ge \mathrm{e}^s$ cannot be used for practical applications. For example, the case where $s = 10$, which is not considered to be large in practical applications, is shown in Figure 3.7.

Hence, we are also interested in the discrepancy of point sets with not too large a cardinality. To analyse this problem systematically, we introduce the following quantity.

Definition 3.53 For integers $s, N \in \mathbb{N}$ let

$$\mathrm{disc}^*(N, s) = \inf_{\mathcal{P}} D_N^*(\mathcal{P}),$$

where the infimum is extended over all point sets $\mathcal{P}$ consisting of N points in the s-dimensional unit-cube. Then $\mathrm{disc}^*(N, s)$ is called the *Nth minimal star* *discrepancy*. Furthermore, for $\varepsilon > 0$ we define

$$N^*(s, \varepsilon) = \min\left\{N \in \mathbb{N} : \mathrm{disc}^*(N, s) \leq \varepsilon\right\},$$

the so-called *inverse of star discrepancy*.

For example, consider point sets consisting of $N = 2^s$ points in the s-dimensional unit-cube (for $s \geq 30$ this is already a huge cardinality). Can we say, then, that in each dimension s there exists a point set of such a cardinality that its star discrepancy tends to zero as s grows to infinity? In terms of Definition 3.53 this would mean whether or not we can say that $\mathrm{disc}^*(2^s, s)$ goes to zero as $s \to \infty$. But from the upper bounds on the star discrepancy of special point sets that we know so far, it is not known how to deduce an answer to such a question.

The best bounds on the star discrepancy that we know are all of asymptotic order $(\log N)^s/N$. If we insert here for the cardinality $N = 2^s$, then we obtain upper bounds of order

$$\frac{(\log 2^s)^s}{2^s} \approx \left(\frac{s}{2}\right)^s$$

which goes rapidly to infinity with s (and also the small constant $c_s = 7/(s2^s)$ from the star discrepancy bound for the van der Corput–Halton sequence cannot invert this behaviour).

As another example (see [198]) consider for an integer $m \geq 2$ the regular lattice Γ_m with $N = m^s$ points in the s-dimensional unit-cube as defined in (3.14). From Proposition 3.32 we know that the star discrepancy of this point set is exactly

$$D_N^*(\Gamma_m) = 1 - \left(1 - \frac{1}{m}\right)^s.$$

Hence, to obtain a star discrepancy of at most $\varepsilon > 0$, one needs a regular lattice with at least

$$\left(\frac{s}{|\log(1-\varepsilon)|}\right)^s$$

points. This number grows superexponentially in the dimension s. For example, N has to be at least $(1.45s)^s$ to obtain a star discrepancy smaller than one half.

Nevertheless, in spite of the negative results that we have found so far, the answer to the initially stated question whether there exist point sets consisting of $N = 2^s$ points in the s-dimensional unit-cube whose star discrepancy tends to zero as s grows to infinity is *Yes*, and even more is possible. This was shown first by Heinrich *et al.* [95]. They showed that there exists a constant $c > 0$ such that

$$\mathrm{disc}^*(N, s) \le c\sqrt{\frac{s}{N}} \tag{3.17}$$

for all $N, s \in \mathbb{N}$ from which it follows that

$$N^*(s, \varepsilon) \le Cs\varepsilon^{-2} \tag{3.18}$$

for some constant $C > 0$. Hence, the inverse of star discrepancy depends only polynomially on s and ε^{-1}. In complexity theory such a behaviour is called *polynomial tractability*.

Furthermore, it is known that the dependence on the dimension s of the upper bound on the Nth minimal star discrepancy in (3.18) cannot be improved. It was shown by Hinrichs [109, Theorem 1] that there exist constants $c, \varepsilon_0 > 0$ such that $N^*(s, \varepsilon) \ge cs/\varepsilon$ for $0 < \varepsilon < \varepsilon_0$ and $\mathrm{disc}^*(N, s) \ge \min(\varepsilon_0, cs/N)$.

In comparison to (3.17) the law of the iterated logarithm for the star discrepancy (see [61, Theorem 1.193]) states that

$$\limsup_{N\to\infty} \frac{\sqrt{2N}\, D_N^*(\mathcal{S})}{\sqrt{\log\log N}} = 1$$

for almost all random sequences $\mathcal{S}$ in $[0, 1)^s$. However, this result gives absolutely no information about the dependence of the star discrepancy on the dimension s.

Here, we show a slightly weaker bound than those given in (3.17). This result, which was also shown first in [95], has the advantage that its proof is more or less elementary and that it contains no unknown constants. Improvements can be found in [57, Theorem 3.2] (see also Exercise 3.28) and in [86, Theorem 2.1]. A similar result for the extreme discrepancy can be found in [86, Theorem 2.2].

Theorem 3.54 *For all $N, s \in \mathbb{N}$, we have*

$$\mathrm{disc}^*(N, s) \le \frac{2\sqrt{2}}{\sqrt{N}}\left(s \log\left(\left\lceil \frac{s\sqrt{N}}{2(\log 2)^{1/2}} \right\rceil + 1\right) + \log 2\right)^{1/2}. \tag{3.19}$$

For all $s \in \mathbb{N}$ and all $\varepsilon > 0$, we have

$$N^*(s, \varepsilon) \le \lceil 8\varepsilon^{-2}(s \log(\lceil 2s/\varepsilon \rceil + 1) + \log 2)\rceil. \tag{3.20}$$

Proof The proof is based on Hoeffding's inequality from probability theory which states the following: assume that $X_1, \ldots, X_n$ are independent random variables with expectation 0 and $X_i \in [a_i, b_i]$ almost sure for $1 \le i \le n$, where $a_i < 0 < b_i$, and let $S_n := X_1 + \cdots + X_n$. Then, for every $t \ge 0$, we have

$$\mathrm{Prob}\,[|S_n| \ge t] \le 2\mathrm{e}^{-2t^2/\sum_{i=1}^n (b_i - a_i)^2}.$$

Now let $\boldsymbol{\tau}_1, \ldots, \boldsymbol{\tau}_N$ be independent, identically and uniformly on $[0,1)^s$ distributed random variables. For $\boldsymbol{x} = (x_1, \ldots, x_s)$ in $[0,1]^s$ and $1 \le i \le N$, let

$$\zeta_{\boldsymbol{x}}^{(i)} := \chi_{[\boldsymbol{0},\boldsymbol{x})}(\boldsymbol{\tau}_i) - x_1 \cdots x_s.$$

Then the expected value of $\zeta_{\boldsymbol{x}}^{(i)}$ is $\mathbb{E}[\zeta_{\boldsymbol{x}}^{(i)}] = 0$ and further, we obviously have $|\zeta_{\boldsymbol{x}}^{(i)}| \le 1$ for all $1 \le i \le N$. Let $\delta > 0$. Using Hoeffding's inequality, it follows that, for all $\boldsymbol{x} \in [0,1]^s$, we have

$$\mathrm{Prob}\left[\left|\frac{1}{N}\sum_{i=1}^{N} \zeta_{\boldsymbol{x}}^{(i)}\right| \ge \delta\right] \le 2\mathrm{e}^{-\delta^2 N/2}.$$

Let Γ_m be the equidistant grid on $[0,1]^s$ with mesh size $1/m$, where $m = \lceil s/\delta \rceil$. Using Proposition 3.17, we now obtain

$$\begin{aligned}
&\mathrm{Prob}\left[D_N^*(\{\boldsymbol{\tau}_1, \ldots, \boldsymbol{\tau}_N\}) \le 2\delta\right] \\
&\ge \mathrm{Prob}\left[\max_{\boldsymbol{x} \in \Gamma_m} \left|\frac{A([\boldsymbol{0},\boldsymbol{x}), N, \{\boldsymbol{\tau}_1, \ldots, \boldsymbol{\tau}_N\})}{N} - x_1 \cdots x_s\right| \le \delta\right] \\
&\ge 1 - 2(m+1)^s \mathrm{e}^{-\delta^2 N/2}.
\end{aligned}$$

The last expression is strictly larger than $c \ge 0$, if

$$\log\frac{2}{1-c} + s\log\left(\left\lceil \frac{s}{\delta}\right\rceil + 1\right) - \delta^2 \frac{N}{2} < 0. \tag{3.21}$$

This inequality holds for all $\delta > \delta_0 = \delta_0(N, s)$ where

$$\delta_0^2 = \frac{2}{N}\left(s\log\left(\left\lceil \frac{s}{\delta_0}\right\rceil + 1\right) + \log\frac{2}{1-c}\right). \tag{3.22}$$

Hence, $\frac{1}{\delta_0} \le \left(\frac{N}{4\log 2}\right)^{1/2}$ and substituting this result back into (3.22), it follows that

$$\delta_0^2 \le \frac{2}{N}\left(s\log\left(\left\lceil \frac{s\sqrt{N}}{2(\log 2)^{1/2}}\right\rceil + 1\right) + \log\frac{2}{1-c}\right).$$

Choosing $c = 0$, it follows that for all $\delta > \delta_0$ there exist $\boldsymbol{\tau}_1, \ldots, \boldsymbol{\tau}_N \in [0,1)^s$ such that $D_N^*(\{\boldsymbol{\tau}_1, \ldots, \boldsymbol{\tau}_N\}) \le 2\delta_0$. Therefore, we obtain (3.19).

We also have that there exist $\boldsymbol{\tau}_1, \ldots, \boldsymbol{\tau}_N \in [0,1)^s$ with $D_N^*(\{\boldsymbol{\tau}_1, \ldots, \boldsymbol{\tau}_N\}) \le \varepsilon$ whenever inequality (3.21) with $c = 0$ is fulfilled with $\delta = \varepsilon/2$. This is the case for

$$N > 8\varepsilon^{-2}(s\log(\lfloor 2s/\varepsilon \rfloor + 1) + \log 2)$$

and hence (3.20) follows. □

Remark 3.55 From the proof of Theorem 3.54 we even obtain a little more. Namely, for $c \in [0,1)$ we have the probability to choose randomly a point set $\mathcal{P}$

consisting of N points in the s-dimensional unit-cube with star discrepancy of at most

$$D_N^*(\mathcal{P}) \le \frac{2\sqrt{2}}{\sqrt{N}}\left(s\log\left(\left\lceil\frac{s\sqrt{N}}{2(\log 2)^{1/2}}\right\rceil+1\right)+\log\frac{2}{1-c}\right)^{1/2}$$

to be strictly larger than c.

The main disadvantage of Theorem 3.54 is that it is purely probabilistic and therefore by no means constructive. A first constructive approach is given in [57] and is further improved in [55]. Here, a deterministic algorithm is presented that constructs point sets $\mathcal{P}_{N,s}$ consisting of N points in the s-dimensional unit-cube satisfying

$$D_N^*(\mathcal{P}_{N,s}) = O\left(\frac{s^{1/2}}{N^{1/2}}(\log(N+1))^{1/2}\right)$$

in run-time $O(s\log(sN)(\sigma N)^s)$, where $\sigma=\sigma(s)=O((\log s)^2/(s\log\log s))\to 0$ as $s\to\infty$ and where the implied constant in the O-notation is independent of s and N. This is far too expensive for high-dimensional applications. An implementation and numerical tests of the algorithm can be found in [59].

A further improvement is presented in [56]. Here a component-by-component approach is used to construct point sets $\mathcal{P}_{N,s}$ consisting of N points in the s-dimensional unit-cube satisfying

$$D_N^*(\mathcal{P}_{N,s}) = O\left(\frac{s^{3/2}}{N^{1/2}}\left(\log\left(\frac{N}{s}+1\right)\right)^{1/2}\right)$$

in run-time $O(c^s N^{(s+3)/2}\left(\log\frac{N}{s}\right)^{-(s+1)/2} s^{1/4-s/2})$, where $c>0$ is a constant and where the implied constant in the O-notation is independent of s and N. The price for improved run-time is a worse dependence of the bound for the star discrepancy on the dimension s. Nevertheless, numerical tests of the CBC algorithm in [58] suggest that the star discrepancy only grows linearly in s rather than with $s^{3/2}$.

An overview of many open questions concerning this topic can be found in [93, 202]. An effective construction of point sets whose star discrepancy satisfies a bound such as in Theorem 3.54 is still not known. An answer to this question would certainly be a major contribution, especially for users of QMC rules.

Let us now turn our attention to this problem but for the L_2-discrepancy instead of the star discrepancy. As for the star discrepancy, we define the following quantity.

Definition 3.56 For integers $s, N \in \mathbb{N}$, let

$$\mathrm{disc}_2(N, s) = \inf_{\mathcal{P}} L_{2,N}(\mathcal{P}),$$

where the infimum is extended over all point sets $\mathcal{P}$ consisting of N points in the s-dimensional unit-cube. Then $\mathrm{disc}_2(N, s)$ is called the *Nth minimal L_2-discrepancy.*

Unlike with the star discrepancy, it makes little sense here to ask for the smallest cardinality of a point set with L_2-discrepancy of at most some $\varepsilon > 0$. The reason for this is that the L_2-discrepancy of the empty point set in the s-dimensional unit-cube is exactly $3^{-s/2}$, which follows from Proposition 2.15, or in other words, $\mathrm{disc}_2(0, s) = 3^{-s/2}$. Thus, for s large enough, the empty set always has an L_2-discrepancy smaller than ε. (This is not the case with the star discrepancy, which is always one for the empty set.) This may suggest that for large s, the L_2-discrepancy is not properly scaled.

We define the following quantity.

Definition 3.57 For $\varepsilon > 0$, we define

$$N_2(s, \varepsilon) = \min \{N \in \mathbb{N} : \mathrm{disc}_2(N, s) \leq \varepsilon\, \mathrm{disc}_2(0, s)\},$$

the so-called *inverse* of the L_2-discrepancy.

Here the situation is quite different. The inverse of L_2-discrepancy depends at least exponentially on the dimension s. This was shown in [249, 266] in a much more general setting. In complexity theory this exponential dependence on the dimension is called *intractability* or the *curse of dimensionality*.

Proposition 3.58 *For $\varepsilon \in (0, 1)$, we have*

$$N_2(s, \varepsilon) \geq (1 - \varepsilon^2) \left(\frac{9}{8}\right)^s.$$

Proof Proposition 2.15 states that for any point set $\mathcal{P} = \{\boldsymbol{x}_0, \ldots, \boldsymbol{x}_{N-1}\}$ in $[0, 1)^s$, we have

$$(L_{2,N}(\mathcal{P}))^2 = \frac{1}{3^s} - \frac{2}{N} \sum_{n=0}^{N-1} \prod_{i=1}^{s} \frac{1 - x_{n,i}^2}{2} + \frac{1}{N^2} \sum_{m,n=0}^{N-1} \prod_{i=1}^{s} \min(1 - x_{m,i}, 1 - x_{n,i}),$$

where $x_{n,i}$ is the ith component of the point $\boldsymbol{x}_n$.

With

$$\kappa_s := \sup_{\boldsymbol{x} \in [0,1]^s} 3^{s/2} \prod_{i=1}^{s} \frac{1 - x_j^2}{2\sqrt{1 - x_i}} \leq \left(\frac{8}{9}\right)^{s/2}$$

(note that the function $x \mapsto (1-x^2)/\sqrt{1-x}$ for $x \in [0,1]$ attains its maximum at $x = 1/3$), we obtain $\prod_{i=1}^{s} \frac{1-x_{n,i}^2}{2} \le \frac{\kappa_s}{3^{s/2}} \prod_{i=1}^{s} \sqrt{1-x_{n,i}}$ and hence,

$$\frac{1}{N}\sum_{n=0}^{N-1}\prod_{i=1}^{s}\frac{1-x_{n,i}^2}{2} \le \frac{\kappa_s}{3^{s/2}}\frac{1}{N}\sum_{n=0}^{N-1}\prod_{i=1}^{s}\sqrt{1-x_{n,i}}$$

$$\le \frac{\kappa_s}{3^{s/2}}\sqrt{\frac{1}{N}\sum_{n=0}^{N-1}\prod_{i=1}^{s}(1-x_{n,i})},$$

where we used Cauchy–Schwarz' inequality for the second estimate.

On the other hand we have

$$\frac{1}{N^2}\sum_{m,n=0}^{N-1}\prod_{i=1}^{s}\min(1-x_{m,i}, 1-x_{n,i}) \ge \frac{1}{N^2}\sum_{n=0}^{N-1}\prod_{i=1}^{s}(1-x_{n,i})\,.$$

Letting $y := \left(\frac{1}{N}\sum_{n=0}^{N-1}\prod_{i=1}^{s}(1-x_{n,i})\right)^{1/2}$, we therefore obtain

$$(L_{2,N}(\mathcal{P}))^2 \ge \frac{1}{3^s} - \frac{2\kappa_s}{3^{s/2}}y + \frac{y^2}{N}.$$

The last term becomes minimal for $y = N\kappa_s 3^{-s/2}$ and hence,

$$(L_{2,N}(\mathcal{P}))^2 \ge \frac{1}{3^s}\left(1 - N\kappa_s^2\right) \ge \frac{1}{3^s}\left(1 - N\left(\frac{8}{9}\right)^s\right).$$

If we assume now that $L_{2,N}(\mathcal{P}) \le \varepsilon \cdot 3^{-s/2}$, then it follows that $\varepsilon^2 \ge 1 - N\,(8/9)^s$, and hence,

$$N \ge \left(1-\varepsilon^2\right)\left(\frac{9}{8}\right)^s. \qquad \square$$

For a more detailed discussion of tractability of various notions of discrepancy, we refer to Novak and Woźniakowski [199, 200, 201, 202].

3.6 Weighted discrepancy

Apart from the classical concept of discrepancy, there is also the idea of weighted discrepancy as introduced by Sloan and Woźniakowski [249], who observed that different coordinates may have a different influence on the quality of approximation of an integral by a QMC rule.

We assume that we are given non-negative real numbers $\gamma_{\mathfrak{u},s}$ for $\mathfrak{u} \subseteq \mathcal{I}_s$, the so-called *weights* corresponding to the projection on the coordinates whose indices are in $\mathfrak{u}$. We collect these weights in the set $\boldsymbol{\gamma} = \{\gamma_{\mathfrak{u},s} : \mathfrak{u} \subseteq \mathcal{I}_s\}$.

Definition 3.59 For a point set $\mathcal{P}$ consisting of N points in the s-dimensional unit-cube and given weights $\boldsymbol{\gamma}$, the weighted star discrepancy $D^*_{N,\boldsymbol{\gamma}}$ is given by

$$D^*_{N,\boldsymbol{\gamma}}(\mathcal{P}) = \sup_{\boldsymbol{z}\in(0,1]^s} \max_{\emptyset\neq\mathfrak{u}\subseteq\mathcal{I}_s} \gamma_{\mathfrak{u},s}|\Delta_{\mathcal{P}}((\boldsymbol{z}_{\mathfrak{u}},1))|.$$

For $1 \leq q < \infty$, the weighted L_q-discrepancy $L_{q,N,\boldsymbol{\gamma}}$ of $\mathcal{P}$ is given by

$$L_{q,N,\boldsymbol{\gamma}}(\mathcal{P}) = \left(\sum_{\emptyset\neq\mathfrak{u}\subseteq\mathcal{I}_s} \gamma_{\mathfrak{u},s} \int_{[0,1]^{|\mathfrak{u}|}} |\Delta_{\mathcal{P}}((\boldsymbol{z}_{\mathfrak{u}},1))|^q \,\mathrm{d}\boldsymbol{z}_{u} \right)^{1/q}.$$

Here, $\Delta_{\mathcal{P}}$ is the discrepancy function of $\mathcal{P}$ as defined in Definition 2.13.

In the literature, mainly the following kinds of weights are studied:

- *Product weights* which are weights of the form $\gamma_{\mathfrak{u},s} = \prod_{i\in\mathfrak{u}} \gamma_{i,s}$, for $\emptyset \neq \mathfrak{u} \subseteq \mathcal{I}_s$, where $\gamma_{i,s}$ is the weight associated with the ith component. In this case we simply write $\boldsymbol{\gamma} = (\gamma_{i,s})_{i=1}^s$. Often the weights $\gamma_{i,s}$ have no dependence on s, i.e. $\gamma_{i,s} = \gamma_i$.
- *Finite-order weights* of fixed order $k \in \mathbb{N}$ which are weights with $\gamma_{\mathfrak{u},s} = 0$ for all $\mathfrak{u} \subseteq \mathcal{I}_s$ with $|\mathfrak{u}| > k$.

Here, we restrict ourselves mainly to the case of product weights.

If it is not important, we suppress a possible dependence of the weights on the dimension s in the following and we simply write $\gamma_{\mathfrak{u}}$ instead of $\gamma_{\mathfrak{u},s}$.

Note that for $\gamma_{\mathcal{I}_s,s} = 1$ and $\gamma_{\mathfrak{u},s} = 0$ for all $\mathfrak{u} \subsetneq \mathcal{I}_s$, we obtain the usual definitions of L_q- or star discrepancy. Hence, Definition 3.59 is a generalisation of Definition 2.14 and Definition 3.19, respectively. Furthermore, in the case of product weights, we also have $D^*_{N,\mathbf{1}} = D^*_N$ when $\mathbf{1} = (1)_{i\geq 1}$, the sequence of weights where every weight is equal to one.

The two most important cases for weighted discrepancies are those of the weighted L_2-discrepancy and the weighted star discrepancy. Many results for the classical definitions can easily be generalised to results for the weighted discrepancies. For example, we also have here a compact formula for the evaluation of the weighted L_2-discrepancy of a finite point set (see Proposition 2.15 for the unweighted case).

Proposition 3.60 *For any point set $\mathcal{P} = \{\boldsymbol{x}_0, \ldots, \boldsymbol{x}_{N-1}\}$ in $[0,1)^s$, we have*

$$(L_{2,N,\boldsymbol{\gamma}}(\mathcal{P}))^2 = \sum_{\emptyset\neq\mathfrak{u}\subseteq\mathcal{I}_s} \gamma_{\mathfrak{u},s}$$
$$\times \left[\frac{1}{3^{|\mathfrak{u}|}} - \frac{2}{N} \sum_{n=0}^{N-1} \prod_{i\in\mathfrak{u}} \frac{1-x_{n,i}^2}{2} + \frac{1}{N^2} \sum_{m,n=0}^{N-1} \prod_{i\in\mathfrak{u}} \min\left(1-x_{m,i}, 1-x_{n,i}\right) \right],$$

where $x_{n,i}$ is the ith component of the point $\boldsymbol{x}_n$.

For the weighted star discrepancy, we have the following generalisation of Theorem 3.28.

Theorem 3.61 *Let* $\mathcal{P} = \{\boldsymbol{x}_0, \ldots, \boldsymbol{x}_{N-1}\}$ *be a point set in* $[0,1)^s$ *with* $\boldsymbol{x}_n$ *of the form* $\boldsymbol{x}_n = \{\boldsymbol{y}_n / b^m\}$ *with* $\boldsymbol{y}_n \in \mathbb{Z}^s$ *and integers* $m \geq 1$ *and* $b \geq 2$. *Then we have*

$$D^*_{N,\boldsymbol{\gamma}}(\mathcal{P}) \leq \max_{\emptyset \neq \mathfrak{u} \subseteq \mathcal{I}_s} \gamma_{\mathfrak{u},s} \left(1 - \left(1 - \frac{1}{b^m}\right)^{|\mathfrak{u}|}\right)$$
$$+ \max_{\emptyset \neq \mathfrak{u} \subseteq \mathcal{I}_s} \gamma_{\mathfrak{u},s} \sum_{\substack{\boldsymbol{k} \in \mathbb{N}_0^{|\mathfrak{u}|} \\ 0 < |\boldsymbol{k}|_\infty < b^m}} \rho_b(\boldsymbol{k}) \left| \frac{1}{N} \sum_{n=0}^{N-1} {}_b\mathrm{wal}_{\boldsymbol{k}}(\boldsymbol{x}_{n,\mathfrak{u}}) \right|,$$

where $\boldsymbol{x}_{n,\mathfrak{u}}$ *is the projection of* $\boldsymbol{x}_n$ *to the coordinates given by* $\mathfrak{u}$.

Proof We have

$$D^*_{N,\boldsymbol{\gamma}}(\mathcal{P}) = \sup_{\boldsymbol{z} \in (0,1]^s} \max_{\emptyset \neq \mathfrak{u} \subseteq \mathcal{I}_s} \gamma_{\mathfrak{u},s} |\Delta_{\mathcal{P}}((\boldsymbol{z}_{\mathfrak{u}}, 1))| \leq \max_{\emptyset \neq \mathfrak{u} \subseteq \mathcal{I}_s} \gamma_{\mathfrak{u},s} D^*_N(\mathcal{P}_{\mathfrak{u}}),$$

where $\mathcal{P}_{\mathfrak{u}} = \{\boldsymbol{x}_{0,\mathfrak{u}}, \ldots, \boldsymbol{x}_{N-1,\mathfrak{u}}\}$ in $[0,1)^{|\mathfrak{u}|}$ consists of the points of $\mathcal{P}$ projected to the components whose indices are in $\mathfrak{u}$. For any $\emptyset \neq \mathfrak{u} \subseteq \mathcal{I}_s$ we have from Theorem 3.28 that

$$D^*_N(\mathcal{P}_{\mathfrak{u}}) \leq 1 - \left(1 - \frac{1}{b^m}\right)^{|\mathfrak{u}|} + \sum_{\substack{\boldsymbol{k} \in \mathbb{N}_0^{|\mathfrak{u}|} \\ 0 < |\boldsymbol{k}|_\infty < b^m}} \rho_b(\boldsymbol{k}) \left| \frac{1}{N} \sum_{n=0}^{N-1} {}_b\mathrm{wal}_{\boldsymbol{k}}(\boldsymbol{x}_{n,\mathfrak{u}}) \right|,$$

and the result follows. □

One of the reasons for introducing a weighted L_2-discrepancy is that with this concept one can overcome the curse of dimensionality for the L_2-discrepancy under suitable conditions on the weights $\boldsymbol{\gamma}$. Also, for the weighted star discrepancy one can obtain a weaker dependence on the dimension for suitable choices of weights.

Definition 3.62 For integers $s, N \in \mathbb{N}$ let

$$\mathrm{disc}^*_{\boldsymbol{\gamma}}(N,s) = \inf_{\mathcal{P}} D^*_{N,\boldsymbol{\gamma}}(\mathcal{P}),$$

and let

$$\mathrm{disc}_{2,\boldsymbol{\gamma}}(N,s) = \inf_{\mathcal{P}} L_{2,N,\boldsymbol{\gamma}}(\mathcal{P}),$$

where the infimum is in both cases extended over all point sets $\mathcal{P}$ consisting of N points in the s-dimensional unit-cube. Then $\mathrm{disc}^*_{\boldsymbol{\gamma}}(N,s)$ is called the *Nth minimal weighted star discrepancy* and $\mathrm{disc}_{2,\boldsymbol{\gamma}}(N,s)$ is called the *Nth minimal weighted*

L_2*-discrepancy*. Furthermore, for $\varepsilon > 0$ define

$$N^*_{\boldsymbol{\gamma}}(s,\varepsilon) = \min\{N \in \mathbb{N} : \mathrm{disc}^*_{\boldsymbol{\gamma}}(N,s) \le \varepsilon\}$$

and

$$N_{2,\boldsymbol{\gamma}}(s,\varepsilon) = \min\{N \in \mathbb{N} : \mathrm{disc}_{2,\boldsymbol{\gamma}}(N,s) \le \varepsilon \cdot \mathrm{disc}_{2,\boldsymbol{\gamma}}(0,s)\},$$

the *inverse* of weighted star and weighted L_2-discrepancy, respectively.

Note that $\mathrm{disc}_{2,\boldsymbol{\gamma}}(0,s) = \sum_{\emptyset \ne \mathfrak{u} \subseteq \mathcal{I}_s} \frac{\gamma_{\mathfrak{u},s}}{3^{|\mathfrak{u}|}}$ and $\mathrm{disc}^*_{\boldsymbol{\gamma}}(0,s) = \max_{\emptyset \ne \mathfrak{u} \subseteq \mathcal{I}_s} \gamma_{\mathfrak{u},s}$.

Definition 3.63 We say that the weighted star discrepancy and the weighted L_2-discrepancy, respectively, is *polynomially tractable*, if there exist non-negative C, α and β such that

$$N^*_{\boldsymbol{\gamma}}(s,\varepsilon) \le C s^{\alpha} \varepsilon^{-\beta} \quad \text{and} \quad N_{2,\boldsymbol{\gamma}}(s,\varepsilon) \le C s^{\alpha} \varepsilon^{-\beta},$$

respectively hold for all dimensions $s \in \mathbb{N}$ and for all $\varepsilon \in (0,1)$. This behaviour is also called *tractability*. The infima of α and β such that this type of inequality holds are called the s*-exponent* and the ε*-exponent* of tractability. We say that the weighted star and the weighted L_2-discrepancy, respectively, are *strongly tractable*, if the above inequality holds with $\alpha = 0$. In this context one also speaks of *strong tractability*.

We consider the case of the weighted L_2-discrepancy first.

Theorem 3.64 *Assume that the weights $\boldsymbol{\gamma}$ are such that*

$$B_{\boldsymbol{\gamma}} := \sup_{s \in \mathbb{N}} \frac{\sum_{\emptyset \ne \mathfrak{u} \subseteq \mathcal{I}_s} \gamma_{\mathfrak{u},s} \left(\frac{1}{2^{|\mathfrak{u}|}} - \frac{1}{3^{|\mathfrak{u}|}}\right)}{\sum_{\emptyset \ne \mathfrak{u} \subseteq \mathcal{I}_s} \gamma_{\mathfrak{u},s} \frac{1}{3^{|\mathfrak{u}|}}} < \infty,$$

then the weighted L_2-discrepancy is strongly tractable and the ε-exponent is at most two. Moreover, in the case of product weights (independent of s) with decreasing weights, the weighted L_2-discrepancy is strongly tractable if and only if $\sum_{i=1}^{\infty} \gamma_i < \infty$.

Proof Averaging the squared weighted L_2-discrepancy over all $\boldsymbol{\tau}_1, \ldots, \boldsymbol{\tau}_N$ from the s-dimensional unit-cube yields

$$\int_{[0,1]^{sN}} \left(L_{2,N,\boldsymbol{\gamma}}(\{\boldsymbol{\tau}_1,\ldots,\boldsymbol{\tau}_N\})\right)^2 \,\mathrm{d}\boldsymbol{\tau}_1 \cdots \mathrm{d}\boldsymbol{\tau}_N = \frac{1}{N} \sum_{\emptyset \ne \mathfrak{u} \subseteq \mathcal{I}_s} \gamma_{\mathfrak{u},s} \left(\frac{1}{2^{|\mathfrak{u}|}} - \frac{1}{3^{|\mathfrak{u}|}}\right).$$

Hence, there exists a point set $\mathcal{P}$ consisting of N points in the s-dimensional unit-cube such that

$$L_{2,N,\boldsymbol{\gamma}}(\mathcal{P}) \le \frac{1}{\sqrt{N}} \left(\sum_{\emptyset \ne \mathfrak{u} \subseteq \mathcal{I}_s} \gamma_{\mathfrak{u},s} \left(\frac{1}{2^{|\mathfrak{u}|}} - \frac{1}{3^{|\mathfrak{u}|}}\right)\right)^{1/2} \le \frac{\sqrt{B_{\boldsymbol{\gamma}}}}{\sqrt{N}} \left(\sum_{\emptyset \ne \mathfrak{u} \subseteq \mathcal{I}_s} \frac{\gamma_{\mathfrak{u},s}}{3^{|\mathfrak{u}|}}\right)^{1/2}.$$

The last term is smaller than $\varepsilon\left(\sum_{\emptyset\neq\mathfrak{u}\subseteq\mathcal{I}_s}\frac{\gamma_{\mathfrak{u},s}}{3^{|\mathfrak{u}|}}\right)^{1/2}$ if $N \geq B_{\boldsymbol{\gamma}}\varepsilon^{-2}$. This means that $N_{2,\boldsymbol{\gamma}}(s,\varepsilon) \leq \lceil B_{\boldsymbol{\gamma}}\varepsilon^{-2}\rceil$ and hence, we have strong tractability with ε-exponent of at most two.

Assume that we are given product weights which are independent of the dimension s, i.e. $\gamma_{\mathfrak{u},s} = \prod_{i\in\mathfrak{u}}\gamma_i$ with a sequence $\gamma_1, \gamma_2, \ldots \geq 0$. In this case we have

$$\begin{aligned}\frac{\sum_{\emptyset\neq\mathfrak{u}\subseteq\mathcal{I}_s}\gamma_{\mathfrak{u},s}\left(\frac{1}{2^{|\mathfrak{u}|}}-\frac{1}{3^{|\mathfrak{u}|}}\right)}{\sum_{\emptyset\neq\mathfrak{u}\subseteq\mathcal{I}_s}\gamma_{\mathfrak{u},s}\frac{1}{3^{|\mathfrak{u}|}}} &= \frac{\prod_{i=1}^s\left(1+\frac{\gamma_i}{2}\right)-\prod_{i=1}^s\left(1+\frac{\gamma_i}{3}\right)}{\prod_{i=1}^s\left(1+\frac{\gamma_i}{3}\right)}\\ &= \frac{\prod_{i=1}^s\left(1+\frac{\gamma_i}{2}\right)}{\prod_{i=1}^s\left(1+\frac{\gamma_i}{3}\right)} - 1 \leq \prod_{i=1}^s\left(1+\frac{\gamma_i}{6}\right)\\ &\leq \mathrm{e}^{\sum_{i=1}^s\log(1+\gamma_i/6)} \leq \mathrm{e}^{(\sum_{i=1}^s\gamma_i)/6}.\end{aligned}$$

Hence, $B_{\boldsymbol{\gamma}} < \infty$ if $\sum_{i=1}^\infty\gamma_i < \infty$ and we obtain strong tractability.

On the other hand, using the lower bound on the unweighted L_2-discrepancy from the proof of Proposition 3.58, we have

$$\begin{aligned}(L_{2,N,\boldsymbol{\gamma}}(\mathcal{P}))^2 &\geq \sum_{\emptyset\neq\mathfrak{u}\subseteq\mathcal{I}_s}\gamma_{\mathfrak{u},s}\frac{1}{3^{|\mathfrak{u}|}}\left(1-N\left(\frac{8}{9}\right)^{|\mathfrak{u}|}\right)\\ &= -1+\prod_{i=1}^s\left(1+\frac{\gamma_i}{3}\right)+N-N\prod_{i=1}^s\left(1+\frac{8\gamma_i}{27}\right).\end{aligned}$$

Assume that we have strong tractability, i.e. that there exist non-negative C and β with the property that $N_{2,\boldsymbol{\gamma}}(s,\varepsilon) \leq C\varepsilon^{-\beta}$ for all $s \in \mathbb{N}$ and all $\varepsilon > 0$. Then, for $N = N_{2,\boldsymbol{\gamma}}(s,\varepsilon)$, we have

$$\begin{aligned}\varepsilon^2\prod_{i=1}^s\left(1+\frac{\gamma_i}{3}\right) &\geq -1+\prod_{i=1}^s\left(1+\frac{\gamma_i}{3}\right)+N-N\prod_{i=1}^s\left(1+\frac{8\gamma_i}{27}\right)\\ &\geq \prod_{i=1}^s\left(1+\frac{\gamma_i}{3}\right)-N\prod_{i=1}^s\left(1+\frac{8\gamma_i}{27}\right).\end{aligned}$$

Hence, for $0 < \varepsilon < 1$, we have

$$C\varepsilon^{-\beta} \geq N \geq (1-\varepsilon^2)\prod_{i=1}^s\frac{1+\frac{\gamma_i}{3}}{1+\frac{8\gamma_i}{27}} = (1-\varepsilon^2)\prod_{i=1}^s\left(1+\frac{\gamma_i}{27+8\gamma_i}\right).$$

Obviously, the sequence $(\gamma_i)_{i\geq 1}$ must be bounded, since otherwise we would have $\frac{\gamma_i}{27+8\gamma_i} \geq \frac{1}{16}$ for infinitely many $i \in \mathbb{N}$ and hence $C\varepsilon^{-\beta} \geq (1-\varepsilon^2)\left(1+\frac{1}{16}\right)^d$ for infinitely many $d \in \mathbb{N}$ which is certainly a contradiction.

For bounded γ_i's, say $\gamma_i \leq M$ for all $i \in \mathbb{N}$, we obtain

$$C\varepsilon^{-\beta} \geq (1-\varepsilon^2)\prod_{i=1}^{s}\left(1+\frac{1}{27+8M}\gamma_i\right) \geq (1-\varepsilon^2)\frac{1}{27+8M}\sum_{i=1}^{s}\gamma_i$$

and thus we must have $\sum_{i=1}^{\infty}\gamma_i < \infty$. □

For the star discrepancy we have tractability already for the unweighted case (with s-exponent of, at most, one and ε-exponent of, at most, two). From this it follows immediately that the weighted star discrepancy is also tractable with s-exponent of, at most, one and ε-exponent of, at most, two as long as the weights are bounded. However, under a very mild condition on the weights, one can even obtain tractability with s-exponent equal to zero. The following result was first proved in [110].

Theorem 3.65 *If*

$$C_{\boldsymbol{\gamma}} := \sup_{s=1,2,\ldots} \max_{\emptyset \neq \mathfrak{u} \subseteq \mathcal{I}_s} \gamma_{\mathfrak{u},s}\sqrt{|\mathfrak{u}|} < \infty, \tag{3.23}$$

then, for all $N, s \in \mathbb{N}$, we have

$$\mathrm{disc}^*_{\boldsymbol{\gamma}}(N,s) \leq \frac{2\sqrt{2}C_{\boldsymbol{\gamma}}}{\sqrt{N}}\left(\log\left(\left\lceil \rho_s\sqrt{N}\right\rceil+1\right)+\log\left(2(\mathrm{e}-1)s\right)\right)^{1/2}, \tag{3.24}$$

where $\rho_s = \frac{s}{2(\log 2)^{1/2}}$. Hence, for any $0 < \delta < 1$, there exists a $c_\delta > 0$ such that

$$N^*_{\boldsymbol{\gamma}}(s,\varepsilon) \leq \left\lceil c_\delta \varepsilon^{-2/(1-\delta)}(\log s+1)^{1/(1-\delta)}\right\rceil, \tag{3.25}$$

i.e. the weighted star discrepancy is tractable with s-exponent equal to zero and with ε-exponent at most two.

We stress that we do not have strong tractability in this case as we still have the logarithmic dependence on the dimension s.

Note that condition (3.23) is a very mild condition on the weights. For example, for bounded finite order weights it is always fulfilled. In the case of product weights (independent of s) it is enough that the weights γ_i are decreasing and that $\gamma_i < 1$ for an index $i \in \mathbb{N}$. In fact, we have

$$\max_{\emptyset \neq \mathfrak{u} \subseteq \mathcal{I}_s} \gamma_{\mathfrak{u},s}\sqrt{|\mathfrak{u}|} = \max_{u=1,\ldots,s} \sqrt{u}\prod_{i=1}^{u}\gamma_i$$

and hence, $C_{\boldsymbol{\gamma}} = \sup_{s=1,2,\ldots} \sqrt{s}\prod_{i=1}^{s}\gamma_i$. We have

$$\frac{\sqrt{s}\prod_{i=1}^{s}\gamma_i}{\sqrt{s+1}\prod_{i=1}^{s+1}\gamma_i} = \sqrt{\frac{s}{s+1}\frac{1}{\gamma_{s+1}}} > 1$$

for s large enough and therefore it follows that $C_\gamma < \infty$. For example, if $\gamma_i = 1/\log(i+1)$, then $C_\gamma = \sqrt{2}/(\log 2 \log 3)$.

Proof of Theorem 3.65 For a given number of points N and dimension s and $0 < c_{\mathfrak{u}} \leq 1$ for all $\emptyset \neq \mathfrak{u} \subseteq \mathcal{I}_s$, we consider the set

$$A := \Bigg\{ \mathcal{P}_{N,s} \subseteq [0,1)^s \, : \, |\mathcal{P}_{N,s}| = N \text{ and for all } \emptyset \neq \mathfrak{u} \subseteq \mathcal{I}_s$$
$$D_N^*(\mathcal{P}_{N,s,\mathfrak{u}}) \leq \frac{2\sqrt{2}}{\sqrt{N}} \left(|\mathfrak{u}| \log\left(\left\lceil \rho_{|\mathfrak{u}|} \sqrt{N} \right\rceil + 1 \right) + \log\left(\frac{2}{c_{\mathfrak{u}}} \right) \right)^{1/2} \Bigg\},$$

where $\mathcal{P}_{N,s,\mathfrak{u}} := \{\boldsymbol{x}_{0,\mathfrak{u}}, \ldots, \boldsymbol{x}_{N-1,\mathfrak{u}}\}$ if $\mathcal{P}_{N,s} = \{\boldsymbol{x}_0, \ldots, \boldsymbol{x}_{N-1}\}$ and where $\rho_{|\mathfrak{u}|} = \frac{|\mathfrak{u}|}{2(\log 2)^{1/2}}$. Furthermore, for $\emptyset \neq \mathfrak{u} \subseteq \mathcal{I}_s$, we define

$$\begin{aligned} A_{\mathfrak{u}} &= A_{\mathfrak{u}}(c_{\mathfrak{u}}) \\ &:= \Bigg\{ \mathcal{P}_{N,s} \subseteq [0,1)^s \, : \, |\mathcal{P}_{N,s}| = N \text{ and} \\ &\qquad D_N^*(\mathcal{P}_{N,s,\mathfrak{u}}) \leq \frac{2\sqrt{2}}{\sqrt{N}} \left(|\mathfrak{u}| \log\left(\left\lceil \rho_{|\mathfrak{u}|} \sqrt{N} \right\rceil + 1 \right) + \log\left(\frac{2}{c_{\mathfrak{u}}} \right) \right)^{1/2} \Bigg\}. \end{aligned}$$

From Remark 3.55, we know that $\mathrm{Prob}[A_{\mathfrak{u}}(c_{\mathfrak{u}})] > 1 - c_{\mathfrak{u}}$. Then we have $A = \bigcap_{\emptyset \neq \mathfrak{u} \subseteq \mathcal{I}_s} A_{\mathfrak{u}}$ and hence

$$\begin{aligned} \mathrm{Prob}[A] &= \mathrm{Prob}\Bigg[\bigcap_{\emptyset \neq \mathfrak{u} \subseteq \mathcal{I}_s} A_{\mathfrak{u}} \Bigg] = 1 - \mathrm{Prob}\Bigg[\bigcup_{\emptyset \neq \mathfrak{u} \subseteq \mathcal{I}_s} A_{\mathfrak{u}}^c \Bigg] \\ &\geq 1 - \sum_{\emptyset \neq \mathfrak{u} \subseteq \mathcal{I}_s} \mathrm{Prob}\left[A_{\mathfrak{u}}^c \right] \geq 1 - \sum_{\emptyset \neq \mathfrak{u} \subseteq \mathcal{I}_s} c_{\mathfrak{u}}. \end{aligned}$$

If we choose $c_{\mathfrak{u}} := cs^{-|\mathfrak{u}|}$ with a constant $0 < c \leq (\mathrm{e}-1)^{-1}$, then we obtain

$$\mathrm{Prob}[A] \geq 1 - \sum_{u=1}^{s} \binom{s}{u} \frac{c}{s^u} = 1 + c - c\left(1 + \frac{1}{s}\right)^s > 1 + c - c \cdot \mathrm{e} \geq 0.$$

Thus, we have shown that there exists a point set $\mathcal{P}_{N,s} \subseteq [0,1)^s$ such that for each $\emptyset \neq \mathfrak{u} \subseteq \mathcal{I}_s$, we have

$$\begin{aligned} D_N^*(\mathcal{P}_{N,s,\mathfrak{u}}) &\leq \frac{2\sqrt{2}}{\sqrt{N}} \left(|\mathfrak{u}| \log\left(\left\lceil \rho_{|\mathfrak{u}|} \sqrt{N} \right\rceil + 1 \right) + \log\left(2(\mathrm{e}-1) s^{|\mathfrak{u}|} \right) \right)^{1/2} \\ &\leq \frac{2\sqrt{2}\sqrt{|\mathfrak{u}|}}{\sqrt{N}} \left(\log\left(\left\lceil \rho_{|\mathfrak{u}|} \sqrt{N} \right\rceil + 1 \right) + \log\left(2(\mathrm{e}-1)s \right) \right)^{1/2}. \end{aligned}$$

For the weighted star discrepancy of this point set, we obtain

$$D^*_{N,\gamma}(\mathcal{P}_{N,s})$$
$$\leq \frac{2\sqrt{2}}{\sqrt{N}}\left(\log\left(\left\lceil \rho_{|\mathfrak{u}|}\sqrt{N}\right\rceil+1\right)+\log\left(2(\mathrm{e}-1)s\right)\right)^{1/2} \max_{\emptyset\neq\mathfrak{u}\subseteq\mathcal{I}_s} \gamma_{\mathfrak{u},s}\sqrt{|\mathfrak{u}|}.$$

Assume now that $C_\gamma := \sup_{s=1,2,\ldots} \max_{\emptyset\neq\mathfrak{u}\subseteq\mathcal{I}_s} \gamma_{\mathfrak{u},s}\sqrt{|\mathfrak{u}|} < \infty$. Then we obtain

$$D^*_{N,\gamma}(\mathcal{P}_{N,s}) \leq \frac{2\sqrt{2}C_\gamma}{\sqrt{N}}\left(\log\left(\left\lceil \rho_{|\mathfrak{u}|}\sqrt{N}\right\rceil+1\right)+\log\left(2(\mathrm{e}-1)s\right)\right)^{1/2}$$

and (3.24) follows.

For any $\delta > 0$, there exists a $c_\delta > 0$ such that

$$C_\gamma 2\sqrt{2}\left(\log\left(\left\lceil \rho_s\sqrt{N}\right\rceil+1\right)+\log\left(2(\mathrm{e}-1)s\right)\right)^{1/2} \leq \left(c_\delta N^\delta(\log s+1)\right)^{1/2}.$$

Hence, it follows from (3.24) that $N \geq c_\delta \varepsilon^{-2/(1-\delta)}(\log s+1)^{1/(1-\delta)}$ implies $\mathrm{disc}^*_\gamma(N,s) \leq \varepsilon$ and therefore

$$N^*_\gamma(s,\varepsilon) \leq \left\lceil c_\delta \varepsilon^{-2/(1-\delta)}(\log s+1)^{1/(1-\delta)}\right\rceil. \qquad \square$$

We close this section by showing that the logarithmic factor in the dimension in the tractability result from Theorem 3.65 is indeed necessary for a large class of weights. This implies that the star discrepancy is not strongly tractable for such weights. In particular, this includes finite order weights of order $k \geq 2$ if all the weights of order 2 are bounded below by a constant $c > 0$.

To prove this lower bound, we need an elementary lemma. For $\mathfrak{u} \subseteq \mathcal{I}_s$ and $k \in \{0,1\}$, let

$$B_k(\mathfrak{u}) = \left\{\boldsymbol{x} = (x_1,\ldots,x_s) \in [0,1)^s \,:\, x_i \in \left[\frac{k}{2},\frac{k+1}{2}\right) \text{ for } i \in \mathfrak{u}\right\}.$$

Lemma 3.66 *Let $\mathcal{P}_{N,s} \subseteq [0,1)^s$ with $|\mathcal{P}_{N,s}| = N$. Then there exists $\mathfrak{u} \subseteq \mathcal{I}_s$ with cardinality at least $s/2^N$ such that one of the sets $B_0(\mathfrak{u})$ and $B_1(\mathfrak{u})$ contains at least half of the points of $\mathcal{P}_{N,s}$.*

Proof There exists $\mathfrak{u}_0 \subseteq \mathcal{I}_s$ with cardinality at least $s/2$ and $k_0 \in \{0,1\}$ such that $\boldsymbol{x}_0 \in B_{k_0}(\mathfrak{u}_0)$. Inductively, for $1 \leq h < N$, we can choose $\mathfrak{u}_h \subseteq \mathfrak{u}_{h-1}$ with cardinality at least $s/2^{h+1}$ and $k_h \in \{0,1\}$ such that $\boldsymbol{x}_h \in B_{k_h}(\mathfrak{u})$. Set $\mathfrak{u} = \mathfrak{u}_{N-1}$ and let $k \in \{0,1\}$ be such that at least half of the k_h, $0 \leq h < N$ are equal to k. Then the cardinality of $\mathfrak{u}$ is at least $s/2^N$ and at least half of the points $\boldsymbol{x}_0,\ldots,\boldsymbol{x}_{N-1}$ are in $B_k(\mathfrak{u})$. $\square$

Now we give the announced lower bound for the weighted star discrepancy which was first proved in [110].

Theorem 3.67 *If the weights* $\boldsymbol{\gamma} = \{\gamma_{\mathfrak{u},s} : \mathfrak{u} \subseteq \mathcal{I}_s\}$ *are such that there exists a constant* $c > 0$ *with* $\gamma_{\mathfrak{u},s} \geq c$ *for all* $\mathfrak{u} \subseteq \mathcal{I}_s$ *with cardinality two, then for all* $N, s \in \mathbb{N}$ *with* $s \geq 2^{N+1}$, *we have*

$$\mathrm{disc}^*_{\boldsymbol{\gamma}}(N, s) \geq \frac{c}{12}.$$

In particular, the weighted star discrepancy is not strongly tractable for such weights.

Proof Let $\mathcal{P}$ be a point set consisting of N points in the s-dimensional unit-cube where $s \geq 2^{N+1}$. With Lemma 3.66 we find $\mathfrak{u}_0 \subseteq \mathcal{I}_s$ with cardinality 2 such that one of the sets $B_0(\mathfrak{u}_0)$ or $B_1(\mathfrak{u}_0)$ contains at least $N/2$ points of $\mathcal{P}$. Without loss of generality we assume that $\mathfrak{u}_0 = \{1, 2\}$. Let $\boldsymbol{z}^{(0)} = (1/2, 1/2, 1/2, \ldots, 1/2)$, $\boldsymbol{z}^{(1)} = (1, 1/2, 1/2, \ldots, 1/2)$ and $\boldsymbol{z}^{(2)} = (1/2, 1, 1/2, \ldots, 1/2)$. Furthermore, let n_0, n_1, n_2 be the number of points in the point set $\mathcal{P}$ that are contained in the boxes $I_1 \times I_2 \times [0, 1)^{s-2}$ for $I_1 = I_2 = [0, 1/2)$, $I_1 = [1/2, 1)$, $I_2 = [0, 1/2)$ and $I_1 = [0, 1/2)$, $I_2 = [1/2, 1)$, respectively.

Let us first assume that the set $B_0(\mathfrak{u}_0)$ contains at least $N/2$ points. Then

$$\Delta_{\mathcal{P}}(\boldsymbol{z}^{(0)}_{\mathfrak{u}_0}, 1) = \frac{A(B_0(\mathfrak{u}_0), N, \mathcal{P})}{N} - \frac{1}{4} \geq \frac{1}{4}$$

which implies that

$$D^*_{N,\boldsymbol{\gamma}}(\mathcal{P}) \geq \frac{c}{4}.$$

We now treat the case that the set $B_1(\mathfrak{u}_0)$ contains at least $N/2$ points so that its complement contains at most $N/2$ points, i.e.

$$n_0 + n_1 + n_2 \leq N/2.$$

Then at least one of the following three inequalities holds

$$n_0 + n_1 \leq \frac{5N}{12}, \quad n_0 + n_2 \leq \frac{5N}{12}, \quad n_0 \geq \frac{N}{3}.$$

If the first inequality holds, then it follows that

$$\Delta_{\mathcal{P}}(\boldsymbol{z}^{(1)}_{\mathfrak{u}_0}, 1) = \frac{n_0 + n_1}{N} - \frac{1}{2} \leq -\frac{1}{12}.$$

If the second inequality holds, we have

$$\Delta_{\mathcal{P}}(\boldsymbol{z}^{(2)}_{\mathfrak{u}_0}, 1) = \frac{n_0 + n_2}{N} - \frac{1}{2} \leq -\frac{1}{12}.$$

If the third inequality is true, then

$$\Delta_{\mathcal{P}}(z_{u_0}^{(0)}, 1) = \frac{n_0}{N} - \frac{1}{4} \geq \frac{1}{12}.$$

In any case $D_{N,\gamma}^*(\mathcal{P}) \geq \frac{c}{12}$ and the result follows. □

Again we refer to Novak and Woźniakowski [199, 200, 201, 202] for a more detailed discussion of the tractability of various notions of discrepancy.

Exercises

3.1 Show that a uniformly distributed sequence is dense in the unit-cube and explain why the converse is not true.

3.2 Which one-dimensional point set $\mathcal{P}$ consisting of N points in $[0, 1)$ minimises $D_N^*(\mathcal{P})$, i.e. for which $\mathcal{P}$ do we have $D_N^*(\mathcal{P}) = \min_{\mathcal{P}'} D_N^*(\mathcal{P}')$, where the minimum is taken over all point sets $\mathcal{P}'$ consisting of N points? Which point set $\mathcal{P}$ consisting of N points minimises $L_{2,N}(\mathcal{P})$? What is the value of $D_N^*(\mathcal{P})$ and $L_{2,N}(\mathcal{P})$ for this point set?
Hint: Draw the graph of the discrepancy function $\Delta_{\mathcal{P}}$.

3.3 Give a rigorous proof of Theorem 3.3.
Hint: See [130, Chapter 1, Corollary 1.1].

3.4 Give a proof of Theorem 3.4.
Hint: See [130, Chapter 1, Corollary 1.2].

3.5 Show that for uniform distribution of the sequence $(\{n\boldsymbol{\alpha}\})_{n\geq 0}$, we necessarily need that $1, \alpha_1, \ldots, \alpha_s$ are linearly independent over $\mathbb{Q}$.

3.6 Show that the b-adic van der Corput sequence is uniformly distributed modulo one just by counting elements of the sequence in intervals, i.e. without the use of Theorem 3.7.
Hint: Consider elementary b-adic intervals first.

3.7 For $b \geq 2$ the *b-adic diaphony* $F_{b,N}$ (see [88] or [99]) of the first N elements of a sequence $\mathcal{S} = (\boldsymbol{x}_n)_{n\geq 0}$ is defined by

$$F_{b,N}(\mathcal{S}) = \left(\frac{1}{(b+1)^s - 1} \sum_{\substack{\boldsymbol{k}\in\mathbb{N}_0^s \\ \boldsymbol{k}\neq\boldsymbol{0}}} \frac{1}{\psi_b(\boldsymbol{k})^2} \left| \frac{1}{N} \sum_{n=0}^{N-1} {}_b\mathrm{wal}_{\boldsymbol{k}}(\boldsymbol{x}_n) \right|^2 \right)^{1/2},$$

where for $\boldsymbol{k} = (k_1, \ldots, k_s) \in \mathbb{N}_0^s$ it is $\psi_b(\boldsymbol{k}) = \prod_{i=1}^s \psi_b(k_i)$ and for $k \in \mathbb{N}_0$,

$$\psi_b(k) = \begin{cases} 1 & \text{if } k = 0, \\ b^r & \text{if } b^r \leq k < b^{r+1} \text{ where } r \in \mathbb{N}_0. \end{cases}$$

Show that a sequence $\mathcal{S}$ is uniformly distributed modulo one if and only if $\lim_{N\to\infty} F_{b,N}(\mathcal{S}) = 0$ for $b \geq 2$.

Note: Compare the b-adic diaphony with the worst-case error for a QMC rule in the Walsh space $\mathscr{H}_{\mathrm{wal},s,b,\alpha,\boldsymbol{\gamma}}$ as given in Exercise 2.15 (especially in the unweighted case and with $\alpha = 2$).

Hint: See [99, Theorem 3.1].

3.8 For $b \ge 2$ the *b-adic spectral test* $\sigma_{b,N}(\mathcal{S})$ (see [97]) of the first N elements of a sequence $\mathcal{S} = (\boldsymbol{x}_n)_{n\ge 0}$ is defined by

$$\sigma_{b,N}(\mathcal{S}) = \sup_{\substack{\boldsymbol{k}\in\mathbb{N}_0^s\\ \boldsymbol{k}\neq\boldsymbol{0}}} \frac{1}{\psi_b(\boldsymbol{k})}\left|\frac{1}{N}\sum_{n=0}^{N-1} {}_b\mathrm{wal}_{\boldsymbol{k}}(\boldsymbol{x}_n)\right|,$$

where ψ_b is defined as in Exercise 3.7. Show that a sequence $\mathcal{S}$ is uniformly distributed modulo one if and only if $\lim_{N\to\infty} \sigma_{b,N}(\mathcal{S}) = 0$ for $b \ge 2$.

3.9 Show that a sequence $\mathcal{S}$ is uniformly distributed modulo one if and only if $\lim_{N\to\infty} D_N(\mathcal{S}) = 0$.

Hint: See [130, Chapter 2, Theorem 1.1].

3.10 Give a rigorous proof of the right-hand inequality in Proposition 3.14 (draw a picture).

3.11 Prove Proposition 3.16.

Hint: See [130, Chapter 2, Theorem 2.6].

3.12 Let $u_i, v_i, \delta_i \in [0,1]$ be such that $|u_i - v_i| \le \delta_i$ for $1 \le i \le s$. Show that

$$\left|\prod_{i=1}^s u_i - \prod_{i=1}^s v_i\right| \le 1 - \prod_{i=1}^s (1-\delta_i) \le s \max_{1\le i\le s} \delta_i .$$

3.13 A finite set $\Gamma \subseteq [0,1]^s$ is a *δ-cover* of $[0,1]^s$ if for every $\boldsymbol{x} = (x_1,\ldots,x_s) \in [0,1]^s$ there exist $\boldsymbol{y}_1 = (y_{1,1},\ldots,y_{1,s})$, $\boldsymbol{y}_2 = (y_{2,1},\ldots,y_{2,s}) \in \Gamma \cup \{\boldsymbol{0}\}$ with $\lambda_s([\boldsymbol{0},\boldsymbol{y}_2)) - \lambda_s([\boldsymbol{0},\boldsymbol{y}_1)) \le \delta$ and $y_{1,i} \le x_i \le y_{2,i}$ for all $1 \le i \le s$.

Let Γ be a δ-cover of $[0,1]^s$. Show that for any N-point set $\mathcal{P} \subseteq [0,1)^s$, we then have

$$D_N^*(\mathcal{P}) \le \max_{\boldsymbol{y}\in\Gamma} |\Delta_{\mathcal{P}}(\boldsymbol{y})| + \delta .$$

3.14 Prove a similar formula to that in Proposition 2.15 for the L_q-discrepancy with an even integer q.

3.15 Show that

$$\int_{[0,1]^{sN}} (L_{2,N}(\{\boldsymbol{\tau}_1,\ldots,\boldsymbol{\tau}_N\}))^2 \,\mathrm{d}\boldsymbol{\tau}_1\cdots\mathrm{d}\boldsymbol{\tau}_N = \frac{1}{N}\left(\frac{1}{2^s} - \frac{1}{3^s}\right).$$

Thus, there exists a point set $\mathcal{P}$ consisting of N points in the s-dimensional unit-cube such that

$$L_{2,N}(\mathcal{P}) \le \frac{1}{\sqrt{N}}\left(\frac{1}{2^s} - \frac{1}{3^s}\right)^{1/2}.$$

Hint: Use Proposition 2.15.

3.16 Let $\mathcal{T}_{s,N}(\alpha)$ be the set of all tuples $(\boldsymbol{\tau}_1, \ldots, \boldsymbol{\tau}_N)$ with $\boldsymbol{\tau}_j \in [0,1]^s$ for $1 \le j \le N$ such that

$$L_{2,N}(\{\boldsymbol{\tau}_1, \ldots, \boldsymbol{\tau}_N\}) \le \frac{\alpha}{\sqrt{N}} \left(\frac{1}{2^s} - \frac{1}{3^s} \right)^{1/2}.$$

Use Exercise 3.15 to show that for all $\alpha \ge 1$, we have

$$\lambda_{sN}\left(\mathcal{T}_{s,N}(\alpha)\right) > 1 - \alpha^{-2}.$$

3.17 Use Theorem 3.26 to show that the point set $\{0, 1/N, \ldots, (N-1)/N\}$ in the unit-interval has extreme discrepancy of order $1/N$.

3.18 Prove a similar result to that of Theorem 3.28 also for the extreme discrepancy. *Hint:* See [96, Theorem 1].

3.19 For integers $m_1, \ldots, m_s \ge 2$, let

$$\Gamma_{m_1,\ldots,m_s} = \left\{ \left(\frac{n_1}{m_1}, \ldots, \frac{n_s}{m_s} \right) : 0 \le n_i < m_j \text{ for } 1 \le i \le s \right\}$$

be the regular lattice consisting of $N = m_1 \cdots m_s$ points. Show that then

$$D_N^*(\Gamma_{m_1,\ldots,m_s}) = 1 - \prod_{i=1}^{s} \left(1 - \frac{1}{m_i} \right).$$

3.20 Let $\mathcal{P}_s = \left\{ \left(\frac{a_1}{4}, \ldots, \frac{a_s}{4} \right) : a_i \in \{1,3\} \text{ for all } 1 \le i \le s \right\}$ be the centred regular lattice consisting of 2^s points in $[0,1)^s$. Show that $\lim_{s\to\infty} D_{2^s}^*(\mathcal{P}_s) = 1$.

3.21 Let Γ_m be the regular lattice defined by (3.14). Use Theorem 3.27 to show that the extreme discrepancy of Γ_m is given by $D_N(\Gamma_m) = 1 - (1 - 1/m)^s$.

3.22 Show that the star discrepancy of the centred regular lattice Γ_m^{c} consisting of $N = m^s$ points defined by (1.1) is

$$D_N^*(\Gamma_m^{\mathrm{c}}) = 1 - \left(1 - \frac{1}{2m} \right)^s.$$

3.23 In dimensions $s = 1$ and $s = 2$, draw a picture to make the result from Lemma 3.40 more plausible.

3.24 Let $b_1, \ldots, b_s \ge 2$ be pairwise relatively prime integers and let $\mathcal{S}$ be the van der Corput–Halton sequence with bases $b_1, \ldots, b_s$. Show that for any $N \ge 2$, we have

$$D_N(\mathcal{S}) \le \widetilde{c}(b_1, \ldots, b_s) \frac{(\log N)^s}{N} + O\left(\frac{(\log N)^{s-1}}{N} \right),$$

with

$$\widetilde{c}(b_1, \ldots, b_s) = \frac{2^s}{s!} \prod_{i=1}^{s} \frac{\lfloor b_i/2 \rfloor}{\log b_i}.$$

Show, further, that if $b_1, \ldots, b_s$ are the first s prime numbers, then $\widetilde{c}(b_1, \ldots, b_s) = O(s^{-1})$.

3.25 For integers $s \geq 2$ and $N \geq 2$, consider a generating vector of the form $\boldsymbol{g} = (1, g, g^2, \ldots, g^{s-1}) \in \mathbb{Z}^s$. Such a choice was first proposed by Korobov [124] and therefore such lattice points are often called *Korobov vectors* or *Korobov lattice points*. A lattice point set which is generated by a Korobov vector is often called a *Korobov lattice point set*.

Show, by averaging over all $g \in G_N$, that there exists a Korobov vector for which we have

$$R_N((1, g, g^2, \ldots, g^{s-1})) \leq \frac{s-1}{N-1}(1 + S_N)^s.$$

Hint: Recall that any non-zero polynomial of degree k over an integral domain has, at most, k zeros.

3.26 Let $\mathcal{P}$ be a lattice point set consisting of N points in $[0, 1)^s$ with generating vector $\boldsymbol{g} \in \mathbb{Z}^s$. Show that the worst-case error for the lattice rule based on $\mathcal{P}$ in the s-dimensional Korobov space $\mathscr{H}_{\mathrm{kor},s,\alpha}$ from Exercise 2.13 is given by

$$e^2(\mathscr{H}_{\mathrm{kor},s,\alpha}, \mathcal{P}) = \sum_{\substack{\boldsymbol{h} \in \mathbb{Z}^s \setminus \{\boldsymbol{0}\} \\ \boldsymbol{g} \cdot \boldsymbol{h} \equiv 0 \pmod{N}}} \frac{1}{r_\alpha(\boldsymbol{h})},$$

where $r_\alpha(\boldsymbol{h})$ is as in Exercise 2.13.

3.27 Let $e_\alpha^2(\boldsymbol{g}, N)$ be the worst-case integration error for a lattice rule in the s-dimensional Korobov space $\mathscr{H}_{\mathrm{kor},s,\alpha}$ for a lattice point set consisting of N points in $[0, 1)^s$ with generating vector $\boldsymbol{g} \in \mathbb{Z}^s$. Let N be a prime. Show that

$$\frac{1}{N^s} \sum_{\boldsymbol{g} \in \{0,\ldots,N-1\}^s} e_\alpha^2(\boldsymbol{g}, N) = \frac{1}{N}\left(-1 + (1 + 2\zeta(\alpha))^s\right).$$

Deduce from this result that for any $1/\alpha < \lambda \leq 1$, there exists a generating vector $\boldsymbol{g} \in \{0, \ldots, N-1\}^s$ such that

$$e_\alpha^2(\boldsymbol{g}, N) \leq \frac{1}{N^{1/\lambda}}\left(-1 + (1 + 2\zeta(\alpha\lambda))^s\right)^{1/\lambda}.$$

Hint: Use Jensen's inequality which states that for a sequence (a_k) of non-negative reals and for any $0 < \lambda < 1$, we have $\left(\sum a_k\right)^\lambda \leq \sum a_k^\lambda$.

3.28 It has been shown in [57, Theorem 2.3] that there exists a δ-cover Γ of $[0, 1]^s$ such that $|\Gamma| \leq \left(\left\lceil \frac{s}{s-1} \frac{\log s}{\delta} \right\rceil + 1\right)^d$. Use this result together with Exercise 3.13 to show that

$$\mathrm{disc}^*(N, s) \leq \sqrt{2} n^{-1/2}(s \log(\lceil \rho n^{1/2} \rceil + 1) + \log 2),$$

where $\rho = \frac{3 \log 3}{\sqrt{2(3 \log 3 + \log 2)}}$.

Hint: Follow the proof of Theorem 3.54.

Note: This is [57, Theorem 3.2]. Smaller δ-covers such as that from [57, Theorem 2.3] have been constructed in [86].

3.29 Prove Proposition 3.60.

3.30 Prove a similar formula to that of Proposition 3.60 for the weighted L_q-discrepancy with an even integer q.
Hint: See [156, Theorem 2.1].

3.31 Generalise Proposition 3.16 to the case of weighted star discrepancy.

3.32 For product weights, show that the weighted L_2-discrepancy is tractable if and only if

$$\limsup_{s \to \infty} \frac{\sum_{j=1}^{s} \gamma_j}{\log s} < \infty.$$

4

Nets and sequences

In this chapter we give an introduction to the concept of (t, m, s)-nets and $(\mathbf{T}, s)$-sequences. Compared to classical types of point sets and sequences, like Hammersley point sets or van der Corput–Halton sequences, the general concept of (t, m, s)-nets and $(\mathbf{T}, s)$-sequences is a more natural one. Whereas in former examples a certain generation algorithm was the centre and origin of the investigation, here the starting point is the central property of uniform distribution modulo one that all intervals have to contain the correct proportion of points of a sequence. With this definition in mind we search for a reasonably large class of intervals which are 'fair' in this sense with respect to a finite point set. This leads to the definition of (t, m, s)-nets and their infinite analogues, to $(\mathbf{T}, s)$-sequences.

The generation of such point sets and sequences is based mainly on the digital construction scheme which leads to the notion of digital nets and sequences. Although such constructions go back to Sobol′ [253] and Faure [68] the detailed introduction and investigation of the general concept was given by Niederreiter [172]. This paper can be regarded nowadays as the initiation of the whole theory of (t, m, s)-nets and $(\mathbf{T}, s)$-sequences. An introduction can also be found in [177, Chapter 4].

4.1 Motivation, fair intervals

The origin of studying (t, m, s)-nets, and, more generally, 'fair intervals', is the property of uniform distribution modulo one (see Definition 3.1). For a finite point set $\mathcal{P} = \{\boldsymbol{x}_0, \ldots, \boldsymbol{x}_{N-1}\}$ in $[0, 1)^s$ it is never possible that it be absolutely uniformly distributed; that is, there are always subsets J, moreover, there are always even intervals J in $[0, 1)^s$, for which

$$\frac{A(J, N, \mathcal{P})}{N} = \lambda_s(J)$$

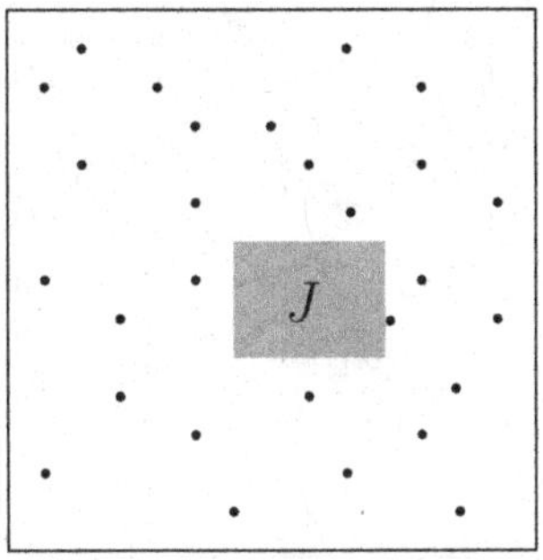

Figure 4.1 An interval J containing no point of $\mathcal{P}$.

does not hold. For instance, take an interval J of positive volume containing none of the points $\boldsymbol{x}_0, \ldots, \boldsymbol{x}_{N-1}$ (see Figure 4.1). Then $A(J, N, \mathcal{P})/N = 0 < \lambda_s(J)$. If $\mathcal{P}$ is finite, such intervals J can always be found.

Let us use the following notation.

Definition 4.1 For a given set $\mathcal{P}$ consisting of N points in $[0, 1)^s$, we say for a subset J of $[0, 1)^s$ that it is *fair* (with respect to $\mathcal{P}$), if

$$\frac{A(J, N, \mathcal{P})}{N} = \lambda_s(J).$$

This notation is also used the other way round.

Definition 4.2 For a given subset J of $[0, 1)^s$, we say that a set $\mathcal{P}$ consisting of N points in $[0, 1)^s$ is *fair* (with respect to J), if

$$\frac{A(J, N, \mathcal{P})}{N} = \lambda_s(J).$$

As we have seen, it is never possible that all intervals J are fair with respect to a given finite point set $\mathcal{P}$. Indeed, from the result of Roth, see Theorem 3.20, it follows that there even always exists an interval J with

$$\left| \frac{A(J, N, \mathcal{P})}{N} - \lambda_s(J) \right| \geq c_s \frac{(\log N)^{(s-1)/2}}{N}$$

with a constant $c_s > 0$, depending only on the dimension s. However, for given s and N we could try to consider a certain class $\mathcal{C}$ of intervals J in $[0, 1)^s$ and to find point sets $\mathcal{P}$ in $[0, 1)^s$ such that any $J \in \mathcal{C}$ is fair with respect to $\mathcal{P}$.

Definition 4.3 For a given set $\mathcal{C}$ of subsets J of $[0, 1)^s$, $\mathcal{C} \subseteq \{J : J \subseteq [0, 1)^s\}$, we say that a set $\mathcal{P}$ consisting of N points in $[0, 1)^s$ is *fair* (with respect to $\mathcal{C}$), if

$$\frac{A(J, N, \mathcal{P})}{N} = \lambda_s(J) \quad \text{for all } J \in \mathcal{C}.$$

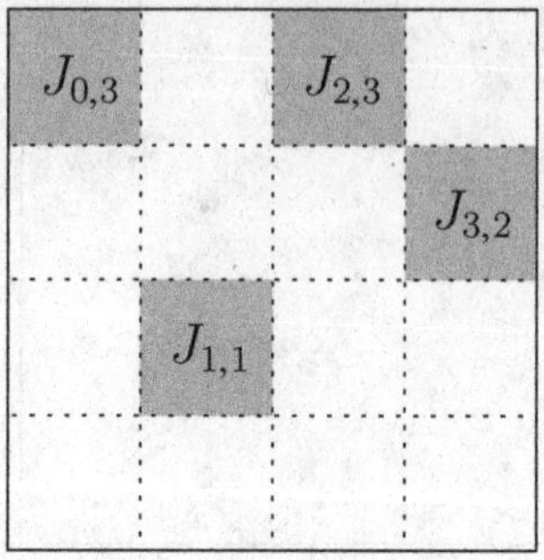

Figure 4.2 Intervals $J_{0,1}$, $J_{1,1}$, $J_{2,3}$, $J_{3,2}$ from the class $\mathcal{C}$ for $s = 2$ and $N = 16$.

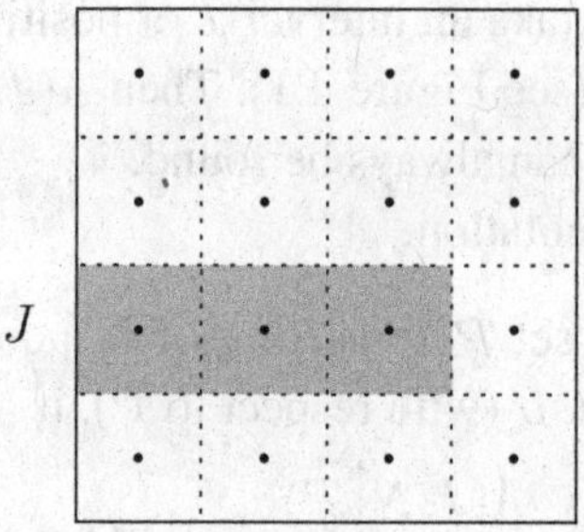

Figure 4.3 The class $\mathcal{C}$ for $s = 2$ and $N = 16$ and the regular lattice with 16 points.

Of course, we would like to consider classes $\mathcal{C}$ of intervals as large as possible, with the hope that then for all intervals J in $[0, 1)^s$ the fraction $A(J, N, \mathcal{P})/N$ is at least approximately equal to $\lambda_s(J)$.

Let us consider one concrete example. Choose $s = 2$, $N = 16$ and

$$\mathcal{C} = \{J_{A,B} = [A/4, (A+1)/4) \times [B/4, (B+1)/4) \, : \, A, B \in \{0, 1, 2, 3\}\};$$

see Figure 4.2. We remark that the choice of half-open intervals here and in the following is of minor importance.

If we choose for $\mathcal{P} = \{\boldsymbol{x}_0, \ldots, \boldsymbol{x}_{15}\}$ the regular lattice (for convenience with the points centred in the intervals, see Figure 4.3), then clearly every $J_{A,B} \in \mathcal{C}$ is fair with respect to $\mathcal{P}$, i.e.

$$\frac{A(J_{A,B}, 16, \mathcal{P})}{16} = \frac{1}{16} = \lambda_2(J_{A,B}).$$

Trivially, any interval J, which is a union of some of the disjoint intervals $J_{A,B}$, is fair also. Consider, for example, $J := J_{0,1} \cup J_{1,1} \cup J_{2,1}$, for which we have $A(J, 16, \mathcal{P})/16 = 3/16 = \lambda_2(J)$.

Instead of $\mathcal{C}$, we could even choose the larger class

$$\mathcal{C}_1 = \{[A/4, C/4) \times [B/4, D/4) \, : \, 0 \le A < C \le 4, 0 \le B < D \le 4\}$$

containing all intervals, which are unions of intervals of $\mathcal{C}$. Every interval in $\mathcal{C}_1$ is fair with respect to the regular lattice $\mathcal{P} = \{\boldsymbol{x}_0, \ldots, \boldsymbol{x}_{15}\}$. But this fact does not give more information than the fact that the set $\mathcal{C}$ of 'more elementary' intervals is fair. This consideration can be extended to arbitrary dimension s and to arbitrary N of the form $N = b^s$ with an integer $b \geq 2$. The regular lattice $\mathcal{P} = \{\boldsymbol{x}_0, \ldots, \boldsymbol{x}_{b^s-1}\}$ then has the property that

$$\mathcal{C} := \left\{ \prod_{i=1}^{s} \left[\frac{A_i}{b}, \frac{A_i+1}{b} \right) : 0 \leq A_i < b \text{ for } 1 \leq i \leq s \right\}$$

and therefore

$$\mathcal{C}_1 := \left\{ \prod_{i=1}^{s} \left[\frac{A_i}{b}, \frac{B_i}{b} \right) : 0 \leq A_i < B_i \leq b \text{ for } 1 \leq i \leq s \right\}$$

is fair with respect to $\mathcal{P}$. Thus, we have a reasonably large class of fair intervals for the regular lattice.

However, we have already seen that the (star) discrepancy, of the regular lattice (centred or not) is rather large (see Proposition 3.32 and Remark 3.33). Consider, for example, the rather large intervals $J_1 = [0, \frac{1}{8}) \times [0, 1)$ or $J_2 = [0, 1) \times (\frac{3}{8}, \frac{5}{8})$, which do not contain any point and so they are, by far, not fair (we should have $A(J_1, 16, \mathcal{P}) = 2$ and $A(J_2, 16, \mathcal{P}) = 4$). In general, the interval

$$J = \prod_{i=1}^{s-1} [0, 1) \times \left(\frac{1}{2}\frac{1}{b}, \frac{3}{2}\frac{1}{b} \right)$$

is empty, whereas we should have $A(J, b^s, \mathcal{P}) = b^{s-1}$, and hence we have

$$D_N(\mathcal{P}) \geq \left| \frac{A(J, N, \mathcal{P})}{N} - \lambda_s(J) \right| = \left| 0 - \frac{1}{b} \right| = \frac{1}{b} = \frac{1}{N^{1/s}}.$$

This means that to obtain point sets with a small (star) discrepancy, we certainly have to demand fairness for larger, and in some sense, finer classes $\mathcal{C}$ of intervals.

Now let us try to extend $\mathcal{C}$ to a class $\widetilde{\mathcal{C}}$ such that fairness can still be attained with respect to certain point sets.

For simplicity let us again restrict ourselves to half-open intervals. Since for $J \in \widetilde{\mathcal{C}}$ we demand $A(J, 16, \mathcal{P})/16 = \lambda_s(J)$, we must have $\lambda_s(J) = k/16$ for an integer $k \geq 1$. Since any interval J of volume $k/16$ can be represented by the union of disjoint intervals of volume $1/16$, let us restrict ourselves to intervals of volume $1/16$.

Examples of such intervals are intervals of the 'elementary' form $[0, 1) \times [\frac{B}{16}, \frac{B+1}{16})$ or $[\frac{A}{2}, \frac{A+1}{2}) \times [\frac{B}{8}, \frac{B+1}{8})$ or $[\frac{A}{4}, \frac{A+1}{4}) \times [\frac{B}{4}, \frac{B+1}{4})$ and similar ones (see Figure 4.4).

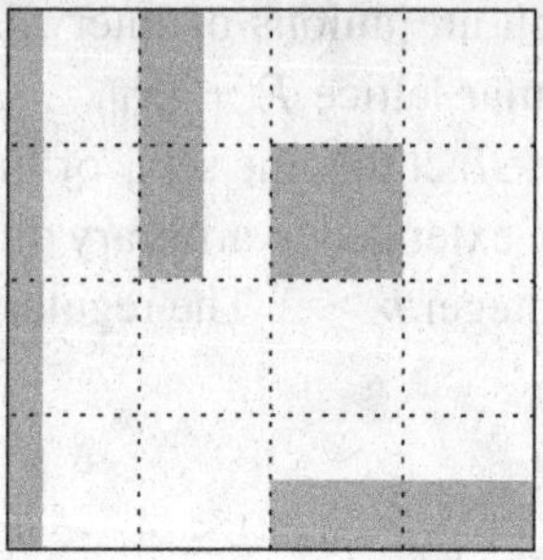

Figure 4.4 'Elementary' intervals of area 1/16.

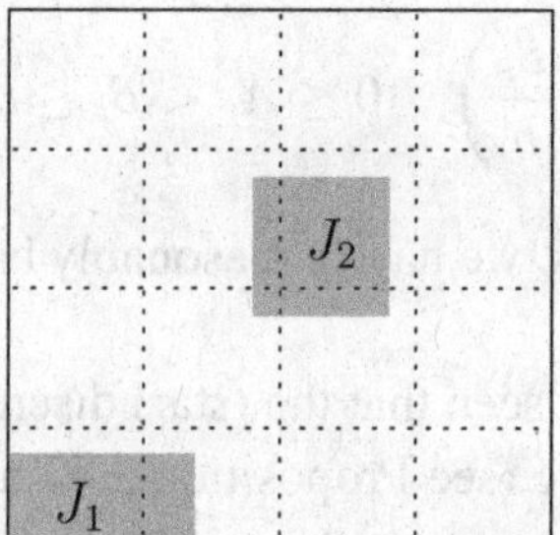

Figure 4.5 The intervals J_1 and J_2.

Considering these intervals means a considerable extension of the class $\mathcal{C}$. Obviously there are many other intervals of volume 1/16, for example $J_1 := [0, \frac{1}{\pi}) \times [0, \frac{\pi}{16})$ or $J_2 := [\frac{7}{16}, \frac{7}{16} + \frac{1}{4}) \times [\frac{7}{16}, \frac{7}{16} + \frac{1}{4})$; see Figure 4.5.

It is quite obvious that including intervals of the 'J_1-type' (any interval of prescribed volume) together with the 'elementary' intervals in $\widetilde{\mathcal{C}}$ would cause problems with finding a point set $\mathcal{P}$ in $[0, 1)^s$, which is fair for all these $J \in \widetilde{\mathcal{C}}$. Although it is not so obvious, to also include intervals of the form J_2 (all translates of intervals from $\widetilde{\mathcal{C}}$) together with the elementary intervals in $\widetilde{\mathcal{C}}$, at least in most cases, is a too restrictive demand (see the example below).

Let us consider

$$\widetilde{\mathcal{C}} := \left\{ \left[\frac{A}{2^d}, \frac{A+1}{2^d}\right) \times \left[\frac{B}{2^{4-d}}, \frac{B+1}{2^{4-d}}\right) : \right.$$
$$\left. d \in \{0, 1, 2, 3, 4\},\ 0 \leq A < 2^d,\ 0 \leq B < 2^{4-d} \right\}.$$

Obviously $\mathcal{C} \subseteq \widetilde{\mathcal{C}}$. The question is as follows. Is there a point set $\mathcal{P} = \{\boldsymbol{x}_0, \ldots, \boldsymbol{x}_{15}\}$ in $[0, 1)^2$ which is fair with respect to $\widetilde{\mathcal{C}}$; that is, such that any $J \in \widetilde{\mathcal{C}}$ contains exactly one point of $\mathcal{P}$? The answer is *yes*! Take, for example, the two-dimensional 16-point Hammersley point set in base 2 from Definition 3.44; see Figure 4.6.

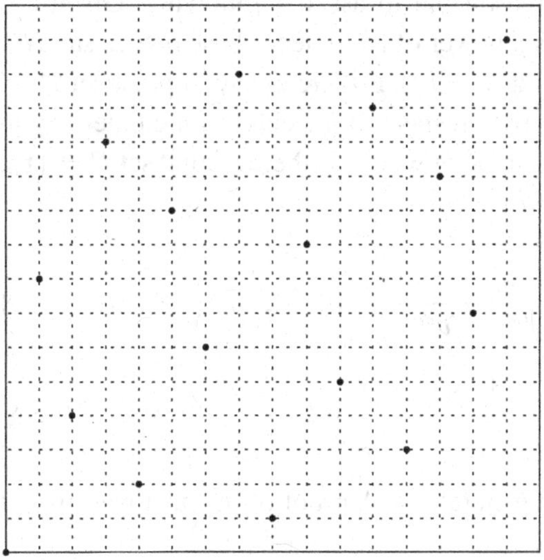

Figure 4.6 The 16-point Hammersley point set in base 2.

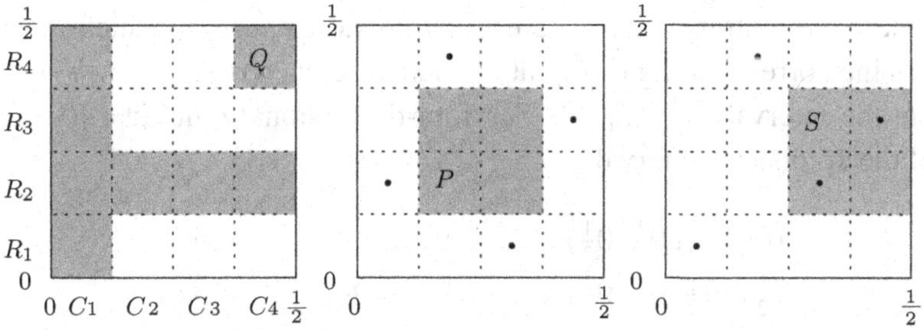

Figure 4.7 Placing four points in $[0, 1/2)^2$ which are fair with respect to R_1, R_2, R_3, R_4 and to C_1, C_2, C_3, C_4.

We shall now show that it is not possible to satisfy the fairness condition if we also include intervals of the type J_2 in $\widetilde{\mathcal{C}}$.

Consider the left lower quarter $[0, 1/2)^2$ of the unit square. It must contain exactly four points. Any of the four (right half-open) rows R_1, R_2, R_3, R_4 and any of the four (right half-open) columns C_1, C_2, C_3, C_4, indicated in Figure 4.7, must contain exactly one point.

In whichever way one tries to place four points in the above square (see again Figure 4.7), there are either two small sub-squares of type Q, containing one point each, which are joined at one vertex, or the square P remains empty. The intervals S and P are of type J_2, of volume $1/16$, and therefore should contain exactly one point. Hence, it is useless to demand the fairness condition for a class of intervals containing the elementary as well as the J_2-type intervals.

In general it is reasonable to ask the following. Given a dimension s and a number N, which is a power of any integer base $b \geq 2$, say $N = b^m$ (in the above example we restricted $N = b^s$), is there always a point set $\mathcal{P} = \{\boldsymbol{x}_0, \ldots, \boldsymbol{x}_{N-1}\}$ in $[0, 1)^s$ which is fair with respect to the class $\widetilde{\mathcal{C}}$ of elementary intervals of order m (see Definition 3.8)? In other words, is there a point set $\mathcal{P} = \{\boldsymbol{x}_0, \ldots, \boldsymbol{x}_{N-1}\}$ which is fair with respect to

$$\widetilde{\mathcal{C}} = \left\{ \prod_{i=1}^{s} \left[\frac{A_i}{b^{d_i}}, \frac{A_i + 1}{b^{d_i}} \right) : d_1, \ldots, d_s \in \mathbb{N}_0,\ d_1 + \cdots + d_s = m, \right.$$
$$\left. 0 \leq A_i < b^{d_i} \text{ for } 1 \leq i \leq s \right\}?$$

The answer is, in general, *no*. A proof of this fact was given by Sobol′ [253].

Example 4.4 We show that even for $s = 4$ and $N = 2^2$ ($b = 2$ and $m = 2$) such a point set does not exist. In our argument we follow the proof of this result in [253, Section 5.5].

Assume to the contrary that there are four points $\boldsymbol{x}_0, \boldsymbol{x}_1, \boldsymbol{x}_2, \boldsymbol{x}_3$ which are fair with respect to the corresponding $\widetilde{\mathcal{C}}$. For abbreviation let us write $(k_1 l_1, k_2 l_2, k_3 l_3, k_4 l_4)$ to denote the interval $\prod_{i=1}^{4} [k_i, l_i)$. The four-dimensional unit-cube $[0, 1)^4$ is the union of the 16 disjoint intervals

$(0\tfrac{1}{2}, 0\tfrac{1}{2}, 0\tfrac{1}{2}, 0\tfrac{1}{2})$	type 0
$(\tfrac{1}{2}1, 0\tfrac{1}{2}, 0\tfrac{1}{2}, 0\tfrac{1}{2}), \ldots, (0\tfrac{1}{2}, 0\tfrac{1}{2}, 0\tfrac{1}{2}, \tfrac{1}{2}1)$	type 1
$(\tfrac{1}{2}1, \tfrac{1}{2}1, 0\tfrac{1}{2}, 0\tfrac{1}{2}), \ldots, (0\tfrac{1}{2}, 0\tfrac{1}{2}, \tfrac{1}{2}1, \tfrac{1}{2}1)$	type 2
$(\tfrac{1}{2}1, \tfrac{1}{2}1, \tfrac{1}{2}1, 0\tfrac{1}{2}), \ldots, (0\tfrac{1}{2}, \tfrac{1}{2}1, \tfrac{1}{2}1, \tfrac{1}{2}1)$	type 3
$(\tfrac{1}{2}1, \tfrac{1}{2}1, \tfrac{1}{2}1, \tfrac{1}{2}1)$	type 4

Because of symmetry we can assume without loss of generality that $\boldsymbol{x}_0 \in (0\tfrac{1}{2}, 0\tfrac{1}{2}, 0\tfrac{1}{2}, 0\tfrac{1}{2})$.

1. Assume that $\boldsymbol{x}_1$ is also an element of the type 0 interval or $\boldsymbol{x}_1$ is an element of a type 1 interval, without restriction of generality say $\boldsymbol{x}_1 \in (\tfrac{1}{2}1, 0\tfrac{1}{2}, 0\tfrac{1}{2}, 0\tfrac{1}{2})$ or of a type 2 interval, without restriction of generality say $\boldsymbol{x}_1 \in (\tfrac{1}{2}1, \tfrac{1}{2}1, 0\tfrac{1}{2}, 0\tfrac{1}{2})$. Then there are at least two points in the elementary interval $(01, 01, 0\tfrac{1}{2}, 0\tfrac{1}{2})$ of volume $\tfrac{1}{4}$ which must contain exactly one point.
2. Assume that $\boldsymbol{x}_1$ is an element of the type 4 interval $(\tfrac{1}{2}1, \tfrac{1}{2}1, \tfrac{1}{2}1, \tfrac{1}{2}1)$. Then with the same argument as above, none of the points $\boldsymbol{x}_2$ and $\boldsymbol{x}_3$ can be contained in a type 4 interval or a type 3 interval, and so there is no space at all for $\boldsymbol{x}_2$ and $\boldsymbol{x}_3$.

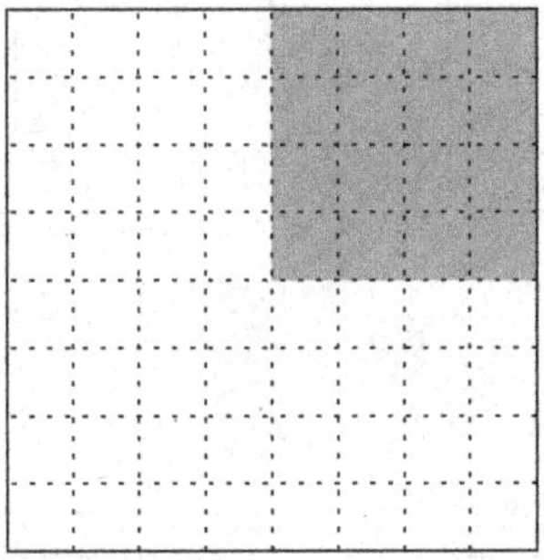

Figure 4.8 A disjoint union of elementary intervals.

3. Therefore, $\boldsymbol{x}_1$ and $\boldsymbol{x}_2$ (and also $\boldsymbol{x}_3$) must be contained in type 3 intervals, without loss of generality assume they are contained in $(0\frac{1}{2}, \frac{1}{2}1, \frac{1}{2}1, \frac{1}{2}1) \cup (\frac{1}{2}1, 0\frac{1}{2}, \frac{1}{2}1, \frac{1}{2}1)$. Then there are at least two points in the elementary interval $(01, 01, \frac{1}{2}1, \frac{1}{2}1)$ of volume $\frac{1}{4}$ which must contain exactly one point.

Hence, a fair distribution of four points in $[0, 1)^4$, in the above sense, is not possible.

The answer to the question as to when a fair distribution can be attained depends on the parameters b and s (and not on m) as is shown in the next section. Alas, in general, the demand for fairness for all intervals in $\widetilde{\mathcal{C}}$ must be weakened. A quite reasonable way to do this is as follows. If $\mathcal{P} = \{\boldsymbol{x}_0, \ldots, \boldsymbol{x}_{N-1}\}$ is fair with respect to all elementary intervals

$$\prod_{i=1}^{s} \left[\frac{A_i}{b^{d_i}}, \frac{A_i + 1}{b^{d_i}} \right)$$

of volume b^{-m} in $\widetilde{\mathcal{C}}$, i.e. $d_1 + \cdots + d_s = m$, then of course it is also fair with respect to all intervals $\prod_{i=1}^{s}[\frac{A_i}{b^{d_i}}, \frac{A_i+1}{b^{d_i}})$ with $d_1 + \cdots + d_s \leq m$, since any such interval is a disjoint union of elementary intervals of volume b^{-m}. For example,

$$\left[\frac{1}{2}, 1\right) \times \left[\frac{1}{2}, 1\right) = \bigcup_{k=1}^{4} \left(\left[\frac{1}{2}, 1\right) \times \left[\frac{3+k}{8}, \frac{4+k}{8}\right) \right);$$

see Figure 4.8.

To weaken the original condition

'fairness with respect to all $J = \prod_{i=1}^{s}[\frac{A_i}{b^{d_i}}, \frac{A_i+1}{b^{d_i}})$ with $d_1 + \cdots + d_s = m$',

i.e. to all b-adic elementary intervals of order m (see Definition 3.8), we could instead demand

'fairness with respect to all $J = \prod_{i=1}^{s}[\frac{A_i}{b^{d_i}}, \frac{A_i+1}{b^{d_i}})$ with $d_1 + \cdots + d_s = m - 1$',

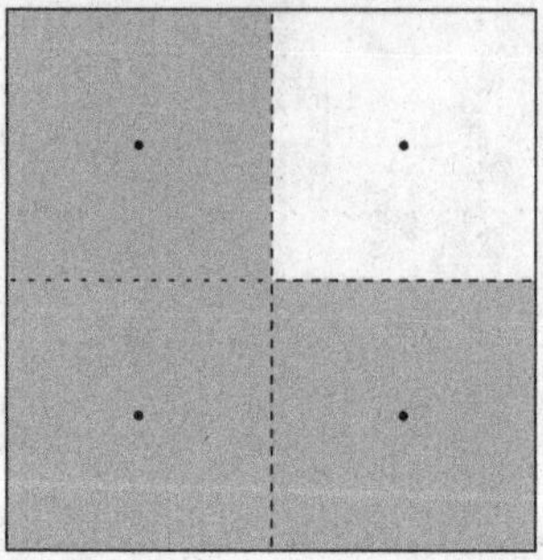

Figure 4.9 An example for $s = 2, b = 2$ and $N = 2^2$.

i.e. to all b-adic elementary intervals of order $m - 1$. Obviously, the first condition does contain the second condition, whereas the second condition does not contain the first one. To illustrate this, consider the example in Figure 4.9 for $s = 2, b = 2$ and $N = 2^2$. The four points are fair to all 2-adic elementary intervals of order 1 (area 1/2), but there is no point in the elementary interval $[0, \frac{1}{4}) \times [0, 1)$ of order 2 (area $1/2^2$). If this condition still cannot be satisfied, then we can again replace the order $m - 1$ by $m - t$ for some $2 \leq t \leq m$. Finally, by choosing $t = m$, we obtain the condition that $\boldsymbol{x}_0, \ldots, \boldsymbol{x}_{N-1}$, with $N = b^m$, is fair with respect to $[0, 1)^s$, which is trivially satisfied.

We motivated these considerations by starting with the (centred) regular lattice. Let us finish this section with an example by considering the regular lattice (centred or not) once more with respect to the above condition on elementary intervals.

Let a dimension s and a base b be given and let $N = b^m$ be such that we can generate a (centred) regular lattice with N points. This is certainly possible if $m = Ls$ for a positive integer L. Then, for points of the centred regular lattice, we can choose the centres of the sub-cubes $\prod_{i=1}^{s}[\frac{A_i}{b^L}, \frac{A_i+1}{b^L})$, $0 \leq A_i < b^L$ for $1 \leq i \leq s$.

Example 4.5 For $s = b = L = 2$, we arrive at the point set from Figure 4.10. This point set is not fair with respect to all 2-adic intervals of order 4 or of order 3. For example, the elementary interval $[0, \frac{1}{8}) \times [0, 1)$ of order 3 (area $1/2^3$) contains no point of the (centred) regular lattice. However, it is fair with respect to all elementary intervals of order 2 (area $1/2^2$) and of lower order, since any elementary interval of order 2 is a (disjoint) union of sub-cubes $[\frac{A_1}{4}, \frac{A_1+1}{4}) \times [\frac{A_2}{4}, \frac{A_2+1}{4})$ with $0 \leq A_1, A_2 < 4$, all of which contain one point, have area $1/2^4$ and are therefore fair (see Figure 4.10).

In general we have the following result.

Lemma 4.6 *The (centred) regular lattice of b^{Ls} points in $[0, 1)^s$ is fair for the class of all b-adic elementary intervals of order L. It is not fair for the class of all b-adic elementary intervals of order $L + 1$.*

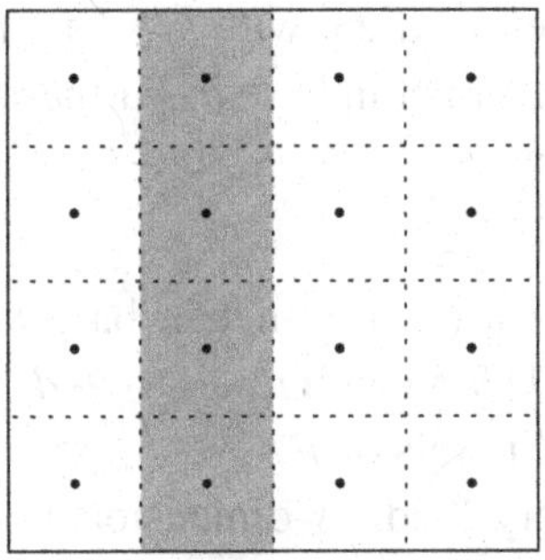

Figure 4.10 Centred regular lattice Γ_4^c with 16 points and an elementary interval of order 2.

Proof The b-adic elementary interval $[0, \frac{1}{b^{L+1}}) \times \prod_{i=2}^{s}[0, 1)$ of order $L+1$ is not fair with respect to the regular lattice. Any b-adic elementary interval J of order L, say $J = \prod_{i=1}^{s}[\frac{A_i}{b^{d_i}}, \frac{A_i+1}{b^{d_i}})$ with $d_1 + \cdots + d_s = L$ and $0 \le A_i < b^{d_i}$ for $1 \le i \le s$, can be represented as the disjoint union of fair sub-cubes by

$$J = \bigcup_{B_1=b^{L-d_1}A_1}^{b^{L-d_1}(A_1+1)-1} \cdots \bigcup_{B_s=b^{L-d_s}A_s}^{b^{L-d_s}(A_s+1)-1} \prod_{i=1}^{s} \left[\frac{B_i}{b^L}, \frac{B_i+1}{b^L}\right).$$

Therefore, J is fair and the result follows. □

In this section we have provided the motivation for the definition of a (t, m, s)-net in base b, which is given in the next section.

4.2 (t, m, s)-nets and their basic properties

Motivated by the discussion in the previous section, we give the following definitions (thereby we essentially follow the general definitions given for the first time by Niederreiter [172]).

Recall that, according to Definition 3.8, for a given dimension $s \ge 1$, an integer base $b \ge 2$ and a non-negative integer k, a b-adic s-dimensional elementary interval of order k is an interval of the form

$$J = \prod_{i=1}^{s}\left[\frac{A_i}{b^{d_i}}, \frac{A_i+1}{b^{d_i}}\right),$$

where $d_1, \ldots, d_s \in \mathbb{N}_0$ with $d_1 + \cdots + d_s = k$ and $0 \le A_i < b^{d_i}$ for $1 \le i \le s$.

Definition 4.7 For a given dimension $s \ge 1$, an integer base $b \ge 2$, a positive integer m and an integer t with $0 \le t \le m$, a point set $\mathcal{P}$ of b^m points in $[0, 1)^s$ is called a *(t, m, s)-net in base b* if the point set $\mathcal{P}$ is fair with respect to all b-adic s-dimensional elementary intervals of order $m - t$.

Definition 4.8 A (t, m, s)-net in base b with $t \geq 1$ is called a *strict* (t, m, s)-net in base b if it is not a $(t-1, m, s)$-net in base b. Furthermore, a $(0, m, s)$-net in base b is called strict by definition.

Remark 4.9

1. The property for $\mathcal{P}$ to be a (t, m, s)-net in base b means that every interval $J = \prod_{i=1}^{s} [A_i/b^{d_i}, (A_i + 1)/b^{d_i})$ with $d_1 + \cdots + d_s = m - t$, that is, of volume b^{-m+t}, contains exactly b^t points of $\mathcal{P}$.
2. Since for every $k \geq 1$ every b-adic s-dimensional elementary interval of order $k-1$ (volume b^{-k+1}) is the union of b disjoint b-adic s-dimensional elementary intervals of order k, every (t, m, s)-net in base b with $t \leq m-1$ is also a $(t+1, m, s)$-net in base b.
3. Every point set of b^m points in $[0, 1)^s$ is an (m, m, s)-net in base b. The condition then is that the interval $J = [0, 1)^s$ contains b^m points of the set, which is trivially satisfied.
4. It does not make sense to define the notion of (t, m, s)-nets in base b for negative t, since a point set of b^m points can never be fair with respect to an interval of volume less than b^{-m}.
5. We call t the *quality parameter* of the (t, m, s)-net.

4.2.1 First examples

We provide two examples for (t, m, s)-nets.

Example 4.10 As a first non-trivial example, let us consider a (centred) regular lattice $\mathcal{P} = \{\boldsymbol{x}_0, \ldots, \boldsymbol{x}_{N-1}\}$ of $N = b^{sL}$ points in $[0, 1)^s$. Letting $m = sL$, the point set is in any case an (m, m, s)-net in base b. But, by Lemma 4.6, we have that $\mathcal{P}$ is fair with respect to every b-adic s-dimensional elementary interval of order L, and this order L is optimal. Consequently, we get the following corollary from Lemma 4.6.

Corollary 4.11 *The (centred) regular lattice of b^m points, with $m = sL$, in $[0, 1)^s$ is a strict $(m(1 - \frac{1}{s}), m, s)$-net in base b.*

Remark 4.12 Intuitively, the strict quality parameter $t = m(1 - 1/s)$ in the scale between 0 and m is rather large for dimension $s \geq 3$. This fits with the bad order of magnitude of the (star) discrepancy of the regular lattice in dimensions larger than or equal to three. For $s = 1$ we obtain an equidistant point set in $[0, 1)$ of optimal star discrepancy $1/(2N)$, which fits with the optimal quality parameter $t = 0$. For $s = 2$, the regular lattice has a discrepancy of order $1/\sqrt{N}$, an order which essentially coincides with the average order of the discrepancy of N-element point sets in $[0, 1)^2$. This again fits with the median value $m/2$ for the quality parameter t. (We remark that these results also hold for the 'non-centred' regular lattice.)

As a second example, let us consider a two-dimensional Hammersley point set in base b; see Definition 3.44.

Lemma 4.13 *For a given base b and a given positive integer m, the two-dimensional Hammersley point set $\mathcal{P} = \{\boldsymbol{x}_0, \ldots, \boldsymbol{x}_{N-1}\}$ with $N = b^m$ and $\boldsymbol{x}_k = (k/N, \varphi_b(k))$ for $0 \le k \le N-1$ is a $(0, m, 2)$-net in base b.*

Proof First recall the definition of the b-adic radical inverse function φ_b. For a non-negative integer k with b-adic expansion $k = \kappa_{r-1} b^{r-1} + \kappa_{r-2} b^{r-2} + \cdots + \kappa_1 b + \kappa_0$ we define

$$\varphi_b(k) := \frac{\kappa_0}{b} + \frac{\kappa_1}{b^2} + \cdots + \frac{\kappa_{r-1}}{b^r} \in [0, 1).$$

For a b-adic elementary two-dimensional interval J of order m, i.e.

$$J = \left[\frac{A_1}{b^d}, \frac{A_1 + 1}{b^d}\right) \times \left[\frac{A_2}{b^{m-d}}, \frac{A_2 + 1}{b^{m-d}}\right)$$

with $0 \le A_1 < b^d$ and $0 \le A_2 < b^{m-d}$, we have to determine the number of $\boldsymbol{x}_k$ contained in J. Recall that this number should be one.

Note that for k with $0 \le k < b^m$ and b-adic representation $k = \kappa_{m-1} b^{m-1} + \cdots + \kappa_0$, the point $\boldsymbol{x}_k$ belongs to J if and only if

$$\frac{k}{b^m} \in \left[\frac{A_1}{b^d}, \frac{A_1 + 1}{b^d}\right) \quad \text{and} \quad \varphi_b(k) \in \left[\frac{A_2}{b^{m-d}}, \frac{A_2 + 1}{b^{m-d}}\right).$$

This is the case if and only if

$$A_1 b^{m-d} \le \kappa_{m-1} b^{m-1} + \cdots + \kappa_0 < A_1 b^{m-d} + b^{m-d}$$

and

$$A_2 b^d \le \kappa_0 b^{m-1} + \cdots + \kappa_{m-1} < A_2 b^d + b^d.$$

By the first condition the digits $\kappa_{m-d}, \ldots, \kappa_{m-1}$ are uniquely determined (whereas the digits $\kappa_{m-d-1}, \ldots, \kappa_0$ can be chosen arbitrarily). By the second condition the digits $\kappa_0, \ldots, \kappa_{m-d-1}$ are uniquely determined (whereas the digits $\kappa_{m-d}, \ldots, \kappa_{m-1}$ can be chosen arbitrarily). Hence, there is a uniquely determined k such that $\boldsymbol{x}_k \in J$. □

A $(0, m, s)$-net in base b does not exist for all parameters m, s and b. For instance, in Example 4.4 it was shown that there does not exist a $(0, 2, 4)$-net in base 2. Consequently, we show below that there does not exist a $(0, m, s)$-net in base 2 for any $m \ge 2$ and $s \ge 4$. Before we do so, we convince ourselves of several, so-called *propagation rules* for (t, m, s)-nets. Here, a propagation rule is a method of constructing new (t, m, s)-nets from other, given (t, m, s)-nets.

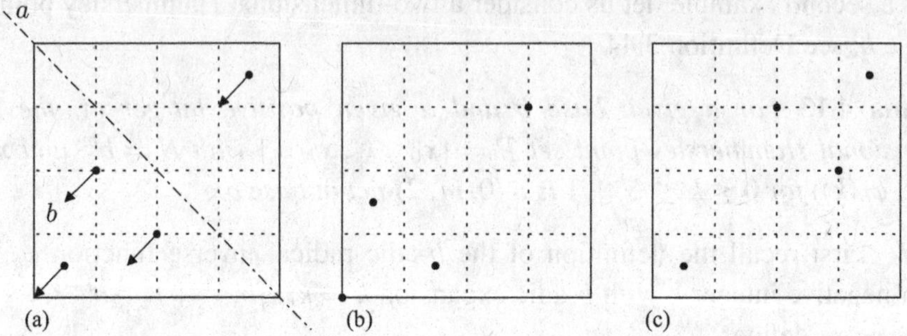

Figure 4.11 (0, 2, 2)-net in base 2 with elementary movements.

4.2.2 Propagation rules for nets

Note that a (t, m, s)-net in base b easily loses its quality by elementary movements. It does not lose its net property entirely, since any point set of b^m points in $[0, 1)^s$ is a (m, m, s)-net in base b. However, its quality parameter t has no stability with respect to even simple movements. For instance, consider the (0, 2, 2)-net in base 2 from Figure 4.11(a) and apply a translation along b or a reflection on a, considered modulo one in each coordinate. Then, both new point sets are now strict (2, 2, 2)-nets in base 2. As we see below, more stability can be found for so-called digital nets (see Lemma 4.63 in Section 4.4).

We may ask what happens with the net structure if we merge (t, m, s)-nets in base b to one point set. Assume that we have r point sets $\mathcal{P}_1, \ldots, \mathcal{P}_r$, where $\mathcal{P}_i$ is a (t_i, m_i, s)-net in base b. Assume, further, that $b^{m_1} + \cdots + b^{m_r} = b^m$ for some integer m. Then the multiset union $\mathcal{P} := \mathcal{P}_1 \cup \ldots \cup \mathcal{P}_r$ is of course a (t, m, s)-net in base b, at least for $t = m$. But we can say even more.

Lemma 4.14 *For $1 \leq j \leq r$ let $\mathcal{P}_j$ be (t_j, m_j, s)-nets in base b, with $m_1, \ldots, m_r$ such that $b^{m_1} + \cdots + b^{m_r} = b^m$ for some integer m. Then the multiset union $\mathcal{P} := \mathcal{P}_1 \cup \ldots \cup \mathcal{P}_r$ is a (t, m, s)-net in base b with*

$$t = m - \min_{1 \leq j \leq r} (m_j - t_j).$$

Proof Let J be an elementary interval in base b of order $w := \min_{1 \leq j \leq r}(m_j - t_j)$. For every $1 \leq j \leq r$, J contains exactly $b^{m_j - w}$ of the elements of $\mathcal{P}_j$. Note that any interval of order less than or equal to $m_j - t_j$ is fair with respect to $\mathcal{P}_j$ and that $w \leq m_j - t_j$. Hence, J contains exactly $\sum_{j=1}^{r} b^{m_j - w} = b^{m-w}$ elements of $\mathcal{P}$ and is therefore fair with respect to $\mathcal{P}$. Consequently, the strict quality parameter t of $\mathcal{P}$ is at most $m - w$ and the result follows. □

Remark 4.15 For example, the superposition of b^r copies of a (t, m, s)-net in base b yields a $(t + r, m + r, s)$-net in base b. This is [192, Lemma 10].

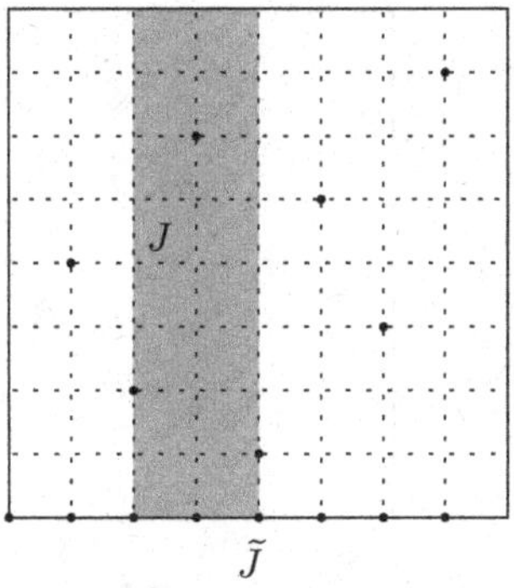

Figure 4.12 Projection of a (0, 3, 2)-net in base 2 to the first components.

Let $\mathcal{P} = \{\boldsymbol{x}_0, \ldots, \boldsymbol{x}_{b^m-1}\}$ be a (t, m, s)-net in base b and let $1 \le n \le s$. Now fix any n of the s dimensions, without restriction of generality, say, the first n dimensions. For every $\boldsymbol{x}_k$, we now consider only the first n coordinates. We obtain an n-dimensional point set, say, $\widetilde{\mathcal{P}} = \{\boldsymbol{y}_0, \ldots, \boldsymbol{y}_{b^m-1}\}$. We then have the following lemma.

Lemma 4.16 *Let $\mathcal{P}$ be a (t, m, s)-net in base b and let $\widetilde{\mathcal{P}}$ be defined as above. Then the point set $\widetilde{\mathcal{P}}$ is a (t, m, n)-net in base b.*

Proof Let $\widetilde{J}$ be a b-adic n-dimensional elementary interval of order $m - t$, then $J := \widetilde{J} \times [0, 1)^{s-n}$ is a b-adic s-dimensional elementary interval of order $m - t$ and hence, J contains exactly b^t of the $\boldsymbol{x}_h$, $0 \le h < b^m$. Since J puts no conditions on the last $s - n$ coordinates, this means that $\widetilde{J}$ contains exactly b^t points of the point set $\widetilde{\mathcal{P}}$ (see Figure 4.12 for an example). □

The above result cannot be improved in the following sense. If $\mathcal{P}$ is a strict (t, m, s)-net in base b, then we cannot conclude that $\widetilde{\mathcal{P}}$ is also a strict (t, m, n)-net in base b. An extreme example is the following.

Let $\mathcal{P} = \{\boldsymbol{x}_0, \ldots, \boldsymbol{x}_{b^m-1}\}$ be defined by $\boldsymbol{x}_k = (0, \frac{k}{b^m})$ for $0 \le k < b^m$. Then $\mathcal{P}$ is a strict $(m, m, 2)$-net in base b. Its first projection is a strict $(m, m, 1)$-net in base b and its second projection is a $(0, m, 1)$-net in base b (see Figure 4.13).

We now have propagation rules concerning t and s (see also the collection of the propagation rules in Chapter 9). In the following we provide a propagation rule concerning m.

In general, the first b^r points $\{\boldsymbol{x}_0, \ldots, \boldsymbol{x}_{b^r-1}\}$ of a (t, m, s)-net $\mathcal{P} = \{\boldsymbol{x}_0, \ldots, \boldsymbol{x}_{b^m-1}\}$ may not be a (t, r, s)-net for $t < r < m$. (Note that the case $r \le t$ is trivial, since every point set of b^r points is a (r, r, s)-net in base b.)

The question now arises as to how to propagate in this case. We use the following approach (for an illustration, see Figure 4.14):

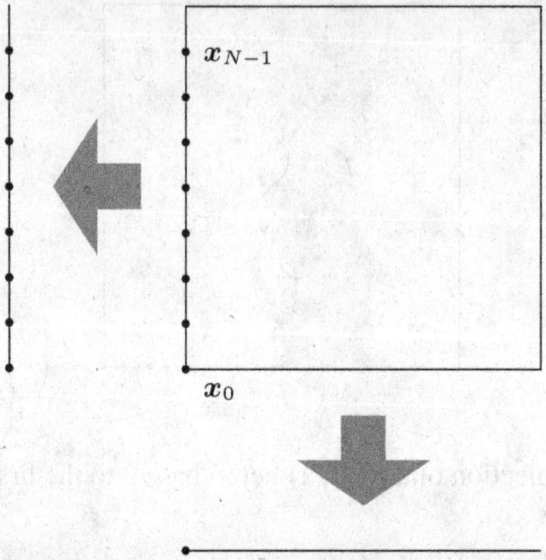

Figure 4.13 Projection of a $(m, m, 2)$-net to the first and second components.

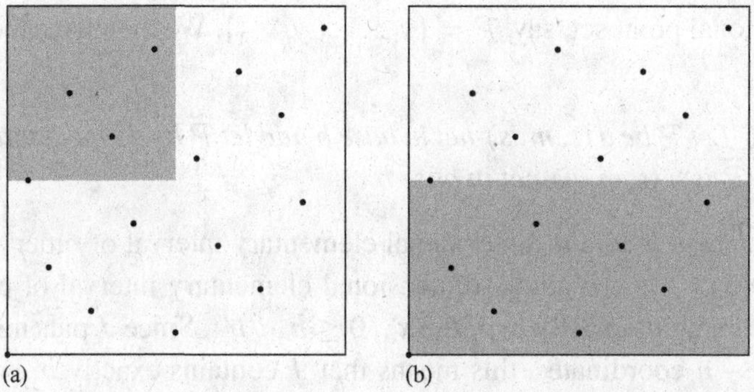

(a) (b)

Figure 4.14 A $(0, 4, 2)$-net in base 2. The points in the elementary interval yield (a) a $(0, 2, 2)$-net in base 2 after doubling both coordinates; (b) a $(0, 3, 2)$-net in base 2 after doubling the second coordinate.

1. Let $\mathcal{P} = \{\boldsymbol{x}_0, \ldots, \boldsymbol{x}_{b^m-1}\}$ be a (t, m, s)-net in base b and let $t < r < m$.
2. Take any elementary interval $J = \prod_{i=1}^{s} [\frac{A_i}{b^{d_i}}, \frac{A_i+1}{b^{d_i}})$ of order $m - r$, i.e. with $d_1 + \cdots + d_s = m - r$. Since $m - r < m - t$, this interval contains exactly b^r elements of the net $\mathcal{P}$.
3. We now translate the point $(\frac{A_1}{b^{d_1}}, \ldots, \frac{A_s}{b^{d_s}})$ of J to the origin and blow up the translated J and the translated net-points in J to the unit-cube; that is, we apply the affine transformation $T : \mathbb{R}^s \to \mathbb{R}^s$,
$$\boldsymbol{x} := (x_1, \ldots, x_s) \mapsto \left(b^{d_1} \left(x_1 - \frac{A_1}{b^{d_1}} \right), \ldots, b^{d_s} \left(x_s - \frac{A_s}{b^{d_s}} \right) \right)$$
to J and to the net points in J.
4. The point set obtained in this way, consisting of b^r points, is denoted by $\widetilde{\mathcal{P}} = \{\boldsymbol{y}_0, \ldots, \boldsymbol{y}_{b^r-1}\}$.

We claim that $\widetilde{\mathcal{P}}$ forms a (t, r, s)-net in base b (see also [177, Lemma 4.4]).

Lemma 4.17 *Let $\mathcal{P}$ be a (t, m, s)-net in base b, let $t < r < m$ and let J be an elementary interval of order $m - r$. Let T be an affine transformation of J onto $[0, 1)^s$. Then, the points of $\mathcal{P}$ that belong to J are transformed by T into a (t, r, s)-net $\widetilde{\mathcal{P}}$ in base b.*

Proof Let J' be a b-adic s-dimensional elementary interval of order $r - t$. The number of points $\boldsymbol{y}_k$ from $\widetilde{\mathcal{P}}$ contained in J' equals the number of points $\boldsymbol{x}_k$ from $\mathcal{P}$ contained in the b-adic s-dimensional elementary interval $T^{-1}(M')$ of order $(r - t) + (m - r) = m - t$. This number is exactly b^t, since $\mathcal{P}$ is a (t, m, s)-net in base b. □

4.2.3 Existence of $(0, m, s)$-nets in base b

As a corollary from Lemma 4.16 and Lemma 4.17, we obtain the following corollary.

Corollary 4.18 *A $(0, m, s)$-net in base 2 cannot exist if $m \geq 2$ and $s \geq 4$.*

Proof If a $(0, m, s)$-net in base 2 with $m \geq 2$ and $s \geq 4$ exists, then, by the above propagation rules (Lemmas 4.16 and 4.17) on m and s, a $(0, 2, 4)$-net in base 2 would exist, which is a contradiction in view of Example 4.4. □

Obviously, the point set $\{\boldsymbol{x}_0 = (0, \ldots, 0), \boldsymbol{x}_1 = (\frac{1}{2}, \ldots, \frac{1}{2})\}$ forms a $(0, 1, s)$-net in base 2 for all s. For $s = 2$, the two-dimensional Hammersley point set with 2^m points gives, for any integer $m \geq 1$, a $(0, m, 2)$-net in base 2 by Lemma 4.13. Hence, concerning the existence of $(0, m, s)$-nets in base 2, the only question remaining is whether there exist $(0, m, 3)$-nets in base 2 for all $m \geq 2$. This question was answered in the affirmative by Sobol′ [253]. Concrete examples of $(0, m, 3)$-nets in base 2 for any $m \geq 2$ are given in Section 4.4. (The examples given there are also special cases of nets obtained from Sobol′-, Faure- and Niederreiter sequences; see Chapter 8).

In arbitrary base $b \geq 2$ we have the following result, which for the first time in this form was shown by Niederreiter [177, Corollary 4.21].

Corollary 4.19 *A $(0, m, s)$-net in base b cannot exist if $m \geq 2$ and $s \geq b + 2$.*

This corollary is a consequence of the following lemma:

Lemma 4.20 *A $(0, 2, b + 2)$-net in base $b \geq 2$ cannot exist.*

Proof Assume to the contrary that a $(0, 2, b+2)$-net $\mathcal{P} = \{\boldsymbol{x}_0, \ldots, \boldsymbol{x}_{b^2-1}\}$ in base b exists. Then any elementary interval of the form

$$[0,1)^i \times \left[\frac{A}{b}, \frac{A+1}{b}\right) \times [0,1)^j \times \left[\frac{B}{b}, \frac{B+1}{b}\right) \times [0,1)^{b-i-j}$$

of volume b^{-2} contains, by the net property, exactly one point of $\mathcal{P}$. We call this the 'orthogonality property' of this net.

Let us check in which interval of the form $[A/b, (A+1)/b)$ of length b^{-1}, where $A \in \{0, \ldots, b-1\}$, each coordinate of each net point $\boldsymbol{x}_n$ is contained; that is, we describe any $\boldsymbol{x}_n$ by a vector

$$\boldsymbol{x}_n \leftrightarrow \begin{pmatrix} a_n^{(1)} \\ \vdots \\ a_n^{(b+2)} \end{pmatrix},$$

where $a_n^{(i)} \in \{0, 1, \ldots, b-1\}$ is chosen such that the ith coordinate $x_{n,i}$ of $\boldsymbol{x}_n$ is contained in the interval $[a_n^{(i)}/b, (a_n^{(i)}+1)/b)$.

Let us set these b^2 column vectors side by side, so we get an array of numbers of the form

$$\begin{array}{cccc} \boldsymbol{x}_0 & \boldsymbol{x}_1 & \ldots & \boldsymbol{x}_{b^2-1} \\ \updownarrow & \updownarrow & & \updownarrow \\ a_0^{(1)} & a_1^{(1)} & \ldots & a_{b^2-1}^{(1)} \\ \vdots & \vdots & & \vdots \\ a_0^{(b+2)} & a_1^{(b+2)} & \ldots & a_{b^2-1}^{(b+2)} \end{array} \tag{4.1}$$

Let us now take any two of the rows of the above array, say

$$\begin{array}{cccc} a_0^{(i)} & a_1^{(i)} & \ldots & a_{b^2-1}^{(i)}, \\ a_0^{(j)} & a_1^{(j)} & \ldots & a_{b^2-1}^{(j)}, \end{array}$$

then the 'orthogonality property' of the net is equivalent to the fact that the above b^2 two-dimensional columns

$$\begin{pmatrix} a_k^{(i)} \\ a_k^{(j)} \end{pmatrix}_{k=0,\ldots,b^2-1}$$

attain any possible value $\begin{pmatrix} n \\ r \end{pmatrix}$, with $n, r \in \{0, \ldots, b-1\}$, exactly once. Therefore, in particular, any possible value $n \in \{0, \ldots, b-1\}$ must occur in any row exactly b-times.

However, we show that this property cannot be satisfied for all possible pairs of rows.

Assume to the contrary that any two of the $b+2$-rows satisfy the orthogonality property. Without restriction of generality, we can assume that in array (4.1) the values of the first column all equal 1 (a permutation of the values $r \in \{0, \ldots, b-1\}$ in a single row of the array does not affect the 'orthogonal property').

Then, in any of the remaining $b^2 - 1$ columns, 1 can occur at most, once. However, since in each row, 1 must occur b-times, we would need a place for the $(b-1)(b+2)$ remaining 1's in these $b^2 - 1$ columns. Since $(b-1)(b+2) = b^2 + b - 2 > b^2 - 1$, we have a contradiction. □

Again, it is easy to provide a $(0, 1, s)$-net in base b for any dimension s. Faure- and Niederreiter sequences (see Chapter 8) provide, for any prime-power base b, any $m \geq 2$ and any $s \leq b+1$, examples of $(0, m, s)$-nets in base b. Hence, the question concerning the existence of $(0, m, s)$-nets in base b is solved for all prime-power bases b. In general, it is not solved for composite bases b. It is known that the maximal dimension s for which there exists a $(0, m, s)$-net in base b with $m \geq 2$, for composite b, is much smaller than $b+1$. For more information, see [141, Section 3] and the MinT database to be found at

http://mint.sbg.ac.at/

We note the following singular result.

Lemma 4.21 *There does not exist a* $(0, 2, 4)$*-net in base* 6.

The above considerations can be formulated and proved more elegantly in terms of combinatorial objects such as orthogonal Latin squares or ordered orthogonal arrays. This is done in Chapter 6.

4.2.4 Further propagation rules for nets

We have already shown propagation rules for the parameters t, m and s of a (t, m, s)-net in base b. In the following, we consider possible propagation rules for the parameter b, the base of the net.

Such propagation rules principally should be of the following form.

1. Any (t, m, s)-net in base b is a (t', m', s')-net in base b', or
2. if there exist (t_j, m_j, s_j)-nets in bases b_j for $1 \leq j \leq l$, then there exists a (t', m', s')-net in base b'.

Note that for results of the first form, there must be a principal connection between the compared bases b and b', since the number of points b^m, respectively $b'^{m'}$ remains unchanged; that is, $b^m = b'^{m'}$. Therefore, b and b' must have the same prime divisors, say $b = p_1^{\alpha_1} \cdots p_r^{\alpha_r}$ and $b' = p_1^{\beta_1} \cdots p_r^{\beta_r}$ with $\alpha_i, \beta_i \geq 1$ for

$1 \leq i \leq r$. Since $b^m = b'^{m'}$, we get $m\alpha_i = m'\beta_i$ for $1 \leq i \leq r$. Let d denote the greatest common divisor of m and m'. Then the integer $\widetilde{m} := m/d$ divides β_i, the integer $\widetilde{m}' := m'/d$ divides α_i and $\gamma_i := \alpha_i/\widetilde{m}' = \beta_i/\widetilde{m}$ is a positive integer. Let $c = p_1^{\gamma_1} \cdots p_r^{\gamma_r}$, then $b = c^{\widetilde{m}'}$ and $b' = c^{\widetilde{m}}$. Therefore, a simple propagation rule of the first kind can only exist if b and b' are powers of a common 'base' c, say $b = c^L$ and $b' = c^{L'}$ with L and L' relatively prime. Further, since then $c^{Lm} = b^m = b'^{m'} = c^{L'm'}$, that is, $Lm = L'm'$, with $\gcd(L, L') = 1$ we must have $m = \mu L'$ and $m' = \mu L$ for some positive integer μ.

Consequently, propagation rules of the first kind have to be of the following principal form. Any $(t, \mu L', s)$-net in base c^L is a $(t', \mu L, s)$-net in base $c^{L'}$.

We do not give base-propagation rules of the second type here. But also, the base-propagation rules of the first kind are of a more complex nature than the propagation rules on m, s and t.

The simplest base propagation rule is based on the following fact concerning elementary intervals.

Lemma 4.22 *Let the integers $b, k \geq 2$ be given. Any b^k-adic s-dimensional elementary interval of order n is a b-adic s-dimensional elementary interval of order nk.*

Proof Let $J = \prod_{i=1}^{s} [\frac{A_i}{(b^k)^{d_i}}, \frac{A_i+1}{(b^k)^{d_i}})$ with $d_i \geq 0$ and $0 \leq A_i < (b^k)^{d_i}$ for $1 \leq i \leq s$ and $d_1 + \cdots + d_s = n$ be an arbitrary b^k-adic s-dimensional elementary interval of order n. Define $d_i' := kd_i$, then $J = \prod_{i=1}^{s} [A_i/b^{d_i'}, (A_i + 1)/b^{d_i'})$ with $d_i' \geq 0$, $0 \leq A_i < b^{d_i'}$ for $1 \leq i \leq s$ and $d_1' + \cdots + d_s' = nk$ is a b-adic s-dimensional elementary interval of order nk. $\square$

The converse, in general, does not hold. For instance the 2-adic two-dimensional elementary intervals of order 2 are the intervals

$$\begin{array}{llll} [0,1) \times [0, \frac{1}{4}), & [0,1) \times [\frac{1}{4}, \frac{1}{2}), & [0,1) \times [\frac{1}{2}, \frac{3}{4}), & [0,1) \times [\frac{3}{4}, 1), \\ [0, \frac{1}{2}) \times [0, \frac{1}{2}), & [0, \frac{1}{2}) \times [\frac{1}{2}, 1), & [\frac{1}{2}, 1) \times [0, \frac{1}{2}), & [\frac{1}{2}, 1) \times [\frac{1}{2}, 1), \\ [0, \frac{1}{4}) \times [0, 1), & [\frac{1}{4}, \frac{1}{2}) \times [0, 1), & [\frac{1}{2}, \frac{3}{4}) \times [0, 1), & [\frac{3}{4}, 1) \times [0, 1), \end{array}$$

whereas the 4-adic two-dimensional elementary intervals of order 1 are just the intervals in the first and third lines above.

Consequently we immediately obtain the following result.

Corollary 4.23 *Any $(t, \mu k, s)$-net in base b is a $(\lceil t/k \rceil, \mu, s)$-net in base b^k. The converse, in general, is not true.*

Proof Any b^k-adic s-dimensional elementary interval of order $\mu - \lceil t/k \rceil$ is a b-adic s-dimensional elementary interval of order $k(\mu - \lceil t/k \rceil) \leq k\mu - t$. Hence, it is fair with respect to the $(t, \mu k, s)$-net in base b.

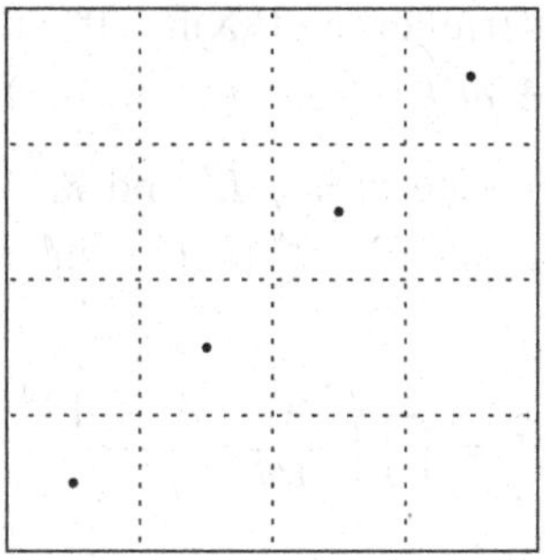

Figure 4.15 A (0, 1, 2)-net in base 4 which is not a (0, 2, 2)-net in base 2.

To provide a counterexample for the converse assertion, consider the (0, 1, 2)-net in base 4 given in Figure 4.15, which is not a (0, 2, 2)-net in base 2 (consider the corresponding elementary 2-adic and 4-adic intervals listed above), and hence the result follows . □

However, it is obvious that some relation must also hold in the converse direction and therefore, in general, between the quality parameters of a $(t, \mu L', s)$-net in base c^L and a $(t', \mu L, s)$-net in base $c^{L'}$.

The following base propagation rule was first given in [217]; see also [218].

Theorem 4.24 *For given integers $c \geq 2$, L and $L' \geq 1$ with $\gcd(L, L') = 1$, for every dimension s, and all positive integers μ we have that every $(t, \mu L', s)$-net in base c^L is a $(t', \mu L, s)$-net in base $c^{L'}$, where*

$$t' = \min\left(\left\lceil \frac{Lt + \mu L(-L' \pmod{L})}{L' + (-L' \pmod{L})} \right\rceil, \left\lceil \frac{Lt + (s-1)(L-1)}{L'} \right\rceil\right).$$

Remark 4.25 Before we prove the theorem, let us consider some special cases. For the trivial case of equal bases, i.e. for $L = L' = 1$, by the above estimate for t', we achieve the best possible result $t = t'$. For the case considered in Corollary 4.23, i.e. $L = 1$, by the above estimate for t', we get the best possible result $t' = \lceil t/L' \rceil$. For $L' = 1$, we rewrite the above result and state it as a corollary on its own.

Corollary 4.26 *For a given base $b \geq 2$ and any integer $k \geq 1$, every (t, m, s)-net in base b^k is a (t', mk, s)-net in base b with*

$$t' = \min(t + m(k-1), kt + (s-1)(k-1)).$$

This result, for some cases, improves the corresponding result given by Niederreiter and Xing [192, Lemma 9], verifying a quality parameter $t' = \min(km, kt + (s-1)(k-1))$. Of course, $t + m(k-1) \leq km$ always. The result of the corollary is better than that of Niederreiter and Xing if and only if $t + m(k-1) < kt + (s-1)(k-1)$ and if $t + m(k-1) < km$, i.e. if $m < s - 1 + t$ and if $t < m$.

Proof of Theorem 4.24 We write $m = \mu L'$ and $m' = \mu L$. Take an elementary interval $\widetilde{J}$ in base $c^{L'}$ of order, say $m' - t''$ (with some non-negative integer t''), i.e. of volume $c^{-L'(m'-t'')}$, say

$$\widetilde{J} = \prod_{i=1}^{s} \left[\frac{A_i}{c^{L'd_i'}}, \frac{A_i + 1}{c^{L'd_i'}} \right)$$

with $d_1' + \cdots + d_s' = m' - t''$. For every $1 \le i \le s$, we set $L'd_i' = Ld_i - r_i$ with $0 \le r_i < L$, then

$$\begin{aligned} \widetilde{J} &= \prod_{i=1}^{s} \left[\frac{A_i c^{r_i}}{c^{Ld_i}}, \frac{A_i c^{r_i} + c^{r_i}}{c^{Ld_i}} \right) \\ &= \prod_{i=1}^{s} \bigcup_{k_i=0}^{c^{r_i}-1} \left[\frac{A_i c^{r_i} + k_i}{c^{Ld_i}}, \frac{A_i c^{r_i} + k_i + 1}{c^{Ld_i}} \right) \\ &= \bigcup_{k_1=0}^{c^{r_1}-1} \cdots \bigcup_{k_s=0}^{c^{r_s}-1} \prod_{i=1}^{s} \left[\frac{A_i c^{r_i} + k_i}{(c^L)^{d_i}}, \frac{A_i c^{r_i} + k_i + 1}{(c^L)^{d_i}} \right). \end{aligned}$$

Therefore, $\widetilde{J}$ is the union of elementary intervals in base c^L of order $d_1 + \cdots + d_s$ each. Therefore, $\widetilde{J}$ is fair with respect to a (t, m, s)-net $\mathcal{P}$ in base c^L if

$$d_1 + \cdots + d_s \le m - t.$$

Substituting $L^{-1}(L'd_i' - r_i)$ for d_i, this is equivalent to

$$L' \sum_{i=1}^{s} d_i' + \sum_{i=1}^{s} r_i \le L(m - t)$$

and therefore to

$$L'm' - L't'' + \sum_{i=1}^{s} r_i \le Lm - Lt.$$

But, since $L'm' = L'L\mu = Lm$, the last inequality is equivalent to

$$L't'' - \sum_{i=1}^{s} r_i \ge Lt.$$

Hence, if t'' is such that for all $d_1', \ldots, d_s' \in \mathbb{N}_0$ with $d_1' + \cdots + d_s' = m' - t''$, we have

$$L't'' - \sum_{i=1}^{s} r_i \ge Lt,$$

then $\mathcal{P}$ is a (t'', m', s)-net in base $c^{L'}$; that is, we can set

$$t' = \min\{t'' : L't'' - M(t'') \geq Lt\}, \tag{4.2}$$

where

$$M(t'') = \max\left\{\sum_{i=1}^{s}(-L'd_i' \pmod L) : d_1', \ldots, d_s' \in \mathbb{N}_0 \text{ and } \sum_{i=1}^{s} d_i' = m' - t''\right\}.$$

In the following, in order to obtain the desired estimate for t', we estimate $M(t'')$ in two different ways.

1. First, we have

$$\begin{aligned} M(t'') &= \max\left\{\sum_{i=1}^{s}(-L'd_i' \pmod L) : d_1', \ldots, d_s' \in \mathbb{N}_0 \right. \\ &\qquad\qquad \left. \text{and } \sum_{i=1}^{s} d_i' = m' - t''\right\} \\ &\leq \max\left\{\sum_{i=1}^{s}(-L' \pmod L)d_i' : d_1', \ldots, d_s' \in \mathbb{N}_0 \right. \\ &\qquad\qquad \left. \text{and } \sum_{i=1}^{s} d_i' = m' - t''\right\} \\ &= (-L' \pmod L)(m' - t''). \end{aligned} \tag{4.3}$$

Now, from (4.2), it follows that

$$t' \leq \min\{t'' : L't'' - (-L' \pmod L)(m' - t'') \geq Lt\},$$

which is satisfied for all t'' with

$$t'' \geq \left\lceil \frac{Lt + \mu L(-L' \pmod L)}{L' + (-L' \pmod L)} \right\rceil.$$

2. Further, if we define

$$\begin{aligned} N(t'') := \max\Bigg\{ &\sum_{i=1}^{s}(L'k_i \pmod L) : \\ &k_i \in \{0, \ldots, L-1\} \text{ and } \sum_{i=1}^{s} k_i \equiv t'' \pmod L\Bigg\}, \end{aligned}$$

then $M(t'') \leq N(t'')$ always.

For $N(t'')$, by its definition, we conclude the properties

$$N(t'') \leq \sum_{i=1}^{s}(L-1) = s(L-1) \tag{4.4}$$

and

$$N(t'') = L't'' + kL \tag{4.5}$$

for some integer k.

Now take $k_1, \ldots, k_{s-1}$ such that $L'k_i \equiv L-1 \pmod{L}$ for $1 \leq i < s$ and k_s such that $\sum_{i=1}^{s} k_i \equiv t'' \pmod{L}$; that is, $L'k_s \equiv L't'' + s - 1 \pmod{L}$. Then

$$\sum_{i=1}^{s}(L'k_i \pmod{L}) = (s-1)(L-1) + (L't'' + s - 1 \pmod{L}).$$

If $N(t'')$ were larger than the right-hand side of the above equation, then, by (4.5), we have

$$N(t'') \geq (s-1)(L-1) + L > s(L-1),$$

which contradicts (4.4). Therefore, we get as a second estimate for $M(t'')$ that

$$M(t'') \leq (s-1)(L-1) + (L't'' + s - 1 \pmod{L}).$$

Again, from (4.2), it follows that

$$t' \leq \min\{t'' : L't'' - (s-1)(L-1) - (L't'' + s - 1 \pmod{L}) \geq Lt\}.$$

We show now that the smallest t'' satisfying the second condition is

$$t'' = \left\lceil \frac{Lt + (s-1)(L-1)}{L'} \right\rceil,$$

which implies the statement of the theorem.

Let $L't'' = Lt + (s-1)(L-1) + F$ for some integer F. Then

$$L't'' - (s-1)(L-1) - (L't'' + s - 1 \pmod{L}) = Lt + F - (F \pmod{L})$$

and this is $\geq Lt$ if and only if $F \geq 0$. Hence, the minimal t'' is given by

$$\left\lceil \frac{Lt + (s-1)(L-1)}{L'} \right\rceil,$$

and the result follows. □

4.3 (T, s)- and (t, s)-sequences and their basic properties

A disadvantage of nets in base b is that the number of points is restricted to a power of b. At first glance, one could argue that we can always choose b arbitrarily large and $m = 1$, which would mean that there is no restriction at all. However, it is intuitively obvious (and is supported by the discrepancy estimates in Chapter 5) that the structure of a (t, m, s)-net in base b becomes strong only if m is large compared with b. Hence, for a given number N of points, it is sometimes better to realize the point set with a small base b, i.e. a larger value for m, and with a sub-optimal quality parameter t, than to choose a large base b (e.g. $b = N$) (and therefore a small m, for instance $m = 1$), in order to obtain an optimal quality parameter t (e.g. $t = 0$). (As we have already seen in Section 4.2, the $(0, 1, s)$-net in base b given by the points $\boldsymbol{x}_n = (n/b, \ldots, n/b)$ with $n = 0, \ldots, b-1$ has no favourable distribution property at all.)

To overcome this problem, i.e. in order to obtain net-like point sets of high distribution quality for any given number N of points, the following principal idea was born.

Try to patch up a whole infinite sequence $(\boldsymbol{x}_n)_{n\geq 0}$ in $[0, 1)^s$ from $(0, m, s)$-nets in a given base b, in the sense that for any $m \geq 1$, any subsequence of the form $\boldsymbol{x}_n, \ldots, \boldsymbol{x}_{n+b^m-1}$ of length b^m is a $(0, m, s)$-net in base b.

Such a sequence intuitively would show outstanding distribution properties. However, this demand certainly cannot be satisfied in general, for two reasons. The first reason is obvious: $(0, m, s)$-nets in a base b do not exist for all s and m. We may, however, replace in the property above '$(0, m, s)$-net' by '(t, m, s)-net with t as small as possible'. The second reason is that, in general, it is not possible to obtain the (non-trivial) net property for all blocks of length b^m, because there is too much interference between overlapping blocks. This can be illustrated by the following example.

Example 4.27 Try to construct four points $\boldsymbol{x}_0, \boldsymbol{x}_1, \boldsymbol{x}_2, \boldsymbol{x}_3$ in $[0, 1)^2$ such that they form a $(0, 2, 2)$-net in base 2 and such that every subset of the form $\{\boldsymbol{x}_i, \boldsymbol{x}_{i+1}\}$; $i \in \{0, 1, 2\}$ is a $(0, 1, 2)$-net in base 2. For our purpose it suffices to place the $\boldsymbol{x}_i$ anywhere in the subcubes of the form $[A/4, (A+1)/4) \times [B/4, (B+1)/4)$, the exact place in the subcube is irrelevant. Without loss of generality let us start with $\boldsymbol{x}_0$ in $[0, 1/4) \times [0, 1/4)$, and note that the four points $\boldsymbol{x}_0, \boldsymbol{x}_1, \boldsymbol{x}_2, \boldsymbol{x}_3$ then finally must show one of the patterns shown in Figure 4.16.

Two successive points must always show one of the patterns shown in Figure 4.17. Hence, in the patterns of Figure 4.16 the point $\boldsymbol{x}_1$ is also prescribed. However, then there is no possible choice for $\boldsymbol{x}_2$ to satisfy one of the patterns in Figure 4.17 with $\boldsymbol{x}_1, \boldsymbol{x}_2$.

Therefore, we have to weaken the condition in this aspect also. We could try this by replacing '... any sub-block of length b^m ...' by '... all successive non-overlapping sub-blocks of length b^m'.

This now leads to the definition of a (t, s)-sequence in base b.

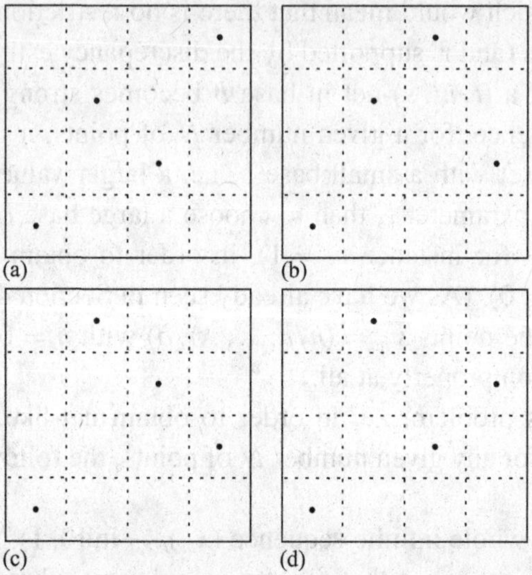

Figure 4.16 Four possible configurations for $\boldsymbol{x}_0, \boldsymbol{x}_1, \boldsymbol{x}_2, \boldsymbol{x}_3$.

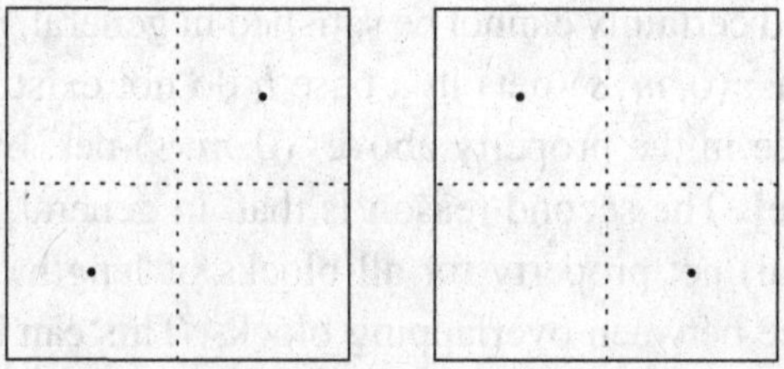

Figure 4.17 Configurations of two successive points.

Definition 4.28 For a given dimension $s \geq 1$, an integer base $b \geq 2$ and a non-negative integer t, a sequence $(\boldsymbol{x}_0, \boldsymbol{x}_1, \ldots)$ of points in $[0, 1)^s$ is called a (t, s)-*sequence in base b* if for all integers $m > t$ and $k \geq 0$, the point set consisting of the points $\boldsymbol{x}_{kb^m}, \ldots, \boldsymbol{x}_{kb^m+b^m-1}$ forms a (t, m, s)-net in base b.

Definition 4.29 A (t, s)-sequence in base b with $t \geq 1$ is called a *strict* (t, s)-*sequence in base b* if it is not a $(t-1, s)$-sequence in base b. Again, we call a $(0, s)$-sequence strict by definition.

Again, we call t the *quality parameter* of the (t, s)-sequence. The notion of a (t, s)-sequence in the above form was introduced by Niederreiter [172] for the first time. Special cases, so-called binary LP_τ-sequences, however, had already been investigated by Sobol′ [253]. Another special case was introduced by Faure [68].

In [140] a generalised concept was introduced by Larcher and Niederreiter, the concept of $(\mathbf{T}, s)$-sequences in a base b.

Definition 4.30 For a given dimension $s \geq 1$, an integer base $b \geq 2$, and a function $\mathbf{T} : \mathbb{N}_0 \to \mathbb{N}_0$ with $\mathbf{T}(m) \leq m$ for all $m \in \mathbb{N}_0$, a sequence $(\boldsymbol{x}_0, \boldsymbol{x}_1, \ldots)$ of points in $[0, 1)^s$ is called a $(\mathbf{T}, s)$-*sequence in base* b if for all integers $m \geq 0$ and $k \geq 0$, the point set consisting of the points $\boldsymbol{x}_{kb^m}, \ldots, \boldsymbol{x}_{kb^m+b^m-1}$ forms a $(\mathbf{T}(m), m, s)$-net in base b.

Definition 4.31 A $(\mathbf{T}, s)$-sequence in base b is called a *strict* $(\mathbf{T}, s)$-*sequence in base* b if for all functions $\mathbf{U} : \mathbb{N}_0 \to \mathbb{N}_0$ with $\mathbf{U}(m) \leq m$ for all $m \in \mathbb{N}_0$ and with $\mathbf{U}(m) < \mathbf{T}(m)$ for at least one $m \in \mathbb{N}_0$, it is not a $(\mathbf{U}, s)$-sequence in base b.

The concept of (t, s)-sequences in base b is contained in the concept of $(\mathbf{T}, s)$-sequences in a base b. We just have to take for $\mathbf{T}$ the constant function $\mathbf{T}(m) = t$ for all m (resp. $\mathbf{T}(m) = m$ for $m \leq t$).

By the condition $\mathbf{T}(m) \leq m$ for all m, we necessarily have $\mathbf{T}(0) = 0$, and therefore, $\mathbf{T}$ is sometimes only defined for $m \geq 1$. A suitable function $\mathbf{T}$ is called a *quality function*.

If $\mathbf{T}$ is the quality function of a strict $(\mathbf{T}, s)$-sequence $(\boldsymbol{x}_0, \boldsymbol{x}_1, \ldots)$ in base b, then for all m we have

$$\mathbf{T}(m+1) \leq \mathbf{T}(m) + 1,$$

hence, the function $S(m) := m - \mathbf{T}(m)$ is non-decreasing. This property follows by considering a sub-block of b^{m+1} successive points of the form $\boldsymbol{x}_{kb^{m+1}}, \ldots, \boldsymbol{x}_{kb^{m+1}+b^{m+1}-1}$, and an elementary interval of order $m - \mathbf{T}(m) = (m + 1) - (\mathbf{T}(m) + 1)$. Since $(\boldsymbol{x}_0, \boldsymbol{x}_1, \ldots)$ is a $(\mathbf{T}, s)$-sequence, the interval contains exactly $b^{\mathbf{T}(m)}$ points of

$$\boldsymbol{x}_{kb^{m+1}+lb^m}, \ldots, \boldsymbol{x}_{kb^{m+1}+lb^m+b^m-1}$$

for all $0 \leq l \leq b - 1$, and so it contains exactly $b^{\mathbf{T}(m)+1}$ of the elements of

$$\boldsymbol{x}_{kb^{m+1}}, \ldots, \boldsymbol{x}_{kb^{m+1}+b^{m+1}-1}.$$

Therefore, any sub-block of length b^{m+1} is fair with respect to intervals of order $(m + 1) - (\mathbf{T}(m) + 1)$ and consequently, $\mathbf{T}(m + 1) \leq \mathbf{T}(m) + 1$.

What does the (t, s)-sequence property in base b mean for the first N elements of a (t, s)-sequence $(\boldsymbol{x}_0, \boldsymbol{x}_1, \ldots)$?

1. Trivially, by definition, if N is a power of b, say $N = b^m$ for some positive integer m, then $\{\boldsymbol{x}_0, \ldots, \boldsymbol{x}_{N-1}\}$ is a (t, m, s)-net in base b; that is, in any elementary b-adic interval of volume $\frac{b^t}{N}$, there are exactly b^t points of the point set.
2. If N is a multiple of a power of b, say $N = kb^m$ for some positive integers $m \geq t$ and k, then $\{\boldsymbol{x}_0, \ldots, \boldsymbol{x}_{N-1}\}$ is a combination of k (t, m, s)-nets in base b; that is, in any elementary b-adic interval of volume $\frac{b^t}{N}$, there are exactly kb^t points of the point set.

3. In general, represent N in base b, say

$$N = a_m b^m + a_{m-1} b^{m-1} + \cdots + a_1 b + a_0$$

with $a_i \in \{0, 1, \ldots, b-1\}$ for $0 \le i \le m$. Then $\{\boldsymbol{x}_0, \ldots, \boldsymbol{x}_{N-1}\}$ is a combination of

$$\begin{array}{ll} a_m & (t, m, s)\text{-nets in base } b, \\ a_{m-1} & (t, m-1, s)\text{-nets in base } b \text{ and} \\ \vdots & \vdots \\ a_{t+1} & (t, t+1, s)\text{-nets in base } b \end{array}$$

and, further, $a_0 + a_1 b + \cdots + a_t b^t$ points without a special prescribed structure; that is, if the quality parameter t is small, then $\{\boldsymbol{x}_0, \ldots, \boldsymbol{x}_{N-1}\}$ is a superposition of large point sets with strong distribution properties, smaller point sets with less restrictive distribution properties and small point sets without any prescribed distribution properties. This framework of (t, s)-sequences is the basis for the derivation of the discrepancy estimates for (t, s)-sequences, which are presented in Chapter 5.

The more general concept of $(\mathbf{T}, s)$-sequences in base b was introduced for two reasons.

1. First, a quality function $\mathbf{T}$ is a more sensitive measure than a quality parameter t. For instance, a (t, s)-sequence in base b may be a strict (t, s)-sequence, (i.e. t cannot be replaced by $t-1$), but if we consider it as a $(\mathbf{T}, s)$-sequence in base b, with $\mathbf{T}(m) = t$ for all $m \ge t$, it does not have to be strict (i.e. $\mathbf{T}(m) = t$ for some $m \ge t$ can be replaced by $\mathbf{T}(m) = t - 1$ and by even smaller values). Indeed, in many concrete examples of (t, s)-sequences, in base b we have a quality parameter t which is obtained by theoretical considerations. If we consider these sequences as $(\mathbf{T}, s)$-sequences, then it turns out that the real (strict) quality function $\mathbf{T}(m)$ for smaller values of m is often essentially smaller than t, and only for large m does $\mathbf{T}(m)$ approach t.

   However, in most cases it is very difficult to obtain good estimates for the strict quality function $\mathbf{T}$ by theoretical means. Therefore, the determination of the strict quality function $\mathbf{T}$ of a $(\mathbf{T}, s)$-sequence relies in most cases on computational work.
2. The second reason for introducing quality functions is of a more theoretical nature. For certain classes of sequences (especially digital sequences, see Chapter 4.4, or Kronecker type sequences, see [135]) it turned out that their average behaviour cannot be described with a constant and therefore a bounded quality parameter t, but it can be described with a quality function $\mathbf{T}$, which may be unbounded. For corresponding results, see Section 4.4.5.

Since any (t, m, s)-net in base b with $t \leq m - 1$ is also a $(t + 1, m, s)$-net in base b, any (t, s)-sequence in base b is also a $(t + 1, s)$-sequence in base b.

Generally, any $(\mathbf{T}, s)$-sequence in base b is also a $(\mathbf{U}, s)$-sequence in base b for all quality functions $\mathbf{U}$ with $\mathbf{U}(m) \geq \mathbf{T}(m)$ for all m.

Every point set of b^m points in $[0, 1)^s$ is a (m, m, s)-net in base b. Hence, with $\mathbf{M}(m) := m$ for all m, every sequence in $[0, 1)^s$ is a $(\mathbf{M}, s)$-sequence in base b.

4.3.1 Distribution properties of $(\mathbf{T}, s)$-sequences

Now consider $(\mathbf{T}, s)$-sequences and (t, s)-sequences. We may ask under which conditions they are uniformly distributed modulo one (see Definition 3.1). The answer is given in the following theorem.

Theorem 4.32 *A strict $(\mathbf{T}, s)$-sequence in any base b is uniformly distributed modulo one if*

$$\lim_{m \to \infty} m - \mathbf{T}(m) = \infty.$$

In particular, every (t, s)-sequence is uniformly distributed modulo one.

Remark 4.33 Recall that $m - \mathbf{T}(m)$ is non-decreasing.

Proof of Theorem 4.32 Let $\mathcal{S}$ be a strict $(\mathbf{T}, s)$-sequence in base b such that $\lim_{m\to\infty} m - \mathbf{T}(m) = \infty$. Further, let

$$J := \prod_{i=1}^{s} [\alpha_i, \beta_i)$$

with $0 \leq \alpha_i < \beta_i \leq 1$, be an arbitrary sub-interval of $[0, 1)^s$, and let $\varepsilon > 0$ be given. We show that

$$\left| \frac{A(J, N, \mathcal{S})}{N} - \lambda_s(J) \right| < \varepsilon$$

for all N large enough. Then the result follows (see Definition 3.1). Let $l := rs$ with $r, s \in \mathbb{N}$ be fixed such that $\frac{2s}{b^r} < \varepsilon/2$ and let m be fixed such that $m - \mathbf{T}(m) \geq l$. Let

$$\tfrac{A_i}{b^r} \leq \alpha_i < \tfrac{A_i+1}{b^r} \quad \text{and} \quad \tfrac{B_i}{b^r} \leq \beta_i < \tfrac{B_i+1}{b^r}$$

for $1 \leq i \leq s$. Then, for

$$J_1 := \prod_{i=1}^{s} \left[\frac{A_i + 1}{b^r}, \frac{B_i}{b^r}\right) \quad \text{and} \quad J_2 := \prod_{i=1}^{s} \left[\frac{A_i}{b^r}, \frac{B_i + 1}{b^r}\right),$$

we have

$$J_1 \subseteq J \subseteq J_2 \subseteq [0, 1)^s;$$

both are unions of, at most, b^l elementary intervals of order l, and by Lemma 3.18, $\lambda_s(J_2 \setminus J_1) \leq 2s/b^r$. Hence, the intervals J_1, J_2 are fair with respect to subsequences of length b^m. Therefore, for all positive integers N, we have

$$\begin{aligned}
A(J, N, \mathcal{S}) - N\lambda_s(J) &\leq A(J_2, N, \mathcal{S}) - N\lambda_s(J_2) + N\frac{2s}{b^r} \\
&\leq A(J_2, \lfloor N/b^m \rfloor b^m, \mathcal{S}) - \left\lfloor \frac{N}{b^m} \right\rfloor b^m \lambda_s(J_2) + b^m + N\frac{2s}{b^r} \\
&= b^m + N\frac{2s}{b^r}
\end{aligned}$$

and

$$\begin{aligned}
A(J, N, \mathcal{S}) - N\lambda_s(J) &\geq A(J_1, N, \mathcal{S}) - N\lambda_s(J_1) - N\frac{2s}{b^r} \\
&\geq A(J_1, \lceil N/b^m \rceil b^m, \mathcal{S}) - \left\lceil \frac{N}{b^m} \right\rceil b^m \lambda_s(J_1) - b^m - N\frac{2s}{b^r} \\
&= -b^m - N\frac{2s}{b^r},
\end{aligned}$$

such that

$$\left| \frac{A(J, N, \mathcal{S})}{N} - \lambda_s(J) \right| \leq \frac{b^m}{N} + \frac{2s}{b^r} < \varepsilon$$

for N large enough. Hence, the result follows. □

Note that the condition is not an ‘if and only if’-condition, since there are uniformly distributed sequences, having no non-trivial net-property at all. For so-called digital sequences (see Section 4.4.5), the above sufficient condition is also necessary and hence the above result cannot be improved.

We even have that all $(\mathbf{T}, s)$-sequences considered in Theorem 4.32 are well-distributed. This is an important fact for many forms of applications where the sequence in use is not used from the first point on. Sometimes, for a variety of reasons, a first sub-block of the sequence is deleted (see [225]). We prove the following result, which is, for the special case $\mathbf{T}(m) = t$ for all $m \geq t$, also proved in [100, Theorem 1], but in a less elementary way.

Theorem 4.34 *A strict* $(\mathbf{T}, s)$*-sequence in any base* b *is well-distributed modulo one if*

$$\lim_{m\to\infty} m - \mathbf{T}(m) = +\infty.$$

In particular, every (t, s)*-sequence is well-distributed modulo one.*

Proof For an interval $B \subseteq [0, 1]^s$, now let

$$A(B, k, N, \mathcal{S}) := \#\{n \in \mathbb{N}_0 : k \le n < k + N \text{ and } \boldsymbol{x}_n \in B\}.$$

We use the notation of the proof of Theorem 4.32. We have to show that for all $\varepsilon > 0$, there is an $N(\varepsilon)$, such that $\left|\frac{A(J,k,N,\mathcal{S})}{N} - \lambda_s(J)\right| < \varepsilon$ for all k and all $N \ge N(\varepsilon)$. Choose again $l := rs$ with $r, s \in \mathbb{N}$ such that $2s/b^r < \varepsilon/2$ and m fixed such that $m - \mathbf{T}(m) \ge l$. Consider again J_1 and J_2. Note that

$$\begin{aligned}
&A(J, k, N, \mathcal{S}) - N\lambda_s(J)\\
&\le A(J_2, k, N, \mathcal{S}) - N\lambda_s(J_2) + N\frac{2s}{b^r}\\
&\le A(J_2, \lfloor (N+k)/b^m \rfloor b^m, \mathcal{S}) - \left\lfloor \frac{N+k}{b^m} \right\rfloor b^m \lambda_s(J_2)\\
&\quad - \left(A(J_2, (\lfloor k/b^m \rfloor + 1)b^m, \mathcal{S}) - (\lfloor k/b^m \rfloor + 1)b^m \lambda_s(J_2)\right) + 2b^m + N\frac{2s}{b^r}\\
&= 2b^m + N\frac{2s}{b^r}
\end{aligned}$$

and

$$\begin{aligned}
&A(J, k, N, \mathcal{S}) - N\lambda_s(J)\\
&\ge A(J_1, k, N, \mathcal{S}) - N\lambda_s(J_1) - N\frac{2s}{b^r}\\
&\ge A(J_1, \lceil (N+k)/b^m \rceil b^m, \mathcal{S}) - \left\lceil \frac{N+k}{b^m} \right\rceil b^m \lambda_s(J_1)\\
&\quad - \left(A(J_1, (\lceil k/b^m \rceil - 1)b^m, \mathcal{S}) - (\lceil k/b^m \rceil - 1)b^m \lambda_s(J_1)\right) - 2b^m - N\frac{2s}{b^r}\\
&= -2b^m - N\frac{2s}{b^r}.
\end{aligned}$$

Hence, we obtain that

$$\left|\frac{A(J, k, N, \mathcal{S})}{N} - \lambda_s(J)\right| \le \frac{2b^m}{N} + \frac{2s}{b^r} < \varepsilon$$

for all k and all $N \ge 4b^m\varepsilon^{-1}$. Therefore, the result follows. □

4.3.2 A first example

As a first non-trivial example, let us try to artificially generate a $(\mathbf{T}, s)$-sequence in base b from regular lattices. We restrict ourselves to base $b = 2$. The points

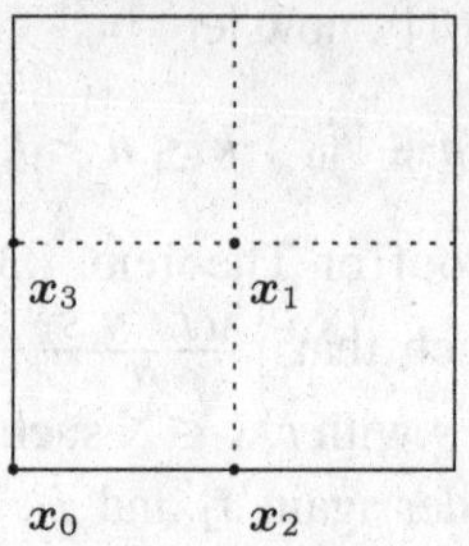

Figure 4.18 The four start points $\boldsymbol{x}_0, \boldsymbol{x}_1, \boldsymbol{x}_2, \boldsymbol{x}_3$.

$\boldsymbol{x}_0, \boldsymbol{x}_1, \ldots$ have the following form:

$$\begin{array}{ll} \boldsymbol{x}_0 = (0, \ldots, 0), & \boldsymbol{x}_1 = (1/2, \ldots, 1/2), \\ \boldsymbol{x}_2 = (1/2, 0, \ldots, 0), & \boldsymbol{x}_3 = (0, 1/2, \ldots, 1/2), \\ \cdots\cdots & \cdots\cdots \\ \boldsymbol{x}_{2^s-2} = (1/2, \ldots, 1/2, 0), & \boldsymbol{x}_{2^s-1} = (0, \ldots, 0, 1/2). \end{array}$$

The points are ordered such that $\boldsymbol{x}_{2j} + \boldsymbol{x}_{2j+1} = (1/2, \ldots, 1/2)$ for all $0 \le j \le 2^{s-1} - 1$. Now let $\boldsymbol{y}_j^{(k)} := \boldsymbol{x}_j / 2^{k-1}$ for all $0 \le j \le 2^s - 1$, i.e.

$$\begin{array}{ll} \boldsymbol{y}_0^{(k)} = (0, \ldots, 0), & \boldsymbol{y}_1^{(k)} = (1/2^k, \ldots, 1/2^k), \\ \boldsymbol{y}_2^{(k)} = (1/2^k, 0, \ldots, 0), & \boldsymbol{y}_3^{(k)} = (0, 1/2^k, \ldots, 1/2^k), \\ \cdots\cdots & \cdots\cdots \\ \boldsymbol{y}_{2^s-2}^{(k)} = (1/2^k, \ldots, 1/2^k, 0), & \boldsymbol{y}_{2^s-1}^{(k)} = (0, \ldots, 0, 1/2^k). \end{array}$$

If we have already constructed the points $\boldsymbol{x}_0, \ldots, \boldsymbol{x}_{2^{sk}-1}$, we obtain the following $2^{s(k+1)} - 2^{sk}$ points by:

$$\begin{array}{lll} \boldsymbol{x}_{2^{sk}} := \boldsymbol{x}_0 + \boldsymbol{y}_1^{(k+1)}, & \ldots, & \boldsymbol{x}_{2 \cdot 2^{sk}-1} := \boldsymbol{x}_{2^{sk}-1} + \boldsymbol{y}_1^{(k+1)}, \\ \boldsymbol{x}_{2 \cdot 2^{sk}} := \boldsymbol{x}_0 + \boldsymbol{y}_2^{(k+1)}, & \ldots, & \boldsymbol{x}_{3 \cdot 2^{sk}-1} := \boldsymbol{x}_{2^{sk}-1} + \boldsymbol{y}_2^{(k+1)}, \\ \cdots\cdots & & \cdots\cdots \\ \boldsymbol{x}_{(2^s-1) \cdot 2^{sk}} := \boldsymbol{x}_0 + \boldsymbol{y}_{2^s-1}^{(k+1)}, & \ldots, & \boldsymbol{x}_{2^{s(k+1)}-1} := \boldsymbol{x}_{2^{sk}-1} + \boldsymbol{y}_{2^s-1}^{(k+1)}, \end{array}$$

for all $k \in \mathbb{N}$.

We illustrate the generation procedure in dimension 2. We start with the four points $\boldsymbol{x}_0, \boldsymbol{x}_1, \boldsymbol{x}_2, \boldsymbol{x}_3$ as indicated in Figure 4.18.

This four-scheme always occurs in the subsequent procedure. Then we repeat this four-scheme consecutively in the four subsquares according to their numbering by $\boldsymbol{x}_0, \boldsymbol{x}_1, \boldsymbol{x}_2, \boldsymbol{x}_3$; see Figure 4.19.

Then we repeat this four-scheme consecutively in the 4^2 subsquares according to their numbering by $\boldsymbol{x}_0, \ldots, \boldsymbol{x}_{15}$, and we get Figure 4.20.

For $s = 1$ we obtain the van der Corput sequence in base 2 (see Definition 3.10) in this way. We have the following result.

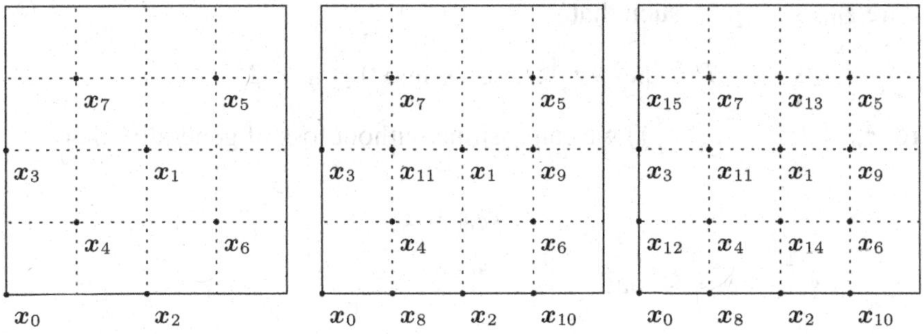

Figure 4.19 Construction of $\boldsymbol{x}_0, \ldots, \boldsymbol{x}_{15}$.

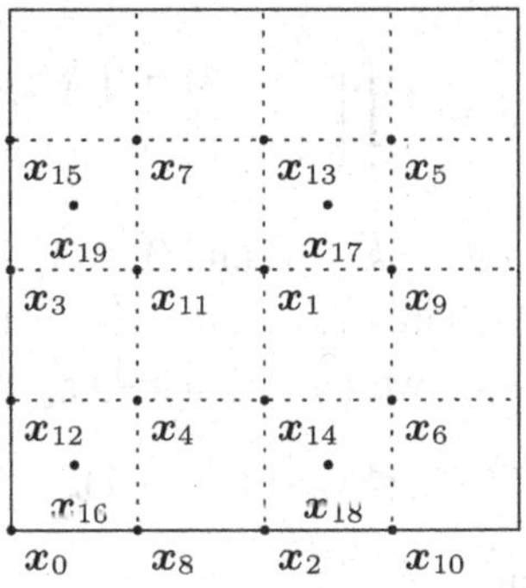

Figure 4.20 Construction of $\boldsymbol{x}_0, \ldots, \boldsymbol{x}_{19}$.

Proposition 4.35 *The above generated sequence* $(\boldsymbol{x}_0, \boldsymbol{x}_1, \ldots)$ *in* $[0, 1)^s$ *is a strict* $(\mathbf{T}, s)$*-sequence in base* 2 *with* $\mathbf{T}(m) = m - \lceil m/s \rceil$*. In particular, the van der Corput sequence in base* 2 *is a* (0, 1)*-sequence in base 2.*

Proof For $k \in \mathbb{N}$ let $\mathcal{S}_k$ denote the first 2^{sk} points of the sequence, hence

$$\mathcal{S}_k = \left\{ \left(\frac{a_1}{2^k}, \ldots, \frac{a_s}{2^k} \right) : 0 \leq a_i < 2^k \right\}.$$

The first 2^{sk} points of the sequence are fair with respect to any elementary interval of order k, because of the net property of the regular lattice shown in Corollary 4.11. Now we show the fairness of a point set $\mathcal{P}$ of the form

$$\mathcal{P} = \{\boldsymbol{x}_{p2^{sk+j}}, \ldots, \boldsymbol{x}_{p2^{sk+j}+2^{sk+j}-1}\}, \tag{4.6}$$

for arbitrarily chosen $p \in \mathbb{N}$ and $j \in \mathbb{N}_0$, with respect to all 2-adic elementary intervals of order $k + 1$.

The case $j = 0$ follows from the above considerations concerning $\mathcal{S}_k$. Now let $j \in \mathbb{N}$. By the construction method for the sequence $(\boldsymbol{x}_0, \boldsymbol{x}_1, \ldots)$ it follows that there are $z_0, \ldots, z_{2^j-1}$, such that

$$\mathcal{P} = \{\boldsymbol{x} + \boldsymbol{z}_q \,:\, \boldsymbol{x} \in \mathcal{S}_k \text{ and } 0 \le q < 2^j\}$$

and for $\boldsymbol{z}_q = (z_{q,1}, \ldots, z_{q,s})$ we can assume without loss of generality that

$$0 \le z_{q,i} < \frac{1}{2^k}$$

for $1 \le i \le s$, $0 \le q < 2^j$ and

$$|z_{2r+1,i} - z_{2r,i}| = \frac{1}{2^{k+1}}$$

for $1 \le i \le s$, $0 \le r \le 2^{j-1} - 1$. Let

$$J = \prod_{i=1}^{s} \left[\frac{A_i}{2^{d_i}}, \frac{A_i + 1}{2^{d_i}} \right),$$

where $d_1, \ldots, d_s \in \mathbb{N}_0$, $\sum_{i=1}^{s} d_i = k + 1$, and $0 \le A_i < 2^{d_i}$ for all $1 \le i \le s$.

First, we consider the case where $d_1, \ldots, d_s \le k$. For $\boldsymbol{x} = (x_1/2^k, \ldots, x_s/2^k) \in J$, where $x_1, \ldots, x_s$ are integers, we have that $\boldsymbol{x} + \boldsymbol{z}_q \in J$ also. This holds, since

$$A_i 2^{k-d_i} \le x_i < (A_i + 1) 2^{k-d_i}$$

and $0 \le z_{q,i} 2^k < 1$ imply that

$$A_i 2^{k-d_i} \le x_i + z_{q,i} 2^k < (A_i + 1) 2^{k-d_i}.$$

Hence, there are exactly $2^{sk-k-1+j}$ points of $\mathcal{P}$ in J. (Recall that any interval of the form $\prod_{i=1}^{s}[B/2^k, (B+1)/2^k)$ contains exactly one point of $\mathcal{S}_k$.)

For the second case we can assume without loss of generality that $d_1 = k + 1$ and $d_2 = \cdots = d_s = 0$. For $\boldsymbol{x} = (x_1/2^k, \ldots, x_s/2^k)$, where $x_1, \ldots, x_s$ are integers, with $x_1 = \lfloor A_1/2 \rfloor$ and $0 \le x_i < 2^k$ for $2 \le i \le s$, we have that $\boldsymbol{x} + \boldsymbol{z}_q \in J$ if and only if $\boldsymbol{z}_q$ is of the following form

$$z_{q,1} < \frac{1}{2^{k+1}}$$

if A_1 is even, or

$$z_{q,1} \ge \frac{1}{2^{k+1}}$$

if A_1 is odd.

In either case there are 2^{j-1} elements $\boldsymbol{z}_q$ with $\boldsymbol{x} + \boldsymbol{z}_q \in J$, so altogether we have $2^{sk-k+j-1}$ points of $\mathcal{P}$ in J.

These two cases show that the point set $\mathcal{P}$ from (4.6) is a $(sk + j - k - 1, sk + j, s)$-net in base 2 for all p and j. If we write m as $m = sk + j$, then we find that a point set of the form $\{\boldsymbol{x}_{p2^m}, \ldots, \boldsymbol{x}_{p2^m+2^m-1}\}$ is, for all p and m, a $(m - \lceil \frac{m}{s} \rceil, m, s)$-net in base 2.

To prove strictness, it suffices to show that the point set $\{\boldsymbol{x}_0, \ldots, \boldsymbol{x}_{2^m-1}\}$ is a strict $(m - \lceil \frac{m}{s} \rceil, m, s)$-net in base 2 for all m. Choose any $m = sk + j$ and consider the elementary interval J of order $k + 2$,

$$J = \left[0, \frac{1}{2^{k+2}}\right) \times \prod_{i=1}^{s} [0, 1).$$

If $\{\boldsymbol{x}_0, \ldots, \boldsymbol{x}_{2^m-1}\}$ would be a $(m - \lceil \frac{m}{s} \rceil - 1, m, s)$-net in base 2, then there should be $2^{sk-k+j-2}$ points of the point set in J. But for the first components $x_{n,1}$ of $\boldsymbol{x}_n \in J, 0 \le n \le 2^{sk} - 1$, we have $0 \le x_{n,1} < 1/4$. Hence, there are $2^{(s-1)k}$ points from $\{\boldsymbol{x}_0, \ldots, \boldsymbol{x}_{2^{sk}-1}\}$ in J and from the construction method for the $\boldsymbol{x}_n$, it follows that there are even $2^{sk-k+j-1}$ points from $\{\boldsymbol{x}_0, \ldots, \boldsymbol{x}_{2^{sk+j}-1}\}$ in J. As $2^{sk-k+j-1} > 2^{sk-k+j-2}$, we obtain a contradiction and hence the result follows. □

Further examples of $(\mathbf{T}, s)$-sequences and (t, s)-sequences are given in the subsequent section and in Chapter 8.

4.3.3 Existence of $(0, s)$-sequences in base b

As for $(0, m, s)$-nets in base b, it is clear that a $(0, s)$-sequence in base b cannot exist for all dimensions s. We have the following result.

Corollary 4.36 *A $(0, s)$-sequence in base b cannot exist if $s \ge b + 1$.*

This corollary is a consequence of Corollary 4.19 in Section 4.2 and of the following corollary (see [177, Lemma 4.22]).

Corollary 4.37 *If there exists a (t, s)-sequence in base b, then, for every $m \ge t$, there exists a $(t, m, s + 1)$-net in base b.*

This is again a consequence of the following lemma.

Lemma 4.38 *Let $(\boldsymbol{x}_0, \boldsymbol{x}_1, \ldots)$ be a $(\mathbf{T}, s)$-sequence in base b. Then, for every m, the point set $\{\boldsymbol{y}_0, \boldsymbol{y}_1, \ldots, \boldsymbol{y}_{b^m-1}\}$ with $\boldsymbol{y}_k := (k/b^m, \boldsymbol{x}_k)$, $0 \le k < b^m$, is an $(r(m), m, s + 1)$-net in base b with $r(m) := \max\{\mathbf{T}(0), \ldots, \mathbf{T}(m)\}$.*

Proof Let $J = \prod_{i=1}^{s+1} \left[\frac{A_i}{b^{d_i}}, \frac{A_i+1}{b^{d_i}}\right)$ be an elementary interval of order $m - r(m)$. Then $\boldsymbol{y}_k \in J$ if and only if

$$\frac{k}{b^m} \in \left[\frac{A_1}{b^{d_1}}, \frac{A_1 + 1}{b^{d_1}}\right) \quad \text{and} \quad \boldsymbol{x}_k \in \prod_{i=2}^{s+1} \left[\frac{A_i}{b^{d_i}}, \frac{A_i + 1}{b^{d_i}}\right).$$

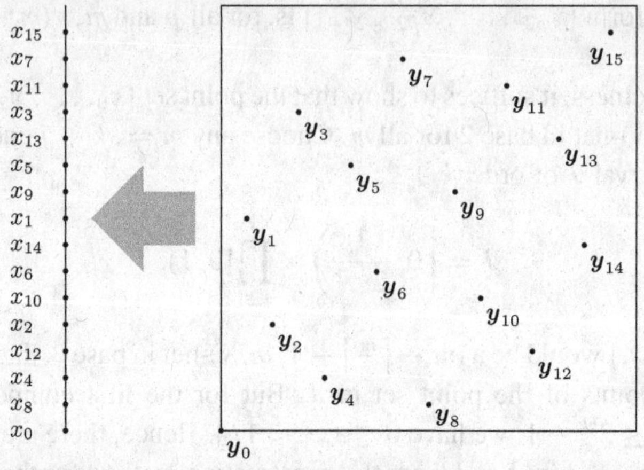

Figure 4.21 Hammersley point set in base 2 with 16 points. The projection to the second coordinate gives the first 16 elements of the van der Corput sequence in base 2.

The first condition leads to

$$A_1 b^{m-d_1} \leq k < A_1 b^{m-d_1} + b^{m-d_1}.$$

Since $(\boldsymbol{x}_0, \boldsymbol{x}_1, \ldots)$ is a $(\mathbf{T}, s)$-sequence in base b, the points $\boldsymbol{x}_{A_1 b^{m-d_1}+l}$, $0 \leq l \leq b^{m-d_1} - 1$, form an $(r(m), m - d_1, s)$-net in base b, because $r(m) \geq \mathbf{T}(m - d_1)$. The interval $\prod_{i=2}^{s+1} [A_i/b^{d_i}, (A_i + 1)/b^{d_i})$ has volume $b^{-d_2-\cdots-d_{s+1}} = b^{-m+d_1+r(m)}$ and therefore contains exactly $b^{r(m)}$ of the points $\boldsymbol{x}_{A_1 b^{m-d_1}+l}$, $0 \leq l \leq b^{m-d_1} - 1$. Consequently, J contains exactly $b^{r(m)}$ of the points $\boldsymbol{y}_k$, $0 \leq k \leq b^m - 1$, and the result follows. □

Example 4.39 Let $(x_0, x_1, \ldots)$ be the van der Corput sequence in base b, which is an example of a $(0, 1)$-sequence in base b. Then the point set $\{\boldsymbol{y}_0, \ldots, \boldsymbol{y}_{b^m-1}\}$, where $\boldsymbol{y}_k := (k/b^m, x_k)$ for $0 \leq k \leq b^m - 1$, is the Hammersley point set in base b with b^m points and hence a $(0, m, 2)$-net in base b (see Figure 4.21).

The advantage of (t, s)-sequences is that sub-sequences also show favourable distribution properties (and even net properties).

Faure and Niederreiter sequences provide, for every prime power base b and any $s \leq b$, a $(0, s)$-sequence in base b; see Chapter 8. Consequently, we obtain the following result.

Corollary 4.40 *A $(0, s)$-sequence in a prime power base b exists if and only if $s \leq b$.*

Again, it is more difficult to give sharp existence results for $(0, s)$-sequences in composite bases b. As a singular result from Lemma 4.21 in Section 4.2 and Corollary 4.37, it follows that:

Corollary 4.41 *There does not exist a* $(0, 3)$*-sequence in base* 6.

4.3.4 Propagation rules for sequences

Base propagation rules for (t, s)- and $(\mathbf{T}, s)$-sequences can be transferred from the corresponding rules for (t, m, s)-nets. Thus, as a consequence from Corollary 4.23 in Section 4.2, we obtain the following result.

Corollary 4.42 *Any* $(\mathbf{T}, s)$*-sequence* $(\boldsymbol{x}_0, \boldsymbol{x}_1, \ldots)$ *in base* b *is a* $(\mathbf{U}, s)$*-sequence in base* b^k*, where*

$$\mathbf{U}(m) := \left\lceil \frac{\mathbf{T}(km)}{k} \right\rceil.$$

Proof Take any sub-sequence of the form

$$(\boldsymbol{x}_{l(b^k)^m}, \boldsymbol{x}_{l(b^k)^m+1}, \ldots, \boldsymbol{x}_{l(b^k)^m+(b^k)^m-1}),$$

where $l \geq 0$, of the sequence $(\boldsymbol{x}_0, \boldsymbol{x}_1, \ldots)$ which is a $(\mathbf{T}, s)$-sequence in base b. Then the elements of this sub-sequence form a $(\mathbf{T}(km), km, s)$-net in base b and therefore, by Corollary 4.23 in Section 4.2, a $(\lceil \mathbf{T}(km)/k \rceil, m, s)$-net in base b^k. The result follows by the definition of a $(\mathbf{U}, s)$-sequence in base b^k. □

We also have the following result; see [192, Proposition 5].

Corollary 4.43 *Any* (t, s)*-sequence in base* b *is a* $(\lceil t/k \rceil, s)$*-sequence in base* b^k.

Again, a similar converse assertion does not hold in general. As a counter-example serves, for instance, the van der Corput sequence in base 4 which is a $(0, 1)$-sequence in base 4, but certainly not a $(0, 1)$-sequence in base 2. This assertion can be shown by observing that for any integer $k \geq 1$, the two points $x_{4^k} = \frac{1}{4^{k+1}}$ and $x_{4^k+1} = \frac{1}{4} + \frac{1}{4^{k+1}}$ are both contained in $[0, \frac{1}{2})$. Hence, they do not form a $(0, 1, 1)$-net in base 2 and therefore $(x_0, x_1, \ldots)$ is not a $(0, 1)$-sequence in base 2.

However, we can use Theorem 4.24 from Section 4.2 to obtain a base change result for $(\mathbf{T}, s)$- and (t, s)-sequences.

Theorem 4.44 *For given integers* $c \geq 2$*,* L *and* $L' \geq 1$ *with* $\gcd(L, L') = 1$ *we have that every* $(\mathbf{T}, s)$*-sequence* $(\boldsymbol{x}_0, \boldsymbol{x}_1, \ldots)$ *in base* c^L *is a* $(\mathbf{U}, s)$*-sequence in base* $c^{L'}$*, where*

$$\mathbf{U}(m) = m \pmod{L} + \min(V(m), W(m)),$$

with

$$V(m) := \left\lceil \frac{L\mathbf{T}(L'\lfloor m/L \rfloor) + \lfloor m/L \rfloor L((-L') \pmod{L})}{L' + ((-L') \pmod{L})} \right\rceil$$

and

$$W(m) := \left\lceil \frac{L\mathbf{T}(L'\lfloor m/L \rfloor) + (s-1)(L-1)}{L'} \right\rceil.$$

Before we prove the theorem, let us again consider the special cases $L = 1$, $L' = 1$ and $\mathbf{T} \equiv t$. For $L = 1$, we obtain $\mathbf{U}(m) = \left\lceil \frac{\mathbf{T}(L'm)}{L'} \right\rceil$ and therefore Corollary 4.42 again. For $L' = 1$, we obtain the following corollary, which is a generalisation of [192, Proposition 4].

Corollary 4.45 *For a given base $b \geq 2$ and any integer $L \geq 1$, every $(\mathbf{T}, s)$-sequence in base b^L is a $(\mathbf{U}, s)$-sequence in base b with*

$$\mathbf{U}(m) = m \pmod{L} + \min(V(m), W(m))$$

with

$$V(m) := \mathbf{T}(\lfloor m/L \rfloor) + \lfloor m/L \rfloor (L-1)$$

and

$$W(m) := L\mathbf{T}(\lfloor m/L \rfloor) + (s-1)(L-1).$$

For $\mathbf{T} \equiv t$, we obtain the following result; see [192, Proposition 4].

Corollary 4.46 *For given integers $c \geq 2$, L and $L' \geq 1$ with $\gcd(L, L') = 1$, we have that every (t, s)-sequence in base c^L is a (n, s)-sequence in base $c^{L'}$, where*

$$n = L - 1 + \left\lceil \frac{Lt + (s-1)(L-1)}{L'} \right\rceil.$$

Proof of Theorem 4.44 Consider a sub-sequence of $(c^{L'})^m$ elements of the sequence $(\boldsymbol{x}_0, \boldsymbol{x}_1, \ldots)$ of the form

$$(\boldsymbol{x}_{k(c^{L'})^m}, \ldots, \boldsymbol{x}_{k(c^{L'})^m + (c^{L'})^m - 1}).$$

Represent m in the form $m = pL + r$ with $0 \leq r < L$, then the above sub-sequence is

$$(\boldsymbol{x}_{kc^{rL'}(c^L)^{pL'}}, \ldots, \boldsymbol{x}_{kc^{rL'}(c^L)^{pL'} + c^{rL'}(c^L)^{pL'} - 1})$$

and so a multi-set-union of $(c^{L'})^r$ sub-sequences of length $(c^L)^{pL'}$. Any such sub-sequence, by the $(\mathbf{T}, s)$-sequence property in base c^L of $(\boldsymbol{x}_0, \boldsymbol{x}_1, \ldots)$, forms a

$(\mathbf{T}(pL'), pL', s)$-net in base c^L and therefore by Theorem 4.24 in Section 4.2 (note that $p = \lfloor m/L \rfloor$) is a (q, pL, s)-net in base $c^{L'}$ with $q = \min(v, w)$, where

$$v = \left\lceil \frac{L\,\mathbf{T}(L'\lfloor m/L \rfloor) + \lfloor m/L \rfloor L((-L') \pmod{L})}{L' + ((-L') \pmod{L})} \right\rceil$$

and

$$w = \left\lceil \frac{L\,\mathbf{T}(L'\lfloor m/L \rfloor) + (s-1)(L-1)}{L'} \right\rceil.$$

By Lemma 4.14, concerning the combination of (t, m, s)-nets, now the original sub-block as a combination of $(c^{L'})^r$ (q, pL, s)-nets in base $c^{L'}$ forms a $(q + r, pL + r, s) = (q + r, m, s)$-net in base $c^{L'}$. Note that $r \equiv m \pmod{L}$. Hence, the result follows by definition of a $(\mathbf{U}, s)$-sequence in base $c^{L'}$. □

4.4 Digital (t, m, s)-nets and digital $(\mathbf{T}, s)$- and (t, s)-sequences

The concept of digital (t, m, s)-nets, and digital $(\mathbf{T}, s)$- and (t, s)-sequences is a general framework for the construction of (t, m, s)-nets and $(\mathbf{T}, s)$- and (t, s)-sequences. In fact, until now, essentially all concrete (t, m, s)-nets, and $(\mathbf{T}, s)$- and (t, s)-sequences which are of relevance for applications are digital (t, m, s)-nets, and digital $(\mathbf{T}, s)$- and (t, s)-sequences. For brevity, in the following we speak of digital point sets. In particular, all relevant examples provided so far can be introduced in terms of digital point sets.

Using the framework of digital point sets, allows us to:

- provide the (t, m, s)-net, the $(\mathbf{T}, s)$- or (t, s)-sequence in an easy way (in the form of s matrices);
- determine the quality parameter t or $\mathbf{T}$ in a rather fast way;
- describe the properties of point sets in question in terms of properties of the matrices mentioned above, i.e. the search for point sets of high quality can be restricted to the search for matrices with certain properties.

Although one can introduce digital nets in arbitrary integer bases $b \geq 2$, we restrict ourselves to *prime power* bases b only in the following. The main motivation for this restriction is that there exists a finite field of order b if and only if b is a prime power. This leads to a simpler and clearer construction of digital point sets. Some points of the analysis of digital nets in arbitrarily chosen bases are much more involved compared with the prime power base case, where the construction principle is much simpler. Furthermore, the prime power base case (and even the prime base case) is also for practical applications the most important one.

Most of the results and ideas which we give below can be generalised to digital nets in arbitrary integer bases $b \geq 2$. For a detailed treatment of the general case, see [141, Section 1] and [177, Section 4].

4.4.1 Digital (t, m, s)-nets

To construct a digital (t, m, s)-net in a prime power base b, we use the finite field $\mathbb{F}_b$ with b elements and a bijection $\varphi : \{0, \ldots, b-1\} \to \mathbb{F}_b$ with $\varphi(0) = \overline{0}$, the neutral element of addition in $\mathbb{F}_b$. We speak then of a 'digital (t, m, s)-net over the field $\mathbb{F}_b$' instead of 'digital (t, m, s)-net in base b'. (For arbitrary b, one has to choose a finite commutative ring R with identity of order b; see [137, 141, 177] for more information.)

The elements of $\mathbb{F}_b$ are denoted by $\overline{0}, \overline{1}, \ldots, \overline{b-1}$, respectively, and we use the bijection $\varphi(j) := \overline{j}$ for $j \in \{0, \ldots, b-1\}$. If b is a prime, then we identify $\mathbb{F}_b$ with $\mathbb{Z}_b$, the set of residue classes modulo b with addition and multiplication modulo b, which in turn we identify with the elements of $\{0, \ldots, b-1\}$. Therefore, we omit the bijection φ and the bar in this case.

Let us explain the concept of digital (t, m, s)-nets over $\mathbb{F}_b$. We want to construct a (t, m, s)-net $\{\boldsymbol{x}_0, \boldsymbol{x}_1, \ldots, \boldsymbol{x}_{b^m-1}\}$ in base b by the digital method. To generate such a point set, we first have to choose $m \times m$ matrices $C_1, \ldots, C_s$ (one for each component) over $\mathbb{F}_b$, that is, with entries from $\mathbb{F}_b$. For example, to generate a $(t, 4, 2)$-net over $\mathbb{Z}_2$, take the matrices

$$C_1 = \begin{pmatrix} 1 & 0 & 0 & 0 \\ 0 & 1 & 0 & 0 \\ 0 & 0 & 1 & 0 \\ 0 & 0 & 0 & 1 \end{pmatrix} \quad \text{and} \quad C_2 = \begin{pmatrix} 0 & 0 & 0 & 1 \\ 0 & 0 & 1 & 0 \\ 0 & 1 & 0 & 0 \\ 1 & 0 & 0 & 0 \end{pmatrix}. \tag{4.7}$$

To now generate one of the points $\boldsymbol{x}_n = (x_{n,1}, \ldots, x_{n,s})$, with $0 \leq n < b^m$, of the net, we first write n in its b-adic (i.e. base b) expansion $n = \sum_{j=0}^{m-1} a_j b^j$, with digits $a_j \in \{0, \ldots, b-1\}$. Note that $0 \leq n < b^m$ and therefore it suffices to consider only j with $0 \leq j \leq m-1$. Then take the m-dimensional column vector

$$\mathbf{n} := \begin{pmatrix} \varphi(a_0) \\ \varphi(a_1) \\ \vdots \\ \varphi(a_{m-1}) \end{pmatrix} \in (\mathbb{F}_b^m)^\top.$$

For example, to generate the point $\boldsymbol{x}_{11} = (x_{11,1}, x_{11,2})$ of the $(t, 4, 2)$-net over $\mathbb{Z}_2$ from above, write

$$11 = 1 \cdot 2^0 + 1 \cdot 2^1 + 0 \cdot 2^2 + 1 \cdot 2^3,$$

which corresponds to the vector

$$\mathbf{n} = \begin{pmatrix} 1 \\ 1 \\ 0 \\ 1 \end{pmatrix}$$

or to generate the point $\boldsymbol{x}_7 = (x_{7,1}, x_{7,2})$, write

$$7 = 1 \cdot 2^0 + 1 \cdot 2^1 + 1 \cdot 2^2 + 0 \cdot 2^3,$$

which corresponds to the vector

$$\mathbf{n} = \begin{pmatrix} 1 \\ 1 \\ 1 \\ 0 \end{pmatrix}.$$

To generate the point $\boldsymbol{x}_n = (x_{n,1}, \ldots, x_{n,s})$ we explain how to generate the ith coordinate: the ith coordinate $x_{n,i}$ is obtained by multiplying the ith matrix C_i by $\mathbf{n}$ over $\mathbb{F}_b$, which gives as result an m-dimensional vector of elements of $\mathbb{F}_b$, say

$$C_i \mathbf{n} = \begin{pmatrix} \overline{y}_{n,i,1} \\ \vdots \\ \overline{y}_{n,i,m} \end{pmatrix} \in (\mathbb{F}_b^m)^\top.$$

The elements $\varphi^{-1}(\overline{y}_{n,i,j}) \in \{0, \ldots, b-1\}$ are now the b-adic digits of $x_{n,i}$, i.e.

$$x_{n,i} = \frac{\varphi^{-1}(\overline{y}_{n,i,1})}{b} + \frac{\varphi^{-1}(\overline{y}_{n,i,2})}{b^2} + \cdots + \frac{\varphi^{-1}(\overline{y}_{n,i,m})}{b^m}.$$

Definition 4.47 We call the point set $\{\boldsymbol{x}_0, \ldots, \boldsymbol{x}_{b^m-1}\}$ constructed as introduced above a *digital net over* $\mathbb{F}_b$ *with generating matrices* $C_1, \ldots, C_s$ or, in short, a *digital net*.

Since any point set consisting of b^m points in $[0, 1)^s$ is a (t, m, s)-net in base b with a certain quality parameter t, we also speak of a *digital* (t, m, s)*-net over* $\mathbb{F}_b$.

Therefore, to provide the b^m points in dimension s, it suffices to provide s matrices of size $m \times m$ over $\mathbb{F}_b$. This of course simplifies storage of the point sets.

As already mentioned, in most cases the finite field $\mathbb{Z}_b$ with b prime is chosen for practical applications, and indeed $\mathbb{Z}_2$ is the most usual choice. We remark again that in this case we can omit the bijection φ as we identify $\mathbb{Z}_b$ with the elements $\{0, \ldots, b-1\}$.

Example 4.48 Consider again the $(t, 4, 2)$-net over $\mathbb{Z}_2$ with generating matrices (4.7). To construct, for instance, $\boldsymbol{x}_{11}$, we have $n = 11$ and therefore,

$$C_1\mathbf{n} = \begin{pmatrix} 1 & 0 & 0 & 0 \\ 0 & 1 & 0 & 0 \\ 0 & 0 & 1 & 0 \\ 0 & 0 & 0 & 1 \end{pmatrix} \begin{pmatrix} 1 \\ 1 \\ 0 \\ 1 \end{pmatrix} = \begin{pmatrix} 1 \\ 1 \\ 0 \\ 1 \end{pmatrix}$$

$$C_2\mathbf{n} = \begin{pmatrix} 0 & 0 & 0 & 1 \\ 0 & 0 & 1 & 0 \\ 0 & 1 & 0 & 0 \\ 1 & 0 & 0 & 0 \end{pmatrix} \begin{pmatrix} 1 \\ 1 \\ 0 \\ 1 \end{pmatrix} = \begin{pmatrix} 1 \\ 0 \\ 1 \\ 1 \end{pmatrix}.$$

Hence, $x_{11,1} = \frac{1}{2} + \frac{1}{4} + \frac{1}{16} = \frac{13}{16}$ and $x_{11,2} = \frac{1}{2} + \frac{1}{8} + \frac{1}{16} = \frac{11}{16}$, and thus, $\boldsymbol{x}_{11} = \left(\frac{13}{16}, \frac{11}{16}\right)$.

For $n = 7$, we have

$$C_1\mathbf{n} = \begin{pmatrix} 1 & 0 & 0 & 0 \\ 0 & 1 & 0 & 0 \\ 0 & 0 & 1 & 0 \\ 0 & 0 & 0 & 1 \end{pmatrix} \begin{pmatrix} 1 \\ 1 \\ 1 \\ 0 \end{pmatrix} = \begin{pmatrix} 1 \\ 1 \\ 1 \\ 0 \end{pmatrix}$$

$$C_2\mathbf{n} = \begin{pmatrix} 0 & 0 & 0 & 1 \\ 0 & 0 & 1 & 0 \\ 0 & 1 & 0 & 0 \\ 1 & 0 & 0 & 0 \end{pmatrix} \begin{pmatrix} 1 \\ 1 \\ 1 \\ 0 \end{pmatrix} = \begin{pmatrix} 0 \\ 1 \\ 1 \\ 1 \end{pmatrix}.$$

Hence, $x_{7,1} = \frac{1}{2} + \frac{1}{4} + \frac{1}{8} = \frac{7}{8}$ and $x_{7,2} = \frac{1}{4} + \frac{1}{8} + \frac{1}{16} = \frac{7}{16}$, and thus, $\boldsymbol{x}_7 = \left(\frac{7}{8}, \frac{7}{16}\right)$. Determining all 16 points shows that this example just gives the 16-point Hammersley point set in base 2.

Example 4.49 To illustrate the generation procedure, we provide one example of a digital $(t, 3, 2)$-net over $\mathbb{F}_4$, the finite field of order 4. Let $\mathbb{F}_4 = \{\bar{0}, \bar{1}, \bar{2}, \bar{3}\}$. We identify the elements $\bar{0}, \bar{1}, \bar{2}, \bar{3}$ of $\mathbb{F}_4$ with the 4-adic digits 0, 1, 2, 3 respectively, i.e. $\varphi(i) = \bar{i}$ for $i \in \{0, 1, 2, 3\}$. Addition and multiplication in $\mathbb{F}_4$ are defined by the following tables:

$+$	$\bar{0}$	$\bar{1}$	$\bar{2}$	$\bar{3}$
$\bar{0}$	$\bar{0}$	$\bar{1}$	$\bar{2}$	$\bar{3}$
$\bar{1}$	$\bar{1}$	$\bar{0}$	$\bar{3}$	$\bar{2}$
$\bar{2}$	$\bar{2}$	$\bar{3}$	$\bar{0}$	$\bar{1}$
$\bar{3}$	$\bar{3}$	$\bar{2}$	$\bar{1}$	$\bar{0}$

$\cdot$	$\bar{0}$	$\bar{1}$	$\bar{2}$	$\bar{3}$
$\bar{0}$	$\bar{0}$	$\bar{0}$	$\bar{0}$	$\bar{0}$
$\bar{1}$	$\bar{0}$	$\bar{1}$	$\bar{2}$	$\bar{3}$
$\bar{2}$	$\bar{0}$	$\bar{2}$	$\bar{3}$	$\bar{1}$
$\bar{3}$	$\bar{0}$	$\bar{3}$	$\bar{1}$	$\bar{2}$

Choose the 3×3 matrices C_1 and C_2 over $\mathbb{F}_4$ by

$$C_1 = \begin{pmatrix} \bar{1} & \bar{0} & \bar{0} \\ \bar{0} & \bar{1} & \bar{0} \\ \bar{0} & \bar{2} & \bar{2} \end{pmatrix} \text{ and } C_2 = \begin{pmatrix} \bar{2} & \bar{3} & \bar{1} \\ \bar{0} & \bar{0} & \bar{1} \\ \bar{0} & \bar{1} & \bar{0} \end{pmatrix}.$$

To demonstrate how to generate the $4^3 = 64$ points $\boldsymbol{x}_n = (x_{n,1}, x_{n,2}) \in [0, 1)^2$, let us generate $\boldsymbol{x}_{35}$. We have

$$35 = 3 \cdot 4^0 + 0 \cdot 4^1 + 2 \cdot 4^2$$

which corresponds to the vector

$$\mathbf{n} = \begin{pmatrix} \bar{3} \\ \bar{0} \\ \bar{2} \end{pmatrix} \in (\mathbb{F}_4^3)^\top.$$

Now

$$C_1 \begin{pmatrix} \bar{3} \\ \bar{0} \\ \bar{2} \end{pmatrix} = \begin{pmatrix} \bar{1} & \bar{0} & \bar{0} \\ \bar{0} & \bar{1} & \bar{0} \\ \bar{0} & \bar{2} & \bar{2} \end{pmatrix} \begin{pmatrix} \bar{3} \\ \bar{0} \\ \bar{2} \end{pmatrix} = \begin{pmatrix} \bar{3} \\ \bar{0} \\ \bar{3} \end{pmatrix} \in (\mathbb{F}_4^3)^\top$$

and hence, $x_{35,1} = \frac{3}{4} + \frac{0}{16} + \frac{3}{64} = \frac{51}{64}$. Further,

$$C_2 \begin{pmatrix} \bar{3} \\ \bar{0} \\ \bar{2} \end{pmatrix} = \begin{pmatrix} \bar{2} & \bar{3} & \bar{1} \\ \bar{0} & \bar{0} & \bar{1} \\ \bar{0} & \bar{1} & \bar{0} \end{pmatrix} \begin{pmatrix} \bar{3} \\ \bar{0} \\ \bar{2} \end{pmatrix} = \begin{pmatrix} \bar{3} \\ \bar{2} \\ \bar{0} \end{pmatrix} \in (\mathbb{F}_4^3)^\top$$

and hence, $x_{35,2} = \frac{3}{4} + \frac{2}{16} + \frac{0}{64} = \frac{7}{8}$. Therefore, we have $\boldsymbol{x}_{35} = \left(\frac{51}{64}, \frac{7}{8}\right)$.

4.4.2 The quality parameter of digital nets

Trivially, since the number of points N is b^m, the resulting point set is a (t, m, s)-net in base b (every set of b^m points in $[0, 1)^s$ is an (m, m, s)-net at least). But what is the real, strict quality parameter t of the point set, generated in the above way? The answer is given with the help of the following quantity ρ which, in some sense, 'measures' the 'linear independence of the s matrices $C_1, \ldots, C_s$'.

Definition 4.50 Let b be a prime power and let $C_1, \ldots, C_s$ be $m \times m$ matrices with entries from the finite field $\mathbb{F}_b$. Let $\rho = \rho(C_1, \ldots, C_s)$ be the largest integer such that for any choice of $d_1, \ldots, d_s \in \mathbb{N}_0$, with $d_1 + \cdots + d_s = \rho$, the following holds:

the first d_1 row vectors of C_1 together with
the first d_2 row vectors of C_2 together with
$\vdots$
the first d_s row vectors of C_s,

(these are, together, ρ vectors in $\mathbb{F}_b^m$) are linearly independent over the finite field $\mathbb{F}_b$. We call ρ the *linear independence parameter* of the matrices $C_1, \ldots, C_s$.

Example 4.51 Consider C_1, C_2 over $\mathbb{Z}_2$ from the example above,

$$C_1 = \begin{pmatrix} 1 & 0 & 0 & 0 \\ 0 & 1 & 0 & 0 \\ 0 & 0 & 1 & 0 \\ 0 & 0 & 0 & 1 \end{pmatrix} \quad \text{and} \quad C_2 = \begin{pmatrix} 0 & 0 & 0 & 1 \\ 0 & 0 & 1 & 0 \\ 0 & 1 & 0 & 0 \\ 1 & 0 & 0 & 0 \end{pmatrix}.$$

Clearly, ρ is at most 4, since there never exist more than four linearly independent four-dimensional vectors over $\mathbb{Z}_2$. However, ρ is indeed 4 in this example, since for every choice of $d_1, d_2 \geq 0$ with $d_1 + d_2 = 4$, the first d_1 rows of C_1 together with the first d_2 rows of C_2 provide the system of the four canonical row-vectors $(1, 0, 0, 0)$, $(0, 1, 0, 0)$, $(0, 0, 1, 0)$, $(0, 0, 0, 1)$, which are linearly independent over $\mathbb{Z}_2$.

Now we can determine the strict quality parameter t of a digital net generated by matrices $C_1, \ldots, C_s$ over $\mathbb{Z}_b$. This is a special case of [177, Theorem 4.28].

Theorem 4.52 *Let b be a prime power. The point set constructed by the digital method with the $m \times m$ matrices $C_1, \ldots, C_s$ over a finite field $\mathbb{F}_b$ is a strict $(m - \rho, m, s)$-net in base b, where $\rho = \rho(C_1, \ldots, C_s)$ is the linear independence parameter defined in Definition 4.50.*

Proof First, we have to show that every elementary interval of order ρ, i.e. of volume $b^{-\rho}$, contains exactly $b^{m-\rho}$ of the generated points. Let

$$J = \prod_{i=1}^{s} \left[\frac{A_i}{b^{d_i}}, \frac{A_i + 1}{b^{d_i}} \right)$$

with $d_1, \ldots, d_s \in \mathbb{N}_0$ such that $d_1 + \cdots + d_s = \rho$ and $0 \leq A_i < b^{d_i}$ for $1 \leq i \leq s$ be such an interval. We ask for which n is $\boldsymbol{x}_n = (x_{n,1}, \ldots, x_{n,s})$ contained in J, i.e. for which n is $x_{n,i} \in \left[A_i/b^{d_i}, (A_i + 1)/b^{d_i}\right)$ for all $1 \leq i \leq s$ satisfied. We find that $x_{n,i} \in \left[A_i/b^{d_i}, (A_i + 1)/b^{d_i}\right)$ means that the first d_i digits in the b-adic representation of $x_{n,i}$ are determined. In detail, let

$$\frac{A_i}{b^{d_i}} = \frac{e_1^{(i)}}{b} + \cdots + \frac{e_{d_i}^{(i)}}{b^{d_i}},$$

then

$$\frac{e_1^{(i)}}{b} + \cdots + \frac{e_{d_i}^{(i)}}{b^{d_i}} \leq x_{n,i} < \frac{e_1^{(i)}}{b} + \cdots + \frac{e_{d_i}^{(i)}}{b^{d_i}} + \frac{1}{b^{d_i}},$$

that is

$$x_{n,i} = \frac{e_1^{(i)}}{b} + \cdots + \frac{e_{d_i}^{(i)}}{b^{d_i}} + \cdots .$$

Recall that by definition of digital point sets, the jth digit of $x_{n,i}$ is given by φ^{-1} applied to the product $\mathbf{c}_j^{(i)}\mathbf{n}$ of the jth row $\mathbf{c}_j^{(i)}$ of C_i with the n-column vector $\mathbf{n} \in (\mathbb{F}_b^m)^\top$, where φ is the bijection used in the construction. Hence, $\boldsymbol{x}_n \in J$ if and only if the following system of equations over $\mathbb{F}_b$ is satisfied:

$$\left.\begin{aligned}
\mathbf{c}_1^{(1)}\mathbf{n} &= \varphi(e_1^{(1)}) \\
\vdots \quad & \quad \vdots \quad \vdots \\
\mathbf{c}_{d_1}^{(1)}\mathbf{n} &= \varphi(e_{d_1}^{(1)}) \\
\mathbf{c}_1^{(2)}\mathbf{n} &= \varphi(e_2^{(1)}) \\
\vdots \quad & \quad \vdots \quad \vdots \\
\mathbf{c}_{d_2}^{(2)}\mathbf{n} &= \varphi(e_{d_2}^{(1)}) \\
\vdots \quad & \quad \vdots \quad \vdots \\
\vdots \quad & \quad \vdots \quad \vdots \\
\mathbf{c}_1^{(s)}\mathbf{n} &= \varphi(e_1^{(s)}) \\
\vdots \quad & \quad \vdots \quad \vdots \\
\mathbf{c}_{d_s}^{(s)}\mathbf{n} &= \varphi(e_{d_s}^{(s)})
\end{aligned}\right\} \tag{4.8}$$

We ask, how many m-variable vectors $\mathbf{n}$ satisfy this system of $d_1 + \cdots + d_s = \rho$ equations?

Since the system of row vectors $\mathbf{c}_j^{(i)}$ by definition of ρ is linearly independent, the linear system (4.8) has exactly $b^{m-\rho}$ solutions and the result is shown.

Let us now prove the strictness of the quality parameter. If $\rho = m$, then there is nothing to prove, since any $(0, m, s)$-net is strict by definition. If $\rho \leq m - 1$, then, by definition of ρ, there are $d_1, \ldots, d_s \in \mathbb{N}_0$ with $d_1 + \cdots + d_s = \rho + 1$ and such that

$$\mathbf{c}_1^{(1)}, \ldots, \mathbf{c}_{d_1}^{(1)}, \mathbf{c}_1^{(2)}, \ldots, \mathbf{c}_{d_2}^{(2)}, \ldots, \mathbf{c}_1^{(s)}, \ldots, \mathbf{c}_{d_s}^{(s)},$$

are linearly dependent over $\mathbb{F}_b$. But then the linear system (4.8) with $e_j^{(i)} = 0$ for all $1 \leq j \leq d_i$ and $1 \leq i \leq s$, also has $b^{m-\rho}$ solutions $\mathbf{n} \in (\mathbb{F}_b^m)^\top$ (although it consists of $\rho + 1$ equations in m variables over $\mathbb{F}_b$). This means that the elementary interval

$\prod_{i=1}^{s}\left[0, \frac{1}{b^{d_i}}\right)$ of volume $b^{-\rho-1}$ (i.e. of order $\rho+1$) contains $b^{m-\rho}$ points of the net and is therefore not fair. Hence, the net has strict quality parameter $m-\rho$. □

Remark 4.53 According to Theorem 4.52 the strict quality parameter t of a digital net is $m-\rho$. The quantity $\rho = m-t$ is often referred to as the *strength* of a digital net.

As a consequence of Theorem 4.52, we obtain the following result.

Corollary 4.54 *Let b be a prime power. A digital net over a finite field $\mathbb{F}_b$ generated by the $m \times m$ matrices $C_1, \ldots, C_s$ is a $(0, m, s)$-net in base b if and only if for all $d_1, \ldots, d_s \in \mathbb{N}_0$ with $d_1 + \cdots + d_s = m$, the $m \times m$ matrix formed by*

the first d_1 rows of C_1 and
the first d_2 rows of C_2 and
$\vdots$
the first d_s rows of C_s

has a determinant different from zero.

Therefore, the task of determining the quality parameter t is turned into determining the independence parameter ρ of the s-tuple of matrices. The advantage now is that various tools from linear algebra can be used for carrying out this task.

Example 4.55 The $(t, 4, 2)$-net over $\mathbb{Z}_2$ considered in Example 4.48 is a $(0, 4, 2)$-net over $\mathbb{Z}_2$ by Theorem 4.52.

Example 4.56 For any prime b and any $m \in \mathbb{N}$ the two $m \times m$ matrices over $\mathbb{Z}_b$ given by

$$C_1 = \begin{pmatrix} 1 & 0 & \cdots & 0 & 0 \\ 0 & 1 & \ddots & & 0 \\ \vdots & \ddots & \ddots & \ddots & \vdots \\ 0 & & \ddots & 1 & 0 \\ 0 & 0 & \cdots & 0 & 1 \end{pmatrix}, \quad C_2 = \begin{pmatrix} 0 & 0 & \cdots & 0 & 1 \\ 0 & & \iddots & 1 & 0 \\ \vdots & \iddots & \iddots & \iddots & \vdots \\ 0 & 1 & \iddots & & 0 \\ 1 & 0 & \cdots & 0 & 0 \end{pmatrix}$$

generate a digital $(0, m, 2)$-net over $\mathbb{Z}_b$. For every choice of $0 \le d \le m$, the system of vectors

$$\mathbf{c}_1^{(1)}, \ldots, \mathbf{c}_d^{(1)}, \mathbf{c}_1^{(2)}, \ldots, \mathbf{c}_{m-d}^{(2)},$$

where $\mathbf{c}_j^{(i)}$ denotes the jth row vector of the matrix C_i, is linearly independent over $\mathbb{Z}_b$. Hence, the quality parameter $t = 0$. Indeed, the resulting digital $(0, m, 2)$-net over $\mathbb{Z}_b$ is just the two-dimensional Hammersley point set in base b.

Example 4.57 We now show that the following three $m \times m$ matrices C_1, C_2 and C_3 over $\mathbb{Z}_2$ provide, for all $m \geq 1$, a digital $(0, m, 3)$-net over $\mathbb{Z}_2$. Let

$$C_1 = \begin{pmatrix} 1 & 0 & \dots & 0 & 0 \\ 0 & 1 & \ddots & & 0 \\ \vdots & \ddots & \ddots & \ddots & \vdots \\ 0 & & \ddots & 1 & 0 \\ 0 & 0 & \dots & 0 & 1 \end{pmatrix}, \quad C_2 = \begin{pmatrix} 0 & 0 & \dots & 0 & 1 \\ 0 & & \cdot^{\cdot^{\cdot}} & 1 & 0 \\ \vdots & \cdot^{\cdot^{\cdot}} & \cdot^{\cdot^{\cdot}} & \cdot^{\cdot^{\cdot}} & \vdots \\ 0 & 1 & \cdot^{\cdot^{\cdot}} & & 0 \\ 1 & 0 & \dots & 0 & 0 \end{pmatrix}$$

and

$$C_3 = \begin{pmatrix} \binom{0}{0} & \binom{1}{0} & \dots & \dots & \binom{m-1}{0} \\ 0 & \binom{1}{1} & \dots & \dots & \binom{m-1}{1} \\ \vdots & \ddots & \ddots & & \vdots \\ 0 & \dots & 0 & \binom{m-2}{m-2} & \binom{m-1}{m-2} \\ 0 & \dots & \dots & 0 & \binom{m-1}{m-1} \end{pmatrix},$$

where the binomial coefficients are taken modulo 2. This example was first provided by Sobol′ [253]. See also [172, Proof of Theorem 6.2]. We have to show that for any choice of $d_1, d_2 \in \mathbb{N}_0$ with $d_1 + d_2 \leq m$, the vectors

$$\begin{array}{llllllll} (1, & 0, & \dots & \dots & \dots & \dots & \dots, & 0) \\ (0, & 1, & 0, & \dots & \dots & \dots & \dots, & 0) \\ \vdots & \ddots & \ddots & \ddots & & & & \vdots \\ (0, & \dots, & 0, & 1, & 0, & \dots & \dots, & 0) \\ & & & \uparrow & & & & \\ & & & d_1 & & & & \\ (0, & \dots & \dots & \dots & \dots & \dots & 0, & 1) \\ (0, & \dots & \dots & \dots & \dots & 0, & 1, & 0) \\ \vdots & & & & \cdot^{\cdot^{\cdot}} & \cdot^{\cdot^{\cdot}} & \cdot^{\cdot^{\cdot}} & \vdots \\ (0, & \dots & \dots & 0, & 1, & 0, & \dots, & 0) \\ & & & & \uparrow & & & \\ & & & & m - d_2 + 1 & & & \\ (\binom{0}{0}, & \binom{1}{0}, & \dots & \dots & \dots & & \dots, & \binom{m-1}{0}) \\ (0, & \binom{1}{1}, & \binom{2}{1}, & \dots & \dots & & \dots & \binom{m-1}{1}) \\ \vdots & \ddots & \ddots & \ddots & & & & \vdots \\ (0, & \dots, & 0, & \binom{d_3-1}{d_3-1}, & \binom{d_3}{d_3-1}, & & \dots, & \binom{m-1}{d_3-1}) \end{array}$$

are linearly independent over $\mathbb{Z}_2$ (here, $d_3 := m - d_1 - d_2$). To do this, we show that the $m \times m$ matrix

$$C = \begin{pmatrix} 1 & 0 & \dots & \dots & \dots & \dots & \dots & \dots & 0 \\ 0 & 1 & 0 & \dots & \dots & \dots & \dots & \dots & 0 \\ \vdots & \ddots & \ddots & \ddots & & & & & \vdots \\ 0 & \dots & 0 & 1 & 0 & \dots & \dots & \dots & 0 \\ 0 & \dots & \dots & \dots & \dots & \dots & \dots & 0 & 1 \\ 0 & \dots & \dots & \dots & \dots & \dots & 0 & 1 & 0 \\ \vdots & & & & & \iddots & \iddots & \iddots & \vdots \\ 0 & \dots & \dots & \dots & 0 & 1 & 0 & \dots & 0 \\ \binom{0}{0} & \binom{1}{0} & \dots & \dots & \dots & \dots & \dots & \binom{m-2}{0} & \binom{m-1}{0} \\ \vdots & \vdots & & & & & & \vdots & \vdots \\ \binom{0}{d_3-1} & \binom{1}{d_3-1} & \dots & \dots & \dots & \dots & \dots & \binom{m-2}{d_3-1} & \binom{m-1}{d_3-1} \end{pmatrix},$$

where we define $\binom{a}{b} := 0$ if $b > a$, over $\mathbb{Z}_2$ has a determinant of 1. Developing the determinant of C along the first $d_1 + d_2$ rows yields that $|\det C| = |\det C'|$ with

$$C' = \begin{pmatrix} \binom{d_1}{0} & \dots & \binom{m-d_2-1}{0} \\ \vdots & & \vdots \\ \binom{d_1}{d_3-1} & \dots & \binom{m-d_2-1}{d_3-1} \end{pmatrix} \in \mathbb{Z}_2^{d_3 \times d_3}.$$

For any non-negative integers a and k let us now consider the determinant of the matrix

$$D_{a,k} = \begin{pmatrix} \binom{a}{0} & \dots & \binom{a+k}{0} \\ \vdots & & \vdots \\ \binom{a}{k} & \dots & \binom{a+k}{k} \end{pmatrix} \in \mathbb{Z}_2^{(k+1)\times k+1)}.$$

For $j = k, k-1, \dots, 1$ we successively subtract the jth column of $D_{a,k}$ from the $j+1$st column and by using the fact that $\binom{a+j}{i} - \binom{a+j-1}{i} = \binom{a+j-1}{i-1}$, we arrive at the matrix

$$D'_{a,k} = \begin{pmatrix} 1 & 0 & 0 & \dots & 0 \\ \binom{a}{1} & \binom{a}{0} & \binom{a+1}{0} & \dots & \binom{a+k-1}{0} \\ \vdots & \vdots & \vdots & & \vdots \\ \binom{a}{k} & \binom{a}{k-1} & \binom{a+1}{k-1} & \dots & \binom{a+k-1}{k-1} \end{pmatrix},$$

so that, by developing the determinant of the above matrix along the first row, we obtain $\det(D_{a,k}) = \det(D'_{a,k}) = \det(D_{a,k-1})$ and by proceeding in this way we obtain $\det(D_{a,k}) = \det(D_{a,0}) = \binom{a}{0} = 1$. The result then follows from Corollary 4.54. □

For later use, we introduce a further quantity.

Definition 4.58 Let $C_1, \ldots, C_s$ be $m \times m$ matrices over $\mathbb{F}_b$. Define $\delta = \delta(C_1, \ldots, C_s)$ to be the least integer t, with $0 \le t \le m$, such that for any $d_1, \ldots, d_s \in \mathbb{N}_0$ with $d_1 + \cdots + d_s = m - t$ and any $\overline{e}_j^{(i)} \in \mathbb{F}_b$, for $1 \le j \le d_i$ and $1 \le i \le s$, the system

$$\left.\begin{array}{rcl} \mathbf{c}_1^{(1)}\mathbf{n} & = & \overline{e}_1^{(1)} \\ & \vdots & \\ \mathbf{c}_{d_1}^{(1)}\mathbf{n} & = & \overline{e}_{d_1}^{(1)} \\ \mathbf{c}_1^{(2)}\mathbf{n} & = & \overline{e}_1^{(2)} \\ & \vdots & \\ \mathbf{c}_{d_2}^{(2)}\mathbf{n} & = & \overline{e}_{d_2}^{(2)} \\ & \vdots & \\ \mathbf{c}_1^{(s)}\mathbf{n} & = & \overline{e}_1^{(s)} \\ & \vdots & \\ \mathbf{c}_{d_s}^{(s)}\mathbf{n} & = & \overline{e}_{d_s}^{(s)} \end{array}\right\} \tag{4.9}$$

where $\mathbf{c}_j^{(i)}$ denotes the jth row vector of C_i, has exactly b^t solutions $\mathbf{n} \in (\mathbb{F}_b^m)^\top$.

Obviously, in the above definition, it suffices to consider the homogeneous system only, i.e. $\overline{e}_j^{(i)} = 0$ for all i and j. This system has exactly b^t solutions if and only if each system in (4.9) has exactly b^t solutions. This follows from elementary properties of systems of linear equations.

The proof of the following result is left as an exercise (see Exercise 4.6).

Lemma 4.59 *Let b be a prime power. Any $m \times m$ matrices $C_1, \ldots, C_s$ over $\mathbb{F}_b$ generate a strict digital (δ, m, s)-net over $\mathbb{F}_b$.*

4.4.3 Propagation rules for digital nets

We have seen several propagation rules for (t, m, s)-nets in Section 4.2. We show now that certain propagation rules also hold for digital nets. For instance:

- Any digital (t, m, s)-net over $\mathbb{F}_b$ is a digital (t', m, s)-net over $\mathbb{F}_b$ for all $t' \ge t$.
- If the matrices $C_1, \ldots, C_s$ generate a digital (t, m, s)-net over $\mathbb{F}_b$ and if we take any $s' \le s$ of these matrices, then these matrices form a digital (t, m, s')-net over $\mathbb{F}_b$.

Again, it is more subtle to provide suitable propagation rules for digital (t, m, s)-nets concerning the parameter m. The following propagation rule was first given (for arbitrary bases b) in [236, Lemma 3].

Theorem 4.60 *Let b be a prime power. If there exists a digital (t, m, s)-net over $\mathbb{F}_b$, then for each n with $t \le n \le m$, there exists a digital (t, n, s)-net over $\mathbb{F}_b$.*

For the proof of this result, we need the following lemmas.

Lemma 4.61 *Let b be a prime power and let a (strict) digital (t, m, s)-net over $\mathbb{F}_b$ be generated by the $m \times m$ matrices $C_1, \ldots, C_s$. Let Z be a non-singular $m \times m$ matrix over $\mathbb{F}_b$. Then the matrices $C_1', \ldots, C_s'$ with $C_i' := C_i Z$ also generate a (strict) digital (t, m, s)-net over $\mathbb{F}_b$. Indeed, they generate the same digital net, only with the order of the points changed.*

The proof of this result is left as an exercise (see Exercise 4.7).

Lemma 4.62 *Let b be a prime power. If there exists a digital (t, m, s)-net over $\mathbb{F}_b$, then for any given non-singular $m \times m$ matrix Y_s over $\mathbb{F}_b$, there are non-singular $m \times m$ matrices $D_1, \ldots, D_s$ over $\mathbb{F}_b$ with $D_s = Y_s$, generating a digital (t, m, s)-net over $\mathbb{F}_b$.*

Proof Let $C_1, \ldots, C_s$ be an s-tuple of $m \times m$ matrices generating a digital (t, m, s)-net over $\mathbb{F}_b$. Theorem 4.52 implies that the linear independence parameter ρ of $C_1, \ldots, C_s$ satisfies $\rho = m - t$, and hence, for each C_i the first $m - t$ rows are linearly independent. We now generate new $m \times m$ matrices $\widetilde{C}_i$ by removing the last t rows of C_i and by completing the remaining $m - t$ rows by t arbitrary rows, such that all m rows of the new matrix $\widetilde{C}_i$ are linearly independent. This is possible since $\mathbb{F}_b$ is a field. The matrices $\widetilde{C}_1, \ldots, \widetilde{C}_s$ again generate a (t, m, s)-net over $\mathbb{F}_b$. Since $\widetilde{C}_s$ is invertible, there exists a non-singular $m \times m$ matrix Z over $\mathbb{F}_b$ such that $\widetilde{C}_s Z = Y_s$. Let the $m \times m$ matrices $D_1, \ldots, D_s$ be defined by $D_i = \widetilde{C}_i Z$, i.e. in particular, $D_s = Y_s$. By Lemma 4.61 the matrices $D_1, \ldots, D_s$ again generate a digital (t, m, s)-net over $\mathbb{F}_b$. □

Proof of Theorem 4.60 By Lemma 4.62 we may assume that the given digital (t, m, s)-net over $\mathbb{F}_b$ is generated by the non-singular $m \times m$ matrices $C_1, \ldots, C_s$ over $\mathbb{F}_b$, where

$$C_s = E_m' := \begin{pmatrix} 0 & 0 & \ldots & 0 & 1 \\ 0 & & \cdot^{\cdot^{\cdot}} & 1 & 0 \\ \vdots & \cdot^{\cdot^{\cdot}} & \cdot^{\cdot^{\cdot}} & \cdot^{\cdot^{\cdot}} & \vdots \\ 0 & 1 & \cdot^{\cdot^{\cdot}} & & 0 \\ 1 & 0 & \ldots & 0 & 0 \end{pmatrix} \in \mathbb{F}_b^{m \times m}.$$

Now define $n \times n$ matrices $D_1, \ldots, D_s$ over $\mathbb{F}_b$ by setting $D_i := C_i^{(n)}$ (i.e. the left upper $n \times n$ sub-matrix of C_i) for $1 \le i \le s - 1$ and $D_s := E_n'$. We show that $D_1, \ldots, D_s$ generate a digital (t, n, s)-net over $\mathbb{F}_b$.

Let $d_1, \ldots, d_s \in \mathbb{N}_0$ with $d_1 + \cdots + d_s = n - t$ be arbitrarily given. Take the system of the first d_1 rows of D_1, the first d_2 rows of D_2, ..., the first d_s rows of D_s. For simplicity we set $d_1 + \cdots + d_{s-1} =: d$ and denote the first d vectors above by $\mathbf{a}_j^{(n)} \in \mathbb{F}_b^n$ for $1 \le j \le d$. They are the projection of the corresponding m-dimensional vectors $\mathbf{a}_j$ from the matrices C_i from above. We write $\mathbf{a}_j = (a_{j,1}, \ldots, a_{j,n}, |a_{j,n+1}, \ldots, a_{j,m}) = (\mathbf{a}_j^{(n)} | \widetilde{\mathbf{a}}_j^{(m-n)})$. Since $C_1, \ldots, C_{s-1}$ and $C_s = E_m'$ generate a (t, m, s)-net over $\mathbb{F}_b$, the system of $m - t$ vectors from $\mathbb{F}_b^m$ given by

$$\begin{array}{llllll|llll}
(a_{1,1}, & \ldots, & \ldots, & \ldots, & \ldots, & a_{1,n}, & a_{1,n+1}, & \ldots, & \ldots, & a_{1,m}), \\
\vdots & & & & & \vdots & \vdots & & & \vdots \\
(a_{d,1}, & \ldots, & \ldots, & \ldots, & \ldots, & a_{d,n}, & a_{d,n+1}, & \ldots, & \ldots, & a_{d,m}), \\
(0, & \ldots, & \ldots, & \ldots, & \ldots, & 0, & 0, & \ldots, & 0, & 1), \\
(0, & \ldots, & \ldots, & \ldots, & \ldots, & \vdots, & \vdots & \iddots & 1, & 0), \\
\vdots & & & & & \vdots & 0, & \iddots & \iddots & \vdots \\
(0, & \ldots, & \ldots, & \ldots, & \ldots, & 0, & 1, & 0, & \ldots, & 0), \\
(0, & \ldots, & \ldots, & \ldots & 0, & 1, & 0, & \ldots, & \ldots, & 0), \\
\vdots & & & \iddots & \iddots & \iddots & \vdots & & & \vdots \\
(0, & \ldots, & 0, & 1, & 0, & \ldots, & 0, & \ldots, & \ldots, & 0),
\end{array}$$

where the '1' in the last vector is the $t + d +$ first component, is linearly independent over $\mathbb{F}_b$ (note that $d \le n - t$ and therefore, $t + d \le n$). But then, as it is obvious by the above scheme, $\mathbf{a}_1^{(n)}, \ldots, \mathbf{a}_d^{(n)}$ and the first $n - t - d$ rows of E_n' must be linearly independent over $\mathbb{F}_b$ and the result follows. □

More detailed propagation rules for digital nets are presented in Chapter 9.

4.4.4 Structural results for digital nets

In the following we give some general structural results for digital nets. We have seen in the example shown in Figure 4.11 in Section 4.2 that the addition modulo 1 of a fixed s-dimensional point $\boldsymbol{x}$ to all the points of a (t, m, s)-net in base b, although not disturbing the net property, does change in general the (strict) quality parameter t. The principal *digital net* property, however, by shifting the net in general is destroyed. This, for example, can be seen by the fact that any coordinate of any point of a digital (t, m, s)-net in base b is of the form a/b^m, where a is an integer. Hence, for example, the addition of a vector whose coordinates are not all of this form destroys the digital net property. Another reason is that any digital net contains the origin. Hence, shifting the net in a way which removes the origin from the point set destroys the digital net property. Any elementary interval in base b is half open at the right-upper boundary. The right-upper boundary of an elementary interval in base b of order less than or equal to m (i.e. of volume larger than or equal to b^{-m}) in all coordinates is of the form a/b^m. Therefore, any element of a digital (t, m, s)-net in base b has a distance from the right-upper boundary of any elementary interval of order less than or equal to m, of at least b^{-m}. From this fact the following stability result for digital (t, m, s)-nets in a base b follows.

Lemma 4.63 *Let b be a prime power and let $\{\boldsymbol{x}_0, \ldots, \boldsymbol{x}_{b^m-1}\}$ with $\boldsymbol{x}_n := (x_{n,1}, \ldots, x_{n,s})$ be a strict digital (t, m, s)-net over $\mathbb{F}_b$. Let $\varepsilon_{n,i}$ for $1 \leq i \leq s$ and $0 \leq n \leq b^m - 1$ be non-negative reals with $\varepsilon_{n,i} < b^{-m}$ for all n and i. Then $\{\boldsymbol{y}_0, \ldots, \boldsymbol{y}_{b^m-1}\}$ with $\boldsymbol{y}_n := (x_{n,1} + \varepsilon_{n,1}, \ldots, x_{n,s} + \varepsilon_{n,s})$ is a strict (t, m, s)-net in base b.*

Remark 4.64 Indeed, this property holds for all (t, m, s)-nets in base b whose points have coordinates of the form a/b^m with integers $0 \leq a < b^m$.

Another form of shifting a digital net is of higher relevance. Recall the scheme for generating a digital (t, m, s)-net over $\mathbb{F}_b$. Let the integer n be such that $0 \leq n \leq b^m - 1$. Then

$$n \to \mathbf{n} \in (\mathbb{F}_b^m)^\top \to C_i\mathbf{n} = \begin{pmatrix} \overline{y}_{n,i,1} \\ \vdots \\ \overline{y}_{n,i,m} \end{pmatrix} \in (\mathbb{F}_b^m)^\top \to x_{n,i} \in [0, 1).$$

Instead of shifting $x_{n,i}$ as above, let us now shift the column vector

$$\begin{pmatrix} \overline{y}_{n,i,1} \\ \vdots \\ \overline{y}_{n,i,m} \end{pmatrix} \in (\mathbb{F}_b^m)^\top$$

by a fixed column vector over $\mathbb{F}_b$, say

$$\begin{pmatrix} \overline{\sigma}_{i,1} \\ \vdots \\ \overline{\sigma}_{i,m} \end{pmatrix} \in (\mathbb{F}_b^m)^\top.$$

That is, instead of $x_{n,i}$ consider $z_{n,i}$, which is obtained by

$$\begin{pmatrix} \overline{z}_{n,i,1} \\ \vdots \\ \overline{z}_{n,i,m} \end{pmatrix} = \begin{pmatrix} \overline{y}_{n,i,1} + \overline{\sigma}_{i,1} \\ \vdots \\ \overline{y}_{n,i,m} + \overline{\sigma}_{i,m} \end{pmatrix}$$

and

$$z_{n,i} = \frac{\varphi^{-1}(\overline{z}_{n,i,1})}{b} + \cdots + \frac{\varphi^{-1}(\overline{z}_{n,i,m})}{b^m}.$$

We introduce a slightly more general concept here.

Definition 4.65 Let b be a prime power and $\varphi : \{0, \ldots, b-1\} \to \mathbb{F}_b$ be a bijection with $\varphi(0) = \overline{0}$. For $x = \sum_{i=1}^{\infty} \xi_i b^{-i} \in [0, 1)$ and $\sigma = \sum_{i=1}^{\infty} \varsigma_i b^{-i} \in [0, 1)$, where $\xi_i, \varsigma_i \in \{0, \ldots, b-1\}$, we define the ($b$-adic) *digitally shifted point* y by $y = x \oplus_{b,\varphi} \sigma := \sum_{i=1}^{\infty} \eta_i b^{-i}$ where $\eta_i = \varphi^{-1}(\varphi(\xi_i) + \varphi(\varsigma_i))$, and where the '+' is addition in $\mathbb{F}_b$.

For higher dimensions $s > 1$, let $\boldsymbol{\sigma} = (\sigma_1, \ldots, \sigma_s) \in [0, 1)^s$. For $\boldsymbol{x} = (x_1, \ldots, x_s) \in [0, 1)^s$ we define the (b-adic) *digitally shifted point* $\boldsymbol{y}$ by $\boldsymbol{y} = \boldsymbol{x} \oplus_{b,\varphi} \boldsymbol{\sigma} = (x_1 \oplus_{b,\varphi} \sigma_1, \ldots, x_s \oplus_{b,\varphi} \sigma_s)$.

In the following, b and the bijection φ are considered to be fixed and therefore, we simply write $\oplus$ instead of $\oplus_{b,\varphi}$.

Definition 4.66 Let b be a prime power and $\varphi : \{0, \ldots, b-1\} \to \mathbb{F}_b$ be a bijection with $\varphi(0) = \overline{0}$. For a point set $\mathcal{P} = \{\boldsymbol{x}_0, \ldots, \boldsymbol{x}_{N-1}\}$ in $[0, 1)^s$ and a $\boldsymbol{\sigma} \in [0, 1)^s$ the point set $\mathcal{P}_{\boldsymbol{\sigma}} = \{\boldsymbol{x}_0 \oplus \boldsymbol{\sigma}, \ldots, \boldsymbol{x}_{N-1} \oplus \boldsymbol{\sigma}\}$ is called the (b-adic) *digitally shifted point set* $\mathcal{P}$, or the (b-adic) *digitally shifted version of* $\mathcal{P}$. The vector $\boldsymbol{\sigma} \in [0, 1)^s$ is called a (b-adic) *digital shift*.

If we use a digital shift in conjunction with a (t, m, s)-net, then they are always assumed to be in the same base b. Therefore, if it is clear with respect to which base b a point is shifted, we may omit the phrase 'b-adic'.

We show now that a digital shift preserves the (t, m, s)-net structure.

Lemma 4.67 *Let b be a prime power, $\varphi : \{0, \ldots, b-1\} \to \mathbb{F}_b$ a bijection with $\varphi(0) = \overline{0}$ and let $\{\boldsymbol{x}_0, \ldots, \boldsymbol{x}_{b^m-1}\}$ be a (strict) (t, m, s)-net in base b, $\boldsymbol{x}_n = (x_{n,1}, \ldots, x_{n,s})$ for $0 \le n < b^m$, and let $\boldsymbol{\sigma} = (\sigma_1, \ldots, \sigma_s) \in [0, 1)^s$. Then the digitally shifted point set formed by the points $\boldsymbol{y}_n = \boldsymbol{x}_n \oplus \boldsymbol{\sigma}$, $0 \le n < b^m$, is again a (strict) (t, m, s)-net in base b with probability one with respect to the Lebesgue measure of $\boldsymbol{\sigma}$'s. (If the σ_i's have only finitely many b-adic digits different from zero, then the assertion is always true.)*

Proof First, we note that for any $x \in [0, 1)$ the set of all $\sigma \in [0, 1)$, for which the b-adic expansion of $x \oplus \sigma$ has only finitely many digits different from $b-1$, is countable. In fact, if ξ_j denotes the digits in the b-adic expansion of x and ς_j denotes the digits in the b-adic expansion of σ, then $x \oplus \sigma$ has only finitely many digits different from $b-1$ if and only if there is an index j_0 such that for all $j \ge j_0$, we have $\varphi(\xi_j) + \varphi(\varsigma_j) = \varphi(b-1) \in \mathbb{F}_b$ and this holds if and only if

$\varsigma_j = \varphi^{-1}(\varphi(b-1) - \varphi(\xi_j)) \in \mathbb{F}_b$ for all $j \geq j_0$. Thus, the Lebesgue measure of this set is zero and the probability that this case occurs is zero also.

For $1 \leq i \leq s$ let $\sigma_i = \varsigma_{i,1}b^{-1} + \varsigma_{i,2}b^{-2} + \cdots$. Further, for $0 \leq n < b^m$ and $1 \leq i \leq s$ let $x_{n,i} = \xi_{n,i,1}b^{-1} + \xi_{n,i,2}b^{-2} + \cdots$ and $y_{n,i} = \eta_{n,i,1}b^{-1} + \eta_{n,i,2}b^{-2} + \cdots$, where for $k \geq 1$,

$$\eta_{n,i,k} = \varphi^{-1}(\varphi(\xi_{n,i,k}) + \varphi(\varsigma_{i,k})).$$

In the following we assume that infinitely many of the $\eta_{n,i,1}, \eta_{n,i,2}, \ldots$ are different from $b-1$. As shown above, this occurs with probability one. Let

$$J = \prod_{i=1}^{s} \left[\frac{A_i}{b^{d_i}}, \frac{A_i + 1}{b^{d_i}} \right)$$

be an elementary interval of volume b^{t-m}, i.e. $d_1, \ldots, d_s \in \mathbb{N}_0$ with $d_1 + \cdots + d_s = m - t$ and integers $A_1, \ldots, A_s$ with $0 \leq A_i < b^{d_i}$ for $1 \leq i \leq s$, and let

$$\frac{A_i}{b^{d_i}} = \frac{A_{i,1}}{b} + \cdots + \frac{A_{i,d_i}}{b^{d_i}}.$$

Then the point $\boldsymbol{y}_n$ is contained in J if and only if

$$\eta_{n,i,k} = A_{i,k} \quad \text{for all } 1 \leq k \leq d_i \text{ and } 1 \leq i \leq s,$$

and this is true if and only if

$$\xi_{n,i,k} = \varphi^{-1}(\varphi(A_{i,k}) - \varphi(\varsigma_{i,k})) \quad \text{for all } 1 \leq k \leq d_i \text{ and } 1 \leq i \leq s. \tag{4.10}$$

Now let $\overline{B}_{i,k} \in \mathbb{F}_b$ such that

$$\overline{B}_{i,k} = \varphi(A_{i,k}) - \varphi(\varsigma_{i,k}),$$

and let

$$\frac{B_i}{b^{d_i}} = \frac{B_{i,1}}{b} + \cdots + \frac{B_{i,d_i}}{b^{d_i}},$$

where $B_{i,k} = \varphi^{-1}(\overline{B}_{i,k})$ for $1 \leq k \leq d_i$ and $1 \leq i \leq s$. Then (4.10) is equivalent to

$$\boldsymbol{x}_n \in M := \prod_{i=1}^{s} \left[\frac{B_i}{b^{d_i}}, \frac{B_i + 1}{b^{d_i}} \right).$$

Now M is again an elementary interval of volume b^{t-m}. Since $\{\boldsymbol{x}_0, \ldots, \boldsymbol{x}_{b^m-1}\}$ forms a (t, m, s)-net in base b, it follows that M contains exactly b^t points of $\{\boldsymbol{x}_0, \ldots, \boldsymbol{x}_{b^m-1}\}$. Therefore, J contains exactly b^t points of $\{\boldsymbol{y}_0, \ldots, \boldsymbol{y}_{b^m-1}\}$ and hence, this point set is a (t, m, s)-net in base b.

If $t = 0$, then the $\boldsymbol{y}_n$, $0 \leq n < b^m$ form a strict net. If $t \geq 1$, then let

$$M := \prod_{i=1}^{s} \left[\frac{B_i}{b^{d_i}}, \frac{B_i + 1}{b^{d_i}} \right)$$

now be an elementary interval of order $m - t + 1$, such that M does not contain exactly b^{t-1} of the elements of the strict (t, m, s)-net $\{\boldsymbol{x}_0, \ldots, \boldsymbol{x}_{b^m-1}\}$. Let $B_i = \frac{B_{i,1}}{b} + \cdots + \frac{B_{i,d_i}}{b^{d_i}}$. Now defining in the opposite way $A_i = \frac{A_{i,1}}{b} + \cdots + \frac{A_{i,d_i}}{b^{d_i}}$ such that $\varphi(A_{i,k}) = \varphi(B_{i,k}) + \varphi(\varsigma_{i,k}) \in \mathbb{F}_b$ for $1 \leq k \leq d_i$ and $1 \leq i \leq s$, then as above

$$\boldsymbol{x}_n \in M \quad \text{if and only if} \quad \boldsymbol{x}_n \in J := \prod_{i=1}^{s} \left[\tfrac{A_i}{b^{d_i}}, \tfrac{A_i+1}{b^{d_i}} \right).$$

Therefore, the strictness of the net $\{\boldsymbol{y}_0, \ldots, \boldsymbol{y}_{b^m-1}\}$ follows. □

Remark 4.68 Note that for a given net the digital shift $\boldsymbol{\sigma} \in [0, 1)^s$ can be chosen such that the origin is not contained in the shifted version of the net any more. Hence, in general, the digitally shifted version of a digital net is not a digital net.

There are several variants of digital shifts. We introduce the so-called digital shift of depth m and a simplified digital shift for digital nets. Such shifts are used later in Chapter 16, when we show the existence of digital nets which achieve the best possible order of the L_2-discrepancy.

Definition 4.69 Let b be a prime power and let $\varphi : \{0, \ldots, b-1\} \to \mathbb{F}_b$ be a bijection with $\varphi(0) = \overline{0}$. Let $\mathcal{P}_{b^m} = \{x_0, \ldots, x_{b^m-1}\}$ be a digital $(t, m, 1)$-net over $\mathbb{F}_b$ and let

$$x_n = \frac{x_{n,1}}{b} + \frac{x_{n,2}}{b^2} + \cdots + \frac{x_{n,m}}{b^m}$$

be the b-adic digit expansion of x_n. Choose $\sigma = \frac{\varsigma_1}{b} + \cdots + \frac{\varsigma_m}{b^m}$ with $\varsigma_i \in \mathbb{F}_b$ and define

$$z_{n,i} := \varphi^{-1}(\varphi(x_{n,i}) + \varphi(\varsigma_i)) \qquad \text{for } 1 \leq i \leq m.$$

Further, for $0 \leq n < b^m$, choose $\delta_n \in [0, b^{-m})$. Then the digitally shifted point set $\widetilde{\mathcal{P}}_{b^m} = \{z_0, \ldots, z_{b^m-1}\}$ is defined by

$$z_n = \frac{z_{n,1}}{b} + \cdots + \frac{z_{n,m}}{b^m} + \delta_n.$$

Such a digital shift is called a *digital shift of depth m*.

For higher dimensions $s > 1$, each coordinate is shifted independently by a digital shift of depth m.

This means that one applies the same digital shift to the first m digits, whereas the following digits are shifted independently of each x_n. In other words, a digital shift of depth m is a combination of a digital shift $\boldsymbol{\sigma} = (\sigma_1, \ldots, \sigma_s)$ where the σ_i's are of the form $\sigma_i = \varsigma_{i,1}/b + \cdots + \varsigma_{i,m}/b^m$ with $\varsigma_{i,j} \in \mathbb{F}_b$ for $1 \leq j \leq m$ and $1 \leq i \leq s$, and a geometric shift as used in Lemma 4.63.

We also introduce a simplified version of a digital shift (of depth m).

Definition 4.70 With the notation from Definition 4.69 above, we define a digitally shifted point set $\widehat{\mathcal{P}}_{b^m} = \{z_0, \ldots, z_{b^m-1}\}$ by

$$z_n = \frac{z_{n,1}}{b} + \cdots + \frac{z_{n,m}}{b^m} + \frac{1}{2b^m}.$$

Such a shift is called a *simplified digital shift (of depth m)*.

For higher dimensions $s > 1$, each coordinate is shifted independently by a simplified digital shift. This means that we apply the same digital shift to the first m digits and then we add to each point the quantity $1/(2b^m)$.

Geometrically, the simplified digital shift of depth m means that the shifted points are no longer on the left boundary of elementary intervals of the form $\prod_{i=1}^{s}[A_i/b^m, (A_i+1)/b^m)$, but they are moved to the midpoints of such intervals. Note that for the simplified digital shift, we only have b^m possibilities, which means only sm digits need to be selected in performing a simplified digital shift. In comparison, the digital shift of depth m requires infinitely many digits.

It can be shown that a (strict) digital (t, m, s)-net over $\mathbb{F}_b$, which is shifted by a digital shift of depth m or a simplified digital shift independently in each coordinate, is again a (strict) (t, m, s)-net in base b with the same quality parameter t (with probability one in the case of a digital shift of depth m). See Exercise 4.9 and Exercise 4.10.

Example 4.71 Consider the eight elements of the digital $(0, 3, 2)$-net over $\mathbb{Z}_2$ shown in Figure 4.22(a) that are generated by

$$C_1 = \begin{pmatrix} 0 & 0 & 1 \\ 0 & 1 & 0 \\ 1 & 0 & 0 \end{pmatrix} \quad \text{and} \quad C_2 = \begin{pmatrix} 1 & 1 & 1 \\ 0 & 1 & 0 \\ 0 & 0 & 1 \end{pmatrix}.$$

Applying a 2-adic digital shift $\boldsymbol{\sigma} = (\sigma_1, \sigma_2)$ with $\sigma_1 = 1/2$ and $\sigma_2 = 7/8$ then gives, for example, $\boldsymbol{y}_3 = (y_{3,1}, y_{3,2})$, where

$$y_{3,1} \leftarrow \begin{pmatrix} 0 & 0 & 1 \\ 0 & 1 & 0 \\ 1 & 0 & 0 \end{pmatrix}\begin{pmatrix} 1 \\ 1 \\ 0 \end{pmatrix} + \begin{pmatrix} 1 \\ 0 \\ 0 \end{pmatrix} = \begin{pmatrix} 0 \\ 1 \\ 1 \end{pmatrix} + \begin{pmatrix} 1 \\ 0 \\ 0 \end{pmatrix} = \begin{pmatrix} 1 \\ 1 \\ 1 \end{pmatrix}$$

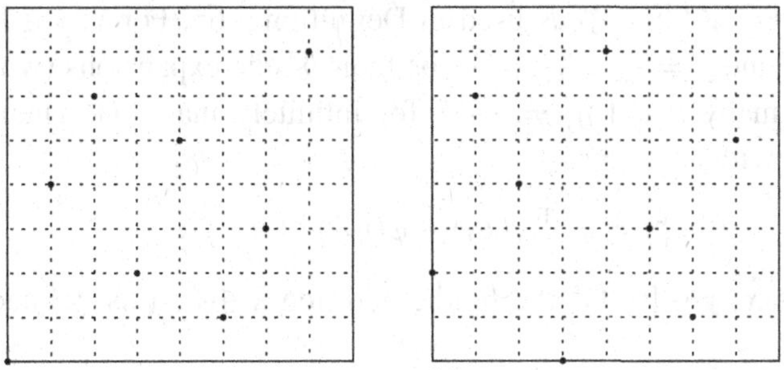

Figure 4.22 (a) A digital (0, 3, 2)-net over $\mathbb{Z}_2$ and (b) its digitally shifted version.

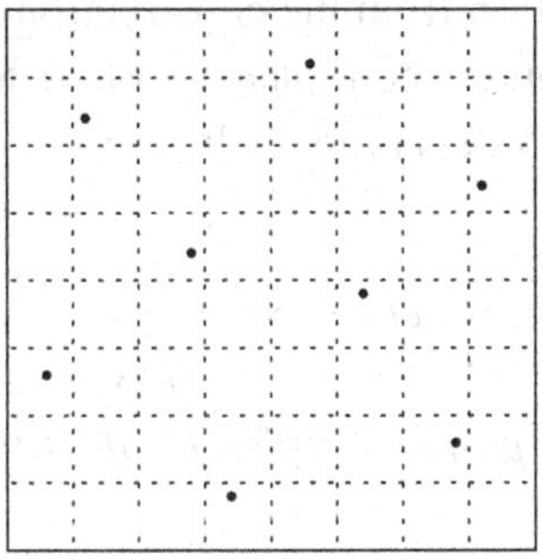

Figure 4.23 A digital shift of depth 3 applied to a digital (0, 3, 2)-net in base 2.

and

$$y_{3,2} \leftarrow \begin{pmatrix} 1 & 1 & 1 \\ 0 & 1 & 0 \\ 0 & 0 & 1 \end{pmatrix} \begin{pmatrix} 1 \\ 1 \\ 0 \end{pmatrix} + \begin{pmatrix} 1 \\ 1 \\ 1 \end{pmatrix} = \begin{pmatrix} 0 \\ 1 \\ 0 \end{pmatrix} + \begin{pmatrix} 1 \\ 1 \\ 1 \end{pmatrix} = \begin{pmatrix} 1 \\ 0 \\ 1 \end{pmatrix}$$

and hence $\boldsymbol{y}_3 = (7/8, 5/8)$.

We obtain the point set shown in Figure 4.22(b) that obviously cannot be obtained by the original digital net by an ordinary translation, and which is not a digital net any more (as it does not contain the origin).

Now let us disturb this point set in the 'positive direction' by individual quantities $\delta_{n,i}$ less than $1/8$ in each coordinate i for $0 \leq n < 8$ (that is, we have a digital shift of depth 3). Then we arrive, for example, at the point set shown in Figure 4.23 that is still a strict (0, 3, 2)-net in base 2.

A further very important structural property of digital nets is their group structure, which was first used by Larcher *et al.* [141].

Let b be a prime power and let $\varphi : \{0, \ldots, b-1\} \to \mathbb{F}_b$ be a bijection with $\varphi(0) = \overline{0}$. The s-dimensional unit-cube is an abelian group with respect to the digitwise b-adic addition $\oplus$ as used in Definition 4.65. For $x, y \in [0,1)$ let $x = \frac{\xi_1}{b} + \frac{\xi_2}{b^2} + \cdots$ and $y = \frac{\eta_1}{b} + \frac{\eta_2}{b^2} + \cdots$ be their b-adic expansions (with $\xi_i \neq b-1$ for infinitely many i and $\eta_j \neq b-1$ for infinitely many j). Then $x \oplus_{b,\varphi} y := \frac{\zeta_1}{b} + \frac{\zeta_2}{b^2} + \cdots$ with

$$\zeta_j = \varphi^{-1}(\varphi(\xi_j) + \varphi(\eta_j)) \quad \text{for} \quad j \in \mathbb{N}.$$

For vectors $\boldsymbol{x}, \boldsymbol{y} \in [0,1)^s$ the b-adic addition $\boldsymbol{x} \oplus_{b,\varphi} \boldsymbol{y}$ is defined component wise.

As before, the base b and the bijection φ are considered to be fixed and therefore we simply write $\oplus$ instead of $\oplus_{b,\varphi}$. If we use the b-adic addition $\oplus = \oplus_{b,\varphi}$ in conjunction with a digital net, then we always assume that b is the base of the digital net and φ is the bijection from the construction of the digital net.

Now we consider the natural continuation of $\oplus$ to $[0,1)^s$ which we denote again by $\oplus$. Obviously $([0,1)^s, \oplus)$ is an abelian group. We then have the following lemma.

Lemma 4.72 *Let b be a prime power and let $\varphi : \{0, \ldots, b-1\} \to \mathbb{F}_b$ be a bijection with $\varphi(0) = \overline{0}$. Any digital (t, m, s)-net over $\mathbb{F}_b$ is a subgroup of $([0,1)^s, \oplus)$. If the points of the digital net are pairwise different, then this subgroup is isomorphic to $\mathbb{F}_b^m$.*

Proof Any column vector

$$\mathbf{n} = \begin{pmatrix} \overline{n}_0 \\ \vdots \\ \overline{n}_{m-1} \end{pmatrix} \in (\mathbb{F}_b^m)^\top$$

uniquely represents an integer $n := n_0 + n_1 b + \cdots + n_{m-1} b^{m-1}$ from $\{0, \ldots, b^m - 1\}$ via $n_i = \varphi^{-1}(\overline{n}_i)$ for $0 \leq i < m$, and to any such integer belongs a net element $\boldsymbol{x}_n$.

We show that the mapping

$$\Psi : (\mathbb{F}_b^m)^\top \to \{\boldsymbol{x}_0, \ldots, \boldsymbol{x}_{b^m-1}\}, \ \mathbf{n} \mapsto \boldsymbol{x}_n$$

is a group-isomorphism from the additive group of $\mathbb{F}_b^m$ to $(\{\boldsymbol{x}_0, \ldots, \boldsymbol{x}_{b^m-1}\}, \oplus)$. Let

$$\mathbf{n} := \begin{pmatrix} \overline{n}_0 \\ \vdots \\ \overline{n}_{m-1} \end{pmatrix} \text{ and } \mathbf{l} := \begin{pmatrix} \overline{l}_0 \\ \vdots \\ \overline{l}_{m-1} \end{pmatrix}$$

be two elements from $(\mathbb{F}_b^m)^\top$. Then the property $\Psi(\mathbf{n} + \mathbf{l}) = \Psi(\mathbf{n}) \oplus \Psi(\mathbf{l})$ easily follows from the fact that for any $m \times m$ matrix C over $\mathbb{F}_b$, we have $C(\mathbf{n} + \mathbf{l}) = C\mathbf{n} + C\mathbf{l}$. If the points of the digital net are pairwise different, then the mapping

Ψ is surjective and therefore also injective, because $|\mathbb{F}_b^m| = |\{\boldsymbol{x}_0, \ldots, \boldsymbol{x}_{b^m-1}\}|$. The result follows. □

Remark 4.73 With the notation of the b-adic addition, we may interpret the digitally b-adic digital shifting of a digital net as a translation of the digital net with respect to $\oplus$ along a certain translation vector of $[0, 1)^s$. From the group structure of the digital net, it follows that a digital net remains unchanged by translation with respect to $\oplus$ if and only if the translation vector is an element of the digital net.

Example 4.74 In the shifting example above, the translation vector was given by $(1/2, 7/8)$ in $[0, 1)^2$. This point does not belong to the original digital net, so that the digitally shifted net is different from the original one.

For the following let b be a prime number and identify the finite field $\mathbb{F}_b$ with $\mathbb{Z}_b$. In this case we show how b-adic Walsh functions are linked to digital nets over $\mathbb{Z}_b$. This connection is very important for the analysis of the discrepancy of digital nets and of the worst-case error of QMC rules using digital nets in certain function spaces.

Let $\{\boldsymbol{x}_0, \ldots, \boldsymbol{x}_{b^m-1}\}$ be a digital (t, m, s)-net over $\mathbb{Z}_b$. By Corollary A.7, for all $\boldsymbol{k} \in \mathbb{N}_0^s$, we have

$$ {}_b\mathrm{wal}_{\boldsymbol{k}}(\boldsymbol{x}_h \oplus_b \boldsymbol{x}_i) = {}_b\mathrm{wal}_{\boldsymbol{k}}(\boldsymbol{x}_h)\, {}_b\mathrm{wal}_{\boldsymbol{k}}(\boldsymbol{x}_i) $$

and hence ${}_b\mathrm{wal}_{\boldsymbol{k}}$ is a character on the group $(\{\boldsymbol{x}_0, \ldots, \boldsymbol{x}_{b^m-1}\}, \oplus)$. Now we can prove the following very important character property of Walsh functions.

Lemma 4.75 *Let b be a prime and let $\{\boldsymbol{x}_0, \ldots, \boldsymbol{x}_{b^m-1}\}$ be a digital (t, m, s)-net over $\mathbb{Z}_b$ generated by the $m \times m$ matrices $C_1, \ldots, C_s$ over $\mathbb{Z}_b$. Then, for a $\boldsymbol{k} = (k_1, \ldots, k_s) \in \{0, \ldots, b^m - 1\}^s$, we have*

$$ \sum_{h=0}^{b^m-1} {}_b\mathrm{wal}_{\boldsymbol{k}}(\boldsymbol{x}_h) = \begin{cases} b^m & \text{if } C_1^\top \mathbf{k}_1 + \cdots + C_s^\top \mathbf{k}_s = \mathbf{0}, \\ 0 & \text{otherwise}, \end{cases} $$

where for $k \in \{0, \ldots, b^m - 1\}$ we denote by $\mathbf{k}$ the m-dimensional column vector of b-adic digits of k, i.e. $\mathbf{k} \in (\mathbb{Z}_b^m)^\top$, and $\mathbf{0}$ denotes the zero-vector in $(\mathbb{Z}_b^m)^\top$.

Proof Since ${}_b\mathrm{wal}_{\boldsymbol{k}}$ is a character, we obtain, by using Lemma 4.72, that

$$ \sum_{h=0}^{b^m-1} {}_b\mathrm{wal}_{\boldsymbol{k}}(\boldsymbol{x}_h) = \begin{cases} b^m & \text{if } {}_b\mathrm{wal}_{\boldsymbol{k}}(\boldsymbol{x}_h) = 1 \text{ for all } 0 \le h < b^m, \\ 0 & \text{otherwise.} \end{cases} $$

We have ${}_b\mathrm{wal}_{\boldsymbol{k}}(\boldsymbol{x}_h) = 1$ for all $0 \le h < b^m$ if and only if

$$\sum_{i=1}^{s} \mathbf{k}_i \cdot \mathbf{x}_{h,i} = 0 \text{ for all } 0 \le h < b^m,$$

where $\mathbf{k}_i$ is the m-dimensional column vector of b-adic digits of k_i and $\mathbf{x}_{h,i}$ denotes the m-dimensional column vector of b-adic digits of the ith component of $\boldsymbol{x}_h$. From the construction of the digital net, we find that $\mathbf{x}_{h,i} = C_i\mathbf{h}$ and hence ${}_b\mathrm{wal}_{\boldsymbol{k}}(\boldsymbol{x}_h) = 1$ for all $0 \le h < b^m$ if and only if

$$\sum_{i=1}^{s} \mathbf{k}_i \cdot C_i\mathbf{h} = 0 \text{ for all } 0 \le h < b^m,$$

where $\mathbf{h}$ denotes the column vector of b-adic digits of h. This is satisfied if and only if

$$C_1^\top \mathbf{k}_1 + \cdots + C_s^\top \mathbf{k}_s = \mathbf{0}.$$ □

A generalisation of Lemma 4.75 to the case of digital nets over $\mathbb{F}_b$ with prime power b can be found in [221, Lemma 2.5]. In this case, one requires the more general concept of Walsh functions over the finite field $\mathbb{F}_b$.

Following from Lemma 4.75, we introduce the notion of a so-called dual net, which is, in this form, due to Niederreiter and Pirsic [189].

Definition 4.76 Let b be a prime. For a digital net with generating matrices $C_1, \ldots, C_s$ over $\mathbb{Z}_b$, we call the matrix $C = (C_1^\top | \ldots | C_s^\top) \in \mathbb{Z}_b^{m \times sm}$ the *overall generating matrix* of the digital net. The corresponding *dual net* is defined by

$$\mathcal{D} = \mathcal{D}(C_1, \ldots, C_s) := \{\boldsymbol{k} \in \{0, \ldots, b^m - 1\}^s : C_1^\top \mathbf{k}_1 + \cdots + C_s^\top \mathbf{k}_s = \mathbf{0}\},$$

where $\boldsymbol{k} = (k_1, \ldots, k_s)$ and for $1 \le i \le s$ we denote by $\mathbf{k}_i$ the m-dimensional column vector of b-adic digits of $k_i \in \{0, \ldots, b^m - 1\}$. Furthermore, let

$$\mathcal{D}' = \mathcal{D}'(C_1, \ldots, C_s) := \mathcal{D} \setminus \{\mathbf{0}\}.$$

Remark 4.77 Sometimes, we also use the definition

$$\begin{aligned}\mathcal{D}_\infty = \mathcal{D}_\infty(C_1, \ldots, C_s) &:= \{\boldsymbol{k} \in \mathbb{N}_0^s : \mathrm{tr}_m(\boldsymbol{k}) \in \mathcal{D}(C_1, \ldots, C_s)\} \\ &= \{\boldsymbol{k} \in \mathbb{N}_0^s : C_1^\top \mathrm{tr}_m(\mathbf{k}_1) + \cdots + C_s^\top \mathrm{tr}_m(\mathbf{k}_s) = \mathbf{0}\},\end{aligned}$$

where for $k \in \mathbb{N}_0$ with b-adic expansion $k = \sum_{j \ge 0} \kappa_j b^j$ we write $\mathrm{tr}_m(k) = \kappa_0 + \kappa_1 b + \cdots + \kappa_{m-1} b^{m-1}$ and $\mathrm{tr}_m(\mathbf{k}) := (\kappa_0, \ldots, \kappa_{m-1})^\top \in (\mathbb{Z}_b^m)^\top$ and for $\boldsymbol{k} = (k_1, \ldots, k_s)$ we write $\mathrm{tr}_m(\boldsymbol{k}) = (\mathrm{tr}_m(k_1), \ldots, \mathrm{tr}_m(k_s)) \in \{0, \ldots, b^m - 1\}^s$. Again we speak of the *dual net*.

Duality for digital nets was first introduced and studied by Niederreiter and Pirsic [189] and, in a more specialised setting, by Skriganov [243]; see also [22]. Our definition of a dual net here corresponds to the definitions given in [189]. We are concerned with duality theory for digital nets in more detail in Chapter 7.

4.4.5 Digital (t, s)- and $(\mathbf{T}, s)$-sequences

To construct a digital $(\mathbf{T}, s)$-sequence in prime power base b, we again use a finite field $\mathbb{F}_b$ and a bijection $\varphi : \{0, \ldots, b-1\} \to \mathbb{F}_b$ with $\varphi(0) = \overline{0}$, and we speak then of a 'digital $(\mathbf{T}, s)$-sequence over $\mathbb{F}_b$'. (Again, for arbitrary b, one has to choose a finite commutative ring R with identity of order b; see [137, 141, 177] for more information.) If b is a prime, we identify $\mathbb{F}_b$ with $\mathbb{Z}_b$ and we omit the bijection φ and the bar.

Now let b be a prime power. To generate a digital $(\mathbf{T}, s)$-sequence over $\mathbb{F}_b$, we first have to choose $\mathbb{N} \times \mathbb{N}$ matrices $C_1, \ldots, C_s$ (one for each component) over $\mathbb{F}_b$; that is, matrices of the form

$$C = \begin{pmatrix} c_{11} & c_{12} & c_{13} & \cdots \\ c_{21} & c_{22} & c_{23} & \cdots \\ c_{31} & c_{32} & c_{33} & \cdots \\ \vdots & \vdots & \vdots & \ddots \end{pmatrix} \in \mathbb{F}_b^{\mathbb{N} \times \mathbb{N}}.$$

Example 4.78 For example, to generate a $(\mathbf{T}, 2)$-sequence over $\mathbb{Z}_2$, take the matrices

$$C_1 = \begin{pmatrix} 1 & 0 & 0 & 0 & \cdots \\ 0 & 1 & 0 & 0 & \cdots \\ 0 & 0 & 1 & 0 & \cdots \\ 0 & 0 & 0 & 1 & \cdots \\ \vdots & \vdots & \vdots & \vdots & \ddots \end{pmatrix} \in \mathbb{Z}_2^{\mathbb{N} \times \mathbb{N}}$$

and

$$C_2 = \begin{pmatrix} \binom{0}{0} & \binom{1}{0} & \binom{2}{0} & \binom{3}{0} & \cdots \\ 0 & \binom{1}{1} & \binom{2}{1} & \binom{3}{1} & \cdots \\ 0 & 0 & \binom{2}{2} & \binom{3}{2} & \cdots \\ 0 & 0 & 0 & \binom{3}{3} & \cdots \\ \vdots & \vdots & \ddots & \ddots & \ddots \\ \vdots & \vdots & & \ddots & \ddots \end{pmatrix} = \begin{pmatrix} 1 & 1 & 1 & 1 & 1 & \cdots \\ 0 & 1 & 0 & 1 & 0 & \cdots \\ 0 & 0 & 1 & 1 & 0 & \cdots \\ 0 & 0 & 0 & 1 & 0 & \cdots \\ 0 & 0 & 0 & 0 & 1 & \cdots \\ \vdots & \vdots & & \ddots & \ddots & \ddots \end{pmatrix} \in \mathbb{Z}_2^{\mathbb{N} \times \mathbb{N}},$$

where the binomial coefficients are taken modulo 2.

To now generate one of the points $\boldsymbol{x}_n = (x_{n,1}, \ldots, x_{n,s})$, with $n \in \mathbb{N}_0$, of the $(\mathbf{T}, s)$-sequence, we first write n in its b-adic (i.e. base b) expansion $n = \sum_{i=0}^{\infty} a_i b^i$ with $a_i \in \{0, \ldots, b-1\}$ and $a_i = 0$ for all i large enough. Then take the column vector

$$\mathbf{n} = \begin{pmatrix} \varphi(a_0) \\ \varphi(a_1) \\ \varphi(a_2) \\ \vdots \end{pmatrix} \in (\mathbb{F}_b^{\mathbb{N}})^\top.$$

For example, to generate the point $\boldsymbol{x}_{13} = (x_{13,1}, x_{13,2})$ of a $(\mathbf{T}, s)$-sequence over $\mathbb{Z}_2$, write

$$n = 13 = 1 \cdot 2^0 + 0 \cdot 2^1 + 1 \cdot 2^2 + 1 \cdot 2^3 + 0 \cdot 2^4 + \cdots$$

This corresponds to the vector

$$\mathbf{n} = \begin{pmatrix} 1 \\ 0 \\ 1 \\ 1 \\ 0 \\ 0 \\ \vdots \end{pmatrix}.$$

To generate the point $\boldsymbol{x}_n = (x_{n,1}, \ldots, x_{n,s})$, we explain how to generate the ith coordinate $x_{n,i}$. The value of $x_{n,i}$ is obtained by multiplying the ith matrix C_i by $\mathbf{n}$ in $\mathbb{F}_b^m$, which gives as result a column vector over $\mathbb{F}_b$, say

$$C_i \mathbf{n} = \begin{pmatrix} \overline{y}_{n,i,1} \\ \overline{y}_{n,i,2} \\ \vdots \end{pmatrix} \in (\mathbb{F}_b^{\mathbb{N}})^\top.$$

(Note that for the multiplication, only finitely many entries of $\mathbf{n}$ are different from zero, as we assumed that $\varphi(0) = \overline{0}$.) The elements $\varphi^{-1}(\overline{y}_{n,i,j}) \in \{0, \ldots, b-1\}$, for $j \in \mathbb{N}$, are now the b-adic digits of $x_{n,i}$, i.e.

$$x_{n,i} = \frac{\varphi^{-1}(\overline{y}_{n,i,1})}{b} + \frac{\varphi^{-1}(\overline{y}_{n,i,2})}{b^2} + \cdots.$$

Definition 4.79 We call the sequence $(\boldsymbol{x}_0, \boldsymbol{x}_1, \ldots)$ constructed in this way a *digital sequence over* $\mathbb{F}_b$ *with generating matrices* $C_1, \ldots, C_s$, or for short, a *digital sequence*.

Since any sequence in $[0, 1)^s$ is a $(\mathbf{T}, s)$-sequence in base b with a certain quality function $\mathbf{T}$ (at least for $\mathbf{T}(m) = m$) we also speak of a *digital* $(\mathbf{T}, s)$*-sequence over* $\mathbb{F}_b$.

Example 4.80 In Example 4.78, for $n = 13$, we have

$$C_1\mathbf{n} = \begin{pmatrix} 1 & 0 & 0 & 0 & 0 & 0 & \dots \\ 0 & 1 & 0 & 0 & 0 & 0 & \dots \\ 0 & 0 & 1 & 0 & 0 & 0 & \dots \\ 0 & 0 & 0 & 1 & 0 & 0 & \dots \\ 0 & 0 & 0 & 0 & 1 & 0 & \dots \\ 0 & 0 & 0 & 0 & 0 & 1 & \dots \\ \vdots & \vdots & \vdots & \vdots & \vdots & \vdots & \ddots \end{pmatrix} \begin{pmatrix} 1 \\ 0 \\ 1 \\ 1 \\ 0 \\ 0 \\ \vdots \end{pmatrix} = \begin{pmatrix} 1 \\ 0 \\ 1 \\ 1 \\ 0 \\ 0 \\ \vdots \end{pmatrix}$$

$$C_2\mathbf{n} = \begin{pmatrix} 1 & 1 & 1 & 1 & 1 & 1 & \dots \\ 0 & 1 & 0 & 1 & 0 & 1 & \dots \\ 0 & 0 & 1 & 1 & 0 & 0 & \dots \\ 0 & 0 & 0 & 1 & 0 & 0 & \dots \\ 0 & 0 & 0 & 0 & 1 & 1 & \dots \\ 0 & 0 & 0 & 0 & 0 & 1 & \dots \\ \vdots & \vdots & \vdots & \vdots & \vdots & \vdots & \ddots \end{pmatrix} \begin{pmatrix} 1 \\ 0 \\ 1 \\ 1 \\ 0 \\ 0 \\ \vdots \end{pmatrix} = \begin{pmatrix} 1 \\ 1 \\ 0 \\ 1 \\ 0 \\ 0 \\ \vdots \end{pmatrix},$$

which yields $x_{13,1} = \frac{1}{2} + \frac{1}{8} + \frac{1}{16} = \frac{11}{16}$, $x_{13,2} = \frac{1}{2} + \frac{1}{4} + \frac{1}{16} = \frac{13}{16}$, and hence $\boldsymbol{x}_{13} = \left(\frac{11}{16}, \frac{13}{16}\right)$.

Remark 4.81 Depending on the matrices $C_1, \dots, C_s$, it may happen that the vector $C_i\mathbf{n} =: \mathbf{y}_n$ contains infinitely many entries different from zero. For practical purposes this requires an adaptation of the point generation. Usually, the vector $\mathbf{y}_n$ is truncated at a suitable place.

Further, another theoretical problem may arise. That the vector $\mathbf{y}_n$ contains only finitely many elements different from $\varphi(b - 1)$ should be avoided. Because of the non-uniqueness of representation of the b-adic real numbers represented by such 'digit vectors', the net structure of the sequence in consideration would be destroyed. This does not happen for matrices as in the example above, but it may happen for other choices of matrices. This is the reason for the following additional condition on the matrices $C_1, \dots, C_s$. Let

$$C_i = (c_{j,r}^{(i)})_{j,r\in\mathbb{N}} \in \mathbb{F}_b^{\mathbb{N}\times\mathbb{N}}$$

for $1 \le i \le s$. We demand that for all i and r, we have $c_{j,r}^{(i)} = 0$ for all j large enough.

4.4.6 The quality function of digital sequences

As already mentioned, every sequence in $[0, 1)^s$ is a $(\mathbf{T}, s)$-sequence in base b, with $\mathbf{T}(m) = m$. Therefore, we may ask: what is the strict quality function of the above $(\mathbf{T}, s)$-sequence in base b? The answer is given with the help of the following quantity ρ_m, which in some sense 'measures' the 'linear independence' of the s infinite matrices $C_1, \ldots, C_s$.

Definition 4.82 Let $C_1, \ldots, C_s$ be $\mathbb{N} \times \mathbb{N}$ matrices over the finite field $\mathbb{F}_b$. For any integers $1 \le i \le s$ and $m \ge 1$ by $C_i^{(m)}$ we denote the left upper $m \times m$ sub-matrix of C_i. Then

$$\rho_m = \rho_m(C_1, \ldots, C_s) := \rho(C_1^{(m)}, \ldots, C_s^{(m)}),$$

where ρ is the linear independence parameter defined for s-tuples of $m \times m$ matrices over $\mathbb{F}_b$ in Definition 4.50.

Example 4.83 In Example 4.78 above, for every $m \ge 1$ the matrices $C_1^{(m)}$ and $C_2^{(m)}$ are just the first and the third matrices of Example 4.57. For these matrices the value of ρ always equals m. Hence, $\rho_m(C_1, C_2) = m$ for all $m \in \mathbb{N}$.

Now we can determine the strict quality function $\mathbf{T}$ of a digital sequence over $\mathbb{F}_b$. The proof of the following theorem gives some additional insight into the structure of a digital $(\mathbf{T}, s)$-sequence.

Theorem 4.84 *Let b be a prime power and let $\varphi : \{0, \ldots, b-1\} \to \mathbb{F}_b$ be a bijection with $\varphi(0) = \overline{0}$. The sequence $(\boldsymbol{x}_0, \boldsymbol{x}_1, \ldots)$ constructed by the digital method with the $\mathbb{N} \times \mathbb{N}$ matrices $C_1, \ldots, C_s$ over $\mathbb{F}_b$ is a strict $(\mathbf{T}, s)$-sequence in base b with $\mathbf{T}(m) = m - \rho_m$ for all $m \in \mathbb{N}$, where ρ_m is the quantity defined in Definition 4.82.*

Proof By the definition of a $(\mathbf{T}, s)$-sequence, we have to show that for any $m \in \mathbb{N}$ and any $k \in \mathbb{N}_0$, the point set

$$\{\boldsymbol{x}_{kb^m}, \ldots, \boldsymbol{x}_{kb^m+b^m-1}\}$$

is a strict $(\mathbf{T}(m), m, s)$-net in base b. (In fact, it suffices to show the strictness for at least one of these blocks.) Indeed, for given k and m, and any l between 0 and $b^m - 1$, let $k = \kappa_{r+1}b^r + \cdots + \kappa_1$ and $l = \lambda_{m-1}b^{m-1} + \cdots + \lambda_0$ be the base b representations of k and l. For $n = kb^m + l$, we have

$$\mathbf{n} = (\varphi(\lambda_0), \ldots, \varphi(\lambda_{m-1}), \varphi(\kappa_1), \ldots, \varphi(\kappa_{r+1}), \ldots)^\top \in (\mathbb{F}_b^{\mathbb{N}})^\top$$

and with the following representation of the matrices C_i,

$$C_i = \left(\begin{array}{c|c} C_i^{(m)} & D_i^{(m)} \\ \hline \multicolumn{2}{c}{F_i^{(m)}} \end{array}\right) \in \mathbb{F}_b^{\mathbb{N}\times\mathbb{N}},$$

we have

$$C_i\mathbf{n} = \begin{pmatrix} C_i^{(m)} \begin{pmatrix} \varphi(\lambda_0) \\ \vdots \\ \varphi(\lambda_{m-1}) \end{pmatrix} \\ \overline{0} \\ \overline{0} \\ \vdots \end{pmatrix} + \begin{pmatrix} D_i^{(m)} \begin{pmatrix} \varphi(\kappa_1) \\ \vdots \\ \varphi(\kappa_{r+1}) \\ \overline{0} \\ \vdots \end{pmatrix} \\ \overline{0} \\ \overline{0} \\ \vdots \end{pmatrix} + \begin{pmatrix} \overline{0} \\ \vdots \\ \overline{0} \\ F_i^{(m)}\mathbf{n} \end{pmatrix}.$$

Now we invoke Lemma 4.63 and Lemma 4.67 from Section 4.4.1. For the point set under consideration, the vector

$$\begin{pmatrix} D_i^{(m)} \begin{pmatrix} \varphi(\kappa_1) \\ \vdots \\ \varphi(\kappa_{r+1}) \\ \overline{0} \\ \vdots \end{pmatrix} \\ \overline{0} \\ \overline{0} \\ \vdots \end{pmatrix}$$

is constant. The term

$$\begin{pmatrix} \overline{0} \\ \vdots \\ \overline{0} \\ F_i^{(m)}\mathbf{n} \end{pmatrix}$$

increases the value of each coordinate of the point $\boldsymbol{x}_n$ by a value less than b^{-m} (here we use the additional condition in the definition of digital sequences). Therefore, the point set

$$\{\boldsymbol{x}_{kb^m}, \ldots, \boldsymbol{x}_{kb^m+b^m-1}\}$$

is the digital net over $\mathbb{F}_b$ generated by the matrices $C_1^{(m)}, \ldots, C_s^{(m)}$, which is shifted by a digital shift of depth m. Hence, by Lemmas 4.52, 4.63 and 4.67, this point set is a strict (t, m, s)-net in base b with quality parameter t equal to the quality parameter of the digital net over $\mathbb{F}_b$ generated by the matrices $C_1^{(m)}, \ldots, C_s^{(m)}$. This parameter, by Lemma 4.52 and Definition 4.82, is $m - \rho_m$ and the result follows. □

Example 4.85 According to Example 4.83 and Theorem 4.84, the digital sequence from Example 4.78 provides a digital $(0, 2)$-sequence over $\mathbb{Z}_2$.

4.4.7 Distribution properties of digital sequences

Concerning the uniform distribution of a strict digital $(\mathbf{T}, s)$-sequence over $\mathbb{F}_b$, by Theorem 4.32 in Section 4.3, we again have that it is uniformly distributed if $\lim_{m\to\infty} m - \mathbf{T}(m) = \infty$. In contrast to the general case, however, for digital $(\mathbf{T}, s)$-sequences, this condition can be shown to be a necessary and sufficient one.

Theorem 4.86 *Let b be a prime power. A strict digital $(\mathbf{T}, s)$-sequence over $\mathbb{F}_b$ is uniformly distributed modulo one, if and only if*

$$\lim_{m\to\infty} m - \mathbf{T}(m) = \infty.$$

For the proof of this result, we need the following lemma.

Lemma 4.87 *Let b be a prime power. For integers $m \geq 1$ and t with $0 \leq t < m$, let $\mathbf{c}_1, \ldots, \mathbf{c}_{m-t} \in \mathbb{F}_b^m$ be given. Let L be the number of solutions of the system of linear equations $\mathbf{c}_j\mathbf{z} = 0$ for $1 \leq j \leq m - t$ in unknowns $\mathbf{z} \in (\mathbb{F}_b^m)^\top$. Then b^t divides L.*

Proof Let us consider the additive group of $(\mathbb{F}_b^{m-t})^\top$ and denote it by G. Let $\widehat{G}$ denote the dual group of characters χ of G. Let $\mathbf{c}_j := (c_{j,1}, \ldots, c_{j,m}) \in \mathbb{F}_b^m$ and

$$\mathbf{a}_i := \begin{pmatrix} c_{1,i} \\ \vdots \\ c_{m-t,i} \end{pmatrix} \in (\mathbb{F}_b^{m-t})^\top$$

for $1 \leq i \leq m$. Let H be the subgroup

$$H = \{z_1\mathbf{a}_1 + \cdots + z_m\mathbf{a}_m \;:\; z_1, \ldots, z_m \in \mathbb{F}_b\}$$

in G.

A character $\chi \in \widehat{G}$ is trivial on H if and only if it is trivial on all of the groups $H_i := \{z\mathbf{a}_i \, : \, z \in \mathbb{F}_b\}$.

We have

$$\begin{aligned} L &= \sum_{\substack{z \in (\mathbb{F}_b^m)^\top \\ \mathbf{c}_j z = 0 \\ \forall j \in \{1,\ldots,m-t\}}} 1 \\ &= \sum_{\mathbf{z} \in (\mathbb{F}_b^m)^\top} \frac{1}{b^{m-t}} \sum_{\chi \in \widehat{G}} \chi \begin{pmatrix} \mathbf{c}_1 \mathbf{z} \\ \vdots \\ \mathbf{c}_{m-t} \mathbf{z} \end{pmatrix} \\ &= \frac{1}{b^{m-t}} \sum_{\chi \in \widehat{G}} \sum_{\mathbf{z} \in (\mathbb{F}_b^m)^\top} \chi \begin{pmatrix} \mathbf{c}_1 \mathbf{z} \\ \vdots \\ \mathbf{c}_{m-t} \mathbf{z} \end{pmatrix} \\ &= \frac{1}{b^{m-t}} \sum_{\chi \in \widehat{G}} \prod_{i=1}^{m} \sum_{z_i \in \mathbb{F}_b} \chi(z_i \mathbf{a}_i). \end{aligned}$$

Now

$$\sum_{z_i \in \mathbb{F}_b} \chi(z_i \mathbf{a}_i) = \begin{cases} b & \text{if } \chi \text{ is trivial on } H_i, \\ 0 & \text{otherwise,} \end{cases}$$

thus,

$$\prod_{i=1}^{m} \sum_{z_i \in \mathbb{F}_b} \chi(z_i \mathbf{a}_i) = \begin{cases} b^m & \text{if } \chi \text{ is trivial on } H, \\ 0 & \text{otherwise.} \end{cases}$$

Consequently,

$$L = \frac{1}{b^{m-t}} \sum_{\substack{\chi \in \widehat{G} \\ \chi \text{ trivial on } H}} b^m = b^t \, |\{\chi \in \widehat{G} \, : \, \chi \text{ trivial on } H\}|$$

and hence, b^t divides L. □

Proof of Theorem 4.86 By Theorem 4.32 it suffices to show that the digital sequence $\mathcal{S} = (\boldsymbol{x}_0, \boldsymbol{x}_1, \ldots)$ is not uniformly distributed if $m - \mathbf{T}(m)$ does not tend to infinity. Since $m - \mathbf{T}(m)$ is non-decreasing, this means $m - \mathbf{T}(m) = \kappa$ for some integer $\kappa \geq 0$ and all $m \geq m_0$, for some integer $m_0 \geq 0$. Hence, for all $m \geq m_0$, the point set $\{\boldsymbol{x}_0, \ldots, \boldsymbol{x}_{b^m-1}\}$ is a strict $(m-\kappa, m, s)$-net in base b, in particular, it is never a $(m-\kappa-1, m, s)$-net in base b. Assume that $\mathcal{S}$ is generated by the $\mathbb{N} \times \mathbb{N}$ matrices $C_1, \ldots, C_s$. Let $\mathbf{c}_j^{(i)}$ be the jth row vector of the ith matrix and for $m \in \mathbb{N}$, let $\pi_m(\mathbf{c}_j^{(i)})$ be the vector from $\mathbb{F}_b^m$ consisting of the first m components of $\mathbf{c}_j^{(i)}$.

Hence, there are integers $d_1, \ldots, d_s \geq 0$, which may depend on m, i.e. $d_i = d_i(m)$, with $d_1 + \cdots + d_s = \kappa + 1$ and elements $\overline{e}_j^{(i)} \in \mathbb{F}_b$, $1 \leq j \leq d_i$ and $1 \leq i \leq s$ such that the system

$$\pi_m(\mathbf{c}_j^{(i)})\mathbf{n} = \overline{e}_j^{(i)} \text{ for } 1 \leq j \leq d_i \text{ and } 1 \leq i \leq s$$

has $L \neq b^{m-\kappa-1}$ solutions $\mathbf{n} \in (\mathbb{F}_b^m)^\top$ (see Lemma 4.59 and the proof of Theorem 4.84). Hence, the corresponding homogeneous system of equations

$$\pi_m(\mathbf{c}_j^{(i)})\mathbf{n} = \overline{0} \text{ for } 1 \leq j \leq d_i \text{ and } 1 \leq i \leq s$$

has more than $b^{m-\kappa-1}$ solutions; indeed, by Lemma 4.87, at least $2b^{m-\kappa-1}$ solutions. Therefore, the box

$$J = J(m) = \prod_{i=1}^{s} \left[0, \frac{1}{b^{d_i}}\right)$$

of volume $b^{-\kappa-1}$ contains at least $2b^{m-\kappa-1}$ points (see again the proof of Theorem 4.84). As there is only a finite number of boxes $J(m)$, there is one box, say J^*, such that for infinitely many $m \geq m_0$, we have $J(m) = J^*$. Therefore, we obtain

$$\left| \frac{A(J^*, b^m, \mathcal{S})}{b^m} - \lambda_s(J^*) \right| \geq \frac{1}{b^{\kappa+1}}$$

for infinitely many $m \geq m_0$. Thus, $\mathcal{S} = (\boldsymbol{x}_0, \boldsymbol{x}_1, \ldots)$ is not uniformly distributed modulo one. □

Corollary 4.88 *Let b be a prime power. The $\mathbb{N} \times \mathbb{N}$ matrices $C_1, \ldots, C_s$ over $\mathbb{F}_b$ generate a uniformly distributed sequence in $[0, 1)^s$ if and only if*

$$\lim_{m \to \infty} \rho_m = \infty,$$

where $\rho_m = \rho(C_1^{(m)}, \ldots, C_s^{(m)})$ is the independence quantity defined in Definition 4.82.

Proof This follows from Theorem 4.84 and from Theorem 4.86. □

Remark 4.89 From the above result and from Theorem 4.34, it also follows that a strict digital $(\mathbf{T}, s)$-sequence over $\mathbb{F}_b$ is even well distributed if and only if $\lim_{m\to\infty} m - \mathbf{T}(m) = \infty$.

4.4.8 Propagation rules for digital sequences

For digital $(\mathbf{T}, s)$-sequences, we have the following simple propagation rules:

1. Any digital $(\mathbf{T}, s)$-sequence over $\mathbb{F}_b$ is a digital $(\mathbf{U}, s)$-sequence over $\mathbb{F}_b$ for all $\mathbf{U}$ with $\mathbf{U}(m) \geq \mathbf{T}(m)$ for all m.
2. If the matrices $C_1, \ldots, C_s$ generate a digital $(\mathbf{T}, s)$-sequence over $\mathbb{F}_b$ and if we take any s' (where $s' \leq s$) of these matrices, then these matrices generate a digital $(\mathbf{T}, s')$-sequence over $\mathbb{F}_b$.

4.4.9 Structural results for digital sequences

Note that there is no analogue to Lemma 4.63 for digital $(\mathbf{T}, s)$-sequences over $\mathbb{F}_b$. In general, common addition of a fixed (even very 'small') constant vector can disturb the $(\mathbf{T}, s)$-sequence property (i.e. can destroy its quality). However, digitally shifting using $\oplus_{b,\varphi}$ from Definition 4.65 is possible.

Definition 4.90 Let b be a prime power and let $\varphi : \{0, \ldots, b-1\} \to \mathbb{F}_b$ be a bijection with $\varphi(0) = \overline{0}$. For a sequence $\mathcal{S} = (\boldsymbol{x}_0, \boldsymbol{x}_1, \ldots)$ in $[0, 1)^s$ and a $\boldsymbol{\sigma} \in [0, 1)^s$, the sequence $\mathcal{S}_{\boldsymbol{\sigma}} = (\boldsymbol{x}_0 \oplus \boldsymbol{\sigma}, \boldsymbol{x}_1 \oplus \boldsymbol{\sigma}, \ldots\}$ is called the (b-adic) *digitally shifted sequence* $\mathcal{S}$, or the (b-adic) *digitally shifted version of* $\mathcal{S}$. The vector $\boldsymbol{\sigma} \in [0, 1)^s$ is called a (b-adic) *digital shift*.

If we use a digital shift in conjunction with a $(\mathbf{T}, s)$-sequence, then they are always considered to be in the same base b and with the same bijection φ. Therefore, if it is clear with respect to which base b a point is shifted, we may omit the phrase 'b-adic'.

We show that a digital shift preserves the $(\mathbf{T}, s)$-sequence structure.

Lemma 4.91 *Let b be a prime power and let $\varphi : \{0, \ldots, b-1\} \to \mathbb{F}_b$ be a bijection with $\varphi(0) = \overline{0}$. Let $\mathcal{S} = (\boldsymbol{x}_0, \boldsymbol{x}_1, \ldots)$ be a (strict) digital $(\mathbf{T}, s)$-sequence over $\mathbb{F}_b$ and let $\boldsymbol{\sigma} \in [0, 1)^s$. Then the digitally shifted sequence $\mathcal{S}_{\boldsymbol{\sigma}} = (\boldsymbol{y}_0, \boldsymbol{y}_1, \ldots)$ is a (strict) $(\mathbf{T}, s)$-sequence in base b.*

Remark 4.92 For $\boldsymbol{\sigma} = (\sigma_1, \ldots, \sigma_s) \in [0, 1)^s$ it should be avoided that the σ_i, $1 \leq i \leq s$, contain only finitely many b-adic digits different from $\varphi^{-1}(b-1)$ (see also Remark 4.81).

Proof of Lemma 4.91 We use the notation of the proof of Theorem 4.84. For $1 \leq i \leq s$ and $\sigma_i = \frac{\varsigma_{i,1}}{b} + \frac{\varsigma_{i,2}}{b^2} + \cdots$ with $\varsigma_{i,k} \in \{0, \ldots, b-1\}$ for $k \geq 1$, let $\boldsymbol{\sigma}_i := (\varphi(\varsigma_{i,1}), \varphi(\varsigma_{i,2}), \ldots)^\top \in (\mathbb{F}_b^{\mathbb{N}})^\top$.

The sub-sequence

$$\{\boldsymbol{y}_{kb^m}, \ldots, \boldsymbol{y}_{kb^m+b^m-1}\}$$

is obtained by calculating, for

$$\mathbf{n} = (\varphi(\lambda_0), \ldots, \varphi(\lambda_{m-1}), \varphi(\kappa_1), \ldots, \varphi(\kappa_{r+1}), \overline{0}, \ldots)^\top \in (\mathbb{F}_b^{\mathbb{N}})^\top,$$

the shifted vector

$$C_i\mathbf{n} + \boldsymbol{\sigma}_i = \begin{pmatrix} C_i^{(m)} \begin{pmatrix} \varphi(\lambda_0) \\ \vdots \\ \varphi(\lambda_{m-1}) \end{pmatrix} \\ \overline{0} \\ \overline{0} \\ \vdots \end{pmatrix} + \begin{pmatrix} \varphi(\varsigma_{i,1}) \\ \vdots \\ \varphi(\varsigma_{i,m}) \\ \overline{0} \\ \vdots \end{pmatrix}$$

$$+ \begin{pmatrix} D_i^{(m)} \begin{pmatrix} \varphi(\kappa_1) \\ \vdots \\ \varphi(\kappa_{r+1}) \\ \overline{0} \\ \vdots \\ \overline{0} \end{pmatrix} \\ \overline{0} \\ \vdots \end{pmatrix} + \begin{pmatrix} \overline{0} \\ \vdots \\ \overline{0} \\ F_i^{(m)}\mathbf{n} + \begin{pmatrix} \varphi(\varsigma_{i,m+1}) \\ \varphi(\varsigma_{i,m+2}) \\ \vdots \end{pmatrix} \end{pmatrix}.$$

Using Lemma 4.63 and Lemma 4.67, this yields a (strict) $(\mathbf{T}(m), m, s)$-net in base b and the result follows. □

Like digital (t, m, s)-nets over $\mathbb{F}_b$, also digital $(\mathbf{T}, s)$-sequences over $\mathbb{F}_b$ have a group structure. Recall that $([0, 1)^s, \oplus)$ is an abelian group.

Theorem 4.93 *Let b be a prime power and let $\varphi : \{0, \ldots, b-1\} \to \mathbb{F}_b$ be a bijection with $\varphi(0) = \overline{0}$. Any digital $(\mathbf{T}, s)$-sequence over $\mathbb{F}_b$ is a subgroup of $([0, 1)^s, \oplus)$. If the points of the digital sequence are pairwise different, then this subgroup is isomorphic to the additive group $\widetilde{\mathbb{F}}_b^{\mathbb{N}} := \{(g_1, g_2, \ldots) \in \mathbb{F}_b^{\mathbb{N}} : g_i = \overline{0}$ for almost all $i \in \mathbb{N}\}$.*

Proof Any non-negative integer n is uniquely represented by a vector

$$\mathbf{n} = \begin{pmatrix} \overline{n}_0 \\ \overline{n}_1 \\ \vdots \end{pmatrix} \in (\widetilde{\mathbb{F}}_b^{\mathbb{N}})^\top,$$

where $n := n_0 + n_1 b + \cdots$ via $n_i = \varphi^{-1}(\overline{n}_i)$, and to any such integer belongs an element $\boldsymbol{x}_n$ of the digital sequence. This also holds the other way round; namely, to any point $\boldsymbol{x}_n$ from the digital sequence belongs a unique vector $\mathbf{n} \in (\widetilde{\mathbb{F}_b^{\mathbb{N}}})^\top$ and therefore a uniquely determined non-negative integer n. Hence, the mapping

$$\Psi : (\widetilde{\mathbb{F}_b^{\mathbb{N}}})^\top \to \{\boldsymbol{x}_0, \boldsymbol{x}_1, \ldots\}, \ \mathbf{n} \mapsto \boldsymbol{x}_n$$

is bijective. It can be shown, as in the proof of Lemma 4.72, that Ψ is a group homomorphism. Hence, the result follows. □

Exercises

4.1 Construct a $(0, 2, 2)$-net in base 3 'by hand'.

4.2 Let $b \geq 2$ be an integer. Show that for any $s \geq 2$ and any $m \geq 2$, there is a $(m - 1, m, s)$-net in base 2.

4.3 Show that the van der Corput sequence in base b is a $(0, 1)$-sequence in base b.

4.4 Show that the 4×4 matrices

$$C_1 = \begin{pmatrix} 1 & 0 & 0 & 0 \\ 0 & 1 & 0 & 0 \\ 0 & 0 & 1 & 0 \\ 0 & 0 & 0 & 1 \end{pmatrix}, \quad C_2 = \begin{pmatrix} 0 & 0 & 0 & 1 \\ 0 & 0 & 1 & 0 \\ 0 & 1 & 0 & 0 \\ 1 & 0 & 0 & 0 \end{pmatrix},$$

$$C_3 = \begin{pmatrix} 1 & 1 & 1 & 1 \\ 0 & 1 & 0 & 1 \\ 0 & 0 & 1 & 1 \\ 0 & 0 & 0 & 1 \end{pmatrix}, \quad C_4 = \begin{pmatrix} 0 & 1 & 1 & 0 \\ 1 & 1 & 0 & 1 \\ 0 & 0 & 0 & 1 \\ 0 & 0 & 1 & 0 \end{pmatrix},$$

over $\mathbb{Z}_2$ generate a digital $(1, 4, 4)$-net over $\mathbb{Z}_2$.

4.5 Determine the strict quality parameter t of the digital $(t, 3, 2)$-net over $\mathbb{F}_4$ from Example 4.49.

4.6 Prove Lemma 4.59.

4.7 Prove Lemma 4.61.

4.8 Let b be a prime power, let $s \in \mathbb{N}$ and let $C_1, \ldots, C_s$ be $\mathbb{N} \times \mathbb{N}$ matrices over $\mathbb{F}_b$. For $m \in \mathbb{N}$ let $C_i^{(m)}$ be the left upper $m \times m$ sub-matrix of C_i, $1 \leq i \leq s$. Show that $C_1, \ldots, C_s$ generate a strict digital $(\mathbf{T}, s)$-sequence over $\mathbb{F}_b$ with $\mathbf{T}(m) = \delta(C_1^{(m)}, \ldots, C_s^{(m)})$, where δ is defined as in Definition 4.58.

4.9 Show that a (strict) digital (t, m, s)-net in base b, which is shifted by a digital shift of depth m (Definition 4.69) independently in each coordinate, is, with probability one, a (strict) (t, m, s)-net in base b with the same quality parameter t. (Assume that the shifts are uniformly and independent and identically distributed.)

4.10 Show that a (strict) digital (t, m, s)-net in base b, which is shifted by a simplified digital shift (Definition 4.70), independently in each coordinate, is again a (strict) (t, m, s)-net in base b with the same quality parameter t.

4.11 Let b be a prime power and let the $\mathbb{N} \times \mathbb{N}$ matrices $C_1, \ldots, C_s$ generate a digital $(\mathbf{T}, s)$-sequence over the finite field $\mathbb{F}_b$. For any $m \geq 1$ consider the left upper $m \times m$ sub-matrices $C_1^{(m)}, \ldots, C_s^{(m)}$. Take

$$C_{s+1}^{(m)} := E'_m = \begin{pmatrix} \overline{0} & \overline{0} & \ldots & \overline{0} & \overline{1} \\ \overline{0} & & \cdot^{\cdot^{\cdot}} & \overline{1} & \overline{0} \\ \vdots & \cdot^{\cdot^{\cdot}} & \cdot^{\cdot^{\cdot}} & \cdot^{\cdot^{\cdot}} & \vdots \\ \overline{0} & \overline{1} & \cdot^{\cdot^{\cdot}} & & \overline{0} \\ \overline{1} & \overline{0} & \ldots & \overline{0} & \overline{0} \end{pmatrix} \in \mathbb{F}_b^{m \times m}.$$

Show that the $m \times m$ matrices $C_1^{(m)}, \ldots, C_s^{(m)}, C_{s+1}^{(m)}$ generate a digital $(r(m), m, s+1)$-net over $\mathbb{F}_b$ with $r(m) := \max\{\mathbf{T}(0), \ldots, \mathbf{T}(m)\}$.
Note: Note that this is a 'digital version' of Lemma 4.38. Note also the increase of the dimension from s to $s+1$.

4.12 For $k \in \mathbb{N}$ with b-adic expansion $k = \kappa_0 + \kappa_1 b + \cdots + \kappa_{a-1} b^{a-1}$, where $\kappa_{a-1} \neq 0$, we define $\rho(k) = a$. Furthermore, we define $\rho(0) = 0$. For $\boldsymbol{k} = (k_1, \ldots, k_s) \in \mathbb{N}_0^s$ let $\rho(\boldsymbol{k}) = \sum_{i=1}^{s} \rho(k_i)$. (This weight function is intimately related to the so-called NRT-weight which is introduced and used in Chapter 7 (Definition 7.1). See also Chapter 16, Definition 16.24.)

Show that if a point set $\mathcal{P} = \{\boldsymbol{x}_0, \ldots, \boldsymbol{x}_{b^m-1}\}$ consisting of b^m points in $[0,1)^s$ is a (t, m, s)-net in base b, $b \geq 2$ an arbitrary integer, then we have

$$\sum_{n=0}^{b^m-1} {}_b\mathrm{wal}_{\boldsymbol{k}}(\boldsymbol{x}_n) = 0 \quad \text{for all } \boldsymbol{k} \in \mathbb{N}_0^s \setminus \{\boldsymbol{0}\} \text{ with } 0 < \rho(\boldsymbol{k}) \leq m - t.$$

Note: This is [98, Lemma 1]. Compare with Lemma 4.75, but note that here $\mathcal{P}$ does not need to be a digital net.
Hint: Show that the Walsh function ${}_b\mathrm{wal}_{\boldsymbol{k}}$ for $\boldsymbol{k} = (k_1, \ldots, k_s) \in \mathbb{N}_0^s$ satisfying $0 \leq k_i < b^{g_i}$ for $1 \leq i \leq s$ can be written as a step function of the form ${}_b\mathrm{wal}_{\boldsymbol{k}} = \sum_{\boldsymbol{a}} c_{\boldsymbol{a}} \chi_{J_{\boldsymbol{a}}}$ with coefficients $c_{\boldsymbol{a}} \in \mathbb{R}$, where $J_{\boldsymbol{a}} = \prod_{i=1}^{s} [a_i b^{-g_i}, (a_i+1) b^{-g_i})$ and where the summation is overall possible $\boldsymbol{a} = (a_1, \ldots, a_s) \in \mathbb{N}_0^s$ with $0 \leq a_i < b^{g_i}$ for $1 \leq i \leq s$. Show that $\sum_{\boldsymbol{a}} c_{\boldsymbol{a}} = 0$ whenever $\boldsymbol{k} \neq \boldsymbol{0}$ and use the (t, m, s)-net property of $\mathcal{P}$.

4.13 Show the converse of Exercise 4.12. If $\mathcal{P} = \{\boldsymbol{x}_0, \ldots, \boldsymbol{x}_{b^m-1}\}$ is a point set consisting of b^m points in $[0,1)^s$ such that

$$\sum_{n=0}^{b^m-1} {}_b\mathrm{wal}_{\boldsymbol{k}}(\boldsymbol{x}_n) = 0 \quad \text{for all } \boldsymbol{k} \in \mathbb{N}_0^s \setminus \{\boldsymbol{0}\} \text{ with } 0 < \rho(\boldsymbol{k}) \leq m - t,$$

then $\mathcal{P}$ is a (t, m, s)-net in base b.
Note: This is [98, Lemma 2]. Note that $\mathcal{P}$ is in general not a digital net.
Hint: Consider the Walsh series expansion of the characteristic function of an arbitrary b-adic elementary interval of order $m - t$ and use Lemma 3.9.

4.14 Show that for the b-adic spectral test (see Exercise 3.8) of a (t, m, s)-net $\mathcal{P}$ in base b, we have $\sigma_{b,b^m}(\mathcal{P}) \le b^{t-m-1}$.
Note: This is [98, Theorem 4].

4.15 Show that for the b-adic spectral test of a strict digital (t, m, s)-net $\mathcal{P}$ in base b, we have $\sigma_{b,b^m}(\mathcal{P}) = b^{t-m-1}$.
Note: This is [98, Corollary 8].

5

Discrepancy estimates and average type results

The motivation for introducing and studying the concept of (t, m, s)-nets and $(\mathbf{T}, s)$-sequences was to generate point sets (also sometimes in high dimensions) with as small a discrepancy as possible. In this chapter we give an overview of theoretical results for the discrepancy of (digital) nets and sequences.

While singular results were already given by Sobol′ [253] and by Faure [68], the first systematic study of the discrepancy of nets was given by Niederreiter [168]. These results can also be found in [177, Chapter 4]. Further results on the star discrepancy of digital nets and sequences, mainly for low dimensions, can be found in [40, 71, 72, 74, 125, 126, 144, 145, 213].

After the work of Niederreiter [172, 177], metrical and average results on the discrepancy of nets and net-sequences were given; see, for instance, [134, 135, 136, 138, 140]. Further, the study of weighted discrepancy of net-type point sets also received considerable attention in recent years (see, for example, [49, 146]).

Even though we have many results for the extreme and star discrepancies, very little is known about concrete theoretical estimates for the L_p-discrepancy, especially for net-type point sets. Singular results in this direction can be found in [20, 22, 75, 142, 143, 212, 244] (results concerning the L_2-discrepancy are presented in Chapter 16).

The aims of this chapter are as follows:

1. We illustrate the ideas underlying all discrepancy estimates for (t, m, s)-nets with the help of detailed elaborated and illustrated proofs of a few discrepancy results.
2. We give a collection of concrete discrepancy estimates for net-type point sets with references for their proofs.
3. We give a discussion on these results concerning their value for applications.
4. We give a collection of metrical and average-type estimates for the quality parameter and the discrepancy of net-type point sets.

5.1 Discrepancy estimates for (t, m, s)-nets and $(\mathbf{T}, s)$-sequences

In this section we give a collection of concrete star discrepancy estimates for net-type point sets and sequences and we illustrate the ideas underlying all such estimates.

5.1.1 Star discrepancy estimates for (t, m, s)-nets

The most important and general applicable concrete discrepancy estimates for (t, m, s)-nets are the following two results given by Niederreiter [177, Theorem 4.5 and Theorem 4.6].

Theorem 5.1 *The star discrepancy of a (t, m, s)-net $\mathcal{P}$ in base $b \geq 3$ satisfies*

$$b^m D^*_{b^m}(\mathcal{P}) \leq b^t \sum_{i=0}^{s-1} \binom{s-1}{i} \binom{m-t}{i} \left\lfloor \frac{b}{2} \right\rfloor^i .$$

Theorem 5.2 *The star discrepancy of a (t, m, s)-net $\mathcal{P}$ in an even base b satisfies*

$$b^m D^*_{b^m}(\mathcal{P}) \leq b^t \sum_{i=0}^{s-1} \binom{m-t}{i} \left(\frac{b}{2}\right)^i + \left(\frac{b}{2} - 1\right) b^t \sum_{i=0}^{s-2} \binom{m-t+i+1}{i} \left(\frac{b}{2}\right)^i .$$

For applications the case $b = 2$ is important. For this case we obtain the following corollary from the last result.

Corollary 5.3 *The star discrepancy of a (t, m, s)-net $\mathcal{P}$ in base $b = 2$ satisfies*

$$2^m D^*_{2^m}(\mathcal{P}) \leq 2^t \sum_{i=0}^{s-1} \binom{m-t}{i} .$$

Below, we present a detailed and self-contained proof for this bound.

Both of the above theorems give results for even bases $b \geq 4$. For the special cases $s = 2, 3$ and 4, alternative estimates are given which in some cases improve the results derived from Theorem 5.1.

The corresponding result for $s = 2$ was proved by Dick and Kritzer [41, Theorem 1] (see also [144, Theorem 5] for the special case of digital $(0, m, 2)$-nets over $\mathbb{Z}_2$).

Theorem 5.4 *For $s = 2$, the star discrepancy of a (t, m, s)-net $\mathcal{P}$ in base b satisfies*

$$b^m D^*_{b^m}(\mathcal{P}) \leq b^m D^*_{b^{m-t}}(\mathcal{H}_{b,m-t}) + b^t ,$$

where $\mathcal{H}_{b,m-t}$ denotes the two-dimensional Hammersley point set in base b consisting of b^{m-t} points (see Definition 3.44). If $m - t \geq 2$ we obtain

$$b^m D^*_{b^m}(\mathcal{P}) \leq b^t \left(\frac{b^2}{4(b+1)}(m-t) + \frac{9}{4} + \frac{1}{b} \right),$$

for even bases $b \geq 2$ and

$$b^m D^*_{b^m}(\mathcal{P}) \leq b^t \left(\frac{b-1}{4}(m-t) + \frac{9}{4} + \frac{1}{b} \right),$$

for odd bases $b \geq 3$.

Remark 5.5 This result improves [177, Theorem 4.7], which states that for $s = 2$ the star discrepancy of a (t, m, s)-net $\mathcal{P}$ in base b satisfies

$$b^m D^*_{b^m}(\mathcal{P}) \leq b^t \left\lfloor \frac{b-1}{2}(m-t) + \frac{3}{2} \right\rfloor.$$

Remark 5.6 It follows from Theorem 5.4 that among all $(0, m, 2)$-nets in base b, the two-dimensional Hammersley point set in base b consisting of b^m points (which, of course, is itself a (digital) $(0, m, 2)$-net in base b by Lemma 4.13) has, up to the term b^0, the worst star discrepancy.

The following result for nets in dimension $s = 3$ is [177, Theorem 4.8].

Theorem 5.7 *For $s = 3$, the star discrepancy of a (t, m, s)-net $\mathcal{P}$ in base b satisfies*

$$b^m D^*_{b^m}(\mathcal{P}) \leq b^t \left\lfloor \left(\frac{b-1}{2}\right)^2 (m-t)^2 + \frac{b-1}{2}(m-t) + \frac{9}{4} \right\rfloor.$$

Remark 5.8 For digital $(0, m, 3)$-nets $\mathcal{P}$ over $\mathbb{Z}_2$ we have the improvement $2^m D^*_{2^m}(\mathcal{P}) \leq m^2/6 + O(m)$, by [213, Theorem 1].

The following result for nets in dimension $s = 4$ is [177, Theorem 4.9].

Theorem 5.9 *For $s = 4$, the star discrepancy of a (t, m, s)-net $\mathcal{P}$ in base b satisfies*

$$b^m D^*_{b^m}(\mathcal{P}) \leq b^t \left\lfloor \left(\frac{b-1}{2}\right)^3 (m-t)^3 + \frac{3(b-1)^2}{8}(m-t)^2 + \frac{3(b-1)}{8}(m-t) + \frac{15}{4} \right\rfloor.$$

These estimates are used by Niederreiter [177, Theorem 4.10] to obtain the following asymptotic result for the discrepancy of (t, m, s)-nets in base b.

Theorem 5.10 *The star discrepancy of a (t, m, s)-net $\mathcal{P}$ in base b with $m > 0$ satisfies*

$$b^m D^*_{b^m}(\mathcal{P}) \leq B(s, b) b^t m^{s-1} + O(b^t m^{s-2}), \tag{5.1}$$

where the implied O-constant depends only on b and s. Here, $B(s, b) = \left(\frac{b-1}{2}\right)^{s-1}$ if either $s = 2$ or $b = 2$, $s = 3, 4$; otherwise $B(s, b) = \frac{\lfloor b/2 \rfloor^{s-1}}{(s-1)!}$.

Remark 5.11 Using the same method as Niederreiter, Kritzer [125] improved the values of $B(s, b)$ by a factor of approximately $1/2$.

Proof of Theorem 5.10 For the expression in Theorem 5.1, for large enough m we have

$$\begin{aligned} b^t \sum_{i=0}^{s-1} \binom{s-1}{i} \binom{m-t}{i} \left\lfloor \frac{b}{2} \right\rfloor^i &\leq b^t \left\lfloor \frac{b}{2} \right\rfloor^{s-1} \binom{m-t}{s-1} + b^t \left\lfloor \frac{b}{2} \right\rfloor^{s-2} (m-t)^{s-2} 2^{s-1} \\ &\leq b^t \left\lfloor \frac{b}{2} \right\rfloor^{s-1} \frac{m^{s-1}}{(s-1)!} + O(b^t m^{s-2}) \end{aligned}$$

with an implied O-constant depending only on s and b. For the expression in Theorem 5.2, analogously, we have

$$\begin{aligned} b^t \sum_{i=0}^{s-1} \binom{m-t}{i} \left(\frac{b}{2}\right)^i &+ \left(\frac{b}{2} - 1\right) b^t \sum_{i=0}^{s-2} \binom{m-t+i+1}{i} \left(\frac{b}{2}\right)^i \\ &\leq b^t \binom{m-t}{s-1} \left(\frac{b}{2}\right)^{s-1} + b^t \left(\frac{b}{2}\right)^{s-2} (m-t)^{s-2} s \\ &\quad + \left(\frac{b}{2}\right)^{s-1} b^t s (m-t+s-1)^{s-2} \\ &\leq b^t \left(\frac{b}{2}\right)^{s-1} \frac{m^{s-1}}{(s-1)!} + O(b^t m^{s-2}) \end{aligned}$$

with an implied O-constant depending only on s and b. Hence, the result follows for all cases, apart from either $s = 2$ or $b = 2$, $s = 3, 4$. For the expression in Remark 5.5 (i.e. $s = 2$), we have

$$b^t \left\lfloor \frac{b-1}{2}(m-t) + \frac{3}{2} \right\rfloor \leq b^t \frac{b-1}{2} m + b^t \frac{3}{2} = b^t \frac{b-1}{2} m + O(b^t).$$

For the expression in Theorem 5.7 (i.e. $s = 3$), we have

$$b^t \left[\left(\frac{b-1}{2}\right)^2 (m-t)^2 + \frac{b-1}{2}(m-t) + \frac{9}{4} \right]$$
$$\leq b^t \left(\frac{b-1}{2}\right)^2 m^2 + b^t \left(\frac{b-1}{2} + \frac{9}{2}\right) m$$
$$= b^t \left(\frac{b-1}{2}\right)^2 m^2 + O(b^t m),$$

and finally, for the expression in Theorem 5.9 (i.e. $s = 4$), we have

$$b^t \left[\left(\frac{b-1}{2}\right)^3 (m-t)^3 + \frac{3(b-1)^2}{8}(m-t)^2 + \frac{3(b-1)}{8}(m-t) + \frac{15}{4} \right]$$
$$\leq b^t \left(\frac{b-1}{2}\right)^{s-1} m^{s-1} + O(b^t m^{s-2}).$$

Thus, the result follows. □

For the proofs of Theorems 5.1, 5.2, 5.7, 5.9, and Remark 5.5, see [177, Chapter 4]. The proof of Theorem 5.4 can be found in [41]. To illustrate the fundamental idea of the proofs, we give a detailed and illustrative verification for Corollary 5.3. The intention of this proof is not to be as elegant as possible but to give an insight into *how* (t, m, s)-nets of good quality achieve a low star discrepancy. We prove the general result by carrying out various (sometimes redundant) steps.

Proof of Corollary 5.3 We start by considering the case $s = 1$. For a $(t, m, 1)$-net $\mathcal{P}$ in base 2, we have to show that $2^m D^*_{2^m}(\mathcal{P}) \leq 2^t$. By definition, a $(t, m, 1)$-net in base 2 has the property that every 2-adic elementary interval of the form

$$\left[\frac{a}{2^{m-t}}, \frac{a+1}{2^{m-t}} \right)$$

with $0 \leq a < 2^{m-t}$ contains exactly 2^t points of the net.

Let $J = [0, \alpha)$ be any sub-interval of $[0, 1)$ containing the origin and let the integer a be such that $\frac{a}{2^{m-t}} < \alpha \leq \frac{a+1}{2^{m-t}}$. Then, we have

$$A(J, 2^m, \mathcal{P}) - 2^m \lambda(J)$$
$$\leq A\left(\left[0, \frac{a+1}{2^{m-t}}\right), 2^m, \mathcal{P} \right) - (a+1)2^t + (a+1)2^t - 2^m \lambda(J)$$
$$\leq 2^t$$

and

$$A(J, 2^m, \mathcal{P}) - 2^m\lambda(J) \geq A\left(\left[0, \frac{a}{2^{m-t}}\right), 2^m, \mathcal{P}\right) - a2^t + a2^t - 2^m\lambda(J) \geq -2^t,$$

which implies that

$$\left|\frac{A(J, 2^m, \mathcal{P})}{2^m} - \lambda(J)\right| \leq \frac{1}{2^{m-t}}$$

and this yields the result for $s = 1$.

Let us now consider the case $s = 2$. A $(t, m, 2)$-net $\mathcal{P}$ in base 2 has the property that every elementary interval of the form

$$\left[\frac{a_1}{2^d}, \frac{a_1+1}{2^d}\right) \times \left[\frac{a_2}{2^{m-t-d}}, \frac{a_2+1}{2^{m-t-d}}\right)$$

with $0 \leq d \leq m - t$ contains exactly 2^t points of the net $\mathcal{P}$. Consequently, every interval of the form

$$\left[\frac{a_1}{2^{d_1}}, \frac{a_1+u_1}{2^{d_1}}\right) \times \left[\frac{a_2}{2^{d_2}}, \frac{a_2+u_2}{2^{d_2}}\right), \tag{5.2}$$

with $d_1, d_2 \in \mathbb{N}_0$ and with $d_1 + d_2 \leq m - t$ and integers a_1, a_2, u_1, u_2 with $0 \leq a_1 < a_1 + u_1 \leq 2^{d_1}$ and $0 \leq u_2 < a_2 + u_2 \leq 2^{d_2}$, contains exactly $u_1u_22^{m-d_1-d_2}$ elements of the net $\mathcal{P}$.

Let $J = [0, \alpha) \times [0, \beta)$ be any sub-interval of $[0, 1)^2$ containing the origin. We try to approximate J from the interior and from the exterior as well as possible by unions of elementary intervals of order $m - t$, i.e. by unions of intervals of the form (5.2). To do this, let

$$\alpha = \frac{1}{2^{k_1}} + \frac{1}{2^{k_2}} + \cdots + \frac{1}{2^{k_g}} + \frac{1}{2^{k_{g+1}}} + \cdots$$

and

$$\beta = \frac{1}{2^{l_1}} + \frac{1}{2^{l_2}} + \cdots + \frac{1}{2^{l_h}} + \frac{1}{2^{l_{h+1}}} + \cdots$$

with $1 \leq k_1 < k_2 < \cdots$ and $1 \leq l_1 < l_2 < \cdots$ be the base 2 representations of α and β, respectively. Note that if $k_1 > m - t$, then J is entirely contained in an elementary interval of order $m - t$. Hence, in this case, we have $|A(J, 2^m, \mathcal{P}) - 2^m\lambda_2(J)| \leq 2^t$. Analogously the same applies if $l_1 > m - t$, and the result follows also for this case. Hence, we may now assume that $k_1, l_1 \leq m - t$.

Hence, now let $g, h \geq 1$ be the largest integers such that $k_g, l_h \leq m - t$. Note that $g \leq k_g \leq m - t$. Then let us start by proceeding step by step along the first coordinate. Consider the first part of $[0, \alpha)$, i.e. $[0, 1/2^{k_1})$. Let, for a non-negative integer $k \leq m - t$, the non-negative integer $j(k)$ be such that $k + l_{j(k)} \leq m - t$ and

$k + l_{j(k)+1} > m - t$, if this number exists. Otherwise, set $j(k) := 0$ and for this case we define $\frac{1}{2^{l_1}} + \cdots + \frac{1}{2^{l_{j(k)}}} := 0$. Then

$$C_1 := \left[0, \frac{1}{2^{k_1}}\right) \times \left[0, \frac{1}{2^{l_1}} + \cdots + \frac{1}{2^{l_{j(k_1)}}}\right)$$

is the largest interval of type (5.2), which has first coordinate $\left[0, \frac{1}{2^{k_1}}\right)$ and which is contained in J.

Now we consider the second part $\left[\frac{1}{2^{k_1}}, \frac{1}{2^{k_1}} + \frac{1}{2^{k_2}}\right)$ of $[0, \alpha)$. Then

$$C_2 := \left[\frac{1}{2^{k_1}}, \frac{1}{2^{k_1}} + \frac{1}{2^{k_2}}\right) \times \left[0, \frac{1}{2^{l_1}} + \cdots + \frac{1}{2^{l_{j(k_2)}}}\right)$$

is the largest interval of type (5.2), which has first coordinate $\left[\frac{1}{2^{k_1}}, \frac{1}{2^{k_1}} + \frac{1}{2^{k_2}}\right)$ and which is contained in J. We proceed until we arrive at the 'last part' of the first coordinate in $[0, \alpha)$, namely

$$\left[\frac{1}{2^{k_1}} + \cdots + \frac{1}{2^{k_{g-1}}}, \frac{1}{2^{k_1}} + \cdots + \frac{1}{2^{k_{g-1}}} + \frac{1}{2^{k_g}}\right).$$

Obviously,

$$C_g := \left[\frac{1}{2^{k_1}} + \cdots + \frac{1}{2^{k_{g-1}}}, \frac{1}{2^{k_1}} + \cdots + \frac{1}{2^{k_{g-1}}} + \frac{1}{2^{k_g}}\right) \times \left[0, \frac{1}{2^{l_1}} + \cdots + \frac{1}{2^{l_{j(k_g)}}}\right) \tag{5.3}$$

is the largest interval of type (5.2), which has first coordinate

$$\left[\frac{1}{2^{k_1}} + \cdots + \frac{1}{2^{k_{g-1}}}, \frac{1}{2^{k_1}} + \cdots + \frac{1}{2^{k_{g-1}}} + \frac{1}{2^{k_g}}\right)$$

and which is contained in J. Obviously, some of these intervals may be empty (whenever the corresponding $j(k)$ is zero). All the above intervals are pairwise disjoint and so the union of these intervals of type (5.2),

$$C = C_1 \cup \ldots \cup C_g,$$

is fair with respect to the net $\mathcal{P}$ and is contained in J.

To illustrate the procedure, consider the following example. Let $m = 5$, $t = 1$, $\alpha = \frac{1}{2} + \frac{1}{4} + \frac{1}{8} + \frac{1}{64} = \frac{57}{64}$, and $\beta = \frac{1}{2} + \frac{1}{4} + \frac{1}{32} = \frac{25}{32}$. Then we have

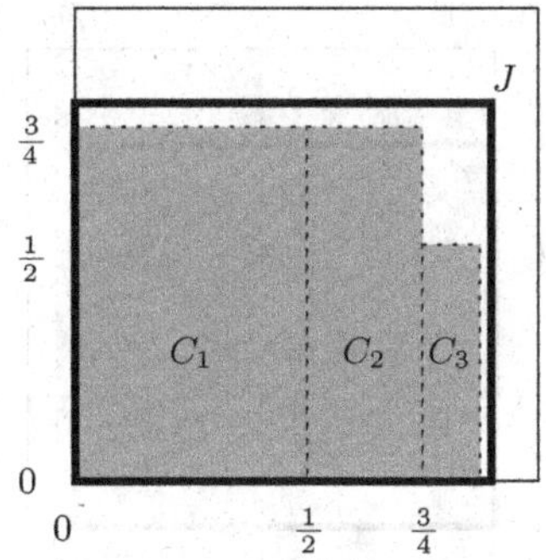

Figure 5.1 The union $C = C_1 \cup C_2 \cup C_3$ for $J = [0, 57/64) \times [0, 25/32)$.

(see Figure 5.1),

$$\begin{aligned} C &= C_1 \cup C_2 \cup C_3 \\ &= \left[0, \frac{1}{2}\right) \times \left[0, \frac{1}{2} + \frac{1}{4}\right) \cup \left[\frac{1}{2}, \frac{1}{2} + \frac{1}{4}\right) \times \left[0, \frac{1}{2} + \frac{1}{4}\right) \\ &\quad \cup \left[\frac{1}{2} + \frac{1}{4}, \frac{1}{2} + \frac{1}{4} + \frac{1}{8}\right) \times \left[0, \frac{1}{2}\right) \\ &= \left[0, \frac{1}{2}\right) \times \left[0, \frac{3}{4}\right) \cup \left[\frac{1}{2}, \frac{3}{4}\right) \times \left[0, \frac{3}{4}\right) \cup \left[\frac{3}{4}, \frac{7}{8}\right) \times \left[0, \frac{1}{2}\right). \end{aligned}$$

To construct a union of elementary intervals of order $m - t$ which is as small as possible and which contains J, we just add at the right border of the second coordinate of C_i the value $\frac{1}{2^{m-t-k_i}}$ and obtain

$$\begin{aligned} C_i' := &\left[\frac{1}{2^{k_1}} + \cdots + \frac{1}{2^{k_{i-1}}}, \frac{1}{2^{k_1}} + \cdots + \frac{1}{2^{k_{i-1}}} + \frac{1}{2^{k_i}}\right) \\ &\times \left[0, \frac{1}{2^{l_1}} + \cdots + \frac{1}{2^{l_{j(k_i)}}} + \frac{1}{2^{m-t-k_i}}\right). \end{aligned}$$

Now the $C_1', \ldots, C_g'$ together overlap J apart from the last part along the first coordinate. This last strip is overlapped by

$$\widetilde{C}' := \left[\frac{1}{2^{k_1}} + \cdots + \frac{1}{2^{k_g}}, \frac{1}{2^{k_1}} + \cdots + \frac{1}{2^{k_g}} + \frac{1}{2^{m-t}}\right) \times [0, 1).$$

Now

$$C' = C_1' \cup \ldots \cup C_g' \cup \widetilde{C}'$$

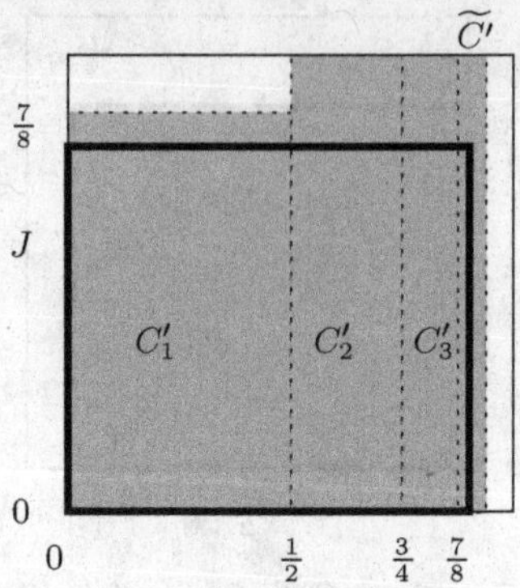

Figure 5.2 The union $C' = C_1' \cup C_2' \cup C_3' \cup \widetilde{C}'$ for $J = [0, 57/64) \times [0, 25/32)$.

is a union of intervals of type (5.2), is fair with respect to the net $\mathcal{P}$, and contains J. For our example, we have (see Figure 5.2),

$$\begin{aligned} C' &= C_1' \cup \ldots \cup C_g' \cup \widetilde{C}' \\ &= \left[0, \frac{1}{2}\right) \times \left[0, \frac{1}{2} + \frac{1}{4} + \frac{1}{8}\right) \cup \left[\frac{1}{2}, \frac{1}{2} + \frac{1}{4}\right) \times [0, 1) \\ &\quad \cup \left[\frac{1}{2} + \frac{1}{4}, \frac{1}{2} + \frac{1}{4} + \frac{1}{8}\right) \times [0, 1) \\ &\quad \cup \left[\frac{1}{2} + \frac{1}{4} + \frac{1}{8}, \frac{1}{2} + \frac{1}{4} + \frac{1}{8} + \frac{1}{16}\right) \times [0, 1) \\ &= \left[0, \frac{1}{2}\right) \times \left[0, \frac{7}{8}\right) \cup \left[\frac{1}{2}, \frac{3}{4}\right) \times [0, 1) \cup \left[\frac{3}{4}, \frac{7}{8}\right) \times [0, 1) \cup \left[\frac{7}{8}, \frac{15}{16}\right) \times [0, 1). \end{aligned}$$

Now we can estimate

$$\begin{aligned} A(J, 2^m, \mathcal{P}) - 2^m \lambda_2(J) &\leq A(C', 2^m, \mathcal{P}) - 2^m \lambda_2(C') + 2^m \lambda_2(C' \setminus C) \\ &= 2^m \lambda_2(C' \setminus C) \end{aligned}$$

and

$$\begin{aligned} A(J, 2^m, \mathcal{P}) - 2^m \lambda_2(J) &\geq A(C, 2^m, \mathcal{P}) - 2^m \lambda_2(C) - 2^m \lambda_2(C' \setminus C) \\ &= -2^m \lambda_2(C' \setminus C). \end{aligned}$$

Thus,

$$\begin{aligned}|A(J, 2^m, \mathcal{P}) - 2^m\lambda_2(J)| &\leq 2^m\lambda_2(C' \setminus C)\\ &= 2^m(\lambda_2(C'_1 \setminus C_1) + \cdots + \lambda_2(C'_g \setminus C_g) + \lambda_2(\widetilde{C}'))\\ &= 2^m\left(\frac{g}{2^{m-t}} + \frac{1}{2^{m-t}}\right)\\ &\leq 2^t(m - t + 1)\\ &= 2^t\sum_{i=0}^{1}\binom{m-t}{i},\end{aligned}$$

and this yields the result for $s = 2$.

The proof proceeds by induction on the dimension s. The general induction step $s \to s + 1$ follows along the same lines as step $2 \to 3$, which is carried out in the following. The general step can then be obtained in the same manner.

Let

$$J = [0, \alpha) \times [0, \beta) \times [0, \gamma)$$

be any sub-interval of $[0, 1)^3$ containing the origin. Let α, β have base 2 representation as above, and let $\gamma = \frac{1}{2^{p_1}} + \frac{1}{2^{p_2}} + \cdots + \frac{1}{2^{p_n}} + \cdots$ with $0 < p_1 < p_2 < \cdots$.

Let us first approximate the two-dimensional interval $J' := [0, \alpha) \times [0, \beta)$ from the interior by a union of intervals of type (5.2), and also from the exterior, in exactly the same way as is done in the case $s = 2$ by C and C'.

From the procedure in dimension $s = 2$ we have obtained that

$$2^m(\lambda_2(C') - \lambda_2(C)) = 2^m\lambda_2(C' \setminus C) \leq 2^t\left(\binom{m-t}{0} + \binom{m-t}{1}\right).$$

The set C is typically a disjoint union of intervals of the form

$$\left[\frac{1}{2^{k_1}} + \cdots + \frac{1}{2^{k_{e-1}}}, \frac{1}{2^{k_1}} + \cdots + \frac{1}{2^{k_{e-1}}} + \frac{1}{2^{k_e}}\right)$$
$$\times \left[\frac{1}{2^{l_1}} + \cdots + \frac{1}{2^{l_{f-1}}}, \frac{1}{2^{l_1}} + \cdots + \frac{1}{2^{l_{f-1}}} + \frac{1}{2^{l_f}}\right)$$

with $k_e + l_f \leq m - t$.

First, we approximate J from the interior by extending the elements of C to three-dimensional fair intervals contained in J. Let for non-negative integers k and l with $k + l \leq m - t$ the non-negative integer $j(k, l)$ be such that $k + l + p_{j(k,l)} \leq m - t$ and $k + l + p_{j(k,l)+1} > m - t$, if this number exists. If this number does not exist, then set $j(k,l) := 0$ and $\frac{1}{2^{p_1}} + \cdots + \frac{1}{2^{p_{j(k_e,l_f)}}} := 0$. Then consider the intervals

$$\left[\frac{1}{2^{k_1}} + \cdots + \frac{1}{2^{k_{e-1}}}, \frac{1}{2^{k_1}} + \cdots + \frac{1}{2^{k_{e-1}}} + \frac{1}{2^{k_e}}\right)$$
$$\times \left[\frac{1}{2^{l_1}} + \cdots + \frac{1}{2^{l_{f-1}}}, \frac{1}{2^{l_1}} + \cdots + \frac{1}{2^{l_{f-1}}} + \frac{1}{2^{l_f}}\right) \tag{5.4}$$
$$\times \left[0, \frac{1}{2^{p_1}} + \cdots + \frac{1}{2^{p_{j(k_e,l_f)}}}\right).$$

The union of all these intervals with $k_e + l_f \leq m - t$, we call it E, is fair with respect to the net $\mathcal{P}$ and approximates J from the interior.

To approximate J from the exterior by fair intervals, we first use $C' \setminus C \times [0,1)$ and instead of the intervals in (5.4) we take, as for $s = 2$, the intervals

$$\left[\frac{1}{2^{k_1}} + \cdots + \frac{1}{2^{k_{e-1}}}, \frac{1}{2^{k_1}} + \cdots + \frac{1}{2^{k_{e-1}}} + \frac{1}{2^{k_e}}\right)$$
$$\times \left[\frac{1}{2^{l_1}} + \cdots + \frac{1}{2^{l_{f-1}}}, \frac{1}{2^{l_1}} + \cdots + \frac{1}{2^{l_{f-1}}} + \frac{1}{2^{l_f}}\right)$$
$$\times \left[0, \frac{1}{2^{p_1}} + \cdots + \frac{1}{2^{p_{j(k_e,l_f)}}} + \frac{1}{2^{m-t-k_e-l_f}}\right).$$

The union of $C' \setminus C \times [0,1)$ with all these intervals (with $k_e + l_f \leq m - t$), we call it E', is fair with respect to the net $\mathcal{P}$ and contains J. Hence, as in the case $s = 2$, we obtain

$$\begin{aligned}
|A(J, 2^m, \mathcal{P}) - 2^m \lambda_3(J)| &\leq 2^m(\lambda_3(E') - \lambda_3(E)) \\
&= 2^m \lambda_2(C' \setminus C) + 2^m \sum_{\substack{k_e, l_f \\ k_e + l_f \leq m-t}} \frac{1}{2^{m-t}} \\
&\leq 2^t \left(\binom{m-t}{0} + \binom{m-t}{1}\right) + 2^t \sum_{\substack{1 \leq k,l \leq m-t \\ k+l \leq m-t}} 1 \\
&= 2^t \left(\binom{m-t}{0} + \binom{m-t}{1} + \binom{m-t}{2}\right),
\end{aligned}$$

and this yields the result for $s = 3$.

The formal details of the general step from dimension s to dimension $s+1$ can be obtained along the same lines as the step from dimension 2 to 3. □

By carrying out the procedure of the above proof in the general case, for arbitrary base b, one would obtain the following easy form of an estimate whose proof is left as an exercise (see Exercise 5.1).

Theorem 5.12 *The star discrepancy of a (t, m, s)-net $\mathcal{P}$ in base b satisfies*

$$b^m D^*_{b^m}(\mathcal{P}) \leq b^t \sum_{i=0}^{s-1} \binom{m-t}{i} (b-1)^i.$$

The results of Theorems 5.1 and 5.2, for $b \geq 3$, in many cases provide improvements compared with the estimate of Theorem 5.12. The basic idea to obtain these improvements, roughly speaking, is that the approximation of the interval J is carried out more carefully; that is, one takes the concrete digit expansion of the boundaries of the interval J into account. Note, also, that the asymptotic results in m, which we obtained from Theorems 5.1 and 5.2 are better than the results that could be obtained from Theorem 5.12.

5.1.2 Star discrepancy estimates for $(\mathbf{T}, s)$-sequences

A similar strategy to the one used for nets is also used by Niederreiter in giving estimates for $(\mathbf{T}, s)$-sequences (as is done, for instance, for (t, s)-sequences in [177, Theorems 4.12–4.16]). Such estimates could be obtained immediately from the above discrepancy estimates for nets, together with Proposition 3.16, which allows us to estimate the discrepancy of a sequence by the discrepancies of its parts, and by the fact that a $(\mathbf{T}, s)$-sequence is, in a certain way, made up of (t, m, s)-nets.

Hence, assume that $\Delta_b(t, m, s)$ is a number for which

$$b^m D^*_{b^m}(\mathcal{P}) \leq \Delta_b(t, m, s)$$

holds for the star discrepancy of any (t, m, s)-net $\mathcal{P}$ in base b. We consider the star discrepancy of the set $\{\boldsymbol{x}_0, \ldots, \boldsymbol{x}_{N-1}\}$ consisting of the first N points of a $(\mathbf{T}, s)$-sequence $\mathcal{S}$ in base b. Let N have b-adic representation $N = a_r b^r + \cdots + a_1 b + a_0$. Then we consider the parts $\mathcal{P}_{m,a} = \{\boldsymbol{x}_{a_r b^r + \cdots + a_{m+1} b^{m+1} + a b^m + k} : 0 \leq k < b^m\}$, for $0 \leq m \leq r$ and $0 \leq a \leq a_m - 1$, of the whole point set.

Every set $\mathcal{P}_{m,a}$ is a $(\mathbf{T}(m), m, s)$-net in base b and b^m-times its star discrepancy is at most $\Delta_b(\mathbf{T}(m), m, s)$. Now we obtain, from the triangle inequality for the star discrepancy (see Proposition 3.16), the following bound on the star discrepancy of the first N elements of $\mathcal{S}$. This result was first shown by Larcher and Niederreiter [140, Lemma 1].

Lemma 5.13 *Let $\mathcal{S}$ be a $(\mathbf{T}, s)$-sequence in base b. Let $N = a_r b^r + \cdots + a_1 b + a_0$ be the b-adic representation of the positive integer N. Let $\Delta_b(t, m, s)$ be such that for the star discrepancy of any (t, m, s)-net $\mathcal{P}$ in base b the inequality*

$b^m D^*_{b^m}(\mathcal{P}) \le \Delta_b(t, m, s)$ *holds. Then*

$$N D^*_N(\mathcal{S}) \le \sum_{m=0}^{r} a_m \Delta_b(\mathbf{T}(m), m, s).$$

Niederreiter [177, Lemma 4.11] gives the following variant (which we state here in a slightly more general form).

Lemma 5.14 *With the notation of Lemma 5.13, we have*

$$N D^*_N(\mathcal{S}) \le \min\Bigg(\sum_{m=n}^{r} a_m \Delta_b(\mathbf{T}(m), m, s), \sum_{m=n}^{r}(b - 1 - a_m)\Delta_b(\mathbf{T}(m), m, s) \\ + \Delta_b(\mathbf{T}(n), n, s) + \Delta_b(\mathbf{T}(r+1), r+1, s)\Bigg),$$

where n is the largest integer such that $b^n | N$.

Proof With $N = a_r b^r + \cdots + a_1 b + a_0$, we have, by Lemma 5.13, that

$$N D^*_N(\mathcal{S}) \le \sum_{m=0}^{r} a_m \Delta_b(\mathbf{T}(m), m, s).$$

We consider now the next $b^{r+1} - N$ points of the $(\mathbf{T}, s)$-sequence, i.e. $\mathcal{P}' = \{\boldsymbol{x}_n : N \le n < b^{r+1}\}$. Let $b^{r+1} - N$ have b-adic expansion $b^{r+1} - N = c_r b^r + \cdots + c_1 b + c_0$. Again we can split up this point set into a union of nets, namely into the nets

$$\mathcal{P}'_{m,c} = \{\boldsymbol{x}_{b^{r+1} - c_r b^r - \cdots - c_{m+1} b^{m+1} - c b^m + k} : 0 \le k < b^m\},$$

for all $0 \le m \le r$ and $0 \le c \le c_m - 1$. Every $\mathcal{P}'_{m,c}$ is a $(\mathbf{T}(m), m, s)$-net in base b and so b^m-times its star discrepancy is at most $\Delta_b(\mathbf{T}(m), m, s)$. From Proposition 3.16 for the star discrepancy of $\mathcal{P}'$ we obtain

$$(b^{r+1} - N) D^*_{b^{r+1}-N}(\mathcal{P}') \le \sum_{m=0}^{r} c_m \Delta_b(\mathbf{T}(m), m, s).$$

The first b^{r+1} points of the $(\mathbf{T}, s)$-sequence build a $(\mathbf{T}(r+1), r+1, s)$-net $\widetilde{\mathcal{P}}$ in base b whose star discrepancy hence satisfies $b^{r+1} D^*_{b^{r+1}}(\widetilde{\mathcal{P}}) \le \Delta_b(\mathbf{T}(r+1), r+1, s)$. The initial point set $\{\boldsymbol{x}_0, \ldots, \boldsymbol{x}_{N-1}\}$, i.e. the first N elements of $\mathcal{S}$, is the difference between the two point sets $\widetilde{\mathcal{P}}$ and $\mathcal{P}'$ and hence, using again Proposition 3.16, we obtain

$$\begin{aligned} N D^*_N(\mathcal{S}) &\le (b^{r+1} - N) D^*_{b^{r+1}-N}(\mathcal{P}') + b^{r+1} D^*_{b^{r+1}}(\widetilde{\mathcal{P}}) \\ &\le \sum_{m=0}^{r} c_m \Delta_b(\mathbf{T}(m), m, s) + \Delta_b(\mathbf{T}(r+1), r+1, s). \end{aligned}$$

Now consider c_m. We have

$$b^{r+1} = b^{r+1} - N + N = \sum_{m=0}^{r} (c_m + a_m) b^m.$$

Hence, $c_0, \ldots, c_i$ are zero as long as $a_0, \ldots, a_i$ are zero; that is, as long as $i \leq n - 1$. Further, $a_n + c_n = b$ and $a_m + c_m = b - 1$ for $n + 1 \leq m \leq r$. Hence, on the one hand

$$N D_N^*(\mathcal{S}) \leq \sum_{m=n}^{r} a_m \Delta_b(\mathbf{T}(m), m, s),$$

and on the other hand

$$\begin{aligned} N D_N^*(\mathcal{S}) \leq & \sum_{m=n}^{r} (b - 1 - a_m) \Delta_b(\mathbf{T}(m), m, s) \\ & + \Delta_b(\mathbf{T}(n), n, s) + \Delta_b(\mathbf{T}(r+1), r+1, s). \end{aligned}$$

Therefore, the result follows. □

As a simple corollary we obtain the following result.

Corollary 5.15 *Let $\mathcal{S}$ be a $(\mathbf{T}, s)$-sequence in base b. Let $\Delta_b(t, m, s)$ be such that for the star discrepancy of any (t, m, s)-net $\mathcal{P}$ in base b we have $b^m D_{b^m}^*(\mathcal{P}) \leq \Delta_b(t, m, s)$. Then*

$$\begin{aligned} N D_N^*(\mathcal{S}) \leq & \frac{b-1}{2} \sum_{m=n}^{r} \Delta_b(\mathbf{T}(m), m, s) \\ & + \frac{1}{2} (\Delta_b(\mathbf{T}(n), n, s) + \Delta_b(\mathbf{T}(r+1), r+1, s)), \end{aligned}$$

where $r \in \mathbb{N}_0$ is such that $b^r \leq N < b^{r+1}$ and n is the largest integer such that $b^n | N$.

Using this corollary and the results of Theorems 5.1 and 5.2, Remark 5.5 and Theorems 5.7 and 5.9, Niederreiter obtains the discrepancy estimates for (t, s)-sequences given in [177, Theorems 4.12–4.16]. For the sake of completeness we shall state these results in the following. First, we shall give one general estimate for $(\mathbf{T}, s)$-sequences, directly originating from Theorem 5.12 and Corollary 5.15.

Theorem 5.16 *Let $\mathcal{S}$ be a $(\mathbf{T}, s)$-sequence in base b. Let $r \in \mathbb{N}_0$ be such that $b^r \leq N < b^{r+1}$ and let n be that largest integer such that $b^n | N$. Then*

$$ND_N^*(\mathcal{S}) \leq \frac{1}{2}\Bigg(\sum_{i=0}^{s-1}(b-1)^{i+1}\sum_{m=n}^{r} b^{\mathbf{T}(m)}\binom{m-\mathbf{T}(m)}{i}$$
$$+ b^{\mathbf{T}(n)}\sum_{i=0}^{s-1}\binom{n-\mathbf{T}(n)}{i}(b-1)^i$$
$$+ b^{\mathbf{T}(r+1)}\sum_{i=0}^{s-1}\binom{r+1-\mathbf{T}(r+1)}{i}(b-1)^i\Bigg).$$

The following estimates for the star discrepancy D_N^* of a (t, s)-sequence were given by Niederreiter [177, Theorems 4.12–4.16].

Theorem 5.17 *The star discrepancy of the first N terms of a (t, s)-sequence $\mathcal{S}$ in base $b \geq 3$ satisfies*

$$ND_N^*(\mathcal{S}) \leq \frac{b-1}{2}b^t\sum_{i=1}^{s}\binom{s-1}{i-1}\binom{k+1-t}{i}\left\lfloor\frac{b}{2}\right\rfloor^{i-1}$$
$$+\frac{1}{2}b^t\sum_{i=0}^{s-1}\binom{s-1}{i}\left(\binom{k+1-t}{i}+\binom{k-t}{i}\right)\left\lfloor\frac{b}{2}\right\rfloor^{i}$$

for $N \geq b^t$, where k is the largest integer with $b^k \leq N$.

Theorem 5.18 *The star discrepancy of the first N terms of a (t, s)-sequence in an even base b satisfies*

$$ND_N^*(\mathcal{S}) \leq (b-1)b^{t-1}\sum_{i=1}^{s}\binom{k+1-t}{i}\left(\frac{b}{2}\right)^i$$
$$+\binom{b-1}{2}b^{t-1}\sum_{i=1}^{s-1}\binom{k+i+1-t}{i}\left(\frac{b}{2}\right)^i$$
$$+\frac{1}{2}b^t\sum_{i=0}^{s-1}\left(\binom{k+1-t}{i}+\binom{k-t}{i}\right)\left(\frac{b}{2}\right)^i$$
$$+\frac{b-2}{4}b^t\sum_{i=0}^{s-2}\left(\binom{k+i+2-t}{i}+\binom{k+i+1-t}{i}\right)\left(\frac{b}{2}\right)^i$$

for $N \geq b^t$, where k is the largest integer with $b^k \leq N$.

Theorem 5.19 *For $s = 2$, the star discrepancy of the first N terms of a (t, s)-sequence $\mathcal{S}$ in base b satisfies*

$$ND_N^*(\mathcal{S}) \leq \frac{(b-1)^2}{8} b^t (k-t)^2 + \frac{(b-1)(b+9)}{8} b^t (k-t) + \frac{3(b+1)}{4} b^t$$

for $N \geq b^t$, where k is the largest integer with $b^k \leq N$.

Theorem 5.20 *For $s = 3$, the star discrepancy of the first N terms of a (t, s)-sequence $\mathcal{S}$ in base b satisfies*

$$ND_N^*(\mathcal{S}) \leq \frac{(b-1)^3}{24} b^t (k-t)^3 + \frac{(b-1)^2(b+5)}{16} b^t (k-t)^2 + \frac{(b-1)(b^2+16b+61)}{48} b^t (k-t) + \frac{b^2+4b+13}{8} b^t$$

for $N \geq b^t$, where k is the largest integer with $b^k \leq N$.

Theorem 5.21 *For $s = 4$, the star discrepancy of the first N terms of a (t, s)-sequence $\mathcal{S}$ in base b satisfies*

$$ND_N^*(\mathcal{S}) \leq \frac{(b-1)^4}{64} b^t (k-t)^4 + \frac{(b-1)^3(b+5)}{32} b^t (k-t)^3 + \frac{(b-1)^2(b^2+16b+13)}{64} b^t (k-t)^2 + \frac{(b-1)(7b^2+b+64)}{32} b^t (k-t) + \frac{b^3+8b+51}{16} b^t$$

for $N \geq b^t$, where k is the largest integer with $b^k \leq N$.

Again, from these estimates we obtain asymptotic results for the star discrepancy of (t, s)-sequences. Niederreiter's [177, Theorem 4.17] states the following result.

Corollary 5.22 *The star discrepancy of the first N terms of a (t, s)-sequence $\mathcal{S}$ in base b satisfies*

$$ND_N^*(\mathcal{S}) \leq C(s, b) b^t (\log N)^s + O(b^t (\log N)^{s-1}),$$

where the implied constant depends only on b and s. Here

$$C(s, b) = \frac{1}{s} \left(\frac{b-1}{2 \log b} \right)^s$$

if either $s = 2$ or $b = 2$, $s = 3, 4$; otherwise

$$C(s, b) = \frac{1}{s!} \frac{b-1}{2\lfloor b/2 \rfloor} \left(\frac{\lfloor b/2 \rfloor}{\log b} \right)^s.$$

Remark 5.23 Using the same method as Niederreiter, Kritzer [125] improved the values of $C(s, b)$ by a factor of approximately $1/2$.

Hence (t, s)-sequences provide sequences $\mathcal{S}$ with star discrepancy of order

$$D_N^*(\mathcal{S}) = O\left(\frac{(\log N)^s}{N}\right),$$

which by a long-standing conjecture in the theory of uniform distribution modulo one (see Section 3.2) is probably the best possible order of the star discrepancy for infinite sequences in $[0, 1)^s$. Hence, a (t, s)-sequence is a so-called low-discrepancy sequence. But other $(\mathbf{T}, s)$-sequences also provide low-discrepancy sequences. In [140, Theorem 1] the following result was shown.

Theorem 5.24 *Let $\mathcal{S}$ be a $(\mathbf{T}, s)$-sequence in base b with a quality function $\mathbf{T}$ satisfying the property that the sequence $\left(\frac{1}{r}\sum_{m=1}^{r} b^{\mathbf{T}(m)}\right)_{r\in\mathbb{N}}$ is bounded. Then, for the star discrepancy of the first $N \geq 2$ elements of $\mathcal{S}$, we have*

$$D_N^*(\mathcal{S}) = O\left(\frac{(\log N)^s}{N}\right).$$

Proof By Lemma 5.13 and by Theorem 5.10 for $N = a_r b^r + \cdots + a_1 b + a_0$, we obtain

$$N D_N^*(\mathcal{S}) \leq \sum_{m=0}^{r} b\Delta_b(\mathbf{T}(m), m, s) \leq \overline{B}(s, b) \sum_{m=0}^{r} b^{\mathbf{T}(m)} m^{s-1} \tag{5.5}$$

with a constant $\overline{B}(s, b)$, depending only on s and b. Now let $\frac{1}{r}\sum_{m=1}^{r} b^{\mathbf{T}(m)} \leq C$ for all r. Then

$$\sum_{m=0}^{r} b^{\mathbf{T}(m)} m^{s-1} \leq r^{s-1} \sum_{m=0}^{r} b^{\mathbf{T}(m)} \leq C r^s \leq \frac{C}{(\log b)^s} (\log N)^s$$

and the result follows. □

Remark 5.25 Indeed, the discrepancy bound from (5.5) is

$$\sum_{m=0}^{r} b^{\mathbf{T}(m)} m^{s-1} = O((\log N)^s)$$

if and only if $\left(\frac{1}{r}\sum_{m=0}^{r} b^{\mathbf{T}(m)}\right)_{r\in\mathbb{N}}$ is bounded (see Exercise 5.2).

5.1.3 Weighted star discrepancy estimates for (t, m, s)-nets

The star discrepancy estimates presented can also be adapted to obtain estimates for the weighted star discrepancy, which we present in the following.

Theorem 5.26 *Let $\Delta_b(t, m, s)$ be such that for the star discrepancy of any (t, m, s)-net $\mathcal{P}$ in base b, the inequality $b^m D^*_{b^m}(\mathcal{P}) \leq \Delta_b(t, m, s)$ holds. Then, for the weighted star discrepancy $D^*_{b^m,\boldsymbol{\gamma}}$, with respect to the weights $\boldsymbol{\gamma} = \{\gamma_{\mathfrak{u},s} : \mathfrak{u} \subseteq \mathcal{I}_s\}$, of a (t, m, s)-net $\mathcal{P}$ in base b, we have*

$$b^m D^*_{b^m,\boldsymbol{\gamma}}(\mathcal{P}) \leq \max_{\emptyset \neq \mathfrak{u} \subseteq \mathcal{I}_s} \gamma_{\mathfrak{u},s} \Delta_b(t, m, |\mathfrak{u}|).$$

Proof This immediately follows from Definition 3.59 of the weighted star discrepancy and the fact that any d-dimensional projection of a (t, m, s)-net in base b (where $d \leq s$) is a (t, m, d)-net in base b (see Lemma 4.16 in Section 4.2). □

Example 5.27 In particular, if we consider product weights of the form $\gamma_{\mathfrak{u},s} = \prod_{j \in \mathfrak{u}} \gamma_{j,s}$ with $\gamma_{1,s} \geq \gamma_{2,s} \geq \cdots \geq \gamma_{s,s}$, then for any (t, m, s)-net $\mathcal{P}$ in base b, we have

$$b^m D^*_{b^m,\boldsymbol{\gamma}}(\mathcal{P}) \leq \max_{1 \leq d \leq s} \Delta_b(t, m, d) \prod_{j=1}^{d} \gamma_{j,s}.$$

Let us consider a $(0, m, s)$-net $\mathcal{P}$ in base $b \geq 3$, where $b \geq s - 1$ is a prime power (explicit constructions of such nets are presented in Chapter 8). We use the discrepancy estimate of Theorem 5.1, which shows that

$$\Delta_b(0, m, d) \leq \sum_{i=0}^{d-1} \binom{d-1}{i} \binom{m}{i} \left\lfloor \frac{b}{2} \right\rfloor^i.$$

Hence,

$$b^m D^*_{b^m,\boldsymbol{\gamma}}(\mathcal{P}) \leq \max_{1 \leq d \leq s} \left(\prod_{j=1}^{d} \gamma_{j,s} \right) \sum_{i=0}^{d-1} \binom{d-1}{i} \binom{m}{i} \left\lfloor \frac{b}{2} \right\rfloor^i.$$

A more detailed investigation of the quality of a (t, m, s)-net, especially the quality of its projections, can give improved estimates for the weighted discrepancy (see Exercise 5.3).

5.2 Some discussion about the discrepancy estimates

As was pointed out by several authors (see the discussion in [177, Chapter 4]), the asymptotic results in N (the number of points) for the discrepancy of (t, m, s)-nets and (t, s)-sequences far exceed what was known about the asymptotic behaviour of the discrepancy of 'classical' sequences and point sets (see Section 3.4). Hence, the order of magnitude of the discrepancies in N are presumptively the best possible and the coefficients $B(s, b)$ and $C(s, b)$ of the leading terms $(\log N)^{s-1}$ and $(\log N)^s$ respectively decrease with growing dimension s extremely quickly. For practical purposes, however, concrete finite point sets and their discrepancies are of course of interest. Let us consider the discrepancy estimates, therefore, with respect to their practical meaning. By doing this, we arrive at a principal problem, namely, that we do not have strong and adequate discrepancy estimates for 'relatively small' point sets in an s-dimensional unit-cube.

As in Section 3.5, let us consider a point set consisting of 2^s points in $[0, 1)^s$. (For dimension, say, $s = 20$, this already becomes a large point set for practical applications in simulation and for $s \geq 30$ such a point set is already hardly manageable anymore.) Hence, at least for, say, $s \geq 20$, we need good discrepancy estimates for point sets with 2^s or less points.

As already pointed out in Section 3.5, it is not known how such estimates could be obtained from the known estimates for regular lattices, Hammersley point sets or good lattice point sets, although it is known that such point sets must exist. Recall from Section 3.5 that there exists an absolute constant $c > 0$ such that for the Nth minimal star discrepancy, we have $\mathrm{disc}^*(N, s) \leq c\sqrt{s/N}$ for all $s, N \in \mathbb{N}$ and therefore $\mathrm{disc}^*(2^s, s) \leq c\sqrt{s/2^s}$. Hence, for any dimension s, there exists a point set $\mathcal{P}$, consisting of $N = 2^s$ points in $[0, 1)^s$, such that $D_N^*(\mathcal{P}) \leq c\sqrt{s/2^s}$.

Let us now check the discrepancy estimate for a (t, m, s)-net $\mathcal{P}$ in base 2 derived in Theorem 5.2, or in Theorem 5.12 above, for 2^s points. For $N = 2^s$, we obtain

$$N D_N^*(\mathcal{P}) \leq 2^t \sum_{i=0}^{s-1} \binom{s-t}{i} = 2^t 2^{s-t} = N,$$

hence, we only obtain $D_N^*(\mathcal{P}) \leq 1$, which is the trivial estimate for the star discrepancy of any point set. Thus, in this context, the above bound is useless.

Let us try another approach. It is known that for every prime power b there exist $(0, m, s)$-nets in base b for all $s \leq b + 1$ (for example, nets from Faure and Niederreiter sequences; see Chapter 8). If we consider such nets with $s = b + 1$ and $m \approx s\frac{\log 2}{\log b}$, so that $N = b^m \approx 2^s$, and if we insert these parameters in the discrepancy estimates of Theorem 5.2 or of Theorem 5.12, we again only obtain trivial estimates, larger or equal to one for the star discrepancy.

The best result that can be shown for the star discrepancy of (t, m, s)-nets in this context is at the moment the following theorem.

Theorem 5.28 *For every dimension s there is a (t, m, s)-net $\mathcal{P}$ in base 2 consisting of 2^{11s} points in $[0, 1)^s$ whose star discrepancy is less then $\frac{s}{2^{1.09s}}$.*

Proof Niederreiter and Xing [194, Theorem 4] have shown that for every dimension s and any m, there exists a (t, m, s)-net in base 2 with $t \leq 5s$. Using this point set with $m = 11s$ and the discrepancy estimate from Theorem 5.12 for $b = 2$, we obtain for the star discrepancy of this net $\mathcal{P}$,

$$N D_N^*(\mathcal{P}) \le 2^{5s} \sum_{i=0}^{s-1} \binom{11s}{i} \le 2^{5s} s \binom{11s}{s} \le 2^{5s} s 11^s \frac{s^s}{s!}.$$

Since $s! \ge \left(\frac{s}{e}\right)^s$ for all s, we obtain

$$N D_N^*(\mathcal{P}) \le s(2^5 e 11)^s < s 2^{9.91 s}$$

and the result follows. □

Thus, although it is known from Section 3.5 that there must exist 'relatively small' point sets with 'small' star discrepancy, and although it is known that the star discrepancy of (t, m, s)-nets is (presumptively) asymptotically the best possible, it is not known whether it can be shown that (t, m, s)-nets are good candidates for 'relatively small' point sets with 'small' star discrepancy; that is, currently it is not known whether it can be shown that there exist, for every m and $s \in \mathbb{N}$, (t, m, s)-nets $\mathcal{P}$ whose star discrepancy satisfies a bound of the form $D_N^*(\mathcal{P}) \le C s^\alpha / N^\beta$ with constants $C, \alpha, \beta > 0$, where $N = b^m$.

5.3 Discrepancy estimates for digital (t, m, s)-nets and digital $(\mathbf{T}, s)$-sequences

All the discrepancy estimates presented in Section 5.1 are valid for arbitrary nets and arbitrary $(\mathbf{T}, s)$-sequences. One may ask if there are sharper discrepancy estimates which only apply for digital (t, m, s)-nets and for digital $(\mathbf{T}, s)$-sequences.

Until now there are no such results which improve the known general estimates in important cases, i.e. for net-type point sets with (nearly) optimal quality. However, in [136, Proposition 1] a discrepancy bound for digital nets and digital sequences was provided, which turned out to be essentially stronger than the general bounds in the cases 'near the average', i.e. for digital point sets whose quality parameter t or $\mathbf{T}$ is of about average value. Further, this bound is better than previous estimates. We give the result and a detailed proof below. In the following we also give an application when we are dealing with metrical and average-type results for the quality parameter and for the discrepancy of net-type sequences. The subsequent results were given by Larcher [136, Proposition 1; 138, Lemma 1 and Lemma 2]. These results provide discrepancy estimates for digital nets and for digital sequences over $\mathbb{Z}_b$ of prime order b in terms of their generating matrices.

5.3.1 Star discrepancy estimates for digital (t, m, s)-nets

We need some further notation before we can state the results. Within this subsection, let b be a prime. A digital (t, m, s)-net over $\mathbb{Z}_b$ is generated by $m \times m$ matrices $C_1, \ldots, C_s$ over $\mathbb{Z}_b$. We denote by $\mathbf{c}_j^{(i)} \in \mathbb{Z}_b^m$ the jth row vector of C_i. For $0 \le w \le s$, a w-tuple $\boldsymbol{d} = (d_1, \ldots, d_w)$ of non-negative integers is called *admissible* with respect to $C_1, \ldots, C_s$ if the system $\{\mathbf{c}_j^{(i)} : 1 \le j \le d_i \text{ and } 1 \le i \le w\}$ of row vectors is linearly independent over $\mathbb{Z}_b$. For $w = 0$ we have the 'zero-tuple' (), which we call admissible by definition. For $w \le s - 1$ and admissible $\boldsymbol{d} = (d_1, \ldots, d_w) \in \mathbb{N}_0^w$, we set

$$h(\boldsymbol{d}) := \max\{h \ge 0 : (d_1, \ldots, d_w, h) \text{ is admissible}\}.$$

For $\boldsymbol{d} = (d_1, \ldots, d_w) \in \mathbb{N}_0^w$ we set $|\boldsymbol{d}|_1 := d_1 + \cdots + d_w$. Note that if $\boldsymbol{d}$ is admissible, then $|\boldsymbol{d}|_1 \le m$ and $0 \le h(\boldsymbol{d}) \le m - |\boldsymbol{d}|_1$.

With these definitions we can state the desired result.

Theorem 5.29 *Let $s, m \in \mathbb{N}$ and let b be a prime. The star discrepancy of a digital net $\mathcal{P}$ over $\mathbb{Z}_b$, generated by the $m \times m$ matrices $C_1, \ldots, C_s$, satisfies*

$$D_{b^m}^*(\mathcal{P}) \le \sum_{w=0}^{s-1} (b-1)^w \sum_{\substack{\boldsymbol{d} \in \mathbb{N}^w \\ \boldsymbol{d} \text{ admissible}}} b^{-|\boldsymbol{d}|_1 - h(\boldsymbol{d})}.$$

Proof Let $\boldsymbol{d} = (d_1, \ldots, d_w)$ be admissible, i.e. the vectors

$$\mathbf{c}_1^{(1)}, \ldots, \mathbf{c}_{d_1}^{(1)}, \ldots, \mathbf{c}_1^{(w)}, \ldots, \mathbf{c}_{d_w}^{(w)} \in \mathbb{Z}_b^m$$

are linearly independent over $\mathbb{Z}_b$. We use the following basic property. For every choice of

$$f_1^{(1)}, \ldots, f_{d_1}^{(1)}, \ldots, f_1^{(w)}, \ldots, f_{d_w}^{(w)} \in \mathbb{Z}_b,$$

the linear system of $|\boldsymbol{d}|_1$ equations in $\mathbf{n} \in (\mathbb{Z}_b^m)^\top$,

$$\mathbf{c}_j^{(i)} \mathbf{n} = f_j^{(i)}$$

with $1 \le j \le d_i$ and $1 \le i \le w$, has exactly $b^{m-|\boldsymbol{d}|_1}$ solutions, and so (as was carried out in the proof of Theorem 4.52 in Section 4.4) any interval of the form

$$\prod_{i=1}^{w} \left[\frac{u_i}{b^{d_i}}, \frac{v_i}{b^{d_i}}\right) \times [0, 1)^{s-w}$$

with $0 \le u_i < v_i < b^{d_i}$ for $1 \le i \le w$, contains exactly $b^{m-|\boldsymbol{d}|_1} \prod_{i=1}^{w} (u_i - v_i)$ elements of the digital net $\mathcal{P}$. We call an interval of this form an *admissible interval*. Hence, an admissible interval is fair with respect to the digital net $\mathcal{P}$.

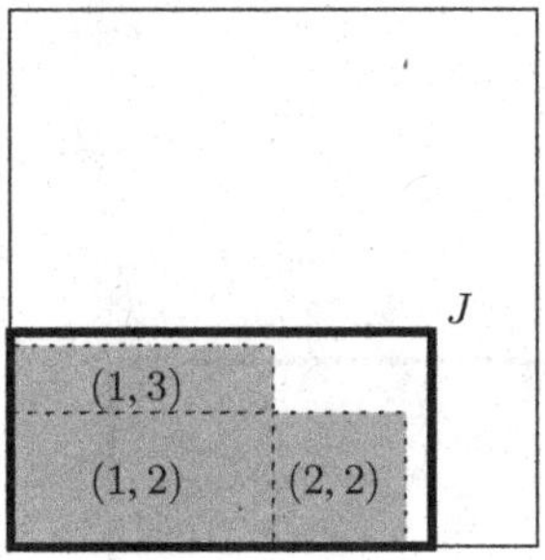

Figure 5.3 The set $\underline{J}$.

Now let $J = \prod_{i=1}^{s}[0, \alpha_i) \subseteq [0, 1)^s$ be an arbitrary interval containing the origin. Assume that for $1 \le i \le s$ the α_i have a b-adic representation of the form

$$\alpha_i = \frac{\alpha_{i,1}}{b} + \frac{\alpha_{i,2}}{b^2} + \cdots .$$

(If α_i is a b-adic fraction, i.e. $\alpha_i = Ab^{-r}$ for some non-negative integers A and r, then we take the infinite representation of α_i.) We again try to approximate J from the interior and from the exterior as closely as possible by unions of admissible intervals. Notice that the following union of admissible intervals

$$\underline{J} := \bigcup_{\substack{\boldsymbol{d}=(d_1,\ldots,d_s)\in\mathbb{N}^s \\ \boldsymbol{d} \text{ admissible}}} \prod_{i=1}^{s} \left[\sum_{j=1}^{d_i-1} \frac{\alpha_{i,j}}{b^j}, \sum_{j=1}^{d_i} \frac{\alpha_{i,j}}{b^j} \right)$$

is a subset of J, and that the single s-dimensional intervals in the above union are pairwise disjoint.

For example, let $s = 2$, $m = 4$, $b = 2$ and consider the following matrices

$$C_1 = \begin{pmatrix} 1 & 0 & 0 & 0 \\ 0 & 1 & 0 & 0 \\ 0 & 0 & 1 & 0 \\ 0 & 0 & 0 & 1 \end{pmatrix} \text{ and } C_2 = \begin{pmatrix} 0 & 0 & 0 & 1 \\ 0 & 0 & 1 & 0 \\ 0 & 1 & 0 & 0 \\ 0 & 0 & 0 & 0 \end{pmatrix}$$

over $\mathbb{Z}_2$ with admissible pairs (d_1, d_2): $(4, 0), (3, 1), (2, 2), (1, 3)$ and all tuples which are less than or equal to these in both coordinates. Let $\alpha_1 = \frac{1}{2} + \frac{1}{4} + \frac{1}{16} + \frac{1}{64} + \cdots$, $\alpha_2 = \frac{1}{4} + \frac{1}{8} + \frac{1}{32} + \cdots$. (Note that J is right-half-open.) Then the admissible pairs $(2, 2)$, $(1, 2)$ and $(1, 3)$ give the intervals $[1/2, 3/4) \times [0, 1/4)$, $[0, 1/2) \times [0, 1/4)$ and $[0, 1/2) \times [1/4, 3/8)$, respectively. All other admissible pairs provide only empty intervals (see Figure 5.3).

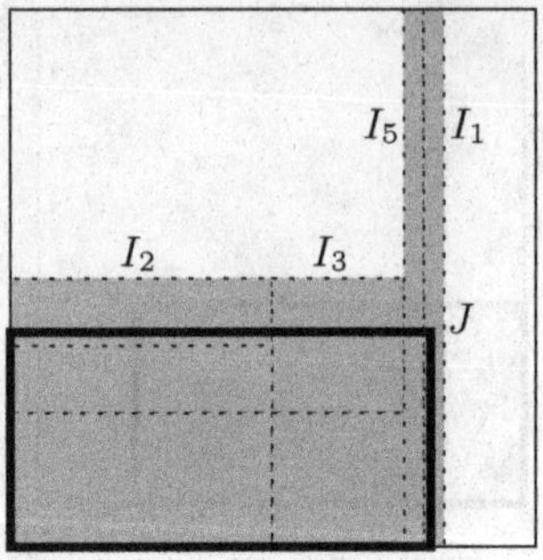

Figure 5.4 The set $\underline{J} \cup \overline{J}$.

Because of the technical complexity of the expressions, it may not be so obvious that

$$J \subseteq \underline{J} \cup \bigcup_{w=0}^{s-1} \bigcup_{\substack{\boldsymbol{d}=(d_1,\ldots,d_w)\in\mathbb{N}^w \\ \boldsymbol{d}\text{ admissible}}} \left(\prod_{i=1}^{w} \left[\sum_{j=1}^{d_i-1} \frac{\alpha_{i,j}}{b^j}, \sum_{j=1}^{d_i} \frac{\alpha_{i,j}}{b^j} \right) \right.$$

$$\left. \times \left[\sum_{j=1}^{h(\boldsymbol{d})} \frac{\alpha_{w+1,j}}{b^j}, \sum_{j=1}^{h(\boldsymbol{d})} \frac{\alpha_{w+1,j}}{b^j} + \frac{1}{b^{h(\boldsymbol{d})}} \right) \times [0,1)^{s-w-1} \right)$$

$$=: \underline{J} \cup \overline{J}. \tag{5.6}$$

Notice that all single s-dimensional intervals occurring in the above union are pairwise disjoint and admissible. Thus, the right-hand side is fair with respect to the net.

Before we show the above inclusion, we illustrate it with the above example. Here we have to consider the following additional intervals (see Figure 5.4):

$$\begin{aligned}
w = 0: \quad & h() = 4 && : \quad I_1 = \left[\tfrac{1}{2} + \tfrac{1}{4} + \tfrac{1}{16}, \tfrac{1}{2} + \tfrac{1}{4} + \tfrac{1}{16} + \tfrac{1}{16}\right) \times [0,1) \\
w = 1: \quad & h(1) = 3 && : \quad I_2 = \left[0, \tfrac{1}{2}\right) \times \left[\tfrac{1}{4} + \tfrac{1}{8}, \tfrac{1}{4} + \tfrac{1}{8} + \tfrac{1}{8}\right) \\
& h(2) = 2 && : \quad I_3 = \left[\tfrac{1}{2}, \tfrac{1}{2} + \tfrac{1}{4}\right) \times \left[\tfrac{1}{4}, \tfrac{1}{4} + \tfrac{1}{4}\right) \\
& h(3) = 1 && : \quad I_4 = \left[\tfrac{1}{2} + \tfrac{1}{4}, \tfrac{1}{2} + \tfrac{1}{4}\right) \times \left[0, \tfrac{1}{2}\right) = \emptyset \\
& h(4) = 0 && : \quad I_5 = \left[\tfrac{1}{2} + \tfrac{1}{4}, \tfrac{1}{2} + \tfrac{1}{4} + \tfrac{1}{16}\right) \times [0,1)
\end{aligned}$$

To show that (5.6) holds, we carry out induction on the dimension s. For $s = 1$ the right-hand side above becomes

$$\bigcup_{\substack{d_1 \in \mathbb{N} \\ d_1 \text{ admissible}}} \left[\sum_{j=1}^{d_1-1} \frac{\alpha_{1,j}}{b^j}, \sum_{j=1}^{d_1} \frac{\alpha_{1,j}}{b^j}\right) \cup \left[\sum_{j=1}^{h()} \frac{\alpha_{1,j}}{b^j}, \sum_{j=1}^{h()} \frac{\alpha_{1,j}}{b^j} + \frac{1}{b^{h()}}\right)$$

$$= \left[0, \sum_{j=1}^{h()} \frac{\alpha_{1,j}}{b^j} + \frac{1}{b^{h()}}\right),$$

which contains $J = [0, \alpha_1)$. Assume now that the assertion is true up to dimension $s - 1$ and consider

$$J = \prod_{i=1}^{s-1} [0, \alpha_i) \times [0, \alpha_s).$$

The induction assumption states that

$$\prod_{i=1}^{s\ 1} [0, \alpha_i) \subseteq \bigcup_{\substack{\boldsymbol{d}=(d_1,\ldots,d_{s-1}) \in \mathbb{N}^{s-1} \\ \boldsymbol{d} \text{ admissible}}} \prod_{i=1}^{s-1} \left[\sum_{j=1}^{d_i-1} \frac{\alpha_{i,j}}{b^j}, \sum_{j=1}^{d_i} \frac{\alpha_{i,j}}{b^j}\right)$$

$$\cup \bigcup_{w=0}^{s-2} \bigcup_{\substack{\boldsymbol{d}=(d_1,\ldots,d_w) \in \mathbb{N}^w \\ \boldsymbol{d} \text{ admissible}}} \left(\prod_{i=1}^{w} \left[\sum_{j=1}^{d_i-1} \frac{\alpha_{i,j}}{b^j}, \sum_{j=1}^{d_i} \frac{\alpha_{i,j}}{b^j}\right)\right.$$

$$\left. \times \left[\sum_{j=1}^{h(\boldsymbol{d})} \frac{\alpha_{w+1,j}}{b^j}, \sum_{j=1}^{h(\boldsymbol{d})} \frac{\alpha_{w+1,j}}{b^j} + \frac{1}{b^{h(\boldsymbol{d})}}\right) \times [0, 1)^{s-w-2}\right).$$

We extend each of the $s - 1$-dimensional intervals K on the right-hand side above to an s-dimensional interval K' such that J is contained in the union of these extensions.

If K is part of the first 'big' union above, that is, if it is of the form

$$\prod_{i=1}^{s-1} \left[\sum_{j=1}^{d_i-1} \frac{\alpha_{i,j}}{b^j}, \sum_{j=1}^{d_i} \frac{\alpha_{i,j}}{b^j}\right)$$

for some admissible $\boldsymbol{d} = (d_1, \ldots, d_{s-1}) \in \mathbb{N}^{s-1}$, then we take

$$K' := \prod_{i=1}^{s-1} \left[\sum_{j=1}^{d_i - 1} \frac{\alpha_{i,j}}{b^j}, \sum_{j=1}^{d_i} \frac{\alpha_{i,j}}{b^j} \right) \times \left(\bigcup_{k=1}^{h(\boldsymbol{d})} \left[\sum_{j=1}^{k-1} \frac{\alpha_{s,j}}{b^j}, \sum_{j=1}^{k} \frac{\alpha_{s,j}}{b^j} \right) \cup \left[\sum_{j=1}^{h(\boldsymbol{d})} \frac{\alpha_{s,j}}{b^j}, \sum_{j=1}^{h(\boldsymbol{d})} \frac{\alpha_{s,j}}{b^j} + \frac{1}{b^{h(\boldsymbol{d})}} \right) \right).$$

If K is part of the second 'big' union, then we just extend by $[0, 1)$.

By inserting, we obtain

$$\begin{aligned} J \subseteq & \bigcup_{\substack{\boldsymbol{d}=(d_1,\ldots,d_{s-1}) \in \mathbb{N}^{s-1} \\ \boldsymbol{d} \text{ admissible}}} \left(\prod_{i=1}^{s-1} \left[\sum_{j=1}^{d_i-1} \frac{\alpha_{i,j}}{b^j}, \sum_{j=1}^{d_i} \frac{\alpha_{i,j}}{b^j} \right) \times \bigcup_{k=1}^{h(\boldsymbol{d})} \left[\sum_{j=1}^{k-1} \frac{\alpha_{s,j}}{b^j}, \sum_{j=1}^{k} \frac{\alpha_{s,j}}{b^j} \right) \right) \\ & \cup \bigcup_{\substack{\boldsymbol{d}=(d_1,\ldots,d_{s-1}) \in \mathbb{N}^{s-1} \\ \boldsymbol{d} \text{ admissible}}} \left(\prod_{i=1}^{s-1} \left[\sum_{j=1}^{d_i-1} \frac{\alpha_{i,j}}{b^j}, \sum_{j=1}^{d_i} \frac{\alpha_{i,j}}{b^j} \right) \times \left[\sum_{j=1}^{h(\boldsymbol{d})} \frac{\alpha_{s,j}}{b^j}, \sum_{j=1}^{h(\boldsymbol{d})} \frac{\alpha_{s,j}}{b^j} + \frac{1}{b^{h(\boldsymbol{d})}} \right) \right) \\ & \cup \bigcup_{w=0}^{s-2} \bigcup_{\substack{\boldsymbol{d}=(d_1,\ldots,d_w) \in \mathbb{N}^w \\ \boldsymbol{d} \text{ admissible}}} \left(\prod_{i=1}^{w} \left[\sum_{j=1}^{d_i-1} \frac{\alpha_{i,j}}{b^j}, \sum_{j=1}^{d_i} \frac{\alpha_{i,j}}{b^j} \right) \right. \\ & \qquad \left. \times \left[\sum_{j=1}^{h(\boldsymbol{d})} \frac{\alpha_{w+1,j}}{b^j}, \sum_{j=1}^{h(\boldsymbol{d})} \frac{\alpha_{w+1,j}}{b^j} + \frac{1}{b^{h(\boldsymbol{d})}} \right) \times [0, 1)^{s-w-1} \right), \end{aligned}$$

and the induction is finished.

Hence, for the number $A(J, b^m, \mathcal{P})$ of net points in J, we obtain

$$\begin{aligned} \frac{A(J, b^m, \mathcal{P})}{b^m} - \lambda_s(J) &\leq \frac{A\left(\underline{J} \cup \overline{J}, b^m, \mathcal{P}\right)}{b^m} - \lambda_s\left(\underline{J} \cup \overline{J}\right) + \lambda_s\left(\underline{J} \cup \overline{J} \setminus J\right) \\ &\leq \lambda_s\left(\overline{J}\right) \end{aligned}$$

and

$$\frac{A(J, b^m, \mathcal{P})}{b^m} - \lambda_s(J) \geq \frac{A\left(\underline{J}, b^m, \mathcal{P}\right)}{b^m} - \lambda_s\left(\underline{J}\right) - \lambda_s\left(J \setminus \underline{J}\right) \geq -\lambda_s\left(\overline{J}\right).$$

Now the result follows from the fact that

$$\lambda_s\left(\overline{J}\right) \le \sum_{w=0}^{s-1} \sum_{\substack{\boldsymbol{d} \in \mathbb{N}^w \\ \boldsymbol{d} \text{ admissible}}} (b-1)^w b^{-|\boldsymbol{d}|_1 - h(\boldsymbol{d})}. \qquad \square$$

Remark 5.30 The above discrepancy estimate also holds for digital nets which are digitally shifted by a digital b-adic shift $\boldsymbol{\sigma} = (\sigma_1, \ldots, \sigma_s) \in [0, 1)^s$ (with probability one if a σ_i has infinitely many digits different from zero) or by a digital shift of depth m. This can be checked by following and adopting the proof of the above theorem (and that of Theorem 4.52, respectively).

Example 5.31 Let us consider one concrete numerical example. We take the same example as above (illustrating the proof of Theorem 5.29) with $s = 2$, $m = 4$, $b = 2$,

$$C_1 = \begin{pmatrix} 1 & 0 & 0 & 0 \\ 0 & 1 & 0 & 0 \\ 0 & 0 & 1 & 0 \\ 0 & 0 & 0 & 1 \end{pmatrix} \quad \text{and} \quad C_2 = \begin{pmatrix} 0 & 0 & 0 & 1 \\ 0 & 0 & 1 & 0 \\ 0 & 1 & 0 & 0 \\ 0 & 0 & 0 & 0 \end{pmatrix}.$$

By Theorem 5.29, the star discrepancy of the 16-point net $\mathcal{P}$ generated by these matrices satisfies

$$\begin{aligned} D_{16}^*(\mathcal{P}) &\le 2^{-h()} + \sum_{d=1}^{4} 2^{-d-h(d)} \\ &= 2^{-4} + 2^{-1-3} + 2^{-2-2} + 2^{-3-1} + 2^{-4} = \frac{5}{16}. \end{aligned}$$

If we apply the estimate of Remark 5.5 for $s = 2$, by noting that the quality parameter t of the net is 1, we obtain

$$D_{16}^*(\mathcal{P}) \le \frac{1}{16}\left(\frac{1}{2}3 + \frac{3}{2}\right)2^1 = \frac{3}{8},$$

which is larger than $\frac{5}{16}$. Let us consider the picture of the net points (see Figure 5.5) and note that for the closed set B we have

$$\frac{A(B, 16, \mathcal{P})}{16} - \lambda(B) = \frac{8}{16} - \frac{80}{256} = \frac{3}{16}$$

so that $D_{16}^*(\mathcal{P}) \ge \frac{3}{16}$.

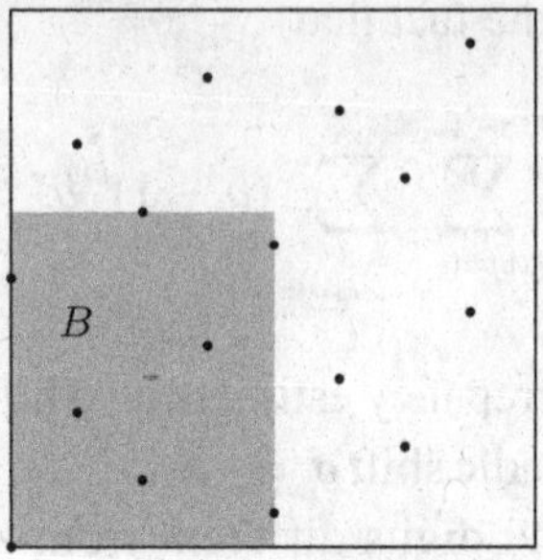

Figure 5.5 The 16-point net $\mathcal{P}$ and the interval B.

5.3.2 Star discrepancy estimates for digital sequences

We now give the corresponding result for digital sequences. The following result is a slight improvement of [138, Lemma 2]. We again use the technique of Niederreiter as already applied in the proof of Lemma 5.13.

Theorem 5.32 *Let $s \in \mathbb{N}$ and let b be a prime. Let $\mathcal{S}$ be a digital sequence generated by the $\mathbb{N} \times \mathbb{N}$ matrices $C_1, \ldots, C_s$ over $\mathbb{Z}_b$ and let $C_i^{(m)}$ denote the left upper $m \times m$ sub-matrix of C_i for $1 \leq i \leq s$. Let $N \in \mathbb{N}$ with b-adic representation $N = \sum_{k=0}^{r} a_k b^k$, where $0 \leq a_k < b$ and $a_r \neq 0$. Then*

$$N D_N^*(\mathcal{S}) \leq \min\left(\sum_{m=n}^{r} a_m \sum_{w=0}^{s-1} (b-1)^w \sum_{\substack{\boldsymbol{d} \in \mathbb{N}^w \\ \boldsymbol{d} \text{ admissible to } m}} b^{m-|\boldsymbol{d}|_1 - h(\boldsymbol{d})}, \right.$$

$$\sum_{m=n}^{r} (b-1-a_m) \sum_{w=0}^{s-1} (b-1)^w \sum_{\substack{\boldsymbol{d} \in \mathbb{N}^w \\ \boldsymbol{d} \text{ admissible to } m}} b^{m-|\boldsymbol{d}|_1 - h(\boldsymbol{d})}$$

$$+ \sum_{w=0}^{s-1} (b-1)^w \sum_{\substack{\boldsymbol{d} \in \mathbb{N}^w \\ \boldsymbol{d} \text{ admissible to } n}} b^{n-|\boldsymbol{d}|_1 - h(\boldsymbol{d})}$$

$$\left. + \sum_{w=0}^{s-1} (b-1)^w \sum_{\substack{\boldsymbol{d} \in \mathbb{N}^w \\ \boldsymbol{d} \text{ admissible to } r+1}} b^{r+1-|\boldsymbol{d}|_1 - h(\boldsymbol{d})} \right).$$

Here, 'admissible to m' means 'admissible with respect to the matrices $C_1^{(m)}, \ldots, C_s^{(m)}$' and n is the largest integer such that $b^n | N$.

Proof We split the set $\{\boldsymbol{x}_0, \ldots, \boldsymbol{x}_{N-1}\}$, consisting of the first N points of the sequence $\mathcal{S}$, into the subsets $\mathcal{P}_{m,a}$ for $a \in \{0, \ldots, a_m - 1\}$ and $0 \leq m \leq r$,

where

$$\mathcal{P}_{m,a} = \left\{ \boldsymbol{x}_n : \sum_{k=m+1}^{r} a_k b^k + a b^m \le n < \sum_{k=m+1}^{r} a_k b^k + (a+1) b^m \right\}.$$

For $1 \le i \le s$, let us divide the matrix C_i into the following parts

$$C_i = \left(\begin{array}{c|c} C_i^{(m)} & D_i^{(m)} \\ \hline \multicolumn{2}{c}{E_i^{(m)}} \end{array} \right).$$

If $n = \sum_{k=m+1}^{r} a_k b^k + a b^m + \sum_{k=0}^{m-1} d_k b^k$, then

$$\mathbf{n} = (d_0, d_1, \ldots, d_{m-1}, a, a_{m+1}, \ldots, a_r, 0, 0, \ldots)^\top \in (\mathbb{Z}_b^{\mathbb{N}})^\top$$

and

$$C_i \mathbf{n} = \begin{pmatrix} C_i^{(m)} \begin{pmatrix} d_0 \\ \vdots \\ d_{m-1} \end{pmatrix} \\ 0 \\ 0 \\ \vdots \end{pmatrix} + \begin{pmatrix} D_i^{(m)} \begin{pmatrix} a \\ a_{m+1} \\ \vdots \\ a_r \\ 0 \\ \vdots \end{pmatrix} \\ 0 \\ 0 \\ \vdots \end{pmatrix} + \begin{pmatrix} 0 \\ \vdots \\ 0 \\ E_i^{(m)} \mathbf{n} \end{pmatrix}.$$

Therefore, $\mathcal{P}_{m,a}$ is a (modulo $\mathbb{Z}_b$) digitally shifted digital net generated by the $m \times m$ matrices $C_1^{(m)}, \ldots, C_s^{(m)}$, which finally is translated by a vector with positive coordinates less than b^{-m} (i.e. a digital shift of depth m). By Proposition 3.16 and Theorem 5.29 (see also Remark 5.30), we have

$$\begin{aligned} N D_N^*(\mathcal{S}) &\le \sum_{m=0}^{r} \sum_{a=0}^{a_m - 1} b^m D_{b^m}^*(\mathcal{P}_{m,a}) \\ &\le \sum_{m=0}^{r} a_m \sum_{w=0}^{s-1} (b-1)^w \sum_{\substack{\boldsymbol{d} \in \mathbb{N}^w \\ \boldsymbol{d} \text{ admissible to } m}} b^{m - |\boldsymbol{d}|_1 - h(\boldsymbol{d})}. \end{aligned}$$

Now let $b^{r+1} - N = \sum_{m=0}^{r} c_m b^m$, then as in the proof of Lemma 5.14, we also obtain

$$N D_N^*(\mathcal{S}) \le \sum_{m=0}^{r} c_m \sum_{w=0}^{s-1} (b-1)^w \sum_{\substack{\boldsymbol{d} \in \mathbb{N}^w \\ \boldsymbol{d} \text{ admissible to } m}} b^{m-|\boldsymbol{d}|_1 - h(\boldsymbol{d})}$$
$$+ \sum_{w=0}^{s-1} (b-1)^w \sum_{\substack{\boldsymbol{d} \in \mathbb{N}^w \\ \boldsymbol{d} \text{ admissible to } r+1}} b^{r+1-|\boldsymbol{d}|_1 - h(\boldsymbol{d})}.$$

Note that $a_0 = \cdots = a_{n-1} = c_0 = \cdots = c_{n-1} = 0$, that $a_n + c_n = b$, and that $a_m + c_m = b - 1$ for $n + 1 \le m \le r$. Hence, the result follows. □

As a consequence, we obtain the following result.

Corollary 5.33 *Let $s \in \mathbb{N}$ and let b be a prime. Let $\mathcal{S}$ be the digital sequence generated by the $\mathbb{N} \times \mathbb{N}$ matrices $C_1, \ldots, C_s$ over $\mathbb{Z}_b$. Let $r \in \mathbb{N}_0$ such that $b^r \le N < b^{r+1}$ and let n be the largest integer such that $b^n | N$. Then we have*

$$N D_N^*(\mathcal{S}) \le \frac{1}{2} \sum_{m=n}^{r} (b-1) \sum_{w=0}^{s-1} (b-1)^w \sum_{\substack{\boldsymbol{d} \in \mathbb{N}^w \\ \boldsymbol{d} \text{ admissible to } m}} b^{m-|\boldsymbol{d}|_1 - h(\boldsymbol{d})}$$
$$+ \frac{1}{2} \sum_{w=0}^{s-1} (b-1)^w \left(\sum_{\substack{\boldsymbol{d} \in \mathbb{N}^w \\ \boldsymbol{d} \text{ admissible to } n}} b^{n-|\boldsymbol{d}|_1 - h(\boldsymbol{d})} + \sum_{\substack{\boldsymbol{d} \in \mathbb{N}^w \\ \boldsymbol{d} \text{ admissible to } r+1}} b^{r+1-|\boldsymbol{d}|_1 - h(\boldsymbol{d})} \right).$$

5.3.3 Weighted star discrepancy estimates for digital (t, m, s)-nets

In the following we use a different approach for the weighted star discrepancy. This method is based on Theorem 3.28. We start with a bound on the unweighted star discrepancy of digital nets. The quantity R_b, defined in the following, is useful for obtaining such a bound as it captures the essential part of the star discrepancy. In detail, for $m \times m$ matrices $C_1, \ldots, C_s$ over $\mathbb{Z}_b$, b a prime, define

$$R_b(C_1, \ldots, C_s) := \sum_{\boldsymbol{k} \in \mathcal{D}'} \rho_b(\boldsymbol{k}), \tag{5.7}$$

where the set $\mathcal{D}'$ is the dual net without the zero vector (see Definition 4.76), that is,

$$\mathcal{D}' = \left\{ \boldsymbol{k} \in \{0, 1, \ldots, b^m - 1\}^s : C_1^\top \mathbf{k}_1 + \cdots + C_s^\top \mathbf{k}_s = \mathbf{0} \right\} \setminus \{\mathbf{0}\}, \tag{5.8}$$

where $\boldsymbol{k} = (k_1, \ldots, k_s)$ and for $1 \le i \le s$, we denote by $\mathbf{k}_i$ the m-dimensional column vector of b-adic digits of $k_i \in \{0, \ldots, b^m - 1\}$. Furthermore,

$\rho_b(\boldsymbol{k}) := \prod_{i=1}^{s} \rho_b(k_i)$ where for $k \in \mathbb{N}_0$ we put

$$\rho_b(k) := \begin{cases} 1 & \text{if } k = 0, \\ \frac{1}{b^{r+1}\sin(\pi\kappa_r/b)} & \text{if } k = \kappa_0 + \kappa_1 b + \cdots + \kappa_r b^r,\ \kappa_r \neq 0. \end{cases} \tag{5.9}$$

Theorem 5.34 *Let $s, m \in \mathbb{N}$ and let b be a prime. For the star discrepancy of the digital net $\mathcal{P}$ over $\mathbb{Z}_b$ with generating matrices $C_1, \ldots, C_s \in \mathbb{Z}_b^{m\times m}$, we have*

$$D_{b^m}^*(\mathcal{P}) \leq 1 - \left(1 - \frac{1}{b^m}\right)^s + R_b(C_1, \ldots, C_s). \tag{5.10}$$

Proof The result follows from Theorem 3.28 by invoking Lemma 4.75. Note that for a digital (t, m, s)-net over $\mathbb{Z}_b$, each component of each point is a rational with denominator b^m. □

Note that $1 - (1 - 1/b^m)^s \leq sb^{-m}$ by the mean value theorem.

The quantity $R_b(C_1, \ldots, C_s)$, defined above, can be represented in terms of Walsh functions. This representation is an important tool when we analyse the average star discrepancy of digital nets later on.

Lemma 5.35 *Let $s, m \in \mathbb{N}$ and let b be a prime. Let $\{\boldsymbol{x}_0, \ldots, \boldsymbol{x}_{b^m-1}\}$ with $\boldsymbol{x}_n = (x_{n,1}, \ldots, x_{n,s})$ for $0 \leq n < b^m$ be a digital net over $\mathbb{Z}_b$ generated by the $m \times m$ matrices $C_1, \ldots, C_s$. Then we have*

$$R_b(C_1, \ldots, C_s) = -1 + \frac{1}{b^m}\sum_{n=0}^{b^m-1}\prod_{i=1}^{s}\left(\sum_{k=0}^{b^m-1} \rho_b(k)\, {}_b\mathrm{wal}_k(x_{n,i})\right).$$

Proof Using Lemma 4.75, we have

$$\begin{aligned} R_b(C_1, \ldots, C_s) &= \sum_{\boldsymbol{k}\in\mathcal{D}'} \rho_b(\boldsymbol{k}) \\ &= -1 + \sum_{\boldsymbol{k}\in\{0,\ldots,b^m-1\}^s} \rho_b(\boldsymbol{k}) \frac{1}{b^m}\sum_{n=0}^{b^m-1} {}_b\mathrm{wal}_{\boldsymbol{k}}(\boldsymbol{x}_n) \\ &= -1 + \frac{1}{b^m}\sum_{n=0}^{b^m-1}\sum_{\boldsymbol{k}\in\{0,\ldots,b^m-1\}^s} \rho_b(\boldsymbol{k})\, {}_b\mathrm{wal}_{\boldsymbol{k}}(\boldsymbol{x}_n), \end{aligned}$$

and the result follows. □

Now we turn to the weighted star discrepancy with weights $\boldsymbol{\gamma} = \{\gamma_{\mathfrak{u},s} : \mathfrak{u} \subseteq \mathcal{I}_s\}$. It follows from Definition 3.59 that for the weighted star discrepancy of a point set

$\mathcal{P}$ in $[0, 1)^s$, we have

$$D^*_{N,\boldsymbol{\gamma}}(\mathcal{P}) = \sup_{\boldsymbol{z}\in(0,1]^s} \max_{\emptyset\neq\mathfrak{u}\subseteq\mathcal{I}_s} \gamma_{\mathfrak{u},s}|\Delta_{\mathcal{P}}(\boldsymbol{z}_{\mathfrak{u}}, 1)| \le \max_{\emptyset\neq\mathfrak{u}\subseteq\mathcal{I}_s} \gamma_{\mathfrak{u},s} \sup_{\boldsymbol{z}_{\mathfrak{u}}\in(0,1]^{|\mathfrak{u}|}} |\Delta_{\mathcal{P}}(\boldsymbol{z}_{\mathfrak{u}}, 1)|$$
$$= \max_{\emptyset\neq\mathfrak{u}\subseteq\mathcal{I}_s} \gamma_{\mathfrak{u},s} D^*_N(\mathcal{P}_{\mathfrak{u}}),$$

where $\mathcal{P}_{\mathfrak{u}}$ in $[0, 1)^{|\mathfrak{u}|}$ consists of the points of $\mathcal{P}$ projected to the components whose indices are in $\mathfrak{u}$.

If we consider a digital net over $\mathbb{Z}_b$, b a prime, generated by $C_1, \ldots, C_s$ over $\mathbb{Z}_b$, then for $\emptyset \neq \mathfrak{u} \subseteq \mathcal{I}_s$ we obtain from (5.10) that

$$D^*_{b^m}(\mathcal{P}_{\mathfrak{u}}) \le 1 - \left(1 - \frac{1}{b^m}\right)^{|\mathfrak{u}|} + R_b((C_i)_{i\in\mathfrak{u}})$$

and that for $\mathfrak{u} = \{u_1, \ldots, u_d\}$, $R_b((C_i)_{i\in\mathfrak{u}})$ is given by

$$R_b((C_i)_{i\in\mathfrak{u}}) = \sum_{\substack{k_1,\ldots,k_d=0 \\ (k_1,\ldots,k_d)\neq(0,\ldots,0) \\ C_{u_1}^\top \mathbf{k}_1+\cdots+C_{u_d}^\top \mathbf{k}_d=\mathbf{0}}}^{2^m-1} \prod_{i=1}^{d} \rho_b(k_i).$$

This yields the following result.

Theorem 5.36 *Let $s, m \in \mathbb{N}$ and let b be a prime. Then for the weighted star discrepancy of a digital net $\mathcal{P}$ over $\mathbb{Z}_b$ generated by the $m \times m$ matrices $C_1, \ldots, C_s$, we have*

$$D^*_{b^m,\boldsymbol{\gamma}}(\mathcal{P}) \le \max_{\emptyset\neq\mathfrak{u}\subseteq\mathcal{I}_s} \gamma_{\mathfrak{u},s}\left(1 - \left(1 - \frac{1}{b^m}\right)^{|\mathfrak{u}|}\right) + R_{\max,b,\boldsymbol{\gamma}}(C_1, \ldots, C_s),$$

where $R_{\max,b,\boldsymbol{\gamma}}(C_1, \ldots, C_s) := \max_{\emptyset\neq\mathfrak{u}\subseteq\mathcal{I}_s} \gamma_{\mathfrak{u},s} R_b((C_i)_{i\in\mathfrak{u}})$.

5.4 Average type and metrical results

We now investigate the average quality parameter and the average star discrepancy for randomly chosen digital nets or digital sequences.

5.4.1 Results on digital nets

We first give the results on digital (t, m, s)-nets. In the 'finite case' it is easy to explain what we mean by 'at random'. For $m, s \in \mathbb{N}$ and for prime b let $\mathcal{C}$ be the set of all s-tuples of $m \times m$ matrices $C_1, \ldots, C_s$ over $\mathbb{Z}_b$. Note that $|\mathcal{C}| = b^{sm^2}$. Every digital (t, m, s)-net over $\mathbb{Z}_b$ is defined by an s-tuple of $m \times m$ matrices over $\mathbb{Z}_b$. Hence, we want to estimate how large the average value of the quality-parameter

t is if we take the average over all digital nets generated by an element from the finite set $\mathcal{C}$, were each s-tuple of generating matrices is chosen as equally likely. We could also state the problem in a slightly modified form. Given t_0 with $0 \le t_0 \le m$, how many s-tuples of $m \times m$ matrices $C_1, \ldots, C_s$ over $\mathbb{Z}_b$ yield a (t, m, s)-net with $t \le t_0$? Instead, for the quality-parameter t, we could also ask the above questions for the star discrepancy.

The following result was first proved (in a more general setting) in [141, Theorem 3].

Theorem 5.37 *Let $m, s \in \mathbb{N}$, let b be a prime, and let α with $0 \le \alpha < 1$ be given. Then, more than $\alpha|\mathcal{C}|$ elements of $\mathcal{C}$ generate a digital (t, m, s)-net over $\mathbb{Z}_b$ with*

$$t \le \left\lceil (s-1)\log_b m + \log_b \frac{1}{1-\alpha} \right\rceil.$$

Remark 5.38 For fixed s by a random choice of matrices we can, roughly speaking, expect a digital (t, m, s)-net over $\mathbb{Z}_b$ with quality parameter t about a constant times $\log_b m$.

Proof of Theorem 5.37 For given m and s we consider the class $\mathcal{C}$ of all s-tuples $(C_1, \ldots, C_s)$ of $m \times m$ matrices over $\mathbb{Z}_b$. By the proof of Theorem 4.52 (see also Lemma 4.59) the matrices from the s-tuple $(C_1, \ldots, C_s)$ do not generate a digital (t, m, s)-net over $\mathbb{Z}_b$ if and only if there exist $d_1, \ldots, d_s \in \mathbb{N}_0$ with $d_1 + \cdots + d_s = m - t$ such that the linear system

$$\mathbf{c}_j^{(i)}\mathbf{n} = 0 \text{ for } 1 \le j \le d_i \text{ and } 1 \le i \le s \tag{5.11}$$

has more than b^t solutions $\mathbf{n} \in (\mathbb{Z}_b^m)^\top$, where $\mathbf{c}_j^{(i)} \in \mathbb{Z}_b^m$ is the jth row vector of the matrix C_i for $1 \le j \le d_i$ and $1 \le i \le s$. By Lemma 4.87, the linear system then has at least $2b^t$ solutions. For $0 \le t < m$ let $M(t)$ be the set of $(C_1, \ldots, C_s) \in \mathcal{C}$ generating no digital (t, m, s)-net over $\mathbb{Z}_b$. Then, for the number $|M(t)|$ of elements $(C_1, \ldots, C_s)$ in $M(t)$, we have

$$\begin{aligned}
|M(t)| &\le \sum_{(C_1,\ldots,C_s)\in\mathcal{C}} \sum_{\substack{\boldsymbol{d}\in\mathbb{N}_0^s\\ |\boldsymbol{d}|_1=m-t}} \frac{1}{b^t}\left(\left|\{\mathbf{n} \in (\mathbb{Z}_b^m)^\top : \mathbf{n} \text{ solves } (5.11)\}\right| - b^t\right)\\
&= \sum_{\substack{\boldsymbol{d}\in\mathbb{N}_0^s\\ |\boldsymbol{d}|_1=m-t}} \left(\frac{1}{b^t} \sum_{\mathbf{n}\in(\mathbb{Z}_b^m)^\top} \sum_{\substack{C\in\mathcal{C}\\ \mathbf{n}\text{ solves }(5.11)}} 1 - \sum_{C\in\mathcal{C}} 1\right).
\end{aligned}$$

For fixed $\boldsymbol{d} \in \mathbb{N}_0^s$, we have

$$\sum_{\mathbf{n}\in(\mathbb{Z}_b^m)^\top} \sum_{\substack{C\in\mathcal{C}\\ \mathbf{n}\text{ solves }(5.11)}} 1 = b^{m^2s-m(m-t)} \sum_{\mathbf{n}\in(\mathbb{Z}_b^m)^\top} \sum_{\substack{\mathbf{c}_1,\ldots,\mathbf{c}_{m-t}\in\mathbb{Z}_b^m\\ \mathbf{n}\text{ solves }(5.12)}} 1,$$

where (5.12) is the linear system

$$\mathbf{c}_k\mathbf{n} = 0 \text{ for } 1 \le k \le m-t. \tag{5.12}$$

To obtain the last equality, note that the linear system (5.11) of equations, $\mathbf{c}_j^{(i)}\mathbf{n} = 0$ for $1 \le j \le d_i$ and $1 \le i \le s$, now considered as a system in the $(m-t)m$ coordinates of the $\mathbf{c}_j^{(i)}$ as unknowns, is independent of the rows $\mathbf{c}_j^{(i)}$ for $d_i < j \le m$, $1 \le i \le s$ of a given s-tuple $(C_1, \ldots, C_s) \in \mathcal{C}$; that is, for any given $\mathbf{c}_1, \ldots, \mathbf{c}_{m-t} \in \mathbb{Z}_b^m$, there are exactly $b^{m^2s-(m-t)m}$ tuples $(C_1, \ldots, C_s) \in \mathcal{C}$ having these $\mathbf{c}_1, \ldots, \mathbf{c}_{m-t}$ as 'first d_i rows'.

Since $|\mathcal{C}| = b^{sm^2}$ and since

$$\sum_{\substack{\boldsymbol{d}\in\mathbb{N}_0^s\\ |\boldsymbol{d}|_1=m-t}} 1 \le (m-t+1)^{s-1},$$

we obtain

$$|M(t)| \le |\mathcal{C}|(m-t+1)^{s-1}\Bigg(b^{-m(m-t)-t} \sum_{\mathbf{n}\in(\mathbb{Z}_b^m)^\top} \sum_{\substack{\mathbf{c}_1,\ldots,\mathbf{c}_{m-t}\in\mathbb{Z}_b^m\\ \mathbf{n}\text{ solves }(5.12)}} 1 - 1\Bigg).$$

We have

$$\sum_{\mathbf{n}\in(\mathbb{Z}_b^m)^\top} \sum_{\substack{\mathbf{c}_1,\ldots,\mathbf{c}_{m-t}\in\mathbb{Z}_b^m\\ \mathbf{n}\text{ solves }(5.12)}} 1 = \sum_{\mathbf{n}\in(\mathbb{Z}_b^m)^\top} \Bigg(\sum_{\substack{\mathbf{c}\in\mathbb{Z}_b^m\\ \mathbf{c}\mathbf{n}=0}} 1\Bigg)^{m-t}.$$

Using

$$\sum_{\substack{\mathbf{c}\in\mathbb{Z}_b^m\\ \mathbf{c}\mathbf{n}=0}} 1 = \begin{cases} b^m & \text{if } \mathbf{n} = \mathbf{0}, \\ b^{m-1} & \text{if } \mathbf{n} \neq \mathbf{0}, \end{cases}$$

we obtain

$$\begin{aligned} |M(t)| &\le |\mathcal{C}|(m-t+1)^{s-1}\left(\frac{b^{(m-t)m} + (b^m-1)b^{(m-1)(m-t)}}{b^{m(m-t)+t}} - 1\right) \\ &\le |\mathcal{C}|(m-t+1)^{s-1}\frac{1}{b^t}. \end{aligned}$$

Let us now determine t_0 such that $(m - t_0 + 1)^{s-1} b^{-t_0} < (1 - \alpha)$. This is certainly satisfied if t_0 is chosen as

$$t_0 = \left\lceil (s-1)\log_b m + \log_b \frac{1}{1-\alpha} \right\rceil.$$

Therefore, the set $M(t_0)$ of s-tuples of $m \times m$ matrices over $\mathbb{Z}_b$ generating no (t_0, m, s)-net over $\mathbb{Z}_b$ has fewer than $(1-\alpha)|\mathcal{C}|$ elements. Hence, the result follows. □

We can use the last result and Theorem 5.10 to obtain an analogous result for the star discrepancy of digital (t, m, s)-nets.

Corollary 5.39 *Let $m, s \in \mathbb{N}$, $m \geq 2$ and let b be a prime. Then, there exists a constant $B(s, b) > 0$, depending only on the dimension s and the base b, with the property that for all given α, with $0 \leq \alpha < 1$, there are more than $\alpha|\mathcal{C}|$ elements of $\mathcal{C}$ generating a digital (t, m, s)-net $\mathcal{P}$ over $\mathbb{Z}_b$ with star discrepancy satisfying*

$$D^*_{b^m}(\mathcal{P}) \leq \frac{B(s,b)}{1-\alpha} \frac{m^{2(s-1)}}{b^m}.$$

Proof The result follows, on combining Theorems 5.10 and 5.37. □

We do not give any details of the proof of Corollary 5.39 since we can improve the result. As it turns out, the order of discrepancy of $(\log N)^{2(s-1)}/N$ is not the best possible. The following result was first proved by Larcher [137, Theorem 10].

Theorem 5.40 *For $m, s \in \mathbb{N}$, $m \geq 2$ and prime base b, let $\mathcal{C}$ be the set of all s-tuples of $m \times m$ matrices over $\mathbb{Z}_b$. Then, there exists a constant $B(s, b) > 0$, depending only on the dimension s and the base b, with the property that for all given α, with $0 \leq \alpha < 1$, there are more than $\alpha|\mathcal{C}|$ elements of $\mathcal{C}$ generating a digital (t, m, s)-net $\mathcal{P}$ over $\mathbb{Z}_b$ with star discrepancy satisfying*

$$\begin{aligned} D^*_{b^m}(\mathcal{P}) &\leq \frac{2}{1-\alpha} \frac{1}{b^m} \sum_{w=0}^{s-1} (b-1)^w \binom{m}{w} \\ &\quad \times \frac{2b - 1 + b\left((s-1)\log_b m + \log_b 2 - \log_b(1-\alpha)\right)}{b-1} \\ &\leq B(s,b) \frac{1}{1-\alpha} \frac{m^{s-1}}{b^m} \log m + O(m^{s-1}). \end{aligned}$$

Here, the implied O-constant depends only on s, b and α.

Proof For $(C_1, \dots, C_s) \in \mathcal{C}$ let $\mathbf{c}_j^{(i)} \in \mathbb{Z}_b^m$ denote the jth row vector of the $m \times m$ matrix C_i for $1 \le j \le m$ and $1 \le i \le s$. For a non-negative integer c let

$$\begin{aligned} M(c) := \{(C_1, \dots, C_s) \in \mathcal{C} : \exists \boldsymbol{d} \in \mathbb{N}_0^s \text{ with } |\boldsymbol{d}|_1 = m - c \text{ such that } \\ \mathbf{c}_j^{(i)},\ 1 \le j \le d_i,\ 1 \le i \le s \text{ are linearly dependent over } \mathbb{Z}_b\}, \end{aligned}$$

where, as usual, $\boldsymbol{d}$ is of the form $\boldsymbol{d} = (d_1, \dots, d_s)$. Then we have

$$|M(c)| \le \sum_{\substack{\boldsymbol{d} \in \mathbb{N}_0^s \\ |\boldsymbol{d}|_1 = m-c}} \sum_{\boldsymbol{\lambda} \in \mathbb{Z}_b^{m-c} \setminus \{\boldsymbol{0}\}} |M(\boldsymbol{\lambda}, \boldsymbol{d})|$$

with

$$M(\boldsymbol{\lambda}, \boldsymbol{d}) := \left\{ (C_1, \dots, C_s) \in \mathcal{C} : \sum_{i=1}^{s} \sum_{j=1}^{d_i} \lambda_{d_1 + \cdots + d_{i-1} + j} \mathbf{c}_j^{(i)} = \boldsymbol{0} \right\},$$

where $\boldsymbol{d} = (d_1, \dots, d_s) \in \mathbb{N}_0^s$ and $\boldsymbol{\lambda} := (\lambda_1, \dots, \lambda_{m-c}) \in \mathbb{Z}_b^{m-c}$. We now determine the number of elements of $M(\boldsymbol{\lambda}, \boldsymbol{d})$. There is an $i \in \{1, \dots, m-c\}$ with $\lambda_i \neq 0$. Assume first that $\lambda_1 \neq 0$. Then, for any choice of

$$\mathbf{c}_2^{(1)}, \dots, \mathbf{c}_m^{(1)}, \mathbf{c}_1^{(2)}, \dots, \mathbf{c}_m^{(2)}, \dots, \mathbf{c}_1^{(s)}, \dots, \mathbf{c}_m^{(s)} \in \mathbb{Z}_b^m,$$

we can find exactly one vector $\mathbf{c}_1^{(1)} \in \mathbb{Z}_b^m$ such that

$$\sum_{i=1}^{s} \sum_{j=1}^{d_i} \lambda_{d_1 + \cdots + d_{i-1} + j} \mathbf{c}_j^{(i)} = \boldsymbol{0}.$$

The same argument holds with λ_1 replaced by $\lambda_{d_1 + \cdots + d_{i-1} + j}$ and $\mathbf{c}_1^{(1)}$ replaced by $\mathbf{c}_j^{(i)}$ for $1 \le j \le d_i$ and $1 \le i \le s$. Therefore, we have $|M(\boldsymbol{\lambda}, \boldsymbol{d})| = b^{-m} |\mathcal{C}|$ and consequently,

$$|M(c)| \le |\mathcal{C}| \frac{1}{b^m} b^{m-c} \sum_{\substack{\boldsymbol{d} \in \mathbb{N}_0^s \\ |\boldsymbol{d}|_1 = m-c}} 1 = |\mathcal{C}| \frac{1}{b^c} \binom{m-c+s-1}{s-1}.$$

For $\overline{M}(c) := \mathcal{C} \setminus M(c)$, we have $|\overline{M}(c)| \ge |\mathcal{C}|(1 - R(c))$ where $R(c) := \frac{1}{b^c} \binom{m-c+s-1}{s-1}$. For a positive integer c, we now consider

$$\Sigma := \frac{1}{|\overline{M}(c)|} \sum_{C \in \overline{M}(c)} D_{b^m}^*(\mathcal{P}_{(C_1, \dots, C_s)}),$$

where $\mathcal{P}_{(C_1,\ldots,C_s)}$ denotes the digital net defined by the s-tuple $(C_1,\ldots,C_s) \in \mathcal{C}$. By the discrepancy estimate for digital nets given in Theorem 5.29, we obtain

$$\begin{aligned}\Sigma &\le \frac{1}{|\overline{M}(c)|} \sum_{(C_1,\ldots,C_s)\in\overline{M}(c)} \sum_{w=0}^{s-1} (b-1)^w \sum_{\substack{\boldsymbol{d}\in\mathbb{N}^w \\ \boldsymbol{d} \text{ admissible to } (C_1,\ldots,C_s)}} b^{-|\boldsymbol{d}|_1 - h(\boldsymbol{d})} \\ &\le \frac{1}{|\overline{M}(c)|} \sum_{(C_1,\ldots,C_s)\in\overline{M}(c)} \sum_{w=0}^{s-1} (b-1)^w \sum_{\substack{\boldsymbol{d}\in\mathbb{N}^w \\ \boldsymbol{d} \text{ admissible to } (C_1,\ldots,C_s)}} b^{-|\boldsymbol{d}|_1} \\ &\quad \times \left(\left(\sum_{k=m-|\boldsymbol{d}|_1-c+1}^{m-|\boldsymbol{d}|_1} \sum\nolimits_{\boldsymbol{\lambda}}^{*} \frac{1}{b-1} \frac{b}{b^k} \right) + \frac{1}{b^{m-|\boldsymbol{d}|_1}} \right).\end{aligned}$$

Here, $\sum_{\boldsymbol{\lambda}}^{*}$ means summation over all $\boldsymbol{\lambda} := (\lambda_1,\ldots,\lambda_{|\boldsymbol{d}|_1+k}) \in \mathbb{Z}_b^{|\boldsymbol{d}|_1+k} \setminus \{\boldsymbol{0}\}$, for which

$$\sum_{i=1}^{w} \sum_{j=1}^{d_i} \lambda_{d_1+\cdots+d_{i-1}+j} \mathbf{c}_j^{(i)} + \sum_{j=1}^{k} \lambda_{|\boldsymbol{d}|_1+j} \mathbf{c}_j^{(w+1)} = \boldsymbol{0} \in \mathbb{Z}_b^m.$$

The summand $\frac{1}{b^{m-|\boldsymbol{d}|_1}}$ results from the case where $h(\boldsymbol{d}) = m - |\boldsymbol{d}|_1$ and the factor $\frac{1}{b-1}$ derives from the fact that, whenever, for given $(C_1,\ldots,C_s)$, w, $\boldsymbol{d}$ and k, there is a possible summand $\boldsymbol{\lambda}$, then there are at least $b-1$ such summands $\boldsymbol{\lambda}$.

Therefore

$$\begin{aligned}\Sigma \le \frac{1}{b^m} \sum_{w=0}^{s-1} (b-1)^w \binom{m}{w} + \frac{1}{|\overline{M}(c)|} \frac{b}{b-1} \sum_{w=0}^{s-1} (b-1)^w \sum_{\substack{\boldsymbol{d}\in\mathbb{N}^w \\ |\boldsymbol{d}|_1 \le m}} b^{-|\boldsymbol{d}|_1} \\ \times \sum_{k=\max(0,m-|\boldsymbol{d}|_1-c+1)}^{m-|\boldsymbol{d}|_1} \frac{1}{b^k} \sum_{\boldsymbol{\lambda}\in\mathbb{Z}_b^{|\boldsymbol{d}|_1+k}\setminus\{\boldsymbol{0}\}} |M(\boldsymbol{\lambda},\boldsymbol{d},w)|,\end{aligned}$$

where $M(\boldsymbol{\lambda},\boldsymbol{d},w)$ is the set of all $(C_1,\ldots,C_s) \in \mathcal{C}$ for which we have

$$\sum_{i=1}^{w} \sum_{j=1}^{d_i} \lambda_{d_1+\cdots+d_{i-1}+j} \mathbf{c}_j^{(i)} + \sum_{j=1}^{k} \lambda_{|\boldsymbol{d}|_1+j} \mathbf{c}_j^{(w+1)} = \boldsymbol{0}.$$

As above, we obtain that $|M(\boldsymbol{\lambda}, \boldsymbol{d}, w)| = b^{-m}|\mathcal{C}|$, and hence,

$$\Sigma \leq \frac{1}{b^m}\sum_{w=0}^{s-1}(b-1)^w\binom{m}{w} + \frac{c}{|\overline{M}(c)|}\frac{b}{b-1}\frac{|\mathcal{C}|}{b^m}\sum_{w=0}^{s-1}(b-1)^w\binom{m}{w}$$

$$\leq \frac{1}{b^m}\sum_{w=0}^{s-1}(b-1)^w\binom{m}{w}\left[1+\frac{cb}{b-1}(1-R(c))^{-1}\right] := A(c).$$

Therefore, for $\gamma \geq 1$, we have

$$A(c) \geq \Sigma$$

$$> \frac{1}{|\overline{M}(c)|}\gamma A(c)|\{(C_1,\ldots,C_s) \in \overline{M}(c) : D^*_{b^m}(\mathcal{P}_{(C_1,\ldots,C_s)}) > \gamma A(c)\}|$$

and hence, the number of $(C_1,\ldots,C_s) \in \mathcal{C}$ such that $D^*_{b^m}(\mathcal{P}_{(C_1,\ldots,C_s)}) \leq \gamma A(c)$ is at least $\left(1-\gamma^{-1}\right)(1-R(c))|\mathcal{C}|$.

Now let $\gamma = \frac{1+\alpha}{1-\alpha}$ with $0 < \alpha < 1$ and choose $c \geq 1$ such that $R(c) \leq \frac{1-\alpha}{2}$, which is satisfied for $c \geq \left\lceil \log_b\left(\frac{2}{(1-\alpha)}m^{s-1}\right)\right\rceil$. Then, $(1-\gamma^{-1})(1-R(c))|\mathcal{C}| \geq \alpha|\mathcal{C}|$ and

$$\gamma A(c) \leq \frac{2}{1-\alpha}\frac{1}{b^m}\sum_{w=0}^{s-1}(b-1)^w\binom{m}{w}$$

$$\times \frac{2b-1+b((s-1)\log_b m + \log_b 2 - \log_b(1-\alpha))}{b-1}.$$

The result follows. □

In view of the best possible order of the star discrepancy of finite sets (see Section 3.2 and note that $N = b^m$), this result shows that most choices of s-tuples of matrices provide digital nets with almost (apart from the $\log m$-term) the smallest possible order of the star discrepancy.

Let us now turn to the weighted star discrepancy. We obtain an upper bound on the average of the weighted star discrepancy over all digital nets constructed over $\mathbb{Z}_b$ with b^m points in $[0,1)^s$. Here we consider only weights of product form that are independent of the dimension; that is, for $\emptyset \neq \mathfrak{u} \subseteq \mathcal{I}_s$, the weights $\gamma_{\mathfrak{u},s}$ are given by $\gamma_{\mathfrak{u},s} = \gamma_{\mathfrak{u}} = \prod_{i\in\mathfrak{u}}\gamma_i$ with non-negative reals γ_i independent of s. Define

$$R_{b,\boldsymbol{\gamma}}(C_1,\ldots,C_s) := \sum_{\emptyset\neq\mathfrak{u}\subseteq\mathcal{I}_s}\gamma_{\mathfrak{u}}R_b((C_i)_{i\in\mathfrak{u}}).$$

Then it follows from Theorem 5.36 that for the weighted star discrepancy of a digital net $\mathcal{P}$ over $\mathbb{Z}_b$ generated by the $m \times m$ matrices $C_1, \ldots, C_s$, we have

$$D^*_{b^m,\boldsymbol{\gamma}}(\mathcal{P}) \leq \sum_{\emptyset \neq \mathfrak{u} \subseteq \mathcal{I}_s} \gamma_{\mathfrak{u}} \left(1 - \left(1 - \frac{1}{b^m}\right)^{|\mathfrak{u}|}\right) + R_{b,\boldsymbol{\gamma}}(C_1, \ldots, C_s). \tag{5.13}$$

The sum in the above expression can be estimated by the following lemma, which was proved by Joe [116, Lemma 1].

Lemma 5.41 *Suppose that the weight sequence $(\gamma_i)_{i \geq 1}$ satisfies $\sum_{i=1}^{\infty} \gamma_i < \infty$, then for any $s, N \in \mathbb{N}$, we have*

$$\sum_{\emptyset \neq \mathfrak{u} \subseteq \mathcal{I}_s} \gamma_{\mathfrak{u}} \left(1 - \left(1 - \frac{1}{N}\right)^{|\mathfrak{u}|}\right) \leq \frac{\max(1, \Gamma)}{N} \mathrm{e}^{\sum_{i=1}^{\infty} \gamma_i},$$

where $\Gamma := \sum_{i=1}^{\infty} \frac{\gamma_i}{1+\gamma_i}$.

Proof We have

$$\begin{aligned}\sum_{\emptyset \neq \mathfrak{u} \subseteq \mathcal{I}_s} \gamma_{\mathfrak{u}} \left(1 - \left(1 - \frac{1}{N}\right)^{|\mathfrak{u}|}\right) &= \prod_{i=1}^{s} (1 + \gamma_i) - \prod_{i=1}^{s} \left(1 + \gamma_i \left(1 - \frac{1}{N}\right)\right) \\ &= \prod_{i=1}^{s} (1 + \gamma_i) \left[1 - \prod_{i=1}^{s} \left(1 - \frac{\gamma_i}{N(1+\gamma_i)}\right)\right].\end{aligned}$$

Now we use an argument from [107, Proof of Theorem 7]. Since $\log(1-x) \geq x(\log(1-a))/a$ for $0 \leq x \leq a < 1$, we obtain

$$\begin{aligned}\log\left(\prod_{i=1}^{s} \left(1 - \frac{\gamma_i}{N(1+\gamma_i)}\right)\right) &= \sum_{i=1}^{s} \log\left(1 - \frac{\gamma_i}{N(1+\gamma_i)}\right) \\ &\geq \log\left(1 - \frac{1}{N}\right) \sum_{i=1}^{s} \frac{\gamma_i}{1+\gamma_i}.\end{aligned}$$

This leads to the estimate

$$\sum_{\emptyset \neq \mathfrak{u} \subseteq \mathcal{I}_s} \gamma_{\mathfrak{u}} \left(1 - \left(1 - \frac{1}{N}\right)^{|\mathfrak{u}|}\right) \leq \prod_{i=1}^{s} (1 + \gamma_i) \left[1 - \left(1 - \frac{1}{N}\right)^{\sum_{i=1}^{s} \frac{\gamma_i}{1+\gamma_i}}\right].$$

Since $\sum_{i=1}^{\infty} \gamma_i < \infty$, it follows that $\Gamma := \sum_{i=1}^{\infty} \frac{\gamma_i}{1+\gamma_i} < \infty$.

If $\Gamma \le 1$, then we have $(1 - 1/N)^\Gamma \ge 1 - 1/N$ and hence,

$$1 - \left(1 - \frac{1}{N}\right)^\Gamma \le \frac{1}{N}.$$

If $\Gamma > 1$, then we obtain from the mean value theorem that

$$1 - \left(1 - \frac{1}{N}\right)^\Gamma \le \frac{\Gamma}{N}.$$

Therefore, we obtain

$$\begin{aligned}\sum_{\emptyset \ne \mathfrak{u} \subseteq \mathcal{I}_s} \gamma_{\mathfrak{u}} \left(1 - \left(1 - \frac{1}{N}\right)^{|\mathfrak{u}|}\right) &\le \prod_{i=1}^{s}(1+\gamma_i)\left[1 - \left(1 - \frac{1}{N}\right)^\Gamma\right] \\ &\le \frac{\max(1,\Gamma)}{N}\prod_{i=1}^{\infty}(1+\gamma_i) \\ &= \frac{\max(1,\Gamma)}{N} \mathrm{e}^{\sum_{i=1}^\infty \log(1+\gamma_i)} \\ &\le \frac{\max(1,\Gamma)}{N} \mathrm{e}^{\sum_{i=1}^\infty \gamma_i}. \qquad \square\end{aligned}$$

Lemma 5.42 *Let $s, m \in \mathbb{N}$ and let b be a prime. For $(C_1, \ldots, C_s) \in \mathcal{C}$, we have*

$$R_{b,\boldsymbol{\gamma}}(C_1, \ldots, C_s) = \sum_{\boldsymbol{k} \in \mathcal{D}'} \prod_{i=1}^{s} \rho_b(k_i, \gamma_i),$$

where $\mathcal{D}'$ is defined as in (5.8) *and $\rho_b(k, \gamma)$ is defined by*

$$\rho_b(k,\gamma) := \begin{cases} 1+\gamma & \text{if } k = 0, \\ \gamma \rho_b(k) & \text{if } k \ne 0, \end{cases}$$

with $\rho_b(k)$ as in (5.9).

Proof Let $\{\boldsymbol{x}_0, \ldots, \boldsymbol{x}_{b^m-1}\}$ be the digital net generated by $C_1, \ldots, C_s$ and write $\boldsymbol{x}_n = (x_{n,1}, \ldots, x_{n,s})$ for $0 \le n < b^m$. From Lemma 5.35, it follows that for $\emptyset \ne \mathfrak{u} \subseteq \mathcal{I}_s$, we have

$$R_b((C_i)_{i \in \mathfrak{u}}) = -1 + \frac{1}{b^m} \sum_{n=0}^{b^m-1} \prod_{i \in \mathfrak{u}} \left(1 + \sum_{k=1}^{b^m-1} \rho_b(k)\, {}_b\mathrm{wal}_k(x_{n,i})\right).$$

Therefore, together with Lemma 4.75, we obtain

$$\begin{aligned}
&R_{b,\boldsymbol{\gamma}}(C_1,\ldots,C_s)\\
&\quad = \sum_{\emptyset\neq\mathfrak{u}\subseteq\mathcal{I}_s} \gamma_{\mathfrak{u}} R_b((C_i)_{i\in\mathfrak{u}})\\
&\quad = -\sum_{\emptyset\neq\mathfrak{u}\subseteq\mathcal{I}_s} \gamma_{\mathfrak{u}} + \sum_{\emptyset\neq\mathfrak{u}\subseteq\mathcal{I}_s} \frac{1}{b^m}\sum_{n=0}^{b^m-1}\prod_{i\in\mathfrak{u}}\gamma_i\left(1+\sum_{k=1}^{b^m-1}\rho_b(k)\,{}_b\mathrm{wal}_k(x_{n,i})\right)\\
&\quad = 1-\prod_{i=1}^{s}(1+\gamma_i)+\frac{1}{b^m}\sum_{n=0}^{b^m-1}\left(-1+\prod_{i=1}^{s}\left(1+\gamma_i+\gamma_i\sum_{k=1}^{b^m-1}\rho_b(k)\,{}_b\mathrm{wal}_k(x_{n,i})\right)\right)\\
&\quad = -\prod_{i=1}^{s}(1+\gamma_i)+\frac{1}{b^m}\sum_{n=0}^{b^m-1}\prod_{i=1}^{s}\left(\sum_{k=0}^{b^m-1}\rho_b(k,\gamma_i)\,{}_b\mathrm{wal}_k(x_{n,i})\right)\\
&\quad = -\prod_{i=1}^{s}(1+\gamma_i)+\sum_{k_1,\ldots,k_s=0}^{b^m-1}\prod_{i=1}^{s}\rho_b(k_i,\gamma_i)\frac{1}{b^m}\sum_{n=0}^{b^m-1}\prod_{i=1}^{s}{}_b\mathrm{wal}_{k_i}(x_{n,i})\\
&\quad = \sum_{\substack{k_1,\ldots,k_s=0\\ \boldsymbol{k}=(k_1,\ldots,k_s)\neq(0,\ldots,0)}}^{b^m-1}\prod_{i=1}^{s}\rho_b(k_i,\gamma_i)\frac{1}{b^m}\sum_{n=0}^{b^m-1}{}_b\mathrm{wal}_{\boldsymbol{k}}(\boldsymbol{x}_n)\\
&\quad = \sum_{\boldsymbol{k}\in\mathcal{D}'}\prod_{i=1}^{s}\rho_b(k_i,\gamma_i).
\end{aligned}$$

□

Let $s, m \in \mathbb{N}$ and b be a prime. Again let $\mathcal{C}$ be the set of all s-tuples $(C_1,\ldots,C_s)$ of $m\times m$ matrices over $\mathbb{Z}_b$. Then we define

$$A_b(m,s) := \frac{1}{|\mathcal{C}|}\sum_{(C_1,\ldots,C_s)\in\mathcal{C}} R_{b,\boldsymbol{\gamma}}(C_1,\ldots,C_s), \tag{5.14}$$

i.e. $A_b(m,s)$ is the average of $R_{b,\boldsymbol{\gamma}}$ taken over all s-tuples of $m\times m$ matrices over $\mathbb{Z}_b$. The following result was first proved in [49, Theorem 8]. A similar result for the unweighted case can be found in [177, Theorem 4.33].

Theorem 5.43 *For $m, s \in \mathbb{N}$ and a prime b, let $A_b(m,s)$ be defined by* (5.14). *Then, for $b = 2$, we have*

$$A_2(m,s) = \frac{1}{2^m}\left(\prod_{i=1}^{s}\left(1+\gamma_i\left(\frac{m}{2}+1\right)\right)-\prod_{i=1}^{s}(1+\gamma_i)\right),$$

and for $b > 2$, we have

$$A_b(m,s) \le \frac{1}{b^m}\left(\prod_{i=1}^{s}\left(1+\gamma_i\left(1+2m\left(\frac{1}{\pi}\log b+\frac{1}{5}\right)\right)\right)-\prod_{i=1}^{s}(1+\gamma_i)\right).$$

Proof We have

$$\begin{aligned} A_b(m,s) &= \frac{1}{b^{m^2 s}} \sum_{(C_1,\ldots,C_s)\in\mathcal{C}} \sum_{\boldsymbol{k}\in\mathcal{D}'} \prod_{i=1}^{s} \rho_b(k_i,\gamma_i) \\ &= \frac{1}{b^{m^2 s}} \sum_{\substack{k_1,\ldots,k_s=0 \\ (k_1,\ldots,k_s)\neq(0,\ldots,0)}}^{b^m-1} \prod_{i=1}^{s} \rho_b(k_i,\gamma_i) \sum_{\substack{(C_1,\ldots,C_s)\in\mathcal{C} \\ C_1^\top \mathbf{k}_1+\cdots+C_s^\top \mathbf{k}_s=\mathbf{0}}} 1. \end{aligned}$$

Let $\mathbf{c}_j^{(i)}$ denote the jth row vector, $1 \le j \le m$, of the matrix C_i, $1 \le i \le s$. Then, for $(k_1,\ldots,k_s) \in \{0,1,\ldots,b^m-1\}^s$, $(k_1,\ldots,k_s) \neq (0,\ldots,0)$, with $k_i = \kappa_{i,0} + \kappa_{i,1}b + \cdots + \kappa_{i,m-1}b^{m-1}$ for $1 \le i \le s$, the condition in the innermost sum of the above expression becomes

$$\sum_{i=1}^{s}\sum_{j=0}^{m-1} \kappa_{i,j}\mathbf{c}_{j+1}^{(i)} = \mathbf{0}. \tag{5.15}$$

Since at least one $k_i \neq 0$, it follows that there is a $\kappa_{i,j} \neq 0$. First, assume that $\kappa_{1,0} \neq 0$. Then, for any choice of

$$\mathbf{c}_2^{(1)},\ldots,\mathbf{c}_m^{(1)},\mathbf{c}_1^{(2)},\ldots,\mathbf{c}_m^{(2)},\ldots,\mathbf{c}_1^{(s)},\ldots,\mathbf{c}_m^{(s)} \in \mathbb{Z}_b^m$$

we can find exactly one vector $\mathbf{c}_1^{(1)}$ such that condition (5.15) is fulfilled. The same argument holds with $\kappa_{1,0}$ replaced by $\kappa_{i,j}$ and $\mathbf{c}_1^{(1)}$ replaced by $\mathbf{c}_{j+1}^{(i)}$.

Therefore, we get

$$\begin{aligned} A_b(m,s) &= \frac{1}{b^m} \sum_{\substack{k_1,\ldots,k_s=0 \\ (k_1,\ldots,k_s)\neq(0,\ldots,0)}}^{b^m-1} \prod_{i=1}^{s} \rho_b(k_i,\gamma_i) \\ &= \frac{1}{b^m}\left(\prod_{i=1}^{s}\sum_{k=0}^{b^m-1} \rho_b(k,\gamma_i) - \prod_{i=1}^{s}(1+\gamma_i)\right) \\ &= \frac{1}{b^m}\left(\prod_{i=1}^{s}\left(1+\gamma_i+\gamma_i\sum_{k=1}^{b^m-1}\rho_b(k)\right) - \prod_{i=1}^{s}(1+\gamma_i)\right) \\ &= \frac{1}{b^m}\left(\prod_{i=1}^{s}\left(1+\gamma_i\sum_{k=0}^{b^m-1}\rho_b(k)\right) - \prod_{i=1}^{s}(1+\gamma_i)\right). \end{aligned}$$

From the definition of ρ_b in (5.9), we find that

$$\sum_{k=0}^{2^m-1} \rho_2(k) = 1 + \sum_{r=0}^{m-1} \sum_{k=2^r}^{2^{r+1}-1} \frac{1}{2^{r+1}} = \frac{m}{2} + 1$$

and that for $b > 2$,

$$\sum_{k=0}^{b^m-1} \rho_b(k) = 1 + \sum_{r=0}^{m-1} \sum_{k=b^r}^{b^{r+1}-1} \frac{1}{b^{r+1} \sin(\pi \kappa_r / b)}$$

$$= 1 + \frac{m}{b} \sum_{\kappa=1}^{b-1} \frac{1}{\sin(\pi\kappa/b)} \leq 1 + m\left(\frac{2}{\pi}\log b + \frac{2}{5}\right),$$

where we have used

$$\sum_{\kappa=1}^{b-1} \frac{1}{\sin(\pi\kappa/b)} \leq \frac{2}{\pi} b \log b + \frac{2}{5} b,$$

which was shown in [167, p. 574]. The result follows. □

We obtain the following metrical result.

Corollary 5.44 *Let $m, s \in \mathbb{N}$, let b be a prime and let $0 \leq \alpha < 1$. Then, for more than $\alpha|\mathcal{C}|$ elements of $\mathcal{C}$, we have*

$$R_{b,\boldsymbol{\gamma}}(C_1, \ldots, C_s) \leq \frac{1}{1-\alpha} \frac{1}{b^m} \left(\prod_{i=1}^{s} (1 + \gamma_i h(p, m)) - \prod_{i=1}^{s} (1 + \gamma_i) \right),$$

where $h(b, m) = 1 + 2m((\log b)/\pi + 1/5)$ if $b \neq 2$ and $h(2, m) = m/2 + 1$.

Proof For $\varepsilon \geq 1$, we have

$$A_b(m, s) > \frac{1}{|\mathcal{C}|} \frac{\varepsilon}{b^m} \left(\prod_{i=1}^{s} (1 + \gamma_i h(p, m)) - \prod_{i=1}^{s} (1 + \gamma_i) \right) T_{b,m,s}(\varepsilon),$$

where $T_{b,m,s}(\varepsilon)$ is the number of $(C_1, \ldots, C_s) \in \mathcal{C}$ for which we have

$$R_{b,\boldsymbol{\gamma}}(C_1, \ldots, C_s) > \frac{\varepsilon}{b^m} \left(\prod_{i=1}^{s} (1 + \gamma_i h(b, m)) - \prod_{i=1}^{s} (1 + \gamma_i) \right).$$

From Theorem 5.43, we obtain then that $|\mathcal{C}|\varepsilon^{-1} > T_{b,m,s}(\varepsilon)$ and the result follows by setting $\varepsilon = (1-\alpha)^{-1}$. □

Corollary 5.45 *Let b be a prime. If $\sum_{i=1}^{\infty} \gamma_i < \infty$, then for any $\delta > 0$, there exists a constant $\widetilde{c}_{\boldsymbol{\gamma},\delta} > 0$ with the property that for any $s, m \in \mathbb{N}$, there exist $m \times m$*

matrices $C_1, \ldots, C_s$ over $\mathbb{Z}_b$ such that the weighted star discrepancy of the digital net $\mathcal{P}$ generated by $C_1, \ldots, C_s$ satisfies

$$D^*_{b^m,\boldsymbol{\gamma}}(\mathcal{P}) \le \frac{\widetilde{c}_{\boldsymbol{\gamma},\delta}}{b^{m(1-\delta)}}. \tag{5.16}$$

Proof Let $c_b := 2\left(\frac{1}{\pi}\log b + \frac{4}{5}\right)$, $N = b^m$ and assume that $\sum_{i=1}^{\infty} \gamma_i < \infty$. Then we have

$$\prod_{i=1}^{s}(1+\gamma_i m c_b) = \prod_{i=1}^{s}\left(1+\gamma_i(\log N)\frac{c_b}{\log b}\right) \le \prod_{i=1}^{s}(1+\gamma_i c \log N),$$

where $c > 1$ is an absolute constant. Now we use an argumentation presented first in [107, Lemma 3]. Let

$$S(\boldsymbol{\gamma}, N) := \prod_{i=1}^{\infty}(1+\gamma_i c \log N)$$

and define $\sigma_d := c\sum_{i=d+1}^{\infty}\gamma_i$ for $d \ge 0$. Then

$$\begin{aligned}
\log S(\boldsymbol{\gamma}, N) &= \sum_{i=1}^{\infty}\log(1+\gamma_i c\log N) \\
&\le \sum_{i=1}^{d}\log(1+\sigma_d^{-1}+\gamma_i c\log N) + \sum_{i=d+1}^{\infty}\log(1+\gamma_i c\log N) \\
&\le d\log(1+\sigma_d^{-1}) + \sum_{i=1}^{d}\log(1+\gamma_i\sigma_d c\log N) \\
&\quad + \sum_{i=d+1}^{\infty}\log(1+\gamma_i c\log N) \\
&\le d\log(1+\sigma_d^{-1}) + \sigma_d c(\log N)\sum_{i=1}^{d}\gamma_i + \sigma_d\log N \\
&\le d\log(1+\sigma_d^{-1}) + \sigma_d(\sigma_0+1)\log N.
\end{aligned}$$

Hence, we obtain

$$S(\boldsymbol{\gamma}, N) \le (1+\sigma_d^{-1})^d b^{m(\sigma_0+1)\sigma_d}.$$

For $\delta > 0$ choose d large enough to make $\sigma_d \le \delta/(\sigma_0+1)$. Then we obtain

$$S(\boldsymbol{\gamma}, N) \le c_{\boldsymbol{\gamma},\delta} b^{\delta m}.$$

The result follows now from (5.13), Lemma 5.41 and Theorem 5.43. □

We can use the above corollary to give conditions on the weights $\boldsymbol{\gamma}$ under which the weighted star discrepancy is strongly tractable (see Definition 3.63).

Corollary 5.46 *Let $N, s \in \mathbb{N}$. For product weights, if $\sum_{i=1}^{\infty} \gamma_i < \infty$, then there exists a point set $\mathcal{P}$ consisting of N points in $[0,1)^s$ such that for any $\delta > 0$, we have*

$$D^*_{N,\boldsymbol{\gamma}}(\mathcal{P}) \leq \frac{C_{\delta,\boldsymbol{\gamma}}}{N^{1-\delta}},$$

where $C_{\delta,\boldsymbol{\gamma}} > 0$ is independent of s and N. Hence, for $\varepsilon > 0$ we have $N^*_{\boldsymbol{\gamma}}(s,\varepsilon) \leq \lceil C'_{\delta,\boldsymbol{\gamma}} \varepsilon^{-1/(1-\delta)} \rceil$ for any $\delta > 0$ with $C'_{\delta,\boldsymbol{\gamma}} > 0$ independent of s and N. Thus, the weighted star discrepancy is strongly tractable with ε-exponent equal to one.

Remark 5.47 We remark that the point set $\mathcal{P}$ considered in Corollary 5.46 is a superposition of digital nets over $\mathbb{Z}_b$. This follows from the proof below. However, the result is (at the moment) still not constructive as we use Corollary 5.45 which is obtained from averaging over all digital nets. A construction of the digital nets used in the superposition is given below in Chapter 10, Algorithm 10.26, and in Chapter 11, Algorithm 11.19. In this context, we refer already here to Corollary 10.30 and Remark 10.31 and to Corollary 11.22 and Remark 11.23, respectively. We remark further that strong tractability results for the weighted star discrepancy can also be obtained from the results of Wang [261, 262]. Wang's results are constructive, but one needs much more restrictive conditions on the weights.

Proof of Corollary 5.46 From Corollary 5.45, we know that under the assumption $\sum_{i=1}^{\infty} \gamma_i < \infty$, for each $\delta > 0$, there exists for each prime b and each $m \in \mathbb{N}$ a digital net over $\mathbb{Z}_b$ with b^m points, say $\mathcal{P}_{b^m,s} \subseteq [0,1)^s$, such that

$$D^*_{b^m,\boldsymbol{\gamma}}(\mathcal{P}_{b^m,s}) \leq \frac{C_{\delta,\boldsymbol{\gamma}}}{b^{m(1-\delta)}},$$

where $C_{\delta,\boldsymbol{\gamma}} > 0$ is independent of s and m.

Now, for simplicity, we consider the case $b = 2$ only. Let $\delta > 0$ and let $N \in \mathbb{N}$ with binary representation $N = 2^{r_1} + \cdots + 2^{r_m}$, where $0 \leq r_1 < r_2 < \cdots < r_m$, i.e. $r_m = \lfloor \log_2 N \rfloor$, where $\log_2$ denotes the logarithm in base 2. For each $1 \leq i \leq m$, there exists a point set $\mathcal{P}_{2^{r_i},s} \subseteq [0,1)^s$ such that

$$D^*_{2^{r_i},\boldsymbol{\gamma}}(\mathcal{P}_{2^{r_i},s}) \leq \frac{C_{\delta,\boldsymbol{\gamma}}}{2^{r_i(1-\delta)}}.$$

Let $\mathcal{P}_{N,s} = \mathcal{P}_{2^{r_1},s} \cup \ldots \cup \mathcal{P}_{2^{r_m},s}$ (here we mean a superposition where the multiplicity of elements matters). Then it follows from a weighted version of the triangle inequality for the star discrepancy (see Proposition 3.16 and Exercise 3.31) that

$$D^*_{N,\gamma}(\mathcal{P}_{N,s}) \le \sum_{i=1}^{m} \frac{2^{r_i}}{N} D^*_{2^{r_i},\gamma}(\mathcal{P}_{2^{r_i},s}) \le \frac{C_{\delta,\gamma}}{N} \sum_{i=1}^{m} 2^{r_i\delta}$$
$$\le \frac{C_{\delta,\gamma}}{N} \sum_{j=0}^{\lfloor \log_2 N \rfloor} 2^{j\delta} \le \frac{\widetilde{C}_{\delta,\gamma}}{N^{1-\delta}}.$$

Hence, for each $s, N \in \mathbb{N}$ there exists a point set $\mathcal{P}_{N,s}$ with $D^*_{N,\gamma}(\mathcal{P}_{N,s}) \le \frac{\widetilde{C}_{\delta,\gamma}}{N^{1-\delta}}$ which shows the desired result. This point set is a superposition of digital nets over $\mathbb{Z}_2$. The results on strong tractability also follow. □

5.4.2 Results on digital sequences

Let us now consider the corresponding results for digital $(\mathbf{T}, s)$-sequences. Contrary to finite nets, digital $(\mathbf{T}, s)$-sequences over $\mathbb{Z}_b$ are generated by s-tuples $(C_1, \ldots, C_s)$ of $\mathbb{N} \times \mathbb{N}$ matrices over $\mathbb{Z}_b$. The set of these s-tuples is infinite and so we have to use a suitable measure on this set to which our average (or metrical) results are related. Let $\mathcal{M}_s$ denote the set of all s-tuples of $\mathbb{N} \times \mathbb{N}$ matrices over $\mathbb{Z}_b$. We define the probability measure μ_s on $\mathcal{M}_s$ as the product measure induced by a certain probability measure μ on the set $\mathcal{M}$ of all infinite matrices over $\mathbb{Z}_b$. We can view $\mathcal{M}$ as the product of denumerably many copies of the sequence space $\mathbb{Z}_b^{\mathbb{N}}$ over $\mathbb{Z}_b$, and so we define μ as the product measure induced by a certain probability measure $\widetilde{\mu}$ on $\mathbb{Z}_b^{\mathbb{N}}$. For $\widetilde{\mu}$, we just take the measure on $\mathbb{Z}_b^{\mathbb{N}}$ induced by the equiprobability measure on $\mathbb{Z}_b$.

Remark 5.48 Let us note the following concerning the measure $\widetilde{\mu}$. We can identify each $\mathbf{c} = (c_1, c_2, \ldots) \in \mathbb{Z}_b^{\mathbb{N}}$ with its generating function $L = \sum_{k=1}^{\infty} c_k z^{-k} \in \mathbb{Z}_b((z^{-1}))$, where $\mathbb{Z}_b((z^{-1}))$ is the field of formal Laurent series over $\mathbb{Z}_b$ in the variable z^{-1}. In this way we can identify $\mathbb{Z}_b^{\mathbb{N}}$ with the set H of all generating functions. Consider the *discrete exponential valuation* ν on H which is defined by $\nu(L) = -w$ if $L \neq 0$ and w is the least index with $c_w \neq 0$. For $L = 0$ we set $\nu(0) = -\infty$. With the topology induced by the discrete exponential valuation ν and with respect to addition, H is a compact abelian group and $\widetilde{\mu}$ is then the unique Haar probability measure on H.

Now we ask how 'large' is the 'average value' of the quality function $\mathbf{T}$ if we compute the average by integration with respect to μ_s over $\mathcal{M}_s$? Or in modified form, given $\mathbf{T}_0 : \mathbb{N} \to \mathbb{N}_0$, how large is the measure of all $(C_1, \ldots, C_s)$ in $\mathcal{M}_s$, which generate a $(\mathbf{T}, s)$-sequence with $\mathbf{T}(m) \le \mathbf{T}_0(m) + O(1)$ for all $m \ge 1$?

Again, analogous questions can be stated for the sequence of discrepancies of the corresponding digital sequences.

The first result was given (in a slightly different form) by Larcher and Niederreiter [140, Theorem 2].

Theorem 5.49 *For given dimension $s \in \mathbb{N}$ and a given prime base b, let $\mathcal{M}_s$ denote the set of all s-tuples of $\mathbb{N} \times \mathbb{N}$ matrices over $\mathbb{Z}_b$. Then we have:*

1. *Let $\mathbf{D} : \mathbb{N} \to [0, \infty)$ be such that*
$$\sum_{m=1}^{\infty} \frac{m^{s-1}}{b^{\mathbf{D}(m)}} < \infty.$$
Then μ_s-almost all s-tuples $(C_1, \dots, C_s) \in \mathcal{M}_s$ generate a digital $(\mathbf{T}, s)$-sequence over $\mathbb{Z}_b$ with $\mathbf{T}(m) \le \mathbf{D}(m) + O(1)$ for all $m \in \mathbb{N}$, where the implied O-constant may depend on the sequence (i.e. for almost all $(C_1, \dots, C_s) \in \mathcal{M}_s$, there is a constant K such that the $(\mathbf{T}, s)$-sequence generated by C satisfies $\mathbf{T}(m) \le \mathbf{D}(m) + K$ for all $m \in \mathbb{N}$).
2. *Let $\mathbf{D} : \mathbb{N} \to [0, \infty)$ be such that*
$$K_b(s, \mathbf{D}) := \sum_{m=1}^{\infty} \frac{m^{s-1}}{b^{\mathbf{D}(m)}} < \infty.$$
Let $0 \le \alpha < 1$. Then the μ_s-measure of the s-tuples $(C_1, \dots, C_s) \in \mathcal{M}_s$ of $\mathbb{N} \times \mathbb{N}$ matrices over $\mathbb{Z}_b$ generating a digital $(\mathbf{T}, s)$-sequence over $\mathbb{Z}_b$ with
$$\mathbf{T}(m) \le \mathbf{D}(m) + \left\lfloor \frac{\log(K_b(s, \mathbf{D})) - \log(1 - \alpha)}{\log b} \right\rfloor + 1$$
for all $m \in \mathbb{N}$, is greater than α.

Example 5.50 For instance, μ_s-almost all s-tuples $(C_1, \dots, C_s) \in \mathcal{M}_s$ generate a digital $(\mathbf{T}, s)$-sequence over $\mathbb{Z}_b$ such that for some constant L we have

$$\mathbf{T}(m) \le s \log_b m + 2 \log_b \log m + L$$

for all integers $m \ge 2$.

Proof of Theorem 5.49 Note that we can assume without loss of generality that $\mathbf{D}(m) \in \mathbb{N}_0$ for all $m \in \mathbb{N}$. Now we put

$$K_b(s, \mathbf{D}) = \sum_{m=1}^{\infty} \frac{m^{s-1}}{b^{\mathbf{D}(m)}}.$$

For $M \in \mathbb{N}$, let $\mathcal{M}_s(\mathbf{D}, M)$ be the set of all $(C_1, \dots, C_s) \in \mathcal{M}_s$ such that $\delta(C_1^{(m)}, \dots, C_s^{(m)}) > \mathbf{D}(m) + M$ for some $m \in \mathbb{N}$, where $C_i^{(m)}$ denotes the left upper sub-matrix of C_i for $1 \le i \le s$ and where $\delta(C_1^{(m)}, \ldots, C_s^{(m)})$ is as defined in Definition 4.58. Note that if $\delta(C^{(m)}) > \mathbf{D}(m) + M$, then there exist $\boldsymbol{d} = (d_1, \ldots, d_s) \in \mathbb{N}_0$ with $|\boldsymbol{d}|_1 = m - \mathbf{D}(m) - M$ such that the system of equations $\pi_m(\mathbf{c}_j^{(i)})\mathbf{z} = 0$ for $1 \le j \le d_i$ and $1 \le i \le s$ (where $\mathbf{c}_j^{(i)}$ denotes the jth row vector of the matrix C_i and $\pi_m(\mathbf{c}_j^{(i)})$ is the row vector from $\mathbb{Z}_b^m$ consisting of the first m elements of $\mathbf{c}_j^{(i)}$), has at least $2b^{\mathbf{D}(m)+M}$ solutions $\mathbf{z} \in (\mathbb{Z}_b^m)^\top$ (see Lemma 4.87). It follows that

$$\mu_s(\mathcal{M}_s(\mathbf{D}, M)) \le \sum_{m=1}^{\infty} \sum_{\substack{\boldsymbol{d} \in \mathbb{N}_0 \\ |\boldsymbol{d}|_1 = m - \mathbf{D}(m) - M}} \frac{A(m, m - \mathbf{D}(m) - M)}{b^{m(m-\mathbf{D}(m)-M)}},$$

where $A(m, m-t)$ is the number of $(m-t)$-tuples $(\mathbf{c}_1, \ldots, \mathbf{c}_{m-t})$ of elements of $\mathbb{Z}_b^m$ such that the system $\mathbf{c}_k\mathbf{z} = 0$ for $1 \le k \le m-t$ has at least $2b^t$ solutions $\mathbf{z} \in (\mathbb{Z}_b^m)^\top$. Now

$$\begin{aligned}
A(m, m-t) &\le \sum_{\mathbf{c}_1, \ldots, \mathbf{c}_{m-t} \in \mathbb{Z}_b^m} \frac{1}{b^t}(|\{\mathbf{z} \in (\mathbb{Z}_b^m)^\top \,:\, \mathbf{c}_k\mathbf{z} = 0 \text{ for } 1 \le k \le m-t\}| - b^t) \\
&= \sum_{\mathbf{c}_1, \ldots, \mathbf{c}_{m-t} \in \mathbb{Z}_b^m} \frac{1}{b^t}\Bigg(\sum_{\substack{\mathbf{z} \in (\mathbb{Z}_b^m)^\top \\ \mathbf{c}_k\mathbf{z}=0 \text{ for } 1 \le k \le m-t}} 1 - b^t \Bigg) \\
&= b^{m(m-t)} \Bigg(b^{-m(m-t)-t} \sum_{\mathbf{z} \in (\mathbb{Z}_b^m)^\top} \sum_{\substack{\mathbf{c}_1, \ldots, \mathbf{c}_{m-t} \in \mathbb{Z}_b^m \\ \mathbf{c}_k\mathbf{z}=0 \text{ for } 1 \le k \le m-t}} 1 - 1 \Bigg)
\end{aligned}$$

and this last quantity is, as it was shown in the proof of Theorem 5.37, at most $b^{m(m-t)}b^{-t}$. Therefore, we obtain

$$\begin{aligned}
\mu_s(\mathcal{M}_s(\mathbf{D}, M)) &\le \sum_{m=1}^{\infty} \sum_{\substack{\boldsymbol{d} \in \mathbb{N}_0^s \\ |\boldsymbol{d}|_1 = m - \mathbf{D}(m) - M}} b^{-\mathbf{D}(m) - M} \\
&\le \sum_{m=1}^{\infty} m^{s-1} b^{-\mathbf{D}(m) - M} = b^{-M} K_b(s, \mathbf{D}).
\end{aligned}$$

Since M can be chosen to be arbitrarily large, it follows that for μ_s-almost all $(C_1, \ldots, C_s) \in M_s$, we have $\delta(C_1^{(m)}, \ldots, C_s^{(m)}) \le \mathbf{D}(m) + O(1)$ for all $m \in \mathbb{N}$. By Theorem 4.84 and Lemma 4.59, the first result follows.

For the second part, we just have to look at the end of the first part of the proof in more detail. The measure of s-tuples $(C_1, \ldots, C_s)$ of $\mathbb{N} \times \mathbb{N}$ matrices over $\mathbb{Z}_b$ generating a digital $(\mathbf{T}, s)$-sequence with $\mathbf{T}(m) \le \mathbf{D}(m) + M$ for all $m \in \mathbb{N}$ is at least $1 - b^{-M}K_b(s, \mathbf{D})$. Let α with $0 \le \alpha < 1$ be given. Then

$$1 - b^{-M}K_b(s, \mathbf{D}) > \alpha$$

provided that

$$M > \frac{\log(K_b(s, \mathbf{D})) - \log(1 - \alpha)}{\log b}$$

and the result follows. □

Finally, we give the corresponding metrical result for the star discrepancy of digital sequences. Again, by simply combining Theorem 5.49 and the star discrepancy estimate given in (5.5), we could obtain such a result. But this result is not the best possible.

Corollary 5.51 *Let $s \in \mathbb{N}$ and let b be a prime. Then, μ_s-almost all s-tuples $(C_1, \ldots, C_s) \in \mathcal{M}_s$ generate a digital sequence $\mathcal{S}$ over $\mathbb{Z}_b$ whose star discrepancy satisfies*

$$ND_N^*(\mathcal{S}) = O\left((\log N)^{2s}(\log\log N)^2\right).$$

Proof For the star discrepancy of the first N elements of a $(\mathbf{T}, s)$-sequence $\mathcal{S}$, we have according to (5.5) that $ND_N^*(\mathcal{S}) \le \overline{B}(s, b)\sum_{m=0}^{r} b^{\mathbf{T}(m)}m^{s-1}$, where $r \in \mathbb{N}_0$ such that $b^r \le N < b^{r+1}$. By Example 5.50, μ_s-almost all s-tuples $(C_1, \ldots, C_s) \in \mathcal{M}_s$ generate a digital $(\mathbf{T}, s)$-sequences over $\mathbb{Z}_b$ with $\mathbf{T}(m) = s\log_b m + 2\log_b \log m + O(1)$. For any such sequence $\mathcal{S}$, we have

$$\begin{aligned} ND_N^*(\mathcal{S}) &= O\left(\sum_{m=0}^{r} b^{s\log_b m + 2\log_b \log m} m^{s-1}\right) \\ &= O\left(\sum_{m=0}^{r} m^{2s-1}(\log m)^2\right) \\ &= O\left((\log N)^{2s}(\log\log N)^2\right). \end{aligned}$$

□

Again, this result can be improved. The following result was shown by Larcher [138, Theorem 1].

Theorem 5.52 *Let $s \in \mathbb{N}$ and let b be a prime. Let $\mathbf{G} : \mathbb{N} \to \mathbb{R}^+$ be monotonically increasing such that*

$$\sum_{m=1}^{\infty} \frac{m^{s-1}\log m}{\mathbf{G}(m)} < \infty.$$

Then, for μ_s-almost all s-tuples $(C_1, \ldots, C_s) \in \mathcal{M}_s$, the digital sequence $\mathcal{S}$ generated by $C_1, \ldots, C_s$ has a star discrepancy satisfying

$$D_N^*(\mathcal{S}) = O\left(\frac{\mathbf{G}(\log N)}{N}\right).$$

Example 5.53 For example, by choosing for some $\varepsilon > 0$, $\mathbf{G}(m) := m^s(\log m)^{2+\varepsilon}$, we obtain for μ_s-almost all $(C_1, \ldots, C_s) \in \mathcal{M}_s$ a star discrepancy estimate for the corresponding sequence $\mathcal{S}$ of the form

$$D_N^*(\mathcal{S}) = O\left(\frac{(\log N)^s(\log\log N)^{2+\varepsilon}}{N}\right).$$

For the proof of Theorem 5.52, we follow reference [138], where we make use of Theorem 5.29 and of the subsequent notation and lemma. Let w with $0 \le w \le s-1$ be fixed. For an arbitrary w-tuple $\boldsymbol{d}$ of positive integers $\boldsymbol{d} := (d_1, \ldots, d_w)$ let $|\boldsymbol{d}|_1 := d_1 + \cdots + d_w$. Let $g = g(m)$ be a non-negative integral-valued function in the variable m. Let

$$\mathcal{M}(g) := \{(C_1, \ldots, C_{w+1}) \in \mathcal{M}_{w+1} : \exists m \ge 1 \text{ and } \boldsymbol{d} \text{ admissible with respect to } m \text{ such that } h(\boldsymbol{d}) < m - |\boldsymbol{d}|_1 - g(m)\}.$$

Recall that $\mathcal{M}_{w+1}$ is the set of all $w+1$-tuples of $\mathbb{N} \times \mathbb{N}$ matrices over $\mathbb{Z}_b$, 'admissible with respect to m' means that $\boldsymbol{d}$ is admissible for the matrices $C_1^{(m)}, \ldots, C_w^{(m)}$, and the function h is also meant with respect to the matrices $C_1^{(m)}, \ldots, C_w^{(m)}, C_{w+1}^{(m)}$ (for the 'admissibility-notation' and the definition of the function h, we refer to the beginning of Section 5.3).

Lemma 5.54 *With the above notation, we have*

$$\mu_{w+1}(\mathcal{M}(g)) \le \sum_{m=1}^{\infty} \frac{m^w}{b^{g(m)}}.$$

Proof Let $\mathbf{c}_j^{(i)}$ denote the jth row vector of the matrix C_i, where $j \in \mathbb{N}$ and $1 \le i \le s$. For $m \in \mathbb{N}$, let $\pi_m(\mathbf{c}_j^{(i)})$ be the row vector from $\mathbb{Z}_b^m$ consisting of the first m components of $\mathbf{c}_j^{(i)}$ (i.e. $\pi_m(\mathbf{c}_j^{(i)}) \in \mathbb{Z}_b^m$ is the jth row vector of the matrix $C_i^{(m)}$). We have

$$\mu_{w+1}(\mathcal{M}(g)) \le \sum_{m=1}^{\infty} \sum_{\substack{\boldsymbol{d}\in\mathbb{N}^w \\ |\boldsymbol{d}|_1 < m-g(m)}} \sum_{\substack{\boldsymbol{\lambda}:=(\lambda_1,\ldots,\lambda_{m-g(m)})\in\mathbb{Z}_b^{m-g(m)} \\ \lambda_{|\boldsymbol{d}|_1+1},\ldots,\lambda_{m-g(m)} \text{ not all } 0}} \mu_{w+1}(\mathcal{M}(\boldsymbol{\lambda}, \boldsymbol{d}, m)),$$

where, for $\boldsymbol{\lambda} := (\lambda_1, \ldots, \lambda_{m-g(m)}) \in \mathbb{Z}_b^{m-g(m)}$ and for $\boldsymbol{d} = (d_1, \ldots, d_w) \in \mathbb{N}^w$, we define $\mathcal{M}(\boldsymbol{\lambda}, \boldsymbol{d}, m)$ as the set of all $w+1$-tuples $(C_1, \ldots, C_{w+1}) \in \mathcal{M}_{w+1}$ for which

$\boldsymbol{d}$ is admissible with respect to $C_1^{(m)}, \ldots, C_{w+1}^{(m)}$ and

$$\sum_{i=1}^{w}\sum_{j=1}^{d_i} \lambda_{d_1+\cdots+d_{i-1}+j}\pi_m(\mathbf{c}_j^{(i)}) + \sum_{j=1}^{m-|\boldsymbol{d}|_1-g(m)} \lambda_{|\boldsymbol{d}|_1+j}\pi_m(\mathbf{c}_j^{(w+1)}) = \mathbf{0}.$$

Since one of $\lambda_{|\boldsymbol{d}|_1+1}, \ldots, \lambda_{m-g(m)}$ is different from zero, say λ_{j_*}, the row vector $\pi_m(\mathbf{c}_{j_*-|\boldsymbol{d}|_1}^{(w+1)})$ is uniquely determined by the other rows. Therefore, $\mu_{w+1}(\mathcal{M}(\boldsymbol{\lambda}, \boldsymbol{d}, m)) = \frac{1}{b^m}$ and hence,

$$\mu_{w+1}(\mathcal{M}(g)) \le \sum_{m=1}^{\infty} \sum_{\substack{\boldsymbol{d}\in\mathbb{N}^w \\ |\boldsymbol{d}|_1<m}} \sum_{\boldsymbol{\lambda}\in\mathbb{Z}_b^{m-g(m)}} \frac{1}{b^m} \le \sum_{m=1}^{\infty} \frac{m^w}{b^{g(m)}}. \qquad \square$$

Proof of Theorem 5.52 Let the integer w with $0 \le w \le s-1$ be fixed, and for g, as in the lemma above, let $\overline{\mathcal{M}} := \mathcal{M}_{w+1} \setminus \mathcal{M}(g)$. Now let $N \in \mathbb{N}$, the number of points, be given and $r \in \mathbb{N}$ be such that $b^{r-1} \le N < b^r$. Since $r \le \frac{\log N}{\log b} + 1$, then, in view of Theorem 5.32, it suffices to show that for μ_{w+1}-almost all $(C_1, \ldots, C_{w+1}) \in \mathcal{M}_{w+1}$, we have

$$\sum_{m-1}^{r-1} \sum_{\substack{\boldsymbol{d}\in\mathbb{N}^w \\ \boldsymbol{d} \text{ admissible to } m}} b^{m-(|\boldsymbol{d}|_1+h(\boldsymbol{p}))} = O(\mathbf{G}(r)).$$

For the positive function $\mathbf{G}(m)$, define

$$H_r(C_1, \ldots, C_{w+1}) := \sum_{m=1}^{r-1} \frac{1}{\mathbf{G}(m)} \sum_{\substack{\boldsymbol{d}\in\mathbb{N}^w \\ \boldsymbol{d} \text{ admissible to } m}} b^{m-|\boldsymbol{d}|_1-h(\boldsymbol{d})}$$

and consider the integral

$$\mathcal{J} := \int_{\overline{\mathcal{M}}} H_r(C_1, \ldots, C_{w+1})\, \mathrm{d}\mu_{w+1}(C_1, \ldots, C_{w+1}).$$

We have

$$\begin{aligned}\mathcal{J} &\le \int_{\overline{\mathcal{M}}} \sum_{m=1}^{r-1} \frac{1}{\mathbf{G}(m)} \sum_{\substack{\boldsymbol{d}\in\mathbb{N}^w \\ \boldsymbol{d} \text{ admissible to } m \\ h(\boldsymbol{d})<m-|\boldsymbol{d}|_1}} b^{m-|\boldsymbol{d}|_1-h(\boldsymbol{d})}\, \mathrm{d}\mu_{w+1}(C_1, \ldots, C_{w+1}) \\ &\quad + \int_{\overline{\mathcal{M}}} \sum_{m=1}^{r-1} \frac{1}{\mathbf{G}(m)} \sum_{\substack{\boldsymbol{d}\in\mathbb{N}^w \\ \boldsymbol{d} \text{ admissible to } m \\ |\boldsymbol{d}|_1\le m}} 1\, \mathrm{d}\mu_{w+1}(C_1, \ldots, C_{w+1}) \\ &=: \mathcal{J}_1 + \mathcal{J}_2.\end{aligned}$$

Here, the second integral estimates the part where $\boldsymbol{d}$ satisfies $h(\boldsymbol{d}) = m - |\boldsymbol{d}|_1$.

We have

$$\mathcal{J}_2 \leq \sum_{m=1}^{r-1} \frac{m^w}{\mathbf{G}(m)}.$$

Hence, it remains to estimate $\mathcal{J}_1$. We have

$$\mathcal{J}_1 \leq \int_{\overline{\mathcal{M}}} \sum_{m=1}^{r-1} \frac{1}{\mathbf{G}(m)}$$

$$\times \sum_{\substack{\boldsymbol{d}\in\mathbb{N}^w \\ \boldsymbol{d} \text{ admissible to } m}} \sum_{k=m-g(m)-|\boldsymbol{d}|_1+1}^{m-|\boldsymbol{d}|_1} \sum_{\boldsymbol{\lambda}} b^{m-|\boldsymbol{d}|_1-k+1} \, \mathrm{d}\mu_{w+1}(C_1, \ldots, C_{w+1}),$$

where summation in the last sum is over all $\boldsymbol{\lambda} = (\lambda_1, \ldots, \lambda_{|\boldsymbol{d}|_1+k}) \in \mathbb{Z}_b^{|\boldsymbol{d}|_1+k} \setminus \{\mathbf{0}\}$ for which

$$\sum_{i=1}^{w} \sum_{j=1}^{d_i} \lambda_{d_1+\cdots+d_{i-1}+j} \pi_m(\mathbf{c}_j^{(i)}) + \sum_{j=1}^{k} \lambda_{|\boldsymbol{d}|_1+j} \pi_m(\mathbf{c}_j^{(w+1)}) = \mathbf{0} \in \mathbb{Z}_b^m. \tag{5.17}$$

Therefore,

$$\mathcal{J}_1 \leq \sum_{m=1}^{r-1} \frac{1}{\mathbf{G}(m)} \sum_{\substack{\boldsymbol{d}\in\mathbb{N}^w \\ |\boldsymbol{d}|_1 \leq m}} \sum_{i=\max(0,m-g(m)-|\boldsymbol{d}|_1+1)}^{m-|\boldsymbol{d}|_1} \sum_{\boldsymbol{\lambda}\in\mathbb{Z}_b^{i+|\boldsymbol{d}|_1}\setminus\{\mathbf{0}\}} b^{m-|\boldsymbol{d}|_1-i+1}$$

$$\times \int 1 \, \mathrm{d}\mu_{w+1}(C_1, \ldots, C_{w+1}),$$

where integration in the last integral is over all $(C_1, \ldots, C_{w+1}) \in \mathcal{M}_{w+1}$ for which (5.17) is satisfied. This integral (by the same argument as in the proof of Lemma 5.54) is $\frac{1}{b^m}$. Consequently,

$$\mathcal{J}_1 \leq b \sum_{m=1}^{r-1} \frac{g(m) m^w}{\mathbf{G}(m)}.$$

For $L > 1$, let g be given by

$$g(m) := \left\lceil \frac{\log L}{\log b} + \frac{(w+2)\log m}{\log b} \right\rceil \geq 1.$$

Then, using that $g(m) = O(\log m)$ as well as the assumption on $\mathbf{G}$ and that $w \leq s-1$, we obtain

$$\mathcal{J} \leq (b+1) \sum_{m=1}^{r-1} \frac{g(m) m^w}{\mathbf{G}(m)} \leq (b+1) \sum_{m=1}^{\infty} \frac{g(m) m^w}{\mathbf{G}(m)} < \infty.$$

Therefore, for all $L > 1$ and for μ_{w+1}-almost all $(C_1, \ldots, C_{w+1}) \in \overline{\mathcal{M}}$, we have that

$$H_r(C_1, \ldots, C_{w+1}) = O(1).$$

Now, since $\mathbf{G}$ is monotonically increasing, it follows that

$$\frac{1}{\mathbf{G}(r)} \sum_{m=1}^{r-1} \sum_{\substack{\boldsymbol{d} \in \mathbb{N}^w \\ \boldsymbol{d} \text{ admissible to } m}} b^{m-|\boldsymbol{d}|_1 - h(\boldsymbol{d})} \leq H_r(C_1, \ldots, C_{w+1})$$

and therefore, we have for all $L > 1$ for μ_{w+1}-almost all $(C_1, \ldots, C_{w+1}) \in \overline{\mathcal{M}}$ that

$$\sum_{m=1}^{r-1} \sum_{\substack{\boldsymbol{d} \in \mathbb{N}^w \\ \boldsymbol{d} \text{ admissible to } m}} b^{m-|\boldsymbol{d}|_1 - h(\boldsymbol{d})} = O(\mathbf{G}(r)).$$

By Lemma 5.54, we have

$$\mu_{w+1}(\mathcal{M}(g)) \leq \frac{1}{L} \frac{\pi^2}{6}.$$

Hence, choosing L arbitrarily large, we also get that for μ_{w+1}-almost all $(C_1, \ldots, C_{w+1}) \in \mathcal{M}_{w+1}$, we have

$$\sum_{m=1}^{r-1} \sum_{\substack{\boldsymbol{d} \in \mathbb{N}^w \\ \boldsymbol{d} \text{ admissible to } m}} b^{m-|\boldsymbol{d}|_1 - h(\boldsymbol{d})} = O(\mathbf{G}(r)).$$

Hence, the result follows. □

Further metrical and average results for special sub-classes of digital nets (so-called polynomial lattice point sets) are presented in Section 10.2.

Exercises

5.1 Prove Theorem 5.12.

5.2 Show that the discrepancy bound from (5.5) is

$$\sum_{m=0}^{r} b^{\mathbf{T}(m)} m^{s-1} = O((\log N)^s)$$

if and only if $\left(\frac{1}{r}\sum_{m=0}^{r} b^{\mathbf{T}(m)}\right)_{r \in \mathbb{N}}$ is bounded.
Hint: Use summation by parts.

5.3 A (t, m, s)-net in base b whose projections onto the coordinates given by $\emptyset \neq \mathfrak{u} \subseteq \mathcal{I}_s$ have quality parameter $t_{\mathfrak{u}}$ is called a $((t_{\mathfrak{u}})_{\emptyset \neq \mathfrak{u} \subseteq \mathcal{I}_s}, m, s)$-net in base b. (The existence of the quality parameters $t_{\mathfrak{u}}$ for all $\emptyset \neq \mathfrak{u} \subseteq \mathcal{I}_s$ is guaranteed by Lemma 4.16.)

Show the following extension of Theorem 5.26 for $((t_{\mathfrak{u}})_{\emptyset \neq \mathfrak{u} \subseteq \mathcal{I}_s}, m, s)$-nets in base b:

Let $\Delta_b(t, m, s)$ be such that for the star discrepancy of any (t, m, s)-net $\mathcal{P}$ in base b the inequality $b^m D^*_{b^m}(\mathcal{P}) \le \Delta_b(t, m, s)$ holds. Then, for the weighted star discrepancy, with respect to the weights $\boldsymbol{\gamma} = \{\gamma_{\mathfrak{u},s} : \mathfrak{u} \subseteq \mathcal{I}_s\}$, of a $((t_{\mathfrak{u}})_{\emptyset \ne \mathfrak{u} \subseteq \mathcal{I}_s}, m, s)$-net $\mathcal{P}$ in base b, we have

$$b^m D^*_{b^m,\boldsymbol{\gamma}}(\mathcal{P}) \le \max_{\emptyset \ne \mathfrak{u} \subseteq \mathcal{I}_s} \gamma_{\mathfrak{u},s} \Delta_b(t_{\mathfrak{u}}, m, |\mathfrak{u}|). \tag{5.18}$$

5.4 Let $s, m \in \mathbb{N}$ and let b be a prime power. Let $C_1, \ldots, C_s$ be $m \times m$ matrices over $\mathbb{F}_b$ where $\mathbf{c}_j^{(i)}$ denotes the jth row vector of the matrix C_i for $1 \le j \le m$ and $1 \le i \le s$. For $\emptyset \ne \mathfrak{u} \subseteq \mathcal{I}_s$, let $\rho_{\mathfrak{u}} := \rho_{\mathfrak{u}}(C_1, \ldots, C_s)$ be the largest integer such that every system $\{\mathbf{c}_j^{(i)} : 1 \le j \le d_i, i \in \mathfrak{u}\}$ with $d_i \in \{0, \ldots, m\}$ for $i \in \mathfrak{u}$ and $\sum_{i \in \mathfrak{u}} d_i = \rho$, is linearly independent over $\mathbb{Z}_b$.

Show that $C_1, \ldots, C_s$ generate a digital $((t_{\mathfrak{u}})_{\emptyset \ne \mathfrak{u} \subseteq \mathcal{I}_s}, m, s)$-net over $\mathbb{F}_b$, where for every $\emptyset \ne \mathfrak{u} \subseteq \mathcal{I}_s$, we have $t_{\mathfrak{u}} = m - \rho_{\mathfrak{u}}(C_1, \ldots, C_s)$.

5.5 From [177, Theorem 4.34], it is known that for any $m \times m$ matrices $C_1, \ldots, C_s$ over $\mathbb{Z}_b$, b a prime, we have

$$R_b(C_1, \ldots, C_s) \le \left(1 - \frac{1}{b}\right) k(b)^s \left((m+1)^s - \binom{\rho + s}{s}\right) \frac{1}{b^\rho},$$

where $k(b) = 1$ if $b = 2$, $k(b) = \csc(\pi/b) + 1$ if $b > 2$ and where $\rho = \rho(C_1, \ldots, C_s)$ is the linear independence parameter of the matrices $C_1, \ldots, C_s$ as given in Definition 4.50.

Use this result to show that

$$\begin{aligned} &R_{\max,b,\boldsymbol{\gamma}}(C_1, \ldots, C_s) \\ &\le \max_{\emptyset \ne \mathfrak{u} \subseteq \mathcal{I}_s} \gamma_{\mathfrak{u},s} \left(1 - \frac{1}{b}\right) k(b)^{|\mathfrak{u}|} \left((m+1)^{|\mathfrak{u}|} - \binom{\rho_{\mathfrak{u}} + |\mathfrak{u}|}{|\mathfrak{u}|}\right) \frac{1}{b^{\rho_{|\mathfrak{u}|}}}, \end{aligned}$$

where $\rho_{|\mathfrak{u}|} = \rho_{|\mathfrak{u}|}(C_1, \ldots, C_s)$ as in Example 5.4.

5.6 Show that for the weighted star discrepancy of a digital $(0, m, s)$-net $\mathcal{P}$ over $\mathbb{Z}_b$, $b \ge s - 1$ a prime, we have

$$b^m D^*_{b^m,\boldsymbol{\gamma}}(\mathcal{P}) \le \max_{\emptyset \ne \mathfrak{u} \subseteq \mathcal{I}_s} (|\mathfrak{u}| \gamma_{\mathfrak{u},s}) + \max_{\emptyset \ne \mathfrak{u} \subseteq \mathcal{I}_s} \gamma_{\mathfrak{u},s} (b(m+1)/2)^{|\mathfrak{u}|}.$$

5.7 It is known that the first b^m points of a Niederreiter sequence (see Chapter 8) form a digital $((t_{\mathfrak{u}})_{\emptyset \ne \mathfrak{u} \subseteq \mathcal{I}_s}, m, s)$-net in base b with $t_{\mathfrak{u}} \le \sum_{i \in \mathfrak{u}} (\log_b i + \log_b \log_b(i + b) + 1)$ for $\emptyset \ne \mathfrak{u} \subseteq \mathcal{I}_s$ (see, for example, [49, Section 6] and the references therein). Show that the weighted star discrepancy for such a digital net $\mathcal{P}$ can be estimated by

$$b^m D^*_{b^m,\boldsymbol{\gamma}}(\mathcal{P}) \le \max_{\emptyset \ne \mathfrak{u} \subseteq \mathcal{I}_s} (|\mathfrak{u}| \gamma_{\mathfrak{u},s}) + \max_{\emptyset \ne \mathfrak{u} \subseteq \mathcal{I}_s} \gamma_{\mathfrak{u},s} \left(\frac{b^2(m+1)}{2}\right)^{|\mathfrak{u}|} \prod_{i \in \mathfrak{u}} i \log_b(i + b).$$

Note: This is [49, Theorem 6].

5.8 In Exercise 5.7, assume that the weights $\gamma_{\mathfrak{u},s}$ are of product form, i.e. $\gamma_{\mathfrak{u},s} = \prod_{i\in\mathfrak{u}} \gamma_{i,s}$, for non-negative $\gamma_{1,s}, \ldots, \gamma_{s,s}$, and assume that

$$\Lambda := \sup_{s\in\mathbb{N}} \max_{\emptyset\neq\mathfrak{u}\subseteq\mathcal{I}_s} \left(\frac{b^2}{2}\right)^{|\mathfrak{u}|} \prod_{i\in\mathfrak{u}} \gamma_{i,s} i \log_b(i+b) < \infty.$$

Show that we have

$$b^m D^*_{b^m,\boldsymbol{\gamma}}(\mathcal{P}) \leq 2\Lambda(m+1)^s.$$

5.9 In Exercise 5.7, assume that the weights $\gamma_{\mathfrak{u},s}$ are finite-order weights of order k, i.e. $\gamma_{\mathfrak{u},s} = 0$ for all $\mathfrak{u} \subseteq \mathcal{I}_s$ with $|\mathfrak{u}| > k$. Set $c_{\boldsymbol{\gamma},s,k} := \max_{\mathfrak{u}\subseteq\mathcal{I}_s, 1\leq|\mathfrak{u}|\leq k} \gamma_{\mathfrak{u},s}$. Show that we have

$$b^m D^*_{b^m,\boldsymbol{\gamma}}(\mathcal{P}) \leq c_{\boldsymbol{\gamma},s,k} s^k (1 + b^2 \log_b(s+b)(m+1)/2)^k.$$

Furthermore, if

$$\Lambda := \sup_{s\in\mathbb{N}} \max_{\substack{\mathfrak{u}\subseteq\mathcal{I}_s \\ 1\leq|\mathfrak{u}|\leq k}} \gamma_{\mathfrak{u},s} \prod_{i\in\mathfrak{u}} i \log_b(i+b) < \infty,$$

then for any $\delta > 0$ there exists a $C_{b,\boldsymbol{\gamma},\delta} > 0$, independent of s and m, such that

$$D^*_{b^m,\boldsymbol{\gamma}}(\mathcal{P}) \leq \frac{C_{b,\boldsymbol{\gamma},\delta}}{b^{m(1-\delta)}}.$$

Note. This is [49, Corollary 4].

5.10 Show that the discrepancy estimate from Theorem 5.29 also holds for digital nets which are digitally shifted by a digital b-adic shift (with probability one) or by a digital shift of depth m (see Remark 5.30).

5.11 Let $R_b(C_1, \ldots, C_s)$ be defined as in (5.7). Show, as in the proof of Theorem 5.43, that

$$\frac{1}{|\mathcal{C}|} \sum_{(C_1,\ldots,C_s)\in\mathcal{C}} R_b(C_1, \ldots, C_s) = O(m^s/b^m).$$

6
Connections to other discrete objects

The problem of constructing point sets with low discrepancy has a certain combinatorial flavour, and this flavour has become more pronounced with the introduction of (t, m, s)-net by Niederreiter in 1987 [170]. First results on the equivalence of nets and certain combinatorial objects have been known since this first paper on the general theory of (t, m, s)-nets. Since 1992, especially by the work of Lawrence [147] and Mullen and Schmid [163], the investigations on combinatorial aspects of (t, m, s)-nets have been extended considerably. This led to existence results and explicit constructions of (t, m, s)-nets in base b. In this chapter we provide the most important equivalences between nets and combinatorial objects.

6.1 Nets and orthogonal squares

The connection between (t, m, s)-nets and the combinatorial theory of orthogonal squares has been established by Niederreiter [172, Section 5] and can also be found in [177, Chapter 4.2].

Definition 6.1 Let $b \geq 2$ be an integer. A *square of order* b is a $b \times b$ array $E = (e_{k,l})_{k,l=0,\ldots,b-1}$ with entries from a set of order b, say from $\{0, \ldots, b-1\}$.

Two squares $E = (e_{k,l})$ and $F = (f_{k,l})$ of the same order b are called *orthogonal* if the b^2 ordered pairs $(e_{k,l}, f_{k,l})_{k,l=0,\ldots,b-1}$ are all distinct. The squares $E_1, \ldots, E_s$ of the same order b are called *mutually orthogonal* if E_i and E_j are orthogonal for all $1 \leq i < j \leq s$.

A square $E = (e_{k,l})_{k,l=0,\ldots,b-1}$ of order b is called a Latin square of order b, if for given integers k_0 and l_0, $0 \leq k_0, l_0 \leq b-1$, the elements $(e_{k,l_0})_{k=0,\ldots,b-1}$ and the elements $(e_{k_0,l})_{l=0,\ldots,b-1}$ are permutations of the set $\{0, \ldots, b-1\}$.

Note that in a Latin square of order b, each row and each column of the square contains every element of $\{0, \ldots, b-1\}$ exactly once.

Example 6.2 The following squares of order three are mutually orthogonal:

$$\begin{pmatrix} 1 & 0 & 0 \\ 1 & 2 & 2 \\ 0 & 1 & 2 \end{pmatrix}, \begin{pmatrix} 1 & 1 & 2 \\ 2 & 0 & 1 \\ 0 & 0 & 2 \end{pmatrix}, \begin{pmatrix} 0 & 1 & 2 \\ 1 & 1 & 2 \\ 0 & 2 & 0 \end{pmatrix}.$$

Two orthogonal Latin squares of order three:

$$\begin{pmatrix} 0 & 1 & 2 \\ 1 & 2 & 0 \\ 2 & 0 & 1 \end{pmatrix}, \begin{pmatrix} 0 & 1 & 2 \\ 2 & 0 & 1 \\ 1 & 2 & 0 \end{pmatrix}.$$

The basic relation between $(0, 2, s)$-nets in base b and mutually orthogonal squares of order b is given by the following result of Niederreiter [172].

Theorem 6.3 *Let $b, s \geq 2$ be given. Then a $(0, 2, s)$-net in base b exists if and only if there exist s mutually orthogonal squares of order b.*

Proof Assume first that a $(0, 2, s)$-net in base b exists. We denote the points of the net by $\boldsymbol{x}_0, \ldots, \boldsymbol{x}_{b^2-1}$, with $\boldsymbol{x}_n := (x_{n,1}, \ldots, x_{n,s})$. We intend to construct s squares $E_1, \ldots, E_s$ of order b with $E_i = (e_{k,l}^{(i)})_{k,l=0,\ldots,b-1}$, which are mutually orthogonal. This is done by defining

$$e_{k,l}^{(i)} := \lfloor b x_{kb+l,i} \rfloor$$

for $0 \leq k, l \leq b-1$ and $1 \leq i \leq s$. It follows that $E_1, \ldots, E_s$ are squares over the same set $\{0, 1, \ldots, b-1\}$. It remains to prove their orthogonality; that is, we have to show that for all i, j with $1 \leq i < j \leq s$, and all $c, d \in \{0, \ldots, b-1\}$, there exist $k, l \in \{0, \ldots, b-1\}$, such that $e_{k,l}^{(i)} = c$ and $e_{k,l}^{(j)} = d$. Now,

$$e_{k,l}^{(i)} = \lfloor b x_{kb+l,i} \rfloor = c \text{ and } e_{k,l}^{(j)} = \lfloor b x_{kb+l,j} \rfloor = d$$

means that the net-point $\boldsymbol{x}_{kb+l}$ has its ith coordinate in the interval $\left[\frac{c}{b}, \frac{c+1}{b}\right)$ and its jth coordinate in $\left[\frac{d}{b}, \frac{d+1}{b}\right)$, i.e. $\boldsymbol{x}_{kb+l}$ is contained in the elementary b-adic interval

$$J = [0, 1)^{i-1} \times \left[\frac{c}{b}, \frac{c+1}{b}\right) \times [0, 1)^{j-i-1} \times \left[\frac{d}{b}, \frac{d+1}{b}\right) \times [0, 1)^{s-j},$$

of volume b^{-2}. Since the $(0, 2, s)$-net has exactly one point in J, it follows that $E_1, \ldots, E_s$ are mutually orthogonal.

Conversely, we now construct a $(0, 2, s)$-net in base b from mutually orthogonal squares $E_1, \ldots, E_s$ of order b.

Let $E_i = (e_{k,l}^{(i)})_{k,l=0,\ldots,b-1}$ for $1 \leq i \leq s$. Then for $0 \leq n \leq b^m - 1$ and $1 \leq i \leq s$ we define

$$x_{n,i} := \frac{1}{b} e_{k,l}^{(i)} + \frac{1}{b^2} \psi_{k,l}^{(i)},$$

with $k = \lfloor n/b \rfloor$ and $l = n - kb$, for $0 \le n \le b-1$ (this part alone would mean the converse construction to the first part of the proof) and where the $\psi_{k,l}^{(i)} \in \{0, \ldots, b-1\}$ have the property that for any given $u \in \{0, \ldots, b-1\}$ and all $1 \le i \le s$, the set $\{\psi_{k,l}^{(i)} : e_{k,l}^{(i)} = u\}$ equals the set $\{0, \ldots, b-1\}$. For $0 \le n \le b^m - 1$, let $\boldsymbol{x}_n = (x_{n,1}, \ldots, x_{n,s})$. We have to show that any elementary b-adic interval of volume b^{-2} contains exactly one of the constructed points $\boldsymbol{x}_0, \ldots, \boldsymbol{x}_{b^m-1}$.

The elementary b-adic intervals in question are either of the form

$$[0,1)^{i-1} \times \left[\frac{c}{b}, \frac{c+1}{b}\right) \times [0,1)^{j-i-1} \times \left[\frac{d}{b}, \frac{d+1}{b}\right) \times [0,1)^{s-j}$$

with $1 \le i < j \le s$ and $0 \le c, d \le b-1$, or of the form

$$[0,1)^{i-1} \times \left[\frac{c}{b^2}, \frac{c+1}{b^2}\right) \times [0,1)^{s-i}$$

with $1 \le i \le s$ and $0 \le c \le b^2 - 1$. The intervals of the first form contain exactly one point, since $\lfloor b x_{n,i} \rfloor = e_{k,l}^{(i)}$ and since $E_1, \ldots, E_s$ are mutually orthogonal.

Let us now consider an interval J of the second form. Let $c = ub + v$ with $0 \le u \le b-1$ and $0 \le v \le b-1$. Choose n such that $e_{k,l}^{(i)} = u$ and such that $\psi_{k,l}^{(i)} = v$. By the definition of $\psi_{k,l}^{(i)}$, there is exactly one such n, and hence $\boldsymbol{x}_n$ is the only point contained in J. □

Example 6.4 To illustrate the second part of the above proof, we construct a (0, 2, 3)-net in base 3 from the mutually orthogonal squares

$$E_1 = \begin{pmatrix} 1 & 0 & 0 \\ 1 & 2 & 2 \\ 0 & 1 & 2 \end{pmatrix}, \quad E_2 = \begin{pmatrix} 1 & 1 & 2 \\ 2 & 0 & 1 \\ 0 & 0 & 2 \end{pmatrix} \quad \text{and } E_3 = \begin{pmatrix} 0 & 1 & 2 \\ 1 & 1 & 2 \\ 0 & 2 & 0 \end{pmatrix}$$

considered in the example above. First, for any $1 \le i \le 3$ we have to construct a suitable $\Psi^{(i)} = (\psi_{k,l}^{(i)})_{k,l=0,\ldots,2}$. For example, we can choose

$$\Psi^{(1)} = \begin{pmatrix} 0 & 0 & 1 \\ 1 & 0 & 1 \\ 2 & 2 & 2 \end{pmatrix}, \quad \Psi^{(2)} = \begin{pmatrix} 0 & 1 & 0 \\ 1 & 0 & 2 \\ 1 & 2 & 2 \end{pmatrix} \quad \text{and } \Psi^{(3)} = \begin{pmatrix} 0 & 0 & 0 \\ 1 & 2 & 1 \\ 1 & 2 & 2 \end{pmatrix}.$$

It is easily checked that the $\Psi^{(i)}$ satisfy the demanded property. For $0 \le n \le 8$, we have

$$\boldsymbol{x}_n = \left(\frac{e_{k,l}^{(1)}}{3} + \frac{\Psi_{k,l}^{(1)}}{9}, \frac{e_{k,l}^{(2)}}{3} + \frac{\Psi_{k,l}^{(2)}}{9}, \frac{e_{k,l}^{(3)}}{3} + \frac{\Psi_{k,l}^{(3)}}{9} \right)$$

and obtain $\boldsymbol{x}_0 = (1/3, 1/3, 0)$, $\boldsymbol{x}_1 = (0, 4/9, 1/3)$, $\boldsymbol{x}_2 = (1/9, 2/3, 2/3)$, $\boldsymbol{x}_3 = (4/9, 7/9, 4/9)$, $\boldsymbol{x}_4 = (2/3, 0, 5/9)$, $\boldsymbol{x}_5 = (7/9, 5/9, 7/9)$, $\boldsymbol{x}_6 = (2/9, 1/9, 1/9)$, $\boldsymbol{x}_7 = (5/9, 2/9, 8/9)$ and $\boldsymbol{x}_8 = (8/9, 8/9, 2/9)$.

The next result provides a connection between mutually orthogonal squares and mutually orthogonal Latin squares.

Lemma 6.5 *There exist s mutually orthogonal squares of order b, if and only if there exist $s-2$ mutually orthogonal Latin squares of order b.*

Proof Assume first that we are given s mutually orthogonal squares of order b, say, $E_1, \ldots, E_s$ with $E_i = (e_{k,l}^{(i)})_{k,l=0,\ldots,b-1}$ for $1 \le i \le s$. In the following, we construct $s-2$ mutually orthogonal Latin squares of order b, say $F_3, \ldots, F_s$, where $F_i = (f_{k,l}^{(i)})_{k,l=0,\ldots,b-1}$ for $3 \le i \le s$. To do so, we construct a bijection

$$\varphi : \{0, \ldots, b-1\}^2 \to \{0, \ldots, b-1\}^2$$

and then set

$$f_{k,l}^{(i)} := e_{\varphi(k,l)}^{(i)} \tag{6.1}$$

for $0 \le k, l < b-1$ and $3 \le i \le s$. The bijection φ is generated with the help of the squares E_0 and E_1 as follows. For $0 \le c, d \le b-1$, let $\varphi(c, d)$ be the place where the pair (c, d) occurs in the orthogonal pair E_0, E_1 of squares. The squares $F_3, \ldots, F_s$ are still mutually orthogonal since they are generated from $E_3, \ldots, E_s$ by an identical permutation of their elements. It only remains to show that $F_3, \ldots, F_s$ are Latin squares. To this end, define F_1 and F_2 using (6.1). Then we have

$$F_1 = \begin{pmatrix} 0 & \ldots & 0 \\ 1 & \ldots & 1 \\ \vdots & & \vdots \\ b-1 & \ldots & b-1 \end{pmatrix} \quad \text{and} \quad F_2 = \begin{pmatrix} 0 & 1 & \ldots & b-1 \\ \vdots & \vdots & & \vdots \\ 0 & 1 & \ldots & b-1 \end{pmatrix}.$$

Each F_i, $3 \le i \le s$, is orthogonal to F_1 and to F_2 and therefore must be a Latin square.

We now prove the converse. To given $s-2$ mutually orthogonal Latin squares $F_3, \ldots, F_s$ of order b, we add the squares

$$F_1 = \begin{pmatrix} 0 & \ldots & 0 \\ 1 & \ldots & 1 \\ \vdots & & \vdots \\ b-1 & \ldots & b-1 \end{pmatrix} \quad \text{and} \quad F_2 = \begin{pmatrix} 0 & 1 & \ldots & b-1 \\ \vdots & \vdots & & \vdots \\ 0 & 1 & \ldots & b-1 \end{pmatrix}.$$

Then it follows that the s squares $F_1, \ldots, F_s$ are mutually orthogonal. □

Corollary 6.6 *Let $s \ge 2$ and $b \ge 2$ be given. A $(0, 2, s)$-net in base b exists if and only if there exist $s-2$ mutually orthogonal Latin squares of order b.*

Remark 6.7 There is also a connection to finite projective planes which has been noted in [176]. It is well known in combinatorics that for $b \geq 2$ the existence of $b - 1$ mutually orthogonal Latin squares is equivalent to the existence of a finite projective plane of order b. See, for example, [162, Theorem 9.3.2]. Hence, there exists a finite projective plane of order b if and only if there exists a $(0, 2, b+1)$-net in base b.

Now we can give an alternative proof of the non-existence result for $(0, m, s)$-nets in base b, which has already been stated in Corollary 4.19. We restate and prove this result in the following form.

Theorem 6.8 *Let $s, m, b \geq 2$ be integers. A $(0, m, s)$-net in base b can only exist if $s \leq b + 1$.*

For the proof of Theorem 6.8, we need an upper bound on the maximal number of mutually orthogonal Latin squares of a given order b. (This upper bound can be shown to be sharp for prime powers b, but it is not sharp for arbitrary order b.)

Lemma 6.9 *Not more than $b - 1$ mutually orthogonal Latin squares of order b can exist.*

Proof Assume that we had b mutually orthogonal Latin squares of order b, say, $F_1, \ldots, F_b$. Note that renaming the elements of one of the F_i in any way does not affect the Latin square property of F_i; nor does it affect its orthogonality relation to the other F_j. Hence, we may assume that the first row of each of the F_i has the form $0 \quad 1 \quad \ldots \quad b-1$. Consider now the first entries in the second rows. None of the entries can be 0 because of the Latin square property. Further, for no $0 \leq i < j \leq b - 1$ can the entries be the same because of the orthogonality of F_i and F_j and because of the special structure of their first rows. This, however, contradicts the assumption of the existence of b mutually orthogonal Latin squares. □

Proof of Theorem 6.8 The starting point for the proof is the fact, shown in Lemma 4.17, that for $m \geq 2$ a $(0, m, s)$-net in a base b can only exist if a $(0, 2, s)$-net in base b exists. By Corollary 6.6, the existence of a $(0, 2, s)$-net in base b is equivalent to the existence of $s - 2$ mutually orthogonal Latin squares of order b. But by Lemma 6.9, there are not more than $b - 1$ mutually orthogonal Latin squares of order b and hence, the result follows. □

These considerations were the starting point for investigations of combinatorial objects in relation to (t, m, s)-nets which led to several generalisations of Theorem 6.3. However, for such results one needs generalisations of orthogonal squares of order b, such as orthogonal hypercubes or generalised orthogonal hypercubes of order b. Mullen and Whittle [166] have generalised Theorem 6.3 to the case of $(t, t+2, s)$-nets in base b and Mullen and Schmid [165] proved a result for $(t, t+k, s)$-nets in base b where $k \geq 2$. We also refer to the survey article of Mullen [164]. A somewhat simpler and more direct approach to these results can be described by using the theory of (ordered) orthogonal arrays, which we consider in the following section.

6.2 Nets and (ordered) orthogonal arrays

The connection between (t, m, s)-nets and the theory of orthogonal arrays has been observed by Niederreiter [176].

Definition 6.10 Let b, s, k, M and λ be integers with $b \geq 2$ and $s \geq k \geq 1$. An *orthogonal array* $\mathrm{OA}(M, s, b, k)$ of size M, s constraints, b levels, strength k and index λ is an $M \times s$ matrix A with entries from a set of b elements, say $\{0, \ldots, b-1\}$, such that any $M \times k$ submatrix of A contains all possible $1 \times k$ rows with the same frequency λ.

It follows from the definition that we always have $M = \lambda b^k$.

Example 6.11 The 9×3 matrix

$$\begin{pmatrix} 1 & 1 & 0 \\ 0 & 1 & 1 \\ 0 & 2 & 2 \\ 1 & 2 & 1 \\ 2 & 0 & 1 \\ 2 & 1 & 2 \\ 0 & 0 & 0 \\ 1 & 0 & 2 \\ 2 & 2 & 0 \end{pmatrix}$$

is an orthogonal array $\mathrm{OA}(9, 3, 3, 2)$ of index one.

Niederreiter [176, Theorem 1] showed the equivalence between $(t, t+2, s)$-nets in base b and orthogonal arrays of strength two.

Theorem 6.12 *Let $s, b \geq 2$, and $t \geq 0$ be integers. Then there exists a $(t, t+2, s)$-net in base b if and only if there exists an orthogonal array $\mathrm{OA}(b^{t+2}, s, b, 2)$ of index b^t.*

A generalisation of this result in the form of an equivalence between $(t, t+k, s)$-nets in base b and orthogonal arrays of strength k for $k > 2$ is not possible. Therefore, one has to use the generalised concept of ordered orthogonal arrays that was introduced by Mullen and Schmid [165] (see also Lawrence [149] and Schmid [233]).

Definition 6.13 Let b, s, k, M, T and λ be integers with $b \geq 2$, $T \geq 1$ and $sT \geq k \geq 1$. An *ordered orthogonal array* $\mathrm{OOA}(M, s, b, T, k)$ of size M, s ordered constraints of heights T, b levels, strength k and index λ is a $M \times sT$ matrix A with entries from a set of b elements, say $\{0, \ldots, b-1\}$, with column labels (i, j) for $1 \leq i \leq s$ and $1 \leq j \leq T$ such that, for any integers $0 \leq d_1, \ldots, d_s \leq T$ with $\sum_{i=1}^{s} d_i = k$, the $M \times k$ submatrix obtained by restriction to the columns (i, j), $1 \leq j \leq d_i$, $1 \leq i \leq s$, contains among its rows every k-tuple over $\{0, \ldots, b-1\}$ with the same frequency λ.

It follows from the definition that we always have $M = \lambda b^k$.

The $M \times sT$ matrix A can be written as $A = (A_1|A_2|\ldots|A_s)$ consisting of $M \times T$ matrices $A_i = (a_{n,r}^{(i)})$, $1 \leq i \leq s$, with entries in $\{0, \ldots, b-1\}$. The condition for an $\mathrm{OOA}(M, s, b, T, k)$ means then that, for any integers $0 \leq d_1, \ldots, d_s \leq T$ with $\sum_{i=1}^{s} d_i = k$, the $M \times k$ matrix consisting of the first d_1 columns of A_1, the first d_2 columns of A_2, ..., the first d_s columns of A_s contains among its rows every k-tuple over $\{0, \ldots, b-1\}$ with the same frequency Mb^{-k}.

For $s \geq k$, it is clear that an $\mathrm{OOA}(M, s, b, 1, k)$ is an $\mathrm{OA}(M, s, b, k)$. Tables for parameters of (ordered) orthogonal arrays can be obtained from the MinT database to be found under http://mint.sbg.ac.at/.

Example 6.14 The 8×4 matrix

$$\begin{pmatrix} 0 & 0 & 0 & 0 \\ 1 & 0 & 0 & 0 \\ 0 & 1 & 0 & 1 \\ 1 & 1 & 0 & 1 \\ 0 & 0 & 1 & 0 \\ 1 & 0 & 1 & 0 \\ 0 & 1 & 1 & 1 \\ 1 & 1 & 1 & 1 \end{pmatrix}$$

is an ordered orthogonal array $\mathrm{OOA}(8, 2, 2, 2, 3)$ of index one.

Theorem 6.15 *Let $s, b, k \geq 2$ and $t \geq 0$ be integers. Then, there exists a $(t, t+k, s)$-net in base b if and only if there exists an ordered orthogonal array $\mathrm{OOA}(b^{t+k}, s, b, k-1, k)$ of index b^t.*

Proof Let $\boldsymbol{x}_n = (x_{n,1}, \ldots, x_{n,s})$ for $0 \leq n \leq b^m - 1$ be the points of a $(t, t+k, s)$-net in base b and let $x_{n,i} = \sum_{r=1}^{\infty} x_{n,i,r} b^{-r}$ be the b-adic expansion of $x_{n,i}$ for $0 \leq n \leq b^m - 1$ and $1 \leq i \leq s$.

We now define a $b^{t+k} \times s(k-1)$ matrix A by setting $A = (A_1|A_2|\ldots|A_s)$, where the $b^{t+k} \times (k-1)$ matrices $A_i = (a_{n,r}^{(i)})$, $1 \le i \le s$, with entries in $\{0, \ldots, b-1\}$, are given by

$$a_{n,r}^{(i)} = x_{n,i,r} \text{ for } 1 \le i \le s,\ 0 \le n \le b^m - 1 \text{ and } 1 \le r \le k-1.$$

Let $d_1, \ldots, d_s$ be arbitrary integers with $0 \le d_i \le k-1$ for $1 \le i \le s$ and $\sum_{i=1}^{s} d_i = k$. Consider now the $M \times k$ matrix $B_{d_1,\ldots,d_s}$ consisting of the first d_1 columns of A_1, the first d_2 columns of A_2, $\ldots$, the first d_s columns of A_s. We have to show that any k-tuple $(c_{1,1}, \ldots, c_{1,d_1}, \ldots, c_{s,1}, \ldots, c_{s,d_s}) \in \{0, \ldots, b-1\}^k$ appears exactly b^t times among the rows of the matrix $B_{d_1,\ldots,d_s}$.

The k-tuple $(c_{1,1}, \ldots, c_{1,d_1}, \ldots, c_{s,1}, \ldots, c_{s,d_s})$ appears as a row in the matrix $B_{d_1,\ldots,d_s}$ if and only if there is an element $\boldsymbol{x}_n = (x_{n,1}, \ldots, x_{n,s})$ for which the ith components have b-adic expansion of the form

$$x_{n,i} = \sum_{r=1}^{d_i} c_{i,r} b^{-r} + \sum_{r=d_i+1}^{\infty} x_{n,i,r} b^{-r}$$

for $1 \le i \le s$. This, however, is equivalent to the condition

$$\boldsymbol{x}_n \in \prod_{i=1}^{s} \left[\frac{c_i}{b^{d_i}}, \frac{c_i+1}{b^{d_i}} \right) =: J$$

where $c_i := c_{i,1} b^{d_i - 1} + \cdots + c_{i,d_i - 1} b + c_{i,d_i}$ for $1 \le i \le s$. Since J is an elementary b-adic interval of volume $b^{-d_1-\cdots-d_s} = b^{-k}$ and since $\boldsymbol{x}_0, \ldots, \boldsymbol{x}_{b^{t+k}-1}$ form a $(t, t+k, s)$-net in base b, it follows that the k-tuple in question appears exactly b^t times among the rows of the matrix $B_{d_1,\ldots,d_s}$. Hence, the matrix A is an ordered orthogonal array $\mathrm{OOA}(b^{t+k}, s, b, k-1, k)$ of index b^t.

Conversely, suppose that the $b^{t+k} \times s(k-1)$ matrix $A = (a_{n,r}^{(i)})$ is an ordered orthogonal array $\mathrm{OOA}(b^{t+k}, s, b, k-1, k)$ of index b^t. Then, for $0 \le n \le b^{t+k} - 1$, we define the points $\boldsymbol{x}_n = (x_{n,1}, \ldots, x_{n,s})$ by

$$x_{n,i} = \sum_{r=1}^{k-1} a_{n,r}^{(i)} b^{-r} + a_{n,1}^{(h(i))} b^{-k}$$

for $1 \le i \le s$ where $h(i) \in \{1, \ldots, s\}$ is arbitrary with $h(i) \ne i$. Now we have to show that the points $\boldsymbol{x}_0, \ldots, \boldsymbol{x}_{b^{t+k}-1}$ form a $(t, t+k, s)$-net in base b, i.e. we have to show that any elementary b-adic interval $J = \prod_{i=1}^{s} \left[\frac{c_i}{b^{d_i}}, \frac{c_i+1}{b^{d_i}}\right)$ of volume b^{-k}, where $0 \le d_i \le k$ and $0 \le c_i < b^{d_i}$ for $1 \le i \le s$ are integers, contains exactly b^t points $\boldsymbol{x}_n$.

Letting $c_i b^{-d_i} = \sum_{r=1}^{d_i} c_{i,r} b^{-r}$, we have that $\boldsymbol{x}_n \in J$ if and only if for each $1 \le i \le s$ we have that $c_{i,1}, \ldots, c_{i,d_i}$ are the first d_i digits of the b-adic representation of $x_{n,i}$. Now we have to distinguish between two cases:

1. If $d_i > 0$ for at least two indices $1 \le i \le s$, then we have $0 \le d_i \le k-1$ for all $1 \le i \le s$. Consider the $b^{t+k} \times k$ matrix $B_{d_1,\dots,d_s}$ consisting of the first d_1 columns of A_1, the first d_2 columns of A_2, $\dots$, the first d_s columns of A_s. Since A is an ordered orthogonal array $\mathrm{OOA}(b^{t+k}, s, b, k-1, k)$ of index b^t, it follows that the k-tuple $(c_{1,1}, \dots, c_{1,d_1}, \dots, c_{s,1}, \dots, c_{s,d_s}) \in \{0, \dots, b-1\}^k$ appears exactly b^t times among the rows of $B_{d_1,\dots,d_s}$ and hence, J contains exactly b^t points $\boldsymbol{x}_n$.
2. If $d_i > 0$ for only one index $1 \le i' \le s$, then we consider the $b^{t+k} \times k$ matrix B consisting of the first $k-1$ columns of $A_{i'}$ and the first column of $A_{h(i')}$. Again, since A is an ordered orthogonal array $\mathrm{OOA}(b^{t+k}, s, b, k-1, k)$ of index b^t, it follows that the k-tuple $(c_{i',1}, \dots, c_{i',k-1}, c_{i',k}) \in \{0, \dots, b-1\}^k$ appears exactly b^t times among the rows of B and hence, J contains exactly b^t points $\boldsymbol{x}_n$. □

Bierbrauer *et al.* [14] used a special family of ordered orthogonal arrays, called linear ordered orthogonal arrays, to prove an equivalence with digital nets over $\mathbb{F}_b$ (see also Martin and Stinson [159]). Furthermore, it should be noted that Lawrence [149] has independently obtained another equivalence between nets and what he calls generalised orthogonal arrays. For an overview of many results concerning the relation of (t, m, s)-nets and ordered orthogonal arrays, see also [240].

Exercises

6.1 Consider the digital $(0, 2, 3)$-net over $\mathbb{Z}_2$ which is generated by the matrices

$$C_1 = \begin{pmatrix} 1 & 0 \\ 0 & 1 \end{pmatrix}, \; C_2 = \begin{pmatrix} 0 & 1 \\ 1 & 0 \end{pmatrix} \text{ and } C_3 = \begin{pmatrix} 1 & 1 \\ 0 & 1 \end{pmatrix}.$$

Construct three corresponding mutually orthogonal squares of order two.

6.2 Construct an orthogonal array OA(8, 4, 2, 3) of index one.

6.3 Show that the orthogonal array OA(9, 3, 3, 2) of index one from Example 6.11 is constructed from the $(0, 2, 3)$-net in base 3 given in Example 6.4.

6.4 Construct an orthogonal array OA(4, 3, 2, 2) of index one from the digital $(0, 2, 3)$-net over $\mathbb{Z}_2$ from Exercise 6.1.

6.5 Let $s \ge 2$, $b \ge 2$ and $t \ge 0$ be integers. It is known (see, for example, [226, Theorem 2.2.1 or Theorem 2.2.4]) that an orthogonal array $OA(b^{t+2}, s, b, 2)$ of index b^t can only exist if $s \le (b^{t+2}-1)/(b-1)$. Deduce from this result that for $m \ge t+2$, a (t, m, s)-net in base b can only exist if $s \le (b^{t+2}-1)/(b-1)$.
Note: This is [176, Corollary 1].

6.6 Let $s \ge 2$, $b \ge 2$ and $t \ge 0$ be integers. Show that a (t, s)-sequence in base b can only exist if $s \le (b^{t+2}-1)/(b-1)-1$.
Note: This is [176, Corollary 2].

6.7 For given integers $b \ge 2$ and $s \ge 2$, let $\tau_b(s)$ be the least value of t for which there exists a (t, m, s)-net in base b for any $m \ge t$. Show that $\tau_b(s) \ge \lceil \log_b(bs-s+1) \rceil - 2$.

6.8 Construct a $(0, 3, 2)$-net in base 2 from the ordered orthogonal array $\mathrm{OOA}(8, 2, 2, 2, 3)$ of index one given in Example 6.14.

6.9 Consider the digital $(0, 3, 3)$-net over $\mathbb{Z}_2$ which is generated by the matrices

$$C_1 = \begin{pmatrix} 1 & 0 & 0 \\ 0 & 1 & 0 \\ 0 & 0 & 1 \end{pmatrix}, \; C_2 = \begin{pmatrix} 0 & 0 & 1 \\ 0 & 1 & 0 \\ 1 & 0 & 0 \end{pmatrix} \text{ and } C_3 = \begin{pmatrix} 1 & 1 & 1 \\ 0 & 1 & 0 \\ 0 & 0 & 1 \end{pmatrix}.$$

Construct the corresponding ordered orthogonal array $\mathrm{OOA}(8, 3, 2, 2, 3)$ of index one.

6.10 Consider the $(1, 4, 4)$-net over $\mathbb{Z}_2$ from Exercise 4.4 and construct the corresponding ordered orthogonal array $\mathrm{OOA}(16, 4, 2, 2, 3)$ of index two.

6.11 Let $s, b, k \geq 2$ and $t \geq 0$ be integers. Show that the existence of an orthogonal array $\mathrm{OA}(b^{t+k}, s(k-1), b, k)$ of index b^t implies the existence of a $(t, t+k, s)$-net in base b.
Hint: Show that an orthogonal array $\mathrm{OA}(b^{t+k}, s(k-1), b, k)$ of index b^t is also an ordered orthogonal array $\mathrm{OOA}(b^{t+k}, s, b, k-1, k)$ of index b^t.
Note: This is [165, Corollary 8].

6.12 Let $b, k \geq 2$, $s \geq k$ and $t \geq 0$ be integers. Show that the existence of a $(t, t+k, s)$-net in base b implies the existence of an orthogonal array $\mathrm{OA}(b^{t+k}, s, b, k)$ of index b^t.
Hint: Show that for $s \geq k$ an ordered orthogonal array $\mathrm{OOA}(b^{t+k}, s, b, k-1, k)$ of index b^t is also an orthogonal array $\mathrm{OA}(b^{t+k}, s, b, k)$ of index b^t.
Note: This is reference [165, Corollary 9], which is also mentioned in a slightly more general form in [206, Section 2.4].

7

Duality theory

In this chapter, we show that the construction of digital (t, m, s)-nets over $\mathbb{F}_b$ can be reduced to the construction of certain $\mathbb{F}_b$-linear subspaces of $\mathbb{F}_b^{sm}$. Using the standard inner product in $\mathbb{F}_b^{sm}$, one can define and study the dual linear subspace. If one defines a special weight on $\mathbb{F}_b^{sm}$, the so-called Niederreiter–Rosenbloom–Tsfasman weight, then the t-parameter of a digital net is closely related to the weight of the corresponding dual linear subspace. This was shown independently by Niederreiter and Pirsic [189] and by Skriganov [243]. This point of view gives new possibilities for the construction of digital nets and it provides a connection to the theory of linear codes. Further information on duality theory for digital nets can be found in the overview articles [183, 184]. The duality theory for digital nets can also be extended to digital sequences. This was first done in [48].

7.1 $\mathbb{F}_b$-linear subspaces

Let $s, m \in \mathbb{N}$ and let $\mathbb{F}_b$ be the finite field of prime power order b. Let $\mathcal{N}$ be an arbitrary $\mathbb{F}_b$-linear subspace of $\mathbb{F}_b^{sm}$. Let H be a matrix over $\mathbb{F}_b$ consisting of sm columns such that the row-space of H is equal to $\mathcal{N}$. Then we define the dual space $\mathcal{N}^\perp \subseteq \mathbb{F}_b^{sm}$ of $\mathcal{N}$ to be the null space of H. In other words, $\mathcal{N}^\perp$ is the orthogonal complement of $\mathcal{N}$ relative to the standard inner product in $\mathbb{F}_b^{sm}$,

$$\mathcal{N}^\perp = \{\mathbf{A} \in \mathbb{F}_b^{sm} : \mathbf{B} \cdot \mathbf{A} = 0 \text{ for all } \mathbf{B} \in \mathcal{N}\}.$$

Note that $\mathcal{N}^\perp$ depends only on the linear space $\mathcal{N}$ and not on the specific matrix H. We have $\dim(\mathcal{N}^\perp) = sm - \dim(\mathcal{N})$ and $(\mathcal{N}^\perp)^\perp = \mathcal{N}$ (see Exercise 7.1).

Now let G be a matrix over $\mathbb{F}_b$ with sm columns such that the row space of G is equal to $\mathcal{N}^\perp$. Then we have $HG^\top = 0$.

We define a weight function on $\mathbb{F}_b^{sm}$ that was first introduced by Niederreiter [169] and later used in an equivalent form in coding theory by Rosenbloom and Tsfasman [227].

Definition 7.1 For $\mathbf{a} = (a_1, \ldots, a_m) \in \mathbb{F}_b^m$ let

$$v_m(\mathbf{a}) = \begin{cases} 0 & \text{if } \mathbf{a} = \mathbf{0}, \\ \max\{j : a_j \neq 0\} & \text{if } \mathbf{a} \neq \mathbf{0}. \end{cases}$$

We extend this definition to $\mathbb{F}_b^{sm}$ by writing $\mathbf{A} \in \mathbb{F}_b^{sm}$ as the concatenation of s vectors of length m, i.e. $\mathbf{A} = (\mathbf{a}_1, \ldots, \mathbf{a}_s) \in \mathbb{F}_b^{sm}$ with $\mathbf{a}_i \in \mathbb{F}_b^m$ for $1 \leq i \leq s$, and putting

$$V_m(\mathbf{A}) = \sum_{i=1}^{s} v_m(\mathbf{a}_i).$$

The weight V_m is called the *Niederreiter–Rosenbloom–Tsfasman (NRT) weight.*

Note that $d_m(\mathbf{A}, \mathbf{B}) = V_m(\mathbf{A} - \mathbf{B})$ for $\mathbf{A}, \mathbf{B} \in \mathbb{F}_b^{sm}$ defines a metric on $\mathbb{F}_b^{sm}$ (see Exercise 7.2).

Definition 7.2 Let $\mathcal{N}$ be an arbitrary subset of $\mathbb{F}_b^{sm}$ containing at least two elements. Then the *minimum distance* of $\mathcal{N}$ is defined by

$$\delta_m(\mathcal{N}) = \min\{V_m(\mathbf{A} - \mathbf{B}) : \mathbf{A}, \mathbf{B} \in \mathcal{N} \text{ and } \mathbf{A} \neq \mathbf{B}\}.$$

Furthermore, we put $\delta_m(\mathcal{N}) = sm + 1$ whenever $|\mathcal{N}| = 1$.

If $\mathcal{N} \neq \{\mathbf{0}\}$ is a $\mathbb{F}_b$-linear subspace of $\mathbb{F}_b^{sm}$, this definition can be rewritten in the form

$$\delta_m(\mathcal{N}) = \min\{V_m(\mathbf{A}) : \mathbf{A} \in \mathcal{N} \setminus \{\mathbf{0}\}\}.$$

Furthermore, we put $\delta_m(\{\mathbf{0}\}) = sm + 1$.

We show a general bound on the minimum distance of a subset of $\mathbb{F}_b^{sm}$.

Proposition 7.3 *For any subset $\mathcal{N}$ of $\mathbb{F}_b^{sm}$ consisting of b^h elements, we have $1 \leq \delta_m(\mathcal{N}) \leq sm - h + 1$. In particular, if $\mathcal{N}$ is a $\mathbb{F}_b$-linear subspace of $\mathbb{F}_b^{sm}$, then we have $1 \leq \delta_m(\mathcal{N}) \leq sm - \dim(\mathcal{N}) + 1$.*

Proof The lower bound holds trivially true. If $h = 0$, then $\mathcal{N}$ consists of one element only and by definition we have $\delta_m(\mathcal{N}) = sm + 1$. Hence, the result holds true in this case. For $h \geq 1$, we define $\pi : \mathcal{N} \to \mathbb{F}_b^h$ to be the transformation which maps $\mathbf{A} \in \mathcal{N}$ to the h-tuple of the last h components of $\mathbf{A}$. Now we consider two cases:

1. If π is surjective, then there exist vectors $\mathbf{A}, \mathbf{B} \in \mathcal{N}$, $\mathbf{A} \neq \mathbf{B}$, with $\pi(\mathbf{A} - \mathbf{B}) = (1, 0, \ldots, 0) \in \mathbb{F}_b^h$. Let $1 \leq k \leq s$ denote the unique integer such that $sm - km < h \leq sm - km + m$. Then we have

$$\mathbf{A} - \mathbf{B} = (\underbrace{x_{1,1}, \ldots, x_{1,m}, \ldots, x_{k-1,1}, \ldots, x_{k-1,m}}_{(k-1)m}, \\ x_{k,1}, \ldots, x_{k,sm-h-(k-1)m}, \underbrace{1, 0, \ldots, 0}_{h})$$

and hence,

$$V_m(\mathbf{A} - \mathbf{B}) \leq (k-1)m + sm - h - (k-1)m + 1 = sm - h + 1.$$

2. If π is not surjective, then there exist vectors $\mathbf{A}, \mathbf{B} \in \mathcal{N}$, $\mathbf{A} \neq \mathbf{B}$ with $\pi(\mathbf{A}) = \pi(\mathbf{B})$ and hence, $\pi(\mathbf{A} - \mathbf{B}) = \mathbf{0} \in \mathbb{F}_b^h$. In the same way as above, we obtain $V_m(\mathbf{A} - \mathbf{B}) \leq sm - h$.

Hence, in any case we have $\delta_m(\mathcal{N}) \leq sm - h + 1$ as desired.

If $\mathcal{N}$ is a $\mathbb{F}_b$-linear subspace of $\mathbb{F}_b^{sm}$, then it consists of exactly $b^{\dim(\mathcal{N})}$ elements. □

The following notion was first considered in [174] and then formally defined in [189].

Definition 7.4 Let k, m, s be positive integers and let d be an integer with $0 \leq d \leq \min(k, ms)$. The system $\{\mathbf{c}_j^{(i)} \in \mathbb{F}_b^k : 1 \leq j \leq m, 1 \leq i \leq s\}$ is called a (d, k, m, s)-*system over* $\mathbb{F}_b$ if for any $d_1, \ldots, d_s \in \mathbb{N}_0$ with $0 \leq d_i \leq m$ for $1 \leq i \leq s$ and $\sum_{i=1}^{s} d_i = d$, the system

$$\{\mathbf{c}_j^{(i)} \in \mathbb{F}_b^k : 1 \leq j \leq d_i, 1 \leq i \leq s\}$$

is linearly independent over $\mathbb{F}_b$. Here, the empty system is considered to be linearly independent over $\mathbb{F}_b$. A (d, m, m, s)-system over $\mathbb{F}_b$ is also called a (d, m, s)-*system over* $\mathbb{F}_b$.

For a given (d, m, s)-system $\{\mathbf{c}_j^{(i)} \in \mathbb{F}_b^m : 1 \leq j \leq m, 1 \leq i \leq s\}$, let C_i, $1 \leq i \leq s$ be the $m \times m$ matrix with the row vectors $\mathbf{c}_1^{(i)}, \ldots, \mathbf{c}_m^{(i)}$. With these $m \times m$ matrices over $\mathbb{F}_b$, we build up the matrix

$$C = (C_1^\top | C_2^\top | \ldots | C_s^\top) \in \mathbb{F}_b^{m \times sm}$$

so that $C_1^\top, \ldots, C_s^\top$ are submatrices of C. Let $\mathcal{C}$ denote the row space of the matrix C. The dual space is then given by

$$\mathcal{C}^\perp = \{\mathbf{A} \in \mathbb{F}_b^{sm} : C\mathbf{A}^\top = \mathbf{0} \in (\mathbb{F}_b^m)^\top\}.$$

The following result was shown by Niederreiter and Pirsic [189, Theorem 1].

Theorem 7.5 *The system* $\{\mathbf{c}_j^{(i)} \in \mathbb{F}_b^m : 1 \le j \le m, 1 \le i \le s\}$ *is a* (d, m, s)*-system over* $\mathbb{F}_b$ *if and only if the dual space* $\mathcal{C}^\perp$ *of the row space* $\mathcal{C}$ *satisfies* $\delta_m(\mathcal{C}^\perp) \ge d + 1$.

Proof For $\mathbf{A} = (\mathbf{a}_1, \ldots, \mathbf{a}_s) \in \mathbb{F}_b^{sm}$ with $\mathbf{a}_i = (a_{i,1}, \ldots, a_{i,m}) \in \mathbb{F}_b^m$ for $1 \le i \le s$, we have

$$\sum_{i=1}^{s} \sum_{j=1}^{m} a_{i,j} \mathbf{c}_j^{(i)} = \mathbf{0} \in \mathbb{F}_b^m$$

if and only if

$$C\mathbf{A}^\top = \mathbf{0} \in (\mathbb{F}_b^m)^\top,$$

i.e. if and only if $\mathbf{A} \in \mathcal{C}^\perp$.

Now let the given system be a (d, m, s)-system over $\mathbb{F}_b$ and consider any non-zero vector $\mathbf{A} \in \mathcal{C}^\perp$. Then, from the above, we get $\sum_{i=1}^{s} \sum_{j=1}^{m} a_{i,j} \mathbf{c}_j^{(i)} = \mathbf{0} \in \mathbb{F}_b^m$. Putting $v_m(\mathbf{a}_i) = v_i$ for $1 \le i \le s$, we have

$$\sum_{i=1}^{s} \sum_{j=1}^{v_i} a_{i,j} \mathbf{c}_j^{(i)} = \mathbf{0} \in \mathbb{F}_b^m.$$

Since not all coefficients $a_{i,j}$ in this relation are equal to 0, the system $\{\mathbf{c}_j^{(i)} \in \mathbb{F}_b^m : 1 \le j \le v_i, 1 \le i \le s\}$ is linearly dependent over $\mathbb{F}_b$. Thus, the definition of a (d, m, s)-system over $\mathbb{F}_b$ implies that $\sum_{i=1}^{s} v_i \ge d + 1$. Therefore, we have

$$V_m(\mathbf{A}) = \sum_{i=1}^{s} v_m(\mathbf{a}_i) = \sum_{i=1}^{s} v_i \ge d + 1$$

and so $\delta_m(\mathcal{C}^\perp) \ge d + 1$.

Conversely, assume that $\delta_m(\mathcal{C}^\perp) \ge d + 1$. Then we have to show that any system $\{\mathbf{c}_j^{(i)} \in \mathbb{F}_b^m : 1 \le j \le d_i, 1 \le i \le s\}$ with $d_1, \ldots, d_s \in \mathbb{N}_0$ and $\sum_{i=1}^{s} d_i = d$ is linearly independent over $\mathbb{F}_b$. Suppose, on the contrary, that such a system was linearly dependent over $\mathbb{F}_b$, i.e. there exist coefficients $a_{i,j} \in \mathbb{F}_b$, not all of them zero, such that

$$\sum_{i=1}^{s} \sum_{j=1}^{d_i} a_{i,j} \mathbf{c}_j^{(i)} = \mathbf{0} \in \mathbb{F}_b^m.$$

Define $a_{i,j} = 0$ for $d_i < j \le m$ and $1 \le i \le s$, then

$$\sum_{i=1}^{s} \sum_{j=1}^{m} a_{i,j} \mathbf{c}_j^{(i)} = \mathbf{0} \in \mathbb{F}_b^m.$$

Hence, we get $\mathbf{A} \in \mathcal{C}^\perp$ and so $V_m(\mathbf{A}) \geq d+1$. But on the other hand, we have $v_m(\mathbf{a}_i) \leq d_i$ for $1 \leq i \leq s$ and so

$$V_m(\mathbf{A}) = \sum_{i=1}^{s} v_m(\mathbf{a}_i) \leq \sum_{i=1}^{s} d_i = d,$$

which is a contradiction. □

7.2 Duality theory for digital nets

It is clear that any system $\{\mathbf{c}_j^{(i)} \in \mathbb{F}_b^m : 1 \leq j \leq m, 1 \leq i \leq s\}$ determines a digital (t, m, s)-net over $\mathbb{F}_b$ with generating matrices $C_1, \ldots, C_s$ where the row vectors of the matrix C_i are given by $\mathbf{c}_1^{(i)}, \ldots, \mathbf{c}_m^{(i)}$ (in this order) for $1 \leq i \leq s$, and vice versa. In this context we also say the system generates the digital net and we call the matrix

$$C = (C_1^\top | C_2^\top | \ldots | C_s^\top) \in \mathbb{F}_b^{m \times sm}$$

the *overall generating matrix* of the digital net. As before, we denote by $\mathcal{C}$ the row space of the matrix C which we call in this context the *row space of the digital net.*

Example 7.6 Consider the generating matrices

$$C_1 = \begin{pmatrix} 1 & 1 & 1 \\ 0 & 1 & 1 \\ 0 & 0 & 1 \end{pmatrix} \quad \text{and} \quad C_2 = \begin{pmatrix} 0 & 0 & 1 \\ 0 & 1 & 0 \\ 1 & 0 & 0 \end{pmatrix}$$

as matrices over $\mathbb{Z}_2$. These matrices generate a digital $(t, 3, 2)$-net over $\mathbb{Z}_2$ with a certain t-parameter (what is t here?). The corresponding overall generating matrix C is given by

$$C = \left(\begin{array}{ccc|ccc} 1 & 0 & 0 & 0 & 0 & 1 \\ 1 & 1 & 0 & 0 & 1 & 0 \\ 1 & 1 & 1 & 1 & 0 & 0 \end{array}\right)$$

and its row space $\mathcal{C}$ in $\mathbb{Z}_2^6$ is the linear span of the three vectors

$$(1, 0, 0|0, 0, 1), (1, 1, 0|0, 1, 0), (1, 1, 1|1, 0, 0).$$

Hence,

$$\mathcal{C} = \{(0, 0, 0|0, 0, 0), (1, 1, 1|1, 0, 0), (1, 1, 0|0, 1, 0), (0, 0, 1|1, 1, 0),$$
$$(1, 0, 0|0, 0, 1), (0, 1, 1|1, 0, 1), (0, 1, 0|0, 1, 1), (1, 0, 1|1, 1, 1)\}$$

and $\dim(\mathcal{C}) = 3$.

The dual space $\mathcal{C}^\perp$ is given by all vectors $\mathbf{A} \in \mathbb{Z}_2^6$ such that $C\mathbf{A}^\top = \mathbf{0} \in (\mathbb{Z}_2^3)^\top$. Those vectors are given by the linear span of the three vectors

$$(0, 0, 1|1, 0, 0), (0, 1, 0|1, 1, 0), (1, 0, 0|1, 1, 1).$$

Hence,

$$\mathcal{C}^\perp = \{(0, 0, 0|0, 0, 0), (0, 0, 1|1, 0, 0), (0, 1, 0|1, 1, 0), (1, 0, 0|1, 1, 1),$$
$$(0, 1, 1|0, 1, 0), (1, 0, 1|0, 1, 1), (1, 1, 0|0, 0, 1), (1, 1, 1|1, 0, 1)\},$$

and $\dim(\mathcal{C}^\perp) = 3$. Together, we have $\dim(\mathcal{C}) + \dim(\mathcal{C}^\perp) = 6 = 2 \cdot 3$.

Now we show how the quality parameter of the digital net is connected to the properties of the corresponding vector system.

Lemma 7.7 *Let $t, m \in \mathbb{N}_0$ such that $m \geq 1$ and $0 \leq t \leq m$. A system $\{\mathbf{c}_j^{(i)} \in \mathbb{F}_b^m : 1 \leq j \leq m, 1 \leq i \leq s\}$ over $\mathbb{F}_b$ generates a digital (t, m, s)-net over $\mathbb{F}_b$ if and only if it is an $(m - t, m, s)$-system over $\mathbb{F}_b$.*

Hence, the construction of a digital (t, m, s)-net over $\mathbb{F}_b$ is the same as the construction of an $(m - t, m, s)$-system over $\mathbb{F}_b$.

Proof of Lemma 7.7 Assume that the system $\{\mathbf{c}_j^{(i)} \in \mathbb{F}_b^m : 1 \leq j \leq m, 1 \leq i \leq s\}$ is an $(m - t, m, s)$-system over $\mathbb{F}_b$. Then, for any $d_1, \ldots, d_s \in \mathbb{N}_0$ with $\sum_{i=1}^s d_i = m - t$, the system $\{\mathbf{c}_j^{(i)} \in \mathbb{F}_b^m : 1 \leq j \leq d_i, 1 \leq i \leq s\}$ is linearly independent over $\mathbb{F}_b$ and hence, we have $\rho(C_1, \ldots, C_s) \geq m - t$ where ρ is the linear independence parameter from Definition 4.50. By Lemma 4.52 the matrices $C_1, \ldots, C_s$ generate a digital (t, m, s)-net over $\mathbb{F}_b$.

On the other hand, assume that the system $\{\mathbf{c}_j^{(i)} \in \mathbb{F}_b^m : 1 \leq j \leq m, 1 \leq i \leq s\}$ generates a digital (t, m, s)-net over $\mathbb{F}_b$. Fix $d_1, \ldots, d_s \in \mathbb{N}_0$ with $\sum_{i=1}^s d_i = m - t$ and consider the elementary interval in base b of the form

$$J = \prod_{i=1}^s \left[\frac{A_i}{b^{d_i}}, \frac{A_i + 1}{b^{d_i}}\right)$$

with integers $0 \leq A_i < b^{d_i}$ for $1 \leq i \leq s$. By the proof of Lemma 4.52, we have that a point $\boldsymbol{x}_n$ of the digital net, $0 \leq n < b^m$, belongs to J if and only if the b-adic digit vector $\mathbf{n} \in (\mathbb{F}_b^m)^\top$ corresponding to n satisfies the linear system (4.8). Since the volume of J is $b^{d_1 + \cdots + d_s} = b^{t-m}$, we have $\boldsymbol{x}_n \in J$ for exactly b^t values of n and hence, the linear system (4.8) has exactly b^t solutions for any possible choice of $0 \leq A_i < b^{d_i}$ for $1 \leq i \leq s$. This means that the matrix $(\mathbf{c}_1^{(1)}, \ldots, \mathbf{c}_{d_1}^{(1)}, \ldots, \mathbf{c}_1^{(s)}, \ldots, \mathbf{c}_{d_s}^{(s)})^\top \in \mathbb{F}_b^{(m-t)\times m}$ has rank $m - t$ and therefore the vectors $\mathbf{c}_j^{(i)}$ for $1 \leq j \leq d_i$ and $1 \leq i \leq j$ are linearly independent over $\mathbb{F}_b$. Since this is true for any choice of $d_1, \ldots, d_s \in \mathbb{N}_0$ with $\sum_{i=1}^s d_i = m - t$, it follows that the system $\{\mathbf{c}_j^{(i)} \in \mathbb{F}_b^m : 1 \le j \le m, 1 \le i \le s\}$ is an $(m-t, m, s)$-system over $\mathbb{F}_b$. □

Combining Theorem 7.5 and Lemma 7.7, we obtain the following result.

Theorem 7.8 *Let $t, m \in \mathbb{N}_0$ such that $m \ge 1$ and $0 \le t \le m$. A system $\{\mathbf{c}_j^{(i)} \in \mathbb{F}_b^m : 1 \le j \le m, 1 \le i \le s\}$ over $\mathbb{F}_b$ generates a digital (t, m, s)-net over $\mathbb{F}_b$ if and only if $\delta_m(\mathcal{C}^\perp) \ge m - t + 1$.*

Corollary 7.9 *A system $\{\mathbf{c}_j^{(i)} \in \mathbb{F}_b^m : 1 \le j \le m, 1 \le i \le s\}$ over $\mathbb{F}_b$ generates a strict digital (t, m, s)-net over $\mathbb{F}_b$ with $t = m - \delta_m(\mathcal{C}^\perp) + 1$.*

Proof By Theorem 7.8, we have $t \ge m - \delta_m(\mathcal{C}^\perp) + 1$. Since $\dim(\mathcal{C}) \le m$, it follows that $\dim(\mathcal{C}^\perp) \ge sm - m$. Hence, $\delta_m(\mathcal{C}^\perp) \le m + 1$ by Proposition 7.3. From this it follows that $m - \delta_m(\mathcal{C}^\perp) + 1$ is contained in the interval $[0, m]$, which means that $m - \delta_m(\mathcal{C}^\perp) + 1$ is a possible value of t. □

Example 7.10 Let us turn again to Example 7.6 and let us determine the NRT weight of $\mathcal{C}^\perp$. We have

$\mathbf{A} \in \mathcal{C}^\perp$	$V_m(\mathbf{A})$
$(0,0,0\|0,0,0)$	0
$(0,0,1\|1,0,0)$	4
$(0,1,0\|1,1,0)$	4
$(1,0,0\|1,1,1)$	4
$(0,1,1\|0,1,0)$	5
$(1,0,1\|0,1,1)$	6
$(1,1,0\|0,0,1)$	5
$(1,1,1\|1,0,1)$	6

and hence, $\delta_m(\mathcal{C}^\perp) = 4$. According to Corollary 7.9, it follows that $\mathcal{C}$ generates a strict digital $(0, 3, 2)$-net over $\mathbb{Z}_2$.

Corollary 7.9 leads to the following procedure for constructing digital nets on the basis of duality theory:

1. Construct a $\mathbb{F}_b$-linear subspace $\mathcal{N}$ of $\mathbb{F}_b^{sm}$ with $\dim(\mathcal{N}) \ge ms - m$ and a large value for the minimum distance $\delta_m(\mathcal{N})$.
2. Dualise $\mathcal{N}$ to get $\mathcal{C}$, which determines the digital net in the sense that $\mathcal{C}$ is the row space of the overall generating matrix C of the digital net. According to Corollary 7.9, this yields a strict digital (t, m, s)-net over $\mathbb{F}_b$ with $t = m - \delta_m(\mathcal{C}^\perp) + 1$ where $\mathcal{C}^\perp = \mathcal{N}$.

Remark 7.11 Trivially, we have $\dim(\mathcal{C}) \le m$ and so we have $\dim(\mathcal{N}) = ms - \dim(\mathcal{C}) \ge ms - m$ as demanded in the first item of the construction procedure.

Corollary 7.12 *Let $m, s \in \mathbb{N}$, $s \geq 2$. Then, from any $\mathbb{F}_b$-linear subspace $\mathcal{N}$ of $\mathbb{F}_b^{sm}$ with $\dim(\mathcal{N}) \geq ms - m$, we can construct a strict digital (t, m, s)-net over $\mathbb{F}_b$ with $t = m - \delta_m(\mathcal{N}) + 1$.*

Note that any $\mathbf{A} = (\mathbf{a}_1, \ldots, \mathbf{a}_s) \in \mathbb{F}_b^{sm}$ can be transferred in a natural way into the s-dimensional unit-cube $[0, 1)^s$ when we apply the mapping

$$\Phi_{m,\varphi} : \mathbb{F}_b^m \to [0, 1), \quad \mathbf{a} = (a_1, \ldots, a_m) \mapsto \frac{\varphi^{-1}(a_1)}{b} + \cdots + \frac{\varphi^{-1}(a_m)}{b^m} \tag{7.1}$$

to each component of $\mathbf{A}$ for some bijection $\varphi : \{0, \ldots, b-1\} \to \mathbb{F}_b$. (If b is a prime, then we always identify $\mathbb{F}_b$ with $\mathbb{Z}_b$ and we use for φ the identity. In this case we simply write Φ_m.)

Proposition 7.13 *Let b be a prime power, let $m, s \in \mathbb{N}$, $s \geq 2$ and let $\varphi : \{0, \ldots, b-1\} \to \mathbb{F}_b$ be a bijection with $\varphi(0) = \overline{0}$. If the $\mathbb{F}_b$-linear subspace $\mathcal{N}$ of $\mathbb{F}_b^{sm}$ has $\dim(\mathcal{N}) = ms - m$, then the corresponding strict digital (t, m, s)-net over $\mathbb{F}_b$ with $t = m - \delta_m(\mathcal{N}) + 1$ is given by $\mathcal{P} = \Phi_{m,\varphi}(\mathcal{N}^\perp)$.*

Proof The generating matrices $C_1, \ldots, C_s$ of the digital net are chosen such that $\mathcal{N}^\perp$ is the row space of the overall generating matrix $(C_1^\top | \ldots | C_s^\top) \in \mathbb{F}_b^{sm}$. Hence, $\mathcal{N}^\perp$ is given by the elements $\mathbf{A}_n = (\mathbf{a}_{1,n}, \ldots, \mathbf{a}_{s,n})$ with $\mathbf{a}_{i,n} = (C_i \mathbf{n})^\top$ for $1 \leq i \leq s$, where $\mathbf{n} \in (\mathbb{F}_b^m)^\top$. Since $\dim(\mathcal{N}) = ms - m$, and hence, $\dim(\mathcal{N}^\perp) = m$, all these elements are different. Applying the map $\Phi_{m,\varphi}$ to these elements gives the digital net (compare with the construction principle given in Section 4.4). □

Theorem 7.14 *Let b be a prime power, let $m, s \in \mathbb{N}$, $s \geq 2$ and let $\varphi : \{0, \ldots, b-1\} \to \mathbb{F}_b$ be a bijection with $\varphi(0) = \overline{0}$. Let $\mathcal{C}$ and $\mathcal{C}^\perp$ in $\mathbb{F}_b^{sm}$ be mutually dual $\mathbb{F}_b$-linear subspaces of dimensions m and $ms - m$, respectively. Then $\Phi_{m,\varphi}(\mathcal{C})$ is a digital (t, m, s)-net over $\mathbb{F}_b$ if and only if $\delta_m(\mathcal{C}^\perp) \geq m - t + 1$.*

We use this principle based on duality theory later on to construct digital (t, m, s)-nets over $\mathbb{F}_b$. Furthermore, from the viewpoint of duality theory one can construct new nets from existing ones. Such methods, which are discussed in Chapter 9, are usually called *propagation rules*.

The following easy example in this vein is the so-called *direct product construction*, which was first introduced by Niederreiter and Xing [194, Theorem 10].

Example 7.15 Assume that we are given a digital (t_1, m_1, s_1)-net and a digital (t_2, m_2, s_2)-net both over $\mathbb{F}_b$. Then those nets correspond to an $(m_1 - t_1, m_1, s_1)$-system $\{\mathbf{c}_j^{(i)} \in \mathbb{F}_b^{m_1} : 1 \leq j \leq m_1, 1 \leq i \leq s_1\}$ and an $(m_2 - t_2, m_2, s_2)$-system $\{\mathbf{d}_j^{(i)} \in \mathbb{F}_b^{m_2} : 1 \leq j \leq m_2, 1 \leq i \leq s_2\}$ over $\mathbb{F}_b$, respectively.

Assume that $m_1 \le m_2$. Now we define the system $\{\mathbf{e}_j^{(i)} \in \mathbb{F}_b^{m_1+m_2} : 1 \le j \le m_1+m_2, 1 \le i \le s_1+s_2\}$ over $\mathbb{F}_b$ by the concatenations

$$\mathbf{e}_j^{(i)} = \begin{cases} (\mathbf{c}_j^{(i)}, \mathbf{0}) \in \mathbb{F}_b^{m_1+m_2} & \text{if } 1 \le j \le m_1, 1 \le i \le s_1, \\ (\mathbf{0}, \mathbf{d}_j^{(i-s_1)}) \in \mathbb{F}_b^{m_1+m_2} & \text{if } 1 \le j \le m_1, s_1 < i \le s_1+s_2, \\ \mathbf{0} \in \mathbb{F}_b^{m_1+m_2} & \text{if } m_1 < j \le m_1+m_2, 1 \le i \le s_1+s_2. \end{cases}$$

We show that the system $\{\mathbf{e}_j^{(i)} \in \mathbb{F}_b^{m_1+m_2} : 1 \le j \le m_1+m_2, 1 \le i \le s_1+s_2\}$ over $\mathbb{F}_b$ is a (d, m_1+m_2, s_1+s_2)-system over $\mathbb{F}_b$ with $d = \min(m_1-t_1, m_2-t_2)$. Assume on the contrary that there are non-negative integers $\delta_1, \dots, \delta_{s_1+s_2}$ with $\sum_{i=1}^{s_1+s_2} \delta_i = d$ and $\lambda_j^{(i)} \in \mathbb{F}_b, 1 \le j \le \delta_i, 1 \le i \le s_1$ and $\mu_j^{(i)} \in \mathbb{F}_b, 1 \le j \le \delta_i, 1 \le i \le s_2$, not all of the $\lambda_j^{(i)}, \mu_j^{(i)}$ zero, such that

$$\sum_{i=1}^{s_1} \sum_{j=1}^{\delta_i} \lambda_j^{(i)} (\mathbf{c}_j^{(i)}, \mathbf{0}) + \sum_{i=s_1+1}^{s_1+s_2} \sum_{j=1}^{\delta_i} \mu_j^{(i-s_1)} (\mathbf{0}, \mathbf{d}_j^{(i-s_1)}) = \mathbf{0} \in \mathbb{F}_b^{m_1+m_2}.$$

Then we must have

$$\sum_{i=1}^{s_1} \sum_{j=1}^{\delta_i} \lambda_j^{(i)} \mathbf{c}_j^{(i)} = \mathbf{0} \in \mathbb{F}_b^{m_1} \quad \text{and} \quad \sum_{i=1}^{s_2} \sum_{j=1}^{\delta_{s_1+i}} \mu_j^{(i)} \mathbf{d}_j^{(i)} = \mathbf{0} \in \mathbb{F}_b^{m_2}.$$

If not all $\lambda_j^{(i)}$ are zero, then we must have $\sum_{i=1}^{s_1} \delta_i > m_1 - t_1$, since $\{\mathbf{c}_j^{(i)} \in \mathbb{F}_b^{m_1} : 1 \le j \le m_1, 1 \le i \le s_1\}$ is an (m_1-t_1, m_1, s_1)-system over $\mathbb{F}_b$. Hence,

$$\min(m_1-t_1, m_2-t_2) = d = \sum_{i=1}^{s_1+s_2} \delta_i > m_1 - t_1,$$

a contradiction. If not all $\mu_j^{(i)}$ are zero, then the same argument also leads to a contradiction (note that here we have an (m_2-t_2, m_2, m_1, s_2)-system over $\mathbb{F}_b$). Hence, the system $\{\mathbf{e}_j^{(i)} \in \mathbb{F}_b^{m_1+m_2} : 1 \le j \le m_1+m_2, 1 \le i \le s_1+s_2\}$ is a (d, m_1+m_2, s_1+s_2)-system over $\mathbb{F}_b$ with $d = \min(m_1-t_1, m_2-t_2)$ and therefore by Lemma 7.7 it generates a digital (t, m_1+m_2, s_1+s_2)-net over $\mathbb{F}_b$ with

$$t = m_1 + m_2 - d = \max(m_1 + t_2, m_2 + t_1).$$

Further, more sophisticated propagation rules for digital nets are presented in Chapter 9.

7.3 Digital nets and linear codes

From Lemma 7.7, we know that constructing a digital (t, m, s)-net over $\mathbb{F}_b$ is equivalent to constructing an $(m-t, m, s)$-system over $\mathbb{F}_b$. On the other hand it has been pointed out in [184] that if we can construct a $(d, k, 1, s)$-system $\{\mathbf{c}^{(i)} : 1 \le i \le s\}$ over $\mathbb{F}_b$, then we obtain a linear code over $\mathbb{F}_b$ of length s, dimension at least $s - k$ and minimum distance at least $d + 1$ if we use the transpose of the vectors $\mathbf{c}^{(1)}, \ldots, \mathbf{c}^{(s)}$ as the columns of a parity-check matrix of the linear code. (The necessary notions from coding theory are explained below.) Thus, there is a close link between digital nets and linear codes via the theory of (d, k, m, s)-systems over $\mathbb{F}_b$.

The general construction principle for obtaining digital nets from linear codes that we are going to present in this section was established by Lawrence *et al.* [150] (see also [233]).

The following result concerning (d, k, m, s)-systems is crucial for the subsequent considerations.

Lemma 7.16 *Let b be a prime power. From any given $(d, t + d, 1, N)$-system over $\mathbb{F}_b$, we can construct a $(d, t + d, s)$-system over $\mathbb{F}_b$ with*

$$s = \begin{cases} \lfloor (N-1)/h \rfloor & \text{if } d = 2h+1, \\ \lfloor N/h \rfloor & \text{if } d = 2h. \end{cases}$$

Proof Suppose that $\mathbf{d}_1, \ldots, \mathbf{d}_N$ are the N vectors from $\mathbb{F}_b^{t+d}$ forming a $(d, t + d, 1, N)$-system over $\mathbb{F}_b$. This means that any d of the vectors $\mathbf{d}_1, \ldots, \mathbf{d}_N$ are linearly independent over $\mathbb{F}_b$. We construct a system

$$\{\mathbf{c}_j^{(i)} \in \mathbb{F}_b^{t+d} : 1 \le j \le t + d, 1 \le i \le s\}$$

in the following way:

- If $d = 2h + 1$, then the $\mathbf{c}_j^{(i)}$ are given by

	$i = 1$	$i = 2$	$i = 3$	$\ldots$	$i = s$
$\mathbf{c}_1^{(i)}$	$\mathbf{d}_1$	$\mathbf{d}_{h+1}$	$\mathbf{d}_{2h+1}$	$\ldots$	$\mathbf{d}_{(s-1)h+1}$
$\vdots$	$\vdots$	$\vdots$	$\vdots$		$\vdots$
$\mathbf{c}_h^{(i)}$	$\mathbf{d}_h$	$\mathbf{d}_{2h}$	$\mathbf{d}_{3h}$	$\ldots$	$\mathbf{d}_{sh}$
$\mathbf{c}_{h+1}^{(i)}$	$\mathbf{d}_{sh+1}$	$\mathbf{d}_{sh+1}$	$\mathbf{d}_{sh+1}$	$\ldots$	$\mathbf{d}_{sh+1}$
$\mathbf{c}_{h+2}^{(i)}$	$\mathbf{d}_{2h}$	$\mathbf{d}_h$	$\mathbf{d}_h$	$\ldots$	$\mathbf{d}_h$
$\mathbf{c}_{h+3}^{(i)}$	$\mathbf{d}_{2h-1}$	$\mathbf{d}_{h-1}$	$\mathbf{d}_{h-1}$	$\ldots$	$\mathbf{d}_{h-1}$
$\vdots$	$\vdots$	$\vdots$	$\vdots$		$\vdots$
$\mathbf{c}_{2h+1}^{(i)}$	$\mathbf{d}_{h+1}$	$\mathbf{d}_1$	$\mathbf{d}_1$	$\ldots$	$\mathbf{d}_1$

The vectors $\mathbf{c}_j^{(i)}$ for $2h + 2 \le j \le t + 2h + 1$ and $1 \le i \le s$ can be chosen arbitrarily in $\mathbb{F}_b^{t+d}$. For this construction, we need $sh + 1$ vectors of $\mathbf{d}_1, \ldots, \mathbf{d}_N$ and therefore, we may choose $s = \lfloor (N-1)/h \rfloor$.

- If $d = 2h$, then the $\mathbf{c}_j^{(i)}$ are given by

	$i = 1$	$i = 2$	$i = 3$	$\dots$	$i = s$
$\mathbf{c}_1^{(i)}$	$\mathbf{d}_1$	$\mathbf{d}_{h+1}$	$\mathbf{d}_{2h+1}$	$\dots$	$\mathbf{d}_{(s-1)h+1}$
$\vdots$	$\vdots$	$\vdots$	$\vdots$		$\vdots$
$\mathbf{c}_h^{(i)}$	$\mathbf{d}_h$	$\mathbf{d}_{2h}$	$\mathbf{d}_{3h}$	$\dots$	$\mathbf{d}_{sh}$
$\mathbf{c}_{h+1}^{(i)}$	$\mathbf{d}_{2h}$	$\mathbf{d}_h$	$\mathbf{d}_h$	$\dots$	$\mathbf{d}_h$
$\mathbf{c}_{h+2}^{(i)}$	$\mathbf{d}_{2h-1}$	$\mathbf{d}_{h-1}$	$\mathbf{d}_{h-1}$	$\dots$	$\mathbf{d}_{h-1}$
$\vdots$	$\vdots$	$\vdots$	$\vdots$		$\vdots$
$\mathbf{c}_{2h}^{(i)}$	$\mathbf{d}_{h+1}$	$\mathbf{d}_1$	$\mathbf{d}_1$	$\dots$	$\mathbf{d}_1$

  The vectors $\mathbf{c}_j^{(i)}$ for $2h + 1 \le j \le t + 2h$ and $1 \le i \le s$ can be chosen arbitrarily in $\mathbb{F}_b^{t+d}$. For this construction, we need sh vectors of $\mathbf{d}_1, \dots, \mathbf{d}_N$ and therefore we may choose $s = \lfloor N/h \rfloor$.

In both cases, for any $d_1, \dots, d_s \in \mathbb{N}_0$ with $\sum_{i=1}^s d_i = d$, the subsystem of d vectors $\{\mathbf{c}_j^{(i)} \in \mathbb{F}_b^{t+d} : 1 \le j \le d_i, 1 \le i \le s\}$ is linearly independent over $\mathbb{F}_b$ and hence, $\{\mathbf{c}_j^{(i)} \in \mathbb{F}_b^{t+d} : 1 \le j \le t + d, 1 \le i \le s\}$ is a $(d, t + d, s)$-system over $\mathbb{F}_b$. □

Combining Lemma 7.16 and Lemma 7.7, we obtain the following result.

Corollary 7.17 *Let b be a prime power. From any given $(d, t + d, 1, N)$-system over $\mathbb{F}_b$, we can construct a digital $(t, t + d, s)$-net over $\mathbb{F}_b$ with*

$$s = \begin{cases} \lfloor (N-1)/h \rfloor & \text{if } d = 2h + 1, \\ \lfloor N/h \rfloor & \text{if } d = 2h. \end{cases}$$

Now we turn to the theory of linear codes and show how one can obtain a $(d, t + d, 1, N)$-system over $\mathbb{F}_b$. An introduction to algebraic coding theory can be found, for example, in [157, Chapter 8].

Definition 7.18 A *linear code* $\mathcal{C}$ over $\mathbb{F}_b$ is a linear subspace of $\mathbb{F}_b^n$, for some $n \in \mathbb{N}$. If $\mathcal{C}$ has dimension k, then the linear code $\mathcal{C}$ is called an $[n, k]$-*code* over $\mathbb{F}_b$; n is called the *length* and k the *dimension* of the code.

The elements of $\mathcal{C}$ are called the *code words*. If we wish also to specify the minimum distance d of an $[n, k]$-code, then we speak of an $[n, k, d]$-code. The minimum distance $\varkappa_n(\mathcal{C})$ of a linear $[n, k]$-code $\mathcal{C}$ over $\mathbb{F}_b$ is equal to the smallest of the weights of the non-zero code words, where the weight of a code word $\mathbf{c} \in \mathbb{F}_b^n$ is the usual Hamming weight $\varkappa_n$ which is defined as the number of non-zero entries of $\mathbf{c}$, i.e.

$$\varkappa_n(\mathcal{C}) := \min\{\varkappa_n(\mathbf{c}) : \mathbf{c} \in \mathcal{C} \setminus \{\mathbf{0}\}\}.$$

A $k \times n$ matrix over $\mathbb{F}_b$ whose rows form a basis of a linear $[n, k]$-code is called a *generating matrix* of the code.

Given an $[n, k]$-code $\mathcal{C}$, its *dual code* $\mathcal{C}^\perp$ is defined as the set of vectors from $\mathbb{F}_b^n$ which are orthogonal to every code word of $\mathcal{C}$, i.e.

$$\mathcal{C}^\perp = \{\mathbf{v} \in \mathbb{F}_b^n : \mathbf{v} \cdot \mathbf{c} = 0 \text{ for all } \mathbf{c} \in \mathcal{C}\}.$$

If $\mathcal{C}$ is an $[n, k]$-code over $\mathbb{F}_b$, then $\mathcal{C}^\perp$ is an $[n, n-k]$-code. A *parity-check matrix* H for an $[n, k]$-code $\mathcal{C}$ is a generating matrix of $\mathcal{C}^\perp$. Hence, H is an $(n-k) \times n$ matrix over $\mathbb{F}_b$. Note that for each codeword $\mathbf{c} \in \mathcal{C}$, we have $H\mathbf{c}^\top = \mathbf{0}$.

The following result provides a connection between the parity check matrix of a linear code and its minimum distance.

Lemma 7.19 *A linear $[n, k]$-code $\mathcal{C}$ over $\mathbb{F}_b$ with parity-check matrix H has minimum distance d if and only if any $d-1$ columns of H are linearly independent over $\mathbb{F}_b$ but some d columns of H are linearly dependent over $\mathbb{F}_b$.*

Proof We show that a linear code $\mathcal{C}$ over $\mathbb{F}_b$ with parity-check matrix H has minimum distance $d \geq s+1$ if and only if any s columns of H are linearly independent over $\mathbb{F}_b$. From this observation we easily obtain the desired result. We follow [157, Lemma 8.14].

Assume that there are s linearly dependent columns of H, then $H\mathbf{c}^\top = \mathbf{0}$ and $\varkappa_n(\mathbf{c}) \leq s$ for suitable $\mathbf{c} \in \mathcal{C} \setminus \{\mathbf{0}\}$ and hence, $d \leq s$. Similarly, if any s columns of H are linearly independent, then there is no $\mathbf{c} \in \mathcal{C} \setminus \{\mathbf{0}\}$ of weight $\varkappa_n(\mathbf{c}) \leq s$ and hence, $d \geq s+1$. □

Corollary 7.20 *Let b be a prime power. Given a linear $[n, k, d]$-code over $\mathbb{F}_b$ with $d \geq 3$, a digital $(n-k-d+1, n-k, s)$-net over $\mathbb{F}_b$ can be constructed with*

$$s = \begin{cases} \lfloor (n-1)/h \rfloor & \text{if } d = 2h+2, \\ \lfloor n/h \rfloor & \text{if } d = 2h+1. \end{cases}$$

Proof If H is the parity-check matrix of the linear $[n, k, d]$-code over $\mathbb{F}_b$, then any $d-1$ columns of H are linearly independent according to Lemma 7.19. Hence, the transpose of the column vectors of H form a $(d-1, n-k, 1, n)$-system over $\mathbb{F}_b$. Now the result follows from Corollary 7.17. □

Remark 7.21 Assume that we have a linear $[n, k, d]$-code $\mathcal{C}$ over $\mathbb{F}_b$. This code consists of b^k different codewords. Now fix some $n-(d-1)$ coordinates and project each code word onto these coordinates. Since d is the minimum distance of $\mathcal{C}$, it follows that the projected code words are all still different and hence we have $b^k = |\mathcal{C}| \leq b^{n-d+1}$ or equivalently $n-k-d+1 \geq 0$ (this is none other than the well-known Singleton bound in coding theory). Hence, the quality parameter of digital nets obtained from $[n, k, d]$-codes over $\mathbb{F}_b$ is non-negative. A quality parameter $t = 0$ can be obtained from so-called MDS codes, where MDS stands for 'maximum distance separable'.

There is a huge amount of literature concerning the construction of digital nets from linear codes. See, for example, [2, 14, 62, 63, 183, 185, 243]. Furthermore, we mention that there is also the notion of generalised linear codes (using the NRT weight) with a connection to digital nets via ordered orthogonal arrays. For more information, see [159, 189] and [240].

7.4 Duality theory for digital sequences

In this section, we extend the duality theory for digital nets to digital sequences. This was first carried out in [48].

A digital sequence over $\mathbb{F}_b$ is fully determined by its generating matrices $C_1, \ldots, C_s \in \mathbb{F}_b^{\mathbb{N}\times\mathbb{N}}$. For $m \in \mathbb{N}$ we denote the $m \times m$ left-upper sub-matrix of C_i by $C_i^{(m)}$. The matrices $C_1^{(m)}, \ldots, C_s^{(m)}$ are then the generating matrices of a digital net. As above, we also define the overall generating matrix of this digital net by

$$C^{(m)} = ((C_1^{(m)})^\top | (C_2^{(m)})^\top | \ldots | (C_s^{(m)})^\top) \in \mathbb{F}_b^{m\times sm}$$

for any $m \in \mathbb{N}$. Hence, a digital sequence can equivalently be described via the sequence $C^{(1)}, C^{(2)}, \ldots$ of matrices or the sequence $\mathcal{C}_1, \mathcal{C}_2, \ldots$ of row spaces thereof. Each $C^{(m)}$ or $\mathcal{C}_m \subseteq \mathbb{F}_b^{sm}$ describes the first b^m points of the digital sequence and each has a dual space $\mathcal{C}_m^\perp \subseteq \mathbb{F}_b^{sm}$ (which is the null space of $C^{(m)}$ in $\mathbb{F}_b^{sm}$) associated with it, as described in Section 7.1. Hence, the dual for a digital sequence now consists of a sequence $(\mathcal{C}_m^\perp)_{m\geq 1}$ of dual spaces which have certain relations to each other.

The following proposition is a direct consequence of Theorem 7.1 and Theorem 4.84.

Proposition 7.22 *For $s \in \mathbb{N}$, $s \geq 2$, the matrices $C_1, \ldots, C_s$ generate a digital $(\mathbf{T}, s)$-sequence if and only if, for all $m \in \mathbb{N}$, we have*

$$\delta_m(\mathcal{C}_m^\perp) \geq m - \mathbf{T}(m) + 1.$$

We recall that the digital $(\mathbf{T}, s)$-sequence $\boldsymbol{x}_0, \boldsymbol{x}_1, \ldots$ over $\mathbb{F}_b$ is a *strict* digital $(\mathbf{T}, s)$-sequence (over $\mathbb{F}_b$) if, for all $m \in \mathbb{N}$, $\mathbf{T}(m)$ is the least t-value for all blocks of (to the first m digits truncated) points $\boldsymbol{x}_h$, $kb^m \leq h < (k+1)b^m$, with $k \in \mathbb{N}_0$.

Corollary 7.23 *For $s \in \mathbb{N}$, $s \geq 2$, the matrices $C_1, \ldots, C_s$ generate a strict digital $(\mathbf{T}, s)$-sequence with*

$$\mathbf{T}(m) = m - \delta_m(\mathcal{C}_m^\perp) + 1 \quad \textit{for all } m \in \mathbb{N}.$$

To generalise the duality theory, we need the quantity

$$U_m(\mathbf{A}) = \max_{1 \le i \le s} v_m(\mathbf{a}_i),$$

where $\mathbf{A} = (\mathbf{a}_1, \ldots, \mathbf{a}_s) \in \mathbb{F}_b^{sm}$ and $\mathbf{a}_i \in \mathbb{F}_b^m$ for $1 \le i \le s$.

The following definition is essential.

Definition 7.24 Let $s \in \mathbb{N}$, $s \ge 2$. For all $m \in \mathbb{N}$, let $\mathcal{M}_m$ be an $\mathbb{F}_b$-linear subspace of $\mathbb{F}_b^{sm}$ with $\dim(\mathcal{M}_m) \ge (s-1)m$. Let $\mathcal{M}_{m+1,m}$ be the projection of the set $\{\mathbf{A} \in \mathcal{M}_{m+1} : U_{m+1}(\mathbf{A}) \le m\}$, where $\mathbf{A} = (\mathbf{a}_1, \ldots, \mathbf{a}_s)$ with all $\mathbf{a}_i \in \mathbb{F}_b^{m+1}$, on the first m coordinates of each $\mathbf{a}_i$ for $1 \le i \le s$. Suppose that $\mathcal{M}_{m+1,m}$ is an $\mathbb{F}_b$-linear subspace of $\mathcal{M}_m$ with $\dim(\mathcal{M}_{m+1,m}) \ge \dim(\mathcal{M}_m) - 1$ for all $m \in \mathbb{N}$. Then the sequence $(\mathcal{M}_m)_{m \ge 1}$ of spaces is called a *dual space chain*.

We show in the following that for given generating matrices $C_1, \ldots, C_s$ of a digital sequence, the sequence $(\mathcal{C}_m^\perp)_{m \ge 1}$ of dual spaces (with $\mathcal{C}_m$ being the mth row space of the digital sequence) is a dual space chain and that, conversely, a dual space chain $(\mathcal{M}_m)_{m \ge 1}$ determines generating matrices $C_1, \ldots, C_s \in \mathbb{F}_b^{\mathbb{N} \times \mathbb{N}}$ of a digital sequence. Therefore, the conditions of a dual space chain are necessary and sufficient to describe a digital sequence. Proposition 7.22 and Corollary 7.23 can be used to obtain the quality function $\mathbf{T}$ from $(\mathcal{M}_m)_{m \ge 1}$ for such a digital sequence. We assume throughout the rest of this section that $s \in \mathbb{N}$, $s \ge 2$.

For $C_1, \ldots, C_s \in \mathbb{F}_b^{\mathbb{N} \times \mathbb{N}}$ and $m \in \mathbb{N}$, the left upper $m \times (m+1)$ submatrix of C_i is denoted by $C_i^{(m \times (m+1))}$ for $1 \le i \le s$. Furthermore, let

$$C^{(m+1,m)} = ((C_1^{(m \times (m+1))})^\top | (C_2^{(m \times (m+1))})^\top | \ldots | (C_s^{(m \times (m+1))})^\top).$$

The row space of $C^{(m+1,m)} \in \mathbb{F}_b^{(m+1) \times sm}$ is denoted by $\mathcal{C}_{m+1,m} \subseteq \mathbb{F}_b^{sm}$.

Theorem 7.25 *For given generating matrices $C_1, \ldots, C_s$ of a digital sequence, the associated sequence $(\mathcal{C}_m^\perp)_{m \ge 1}$ of dual spaces is a dual space chain.*

Proof Let generating matrices $C_1, \ldots, C_s$ be given. They yield the corresponding sequence $(\mathcal{C}_m^\perp)_{m \ge 1}$ of dual spaces. We show that $\mathcal{M}_m := \mathcal{C}_m^\perp$ satisfies all the properties in Definition 7.24.

The dual space $\mathcal{C}_m^\perp$ is obviously a subspace of $\mathbb{F}_b^{sm}$ with $\dim(\mathcal{C}_m^\perp) = sm - \dim(\mathcal{C}_m) \ge sm - m$, as $\mathcal{C}_m$ is the row space of $C^{(m)}$ and hence, $\dim(\mathcal{C}_m) \le m$.

Note that $\mathcal{M}_{m+1,m} = \mathcal{C}_{m+1,m}^\perp$, the dual space of the row space $\mathcal{C}_{m+1,m}$ of $C^{(m+1,m)}$. Since $\mathcal{C}_m \subseteq \mathcal{C}_{m+1,m}$, we have $\mathcal{M}_{m+1,m} \subseteq \mathcal{M}_m$. As $\dim(\mathcal{C}_m) \ge \dim(\mathcal{C}_{m+1,m}) - 1$, $\dim(\mathcal{C}_m^\perp) = sm - \dim(\mathcal{C}_m)$ and $\dim(\mathcal{C}_{m+1,m}^\perp) = sm - \dim(\mathcal{C}_{m+1,m})$, it follows that $\dim(\mathcal{C}_{m+1,m}^\perp) \ge \dim(\mathcal{C}_m^\perp) - 1$. Thus, the theorem is shown. □

We can also show the converse, namely that for a given dual space chain, we can obtain a digital sequence.

Theorem 7.26 *For a given dual space chain $(\mathcal{M}_m)_{m\geq 1}$, one can construct generating matrices $C_1, \ldots, C_s$ of a digital sequence such that for all $m \in \mathbb{N}$ the mth row space $\mathcal{C}_m$ of the digital sequence satisfies $\mathcal{C}_m^\perp = \mathcal{M}_m$.*

Proof We proceed by induction on $m \in \mathbb{N}$. For $m = 1$, we have $\mathcal{M}_1$ as a subspace of $\mathbb{F}_b^s$ with $\dim(\mathcal{M}_1) \geq s-1$. The dual space $\mathcal{M}_1^\perp$ of $\mathcal{M}_1$ therefore has dimension at most 1. The generating vector of this subspace can be used to define $C^{(1)}$ (if the dimension is 0, then $C^{(1)} = \mathbf{0}$).

Now assume that we know $C^{(m)}$ with row space $\mathcal{C}_m = \mathcal{M}_m^\perp$ and we want to construct $C^{(m+1)}$. We first construct $C^{(m+1,m)}$. If $\dim(\mathcal{M}_m) = \dim(\mathcal{M}_{m+1,m})$, then we obtain $C^{(m+1,m)}$ from $C^{(m)}$ by letting the last row of $C^{(m+1,m)}$ be the zero vector. If $\dim(\mathcal{M}_m) = \dim(\mathcal{M}_{m+1,m}) + 1$, then $\dim(\mathcal{M}_m^\perp) = \dim(\mathcal{M}_{m+1,m}^\perp) - 1$, where $\mathcal{M}_m^\perp$ and $\mathcal{M}_{m+1,m}^\perp$ are the dual spaces of $\mathcal{M}_m$ and $\mathcal{M}_{m+1,m}$ in $\mathbb{F}_b^{sm}$, respectively. Note that as $\mathcal{M}_{m+1,m}$ is a subspace of $\mathcal{M}_m$, we have $\mathcal{M}_m^\perp$ as a subspace of $\mathcal{M}_{m+1,m}^\perp$. The space $\mathcal{M}_m^\perp$ is the row space of $C^{(m)}$, and since $\dim(\mathcal{M}_{m+1,m}^\perp) = \dim(\mathcal{M}_m^\perp) + 1$, we can add another row to $C^{(m)}$ to obtain the $(m+1) \times sm$ matrix $C^{(m+1,m)}$ such that its row space is $\mathcal{M}_{m+1,m}^\perp$.

Let $\overline{\mathcal{M}}_{m+1,m} = \{\mathbf{A} \in \mathcal{M}_{m+1} : U_{m+1}(\mathbf{A}) \leq m\}$. Then $\overline{\mathcal{M}}_{m+1,m}$ is a subspace of $\mathcal{M}_{m+1}$ and the projection of $\overline{\mathcal{M}}_{m+1,m}$ onto the first m coordinates of each $\mathbf{a}_i$, $1 \leq i \leq s$, is $\mathcal{M}_{m+1,m}$. By the construction above, the dual space $\mathcal{M}_{m+1,m}^\perp \subseteq \mathbb{F}_b^{sm}$ of $\mathcal{M}_{m+1,m}$ is equal to the row space of $C^{(m+1,m)}$. Now consider the dual space $\overline{\mathcal{M}}_{m+1,m}^\perp \subseteq \mathbb{F}_b^{s(m+1)}$ of $\overline{\mathcal{M}}_{m+1,m}$. For $1 \leq i \leq s$ let $\overline{C}_i^{(m\times(m+1))} \in \mathbb{F}_b^{(m+1)\times(m+1)}$ be obtained from the matrix $C_i^{(m\times(m+1))}$ by adding the zero vector as the last row and let

$$\overline{C}^{(m+1,m)} = ((\overline{C}_1^{(m\times(m+1))})^\top \mid \ldots \mid (\overline{C}_s^{(m\times(m+1))})^\top) \in \mathbb{F}_b^{(m+1)\times s(m+1)}.$$

For $1 \leq i \leq s$, let $\mathbf{V}_i = (v_{i,1}, \ldots, v_{i,s(m+1)})$ with $v_{i,i(m+1)} = 1$ and $v_{i,j} = 0$ for $1 \leq j \leq s(m+1)$ with $j \neq i(m+1)$. Then the rows of $\overline{C}^{(m+1,m)}$ and the vectors $\mathbf{V}_1, \ldots, \mathbf{V}_s$ generate the space $\overline{\mathcal{M}}_{m+1,m}^\perp$.

Now as $\overline{\mathcal{M}}_{m+1,m}$ is a subspace of $\mathcal{M}_{m+1}$, so $\mathcal{M}_{m+1}^\perp$ is a subspace of $\overline{\mathcal{M}}_{m+1,m}^\perp$. On the other hand, $\dim(\mathcal{M}_{m+1}^\perp) = s(m+1) - \dim(\mathcal{M}_{m+1}) \leq s(m+1) - (s-1)(m+1) = m+1$. Thus, there are $m+1$ linear combinations of the rows of $\overline{C}^{(m+1,m)}$ and $\mathbf{V}_1, \ldots, \mathbf{V}_s$ which generate the space $\mathcal{M}_{m+1}^\perp$.

For $1 \leq j \leq m+1$, let $\mathbf{D}_j \in \mathbb{F}_b^{s(m+1)}$ denote the jth row of $\overline{C}^{(m+1,m)}$. It remains to show that there are $\lambda_{i,j} \in \mathbb{F}_b$, $1 \leq i \leq s$ and $1 \leq j \leq m+1$, such that vectors of the form $\mathbf{D}_j + \lambda_{1,j}\mathbf{V}_1 + \cdots + \lambda_{s,j}\mathbf{V}_s$ for $1 \leq j \leq m+1$ generate the space $\mathcal{M}_{m+1}^\perp$. From these vectors, we can then build the matrices $C_i^{(m+1)}$ which contain $C_i^{(m)}$, as the $\lambda_{i,j}$ supply the entries for the final rows of the $C_i^{(m+1)}$.

If $\mathbf{D}_1, \ldots, \mathbf{D}_{m+1}$ are linearly independent, then the result holds as $m+1$ vectors are enough and none of the $\mathbf{D}_j$'s can be left out. Otherwise, there would be a vector in the dual space of the generating vectors of $\mathcal{M}_{m+1}^{\perp}$, with $U_{m+1}(\mathbf{A}) \leq m$, which is not in $\overline{\mathcal{M}}_{m+1,m}$ and hence not in $\mathcal{M}_{m+1}$.

Without loss of generality, assume now that $\{\mathbf{D}_1, \ldots, \mathbf{D}_k\}$ is a maximal linearly independent subset of $\{\mathbf{D}_1, \ldots, \mathbf{D}_{m+1}\}$ for some $k \leq m$. Then $\mathbf{D}_{k+1}, \ldots, \mathbf{D}_{m+1}$ can be represented as linear combinations of $\mathbf{D}_1, \ldots, \mathbf{D}_k$. In this case, as above, none of the vectors $\mathbf{D}_1, \ldots, \mathbf{D}_k$ can be left out, so we can assume that $\mathcal{M}_{m+1}^{\perp}$ is generated by the vectors $\mathbf{D}_1 + \mu_{1,1}\mathbf{V}_1 + \cdots + \mu_{s,1}\mathbf{V}_s, \ldots, \mathbf{D}_k + \mu_{1,k}\mathbf{V}_1 + \cdots + \mu_{s,k}\mathbf{V}_s$, for certain $\mu_{i,j} \in \mathbb{F}_b$, and $m+1-k$ linear combinations of $\mathbf{V}_1, \ldots, \mathbf{V}_s$ given by $\kappa_{1,1}\mathbf{V}_1 + \cdots + \kappa_{s,1}\mathbf{V}_s, \ldots, \kappa_{1,m+1-k}\mathbf{V}_1 + \cdots + \kappa_{s,m+1-k}\mathbf{V}_s$, for certain $\kappa_{i,l} \in \mathbb{F}_b$. But the last $m+1-k$ vectors can now be replaced by vectors of the required form. Let $\mathbf{D}_{k+1} = \alpha_1\mathbf{D}_1 + \cdots + \alpha_k\mathbf{D}_k$ with all $\alpha_j \in \mathbb{F}_b$. Now we add to the vector $\kappa_{1,1}\mathbf{V}_1 + \cdots + \kappa_{s,1}\mathbf{V}_s$ a linear combination of the first k vectors generating $\mathcal{M}_{m+1}^{\perp}$ and apply the equation for $\mathbf{D}_{k+1}$ to obtain $\mathbf{D}_{k+1} + (\alpha_1\mu_{1,1} + \cdots + \alpha_k\mu_{1,k} - \kappa_{1,1})\mathbf{V}_1 + \cdots + (\alpha_1\mu_{s,1} + \cdots + \alpha_k\mu_{s,k} - \kappa_{s,1})\mathbf{V}_s$. The same can be done for the remaining vectors. This completes the proof of the theorem. □

Combining Theorem 7.26 with Corollary 7.23 leads to the following result:

Corollary 7.27 *Let $s \in \mathbb{N}$, $s \geq 2$. From a dual space chain $(\mathcal{M}_m)_{m\geq 1}$, one can construct a digital $(\mathbf{T}, s)$-sequence over $\mathbb{F}_b$ with $\mathbf{T}(m) = m - \delta_m(\mathcal{M}_m) + 1$ for all $m \in \mathbb{N}$.*

In the proof above, the construction of the generating matrices was not unique. For certain dual space chains, uniqueness up to a certain reordering of the points can be achieved, as we show in the next theorem.

Theorem 7.28 *Let $(\mathcal{M}_m)_{m\geq 1}$ be a dual space chain. The generating matrices $C_1, \ldots, C_s$ are unique up to a multiplication of $C_1, \ldots, C_s$ from the right with the same non-singular upper triangular matrix if and only if*

$$\dim(\mathcal{M}_{m+1,m}) = (s-1)m - 1$$

for all $m \in \mathbb{N}$.

Proof We retain the notation in the proof of Theorem 7.26. Note that if the vectors $\mathbf{D}_1, \ldots, \mathbf{D}_{m+1}$ are linearly dependent, then, as can be seen from the last paragraph of the proof of Theorem 7.26, there is more than one possible choice for the $\lambda_{i,j} \in \mathbb{F}_b$, $1 \leq i \leq s$ and $1 \leq j \leq m+1$, such that the vectors $\mathbf{D}_j + \lambda_{1,j}\mathbf{V}_1 + \cdots + \lambda_{s,j}\mathbf{V}_s$ for $1 \leq j \leq m+1$ generate the space $\mathcal{M}_{m+1}^{\perp}$. The vectors $\mathbf{D}_1, \ldots, \mathbf{D}_{m+1}$ are linearly dependent if and only if $\dim(\mathcal{M}_{m+1,m}^{\perp}) < m+1$, which is equivalent to $\dim(\mathcal{M}_{m+1,m}) = sm - \dim(\mathcal{M}^{\perp}_{m+1,m}) > sm - (m+1) = (s-1)m - 1$. Hence, if $\dim(\mathcal{M}_{m+1,m}) > (s-1)m - 1$, then the generating matrices are not unique. This proves the 'only if' part of the theorem.

To prove the 'if' part, observe that if $\dim(\mathcal{M}_{m+1,m}) = (s-1)m - 1$, then it follows from the definition of a dual space chain that $(s-1)m \le \dim(\mathcal{M}_m) \le \dim(\mathcal{M}_{m+1,m}) + 1 = (s-1)m$. Hence, we have $\dim(\mathcal{M}_m) = (s-1)m$ for all $m \in \mathbb{N}$.

We now use induction. The result clearly holds for $m = 1$. The construction of $C^{(m+1,m)}$ from $C^{(m)}$ is not affected by adding a scalar multiple of a previous row to the last row of $C^{(m+1,m)}$. Now to the construction of $C^{(m+1)}$ from $C^{(m+1,m)}$. As $\overline{\mathcal{M}}_{m+1,m}$ is a subspace of $\mathcal{M}_{m+1}$, we can consider the factor space $\mathcal{M}_{m+1}/\overline{\mathcal{M}}_{m+1,m}$. We have $\dim(\mathcal{M}_{m+1}) = \dim(\overline{\mathcal{M}}_{m+1,m}) + \dim(\mathcal{M}_{m+1}/\overline{\mathcal{M}}_{m+1,m})$. From $\dim(\mathcal{M}_{m+1}) = (s-1)(m+1)$ and $\dim(\overline{\mathcal{M}}_{m+1,m}) = (s-1)m - 1$, we obtain $\dim(\mathcal{M}_{m+1}/\overline{\mathcal{M}}_{m+1,m}) = s$. For $1 \le i \le s$ let

$$\mathcal{R}_i = \{\mathbf{A} = (\mathbf{a}_1, \ldots, \mathbf{a}_s) \in \mathcal{M}_{m+1} : v_{m+1}(\mathbf{a}_i) = m+1,\ v_{m+1}(\mathbf{a}_j) \le m\ \forall j \ne i\}.$$

From $\dim(\mathcal{M}_{m+1}/\overline{\mathcal{M}}_{m+1,m}) = s$, we know that none of the $\mathcal{R}_i$ is empty. Now, for $1 \le i \le s$, the matrix $(C_i^{(m+1)})^\top$ can be obtained from $(C_i^{(m\times(m+1))})^\top$ by replacing the $(m+1)$st column with the column (which is initially empty) $-(\overline{C}^{(m+1,m)})^\top \mathbf{A}^\top$ where $\mathbf{A} \in \mathcal{R}_i$ such that $a_{i,m+1} = 1$. Then we have

$$\begin{aligned}
C^{(m+1)}\mathbf{A}^\top &= \sum_{j=1}^{s} (C_i^{(m+1)})^\top \boldsymbol{a}_j^\top \\
&= \sum_{\substack{j=1\\ j\ne i}}^{s} (\overline{C}_j^{(m\times(m+1))})^\top \boldsymbol{a}_j^\top + (C_i^{(m\times(m+1))})^\top \pi_m(\boldsymbol{a}_i)^\top - (\overline{C}^{(m+1,m)})^\top \mathbf{A}^\top \\
&= \sum_{j=1}^{s} (\overline{C}_j^{(m\times(m+1))})^\top \boldsymbol{a}_j^\top - (\overline{C}^{(m+1,m)})^\top \mathbf{A}^\top \\
&= (\overline{C}^{(m+1,m)})^\top \mathbf{A}^\top - (\overline{C}^{(m+1,m)})^\top \mathbf{A}^\top = \mathbf{0},
\end{aligned}$$

where $\pi_m(\boldsymbol{a}_i)$ is the projection of $\boldsymbol{a}_i$ to the first m components. Hence, the elements of $\mathcal{R}_i$ for $1 \le i \le s$ are contained in $\mathcal{C}^{\perp}_{m+1}$ and therefore, $\mathcal{M}_{m+1} = \mathcal{C}^{\perp}_{m+1}$.

By construction, for a given $C^{(m+1,m)}$ the matrix $C^{(m+1)}$ is therefore uniquely determined. Also, if we multiply the matrix $C^{(m+1,m)}$ by a non-singular lower triangular matrix from the left, then the $(m+1)$st column of $(C_i^{(m+1)})^\top$ is also multiplied by the same non-singular lower triangular matrix from the left for each $1 \le i \le s$. But this means that the matrices $C_i^{(m+1)}$ are multiplied from the right with the same non-singular upper triangular matrix. Hence, the proof is complete. □

Remark 7.29 Consider the digital net generated by $C_1^{(m)}, \ldots, C_s^{(m)}$. Among these points, there are $b^{\dim(\mathcal{M}_m^\perp)}$ distinct points, i.e. $b^{sm-\dim(\mathcal{M}_m)}$ distinct points. Hence, if $\dim(\mathcal{M}_m) = (s-1)m$, then $sm - \dim(\mathcal{M}_m) = m$, i.e. all points are distinct. If, on the other hand, $\dim(\mathcal{M}_m) > (s-1)m$, then $\dim(\mathcal{M}_m^\perp) = sm - \dim(\mathcal{M}_m) < sm - (s-1)m = m$, and hence, each point occurs with multiplicity $b^{\dim(\mathcal{M}_m)-(s-1)m}$. Equivalently, the last $\dim(\mathcal{M}_m) - (s-1)m$ rows of $C^{(m)}$ can be chosen as $\mathbf{0}$. This also implies that $\mathbf{T}(m) \geq \dim(\mathcal{M}_m) - (s-1)m$.

Remark 7.29 and Theorem 7.28 lead to the following definition.

Definition 7.30 Let $s \geq 2$. We call a dual space chain $(\mathcal{M}_m)_{m\geq 1}$ *regular* if $\dim(\mathcal{M}_{m+1,m}) = (s-1)m - 1$ for all $m \in \mathbb{N}$.

Remark 7.31 In the duality theory for digital sequences, we need to define suitable subspaces $\mathcal{M}_m$ of $\mathbb{F}_b^{sm}$. We note that it suffices to define $\mathcal{M}_m$ for all sufficiently large m, say for all $m \geq r$ with some positive integer r. The reason is that then, by dualising $\mathcal{M}_r$, the rth row space of the digital sequence is determined, and so a matrix $C^{(r)} \in \mathbb{F}_b^{r\times sr}$ with this row space can be chosen. This determines the matrices $C_i^{(r)} \in \mathbb{F}_b^{r\times r}$ for $1 \leq i \leq s$. By using left upper submatrices of the $C_i^{(r)}$, all matrices $C_i^{(m)} \in \mathbb{F}_b^{m\times m}$, $1 \leq i \leq s$, $1 \leq m < r$, are determined, and so are the matrices $C^{(m)} \in \mathbb{F}_b^{m\times sm}$ for $1 \leq m < r$. Again for $1 \leq m < r$, the dual of the row space of $C^{(m)}$ yields the space $\mathcal{M}_m$. By the proof of Theorem 7.25, the conditions for a dual space chain are automatically satisfied for $1 \leq m < r$, and so it suffices to check the conditions for a dual space chain for $m \geq r$.

Exercises

7.1 Let $\mathcal{N} \subseteq \mathbb{F}_b^{sm}$ be a $\mathbb{F}_b$-linear subspace and let $\mathcal{N}^\perp$ be its orthogonal complement. Show that $\mathcal{N}^\perp$ is a $\mathbb{F}_b$-linear subspace too with $\dim(\mathcal{N}) = sm - \dim(\mathcal{N}^\perp)$ and $(\mathcal{N}^\perp)^\perp = \mathcal{N}$.

7.2 Show that $d_m(\mathbf{A}, \mathbf{B}) = V_m(\mathbf{A} - \mathbf{B})$ for $\mathbf{A}, \mathbf{B} \in \mathbb{F}_b^{sm}$, where V_m is the NRT weight, is a metric on $\mathbb{F}_b^{sm}$.

7.3 Consider the generating matrices

$$C_1 = \begin{pmatrix} 1 & 1 & 1 & 1 \\ 0 & 1 & 0 & 1 \\ 0 & 0 & 1 & 1 \\ 0 & 0 & 0 & 1 \end{pmatrix} \quad \text{and} \quad C_2 = \begin{pmatrix} 0 & 0 & 0 & 1 \\ 0 & 0 & 1 & 0 \\ 0 & 1 & 0 & 0 \\ 1 & 0 & 0 & 0 \end{pmatrix}$$

of a digital $(t, 4, 2)$-net over $\mathbb{Z}_2$. Determine the corresponding row space $\mathcal{C}$ of the corresponding overall generating matrix and its orthogonal complement $\mathcal{C}^\perp$. How large is the parameter t?

7.4 Show that if there exist digital (t_k, m_k, s_k)-nets over $\mathbb{F}_b$ for $1 \le k \le n$, then there exists a digital $(t, \sum_{k=1}^n m_k, \sum_{k=1}^n s_k)$-net over $\mathbb{F}_b$ with $t = \sum_{k=1}^n m_k - \min_{1\le k\le n}(m_k - t_k)$. In particular, if there exists a digital (t, m, s)-net over $\mathbb{F}_b$, then for any $n \in \mathbb{N}$ there exists a $((n-1)m + t, nm, ns)$-net over $\mathbb{F}_b$.

7.5 Give explicitly the generating matrices of the digital $(t, 8, 4)$-net over $\mathbb{Z}_2$ which is obtained from the direct product construction using the digital net from Exercise 7.3. How large is the t-value of this digital net?

7.6 Assume that the points $\boldsymbol{x}_0, \ldots, \boldsymbol{x}_{b^{m_1}-1}$ form a digital (t_1, m_1, s_1)-net and that the points $\boldsymbol{y}_0, \ldots, \boldsymbol{y}_{b^{m_2}-1}$ form a digital (t_2, m_2, s_2)-net both over $\mathbb{F}_b$. Show that the $s_1 + s_2$-dimensional point set consisting of the points $(\boldsymbol{x}_k, \boldsymbol{y}_l)$ for $0 \le k < b^{m_1}$ and $0 \le l < b^{m_2}$ form a digital (t, m, s)-net over $\mathbb{F}_b$ where $m = m_1 + m_2$, $s = s_1 + s_2$ and $t = \max(m_1 + t_2, m_2 + t_1)$. Is the assertion also true for nets not necessarily digital?

7.7 Construct a $[4, 2, 3]$-code over $\mathbb{F}_4$.

7.8 Consider the code whose codewords are the binary representations of the numbers $1, \ldots, 2^m - 1$, that is, $H_m = \{(\kappa_0, \ldots, \kappa_{m-1}) : 1 \le \kappa_0 + \kappa_1 2 + \cdots + \kappa_{m-1} 2^{m-1}\}$. Find the values of n, k, d such that the set H_m is an $[n, k, d]$-code.

7.9 Show that if $\mathcal{C}$ is a linear $[n, k]$-code, then $\mathcal{C}^\perp$ is a linear $[n, n-k]$-code.

7.10 Consider the sequence over $\mathbb{Z}_2$ from Example 4.78 in dimension $s = 2$. Find the corresponding dual space chain.

8

Special constructions of digital nets and sequences

This section is devoted to explicit constructions of digital nets and sequences. Some examples have already appeared in previous chapters. We have seen in Section 4.4 that the construction of a digital (t, s)-sequence is furnished by s matrices of size $\mathbb{N} \times \mathbb{N}$ over a finite field $\mathbb{F}_b$, where b is a prime power. Indeed, the van der Corput sequence can be generated by the digital construction scheme of Section 4.4 using the matrix

$$C_1 = \begin{pmatrix} 1 & 0 & 0 & 0 & \cdots \\ 0 & 1 & 0 & 0 & \cdots \\ 0 & 0 & 1 & 0 & \cdots \\ 0 & 0 & 0 & 1 & \cdots \\ \vdots & \vdots & \vdots & \vdots & \ddots \end{pmatrix}.$$

Unfortunately, the construction of a second generating matrix to obtain a, say digital $(0, 2)$-sequence over $\mathbb{F}_b$ is already nontrivial (one such example was given in Section 4.4; see Example 4.78).

The first examples of the construction of such matrices were given by Sobol′ [253] and Faure [68]. These constructions deal directly with the construction of the generating matrices. Niederreiter's essential insight [173] was that these constructions can be described more neatly using polynomial arithmetic over finite fields. This is explained in the following section.

8.1 Sobol′, Faure and Niederreiter sequences

Although Sobol′ was the first to construct digital (t, s)-sequences in base 2 in 1967 and Faure introduced constructions of digital $(0, s)$-sequences in prime base b with $b \geq s$ in 1982, it now seems most convenient to introduce digital (t, s)-sequences using Niederreiter's unifying approach based on polynomial arithmetic over finite fields. By considering generalised Niederreiter sequences, the constructions of Sobol′ and Faure appear as special cases.

For a prime power b, let $\mathbb{F}_b((x^{-1}))$ be the field of formal Laurent series over $\mathbb{F}_b$. Elements of $\mathbb{F}_b((x^{-1}))$ are formal Laurent series of the form

$$L = \sum_{l=w}^{\infty} t_l x^{-l},$$

where w is an arbitrary integer and all $t_l \in \mathbb{F}_b$. Note that $\mathbb{F}_b((x^{-1}))$ contains the field of rational functions over $\mathbb{F}_b$ as a subfield. Further, let $\mathbb{F}_b[x]$ be the set of all polynomials over $\mathbb{F}_b$. The *discrete exponential valuation* ν on $\mathbb{F}_b((x^{-1}))$ is defined by $\nu(L) = -w$ if $L \neq 0$ and w is the least index with $t_w \neq 0$. For $L = 0$, we set $\nu(0) = -\infty$. Observe that we have $\nu(p) = \deg(p)$ for all non-zero polynomials $p \in \mathbb{F}_b[x]$.

8.1.1 Classical Niederreiter sequence

We introduce the classical construction of (t, s)-sequences due to Niederreiter [173]. We follow reference [177, Section 4.5] in our presentation, which is a slight simplification of the original construction.

Let $s \in \mathbb{N}$, b be a prime power and let $p_1, \ldots, p_s \in \mathbb{F}_b[x]$ be distinct monic irreducible polynomials over $\mathbb{F}_b$. Let $e_i = \deg(p_i)$ for $1 \leq i \leq s$. For integers $1 \leq i \leq s$, $j \geq 1$ and $0 \leq k < e_i$, consider the expansions

$$\frac{x^k}{p_i(x)^j} = \sum_{r=0}^{\infty} a^{(i)}(j, k, r) x^{-r-1} \tag{8.1}$$

over the field of formal Laurent series $\mathbb{F}_b((x^{-1}))$. Then, we define the matrix $C_i = (c_{j,r}^{(i)})_{j \geq 1, r \geq 0}$ by

$$c_{j,r}^{(i)} = a^{(i)}(Q+1, k, r) \in \mathbb{F}_b \quad \text{for } 1 \leq i \leq s,\ j \geq 1,\ r \geq 0, \tag{8.2}$$

where $j - 1 = Qe_i + k$ with integers $Q = Q(i, j)$ and $k = k(i, j)$ satisfying $0 \leq k < e_i$.

Definition 8.1 A digital sequence over $\mathbb{F}_b$ generated by the $\mathbb{N} \times \mathbb{N}$ matrices $C_i = (c_{j,r}^{(i)})_{j \geq 1, r \geq 0}$ for $1 \leq i \leq s$ where the $c_{j,r}^{(i)}$ are given by (8.2) is called a *Niederreiter sequence*.

Theorem 8.2 *The Niederreiter sequence with generating matrices defined as above is a digital (t, s)-sequence over $\mathbb{F}_b$ with*

$$t = \sum_{i=1}^{s} (e_i - 1).$$

Proof According to Theorem 4.84, we need to show that for all integers $m > \sum_{i=1}^{s}(e_i - 1)$ and all $d_1, \ldots, d_s \in \mathbb{N}_0$ with $1 \le \sum_{i=1}^{s} d_i \le m - \sum_{i=1}^{s}(e_i - 1)$, the vectors

$$\pi_m(\mathbf{c}_j^{(i)}) = (c_{j,0}^{(i)}, \ldots, c_{j,m-1}^{(i)}) \in \mathbb{F}_b^m \quad \text{for } 1 \le j \le d_i, 1 \le i \le s,$$

are linearly independent over $\mathbb{F}_b$. Suppose to the contrary that we have

$$\sum_{i=1}^{s}\sum_{j=1}^{d_i} f_j^{(i)} \pi_m(\mathbf{c}_j^{(i)}) = \mathbf{0} \in \mathbb{F}_b^m$$

for some $f_j^{(i)} \in \mathbb{F}_b$, where, without loss of generality, we may assume that $d_i \ge 1$ for all $1 \le i \le s$. By comparing components, we obtain

$$\sum_{i=1}^{s}\sum_{j=1}^{d_i} f_j^{(i)} c_{j,r}^{(i)} = 0 \quad \text{for } 0 \le r \le m-1. \tag{8.3}$$

Consider the rational function

$$L = \sum_{i=1}^{s}\sum_{j=1}^{d_i} f_j^{(i)} \frac{x^{k(i,j)}}{p_i(x)^{Q(i,j)+1}} = \sum_{r=0}^{\infty}\left(\sum_{i=1}^{s}\sum_{j=1}^{d_i} f_j^{(i)} c_{j,r}^{(i)}\right) x^{-r-1}.$$

From (8.3) we obtain that $\nu(L) < -m$, where $\nu(L)$ denotes the discrete exponential evaluation.

If we put $Q_i = \lfloor (d_i - 1)/e_i \rfloor$ for $1 \le i \le s$, then a common denominator of L is $g(x) = \prod_{i=1}^{s} p_i(x)^{Q_i+1}$, which implies that Lg is a polynomial. On the other hand, we have

$$\nu(Lg) < -m + \deg(g) = -m + \sum_{i=1}^{s}(Q_i + 1)e_i \le -m + \sum_{i=1}^{s}(d_i - 1 + e_i) \le 0.$$

Thus, $Lg = 0$, hence $L = 0$, and therefore,

$$\sum_{i=1}^{s}\sum_{j=1}^{d_i} f_j^{(i)} \frac{x^{k(i,j)}}{p_i(x)^{Q(i,j)+1}} = 0.$$

The left-hand side is a partial fraction decomposition of a rational function and hence, it follows from the uniqueness of the partial fraction decomposition that all $f_j^{(i)} = 0$. □

The quality parameter $t = \sum_{i=1}^{s}(e_i - 1)$ is exact, i.e. the Niederreiter sequence is a strict $(\sum_{i=1}^{s}(e_i - 1), s)$-sequence over $\mathbb{F}_b$. This was shown in [47, Theorem 1].

Remark 8.3 For fixed s and b list all monic irreducible polynomials over $\mathbb{F}_b$ in a sequence according to non-decreasing degrees, and let $p_1, \ldots, p_s$ be the first s terms of this sequence. Then, it has been shown by Niederreiter [177, Theorem 4.54], for the strict quality parameter t of the corresponding Niederreiter sequence, we have

$$t \leq s(\log_b s + \log_b \log_b s + 1).$$

8.1.2 Generalised Niederreiter sequence

In this subsection we introduce a generalisation of Niederreiter's sequence owing to Tezuka [255, 256]. This sequence differs from the Niederreiter sequence introduced above, in replacing x^k in (8.1) with polynomials $y_{i,j,k}(x)$, where $1 \leq i \leq s$, $j \geq 1$, and $0 \leq k < e_i$. In order for Theorem 8.2 to apply to these sequences, for each $j \geq 1$ and $1 \leq i \leq s$ the set of polynomials $\{y_{i,j,k}(x) : 0 \leq k < e_i\}$ needs to be linearly independent $\pmod{p_i(x)}$ over $\mathbb{F}_b$. The generalised Niederreiter sequence is then defined by the expansion

$$\frac{y_{i,j,k}(x)}{p_i(x)^j} = \sum_{r=0}^{\infty} a^{(i)}(j,k,r)x^{-r-1}$$

over the field of formal Laurent series $\mathbb{F}_b((x^{-1}))$. Then we define the matrix $C_i = (c_{j,r}^{(i)})_{j \geq 1, r \geq 0}$ by

$$c_{j,r}^{(i)} = a^{(i)}(Q+1,k,r) \in \mathbb{F}_b \quad \text{for } 1 \leq i \leq s,\ j \geq 1,\ r \geq 0, \tag{8.4}$$

where $j - 1 = Qe_i + k$ with integers $Q = Q(i,j)$ and $k = k(i,j)$ satisfying $0 \leq k < e_i$.

Definition 8.4 A digital sequence over $\mathbb{F}_b$ generated by the matrices $C_i = (c_{j,r}^{(i)})_{j \geq 1, r \geq 0}$ for $1 \leq i \leq s$ where the $c_{j,r}^{(i)}$ are given by (8.4) is called a *generalised Niederreiter sequence*.

The proof of Theorem 8.2 still applies, hence a generalised Niederreiter sequence is a digital (t,s)-sequence over $\mathbb{F}_b$ with $t = \sum_{i=1}^{s}(e_i - 1)$.

8.1.3 Sobol′ sequence

Sobol′ [253] was the first to introduce a construction of (t,s)-sequences. This sequence, nowadays referred to as a *Sobol′ sequence*, is the generalised Niederreiter sequence where $b = 2$, $p_1(x) = x$, and $p_i(x)$, $2 \leq i \leq s$, is the $(i-1)$th primitive polynomial in a list of primitive polynomials that is sorted in increasing order according to their degree. Further, there are polynomials $g_{i,0}, \ldots, g_{i,e_i-1}$ with $\deg(g_{i,h}) = e_i - h + 1$ such that $y_{i,j,k} = g_{i,k}$ for all $j \geq 1$, $0 \leq k < e_i$, and $1 \leq i \leq s$.

A Sobol′ sequence can also be generated in the following way: let $p_1, \ldots, p_s \in \mathbb{F}_2[x]$ be primitive polynomials ordered according to their degree and let

$$p_i(x) = x^{e_i} + a_{1,i}x^{e_i-1} + a_{2,i}x^{e_i-2} + \cdots + a_{e_i-1}x + 1 \quad \text{for } 1 \le i \le s.$$

Choose odd natural numbers $1 \le m_{1,i}, \ldots, m_{e_i,i}$ such that $m_{k,i} < 2^k$ for $1 \le k \le e_i$, and for all $k > e_i$, define $m_{k,i}$ recursively by

$$m_{k,i} = 2a_{1,i}m_{k-1,i} \oplus \cdots \oplus 2^{e_i-1}a_{e_i-1}m_{k-e_i+1,i} \oplus 2^{e_i}m_{k-e_i,i} \oplus m_{k-e_i,i},$$

where $\oplus$ is the bit-by-bit exclusive-or operator. The numbers

$$v_{k,i} := \frac{m_{k,i}}{2^k}$$

are called *direction numbers*. Then, for $n \in \mathbb{N}_0$ with base 2 expansion $n = n_0 + 2n_1 + \cdots + 2^{r-1}n_{r-1}$, we define

$$x_{n,i} = n_0 v_{1,i} \oplus n_1 v_{2,i} \oplus \cdots \oplus n_{r-1} v_{r,i}.$$

The Sobol′ sequence is then the sequence of points $\boldsymbol{x}_0, \boldsymbol{x}_1, \ldots,$ where $\boldsymbol{x}_n = (x_{n,1}, \ldots, x_{n,s})$.

For an efficient implementation of Sobol′ sequences, see [3, 18] and for questions concerning the choice of polynomials $g_{i,0}, \ldots, g_{i,e_i-1}$ see, for example, [117].

8.1.4 Faure sequence

Faure [68] introduced a construction of $(0, s)$-sequences over prime fields $\mathbb{F}_b$ with $s \le b$. These sequences, nowadays referred to as *Faure sequences*, correspond to the case where the base b is a prime number such that $b \ge s$, $p_i(x) = x - i + 1$ for $1 \le i \le s$ and all $y_{i,j,k}(x) = 1$.

The generating matrices of Faure sequences can also be written down explicitly in terms of the *Pascal matrix*. The Pascal matrix is given by

$$P = \begin{pmatrix} \binom{0}{0} & \binom{0}{1} & \binom{0}{2} & \cdots \\ \binom{1}{0} & \binom{1}{1} & \binom{1}{2} & \cdots \\ \binom{2}{0} & \binom{2}{1} & \binom{2}{2} & \cdots \\ \vdots & \vdots & \vdots & \ddots \end{pmatrix},$$

where we set $\binom{k}{l} = 0$ for $l > k$.

The generating matrices $C_1, \ldots, C_s$ of the Faure sequence are now given by

$$C_i = (P^\top)^{i-1} \pmod{b} \quad \text{for } 1 \le i \le s.$$

For example, the case $s = 2$ is explicitly represented in Example 4.78.

The implementation of Faure sequences has been discussed in [5] and [80].

8.1.5 Original Niederreiter sequence

The sequence originally introduced by Niederreiter [173] corresponds to the case where $y_{i,j,k}(x) = x^k g_{i,j,k}(x)$, where $\gcd(g_{i,j,k}, p_i) = 1$ for all $j \in \mathbb{N}$, $1 \le i \le s$ and $0 \le k < e_i$.

For questions concerning the implementation of Niederreiter sequences, see [19].

8.2 Niederreiter–Özbudak nets

In this section, we present the constructions of digital (t, m, s)-nets over $\mathbb{F}_b$ due to Niederreiter and Özbudak [186]; see also [197]. These constructions are based on duality theory, i.e. instead of a direct construction of generating matrices as in the constructions presented so far, here one constructs $\mathbb{F}_b$ linear subspaces $\mathcal{N}$ of $\mathbb{F}_b^{sm}$ which correspond to digital (t, m, s)-nets over $\mathbb{F}_b$ using the duality theory as outlined in Section 7.2.

8.2.1 Construction of $(0, m, s)$*-nets*

We begin with the simplest case of the construction by Niederreiter and Özbudak [186], i.e. we start with a construction of a digital $(0, m, s)$-net over $\mathbb{F}_b$ for $m \in \mathbb{N}$ and $2 \le s \le b$. As already mentioned, this construction is based on duality theory.

Let

$$\mathcal{L}_{m,s} = \{f \in \mathbb{F}_b[x] : \deg(f) \le ms - m - 1\}.$$

Note that $\dim(\mathcal{L}_{m,s}) = ms - m$. Now choose distinct elements $a_1, \ldots, a_s \in \mathbb{F}_b$ and set $p_i(x) = x - a_i$ for $1 \le i \le s$. Let

$$f(x) = c_0^{(i)} + c_1^{(i)}(x - a_i) + \cdots + c_{m-1}^{(i)}(x - a_i)^{m-1} + \cdots$$

be the expansion of $f \in \mathcal{L}_{m,s}$ in terms of powers of $x - a_i$. Then we define

$$\theta_{p_i,m}(f) = (c_{m-1}^{(i)}, \ldots, c_1^{(i)}, c_0^{(i)}) \in \mathbb{F}_b^m \quad \text{for } 1 \le i \le s$$

and

$$\theta_m(f) = (\theta_{p_1,m}(f), \ldots, \theta_{p_s,m}(f)) \in \mathbb{F}_b^{ms}.$$

Then $\theta_m : \mathcal{L}_{m,s} \to \mathbb{F}_b^{ms}$ is an $\mathbb{F}_b$-linear map.

Let v_m be the weight function from Definition 7.1. Then for any non-zero $f \in \mathcal{L}_{m,s}$, we have

$$v_m(\theta_{p_i,m}(f)) \ge m - \nu_{p_i}(f) \quad \text{for } 1 \le i \le s,$$

where ν_{p_i} is the valuation associated with the irreducible polynomial $p_i(x) = x - a_i$, i.e. $\nu_{p_i}(f)$ is the largest integer ℓ such that $p_i(x)^\ell$ divides $f(x)$. Thus, we get

$$V_m(\theta_m(f)) = \sum_{i=1}^{s} v_m(\theta_{p_i,m}(f)) \geq ms - \sum_{i=1}^{s} \nu_{p_i}(f). \tag{8.5}$$

By definition of ν_{p_i} we have $p_i(x)^{\nu_i(f)}$ dividing $f(x)$ for $1 \leq i \leq s$, and hence, $\prod_{i=1}^{s} p_i(x)^{\nu_{p_i}(f)}$ dividing $f(x)$. This implies that

$$\sum_{i=1}^{s} \nu_{p_i}(f) \leq \deg(f).$$

Therefore, (8.5) implies that

$$V_m(\theta_m(f)) \geq ms - \deg(f) \geq m + 1. \tag{8.6}$$

Let $\mathcal{N}_m$ be the image of the map θ_m. From (8.6) and the fact that θ_m is $\mathbb{F}_b$-linear, it follows in particular that θ_m is injective as, otherwise, there would be non-zero $f_1, f_2 \in \mathcal{L}_{m,s}$, $f_1 \neq f_2$, such that $\theta_m(f_1) = \theta_m(f_2)$, but then

$$0 = V_m(\theta_m(f_1) - \theta_m(f_2)) = V_m(\theta_m(f_1 - f_2)) \geq ms - \deg(f_1 - f_2) \geq m + 1,$$

which is a contradiction. Hence, we get

$$\dim(\mathcal{N}_m) = \dim(\mathcal{L}_{m,s}) = ms - m.$$

Furthermore, $\delta_m(\mathcal{N}_m) \geq m + 1$ by (8.6), thus $\delta_m(\mathcal{N}_m) = m + 1$ by Proposition 7.3 and $t = m + 1 - \delta_m(\mathcal{N}_m) = 0$, by duality theory (see Corollary 7.12). Hence, $\mathcal{N}_m$ is the dual space of a digital $(0, m, s)$-net over $\mathbb{F}_b$.

8.2.2 *Construction of* $(0, m, s + 1)$*-nets*

One way of obtaining $(0, m, s + 1)$-nets is by including the place at ∞. This can be done in the following way.

Let $p_\infty(x) = 1/x$ and $f \in \mathcal{L}_{m,s+1}$. For $1 \leq i \leq s$, we define $\theta_{p_i,m}(f)$ as above. Now let $f(x) = c_0^{(s+1)} + c_1^{(s+1)} x + \cdots + c_{ms-1}^{(s+1)} x^{ms-1}$ and let ν_{p_∞} be the valuation at ∞, i.e. the valuation associated with $p_\infty(x) = 1/x$. In other words, $\nu_{p_\infty}(f)$ is the largest integer ℓ such that $p_\infty(x)^\ell$ divides $f(x)$. As

$$f(x) = c_{ms-1}^{(s+1)}(1/x)^{-ms+1} + c_{ms-2}^{(s+1)}(1/x)^{-ms+2} + \cdots + c_1^{(s+1)}(1/x)^{-1} + c_0^{(s+1)}$$

the largest integer ℓ such that $p_\infty(x)^\ell$ divides f is $-\deg(f)$, and hence, $\nu_{p_\infty}(f) = -\deg(f)$.

Now we define

$$\theta_{p_\infty,m}(f) = (c_{ms-m}^{(s+1)}, \ldots, c_{ms-2}^{(s+1)}, c_{ms-1}^{(s+1)}) \in \mathbb{F}_b^m.$$

Then we have

$$v_m(\theta_{p_\infty,m}(f)) \geq \deg(f) - (ms - m - 1) = -\nu_{p_\infty}(f) - (ms - m - 1).$$

Let $\theta_m(f) = (\theta_{p_1,m}(f), \ldots, \theta_{p_s,m}(f), \theta_{p_\infty,m}(f)) \in \mathbb{F}_b^{m(s+1)}$. Then we have

$$\begin{aligned} V_m(\theta_m(f)) &= \sum_{i=1}^{s+1} v_m(\theta_{p_i,m}(f)) \\ &\geq ms - \sum_{i=1}^{s} \nu_{p_i}(f) - ms + m + 1 - \nu_{p_\infty}(f) \\ &\geq m + 1, \end{aligned}$$

where the last inequality follows as $\nu_{p_\infty}(f) = -\deg(f)$ and as $\prod_{i=1}^s p_i(x)^{\nu_{p_i}(f)}$ divides $f(x)$, we have $\deg(f) \geq \sum_{i=1}^s \nu_{p_i}(f)$. But the last equality just states that $0 \geq -\deg(f) + \sum_{i=1}^s \nu_{p_i}(f) = \nu_{p_\infty}(f) + \sum_{i=1}^s \nu_{p_i}(f)$. This also follows from Remark B.13 in Appendix B, namely, we have

$$0 = \nu_{p_\infty}(f) + \sum_{p} \nu_p(f) \deg(p(x)) \geq \nu_{p_\infty}(f) + \sum_{i=1}^{s} \nu_{p_i}(f),$$

where the sum over all p is extended over all monic irreducible $p(x) \in \mathbb{F}_b[x]$.

Let $\mathcal{N}_m$ be the image of the map θ_m. This map is again injective, hence

$$\dim(\mathcal{N}_m) = \dim(\mathcal{L}_{m,s+1}) = ms,$$

and $\delta_m(\mathcal{N}_m) \geq m + 1$. Thus, as above by duality theory, $\mathcal{N}_m$ is the dual space of a digital $(0, m, s+1)$-net over $\mathbb{F}_b$.

8.2.3 Construction of (t, m, s)-nets

We now consider a special case of Niederreiter and Özbudak's construction, which is more general than the cases considered above in that we also include those where $s > b + 1$ (and hence, $t > 0$).

Let $s \in \mathbb{N}$ and for $1 \leq i \leq s$, choose $p_i \in \mathbb{F}_b[x] \cup \{1/x\}$, where p_i is irreducible if $p_i(x) \in \mathbb{F}_b[x]$ or $p_i(x) = 1/x$. Let $e_i = \deg(p_i)$ for $p_i(x) \in \mathbb{F}_b[x]$ and $e_i = 1$ if $p_i(x) = 1/x$. Let $m > \sum_{i=1}^s (e_i - 1)$ and $f \in \mathcal{L}_{m,s}$. If $e_i = 1$, then we have already defined $\theta_{p_i,m}(f)$ above. Now consider $1 \leq i \leq s$ with $e_i > 1$. Let $m_i = \lfloor m/e_i \rfloor$ and

$$f(x) = c_0^{(i)}(x) + c_1^{(i)}(x) p_i(x) + \cdots + c_{m_i-1}^{(i)}(x) p_i(x)^{m_i-1} + \cdots$$

where $c_k^{(i)}(x) \in \mathbb{F}_b[x]$ with $\deg(c_k^{(i)}) < e_i$ for all $k \in \mathbb{N}_0$ and $1 \le i \le s$. We can write $c_k^{(i)}(x) = c_{k,0}^{(i)} + \cdots + c_{k,e_i-1}^{(i)} x^{e_i-1}$ with $c_{k,\ell}^{(i)} \in \mathbb{F}_b$ and set

$$\vartheta^{(i)}(c_k^{(i)}) = (c_{k,e_i-1}^{(i)}, \ldots, c_{k,0}^{(i)}) \in \mathbb{F}_b^{e_i}.$$

Now let

$$\theta_{p_i,m}(f) = (0, \ldots, 0, \vartheta^{(i)}(c_{m_i-1}^{(i)}), \ldots, \vartheta^{(i)}(c_0^{(i)})) \in \mathbb{F}_b^m,$$

where we include $r_i = m - e_i m_i$ zeros at the beginning of the vector. Note that $0 \le r_i < e_i$. Hence the case where $e_i = 1$ is included in the above, since then, $\deg(c_k^{(i)}) = 0$ and $r_i = 0$.

Now set

$$\theta_m(f) = (\theta_{p_1,m}(f), \ldots, \theta_{p_s,m}(f)) \in \mathbb{F}_b^{ms}.$$

For any non-zero $f \in \mathcal{L}_{m,s}$, we have

$$v_m(\theta_{p_i,m}(f)) \ge m - e_i \nu_{p_i}(f) - (e_i - 1) \quad \text{for } 1 \le i \le s \text{ with } p_i \text{ irreducible,}$$

and

$$v_m(\theta_{p_\infty,m}(f)) \ge \deg(f) - (m(s-1) - m - 1) = -\nu_{p_\infty}(f) - (m(s-1) - m - 1).$$

If all $p_1, \ldots, p_s$ are irreducible, then $p_i(x)^{\nu_{p_i}(f)}$ divides $f(x)$ and hence, $\prod_{i=1}^s p_i(x)^{\nu_{p_i}(f)}$ divides $f(x)$. Therefore,

$$\sum_{i=1}^s e_i \nu_{p_i}(f) \le \deg(f),$$

and hence,

$$\begin{aligned} V_m(\theta_m(f)) &= \sum_{i=1}^s v_m(\theta_{p_i,m}(f)) \\ &\ge ms - \sum_{i=1}^s e_i \nu_{p_i}(f) - \sum_{i=1}^s (e_i - 1) \\ &\ge ms - \deg(f) - \sum_{i=1}^s (e_i - 1) \\ &\ge m + 1 - \sum_{i=1}^s (e_i - 1). \end{aligned}$$

Otherwise, assume without loss of generality that $p_1(x) = p_\infty(x) = 1/x$. Then $\sum_{i=2}^{s} e_i \nu_{p_i}(f) \le \deg(f) = -\nu_{p_\infty}(f) = -\nu_{p_1}(f)$, hence $\sum_{i=1}^{s} e_i \nu_{p_i}(f) \le 0$ and

$$\begin{aligned} V_m(\theta_m(f)) &= \sum_{i=1}^{s} v_m(\theta_{p_i,m}(f)) \\ &\ge -\nu_{p_1}(f) - (m(s-1) - m - 1) \\ &\quad + m(s-1) - \sum_{i=2}^{s} e_i \nu_{p_i}(f) - \sum_{i=2}^{s}(e_i - 1) \\ &\ge m + 1 - \sum_{i=1}^{s}(e_i - 1). \end{aligned}$$

Thus, in both cases we have $V_m(\theta_m(f)) \ge m + 1 - \sum_{i=1}^{s}(e_i - 1)$.

Let $\mathcal{N}_m$ be the image of the map θ_m. This map is again injective, hence

$$\dim(\mathcal{N}_m) = \dim(\mathcal{L}_{m,s}) = ms - m,$$

and $\delta_m(\mathcal{N}_m) \ge m + 1 - \sum_{i=1}^{s}(e_i - 1)$. Thus, by duality theory, $\mathcal{N}_m$ is the dual space of a digital (t, m, s)-net over $\mathbb{F}_b$ with $t = \sum_{i=1}^{s}(e_i - 1)$.

8.2.4 General construction of Niederreiter and Özbudak

For the following constructions, we need results from the theory of algebraic function fields. A short introduction to the necessary material can be found in Appendix B.

We can now introduce the above construction over arbitrary algebraic function fields with a finite constant field. Let $F/\mathbb{F}_b$ be an algebraic function field with a full constant field $\mathbb{F}_b$ and genus $g = g(F/\mathbb{F}_b)$. Note that the case $g = 0$ corresponds to the construction introduced above (compare with Example B.32).

Choose $s \in \mathbb{N}$ distinct places $P_1, \ldots, P_s$ of F with degrees $e_1, \ldots, e_s$. For $1 \le i \le s$ let ν_{P_i} be the normalised discrete valuation of F corresponding to P_i and let t_i be a local parameter at P_i. Further, for each $1 \le i \le s$, let F_{P_i} be the residue class field of P_i, i.e. $F_{P_i} = O_{P_i}/M_{P_i}$, and let $\vartheta_i : F_{P_i} \to \mathbb{F}_b^{e_i}$ be an $\mathbb{F}_b$-linear vector space isomorphism. Let $m > g + \sum_{i=1}^{s}(e_i - 1)$, choose an arbitrary divisor G of $F/\mathbb{F}_b$ with $\deg(G) = ms - m + g - 1$ and define $a_i := \nu_{P_i}(G)$ for $1 \le i \le s$.

For each $1 \le i \le s$, we define an $\mathbb{F}_b$-linear map

$$\theta_i : \mathcal{L}(G) \to \mathbb{F}_b^m$$

on the Riemann–Roch space

$$\mathcal{L}(G) = \{f \in F^* : \operatorname{div}(f) + G \ge 0\} \cup \{0\},$$

where div(f) denotes the principal divisor of $f \in F^*$. We fix i and repeat the following definitions related to θ_i for each $1 \le i \le s$.

Note that for each $f \in \mathcal{L}(G)$ we have $\nu_{P_i}(f) \ge -a_i$, and so the local expansion of f at P_i has the form

$$f = \sum_{j=-a_i}^{\infty} c_j^{(i)} t_i^j,$$

where all $c_j^{(i)} \in F_{P_i}$. We denote $c_j^{(i)}$ by $f^{(j)}(P_i)$. Hence, we have

$$\nu_{P_i}\left(f - \sum_{j=-a_i}^{w} f^{(j)}(P_i) t_i^j\right) \ge w + 1$$

for any integer $w \ge -a_i$. Again let $m_i = \lfloor m/e_i \rfloor$ and $r_i = m - e_i m_i$. Note that $0 \le r_i < e_i$. For $f \in \mathcal{L}(G)$, the image of f under θ_i, for $1 \le i \le s$, is defined as

$$\theta_i(f) := (0, \ldots, 0, \vartheta_i(f^{(-a_i+m_i-1)}(P_i)), \ldots, \vartheta_i(f^{(-a_i)}(P_i))) \in \mathbb{F}_b^m,$$

where we add the r_i-dimensional zero vector $(0, \ldots, 0) \in \mathbb{F}_b^{r_i}$ in the beginning.

Now we set

$$\theta(f) := (\theta_1(f), \ldots, \theta_s(f)) \in \mathbb{F}_b^{ms}$$

and define the $\mathbb{F}_b$-linear map

$$\theta : \mathcal{L}(G) \to \mathbb{F}_b^{ms}, f \mapsto \theta(f).$$

The image of θ is denoted by $\mathcal{N}_m = \mathcal{N}_m(P_1, \ldots, P_s; G)$. In general, the vector space $\mathcal{N}_m = \mathcal{N}_m(P_1, \ldots, P_s; G)$ also depends on the choice of local parameters $t_1, \ldots, t_s$ and on the choice of the $\mathbb{F}_b$-linear isomorphisms $\vartheta_1, \ldots, \vartheta_s$, but we suppress this dependence in the notation for the sake of simplicity.

In the following theorem, we assume that $s \ge 2$ to avoid the trivial cases where $s = 1$.

Theorem 8.5 *Let $F/\mathbb{F}_b$ be an algebraic function field with full constant field $\mathbb{F}_b$ and genus $g = g(F/\mathbb{F}_b)$. Let $s \in \mathbb{N}$, $s \ge 2$ and let $P_1, \ldots, P_s$ be s distinct places of F with degrees $e_1, \ldots, e_s$, respectively. Let $m > g + \sum_{i=1}^{s}(e_i - 1)$ and let G be a divisor of $F/\mathbb{F}_b$ with* deg$(G) = ms - m + g - 1$. *Then*

$$\dim(\mathcal{N}_m) \ge ms - m$$

and

$$\delta_m(\mathcal{N}_m) \ge m + 1 - g - \sum_{i=1}^{s}(e_i - 1).$$

Proof First, note that according to the Riemann–Roch theorem, we have that $\dim(\mathcal{L}(G)) \geq \deg(G) + 1 - g = ms - m \geq 1$ and hence, $\mathcal{L}(G) \supseteq \mathbb{F}_b$.

Let $f \in \mathcal{L}(G) \setminus \{0\}$. Let $\ell_i = \nu_{P_i}(f)$. Then we have $\ell_i \geq -a_i$ for $1 \leq i \leq s$ and $f^{(j)}(P_i) = 0$ for $-a_i \leq j < \ell_i$, and hence, also, $\vartheta_i(f^{(j)}(P_i)) = \mathbf{0} \in \mathbb{F}_b^{e_i}$ for $-a_i \leq j < \ell_i$. On the other hand, we have $f^{(\ell_i)}(P_i) \neq 0$ and $\vartheta_i(f^{(\ell_i)}(P_i)) \neq \mathbf{0} \in \mathbb{F}_b^{e_i}$. Therefore, we have

$$v_m(\theta_i(f)) \geq m - (\ell_i + a_i)e_i - e_i + 1 \quad \text{for } 1 \leq i \leq s.$$

Thus,

$$V_m(\theta(f)) = \sum_{i=1}^{s} v_m(\theta_i(f)) \geq sm - \sum_{i=1}^{s}(\ell_i + a_i)e_i - \sum_{i=1}^{s}(e_i - 1).$$

For $f \in \mathcal{L}(G) \setminus \{0\}$, we have $\operatorname{div}(f) + G \geq 0$ and therefore, $\nu_P(f) + \nu_P(G) \geq 0$ for all places P of F. Further, we have $\deg(G) = \sum_P \nu_P(G) \deg(P)$ and $\deg(\operatorname{div}(f)) = 0$. Hence,

$$\begin{aligned}\sum_{i=1}^{s}(\ell_i + a_i)e_i &= \sum_{i=1}^{s}(\nu_{P_i}(f) + \nu_{P_i}(G)) \deg(P_i) \\ &\leq \sum_{P}(\nu_P(f) + \nu_P(G)) \deg(P) \\ &= \sum_{P} \nu_P(G) \deg(P) \\ &= \deg(G) = ms - m + g - 1.\end{aligned}$$

Thus, we obtain

$$V_m(\theta(f)) \geq sm - (ms - m + g - 1) - \sum_{i=1}^{s}(e_i - 1) = m + 1 - g - \sum_{i=1}^{s}(e_i - 1)$$

and therefore, $\delta_m(\mathcal{N}_m) \geq m + 1 - g - \sum_{i=1}^{s}(e_i - 1)$.

Next, we show that θ is injective. Let $f_1, f_2 \in \mathcal{L}(G)$ with $f_1 \neq f_2$ but $\theta(f_1) = \theta(f_2)$. Then

$$0 < m + 1 - g - \sum_{i=1}^{s}(e_i - 1) \leq V_m(\theta(f_1 - f_2)) = V_m(\theta(f_1) - \theta(f_2)) = V_m(\mathbf{0}),$$

which is absurd and therefore θ is injective.

Hence,

$$\dim(\mathcal{N}_m) = \dim(\mathcal{L}(G)) \geq \deg(G) + 1 - g = ms - m,$$

which implies the first part and the result is shown. □

By duality theory, the space $\mathcal{N}_m$ is the dual space of a digital (t, m, s)-net with $t = g + \sum_{i=1}^{s}(e_i - 1)$.

Corollary 8.6 *Under the assumptions of Theorem 8.5, there exists a digital (t, m, s)-net over $\mathbb{F}_b$ with*

$$t = g + \sum_{i=1}^{s}(e_i - 1).$$

Remark 8.7 The case introduced at the beginning of this section corresponds to choosing F as the rational function field, which implies that $g = 0$ (see Example B.32), and the divisor G being chosen as $G = (ms - m + 1)P_\infty$ such that $\nu_{P_\infty}(G) = ms - m - 1$ and $\nu_P(G) = 0$ for all other places. Note that in the general result P_i may be chosen as the place at ∞ for some $1 \le i \le s$.

8.3 Niederreiter–Xing sequence

As an example of the use of duality theory for digital sequences, we show how to approach the construction of digital sequences by Niederreiter and Xing [192] via this duality theory. We note that the construction in [192] yields most of the currently best digital (t, s)-sequences with respect to the quality parameter t; see [239]. Beside the duality theory for digital sequences, we again need results from the theory of algebraic function fields which is utilised in [192]. For the necessary material, we refer to Appendix B.

Let b be an arbitrary prime power and let $s \ge 2$ be a given dimension. Let $F/\mathbb{F}_b$ be an algebraic function field with full constant field $\mathbb{F}_b$ such that F has at least $s + 1$ different rational places which are denoted by $Q, P_1, \ldots, P_s$.

We recall that for an arbitrary divisor G of $F/\mathbb{F}_b$, the Riemann–Roch space $\mathcal{L}(G)$ is defined by

$$\mathcal{L}(G) = \{f \in F^* : \operatorname{div}(f) + G \ge 0\} \cup \{0\},$$

where $\operatorname{div}(f)$ denotes the principal divisor associated with $f \in F^*$. Note that $\mathcal{L}(G)$ is a finite-dimensional vector space over $\mathbb{F}_b$ and that by the supplement to the Riemann–Roch theorem (Theorem B.31), we have

$$\dim(\mathcal{L}(G)) = \deg(G) + 1 - g \tag{8.7}$$

whenever $\deg(G) \ge 2g - 1$, where $g = g(F/\mathbb{F}_b)$ is the genus of $F/\mathbb{F}_b$. Furthermore, $\mathcal{L}(G) = \{0\}$ whenever $\deg(G) < 0$ by Remark B.29.

For any $m \in \mathbb{N}$, we define the divisor

$$G_m = (g - 1 - m)Q + \sum_{i=1}^{s} m P_i$$

of F. For any $f \in \mathcal{L}(G_m)$, we then have $\nu_{P_i}(f) \geq -m$ for $1 \leq i \leq s$, where ν_{P_i} is the normalised valuation of F belonging to the place P_i. Therefore, the local expansion of f at P_i has the form

$$f = \sum_{j=-m}^{\infty} f_i^{(j)} t_i^j \qquad \text{for } 1 \leq i \leq s,$$

with t_i being a local parameter of F at P_i and $f_i^{(j)} \in \mathbb{F}_b$ for $1 \leq i \leq s$ and $j \geq -m$ (note that P_i is a rational place and hence, $\deg(P_i) = 1$). For $1 \leq i \leq s$, we define the $\mathbb{F}_b$-linear map $\psi_{m,i} : \mathcal{L}(G_m) \to \mathbb{F}_b^m$ by

$$\psi_{m,i}(f) = (f_i^{(-1)}, f_i^{(-2)}, \ldots, f_i^{(-m)}) \qquad \text{for } f \in \mathcal{L}(G_m).$$

Furthermore, let $\Psi_m : \mathcal{L}(G_m) \to \mathbb{F}_b^{sm}$ be the $\mathbb{F}_b$-linear map defined by

$$\Psi_m(f) = (\psi_{m,1}(f), \ldots, \psi_{m,s}(f)) \qquad \text{for } f \in \mathcal{L}(G_m).$$

The following simple result is crucial.

Lemma 8.8 *Let $g = g(F/\mathbb{F}_b)$ be the genus of $F/\mathbb{F}_b$. Then for any $m \geq \max(g, 1)$, the $\mathbb{F}_b$-linear map Ψ_m is injective.*

Proof Let $f \in \mathcal{L}(G_m)$ with $\Psi_m(f) = \mathbf{0} \in \mathbb{F}_b^{sm}$. Then, $\nu_{P_i}(f) \geq 0$ for $1 \leq i \leq s$ and hence, $f \in \mathcal{L}((g-1-m)Q)$. Note that

$$\deg((g-1-m)Q) = g-1-m < 0.$$

From Remark B.29, we obtain that $\mathcal{L}((g-1-m)Q) = \{0\}$. Hence, $f = 0$ and Ψ_m is injective. □

Next, we define subspaces $\mathcal{M}_m$ of $\mathbb{F}_b^{sm}$ which form a dual space chain (see Definition 7.24). In view of Remark 7.31, it suffices to define $\mathcal{M}_m$ for $m \geq g+1$. We put

$$\mathcal{M}_m = \Psi_m(\mathcal{L}(G_m)) \qquad \text{for } m \geq g+1.$$

Again, by Remark 7.31, we need to check the conditions for a dual space chain only for $m \geq g+1$.

For $m \geq g+1$, the definition of G_m shows that

$$\deg(G_m) = g-1-m+sm \geq g-1+m \geq 2g,$$

(note that $Q, P_1, \ldots, P_s$ are rational places) and so (8.7) yields $\dim(\mathcal{L}(G_m)) = (s-1)m$. Therefore, by Lemma 8.8 we have $\dim(\mathcal{M}_m) = \dim(\mathcal{L}(G_m)) = (s-1)m$ and hence, the condition $\dim(\mathcal{M}_m) \geq (s-1)m$ in Definition 7.24 is satisfied.

We put

$$\overline{\mathcal{M}}_{m+1,m} := \{\mathbf{A} \in \mathcal{M}_{m+1} : U_{m+1}(\mathbf{A}) \le m\} \qquad \text{for } m \ge g+1.$$

A typical element of $\mathcal{M}_{m+1} = \Psi_{m+1}(\mathcal{L}(G_{m+1}))$ is

$$\mathbf{A} = (\psi_{m+1,1}(f), \ldots, \psi_{m+1,s}(f)) \qquad \text{with } f \in \mathcal{L}(G_{m+1}).$$

The condition $U_{m+1}(\mathbf{A}) \le m$ means that the last coordinate of each vector $\psi_{m+1,i}(f) \in \mathbb{F}_b^{m+1}$, $1 \le i \le s$, is 0. Therefore, $f_i^{(-m-1)} = 0$ for $1 \le i \le s$, that is, $\nu_{P_i}(f) \ge -m$ for $1 \le i \le s$, and so

$$f \in \mathcal{L}\Big((g-2-m)Q + \sum_{i=1}^{s} m P_i\Big).$$

In this way we obtain

$$\overline{\mathcal{M}}_{m+1,m} = \Psi_{m+1}\Big(\mathcal{L}\Big((g-2-m)Q + \sum_{i=1}^{s} m P_i\Big)\Big).$$

Now we consider the set $\mathcal{M}_{m+1,m}$ in Definition 7.24. By what we have shown above, the elements of $\overline{\mathcal{M}}_{m+1,m}$ are of the form $\Psi_{m+1}(f)$ with $f \in \mathcal{L}((g-2-m)Q + \sum_{i=1}^{s} m P_i)$. By performing the projection indicated in Definition 7.24, we see that $\Psi_{m+1}(f)$ is projected to $\Psi_m(f)$. Therefore,

$$\mathcal{M}_{m+1,m} = \Psi_m\Big(\mathcal{L}\Big((g-2-m)Q + \sum_{i=1}^{s} m P_i\Big)\Big). \tag{8.8}$$

Since $\mathcal{L}((g-2-m)Q + \sum_{i=1}^{s} m P_i) \subseteq \mathcal{L}(G_m)$, it follows that $\mathcal{M}_{m+1,m}$ is an $\mathbb{F}_b$-linear subspace of $\mathcal{M}_m$. For $m \ge g+1$, we have

$$\deg\Big((g-2-m)Q + \sum_{i=1}^{s} m P_i\Big) = g-2-m+sm \ge g-2+m \ge 2g-1,$$

and so (8.7) yields $\dim(\mathcal{L}((g-2-m)Q + \sum_{i=1}^{s} m P_i)) = (s-1)m - 1$. By Lemma 8.8 and (8.8), we obtain

$$\dim(\mathcal{M}_{m+1,m}) = (s-1)m - 1 = \dim(\mathcal{M}_m) - 1.$$

We have thus demonstrated that for $m \ge g+1$ the sequence $(\mathcal{M}_m)$ of spaces satisfies all conditions in Definition 7.24, and indeed in the stronger form given in Definition 7.30. Thus, in view of Theorem 7.26 and Remark 7.31, the sequence $(\mathcal{M}_m)$ of spaces determines a digital sequence. The following result shows that this digital sequence is a digital (t,s)-sequence over $\mathbb{F}_b$ with the same quality parameter t as in Niederreiter and Xing's construction [192].

Theorem 8.9 *Let $s \in \mathbb{N}$, $s \geq 2$ and let b be a prime power. Let $F/\mathbb{F}_b$ be an algebraic function field with full constant field $\mathbb{F}_b$, genus $g = g(F/\mathbb{F}_b)$ and at least $s+1$ rational places. Then the construction above yields a digital (t, s)-sequence over $\mathbb{F}_b$ with $t = g$.*

Proof We have to show that for the quality function $\mathbf{T}$ of this sequence, we have $\mathbf{T}(m) \leq g$ for all $m \geq g+1$. Since $\mathcal{M}_m$ is the dual of the mth row space of the digital sequence, it suffices to show by Corollary 7.23 that

$$\delta_m(\mathcal{M}_m) \geq m - g + 1 \qquad \text{for all } m \geq g+1. \tag{8.9}$$

Consider a non-zero element of $\mathcal{M}_m$, that is, an element $\Psi_m(f)$ with a non-zero $f \in \mathcal{L}(G_m)$. By the definition of Ψ_m, we have

$$V_m(\Psi_m(f)) = \sum_{i=1}^{s} v_m(\psi_{m,i}(f)).$$

We put $k_i = v_m(\psi_{m,i}(f))$ for $1 \leq i \leq s$ and recall that

$$\psi_{m,i}(f) = (f_i^{(-1)}, f_i^{(-2)}, \ldots, f_i^{(-m)}).$$

If $k_i = 0$, then $\psi_{m,i}(f) = \mathbf{0} \in \mathbb{F}_b^m$ and so $\nu_{P_i}(f) \geq 0$. Otherwise, $1 \leq k_i \leq m$ and $f_i^{(-k_i)} \neq 0$, $f_i^{(-k_i-1)} = \cdots = f_i^{(-m)} = 0$, hence $\nu_{P_i}(f) = -k_i$. In all cases we have $\nu_{P_i}(f) \geq -k_i$ for $1 \leq i \leq s$. Therefore,

$$f \in \mathcal{L}\Big((g-1-m)Q + \sum_{i=1}^{s} k_i P_i\Big).$$

Since $f \neq 0$, this implies that

$$\deg\Big((g-1-m)Q + \sum_{i=1}^{s} k_i P_i\Big) \geq 0,$$

which is equivalent to $\sum_{i=1}^{s} k_i \geq m - g + 1$. Therefore,

$$V_m(\Psi_m(f)) = \sum_{i=1}^{s} k_i \geq m - g + 1,$$

and so (8.9) is shown. □

8.4 Xing–Niederreiter sequence

In this section we present the construction of Xing and Niederreiter [267]. This sequence for the special case of rational places was implemented by

Pirsic [219] and generating matrices of this sequence can be downloaded from Pirsic's website at:

http://www.ricam.oeaw.ac.at/people/page/pirsic/niedxing/

Let $F/\mathbb{F}_b$ be an algebraic function field with full constant field $\mathbb{F}_b$ and genus $g = g(F/\mathbb{F}_b)$. Let

$$\mathcal{L}(G) = \{f \in F : \operatorname{div}(f) + G \geq 0\} \cup \{0\},$$

where $\operatorname{div}(f)$ denotes the principal divisor of f, and let $\ell(G)$ denote the dimension of $\mathcal{L}(G)$.

Let $s \in \mathbb{N}$ be a given dimension. Assume that $F/\mathbb{F}_b$ has at least one rational place P_∞ and let G be a positive divisor of $F/\mathbb{F}_b$ with $\deg(G) = 2g$ and $P_\infty \notin \operatorname{supp}(G)$. Let $P_1, \ldots, P_s$ be s distinct places of $F/\mathbb{F}_b$ with $P_i \neq P_\infty$ for $1 \leq i \leq s$. Put $e_i = \deg(P_i)$ for $1 \leq i \leq s$. Then we have $\ell(G) = g + 1$ by the supplement to the Riemann–Roch theorem (Theorem B.31).

We now choose a basis of $\mathcal{L}(G)$ in the following way. Note that $\ell(G - P_\infty) = g$ by the supplement to the Riemann–Roch theorem (Theorem B.31) and $\ell(G - (2g + 1)P_\infty) = 0$ as a consequence of Remark B.29. Since $\ell(G - kP_\infty)$ decreases at most by one as k increases by one, there exist integers $0 = n_0 < n_1 < \cdots < n_g \leq 2g$ such that

$$\ell(G - n_u P_\infty) = \ell(G - (n_u + 1)P_\infty) + 1 \quad \text{for } 0 \leq u \leq g,$$

and hence, $\mathcal{L}(G - n_u P_\infty) \setminus \mathcal{L}(G - (n_u + 1)P_\infty)$ is not empty for $0 \leq u \leq g$. Choose $w_u \in \mathcal{L}(G - n_u P_\infty) \setminus \mathcal{L}(G - (n_u + 1)P_\infty)$, then

$$\nu_{P_\infty}(w_u) = n_u \quad \text{for } 0 \leq u \leq g. \tag{8.10}$$

Let $a_0, \ldots, a_g \in \mathbb{F}_b$ such that we have $a_0 w_0 + \cdots + a_g w_g = 0$. Let $U \subseteq \{0, \ldots, g\}$ such that $a_u \neq 0$ for $u \in U$. If for $u, v \in U$, we have $\nu_{P_\infty}(a_u w_u) = \nu_{P_\infty}(a_v w_v)$, then we obtain $n_u - n_v = \nu_{P_\infty}(a_v a_u^{-1}) = 0$ since $a_v a_u^{-1} \in \mathbb{F}_b^*$ (see Remark B.22) and this is a contradiction. Hence, for $u, v \in U$, we have $\nu_{P_\infty}(a_u w_u) \neq \nu_{P_\infty}(a_v w_v)$ and therefore, we obtain

$$\begin{aligned}\nu_{P_\infty}(0) = \nu_{P_\infty}\left(\sum_{u \in U} a_u w_u\right) &= \min_{u \in U} \nu_{P_\infty}(a_u w_u)\\ &= \min_{u \in U}(\nu_{P_\infty}(a_u) + \nu_{P_\infty}(w_u)) = \min_{u \in U} n_u \leq 2g\end{aligned}$$

in contradiction to $\nu_{P_\infty}(0) = \infty$. Hence, $a_0 = \cdots = a_g = 0$ and therefore, the system $\{w_0, w_1, \ldots, w_g\} \subseteq \mathcal{L}(G)$ is linearly independent over $\mathbb{F}_b$. Since $\ell(G) = g + 1$, it follows that $\{w_0, w_1, \ldots, w_g\}$ is a basis of $\mathcal{L}(G)$ over $\mathbb{F}_b$.

For each $1 \le i \le s$, we consider the chain

$$\mathcal{L}(G) \subset \mathcal{L}(G + P_i) \subset \mathcal{L}(G + 2P_i) \subset \cdots$$

of vector spaces over $\mathbb{F}_b$. By starting from the basis $\{w_0, w_1, \ldots, w_g\}$ of $\mathcal{L}(G)$ and successively adding basis vectors at each step of the chain, we obtain for each $n \in \mathbb{N}$ a basis

$$\{w_0, w_1, \ldots, w_g, k_1^{(i)}, k_2^{(i)}, \ldots, k_{ne_i}^{(i)}\}$$

of $\mathcal{L}(G + nP_i)$. We note that we then have

$$k_j^{(i)} \in \mathcal{L}\left(G + \left(\left\lfloor \frac{j-1}{e_i} \right\rfloor + 1\right) P_i\right) \quad \text{for } 1 \le i \le s \text{ and } j \ge 1. \tag{8.11}$$

The following lemma was shown in [267, Lemma 2].

Lemma 8.10 *The system $\{w_0, w_1, \ldots, w_g\} \cup \{k_j^{(i)}\}_{1 \le i \le s, j \ge 1}$ of elements of F is linearly independent over $\mathbb{F}_b$.*

Proof Suppose that

$$\sum_{u=0}^{g} a_u w_u + \sum_{i=1}^{s} \sum_{j=1}^{N} b_j^{(i)} k_j^{(i)} = 0$$

for some $N \in \mathbb{N}$ and $a_u, b_j^{(i)} \in \mathbb{F}_b$. For a fixed $1 \le h \le s$, we write

$$k := \sum_{j=1}^{N} b_j^{(h)} k_j^{(h)} = -\sum_{u=0}^{g} a_u w_u - \sum_{\substack{i=1 \\ i \ne h}}^{s} \sum_{j=1}^{N} b_j^{(i)} k_j^{(i)}. \tag{8.12}$$

If $k \ne 0$, then by the construction of the $k_j^{(h)}$, we have $k \notin \mathcal{L}(G)$. By (8.11) we have $\nu_P(k) \ge -\nu_P(G)$ for any place $P \ne P_h$ and hence we obtain that

$$\nu_{P_h}(k) \le -\nu_{P_h}(G) - 1.$$

On the other hand, using (8.11) and (8.12), we have

$$\begin{aligned}
\nu_{P_h}(k) &= \nu_{P_h}\left(-\sum_{u=0}^{g} a_u w_u - \sum_{\substack{i=1 \\ i \ne h}}^{s} \sum_{j=1}^{N} b_j^{(i)} k_j^{(i)} \right) \\
&\ge \min\left(\nu_{P_h}\left(\sum_{u=0}^{g} a_u w_u \right), \min_{\substack{1 \le i \le s \\ i \ne h}} \nu_{P_h}\left(\sum_{j=1}^{N} b_j^{(i)} k_j^{(i)} \right) \right) \\
&\ge -\nu_{P_h}(G)
\end{aligned}$$

since $\sum_{u=0}^{g} a_u w_u \in \mathcal{L}(G)$ and since for $i \neq h$ and $z \in \mathcal{L}(G + nP_i)$ we have $\nu_{P_h}(z) \geq -\nu_{P_h}(G + nP_i) = -\nu_{P_h}(G)$.

Thus, we must have $k = 0$. It follows that $b_j^{(h)} = 0$ for $1 \leq j \leq N$ and, since h was arbitrary, we get $b_j^{(i)} = 0$ for $1 \leq i \leq s$ and $1 \leq j \leq N$, and so also $a_u = 0$ for $0 \leq u \leq g$. □

Let z be a local parameter at P_∞ and let the integers $0 = n_0 < n_1 < \cdots < n_g \leq 2g$ be as in (8.10). For $r \in \mathbb{N}_0$ we put

$$z_r = \begin{cases} z^r & \text{if } r \notin \{n_0, n_1, \ldots, n_g\}, \\ w_u & \text{if } r = n_u \text{ for some } u \in \{0, 1, \ldots, g\}. \end{cases}$$

Note that in this case $\nu_{P_\infty}(z_r) = r$ for all $r \in \mathbb{N}_0$. For $1 \leq i \leq s$ and $j \in \mathbb{N}$ we have $k_j^{(i)} \in \mathcal{L}(G + nP_i)$ for some $n \in \mathbb{N}$ and also $P_\infty \notin \operatorname{supp}(G + nP_i)$, hence $\nu_{P_\infty}(k_j^{(i)}) \geq 0$. Thus, we have the local expansions

$$k_j^{(i)} = \sum_{r=0}^{\infty} a_{j,r}^{(i)} z_r \quad \text{for } 1 \leq i \leq s \text{ and } j \in \mathbb{N}, \tag{8.13}$$

where all coefficients $a_{j,r}^{(i)} \in \mathbb{F}_b$. For $1 \leq i \leq s$ and $j \in \mathbb{N}$, we now define the sequences

$$\begin{aligned} \mathbf{c}_j^{(i)} &= (c_{j,0}^{(i)}, c_{j,1}^{(i)}, \ldots) := (a_{j,n}^{(i)})_{n \in \mathbb{N}_0 \setminus \{n_0, \ldots, n_g\}} \\ &= (\widehat{a_{j,n_0}^{(i)}}, a_{j,1}^{(i)}, \ldots, \widehat{a_{j,n_1}^{(i)}}, a_{j,n_1+1}^{(i)}, \ldots, \widehat{a_{j,n_g}^{(i)}}, a_{j,n_g+1}^{(i)}, \ldots) \in \mathbb{F}_b^{\mathbb{N}}, \end{aligned} \tag{8.14}$$

where the hat indicates that the corresponding term is deleted. We define the matrices $C_1, \ldots, C_s \in \mathbb{F}_b^{\mathbb{N} \times \mathbb{N}}$ by

$$C_i = \begin{pmatrix} \mathbf{c}_1^{(i)} \\ \mathbf{c}_2^{(i)} \\ \mathbf{c}_3^{(i)} \\ \vdots \end{pmatrix} \quad \text{for } 1 \leq i \leq s, \tag{8.15}$$

i.e. the vector $\mathbf{c}_j^{(i)}$ is the jth row vector of C_i for $1 \leq i \leq s$. The matrices $C_1, \ldots, C_s$ are now the generating matrices of the Xing–Niederreiter sequence as introduced in [267].

Regarding the quality parameter t of this sequence, we have the following result.

Theorem 8.11 *Let $s \in \mathbb{N}$ and let b be a prime power. Let $F/\mathbb{F}_b$ be an algebraic function field with full constant field $\mathbb{F}_b$ and genus $g = g(F/\mathbb{F}_b)$ which contains at least one rational place P_∞, and let G be a positive divisor of $F/\mathbb{F}_b$ with* $\deg(G) = 2g$ *and $P_\infty \notin$* $\operatorname{supp}(G)$. *Let $P_1, \ldots, P_s$ be s distinct places of $F/\mathbb{F}_b$ with*

$P_i \neq P_\infty$ for $1 \le i \le s$. Then the matrices $C_1, \ldots, C_s \in \mathbb{F}_b^{\mathbb{N}\times\mathbb{N}}$ given by (8.15) are generating matrices of a digital (t, s)-sequence over $\mathbb{F}_b$ with

$$t = g + \sum_{i=1}^{s}(e_i - 1),$$

where $e_i = \deg(P_i)$ for $1 \le i \le s$.

Proof According to Theorem 4.84, it suffices to show that for all $m > g + \sum_{i=1}^{s}(e_i - 1)$ and any $d_1, \ldots, d_s \in \mathbb{N}_0$ with $1 \le \sum_{i=1}^{s} d_i \le m - g - \sum_{i=1}^{s}(e_i - 1)$, the vectors

$$\pi_m(\mathbf{c}_j^{(i)}) = (c_{j,0}^{(i)}, c_{j,1}^{(i)}, \ldots, c_{j,m-1}^{(i)}) \in \mathbb{F}_b^m \quad \text{for } 1 \le j \le d_i, 1 \le i \le s,$$

are linearly independent over $\mathbb{F}_b$.

Suppose that we have

$$\sum_{i=1}^{s}\sum_{j=1}^{d_i} f_j^{(i)} \pi_m(\mathbf{c}_j^{(i)}) = \mathbf{0} \in \mathbb{F}_b^m \tag{8.16}$$

for some $f_j^{(i)} \in \mathbb{F}_b$, where without loss of generality we assume that $d_i \in \mathbb{N}$ for $1 \le i \le s$. Now consider the element $k \in F$ given by

$$k = \sum_{i=1}^{s}\sum_{j=1}^{d_i} f_j^{(i)} k_j^{(i)} - \sum_{i=1}^{s}\sum_{j=1}^{d_i} f_j^{(i)} \sum_{u=0}^{g} a_{j,n_u}^{(i)} w_u. \tag{8.17}$$

Put $R = \{n_0, n_1, \ldots, n_g\}$ and use (8.13) to obtain

$$k = \sum_{i=1}^{s}\sum_{j=1}^{d_i} f_j^{(i)} \left(\sum_{r=0}^{\infty} a_{j,r}^{(i)} z_r - \sum_{u=0}^{g} a_{j,n_u}^{(i)} z_{n_u} \right) = \sum_{\substack{r=0 \\ r \notin R}}^{\infty} \left(\sum_{i=1}^{s}\sum_{j=1}^{d_i} f_j^{(i)} a_{j,r}^{(i)} \right) z_r.$$

From (8.14) and (8.16), we obtain

$$\sum_{i=1}^{s}\sum_{j=1}^{d_i} f_j^{(i)} a_{j,r}^{(i)} = 0$$

for the first m non-negative integers r that are not in R. Assuming that $\sum_{u=1}^{g}(n_u - n_{u-1} - 1) \ge m$, we would have

$$n_g = g + \sum_{u=1}^{g}(n_u - n_{u-1} - 1) \ge g + m > 2g$$

since $m > g$ and this contradicts the fact that $n_g \le 2g$. Hence, we arrive at

$$\nu_{P_\infty}(k) \ge m + g + 1. \tag{8.18}$$

Furthermore, (8.11) and (8.17) yield

$$k \in \mathcal{L}\left(G + \sum_{i=1}^{s}\left(\left\lfloor \frac{d_i - 1}{e_i} \right\rfloor + 1\right) P_i\right). \tag{8.19}$$

Combining (8.18) and (8.19), we obtain that

$$k \in \mathcal{L}\left(G + \sum_{i=1}^{s}\left(\left\lfloor \frac{d_i - 1}{e_i} \right\rfloor + 1\right) P_i - (m + g + 1)P_\infty\right).$$

But

$$\begin{aligned}
&\deg\left(G + \sum_{i=1}^{s}\left(\left\lfloor \frac{d_i - 1}{e_i} \right\rfloor + 1\right) P_i - (m + g + 1)P_\infty\right) \\
&= 2g + \sum_{i=1}^{s}\left(\left\lfloor \frac{d_i - 1}{e_i} \right\rfloor + 1\right) e_i - (m + g + 1) \\
&\leq g - m - 1 + \sum_{i=1}^{s}(e_i - 1) + \sum_{i=1}^{s} d_i \\
&\leq -1.
\end{aligned}$$

Hence,

$$\mathcal{L}\left(G + \sum_{i=1}^{s}\left(\left\lfloor \frac{d_i - 1}{e_i} \right\rfloor + 1\right) P_i - (m + g + 1)P_\infty\right) = \{0\}$$

by Remark B.29 and therefore we have $k = 0$. From (8.17) and Lemma 8.10 we conclude that $f_j^{(i)} = 0$. □

Exercises

8.1 Consider the first 2^4 points of a Niederreiter sequence in base 2 and dimension 3. Find the smallest value of t such that these points form a digital (t, m, s)-net.

8.2 Show that the Sobol′ sequence defined via the recurrence relation is a special case of a generalised Niederreiter sequence as stated in the section on Sobol′ sequences.

8.3 Let $\mathcal{S}_{\mathfrak{u}}$ be the sequence consisting of the points of a Niederreiter sequence projected onto the components given by $\mathfrak{u}$, where $\emptyset \neq \mathfrak{u} \subseteq \mathcal{I}_s$. Show that this sequence is a digital $(t_{\mathfrak{u}}, |\mathfrak{u}|)$-sequence over $\mathbb{F}_b$ with $t_{\mathfrak{u}} = \sum_{i \in \mathfrak{u}}(e_i - 1)$ (with the notation from Section 8.1).

8.4 Show that the generating matrices of a Faure sequence defined via the polynomials can be written in terms of Pascal matrices as stated in the section on Faure sequences.

8.5 Find the generating matrices of a Niederrieter–Özbudak net where $b = 2, m = 2$ and $s = 3$.

8.6 Find the generating matrices of a Niederreiter–Özbudak net where $b = 2$, $m = 2$ and $s = 4$.

8.7 Consider the construction by Niederreiter–Xing for the case where the genus of the algebraic function field is zero. Prove the result for this case.

8.8 Consider the construction by Niederreiter–Xing for the case where the genus of the algebraic function field is zero. Find the generating matrices for the case where $b = 2$, $m = 2$ and $s = 3$.

8.9 Consider the construction by Xing–Niederreiter for the case where the genus of the algebraic function field is zero. Prove the result for this case.

8.10 Consider the construction by Xing–Niederreiter for the case where the genus of the algebraic function field is zero. Find the generating matrices for the case where $b = 3$, $m = 2$ and $s = 3$.

9

Propagation rules for digital nets

Propagation rules for digital (t, m, s)-nets are methods by which to obtain a new digital (t, m, s)-net from given ones. This leads to new digital nets with improved quality parameters. Indeed, many of the best digital nets are obtained by using some propagation rule, as can be seen from the MINT database:

http://mint.sbg.ac.at/

Some propagation rules already featured in previous chapters are repeated here for convenience.

Theorem 9.1 *Assume that there exists a digital (t, m, s)-net over $\mathbb{F}_b$. Then we have the following:*

Propagation Rule I *There exists a digital (t, u, s)-net over $\mathbb{F}_b$ for $t \leq u \leq m$.*
Propagation Rule II *There exists a digital (t, m, r)-net over $\mathbb{F}_b$ for $1 \leq r \leq s$.*
Propagation Rule III *There exists a $(t + u, m + u, s)$-net over $\mathbb{F}_b$ for all $u \in \mathbb{N}_0$.*

A further more sophisticated propagation rule than those given above is the direct product construction as presented in Example 7.15.

Theorem 9.2 (Propagation Rule IV) *Assume that we are given a digital (t_1, m_1, s_1)-net and a digital (t_2, m_2, s_2)-net both over $\mathbb{F}_b$. Then there exists a digital $(t, m_1 + m_2, s_1 + s_2)$-net over $\mathbb{F}_b$ with*

$$t = m_1 + m_2 - d = \max(m_1 + t_2, m_2 + t_1).$$

In the following, we present some further propagation rules for digital nets. Note that there are also several propagation rules for nets which are not necessarily digital (a propagation rule for nets does not necessarily imply a propagation rule for digital nets, since the procedure involved in the propagation rule for nets, when applied to digital nets, need not output a digital net, although it is, by definition, a net). A list of such rules is stated in [179, Section 3] and restated in

[184, Section 3]; see also [233]. Some propagation rules for nets also appeared in Section 4.2 (see Lemmas 4.14, 4.16 and 4.17, Theorem 4.24 and Corollaries 4.23 and 4.26). Propagation rules for nets (in a more general setting) are also the topic of [9] where most of the following results are generalised to not necessarily digital nets.

9.1 The $(u, u + v)$-construction

There is a construction stemming from coding theory called the $(u, u+v)$-construction which can also be applied to digital nets (see, e.g., Bierbrauer *et al.* [14]).

Let $\mathcal{P}_1$ be a digital (t_1, m_1, s_1)-net over $\mathbb{F}_b$, with generating matrices $C_{1,1}, \ldots, C_{s_1,1}$, and let $\mathcal{P}_2$ be a digital (t_2, m_2, s_2)-net over $\mathbb{F}_b$ with generating matrices $C_{1,2}, \ldots, C_{s_2,2}$. We assume that $s_1 \leq s_2$. From these two digital nets we form a new digital (t, m, s)-net over $\mathbb{F}_b$, where $m = m_1 + m_2$ and $s = s_1 + s_2$. Let $\mathcal{P}$ be the digital net generated by the $m \times m$ matrices $D_1, \ldots, D_s$ over $\mathbb{F}_b$, given by

$$D_j = \begin{pmatrix} C_{j,1} & -C_{j,2} \\ \mathbf{0}^{m_2 \times m_1} & \mathbf{0}^{m_1 \times m_2} \end{pmatrix}, \quad 1 \leq j \leq s_1$$

and

$$D_j = \begin{pmatrix} \mathbf{0}^{m_2 \times m_1} & C_{j-s_1,2} \\ \mathbf{0}^{m_1 \times m_1} & \mathbf{0}^{m_1 \times m_2} \end{pmatrix}, \quad s_1 + 1 \leq j \leq s,$$

where $\mathbf{0}^{k \times l}$ denotes a $k \times l$ matrix consisting only of zeros.

This construction for $D_1, \ldots, D_s$ is called a *$(u, u + v)$-construction*. The $(u, u + v)$-construction can also be applied directly to the points (see Exercise 9.5).

The following propagation rule was shown in [14, Corollary 5.1].

Theorem 9.3 (Propagation Rule V) *Let b be a prime power, let $\mathcal{P}_1$ be a digital (t_1, m_1, s_1)-net over $\mathbb{F}_b$, with generating matrices $C_{1,1}, \ldots, C_{s_1,1}$ and let $\mathcal{P}_2$ be a digital (t_2, m_2, s_2)-net over $\mathbb{F}_b$ with generating matrices $C_{1,2}, \ldots, C_{s_2,2}$. Then, the digital net $\mathcal{P}$ generated by the matrices $D_1, \ldots, D_s$ over $\mathbb{F}_b$ as given above is a digital (t, m, s)-net over $\mathbb{F}_b$, where $m = m_1 + m_2$, $s = s_1 + s_2$, and*

$$t = m + 1 - \min(2(m_1 - t_1 + 1), m_2 - t_2 + 1).$$

Proof The proof is based on the duality theory for digital nets (see Section 7.2). Let $m = m_1 + m_2$ and $s = s_1 + s_2$. For $1 \leq k \leq 2$ and $1 \leq i \leq s_k$, let $C'_{i,k} \in \mathbb{F}_b^{m \times m_k}$ be given by: the first m_k rows of $C_{i,k}$ and $C'_{i,k}$ are the same and the remaining rows of $C'_{i,k}$ are rows of $(0, \ldots, 0) \in \mathbb{F}_b^{m_k}$, i.e.

$$C'_{i,k} = \begin{pmatrix} C_{i,k} \\ \mathbf{0}^{(m-m_k)\times m_k} \end{pmatrix},$$

where $\mathbf{0}^{(m-m_k)\times m_k}$ denotes the $(m-m_k) \times m_k$ zero matrix over $\mathbb{F}_b$. Let

$$C_k = ((C'_{1,k})^\top | (C'_{2,k})^\top | \ldots | (C'_{s_k,k})^\top) \in \mathbb{F}_b^{m_k \times s_k m}.$$

Let $\mathcal{C}_k \subseteq \mathbb{F}_b^{s_k m}$ denote the row space of the matrix C_k and $\mathcal{C}_k^\perp$ denote the dual space of $\mathcal{C}_k$. Let

$$D = (D_1^\top | D_2^\top | \ldots | D_s^\top) \in \mathbb{F}_b^{m \times sm}$$

and let $\mathcal{D} \subseteq \mathbb{F}_b^{sm}$ denote the row space of the matrix D and $\mathcal{D}^\perp$ denote the dual space of $\mathcal{D}$.

For $\mathbf{U} = (\mathbf{u}_1, \ldots, \mathbf{u}_{s_1}) \in \mathcal{C}_1^\perp$ with $\mathbf{u}_l \in \mathbb{F}_b^m$, we define the vector $\overline{\mathbf{U}} = (\mathbf{u}_1, \ldots, \mathbf{u}_{s_1}, 0, \ldots, 0) \in \mathbb{F}_b^{s_2 m}$, i.e. we append $(s_2 - s_1)m$ zeros. Then we have

$$\mathcal{D}^\perp = \{(\mathbf{U}, \overline{\mathbf{U}} + \mathbf{V}) \in \mathbb{F}_b^{(s_1+s_2)m} : \mathbf{U} \in \mathcal{C}_1^\perp, \mathbf{V} \in \mathcal{C}_2^\perp\}, \tag{9.1}$$

since for $\mathbf{U} \in \mathcal{C}_1^\perp$ and $\mathbf{V} \in \mathcal{C}_2^\perp$ we have $C_1\mathbf{U}^\top = \mathbf{0} \in (\mathbb{F}_b^{m_1})^\top$ and $C_2\mathbf{V}^\top = \mathbf{0} \in (\mathbb{F}_b^{m_2})^\top$ and hence,

$$\begin{aligned} D(\mathbf{U}, \overline{\mathbf{U}} + \mathbf{V})^\top &= \begin{pmatrix} C_1\mathbf{U}^\top \\ -C_2^{(s_1)}\mathbf{U}^\top \end{pmatrix} + \begin{pmatrix} \mathbf{0} \\ C_2(\overline{\mathbf{U}} + \mathbf{V})^\top \end{pmatrix} \\ &= \begin{pmatrix} \mathbf{0}^{m_1 \times 1} \\ C_2\overline{\mathbf{U}}^\top - C_2^{(s_1)}\mathbf{U}^\top \end{pmatrix} = \mathbf{0} \in (\mathbb{F}_b^m)^\top, \end{aligned}$$

where $C_2^{(s_1)} = ((C'_{1,2})^\top | \ldots | (C'_{s_1,2})^\top) \in \mathbb{F}_b^{m_2 \times s_1 m}$.

(The right-hand side of (9.1) is normally used to define the $(u, u+v)$-construction, from which its name derives.)

From (9.1), we obtain $\dim \mathcal{D}^\perp = \dim \mathcal{C}_1^\perp + \dim \mathcal{C}_2^\perp$ and hence,

$$\dim \mathcal{D} = m - \dim \mathcal{D}^\perp = m_1 - \dim \mathcal{C}_1^\perp + m_2 - \dim \mathcal{C}_2^\perp = \dim \mathcal{C}_1 + \dim \mathcal{C}_2.$$

Therefore, $\dim \mathcal{D} \leq m_1 + m_2$.

We now obtain a lower bound on $\delta_m(\mathcal{D}^\perp)$. Let $\mathbf{U} = (\mathbf{u}_1, \ldots, \mathbf{u}_{s_1}) \in \mathcal{C}_1^\perp$, $\overline{\mathbf{U}} = (\mathbf{u}_1, \ldots, \mathbf{u}_{s_2}) \in \mathbb{F}_b^{s_2 m}$, where $\mathbf{u}_j \in \mathbb{F}_b^m$ and $\mathbf{u}_j = \mathbf{0} \in \mathbb{F}_b^m$ for $s_1 < j \leq s_2$. Further, let

$\mathbf{V} = (\mathbf{v}_1, \ldots, \mathbf{v}_{s_1}) \in \mathcal{C}_2^\perp$ where $\mathbf{v}_j \in \mathbb{F}_b^m$. For any $(\mathbf{U}, \overline{\mathbf{U}} + \mathbf{V}) \in \mathcal{D}^\perp \setminus \{\mathbf{0}\}$, we have

$$V_m(\mathbf{U}, \overline{\mathbf{U}} + \mathbf{V}) = \sum_{i=1}^{s_1} v_m(\mathbf{u}_i) + \sum_{i=1}^{s_2} v_m(\mathbf{u}_i + \mathbf{v}_i)$$
$$= \sum_{i=1}^{s_1} (v_m(\mathbf{u}_i) + v_m(\mathbf{u}_i + \mathbf{v}_i)) + \sum_{i=s_1+1}^{s_2} v_m(\mathbf{v}_i).$$

If $\mathbf{V} = \mathbf{0}$, then $\mathbf{U} \neq \mathbf{0}$ and hence,

$$V_m(\mathbf{U}, \overline{\mathbf{U}}) = 2 \sum_{i=1}^{s_1} v_m(\mathbf{u}_i) \geq 2(m_1 - t_1 + 1),$$

since $\mathbf{U} \in \mathcal{C}_1^\perp$.

Now assume that $\mathbf{V} \in \mathcal{C}_2^\perp \setminus \{\mathbf{0}\}$. If $\mathbf{u}_i + \mathbf{v}_i = \mathbf{0}$, then $v_m(\mathbf{u}_i) = v_m(\mathbf{v}_i)$, and if $\mathbf{u}_i + \mathbf{v}_i \neq \mathbf{0}$, then either $v_m(\mathbf{u}_i + \mathbf{v}_i) \geq v_m(\mathbf{v}_i)$ or $v_m(\mathbf{u}_i) = v_m(\mathbf{v}_i)$. Therefore, we have $v_m(\mathbf{u}_i) + v_m(\mathbf{u}_i + \mathbf{v}_i) \geq v_m(\mathbf{v}_i)$ and hence,

$$V_m(\mathbf{U}, \overline{\mathbf{U}} + \mathbf{V}) \geq \sum_{i=1}^{s_1} v_m(\mathbf{v}_i) + \sum_{i=s_1+1}^{s_2} v_m(\mathbf{v}_i) \geq m_2 - t_2 + 1,$$

since $\mathbf{V} \in \mathcal{C}_2^\perp$.

Thus, it follows that

$$\delta_m(\mathcal{D}^\top) \geq \min(2(m_1 - t_1 + 1), m_2 - t_2 + 1).$$

The result now follows from Corollary 7.9. □

9.2 The matrix-product construction

The matrix-product construction for digital nets was introduced by Niederreiter and Özbudak [187], and is itself a generalisation of the matrix-product construction of codes in [17]. The $(u, u + v)$-construction considered above is a special case thereof.

For the construction of the generating matrices, we need matrices, which are non-singular by column (NSC matrices; see [17]) which we introduce in the following. Let A be an $M \times M$ matrix over a finite field $\mathbb{F}_b$. For $1 \leq l \leq M$, let A_l denote the matrix which consists of the first l rows of A. For $1 \leq k_1 < \cdots < k_l \leq M$, let $A(k_1, \ldots, k_l)$ denote the $l \times l$ matrix consisting of the columns $k_1, \ldots, k_l$ of A_l.

Definition 9.4 We call an $M \times M$ matrix A defined over a finite field $\mathbb{F}_b$ non-singular by columns (NSC) if $A(k_1, \ldots, k_l)$ is non-singular for each $1 \leq l \leq M$ and $1 \leq k_1 < \cdots < k_l \leq M$. A is then called an NSC matrix.

Explicit constructions of NSC matrices are given in [17, Section 3]. For example, the Vandermonde matrix

$$A_M = \begin{pmatrix} 1 & \ldots & 1 \\ \alpha_1 & \ldots & \alpha_M \\ \vdots & \ddots & \vdots \\ \alpha_1^{M-1} & \ldots & \alpha_M^{M-1} \end{pmatrix},$$

where we assume that $\mathbb{F}_b = \{\alpha_1, \ldots, \alpha_b\}$, is an NSC matrix for all $1 \leq M \leq b$. In [17] it is also shown that an NSC matrix can only exist if $M \leq b$. Further constructions of NSC matrices are given in [17, Section 5.2].

In [187], the matrix product construction was introduced via the dual space. Here we only show how the new generating matrices can be obtained from the generating matrices of the digital nets.

For $1 \leq k \leq M$, let $C_{1,k}, \ldots, C_{s_k,k}$ be the generating matrices of a digital (t_k, m_k, s_k)-net over $\mathbb{F}_b$. Let $m = m_1 + \cdots + m_M$. Let $\sigma_0 = 0$ and for $1 \leq k \leq M$, let $\sigma_k = s_1 + \cdots + s_k$. For $1 \leq k \leq M$ and $\sigma_{k-1} < j \leq \sigma_k$, let $C'_{j,k} \in \mathbb{F}_b^{m \times m_k}$ be given by: the first m_k rows of $C_{j,k}$ and $C'_{j,k}$ are the same and the remaining rows of $C'_{j,k}$ are rows of $(0, \ldots, 0) \in \mathbb{F}_b^{m_k}$, i.e.

$$C'_{j,k} = \begin{pmatrix} C_{j,k} \\ \mathbf{0}^{(m-m_k) \times m_k} \end{pmatrix},$$

where $\mathbf{0}^{(m-m_k)\times m_k}$ denotes the $(m - m_k) \times m_k$ zero matrix over $\mathbb{F}_b$.

Let $A \in \mathbb{F}_b^{M \times M}$ be an NSC matrix. As A is non-singular, it has an inverse matrix $A^{-1} := (d_{k,l})_{1 \leq k,l \leq M}$ in $\mathbb{F}_b$. Then, for $1 \leq k \leq M$ and $\sigma_{k-1} < j \leq \sigma_k$, let

$$D_j = \left(d_{k,1} C'_{j-\sigma_{k-1},1} | \ldots | d_{k,M} C'_{j-\sigma_{k-1},M}\right) \in \mathbb{F}_b^{m \times m}. \tag{9.2}$$

This construction for generating matrices $D_1, \ldots, D_s$ is called *matrix-product construction*. The following propagation rule was shown in [187, Corollary 4.6].

Theorem 9.5 (Propagation Rule VI) *Assume that we are given digital (t_k, m_k, s_k)-nets, $1 \leq k \leq M$, over $\mathbb{F}_b$, and an $M \times M$ NSC matrix A.*

Then, the digital net constructed by the matrix-product construction which is generated by $D_1, \ldots, D_s \in \mathbb{F}_b^{m \times m}$ as in (9.2), where $s = s_1 + \cdots + s_M$ and

$m = m_1 + \cdots + m_M$, *is a digital* (t, m, s)*-net over* $\mathbb{F}_b$, *where*

$$t = m + 1 - \min_{1 \le l \le M} (M - l + 1)(m_l - t_l + 1).$$

Remark 9.6 For $M = 2$ and

$$A = \begin{pmatrix} 1 & 1 \\ 0 & 1 \end{pmatrix}$$

the matrix-product construction yields the $(u, u + v)$-construction.

9.3 A double m construction

In [189], Niederreiter and Pirsic introduced a propagation rule which uses two digital nets, a digital (t_1, m, s)-net and a digital (t_2, m, s)-net, to construct a digital $(t, 2m, s)$-net.

Assume that we are given two digital nets over the same finite field $\mathbb{F}_b$, a digital (t_1, m, s)-net with generating matrices $C_{1,1}, \ldots, C_{s,1} \in \mathbb{F}_b^{m \times m}$ and a digital (t_2, m, s)-net with generating matrices $C_{1,2}, \ldots, C_{s,2} \in \mathbb{F}_b^{m \times m}$. Then we consider the digital $(t, 2m, s)$-net with generating matrices $D_1, \ldots, D_s$ given by

$$D_i = \begin{pmatrix} C_{i,2} & C_{i,1} \\ -C_{i,2} & \mathbf{0}^{m \times m} \end{pmatrix} \in \mathbb{F}_b^{2m \times 2m}, \quad \text{for } 1 \le i \le s. \tag{9.3}$$

This construction for $D_1, \ldots, D_s$ is called the *double m construction*

In [189] the double m construction is described via the dual space, which we repeat in the following. As in the previous sections, for $1 \le k \le 2$, we form the matrices

$$C_k = ((C_{1,k})^\top | \ldots |(C_{s,k})^\top) \in \mathbb{F}_b^{m \times sm}.$$

The row space of C_k is denoted by $\mathcal{C}_k \subseteq \mathbb{F}_b^{ms}$ and the dual space of $\mathcal{C}_k$ is denoted by $\mathcal{C}_k^\perp \subseteq \mathbb{F}_q^{ms}$. We have $\dim(\mathcal{C}_k^\perp) \ge (s - 1)m$.

For $1 \le k \le 2$, let $\mathbf{A}_k = (\mathbf{a}_{1,k}, \ldots, \mathbf{a}_{s,k}) \in \mathcal{C}_k^\perp$ and set

$$\mathbf{N} = (\mathbf{a}_{1,1}, \mathbf{a}_{1,1} + \mathbf{a}_{1,2}, \mathbf{a}_{2,1}, \mathbf{a}_{2,1} + \mathbf{a}_{2,2}, \ldots, \mathbf{a}_{s,1}, \mathbf{a}_{s,1} + \mathbf{a}_{s,2}) \in \mathbb{F}_b^{2ms}.$$

Let the space of vectors $\mathbf{N}$ obtained this way be denoted by $\mathcal{N}$, i.e.

$$\mathcal{N} = \{\mathbf{N} \in \mathbb{F}_b^{2ms} : \mathbf{A}_1 \in \mathcal{C}_1^\perp, \mathbf{A}_2 \in \mathcal{C}_2^\perp\}. \tag{9.4}$$

We have

$$\dim(\mathcal{N}) = \dim(\mathcal{C}_1^\perp) + \dim(\mathcal{C}_2^\perp) \ge 2(sm - m),$$

and hence, $\dim(\mathcal{N}^\perp) \le 2sm - \dim(\mathcal{N}) \le 2m$.

It can be shown (see Exercise 9.6) that $\mathcal{N}$ is the dual space of the row space of the matrix

$$E = (D_1^\top | \ldots | D_s^\top) \in \mathbb{F}_b^{2m \times 2sm},$$

where D_i is given by (9.3) for $1 \leq i \leq s$. (Hence, $\mathcal{N}^\perp$ is the row space of E.)

In order to bound the quality parameter for the digital net with generating matrices $D_1, \ldots, D_s$, we define

$$d(\mathcal{C}_1^\perp, \mathcal{C}_2^\perp) := \max_{1 \leq i \leq s} \max_{R_i} \max(0, v_m(\mathbf{a}_{i,1}) - v_m(\mathbf{a}_{i,1} + \mathbf{a}_{i,2})),$$

where R_i is the set of all ordered pairs $(\mathbf{A}_1, \mathbf{A}_2)$, with $\mathbf{A}_k = (\mathbf{a}_{1,k}, \ldots, \mathbf{a}_{s,k}) \in \mathcal{C}_k^\perp \setminus \{\mathbf{0}\}$, $\mathbf{a}_{j,1} + \mathbf{a}_{j,2} = \mathbf{0}$ for $j \neq i$ and $\mathbf{a}_{i,1} + \mathbf{a}_{i,2} \neq \mathbf{0}$. We define the maximum over R_i to be zero if R_i is empty.

Theorem 9.7 (Propagation Rule VII) *Let $C_{1,1}, \ldots, C_{s,1}$ be the generating matrices of a digital (t_1, m, s)-net and $C_{1,2}, \ldots, C_{s,2}$ be the generating matrices of a digital (t_2, m, s)-net over the same $\mathbb{F}_b$.*

Then, the digital net generated by $D_1, \ldots, D_s$ given by (9.3) *is a digital $(t, 2m, s)$-net over $\mathbb{F}_b$, where*

$$t \leq \max(t_1 \mid d(\mathcal{C}_1^\perp, \mathcal{C}_2^\perp), t_2)$$

if $\mathcal{C}_1^\perp \cap \mathcal{C}_2^\perp = \{\mathbf{0}\}$, and

$$t \leq \max(t_1 + d(\mathcal{C}_1^\perp, \mathcal{C}_2^\perp), t_2, 2m + 1 - \delta_m(\mathcal{C}_1^\perp \cap \mathcal{C}_2^\perp))$$

if $\mathcal{C}_1^\perp \cap \mathcal{C}_2^\perp \neq \{\mathbf{0}\}$.

Proof Using Theorem 7.8, it is sufficient to show that $2m - t + 1$ is a lower bound on $\delta_{2m}(\mathcal{N})$. Hence, we need only show a lower bound on $V_m(\mathbf{N})$ for all non-zero vectors $\mathbf{N}$ in $\mathcal{N}$.

Let $\mathbf{N} \in \mathcal{N}$ be non-zero, then

$$V_{2m}(\mathbf{N}) = \sum_{i=1}^{s} v_{2m}(\mathbf{a}_{i,1}, \mathbf{a}_{i,1} + \mathbf{a}_{i,2}).$$

We consider several cases. If $\mathbf{A}_1 = \mathbf{0}$, then $\mathbf{A}_2 \neq \mathbf{0}$ and therefore,

$$V_{2m}(\mathbf{N}) \geq m + \sum_{i=1}^{s} v_m(\mathbf{a}_{i,2}) \geq m + \delta_m(\mathcal{C}_2^\perp) \geq 2m - t_2 + 1.$$

If $\mathbf{A}_2 = \mathbf{0}$, then $\mathbf{A}_1 \neq \mathbf{0}$ and analogously, we obtain

$$V_{2m}(\mathbf{N}) \geq m + \sum_{i=1}^{s} v_m(\mathbf{a}_{i,1}) \geq m + \delta_m(\mathcal{C}_1^\perp) \geq 2m - t_1 + 1.$$

If $\mathbf{A}_1, \mathbf{A}_2 \neq \mathbf{0}$, but $\mathbf{A}_1 + \mathbf{A}_2 = \mathbf{0}$, then $\mathbf{A}_1 \in \mathcal{C}_1^\perp \cap \mathcal{C}_2^\perp$. If $\mathcal{C}_1^\perp \cap \mathcal{C}_2^\perp = \{\mathbf{0}\}$, then this case is not possible. If $\mathcal{C}_1^\perp \cap \mathcal{C}_2^\perp \neq \{\mathbf{0}\}$, then

$$V_{2m}(\mathbf{N}) = V_m(\mathbf{A}_1) \geq \delta_m(\mathcal{C}_1^\perp \cap \mathcal{C}_2^\perp).$$

The last case is where $\mathbf{A}_1, \mathbf{A}_2 \neq \mathbf{0}$ and $\mathbf{A}_1 + \mathbf{A}_2 \neq \mathbf{0}$. Then

$$V_{2m}(\mathbf{N}) = \sum_{\substack{i=1 \\ \mathbf{a}_{i,1}+\mathbf{a}_{i,2}\neq \mathbf{0}}}^{s} (m + v_m(\mathbf{a}_{i,1} + \mathbf{a}_{i,2})) + \sum_{\substack{i=1 \\ \mathbf{a}_{i,1}+\mathbf{a}_{i,2}=\mathbf{0}}}^{s} v_m(\mathbf{a}_{i,1}).$$

If the first sum in the last expression has at least two terms, then $V_{2m}(\mathbf{N}) \geq 2m + 2$. Otherwise, it has exactly one term, say for $i = i_0$, and then

$$\begin{aligned}
V_{2m}(\mathbf{N}) &= m + v_m(\mathbf{a}_{i_0,1} + \mathbf{a}_{i_0,2}) + \sum_{\substack{i=1 \\ i\neq i_0}}^{s} v_m(\mathbf{a}_{i,1}) \\
&= m + V_m(\mathbf{A}_1) + v_m(\mathbf{a}_{i_0,1} + \boldsymbol{a}_{i_0,2}) - v_m(\mathbf{a}_{i_0,1}) \\
&\geq 2m - t_1 + 1 - \max(0, v_m(\mathbf{a}_{i_0,1}) - v_m(\mathbf{a}_{i_0,1} + \boldsymbol{a}_{i_0,2})) \\
&\geq 2m - t_1 + 1 - d(\mathcal{C}_1^\perp, \mathcal{C}_2^\perp).
\end{aligned}$$

Therefore, we have

$$\delta_{2m}(\mathcal{N}) \geq \min(2m - t_1 + 1 - d(\mathcal{C}_1^\perp, \mathcal{C}_2^\perp), 2m - t_2 + 1)$$

if $\mathcal{C}_1^\perp \cap \mathcal{C}_2^\perp = \{\mathbf{0}\}$, and

$$\delta_{2m}(\mathcal{N}) \geq \min(2m - t_1 + 1 - d(\mathcal{C}_1^\perp, \mathcal{C}_2^\perp), 2m - t_2 + 1, \delta_m(\mathcal{C}_1^\perp \cap \mathcal{C}_2^\perp))$$

if $\mathcal{C}_1^\perp \cap \mathcal{C}_2^\perp \neq \{\mathbf{0}\}$. Thus, the result follows. □

9.4 A base change propagation rule

In this section we introduce the *base change propagation rule* of [194, Theorem 9], which is sometimes also referred to as the *trace code for digital nets*.

Theorem 9.8 (Propagation Rule VIII) *Let b be a prime power and r be a positive integer. If $\mathcal{P}$ is a digital (t, m, s)-net over $\mathbb{F}_{b^r}$, then we can construct a digital $((r-1)m + t, rm, rs)$-net $\mathcal{Q}$ over $\mathbb{F}_b$ from $\mathcal{P}$.*

Proof Let $\mathcal{P}$ be a digital (t, m, s)-net over $\mathbb{F}_{b^r}$, with generating matrices $C_1, \ldots, C_s$, where each matrix C_i, $1 \leq i \leq s$ has row vectors $\mathbf{c}_{1,i}, \ldots, \mathbf{c}_{m,i} \in \mathbb{F}_{b^r}^m$. We now choose an ordered basis $B_1, \ldots, B_r$ of $\mathbb{F}_{b^r}$ over $\mathbb{F}_b$ and an $\mathbb{F}_b$-linear isomorphism $\varphi : \mathbb{F}_{b^r}^m \to \mathbb{F}_b^{rm}$. Then, we consider the generating matrices of a net $\mathcal{Q}$,

$$D_{(i-1)r+k} := \begin{pmatrix} \mathbf{d}_{1,(i-1)r+k} \\ \vdots \\ \mathbf{d}_{rm,(i-1)r+k} \end{pmatrix} \in \mathbb{F}_b^{rm\times rm}, \ 1 \le i \le s, \ 1 \le k \le r,$$

where $\mathbf{d}_{j,(i-1)r+k} = \varphi(B_k \mathbf{c}_{j,i})$ for $1 \le j \le m$, $1 \le i \le s$, $1 \le k \le r$ and $\mathbf{d}_{j,(i-1)r+k} = \mathbf{0}$ for $m < j \le rm, 1 \le i \le s, 1 \le k \le r$. We claim that $\mathcal{Q}$ is a digital $((r-1)m+t, rm, rs)$-net over $\mathbb{F}_b$.

Choose $d_1, \ldots, d_{rs} \in \mathbb{N}_0$ such that

$$d_1 + \cdots + d_{rs} \le rm - (r-1)m - t = m - t$$

and let $\delta_j^{(i,k)} \in \mathbb{F}_b$ be such that

$$\sum_{i=1}^{s} \sum_{k=1}^{r} \sum_{j=1}^{d_{(i-1)r+k}} \delta_j^{(i,k)} \mathbf{d}_{j,(i-1)r+k} = \mathbf{0} \in \mathbb{F}_b^{rm}. \tag{9.5}$$

Due to the definition of the vectors $\mathbf{d}_{j,(i-1)r+k}$ and the fact that $d_i \le m$, (9.5) can be rewritten as

$$\sum_{i=1}^{s} \sum_{k=1}^{r} \sum_{j=1}^{d_{(i-1)r+k}} \delta_j^{(i,k)} \varphi\left(B_k \mathbf{c}_{j,i}\right) = \mathbf{0} \in \mathbb{F}_b^{rm}. \tag{9.6}$$

Now let $e_j^{(i,k)} = 1$ for $1 \le j \le d_{(i-1)r+k}$ and $e_j^{(i,k)} = 0$ for $j > d_{(i-1)r+k}$. Let $d_i' = \max_{1 \le k \le r} d_{(i-1)r+k}$. Then, (9.6) can be written as

$$\begin{aligned} \mathbf{0} &= \sum_{i=1}^{s} \sum_{k=1}^{r} \sum_{j=1}^{d_i'} e_j^{(i,k)} \delta_j^{(i,k)} \varphi\left(B_k \mathbf{c}_{j,i}\right) \\ &= \varphi\left(\sum_{i=1}^{s} \sum_{j=1}^{d_i'} \sum_{k=1}^{r} e_j^{(i,k)} \delta_j^{(i,k)} B_k \mathbf{c}_{j,i} \right) \\ &= \varphi\left(\sum_{i=1}^{s} \sum_{j=1}^{d_i'} \gamma_j^{(i)} \mathbf{c}_{j,i} \right), \end{aligned}$$

where $\gamma_j^{(i)} := \sum_{k=1}^{r} e_j^{(i,k)} \delta_j^{(i,k)} B_k \in \mathbb{F}_{b^r}$ for $1 \le i \le s$ and $1 \le j \le m$. Since φ is an $\mathbb{F}_b$-linear isomorphism, we conclude that

$$\sum_{i=1}^{s} \sum_{j=1}^{d_i'} \gamma_j^{(i)} \mathbf{c}_{j,i} = \mathbf{0} \in \mathbb{F}_{b^r}^{m}.$$

As $d_1' + \cdots + d_s' \le d_1 + \cdots + d_{rs} \le m - t$, it follows that $\gamma_j^{(i)} = 0$ for $1 \le j \le d_i'$ and $1 \le i \le s$. Hence, $\delta_j^{(i,k)} = 0$ for all $1 \le j \le d_{(i-1)r+k}$, $1 \le k \le r$, and $1 \le i \le s$. Hence, $\mathcal{Q}$ is a digital $((r-1)m + t, rm, rs)$-net over $\mathbb{F}_b$. □

9.5 A dual space base change propagation rule

In this section we introduce another propagation rule, first established by Niederreiter and Xing [196], where we change the ground field from $\mathbb{F}_{b^r}$ to $\mathbb{F}_b$, for some prime power b and some positive integer r. The difference from the previous propagation rule is that the $\mathbb{F}_b$-linear transformation from $\mathbb{F}_{b^r}$ to $\mathbb{F}_b^r$ is now applied to the dual space instead of applying it to the generating matrices. The following result, which should be compared to Corollary 4.26 for nets which are not necessarily digital, appeared as [196, Corollary 1].

Theorem 9.9 (Propagation Rule IX) *Given a digital (t, m, s)-net over $\mathbb{F}_{b^r}$, we can construct a digital (t', rm, s)-net over $\mathbb{F}_b$, where*

$$t' \le rt + (r-1)(s-1).$$

Proof Let $\varphi : \mathbb{F}_{b^r} \to \mathbb{F}_b^r$ denote again an $\mathbb{F}_b$-linear isomorphism. Let the matrices $C_1, \ldots, C_s \in \mathbb{F}_{b^r}^{m \times m}$ denote the generating matrices of the digital (t, m, s)-net over $\mathbb{F}_{b^r}$, and let $C = (C_1^\top | \ldots | C_s^\top)$ be its overall generating matrix. The row space of C is denoted by $\mathcal{C} \subseteq \mathbb{F}_{b^r}^{sm}$ and the dual space of $\mathcal{C}$ by $\mathcal{C}^\perp \subseteq \mathbb{F}_{b^r}^{sm}$. For a vector $\mathbf{A} = (\mathbf{a}_1, \ldots, \mathbf{a}_s) \in \mathcal{C}^\perp$, with $\mathbf{a}_j \in \mathbb{F}_{b^r}^m$, let $\overline{\mathbf{a}}_j = \varphi(\mathbf{a}_j) \in \mathbb{F}_b^{rm}$ and $\overline{\mathbf{A}} = (\overline{\mathbf{a}}_1, \ldots, \overline{\mathbf{a}}_s)$, where we extend the $\mathbb{F}_b$-linear isomorphism from $\mathbb{F}_{b^r} \to \mathbb{F}_b^r$ componentwise, to an $\mathbb{F}_b$-linear isomorphism from $\mathbb{F}_{b^r}^m \to \mathbb{F}_b^{rm}$. Then we obtain a linear space $\overline{\mathcal{C}}^\perp \subseteq \mathbb{F}_b^{srm}$, by setting $\overline{\mathcal{C}}^\perp = \{\overline{\mathbf{A}} : \mathbf{A} \in \mathcal{C}^\perp\}$.

Note that $\dim_{\mathbb{F}_b}(\overline{\mathcal{C}}^\perp) = r \dim_{\mathbb{F}_{b^r}}(\mathcal{C}^\perp)$, and $\dim_{\mathbb{F}_{b^r}}(\mathcal{C}^\perp) \ge sm - m$ since $\dim_{\mathbb{F}_{b^r}}(\mathcal{C}) \le m$. Thus, $\dim_{\mathbb{F}_b}(\overline{\mathcal{C}}^\perp) \ge rsm - rm$, and the dual space of $\overline{\mathcal{C}}^\perp$, denoted by $\overline{\mathcal{C}}$, satisfies $\dim_{\mathbb{F}_b}(\overline{\mathcal{C}}) \le rm$. Let $\overline{C} \in \mathbb{F}_b^{rm \times srm}$ be a matrix whose row space is $\overline{\mathcal{C}}$, and let $\overline{C} = (D_1^\top | \ldots | D_s^\top)$, where $D_j \in \mathbb{F}_b^{rm \times rm}$ for $1 \le j \le s$. The matrices $D_1, \ldots, D_s$ now generate a digital net over $\mathbb{F}_b$.

We now investigate the quality of this digital net. Let $\overline{\mathbf{A}} = (\overline{\mathbf{a}}_1, \ldots, \overline{\mathbf{a}}_s) \in \overline{\mathcal{C}}^\perp$ be a non-zero vector. We have $V_{rm}(\overline{\mathbf{A}}) = v_{rm}(\overline{\mathbf{a}}_1) + \cdots + v_{rm}(\overline{\mathbf{a}}_s)$. As $\overline{\mathbf{A}}$ is non-zero, it follows that $\mathbf{A}$ is non-zero. If $v_m(\mathbf{a}_i) = 0$, then $\mathbf{a}_i = \mathbf{0}$ and hence, $\overline{\mathbf{a}}_i = \mathbf{0}$, which implies that $v_{rm}(\overline{\mathbf{a}}_i) = 0$.

Let $v_m(\mathbf{a}_i) > 0$ and $\mathbf{a}_i = (a_{i,1}, \ldots, a_{i,m})$. Let $j_0 > 0$ be the largest index such that $a_{i,j_0} \ne 0$. Then $\overline{\mathbf{a}}_i = (\varphi(a_{i,1}), \ldots, \varphi(a_{i,m}))$ and $\varphi(a_{i,j_0}) \ne \mathbf{0}$, and $\varphi(a_{i,j}) = \mathbf{0}$, for $j > j_0$. Then,

$$v_{rm}(\overline{\mathbf{a}}_i) \ge r(j_0 - 1) + 1 = r v_m(\mathbf{a}_i) - (r-1).$$

The above inequality also holds if $v_m(\mathbf{a}_i) = 0$, hence,

$$\begin{aligned} V_{rm}(\overline{\mathbf{A}}) &\geq \sum_{i=1}^{s} (r v_m(\mathbf{a}_j) - (r-1)) \\ &= r V_m(\mathbf{A}) - s(r-1) \geq r\delta_m(\mathcal{C}^\perp) - s(r-1). \end{aligned}$$

As the last inequality holds for all non-zero $\overline{\mathbf{A}} \in \overline{\mathcal{C}}^\perp$, it follows that $\delta_{rm}(\overline{\mathcal{C}}^\perp) \geq r\delta_m(\mathcal{C}^\perp) - s(r-1) \geq r(m-t+1) - s(r-1)$. Since $rm - t' + 1 = \delta_{rm}(\overline{\mathcal{C}}^\perp)$, we obtain the desired result. □

9.6 A base change propagation rule for projective spaces

In this section, we introduce the propagation rule for digital nets which appears in MINT under the name 'base reduction for projective spaces'. Let $r \in \mathbb{N}$ and let $C_1, \ldots, C_s \in \mathbb{F}_{b^r}^{m \times m}$ be the generating matrices of a digital (t, m, s)-net over $\mathbb{F}_{b^r}$. Note that the linear independence condition in Definition 4.58 stays unchanged if we multiply a row of C_i by some non-zero element in $\mathbb{F}_{b^r}$. Doing so, we can obtain generating matrices $C_1', \ldots, C_s' \in \mathbb{F}_{b^r}^{m \times m}$, which also generate a digital (t, m, s)-net over $\mathbb{F}_{b^r}$, and for which the first column of each C_i' only consists of zeros and ones.

Let $\varphi : \mathbb{F}_{b^r} \to \mathbb{F}_b^r$ be an $\mathbb{F}_b$-linear isomorphism such that $\varphi(1) = (0, \ldots, 0, 1)$. For a vector $\mathbf{c} = (c_1, \ldots, c_m) \in \mathbb{F}_{b^r}^m$, we define $\varphi(\mathbf{c}) = (\varphi(c_1), \ldots, \varphi(c_m)) \in \mathbb{F}_b^{rm}$ and for a matrix $C \in \mathbb{F}_{b^r}^{m \times m}$ with $C = (\mathbf{c}_1, \ldots, \mathbf{c}_m)^\top$, we define $\varphi(C) = (\varphi(\mathbf{c}_1), \ldots, \varphi(\mathbf{c}_m))^\top \in \mathbb{F}_b^{m \times rm}$.

For $1 \leq i \leq s$, now let $D_i' = \varphi(C_i') \in \mathbb{F}_b^{m \times rm}$. Note that the first $r-1$ columns of D_i' are zero for each $1 \leq i \leq s$, as the first column of C_i' consists only of zeros and ones. Let $D_i \in \mathbb{F}_b^{(rm-r+1) \times (rm-r+1)}$ be the matrix obtained by discarding the first $r-1$ columns of D_i' and augmenting $(r-1)(m-1)$ arbitrary row vectors in $\mathbb{F}_b^{rm-r+1}$ at the bottom. Then, because we only discarded zeros, the number of linearly independent rows of D_i is the same as the number of linearly independent rows of D_i'. From the proof of Theorem 9.8, we obtain the number of linearly independent rows of the matrices D_i' as being the same as the number of linearly independent rows of the generating matrices $C_1', \ldots, C_s'$, which in turn is the same as the number of linearly independent rows of the generating matrices $C_1, \ldots, C_s$. Thus, we obtain the following result.

Theorem 9.10 (Propagation Rule X) *Let $r \in \mathbb{N}$. Given a digital (t, m, s)-net over $\mathbb{F}_{b^r}$, using the construction outlined in this section, we can obtain a digital $((r-1)(m-1)+t, rm-r+1, s)$-net over $\mathbb{F}_b$.*

Exercises

9.1 Prove Theorem 9.1.

9.2 Give a proof of Theorem 9.2 without using duality theory.

9.3 Prove Theorem 9.2 for (t, m, s)-nets in base b (not necessarily digital).

9.4 Let $\mathcal{P}_1$ be a digital (t_1, m_1, s_1)-net over $\mathbb{F}_b$ with generating matrices $C_{1,1}, \ldots, C_{s_1,1}$ and let $\mathcal{P}_2$ be a digital (t_2, m_2, s_2)-net over $\mathbb{F}_b$ with generating matrices $C_{1,2}, \ldots, C_{s_2,2}$. Show that the generating matrices $D_1, \ldots, D_{s_1+s_2}$ of the direct product of $\mathcal{P}_1$ and $\mathcal{P}_2$ are given by

$$D_j = \begin{pmatrix} C_{j,1} & \mathbf{0}^{m_1 \times m_2} \\ \mathbf{0}^{m_2 \times m_1} & \mathbf{0}^{m_2 \times m_2} \end{pmatrix}, \quad 1 \le j \le s_1,$$

and

$$D_j = \begin{pmatrix} \mathbf{0}^{m_2 \times m_1} & C_{j-s_1,2} \\ \mathbf{0}^{m_1 \times m_1} & \mathbf{0}^{m_1 \times m_2} \end{pmatrix}, \quad s_1 + 1 \le j \le s_1 + s_2,$$

where $\mathbf{0}^{k \times l}$ denotes a $k \times l$ matrix consisting only of zeros.

9.5 Let $\mathcal{P}_1 = \{\boldsymbol{x}_{0,1}, \ldots, \boldsymbol{x}_{b^{m_1}-1,1}\}$ be a digital (t_1, m_1, s_1)-net over $\mathbb{F}_b$ and let $\mathcal{P}_2 = \{\boldsymbol{x}_{0,2}, \ldots, \boldsymbol{x}_{b^{m_2}-1,2}\}$ be a digital (t_2, m_2, s_2)-net over $\mathbb{F}_b$, where $\boldsymbol{x}_{n,k} = (x_{n,k,1}, \ldots, x_{n,k,s})$ and $x_{n,k,i} = x_{n,k,i,1} b^{-1} + x_{n,k,i,2} b^{-2} + \cdots + x_{n,k,i,m_k} b^{-m_k}$ for $0 \le n < b^{m_k}$, $1 \le i \le s_k$ and $1 \le k \le 2$. Assume that $s_1 \le s_2$ and apply the $(u, u+v)$-construction to $\mathcal{P}_1$ and $\mathcal{P}_2$. Show that the resulting point set $\mathcal{P}$ consists of the $b^{m_1+m_2}$ points $\boldsymbol{z}_h = (z_{h,1}, \ldots, z_{h,s_1+s_2})$ in $[0,1)^{s_1+s_2}$ for $0 \le h < b^{m_1+m_2}$, where for $1 \le i \le s_1$, $0 \le l < b^{m_2}$ and $0 \le h < b^{m_1}$, we have

$$z_{lb^{m_1}+h,i} = \frac{x_{h,i,1,1} \ominus x_{l,i,2,1}}{b} + \cdots + \frac{x_{h,i,1,m} \ominus x_{l,i,2,m}}{b^m}$$

and for $s_1 < i \le s_1 + s_2$, $0 \le l < b^{m_2}$ and $0 \le h < b^{m_1}$, we have

$$z_{lb^{m_1}+h,i} = y_{l,i-s_1}.$$

9.6 Show that the space spanned by the rows of

$$E = (D_1^\top | \ldots | D_s^\top) \in \mathbb{F}_b^{2m \times 2sm},$$

where D_i is given by (9.3) for $1 \le i \le s$, is $\mathcal{N}^\perp$ as given by (9.4).

9.7 Show that for $M = 2$ and

$$A = \begin{pmatrix} 1 & 1 \\ 0 & 1 \end{pmatrix}$$

the matrix-product construction yields the $(u, u+v)$-construction.

9.8 Consider the double m construction.

Find digital (t, m, s)-nets $\mathcal{P}_1, \mathcal{P}_2, \mathcal{P}_3, \mathcal{P}_4$ over $\mathbb{Z}_2$ such that $\mathcal{C}_1^\perp \cap \mathcal{C}_2^\perp = \{\mathbf{0}\}$ and $\mathcal{C}_3^\perp \cap \mathcal{C}_4^\perp \neq \{\mathbf{0}\}$, where $\mathcal{C}_j^\perp$ is the dual net corresponding to the digital net $\mathcal{P}_j$ for $j = 1, \ldots, 4$. Find the t value of the digital net which one obtains from applying the double m construction to $\mathcal{P}_1, \mathcal{P}_2$ and $\mathcal{P}_3, \mathcal{P}_4$.

9.9 Consider the Hammersley net over $\mathbb{F}_4$ with $m = 2$. Use Propagation Rule VIII to obtain a digital $(2, 4, 4)$-net over $\mathbb{Z}_2$.

9.10 Consider the Hammersley net over $\mathbb{F}_4$ with $m = 2$. Use Propagation Rule IX to obtain a digital $(1, 4, 2)$-net over $\mathbb{Z}_2$.

9.11 Consider the Hammersley net over $\mathbb{F}_4$ with $m = 2$. Use Propagation Rule X to obtain a digital $(1, 3, 2)$-net over $\mathbb{Z}_2$.

10

Polynomial lattice point sets

In this section, we introduce and analyse special digital nets whose construction is based on rational functions over finite fields. Nowadays these point sets are known under the name polynomial lattice point sets and QMC rules using them as underlying nodes are called polynomial lattice rules. In its overall structure polynomial lattice point sets are very similar to usual lattice point sets as introduced in Definition 3.47 (see also Niederreiter [177, Chapter 5] or Sloan and Joe [245]). The main difference is that here, one uses polynomial arithmetic in $\mathbb{F}_b[x]$ instead of the usual arithmetic in $\mathbb{Z}$. Hence, many results for polynomial lattice point sets have analogues for lattice point sets and vice versa.

10.1 Polynomial lattice point sets and digital nets

In [175] (see also [177, Section 4.4]) Niederreiter introduced a special family of digital (t, m, s)-nets over $\mathbb{F}_b$. Those nets are obtained from rational functions over finite fields.

We give the general definition of polynomial lattice point sets as special digital nets over $\mathbb{F}_b$. They were introduced in this form in [177, Section 4.4], though the name 'polynomial lattice point sets' appeared only later. The polynomial lattice structure is not immediately obvious from the subsequent definition. However, for prime numbers b, there is an equivalent but more concise definition of polynomial lattice point sets which makes the connection with ordinary lattice point sets obvious. This result is given in Theorem 10.5.

Definition 10.1 Let b be a prime power and let $m, s \in \mathbb{N}$. Choose $p \in \mathbb{F}_b[x]$ with $\deg(p) = m \geq 1$ and let $\boldsymbol{q} = (q_1, \ldots, q_s) \in \mathbb{F}_b[x]^s$. For $1 \leq i \leq s$, consider the expansions

$$\frac{q_i(x)}{p(x)} = \sum_{l=w_i}^{\infty} u_l^{(i)} x^{-l} \in \mathbb{F}_b((x^{-1}))$$

where $w_i \leq 1$. Define the $m \times m$ matrices $C_1, \ldots, C_s$ over $\mathbb{F}_b$ where the elements $c_{j,r+1}^{(i)}$ of the matrix C_i are given by

$$c_{j,r+1}^{(i)} = u_{r+j}^{(i)} \in \mathbb{F}_b, \tag{10.1}$$

for $1 \leq i \leq s$, $1 \leq j \leq m$, $0 \leq r \leq m-1$. Then, $C_1, \ldots, C_s$ are the generating matrices of a digital (t, m, s)-net over $\mathbb{F}_b$. The digital net obtained from the polynomials p and $\boldsymbol{q} = (q_1, \ldots, q_s) \in \mathbb{F}_b[x]^s$, without explicitly specifying the involved bijection φ (see Definition 4.47), is denoted by $\mathcal{P}(\boldsymbol{q}, p)$. The point set $\mathcal{P}(\boldsymbol{q}, p)$ is called a polynomial lattice point set and a QMC rule using it is called a *polynomial lattice rule*.

Remark 10.2 Note that the matrices defined by (10.1) are of the form

$$C_i = C_i(q_i, p) = \begin{pmatrix} u_1^{(i)} & u_2^{(i)} & \ldots & u_m^{(i)} \\ u_2^{(i)} & u_3^{(i)} & \ldots & u_{m+1}^{(i)} \\ \vdots & \vdots & & \vdots \\ u_m^{(i)} & u_{m+1}^{(i)} & \ldots & u_{2m-1}^{(i)} \end{pmatrix},$$

i.e. the matrix C_i is a so-called Hankel matrix associated with the linear recurring sequence $(u_1^{(i)}, u_2^{(i)}, \ldots)$. If $\gcd(q_i, p) = 1$, then p is called the minimal polynomial of the linear recurring sequence (see, for example, [177, Appendix A]) and C_i is non-singular (see [157, Theorem 6.75]).

Remark 10.3 From Remark 10.2 it follows that if $\gcd(q_i, p) = 1$ for all $1 \leq i \leq s$, then each one-dimensional projection of the point set $\mathcal{P}(\boldsymbol{q}, p)$ onto the ith coordinate is a $(0, m, 1)$-net over $\mathbb{F}_b$.

The following result concerning the determination of the Laurent series coefficients of rational functions is useful in obtaining the matrices from the polynomials $\boldsymbol{q}$ and p. It was already stated in [155, 222, 235] for the case $b = 2$.

Proposition 10.4 *Let b be a prime power. For $p \in \mathbb{F}_b[x]$, $p(x) = x^m + a_1 x^{m-1} + \cdots + a_{m-1}x + a_m$ and $q \in \mathbb{F}_b[x]$ with $q(x) = q_1 x^{m-1} + \cdots + q_{m-1}x + q_m$, the coefficients u_l, $l \in \mathbb{N}$, in the Laurent series expansion of*

$$\frac{q(x)}{p(x)} = \sum_{l=1}^{\infty} u_l x^{-l}$$

can be computed as follows: the first m coefficients $u_1, \ldots, u_m$ are obtained by solving the linear system

$$\begin{pmatrix} 1 & 0 & \ldots & \ldots & 0 \\ a_1 & 1 & \ddots & & \vdots \\ \vdots & a_1 & \ddots & \ddots & \vdots \\ a_{m-2} & & \ddots & \ddots & 0 \\ a_{m-1} & a_{m-2} & \ldots & a_1 & 1 \end{pmatrix} \begin{pmatrix} u_1 \\ u_2 \\ \vdots \\ u_m \end{pmatrix} = \begin{pmatrix} q_1 \\ q_2 \\ \vdots \\ q_m \end{pmatrix},$$

and for $l > m$, u_l is obtained from the linear recursion in $\mathbb{F}_b$,

$$u_l + u_{l-1}a_1 + u_{l-2}a_2 + \cdots + u_{l-m}a_m = 0.$$

Proof Consider $q(x) = p(x) \sum_{l=1}^{\infty} u_l x^{-l}$ and compare the coefficients of x^l, $l \in \mathbb{Z}$, on both sides of the equation. □

Where b is a prime, it was shown by Niederreiter [178] that there is an equivalent but simpler form of the construction of the point set $\mathcal{P}(\boldsymbol{q}, p)$. In this case we can identify $\mathbb{Z}_b$ with $\mathbb{F}_b$ and choose the bijection φ to be the identity map; see Definition 4.47. (We always assume this setting in the prime b case.)

For the following we need to introduce some definitions and some notation. For $m \in \mathbb{N}$, let υ_m be the map from $\mathbb{Z}_b((x^{-1}))$ to the interval $[0, 1)$ defined by

$$\upsilon_m\left(\sum_{l=w}^{\infty} t_l x^{-l}\right) = \sum_{l=\max(1,w)}^{m} t_l b^{-l}.$$

We frequently associate a non-negative integer k, with b-adic expansion $k = \kappa_0 + \kappa_1 b + \cdots + \kappa_a b^a$, with the polynomial $k(x) = \kappa_0 + \kappa_1 x + \cdots + \kappa_a x^a \in \mathbb{Z}_b[x]$ and vice versa. Further, for arbitrary $\boldsymbol{k} = (k_1, \ldots, k_s) \in \mathbb{Z}_b[x]^s$ and $\boldsymbol{q} = (q_1, \ldots, q_s) \in \mathbb{Z}_b[x]^s$, we define the 'inner product'

$$\boldsymbol{k} \cdot \boldsymbol{q} = \sum_{i=1}^{s} k_i q_i \in \mathbb{Z}_b[x]$$

and we write $q \equiv 0 \pmod{p}$ if p divides q in $\mathbb{Z}_b[x]$.

With these definitions we can give the following equivalent but simpler form of the construction of $\mathcal{P}(\boldsymbol{q}, p)$.

Theorem 10.5 *Let b be a prime and let $m, s \in \mathbb{N}$. For $p \in \mathbb{Z}_b[x]$ with $\deg(p) = m$ and $\boldsymbol{q} = (q_1, \ldots, q_s) \in \mathbb{Z}_b[x]^s$, the polynomial lattice point set $\mathcal{P}(\boldsymbol{q}, p)$ is the point* *set consisting of the b^m points*

$$x_h = \left(v_m\left(\frac{h(x)q_1(x)}{p(x)}\right), \ldots, v_m\left(\frac{h(x)q_s(x)}{p(x)}\right)\right) \in [0,1)^s,$$

for $h \in \mathbb{Z}_b[x]$ with $\deg(h) < m$.

Proof To prove the result, it is enough to consider only one component of the point set $\mathcal{P}(\boldsymbol{q}, p)$. Hence, for simplicity we omit the sub- and superscripts for the dimension.

Let $q, p \in \mathbb{Z}_b[x]$ with $\deg(p) = m$ and $\frac{q(x)}{p(x)} = \sum_{k=w}^{\infty} u_k x^{-k}$. If $w > 1$ set $u_1 = \cdots = u_{w-1} = 0$. Then, for $h \in \mathbb{Z}_b[x]$ with $h = h_0 + h_1 x + \cdots + h_{m-1}x^{m-1}$, we have

$$\begin{aligned} v_m\left(\frac{h(x)q(x)}{p(x)}\right) &= v_m\left(\left(\sum_{k=w}^{\infty} u_k x^{-k}\right)(h_0 + h_1 x + \cdots + h_{m-1}x^{m-1})\right) \\ &= v_m\left(\sum_{k=1}^{m} x^{-k} \sum_{r=0}^{m-1} u_{k+r}h_r\right) \\ &= \sum_{k=1}^{m} b^{-k} \sum_{r=0}^{m-1} u_{k+r}h_r, \end{aligned}$$

where the innermost sum is evaluated in $\mathbb{Z}_b$. We have

$$\sum_{r=0}^{m-1} u_{k+r}h_r = (u_k, \ldots, u_{k+m-1}) \cdot \mathbf{h},$$

where $\mathbf{h} = (h_0, \ldots, h_{m-1}) \in \mathbb{Z}_b^m$ if h has b-adic expansion $h = h_0 + h_1 b + \cdots + h_{m-1}b^{m-1}$. From this, the result follows. □

The representation of $\mathcal{P}(\boldsymbol{q}, p)$ from Theorem 10.5 is the reason for calling $\mathcal{P}(\boldsymbol{q}, p)$ a polynomial lattice point set and for calling a QMC rule using a polynomial lattice point set a polynomial lattice rule. The vector $\boldsymbol{q}$ is called the *generating vector* of $\mathcal{P}(\boldsymbol{q}, p)$. The polynomial p is referred to as the *modulus*. As already mentioned, in its overall structure a polynomial lattice point set is very similar to an ordinary lattice point set as given in Definition 3.47. The main difference is that here, we use polynomial arithmetic in $\mathbb{F}_b[x]$ instead of the usual arithmetic in $\mathbb{Z}$.

It follows from Definition 10.1 that the point set $\mathcal{P}(\boldsymbol{q}, p)$ is a digital (t, m, s)-net over $\mathbb{F}_b$. We now determine the quality parameter t of such a digital net as a function of $\boldsymbol{q}$ and p. Before we do so, let us express the dual net (see Definition 4.76) of a polynomial lattice point set in terms of $\boldsymbol{q}$ and the modulus p.

For a prime power b, let $\varphi : \{0, \ldots, b-1\} \to \mathbb{F}_b$ be a bijection with $\varphi(0) = 0 \in \mathbb{F}_b$ (for simplicity, we denote the zero element in $\mathbb{F}_b$ by 0 instead of $\overline{0}$, as we have done so far) as used in the construction of a digital net over $\mathbb{F}_b$ (see Definition 4.47). Then, for $k \in \{0, \ldots, b^m - 1\}$ with b-adic expansion $k = \kappa_0 + \kappa_1 b + \cdots + \kappa_{m-1} b^{m-1}$, we recall the notation $\mathbf{k} = (\varphi(\kappa_0), \ldots, \varphi(\kappa_{m-1}))^\top \in (\mathbb{F}_b^m)^\top$. Furthermore, we often associate the integer k with the polynomial $k(x) = \varphi(\kappa_0) + \varphi(\kappa_1)x + \cdots + \varphi(\kappa_{m-1})x^{m-1} \in \mathbb{F}_b[x]$ and vice versa (as we have already done so earlier in the prime b case).

The following lemma was first shown by Niederreiter [175, Proof of Lemma 2] (see also [177, Lemma 4.40]).

Lemma 10.6 *Let b be a prime power and let $m, s \in \mathbb{N}$. Let $C_1, \ldots, C_s$ be the generating matrices of a polynomial lattice point set $\mathcal{P}(\boldsymbol{q}, p)$ as given in Definition 10.1. Then, for $\mathbf{k} = (k_1, \ldots, k_s) \in \{0, \ldots, b^m - 1\}^s$, we have*

$$C_1^\top \mathbf{k}_1 + \cdots + C_s^\top \mathbf{k}_s = \mathbf{0}, \tag{10.2}$$

where $\mathbf{0} = (0, \ldots, 0)^\top \in (\mathbb{F}_b^m)^\top$ if and only if

$$\boldsymbol{k} \cdot \boldsymbol{q} \equiv 0 \pmod{p},$$

where in the last expression $\boldsymbol{k}$ is the associated vector of polynomials in $\mathbb{F}_b[x]$.

Proof For $1 \le i \le s$, let $\frac{q_i(x)}{p(x)} = \sum_{l=w_i}^\infty u_l^{(i)} x^{-l} \in \mathbb{F}_b((x^{-1}))$. For fixed $1 \le i \le s$, we have

$$\frac{k_i(x) q_i(x)}{p(x)} = \left(\sum_{j=0}^{m-1} \varphi(\kappa_{i,j}) x^j \right) \left(\sum_{l=w_i}^{\infty} u_l^{(i)} x^{-l} \right) = \sum_{j=0}^{m-1} \varphi(\kappa_{i,j}) \sum_{l=w_i}^{\infty} u_l^{(i)} x^{j-l}$$

$$= \sum_{j=0}^{m-1} \varphi(\kappa_{i,j}) \sum_{r=w_i-j}^{\infty} u_{j+r}^{(i)} x^{-r},$$

and hence, for $r \in \mathbb{N}$ the coefficient of x^{-r} in $\frac{k_i(x) q_i(x)}{p(x)}$ is $\sum_{j=0}^{m-1} u_{j+r}^{(i)} \varphi(\kappa_{i,j})$. Summing up, we obtain that for $r \in \mathbb{N}$ the coefficient of x^{-r} in $\frac{1}{p} \boldsymbol{k} \cdot \boldsymbol{q}$ is given by $\sum_{i=1}^s \sum_{j=0}^{m-1} u_{j+r}^{(i)} \varphi(\kappa_{i,j})$. However, condition (10.2) is equivalent to

$$\sum_{i=1}^{s} \sum_{j=0}^{m-1} u_{j+r}^{(i)} \varphi(\kappa_{i,j}) = 0 \in \mathbb{F}_b$$

for all $1 \le r \le m$. Therefore, we obtain

$$\frac{1}{p} \boldsymbol{k} \cdot \boldsymbol{q} = g + L$$

for some $g \in \mathbb{F}_b[x]$ and $L \in \mathbb{F}_b((x^{-1}))$ of the form $\sum_{k=m+1}^{\infty} f_k x^{-k}$, i.e. for the discrete exponential valuation of L, we have $\nu(L) < -m$. Equivalently, we have $\boldsymbol{k} \cdot \boldsymbol{q} - gp = Lp$. On the left-hand side, we have a polynomial over $\mathbb{F}_b$, whereas on the right-hand side, we have a Laurent series Lp with $\nu(Lp) < 0$, since $\deg(p) = m$. This is only possible if $Lp = 0$, which means that $\boldsymbol{k} \cdot \boldsymbol{q} - gp = 0$ or equivalently $\boldsymbol{k} \cdot \boldsymbol{q} \equiv 0 \pmod{p}$. □

We introduce some notation. For a prime power b and $m \in \mathbb{N}$, we denote by $G_{b,m}$ the subset of $\mathbb{F}_b[x]$ consisting of all polynomials q with degree smaller than m, i.e.

$$G_{b,m} := \{q \in \mathbb{F}_b[x] : \deg(q) < m\},$$

where we use the convention $\deg(0) = -1$. Furthermore, we define $G_{b,m}^* := G_{b,m} \setminus \{0\}$. Obviously, we have $|G_{b,m}| = b^m$ and $|G_{b,m}^*| = b^m - 1$.

Now Lemma 10.6 motivates the following definition.

Definition 10.7 The *dual net* of a polynomial lattice point set $\mathcal{P}(\boldsymbol{q}, p)$ with $p \in \mathbb{F}_b[x]$, $\deg(p) = m$, and $\boldsymbol{q} \in \mathbb{F}_b[x]^s$ is given by

$$\mathcal{D}_{\boldsymbol{q},p} = \{\boldsymbol{k} \in G_{b,m}^s : \boldsymbol{k} \cdot \boldsymbol{q} \equiv 0 \pmod{p}\}.$$

Furthermore, let $\mathcal{D}'_{\boldsymbol{q},p} := \mathcal{D}_{\boldsymbol{q},p} \setminus \{\boldsymbol{0}\}$.

For the determination of the quality parameter of a polynomial lattice point set, we have to introduce a new quantity, which is often called the 'figure of merit'.

Definition 10.8 Let b be a prime power and let $s, m \in \mathbb{N}$. For $p \in \mathbb{F}_b[x]$ with $\deg(p) = m$, and $\boldsymbol{q} \in \mathbb{F}_b[x]^s$, the *figure of merit* $\rho(\boldsymbol{q}, p)$ is defined as

$$\rho(\boldsymbol{q}, p) = s - 1 + \min_{\boldsymbol{h} \in \mathcal{D}'_{\boldsymbol{q},p}} \sum_{i=1}^{s} \deg(h_i),$$

where $\boldsymbol{h} = (h_1, \ldots, h_s)$.

The figure of merit $\rho(\boldsymbol{q}, p)$ is closely related to the quality parameter t of $\mathcal{P}(\boldsymbol{q}, p)$ considered as a (t, m, s)-net over $\mathbb{F}_b$.

Theorem 10.9 *Let b be a prime power and let $m, s \in \mathbb{N}$. Let $p \in \mathbb{F}_b[x]$ with $\deg(p) = m$ and let $\boldsymbol{q} \in \mathbb{F}_b[x]^s$. Then, the point set $\mathcal{P}(\boldsymbol{q}, p)$ is a strict digital (t, m, s)-net over $\mathbb{F}_b$ with $t = m - \rho(\boldsymbol{q}, p)$.*

Proof We again follow [175, Proof of Lemma 2] (see also [177, Corollary 4.41]). It suffices to show that we have $\rho(C_1, \ldots, C_s) = \rho(\boldsymbol{q}, p)$, where $\rho(C_1, \ldots, C_s)$ is the linear independence parameter as defined in Definition 4.50. The result then follows from Theorem 4.52. Let $\varphi : \{0, \ldots, b-1\} \to \mathbb{F}_b$ with $\varphi(0) = 0$ be the bijection used in the construction of the digital net $\mathcal{P}(\boldsymbol{q}, p)$.

According to the definition of $\rho(C_1, \ldots, C_s)$, there are $d_1, \ldots, d_s \in \mathbb{N}_0$ with $d_1 + \cdots + d_s = \rho(C_1, \ldots, C_s) + 1$ such that the system consisting of the union of the first d_i row vectors $\mathbf{c}_1^{(i)}, \ldots, \mathbf{c}_{d_i}^{(i)}$ of the matrix C_i, where $1 \le i \le s$, is linearly dependent over $\mathbb{F}_b$; that is, there exist $\kappa_{i,j} \in \mathbb{Z}_b$ for $0 \le j < d_i$, $1 \le i \le s$, not all zero, such that

$$\sum_{i=1}^{s} \sum_{j=0}^{d_i-1} \varphi(\kappa_{i,j}) \mathbf{c}_{j+1}^{(i)} = \mathbf{0} \in \mathbb{F}_b^m.$$

Putting $\kappa_{i,j} = 0$ for $d_i \le j \le m-1$ and $1 \le i \le s$ and $k_i = \kappa_{i,0} + \kappa_{i,1} b + \cdots + \kappa_{i,m-1} b^{m-1}$ and correspondingly $\mathbf{k}_i = (\varphi(\kappa_{i,0}), \ldots, \varphi(\kappa_{i,m-1}))^\top \in (\mathbb{F}_b^m)^\top$ for $1 \le i \le s$, we obtain

$$C_1^\top \mathbf{k}_1 + \cdots + C_s^\top \mathbf{k}_s = \mathbf{0} \in (\mathbb{F}_b^m)^\top.$$

By Lemma 10.6 this is equivalent to $\boldsymbol{k} \cdot \boldsymbol{q} \equiv 0 \pmod{p}$ for $\boldsymbol{k} = (k_1, \ldots, k_s) \in \mathbb{F}_b[x]^s \setminus \{\mathbf{0}\}$ where $k_i(x) = \varphi(\kappa_{i,0}) + \varphi(\kappa_{i,1}) x + \cdots + \varphi(\kappa_{i,m-1}) x^{m-1} \in \mathbb{F}_b[x]$. Hence, from the definition of $\rho(\boldsymbol{q}, p)$, we obtain

$$\rho(\boldsymbol{q}, p) \le s - 1 + \sum_{i=1}^{s} \deg(k_i) \le s - 1 + \sum_{i=1}^{s} (d_i - 1) = \rho(C_1, \ldots, C_s).$$

On the other hand, from the definition of $\rho(\boldsymbol{q}, p)$, we find that there exists a non-zero $\boldsymbol{k} = (k_1, \ldots, k_s) \in \mathbb{F}_b[x]^s$ with $\deg(k_i) < m$ for $1 \le i \le s$ and $\boldsymbol{k} \cdot \boldsymbol{q} \equiv 0 \pmod{p}$ such that $\rho(\boldsymbol{q}, p) = s - 1 + \sum_{i=1}^{s} \deg(k_i)$. From Lemma 10.6, we obtain $C_1^\top \mathbf{k}_1 + \cdots + C_s^\top \mathbf{k}_s = \mathbf{0} \in (\mathbb{F}_b^m)^\top$, where $\mathbf{k}_i \in (\mathbb{F}_b^m)^\top$ is determined by the coefficients of the polynomials k_i for $1 \le i \le s$. For $1 \le i \le s$, let $d_i = \deg(k_i) + 1$. Then, the system consisting of the union of the first d_i row vectors of C_i, where $1 \le i \le s$, is linearly dependent over $\mathbb{F}_b$ and hence,

$$\rho(C_1, \ldots, C_s) \le -1 + \sum_{i=1}^{s} d_i = -1 + \sum_{i=1}^{s} (\deg(k_i) + 1) = \rho(\boldsymbol{q}, p). \qquad \square$$

Remark 10.10 Let $\boldsymbol{q} = (q_1, \ldots, q_s) \in \mathbb{F}_b[x]^s$ with $\gcd(q_1, p) = 1$. Then, the condition $\boldsymbol{h} \cdot \boldsymbol{q} = h_1 q_1 + \cdots + h_s q_s \equiv 0 \pmod{p}$ in Definition 10.8 of the figure of merit $\rho(\boldsymbol{q}, p)$ is equivalent to $h_1 + h_2 q_1^* q_2 + \cdots + h_s q_1^* q_s \equiv 0 \pmod{p}$, where $q_1^* \in \mathbb{F}_b[x]$ is such that $q_1^* q_1 \equiv 1 \pmod{p}$ (q_1^* always exists as long as $\gcd(q_1, p) = 1$). Therefore, the figure of merit is the same for $\boldsymbol{q}$ and for $(1, q_1^* q_2, \ldots, q_1^* q_s)$ and hence, it suffices to consider the figure of merit for vectors $\boldsymbol{q}$ of the form $\boldsymbol{q} = (1, q_2, \ldots, q_s) \in \mathbb{F}_b[x]^s$ only.

From Theorem 10.9, we find that to obtain a polynomial lattice point set which is a digital (t, m, s)-net over $\mathbb{F}_b$ with a small quality parameter t, we have to choose $p \in \mathbb{F}_b[x]$ with $\deg(p) = m$ and a vector of polynomials $\boldsymbol{q} = (q_1, \ldots, q_s) \in \mathbb{F}_b[x]^s$ in such a way that the figure of merit $\rho(\boldsymbol{q}, p)$ is large.

For dimension $s = 2$, there is a general construction which yields the maximal value $\rho(\boldsymbol{q}, p) = m$ (and hence, $t = 0$). This construction uses a connection between the figure of merit $\rho(\boldsymbol{q}, p)$ and continued fractions for rational functions over $\mathbb{F}_b$. We briefly outline this construction by following Niederreiter [177, Section 4.4].

Let b be a prime power, let $m \in \mathbb{N}$, let $p \in \mathbb{F}_b[x]$ with $\deg(p) = m$ and let $\boldsymbol{q} = (1, q)$ where $q \in \mathbb{F}_b[x]$ with $\gcd(q, p) = 1$. Let

$$\frac{q}{p} = [A_0; A_1, \ldots, A_l]$$

be the continued fraction expansion of the rational function q/p, with partial quotients $A_n \in \mathbb{F}_b[x]$ satisfying $\deg(A_n) \geq 1$ for $1 \leq n \leq l$. Put

$$K\left(\frac{q}{p}\right) = \max_{1 \leq n \leq l} \deg(A_n).$$

Theorem 10.11 *Let b be a prime power, let $m \in \mathbb{N}$, let $p \in \mathbb{F}_b[x]$ with $\deg(p) = m$ and let $\boldsymbol{q} = (1, q)$ where $q \in \mathbb{F}_b[x]$ with $\gcd(q, p) = 1$. Then we have*

$$\rho(\boldsymbol{q}, p) = m + 1 - K\left(\frac{q}{p}\right).$$

For a proof of this result, we refer to Niederreiter [177, Theorem 4.46].

It follows that, to obtain a large value of $\rho(\boldsymbol{q}, p)$, we have to choose q and p with $\deg(p) = m \geq 1$ such that $K(q/p)$ is small. The smallest value that can be obtained is $K(q/p) = 1$, namely, by choosing the partial quotients $A_0, \ldots, A_m$ with $\deg(A_r) = 1$ for all $1 \leq r \leq m$ (here, A_0 can be chosen arbitrarily and hence, we choose $A_0 = 0$) and letting q/p be the resulting rational function. For this choice and for $\boldsymbol{q} = (1, q)$, we obtain $\rho(\boldsymbol{q}, p) = 1$ and hence, by Theorem 10.9, the polynomial lattice point set $\mathcal{P}(\boldsymbol{q}, p)$ is a digital $(0, m, 2)$-net over $\mathbb{F}_b$.

To get suitable parameters p and $\boldsymbol{q}$ for $s \geq 3$ explicitly, one has to resort to a computer search.

Remark 10.12 From Definition 10.1, it is clear that it is enough to consider generating vectors $\boldsymbol{q} = (q_1, \ldots, q_s) \in G_{b,m}^s$ only, where $m = \deg(p)$.

Despite this restriction, the fundamental problem with search procedures is that even for moderately large s and m, an exhaustive search through all b^{ms} possible s-tuples $\boldsymbol{q} = (q_1, \ldots, q_s) \in G_{b,m}^s$ is infeasible. (Also, the restriction $q_1 = 1$ from Remark 10.10 is only of minor help.) However, we show in the following that the search domain can be restricted to what is in a sense a one-parameter subset of $G_{b,m}^s$. We take our cue from the analogy between the polynomial lattice point sets $\mathcal{P}(\boldsymbol{q}, p)$ and ordinary lattice point sets. In the latter construction, one often restricts the attention to lattice points whose coordinates are successive powers of a single integer (see Exercise 3.25), and a suitable integer for this purpose is called an 'optimal coefficient' relative to a dimension s and an integer modulus (see, for example, Korobov [124]).

In the polynomial case, we consider s-tuples $\boldsymbol{q} = (q_1, \ldots, q_s)$ of polynomials that are obtained by taking a polynomial $q \in G_{b,m}$ and putting $q_i \equiv q^{i-1} \pmod{p}$ with $\deg(q_i) < \deg(p)$ for $1 \le i \le s$. We use the simpler notation $\boldsymbol{v}_s(q) \equiv (1, q, q^2, \ldots, q^{s-1}) \pmod{p}$ for such s-tuples (we say such a vector is a *Korobov vector*). A polynomial q which leads to a large figure of merit $\rho(\boldsymbol{v}_s(q), p)$ is then, by analogy, called an *optimal polynomial*. This informal notion depends, of course, on the dimension s and on the polynomial p.

For irreducible moduli p we can give the following existence results, which were first given for $b = 2$ in [139, Theorem 1] and then generalised (and slightly improved) in [235, Theorem 6].

Theorem 10.13 *Let b be a prime power, let $s, m \in \mathbb{N}$, $s \ge 2$ and let $p \in \mathbb{F}_b[x]$ be irreducible over $\mathbb{F}_b$ with $\deg(p) = m$. For $\rho \in \mathbb{Z}$, define*

$$\Delta_b(s, \rho) = \sum_{d=0}^{s-1} \binom{s}{d} (b-1)^{s-d} \sum_{\gamma=0}^{\rho+d} \binom{s-d+\gamma-1}{\gamma} b^\gamma + 1 - b^{\rho+s}.$$

1. *If $\Delta_b(s, \rho) < b^m$, then there exists a $\boldsymbol{q} = (1, q_2, \ldots, q_s) \in G_{b,m}^s$ with $\rho(\boldsymbol{q}, p) \ge s + \rho$. Therefore, the point set $\mathcal{P}(\boldsymbol{q}, p)$ is a digital (t, m, s)-net over $\mathbb{F}_b$ with $t \le m - s - \rho$.*
2. *If $\Delta_b(s, \rho) < \frac{b^m}{s-1}$, then there exists a $q \in G_{b,m}$ such that $\boldsymbol{v}_s(q) \equiv (1, q, \ldots, q^{s-1}) \pmod{p}$ satisfies $\rho(\boldsymbol{v}_s(q), p) \ge s + \rho$. Therefore, the point set $\mathcal{P}(\boldsymbol{v}_s(q), p)$ is a digital (t, m, s)-net over $\mathbb{F}_b$ with $t \le m - s - \rho$.*

For the proof of these results, we need the following lemma.

Lemma 10.14 *For a prime power b, $l \in \mathbb{N}$, and $k \in \mathbb{Z}$ the number $A_b(l, k)$ of $(h_1, \ldots, h_l) \in \mathbb{F}_b[x]^l$ with $h_i \ne 0$ for $1 \le i \le l$ and $\sum_{i=1}^{l} \deg(h_i) \le k$ is given by*

$$A_b(l, k) = (b-1)^l \sum_{\gamma=0}^{k} \binom{l+\gamma-1}{\gamma} b^\gamma.$$

Proof Let $k \ge 0$ (the case $k < 0$ holds trivially). Then we have

$$A_b(l, k) = \sum_{\gamma=0}^{k} D(l, \gamma)$$

with $D(l, \gamma)$ being the number of $(h_1, \ldots, h_l) \in \mathbb{F}_b[x]^l$ for which $h_i \neq 0$ for $1 \leq i \leq l$ and $\sum_{i=1}^{l} \deg(h_i) = \gamma$. For fixed $\gamma \geq 0$, there are $\binom{l+\gamma-1}{\gamma}$ tuples $(d_1, \ldots, d_l)$ of non-negative integers with $\sum_{i=1}^{l} d_i = \gamma$, and for each such l-tuple $(d_1, \ldots, d_l)$ the number of $(h_1, \ldots, h_l) \in \mathbb{F}_b[x]^l$ with $\deg(h_i) = d_i$ for $1 \leq i \leq l$ is $(b-1)^l b^{d_1+\cdots+d_l} = (b-1)^l b^\gamma$. Thus,

$$D(l, \gamma) = \binom{l+\gamma-1}{\gamma}(b-1)^l b^\gamma,$$

and the result follows. □

Proof of Theorem 10.13 We can assume that $-s \leq \rho \leq m - s$. Let $M(s, \rho)$ be the number of $(h_1, \ldots, h_s) \in \mathbb{F}_b[x]^s$ with $(h_2, \ldots, h_s) \neq (0, \ldots, 0)$ and $\sum_{i=1}^{s} \deg(h_i) \leq \rho$. Since $\rho \leq m - s$, it follows from $\sum_{i=1}^{s} \deg(h_i) \leq \rho$ that $\deg(h_i) < m$ for $1 \leq i \leq s$. Using the notation and the result of Lemma 10.14, we get

$$M(s, \rho) = \sum_{d=0}^{s-1} \binom{s}{d} A_b(s-d, \rho+d) + 1 - b^{\rho+s} = \Delta(s, \rho).$$

(Recall the convention $\deg(0) = -1$.)

1. Since p is irreducible, for a given non-zero s-tuple $(h_1, \ldots, h_s) \in G_{b,m}^s$, the congruence

$$h_1 + h_2 q_2 + \cdots + h_s q_s \equiv 0 \pmod{p}$$

has no solution if $h_2 = h_3 = \cdots = h_s = 0$, and it has exactly $b^{m(s-2)}$ solutions $\boldsymbol{q} = (1, q_2, \ldots, q_s) \in G_{b,m}^s$ otherwise. Therefore, to all non-zero $(h_1, \ldots, h_s)$ with $\sum_{i=1}^{s} \deg(h_i) \leq \rho$, there are assigned altogether at most $M(s, \rho) b^{m(s-2)}$ different solutions $\boldsymbol{q} = (1, q_2, \ldots, q_s) \in G_{b,m}^s$ satisfying the above congruence. Now the total number of $\boldsymbol{q} = (1, q_2, \ldots, q_s) \in G_{b,m}^s$ is $b^{m(s-1)}$. Thus, if $M(s, \rho) b^{m(s-2)} < b^{m(s-1)}$, that is, if $\Delta_b(s, \rho) < b^m$, then there exists at least one $\boldsymbol{q} = (1, q_2, \ldots, q_s) \in G_{b,m}^s$ such that

$$h_1 + h_2 q_2 + \cdots + h_s q_s \not\equiv 0 \pmod{p}$$

for all non-zero $(h_1, \ldots, h_s)$ with $\sum_{i=1}^{s} \deg(h_i) \leq \rho$. For this $\boldsymbol{q}$, we then have $\rho(\boldsymbol{q}, p) \geq s + \rho$. By Theorem 10.9 the point set $\mathcal{P}(\boldsymbol{q}, p)$ is a digital (t, m, s)-net over $\mathbb{F}_b$ with $t \leq m - s - \rho$.

2. We proceed as above, but we note that for an irreducible p and a non-zero $(h_1, \ldots, h_s) \in G_{b,m}^s$, the congruence

$$h_1 + h_2 q + \cdots + h_s q^{s-1} \equiv 0 \pmod{p}$$

has no solution if $h_2 = \cdots = h_s = 0$, and it has at most $s - 1$ solutions $q \in G_{b,m}$ otherwise. □

Corollary 10.15 *Let b be a prime power and let $s, m \in \mathbb{N}$, where $s \geq 2$ and where m is sufficiently large. Let $p \in \mathbb{F}_b[x]$ be irreducible with* $\deg(p) = m$.

1. *There exists a vector $\boldsymbol{q} = (1, q_2, \ldots, q_s) \in G_{b,m}^s$ with*
$$\rho(\boldsymbol{q}, p) \geq \left\lfloor m - (s-1)(\log_b m - 1) + \log_b \frac{(s-1)!}{(b-1)^{s-1}} \right\rfloor .$$
2. *There exists a polynomial $q \in G_{b,m}$ such that $\boldsymbol{v}_s(q) \equiv (1, q, \ldots, q^{s-1}) \pmod{p}$ satisfies*
$$\rho(\boldsymbol{v}_s(q), p) \geq \left\lfloor m - (s-1)(\log_b m - 1) + \log_b \frac{(s-2)!}{(b-1)^{s-1}} \right\rfloor .$$

Proof

1. For $\rho \geq 1$, we have
$$\begin{aligned}\Delta_b(s, \rho) &\leq \sum_{d=0}^{s-1} \binom{s}{d} (b-1)^{s-d} \binom{\rho + s - 1}{s - d - 1} \frac{b^{\rho+d+1}}{b-1} \\ &\leq b^{\rho+1} \sum_{d=0}^{s-1} \binom{s}{d} (b-1)^{s-d-1} \frac{(\rho + s - 1)^{s-d-1}}{(s-d-1)!} \\ &= \frac{\rho^{s-1}}{(s-1)!} b^{\rho+1} (b-1)^{s-1} \left(1 + O_s\left(\frac{1}{\rho}\right)\right),\end{aligned}$$
where O_s indicates that the implied constant depends only on s. Now let
$$\rho = \left\lfloor m - (s-1)\log_b m + \log_b \frac{(s-1)!}{(b-1)^{s-1}} - 1 \right\rfloor ,$$
which is in $\mathbb{N}$ for sufficiently large m. Then
$$\begin{aligned}&\Delta_b(s, \rho) \\ &\leq b^m \left(1 - (s-1)\frac{\log_b m}{m} + \frac{1}{m} \log_b \frac{(s-1)!}{(b-1)^{s-1}}\right)^{s-1} \left(1 + O_s\left(\frac{1}{m}\right)\right) < b^m\end{aligned}$$
for sufficiently large m, and the result follows from the first part of Theorem 10.13.
2. The second assertion is deduced in a similar way from the second part of Theorem 10.13. □

We remark that establishing similar existence results for not necessarily irreducible polynomials involves several technical difficulties. Until now, very little is known for reducible p. There is only one singular result for

$p(x) = x^m \in \mathbb{Z}_2[x]$ shown in [139, Corollary 2] which states that there exists a vector $\boldsymbol{q} = (1, q_2, \ldots, q_s) \in G_{2,m}^s$ such that

$$\rho(\boldsymbol{q}, x^m) \geq \lfloor m - (s-1)(\log_2 m - 1) + \log_2(s-1)! \rfloor.$$

10.2 Discrepancy of polynomial lattice point sets

In this section we deal with the classical star discrepancy as well as the weighted star discrepancy of polynomial lattice point sets $\mathcal{P}(\boldsymbol{q}, p)$. All the discrepancy estimates are based on Theorem 5.34 and hence, we only consider the case where b is a prime. As always in this case, we identify $\mathbb{F}_b$ with $\mathbb{Z}_b$ and choose the bijection $\varphi : \mathbb{Z}_b \to \mathbb{F}_b$ to be the identity map.

It follows from Lemma 10.6 that the quantity $R_b(C_1, \ldots, C_s)$ as defined in (5.7) can be written as

$$R_b(C_1, \ldots, C_s) = \sum_{\boldsymbol{h} \in \mathcal{D}'_{\boldsymbol{q},p}} \prod_{i=1}^{s} \rho_b(h_i),$$

where we use the association of the non-negative integers h_i with their corresponding polynomials in $\mathbb{Z}_b[x]$ again, and where $\mathcal{D}'_{\boldsymbol{q},p}$ is as in Definition 10.7. For this reason we write in the following $R_b(\boldsymbol{q}, p)$ instead of $R_b(C_1, \ldots, C_s)$. With this notation we can rewrite Theorem 5.34 in the following way.

Corollary 10.16 *Let b be a prime and let $s, m \in \mathbb{N}$. Let $p \in \mathbb{Z}_b[x]$ with $\deg(p) = m$ and let $\boldsymbol{q} \in G_{b,m}^s$. For the star discrepancy of the polynomial lattice point set $\mathcal{P}(\boldsymbol{q}, p)$, we have*

$$D_{b^m}^*(\mathcal{P}(\boldsymbol{q}, p)) \leq 1 - \left(1 - \frac{1}{b^m}\right)^s + R_b(\boldsymbol{q}, p),$$

where

$$R_b(\boldsymbol{q}, p) = \sum_{\boldsymbol{h} \in \mathcal{D}'_{\boldsymbol{q},p}} \rho_b(\boldsymbol{h}).$$

Here, for $\boldsymbol{h} = (h_1, \ldots, h_s) \in G_{b,m}^s$, we put $\rho_b(\boldsymbol{h}) = \rho_b(h_1) \cdots \rho_b(h_s)$ and for $h \in G_{b,m}$, we put

$$\rho_b(h) = \begin{cases} 1 & \text{if } h = 0, \\ \frac{1}{b^{r+1} \sin(\pi \kappa_r / b)} & \text{if } h = \kappa_0 + \kappa_1 x + \cdots + \kappa_r x^r,\ \kappa_r \neq 0. \end{cases}$$

In the following we deal with a slightly weaker bound on the star discrepancy. We explain the reason for this change for the worse in a moment.

Corollary 10.17 *Let b be a prime and let $s, m \in \mathbb{N}$. Let $p \in \mathbb{Z}_b[x]$ with $\deg(p) = m$ and let $\boldsymbol{q} \in G_{b,m}^s$. For the star discrepancy of the polynomial lattice point set*

$\mathcal{P}(\boldsymbol{q}, p)$, *we have*

$$D^*_{b^m}(\mathcal{P}(\boldsymbol{q}, p)) \leq 1 - \left(1 - \frac{1}{b^m}\right)^s + R'_b(\boldsymbol{q}, p),$$

where

$$R'_b(\boldsymbol{q}, p) = \sum_{\boldsymbol{h} \in \mathcal{D}'_{q,p}} r_b(\boldsymbol{h}). \tag{10.3}$$

Here, for $\boldsymbol{h} = (h_1, \ldots, h_s) \in G^s_{b,m}$, *we put* $r_b(\boldsymbol{h}) = r_b(h_1) \cdots r_b(h_s)$ *and for* $h \in G_{b,m}$, *we put*

$$r_b(h) = \begin{cases} 1 & \text{if } h = 0, \\ \frac{1}{b^{r+1} \sin^2(\pi \kappa_r / b)} & \text{if } h = \kappa_0 + \kappa_1 x + \cdots + \kappa_r x^r,\ \kappa_r \neq 0. \end{cases}$$

Proof The result follows immediately from Corollary 10.16 by invoking the fact that $\sin^{-1}(x) \leq \sin^{-2}(x)$ for $0 \leq x < \pi$. □

Similar results can be given for the weighted star discrepancy. We consider only weights of product form which are independent of the dimension s. Let $\boldsymbol{\gamma} = (\gamma_i)_{i \geq 1}$ be a sequence of non-negative real numbers. Then for $\emptyset \neq \mathfrak{u} \subseteq \mathcal{I}_s$ the weight $\gamma_{\mathfrak{u}}$ is given by $\gamma_{\mathfrak{u}} = \prod_{j \in \mathfrak{u}} \gamma_j$. Using (5.13), Lemma 5.42 and Lemma 10.6, we obtain the following result.

Corollary 10.18 *Let b be a prime and let $s, m \in \mathbb{N}$. Let $p \in \mathbb{Z}_b[x]$ with* $\deg(p) = m$ *and let $\boldsymbol{q} \in G^s_{b,m}$. Let $\boldsymbol{\gamma} = (\gamma_i)_{i \geq 1}$ be a sequence of weights. For the weighted star discrepancy of the polynomial lattice point set $\mathcal{P}(\boldsymbol{q}, p)$, we have*

$$D^*_{b^m,\boldsymbol{\gamma}}(\mathcal{P}(\boldsymbol{q}, p)) \leq \sum_{\emptyset \neq \mathfrak{u} \subseteq \mathcal{I}_s} \gamma_{\mathfrak{u}} \left(1 - \left(1 - \frac{1}{b^m}\right)^{|\mathfrak{u}|}\right) + R'_{b,\boldsymbol{\gamma}}(\boldsymbol{q}, p),$$

where

$$R'_{b,\boldsymbol{\gamma}}(\boldsymbol{q}, p) = \sum_{\boldsymbol{h} \in \mathcal{D}'_{q,p}} r_b(\boldsymbol{h}, \boldsymbol{\gamma}).$$

Here, for $\boldsymbol{h} = (h_1, \ldots, h_s) \in G^s_{b,m}$, *we put* $r_b(\boldsymbol{h}, \boldsymbol{\gamma}) = r_b(h_1, \gamma_1) \cdots r_b(h_s, \gamma_s)$ *and for* $h \in G_{b,m}$, *we put*

$$r_b(h, \gamma) = \begin{cases} 1 + \gamma & \text{if } h = 0, \\ \gamma r_b(h) & \text{if } h \neq 0. \end{cases}$$

Remark 10.19 Of course, the result for the weighted star discrepancy can also be stated in terms of ρ_b instead of r_b which would be slightly better.

Now we explain why we deal with the slightly worse bounds on the (weighted) star discrepancy. The reason for this is that the quantities $R'_b(\boldsymbol{q}, p)$ and $R'_{b,\boldsymbol{\gamma}}(\boldsymbol{q}, p)$ can be computed efficiently whereas this is not the case for $R_b(\boldsymbol{q}, p)$.

Let $p \in \mathbb{Z}_b[x]$, with $\deg(p) = m$, $\boldsymbol{q} \in G_{b,m}^s$, and $\mathcal{P}(\boldsymbol{q}, p) = \{\boldsymbol{x}_0, \ldots, \boldsymbol{x}_{b^m-1}\}$ where $\boldsymbol{x}_n = (x_{n,1}, \ldots, x_{n,s})$. First, we note that it can be shown as in Lemma 8.8 that

$$R_b'(\boldsymbol{q}, p) = -1 + \frac{1}{b^m} \sum_{n=0}^{b^m-1} \prod_{i=1}^{s} \left(\sum_{k=0}^{b^m-1} r_b(k)\, {}_b\mathrm{wal}_k(x_{n,i}) \right).$$

We define

$$\phi_{b,m}(x) := \sum_{h=0}^{b^m-1} r_b(h)\, {}_b\mathrm{wal}_h(x).$$

Then

$$R_b'(\boldsymbol{q}, p) = -1 + \frac{1}{b^m} \sum_{n=0}^{b^m-1} \prod_{i=1}^{s} \phi_{b,m}(x_{n,i}). \tag{10.4}$$

We further have

$$\begin{aligned} R_{b,\boldsymbol{\gamma}}'(\boldsymbol{q}, p) &= \sum_{\emptyset \neq \mathfrak{u} \subseteq \mathcal{I}_s} \gamma_{\mathfrak{u}} R_b'(\boldsymbol{q}_{\mathfrak{u}}, p) \\ &= -\sum_{\emptyset \neq \mathfrak{u} \subseteq \mathcal{I}_s} \gamma_{\mathfrak{u}} + \frac{1}{b^m} \sum_{n=0}^{b^m-1} \sum_{\emptyset \neq \mathfrak{u} \subseteq \mathcal{I}_s} \gamma_{\mathfrak{u}} \prod_{i \in \mathfrak{u}} \phi_{b,m}(x_{n,i}) \\ &= -\prod_{i=1}^{s} (1 + \gamma_i) + \frac{1}{b^m} \sum_{n=0}^{b^m-1} \prod_{i=1}^{s} (1 + \gamma_i \phi_{b,m}(x_{n,i})). \end{aligned} \tag{10.5}$$

In the following we show that the function $\phi_{b,m}$ can be simplified. Let $h = h_0 + h_1 b + \cdots + h_d b^d$ with $h_d \neq 0$. For $0 \leq d < m$ and $1 \leq h_d < b$, let

$$D_{d,h_d,b,m}(x) := \sum_{h=h_d b^d}^{h_d b^d + b^d - 1} {}_b\mathrm{wal}_h(x),$$

then it follows that

$$\phi_{b,m}(x) = 1 + \sum_{d=0}^{m-1} \sum_{h_d=1}^{b-1} r_b(h_d b^d) D_{d,h_d,b,m}(x).$$

Let $\omega_b = \mathrm{e}^{2\pi \mathrm{i}/b}$ and $x = \xi_1 b^{-1} + \xi_2 b^2 + \cdots$. We have

$$D_{d,h_d,b,m}(x) = \sum_{h=h_d b^d}^{h_d b^d + b^d - 1} {}_b\mathrm{wal}_h(x) = \omega_b^{h_d \xi_{d+1}} \sum_{h_{d-1}=0}^{b-1} \omega_b^{h_{d-1}\xi_d} \cdots \sum_{h_0=0}^{b-1} \omega_b^{h_0 \xi_1}.$$

As $\sum_{h_i=0}^{b-1} \omega_b^{h_i \xi_{i+1}} = 0$ if $\xi_{i+1} \neq 0$ and $\sum_{h_i=0}^{b-1} \omega_b^{h_i \xi_{i+1}} = b$ if $\xi_{i+1} = 0$, we have

$$D_{d,h_d,b,m}(x) = \begin{cases} \omega_b^{h_d \xi_{d+1}} b^d & \text{if } \xi_1 = \cdots = \xi_d = 0 \text{ or if } d = 0, \\ 0 & \text{otherwise.} \end{cases}$$

We have $r_b(0) = 1$ and for $h > 0$ with $h = h_0 + h_1 b + \cdots + h_d b^d$ and $h_d \neq 0$, we have $r_b(h) = b^{-d-1} \sin^{-2}(h_d \pi / b)$.

First, let $\xi_1 = \cdots = \xi_m = 0$, then we have

$$\begin{aligned} \phi_{b,m}(x) &= 1 + \sum_{d=0}^{m-1} b^d \sum_{h_d=1}^{b-1} \frac{1}{b^{d+1}} \frac{1}{\sin^2(h_d \pi / b)} \\ &= 1 + \frac{1}{b} \sum_{d=0}^{m-1} \frac{b^2-1}{3} = 1 + m \frac{b^2-1}{3b}, \end{aligned}$$

where we used Corollary A.23 in Appendix A.

Let $i_0 = i_0(x)$ be such that $\xi_1 = \cdots = \xi_{i_0-1} = 0$ and $\xi_{i_0} \neq 0$ with $1 \leq i_0 \leq m$. Then we have

$$\phi_{b,m}(x) = 1 + \sum_{d=0}^{i_0-2} \sum_{h_d=1}^{b-1} r_b(h_d b^d) b^d + \sum_{h_{i_0-1}=1}^{b-1} r_b(h_{i_0-1} b^{i_0-1}) b^{i_0-1} \omega_b^{h_{i_0-1} \xi_{i_0}}.$$

Now

$$\begin{aligned} \sum_{d=0}^{i_0-2} \sum_{h_d=1}^{b-1} r_b(h_d b^d) b^d &= \sum_{d=0}^{i_0-2} \sum_{h_d=1}^{b-1} b^d \frac{1}{b^{d+1}} \frac{1}{\sin^2(h_d \pi / b)} \\ &= \frac{1}{b} \sum_{d=0}^{i_0-2} \sum_{h_d=1}^{b-1} \frac{1}{\sin^2(h_d \pi / b)} \\ &= \frac{1}{b} \sum_{d=0}^{i_0-2} \frac{b^2-1}{3} = \frac{b^2-1}{3b}(i_0 - 1), \end{aligned}$$

where we used Corollary A.23 again. Further, we have

$$\begin{aligned} \sum_{h_{i_0-1}=1}^{b-1} r_b(h_{i_0-1} b^{i_0-1}) b^{i_0-1} \omega_b^{h_{i_0-1} \xi_{i_0}} &= \sum_{k=1}^{b-1} b^{i_0-1} \omega_b^{k \xi_{i_0}} \frac{1}{b^{i_0}} \frac{1}{\sin^2(k\pi/b)} \\ &= \frac{1}{b} \sum_{k=1}^{b-1} \frac{\omega_b^{k \xi_{i_0}}}{\sin^2(k\pi/b)} \\ &= \frac{1}{b} \left(2\xi_{i_0}(\xi_{i_0} - b) + \frac{b^2-1}{3} \right), \end{aligned}$$

where we used Corollary A.23. It follows that

$$\phi_{b,m}(x) = 1 + i_0 \frac{b^2-1}{3b} + \frac{2}{b}\xi_{i_0}(\xi_{i_0} - b).$$

Thus, we have

$$\phi_{b,m}(x) = \begin{cases} 1 + i_0\frac{b^2-1}{3b} + \frac{2}{b}\xi_{i_0}(\xi_{i_0}-b) & \text{if } \xi_1 = \cdots = \xi_{i_0-1} = 0 \text{ and} \\ & \xi_{i_0} \neq 0 \text{ with } 1 \leq i_0 \leq m, \\ 1 + m\frac{b^2-1}{3b} & \text{otherwise.} \end{cases} \tag{10.6}$$

We summarise:

Proposition 10.20 *Let b be a prime and let $s, m \in \mathbb{N}$. Let $p \in \mathbb{Z}_b[x]$, with $\deg(p) = m$, and $\boldsymbol{q} \in G_{b,m}^s$. Using (10.4), (10.5) and (10.6), one can compute the quantities $R_b'(\boldsymbol{q}, p)$ and $R_{b,\boldsymbol{\gamma}}'(\boldsymbol{q}, p)$ in $O(b^m s)$ operations.*

Hence, $R_b'(\boldsymbol{q}, p)$ and $R_{b,\boldsymbol{\gamma}}'(\boldsymbol{q}, p)$ and therefore upper bounds on the (weighted) star discrepancy of $\mathcal{P}(\boldsymbol{q}, p)$ can be computed with reasonable effort. We exploit this fact later for a construction of vectors $\boldsymbol{q}$ (for given p) which yields a polynomial lattice point set with appropriate (weighted) star discrepancy. But first let us show some existence results.

10.2.1 Existence results

We show that for a given polynomial p, there always exists at least one vector $\boldsymbol{q}$ such that $\mathcal{P}(\boldsymbol{q}, p)$ has appropriate (weighted) star discrepancy. This was first carried out by Niederreiter [177, Theorem 4.43] (in the unweighted case) by an averaging argument. Here, we state a similar result which was proved in [46, Theorem 2.3]. The bound on the average in the subsequent theorem serves as a benchmark for constructions of polynomial lattices with low star discrepancy.

Theorem 10.21 *Let b be a prime, let $s, m \in \mathbb{N}$ and let $p \in \mathbb{Z}_b[x]$ be irreducible with $\deg(p) = m$. Then we have*

$$\frac{1}{|G_{b,m}^*|^s} \sum_{\boldsymbol{q} \in (G_{b,m}^*)^s} R_b'(\boldsymbol{q}, p) = \frac{1}{b^m - 1}\left(\left(1 + m\frac{b^2-1}{3b}\right)^s - 1 - sm\frac{b^2-1}{3b}\right).$$

Proof First, observe that $|G_{b,m}^*| = b^m - 1$. We have

$$\frac{1}{|G_{b,m}^*|^s} \sum_{\boldsymbol{q} \in (G_{b,m}^*)^s} R_b'(\boldsymbol{q}, p) = \frac{1}{(b^m - 1)^s} \sum_{\boldsymbol{q} \in (G_{b,m}^*)^s} \sum_{\boldsymbol{h} \in \mathcal{D}'_{\boldsymbol{q},p}} r_b(\boldsymbol{h})$$

$$= \frac{1}{(b^m - 1)^s} \sum_{\boldsymbol{h} \in G_{b,m}^s \setminus \{\boldsymbol{0}\}} r_b(\boldsymbol{h}) \sum_{\substack{\boldsymbol{q} \in (G_{b,m}^*)^s \\ \boldsymbol{h} \in \mathcal{D}'_{\boldsymbol{q},p}}} 1,$$

where we used (10.3) to substitute for $R_b'(\boldsymbol{q}, p)$ and changed the order of summation. The last summation is extended over all $\boldsymbol{q} \in (G_{b,m}^*)^s$ for which $\boldsymbol{h} \in \mathcal{D}'_{\boldsymbol{q},p}$. Hence, for a fixed $\boldsymbol{h} \in G_{b,m}^s \setminus \{\boldsymbol{0}\}$, we have

$$\sum_{\substack{\boldsymbol{q} \in (G_{b,m}^*)^s \\ \boldsymbol{h} \in \mathcal{D}'_{\boldsymbol{q},p}}} 1 = |\{\boldsymbol{q} \in (G_{b,m}^*)^s : \boldsymbol{h} \cdot \boldsymbol{q} \equiv 0 \pmod{p}\}|.$$

If $\boldsymbol{h} = (0, \ldots, 0, h_i, 0, \ldots, 0)$, with $h_i \neq 0$, then there is no polynomial $\boldsymbol{q} \in (G_{b,m}^*)^s$ such that $\boldsymbol{h} \cdot \boldsymbol{q} = h_i q_i \equiv 0 \pmod{p}$, as $q_i \neq 0$ and p is irreducible. Otherwise, the number of polynomials $\boldsymbol{q} \in (G_{b,m}^*)^s$ is $(b^m - 1)^{s-1}$. Therefore, we have

$$\frac{1}{|G_{b,m}^*|^s} \sum_{\boldsymbol{q} \in (G_{b,m}^*)^s} R_b'(\boldsymbol{q}, p)$$

$$= \frac{1}{b^m - 1} \sum_{\boldsymbol{h} \in G_{b,m}^s \setminus \{\boldsymbol{0}\}} r_b(\boldsymbol{h}) - \frac{1}{b^m - 1} \sum_{i=1}^{s} \sum_{h_i \in G_{b,m} \setminus \{0\}} r_b(h_i) \prod_{\substack{j=1 \\ j \neq i}}^{s} r_b(0).$$

The result now follows from the subsequent Lemma 10.22. □

Lemma 10.22 *For any prime number b, we have*

$$\sum_{\boldsymbol{h} \in G_{b,m}^s} r_b(\boldsymbol{h}) = \left(1 + m\frac{b^2 - 1}{3b}\right)^s.$$

Proof We have

$$\sum_{\boldsymbol{h} \in G_{b,m}^s} r_b(\boldsymbol{h}) = \sum_{\boldsymbol{h} \in G_{b,m}^s} \prod_{i=1}^{s} r_b(h_i) = \prod_{i=1}^{s} \sum_{h_i \in G_{b,m}} r_b(h_i) = \left(\sum_{h \in G_{b,m}} r_b(h) \right)^s.$$

Now for $h \in G_{b,m}$, with $\deg(h) = a - 1$, we write $h = h_0 + h_1 x + \cdots + h_{a-1}x^{a-1}$, where $h_{a-1} \neq 0$. Then

$$\begin{aligned}\sum_{h \in G_{b,m}} r_b(h) &= 1 + \sum_{a=1}^{m} \sum_{\substack{h \in G_{b,m} \\ \deg(h)=a-1}} r_b(h) \\ &= 1 + \sum_{a=1}^{m} \frac{1}{b^a} \sum_{\substack{h \in G_{b,m} \\ \deg(h)=a-1}} \frac{1}{\sin^2(h_{a-1}\pi/b)} \\ &= 1 + \sum_{a=1}^{m} \frac{1}{b^a} \sum_{h_{a-1}=1}^{b-1} b^{a-1} \frac{1}{\sin^2(h_{a-1}\pi/b)} \\ &= 1 + \frac{1}{b} \sum_{a=1}^{m} \sum_{h_{a-1}=1}^{b-1} \frac{1}{\sin^2(h_{a-1}\pi/b)}.\end{aligned}$$

From Corollary A.23 in Appendix A, we obtain $\sum_{h=1}^{b-1} \sin^{-2}(h\pi/b) = (b^2 - 1)/3$ and hence, the result follows. □

It is also possible to prove a result similar to Theorem 10.21 for polynomials p that are not necessarily irreducible, but one has to overcome some technical difficulties. For a general result, see [177, Theorem 4.43] or see [43, Theorem 5].

As a consequence of Theorem 10.21, we obtain the following existence result.

Corollary 10.23 *Let b be a prime, let $s, m \in \mathbb{N}$ and let $p \in \mathbb{Z}_b[x]$ be irreducible with $\deg(p) = m$. Then, for $0 \leq \alpha < 1$, there are more than $\alpha |G_{b,m}^*|^s$ vectors of polynomials $\boldsymbol{q} \in (G_{b,m}^*)^s$ such that*

$$D_{b^m}^*(\mathcal{P}(\boldsymbol{q}, p)) \leq \frac{s}{b^m} + \frac{1}{1-\alpha} \frac{1}{b^m - 1} \left(1 + m\frac{b^2-1}{3b}\right)^s.$$

Proof For $\varepsilon > 0$, we have

$$\begin{aligned}\sum_{\boldsymbol{q} \in (G_{b,m}^*)^s} R_b'(\boldsymbol{q}, p) &> \frac{\varepsilon}{b^m - 1} \left(1 + m\frac{b^2-1}{3b}\right)^s \\ &\times \left| \left\{ \boldsymbol{q} \in (G_{b,m}^*)^s \, : \, R_b'(\boldsymbol{q}, p) > \frac{\varepsilon}{b^m - 1} \left(1 + m\frac{b^2-1}{3b}\right)^s \right\} \right|.\end{aligned}$$

Hence, with Theorem 10.21 we obtain,

$$\left| \left\{ \boldsymbol{q} \in (G_{b,m}^*)^s \, : \, R_b'(\boldsymbol{q}, p) \leq \frac{\varepsilon}{b^m - 1} \left(1 + m\frac{b^2-1}{3b}\right)^s \right\} \right| > |G_{b,m}^*|^s \left(1 - \frac{1}{\varepsilon}\right),$$

and the result follows by substituting $\varepsilon = (1-\alpha)^{-1}$ and invoking Corollary 10.17. □

Hence, on average we get a star discrepancy of polynomial lattice point sets of order $O((\log N)^s/N)$ where $N = b^m$. If p is specialised to $p(x) = x^m$, then Larcher [134] proved that there exists a choice of $\boldsymbol{q} \in \mathbb{F}_b[x]^s$ for which the star discrepancy of the resulting point set $\mathcal{P}(\boldsymbol{q}, x^m)$ even satisfies

$$D_N^*(\mathcal{P}(\boldsymbol{q}, x^m)) < c\frac{(\log N)^{s-1} \log\log N}{N}$$

with a constant $c > 0$ only depending on b and s.

We turn to the weighted star discrepancy and compute the average of $R'_{b,\boldsymbol{\gamma}}(\boldsymbol{q}, p)$ over all $\boldsymbol{q} \in (G^*_{b,m})^s$.

Theorem 10.24 *Let b be a prime, let $s, m \in \mathbb{N}$ and let $p \in \mathbb{Z}_b[x]$ be irreducible with* $\deg(p) = m$. *Then we have*

$$\frac{1}{|G^*_{b,m}|^s} \sum_{\boldsymbol{q} \in (G^*_{b,m})^s} R'_{b,\boldsymbol{\gamma}}(\boldsymbol{q}, p) = \frac{1}{b^m - 1} \sum_{\substack{\mathfrak{u} \subseteq \mathcal{I}_s \\ |\mathfrak{u}| \geq 2}} \prod_{i \in \mathfrak{u}} \left(\gamma_i \left(m\frac{b^2-1}{3b}\right)\right) \prod_{i \notin \mathfrak{u}} (1 + \gamma_i).$$

The proof of this result follows exactly along the lines of the proof of Theorem 10.21 and is left to the reader as an exercise (see Exercise 10.8). The corresponding result without the restriction that p has to be irreducible can be found in [43, Theorem 1].

Corollary 10.25 *Let b be a prime, let $s, m \in \mathbb{N}$ and let $p \in \mathbb{Z}_b[x]$ be irreducible with* $\deg(p) = m$. *Then, for $0 \leq \alpha < 1$, there are more than $\alpha|G^*_{b,m}|^s$ vectors of polynomials $\boldsymbol{q} \in (G^*_{b,m})^s$ such that*

$$D^*_{b^m,\boldsymbol{\gamma}}(\mathcal{P}(\boldsymbol{q}, p)) \leq \sum_{\emptyset \neq \mathfrak{u} \subseteq \mathcal{I}_s} \gamma_{\mathfrak{u}} \left(1 - \left(1 - \frac{1}{b^m}\right)^{|\mathfrak{u}|}\right) + \frac{1}{1-\alpha}\frac{1}{b^m - 1} \prod_{i=1}^{s} \left(1 + \gamma_i \left(1 + m\frac{b^2-1}{3b}\right)\right).$$

This result can be proven in the same way as Corollary 10.23 and is therefore left as an exercise (see Exercise 10,9).

10.2.2 The component-by-component construction

Now that we know that for any given irreducible polynomial $p \in \mathbb{Z}_b[x]$ there exist a sufficiently large number of good vectors $\boldsymbol{q}$ of polynomials which yield polynomial lattice point sets with reasonably low (weighted) star discrepancy, we want to find such vectors by computer search. Unfortunately, a full search is not possible (except maybe for small values of m, s), since we have to check b^{ms} vectors of polynomials.

But at this point we get our cue from the analogy between polynomial lattice point sets and ordinary lattice point sets where the component-by-component (CBC) construction approach works very well (see Algorithm 3.50). We use the same idea for the polynomial case. This was carried out first in [45] for a different quality measure of polynomial lattice point sets (see Section 12.4).

We state the algorithm for the star- and the weighted star discrepancies.

Algorithm 10.26 *Given a prime b, $s, m \in \mathbb{N}$, and a polynomial $p \in \mathbb{Z}_b[x]$, with $\deg(p) = m$ (and a sequence $\boldsymbol{\gamma} = (\gamma_i)_{i \geq 1}$ of weights).*

1. *Choose $q_1 = 1$.*
2. *For $d > 1$, assume that we have already constructed $q_1, \ldots, q_{d-1} \in G^*_{b,m}$. Then find $q_d \in G^*_{b,m}$ which minimises the quantity $R'_b((q_1, \ldots, q_{d-1}, q_d), p)$ (or $R'_{b,\boldsymbol{\gamma}}((q_1, \ldots, q_{d-1}, q_d), p)$ in the weighted case) as a function of q_d.*

Remark 10.27 We have shown in Proposition 10.20 that the quantities $R'_b(\boldsymbol{q}, p)$ and $R'_{b,\boldsymbol{\gamma}}(\boldsymbol{q}, p)$ can be calculated in $O(b^m s)$ operations. Hence, the cost of Algorithm 10.26 is of $O(b^{2m} s^2)$ operations.

In the following theorem, we show that Algorithm 10.26 is guaranteed to find a good generating vector where the polynomial p is irreducible. A similar result for not necessarily irreducible polynomials is proven, but with much more technical effort, in [43, Theorem 2 and Theorem 6].

Theorem 10.28 *Let b be prime, let $s, m \in \mathbb{N}$, let $p \in \mathbb{Z}_b[x]$ be irreducible with $\deg(p) = m$ and let $\boldsymbol{\gamma} = (\gamma_i)_{i \geq 1}$ be a sequence of weights. Suppose that $\boldsymbol{q} = (q_1, \ldots, q_s) \in (G^*_{b,m})^s$ is constructed according to Algorithm 10.26 using R'_b (or $R'_{b,\boldsymbol{\gamma}}$ in the weighted case). Then, for all $1 \leq d \leq s$, we have*

$$R'_b((q_1, \ldots, q_d), p) \leq \frac{1}{b^m - 1}\left(1 + m\frac{b^2 - 1}{3b}\right)^d,$$

and

$$R'_{b,\boldsymbol{\gamma}}((q_1, \ldots, q_d), p) \leq \frac{1}{b^m - 1}\prod_{i=1}^{d}\left(1 + \gamma_i\left(1 + m\frac{b^2 - 1}{3b}\right)\right),$$

respectively.

Proof We prove the result only for the unweighted case. The weighted case can be shown in the same way and is left as an exercise (see Exercise 10.10).

Since p is irreducible, it follows that $R_b'(1, p) = 0$ and the result follows for $d = 1$. Suppose now that for some $2 \le d < s$, we have already constructed $\boldsymbol{q} \in (G_{b,m}^*)^d$ and

$$R_b'(\boldsymbol{q}, p) \le \frac{1}{b^m - 1}\left(1 + m\frac{b^2-1}{3b}\right)^d.$$

Now we consider $(\boldsymbol{q}, q_{d+1}) := (q_1, \ldots, q_d, q_{d+1})$. We have

$$\begin{aligned}
R_b'((\boldsymbol{q}, q_{d+1}), p) &= \sum_{(\boldsymbol{h}, h_{d+1}) \in \mathcal{D}'_{(\boldsymbol{q}, q_{d+1}), p}} r_b(\boldsymbol{h}) r_b(h_{d+1}) \\
&= \sum_{\boldsymbol{h} \in \mathcal{D}'_{\boldsymbol{q}, p}} r_b(\boldsymbol{h}) + \theta(q_{d+1}) \\
&= R_b'(\boldsymbol{q}, p) + \theta(q_{d+1}),
\end{aligned}$$

where we have separated out the $h_{d+1} = 0$ terms, and

$$\theta(q_{d+1}) = \sum_{h_{d+1} \in G_{b,m}^*} r_b(h_{d+1}) \sum_{\substack{\boldsymbol{h} \in G_{b,m}^d \\ (\boldsymbol{h}, h_{d+1}) \in \mathcal{D}'_{(\boldsymbol{q}, q_{d+1}), p}}} r_b(\boldsymbol{h}).$$

Here, the last summation is over all $\boldsymbol{h} \in G_{b,m}^d$ for which $(\boldsymbol{h}, h_{d+1}) \in \mathcal{D}'_{(\boldsymbol{q}, q_{d+1}), p}$.

Since q_{d+1} is a minimiser of $R_b'((\boldsymbol{q}, \cdot), p)$ and since the only dependence on q_{d+1} is in θ, it follows that q_{d+1} is also a minimiser of θ and hence, we obtain

$$\begin{aligned}
\theta(q_{d+1}) &\le \frac{1}{b^m - 1} \sum_{z \in G_{b,m}^*} \theta(z) \\
&\le \frac{1}{b^m - 1} \sum_{z \in G_{b,m}^*} \sum_{h_{d+1} \in G_{b,m}^*} r_b(h_{d+1}) \sum_{\substack{\boldsymbol{h} \in G_{b,m}^d \\ (\boldsymbol{h}, h_{d+1}) \in \mathcal{D}'_{(\boldsymbol{q}, z), p}}} r_b(\boldsymbol{h}) \\
&= \frac{1}{b^m - 1} \sum_{h_{d+1} \in G_{b,m}^*} r_b(h_{d+1}) \sum_{\boldsymbol{h} \in G_{b,m}^d} r_b(\boldsymbol{h}) \sum_{\substack{z \in G_{b,m}^* \\ (\boldsymbol{h}, h_{d+1}) \in \mathcal{D}'_{(\boldsymbol{q}, z), p}}} 1.
\end{aligned}$$

The condition $(\boldsymbol{h}, h_{d+1}) \in \mathcal{D}'_{(\boldsymbol{q}, z), p}$ is equivalent to the equation

$$z h_{d+1} \equiv -\boldsymbol{h} \cdot \boldsymbol{q} \pmod{p}.$$

Since $\gcd(h_{d+1}, p) = 1$, it follows that this congruence has exactly one solution $z \in G_{b,m}^*$ if $-\boldsymbol{h} \cdot \boldsymbol{q} \not\equiv 0 \pmod{p}$ and no solution if $-\boldsymbol{h} \cdot \boldsymbol{q} \equiv 0 \pmod{p}$. Therefore, we obtain

$$\begin{aligned}\theta(q_{d+1}) &\leq \frac{1}{b^m-1}\sum_{h_{d+1}\in G^*_{b,m}} r_b(h_{d+1}) \sum_{\boldsymbol{h}\in G^d_{b,m}} r_b(\boldsymbol{h})\\ &= \frac{1}{b^m-1}\left(1+m\frac{b^2-1}{3b}\right)^d \sum_{h_{d+1}\in G^*_{b,m}} r_b(h_{d+1}),\end{aligned}$$

where we have used Lemma 10.22. Now we obtain

$$\begin{aligned}R'_b((\boldsymbol{q},q_{d+1}),p) &\leq R'_b(\boldsymbol{q},p) + \frac{1}{b^m-1}\left(1+m\frac{b^2-1}{3b}\right)^d \sum_{h_{d+1}\in G^*_{b,m}} r_b(h_{d+1})\\ &\leq \frac{1}{b^m-1}\left(1+m\frac{b^2-1}{3b}\right)^d \sum_{h_{d+1}\in G_{b,m}} r_b(h_{d+1})\\ &= \frac{1}{b^m-1}\left(1+m\frac{b^2-1}{3b}\right)^{d+1},\end{aligned}$$

where we have used Lemma 10.22 again. The result follows by induction. □

From Corollary 10.17, Corollary 10.18 and Theorem 10.28, we obtain the following result.

Corollary 10.29 *Let b be prime, let $s,m\in\mathbb{N}$, let $p\in\mathbb{Z}_b[x]$ be irreducible with $\deg(p)=m$ and let $\boldsymbol{\gamma}=(\gamma_i)_{i\geq 1}$ be a sequence of weights. Suppose that $\boldsymbol{q}=(q_1,\ldots,q_s)\in(G^*_{b,m})^s$ is constructed according to Algorithm 10.26 using R'_b (or $R'_{b,\boldsymbol{\gamma}}$ in the weighted case). Then we have*

$$D^*_{b^m}(\mathcal{P}(\boldsymbol{q},p)) \leq \frac{s}{b^m} + \frac{1}{b^m-1}\left(1+m\frac{b^2-1}{3b}\right)^s,$$

and

$$\begin{aligned}D^*_{b^m,\boldsymbol{\gamma}}(\mathcal{P}(\boldsymbol{q},p)) &\leq \sum_{\emptyset\neq\mathfrak{u}\subseteq\mathcal{I}_s} \gamma_{\mathfrak{u}}\left(1-\left(1-\frac{1}{b^m}\right)^{|\mathfrak{u}|}\right)\\ &\quad + \frac{1}{b^m-1}\prod_{i=1}^s\left(1+\gamma_i\left(1+m\frac{b^2-1}{3b}\right)\right),\end{aligned}$$

respectively.

The following result can be proven in the same way as Corollary 5.45 (see Exercise 10.11).

Corollary 10.30 *Let b be prime, let $s, m \in \mathbb{N}$, let $p \in \mathbb{Z}_b[x]$ be irreducible with $\deg(p) = m$ and let $\boldsymbol{\gamma} = (\gamma_i)_{i \geq 1}$ be a sequence of weights.*

If $\sum_{i=1}^{\infty} \gamma_i < \infty$, then for any $\delta > 0$ there exists a constant $\widetilde{c}_{\boldsymbol{\gamma},\delta} > 0$, independent of s and m, such that the weighted star discrepancy of the polynomial lattice point set $\mathcal{P}(\boldsymbol{q}, p)$ whose generating vector $\boldsymbol{q} \in (G_{b,m}^*)^s$ is constructed according to Algorithm 10.26 using $R'_{b,\boldsymbol{\gamma}}$ satisfies

$$D_{b^m,\boldsymbol{\gamma}}^*(\mathcal{P}(\boldsymbol{q}, p)) \leq \frac{\widetilde{c}_{\boldsymbol{\gamma},\delta}}{b^{m(1-\delta)}}. \tag{10.7}$$

Remark 10.31 In the same way as in Corollary 5.46, we can use a superposition of polynomial lattice point sets $\mathcal{P}(\boldsymbol{q}, p)$ whose generating vectors $\boldsymbol{q} \in (G_{b,m}^*)^s$ are constructed according to Algorithm 10.26 using $R'_{b,\boldsymbol{\gamma}}$. In this way we can obtain, for any $s, N \in \mathbb{N}$, a point set $\mathcal{P}$ in $[0, 1)^s$ of cardinality N which satisfies $D_{N,\boldsymbol{\gamma}}^*(\mathcal{P}) \leq C_{\boldsymbol{\gamma},\delta} N^{-1+\delta}$, where $C_{\boldsymbol{\gamma},\delta}$ is independent of s and N whenever $\sum_{i=1}^{\infty} \gamma_i < \infty$. Hence, we have a constructive version of the strong tractability result for the weighted star discrepancy given in Corollary 5.46.

10.2.3 The construction of Korobov vectors

As already mentioned in Section 10.1, one can reduce the search space for generating vectors $\boldsymbol{q}$ by considering so-called Korobov vectors. Here one considers s-tuples $\boldsymbol{q} = (q_1, \ldots, q_s)$ of polynomials that are obtained by taking a polynomial $q \in G_{b,m}^*$ and putting $q_i \equiv q^{i-1} \pmod{p}$ with $\deg q_i < m = \deg(p)$, for $1 \leq i \leq s$. As before, we use the notation $\boldsymbol{v}_s(q) \equiv (1, q, q^2, \ldots, q^{s-1}) \pmod{p}$ for such s-tuples.

Algorithm 10.32 *Given a prime b, $s, m \in \mathbb{N}$, $s \geq 2$, and a polynomial $p \in \mathbb{Z}_b[x]$ with $\deg(p) = m$ (and a sequence $\boldsymbol{\gamma} = (\gamma_i)_{i \geq 1}$ of weights). Find $q \in G_{b,m}^*$ by minimising $R'_b(\boldsymbol{v}_s(q), p)$ (or $R'_{b,\boldsymbol{\gamma}}(\boldsymbol{v}_s(q), p)$ in the weighted case).*

Remark 10.33 We have shown in Proposition 10.20 that the quantities $R'_b(\boldsymbol{q}, p)$ and $R'_{b,\boldsymbol{\gamma}}(\boldsymbol{q}, p)$ can be calculated in $O(b^m s)$ operations. Hence, the cost of Algorithm 10.32 is of $O(b^{2m} s)$ operations. Note that, compared to Algorithm 10.26, the search cost is reduced by a factor s.

In the following theorem we show that Algorithm 10.32 is guaranteed to find a good generating vector where the polynomial p is irreducible. A similar result where p is the product of different monic irreducible polynomials is proved, but with much more technical effort, in [43, Theorem 4 and Theorem 8].

Theorem 10.34 *Let b be prime, let $s, m \in \mathbb{N}$, let $p \in \mathbb{Z}_b[x]$ be irreducible with $\deg(p) = m$ and let $\boldsymbol{\gamma} = (\gamma_i)_{i \geq 1}$ be a sequence of weights. Suppose that $q \in G_{b,m}^*$*

is constructed according to Algorithm 10.32 by using R'_b (or $R'_{b,\gamma}$ in the weighted case). Then we have

$$R'_b(\boldsymbol{v}_s(q), p) \leq \frac{s-1}{b^m-1}\left(1+m\frac{b^2-1}{3b}\right)^s,$$

and

$$R'_{b,\boldsymbol{\gamma}}(\boldsymbol{v}_s(q), p) \leq \frac{s-1}{b^m-1}\prod_{i=1}^{s}\left(1+\gamma_i\left(1+m\frac{b^2-1}{3b}\right)\right),$$

respectively.

Proof We prove the result only for the unweighted case. The weighted case can be shown in the same way and is left as an exercise (see Exercise 10.13).

Define

$$M_s(p) := \frac{1}{b^m-1}\sum_{z\in G^*_{b,m}} R'_b(\boldsymbol{v}_s(z), p).$$

It follows from Algorithm 10.32 that $R'_b(\boldsymbol{v}_s(q), p) \leq M_s(p)$. Hence, it suffices to show that $M_s(p)$ satisfies the bound. We have

$$\begin{aligned} M_s(p) &= \frac{1}{b^m-1}\sum_{z\in G^*_{b,m}}\sum_{\boldsymbol{h}\in\mathcal{D}'_{\boldsymbol{v}_s(z),p}} r_b(\boldsymbol{h}) \\ &= \frac{1}{b^m-1}\sum_{\boldsymbol{h}\in G^s_{b,m}\setminus\{\boldsymbol{0}\}} r_b(\boldsymbol{h}) \sum_{\substack{z\in G^*_{b,m} \\ \boldsymbol{h}\in\mathcal{D}'_{\boldsymbol{v}_s(z),p}}} 1. \end{aligned}$$

The condition $\boldsymbol{h} \in \mathcal{D}'_{\boldsymbol{v}_s(z),p}$, where $\boldsymbol{h} = (h_1, \ldots, h_s) \in G^s_{b,m} \setminus \{\boldsymbol{0}\}$, is equivalent to $h_1 + h_2 z + \cdots + h_s z^{s-1} \equiv 0 \pmod{p}$.

Now we recall that for an irreducible polynomial $p \in \mathbb{Z}_b[x]$, with $\deg(p) = m \geq 1$, and a non-zero $(h_1, \ldots, h_s) \in \mathbb{Z}_b[x]^s$ with $\deg(h_i) < m$ for $1 \leq i \leq s$, the congruence

$$h_1 + h_2 z + \cdots + h_s z^{s-1} \equiv 0 \pmod{p}$$

has at most $s-1$ solutions $z \in G^*_{b,m}$. Thus, we have

$$M_s(p) \leq \frac{s-1}{b^m-1}\sum_{\boldsymbol{h}\in G^s_{b,m}} r_b(\boldsymbol{h}).$$

Hence, the result follows from Lemma 10.22. □

From Corollary 10.17, Corollary 10.18 and Theorem 10.34, we obtain the following result.

Corollary 10.35 *Let b be prime, let $s, m \in \mathbb{N}$, let $p \in \mathbb{Z}_b[x]$ be irreducible with $\deg(p) = m$ and let $\boldsymbol{\gamma} = (\gamma_i)_{i \geq 1}$ be a sequence of weights. Suppose that $q \in G_{b,m}^*$ is constructed according to Algorithm 10.32 by using R_b' (or $R_{b,\boldsymbol{\gamma}}'$ in the weighted case). Then we have*

$$D_{b^m}^*(\mathcal{P}(\boldsymbol{v}_s(q), p)) \leq \frac{s}{b^m} + \frac{s-1}{b^m - 1}\left(1 + m\frac{b^2-1}{3b}\right)^s,$$

and

$$D_{b^m,\boldsymbol{\gamma}}^*(\mathcal{P}(\boldsymbol{v}_s(q), p)) \leq \sum_{\emptyset \neq \mathfrak{u} \subseteq \mathcal{I}_s} \gamma_{\mathfrak{u}} \left(1 - \left(1 - \frac{1}{b^m}\right)^{|\mathfrak{u}|}\right)$$
$$+ \frac{s-1}{b^m - 1} \prod_{i=1}^{s} \left(1 + \gamma_i \left(1 + m\frac{b^2-1}{3b}\right)\right),$$

respectively.

10.3 Fast CBC-construction of polynomial lattice point sets

In the previous section we showed how to construct, for a given modulus p, a generating vector $\boldsymbol{q}$ which yields a polynomial lattice point set $\mathcal{P}(\boldsymbol{q}, p)$ with small (weighted) star discrepancy using a component-by-component algorithm. The cost of the algorithm for a polynomial lattice point set in dimension s and of cardinality b^m was at least of order $O(s^2 b^{2m})$ operations. Hence, the CBC-algorithm can only be applied for moderately large values of b^m. However, we are interested in polynomial lattice point sets with a large number of points. Thus, we need to reduce the factor b^{2m} in the construction cost to get an applicable construction method also for large values of b^m.

A breakthrough for this problem was first achieved by Nuyens and Cools [204] using fast Fourier transform (FFT) methods for the construction of classical lattice point sets. Due to the similarities between ordinary and polynomial lattice point sets, it transpires that their methods can also be carried over to the polynomial case (see [205]). In this way it is possible to construct, for a given polynomial p with $\deg(p) = m$, an s-dimensional generating vector $\boldsymbol{q}$ in $O(smb^m)$ operations, compared to $O(s^2 b^{2m})$ operations for the usual CBC-algorithm.

In the following, we explain this so-called, *fast component-by-component construction* by example of the construction of polynomial lattice point sets, where we use the star discrepancy as a quality measure. The same ideas also apply to the weighted star discrepancy and other quality measures. Our intention is not to give a ready-to-use algorithm. We just want to explain the basic ideas leading to the drastic speed-up of the CBC algorithm. Implementations of the fast algorithm using Matlab can be found in [203, 205].

Let b be a prime. Throughout this section, we consider the polynomial $p \in \mathbb{Z}_b[x]$ with $\deg(p) = m$ to be irreducible.

Using Algorithm 10.26, we construct, component by component, a generating vector $\boldsymbol{q} = (q_1, \ldots, q_s) \in (G_{b,m}^*)^s$ such that for all $1 \le d \le s$, the quantity $R_b'((q_1, \ldots, q_d), p)$ is minimised with respect to q_d for fixed $q_1, \ldots, q_{d-1}$.

Assume that $q_1, \ldots, q_{d-1}$ are already constructed. Then we have to find $q \in G_{b,m}^*$, which minimises

$$R_b'(q) := R_b'((q_1, \ldots, q_{d-1}, q), p) = -1 + \frac{1}{b^m} \sum_{n=0}^{b^m-1} \prod_{i=1}^{d} \phi_{b,m}(x_{n,i})$$

$$= -1 + \frac{1}{b^m} \sum_{n=0}^{b^m-1} \prod_{i=1}^{d-1} \phi_{b,m}(x_{n,i})\, \phi_{b,m}\left(\upsilon_m\left(\frac{q(x)n(x)}{p(x)}\right)\right).$$

We now have a closer look at the last formula. First notice that $\phi_{b,m}(x_{n,i}) = \phi_{b,m}\left(\upsilon_m\left(\frac{q_i(x)n(x)}{p(x)}\right)\right)$ takes on, at most, b^m different values, since $x_{n,i} \in \{0, b^{-m}, 2b^{-m}, \ldots, (b^m-1)b^{-m}\}$ for all $0 \le n < b^m$ and $1 \le i \le s$. These values are used in each iteration step; hence, they can be computed and stored in a table before using Algorithm 10.26. As this table can be computed in $O(mb^m)$ operations, it follows that the computational cost of this step is lower than the cost of Algorithm 10.26 (even taking into account the speed-ups which we introduce below).

For $n = 0$, we have $\phi_{b,m}\left(\upsilon_m\left(\frac{q(x)n(x)}{p(x)}\right)\right) = \phi_{b,m}(0)$, which does not depend on q. Hence, we can write

$$R_b'(q) = -1 + \frac{(\phi_{b,m}(0))^d}{b^m} + \frac{1}{b^m} \sum_{n=1}^{b^m-1} \prod_{i=1}^{d-1} \phi_{b,m}(x_{n,i})\, \phi_{b,m}\left(\upsilon_m\left(\frac{q(x)n(x)}{p(x)}\right)\right).$$

Note that the product $\prod_{i=1}^{d-1} \phi_{b,m}(x_{n,i}) = \prod_{i=1}^{d-1} \phi_{b,m}\left(\upsilon_m\left(\frac{q_i(x)n(x)}{p(x)}\right)\right)$ does not depend on q as well and hence, it remains fixed in the iteration from dimension $d-1$ to d in Algorithm 10.26. We collect these products in a column vector $\boldsymbol{\eta}_{d-1} = (\eta_{d-1}(1), \ldots, \eta_{d-1}(b^m-1))^\top$, where $\eta_{d-1}(n) = \prod_{i=1}^{d-1} \phi_{b,m}(x_{n,i})$. This allows us to write

$$R_b'(q) = -1 + \frac{(\phi_{b,m}(0))^d}{b^m} + \frac{1}{b^m} \sum_{n=1}^{b^m-1} \eta_{d-1}(n) \phi_{b,m}\left(\upsilon_m\left(\frac{q(x)n(x)}{p(x)}\right)\right).$$

Note that the vector $\boldsymbol{\eta}_{d-1}$ remains fixed for fixed d.

Set $\boldsymbol{\eta}_0 = (1, \ldots, 1) \in \mathbb{R}^{b^m-1}$. Before the iteration step in which we find q_d, we compute $\eta_{d-1}(n) = \eta_{d-2}(n)\phi_{b,m}(x_{n,d-1})$ for $n = 1, \ldots, b^m - 1$. Hence, the cost of computing $\boldsymbol{\eta}_1, \ldots, \boldsymbol{\eta}_{d-1}$ is of $O(db^m)$ operations. The cost of calculating $\boldsymbol{\eta}_1, \ldots, \boldsymbol{\eta}_{d-1}$ is therefore less than the cost of Algorithm 10.26 and is not significant in the computational cost of the component-by-component algorithm.

Let us estimate the number of operations needed for Algorithm 10.26. The main part is the computation of the sum

$$\sum_{n=1}^{b^m-1} \eta_{d-1}(n)\phi_{b,m}\left(v_m\left(\frac{q(x)n(x)}{p(x)}\right)\right),$$

which needs to be calculated for $q = 1, \ldots, b^m - 1$. Hence, we require $O(sb^{2m})$ operations for this part.

Therefore, we obtain that the simple modifications introduced above already result in a reduced construction cost of Algorithm 10.26 of $O(sb^{2m})$ operations by using $O(b^m)$ memory space (this method was already applied in [46, Section 5]).

For brevity, hereforth we write $\omega := \phi_{b,m} \circ v_m$. We define the $(b^m - 1) \times (b^m - 1)$ matrix

$$\Omega_p := \left(\omega\left(\frac{q(x)n(x)}{p(x)}\right)\right)_{\substack{q=1,\ldots,b^m-1\\ n=1,\ldots,b^m-1}}.$$

Further let $\boldsymbol{R}'_b = (R'_b(1), \ldots, R'_b(b^m - 1))^\top$ be the column vector collecting the quantities $R'_b(q)$ and $\boldsymbol{1}$ be the $(b^m - 1)$-dimensional column-vector whose components are all one. Then we have

$$\boldsymbol{R}'_b = \left(-1 + \frac{(\phi_{b,m}(0))^d}{b^m}\right)\boldsymbol{1} + \frac{1}{b^m}\Omega_p\boldsymbol{\eta}_{d-1}.$$

As we are only interested in which q minimises $R'_b(q)$, but not the value of $R'_b(q)$ itself, we need only to compute $\Omega_p\boldsymbol{\eta}_{d-1}$. We can now rewrite Algorithm 10.26 in matrix form.

Algorithm 10.36

1. *Compute the values* $\omega\left(\frac{n(x)}{p(x)}\right)$ *for* $n = 0, 1, \ldots, b^m - 1$ *and store them in a table* T.
2. *Determine* Ω_p *using table* T.
3. *For* $d = 1, \ldots, s$ *do:*
   (a) *if* $d = 1$ *set* $\eta_0 = \boldsymbol{1} = (1, \ldots, 1)^\top$, *and if* $d > 1$ *set* $\eta_{d-1}(n) := \eta_{d-2}(n)\omega\left(\frac{q_{d-1}(x)n(x)}{p(x)}\right)$ *for all* $0 \le n < b^m$ *and store the vector* $\boldsymbol{\eta}_{d-1} = (\eta_{d-1}(0), \ldots, \eta_{d-1}(b^m - 1))^\top$.

(b) *compute* $\boldsymbol{A} = \Omega_p \boldsymbol{\eta}_{d-1}$, *where* $\boldsymbol{A} = (a(1), \ldots, a(b^m - 1))^\top$;
(c) *set* $q_d := \operatorname{argmin}_{1 \le q < b^m} a(q)$;
(d) *if* $d < s$ *increase* d *by* 1, *otherwise exit;*

In total we end up with $O(sb^{2m})$ operations for the generation of the s-dimensional vector $\boldsymbol{q}$. However, from the formulation of Algorithm 10.36 it is evident that the construction cost of $O(sb^{2m})$ operations could be reduced if we find an algorithm for the matrix-vector multiplication $\Omega_p \boldsymbol{\eta}_{d-1}$ costing less than $O(b^{2m})$ operations.

Hence, let us look more closely at the matrix-vector product $\Omega_p \boldsymbol{\eta}$. The entries of this matrix are of the form $\omega\left(\frac{q(x)n(x)}{p(x)}\right)$, where the product of the non-zero polynomials q and n has to be evaluated in the field $\mathbb{Z}_b[x]/(p)$, and thus modulo p. Since the multiplicative group of every finite field is cyclic, we can find a primitive element g which generates all elements of $(\mathbb{Z}_b[x]/(p))^*$; that is, there is a $g \in (\mathbb{Z}_b[x]/(p))^*$ such that $(\mathbb{Z}_b[x]/(p))^* = \{g^0, g^1, g^2, \ldots, g^{b^m-1}\}$. Thus, we can write the product of any non-zero polynomials $q, n \in \mathbb{Z}_b[x]/(p)$ as a power of the polynomial g. Nuyens and Cools [204, 205] suggest permuting the rows of Ω_p by the positive powers of the primitive polynomial g and the columns by the negative powers of the same primitive polynomial at this stage. This procedure is often called Rader's transform, since it goes back to an idea of Rader's [224].

We describe the Rader transform now in detail. Let $g(x)$ be a primitive element in $(\mathbb{Z}_b[x]/(p))^*$. We define a $(b^m - 1) \times (b^m - 1)$ matrix $\Pi(g) = (\pi_{k,l}(g))_{1 \le k,l < b^m}$ where

$$\pi_{k,l}(g) = \begin{cases} 1 & \text{if } k(x) \equiv g(x)^l \pmod{p(x)}, \\ 0 & \text{otherwise.} \end{cases}$$

Here, $k(x)$ denotes the polynomial which is associated with the integer k. Since g is a primitive element, it follows that each row and each column of $\Pi(g)$ has exactly one entry which is 1 and the remaining entries are 0. Further, $\Pi(g)\Pi(g)^\top = I$, the identity matrix. In fact, the matrix $\Pi(g)$ is a permutation matrix; that is, for any $(b^m - 1) \times (b^m - 1)$ matrix C, $\Pi(g)C$ just changes the order of the rows of C and $C\Pi(g)$ only changes the order of the columns of C.

Let $C = (c_{k,l})_{1 \le k,l < b^m}$ and

$$C = \Pi(g)\Omega_p\Pi(g^{-1}).$$

Then

$$c_{k,l} = \sum_{u,v=1}^{b^m-1} \pi_{u,k}(g)\omega\left(\frac{u(x)v(x)}{p(x)}\right)\pi_{v,l}(g^{-1}) = \omega\left(\frac{g(x)^k g(x)^{-l}}{p(x)}\right).$$

Let $c_r = \omega\left(\frac{g(x)^r}{p(x)}\right)$. Note that $c_r = c_{r'}$ for all $r, r' \in \mathbb{Z}$ with $r \equiv r' \pmod{b^m - 1}$, since $g(x)^{b^m-1} = 1$. Then we have $c_{k,l} = c_{k-l}$ and therefore we obtain

$$C = \begin{pmatrix} c_0 & c_{-1} & \cdots & \cdots & c_2 & c_1 \\ c_1 & c_0 & c_{-1} & \cdots & \cdots & c_2 \\ \vdots & \ddots & \ddots & \ddots & & \vdots \\ \vdots & & \ddots & \ddots & \ddots & \vdots \\ c_{-2} & \cdots & \cdots & c_1 & c_0 & c_{-1} \\ c_{-1} & c_{-2} & \cdots & \cdots & c_1 & c_0 \end{pmatrix}. \tag{10.8}$$

Matrices of the form C are called *circulant*. In general, a circulant matrix $C_n = \mathrm{circ}(\boldsymbol{c})$ of order n is a $n \times n$ matrix defined by the n elements of a vector $\boldsymbol{c} = (c_0, c_1, \ldots, c_{n-1})^\top$ as

$$C_n = \begin{pmatrix} c_0 & c_{n-1} & \cdots & \cdots & c_2 & c_1 \\ c_1 & c_0 & c_{n-1} & \cdots & \cdots & c_2 \\ \vdots & \ddots & \ddots & \ddots & & \vdots \\ \vdots & & \ddots & \ddots & \ddots & \vdots \\ c_{n-2} & \cdots & \cdots & c_1 & c_0 & c_{n-1} \\ c_{n-1} & c_{n-2} & \cdots & \cdots & c_1 & c_0 \end{pmatrix}.$$

For such a matrix, we set $c_{k'} = c_k$ for all $k, k' \in \mathbb{Z}$ such that $k \equiv k' \pmod{n}$.

Note that the circulant matrix C_n is fully determined by its first column $\boldsymbol{c}$. Such matrices have a similarity transform which has the Fourier matrix as its eigenvectors.

For $n \in \mathbb{N}$, let $F_n := \frac{1}{\sqrt{n}}(f_{k,l})_{k,l=0}^{n-1}$ be the Fourier matrix of order n given by $f_{k,l} = \omega_n^{kl}$, where $\omega_n = \mathrm{e}^{2\pi \mathrm{i}/n}$. Note that F_n is symmetric and $F_n\overline{F}_n = I$, the identity matrix.

Furthermore, let $\mathrm{diag}(a_1, \ldots, a_n)$ be the $n \times n$ diagonal matrix $A = (A_{i,j})_{i,j=1}^n$ with $A_{i,i} = a_i$ for $1 \le i \le n$ and $A_{i,j} = 0$ for $i \neq j$.

We need the subsequent lemma (see also [30, Theorem 3.2.2]).

Lemma 10.37 *A circulant matrix $C_n = \mathrm{circ}(\boldsymbol{c})$, with first column $\boldsymbol{c} = (c_0, c_{n-1}, c_{n-2}, \ldots, c_1)^\top$, of order n, has a similarity transform $C_n = F_n^{-1} D F_n$, where the diagonal matrix $D = \mathrm{diag}(p_{\boldsymbol{c}}(1), p_{\boldsymbol{c}}(\omega_n), \ldots, p_{\boldsymbol{c}}(\omega_n^{n-1}))$, and where $p_{\boldsymbol{c}}(z) := c_0 + c_1 z + \cdots + c_{n-1} z^{n-1}$.*

Proof Let $D = (d_{k,l})_{0 \le k,l < n}$ and

$$D = F_n C_n \overline{F}_n.$$

Then we have

$$d_{k,l} = \frac{1}{n} \sum_{u,v=0}^{n-1} \omega_n^{ku} c_{u-v} \omega_n^{-lv} = \frac{1}{n} \sum_{u=0}^{n-1} \omega_n^{u(k-l)} \sum_{v=0}^{n-1} c_{u-v} \omega_n^{l(u-v)}.$$

We have $\sum_{v=0}^{n-1} c_{u-v} \omega_n^{l(u-v)} = p_c(\omega_n^l)$ and therefore

$$d_{k,l} = p_c(\omega_n^l) \frac{1}{n} \sum_{u=0}^{n-1} \omega_n^{u(l-k)}.$$

The result now follows by noting that $\frac{1}{n} \sum_{u=0}^{n-1} \omega_n^{u(l-k)} = 1$ if $l = k$ and 0 otherwise. □

Hence, we have shown that

$$\Omega_p = \Pi(g)^\top \overline{F}_{b^m-1} D F_{b^m-1} \Pi(g^{-1})^\top,$$

where $\Pi(g)^\top, \Pi(g^{-1})^\top$ are permutation matrices, F_{b^m-1} is a Fourier matrix, $\overline{F}_{b^m-1}$ its complex conjugate and D is a diagonal matrix.

For any vector $\boldsymbol{x} = (x_1, \ldots, x_{b^m-1})^\top \in (\mathbb{C}^n)^\top$ the matrix-vector multiplications $\Pi(g)^\top \boldsymbol{x}$, $D\boldsymbol{x}$ and $\Pi(g^{-1})^\top \boldsymbol{x}$ can be done in $O(n)$ operations. Hence, it only remains to show that $F_{b^m-1}\boldsymbol{x}$ and $\overline{F}_{b^m-1}\boldsymbol{x}$ can be computed in $O(n \log n)$ operations. Since $\overline{F}_{b^m-1}\boldsymbol{x} = \overline{F_{b^m-1}\overline{\boldsymbol{x}}}$, it is enough to show that $F_{b^m-1}\boldsymbol{x}$ can be computed in $O(n \log n)$ operations. This can be done using the fast Fourier transform; see for instance [25, 83].

We illustrate this procedure for $b = 2$, the general case is given as exercise (Exercise 10.15). Note that the matrix C given in (10.8) is a $(2^m - 1) \times (2^m - 1)$ matrix. We extend this matrix by one row and one column to obtain

$$T = \begin{pmatrix} c_0 & c_{-1} & \cdots & \cdots & c_2 & c_1 & 0 \\ c_1 & c_0 & c_{-1} & \cdots & \cdots & c_2 & c_1 \\ \vdots & \ddots & \ddots & \ddots & & \vdots & c_2 \\ \vdots & & \ddots & \ddots & \ddots & \vdots & \vdots \\ & & & & & & \vdots \\ c_{-2} & \cdots & \cdots & c_1 & c_0 & c_{-1} & \vdots \\ c_{-1} & c_{-2} & \cdots & \cdots & c_1 & c_0 & c_{-1} \\ 0 & c_{-1} & c_{-2} & \cdots & \cdots & c_1 & c_0 \end{pmatrix}.$$

The $2^m \times 2^m$ matrix T is not a circulant matrix anymore, but it is still a Toeplitz matrix. To obtain a circulant matrix again, let

$$R = \begin{pmatrix} 0 & 0 & c_{-1} & \dots & \dots & c_2 & c_1 \\ 0 & 0 & 0 & c_{-1} & \dots & \dots & c_2 \\ c_1 & \ddots & \ddots & \ddots & \ddots & \vdots & \vdots \\ \vdots & \ddots & \ddots & \ddots & \ddots & c_{-1} & \vdots \\ \vdots & \dots & c_1 & 0 & 0 & 0 & c_{-1} \\ c_{-2} & \dots & \dots & c_1 & 0 & 0 & 0 \\ c_{-1} & c_{-2} & \dots & \dots & c_1 & 0 & 0 \end{pmatrix}.$$

Then the matrix

$$C' = \begin{pmatrix} T & R \\ R & T \end{pmatrix}$$

is a circulant matrix of size $2^{m+1} \times 2^{m+1}$.

Let $\boldsymbol{x} = (x_0, \dots, x_{2^m-1})^\top \in (\mathbb{C}^{2^m-1})^\top$ be a column vector and assume that we want to multiply the matrix C, given by (10.8), by $\boldsymbol{x}$. Then we can do so by multiplying the matrix C' by the vector $\boldsymbol{x}' = (x_0, \dots, x_{2^m-1}, 0, \dots, 0)^\top \in (\mathbb{C}^{2^{m+1}})^\top$. Let $\boldsymbol{y}' = (y_0, \dots, y_{2^{m+1}})^\top = C'\boldsymbol{x}'$. Then $\boldsymbol{y} = (y_0, \dots, y_{2^m-1})^\top = C\boldsymbol{x}$. Hence, we can use Lemma 10.37 with $n = 2^{m+1}$ (rather than $n = 2^m - 1$). This simplifies the FFT algorithm. The following result was shown by Cooley and Tukey [25].

Theorem 10.38 *Let $F_{2^{m+1}} = 2^{-(m+1)/2}(\omega_{2^{m+1}}^{kl})_{0 \le k,l < 2^{m+1}}$ be a Fourier matrix. Let $\boldsymbol{u} = (u_0, \dots, u_{2^{m+1}-1})^\top \in (\mathbb{C}^{2^{m+1}})^\top$ be given. Then the matrix-vector product $F_{2^{m+1}}\boldsymbol{u}$ can be computed in $O((m+1)2^{m+1})$ operations.*

Proof Let $\boldsymbol{z} = (z_0, \dots, z_{2^{m+1}-1})^\top = F_{2^{m+1}}\boldsymbol{u}$, where $\boldsymbol{u} = (u_0, \dots, u_{2^{m+1}-1})^\top \in (\mathbb{C}^{2^{m+1}})^\top$. Then

$$2^{(m+1)/2} z_k = \sum_{l=0}^{2^{m+1}-1} \omega_{2^{m+1}}^{kl} u_l \quad \text{for } 0 \le k < 2^{m+1}.$$

Let $k = \kappa_0 + \kappa_1 2 + \dots + \kappa_m 2^m$ and $l = \lambda_0 + \lambda_1 2 + \dots + \lambda_m 2^m$, where $0 \le \kappa_0, \dots, \kappa_m, \lambda_0, \dots, \lambda_m \le 1$. Further, let

$$G_0(\lambda_0, \dots, \lambda_{m-1}, \kappa_0) = \sum_{\lambda_m=0}^{1} \omega_2^{\kappa_0 \lambda_m} u_{\lambda_0 + \lambda_1 2 + \dots + \lambda_m 2^m}, \tag{10.9}$$

and for $0 < r \leq m$, let

$$G_r(\lambda_0, \ldots, \lambda_{m-r-1}, \kappa_0, \ldots, \kappa_r) \tag{10.10}$$
$$= \sum_{\lambda_{m-r}=0}^{1} \omega_{2^{r+1}}^{(\kappa_0+\cdots+\kappa_r 2^r)(\lambda_{m-r}+\cdots+\lambda_m 2^r)} G_{r-1}(\lambda_0, \ldots, \lambda_{m-r}, \kappa_0, \ldots, \kappa_{r+1}).$$

Then we have

$$G_r(\lambda_0, \ldots, \lambda_{m-r-1}, \kappa_0, \ldots, \kappa_r) = \sum_{\lambda_{m-r}=0}^{1} \cdots \sum_{\lambda_m=0}^{1} \omega_{2^{m+1}}^{kl} u_{\lambda_0+\cdots+\lambda_m 2^m}$$

and hence,

$$z_k = 2^{-(m+1)/2} G_m(\kappa_0, \ldots, \kappa_m),$$

for all $0 \leq k = \kappa_0 + \cdots + \kappa_m 2^m < 2^{m+1}$.

We now compute G_r recursively.

For $r = 0, \ldots, m$ compute $G_r(\lambda_0, \ldots, \lambda_{m-r-1}, \kappa_0, \ldots, \kappa_r)$ for all $0 \leq \lambda_0, \ldots, \lambda_{m-r-1}, \kappa_0, \ldots, \kappa_r \leq 1$ using (10.10). For each r, this also requires $O(2^{m+1})$ operations.

Overall we require $O((m+1)2^{m+1})$ operations to compute G_m. Hence, we can compute z in $O((m+1)2^{m+1})$ operations. □

Thus, we obtain the following result.

Corollary 10.39 *Let Ω_p be defined as above and let $\boldsymbol{x} \in (\mathbb{C}^n)^\top$ be a column vector. Then the matrix-vector product $\Omega_p \boldsymbol{x}$ can be computed in $O(mb^m)$ operations.*

Therefore, Algorithm 10.36 requires only $O(smb^m)$ operations by using $O(b^m)$ memory space (compared to $O(sb^{2m})$ operations). This is a significant speed-up compared to a straightforward implementation of Algorithm 10.36. Only through this reduction of the construction cost does the CBC algorithm become applicable for the generation of polynomial lattice point sets with reasonably large cardinality.

10.4 Extensible polynomial lattice point sets

A disadvantage of polynomial lattice rules used to be that the number of quadrature points has to be fixed in advance. The same problem also appears for ordinary lattice rules. Hickernell and Hong [105] introduced a way out by modifying lattice rules in such a way that they can be extended arbitrarily in the number of quadrature points. Such lattice rules are called extensible lattice rules. The existence of such rules of good quality has been shown by Hickernell and Niederreiter [107]. Extensible polynomial lattice rules, on the other hand, were first mentioned in [153] and the existence of good extensible polynomial lattice rules was shown by Niederreiter [182].

To define extensible polynomial lattices, we follow [182]. We call a sequence $P = (p_k)_{k\geq 1}$ of polynomials from $\mathbb{Z}_b[x]$, b a prime, a *divisibility chain* in $\mathbb{Z}_b[x]$ if p_k divides p_{k+1} and $1 \leq \deg(p_k) < \deg(p_{k+1})$ for all $k \in \mathbb{N}$.

With a given divisibility chain P, we now associate the set Y_P of all P-adic polynomials; that is, Y_P is the set of all formal sums

$$A = \sum_{k=0}^{\infty} a_k p_k$$

with $p_0 = 1$, $a_k \in \mathbb{Z}_b[x]$ and $\deg(a_k) < \deg(p_{k+1}/p_k)$ for all $k \in \mathbb{N}_0$. Note that if $a_k = 0$ for all sufficiently large k, then A is just a polynomial in $\mathbb{Z}_b[x]$ and thus $\mathbb{Z}_b[x] \subseteq Y_P$. Subsequently, we call the polynomials a_k the *coefficients of* A or simply *coefficients*.

Note that by taking the residue class ring of all elements of Y_P taken modulo p_k, for $k \in \mathbb{N}$, we obtain all polynomials in $\mathbb{Z}_b[x]$ with degree smaller than $\deg(p_k)$. We use the following notation. Let $\boldsymbol{Q} = (Q_1, \ldots, Q_s) \in Y_P^s$, then by $\boldsymbol{q}_k$ we denote the vector obtained by $\boldsymbol{q}_k \equiv \boldsymbol{Q} \pmod{p_k}$ for $k \in \mathbb{N}$, i.e. $\boldsymbol{q}_k = (q_{1,k}, \ldots, q_{s,k})$ with $q_{i,k} \equiv Q_i \pmod{p_k}$ and where $\deg(q_{i,k}) < \deg(p_k)$ for all $1 \leq i \leq s$ and all $k \in \mathbb{N}$.

Thus, for a given divisibility chain P and a generating vector $\boldsymbol{Q} \in Y_P^s$, we obtain for each $k \in \mathbb{N}$ a polynomial lattice $\mathcal{P}(\boldsymbol{q}_k, p_k)$ such that

$$\mathcal{P}(\boldsymbol{q}_k, p_k) \subseteq \mathcal{P}(\boldsymbol{q}_{k+1}, p_{k+1}) \text{ for all } k \in \mathbb{N}.$$

Finally, we can give the following definition.

Definition 10.40 The set

$$\mathcal{P}(\boldsymbol{Q}, P) := \bigcup_{k=1}^{\infty} \mathcal{P}(\boldsymbol{q}_k, p_k)$$

is called an *extensible polynomial lattice point set*. A sequence of quadrature rules that uses $\mathcal{P}(\boldsymbol{q}_k, p_k)$ as quadrature points is called an *extensible polynomial lattice rule*.

As a quality measure for an extensible polynomial lattice, we use in the following the quantity $R'_{b,\boldsymbol{\gamma}}$ (but of course we could also use R'_b) where the weights should be of product form. First, we extend the definition of $R'_{b,\boldsymbol{\gamma}}$ by setting

$$R'_{b,\boldsymbol{\gamma}}(\boldsymbol{Q}, p_k) := R'_{b,\boldsymbol{\gamma}}(\boldsymbol{q}_k, p_k).$$

For $\mathbf{A} = (A_1, A_2, \ldots) \in Y_P^{\infty}$ and $s \in \mathbb{N}$, we define the projection

$$\mathbf{A}^{(s)} := (A_1, \ldots, A_s) \in Y_P^s.$$

Though Niederreiter's existence result as well as the construction algorithm below would also work in a more general setting, in the following, we assume that $p_k = p^k$, where p is an irreducible polynomial in $\mathbb{Z}_b[x]$ (for example $p(x) = x$ would be a possible choice). This simplifies the notation somewhat. The number of points in $\mathcal{P}(\boldsymbol{q}_k, p^k)$ is in this case given by $b^{k \deg(p)}$. Before we state Niederreiter's existence result for extensible polynomial lattices, we need to introduce some probability measures. Let Y_P be the set of P-adic polynomials and let Y_P^* be the subset of all non-zero polynomials which are not divisible by p. Let $V_{P,k}$ denote the subset of Y_P^* of all P-adic polynomials $A = \sum_{k=0}^{\infty} a_k p^k$ for which the first k coefficients $a_0, \ldots, a_{k-1}$ are prescribed, or equivalently with $A \pmod{p^k}$ specified. Then we set $\mu_P(V_{P,k}) = (b^{\deg(p)} - 1)^{-1} b^{-(k-1)\deg(p)}$. For $s \in \mathbb{N} \cup \{\infty\}$ let now $\mu_P^{(s)}$ denote the complete product measure on $(Y_P^*)^s$ induced by μ_P.

The subsequent theorem guarantees that there exist extensible polynomial lattice point sets $\mathcal{P}(\boldsymbol{Q}, P)$ of good quality with respect to the quality measure $R'_{b,\boldsymbol{\gamma}}$. It was first proved by Niederreiter [182] in a much more general setting.

Theorem 10.41 *Let b be a prime, let $m \in \mathbb{N}$, let $p \in \mathbb{Z}_b[x]$ be an irreducible polynomial with $\deg(p) = m$ and let $P = (p^k)_{k \geq 1}$. Then, for any given $\varepsilon > 0$, there exists a $\mu_P^{(\infty)}$-measurable set $E \subseteq (Y_P^*)^{\infty}$ such that for all $\mathbf{A} \in (Y_P^*)^{\infty} \setminus E$, we have*

$$R'_{b,\boldsymbol{\gamma}}(\mathbf{A}^{(s)}, p^k) \leq \frac{c_\varepsilon s (\log(s+1))^{1+\varepsilon} k (\log(k+1))^{1+\varepsilon}}{b^{km}} \times \prod_{i=1}^{s} \left(1 + \gamma_i \left(1 + m(k+1)\frac{b^2-1}{3b}\right)\right)$$

for all $k \in \mathbb{N}$ and $s \in \mathbb{N}$, where $c_\varepsilon > 0$ depends only on ε. Furthermore, we can make $\mu_P^{(\infty)}(E)$ arbitrarily close to zero by choosing c_ε large enough.

For the proof of Theorem 10.41, we need an extension of results derived in Section 10.2. We omit the very technical and tedious proof of the subsequent lemma and refer the reader to [43, Theorem 2], of which the result serves as a special case.

Lemma 10.42 *Let b be a prime, let $s, m, k \in \mathbb{N}$ and let $p \in \mathbb{Z}_b[x]$ be an irreducible polynomial with $\deg(p) = m$. Then we have*

$$\frac{1}{(b^m-1)^s b^{s(k-1)m}} \sum_{\substack{\boldsymbol{q} \in G_{b,km}^s \\ \gcd(q_i,p)=1\ \forall 1 \le i \le s}} R'_{b,\boldsymbol{\gamma}}(\boldsymbol{q}, p^k) \le \frac{1}{b^{km}} \prod_{i=1}^{s} \left(1 + \gamma_i \left(1 + m(k+1)\frac{b^2-1}{3b}\right)\right).$$

Remark 10.43 If we compare the bound from Theorem 10.41 with that from Lemma 10.42, which only holds for fixed s and k, then we see that the price of having an $\mathbf{A} \in (Y_P^*)^\infty \setminus E$ which works well simultaneously for all k and s in $\mathbb{N}$ is an extra factor of $s(\log(s+1))^{1+\varepsilon} k(\log(k+1))^{1+\varepsilon}$.

Proof of Theorem 10.41 We want to show the existence of polynomial lattice rules which work well for all $k, s \in \mathbb{N}$. The argument below is based on an extension of the following simple principle. Let $A, B \subseteq \{1, \ldots, K\}$. Let $|A|$ denote the number of elements of A and analogously for B. If $|A|, |B| > K/2$, then $|A \cap B| > 0$.

Let $p \in \mathbb{Z}_b[x]$, b a prime, be irreducible with $\deg(p) = m$ and let $P = (p^k)_{k \ge 1}$. For $\boldsymbol{Q} \in (Y_P^*)^\infty$ let $\boldsymbol{Q}_s$ be the projection of $\boldsymbol{Q}$ onto the first s coordinates.

For $k, s \in \mathbb{N}$ we define the set

$$\mathcal{Q}_{s,b^{km}}^{(\infty)}(c) = \left\{ \boldsymbol{Q} \in (Y_P^*)^\infty : R'_{b,\boldsymbol{\gamma}}(\boldsymbol{Q}_s, p^k) \le \frac{c}{b^{km}} \prod_{i=1}^{s} \left(1 + \gamma_i \left(1 + km\frac{b^2-1}{3b}\right)\right)\right\}.$$

Note that the set $\mathcal{Q}_{s,b^{km}}^{(\infty)}(c)$ is $\mu_P^{(\infty)}$-measurable, since we only impose a condition on the first s coordinates. From Lemma 10.42 and an application of Markov's inequality, we obtain

$$\mu_P^{(\infty)}\left(\mathcal{Q}_{s,b^{km}}^{(\infty)}(c)\right) > 1 - \frac{1}{c}. \tag{10.11}$$

In order to obtain a generating vector which works well for all choices of $k, s \in \mathbb{N}$, we need to show that the intersection $\bigcap_{s=1}^\infty \bigcap_{k=1}^\infty \mathcal{Q}_{s,b^{km}}^{(\infty)}(c)$ is not empty, or equivalently, has measure greater than zero (note that a countable intersection of measurable sets is itself measurable). To this end choose for each $k \in \mathbb{N}$ a

$0 < c_k < 1$. Then we have

$$\begin{aligned}\mu_P^{(\infty)}\left(\bigcap_{s=1}^{\infty}\bigcap_{k=1}^{\infty}\mathcal{Q}_{s,b^{km}}^{(\infty)}(c_s c_k)\right) &\geq 1-\mu_P^{(\infty)}\left(\bigcup_{s=1}^{\infty}\bigcup_{k=1}^{\infty}\overline{\mathcal{Q}}_{s,b^{km}}^{(\infty)}(c_s c_k)\right)\\ &\geq 1-\sum_{s=1}^{\infty}\sum_{k=1}^{\infty}\mu_P^{(\infty)}(\overline{\mathcal{Q}}_{s,b^{km}}^{(\infty)}(c_s c_k))\\ &> 1-\sum_{s=1}^{\infty}\sum_{k=1}^{\infty}\frac{1}{c_s c_k}\\ &= 1-\left(\sum_{k=1}^{\infty}\frac{1}{c_k}\right)^2,\end{aligned}$$

where $\overline{\mathcal{Q}}_{s,b^{km}}^{(\infty)}(c)$ stands for the complement of $\mathcal{Q}_{s,b^{km}}^{(\infty)}(c)$, i.e. $\overline{\mathcal{Q}}_{s,b^{km}}^{(\infty)}(c) = (Y_P^*)^{\infty} \setminus \mathcal{Q}_{s,b^{km}}^{(\infty)}(c)$ and where we used inequality (10.11). Thus, by choosing c_k, $k \in \mathbb{N}$, such that

$$\sum_{k\in\mathbb{N}}\frac{1}{c_k} \leq 1$$

it follows that the measure of $\bigcap_{s=1}^{\infty}\bigcap_{k=1}^{\infty}\mathcal{Q}_{s,b^{km}}^{(\infty)}(c_s c_k)$ is greater than zero and hence, this set is not empty. This implies that there is a generating vector which works well for all $k, s \in \mathbb{N}$.

The particular bound in Theorem 10.41 can be obtained by choosing, for a given $\varepsilon > 0$, $c_k := c_\varepsilon k(\log(k+1))^{1+\varepsilon}$ for $k \in \mathbb{N}$ where c_ε is chosen such that

$$c_\varepsilon > \sum_{k=1}^{\infty}\frac{1}{k(\log(k+1))^{1+\varepsilon}}.$$

Now set $E = (Y_P^*)^{\infty} \setminus \bigcap_{s=1}^{\infty}\bigcap_{k=1}^{\infty}\mathcal{Q}_{s,b^{km}}^{(\infty)}(c_s c_k)$. Then we also see that we can make $\mu_P^{(\infty)}(E)$ arbitrarily close to zero by choosing c_ε large enough. This completes the proof. □

From Theorem 10.41 we obtain a bound on the weighted star discrepancy of extensible lattice point sets.

Corollary 10.44 *Let b be a prime, let $m \in \mathbb{N}$, let $p \in \mathbb{Z}_b[x]$ be an irreducible polynomial of* $\deg(p) = m$ *and let $P = (p^k)_{k\geq 1}$. For $\varepsilon > 0$, let E be the set from Theorem 10.41. For $\mathbf{A} \in (Y_P^*)^{\infty} \setminus E$ let $\boldsymbol{q}_k^{(s)} \equiv \mathbf{A}^{(s)} \pmod{p^k}$. Then the point set*

$\mathcal{P}(\boldsymbol{q}_k^{(s)}, p^k)$ of cardinality b^{km} has weighted star discrepancy

$$D^*_{b^{km},\boldsymbol{\gamma}}(\mathcal{P}(\boldsymbol{q}_k^{(s)}, p^k)) \leq c'_\varepsilon \frac{s(\log(s+1))^{1+\varepsilon} k(\log(k+1))^{1+\varepsilon}}{b^{km}} \prod_{i=1}^{s}\left(1+\gamma_i\left(1+m(k+1)\frac{b^2-1}{3b}\right)\right),$$

where $c'_\varepsilon > 0$ depends only on ε.

Proof From Corollary 10.18, we have

$$D^*_{b^{km},\boldsymbol{\gamma}}(\mathcal{P}(\boldsymbol{q}_k^{(s)}, p^k)) \leq \sum_{\emptyset \neq \mathfrak{u} \subseteq \mathcal{I}_s} \gamma_{\mathfrak{u}} \left(1-\left(1-\frac{1}{b^{km}}\right)\right)^{|\mathfrak{u}|} + R'_{b,\boldsymbol{\gamma}}(\mathcal{P}(\boldsymbol{q}_k^{(s)}, p^k)).$$

For product weights, we have

$$\sum_{\emptyset \neq \mathfrak{u} \subseteq \mathcal{I}_s} \gamma_{\mathfrak{u}} \left(1-\left(1-\frac{1}{b^{km}}\right)\right)^{|\mathfrak{u}|} \leq \sum_{\emptyset \neq \mathfrak{u} \subseteq \mathcal{I}_s} \gamma_{\mathfrak{u}} \frac{|\mathfrak{u}|}{b^{km}} \leq \frac{s}{b^{km}} \prod_{j=1}^{s}(1+\gamma_j).$$

Now the result follows by invoking Theorem 10.41. □

Observe that under the assumption $\sum_{i=1}^\infty \gamma_i < \infty$, we can obtain an upper bound on the weighted star discrepancy which depends only polynomially on the dimension s from Corollary 10.44 (see Exercise 10.17).

We now turn the proof of Theorem 10.41 into an algorithm for finding extensible polynomial lattices. Since we can only calculate with finite-dimensional vectors, we define, for $k, s \in \mathbb{N}$, the set

$$\begin{aligned} &\mathcal{Q}_{s,b^{km}}(c) \\ &= \left\{ \boldsymbol{Q}_s \in (Y_P^*)^s : R'_{b,\boldsymbol{\gamma}}(\boldsymbol{Q}_s, p^k) \leq \frac{c}{b^{km}} \prod_{i=1}^{s}\left(1+\gamma_i\left(1+km\frac{b^2-1}{3b}\right)\right)\right\} \\ &= \{\boldsymbol{Q}_s \in (Y_P^*)^s : \boldsymbol{Q} \in \mathcal{Q}^{(\infty)}_{s,b^{km}}(c)\}. \end{aligned}$$

For brevity we write $\boldsymbol{Q}$ instead of $\boldsymbol{Q}_s$ for elements in $\mathcal{Q}_{s,b^{km}}(c)$ in the following.

A straightforward algorithm would now find sets $\mathcal{Q}_{s,b^{km}}(c_k)$ for all $u < k \leq v$ and then search for a vector which lies in all of those sets. Note that for a vector $\boldsymbol{Q}$ in a set $\mathcal{Q}_{s,b^{km}}(c)$, only the first k coefficients in each coordinate matter, i.e. for any other vector $\boldsymbol{L} \in (Y_P^*)^s$ with $\boldsymbol{L} \equiv \boldsymbol{Q} \pmod{p^k}$ we have $R'_{b,\boldsymbol{\gamma}}(\boldsymbol{L}, p^k) = R'_{b,\boldsymbol{\gamma}}(\boldsymbol{Q}, p^k)$. Hence, there is only a finite set of relevant coefficients for each vector in $\mathcal{Q}_{s,b^{km}}(c)$ and the remaining coefficients can be chosen arbitrarily. On the other hand the number of vectors in $\mathcal{Q}_{s,b^{km}}(c)$ is of course infinite.

Our method here uses a sieve, where the generating vectors are extended by one coefficient in each component at each step and where one keeps a certain number of good ones and discards the rest.

Let us start with $k = u + 1$. Then we use a computer search to find $(1 - c_{u+1}^{-1})b^{s(u+1)m}$ vectors which satisfy the desired bound. Next we want to find vectors which are in the intersection $\mathcal{Q}_{s,b^{(u+1)m}}(c_{u+1}) \cap \mathcal{Q}_{s,b^{(u+2)m}}(c_{u+2})$. As the vectors now also need to lie in $\mathcal{Q}_{s,b^{(u+1)m}}(c_{u+1})$ we only need to extend the vectors from the previous search by one new coefficient in each coordinate. Out of those newly obtained vectors we keep at least $\lfloor (1 - c_{u+1}^{-1} - c_{u+2}^{-1})b^{s(u+1)m} + 1 \rfloor$ new vectors which satisfy the desired bound and discard the rest of them. The existence of a sufficient number of good generating vectors is secured by the above arguments.

We continue in this way, always adding coefficients to the remaining set of vectors which are left over from the previous step until we finally obtain a vector which lies in the set $\bigcap_{k=u+1}^{v} \mathcal{Q}_{s,b^{km}}(c_k)$. We call this procedure the *sieve algorithm.* The sieve algorithm was first introduced for ordinary lattice point sets in [53] and for polynomial lattice point sets in [34].

The following theorem is now implied by the observations above.

Theorem 10.45 *Let $u < v \in \mathbb{N}$. Let $\boldsymbol{q}^* \in (Y_p^*)^s$ be constructed by the sieve algorithm. Then, for all $u < k \le v$, we have*

$$R'_{b,\boldsymbol{\gamma}}(\boldsymbol{q}^*, p^k) \le \frac{c_k}{b^{km}} \prod_{i=1}^{s} \left(1 + \gamma_i \left(1 + m(k+1)\frac{b^2-1}{3b}\right)\right).$$

Using the sieve algorithm based on $R'_{b,\boldsymbol{\gamma}}$ we can now obtain polynomial lattice point sets with a small weighted star discrepancy as implied by Corollary 10.18 and Theorem 10.45. Note that here (in contrast to the result in Corollary 10.44) we can even obtain an upper bound on the weighted star discrepancy which is independent of the dimension s whenever $\sum_{i=1}^{\infty} \gamma_i < \infty$ (see Exercise 10.18).

The sieve algorithm has the drawback that the search spaces involved might be very large which makes it inapplicable. Hence, we show now that it can be combined with the CBC construction as introduced in Section 10.2. We call this algorithm the *component-by-component sieve algorithm.*

Before we can introduce this algorithm, we need some further details. In the following, we write $R'_{b,\boldsymbol{\gamma},d}$ instead of $R'_{b,\boldsymbol{\gamma}}$ to stress its dependence on the dimension d.

First note that for given $d \in \mathbb{N}$ and $Q_1, \ldots, Q_d \in Y_p^*$ with $\boldsymbol{q}_k = (q_{1,k}, \ldots, q_{d,k})$ where $q_{i,k} \equiv Q_i \pmod{p^k}$ for $1 \le i \le d$, we can write

$$\begin{aligned} R'_{b,\boldsymbol{\gamma},d}(\boldsymbol{q}_k, p^k) &= (1 + \gamma_d) R'_{b,\boldsymbol{\gamma},d-1}((q_{1,k}, \ldots, q_{d-1,k}), p^k) \\ &\quad + S_{b,\boldsymbol{\gamma},d}((q_{1,k}, \ldots, q_{d-1,k}, q_{d,k}), p^k), \end{aligned} \tag{10.12}$$

where

$$S_{b,\boldsymbol{\gamma},d}((q_{1,k},\ldots,q_{d-1,k},q_{d,k}),p^k) = \sum_{\substack{(\boldsymbol{h},h_d)\in G_{b,km}^{d-1}\times G_{b,km}^*\\ (\boldsymbol{h},h_d)\cdot\boldsymbol{q}_k\equiv 0 \pmod{p^k}}} r_b(\boldsymbol{h},\boldsymbol{\gamma})r_b(h_d,\gamma_d).$$

We need a further extension of results derived in Section 10.2 and again we omit the very technical and tedious proof. From the proof of [43, Theorem 2] we obtain that for any $k, d \in \mathbb{N}$, $d \geq 2$, and fixed $\boldsymbol{Q} \in (Y_P^*)^{d-1}$ with $\boldsymbol{q}_k \equiv \boldsymbol{Q} \pmod{p^k}$, we have

$$\frac{1}{(b^m-1)b^{(k-1)m}} \sum_{\substack{q\in G_{b,km}^*\\ \gcd(q,p)=1}} S_{b,\boldsymbol{\gamma},d}((\boldsymbol{q}_k,q),p^k)$$

$$\leq \frac{1}{b^{km}}\gamma_d m(k+1)\frac{b^2-1}{3b}\prod_{i=1}^{d-1}\left(1+\gamma_i\left(1+km\frac{b^2-1}{3b}\right)\right).$$

For $d \geq 2$ and given that $\boldsymbol{Q} \in (Y_P^*)^{d-1}$, now let $\mathcal{Q}_{d,b^{km}}(\boldsymbol{Q},c)$ denote the set consisting of all $Q_d \in Y_P^*$ for which we have

$$S_{b,\boldsymbol{\gamma},d}((\boldsymbol{q}_k,q_{d,k}),p^k) \leq \frac{c}{b^{km}}\gamma_d m(k+1)\frac{b^2-1}{3b}\prod_{i=1}^{d-1}\left(1+\gamma_i\left(1+km\frac{b^2-1}{3b}\right)\right),$$

where $\boldsymbol{q}_k \equiv \boldsymbol{Q} \pmod{p^k}$ and $q_{d,k} \equiv Q_d \pmod{p^k}$.

The CBC sieve algorithm now works in the following way. Again choose u and v as for the sieve algorithm. We start with dimension $s = 1$. As we assumed that p is irreducible, we may without loss of generality choose $Q_1^* = 1$. This is because in dimension $s = 1$ any polynomial Q_1 which is not divisible by p yields the same polynomial lattice. Note that in this case it follows that $R'_{b,\boldsymbol{\gamma},1}((q_{1,k}^*),p^k) = 0$. Now with $Q_1^* = 1$ fixed, we seek the next coordinate Q_2, but here we can just employ the sieve algorithm from the previous section where Q_1^* is fixed and the sets $\mathcal{Q}_{2,b^{km}}(c_k)$ are replaced by $\mathcal{Q}_{2,b^{km}}((Q_1^*),c)$ and the quality measure $R'_{b,\boldsymbol{\gamma},2}(\boldsymbol{q}_k,p^k)$ is replaced by $S_{b,\boldsymbol{\gamma},2}((q_{1,k}^*),p^k)$. Note that the latter can be computed using identity (10.12). This way, we obtain a Q_2^* which lies in the set $\bigcap_{k=u+1}^{v}\mathcal{Q}_{2,b^{km}}((Q_1^*),c_k)$. Now with Q_1^*, Q_2^* fixed, using the sieve algorithm again, we can obtain a Q_3^* which lies in the set $\bigcap_{k=u+1}^{v}\mathcal{Q}_{3,b^{km}}((Q_1^*,Q_2^*),c_k)$. In general, for $2 \leq d \leq s$ we can use the sieve algorithm to obtain polynomials Q_d^* which lie in the intersection of the sets $\mathcal{Q}_{d-1,b^{km}}((Q_1^*,\ldots,Q_{d-1}^*),c_k)$. The construction cost is now much reduced because the size of the set $\mathcal{Q}_{d-1,b^{km}}((Q_1^*,\ldots,Q_{d-1}^*),c_k)$ is much smaller compared to the size of $\mathcal{Q}_{s,b^{km}}(c_k)$.

The following theorem is now implied by the construction of the vector $\boldsymbol{Q}^* = (Q_1^*,\ldots,Q_s^*)$.

Theorem 10.46 *Let $u < v \in \mathbb{N}$. Let $Q^* \in (Y_p^*)^s$ be constructed by the CBC sieve algorithm. Then, for all $u < k \leq v$, we have*

$$R'_{b,\gamma,s}(Q^*, p^k) \leq \frac{c_k}{b^{mk}} \prod_{i=1}^{s} \left(1 + \gamma_i \left(1 + m(k+1)\frac{b^2-1}{3b}\right)\right).$$

Using the CBC sieve algorithm based on $R'_{b,\gamma}$ we can now obtain polynomial lattice point sets with a small weighted star discrepancy as implied by Corollary 10.18 and Theorem 10.46. Again, we can obtain an upper bound on the weighted star discrepancy which is independent of the dimension as long as $\sum_{i=1}^{\infty} \gamma_i < \infty$ (see Exercise 10.18).

Note that if we choose the c_k's such that $\sum_{k=u+1}^{v} c_k^{-1} < 1$, then one can continue the (CBC) sieve algorithm at a later stage if necessary. Further, it is clear from the (CBC) sieve algorithm that one does not necessarily have to increase the number of points by a factor of $b^{\deg(p)}$ in each step. Because of the probabilistic arguments involved, one can actually choose arbitrary powers of $b^{\deg(p)}$. (Note that the smallest possible value of $b^{\deg(p)}$ is 2, which is, for example, obtained by choosing $b = 2$ and $p(x) = x$.) Hence, we do not need to let k run from $u + 1$ to v, but we could choose a finite subset $K \subset \mathbb{N}$ and construct a generating vector which works well for all choices k in K.

A simple way of choosing the values of c_k would be $c_k = v - u$ for all $u < k \leq v$. On the other hand, this might give a suboptimal bound for small k. Hence, one strategy of choosing c_k would be to obtain a balance of the bound in Theorem 10.45 across all choices of k. Further, note that the (CBC) sieve algorithm does not necessarily have to start with the smallest value of k, but can start at any value $k \in K$. In order to speed up the algorithm, it would of course be advantageous to order the values of $k \in K$ such that the number of vectors which one needs to consider in the (CBC) sieve algorithm is minimised.

Using the fact that there are different generating vectors which yield the same polynomial lattice rule, the number of generating vectors in the (CBC) sieve algorithm can be reduced even more, which makes the construction faster. A further speed-up can be achieved by using the fast CBC algorithm introduced in Section 10.3. See [26, 53] for such an algorithm. We also remark that in the sieve algorithm, the set K does not have to be finite, in which case one obtains polynomial lattice rules with an arbitrarily high number of quadrature points. A major drawback is that it is not known how the CBC algorithm can be used in this case; see [53]. Hence, if K is an infinite set, this method is only feasible for very small s.

Alternatively, we present an algorithm due to Niederreiter and Pillichshammer [188] which yields polynomial lattices that are arbitrarily extensible. The disadvantage of this result is that one obtains weaker bounds on the star discrepancy as anticipated by Theorem 10.41. The algorithm is based on the quantity R'_b as quality criterion.

Algorithm 10.47 *Let $p \in \mathbb{Z}_b[x]$ with $\deg(p) = m$ be monic and irreducible.*

1. *Find $\boldsymbol{q}_1 := \boldsymbol{q}$ by minimising $R'_b(\boldsymbol{q}, p)$ over all $\boldsymbol{q} \in G_{b,m}^s$.*
2. *For $n = 2, 3, \ldots$ find $\boldsymbol{q}_n := \boldsymbol{q}_{n-1} + p^{n-1}\boldsymbol{q}$ by minimising $R'_b(\boldsymbol{q}_{n-1} + p^{n-1}\boldsymbol{q}, p^n)$ over all $\boldsymbol{q} \in G_{b,m}^s$.*

Theorem 10.48 *Let $s, n \in \mathbb{N}$, b be a prime, and $p \in \mathbb{Z}_b[x]$ be monic and irreducible with $\deg(p) = m$. Assume that $\boldsymbol{q}_n \in G_{b,nm}^s$ is constructed according to Algorithm 10.47. Then we have*

$$R'_b(\boldsymbol{q}_n, p^n) = O\left(b^{-mn}\left(\left(1 + m\frac{b^2-1}{3b}\right)^s + 1\right)^n\right)$$

with an implied constant depending only on s, b and p.

From Corollary 10.17 and Theorem 10.48 we immediately obtain a bound on the star discrepancy of $\mathcal{P}(\boldsymbol{q}_n, p^n)$. This bound is good only for small b and polynomials p of large degree.

Corollary 10.49 *Let $s, n \in \mathbb{N}$, b be a prime, and $p \in \mathbb{Z}_b[x]$ be monic and irreducible with $\deg(p) = m$. Assume that $\boldsymbol{q}_n \in G_{b,nm}^s$ is constructed according to Algorithm 10.47. Then we have*

$$D^*_{b^{\deg(p)n}}(\mathcal{P}(\boldsymbol{q}_n, p^n)) = O\left(b^{-mn}\left(\left(1 + m\frac{b^2-1}{3b}\right)^s + 1\right)^n\right)$$

with an implied constant depending only on s, b and p.

Proof of Theorem 10.48 For the sake of convenience we use the abbreviation $\nu_{b,m} := m\frac{b^2-1}{3b}$.

First we show the result for $n = 1$. We have

$$\begin{aligned} R'_b(\boldsymbol{q}_1, p) &\le \frac{1}{b^{sm}} \sum_{\boldsymbol{q} \in G_{b,m}^s} R'_b(\boldsymbol{q}, p) = \frac{1}{b^{sm}} \sum_{\boldsymbol{h} \in G_{b,m}^s \setminus \{\boldsymbol{0}\}} r_b(\boldsymbol{h}) \sum_{\substack{\boldsymbol{q} \in G_{b,m}^s \\ \boldsymbol{h} \in \mathcal{D}'_{\boldsymbol{q},p}}} 1 \\ &= \frac{1}{b^m} \sum_{\boldsymbol{h} \in G_{b,m}^s \setminus \{\boldsymbol{0}\}} r_b(\boldsymbol{h}) = \frac{1}{b^m}\left((1 + \nu_{b,m})^s - 1\right), \end{aligned}$$

where we used Lemma 10.22 for the last equality.

Now let $n \geq 2$. Then we have

$$R'_b(\boldsymbol{q}_n, p^n) \leq \frac{1}{b^{sm}} \sum_{\boldsymbol{q} \in G^s_{b,m}} R'_b(\boldsymbol{q}_{n-1} + p^{n-1}\boldsymbol{q}, p^n)$$

$$= \frac{1}{b^{sm}} \sum_{\boldsymbol{h} \in G^s_{b,nm} \setminus \{\boldsymbol{0}\}} r_b(\boldsymbol{h}) \sum_{\substack{\boldsymbol{q} \in G^s_{b,m} \\ \boldsymbol{h} \in \mathcal{D}'_{\boldsymbol{q}_{n-1}+p^{n-1}\boldsymbol{q}, p^n}}} 1.$$

The inner sum is equal to the number of $\boldsymbol{q} \in G^s_{b,m}$ with $p^{n-1}\boldsymbol{h} \cdot \boldsymbol{q} \equiv -\boldsymbol{h} \cdot \boldsymbol{q}_{n-1} \pmod{p^n}$. For this we must have $\boldsymbol{h} \cdot \boldsymbol{q}_{n-1} \equiv 0 \pmod{p^{n-1}}$, and then $\boldsymbol{h} \cdot \boldsymbol{q} \equiv -\frac{1}{p^{n-1}}\boldsymbol{h} \cdot \boldsymbol{q}_{n-1} \pmod{p}$. Thus,

$$R'_b(\boldsymbol{q}_n, p^n) \leq \frac{1}{b^{sm}} \sum_{\substack{\boldsymbol{h} \in G^s_{b,nm} \setminus \{\boldsymbol{0}\} \\ \boldsymbol{h} \cdot \boldsymbol{q}_{n-1} \equiv 0 \pmod{p^{n-1}}}} r_b(\boldsymbol{h}) \sum_{\substack{\boldsymbol{q} \in G^s_{b,m} \\ \boldsymbol{h} \cdot \boldsymbol{q} \equiv -\frac{1}{p^{n-1}}\boldsymbol{h} \cdot \boldsymbol{q}_{n-1} \pmod{p}}} 1.$$

Consider the inner sum. If $\boldsymbol{h} \not\equiv \boldsymbol{0} \pmod{p}$, then the inner sum is equal to $b^{(s-1)m}$. If $\boldsymbol{h} \equiv \boldsymbol{0} \pmod{p}$, then the inner sum is equal to 0 if $\boldsymbol{h} \cdot \boldsymbol{q}_{n-1} \not\equiv 0 \pmod{p^n}$ and equal to b^{sm} if $\boldsymbol{h} \cdot \boldsymbol{q}_{n-1} \equiv 0 \pmod{p^n}$. Thus,

$$R'_b(\boldsymbol{q}_n, p^n) \leq \frac{1}{b^m} \sum_{\substack{\boldsymbol{h} \in G^s_{b,nm} \setminus \{\boldsymbol{0}\},\, \boldsymbol{h} \not\equiv \boldsymbol{0} \pmod{p} \\ \boldsymbol{h} \cdot \boldsymbol{q}_{n-1} \equiv 0 \pmod{p^{n-1}}}} r_b(\boldsymbol{h}) + \sum_{\substack{\boldsymbol{h} \in G^s_{b,nm} \setminus \{\boldsymbol{0}\},\, \boldsymbol{h} \equiv \boldsymbol{0} \pmod{p} \\ \boldsymbol{h} \cdot \boldsymbol{q}_{n-1} \equiv 0 \pmod{p^n}}} r_b(\boldsymbol{h})$$

$$\leq \frac{1}{b^m} \sum_{\substack{\boldsymbol{h} \in G^s_{b,nm} \setminus \{\boldsymbol{0}\} \\ \boldsymbol{h} \cdot \boldsymbol{q}_{n-1} \equiv 0 \pmod{p^{n-1}}}} r_b(\boldsymbol{h}) + \sum_{\substack{\boldsymbol{h} \in G^s_{b,(n-1)m} \setminus \{\boldsymbol{0}\} \\ \boldsymbol{h} \cdot \boldsymbol{q}_{n-1} \equiv 0 \pmod{p^{n-1}}}} r_b(p\boldsymbol{h}).$$

Since p is monic, we find that $r_b(p\boldsymbol{h}) \leq b^{-m} r_b(\boldsymbol{h})$ for $\boldsymbol{h} \in \mathbb{Z}_b[x]^s$ with $\boldsymbol{h} \neq \boldsymbol{0}$. Hence, we obtain

$$R'_b(\boldsymbol{q}_n, p^n) \leq \frac{2}{b^m} R'_b(\boldsymbol{q}_{n-1}, p^{n-1}) + \frac{1}{b^m}\Sigma \tag{10.13}$$

with

$$\Sigma := \sum_{\substack{\boldsymbol{h} \in G^s_{b,nm} \setminus G^s_{b,(n-1)m} \\ \boldsymbol{h} \cdot \boldsymbol{q}_{n-1} \equiv 0 \pmod{p^{n-1}}}} r_b(\boldsymbol{h}).$$

Any $\boldsymbol{h} \in G^s_{b,nm} \setminus G^s_{b,(n-1)m}$ can be represented uniquely in the form

$$\boldsymbol{h} = \widetilde{\boldsymbol{h}} + p^{n-1}\boldsymbol{c} \quad \text{with} \quad \widetilde{\boldsymbol{h}} \in G^s_{b,(n-1)m} \text{ and } \boldsymbol{c} \in G^s_{b,m} \setminus \{\boldsymbol{0}\}.$$

Therefore,

$$\begin{aligned}\Sigma &= \sum_{\substack{\boldsymbol{h}\in G^s_{b,(n-1)m}\\ \boldsymbol{h}\cdot\boldsymbol{q}_{n-1}\equiv 0 \pmod{p^{n-1}}}} \sum_{\boldsymbol{c}\in G^s_{b,m}\setminus\{\boldsymbol{0}\}} r_b(\boldsymbol{h}+p^{n-1}\boldsymbol{c})\\ &= \sum_{\boldsymbol{c}\in G^s_{b,m}\setminus\{\boldsymbol{0}\}} r_b(p^{n-1}\boldsymbol{c}) + \sum_{\boldsymbol{h}\in\mathcal{D}'_{\boldsymbol{q}_{n-1},p^{n-1}}} \sum_{\boldsymbol{c}\in G^s_{b,m}\setminus\{\boldsymbol{0}\}} r_b(\boldsymbol{h}+p^{n-1}\boldsymbol{c})\\ &=: \Sigma_1+\Sigma_2.\end{aligned}$$

First we deal with Σ_1. We have

$$\begin{aligned}\Sigma_1 &= \left(\sum_{c\in G_{b,m}} r_b(p^{n-1}c)\right)^s - 1 = \left(1+\frac{1}{b^{\deg(p^{n-1})}}\sum_{c\in G_{b,m}\setminus\{0\}} r_b(c)\right)^s - 1\\ &= \left(1+\frac{\nu_{b,m}}{b^{\deg(p^{n-1})}}\right)^s - 1 \le \frac{s\nu_{b,m}}{b^{\deg(p^{n-1})}}\left(1+\frac{\nu_{b,m}}{b^{\deg(p^{n-1})}}\right)^{s-1}.\end{aligned}$$

Now we turn to Σ_2. For $\boldsymbol{h}\in\mathcal{D}'_{\boldsymbol{q}_{n-1},p^{n-1}}$ of the form $\boldsymbol{h}=(h_1,\ldots,h_s)$, we have

$$\begin{aligned}\Sigma_3 &:= \sum_{\boldsymbol{c}\in G^s_{b,m}\setminus\{\boldsymbol{0}\}} r_b(\boldsymbol{h}+p^{n-1}\boldsymbol{c})\\ &= \sum_{\boldsymbol{c}\in G^s_{b,m}} r_b(\boldsymbol{h}+p^{n-1}\boldsymbol{c}) - r_b(\boldsymbol{h})\\ &= \prod_{i=1}^s\left(\sum_{c\in G_{b,m}} r_b(h_i+p^{n-1}c)\right) - r_b(\boldsymbol{h}).\end{aligned}$$

If $h_i=0$, then by Lemma 10.22 and since p is monic,

$$\begin{aligned}\sum_{c\in G_{b,m}} r_b(h_i+p^{n-1}c) &= \sum_{c\in G_{b,m}} r_b(p^{n-1}c)\\ &= 1+\frac{\nu_{b,m}}{b^{\deg(p^{n-1})}} = r_b(h_i)+\frac{\nu_{b,m}}{b^{\deg(p^{n-1})}}.\end{aligned}$$

If $h_i\ne 0$, then $0\le\deg(h_i)<\deg(p^{n-1})$ and

$$\begin{aligned}\sum_{c\in G_{b,m}} r_b(h_i+p^{n-1}c) &= r_b(h_i)+\sum_{c\in G_{b,m}\setminus\{0\}} r_b(h_i+p^{n-1}c)\\ &= r_b(h_i)+\sum_{c\in G_{b,m}\setminus\{0\}} r_b(p^{n-1}c)\\ &= r_b(h_i)+\frac{\nu_{b,m}}{b^{\deg(p^{n-1})}},\end{aligned}$$

where we again used Lemma 10.22 and the assumption that p is monic.

Now we obtain

$$\Sigma_3 \leq \prod_{i=1}^{s} \left(r_b(h_i) + \frac{\nu_{b,m}}{b^{\deg(p^{n-1})}} \right) - r_b(\boldsymbol{h}).$$

Since $r_b(h_i) \geq \frac{1}{b^{\deg(h_i)+1}} \geq \frac{1}{b^{\deg(p^{n-1})}}$, it follows now that

$$\Sigma_3 \leq \prod_{i=1}^{s} r_b(h_i) \left(1 + \nu_{b,m}\right) - r_b(\boldsymbol{h}) = r_b(\boldsymbol{h}) \left(\left(1 + \nu_{b,m}\right)^s - 1 \right)$$

and hence,

$$\Sigma_2 \leq \left(\left(1 + \nu_{b,m}\right)^s - 1 \right) R_b'(\boldsymbol{q}_{n-1}, p^{n-1}).$$

Altogether, we find that

$$\begin{aligned} \Sigma &= \Sigma_1 + \Sigma_2 \\ &\leq \frac{s\nu_{b,m}}{b^{\deg(p^{n-1})}} \left(1 + \frac{\nu_{b,m}}{b^{\deg(p^{n-1})}}\right)^{s-1} + \left(\left(1 + \nu_{b,m}\right)^s - 1 \right) R_b'(\boldsymbol{q}_{n-1}, p^{n-1}) \end{aligned}$$

and hence,

$$\begin{aligned} &R_b'(\boldsymbol{q}_n, p^n) \\ &\leq \frac{1}{b^m} \left(\left(1 + \nu_{b,m}\right)^s + 1 \right) R_b'(\boldsymbol{q}_{n-1}, p^{n-1}) + \frac{s\nu_{b,m}}{b^{\deg(p^n)}} \left(1 + \frac{\nu_{b,m}}{b^{\deg(p^{n-1})}}\right)^{s-1}. \end{aligned}$$

Iterating this inequality we get for all $n \geq 2$,

$$\begin{aligned} R_b'(\boldsymbol{q}_n, p^n) \leq& \frac{1}{b^{m(n-1)}} \left(\left(1 + \nu_{b,m}\right)^s + 1 \right)^{n-1} R_b'(\boldsymbol{q}_1, p) \\ &+ s\nu_{b,m} \sum_{j=0}^{n-2} \left(\frac{\left(\left(1 + \nu_{b,m}\right)^s + 1\right)}{b^m} \right)^j \frac{1}{b^{m(n-j)}} \left(1 + \frac{\nu_{b,m}}{b^{m(n-1-j)}}\right)^{s-1} \\ \leq& \frac{1}{b^{mn}} \left((1+\nu_{b,m})^s + 1 \right)^n + \frac{s\nu_{b,m}}{b^{mn}} \left(1 + \frac{\nu_{b,m}}{b^m}\right)^{s-1} \sum_{j=0}^{n-2} \left((1+\nu_{b,m})^s + 1 \right)^j. \end{aligned}$$

Hence,

$$R_b'(\boldsymbol{q}_n, p^n) = O\left(\frac{\left(\left(1 + \nu_{b,m}\right)^s + 1 \right)^n}{b^{mn}} \right)$$

with an implied constant depending only on s, b and p. □

Exercises

10.1 For $m \in \mathbb{N}$, give the $m \times m$ matrix over $\mathbb{Z}_b$ defined by (10.1) for the special polynomials $p, q \in \mathbb{Z}_b[x]$, where $p(x) = x^m$ and $q(x) = q_1 x^{m-1} + \cdots + q_{m-1}x + q_m$.

10.2 Let b be a prime and let $s \in \mathbb{N}$, $s \geq 2$. Let $p \in \mathbb{Z}_b[x]$ and $\boldsymbol{q} \in \mathbb{Z}_b[x]^s$. Show that for the polynomial lattice point set $\mathcal{P}(\boldsymbol{q}, p)$, we have

$$\sum_{\boldsymbol{x} \in \mathcal{P}(\boldsymbol{q},p)} {}_b\mathrm{wal}_{\boldsymbol{k}}(\boldsymbol{x}) = \begin{cases} b^m & \text{if } \boldsymbol{k} \cdot \boldsymbol{q} \equiv 0 \pmod{p}, \\ 0 & \text{otherwise.} \end{cases}$$

10.3 Let $\emptyset \neq \mathfrak{u} \subseteq \mathcal{I}_s$. Determine the quality parameter $t_{\mathfrak{u}}$ of the projection of $\mathcal{P}(\boldsymbol{q}, p)$ to the coordinates given by $\emptyset \neq \mathfrak{u} \subseteq \mathcal{I}_s$.

10.4 Prove Lemma 10.6.
Hint: See [177, Lemma 4.40].

10.5 Give a detailed proof of the second part of Theorem 10.13.

10.6 Give a detailed proof of the second part of Corollary 10.15.

10.7 Prove Corollary 10.18.
Hint: Use (5.13), Lemma 5.42 and Lemma 10.6.

10.8 Prove Theorem 10.24.

10.9 Prove Corollary 10.25.

10.10 Prove Theorem 10.28 for the weighted case.

10.11 Prove Corollary 10.30.
Hint: Compare with the proof of Corollary 5.45.

10.12 Let $\sum_{i=1}^{\infty} \gamma_i < \infty$. Show that for any $\delta > 0$, there exists a $C_{\boldsymbol{\gamma},\delta}$ such that for every $N, s \in \mathbb{N}$ there exists a superposition $\mathcal{P}$ of polynomial lattice point sets (which can be constructed with Algorithm 10.26) of cardinality N such that

$$D^*_{N,\boldsymbol{\gamma}}(\mathcal{P}) \leq C_{\boldsymbol{\gamma},\delta} N^{\delta-1}.$$

10.13 Prove Theorem 10.34 for the weighted case.

10.14 Let b be prime, $s, m \in \mathbb{N}$, $p \in \mathbb{Z}_b[x]$ be irreducible, with $\deg(p) = m$ and $\boldsymbol{\gamma} = (\gamma_i)_{i \geq 1}$ be a sequence of weights. Show that, for given $0 \leq \alpha < 1$, there are more than $\alpha |G^*_{b,m}|$ polynomials $q \in G^*_{b,m}$ such that

$$D^*_{b^m}(\mathcal{P}(\boldsymbol{v}_s(q), p)) \leq \frac{s}{b^m} + \frac{1}{1-\alpha} \frac{s-1}{b^m - 1} \left(1 + m \frac{b^2-1}{3b}\right)^s,$$

and

$$D^*_{b^m,\boldsymbol{\gamma}}(\mathcal{P}(\boldsymbol{v}_s(q), p)) \leq \sum_{\emptyset \neq \mathfrak{u} \subseteq \mathcal{I}_s} \gamma_{\mathfrak{u}} \left(1 - \left(1 - \frac{1}{b^m}\right)^{|\mathfrak{u}|}\right)$$
$$+ \frac{1}{1-\alpha} \frac{s-1}{b^m - 1} \prod_{i=1}^{s} \left(1 + \gamma_i \left(1 + m \frac{b^2-1}{3b}\right)\right),$$

respectively.

10.15 For arbitrary base $b \geq 2$, embed the matrix C given in (10.8) into a circulant matrix of size $b^{m+1} \times b^{m+1}$. Use the procedure given in Section 10.3 for the case $b = 2$.

10.16 Generalise Theorem 10.38 to arbitrary base $b \geq 2$.

10.17 Let $p \in \mathbb{Z}_b[x]$, b a prime, be an irreducible polynomial of degree $\deg(p) = m$ and let $P = (p^k)_{k \geq 1}$. For $\varepsilon > 0$, let E be the set from Theorem 10.41. For $\mathbf{A} \in (Y_P^*)^\infty \setminus E$ let $\boldsymbol{q}_k^{(s)} \equiv \mathbf{A}^{(s)} \pmod{p^k}$. Assume that the weights $\boldsymbol{\gamma} = (\gamma_i)_{i \geq 1}$ satisfy $\sum_{i=1}^{\infty} \gamma_i < \infty$. Show that for any $\delta_1 > 0$ and $\delta_2 > 0$, there is a $C_{\varepsilon,b,\boldsymbol{\gamma},\delta_1,\delta_2} > 0$ such that the weighted star discrepancy of the point set $\mathcal{P}(\boldsymbol{q}_k^{(s)}, p^k)$ of cardinality b^{km} satisfies

$$D_{b^{km},\boldsymbol{\gamma}}^*(\mathcal{P}(\boldsymbol{q}_k^{(s)}, p^k)) \leq C_{\varepsilon,b,\boldsymbol{\gamma},\delta_1,\delta_2} s^{1+\delta_1} b^{km(\delta_2-1)}.$$

10.18 Let $p \in \mathbb{Z}_b[x]$, b a prime, be an irreducible polynomial of degree $\deg(p) = m$ and let $P = (p^k)_{k \geq 1}$. Let $u < v \in \mathbb{N}$ and let $\boldsymbol{Q}^* \in (Y_P^*)^s$ be constructed by the (CBC) sieve algorithm. Assume that the weights $\boldsymbol{\gamma} = (\gamma_i)_{i \geq 1}$ satisfy $\sum_{i=1}^{\infty} \gamma_i < \infty$. Show that for any $\delta > 0$, there is a $C_{b,\boldsymbol{\gamma},\delta} > 0$ such that the weighted star discrepancy of the point set $\mathcal{P}(\boldsymbol{Q}^*, p^k)$ of cardinality b^{km} for $u < k \leq v$ satisfies

$$D_{b^{km},\boldsymbol{\gamma}}^*(\mathcal{P}(\boldsymbol{Q}^*, p^k)) \leq C_{b,\boldsymbol{\gamma},\delta} c_k b^{km(\delta-1)}.$$

11

Cyclic digital nets and hyperplane nets

Many constructions of digital nets are inspired by a close connection between coding theory and the theory of digital nets (see Section 7.3). Examples for such constructions are the so-called $(u, u+v)$-construction (see Section 9.1), its generalisation, the matrix-product construction (see Section 9.2) and the Kronecker-product construction (see [14, 190]). Here we deal in more detail with a construction of digital nets that is an analogue to a special construction of codes, namely so-called cyclic codes. These codes are well known in coding theory. This construction of digital nets has been introduced by Niederreiter [183], who adopted the view that cyclic codes can be defined by prescribing roots of polynomials. Later, in [221], this construction was generalised to so-called hyperplane nets.

11.1 Cyclic nets, hyperplane nets and their generating matrices

We start with the definition of cyclic nets as given by Niederreiter [183].

Definition 11.1 Let b be a prime power and let $s, m \in \mathbb{N}$ be given. Let $\mathbb{F}_{b^m}$ be a finite field of b^m elements and fix an element $\alpha \in \mathbb{F}_{b^m}$. Let $\mathcal{F} := \{f \in \mathbb{F}_{b^m}[x] : \deg(f) < s\}$ and consider the subset of polynomials

$$\mathcal{F}_\alpha := \{f \in \mathcal{F} : f(\alpha) = 0\}.$$

For each $1 \le i \le s$, choose an ordered basis $\mathcal{B}_i$ of $\mathbb{F}_{b^m}$ over $\mathbb{F}_b$ and define the mapping $\phi : \mathcal{F} \to (\mathbb{F}_b^{ms})^\top$ by

$$f(x) = \sum_{i=1}^{s} \gamma_i x^{i-1} \mapsto (\gamma_{1,1}, \ldots, \gamma_{1,m}, \ldots, \gamma_{s,1}, \ldots, \gamma_{s,m})^\top,$$

where $(\gamma_{i,1}, \ldots, \gamma_{i,m}) \in \mathbb{F}_b^m$ is the coordinate vector of $\gamma_i \in \mathbb{F}_{b^m}$ with respect to the chosen basis $\mathcal{B}_i$ for all $1 \le i \le s$.

Denote by $\mathcal{C}_\alpha$ the orthogonal subspace in $(\mathbb{F}_b^{ms})^\top$ of the image $\mathcal{N}_\alpha := \phi(\mathcal{F}_\alpha)$ and let

$$C_\alpha = (C_1^\top \mid \ldots \mid C_s^\top) \in \mathbb{F}_b^{m \times sm}$$

be a matrix whose row space is the transpose of $\mathcal{C}_\alpha$. Then the $m \times m$ matrices $C_1, \ldots, C_s$ are the generating matrices of a *cyclic net over* $\mathbb{F}_b$ *with respect to* $\mathcal{B}_1, \ldots, \mathcal{B}_s$ and C_α is its overall generating matrix. This cyclic net is denoted by $\mathcal{P}_\alpha$ and we say $\mathcal{P}_\alpha$ is the *cyclic net associated with* α. We shall assume that the choice of bases $\mathcal{B}_1, \ldots, \mathcal{B}_s$ is made before the choice of α.

In the following, we employ linear representations. To be more precise, let $\mathbb{F}_{b^m} = \mathbb{F}_b[\omega]$, such that $\{1, \omega, \omega^2, \ldots, \omega^{m-1}\}$ forms a basis of $\mathbb{F}_{b^m}$ as a vector space over $\mathbb{F}_b$. Let ω^m have the basis representation $\omega^m = \beta_0 + \cdots + \beta_{m-1}\omega^{m-1}$ with $\beta_0, \ldots, \beta_{m-1} \in \mathbb{F}_b$ and let P be the matrix

$$P := \begin{pmatrix} 0 & \ldots & \ldots & 0 & \beta_0 \\ 1 & 0 & \ldots & 0 & \beta_1 \\ 0 & \ddots & \ddots & \vdots & \vdots \\ \vdots & \ddots & \ddots & 0 & \vdots \\ 0 & \ldots & 0 & 1 & \beta_{m-1} \end{pmatrix} \in \mathbb{F}_b^{m \times m}. \tag{11.1}$$

Now we define $\psi : \mathbb{F}_{b^m} \to (\mathbb{F}_b^m)^\top$ and $\Psi : \mathbb{F}_{b^m} \to \mathbb{F}_b^{m \times m}$. If the representation of α in $\mathbb{F}_{b^m}$ is given by $\alpha = \sum_{l=0}^{m-1} a_l \omega^l$, where $a_0, \ldots, a_{m-1} \in \mathbb{F}_b$, then we define

$$\psi(\alpha) := (a_0, \ldots, a_{m-1})^\top \in (\mathbb{F}_b^m)^\top \quad \text{and} \quad \Psi(\alpha) := \sum_{l=0}^{m-1} a_l P^l \in \mathbb{F}_b^{m \times m}.$$

Then, for any $\alpha, x \in \mathbb{F}_{b^m}$, we have

$$\Psi(\alpha)\psi(x) = \psi(\alpha x).$$

This can be seen by showing the identity first for α and x which are powers of ω and then using linearity. The details are left as an exercise (see Exercise 11.1). Note that for any $\alpha, x \in \mathbb{F}_{b^m} \setminus \{0\} =: \mathbb{F}_{b^m}^*$, we have $\alpha x \neq 0 \in \mathbb{F}_{b^m}$ and hence, $\Psi(\alpha)\psi(x) = \psi(\alpha x) \neq \mathbf{0} \in \mathbb{F}_b^m$. Therefore, it follows that for any $\alpha \in \mathbb{F}_{b^m}^*$, we have the matrix $\Psi(\alpha)$ as non-singular.

Furthermore, let the definition of ψ be extended to vectors over $\mathbb{F}_{b^m}$, i.e. such that for arbitrary $r \in \mathbb{N}$, vectors in $\mathbb{F}_{b^m}^r$ get mapped to vectors in $(\mathbb{F}_b^{rm})^\top$. By linearity we can also extend the mapping Ψ to matrices by applying it to the matrix entries and letting the matrices run together, i.e. with some abuse of notation

$$\Psi(A) := (\Psi(a_{i,j}))_{\substack{i=1,\ldots,r_1 \\ j=1,\ldots,r_2}} \in \mathbb{F}_b^{r_1 m \times r_2 m}$$

for $A = (a_{i,j})_{\substack{i=1,\dots,r_1 \\ j=1,\dots,r_2}} \in \mathbb{F}_{b^m}^{r_1 \times r_2}$. Again by linearity we obtain

$$\Psi(A)\psi(\mathbf{x}) = \psi(A\mathbf{x})$$

for $A \in \mathbb{F}_{b^m}^{r_1 \times r_2}$ and $\mathbf{x} \in (\mathbb{F}_{b^m}^{r_2})^\top$ where $r_1, r_2 \in \mathbb{N}$.

Now we can express the generating matrices of a cyclic net in terms of α. The following theorem was first proved in [221, Theorem 2.7].

Theorem 11.2 *Let b be a prime power, let $s, m \in \mathbb{N}$ and let $\alpha \in \mathbb{F}_{b^m} = \mathbb{F}_b[\omega]$, $\alpha \neq 0$, be given. Define the $m \times m$ matrices $B_i = (\psi(b_{i,1}), \dots, \psi(b_{i,m}))$, where $b_{i,1}, \dots, b_{i,m}$ constitute the chosen basis $\mathcal{B}_i$ for $1 \le i \le s$. Then the matrices*

$$C_i = (\Psi(\alpha^{i-1})B_i)^\top = (\Psi(\alpha)^{i-1}B_i)^\top,$$

$1 \le i \le s$, can be chosen as generating matrices of the cyclic net $\mathcal{P}_\alpha$ over $\mathbb{F}_b$. Furthermore, it follows that C_i is non-singular for $1 \le i \le s$.

Proof Let ϕ_1 be the (additive) isomorphism between $\mathcal{F} \subseteq \mathbb{F}_{b^m}[x]$ and $(\mathbb{F}_{b^m}^s)^\top$, i.e. $\phi_1(f) = (\gamma_1, \dots, \gamma_s)^\top \in (\mathbb{F}_{b^m}^s)^\top$ whenever $f(x) = \sum_{i=1}^s \gamma_i x^{i-1}$. To obtain the mapping ϕ of Definition 11.1, we have to account for the choice of arbitrary bases $\mathcal{B}_1, \dots, \mathcal{B}_s$. We do this by multiplying by the transformation matrix B^{-1}, where B is a square, block diagonal matrix with the matrices $B_1, \dots, B_s$ of the statement of the theorem in its diagonal. This can be verified as follows. Fix $1 \le i \le s$ and let $\gamma_i \in \mathbb{F}_{b^m}$ with $\gamma_i = \sum_{r=1}^m \gamma_{i,r} b_{i,r}$, where $b_{i,1}, \dots, b_{i,m}$ constitute the chosen basis $\mathcal{B}_i$. Hence, $\gamma_i = \sum_{l=0}^{m-1} \left(\sum_{r=1}^m \gamma_{i,r}\beta_{i,r,l}\right)\omega^l$ whenever $b_{i,r} = \sum_{l=0}^{m-1} \beta_{i,r,l}\omega^l$ for $1 \le r \le m$. Therefore, we have

$$\psi(\gamma_i) = \begin{pmatrix} \beta_{i,1,0} & \dots & \beta_{i,m,0} \\ \vdots & & \vdots \\ \beta_{i,1,m-1} & \dots & \beta_{i,m,m-1} \end{pmatrix} \begin{pmatrix} \gamma_{i,1} \\ \vdots \\ \gamma_{i,m} \end{pmatrix}$$

$$= (\psi(b_{i,1}), \dots, \psi(b_{i,m})) \begin{pmatrix} \gamma_{i,1} \\ \vdots \\ \gamma_{i,m} \end{pmatrix}.$$

Together, we have $\phi(f) = B^{-1}\psi(\phi_1(f))$ for $f \in \mathcal{F}$. We summarise these relations in the following diagrams.

$$\begin{array}{ccc} \mathcal{F} & \xrightarrow{\phi_1} & (\mathbb{F}_{b^m}^s)^\top \\ \phi \downarrow & & \downarrow \psi, \Psi \\ (\mathbb{F}_b^{ms})^\top & \xleftarrow[B^{-1}]{} & (\mathbb{F}_b^{ms})^\top \end{array} \qquad \begin{array}{ccc} \mathcal{F}_\alpha & \xrightarrow{\phi_1} & \phi_1(\mathcal{F}_\alpha) \\ \phi \downarrow & & \downarrow \psi \\ \mathcal{N}_\alpha & \xleftarrow[B^{-1}]{} & \mathcal{N}_\alpha^\circ \end{array}$$

Our first goal is to describe $\mathcal{N}_\alpha^\circ := \psi(\phi_1(\mathcal{F}_\alpha))$. Clearly, $\phi_1(\mathcal{F}_\alpha)$ is the space of all column vectors orthogonal to $(1, \alpha, \dots, \alpha^{s-1})^\top$. Hence, $\mathbf{x} \in \phi_1(\mathcal{F}_\alpha)$ if and only if $0 = (1, \alpha, \dots, \alpha^{s-1})\mathbf{x}$, which is equivalent to

$$\mathbf{0} = \psi((1, \alpha, \dots, \alpha^{s-1})\mathbf{x}) = \Psi((1, \alpha, \dots, \alpha^{s-1}))\psi(\mathbf{x}).$$

Hence, $\mathcal{N}_\alpha^\circ$ is the orthogonal space to $\mathcal{C}_\alpha^\circ$, the transpose of the row space of the matrix

$$C_\alpha^\circ := \Psi((1, \alpha, \dots, \alpha^{s-1})) = (\Psi(1), \Psi(\alpha), \dots, \Psi(\alpha^{s-1})) \in \mathbb{F}_b^{m \times sm}.$$

If the bases $\mathcal{B}_1, \dots, \mathcal{B}_s$ are again taken into account, we have $\mathcal{N}_\alpha$ as the image of $\mathcal{N}_\alpha^\circ$ under the automorphism $\mathbf{x} \mapsto B^{-1}\mathbf{x}$; accordingly its orthogonal space is the image under $\mathbf{x} \mapsto B^\top \mathbf{x}$, since $\mathcal{C}_\alpha = \mathcal{N}_\alpha^\perp = (B^{-1}\mathcal{N}_\alpha^\circ)^\perp = B^\top(\mathcal{N}_\alpha^\circ)^\perp = B^\top \mathcal{C}_\alpha^\circ$ (see Exercise 11.3). Thus, $C_\alpha^\top := B^\top (C_\alpha^\circ)^\top$ is the transpose of the overall generating matrix of the cyclic digital net and $C_i := (\Psi(\alpha^{i-1})B_i)^\top$, for $1 \le i \le s$, are its generating matrices by the duality theory of digital nets (see Chapter 7). As the mapping Ψ is a ring homomorphism, we also have $\Psi(\alpha^i) = \Psi(\alpha)^i$ (see Exercise 11.2).

In order to show that the matrices $C_1, \dots, C_s$ are non-singular, recall that for any $\alpha \in \mathbb{F}_{b^m}^*$, the matrix $\Psi(\alpha)$ is non-singular and the matrices $B_1, \dots, B_s$ are non-singular as well, hence it follows that $C_1, \dots, C_s$ have to be non-singular. □

Remark 11.3 Note that every digital net with non-singular generating matrices $C_1, \dots, C_s$ is cyclic with respect to some choice of bases $\mathcal{B}_1, \dots, \mathcal{B}_s$. This is clear since any given non-singular matrices $C_1, \dots, C_s$ can be considered as cyclic net generating matrices by choosing B_i such that $B_i^{-1} = \Psi(\alpha)^{-i+1}C_i^\top$ for $1 \le i \le s$. However, the bases $\mathcal{B}_1, \dots, \mathcal{B}_s$ are to be understood as parameters that are chosen before α and completely independent of it.

On the other hand, in many cases it is preferable to consider a restricted version of the original definition of cyclic nets where only a constant fixed basis $\mathcal{B}_i = \mathcal{B}$, $1 \le i \le s$, is allowed. This was proposed by Niederreiter [184].

A generalisation of the cyclic net construction is the concept of hyperplane nets which was introduced in reference [221].

Definition 11.4 Let b be a prime power and let $s, m \in \mathbb{N}$. Let $\mathbb{F}_{b^m}$ be a finite field of b^m elements and fix an element $\boldsymbol{\alpha} = (\alpha_1, \dots, \alpha_s) \in \mathbb{F}_{b^m}^s$. Let $\mathcal{F}$ be the space of polynomials (which are understood as linear forms)

$$\mathcal{F} := \{f(x_1, \dots, x_s) = x_1\gamma_1 + \dots + x_s\gamma_s \,:\, \gamma_1, \dots, \gamma_s \in \mathbb{F}_{q^m}\} \subseteq \mathbb{F}_{q^m}[x_1, \dots, x_s]$$

and consider the subset

$$\mathcal{F}_{\boldsymbol{\alpha}} = \{f \in \mathcal{F} : f(\alpha_1, \ldots, \alpha_s) = 0\}.$$

For each $1 \le i \le s$, choose an ordered basis $\mathcal{B}_i$ of $\mathbb{F}_{b^m}$ over $\mathbb{F}_b$ and define the mapping $\phi : \mathcal{F} \to (\mathbb{F}_b^{ms})^\top$ by

$$f(x_1, \ldots, x_s) = \sum_{i=1}^{s} \gamma_i x_i \mapsto (\gamma_{1,1}, \ldots, \gamma_{1,m}, \ldots, \gamma_{s,1}, \ldots, \gamma_{s,m})^\top,$$

where $(\gamma_{i,1}, \ldots, \gamma_{i,m}) \in \mathbb{F}_b^m$ is the coordinate vector of $\gamma_i \in \mathbb{F}_{b^m}$ with respect to the chosen basis $\mathcal{B}_i$ for all $1 \le i \le s$.

Denote by $\mathcal{C}_{\boldsymbol{\alpha}}$ the orthogonal subspace in $(\mathbb{F}_b^{ms})^\top$ of the image $\mathcal{N}_{\boldsymbol{\alpha}} := \phi(\mathcal{F}_{\boldsymbol{\alpha}})$. Let

$$C_{\boldsymbol{\alpha}} = (C_1^\top \mid \ldots \mid C_s^\top) \in \mathbb{F}_b^{m \times sm}$$

be a matrix whose row space is the transpose of $\mathcal{C}_{\boldsymbol{\alpha}}$. Then $C_1, \ldots, C_s$ are the generating matrices of a *hyperplane net over* $\mathbb{F}_b$ *with respect to* $\mathcal{B}_1, \ldots, \mathcal{B}_s$ and $C_{\boldsymbol{\alpha}}$ is its overall generating matrix. This hyperplane net is denoted by $\mathcal{P}_{\boldsymbol{\alpha}}$ and we say $\mathcal{P}_{\boldsymbol{\alpha}}$ is the *hyperplane net associated with* $\boldsymbol{\alpha}$. We shall assume that the choice of bases $\mathcal{B}_1, \ldots, \mathcal{B}_s$ is made before the choice of $\boldsymbol{\alpha}$.

The definition of hyperplane nets implies that cyclic nets are hyperplane nets with $\boldsymbol{\alpha}$ of the form $\boldsymbol{\alpha} = (1, \alpha, \ldots, \alpha^{s-1})$ where $\alpha \in \mathbb{F}_{b^m}$.

Similarly as for cyclic nets, we can express the generating matrices of a hyperplane net in terms of $\boldsymbol{\alpha} = (\alpha_1, \ldots, \alpha_s) \in \mathbb{F}_{b^m}^s$.

Theorem 11.5 *Let b be a prime power, let $s, m \in \mathbb{N}$ and assume that $\mathbb{F}_{b^m} = \mathbb{F}_b[\omega]$. Let $\boldsymbol{\alpha} \in \mathbb{F}_{b^m}$, $\boldsymbol{\alpha} = (\alpha_1, \ldots, \alpha_s)$, be given. Define the $m \times m$ matrices $B_i = (\psi(b_{i,1}), \ldots, \psi(b_{i,m}))$, where $b_{i,1}, \ldots, b_{i,m}$ constitute the chosen basis $\mathcal{B}_i$ for $1 \le i \le s$. Then the matrices*

$$C_i = (\Psi(\alpha_i) B_i)^\top,$$

for all $1 \le i \le s$ can be chosen as the generating matrices of the hyperplane net $\mathcal{P}_{\boldsymbol{\alpha}}$ over $\mathbb{F}_b$. Furthermore, it follows that C_i is non-singular whenever $\alpha_i \neq 0$.

The proof of this result is similar to that of Theorem 11.2 and is therefore left as an exercise (see Exercise 11.4).

Remark 11.6 Note that for $\alpha_i = 0$, we obtain that $C_i = \mathbf{0} \in \mathbb{F}_b^{m \times m}$, the matrix consisting only of $0 \in \mathbb{F}_b$. As a consequence, by Remark 11.3 a hyperplane net with non-singular generating matrices can also be considered as a cyclic net for some choice of bases $\mathcal{B}_1, \ldots, \mathcal{B}_s$. It is therefore really meaningful to consider hyperplane nets as a generalisation of cyclic nets when the same choice of bases $\mathcal{B}_1, \ldots, \mathcal{B}_s$ is made for both.

We show now that hyperplane nets can be viewed as a generalisation of polynomial lattice point sets as introduced in Definition 10.1. This was first shown by Pirsic [220, Theorem 2].

For $m \in \mathbb{N}$, $p \in \mathbb{F}_b[x]$ with $\deg(p) = m$ and $\boldsymbol{q} = (q_1, \ldots, q_s) \in \mathbb{F}_b[x]^s$ with $\deg(q_i) < m$ for all $1 \le i \le s$, the polynomial lattice $\mathcal{P}(\boldsymbol{q}, p)$ is a digital net whose generating matrices are given by

$$C_i = \begin{pmatrix} u_1^{(i)} & u_2^{(i)} & \ldots & u_m^{(i)} \\ u_2^{(i)} & u_3^{(i)} & \ldots & u_{m+1}^{(i)} \\ \vdots & \vdots & & \vdots \\ u_m^{(i)} & u_{m+1}^{(i)} & \ldots & u_{2m-1}^{(i)} \end{pmatrix} \in \mathbb{F}_b^{m \times m},$$

where $q_i(x)/p(x) = \sum_{l=1}^{\infty} u_l^{(i)} x^{-l} \in \mathbb{F}_b((x^{-1}))$ is the Laurent series expansion in $1/x$. Note that $\mathcal{P}(a\boldsymbol{q}, ap) = \mathcal{P}(\boldsymbol{q}, p)$ for any $a \in \mathbb{F}_b^*$. Hence, we assume that the polynomial p is monic.

For a Laurent series $L = \sum_{l=w}^{\infty} t_l x^{-l}$, let $\iota_m(L)$ denote the truncation map of the series to the vector of the first m positively indexed coefficients, i.e. $\iota_m(L) = (t_1, \ldots, t_m)^\top \in (\mathbb{F}_b^m)^\top$, where we set $t_1 = \cdots = t_{w-1} = 0$ if $w > 1$. Hence, the jth column vector of the matrix C_i, $1 \le j \le m$, $1 \le i \le s$, is given by $\iota_m\left(x^{j-1} q_i(x)/p(x)\right)$, i.e.

$$C_i = \left(\iota_m\left(\frac{q_i(x)}{p(x)}\right), \iota_m\left(\frac{x q_i(x)}{p(x)}\right), \ldots, \iota_m\left(\frac{x^{m-1} q_i(x)}{p(x)}\right) \right).$$

Let $M_p \in \mathbb{F}_b^{m \times m}$ be the Hankel matrix associated with $1/p(x) = x^{-m} + \sum_{j>m} p_{j-m} x^{-j}$, i.e.

$$M_p = \left(\iota_m\left(\frac{1}{p(x)}\right), \iota_m\left(\frac{x}{p(x)}\right), \ldots, \iota_m\left(\frac{x^{m-1}}{p(x)}\right) \right)$$

$$= \begin{pmatrix} 0 & 0 & \ldots & 0 & 1 \\ 0 & & \cdot^{\cdot^{\cdot}} & 1 & p_1 \\ \vdots & \cdot^{\cdot^{\cdot}} & \cdot^{\cdot^{\cdot}} & \cdot^{\cdot^{\cdot}} & \vdots \\ 0 & 1 & \cdot^{\cdot^{\cdot}} & & p_{m-2} \\ 1 & p_1 & \ldots & p_{m-2} & p_{m-1} \end{pmatrix} \in \mathbb{F}_b^{m \times m}.$$

Assume that $q_i(x) = \sum_{j=0}^{m-1} q_{i,j} x^j$ for $1 \le i \le s$. Then we have (see Exercise 11.5)

$$\begin{aligned}
\iota_m\left(\frac{q_i(x)}{p(x)}\right) &= \iota_m\left(\frac{q_{i,0} + q_{i,1}x + \cdots + q_{i,m-1}x^{m-1}}{p(x)}\right) \\
&= \sum_{j=0}^{m-1} q_{i,j}\iota_m\left(\frac{x^j}{p(x)}\right) \\
&= M_p\,(q_{i,0}, q_{i,1}, \ldots, q_{i,m-1})^\top \\
&= M_p\,\vartheta_m(q_i(x) \bmod p(x)),
\end{aligned}$$

where ϑ_m maps a polynomial $a(x) = a_0 + a_1x + \cdots + a_{m-1}x^{m-1}$ of degree at most $m-1$ to the m-dimensional vector of its coefficients, i.e. $\vartheta_m(a) = (a_0, \ldots, a_{m-1})^\top$.

As ι_m also cuts off the polynomial part of a Laurent series, we obtain for all $j \in \mathbb{N}_0$ that

$$\iota_m\left(\frac{x^j q_i(x)}{p(x)}\right) = M_p\,\vartheta_m(x^j q_i(x) \bmod p(x)).$$

Assume that $\mathbb{F}_{b^m} = \mathbb{F}_b[\omega]$, where ω is the residue class of x in $\mathbb{F}_b[x]/(p)$ and write the polynomial p as $p(x) = x^m - \beta_{m-1}x^{m-1} - \cdots - \beta_1 x - \beta_0$. Hence, we have $\omega^m = \beta_0 + \cdots + \beta_{m-1}\omega^{m-1}$. Define the matrix P as in (11.1). Then we have $q_i(\omega) \in \mathbb{F}_{b^m}$ and

$$\begin{aligned}
\Psi(q_i(\omega)) &= \sum_{j=0}^{m-1} q_{i,j} P^j \\
&= \left(\vartheta_m(q_i(x) \bmod p(x)), \ldots, \vartheta_m(x^{m-1}q_i(x) \bmod p(x))\right).
\end{aligned}$$

Hence, for all $1 \le i \le s$, we have

$$C_i = M_p\Psi(q_i(\omega)) = \Psi(q_i(\omega))^\top M_p^\top = \Psi(q_i(\omega))^\top M_p,$$

since C_i and M_p are both symmetric with respect to their first diagonals. However, M_p is a non-singular matrix and hence, by Lemma 4.61 its effect is only a reordering of the point set associated with the generating matrices $\Psi(q_i(\omega))^\top$, $1 \le i \le s$.

We summarise these considerations in the following theorem.

Theorem 11.7 *Let b be a prime power, let $m \in \mathbb{N}$, let $p \in \mathbb{F}_b[x]$ be a (not necessarily irreducible) monic polynomial with $\deg(p) = m$. Let ω be the residue class of x in $\mathbb{F}_b[x]/(p)$ and let $\mathbb{F}_{b^m} = \mathbb{F}_b[\omega]$. Then the polynomial lattice point set $\mathcal{P}(\boldsymbol{q}, p)$, where $\boldsymbol{q} = (q_1, .., q_s) \in \mathbb{F}_b[x]^s$ with $\deg(q_i) < m$ for all $1 \le i \le s$, is generated by the matrices $\Psi(q_i(\omega))^\top$, $1 \le i \le s$. Hence, $\mathcal{P}(\boldsymbol{q}, p)$ is the same as* *the hyperplane net associated with the vector* $\boldsymbol{\alpha} := (q_1(\omega), \ldots, q_s(\omega)) \in \mathbb{F}_{b^m}^s$ *and with the powers of* ω *as the choice for the ordered bases* $\mathcal{B}_1 = \cdots = \mathcal{B}_s$ *(hence,* $B_1 = \cdots = B_s$ *are all equal to the identity matrix).*

For hyperplane nets, we can express the dual net (see Definition 4.76) in terms of $\boldsymbol{\alpha} = (\alpha_1, \ldots, \alpha_s)$. The subsequent Lemma 11.8 should be compared with Lemma 10.6, where we expressed the dual net of a polynomial lattice $\mathcal{P}(\boldsymbol{q}, p)$ in terms of its generating vector $\boldsymbol{q}$ and its modulus p.

Let $\varphi : \mathbb{Z}_b \to \mathbb{F}_b$ be a bijection with $\varphi(0) = 0 \in \mathbb{F}_b$ as used in the construction of a digital net (see Definition 4.47). Assuming again that $\mathbb{F}_{b^m} = \mathbb{F}_b[\omega]$, for $0 \le k < b^m$ with b-adic expansion $k = \sum_{l=0}^{m-1} \kappa_l b^l$ where $\kappa_0, \ldots, \kappa_{m-1} \in \mathbb{Z}_b$, define

$$\varphi'(k) := \sum_{l=0}^{m-1} \varphi(\kappa_l)\omega^l \in \mathbb{F}_{b^m}$$

and

$$\psi'(k) := \psi(\varphi'(k)) = (\varphi(\kappa_0), \ldots, \varphi(\kappa_{m-1}))^\top =: \mathbf{k} \in (\mathbb{F}_b^m)^\top$$

and define all extensions to vectors and matrices. We have the following commutative diagram:

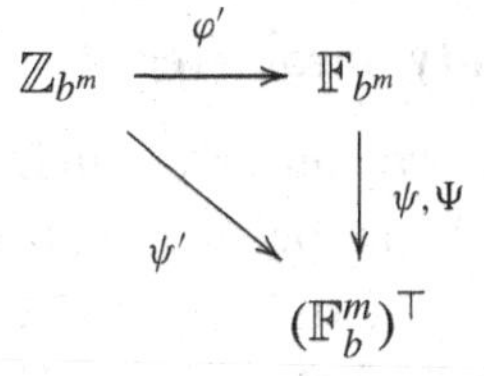

Lemma 11.8 *Let* b *be a prime power and let* $s, m \in \mathbb{N}$. *Assume that the* $m \times m$ *matrices* $C_1, \ldots, C_s$ *as given in Theorem 11.5 are generating matrices of a hyperplane net* $\mathcal{P}_{\boldsymbol{\alpha}}$ *over* $\mathbb{F}_b$, *where* $\boldsymbol{\alpha} = (\alpha_1, \ldots, \alpha_s) \in \mathbb{F}_{b^m}^s$. *Then, for any integers* $k_1, \ldots, k_s \in \{0, \ldots, b^m - 1\}$ *with corresponding* b*-adic digit vectors* $\mathbf{k}_1, \ldots, \mathbf{k}_s \in (\mathbb{F}_b^m)^\top$, *we have*

$$C_1^\top \mathbf{k}_1 + \cdots + C_s^\top \mathbf{k}_s = \mathbf{0} \in (\mathbb{F}_b^m)^\top$$

if and only if

$$\alpha_1 \varphi'(\tau_1(k_1)) + \cdots + \alpha_s \varphi'(\tau_s(k_s)) = 0 \in \mathbb{F}_{b^m}$$

with permutations $\tau_i(k) = \psi'^{-1}(B_i \psi'(k))$, *and* B_i *as in Theorem 11.2, for all* $1 \le i \le s$.

Proof By Theorem 11.5 we have

$$\begin{aligned}\sum_{i=1}^{s} C_i^\top \mathbf{k}_i &= \sum_{i=1}^{s} C_i^\top \psi'(k_i) = \sum_{i=1}^{s} \Psi(\alpha_i) B_i \psi'(k_i)\\ &= \sum_{i=1}^{s} \Psi(\alpha_i)\psi'(\tau_i(k_i)) = \sum_{i=1}^{s} \psi(\alpha_i \varphi'(\tau_i(k_i)))\\ &= \psi\left(\sum_{i=1}^{s} \alpha_i \varphi'(\tau_i(k_i))\right).\end{aligned}$$

Hence, $\sum_{i=1}^{s} C_i^\top \mathbf{k}_i = \mathbf{0}$ if and only if $\sum_{i=1}^{s} \alpha_i \varphi'(\tau_i(k_i)) = 0$. □

Lemma 11.8 prompts the following definition.

Definition 11.9 The *dual net* of a hyperplane net $\mathcal{P}_{\boldsymbol{\alpha}}$ over $\mathbb{F}_b$ is given by

$$\mathcal{D}_{\boldsymbol{\alpha}} := \left\{ \boldsymbol{k} \in \{0, \ldots, b^m - 1\}^s : \sum_{i=1}^{s} \alpha_i \varphi'(\tau_i(k_i)) = 0 \right\},$$

where $\boldsymbol{k} = (k_1, \ldots, k_s)$ and where τ_i for $1 \le i \le s$ is as in Lemma 11.8. Furthermore, let $\mathcal{D}'_{\boldsymbol{\alpha}} = \mathcal{D}_{\boldsymbol{\alpha}} \setminus \{\mathbf{0}\}$.

11.2 The quality parameter of hyperplane nets

For polynomial lattice point sets, we introduced in Definition 10.8 a so-called figure of merit which was based on the associated dual net. With Lemma 11.8 we can define in the same way a figure of merit for the more general concept of hyperplane nets. The following definition was first given in [215, Definition 5].

Definition 11.10 For $\boldsymbol{\alpha} = (\alpha_1, \ldots, \alpha_s) \in \mathbb{F}_{b^m}^s$ the figure of merit $\rho(\boldsymbol{\alpha})$ is defined as

$$\rho(\boldsymbol{\alpha}) = s - 1 + \min_{\boldsymbol{k} \in \mathcal{D}'_{\boldsymbol{\alpha}}} \sum_{i=1}^{s} \lfloor \log_b(k_i) \rfloor,$$

where $\boldsymbol{k} = (k_1, \ldots, k_s)$, where $\log_b$ is the logarithm in base b, and where we use the convention $\lfloor \log_b(0) \rfloor := -1$.

With this figure of merit at hand, we may now give a formula for the quality parameter of a hyperplane net.

Theorem 11.11 *Let b be a prime power and let $s, m \in \mathbb{N}$. Then the hyperplane net $\mathcal{P}_{\boldsymbol{\alpha}}$ associated with $\boldsymbol{\alpha} \in \mathbb{F}_{b^m}^s$ is a strict digital (t, m, s)-net over $\mathbb{F}_b$ with $t = m - \rho(\boldsymbol{\alpha})$.*

Proof Let $C_1, \ldots, C_s$ be the generating matrices of the hyperplane net $\mathcal{P}_{\boldsymbol{\alpha}}$ and let $\varphi : \mathbb{Z}_b \to \mathbb{F}_b$ with $\varphi(0) = 0$ be the bijection used in the construction. It is enough to show that $\rho(\boldsymbol{\alpha}) = \rho(C_1, \ldots, C_s)$, where the later quantity is the linear independence parameter of the matrices $C_1, \ldots, C_s$ as defined in Definition 4.50. The result then follows from Lemma 4.52. To show this equality, we follow the proof of Theorem 10.9.

According to the definition of $\rho(C_1, \ldots, C_s)$ there are $d_1, \ldots, d_s \in \mathbb{N}_0$ with $d_1 + \cdots + d_s = \rho(C_1, \ldots, C_s) + 1$ such that the system consisting of the first d_i row vectors $\mathbf{c}_1^{(i)}, \ldots, \mathbf{c}_{d_i}^{(i)}$ of the matrix C_i for $1 \le i \le s$, is linearly dependent over $\mathbb{F}_b$; that is, there exist $\kappa_{i,j} \in \mathbb{Z}_b$ for $0 \le j < d_i$ and $1 \le i \le s$, not all zero, such that

$$\sum_{i=1}^{s} \sum_{j=0}^{d_i - 1} \varphi(\kappa_{i,j}) \mathbf{c}_{j+1}^{(i)} = \mathbf{0} \in \mathbb{F}_b^m.$$

Putting $\kappa_{i,j} = 0$ for $d_i \le j < m$ and $1 \le i \le s$ and $k_i = \kappa_{i,0} + \kappa_{i,1} b + \cdots + \kappa_{i,m-1} b^{m-1}$ and correspondingly $\mathbf{k}_i = (\varphi(\kappa_{i,0}), \ldots, \varphi(\kappa_{i,m-1}))^\top$ for $1 \le i \le s$, we obtain

$$C_1^\top \mathbf{k}_1 + \cdots + C_s^\top \mathbf{k}_s = \mathbf{0} \in (\mathbb{F}_b^m)^\top.$$

Hence, from Lemma 11.8 we obtain $\alpha_1 \varphi'(\tau_1(k_1)) + \cdots + \alpha_s \varphi'(\tau_s(k_s)) = 0$ and therefore,

$$\rho(\boldsymbol{\alpha}) \le s - 1 + \sum_{i=1}^{s} \lfloor \log_b(k_i) \rfloor \le s - 1 + \sum_{i=1}^{s} (d_i - 1) = \rho(C_1, \ldots, C_s).$$

On the other hand, there exist $k_1, \ldots, k_s \in \{0, \ldots, b^m - 1\}$, not all zero, satisfying $\alpha_1 \varphi'(\tau_1(k_1)) + \cdots + \alpha_s \varphi'(\tau_s(k_s)) = 0$ such that $\rho(\boldsymbol{\alpha}) = s - 1 + \sum_{i=1}^{s} \lfloor \log_b(k_i) \rfloor$. Hence, by Lemma 11.8 we obtain $C_1^\top \mathbf{k}_1 + \cdots + C_s^\top \mathbf{k}_s = \mathbf{0} \in (\mathbb{F}_b^m)^\top$ or equivalently, $\sum_{i=1}^{s} \sum_{j=1}^{m} \varphi(\kappa_{i,j-1}) \mathbf{c}_j^{(i)} = \mathbf{0} \in \mathbb{F}_b^m$, where $k_i = \kappa_{i,0} + \kappa_{i,1} b + \cdots + \kappa_{i,m-1} b^{m-1}$ for $1 \le i \le s$. For $1 \le i \le s$, let $d_i = \lfloor \log_b(k_i) \rfloor + 1$. Then the system consisting of the first d_i row vectors of the matrix C_i for $1 \le i \le s$, is linearly dependent over $\mathbb{F}_b$ and hence,

$$\rho(C_1, \ldots, C_s) \le -1 + \sum_{i=1}^{s} d_i = s - 1 + \sum_{i=1}^{s} \lfloor \log_b(k_i) \rfloor = \rho(\boldsymbol{\alpha}). \qquad \square$$

From the definition of the figure of merit $\rho(\boldsymbol{\alpha})$ and from Theorem 11.11, we see that it is enough to consider vectors $\boldsymbol{\alpha}$ of the form $\boldsymbol{\alpha} = (1, \alpha_2, \ldots, \alpha_s)$ only. The following existence result given in [215, Theorem 2] is the analogue of Theorem 10.13 for hyperplane nets.

Theorem 11.12 *Let b be a prime power and let $s, m \in \mathbb{N}$, $s \geq 2$. Choose ordered bases $\mathcal{B}_1, \ldots, \mathcal{B}_s$ of $\mathbb{F}_{b^m}$ over $\mathbb{F}_b$. For $\rho \in \mathbb{Z}$ define*

$$\Delta_b(s, \rho) = \sum_{d=0}^{s-1} \binom{s}{d} (b-1)^{s-d} \sum_{\gamma=0}^{\rho+d} \binom{s-d+\gamma-1}{\gamma} b^\gamma + 1 - b^{\rho+s}.$$

1. *If $\Delta_b(s, \rho) < b^m$, then there exists an element $\boldsymbol{\alpha} \in \mathbb{F}_{b^m}^s$ of the form $\boldsymbol{\alpha} = (1, \alpha_2, \ldots, \alpha_s)$ with $\rho(\boldsymbol{\alpha}) \geq s + \rho$. Therefore, the hyperplane net $\mathcal{P}_{\boldsymbol{\alpha}}$ is a digital (t, m, s)-net over $\mathbb{F}_b$ with $t \leq m - s - \rho$.*
2. *If $\Delta_b(s, \rho) < \frac{b^m}{s-1}$, then there exists an element $\alpha \in \mathbb{F}_{b^m}$ such that $\boldsymbol{\alpha} = (1, \alpha, \ldots, \alpha^{s-1})$ satisfies $\rho(\boldsymbol{\alpha}) \geq s + \rho$. Therefore, the cyclic net $\mathcal{P}_\alpha$ is a digital (t, m, s)-net over $\mathbb{F}_b$ with $t \leq m - s - \rho$.*

We obtain the following corollary whose proof is identical to that of Corollary 10.15.

Corollary 11.13 *Let b be a prime power and let $s, m \in \mathbb{N}$ where $s \geq 2$ and where m is sufficiently large.*

1. *There exists a vector $\boldsymbol{\alpha} \in \mathbb{F}_{b^m}^s$ with*
$$\rho(\boldsymbol{\alpha}) \geq \lfloor m - (s-1)(\log_b m - 1) + \log_b (s-1)! \rfloor.$$
2. *There exists an element $\alpha \in \mathbb{F}_{b^m}$ such that $\boldsymbol{\alpha} = (1, \alpha, \ldots, \alpha^{s-1})$ satisfies*
$$\rho(\boldsymbol{\alpha}) \geq \lfloor m - (s-1)(\log_b m - 1) + \log_b (s-2)! \rfloor.$$

The proof of Theorem 11.12 is nearly the same as that of Theorem 10.13. However, to see the differences, we present the proof of the first assertion. To this end we need the following result.

Lemma 11.14 *Let b be a prime power and let $l \in \mathbb{N}$ and $k \in \mathbb{N}_0$. Then the number $A_b(l, k)$ of $(h_1, \ldots, h_l) \in \{1, \ldots, b^m - 1\}^l$ such that $\sum_{i=1}^l \lfloor \log_b(h_i) \rfloor \leq k$ is given by*

$$A_b(l, k) = (b-1)^l \sum_{\gamma=0}^{k} \binom{l+\gamma-1}{\gamma} b^\gamma.$$

Proof The proof of this result is identical to that of Lemma 10.14. □

Proof of Theorem 11.12 Let $M_b(s, \rho)$ be the number of $(k_1, \ldots, k_s) \in \mathbb{Z}_{b^m}^s$ with $(k_2, \ldots, k_s) \neq (0, \ldots, 0)$ and $\sum_{i=1}^s \lfloor \log_b(k_i) \rfloor \leq \rho$. Using the notation and the result of Lemma 11.14, we get

$$M_b(s, \rho) = \sum_{d=0}^{s-1} \binom{s}{d} A_b(s-d, \rho+d) + 1 - b^{\rho+s} = \Delta_b(s, \rho).$$

(Recall the convention that $\lfloor \log_b(0) \rfloor = -1$.)

For a given non-zero element $(k_1, \dots, k_s) \in \{0, \dots, b^m - 1\}^s$ the equation $\varphi'(\tau_1(k_1)) + \alpha_2\varphi'(\tau_2(k_2)) + \cdots + \alpha_s\varphi'(\tau_s(k_s)) = 0$ has no solution if $k_2 = \cdots = k_s = 0$ (note that $\varphi'(\tau_i(0)) = 0$ for all $1 \le i \le s$), and it has exactly $b^{m(s-2)}$ solutions $\boldsymbol{\alpha} = (1, \alpha_2, \dots, \alpha_s) \in \mathbb{F}_{b^m}^s$ otherwise (note that $\varphi' \circ \tau_i$ are bijections for all $1 \le i \le s$). Therefore, to all non-zero $(k_1, \dots, k_s)$ with $\sum_{i=1}^s \lfloor \log_b(k_i) \rfloor \le \rho$, there are assigned altogether at most $M_b(s, \rho)b^{m(s-2)}$ different solutions $\boldsymbol{\alpha} = (1, \alpha_2, \dots, \alpha_s) \in \mathbb{F}_{b^m}^s$ of the above equation. Now the total number of $\boldsymbol{\alpha} = (1, \alpha_2, \dots, \alpha_s) \in \mathbb{F}_{b^m}^s$ is $b^{m(s-1)}$. Thus, if $M_b(s, \rho)b^{m(s-2)} < b^{m(s-1)}$, that is, if $\Delta_b(s, \rho) < b^m$, then there exists at least one $\boldsymbol{\alpha} = (1, \alpha_2, \dots, \alpha_s) \in \mathbb{F}_{b^m}^s$ such that $\varphi'(\tau_1(k_1)) + \alpha_2\varphi'(\tau_2(k_2)) + \cdots + \alpha_s\varphi'(\tau_s(k_s)) = 0$ for all non-zero $(k_1, \dots, k_s) \in \{0, \dots, b^m - 1\}^s$ with $\sum_{i=1}^s \lfloor \log_b(k_i) \rfloor \le \rho$. For this $\boldsymbol{\alpha}$, we then have $\rho(\boldsymbol{\alpha}) \ge s + \rho$. By Theorem 11.11, the hyperplane net $\mathcal{P}_{\boldsymbol{\alpha}}$ is a digital (t, m, s)-net over $\mathbb{F}_b$ with $t \le m - s - \rho$. □

11.3 Discrepancy of hyperplane nets

Now let us turn to the (weighted) star discrepancy of hyperplane nets. In Section 10.2 we used the representation of the dual net of a polynomial lattice $\mathcal{P}(\boldsymbol{q}, p)$ in terms of $\boldsymbol{q}$ and p to give bounds for the (weighted) star discrepancy of polynomial lattices. With these bounds we were able to give an upper bound on the average (weighted) star discrepancy of polynomial lattices with fixed modulus p and we were even able to give a CBC construction and a construction of a Korobov vector for reasonably good polynomial lattice point sets. Based on Lemma 11.8, one can obtain similar results for hyperplane nets and cyclic nets. This was first done in [214]. In most cases, we skip the proofs since they are identical to those for the analogous results concerning polynomial lattices.

In the following, we only consider the case where b is a prime number. Thus, we can identify $\mathbb{F}_b$ with $\mathbb{Z}_b$ and choose the bijection $\varphi : \mathbb{Z}_b \to \mathbb{F}_b$ to be the identity map. For the general prime power b case, see [214]. First, we apply Lemma 11.8 to rewrite the bound for the star discrepancy of digital nets given in Theorem 5.34.

Corollary 11.15 *Let b be a prime and let $s, m \in \mathbb{N}$. For the star discrepancy of the hyperplane net $\mathcal{P}_{\boldsymbol{\alpha}}$ over $\mathbb{Z}_b$, where $\boldsymbol{\alpha} = (\alpha_1, \dots, \alpha_s) \in \mathbb{F}_{b^m}^s$, we have*

$$D_{b^m}^*(\mathcal{P}) \le 1 - \left(1 - \frac{1}{b^m}\right)^s + R_b'(\boldsymbol{\alpha}),$$

where

$$R_b'(\boldsymbol{\alpha}) = \sum_{\boldsymbol{k} \in \mathcal{D}_{\boldsymbol{\alpha}}'} r_b(\boldsymbol{k}),$$

where for $\boldsymbol{k} = (k_1, \ldots, k_s) \in \{0, \ldots, b^m - 1\}^s$, *we put* $r_b(\boldsymbol{k}) = r_b(k_1) \cdots r_b(k_s)$ *and where for* $k \in \{0, \ldots, b^m - 1\}$, *we put*

$$r_b(k) = \begin{cases} 1 & \text{if } k = 0, \\ \frac{1}{b^{r+1} \sin^2(\pi \kappa_r / b)} & \text{if } k = \kappa_0 + \kappa_1 b + \cdots + \kappa_r b^r,\ \kappa_r \neq 0. \end{cases}$$

An analogous result holds for the weighted star discrepancy where the weights are of product form.

Corollary 11.16 *Let* b *be a prime, let* $s, m \in \mathbb{N}$ *and let* $\boldsymbol{\gamma} = (\gamma_i)_{i \geq 1}$ *be a sequence of weights. For the weighted star discrepancy of the hyperplane net* $\mathcal{P}_{\boldsymbol{\alpha}}$ *over* $\mathbb{Z}_b$, *where* $\boldsymbol{\alpha} = (\alpha_1, \ldots, \alpha_s) \in \mathbb{F}_{b^m}^s$, *we have*

$$D^*_{b^m, \boldsymbol{\gamma}}(\mathcal{P}_{\boldsymbol{\alpha}}) \leq \sum_{\emptyset \neq \mathfrak{u} \subseteq \mathcal{I}_s} \gamma_{\mathfrak{u}} \left(1 - \left(1 - \frac{1}{b^m}\right)^{|\mathfrak{u}|}\right) + R'_{b, \boldsymbol{\gamma}}(\boldsymbol{\alpha}),$$

where

$$R'_{b, \boldsymbol{\gamma}}(\boldsymbol{\alpha}) = \sum_{\boldsymbol{k} \in \mathcal{D}'_{\boldsymbol{\alpha}}} r_b(\boldsymbol{k}, \boldsymbol{\gamma}),$$

where for $\boldsymbol{k} = (k_1, \ldots, k_s) \in \{0, \ldots, b^m - 1\}^s$, *we put* $r_b(\boldsymbol{k}, \boldsymbol{\gamma}) = r_b(k_1, \gamma_1) \cdots \cdots r_b(k_s, \gamma_s)$ *and where for* $k \in \{0, \ldots, b^m - 1\}$, *we put*

$$r_b(k, \gamma) = \begin{cases} 1 + \gamma & \text{if } k = 0, \\ \gamma r_b(k) & \text{if } k \neq 0. \end{cases}$$

It can be shown that for $\boldsymbol{\alpha} \in \mathbb{F}_{b^m}^s$ one can compute $R'_b(\boldsymbol{\alpha})$ and $R'_{b,\boldsymbol{\gamma}}(\boldsymbol{\alpha})$, respectively, at a cost of $O(sb^m)$ operations (see Exercises 11.7 and 11.8).

Now we can determine the average value of $R'_b(\boldsymbol{\alpha})$ and $R'_{b,\boldsymbol{\gamma}}(\boldsymbol{\alpha})$ over all possible $\boldsymbol{\alpha} \in (\mathbb{F}_{b^m}^*)^s$.

Theorem 11.17 *Let* s *be a prime and let* $s, m \in \mathbb{N}$. *Then we have*

$$\frac{1}{|\mathbb{F}_{b^m}^*|^s} \sum_{\boldsymbol{\alpha} \in (\mathbb{F}_{b^m}^*)^s} R'_b(\boldsymbol{\alpha}) = \frac{1}{b^m - 1} \left(\left(1 + m \frac{b^2 - 1}{3b}\right)^s - 1 - sm \frac{b^2 - 1}{3b} \right)$$

and

$$\frac{1}{|\mathbb{F}_{b^m}^*|^s} \sum_{\boldsymbol{\alpha} \in (\mathbb{F}_{b^m}^*)^s} R'_{b,\boldsymbol{\gamma}}(\boldsymbol{\alpha}) = \frac{1}{b^m - 1} \sum_{\substack{\mathfrak{u} \subseteq \mathcal{I}_s \\ |\mathfrak{u}| \geq 2}} \prod_{i \in \mathfrak{u}} \left(\gamma_i \left(m \frac{b^2 - 1}{3b} \right) \right) \prod_{i \notin \mathfrak{u}} (1 + \gamma_i).$$

Proof We provide the proof only for the unweighted case. First, observe that $|\mathbb{F}_{b^m}^*| = b^m - 1$. We have

$$\frac{1}{|\mathbb{F}_{b^m}^*|^s} \sum_{\boldsymbol{\alpha} \in (\mathbb{F}_{b^m}^*)^s} R_b'(\boldsymbol{\alpha}) = \frac{1}{(b^m - 1)^s} \sum_{\boldsymbol{\alpha} \in (\mathbb{F}_{b^m}^*)^s} \sum_{\boldsymbol{k} \in \mathcal{D}_{\boldsymbol{\alpha}}} r_b(\boldsymbol{k})$$

$$= \frac{1}{(b^m - 1)^s} \sum_{\boldsymbol{k} \in \mathbb{Z}_{b^m}^s \setminus \{\boldsymbol{0}\}} r_b(\boldsymbol{k}) \sum_{\substack{\boldsymbol{\alpha} \in (\mathbb{F}_{b^m}^*)^s \\ \boldsymbol{k} \in \mathcal{D}_{\boldsymbol{\alpha}}}} 1,$$

where we inserted for $R_b'(\boldsymbol{\alpha})$ and changed the order of summation. Note that τ_i is a permutation and that $\tau_i(k) = 0$ if and only if $k = 0$ for all $1 \le i \le s$.

If $\boldsymbol{k} \in \{0, \ldots, b^m - 1\}^s$, $\boldsymbol{k} \neq \boldsymbol{0}$, is of the form $\boldsymbol{k} = (0, \ldots, 0, k_i, 0, \ldots, 0)$ with $k_i \neq 0$, then there is no $\boldsymbol{\alpha} \in (\mathbb{F}_{b^m}^*)^s$ such that $\alpha_1 \varphi'(\tau_1(k_1)) + \cdots + \alpha_s \varphi'(\tau_s(k_s)) = \alpha_i \varphi(\tau_i(k_i)) = 0$, since $\mathbb{F}_{b^m}$ is an integral domain. Otherwise, the number of $\boldsymbol{\alpha} \in (\mathbb{F}_{b^m}^*)^s$ that satisfy $\alpha_1 \varphi'(\tau_1(k_1)) + \cdots + \alpha_s \varphi'(\tau_s(k_s)) = 0$ is exactly $(b^m - 1)^{s-1}$. Therefore, we have

$$\frac{1}{|\mathbb{F}_{b^m}^*|^s} \sum_{\boldsymbol{\alpha} \in (\mathbb{F}_{b^m}^*)^s} R_b'(\boldsymbol{\alpha}) = \frac{1}{b^m - 1} \sum_{\boldsymbol{k} \in \mathbb{Z}_{b^m}^s \setminus \{\boldsymbol{0}\}} r_b(\boldsymbol{k})$$

$$- \frac{1}{b^m - 1} \sum_{i=1}^{s} \sum_{k_i \in \mathbb{Z}_{b^m}^*} r_b(k_i) \prod_{\substack{j=1 \\ j \neq i}}^{s} r_b(0).$$

Now the result follows from Lemma 10.22. □

We obtain the following corollary to Theorem 11.17. The proof of this result is exactly the same as that of Corollary 10.23.

Corollary 11.18 *Let b be a prime and let $s, m \in \mathbb{N}$. Then, for $0 \le \delta < 1$, there are more than $\delta |\mathbb{F}_{b^m}^*|^s$ vectors $\boldsymbol{\alpha} \in (\mathbb{F}_{b^m}^*)^s$ such that*

$$D_{b^m}^*(\mathcal{P}_{\boldsymbol{\alpha}}) \le \frac{s}{b^m} + \frac{1}{1 - \delta} \frac{1}{b^m - 1} \left(1 + m \frac{b^2 - 1}{3b}\right)^s,$$

and

$$D_{b^m, \boldsymbol{\gamma}}^*(\mathcal{P}_{\boldsymbol{\alpha}}) \le \sum_{\emptyset \neq \mathfrak{u} \subseteq \mathcal{I}_s} \gamma_{\mathfrak{u}} \left(1 - \left(1 - \frac{1}{b^m}\right)^{|\mathfrak{u}|}\right)$$

$$+ \frac{1}{1 - \delta} \frac{1}{b^m - 1} \prod_{i=1}^{s} \left(1 + \gamma_i \left(1 + m \frac{b^2 - 1}{3b}\right)\right),$$

respectively.

From the previous results, it follows that there exist a sufficiently large number of vectors $\boldsymbol{\alpha} \in (\mathbb{F}_{b^m}^*)^s$ that yield hyperplane nets of good quality with respect to the (weighted) star discrepancy. As for polynomial lattices, such vectors can be found by computer search using a CBC construction. We state the algorithm for the star- and the weighted star discrepancies.

Algorithm 11.19 *Given $s, m \in \mathbb{N}$, a prime b, a sequence of ordered bases $(\mathcal{B}_i)_{i\geq 1}$ of $\mathbb{F}_{b^m}$ over $\mathbb{Z}_b$ and a sequence $\boldsymbol{\gamma} = (\gamma_i)_{i\geq 1}$ of weights:*

1. *Choose $\alpha_1 = 1$.*
2. *For $d > 1$, assume that we have already constructed $\alpha_1, \ldots, \alpha_{d-1} \in \mathbb{F}_{b^m}^*$. Then find $\alpha_d \in \mathbb{F}_{b^m}^*$ which minimises the quantity $R_b'((\alpha_1, \ldots, \alpha_{d-1}, \alpha_d))$ (or $R_{b,\boldsymbol{\gamma}}'((\alpha_1, \ldots, \alpha_{d-1}, \alpha_d))$ in the weighted case) as a function of α_d.*

Since $R_b'(\boldsymbol{\alpha})$ and $R_{b,\boldsymbol{\gamma}}'(\boldsymbol{\alpha})$ can be computed at a cost of $O(sb^m)$ operations, it follows that the cost of Algorithm 11.19 is of $O(s^2 b^{2m})$ operations.

In the following theorem, we show that Algorithm 11.19 is guaranteed to find a good vector $\boldsymbol{\alpha} \in (\mathbb{F}_{b^m}^*)^s$.

Theorem 11.20 *Let b be prime, let $s, m \in \mathbb{N}$ and let $\boldsymbol{\gamma} = (\gamma_i)_{i\geq 1}$ be a sequence of weights. Suppose that $\boldsymbol{\alpha} = (\alpha_1, \ldots, \alpha_s) \in (\mathbb{F}_{b^m}^*)^s$ is constructed according to Algorithm 11.19 using R_b' (or $R_{b,\boldsymbol{\gamma}}'$ in the weighted case). Then, for all $1 \leq d \leq s$, we have*

$$R_b'((\alpha_1, \ldots, \alpha_d)) \leq \frac{1}{b^m - 1}\left(1 + m\frac{b^2 - 1}{3b}\right)^d,$$

and

$$R_{b,\boldsymbol{\gamma}}'((\alpha_1, \ldots, \alpha_d)) \leq \frac{1}{b^m - 1}\prod_{i=1}^{d}\left(1 + \gamma_i\left(1 + m\frac{b^2 - 1}{3b}\right)\right),$$

respectively.

The proof of Theorem 11.20 is identical to that of Theorem 10.28 and is therefore left as an exercise (see Exercise 11.11).

The subsequent bound for the (weighted) star discrepancy of hyperplane nets, which are constructed according to Algorithm 11.19, follows from Corollary 11.15 by invoking Theorem 11.20.

Corollary 11.21 *Let b be prime, let $s, m \in \mathbb{N}$ and let $\boldsymbol{\gamma} = (\gamma_i)_{i\geq 1}$ be a sequence of weights. Suppose that $\boldsymbol{\alpha} = (\alpha_1, \ldots, \alpha_s) \in (\mathbb{F}_{b^m}^*)^s$ is constructed according to Algorithm 11.19 using R_b' (or $R_{b,\boldsymbol{\gamma}}'$ in the weighted case). Then, for the (weighted)* *star discrepancy of the hyperplane net $\mathcal{P}_{\boldsymbol{\alpha}}$, we have*

$$D^*_{b^m}(\mathcal{P}_{\boldsymbol{\alpha}}) \le \frac{s}{b^m} + \frac{1}{b^m - 1}\left(1 + m\frac{b^2-1}{3b}\right)^s,$$

and

$$D^*_{b^m;\boldsymbol{\gamma}}(\mathcal{P}_{\boldsymbol{\alpha}}) \le \sum_{\emptyset \ne \mathfrak{u} \subseteq \mathcal{I}_s} \gamma_{\mathfrak{u}} \left(1 - \left(1 - \frac{1}{b^m}\right)^{|\mathfrak{u}|}\right) + \frac{1}{b^m - 1}\prod_{i=1}^{s}\left(1 + \gamma_i\left(1 + m\frac{b^2-1}{3b}\right)\right),$$

respectively.

The following result can be proved in the same way as Corollary 5.45.

Corollary 11.22 *Let b be prime, let $s, m \in \mathbb{N}$ and let $\boldsymbol{\gamma} = (\gamma_i)_{i\ge 1}$ be a sequence of weights. If $\sum_{i=1}^{\infty} \gamma_i < \infty$, then for any $\delta > 0$ there exists a constant $\widetilde{c}_{\boldsymbol{\gamma},\delta} > 0$, independent of s and m, such that the weighted star discrepancy of the hyperplane net $\mathcal{P}_{\boldsymbol{\alpha}}$, where $\boldsymbol{\alpha} \in (\mathbb{F}^*_{b^m})^s$ is constructed according to Algorithm 11.19 using $R'_{b,\boldsymbol{\gamma}}$, satisfies*

$$D^*_{b^m,\boldsymbol{\gamma}}(\mathcal{P}_{\boldsymbol{\alpha}}) \le \frac{\widetilde{c}_{\boldsymbol{\gamma},\delta}}{b^{m(1-\delta)}}. \tag{11.2}$$

Remark 11.23 In the same way as in Corollary 5.46, we can use a superposition of hyperplane nets $\mathcal{P}_{\boldsymbol{\alpha}}$, where $\boldsymbol{\alpha} \in (\mathbb{F}^*_{b^m})^s$ is constructed according to Algorithm 11.19 using $R'_{b,\boldsymbol{\gamma}}$, such that we obtain for any $N, s \in \mathbb{N}$ a point set $\mathcal{P}$ in $[0,1)^s$ of cardinality N and with weighted star discrepancy $D^*_{N,\boldsymbol{\gamma}}(\mathcal{P}) \le c_{\boldsymbol{\gamma},\delta} N^{-1+\delta}$, where $c_{\boldsymbol{\gamma},\delta} > 0$ is independent of s and N whenever $\sum_{i=1}^{\infty}\gamma_i < \infty$. Hence, we again have a constructive version of the strong tractability result for the weighted star discrepancy given in Corollary 5.46.

Obviously, we can restrict the search space for $\boldsymbol{\alpha} \in (\mathbb{F}^*_{b^m})^s$ when we search for cyclic nets only. In the following, we write $R'_b(\alpha)$ (and $R'_{b,\boldsymbol{\gamma}}(\alpha)$) instead of $R'_b((1,\alpha,\ldots,\alpha^{s-1}))$ (and $R'_{b,\boldsymbol{\gamma}}((1,\alpha,\ldots,\alpha^{s-1}))$).

Algorithm 11.24 *Given $s, m \in \mathbb{N}$, a prime b, a sequence of ordered bases $(\mathcal{B}_i)_{i\ge1}$ of $\mathbb{F}_{b^m}$ over $\mathbb{Z}_b$ and a sequence $\boldsymbol{\gamma} = (\gamma_i)_{i\ge 1}$ of weights, find $\alpha \in \mathbb{F}^*_{b^m}$ by minimising the quantity $R'_b(\alpha)$ (or $R'_{b,\boldsymbol{\gamma}}(\alpha)$ in the weighted case).*

The cost of the algorithm is of $O(sb^{2m})$ operations.

We show that Algorithm 11.24 is guaranteed to find a good $\alpha \in \mathbb{F}^*_{b^m}$.

Theorem 11.25 *Let b be prime, let $s, m \in \mathbb{N}$ and let $\boldsymbol{\gamma} = (\gamma_i)_{i\geq 1}$ be a sequence of weights. Suppose that $\alpha \in \mathbb{F}_{b^m}^*$ is constructed according to Algorithm 11.24 by using R_b' (or $R_{b,\boldsymbol{\gamma}}'$ in the weighted case). Then we have*

$$R_b'(\alpha) \leq \frac{s-1}{b^m-1}\left(1+m\frac{b^2-1}{3b}\right)^s,$$

and

$$R_{b,\boldsymbol{\gamma}}'(\alpha) \leq \frac{s-1}{b^m-1}\prod_{i=1}^{s}\left(1+\gamma_i\left(1+m\frac{b^2-1}{3b}\right)\right),$$

respectively.

The proof of this result follows exactly along the lines of the proof of Theorem 10.34 and is therefore left as an exercise (Exercise 11.12).

From Corollary 11.15 and Theorem 11.25, we obtain the following bound on the (weighted) star discrepancy.

Corollary 11.26 *Let b be a prime, let $s, m \in \mathbb{N}$ and let $\boldsymbol{\gamma} = (\gamma_i)_{i\geq 1}$ be a sequence of weights. Suppose that $\alpha \in \mathbb{F}_{b^m}^*$ is constructed according to Algorithm 11.24 by using R_b' (or $R_{b,\boldsymbol{\gamma}}'$ in the weighted case). Then, for the (weighted) star discrepancy of the cyclic net $\mathcal{P}_\alpha$, we have*

$$D_{b^m}^*(\mathcal{P}_\alpha) \leq \frac{s}{b^m} + \frac{s-1}{b^m-1}\left(1+m\frac{b^2-1}{3b}\right)^s,$$

and

$$D_{b^m,\boldsymbol{\gamma}}^*(\mathcal{P}_\alpha) \leq \sum_{\emptyset\neq \mathfrak{u}\subseteq \mathcal{I}_s}\gamma_{\mathfrak{u}}\left(1-\left(1-\frac{1}{b^m}\right)^{|\mathfrak{u}|}\right) + \frac{s-1}{b^m-1}\prod_{i=1}^{s}\left(1+\gamma_i\left(1+m\frac{b^2-1}{3b}\right)\right),$$

respectively.

Exercises

11.1 Show that for any $\alpha, x \in \mathbb{F}_{b^m}$, we have $\Psi(\alpha)\psi(x) = \psi(\alpha x)$.

11.2 Show that for any $\alpha \in \mathbb{F}_{b^m}$ and any $j \in \mathbb{N}_0$, we have $\Psi(\alpha^j) = \Psi(\alpha)^j$.

11.3 Let b be a prime power, $r \in \mathbb{N}$ and let A be a non-singular $r \times r$ matrix over $\mathbb{F}_b$. Let $\mathcal{X} \subseteq \mathbb{F}_b^r$ be a linear subspace of $\mathbb{F}_b^r$. Show that $(A\mathcal{X})^\perp = (A^{-1})^\top \mathcal{X}^\perp$.

11.4 Give a proof of Theorem 11.5.
Hint: This is just an adaptation of the proof of Theorem 11.2.

11.5 For a Laurent series $L \in \mathbb{F}_b((x^{-1}))$ and $m \in \mathbb{N}$, let $\iota_m(L)$ be defined as in Section 11.1. Let $p \in \mathbb{F}_b[x]$ and $u, v \in \mathbb{F}_b$ and $0 \leq l < k$ be integers. Show that we have

$$\iota_m\left(\frac{ux^l + vx^k}{p(x)}\right) = u\iota_m\left(\frac{x^l}{p(x)}\right) + v\iota_m\left(\frac{x^k}{p(x)}\right).$$

11.6 Let b be a prime power and let $p \in \mathbb{F}_b[x]$ be an irreducible polynomial. Let ω be the residue class of x in $\mathbb{F}_b[x]/(p)$ and let $\mathbb{F}_{b^m} = \mathbb{F}_b[\omega]$. Show that the polynomial lattice point set whose generating vector is of Korobov form $\boldsymbol{v}_s(q)$ with $q \in \mathbb{F}_b[x]$ and $\deg(q) < \deg(p)$ (see Chapter 10, Section 10.1) is the same as the cyclic net associated with $\alpha = q(\omega) \in \mathbb{F}_{b^m}$ with the powers of ω as choice for the ordered bases $\mathcal{B}_1 = \cdots = \mathcal{B}_s$.

11.7 For $\boldsymbol{\alpha} \in \mathbb{F}_{b^m}^s$, b a prime, let $\mathcal{P}_{\boldsymbol{\alpha}} = \{\boldsymbol{x}_0, \ldots, \boldsymbol{x}_{b^m-1}\}$ be the corresponding hyperplane net over $\mathbb{Z}_b$. Show that we have

$$R_b'(\boldsymbol{\alpha}) = -1 + \sum_{n=0}^{b^m-1} \prod_{i=1}^{s} \phi_{b,m}(x_{n,i}),$$

where $x_{n,i}$ is the ith component of $\boldsymbol{x}_n$ for $1 \leq i \leq s$ and $0 \leq n < b^m$ and where $\phi_{b,m}$ is as in (10.6). Hence, $R_b(\boldsymbol{\alpha})$ can be computed at a cost of $O(sb^m)$ operations.

11.8 With the notation of Exercise 11.7, show that we have

$$R_{b,\boldsymbol{\gamma}}'(\boldsymbol{\alpha}) = -\prod_{i=1}^{s}(1 + \gamma_i) + \sum_{n=0}^{b^m-1} \prod_{i=1}^{s}(1 + \gamma_i \phi_{b,m}(x_{n,i})).$$

11.9 Give a proof of the second assertion in Theorem 11.12.

11.10 Give a proof of Theorem 11.17 for the weighted case.

11.11 Give a proof of Theorem 11.20.

11.12 Give a proof of Theorem 11.25.

11.13 Let b be a prime, let $m \in \mathbb{N}$ and let $(\mathcal{B}_i)_{i\geq 1}$ be a sequence of ordered bases of $\mathbb{F}_{b^m}$ over $\mathbb{Z}_b$. Show that for $c > \sum_{s=1}^{\infty}(s(\log(1+s))^2)^{-1}$ there exists an element $\alpha \in \mathbb{F}_{b^m}^*$ such that for all $s \in \mathbb{N}$, we have

$$R_b'(\alpha) \leq \frac{cs(s-1)(\log(s+1))^2}{b^m - 1}\left(1 + m\frac{b^2-1}{3b}\right).$$

Hint: Show that

$$E_s := \left\{\alpha \in \mathbb{F}_{b^m}^* \,:\, R_b'(\alpha) > \frac{cs(s-1)(\log(s+1))^2}{b^m - 1}\left(1 + m\frac{b^2-1}{3b}\right)\right\}$$

has no more than $\frac{b^m-1}{cs(\log(s+1))^2}$ elements and deduce that $E := \bigcup_{s\in\mathbb{N}} E_s$ does not contain all elements from $\mathbb{F}_{b^m}^*$.

11.14 With the notation of Exercise 11.13 and with a sequence of weights $\boldsymbol{\gamma} = (\gamma_i)_{i\geq 1}$, show that for $c > \sum_{s=1}^{\infty}(s(\log(1+s))^2)^{-1}$ there exists an element $\alpha \in \mathbb{F}_{b^m}^*$ such that for all $s \in \mathbb{N}$, we have

$$R_b'(\alpha, \boldsymbol{\gamma}) \leq \frac{cs(s-1)(\log(s+1))^2}{b^m - 1} \prod_{i=1}^{s}\left(1 + \gamma_i\left(1 + m\frac{b^2-1}{3b}\right)\right).$$

12

Multivariate integration in weighted Sobolev spaces

In this chapter we consider the integration problem in weighted Sobolev spaces consisting of functions whose mixed partial derivatives of order up to one are square integrable. We use digitally shifted digital nets over $\mathbb{Z}_b$ as underlying point sets for the QMC algorithms. The analysis of the mean square worst-case error over all possible digital shifts for this integration problem leads to existence results for digital nets yielding a reasonably small mean square worst-case error. Examples of such digital nets are polynomial lattices, which can be constructed with a CBC algorithm, or Korobov-type polynomial lattices. The main tool for the error analysis is a so-called digital shift invariant kernel associated with the reproducing kernel of the given weighted Sobolev space. This digital shift invariant kernel can be represented in terms of Walsh functions, which gives the link to digital nets. The idea of using Walsh functions for the analysis of QMC algorithms based on digital nets stems from Larcher [133]; see also Larcher and Traunfellner [148] or the survey article [147].

12.1 Digital shift invariant kernels

In this section, we introduce 'digital b-adic shift invariant kernels' associated with a given reproducing kernel K. Throughout this section, we assume that b is a prime number.

For $\boldsymbol{x}, \boldsymbol{\sigma} \in [0,1)^s$, the digital b-adic shifted point $\boldsymbol{x} \oplus \boldsymbol{\sigma}$ is defined as in Definition 4.65. Although we only write $\oplus$ instead of $\oplus_{b,\varphi}$, we remark again that a digital shift depends on the chosen base b (as we consider the case of prime bases b only, we use the identity for the bijection φ in Definition 4.65).

A reproducing kernel K with the property that $K(\boldsymbol{x} \oplus \boldsymbol{\sigma}, \boldsymbol{y} \oplus \boldsymbol{\sigma}) = K(\boldsymbol{x}, \boldsymbol{y})$, for all $\boldsymbol{x}$, $\boldsymbol{y}$, and all $\boldsymbol{\sigma}$, is called a *digital b-adic shift invariant reproducing kernel* or, for short, a *digital shift invariant kernel*.

For an arbitrary reproducing kernel K, we associate a digital shift invariant kernel with K in the following definition, which was first given in reference [50, Section 6.1].

Definition 12.1 *For an arbitrary reproducing kernel K, we define the* associated digital shift invariant kernel *K_{ds} by*

$$K_{\mathrm{ds}}(\boldsymbol{x}, \boldsymbol{y}) := \int_{[0,1]^s} K(\boldsymbol{x} \oplus \boldsymbol{\sigma}, \boldsymbol{y} \oplus \boldsymbol{\sigma}) \, \mathrm{d}\boldsymbol{\sigma}.$$

Notice that the kernel K_{ds} is indeed digital shift invariant as

$$\begin{aligned} K_{\mathrm{ds}}(\boldsymbol{x} \oplus \boldsymbol{\sigma}, \boldsymbol{y} \oplus \boldsymbol{\sigma}) &= \int_{[0,1]^s} K(\boldsymbol{x} \oplus \boldsymbol{\sigma} \oplus \boldsymbol{\Delta}, \boldsymbol{y} \oplus \boldsymbol{\sigma} \oplus \boldsymbol{\Delta}) \, \mathrm{d}\boldsymbol{\Delta} \\ &= \int_{[0,1]^s} K(\boldsymbol{x} \oplus \boldsymbol{\Delta}, \boldsymbol{y} \oplus \boldsymbol{\Delta}) \, \mathrm{d}\boldsymbol{\Delta} \\ &= K_{\mathrm{ds}}(\boldsymbol{x}, \boldsymbol{y}). \end{aligned}$$

Recall that for a reproducing kernel $K : [0, 1]^s \times [0, 1]^s \to \mathbb{C}$, we have $K(\boldsymbol{x}, \boldsymbol{y}) = \overline{K(\boldsymbol{y}, \boldsymbol{x})}$; see Remark 2.7. Therefore, in order to obtain a simple notation, we define, for a reproducing kernel $K \in L_2([0, 1]^{2s})$ and for $\boldsymbol{k}, \boldsymbol{k}' \in \mathbb{N}_0^s$,

$$\widehat{K}(\boldsymbol{k}, \boldsymbol{k}') = \int_{[0,1]^s} \int_{[0,1]^s} K(\boldsymbol{x}, \boldsymbol{y}) \, \overline{{}_b\mathrm{wal}_{\boldsymbol{k}}(\boldsymbol{x})} \, {}_b\mathrm{wal}_{\boldsymbol{k}'}(\boldsymbol{y}) \, \mathrm{d}\boldsymbol{x} \, \mathrm{d}\boldsymbol{y}.$$

From $K(\boldsymbol{x}, \boldsymbol{y}) = \overline{K(\boldsymbol{y}, \boldsymbol{x})}$ it then follows that $\widehat{K}(\boldsymbol{k}, \boldsymbol{k}') = \overline{\widehat{K}(\boldsymbol{k}, \boldsymbol{k}')}$ and therefore $\widehat{K}(\boldsymbol{k}, \boldsymbol{k}') \in \mathbb{R}$. In the following lemma, we show how the digital shift invariant kernel can be expressed in terms of $\widehat{K}(\boldsymbol{k}, \boldsymbol{k})$.

Lemma 12.2 *Let the reproducing kernel $K \in L_2([0, 1]^{2s})$ be continuous and for $\boldsymbol{k} \in \mathbb{N}_0^s$, let*

$$\widehat{K}(\boldsymbol{k}, \boldsymbol{k}) = \int_{[0,1]^s} \int_{[0,1]^s} K(\boldsymbol{x}, \boldsymbol{y}) \, \overline{{}_b\mathrm{wal}_{\boldsymbol{k}}(\boldsymbol{x})} \, {}_b\mathrm{wal}_{\boldsymbol{k}}(\boldsymbol{y}) \, \mathrm{d}\boldsymbol{x} \, \mathrm{d}\boldsymbol{y}.$$

If

$$\sum_{\boldsymbol{k} \in \mathbb{N}_0^s} |\widehat{K}(\boldsymbol{k}, \boldsymbol{k})| < \infty,$$

then the digital shift invariant kernel K_{ds} is given by

$$K_{\mathrm{ds}}(\boldsymbol{x}, \boldsymbol{y}) = \sum_{\boldsymbol{k} \in \mathbb{N}_0^s} \widehat{K}(\boldsymbol{k}, \boldsymbol{k}) \, {}_b\mathrm{wal}_{\boldsymbol{k}}(\boldsymbol{x}) \, \overline{{}_b\mathrm{wal}_{\boldsymbol{k}}(\boldsymbol{y})}.$$

Proof Using the definition of the digital shift invariant kernel, we have for any $\boldsymbol{k}, \boldsymbol{k}' \in \mathbb{N}_0^s$ that

$$\begin{aligned}
&\widehat{K}_{\mathrm{ds}}(\boldsymbol{k}, \boldsymbol{k}') \\
&:= \int_{[0,1]^{2s}} K_{\mathrm{ds}}(\boldsymbol{x}, \boldsymbol{y}) \overline{{}_b\mathrm{wal}_{\boldsymbol{k}}(\boldsymbol{x})}\, {}_b\mathrm{wal}_{\boldsymbol{k}'}(\boldsymbol{y}) \,\mathrm{d}\boldsymbol{x}\,\mathrm{d}\boldsymbol{y} \\
&= \int_{[0,1]^{2s}} \int_{[0,1]^s} K(\boldsymbol{x} \oplus \boldsymbol{\sigma}, \boldsymbol{y} \oplus \boldsymbol{\sigma}) \,\mathrm{d}\boldsymbol{\sigma}\, \overline{{}_b\mathrm{wal}_{\boldsymbol{k}}(\boldsymbol{x})}\, {}_b\mathrm{wal}_{\boldsymbol{k}'}(\boldsymbol{y}) \,\mathrm{d}\boldsymbol{x}\,\mathrm{d}\boldsymbol{y} \\
&= \int_{[0,1]^s} \int_{[0,1]^{2s}} K(\boldsymbol{x} \oplus \boldsymbol{\sigma}, \boldsymbol{y} \oplus \boldsymbol{\sigma}) \overline{{}_b\mathrm{wal}_{\boldsymbol{k}}(\boldsymbol{x})}\, {}_b\mathrm{wal}_{\boldsymbol{k}'}(\boldsymbol{y}) \,\mathrm{d}\boldsymbol{x}\,\mathrm{d}\boldsymbol{y}\,\mathrm{d}\boldsymbol{\sigma} \\
&= \int_{[0,1]^s} \int_{[0,1]^{2s}} K(\boldsymbol{x}, \boldsymbol{y}) \overline{{}_b\mathrm{wal}_{\boldsymbol{k}}(\boldsymbol{x} \oplus \boldsymbol{\sigma})}\, {}_b\mathrm{wal}_{\boldsymbol{k}'}(\boldsymbol{y} \oplus \boldsymbol{\sigma}) \,\mathrm{d}\boldsymbol{x}\,\mathrm{d}\boldsymbol{y}\,\mathrm{d}\boldsymbol{\sigma} \\
&= \int_{[0,1]^s} \int_{[0,1]^{2s}} K(\boldsymbol{x}, \boldsymbol{y}) \overline{{}_b\mathrm{wal}_{\boldsymbol{k}}(\boldsymbol{x})}\, {}_b\mathrm{wal}_{\boldsymbol{k}'}(\boldsymbol{y})\, {}_b\mathrm{wal}_{\boldsymbol{k}}(\boldsymbol{\sigma}) \overline{{}_b\mathrm{wal}_{\boldsymbol{k}'}(\boldsymbol{\sigma})} \,\mathrm{d}\boldsymbol{x}\,\mathrm{d}\boldsymbol{y}\,\mathrm{d}\boldsymbol{\sigma} \\
&= \int_{[0,1]^{2s}} K(\boldsymbol{x}, \boldsymbol{y}) \overline{{}_b\mathrm{wal}_{\boldsymbol{k}}(\boldsymbol{x})}\, {}_b\mathrm{wal}_{\boldsymbol{k}}(\boldsymbol{y}) \,\mathrm{d}\boldsymbol{x}\,\mathrm{d}\boldsymbol{y} \int_{[0,1]^s} {}_b\mathrm{wal}_{\boldsymbol{k}}(\boldsymbol{\sigma}) \overline{{}_b\mathrm{wal}_{\boldsymbol{k}'}(\boldsymbol{\sigma})} \,\mathrm{d}\boldsymbol{\sigma},
\end{aligned}$$

where we used Corollary A.5 and Corollary A.13.

Using Proposition A.10 we obtain for all $\boldsymbol{k}, \boldsymbol{k}' \in \mathbb{N}_0^s$ that

$$\widehat{K}_{\mathrm{ds}}(\boldsymbol{k}, \boldsymbol{k}') = \begin{cases} \widehat{K}(\boldsymbol{k}, \boldsymbol{k}) & \text{if } \boldsymbol{k} = \boldsymbol{k}', \\ 0 & \text{if } \boldsymbol{k} \neq \boldsymbol{k}'. \end{cases}$$

Under the assumption that $\sum_{\boldsymbol{k} \in \mathbb{N}_0^s} |\widehat{K}(\boldsymbol{k}, \boldsymbol{k})| < \infty$, we have that

$$\sum_{\boldsymbol{k} \in \mathbb{N}_0^s} \widehat{K}_{\mathrm{ds}}(\boldsymbol{k}, \boldsymbol{k})\, {}_b\mathrm{wal}_{\boldsymbol{k}}(\boldsymbol{x})$$

converges for every $\boldsymbol{x} \in [0, 1)^s$.

We show now that K_{ds} is continuous. Let $\boldsymbol{x}, \boldsymbol{y}, \boldsymbol{\sigma} \in [0, 1)^s$ with $\boldsymbol{x} = (x_1, \ldots, x_s)$, $\boldsymbol{y} = (y_1, \ldots, y_s)$, $\boldsymbol{\sigma} = (\sigma_1, \ldots, \sigma_s)$, $x_i = \xi_{i,1} b^{-1} + \xi_{i,2} b^{-2} + \cdots$, $y_i = \eta_{i,1} b^{-1} + \eta_{i,2} b^{-2} + \cdots$ and $\sigma_i = \sigma_{i,1} b^{-1} + \sigma_{i,2} b^{-2} + \cdots$. Assume that $|\boldsymbol{x} - \boldsymbol{y}|_\infty < \delta$ for some $0 < \delta \le b^{-1}$, where $|\boldsymbol{x}|_\infty = \max_{1 \le i \le s} |x_i|$. Let $a \in \mathbb{N}$ be such that $b^{-a-1} < \delta \le b^{-a}$. Then it follows that $\xi_{i,k} = \eta_{i,k}$ for all $1 \le i \le s$ and $1 \le k \le a$. Hence, $\xi_{i,k} \oplus \sigma_{i,k} = \eta_{i,k} \oplus \sigma_{i,k}$ for all $1 \le i \le s$ and $1 \le k \le a$ and therefore, $|(\boldsymbol{x} \oplus \boldsymbol{\sigma}) - (\boldsymbol{y} \oplus \boldsymbol{\sigma})|_\infty \le b^{-a} < b\delta$.

Hence, the continuity of $K(\boldsymbol{x}, \boldsymbol{y})$ implies also that $K(\boldsymbol{x} \oplus \boldsymbol{\sigma}, \boldsymbol{y} \oplus \boldsymbol{\sigma})$ is continuous as a function of $\boldsymbol{x}, \boldsymbol{y}$ for each fixed $\boldsymbol{\sigma} \in [0, 1)^s$ and subsequently, also, the continuity of K_{ds}. Indeed, for given $\boldsymbol{x}, \boldsymbol{y} \in [0, 1)^s$ and $\varepsilon > 0$, let $\delta > 0$ be such that $|K(\boldsymbol{x}, \boldsymbol{y}) - K(\boldsymbol{x}', \boldsymbol{y}')| < \varepsilon$ for all $\boldsymbol{x}', \boldsymbol{y}' \in [0, 1)^s$ such that $|(\boldsymbol{x}, \boldsymbol{y}) - (\boldsymbol{x}', \boldsymbol{y}')|_\infty < \delta$. Then, $|K(\boldsymbol{x} \oplus \boldsymbol{\sigma}, \boldsymbol{y} \oplus \boldsymbol{\sigma}) - K(\boldsymbol{x}' \oplus \boldsymbol{\sigma}, \boldsymbol{y}' \oplus \boldsymbol{\sigma})| < \varepsilon$ for all $\boldsymbol{x}', \boldsymbol{y}' \in [0, 1)^s$ such that $|(\boldsymbol{x}, \boldsymbol{y}) - (\boldsymbol{x}', \boldsymbol{y}')|_\infty < \delta b^{-1}$. Hence,

$$|K_{\mathrm{ds}}(\boldsymbol{x}, \boldsymbol{y}) - K_{\mathrm{ds}}(\boldsymbol{x}', \boldsymbol{y}')| \le \int_{[0,1]^s} |K(\boldsymbol{x} \oplus \boldsymbol{\sigma}, \boldsymbol{y} \oplus \boldsymbol{\sigma}) - K(\boldsymbol{x}' \oplus \boldsymbol{\sigma}, \boldsymbol{y}' \oplus \boldsymbol{\sigma})| \,\mathrm{d}\boldsymbol{\sigma}$$
$$< \int_{[0,1]^s} \varepsilon \,\mathrm{d}\boldsymbol{\sigma} = \varepsilon,$$

for all $\boldsymbol{x}', \boldsymbol{y}' \in [0, 1)^s$ such that $|(\boldsymbol{x}, \boldsymbol{y}) - (\boldsymbol{x}', \boldsymbol{y}')|_\infty < \delta b^{-1}$. Therefore, K_{ds} is continuous.

Hence, we obtain from Section A.3 that

$$K_{\mathrm{ds}}(\boldsymbol{x}, \boldsymbol{y}) = \sum_{\boldsymbol{k} \in \mathbb{N}_0^s} \widehat{K}(\boldsymbol{k}, \boldsymbol{k}) \,{}_b\mathrm{wal}_{\boldsymbol{k}}(\boldsymbol{x}) \overline{{}_b\mathrm{wal}_{\boldsymbol{k}}(\boldsymbol{y})}. \qquad \square$$

Remark 12.3 *Notice that we do not require that the reproducing kernel K can be represented by its Walsh series, i.e. we do not require that*

$$K(\boldsymbol{x}, \boldsymbol{y}) = \sum_{\boldsymbol{k}, \boldsymbol{k}' \in \mathbb{N}_0^s} \widehat{K}(\boldsymbol{k}, \boldsymbol{k}') \,{}_b\mathrm{wal}_{\boldsymbol{k}}(\boldsymbol{x}) \overline{{}_b\mathrm{wal}_{\boldsymbol{k}'}(\boldsymbol{y})}.$$

Let b be a prime. For a point set $\mathcal{P}$ in $[0, 1)^s$ and $\boldsymbol{\sigma} \in [0, 1)^s$, let $\mathcal{P}_{\boldsymbol{\sigma}} = \{\boldsymbol{x}_0 \oplus \boldsymbol{\sigma}, \ldots, \boldsymbol{x}_{N-1} \oplus \boldsymbol{\sigma}\}$ be the digitally b-adic shifted version of $\mathcal{P}$ as defined in Definition 4.66. We recall that if we use a digital shift in conjunction with a digital net, then the shift and the net are always considered to be in the same base b. Therefore, if it is clear with respect to which base b a point is shifted, we may omit the phrase 'b-adic'.

According to Definition 2.10, for a reproducing kernel Hilbert space $\mathscr{H}$ with reproducing kernel K, the worst-case error for a QMC rule based on the quadrature points $\mathcal{P} = \{\boldsymbol{x}_0, \ldots, \boldsymbol{x}_{N-1}\}$ is defined as

$$e(\mathscr{H}, \mathcal{P}) := \sup_{f \in \mathscr{H}, \|f\| \le 1} |I(f) - Q_N(f)|.$$

The initial error is defined as $e(\mathscr{H}, 0) := \sup_{f \in \mathscr{H}, \|f\| \le 1} |I(f)| = \|I\|$.

We further define the *mean square worst-case error* $\widehat{e}^2_{\mathrm{ds}}(\mathscr{H}, \mathcal{P})$ over all digitally shifted versions of $\mathcal{P}$ by

$$\widehat{e}^2_{\mathrm{ds}}(\mathscr{H}, \mathcal{P}) := \mathbb{E}[e^2(\mathscr{H}, \mathcal{P}_{\boldsymbol{\sigma}})] = \int_{[0,1]^s} e^2(\mathscr{H}, \mathcal{P}_{\boldsymbol{\sigma}}) \,\mathrm{d}\boldsymbol{\sigma}.$$

In the following theorem, we show that the mean square worst-case error for integration in a reproducing kernel Hilbert space with kernel K is the same as the worst-case error for integration in the reproducing kernel Hilbert space with kernel K_{ds}, the associated digital shift invariant kernel. To stress the dependence on the reproducing kernel K, we write in the following $e(K, \mathcal{P})$ and $\widehat{e}^2_{\mathrm{ds}}(K, \mathcal{P})$ instead of $e(\mathscr{H}, \mathcal{P})$ and $\widehat{e}^2_{\mathrm{ds}}(\mathscr{H}, \mathcal{P})$.

Theorem 12.4 *For any reproducing kernel $K \in L_2([0,1]^{2s})$ and point set $\mathcal{P}$, we have*

$$\mathbb{E}[e^2(K, \mathcal{P}_{\boldsymbol{\sigma}})] = e^2(K_{\mathrm{ds}}, \mathcal{P}).$$

Proof According to (2.11), we have

$$e^2(K, \mathcal{P}) = \int_{[0,1]^{2s}} K(\boldsymbol{x}, \boldsymbol{y}) \,\mathrm{d}\boldsymbol{x} \,\mathrm{d}\boldsymbol{y} - \frac{2}{N} \sum_{n=0}^{N-1} \int_{[0,1]^s} K(\boldsymbol{x}_n, \boldsymbol{y}) \,\mathrm{d}\boldsymbol{y} + \frac{1}{N^2} \sum_{n,m=0}^{N-1} K(\boldsymbol{x}_n, \boldsymbol{x}_m).$$

Therefore, we have

$$\begin{aligned}
&\int_{[0,1]^s} e^2(K, \mathcal{P}_{\boldsymbol{\sigma}}) \,\mathrm{d}\boldsymbol{\sigma} \\
&= \int_{[0,1]^{2s}} K(\boldsymbol{x}, \boldsymbol{y}) \,\mathrm{d}\boldsymbol{x} \,\mathrm{d}\boldsymbol{y} - \frac{2}{N} \sum_{n=0}^{N-1} \int_{[0,1]^s} \int_{[0,1]^s} K(\boldsymbol{x}_n \oplus \boldsymbol{\sigma}, \boldsymbol{y}) \,\mathrm{d}\boldsymbol{y} \,\mathrm{d}\boldsymbol{\sigma} \\
&\quad + \frac{1}{N^2} \sum_{n,m=0}^{N-1} \int_{[0,1]^s} K(\boldsymbol{x}_n \oplus \boldsymbol{\sigma}, \boldsymbol{x}_m \oplus \boldsymbol{\sigma}) \,\mathrm{d}\boldsymbol{\sigma} \\
&= \int_{[0,1]^s} \int_{[0,1]^{2s}} K(\boldsymbol{x} \oplus \boldsymbol{\sigma}, \boldsymbol{y} \oplus \boldsymbol{\sigma}) \,\mathrm{d}\boldsymbol{x} \,\mathrm{d}\boldsymbol{y} \,\mathrm{d}\boldsymbol{\sigma} \\
&\quad - \frac{2}{N} \sum_{n=0}^{N-1} \int_{[0,1]^s} \int_{[0,1]^s} K(\boldsymbol{x}_n \oplus \boldsymbol{\sigma}, \boldsymbol{y} \oplus \boldsymbol{\sigma}) \,\mathrm{d}\boldsymbol{y} \,\mathrm{d}\boldsymbol{\sigma} \\
&\quad + \frac{1}{N^2} \sum_{n,m=0}^{N-1} \int_{[0,1]^s} K(\boldsymbol{x}_n \oplus \boldsymbol{\sigma}, \boldsymbol{x}_m \oplus \boldsymbol{\sigma}) \,\mathrm{d}\boldsymbol{\sigma} \\
&= \int_{[0,1]^{2s}} \int_{[0,1]^s} K(\boldsymbol{x} \oplus \boldsymbol{\sigma}, \boldsymbol{y} \oplus \boldsymbol{\sigma}) \,\mathrm{d}\boldsymbol{\sigma} \,\mathrm{d}\boldsymbol{x} \,\mathrm{d}\boldsymbol{y} \\
&\quad - \frac{2}{N} \sum_{n=0}^{N-1} \int_{[0,1]^s} \int_{[0,1]^s} K(\boldsymbol{x}_n \oplus \boldsymbol{\sigma}, \boldsymbol{y} \oplus \boldsymbol{\sigma}) \,\mathrm{d}\boldsymbol{\sigma} \,\mathrm{d}\boldsymbol{y} \\
&\quad + \frac{1}{N^2} \sum_{n,m=0}^{N-1} \int_{[0,1]^s} K(\boldsymbol{x}_n \oplus \boldsymbol{\sigma}, \boldsymbol{x}_m \oplus \boldsymbol{\sigma}) \,\mathrm{d}\boldsymbol{\sigma}
\end{aligned}$$

and hence, the result follows from $\int_{[0,1]^s} K(\boldsymbol{x} \oplus \boldsymbol{\sigma}, \boldsymbol{y} \oplus \boldsymbol{\sigma}) \,\mathrm{d}\boldsymbol{\sigma} = K_{\mathrm{ds}}(\boldsymbol{x}, \boldsymbol{y})$. □

12.2 Weighted Sobolev spaces

In this section we introduce the weighted version of the unanchored Sobolev space from Section 2.5. This variant of the standard Sobolev space of functions defined over the s-dimensional unit-cube $[0,1]^s$ is also presented in [200, Appendix A.2.3]. We consider product weights that are independent of the dimension s, i.e. $\gamma_{\mathfrak{u},s} = \gamma_{\mathfrak{u}} = \prod_{i \in \mathfrak{u}} \gamma_i$ for $\mathfrak{u} \subseteq \mathcal{I}_s$ and for a sequence $\boldsymbol{\gamma} = (\gamma_i)_{i \geq 1}$ of non-negative real numbers. We denote the function space under consideration by $\mathscr{H}_{\mathrm{sob},s,\boldsymbol{\gamma}}$. Its reproducing kernel is given by (see [54, 200, 251])

$$K(\boldsymbol{x}, \boldsymbol{y}) = \prod_{j=1}^{s} K_j(x_j, y_j) = \prod_{j=1}^{s} (1 + \gamma_j (\tfrac{1}{2} B_2(\{x_j - y_j\}) + (x_j - \tfrac{1}{2})(y_j - \tfrac{1}{2})), \tag{12.1}$$

where $B_2(x) = x^2 - x + \frac{1}{6}$ is the second Bernoulli polynomial and $\{x\} = x - \lfloor x \rfloor$. The inner product in $\mathscr{H}_{\mathrm{sob},s,\boldsymbol{\gamma}}$ is given by

$$\langle f, g \rangle := \sum_{\mathfrak{u} \subseteq \mathcal{I}_s} \prod_{j \in \mathfrak{u}} \gamma_j^{-1} \int_{[0,1]^{|\mathfrak{u}|}} \left(\int_{[0,1]^{s-|\mathfrak{u}|}} \frac{\partial^{|\mathfrak{u}|} f}{\partial \boldsymbol{x}_{\mathfrak{u}}}(\boldsymbol{x}) \, \mathrm{d}\boldsymbol{x}_{\mathcal{I}_s \setminus \mathfrak{u}} \right)$$
$$\times \left(\int_{[0,1]^{s-|\mathfrak{u}|}} \frac{\partial^{|\mathfrak{u}|} g}{\partial \boldsymbol{x}_{\mathfrak{u}}}(\boldsymbol{x}) \, \mathrm{d}\boldsymbol{x}_{\mathcal{I}_s \setminus \mathfrak{u}} \right) \mathrm{d}\boldsymbol{x}_{\mathfrak{u}}.$$

The weighted Sobolev space $\mathscr{H}_{\mathrm{sob},s,\boldsymbol{\gamma}}$ contains all functions on $[0,1]^s$ where the first mixed partial derivatives are square integrable. It is easy to check that the initial error for the space $\mathscr{H}_{\mathrm{sob},s,\boldsymbol{\gamma}}$ is $e(\mathscr{H}_{\mathrm{sob},s,\boldsymbol{\gamma}}, 0) = 1$; see Exercise 12.1.

In the following theorem, we determine the digital shift invariant kernel in base $b \geq 2$.

Proposition 12.5 *Let K be the reproducing kernel given by* (12.1). *Then the corresponding digital shift invariant kernel in prime base $b \geq 2$ is given by*

$$K_{\mathrm{ds}}(\boldsymbol{x}, \boldsymbol{y}) = \sum_{\boldsymbol{k} \in \mathbb{N}_0^s} r_{\mathrm{sob},b}(\boldsymbol{k}, \boldsymbol{\gamma}) \, {}_b\mathrm{wal}_{\boldsymbol{k}}(\boldsymbol{x}) \, \overline{{}_b\mathrm{wal}_{\boldsymbol{k}}(\boldsymbol{y})}, \tag{12.2}$$

where for $\boldsymbol{k} = (k_1, \ldots, k_s)$ we put $r_{\mathrm{sob},b}(\boldsymbol{k}, \boldsymbol{\gamma}) = \prod_{i=1}^{s} r_{\mathrm{sob},b}(k_i, \gamma_i)$, and for $k = \kappa_{a-1} b^{a-1} + \cdots + \kappa_1 b + \kappa_0$ with $\kappa_{a-1} \neq 0$, we put

$$r_{\mathrm{sob},b}(k, \gamma) = \begin{cases} 1 & \text{if } k = 0, \\ \frac{\gamma}{2b^{2a}} \left(\frac{1}{\sin^2(\kappa_{a-1}\pi/b)} - \frac{1}{3} \right) & \text{if } k > 0. \end{cases}$$

Proof Note that the reproducing kernel (12.1) is in $L_2([0,1]^s)$. We use Lemma 12.2 to calculate the digital shift invariant kernel.

As the Sobolev space $\mathscr{H}_{\mathrm{sob},s,\boldsymbol{\gamma}}$ is a tensor product of one-dimensional Hilbert spaces and the reproducing kernel is the product of the kernels K_i, we only need to find the digital shift invariant kernels $K_{\mathrm{ds},j}$ associated with K_j. The digital shift invariant kernel in higher dimension $s > 1$ is then just the product of the $K_{\mathrm{ds},j}$.

Omitting the index j, we have to determine

$$\begin{aligned}
&K_{\mathrm{ds}}(x, y)\\
&\quad = \int_0^1 K(x \oplus \sigma, y \oplus \sigma)\,\mathrm{d}\sigma\\
&\quad = \int_0^1 (1 + \gamma(\tfrac{1}{2}B_2(\{(x \oplus \sigma) - (y \oplus \sigma)\}) + ((x \oplus \sigma) - \tfrac{1}{2})((y \oplus \sigma) - \tfrac{1}{2}))\,\mathrm{d}\sigma,
\end{aligned} \tag{12.3}$$

where the digital shift is in base b.

It is convenient for our analysis to represent the kernel K in terms of Walsh functions in base b. Hence, we need to find the Walsh coefficients $\widehat{K}(k, k)$ of K.

From Lemma A.22 we know that the Walsh representation of the function $x \mapsto x - 1/2$ for $x \in [0, 1)$ is given by

$$\begin{aligned}
x - \frac{1}{2} &= \sum_{a=1}^{\infty} \sum_{\kappa=1}^{b-1} \frac{1}{b^a(\omega_b^{-\kappa} - 1)}\, {}_b\mathrm{wal}_{\kappa b^{a-1}}(x)\\
&= \sum_{a=1}^{\infty} \sum_{\kappa=1}^{b-1} \frac{1}{b^a(\omega_b^{\kappa} - 1)}\, \overline{{}_b\mathrm{wal}_{\kappa b^{a-1}}(x)},
\end{aligned} \tag{12.4}$$

as $x - 1/2 = \overline{x - 1/2}$, where $\omega_b = \mathrm{e}^{2\pi \mathrm{i}/b}$.

Using these equalities, we get for all $x, y \in [0, 1)$ that

$$\begin{aligned}
&(x - \tfrac{1}{2})(y - \tfrac{1}{2})\\
&\quad = \sum_{a=1}^{\infty} \sum_{\kappa=1}^{b-1} \sum_{a'=1}^{\infty} \sum_{\kappa'=1}^{b-1} \frac{1}{b^{a+a'}(\omega_b^{-\kappa} - 1)(\omega_b^{\kappa'} - 1)}\, {}_b\mathrm{wal}_{\kappa b^{a-1}}(x)\, \overline{{}_b\mathrm{wal}_{\kappa' b^{a'-1}}(y)}.
\end{aligned}$$

Note that Lemma 12.2 is true for any function in $L_2([0, 1]^{2s})$ which can be represented by its Walsh series. Hence,

$$\begin{aligned}
&\int_0^1 ((x \oplus \sigma) - \tfrac{1}{2})((y \oplus \sigma) - \tfrac{1}{2})\,\mathrm{d}\sigma\\
&\quad = \sum_{a=1}^{\infty} \sum_{\kappa=1}^{b-1} \frac{1}{b^{2a}|\omega_b^{\kappa} - 1|^2}\, {}_b\mathrm{wal}_{\kappa b^{a-1}}(x)\, \overline{{}_b\mathrm{wal}_{\kappa b^{a-1}}(y)}.
\end{aligned} \tag{12.5}$$

We have $B_2(x) = x^2 - x + \frac{1}{6}$ and it can be shown that $B_2(\{x\}) = B_2(|x|)$ for all $x \in (-1, 1)$. For our investigations here, we use $B_2(|x - y|)$ instead of $B_2(\{x - y\})$.

By using (12.4), we obtain

$$
\begin{aligned}
&|x-y|^2\\
&=\left(\sum_{a=1}^{\infty}\sum_{\kappa=1}^{b-1}\frac{1}{b^a(\omega_b^{-\kappa}-1)}\,{}_b\mathrm{wal}_{\kappa b^{a-1}}(x)-\sum_{a=1}^{\infty}\sum_{\kappa=1}^{b-1}\frac{1}{b^a(\omega_b^{-\kappa}-1)}\,{}_b\mathrm{wal}_{\kappa b^{a-1}}(y)\right)^2\\
&=\sum_{a=1}^{\infty}\sum_{\kappa=1}^{b-1}\sum_{a'=1}^{\infty}\sum_{\kappa'=1}^{b-1}\frac{1}{b^{a+a'}(\omega_b^{-\kappa}-1)(\omega_b^{\kappa'}-1)}\,{}_b\mathrm{wal}_{\kappa b^{a-1}}(x)\,\overline{{}_b\mathrm{wal}_{\kappa' b^{a'-1}}(x)}\\
&\quad+\sum_{a=1}^{\infty}\sum_{\kappa=1}^{b-1}\sum_{a'=1}^{\infty}\sum_{\kappa'=1}^{b-1}\frac{1}{b^{a+a'}(\omega_b^{-\kappa}-1)(\omega_b^{\kappa'}-1)}\,{}_b\mathrm{wal}_{\kappa b^{a-1}}(y)\,\overline{{}_b\mathrm{wal}_{\kappa' b^{a'-1}}(y)}\\
&\quad-2\sum_{a=1}^{\infty}\sum_{\kappa=1}^{b-1}\sum_{a'=1}^{\infty}\sum_{\kappa'=1}^{b-1}\frac{1}{b^{a+a'}(\omega_b^{-\kappa}-1)(\omega_b^{\kappa'}-1)}\,{}_b\mathrm{wal}_{\kappa b^{a-1}}(x)\,\overline{{}_b\mathrm{wal}_{\kappa' b^{a'-1}}(y)}.
\end{aligned}
\tag{12.6}
$$

By using Lemma 12.2 again, we obtain

$$
\begin{aligned}
&\int_0^1 |(x\oplus\sigma)-(y\oplus\sigma)|^2\,\mathrm{d}\sigma\\
&=2\sum_{a=1}^{\infty}\sum_{\kappa=1}^{b-1}\frac{1}{b^{2a}|\omega_b^{\kappa}-1|^2}-2\sum_{a=1}^{\infty}\sum_{\kappa=1}^{b-1}\frac{1}{b^{2a}|\omega_b^{\kappa}-1|^2}\,{}_b\mathrm{wal}_{\kappa b^{a-1}}(x)\,\overline{{}_b\mathrm{wal}_{\kappa b^{a-1}}(y)}\\
&=\frac{1}{6}-2\sum_{a=1}^{\infty}\sum_{\kappa=1}^{b-1}\frac{1}{b^{2a}|\omega_b^{\kappa}-1|^2}\,{}_b\mathrm{wal}_{\kappa b^{a-1}}(x)\,\overline{{}_b\mathrm{wal}_{\kappa b^{a-1}}(y)},
\end{aligned}
\tag{12.7}
$$

where the last equality follows from

$$
2\sum_{a=1}^{\infty}\sum_{\kappa=1}^{b-1}\frac{1}{b^{2a}|\omega_b^{\kappa}-1|^2}=\int_0^1\int_0^1|x-y|^2\,\mathrm{d}x\,\mathrm{d}y=\frac{1}{6},
\tag{12.8}
$$

which in turn follows from (12.6) in combination with the orthogonality properties of the Walsh functions (see Proposition A.10).

For the last part, namely $\int_0^1 |(x\oplus\sigma)-(y\oplus\sigma)|\,\mathrm{d}\sigma$, we cannot use the argument above. Instead, by Lemma 12.2, there are $\tau_b(k)$ such that

$$
\int_0^1 |(x\oplus\sigma)-(y\oplus\sigma)|\,\mathrm{d}\sigma=\sum_{k=0}^{\infty}\tau_b(k)\,{}_b\mathrm{wal}_k(x)\,\overline{{}_b\mathrm{wal}_k(y)}.
\tag{12.9}
$$

For $k \in \mathbb{N}_0$, we have

$$\begin{aligned}\tau_b(k) &= \int_0^1 \int_0^1 \int_0^1 |(x \oplus \sigma) - (y \oplus \sigma)| \overline{{}_b\mathrm{wal}_k(x)}\, {}_b\mathrm{wal}_k(y) \,\mathrm{d}\sigma \,\mathrm{d}x \,\mathrm{d}y \\ &= \int_0^1 \int_0^1 \int_0^1 |x - y| \overline{{}_b\mathrm{wal}_k(x \ominus \sigma)}\, {}_b\mathrm{wal}_k(y \ominus \sigma) \,\mathrm{d}\sigma \,\mathrm{d}x \,\mathrm{d}y \\ &= \int_0^1 \int_0^1 |x - y| \overline{{}_b\mathrm{wal}_k(x)}\, {}_b\mathrm{wal}_k(y) \,\mathrm{d}x \,\mathrm{d}y.\end{aligned}$$

First, one can show that $\int_0^1 \int_0^1 |x - y| \,\mathrm{d}x \,\mathrm{d}y = \frac{1}{3}$ and therefore, $\tau_b(0) = \frac{1}{3}$. For $k \in \mathbb{N}$, let $k = \kappa_{a-1} b^{a-1} + \cdots + \kappa_1 b + \kappa_0$, where a is such that $\kappa_{a-1} \neq 0$, $u = u_{a-1} b^{a-1} + \cdots + u_1 b + u_0$ and $v = v_{a-1} b^{a-1} + \cdots + v_1 b + v_0$. Then

$$\begin{aligned}\tau_b(k) &= \int_0^1 \int_0^1 |x - y| \overline{{}_b\mathrm{wal}_k(x)}\, {}_b\mathrm{wal}_k(y) \,\mathrm{d}x \,\mathrm{d}y \\ &= \sum_{u=0}^{b^a-1} \sum_{v=0}^{b^a-1} \omega_b^{\kappa_0(u_{a-1}-v_{a-1})+\cdots+\kappa_{a-1}(u_0-v_0)} \\ &\quad \times \int_{u/b^a}^{(u+1)/b^a} \int_{v/b^a}^{(v+1)/b^a} |x - y| \,\mathrm{d}x \,\mathrm{d}y.\end{aligned}$$

We have the following equalities: let $0 \le u < b^a$, then

$$\int_{u/b^a}^{(u+1)/b^a} \int_{u/b^a}^{(u+1)/b^a} |x - y| \,\mathrm{d}x \,\mathrm{d}y = \frac{1}{3b^{3a}}$$

and for $0 \le u, v < b^a$, $u \neq v$, we have

$$\int_{u/b^a}^{(u+1)/b^a} \int_{v/b^a}^{(v+1)/b^a} |x - y| \,\mathrm{d}x \,\mathrm{d}y = \frac{|u - v|}{b^{3a}}.$$

Thus,

$$\begin{aligned}\tau_b(k) &= \sum_{u=0}^{b^a-1} \frac{1}{3b^{3a}} + \sum_{u=0}^{b^a-1} \sum_{\substack{v=0 \\ u \neq v}}^{b^a-1} \omega_b^{\kappa_0(u_{a-1}-v_{a-1})+\cdots+\kappa_{a-1}(u_0-v_0)} \frac{|u - v|}{b^{3a}} \\ &= \frac{1}{3b^{2a}} + \frac{2}{b^{3a}} \sum_{u=0}^{b^a-2} \sum_{v=u+1}^{b^a-1} (v - u) \omega_b^{\kappa_0(u_{a-1}-v_{a-1})+\cdots+\kappa_{a-1}(u_0-v_0)}. \qquad (12.10)\end{aligned}$$

In the following, we determine the values of $\tau_b(k)$ for any $k \in \mathbb{N}$. Let

$$\theta(u, v) = (v - u) \omega_b^{\kappa_0(u_{a-1}-v_{a-1})+\cdots+\kappa_{a-1}(u_0-v_0)}.$$

In order to find the value of the double sum in the expression for $\tau_b(k)$, let $u = u_{a-1}b^{a-1} + \cdots + u_1 b$ and let $v = v_{a-1}b^{a-1} + \cdots + v_1 b$, where $v > u$. Observe that u and v are divisible by b, that is $u_0 = v_0 = 0$, and that $k = \kappa_{a-1}b^{a-1} + \cdots + \kappa_1 b + \kappa_0$, where a is such that $\kappa_{a-1} \neq 0$. We have

$$\left|\sum_{u_0=0}^{b-1}\sum_{v_0=0}^{b-1} \theta(u+u_0, v+v_0)\right| = \left|\sum_{u_0=0}^{b-1}\sum_{v_0=0}^{b-1}(v_0-u_0)\omega_b^{\kappa_{a-1}(u_0-v_0)}\right|, \tag{12.11}$$

as $|\omega_b^{\kappa_0(u_{a-1}-v_{a-1})+\cdots+\kappa_{a-2}(u_1-v_1)}| = 1$ and $\sum_{u_0=0}^{b-1}\sum_{v_0=0}^{b-1}(v-u)\omega_b^{\kappa_{a-1}(u_0-v_0)} = 0$. We show that the sum (12.11) is indeed 0. This can be seen by the following:

$$\begin{aligned}
&\sum_{u_0=0}^{b-1}\sum_{v_0=0}^{b-1}(v_0-u_0)\omega_b^{\kappa_{a-1}(u_0-v_0)} \\
&= \sum_{u_0=0}^{b-1}\sum_{\substack{v_0=0\\ v_0\neq u_0}}^{b-1}(v_0-u_0)\omega_b^{\kappa_{a-1}(u_0-v_0)} \\
&= \sum_{u_0=0}^{b-2}\sum_{v_0=u_0+1}^{b-1}(v_0-u_0)\omega_b^{\kappa_{a-1}(u_0-v_0)} + \sum_{v_0=0}^{b-2}\sum_{u_0=v_0+1}^{b-1}(v_0-u_0)\omega_b^{\kappa_{a-1}(u_0-v_0)} \\
&= \sum_{u_0=0}^{b-2}\sum_{v_0=u_0+1}^{b-1}(v_0-u_0)(\omega_b^{\kappa_{a-1}(u_0-v_0)} - \omega_b^{-\kappa_{a-1}(u_0-v_0)}) \\
&= 2\mathrm{i}\sum_{u_0=0}^{b-2}\sum_{v_0=u_0+1}^{b-1}(v_0-u_0)\sin(2\pi\kappa_{a-1}(u_0-v_0)/b).
\end{aligned}$$

Let $M = \{(u_0, v_0) : 0 \le u_0 < v_0 \le b-1\}$. For $c \in \{1, \ldots, b-1\}$, consider the sets $J_c = \{(u_0, v_0) \in M : v_0 - u_0 = c\}$. Let $|J_c|$ be the number of elements in the set J_c, then $|J_c| = b - c$. Further, we have $\sin(2\pi\kappa_{a-1}c/b) = -\sin(-2\pi\kappa_{a-1}c/b) = -\sin(2\pi\kappa_{a-1}(b-c)/b)$. If $c = b - c$, that is $b = 2c$, we have $\sin(2\pi\kappa_{a-1}c/b) = \sin(\pi\kappa_{a-1}) = 0$ and for $c \in \{1, \ldots, b-1\}$ with $c \neq b - c$, we have

$$\begin{aligned}
\sum_{(u_0,v_0)\in J_c}(v_0-u_0) - \sum_{(u_0,v_0)\in J_{b-c}}(v_0-u_0) &= |J_c|c - |J_{b-c}|(b-c) \\
&= (b-c)c - c(b-c) = 0.
\end{aligned}$$

Thus, it follows that

$$\sum_{u_0=0}^{b-1}\sum_{v_0=0}^{b-1}\theta(u+u_0, v+v_0) = 0 \tag{12.12}$$

for any $0 \le u < v \le b^a - 1$ which are divisible by b.

Therefore, most terms in the double sum in (12.10) cancel out. We are left with the following terms: $\theta(u + u_0, u + v_0)$ for $u = 0, \ldots, b^a - b$, where $b|u$, and $0 \le u_0 < v_0 \le b - 1$. We have

$$\begin{aligned}\theta(u + u_0, u + v_0) &= (u + v_0 - u - u_0)\omega_b^{\kappa_0(u_{a-1}-u_{a-1})+\cdots+\kappa_{a-2}(u_1-u_1)+\kappa_{a-1}(u_0-v_0)} \\ &= (v_0 - u_0)\omega_b^{\kappa_{a-1}(u_0-v_0)} \\ &= \theta(u_0, v_0). \end{aligned} \tag{12.13}$$

The sum over all remaining $\theta(u_0, v_0)$ can be calculated using geometric series. By doing that, we obtain

$$\sum_{u_0=0}^{b-2} \sum_{v_0=u_0+1}^{b-1} \theta(u_0, v_0) = \frac{2b\omega_b^{\kappa_{a-1}}}{(\omega_b^{\kappa_{a-1}} - 1)^2} = -\frac{b}{2\sin^2(\kappa_{a-1}\pi/b)}. \tag{12.14}$$

Combining (12.10), (12.12), (12.13) and (12.14), we obtain for $k \in \mathbb{N}$ that

$$\tau_b(k) = \frac{1}{3b^{2a}} - \frac{2}{b^{3a}} \frac{b^a}{2\sin^2(\kappa_{a-1}\pi/b)} = \frac{1}{b^{2a}}\left(\frac{1}{3} - \frac{1}{\sin^2(\kappa_{a-1}\pi/b)}\right), \tag{12.15}$$

where $k = \kappa_{a-1}b^{a-1} + \cdots + \kappa_1 b + \kappa_0$, with $\kappa_{a-1} \neq 0$. Further, we repeat that $\tau_b(0) = \frac{1}{3}$.

Therefore, we obtain from (12.3), (12.5), (12.7), (12.9) and (12.15) that $\widehat{K}(k, k) = r_{\mathrm{sob},b}(k, \gamma)$, where $r_{\mathrm{sob},b}(k, \gamma)$ is as stated in the assertion. It can be checked that $\sum_{k=0}^{\infty} r_{\mathrm{sob},b}(k, \gamma) < \infty$ (this is Exercise 12.2). Further, K is also continuous. Hence, it follows from Section A.3 and Lemma 12.2 that the digital shift invariant kernel K_{ds} associated with K is given by

$$\begin{aligned} K_{\mathrm{ds}}(x, y) &= 1 + \gamma\left(\sum_{k=1}^{\infty} \frac{-\tau_b(k)}{2}\, {}_b\mathrm{wal}_k(x)\, \overline{{}_b\mathrm{wal}_k(y)}\right) \\ &= \sum_{k=0}^{\infty} r_{\mathrm{sob},b}(k, \gamma)\, {}_b\mathrm{wal}_k(x)\, \overline{{}_b\mathrm{wal}_k(y)}. \end{aligned} \tag{12.16}$$

For the multivariate case, we have

$$\begin{aligned} K_{\mathrm{ds}}(\boldsymbol{x}, \boldsymbol{y}) &= \prod_{i=1}^{s}\left(\sum_{k=0}^{\infty} r_{\mathrm{sob},b}(k, \gamma_i)\, {}_b\mathrm{wal}_k(x_i)\, \overline{{}_b\mathrm{wal}_k(y_i)}\right) \\ &= \sum_{\boldsymbol{k}\in\mathbb{N}_0^s} r_{\mathrm{sob},b}(\boldsymbol{k}, \boldsymbol{\gamma})\, {}_b\mathrm{wal}_{\boldsymbol{k}}(\boldsymbol{x})\, \overline{{}_b\mathrm{wal}_{\boldsymbol{k}}(\boldsymbol{y})}. \end{aligned}$$

□

In the next proposition, we show how the digital shift invariant kernel can be simplified. For $x = \xi_1 b^{-1} + \xi_2 b^{-2} + \cdots$ and $y = \eta_1 b^{-1} + \eta_2 b^{-2} + \cdots$ we define

$$\phi_{\mathrm{ds}}(x, y) = \begin{cases} \frac{1}{6} & \text{if } x = y, \\ \frac{1}{6} - \frac{|\xi_{i_0} - \eta_{i_0}|(b - |\xi_{i_0} - \eta_{i_0}|)}{b^{i_0+1}} & \text{if } \xi_{i_0} \neq \eta_{i_0}, \\ & \text{and } \xi_i = \eta_i \text{ for } i = 1, \ldots, i_0 - 1. \end{cases} \tag{12.17}$$

Proposition 12.6 *Let K be the reproducing kernel given by (12.1). Then the associated digital shift invariant kernel in prime base $b \geq 2$ is given by*

$$K_{\mathrm{ds}}(\boldsymbol{x}, \boldsymbol{y}) = \prod_{i=1}^{s} (1 + \gamma_i \phi_{\mathrm{ds}}(x_i, y_i)), \tag{12.18}$$

where $\boldsymbol{x} = (x_1, \ldots, x_s)$ and $\boldsymbol{y} = (y_1, \ldots, y_s)$.

Proof Again it is enough to consider the one-dimensional case.

For $a \geq 1$ and $1 \leq \kappa \leq b - 1$, we define

$$D_{a,\kappa}(x, y) := \sum_{k=\kappa b^{a-1}}^{(\kappa+1)b^{a-1}-1} {}_b\mathrm{wal}_k(x) \overline{{}_b\mathrm{wal}_k(y)}.$$

Now let $x = \xi_1 b^{-1} + \xi_2 b^{-2} + \cdots$, $y = \eta_1 b^{-1} + \eta_2 b^{-2} + \cdots$ and $k = \kappa_{a-1} b^{a-1} + \cdots + \kappa_1 b + \kappa_0$ with $\kappa_{a-1} \neq 0$. Then, for $1 \leq \kappa_{a-1} \leq b - 1$, we have

$$\begin{aligned} D_{a,\kappa_{a-1}}(x, y) &= \sum_{k=\kappa_{a-1} b^{a-1}}^{(\kappa_{a-1}+1)b^{a-1}-1} {}_b\mathrm{wal}_k(x) \overline{{}_b\mathrm{wal}_k(y)} \\ &= \sum_{k=\kappa_{a-1} b^{a-1}}^{(\kappa_{a-1}+1)b^{a-1}-1} \omega_b^{\kappa_0(\xi_1 - \eta_1) + \cdots + \kappa_{a-1}(\xi_a - \eta_a)} \\ &= \omega_b^{\kappa_{a-1}(\xi_a - \eta_a)} \sum_{\kappa_0=0}^{b-1} \omega_b^{\kappa_0(\xi_1 - \eta_1)} \cdots \sum_{\kappa_{a-2}=0}^{b-1} \omega_b^{\kappa_{a-2}(\xi_{a-1} - \eta_{a-1})} \\ &= \begin{cases} b^{a-1} \omega_b^{\kappa_{a-1}(\xi_a - \eta_a)} & \text{if } \xi_i = \eta_i \text{ for all } i \in \{1, \ldots, a-1\}, \\ 0 & \text{otherwise.} \end{cases} \end{aligned}$$

For $x = y$, we obtain $D_{a,\kappa_{a-1}}(x, x) = b^{a-1}$ for all a and κ_{a-1}. Therefore, by using the identity $\sum_{\kappa=1}^{b-1} \sin^{-2}(\kappa\pi/b) = (b^2 - 1)/3$ given in Corollary A.23, we obtain

$$\begin{aligned} \sum_{k=1}^{\infty} \frac{-\tau_b(k)}{2} {}_b\mathrm{wal}_k(x) \overline{{}_b\mathrm{wal}_k(x)} &= \sum_{a=1}^{\infty} \sum_{\kappa=1}^{b-1} \frac{1}{b^{2a}} \left(\frac{1}{2\sin^2(\kappa\pi/b)} - \frac{1}{6} \right) D_{a,\kappa}(x, x) \\ &= \sum_{a=1}^{\infty} \frac{b^2 - b}{6b^{2a}} b^{a-1} = \frac{1}{6}. \end{aligned}$$

Now let $x \neq y$, more precisely, let $\xi_i = \eta_i$ for $i = 1, \ldots, i_0 - 1$ and $\xi_{i_0} \neq \eta_{i_0}$. Then we have

$$\begin{aligned}
\sum_{k=1}^{\infty} \frac{-\tau_b(k)}{2} {}_b\mathrm{wal}_k(x) \overline{{}_b\mathrm{wal}_k(y)} &= \sum_{a=1}^{\infty} \sum_{\kappa=1}^{b-1} \frac{1}{b^{2a}} \left(\frac{1}{2\sin^2(\kappa\pi/b)} - \frac{1}{6} \right) D_{a,\kappa}(x, y) \\
&= \sum_{a=1}^{i_0-1} \sum_{\kappa=1}^{b-1} \frac{1}{b^{2a}} \left(\frac{1}{2\sin^2(\kappa\pi/b)} - \frac{1}{6} \right) D_{a,\kappa}(x, y) \\
&\quad + \sum_{\kappa=1}^{b-1} \frac{1}{b^{2i_0}} \left(\frac{1}{2\sin^2(\kappa\pi/b)} - \frac{1}{6} \right) D_{i_0,\kappa}(x, y) \\
&= \sum_{a=1}^{i_0-1} \frac{1}{b^{a+1}} \sum_{\kappa=1}^{b-1} \left(\frac{1}{2\sin^2(\kappa\pi/b)} - \frac{1}{6} \right) \\
&\quad + \frac{1}{b^{i_0+1}} \sum_{\kappa=1}^{b-1} \left(\frac{\omega_b^{\kappa(\xi_{i_0} - \eta_{i_0})}}{2\sin^2(\kappa\pi/b)} - \frac{\omega_b^{\kappa(\xi_{i_0} - \eta_{i_0})}}{6} \right).
\end{aligned}$$

It follows from Corollary A.23 that

$$\sum_{\kappa=1}^{b-1} \frac{\omega_b^{\kappa(\xi_{i_0} - \eta_{i_0})}}{\sin^2(\kappa\pi/b)} = 2|\xi_{i_0} - \eta_{i_0}|(|\xi_{i_0} - \eta_{i_0}| - b) + \frac{b^2 - 1}{3}$$

and $\sum_{\kappa=1}^{b-1} \sin^{-2}(\kappa_{a-1}\pi/b) = (b^2 - 1)/3$. Further, as $\xi_{i_0} \neq \eta_{i_0}$, we have $\sum_{\kappa=1}^{b-1} \omega_b^{\kappa(\xi_{i_0} - \eta_{i_0})} = -1$. Therefore, we obtain

$$\begin{aligned}
&\sum_{k=1}^{\infty} \frac{-\tau_b(k)}{2} {}_b\mathrm{wal}_k(x) \overline{{}_b\mathrm{wal}_k(y)} \\
&\quad = \sum_{a=1}^{i_0-1} \frac{b^2 - b}{6b^{a+1}} + \frac{1}{b^{i_0+1}} \left(|\xi_{i_0} - \eta_{i_0}|(|\xi_{i_0} - \eta_{i_0}| - b) + \frac{b^2}{6} \right) \\
&\quad = \frac{1}{6} - \frac{|\xi_{i_0} - \eta_{i_0}|(b - |\xi_{i_0} - \eta_{i_0}|)}{b^{i_0+1}}.
\end{aligned}$$

Thus,

$$\sum_{k=1}^{\infty} \frac{-\tau_b(k)}{2} {}_b\mathrm{wal}_k(x) \overline{{}_b\mathrm{wal}_k(y)} = \phi_{\mathrm{ds}}(x, y)$$

as defined in (12.17) and hence the result follows with (12.16). □

12.3 A formula for the mean square worst-case error and existence results for good nets

Using Theorem 12.4 and the representation of the digital shift invariant kernel, we can now give a formula for the mean square worst-case error of a QMC rule using a digitally shifted point set in the weighted Sobolev space $\mathscr{H}_{\mathrm{sob},s,\boldsymbol{\gamma}}$.

Theorem 12.7 *The mean square worst-case error $\widehat{e}^2_{\mathrm{ds}}(\mathscr{H}_{\mathrm{sob},s,\boldsymbol{\gamma}}, \mathcal{P})$ of a QMC rule in the weighted Sobolev space $\mathscr{H}_{\mathrm{sob},s,\boldsymbol{\gamma}}$ by using a random digital shift in prime base $b \geq 2$ on the point set $\mathcal{P} = \{\boldsymbol{x}_0, \ldots, \boldsymbol{x}_{N-1}\}$, with $\boldsymbol{x}_n = (x_{n,1}, \ldots, x_{n,s})$, is given by*

$$\widehat{e}^2_{\mathrm{ds}}(\mathscr{H}_{\mathrm{sob},s,\boldsymbol{\gamma}}, \mathcal{P}) = -1 + \frac{1}{N^2} \sum_{n,m=0}^{N-1} \sum_{\boldsymbol{k} \in \mathbb{N}_0^s} r_{\mathrm{sob},b}(\boldsymbol{k}, \boldsymbol{\gamma})\, {}_b\mathrm{wal}_{\boldsymbol{k}}(\boldsymbol{x}_n)\, \overline{{}_b\mathrm{wal}_{\boldsymbol{k}}(\boldsymbol{x}_m)}$$

$$= -1 + \frac{1}{N^2} \sum_{n,m=0}^{N-1} \prod_{j=1}^{s} \left(1 + \gamma_j \phi_{\mathrm{ds}}(x_{n,j}, x_{m,j})\right),$$

where the function ϕ_{ds} is given by (12.17).

Proof From Theorem 12.4 and from Proposition 2.11, we obtain that

$$\begin{aligned}\widehat{e}^2_{\mathrm{ds}}(\mathscr{H}_{\mathrm{sob},s,\boldsymbol{\gamma}}, \mathcal{P}) &= e^2(K_{\mathrm{ds}}, \mathcal{P}) \\ &= \int_{[0,1]^{2s}} K_{\mathrm{ds}}(\boldsymbol{x}, \boldsymbol{y})\,\mathrm{d}\boldsymbol{x}\,\mathrm{d}\boldsymbol{y} - \frac{2}{N} \sum_{n=0}^{N-1} \int_{[0,1]^s} K_{\mathrm{ds}}(\boldsymbol{x}_n, \boldsymbol{y})\,\mathrm{d}\boldsymbol{y} \\ &\quad + \frac{1}{N^2} \sum_{n,m=0}^{N-1} K_{\mathrm{ds}}(\boldsymbol{x}_n, \boldsymbol{x}_m) \\ &= -1 + \frac{1}{N^2} \sum_{n,m=0}^{N-1} K_{\mathrm{ds}}(\boldsymbol{x}_n, \boldsymbol{x}_m),\end{aligned}$$

as $\int_{[0,1]^s} K_{\mathrm{ds}}(\boldsymbol{x}, \boldsymbol{y})\,\mathrm{d}\boldsymbol{x} = \int_{[0,1]^s} K_{\mathrm{ds}}(\boldsymbol{x}, \boldsymbol{y})\,\mathrm{d}\boldsymbol{y} = 1$ which follows from Proposition 12.5 together with the orthogonality properties of the Walsh functions (see Proposition A.10). Now the desired result follows from Proposition 12.5 and Proposition 12.6. □

The formula from Theorem 12.7 can be simplified further when we assume that the underlying point set $\mathcal{P}$ is a digital (t, m, s)-net over $\mathbb{Z}_b$. We recall here that when we use a digital shift in conjunction with a digital net, then both are in the same base b.

Before we state the result, we need to introduce some notation. For a non-negative integer k with base b representation $k = \sum_{j=0}^{\infty} \kappa_j b^j$, we write

$$\mathrm{tr}_m(k) := \kappa_0 + \kappa_1 b + \cdots + \kappa_{m-1} b^{m-1}$$

and

$$\mathrm{tr}_m(\mathbf{k}) := (\kappa_0, \ldots, \kappa_{m-1})^\top \in (\mathbb{Z}_b^m)^\top.$$

Note that for $k \in \mathbb{N}_0$, we have $\mathrm{tr}_m(k) \in \{0, \ldots, b^m - 1\}$. For a vector $\boldsymbol{k} = (k_1, \ldots, k_s) \in \mathbb{N}_0^s$, we write $\mathrm{tr}_m(\boldsymbol{k}) := (\mathrm{tr}_m(k_1), \ldots, \mathrm{tr}_m(k_s))$ and hence, $\mathrm{tr}_m(\boldsymbol{k}) \in \{0, \ldots, b^m - 1\}^s$.

Theorem 12.8 *Let b be a prime and let $\mathcal{P} = \{\boldsymbol{x}_0, \ldots, \boldsymbol{x}_{b^m-1}\}$ be a digital (t, m, s)-net over $\mathbb{Z}_b$ generated by the $m \times m$ matrices $C_1, \ldots, C_s$ over $\mathbb{Z}_b$.*

1. *The mean square worst-case error of a QMC rule in the weighted Sobolev space $\mathcal{H}_{\mathrm{sob},s,\boldsymbol{\gamma}}$ using the randomly b-adic digitally shifted point set $\mathcal{P}$ is given by*

$$\widehat{e}_{\mathrm{ds}}^2(\mathcal{H}_{\mathrm{sob},s,\boldsymbol{\gamma}}, \mathcal{P}) = \sum_{\boldsymbol{k} \in \mathcal{D}'_\infty(C_1,\ldots,C_s)} r_{\mathrm{sob},b}(\boldsymbol{k}, \boldsymbol{\gamma}),$$

where $\mathcal{D}'_\infty(C_1, \ldots, C_s)$ is the dual net without the zero-vector as given in Remark 4.77, i.e. $\mathcal{D}'_\infty(C_1, \ldots, C_s) = \mathcal{D}_\infty(C_1, \ldots, C_s) \setminus \{\boldsymbol{0}\}$ and

$$\mathcal{D}_\infty(C_1, \ldots, C_s) = \{\boldsymbol{k} \in \mathbb{N}_0^s : C_1^\top \mathrm{tr}_m(\mathbf{k}_1) + \cdots + C_s^\top \mathrm{tr}_m(\mathbf{k}_s) = \mathbf{0}.\}$$

2. *Let $\boldsymbol{x}_n = (x_{n,1}, \ldots, x_{n,s})$ for $0 \le n < b^m$, then we have*

$$\widehat{e}_{\mathrm{ds}}^2(\mathcal{H}_{\mathrm{sob},s,\boldsymbol{\gamma}}, \mathcal{P}) = -1 + \frac{1}{b^m} \sum_{n=0}^{b^m-1} \prod_{i=1}^{s} \left(1 + \gamma_i \phi_{\mathrm{ds}}(x_{n,i}, 0)\right),$$

where ϕ_{ds} is given by (12.17). In particular, $\widehat{e}_{\mathrm{ds}}^2(\mathcal{H}_{\mathrm{sob},s,\boldsymbol{\gamma}}, \mathcal{P})$ can be calculated in $O(sb^m)$ operations.

Proof From the first part of Theorem 12.7, we have

$$\begin{aligned}
\widehat{e}_{\mathrm{ds}}^2(\mathcal{H}_{\mathrm{sob},s,\boldsymbol{\gamma}}, \mathcal{P}) &= -1 + \frac{1}{b^{2m}} \sum_{n,h=0}^{b^m-1} \sum_{\boldsymbol{k} \in \mathbb{N}_0^s} r_{\mathrm{sob},b}(\boldsymbol{k}, \boldsymbol{\gamma})\, {}_b\mathrm{wal}_{\boldsymbol{k}}(\boldsymbol{x}_n) \overline{{}_b\mathrm{wal}_{\boldsymbol{k}}(\boldsymbol{x}_h)} \\
&= -1 + \frac{1}{b^{2m}} \sum_{h=0}^{b^m-1} \left(\sum_{n=0}^{b^m-1} \sum_{\boldsymbol{k} \in \mathbb{N}_0^s} r_{\mathrm{sob},b}(\boldsymbol{k}, \boldsymbol{\gamma})\, {}_b\mathrm{wal}_{\boldsymbol{k}}(\boldsymbol{x}_n \ominus \boldsymbol{x}_h) \right).
\end{aligned}$$

Due to the group structure of digital nets, see Lemma 4.72, each term in the sum over h has the same value. Therefore,

$$\widehat{e}_{\rm ds}^2(\mathscr{H}_{{\rm sob},s,\boldsymbol{\gamma}}, \mathcal{P}) = -1 + \frac{1}{b^m} \sum_{n=0}^{b^m-1} \sum_{\boldsymbol{k}\in\mathbb{N}_0^s} r_{{\rm sob},b}(\boldsymbol{k}, \boldsymbol{\gamma}) \, {}_b{\rm wal}_{\boldsymbol{k}}(\boldsymbol{x}_n)$$

$$= -1 + \sum_{\boldsymbol{k}\in\mathbb{N}_0^s} r_{{\rm sob},b}(\boldsymbol{k}, \boldsymbol{\gamma}) \frac{1}{b^m} \sum_{n=0}^{b^m-1} {}_b{\rm wal}_{\boldsymbol{k}}(\boldsymbol{x}_n).$$

Now apply Lemma 4.75 and the first part of the result follows.

The second part follows from the second part of Theorem 12.7, from the fact that $\phi_{\rm ds}(x_{n,j}, x_{h,j}) = \phi_{\rm ds}(x_{n,j} \ominus x_{h,j}, 0)$ and the group structure of digital nets (see Lemma 4.72 again). □

The formula from part two of Theorem 12.8 guarantees that the mean square worst-case error $\widehat{e}_{\rm ds}^2(\mathscr{H}_{{\rm sob},s,\boldsymbol{\gamma}}, \mathcal{P})$ can be computed with reasonable effort. We exploit this fact later for explicit constructions of good point sets $\mathcal{P}$. But first let us use the formula from part one of Theorem 12.8 to show the existence of digital nets which yield a reasonably small mean square worst-case error.

Before we do so, we have to determine the upper bounds on the sum of $r_{{\rm sob},b}(k, \gamma)^\lambda$ over all $k \in \mathbb{N}$. For any $b \geq 2$, we have

$$\sum_{k=1}^{\infty} r_{{\rm sob},b}(k, \gamma) = \sum_{a=1}^{\infty} \sum_{k=b^{a-1}}^{b^a-1} r_{{\rm sob},b}(k, \gamma)$$

$$= \sum_{a=1}^{\infty} \frac{\gamma b^{a-1}}{2b^{2a}} \sum_{\kappa_{a-1}=1}^{b-1} \left(\frac{1}{\sin^2(\kappa_{a-1}\pi/b)} - \frac{1}{3} \right).$$

We have $\sum_{a=1}^{\infty} b^{-a} = 1/(b-1)$ and $\sum_{\kappa_{a-1}=1}^{b-1} \sin^{-2}(\kappa_{a-1}\pi/b) = (b^2-1)/3$ by Corollary A.23. Thus, we obtain

$$\sum_{k=1}^{\infty} r_{{\rm sob},b}(k, \gamma) = \frac{\gamma}{2b(b-1)} \left(\frac{b^2-1}{3} - \frac{b-1}{3} \right) = \frac{\gamma}{6}.$$

Further, we have $r_{{\rm sob},2}(k, \gamma) = \frac{\gamma}{3 \cdot 2^{2a}}$ for $k \in \mathbb{N}$ and therefore,

$$\sum_{k=1}^{\infty} r_{{\rm sob},2}(k, \gamma)^\lambda = \sum_{a=1}^{\infty} \sum_{k=2^{a-1}}^{2^a-1} r_{{\rm sob},2}(k, \gamma)^\lambda$$

$$= \sum_{a=1}^{\infty} \frac{\gamma^\lambda 2^{a-1}}{3^\lambda 2^{2a\lambda}} = \frac{\gamma^\lambda}{2 \cdot 3^\lambda} \sum_{a=1}^{\infty} \frac{1}{2^{a(2\lambda-1)}} = \frac{\gamma^\lambda}{3^\lambda(2^{2\lambda}-2)},$$

for any $1/2 < \lambda \le 1$. For $b > 2$, we estimate $\sin(\kappa_{a-1}\pi/b) \ge \sin(\pi/b) \ge \frac{3\sqrt{3}}{2b}$ and therefore,

$$\frac{1}{\sin^2(\kappa_{a-1}\pi/b)} - \frac{1}{3} \le \frac{4b^2-9}{27}.$$

Using this estimation, we get

$$\begin{aligned}\sum_{k=1}^{\infty} r_{\mathrm{sob},b}(k,\gamma)^{\lambda} &= \sum_{a=1}^{\infty}\sum_{k=b^{a-1}}^{b^a-1} r_{\mathrm{sob},b}(k,\gamma)^{\lambda}\\ &\le \sum_{a=1}^{\infty} \frac{\gamma^{\lambda} b^{a-1}(b-1)(4b^2-9)^{\lambda}}{2^{\lambda} b^{2\lambda a} 27^{\lambda}} = \frac{\gamma^{\lambda}(b-1)(4b^2-9)^{\lambda}}{54^{\lambda}(b^{2\lambda}-b)},\end{aligned}$$

for any $1/2 < \lambda \le 1$. We note that the inequality becomes an equality for $b = 3$.

In the following, let $\mu_b(1) := 1/6$ and for $1/2 < \lambda < 1$, we define

$$\mu_b(\lambda) := \begin{cases} \frac{1}{3^{\lambda}(2^{2\lambda}-2)} & \text{if } b = 2, \\ \frac{(b-1)(4b^2-9)^{\lambda}}{54^{\lambda}(b^{2\lambda}-b)} & \text{if } b \ne 2. \end{cases} \tag{12.19}$$

Using this notation, we have shown that for all $b \ge 2$ and all $1/2 < \lambda \le 1$, we have

$$\sum_{k=1}^{\infty} r_{\mathrm{sob},b}(k,\gamma)^{\lambda} \le \gamma^{\lambda}\mu_b(\lambda). \tag{12.20}$$

For the following, we define the quantity

$$\widehat{c}_{s,b,\boldsymbol{\gamma},\lambda} := 2^{1/\lambda} \prod_{j=1}^{s} (1 + \gamma_j^{\lambda}\mu_b(\lambda))^{1/\lambda}, \tag{12.21}$$

where μ_b is defined as in (12.19).

We are ready to give upper bounds on the mean square worst-case error.

Theorem 12.9 *Let b be a prime and let $s, m \in \mathbb{N}$.*

1. *There exist generating matrices $C_1, \ldots, C_s$ of size $m \times m$ over $\mathbb{Z}_b$ of a digital net $\mathcal{P}$ over $\mathbb{Z}_b$ such that the mean square worst-case error of QMC integration in the weighted Sobolev space $\mathscr{H}_{\mathrm{sob},s,\boldsymbol{\gamma}}$ is for any $1/2 < \lambda \le 1$ bounded by*

$$\widehat{e}^{\,2}_{\mathrm{ds}}(\mathscr{H}_{\mathrm{sob},s,\boldsymbol{\gamma}}, \mathcal{P}) \le \widehat{c}_{s,b,\boldsymbol{\gamma},\lambda} b^{-m/\lambda},$$

   where $\widehat{c}_{s,b,\boldsymbol{\gamma},\lambda}$ is defined as in (12.21).
2. *For some $\lambda \in (1/2, 1]$, assume that*

$$\sum_{i=1}^{\infty} \gamma_i^{\lambda} < \infty. \tag{12.22}$$

Then, $\widehat{c}_{s,b,\boldsymbol{\gamma},\lambda} \le \widehat{c}_{\infty,b,\boldsymbol{\gamma},\lambda} < \infty$ *and we have*

$$\widehat{e}^2_{\rm ds}(\mathscr{H}_{{\rm sob},s,\boldsymbol{\gamma}}, \mathcal{P}) \le \widehat{c}_{\infty,b,\boldsymbol{\gamma},\lambda} b^{-m/\lambda} \quad \textit{for all } s \ge 1.$$

Thus, assuming (12.22), for any $s, m \in \mathbb{N}$ *there exists a digital net over* $\mathbb{Z}_b$ *such that the mean square worst-case error is bounded independently of the dimension* s.

3. *Under the assumption*

$$A := \limsup_{s\to\infty} \frac{\sum_{i=1}^s \gamma_i}{\log s} < \infty, \tag{12.23}$$

we obtain $\widehat{c}_{s,b,\boldsymbol{\gamma},1} \le \widetilde{c}_\delta s^{\mu_b(1)(A+\delta)}$ *and therefore,*

$$\widehat{e}^2_{\rm ds}(\mathscr{H}_{{\rm sob},s,\boldsymbol{\gamma}}) \le \widetilde{c}_\delta s^{\mu_b(1)(A+\delta)} b^{-m}$$

for any $\delta > 0$, *where the constant* $\widetilde{c}_\delta$ *depends only on* δ. *Thus, assuming* (12.23), *for any* $m, s \in \mathbb{N}$ *there exists a digital net over* $\mathbb{Z}_b$ *such that the mean square worst-case error satisfies a bound which depends only polynomially on the dimension* s.

Proof Let $1/2 < \lambda \le 1$. From Theorem 12.8 and by applying Jensen's inequality, which states that for a sequence (a_k) of non-negative real numbers, we have $\left(\sum a_k\right)^\lambda \le \sum a_k^\lambda$, for any $0 < \lambda \le 1$, we get

$$\widehat{e}^2_{\rm ds}(\mathscr{H}_{{\rm sob},s,\boldsymbol{\gamma}}, \mathcal{P}) \le \left(\sum_{\boldsymbol{k}\in\mathcal{D}'_\infty(C_1,\ldots,C_s)} r_{{\rm sob},b}(\boldsymbol{k},\boldsymbol{\gamma})^\lambda \right)^{1/\lambda}. \tag{12.24}$$

Let $\mathcal{C}$ be the set of all s-tuples $(C_1,\ldots,C_s)$ of $m\times m$ matrices over $\mathbb{Z}_b$. We average the above sum over all possible choices $(C_1,\ldots,C_s)\in\mathcal{C}$, that is,

$$\begin{aligned}&\frac{1}{b^{m^2 s}} \sum_{(C_1,\ldots,C_s)\in\mathcal{C}} \sum_{\boldsymbol{k}\in\mathcal{D}'_\infty(C_1,\ldots,C_s)} r_{{\rm sob},b}(\boldsymbol{k},\boldsymbol{\gamma})^\lambda \\ &= \frac{1}{b^{m^2 s}} \sum_{\boldsymbol{k}\in\mathbb{N}_0^s\setminus\{\boldsymbol{0}\}} r_{{\rm sob},b}(\boldsymbol{k},\boldsymbol{\gamma})^\lambda \sum_{\substack{(C_1,\ldots,C_s)\in\mathcal{C}\\ \boldsymbol{k}\in\mathcal{D}'_\infty(C_1,\ldots,C_s)}} 1.\end{aligned}$$

The condition $\boldsymbol{k}\in\mathcal{D}'_\infty(C_1,\ldots,C_s)$ is equivalent to the equation

$$C_1^\top {\rm tr}_m(\mathbf{k}_1) + \cdots + C_s^\top {\rm tr}_m(\mathbf{k}_s) = \mathbf{0} \in (\mathbb{Z}_b^m)^\top.$$

For $\boldsymbol{k}\in\mathbb{N}_0^s\setminus\{\boldsymbol{0}\}$, we have to consider two cases:

1. Assume that $\boldsymbol{k} = b^m \boldsymbol{l}$ with $\boldsymbol{l}\in\mathbb{N}_0^s\setminus\{\boldsymbol{0}\}$. In this case we have ${\rm tr}_m(k_j) = 0$ for $1\le j\le s$ and the condition

$$C_1^\top {\rm tr}_m(\mathbf{k}_1) + \cdots + C_s^\top {\rm tr}_m(\mathbf{k}_s) = \mathbf{0}$$

is trivially fulfilled for any choice of $(C_1,\ldots,C_s)\in\mathcal{C}$.

2. Assume that $\boldsymbol{k} = \boldsymbol{k}^* + b^m \boldsymbol{l}$ with $\boldsymbol{l} \in \mathbb{N}_0^s$, $\boldsymbol{k}^* = (k_1^*, \ldots, k_s^*) \neq \boldsymbol{0}$, and $0 \le k_i^* \le b^m - 1$ for all $1 \le i \le s$. In this case we have $\mathrm{tr}_m(\mathbf{k}_i) = \mathbf{k}_i^*$ for all $1 \le i \le s$ and our condition becomes
$$C_1^\top \mathbf{k}_1^* + \cdots + C_s^\top \mathbf{k}_s^* = \mathbf{0} \in (\mathbb{Z}_b^m)^\top. \tag{12.25}$$
Let $\mathbf{c}_j^{(i)}$ denote the jth row vector, $1 \le j \le m$, of the matrix C_i, $1 \le i \le s$. Then condition (12.25) becomes
$$\sum_{i=1}^{s} \sum_{j=0}^{m-1} \kappa_{i,j}^* \mathbf{c}_{j+1}^{(i)} = \mathbf{0} \in \mathbb{Z}_b^m, \tag{12.26}$$
where k_i^* has the b-adic representation $k_i^* = \kappa_{i,0}^* + \kappa_{i,1}^* b + \cdots + \kappa_{i,m-1}^* b^{m-1}$. Since at least one $k_i^* \neq 0$, it follows that there is a $\kappa_{i,j}^* \neq 0$. First assume that $\kappa_{1,0}^* \neq 0$. Then for any choice of
$$\mathbf{c}_2^{(1)}, \ldots, \mathbf{c}_m^{(1)}, \mathbf{c}_1^{(2)}, \ldots, \mathbf{c}_m^{(2)}, \ldots, \mathbf{c}_1^{(s)}, \ldots, \mathbf{c}_m^{(s)} \in \mathbb{Z}_b^m,$$
we can find exactly one vector $\mathbf{c}_1^{(1)} \in \mathbb{Z}_b^m$ such that condition (12.26) is fulfilled. The same argument holds with $\kappa_{1,0}^*$ replaced by $\kappa_{j,i}^*$ and $\mathbf{c}_1^{(1)}$ replaced by $\mathbf{c}_{i+1}^{(j)}$.

Now we have
$$\begin{aligned}
&\frac{1}{b^{m^2 s}} \sum_{(C_1,\ldots,C_s)\in\mathcal{C}} \sum_{\boldsymbol{k}\in\mathcal{D}'_\infty(C_1,\ldots,C_s)} r_{\mathrm{sob},b}(\boldsymbol{k},\boldsymbol{\gamma})^\lambda \\
&\le \frac{1}{b^{m^2 s}} \sum_{\boldsymbol{l}\in\mathbb{N}_0^s\setminus\{\boldsymbol{0}\}} r_{\mathrm{sob},b}(b^m\boldsymbol{l},\boldsymbol{\gamma})^\lambda b^{m^2 s} \\
&\quad + \frac{1}{b^{m^2 s}} \sum_{\boldsymbol{l}\in\mathbb{N}_0^s} \sum_{\substack{\boldsymbol{k}^*\in\mathbb{N}_0^s\setminus\{\boldsymbol{0}\} \\ \|\boldsymbol{k}^*\|_\infty < b^m}} r_{\mathrm{sob},b}(\boldsymbol{k}^* + b^m\boldsymbol{l},\boldsymbol{\gamma})^\lambda b^{m^2 s - m} \\
&= -1 + \sum_{\boldsymbol{l}\in\mathbb{N}_0^s} r_{\mathrm{sob},b}(b^m\boldsymbol{l},\boldsymbol{\gamma})^\lambda + \frac{1}{b^m} \sum_{\boldsymbol{l}\in\mathbb{N}_0^s} \sum_{\substack{\boldsymbol{k}^*\in\mathbb{N}_0^s\setminus\{\boldsymbol{0}\} \\ |\boldsymbol{k}^*|_\infty < b^m}} r_{\mathrm{sob},b}(\boldsymbol{k}^* + b^m\boldsymbol{l},\boldsymbol{\gamma})^\lambda \\
&= -1 + \left(1 - \frac{1}{b^m}\right) \sum_{\boldsymbol{l}\in\mathbb{N}_0^s} r_{\mathrm{sob},b}(b^m\boldsymbol{l},\boldsymbol{\gamma})^\lambda + \frac{1}{b^m} \sum_{\boldsymbol{l}\in\mathbb{N}_0^s} r_{\mathrm{sob},b}(\boldsymbol{l},\boldsymbol{\gamma})^\lambda \\
&\le -1 + \left(1 - \frac{1}{b^m}\right) \prod_{i=1}^{s} \left(1 + \frac{1}{b^{2\lambda m}} \gamma_i^\lambda \mu_b(\lambda)\right) + \frac{1}{b^m} \prod_{i=1}^{s} (1 + \gamma_i^\lambda \mu_b(\lambda)) \\
&\le \frac{2}{b^m} \prod_{i=1}^{s} (1 + \gamma_i^\lambda \mu_b(\lambda)),
\end{aligned} \tag{12.27}$$
where we used the fact that $r_{\mathrm{sob},b}(\boldsymbol{0},\boldsymbol{\gamma}) = 1$.

As the average over all choices $(C_1, \ldots, C_s) \in \mathcal{C}$ satisfies the bound (12.27), it is clear that there must exist $(C_1, \ldots, C_s) \in \mathcal{C}$ such that

$$\sum_{\boldsymbol{k}\in\mathcal{D}'_\infty(C_1,\ldots,C_s)} r_{\mathrm{sob},b}(\boldsymbol{k},\boldsymbol{\gamma})^\lambda \leq \frac{2}{b^m}\prod_{i=1}^{s}\left(1+\gamma_i^\lambda \mu_b(\lambda)\right)$$

and for these matrices, we obtain from (12.24) that

$$\widehat{e}_{\mathrm{ds}}^2(\mathscr{H}_{\mathrm{sob},s,\boldsymbol{\gamma}}, \mathcal{P}) \leq \frac{2^{1/\lambda}}{b^{m/\lambda}}\prod_{i=1}^{s}\left(1+\gamma_i^\lambda \mu_b(\lambda)\right)^{1/\lambda} = \frac{\widehat{c}_{s,b,\boldsymbol{\gamma},\lambda}}{b^{m/\lambda}}.$$

For the second part of the theorem, we have

$$\begin{aligned}
\widehat{c}_{\infty,b,\boldsymbol{\gamma},\lambda} &= 2^{1/\lambda}\prod_{i=1}^{\infty}\left(1+\gamma_i^\lambda \mu_b(\lambda)\right)^{1/\lambda}\\
&= 2^{1/\lambda}\exp\left(\frac{1}{\lambda}\sum_{i=1}^{\infty}\log\left(1+\gamma_i^\lambda \mu_b(\lambda)\right)\right)\\
&\leq 2^{1/\lambda}\exp\left(\frac{\mu_b(\lambda)}{\lambda}\sum_{i=1}^{\infty}\gamma_i^\lambda\right) < \infty,
\end{aligned}$$

provided that $\sum_{i=1}^{\infty}\gamma_i^\lambda < \infty$.

For the third part of the theorem, observe that $A < \infty$ and therefore, for any positive δ, there exists a positive s_δ such that

$$\sum_{i=1}^{s}\gamma_i \leq (A+\delta)\log s \quad \text{for all} \quad s \geq s_\delta.$$

Hence,

$$\begin{aligned}
\widehat{c}_{s,b,\boldsymbol{\gamma},1} &= 2\prod_{i=1}^{s}\left(1+\gamma_i\mu_b(1)\right) = 2s^{\sum_{i=1}^{s}\frac{\log(1+\gamma_i\mu_b(1))}{\log s}}\\
&\leq 2s^{\mu_b(1)\sum_{i=1}^{s}\gamma_i/\log s} \leq 2s^{\mu_b(1)(A+\delta)},
\end{aligned}$$

for any $\delta > 0$ and all $s \geq s_\delta$. Thus, there is a constant $\widetilde{c}_\delta > 0$ such that

$$c_{s,b,\boldsymbol{\gamma},1} \leq \widetilde{c}_\delta s^{(A+\delta)\mu_b(1)}.$$

From this the result follows. □

In part one of the theorem above, we showed that the average over all possible shifts satisfies a certain error bound. From this result we can also deduce that there exists a shift $\boldsymbol{\sigma} \in [0,1)^s$ such that this error bound is satisfied. We have the following corollary.

Corollary 12.10 *Let b be a prime and let $s, m \in \mathbb{N}$. Then there exists a digital shift $\boldsymbol{\sigma} \in [0,1)^s$ and $m \times m$ matrices $C_1, \ldots, C_s$ over $\mathbb{Z}_b$, such that the worst-case error for QMC integration in the weighted Sobolev space $\mathscr{H}_{\mathrm{sob},s,\boldsymbol{\gamma}}$ using the digitally shifted digital net $\mathcal{P}_{\boldsymbol{\sigma}}$ generated by $C_1, \ldots, C_s$ is, for any $1/2 < \lambda \leq 1$, bounded by*

$$e^2(\mathscr{H}_{\mathrm{sob},s,\boldsymbol{\gamma}}, \mathcal{P}_{\boldsymbol{\sigma}}) \leq \widehat{c}_{s,b,\boldsymbol{\gamma},\lambda} b^{-m/\lambda},$$

where $\widehat{c}_{s,b,\boldsymbol{\gamma},\lambda}$ is defined as in (12.21).

Corollary 12.11 *Let $s, N \in \mathbb{N}$. For some $\lambda \in (1/2, 1]$, assume that* (12.22) *holds. Then there exists a point set $\mathcal{P}$ consisting of N points in $[0,1)^s$ such that*

$$e^2(\mathscr{H}_{\mathrm{sob},s,\boldsymbol{\gamma}}, \mathcal{P}) \leq \widehat{c}_{\infty,b,\boldsymbol{\gamma},\lambda} N^{-1/\lambda}.$$

The proof of this result is given as Exercise 12.9.

From Corollary 12.11, we find that the minimal number $N_{\mathrm{sob}}(s, \varepsilon)$ of function evaluations needed to obtain a worst-case error smaller or equal to ε for $0 < \varepsilon < 1$ (recall that the initial error for the space $\mathscr{H}_{\mathrm{sob},s,\boldsymbol{\gamma}}$ is equal to one) is bounded by $N_{\mathrm{sob}}(s, \varepsilon) \leq \lceil \widehat{c}^{\lambda}_{\infty,b,\boldsymbol{\gamma},\lambda} \varepsilon^{-2\lambda} \rceil$. Hence, a sufficient condition for strong tractability of the integration problem in $\mathscr{H}_{\mathrm{sob},s,\boldsymbol{\gamma}}$ is that $\sum_{i=1}^{\infty} \gamma_i < \infty$. (The notion of strong tractability here is defined in the same way as for the weighted star discrepancy in Definition 3.63 but with $N^*_{\boldsymbol{\gamma}}(s, \varepsilon)$ replaced by $N_{\mathrm{sob}}(s, \varepsilon)$.) In a similar way one can give a sufficient condition for polynomial tractability; see Exercise 12.10.

12.4 Constructions of polynomial lattices

So far, we have only provided existence results for digital nets which yield a reasonably small mean square worst-case error for integration in the weighted Sobolev space $\mathscr{H}_{\mathrm{sob},s,\boldsymbol{\gamma}}$. Now we are going to give explicit constructions of such nets, where we restrict ourselves to the subclass of polynomial lattices. To this end we rewrite the worst-case error formula from Theorem 12.8. As usual, we often associate a non-negative integer $k = \kappa_0 + \kappa_1 b + \cdots + \kappa_a b^a$ with the polynomial $k(x) = \kappa_0 + \kappa_1 x + \cdots + \kappa_a x^a \in \mathbb{Z}_b[x]$ and vice versa.

Lemma 12.12 *Let b be a prime, let $s, m \in \mathbb{N}$, let $p \in \mathbb{Z}_b[x]$ with* $\deg(p) = m$ *and let $\boldsymbol{q} \in \mathbb{Z}_b[x]^s$.*

Then the mean square worst-case error $\widehat{e}^2_{\mathrm{ds}}(\mathscr{H}_{\mathrm{sob},s,\boldsymbol{\gamma}}, \mathcal{P}(\boldsymbol{q}, p))$ of QMC integration in the Sobolev space $\mathscr{H}_{\mathrm{sob},s,\boldsymbol{\gamma}}$ using the point set $\mathcal{P}(\boldsymbol{q}, p)$ is given by

$$\widehat{e}^2_{\mathrm{ds}}(\mathscr{H}_{\mathrm{sob},s,\boldsymbol{\gamma}}, \mathcal{P}(\boldsymbol{q}, p)) = \sum_{\substack{\boldsymbol{k} \in \mathbb{N}_0^s \setminus \{\boldsymbol{0}\} \\ \mathrm{tr}_m(\boldsymbol{k}) \in \mathcal{D}_{\boldsymbol{q},p}}} r_{\mathrm{sob},b}(\boldsymbol{k}, \boldsymbol{\gamma}),$$

where $\mathcal{D}_{\boldsymbol{q},p}$ is the set from Definition 10.7, i.e.

$$\mathcal{D}_{\boldsymbol{q},p} = \{\boldsymbol{k} \in G_{b,m}^s \,:\, \boldsymbol{k} \cdot \boldsymbol{q} \equiv 0 \pmod{p}\}.$$

Proof The result follows from Theorem 12.8 together with Lemma 10.6. □

We use the following CBC construction for the search of suitable polynomial lattices with reasonably small mean square worst-case error.

Algorithm 12.13 *Given a prime b, and $s, m \in \mathbb{N}$, a polynomial $p \in \mathbb{Z}_b[x]$ with $\deg(p) = m$ and weights $\boldsymbol{\gamma} = (\gamma_i)_{i \geq 1}$:*

1. *Set $q_1 = 1$.*
2. *For $d = 2, 3, \ldots, s$, find $q_d \in G_{b,m}^*$ by minimising the square worst-case error $\widehat{e}_{\mathrm{ds}}^2(\mathscr{H}_{\mathrm{sob},d,\boldsymbol{\gamma}}, \mathcal{P}((q_1, \ldots, q_d), p))$ as a function of q_d.*

In the following theorem we show that Algorithm 12.13 is guaranteed to find a good generating vector provided that the polynomial p is irreducible. A similar result for not necessarily irreducible polynomials p can be shown using the method from [129].

Theorem 12.14 *Let b be a prime, let $s, m \in \mathbb{N}$ and let $p \in \mathbb{Z}_b[x]$ be irreducible with $\deg(p) = m$. Suppose that $(q_1^*, \ldots, q_s^*) \in (G_{b,m}^*)^s$ is constructed by Algorithm 12.13. Then, for all $1 \leq d \leq s$ and for all $1/2 < \lambda \leq 1$, we have*

$$\widehat{e}_{\mathrm{ds}}^2(\mathscr{H}_{\mathrm{sob},d,\boldsymbol{\gamma}}, \mathcal{P}((q_1^*, \ldots, q_d^*), p)) \leq \widehat{c}_{d,b,\boldsymbol{\gamma},\lambda} b^{-m/\lambda},$$

where $\widehat{c}_{d,b,\boldsymbol{\gamma},\lambda}$ is defined as in (12.21).

Proof For $d = 1$, we have $q_1^* = 1$ and hence,

$$\widehat{e}_{\mathrm{ds}}^2(\mathscr{H}_{\mathrm{sob},1,\boldsymbol{\gamma}}, \mathcal{P}((1), p)) = \sum_{\substack{k=1 \\ \mathrm{tr}_m(k) \equiv 0 \pmod{p}}}^{\infty} r_{\mathrm{sob},b}(k).$$

Since p is irreducible with $\deg(p) = m$, the only solutions of $\mathrm{tr}_m(k) \equiv 0 \pmod{p}$ are those k for which $\mathrm{tr}_m(k) = 0$, i.e. k of the form $k = lb^m$. Together with Jensen's inequality and with (12.20), we therefore obtain

$$\widehat{e}_{\mathrm{ds}}^2(\mathscr{H}_{\mathrm{sob},1,\boldsymbol{\gamma}}, \mathcal{P}((1), p)) \leq \left(\sum_{l=1}^{\infty} r_{\mathrm{sob},b}(lb^m)^\lambda\right)^{1/\lambda} \leq \left(\frac{1}{b^{2\lambda m}} \gamma^\lambda \mu_b(\lambda)\right)^{1/\lambda},$$

and hence, the result follows for $d = 1$.

Suppose that, for some $1 \leq d < s$, we have $\boldsymbol{q}^* \in (G_{b,m}^*)^d$ and

$$e^2(\mathscr{H}_{\mathrm{sob},d,\boldsymbol{\gamma}}, \mathcal{P}(\boldsymbol{q}^*, p)) \leq \widehat{c}_{d,b,\boldsymbol{\gamma},\lambda} b^{-m/\lambda}, \tag{12.28}$$

for all $1/2 < \lambda \le 1$. Now we consider $(\boldsymbol{q}^*, q_{d+1}) := (q_1^*, \ldots, q_d^*, q_{d+1})$. It follows from Lemma 12.12 that

$$\begin{aligned} & e^2(\mathcal{H}_{\mathrm{sob},d+1,\boldsymbol{\gamma}}, \mathcal{P}((\boldsymbol{q}^*, q_{d+1}), p)) \\ &= \sum_{\substack{(\boldsymbol{k},k_{d+1}) \in \mathbb{N}_0^{d+1}\setminus\{\boldsymbol{0}\} \\ \mathrm{tr}_m(\boldsymbol{k},k_{d+1}) \in \mathcal{D}_{(\boldsymbol{q}^*, q_{d+1}),p}}} r_{\mathrm{sob},b}(\boldsymbol{k}, \boldsymbol{\gamma}) r_{\mathrm{sob},b}(k_{d+1}, \gamma_{d+1}) \\ &= e^2(\mathcal{H}_{\mathrm{sob},d,\boldsymbol{\gamma}}, \mathcal{P}(\boldsymbol{q}^*, p)) + \theta(q_{d+1}), \end{aligned} \tag{12.29}$$

where we have separated out the $k_{d+1} = 0$ terms, and where

$$\theta(q_{d+1}) = \sum_{k_{d+1}=1}^{\infty} r_{\mathrm{sob},b}(k_{d+1}, \gamma_{d+1}) \sum_{\substack{\boldsymbol{k} \in \mathbb{N}_0^d \\ \mathrm{tr}_m(\boldsymbol{k},k_{d+1}) \in \mathcal{D}_{(\boldsymbol{q}^*, q_{d+1}),p}}} r_{\mathrm{sob},b}(\boldsymbol{k}, \boldsymbol{\gamma}).$$

According to the algorithm, q_{d+1}^* is chosen such that the mean square worst-case error $e^2(\mathcal{H}_{\mathrm{sob},d+1,\boldsymbol{\gamma}}, \mathcal{P}((\boldsymbol{q}^*, q_{d+1}), p))$ is minimised. Since the only dependency on q_{d+1} is in $\theta(q_{d+1})$, we have $\theta(q_{d+1}^*) \le \theta(q_{d+1})$ for all $q_{d+1} \in G_{b,m}^*$, which implies that for any $\lambda \le 1$, we have $\theta(q_{d+1}^*)^\lambda \le \theta(q_{d+1})^\lambda$ for all $q_{d+1} \in G_{b,m}^*$. This leads to

$$\theta(q_{d+1}^*) \le \left(\frac{1}{b^m - 1} \sum_{q_{d+1} \in G_{b,m}^*} \theta(q_{d+1})^\lambda \right)^{1/\lambda}. \tag{12.30}$$

We obtain a bound on $\theta(q_{d+1}^*)$ through this last inequality.

For λ satisfying $1/2 < \lambda \le 1$, it follows from Jensen's inequality that

$$\theta(q_{d+1})^\lambda \le \sum_{k_{d+1}=1}^{\infty} r_{\mathrm{sob},b}(k_{d+1}, \gamma_{d+1})^\lambda \sum_{\substack{\boldsymbol{k} \in \mathbb{N}_0^d \\ \mathrm{tr}_m(\boldsymbol{k},k_{d+1}) \in \mathcal{D}_{(\boldsymbol{q}^*, q_{d+1}),p}}} r_{\mathrm{sob},b}(\boldsymbol{k}, \boldsymbol{\gamma})^\lambda.$$

The condition $\mathrm{tr}_m(\boldsymbol{k}, k_{d+1}) \in \mathcal{D}_{(\boldsymbol{q}^*, q_{d+1}),p}$ is equivalent to the equation

$$\mathrm{tr}_m(k_1) q_1^* + \cdots + \mathrm{tr}_m(k_d) q_d^* \equiv -\mathrm{tr}_m(k_{d+1}) q_{d+1} \pmod{p}.$$

If k_{d+1} is a multiple of b^m, then $\mathrm{tr}_m(k_{d+1}) = 0$ and the corresponding term in the sum is independent of q_{d+1}. If k_{d+1} is not a multiple of b^m, then $\mathrm{tr}_m(k_{d+1})$ can have any value between 1 and $b^m - 1$. Moreover, since $q_{d+1} \neq 0$ and p is irreducible, $\mathrm{tr}_m(k_{d+1})q_{d+1}$ is never a multiple of p.

By averaging over all $q_{d+1} \in G^*_{b,m}$, with the above discussion in mind, we obtain

$$\begin{aligned}
&\frac{1}{b^m - 1} \sum_{q_{d+1} \in G^*_{b,m}} \theta(q_{d+1})^\lambda \\
&\le \sum_{\substack{k_{d+1}=1 \\ b^m | k_{d+1}}}^{\infty} r_{\mathrm{sob},b}(k_{d+1}, \gamma_{d+1})^\lambda \sum_{\substack{\boldsymbol{k} \in \mathbb{N}_0^d \\ \mathrm{tr}_m(\boldsymbol{k}) \cdot \boldsymbol{q} \equiv 0 \pmod p}} r_{\mathrm{sob},b}(\boldsymbol{k}, \boldsymbol{\gamma})^\lambda \\
&\quad + \frac{1}{b^m - 1} \sum_{\substack{k_{d+1}=1 \\ b^m \nmid k_{d+1}}}^{\infty} r_{\mathrm{sob},b}(k_{d+1}, \gamma_{d+1})^\lambda \sum_{\substack{\boldsymbol{k} \in \mathbb{N}_0^d \\ \mathrm{tr}_m(\boldsymbol{k}) \cdot \boldsymbol{q} \not\equiv 0 \pmod p}} r_{\mathrm{sob},b}(\boldsymbol{k}, \boldsymbol{\gamma})^\lambda \\
&\le \frac{\gamma_{d+1}^\lambda \mu_b(\lambda)}{b^m - 1} \prod_{j=1}^{d} \left(1 + \gamma_j^\lambda \mu_b(\lambda)\right), \qquad (12.31)
\end{aligned}$$

where the first inequality follows from the fact that if k_{d+1} is not a multiple of b^m, then

$$\sum_{q_{d+1} \in G^*_{b,m}} \sum_{\substack{\boldsymbol{k} \in \mathbb{N}_0^d \\ \mathrm{tr}_m(\boldsymbol{k}) \cdot \boldsymbol{q} \equiv -\mathrm{tr}_m(k_{d+1}) q_{d+1} \pmod p}} r_{\mathrm{sob},b}(\boldsymbol{k}, \boldsymbol{\gamma})^\lambda = \sum_{\substack{\boldsymbol{k} \in \mathbb{N}_0^d \\ \mathrm{tr}_m(\boldsymbol{k}) \cdot \boldsymbol{q} \not\equiv 0 \pmod p}} r_{\mathrm{sob},b}(\boldsymbol{k}, \boldsymbol{\gamma})^\lambda,$$

and the second inequality is obtained using

$$\sum_{\substack{k_{d+1}=1 \\ b^m | k_{d+1}}}^{\infty} r_{\mathrm{sob},b}(k_{d+1}, \gamma_{d+1})^\lambda \le \frac{\gamma_{d+1}^\lambda \mu_b(\lambda)}{b^{2\lambda m}},$$

$$\sum_{\substack{k_{d+1}=1 \\ b^m \nmid k_{d+1}}}^{\infty} r_{\mathrm{sob},b}(k_{d+1}, \gamma_{d+1})^\lambda \le \sum_{k_{d+1}=1}^{\infty} r_{\mathrm{sob},b}(k_{d+1}, \gamma_{d+1})^\lambda \le \gamma_{d+1}^\lambda \mu_b(\lambda)$$

and

$$\sum_{\substack{\boldsymbol{k} \in \mathbb{N}_0^d \\ \mathrm{tr}_m(\boldsymbol{k}) \cdot \boldsymbol{q} \not\equiv 0 \pmod p}} r_{\mathrm{sob},b}(\boldsymbol{k}, \boldsymbol{\gamma})^\lambda \le \prod_{j=1}^{d} \left(1 + \gamma_j^\lambda \mu_b(\lambda)\right) - \sum_{\substack{\boldsymbol{k} \in \mathbb{N}_0^d \\ \mathrm{tr}_m(\boldsymbol{k}) \cdot \boldsymbol{q} \equiv 0 \pmod p}} r_{\mathrm{sob},b}(\boldsymbol{k}, \boldsymbol{\gamma})^\lambda.$$

Thus, from (12.30), (12.31) and since $b^m - 1 \geq b^m/2$, we obtain

$$\theta(q_{d+1}^*) \leq \frac{\gamma_{d+1}\mu_b(\lambda)^{1/\lambda}}{(b^m-1)^{1/\lambda}} \prod_{j=1}^{d} \left(1+\gamma_j^\lambda \mu_b(\lambda)\right)^{1/\lambda}$$
$$\leq \gamma_{d+1}\mu_b(\lambda)^{1/\lambda} \widehat{c}_{d,b,\boldsymbol{\gamma},\lambda} b^{-m/\lambda},$$

which, together with (12.28) and (12.29), yields

$$\begin{aligned} e^2(\mathscr{H}_{\mathrm{sob},d+1,\boldsymbol{\gamma}}, \mathcal{P}((\boldsymbol{q}^*, q_{d+1}^*), p)) &= e^2(\mathscr{H}_{\mathrm{sob},d,\boldsymbol{\gamma}}, \mathcal{P}(\boldsymbol{q}^*, p)) + \theta(q_{d+1}^*) \\ &\leq \left(1+\gamma_{d+1}\mu_b(\lambda)^{1/\lambda}\right) \widehat{c}_{d,b,\boldsymbol{\gamma},\lambda} b^{-m/\lambda} \\ &\leq \left(1+\gamma_{d+1}^\lambda \mu_b(\lambda)\right)^{1/\lambda} \widehat{c}_{d,b,\boldsymbol{\gamma},\lambda} b^{-m/\lambda} \\ &= \widehat{c}_{d+1,b,\boldsymbol{\gamma},\lambda} b^{-m/\lambda}. \end{aligned}$$

Hence, the result follows for all $1 \leq d \leq s$ by induction. □

Remark 12.15 *Theorem 12.14 shows that a vector $\boldsymbol{q}^* \in (G_{b,m}^*)^s$, which is constructed by Algorithm 12.13, leads to an error bound as stated in part one of Theorem 12.9. Parts two and three of Theorem 12.9 apply accordingly.*

We can also obtain results for Korobov vectors. As before, we use the notation $\boldsymbol{v}_s(q) \equiv (1, q, q^2, \ldots, q^{s-1}) \pmod{p}$. We have the following algorithm.

Algorithm 12.16 *Given a prime b and $s, m \in \mathbb{N}$, a polynomial $p \in \mathbb{Z}_b[x]$ with $\deg(p) = m$ and weights $\boldsymbol{\gamma} = (\gamma_i)_{i\geq 1}$, find $q^* \in G_{b,m}^*$ by minimising $\widehat{e}_{\mathrm{ds}}^2(\mathscr{H}_{\mathrm{sob},s,\boldsymbol{\gamma}}, \mathcal{P}(\boldsymbol{v}_s(q), p))$ over all $q \in G_{b,m}^*$.*

In the following theorem we show that Algorithm 12.13 is guaranteed to find a good generating vector, provided that the polynomial p is irreducible.

Theorem 12.17 *Let b be a prime, let $s, m \in \mathbb{N}$ and let $p \in \mathbb{Z}_b[x]$ be irreducible with $\deg(p) = m$. Suppose that $q^* \in G_{b,m}^*$ is constructed by Algorithm 12.16. Then, for all $1/2 < \lambda \leq 1$, we have*

$$\widehat{e}_{\mathrm{ds}}^2(\mathscr{H}_{\mathrm{sob},s,\boldsymbol{\gamma}}, \mathcal{P}(\boldsymbol{v}_s(q^*), p)) \leq \widehat{c}_{s,b,\boldsymbol{\gamma},\lambda} \left(s/b^m\right)^{1/\lambda},$$

where $\widehat{c}_{s,b,\boldsymbol{\gamma},\lambda}$ is defined as in (12.21).

Proof Let q^* be a minimiser of $\widehat{e}_{\mathrm{ds}}^2(\mathscr{H}_{\mathrm{sob},s,\boldsymbol{\gamma}}, \mathcal{P}(\boldsymbol{v}_s(q), p))$. We are interested in how small $\widehat{e}_{\mathrm{ds}}^2(\mathscr{H}_{\mathrm{sob},s,\boldsymbol{\gamma}}, \mathcal{P}(\boldsymbol{v}_s(q^*), p))$ is. To this end, for $1/2 < \lambda \leq 1$, we define

$$M_{s,\lambda}(p) := \frac{1}{b^m - 1} \sum_{q \in G_{b,m}^*} \widehat{e}_{\rm ds}^{2\lambda}(\mathscr{H}_{{\rm sob},s,\boldsymbol{\gamma}}, \mathcal{P}(\boldsymbol{v}_s(q), p)).$$

From Lemma 12.12 and Jensen's inequality, we obtain

$$\begin{aligned} M_{s,\lambda}(p) &\le \frac{1}{b^m - 1} \sum_{q \in G_{b,m}^*} \sum_{\substack{\boldsymbol{k} \in \mathbb{N}_0^s \setminus \{\boldsymbol{0}\} \\ \operatorname{tr}_m(\boldsymbol{k}) \in \mathcal{D}_{\boldsymbol{v}_s(q),p}}} r_{{\rm sob},b}(\boldsymbol{k}, \boldsymbol{\gamma})^\lambda \\ &= \frac{1}{b^m - 1} \sum_{\boldsymbol{k} \in \mathbb{N}_0^s \setminus \{\boldsymbol{0}\}} r_{{\rm sob},b}(\boldsymbol{k}, \boldsymbol{\gamma})^\lambda \sum_{\substack{q \in G_{b,m}^* \\ \operatorname{tr}_m(\boldsymbol{k}) \in \mathcal{D}_{\boldsymbol{v}_s(q),p}}} 1. \end{aligned}$$

The condition $\operatorname{tr}_m(\boldsymbol{k}) \in \mathcal{D}_{\boldsymbol{v}_s(q),p}$ is equivalent to the equation

$$\operatorname{tr}_m(k_1) + \operatorname{tr}_m(k_2) q + \cdots + \operatorname{tr}_m(k_s) q^{s-1} \equiv 0 \pmod{p}.$$

Now we recall that for an irreducible polynomial $p \in \mathbb{Z}_b[x]$ with $\deg(p) = m$, and a non-zero $(k_1, \ldots, k_s) \in \mathbb{Z}_b[x]^s$ with $\deg(k_i) < m$ for $1 \le i \le s$, the congruence

$$k_1 + k_2 q + \cdots + k_s q^{s-1} \equiv 0 \pmod{p}$$

has no solution if $k_2 = \cdots = k_s = 0$, and it has at most $s - 1$ solutions $q \in G_{b,m}^*$ otherwise.

For $\boldsymbol{k} = (k_1, \ldots, k_s) \in \mathbb{N}_0^s \setminus \{\boldsymbol{0}\}$, we consider two cases:

1. For $2 \le i \le s$, let $k_i = l_i b^m$ for some $l_i \in \mathbb{N}_0$. In this case we have $\operatorname{tr}_m(k_i) = 0$ for $2 \le i \le s$ and therefore,

$$\sum_{\substack{q \in G_{b,m}^* \\ \operatorname{tr}_m(\boldsymbol{k}) \in \mathcal{D}_{\boldsymbol{v}_s(q),p}}} 1 = 0.$$

2. For $2 \le i \le s$, let $k_i = k_i^* + l_i b^m$ for some $l_i \in \mathbb{N}_0$, $0 \le k_i^* \le b^m - 1$ and $(k_2^*, \ldots, k_s^*) \ne (0, \ldots, 0)$. Then we obtain

$$\sum_{\substack{q \in G_{b,m}^* \\ \operatorname{tr}_m(\boldsymbol{k}) \in \mathcal{D}_{\boldsymbol{v}_s(q),p}}} 1 \le s - 1.$$

Now we have

$$M_{s,\lambda}(p) \le \sum_{\boldsymbol{k}\in\mathbb{N}_0^s\setminus\{\boldsymbol{0}\}} r_{\mathrm{sob},b}(b^m\boldsymbol{k},\boldsymbol{\gamma})^\lambda + \frac{s-1}{b^m-1}\sum_{k_1=0}^{\infty} r_{\mathrm{sob},b}(k_1,\gamma_1)^\lambda$$

$$\times \sum_{l_2,\ldots,l_s=0}^{\infty} \sum_{\substack{k_2^*,\ldots,k_s^*=0\\(k_2^*,\ldots,k_s^*)\neq(0,\ldots,0)}}^{b^m-1} \prod_{j=2}^{s} r_{\mathrm{sob},b}(k_j^*+l_jb^m,\gamma_j)^\lambda$$

$$\le \prod_{j=1}^{s}\left(1+\gamma_j^\lambda\frac{\mu_b(\lambda)}{b^{2\lambda m}}\right) - 1 + \frac{s-1}{b^m-1}(1+\gamma_1^\lambda\mu_b(\lambda))$$

$$\times\left[\sum_{k_2,\ldots,k_s=0}^{\infty}\prod_{j=2}^{s} r_{\mathrm{sob},b}(k_j,\gamma_j)^\lambda - \sum_{l_2,\ldots,l_s=0}^{\infty}\prod_{j=2}^{s} r_{\mathrm{sob},b}(l_jb^m,\gamma_j)^\lambda\right]$$

$$\le \frac{1}{b^{2\lambda m}}\prod_{j=1}^{s}(1+\gamma_j^\lambda\mu_b(\lambda)) + \frac{s-1}{b^m-1}(1+\gamma_1^\lambda\mu_b(\lambda))\prod_{j=2}^{s}(1+\gamma_j^\lambda\mu_b(\lambda)),$$

and therefore,

$$M_{s,\lambda}(p) \le \frac{s}{b^m-1}\prod_{j=1}^{s}(1+\gamma_j^\lambda\mu_b(\lambda)).$$

Hence, there exists a $q^* \in G_{b,m}^*$ for which

$$\widehat{e}_{\mathrm{ds}}^{2\lambda}(\mathscr{H}_{\mathrm{sob},s,\boldsymbol{\gamma}}, \mathcal{P}(\boldsymbol{v}_s(q^*),p)) \le \frac{s}{b^m-1}\prod_{j=1}^{s}(1+\gamma_j^\lambda\mu_b(\lambda)) \le \widehat{c}_{s,b,\boldsymbol{\gamma},\lambda}^{\lambda}\frac{s}{b^m}. \qquad \square$$

Using the same argument as in the proof of the third part of Theorem 12.9, we obtain the following corollary.

Corollary 12.18 *Let b be a prime, let $s, m \in \mathbb{N}$ and let $p \in \mathbb{Z}_b[x]$ be irreducible with $\deg(p) = m$. Suppose that $q^* \in G_{b,m}^*$ is constructed by Algorithm 12.16. Assume that*

$$A := \limsup_{s\to\infty}\frac{\sum_{j=1}^{s}\gamma_j}{\log s} < \infty. \tag{12.32}$$

Then, for any $\delta > 0$, there exists a $\widetilde{c}_\delta > 0$, which depends only on δ, such that

$$\widehat{e}_{\mathrm{ds}}^{2}(\mathscr{H}_{\mathrm{sob},s,\boldsymbol{\gamma}}, \mathcal{P}(\boldsymbol{v}_s(q^*),p)) \le \widetilde{c}_\delta s^{1+\mu_b(1)(A+\delta)}b^{-m}.$$

Thus, assuming that (12.32), the bound on the mean square worst-case error $\widehat{e}_{\mathrm{ds}}^{2}(\mathscr{H}_{\mathrm{sob},s,\boldsymbol{\gamma}}, \mathcal{P}(\boldsymbol{v}_s(q^*),p))$ depends only polynomially on the dimension s.

Exercises

12.1 Show that the initial error for the space $\mathscr{H}_{\mathrm{sob},s,\boldsymbol{\gamma}}$ is $e(\mathscr{H}_{\mathrm{sob},s,\boldsymbol{\gamma}}, 0) = 1$.

12.2 Show that $\sum_{k=0}^{\infty} r_{\mathrm{sob},b}(k,\gamma) < \infty$, where $r_{\mathrm{sob},b}(k,\gamma)$ is defined in Proposition 12.5.

12.3 Consider the weighted anchored Sobolev space $\mathscr{H}'_{\mathrm{sob},s,\boldsymbol{w},\boldsymbol{\gamma}}$ with a reproducing kernel given by

$$K'(\boldsymbol{x},\boldsymbol{y}) = \prod_{j=1}^{s}(1+\gamma_j \nu_{w_j}(x_j,y_j)),$$

where $w_j \in [0,1]$ for $j = 1,\ldots,s$ and

$$\nu_w(x,y) = \frac{|x-w|+|y-w|-|x-y|}{2} = \begin{cases} \min(|x-w|,|y-w|) & \text{if } (x-w)(y-w) \geq 0, \\ 0 & \text{otherwise.} \end{cases}$$

This weighted Sobolev space has been considered in several papers; see, for instance, references [33, 131, 246, 247]. The inner product in $\mathscr{H}'_{\mathrm{sob},s,\boldsymbol{w},\boldsymbol{\gamma}}$ is given by

$$\langle f,g\rangle_{\mathscr{H}'_{\mathrm{sob},s,\boldsymbol{w},\boldsymbol{\gamma}}} := \sum_{\mathfrak{u}\subseteq\mathcal{I}_s} \gamma_{\mathfrak{u}}^{-1} \int_{[0,1]^{|\mathfrak{u}|}} \frac{\partial^{|\mathfrak{u}|} f}{\partial \boldsymbol{x}_{\mathfrak{u}}}(\boldsymbol{x}_{\mathfrak{u}},\boldsymbol{w}_{\mathcal{I}_s\setminus\mathfrak{u}}) \frac{\partial^{|\mathfrak{u}|} g}{\partial \boldsymbol{x}_{\mathfrak{u}}}(\boldsymbol{x}_{\mathfrak{u}},\boldsymbol{w}_{\mathcal{I}_s\setminus\mathfrak{u}})\,\mathrm{d}\boldsymbol{x}_{\mathfrak{u}},$$

where, for $\boldsymbol{x} = (x_1,\ldots,x_s)$, we use the notation $(\boldsymbol{x}_{\mathfrak{u}},\boldsymbol{w}_{\mathcal{I}_s\setminus\mathfrak{u}})$ for the s-dimensional vector whose ith component is x_i if $i \in \mathfrak{u}$ and w_i if $i \notin \mathfrak{u}$.

Show that the digital shift invariant kernel associated with the reproducing kernel of K' is given by

$$K'_{\mathrm{ds}}(\boldsymbol{x},\boldsymbol{y}) = \sum_{\boldsymbol{k}\in\mathbb{N}_0^s} r'_{\mathrm{sob},b}(\boldsymbol{k},\boldsymbol{\gamma},\boldsymbol{w})\,{}_b\mathrm{wal}_{\boldsymbol{k}}(\boldsymbol{x})\,\overline{{}_b\mathrm{wal}_{\boldsymbol{k}}(\boldsymbol{y})}, \tag{12.33}$$

where for $\boldsymbol{w} = (w_1,\ldots,w_s) \in [0,1]^s$ and $\boldsymbol{k} = (k_1,\ldots,k_s)$, we put $r'_{\mathrm{sob},b}(\boldsymbol{k},\boldsymbol{\gamma},\boldsymbol{w}) = \prod_{j=1}^{s} r'_{\mathrm{sob},b}(k_j,\gamma_j,w_j)$ and where for $k = \kappa_{a-1}b^{a-1}+\cdots+\kappa_1 b+\kappa_0$ with $\kappa_{a-1} \neq 0$, we put

$$r'_{\mathrm{sob},b}(k,\gamma,w) = \begin{cases} 1+\gamma(w^2-w+\frac{1}{3}) & \text{if } k = 0, \\ \frac{\gamma}{2b^{2a}}\left(\frac{1}{\sin^2(\kappa_{a-1}\pi/b)}-\frac{1}{3}\right) & \text{if } k > 0. \end{cases}$$

12.4 For $x = \xi_1/b+\xi_2/b^2+\cdots$ and $y = \eta_1/b+\eta_2/b^2+\cdots$ define

$$\phi_{\mathrm{ds},w}(x,y) = \begin{cases} w^2-w+\frac{1}{2} & \text{if } x = y, \\ w^2-w+\frac{1}{2}-\frac{|\xi_{i_0}-\eta_{i_0}|(b-|\xi_{i_0}-\eta_{i_0}|)}{b^{i_0+1}} & \text{if } \xi_1 = \eta_1,\ldots,\xi_{i_0-1} = \eta_{i_0-1} \\ & \text{and } \xi_{i_0} \neq \eta_{i_0}. \end{cases}$$

Show that the digital shift invariant kernel (12.33) can be simplified to

$$K'_{\mathrm{ds}}(\boldsymbol{x}, \boldsymbol{y}) = \prod_{i=1}^{s} \left(1 + \gamma_i \phi_{\mathrm{ds},w_i}(x_i, y_i)\right), \tag{12.34}$$

where $\boldsymbol{x} = (x_1, \ldots, x_s)$ and $\boldsymbol{y} = (y_1, \ldots, y_s)$.

12.5 Show that the mean square worst-case error $\widehat{e}^2_{\mathrm{ds}}(\mathscr{H}'_{\mathrm{sob},s,\boldsymbol{w},\boldsymbol{\gamma}}, \mathcal{P})$ for a QMC rule in the weighted anchored Sobolev space $\mathscr{H}'_{\mathrm{sob},s,\boldsymbol{w},\boldsymbol{\gamma}}$ by using a random digital shift in prime base $b \geq 2$ on the point set $\mathcal{P} = \{\boldsymbol{x}_0, \ldots, \boldsymbol{x}_{N-1}\}$, with $\boldsymbol{x}_n = (x_{n,1}, \ldots, x_{n,s})$, is given by

$$\begin{aligned}\widehat{e}^2_{\mathrm{ds}}(\mathscr{H}'_{\mathrm{sob},s,\boldsymbol{w},\boldsymbol{\gamma}}, \mathcal{P}) &= -1 + \frac{1}{N^2} \sum_{n,m=0}^{N-1} \sum_{\boldsymbol{k} \in \mathbb{N}_0^s} r_{\mathrm{sob},b}(\boldsymbol{k}, \boldsymbol{\gamma}, \boldsymbol{w})\, {}_b\mathrm{wal}_{\boldsymbol{k}}(\boldsymbol{x}_n) \overline{{}_b\mathrm{wal}_{\boldsymbol{k}}(\boldsymbol{x}_m)} \\ &= -1 + \frac{1}{N^2} \sum_{n,m=0}^{N-1} \prod_{i=1}^{s} \left(1 + \gamma_i \phi_{\mathrm{ds},w_i}(x_{n,i}, x_{m,i})\right),\end{aligned}$$

where $\boldsymbol{w} = (w_1, \ldots, w_s)$ and where the function $\phi_{\mathrm{ds},w}$ is given as in Exercise 12.4.

12.6 Let b be a prime and let $s, m \in \mathbb{N}$. Let $\mathcal{C}$ be the set of all s-tuples $(C_1, \ldots, C_s)$ of $m \times m$ matrices over $\mathbb{Z}_b$. Define

$$\widehat{A}_{b^m,s} := \frac{1}{b^{m^2 s}} \sum_{(C_1,\ldots,C_s) \in \mathcal{C}} \widehat{e}^2_{\mathrm{ds}}(\mathscr{H}_{\mathrm{sob},s,\boldsymbol{\gamma}}, \mathcal{P}(C_1, \ldots, C_s)).$$

Show that we have

$$\begin{aligned}\widehat{A}_{b^m,s} &= -1 + \frac{1}{b^m} \prod_{j=1}^{s} \left(1 + \frac{\gamma_j}{6}\right) + \left(1 - \frac{1}{b^m}\right) \prod_{j=1}^{s} \left(1 + \frac{\gamma_j}{6b^{2m}}\right) \\ &\leq \frac{2}{b^m} \prod_{j=1}^{s} \left(1 + \frac{\gamma_j}{6}\right).\end{aligned}$$

12.7 Let b be a prime and let $s, m \in \mathbb{N}$. Show that for $0 \leq \alpha < 1$ and $1/2 < \lambda \leq 1$, there are more than $\alpha|\mathcal{C}|$-tuples $(C_1, \ldots, C_s) \in \mathcal{C}$ such that

$$\widehat{e}^2_{\mathrm{ds}}(\mathscr{H}_{\mathrm{sob},s,\boldsymbol{\gamma}}, \mathcal{P}(C_1, \ldots, C_s)) \leq \frac{\widehat{c}_{s,b,\boldsymbol{\gamma},\lambda}}{(1-\alpha)^{1/\lambda}} b^{-m/\lambda}.$$

12.8 Consider the integration problem in $\mathscr{H}'_{\mathrm{sob},s,\boldsymbol{w},\boldsymbol{\gamma}}$ with $\boldsymbol{w} = (w_1, \ldots, w_s) \in [0,1]^s$. Let b be a prime and $p \in \mathbb{Z}_b[x]$ be irreducible, with $\deg(p) = m \geq 1$. Suppose that $(q_1^*, \ldots, q_s^*) \in (G_{b,m}^*)^s$ is constructed with Algorithm 12.13 but with respect to $\widehat{e}^2_{\mathrm{ds}}(\mathscr{H}'_{\mathrm{sob},s,\boldsymbol{w},\boldsymbol{\gamma}}, \mathcal{P})$. Then, for all $1 \leq d \leq s$ and for all $1/2 < \lambda \leq 1$, we have

$$\widehat{e}_{\mathrm{ds}}^2(\mathcal{H}'_{\mathrm{sob},s,\boldsymbol{w},\boldsymbol{\gamma}}, \mathcal{P}((q_1^*,\ldots,q_d^*),p)) \leq (b^m-1)^{-1/\lambda} \prod_{i=1}^{d} \left(\left(1+\gamma_i\left[w_i^2-w_i+\tfrac{1}{3}\right]\right)^{\lambda} + \mu_b(\lambda)\gamma_i^{\lambda} \right)^{1/\lambda}.$$

12.9 Give a proof of Corollary 12.11.
Hint: Proceed as in the proof of Corollary 5.46, but use Lemma 2.12.

12.10 Give a sufficient condition for polynomial tractability of the integration problem in $\mathcal{H}_{\mathrm{sob},s,\boldsymbol{\gamma}}$.

12.11 Consider Exercise 12.8 and show that under the assumption $\sum_{i=1}^{\infty}\gamma_i < \infty$, the mean square worst-case error $\widehat{e}_{\mathrm{ds}}^2(\mathcal{H}'_{\mathrm{sob},s,\boldsymbol{w},\boldsymbol{\gamma}}, \mathcal{P}((q_1^*,\ldots,q_d^*),p))$ satisfies a bound which is independent of the dimension s.

12.12 Let b be a prime, let $s, m \in \mathbb{N}$ and let $p \in \mathbb{Z}_b[x]$ be irreducible with $\deg(p) = m$. Show that there exists a polynomial $q^* \in G_{b,m}^*$ such that for all $1/2 < \lambda \leq 1$, we have

$$\widehat{e}_{\mathrm{ds}}^2(\mathcal{H}'_{\mathrm{sob},s,\boldsymbol{w},\boldsymbol{\gamma}}, \mathcal{P}(\boldsymbol{v}_s(q^*),p)) \leq \left(\frac{s}{b^m-1}\right)^{1/\lambda} \prod_{i=1}^{s} \left(\left(1+\gamma_i\left[w_i^2-w_i+\tfrac{1}{3}\right]\right)^{\lambda} + \mu_b(\lambda)\gamma_i^{\lambda} \right)^{1/\lambda}.$$

12.13 Consider Exercise 12.12 and show that under the assumption $\limsup_{s\to\infty}(\log s)^{-1}\sum_{i=1}^{\infty}\gamma_i < \infty$, the mean square worst-case error $\widehat{e}_{\mathrm{ds}}^2(\mathcal{H}'_{\mathrm{sob},s,\boldsymbol{w},\boldsymbol{\gamma}}, \mathcal{P}(\boldsymbol{v}_s(q^*),p))$ satisfies a bound which depends only polynomially on the dimension s.

12.14 Let b be a prime, let $s, m \in \mathbb{N}$ and let $p \in \mathbb{Z}_b[x]$ be irreducible with $\deg(p) = m$. Let $0 \leq \alpha < 1$ and $1/2 < \lambda \leq 1$. Show that there are more than $\alpha|G_{b,m}^*|$ polynomials $q \in G_{b,m}^*$ such that

$$e^2(\mathcal{H}_{\mathrm{sob},s,\boldsymbol{\gamma}}, \mathcal{P}(\boldsymbol{v}_s(q),p)) \leq \widehat{c}_{s,b,\boldsymbol{\gamma},\lambda}\left(\frac{s}{1-\alpha}\right)^{1/\lambda} b^{-m/\lambda},$$

where $\widehat{c}_{s,b,\boldsymbol{\gamma},\lambda}$ is defined as in (12.21).

12.15 Let $s \in \mathbb{N}$, let $b \geq 2$ be a prime, $\alpha > 1$ a real and $\boldsymbol{\gamma} = (\gamma_i)_{i\geq 1}$ be a sequence of non-negative reals. Consider the Walsh space $\mathcal{H}_{\mathrm{wal},s,b,\alpha,\boldsymbol{\gamma}}$ from Exercise 2.15.

Let $\mathcal{P} = \{\boldsymbol{x}_1,\ldots,\boldsymbol{x}_{b^m}\}$ be a digital (t,m,s)-net over $\mathbb{Z}_b$ generated by the matrices $C_1,\ldots,C_s$. Show that the square worst-case error for integration in the Walsh space $\mathcal{H}_{\mathrm{wal},s,b,\alpha,\boldsymbol{\gamma}}$ is given by

$$e^2(\mathcal{H}_{\mathrm{wal},s,b,\alpha,\boldsymbol{\gamma}}, \mathcal{P}) = \sum_{\boldsymbol{k}\in\mathcal{D}'_{\infty}(C_1,\ldots,C_s)} r_{\mathrm{wal},b,\alpha}(\boldsymbol{k},\boldsymbol{\gamma}),$$

where $\mathcal{D}'_{\infty}(C_1,\ldots,C_s)$ is the dual net without the zero-vector as given in Remark 4.77.
Hint: See [50, Theorem 2].

12.16 For $x = \xi_1 b^{-1} + \xi_2 b^{-2} + \cdots$ and $y = \eta_1 b^{-1} + \eta_2 b^{-2} + \cdots$ define

$$\phi_{\mathrm{wal},\alpha}(x, y) = \begin{cases} \nu_b(\alpha) & \text{if } x = y, \\ \nu_b(\alpha) - b^{(i_0-1)(1-\alpha)}(\mu(\alpha)+1) & \text{if } \xi_1 = \eta_1, \ldots, \xi_{i_0-1} = \eta_{i_0-1} \\ & \text{and } \xi_{i_0} \neq \eta_{i_0}, \end{cases}$$

where $\nu_b(\alpha) = \frac{b^\alpha(b-1)}{b^\alpha - b}$ as in Exercise 2.16. Show that the reproducing kernel $K_{\mathrm{wal},s,b,\alpha,\boldsymbol{\gamma}}$ of the Hilbert space $\mathscr{H}_{\mathrm{wal},s,b,\alpha,\boldsymbol{\gamma}}$ as given in Exercise 2.15 can be simplified to

$$K_{\mathrm{wal},s,b,\alpha,\boldsymbol{\gamma}}(\boldsymbol{x}, \boldsymbol{y}) = \prod_{i=1}^{s}(1 + \gamma_i \phi_{\mathrm{wal},\alpha}(x_i, y_i))$$

for $\boldsymbol{x} = (x_1, \ldots, x_s)$ and $\boldsymbol{y} = (y_1, \ldots, y_s)$.
Hint: See [50, Section 2.2].

12.17 Let $\mathcal{P} = \{\boldsymbol{x}_1, \ldots, \boldsymbol{x}_{b^m}\}$ be a digital (t, m, s)-net over $\mathbb{Z}_b$ and write $\boldsymbol{x}_n = (x_{n,1}, \ldots, x_{n,s})$ for $0 \leq n < b^m$. Show that the square worst-case error of QMC integration in the Walsh space $\mathscr{H}_{\mathrm{wal},s,b,\alpha,\boldsymbol{\gamma}}$ is given by

$$e^2(\mathscr{H}_{\mathrm{wal},s,b,\alpha,\boldsymbol{\gamma}}, \mathcal{P}) = -1 + \frac{1}{b^m}\sum_{n=0}^{b^m-1}\prod_{i=1}^{s}(1 + \gamma_i \phi_{\mathrm{wal},\alpha}(x_{n,i}, 0)).$$

12.18 Let b be a prime and let $s, m \in \mathbb{N}$. Let $\mathcal{C}$ be the set of all s-tuples $(C_1, \ldots, C_s)$ of $m \times m$ matrices over $\mathbb{Z}_b$ and let $\mathcal{P}(C_1, \ldots, C_s)$ be the digital net over $\mathbb{Z}_b$ generated by the s-tuple $(C_1, \ldots, C_s)$. Define

$$A_{b^m,s} := \frac{1}{b^{m^2 s}} \sum_{(C_1,\ldots,C_s)\in\mathcal{C}} e^2(\mathscr{H}_{\mathrm{wal},s,b,\alpha\boldsymbol{\gamma}}, \mathcal{P}(C_1, \ldots, C_s)).$$

Show that we have

$$\begin{aligned} A_{b^m,s} &= -1 + \frac{1}{b^m}\prod_{i=1}^{s}(1 + \gamma_i \nu_b(\alpha)) + \left(1 - \frac{1}{b^m}\right)\prod_{i=1}^{s}\left(1 + \gamma_i \frac{\nu_b(\alpha)}{b^{m\alpha}}\right) \\ &\leq \frac{2}{b^m}\prod_{i=1}^{s}(1 + \gamma_i \nu_b(\alpha)). \end{aligned}$$

Hint: See [50, Lemma 4].

12.19 Let b be a prime and let $s, m \in \mathbb{N}$. Show that for $0 \leq \beta < 1$ and $1/\alpha < \lambda \leq 1$, there are more than $\beta|\mathcal{C}|$ tuples $(C_1, \ldots, C_s) \in \mathcal{C}$ such that

$$e^2(\mathscr{H}_{\mathrm{wal},s,b,\alpha,\boldsymbol{\gamma}}, \mathcal{P}(C_1, \ldots, C_s)) \leq \frac{c_{s,b,\alpha,\boldsymbol{\gamma},\lambda}}{(1-\beta)^{1/\lambda}} b^{-m/\lambda},$$

where $c_{s,b,\alpha,\boldsymbol{\gamma},\lambda} := 2^{1/\lambda}\prod_{i=1}^{s}(1 + \nu_b(\alpha\lambda)\gamma_i^\lambda)^{1/\lambda}$.
Hint: See [50, Theorem 3].

12.20 Let b be a prime and $p \in \mathbb{Z}_b[x]$ be irreducible, with $\deg(p) = m \geq 1$. Suppose that $(q_1^*, \ldots, q_s^*) \in (G_{b,m}^*)^s$ is constructed with Algorithm 12.13 but with respect to $e^2(\mathscr{H}_{\mathrm{wal},s,b,\alpha,\boldsymbol{\gamma}}, \mathcal{P})$. Then, for all $1 \leq d \leq s$ and for all $1/\alpha < \lambda \leq 1$, we have

$$e^2(\mathscr{H}_{\mathrm{wal},s,b,\alpha,\boldsymbol{\gamma}}, \mathcal{P}((q_1^*, \ldots, q_d^*), p)) \leq c_{s,b,\alpha,\boldsymbol{\gamma},\lambda} b^{-m/\lambda}.$$

12.21 Consider Exercise 12.20 and show that under the assumption $\sum_{i=1}^{\infty} \gamma_i < \infty$, the square worst-case error $e^2(\mathscr{H}_{\mathrm{wal},s,b,\alpha,\boldsymbol{\gamma}}, \mathcal{P}((q_1^*, \ldots, q_s^*), p))$ satisfies a bound which is independent of the dimension s.

12.22 Let b be a prime, let $s, m \in \mathbb{N}$ and let $p \in \mathbb{Z}_b[x]$ be irreducible with $\deg(p) = m$. Show that there exists a polynomial $q^* \in G_{b,m}^*$ such that for all $1/\alpha < \lambda \leq 1$, we have

$$e^2(\mathscr{H}_{\mathrm{wal},s,b,\alpha,\boldsymbol{\gamma}}, \mathcal{P}(\boldsymbol{v}_s(q^*), p)) \leq c_{s,b,\alpha,\boldsymbol{\gamma},\lambda}(s/b^m)^{1/\lambda},$$

where $c_{s,b,\alpha,\boldsymbol{\gamma},\lambda}$ is as in Exercise 12.19.

12.23 Consider Exercise 12.22 and show that under the assumption $\limsup_{s\to\infty}(\log s)^{-1} \sum_{i=1}^{s} \gamma_i < \infty$, the square worst-case error $e^2(\mathscr{H}_{\mathrm{wal},s,b,\alpha,\boldsymbol{\gamma}}, \mathcal{P}(\boldsymbol{v}_s(q^*), p))$ satisfies a bound which depends only polynomially on the dimension s.

12.24 Let b be a prime, let $s, m \in \mathbb{N}$ and let $p \in \mathbb{Z}_b[x]$ be irreducible with $\deg(p) = m$. Let $0 \leq \beta < 1$ and $1/\alpha < \lambda \leq 1$. Show that there are more than $\beta|G_{b,m}^*|$ polynomials $q \in G_{b,m}^*$ such that

$$e^2(\mathscr{H}_{\mathrm{wal},s,b,\alpha,\boldsymbol{\gamma}}, \mathcal{P}(\boldsymbol{v}_s(q), p)) \leq c_{s,b,\alpha,\boldsymbol{\gamma},\lambda} \left(\frac{s}{1-\beta}\right)^{1/\lambda} b^{-m/\lambda},$$

where $c_{s,b,\alpha,\boldsymbol{\gamma},\lambda}$ is defined as in Exercise 12.19.

13
Randomisation of digital nets

In this chapter, we consider randomisations of digital nets. The aim of this type of algorithm is to combine random with deterministic algorithms in such a way as to allow one to have the best features of both methods. The advantage of a QMC algorithm based on a digital net is the improved rate of convergence; but there are also some disadvantages compared to Monte Carlo (MC) algorithms (i.e. algorithms where the quadrature points are chosen uniformly and independent and identically distributed in $[0, 1)^s$), for example:

1. The first point of a digital net or sequence is always $\mathbf{0}$, which causes problems in some applications. If the points in $[0, 1]^s$ have to be mapped to $\mathbb{R}^s$ such that they are normally distributed, then the point $\mathbf{0}$ gets mapped to $(-\infty, \ldots, -\infty)$.
2. Approximations of integrals where the integrand has a singularity using deterministic samples in a QMC algorithm can be problematic. Uniform and independent and identically distributed random samples usually avoid this problem (with high probability).
3. Another concern in applications is bias of the estimator $\frac{1}{N}\sum_{n=0}^{N-1} f(\boldsymbol{x}_n)$, i.e. that the estimator consistently underestimates (or overestimates) the correct result. For example, the left rectangle rule $\frac{1}{N}\sum_{n=0}^{N-1} f(n/N)$ consistently underestimates the true value of the integral $\int_0^1 f(x)\,\mathrm{d}x$ for all strictly monotonically increasing integrands $f : [0, 1] \to \mathbb{R}$, i.e.
$$\frac{1}{N}\sum_{n=0}^{N-1} f(n/N) < \int_0^1 f(x)\,\mathrm{d}x \text{ for all } N \in \mathbb{N}.$$
Uniform and independent and identically distributed random samples, on the other hand, satisfy
$$\mathbb{E}\left[\frac{1}{N}\sum_{n=0}^{N-1} f(\boldsymbol{x}_n)\right] = \int_0^1 f(\boldsymbol{x})\,\mathrm{d}\boldsymbol{x}.$$
Only the variance $\mathrm{Var}\left[\frac{1}{N}\sum_{n=0}^{N-1} f(\boldsymbol{x}_n)\right] \neq 0$ in general.

4. An advantage of uniformly and independent and identically distributed chosen random samples over deterministically chosen samples is that, in the former case, a statistical estimate of the error by $\sqrt{(N-1)^{-1}\sum_{n=0}^{N-1}\left(f(\boldsymbol{x}_n)-\frac{1}{N}\sum_{n=0}^{N-1}f(\boldsymbol{x}_n)\right)^2}$ is available. For deterministic quadrature points, such an estimate is not available.

Using randomised digital nets as quadrature points avoids these problems. On the other hand, uniform and independent and identically distributed random choices of the quadrature points yield an unbiased estimator with standard deviation of order $1/\sqrt{N}$, and are therefore inferior to QMC methods in terms of the speed of convergence, provided that the integrand satisfies some smoothness assumptions.

The aim of this chapter is to develop a combination of random choices and deterministic choices of the quadrature points which retain the desirable features of both methods. The strategy is first to construct a deterministic point set (in our case a digital net or digital sequence), and then to apply a randomisation, which on the one hand retains the distribution properties of the point set (i.e. the (t, m, s)-net property) and on the other hand has enough randomness to yield an unbiased estimator. To be more precise, we want to have quadrature points $\boldsymbol{x}_0, \ldots, \boldsymbol{x}_{N-1}$ such that each $\boldsymbol{x}_n$ is uniform and independent and identically distributed and at the same time the point set $\{\boldsymbol{x}_0, \ldots, \boldsymbol{x}_{N-1}\}$ has low discrepancy. This way we can avoid the problems described at the beginning and also obtain a statistical error estimate.

13.1 Randomisation algorithms

Nowadays, various randomisations are known. The simplest method of introducing a randomisation in (t, m, s)-nets is by using a digital shift $\boldsymbol{\sigma} \in [0, 1)^s$ which is uniformly distributed (see Chapter 4 and Chapter 12). This allows one to obtain an unbiased estimator of the integral and also to estimate the standard deviation from the correct result.

There are some variations of this method: for instance, a so-called digital shift of depth m or a simplified digital shift (see Section 4.4). In Chapter 12 we analysed the mean square worst-case error of digitally shifted digital nets and in Section 16.5 we analyse digitally shifted digital nets and show that one obtains the optimal order of the L_2-discrepancy on average for these point sets.

In this chapter we focus on the *scrambling of digital nets* as introduced by Owen [206, 207, 208, 209] and further analysed in [108, 269, 270, 271].

We first introduce *Owen's scrambling algorithm*, which is most easily described for some generic point $\boldsymbol{x} \in [0, 1)^s$, with $\boldsymbol{x} = (x_1, \ldots, x_s)$ and $x_i = x_{i,1}b^{-1} + x_{i,2}b^{-2} + \cdots$ The scrambled point shall be denoted by $\boldsymbol{y} \in [0, 1)^s$, where $\boldsymbol{y} = (y_1, \ldots, y_s)$ and $y_i = y_{i,1}b^{-1} + y_{i,2}b^{-2} + \cdots$. The point $\boldsymbol{y}$ is obtained by applying permutations to each digit of each coordinate of $\boldsymbol{x}$. The permutation applied to $x_{i,l}$ depends on $x_{i,k}$ for $1 \le k < l$. Specifically, $y_{i,1} = \pi_i(x_{i,1})$, $y_{i,2} = \pi_{i,x_{i,1}}(x_{i,2})$, $y_{i,3} = \pi_{i,x_{i,1},x_{i,2}}(x_{i,3})$ and, in general,

$$y_{i,k} = \pi_{i,x_{i,1},\ldots,x_{i,k-1}}(x_{i,k}), \tag{13.1}$$

where $\pi_{i,x_{i,1},\ldots,x_{i,k-1}}$ is a random permutation of $\{0, \ldots, b-1\}$. We assume that permutations with different indices are chosen mutually independent from each other and that each permutation is chosen with the same probability. In this case the scrambled point $\boldsymbol{y}$ is uniformly distributed in $[0, 1)^s$, as shown by Owen [206]. We show this fact after we introduce some further notation.

To describe Owen's scrambling, for $1 \le i \le s$, let

$$\Pi_i = \{\pi_{i,x_{i,1},\ldots,x_{i,k-1}} : k \in \mathbb{N}, x_{i,1}, \ldots, x_{i,k-1} \in \{0, \ldots, b-1\}\},$$

where for $k = 1$, we set $\pi_{i,x_{i,1},\ldots,x_{i,k-1}} = \pi_i$, be a given set of permutations and let $\boldsymbol{\Pi} = (\Pi_1, \ldots, \Pi_s)$. Then, when applying Owen's scrambling using these permutations to some point $\boldsymbol{x} \in [0, 1)^s$, we write $\boldsymbol{y} = \boldsymbol{x}_{\boldsymbol{\Pi}}$, where $\boldsymbol{y}$ is the point obtained by applying Owen's scrambling to $\boldsymbol{x}$ using the permutations $\Pi_1, \ldots, \Pi_s$. For $x \in [0, 1)$, we drop the subscript i and just write $y = x_\Pi$.

Proposition 13.1 *Let $\boldsymbol{x} \in [0, 1)^s$ and let $\boldsymbol{\Pi}$ be a uniformly and independent and identically distributed set of permutations. Then $\boldsymbol{x}_{\boldsymbol{\Pi}}$ is uniformly distributed in $[0, 1)^s$; that is, for any Lebesgue measurable set $G \subseteq [0, 1)^s$, the probability that $\boldsymbol{x}_{\boldsymbol{\Pi}} \in G$, denoted by $\mathrm{Prob}[\boldsymbol{x}_{\boldsymbol{\Pi}} \in G]$, satisfies $\mathrm{Prob}[\boldsymbol{x}_{\boldsymbol{\Pi}} \in G] = \lambda_s(G)$, where λ_s denotes the s-dimensional Lebesgue measure.*

Proof We follow [206, Proof of Proposition 2] in our exposition. We use the notation from above and set $\boldsymbol{y} := \boldsymbol{x}_{\boldsymbol{\Pi}}$. Consider the case $s = 1$ first and let

$$E = \left[\frac{a}{b^l}, \frac{a+1}{b^l}\right)$$

be an elementary interval where $l \ge 0$ and $0 \le a < b^l$. A technical problem which can arise in the proof below is when y is of the form $y_1 = y_{1,1}b^{-1} + \cdots + y_{1,l}b^{-l} + (b-1)b^{-l-1} + (b-1)b^{-l-1} + \cdots$ since then we have $y_1 = y_{1,1}b^{-1} + \cdots + (y_{1,l}+1)b^{-l}$. We show that this only happens with probability zero.

The probability that there are $u \ge j_0 \ge 1$ such that $y_{1,j_0} = y_{1,j_0+1} = \cdots = y_{1,u} = b-1$ is given by $((b-1)!)^{-(u-j_0)}$. Hence, the probability that $y_{1,j_0} = y_{1,j_0+1} = \cdots = b-1$, i.e. all digits of y_1 are $b-1$ from some index j_0 onwards, is 0.

Let $ab^{-l} = a_1 b^{-1} + a_2 b^{-2} + \cdots + a_l b^{-l}$. Then $y_1 \in E$ if and only if $y_1 = a_1, y_2 = a_2, \ldots, y_l = a_l$. Using (13.1), this is equivalent to

$$\pi_{1,x_{1,1},\ldots,x_{1,k-1}}(x_{1,k}) = a_k \quad \text{for } 1 \le k \le l. \tag{13.2}$$

For each $1 \leq k \leq l$, the probability that (13.2) holds is b^{-1}. Hence, the probability that $y_1 \in E$ is b^{-l}. The result therefore holds for all elementary intervals of $[0, 1)$.

We now extend the result to the general case. First, notice that the result also holds for all sub-intervals $[ub^{-l}, vb^{-l})$, where $l \geq 0$ and $0 \leq u < v \leq b^{-l}$. The endpoints of these intervals are dense in $[0, 1)$. A corollary of Chung's [24, p. 28] extends the result $\mathrm{Prob}[y_1 \in B] = \lambda_1(B)$ to all Borel measurable subsets $B \subseteq [0, 1)$. The equality $\mathrm{Prob}[y_1 \in B] = \lambda_1(B)$ extends to Lebesgue measurable sets B, since subsets of sets of measure zero have probability zero of containing y_1.

Consider now $s > 1$. Let $B_1, \ldots, B_s$ be measurable subsets of $[0, 1)$. Because the components $y_1, \ldots, y_s$ of $\boldsymbol{y}$ are independent, it follows that

$$\mathrm{Prob}[y_i \in B_i, 1 \leq i \leq s] = \prod_{i=1}^{s} \lambda_1(B_i). \tag{13.3}$$

Finally, λ_s is the unique measure on $[0, 1)^s$ which satisfies (13.3). □

We illustrate Owen's scrambling algorithm in Figure 13.1. The permutations are applied to each coordinate independently. To illustrate the procedure, we first scrambled the abscissa and then the ordinate in Figure 13.1.

Consider a (t, m, s)-net in base b consisting of points $\boldsymbol{x}_0, \ldots, \boldsymbol{x}_{b^m-1}$, where $\boldsymbol{x}_n = (x_{n,1}, \ldots, x_{n,s})$ and $x_{n,i} = x_{n,i,1}b^{-1} + x_{n,i,2}b^{-2} + \cdots$. We shall denote the scrambled points by $\boldsymbol{y}_0, \ldots, \boldsymbol{y}_{b^m-1}$, where $\boldsymbol{y}_n = (y_{n,1}, \ldots, y_{n,s})$ and $y_{n,i} = y_{n,i,1}b^{-1} + y_{n,i,2}b^{-2} + \cdots$. Specifically, the scrambled points are given by $y_{n,i,k} = \pi_{i,x_{n,i,1},\ldots,x_{n,i,k-1}}(x_{n,i,k})$, for $0 \leq n < b^m$, $1 \leq i \leq s$ and $k \geq 1$.

Similarly, if $(\boldsymbol{x}_0, \boldsymbol{x}_1, \ldots)$ is a (t, s)-sequence, then the scrambled sequence shall be denoted by $(\boldsymbol{y}_0, \boldsymbol{y}_1, \ldots)$, where, using the same notation as above, again $y_{n,i,k} = \pi_{i,x_{n,i,1},\ldots,x_{n,i,k-1}}(x_{n,i,k})$, for all $n \geq 0$, $1 \leq i \leq s$ and $k \geq 1$.

We consider now the expected value of $\frac{1}{N}\sum_{n=0}^{N-1} f(\boldsymbol{y}_n)$. For any measurable function f, we have

$$\mathbb{E}\left[\frac{1}{N}\sum_{n=0}^{N-1} f(\boldsymbol{y}_n)\right] = \frac{1}{N}\sum_{n=0}^{N-1} \mathbb{E}[f(\boldsymbol{y}_n)] = \int_{[0,1]^s} f(\boldsymbol{y})\,\mathrm{d}\boldsymbol{y},$$

since each point $\boldsymbol{y}_n$ is uniformly distributed in $[0, 1)^s$ and hence $\mathbb{E}[f(\boldsymbol{y}_n)] = \int_{[0,1]^s} f(\boldsymbol{y})\,\mathrm{d}\boldsymbol{y}$ for $0 \leq n < N$. In other words, this means that a scrambled point set (note that the above applies even if the underlying point set $\boldsymbol{x}_0, \ldots, \boldsymbol{x}_{N-1}$ is not a digital net) used in a QMC rule yields an unbiased estimator.

The second important property of the randomisation algorithm that we require is that the (t, m, s)-net structure of the points $\boldsymbol{x}_0, \ldots, \boldsymbol{x}_{b^m-1}$ is retained after applying the scrambling algorithm. For some technical reason this does not quite hold, but it

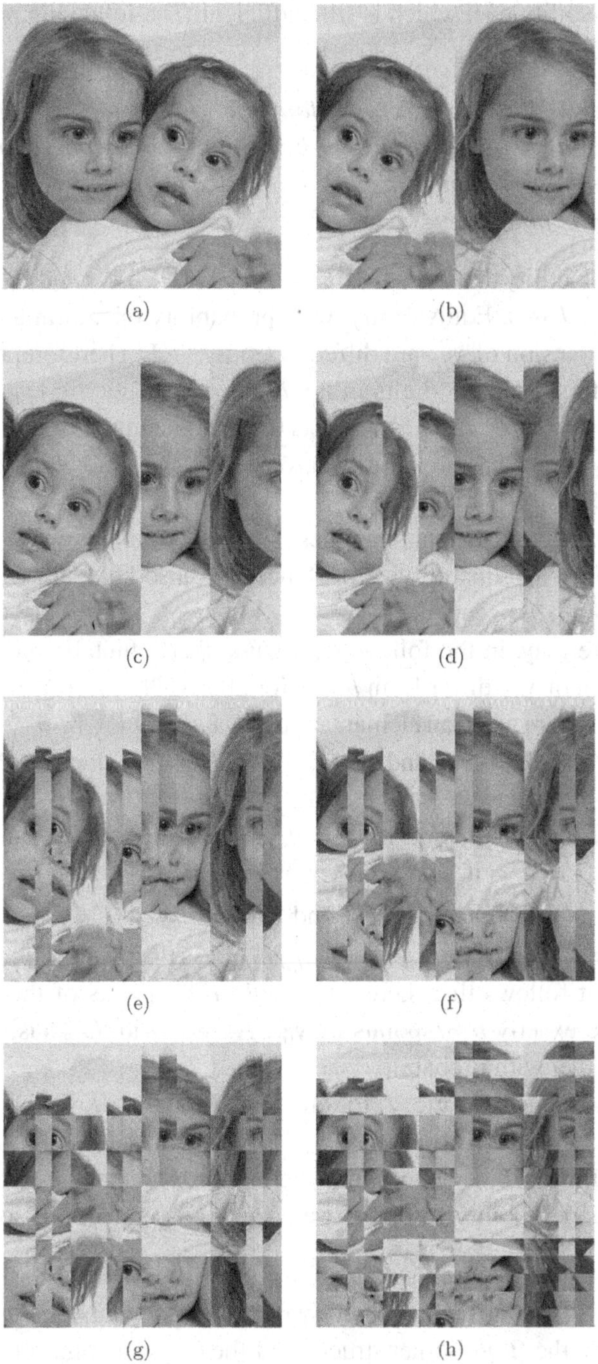

Figure 13.1 Owen's scrambling algorithm in base 2.

holds with probability one, which is still sufficient. The following proposition was first shown by Owen [206].

Proposition 13.2 *If $\boldsymbol{x}_0, \ldots, \boldsymbol{x}_{b^m-1}$ form a (t, m, s)-net in base b, then $\boldsymbol{y}_0, \ldots, \boldsymbol{y}_{b^m-1}$ is a (t, m, s)-net in base b with probability one. If $\boldsymbol{x}_0, \boldsymbol{x}_1, \ldots$ are obtained from a (t, s)-sequence, then the scrambled points $\boldsymbol{y}_0, \boldsymbol{y}_1, \ldots$ form a (t, s)-sequence with probability one.*

Proof The probability that, for some $0 \le n < b^m$, $1 \le i \le s$ and $l \in \mathbb{N}$, all $y_{n,i,k} = b-1$ for all $k \ge l$ is 0. Equivalently, with probability one, infinitely many digits in the b-adic expansion of $y_{n,i}$ are different from $b-1$. Therefore, the probability that $y_{n,i}$ has infinitely many digits in the b-adic expansion of $y_{n,i}$ different from $b-1$ for all $0 \le n < b^m$ and $1 \le i \le s$ is 0, since the union of a finite number of zero probability events has probability zero. Hence, this holds for each component of each point of a (t, m, s)-net.

For a (t, s)-sequence the same applies, since a countable union of probability zero events has itself probability zero. Hence, this also holds for each component of each point of a (t, s)-sequence.

Therefore, we may, in the following, assume that infinitely many digits in the b-adic expansion of $y_{n,i}$ differ from $b-1$ for all $n \in \mathbb{N}_0$ and $1 \le i \le s$.

Assume that we are given an elementary interval $J = \prod_{i=1}^{s} [a_i b^{-d_i}, (a_i + 1) b^{-d_i})$ where $0 \le a_i < b^{d_i}$, $d_i \in \mathbb{N}_0$, and $d_1 + \cdots + d_s \le m - t$. Let $a_i b^{-d_i} = a_{i,1} b^{-1} + a_{i,2} b^{-2} + \cdots + a_{i,d_i} b^{-d_i}$.

Then $\boldsymbol{y}_n \in J$ if and only if $y_{n,i,k} = a_{i,k}$ for all $1 \le k \le d_i$ and all $1 \le i \le s$. Further, $y_{n,i,k} = a_{i,k}$ if and only if $x_{n,i,k} = \pi^{-1}_{i, x_{n,i,1}, \ldots, x_{n,i,k-1}}(a_{i,k})$. Let $a'_{i,k} = \pi^{-1}_{i, x_{n,i,1}, \ldots, x_{n,i,k-1}}(a_{i,k})$. Then $\boldsymbol{y}_n \in J$ if and only if $\boldsymbol{x}_n \in J' = \prod_{i=1}^{s} [a'_i b^{-d_i}, (a'_i + 1) b^{-d_i})$ where $a'_i b^{-d_i} = a'_{i,1} b^{-1} + \cdots + a'_{i,d_i} b^{-d_i}$. As the points $\boldsymbol{x}_0, \ldots, \boldsymbol{x}_{b^m-1}$ form a (t, m, s)-net, it follows that there are exactly b^{m-t} points of this net in J' and hence, there are exactly b^{m-t} points of $\boldsymbol{y}_0, \ldots, \boldsymbol{y}_{b^m-1}$ in J. Thus, $\boldsymbol{y}_0, \ldots, \boldsymbol{y}_{b^m-1}$ form a (t, m, s)-net with probability one.

For a (t, s)-sequence $\boldsymbol{x}_0, \boldsymbol{x}_1, \ldots$ for all $k \in \mathbb{N}_0$ and $m \ge t$, the point set consisting of $\boldsymbol{x}_{kb^m}, \ldots, \boldsymbol{x}_{kb^m + b^m - 1}$ forms a (t, m, s)-net which is again a (t, m, s)-net after scrambling with probability one. Since the union of countably many zero probability events has probability zero, the result for (t, s)-sequences also follows. □

We have shown that Owen's scrambling algorithm has the desired properties that each point is uniformly distributed (which yields an unbiased estimator of the integral) and that the (t, m, s)-net structure of the original point set is retained.

However, in order to facilitate efficient implementation of the scrambling algorithm, various scrambling methods which require fewer permutations for scrambling $(0, m, s)$-nets have been studied [160, 161, 257]. Matoušek [160] also gives various suggestions on the efficient implementation of random scrambling of $(0, m, s)$-nets.

A combination of randomised QMC with antithetic sampling was introduced in [211] which yields further improvements. As pointed out at the beginning, the approximation of integrals where the integrand has a singularity using deterministic QMC algorithms is problematic. This problem has been considered in [91, 210]. More information on randomised QMC can also be found in [153] and in [154], which is also concerned with variance reduction techniques and using randomised QMC in applications.

13.2 Crossed and nested ANOVA decomposition

As in [207], for the analysis of the standard deviation of the integration error, it is useful to introduce the crossed and nested ANOVA decomposition of functions. The crossed ANOVA decomposition of [207] is the same as the ANOVA decomposition introduced in Chapter 2. Hence, we introduce the nested ANOVA decomposition of [207] in the following. We base our analysis on Walsh functions.

For the nested ANOVA decomposition, consider a function $f \in L_2([0,1])$ with Walsh series expansion

$$f(x) \sim \sum_{k=0}^{\infty} \widehat{f}(k)\, {}_b\mathrm{wal}_k(x), \tag{13.4}$$

where

$$\widehat{f}(k) = \int_0^1 f(y)\, \overline{{}_b\mathrm{wal}_k(x)}\, \mathrm{d}x.$$

Notice that we do not necessarily have equality in (13.4), since the function f is only assumed to be in $L_2([0,1])$ (and hence, may, for example, be changed arbitrarily on a set of measure zero without changing $\widehat{f}(k)$ for any $k \geq 0$).

Consider the b^ℓ-term approximation of f given by

$$\sum_{k=0}^{b^\ell-1} \widehat{f}(k)\, {}_b\mathrm{wal}_k(x) = \sum_{k=0}^{b^\ell-1} \int_0^1 f(y)\, {}_b\mathrm{wal}_k(x \ominus y)\, \mathrm{d}y = \int_0^1 f(y) D_\ell(x \ominus y)\, \mathrm{d}y,$$

where D_ℓ is the Walsh–Dirichlet kernel (see Definition A.16 and Lemma A.17) given by

$$D_\ell(z) = \sum_{k=0}^{b^\ell-1} {}_b\mathrm{wal}_k(z) = \begin{cases} b^\ell & \text{if } z \in [0, b^{-\ell}), \\ 0 & \text{otherwise.} \end{cases}$$

Hence, we have

$$\sum_{k=0}^{b^\ell-1} \widehat{f}(k)\,{}_b\mathrm{wal}_k(x) = b^\ell \int_{\lfloor yb^\ell \rfloor = \lfloor xb^\ell \rfloor} f(y)\,\mathrm{d}y,$$

where the integration is over all y such that $\lfloor yb^\ell \rfloor = \lfloor xb^\ell \rfloor$, i.e. the first ℓ digits of x and y coincide. Therefore,

$$\begin{aligned}\beta_\ell(x) &:= \sum_{k=b^{\ell-1}}^{b^\ell-1} \widehat{f}(k)\,{}_b\mathrm{wal}_k(x) \\ &= b^\ell \int_{\lfloor yb^\ell \rfloor = \lfloor xb^\ell \rfloor} f(y)\,\mathrm{d}y - b^{\ell-1} \int_{\lfloor yb^{\ell-1} \rfloor = \lfloor xb^{\ell-1} \rfloor} f(y)\,\mathrm{d}y.\end{aligned}$$

(In [207], this function was defined using Haar wavelets.) We also define $\beta_0 := \int_0^1 f(y)\,\mathrm{d}y$. Notice that β_ℓ is constant on intervals of the form $[ub^{-\ell}, (u+1)b^{-\ell})$, hence, $\beta_\ell(x) = \beta_\ell(\lfloor b^\ell x \rfloor b^{-\ell})$.

Let

$$\sigma_\ell^2(f) := \mathrm{Var}[\beta_\ell]. \tag{13.5}$$

Then, because of the orthogonality of the Walsh functions, we obtain

$$\sigma_\ell^2(f) = \int_0^1 |\beta_\ell(x)|^2\,\mathrm{d}x = \sum_{k=b^{\ell-1}}^{b^\ell-1} |\widehat{f}(k)|^2$$

and also

$$\int_0^1 \beta_\ell(x)\overline{\beta_{\ell'}(x)}\,\mathrm{d}x = 0 \text{ for } \ell \neq \ell'.$$

Since $f \in L_2([0,1])$ and the Walsh function system is complete, we can use Plancherel's identity (see Theorem A.19) to obtain

$$\mathrm{Var}[f] = \int_0^1 |f(y) - \mathbb{E}(f)|^2\,\mathrm{d}y = \sum_{k=1}^\infty |\widehat{f}(k)|^2 = \sum_{\ell=1}^\infty \sigma_\ell^2(f).$$

Therefore, we obtained a decomposition of the variance of f in terms of the variances of β_ℓ, which is called the *nested ANOVA decomposition* of f.

Notice that $\sum_{k=1}^\infty |\widehat{f}(k)|^2 = \mathrm{Var}\left[\sum_{k=0}^\infty \widehat{f}(k)\,{}_b\mathrm{wal}_k\right]$. Hence, as a by-product, we obtain that for any $f \in L_2([0,1])$, the variance of f and the variance of its Walsh series coincide, that is,

$$\mathrm{Var}[f] = \mathrm{Var}\left[\sum_{k=0}^\infty \widehat{f}(k)\,{}_b\mathrm{wal}_k\right]. \tag{13.6}$$

13.3 Variance of the integral estimator using scrambled nets

In this section, we estimate the variance of the estimator

$$\widehat{I}(f) = \frac{1}{N} \sum_{n=0}^{N-1} f(\boldsymbol{y}_n) \tag{13.7}$$

for integrands $f \in L_2([0,1]^s)$ when the points $\boldsymbol{y}_0, \ldots, \boldsymbol{y}_{N-1}$ are obtained by applying Owen's scrambling to a (digital) (t, m, s)-net over $\mathbb{Z}_b$. Throughout this section, let $b \geq 2$ be a prime number.

13.3.1 The one-dimensional case

In the following, let $x_0, \ldots, x_{N-1} \in [0,1)$ be a set of points and let the set of points $y_0, \ldots, y_{N-1} \in [0,1)$ be obtained by applying Owen's scrambling algorithm to $x_0, \ldots, x_{N-1}$.

We also use the following notation: for points $x, y \in [0,1)$, we write their b-adic expansions as $x = \xi_1 b^{-1} + \xi_2 b^{-2} + \cdots$, and $y = \eta_1 b^{-1} + \eta_2 b^{-2} + \cdots$ and analogously for $x', y' \in [0,1)$. Further, let $k = \kappa_0 + \kappa_1 b + \cdots + \kappa_{\ell-1} b^{\ell-1}$ and $k' = \kappa'_0 + \kappa'_1 b + \cdots + \kappa'_{\ell'-1} b^{\ell'-1}$.

We need the following technical lemma which is referred to as Owen's lemma.

Lemma 13.3 *Let $y, y' \in [0,1)$ be two points obtained by applying Owen's scrambling algorithm to the points $x, x' \in [0,1)$. Then we have*

$$\mathbb{E}\left[{}_b\mathrm{wal}_k(y) \overline{{}_b\mathrm{wal}_{k'}(y')} \right] = 0$$

whenever $k \neq k'$. If $k = k'$, then

$$\mathbb{E}\left[{}_b\mathrm{wal}_k(y \ominus y') \right] = \begin{cases} 1 & \text{if } 1 \leq k < b^r, \\ -\frac{1}{b-1} & \text{if } b^r \leq k < b^{r+1}, \\ 0 & \text{if } k \geq b^{r+1}. \end{cases}$$

where r is the largest integer such that $\xi_1 = \xi'_1, \ldots, \xi_r = \xi'_r$, and $\xi_{r+1} \neq \xi'_{r+1}$.

Proof The Walsh function ${}_b\mathrm{wal}_k$ depends only on the first ℓ digits of y and ${}_b\mathrm{wal}_{k'}$ depends only on the first ℓ' digits of y'. To calculate the expectation $\mathbb{E}[{}_b\mathrm{wal}_k(y) \overline{{}_b\mathrm{wal}_{k'}(y')}]$, we therefore only need to average over all choices of permutations $\pi, \pi_{\xi_1}, \pi_{\xi_1,\xi_2}, \ldots, \pi_{\xi_1,\ldots,\xi_\ell}$ and $\pi_{\xi'_1}, \pi_{\xi'_1,\xi'_2}, \ldots, \pi_{\xi'_1,\ldots,\xi'_{\ell'}}$, since the average over the remaining permutations does not change the result.

Assume that $\xi_1 = \xi'_1, \ldots, \xi_r = \xi'_r$ and $\xi_{r+1} \neq \xi'_{r+1}$. Then, $\eta_1 = \eta'_1, \ldots, \eta_r = \eta'_r$, and $\eta_{r+1} = \pi_{\xi_1,\ldots,\xi_r}(\xi_{r+1})$ and $\eta'_{r+1} = \pi_{\xi_1,\ldots,\xi_r}(\xi'_{r+1})$. Further, $\eta_{r+2}, \eta_{r+3}, \ldots$ and $\eta'_{r+2}, \eta'_{r+3}, \ldots$ are independent from each other.

Then,

$$\mathbb{E}\left[\,{}_b\mathrm{wal}_k(y)\,\overline{{}_b\mathrm{wal}_{k'}(y')}\right]$$

$$= \prod_{j=1}^{r} \frac{1}{b} \sum_{\eta_j=0}^{b-1} {}_b\mathrm{wal}_{\kappa_{j-1}\ominus\kappa'_{j-1}}(\eta_j/b) \tag{13.8}$$

$$\times \frac{1}{b(b-1)} \sum_{\substack{\eta_{r+1},\eta'_{r+1}=0 \\ \eta_{r+1}\neq\eta'_{r+1}}}^{b-1} {}_b\mathrm{wal}_{\kappa_r}(\eta_{r+1}/b)\,\overline{{}_b\mathrm{wal}_{\kappa'_r}(\eta'_{r+1}/b)} \tag{13.9}$$

$$\times \prod_{j=r+2}^{\infty} \frac{1}{b} \sum_{\eta_j=0}^{b-1} {}_b\mathrm{wal}_{\kappa_{j-1}}(\eta_j/b) \prod_{j=r+2}^{\infty} \frac{1}{b} \sum_{\eta'_j=0}^{b-1} {}_b\mathrm{wal}_{\kappa'_{j-1}}(\eta'_j/b), \tag{13.10}$$

where we set $\kappa_j = 0$ for $j \geq \ell$ and $\kappa'_j = 0$ for $j \geq \ell'$ (hence, the products in (13.10) are finite).

If there is a $1 \leq j \leq r$ such that $\kappa_{j-1} \neq \kappa'_{j-1}$, then the sum

$$\sum_{\eta_j=0}^{b-1} {}_b\mathrm{wal}_{\kappa_{j-1}\ominus\kappa'_{j-1}}(\eta_j/b) = 0$$

in (13.8). This implies that $\mathbb{E}[\,{}_b\mathrm{wal}_k(y)\,\overline{{}_b\mathrm{wal}_{k'}(y')}] = 0$.

If there is a $j > r+1$ such that $\kappa_{j-1} \neq 0$ or $\kappa'_{j-1} \neq 0$, then one of the sums in (13.10) yields 0, and therefore $\mathbb{E}[\,{}_b\mathrm{wal}_k(y)\,\overline{{}_b\mathrm{wal}_{k'}(y')}] = 0$ also.

Now consider the case where $\kappa_r \neq \kappa'_r$. If $\kappa'_r = 0$, then $\overline{{}_b\mathrm{wal}_{\kappa'_r}(\eta'_{r+1}/b)} = 1$ and (13.9) is given by

$$\frac{1}{b(b-1)} \sum_{\substack{\eta_{r+1},\eta'_{r+1}=0 \\ \eta_{r+1}\neq\eta'_{r+1}}}^{b-1} {}_b\mathrm{wal}_{\kappa_r}(\eta_{r+1}/b) = \frac{1}{b} \sum_{y_{r+1}=0}^{b-1} {}_b\mathrm{wal}_{\kappa_r}(\eta_{r+1}/b) = 0.$$

If $\kappa_r = 0$, then we also obtain 0. If both κ_r and κ'_r are not 0, then

$$\frac{1}{b(b-1)} \sum_{\substack{\eta_{r+1},\eta'_{r+1}=0 \\ \eta_{r+1}\neq\eta'_{r+1}}}^{b-1} {}_b\mathrm{wal}_{\kappa_r}(\eta_{r+1}/b)\,\overline{{}_b\mathrm{wal}_{\kappa'_r}(\eta'_{r+1}/b)}$$

$$= \frac{1}{b(b-1)} \sum_{\eta_{r+1}=0}^{b-1} {}_b\mathrm{wal}_{\kappa_r}(\eta_{r+1}/b) \sum_{\substack{\eta'_{r+1}=0 \\ \eta'_{r+1}\neq\eta_{r+1}}}^{b-1} \overline{{}_b\mathrm{wal}_{\kappa'_r}(\eta'_{r+1}/b)}$$

$$= -\frac{1}{b(b-1)} \sum_{\eta_{r+1}=0}^{b-1} {}_b\mathrm{wal}_{\kappa_r\ominus\kappa'_r}(\eta_{r+1}/b) = 0.$$

Therefore, also in this case we get $\mathbb{E}[{}_b\mathrm{wal}_k(y)\overline{{}_b\mathrm{wal}_{k'}(y')}] = 0$.

Now let $k = k'$. We have already shown the case where $k \geq b^{r+1}$. If $1 \leq k < b^r$, then ${}_b\mathrm{wal}_{\kappa_{j-1}\ominus\kappa'_{j-1}}(\eta_j/b) = 1$ in (13.8) and also, the products in (13.9) and (13.10) are 1, hence $\mathbb{E}[{}_b\mathrm{wal}_k(y \ominus y')] = 1$ in this case.

Finally, consider $b^r \leq k < b^{r+1}$. Then (13.8) and (13.10) are both 1, and (13.9) is

$$\begin{aligned}
&\frac{1}{b(b-1)} \sum_{\substack{\eta_{r+1},\eta'_{r+1}=0 \\ \eta_{r+1}\neq\eta'_{r+1}}}^{b-1} {}_b\mathrm{wal}_{\kappa_r}((\eta_{r+1} \ominus \eta'_{r+1})/b) \\
&= \frac{1}{b(b-1)} \sum_{\eta_{r+1}=0}^{b-1} {}_b\mathrm{wal}_{\kappa_r}(\eta_{r+1}/b) \sum_{\substack{\eta'_{r+1}=0 \\ \eta'_{r+1}\neq\eta_{r+1}}}^{b-1} \overline{{}_b\mathrm{wal}_{\kappa_r}(\eta'_{r+1}/b)} \\
&= -\frac{1}{b(b-1)} \sum_{\eta_{r+1}=0}^{b-1} {}_b\mathrm{wal}_{\kappa_r}(\eta_{r+1}/b)\overline{{}_b\mathrm{wal}_{\kappa_r}(\eta_{r+1}/b)} \\
&= -\frac{1}{b-1},
\end{aligned}$$

which implies the result. □

The second part of the above lemma can also be written as

$$\begin{aligned}
\mathbb{E}\left[{}_b\mathrm{wal}_k(y \ominus y')\right] &= \begin{cases} 1 & \text{if } 1 \leq \ell \leq r, \\ -\frac{1}{b-1} & \text{if } \ell = r+1, \\ 0 & \text{if } \ell > r+1, \end{cases} \\
&= \frac{b}{b-1}\chi_{\lfloor b^\ell x\rfloor = \lfloor b^\ell x'\rfloor} - \frac{1}{b-1}\chi_{\lfloor b^{\ell-1} x\rfloor = \lfloor b^{\ell-1} x'\rfloor},
\end{aligned}$$

where $\chi_{A=B}$ is 1 whenever $A = B$ and 0 otherwise.

For $w \geq 0$ and points $x_0, \ldots, x_{N-1} \in [0, 1)$, we define

$$M_w := \sum_{n,n'=0}^{N-1} \chi_{\lfloor b^w x_n\rfloor = \lfloor b^w x_{n'}\rfloor} = \sum_{n,n'=0}^{N-1} \chi_{\lfloor b^w y_n\rfloor = \lfloor b^w y_{n'}\rfloor},$$

and hence, we can write

$$\sum_{n,n'=0}^{N-1} \mathbb{E}\left[{}_b\mathrm{wal}_k(y_n \ominus y_{n'})\right] = \frac{bM_\ell - M_{\ell-1}}{b-1}.$$

We consider now the variance of the estimator $\widehat{I}(f)$.

Corollary 13.4 *Let $f \in L_2([0, 1])$, let $\sigma_\ell^2(f)$ be as in (13.5) and let $\widehat{I}(f)$ be as in (13.7). Let the points $y_0, \ldots, y_{N-1} \in [0, 1)$ be obtained by applying Owen's* *scrambling algorithm to the points* $x_0, \ldots, x_{N-1} \in [0, 1)$. *Then*

$$\mathrm{Var}[\widehat{I}(f)] = \frac{1}{N^2} \sum_{\ell=1}^{\infty} \frac{bM_\ell - M_{\ell-1}}{b-1} \sigma_\ell^2(f).$$

Proof Using Proposition 13.1 and (13.6), we obtain

$$\mathrm{Var}[\widehat{I}(f)] = \mathbb{E}\left[\frac{1}{N^2} \sum_{n,n'=0}^{N-1} \sum_{\substack{k,k'=0 \\ (k,k') \neq (0,0)}}^{\infty} \widehat{f}(k)\overline{\widehat{f}(k')}\, {}_b\mathrm{wal}_k(y_n)\, \overline{{}_b\mathrm{wal}_{k'}(y_{n'})}\right]$$

$$= \frac{1}{N^2} \sum_{n,n'=0}^{N-1} \sum_{\substack{k,k'=0 \\ (k,k') \neq (0,0)}}^{\infty} \widehat{f}(k)\overline{\widehat{f}(k')} \mathbb{E}\left[{}_b\mathrm{wal}_k(y_n)\, \overline{{}_b\mathrm{wal}_{k'}(y_{n'})}\right].$$

Using Lemma 13.3, the terms where $k \neq k'$ are all 0 and hence,

$$\mathrm{Var}[\widehat{I}(f)] = \frac{1}{N^2} \sum_{n,n'=0}^{N-1} \sum_{k=1}^{\infty} \widehat{f}(k)\overline{\widehat{f}(k)} \mathbb{E}\left[{}_b\mathrm{wal}_k(y_n)\, \overline{{}_b\mathrm{wal}_k(y_{n'})}\right]$$

$$= \sum_{k=1}^{\infty} |\widehat{f}(k)|^2 \frac{1}{N^2} \sum_{n,n'=0}^{N-1} \mathbb{E}\left[{}_b\mathrm{wal}_k(y_n \ominus y_{n'})\right]$$

$$= \frac{1}{N^2} \sum_{\ell=1}^{\infty} \frac{bM_\ell - M_{\ell-1}}{b-1} \sum_{k=b^{\ell-1}}^{b^\ell - 1} |\widehat{f}(k)|^2. \qquad \square$$

Theorem 13.5 *Let* $f \in L_2([0, 1])$ *and* $\widehat{I}(f)$ *be given by* (13.7). *If* $x_0, \ldots, x_{b^m-1}$ *is a* $(0, m, 1)$*-net in base b, then*

$$\mathrm{Var}[\widehat{I}(f)] = b^{-m} \sum_{\ell > m} \sigma_\ell^2(f).$$

If $x_0, \ldots, x_{b^m-1}$ *is a* $(t, m, 1)$*-net in base b, then*

$$\mathrm{Var}[\widehat{I}(f)] \leq b^{t-m} \sum_{\ell > m-t} \sigma_\ell^2(f).$$

Proof Let $x_0, \ldots, x_{b^m-1}$ be a $(0, m, 1)$-net. Then, for $0 \leq \ell \leq m$, for each $0 \leq n < b^m$ there are exactly $b^{m-\ell}$ points $x_{n'}$ such that $\lfloor b^\ell x_n \rfloor = \lfloor b^\ell x_{n'} \rfloor$. Hence, $M_\ell = b^{2m-\ell}$ for $0 \leq \ell \leq m$. For $\ell > m$, for each n, there is exactly one point $x_{n'}$ such that $\lfloor b^\ell x_n \rfloor = \lfloor b^\ell x_{n'} \rfloor$, namely the point $x_{n'} = x_n$. Therefore, $M_\ell = b^m$ for $\ell > m$. Hence, $M_\ell = b^{m+(m-\ell)_+}$, where $(m-\ell)_+ = \max(m-\ell, 0)$.

Therefore,

$$\frac{bM_\ell - M_{\ell-1}}{b-1} = \begin{cases} 0 & \text{if } 0 \le \ell \le m, \\ b^m & \text{if } \ell > m. \end{cases}$$

Hence, Corollary 13.4 yields

$$\mathrm{Var}[\widehat{I}(f)] = b^{-m} \sum_{\ell=m+1}^{\infty} \sigma_\ell^2.$$

If $x_0, \ldots, x_{b^m-1}$ is a $(t, m, 1)$-net on the other hand, then

$$\frac{bM_\ell - M_{\ell-1}}{b-1} \begin{cases} = 0 & \text{if } 0 \le \ell \le m-t, \\ \le b^{m+t} & \text{if } \ell > m-t. \end{cases}$$

Therefore, Corollary 13.4 yields

$$\mathrm{Var}[\widehat{I}(f)] \le b^{t-m} \sum_{\ell=m-t+1}^{\infty} \sigma_\ell^2. \qquad \square$$

We compare the last theorem to MC. From Theorem 1.5 we know that for uniformly and independent and identically distributed chosen quadrature points, i.e. the MC algorithm, we have

$$\mathrm{Var}[\widehat{I}(f)] = \frac{1}{N} \sum_{\ell=1}^{\infty} \sigma_\ell^2,$$

where N is the number of quadrature points. Hence, $\mathrm{Var}[\widehat{I}(f)]$ for a scrambled $(0, m, 1)$-net is always smaller than the variance of a MC algorithm. Further, for scrambled $(t, m, 1)$-nets, we have

$$b^m \mathrm{Var}[\widehat{I}(f)] \le b^t \sum_{\ell=m+1-t}^{\infty} \sigma_\ell^2 \to 0 \quad \text{as } m \to \infty.$$

Therefore, scrambled $(t, m, 1)$-nets outperform MC with respect to $\mathrm{Var}[\widehat{I}(f)]$ asymptotically, as for MC we have $N\mathrm{Var}[\widehat{I}(f)] = \sum_{\ell=1}^{\infty} \sigma_\ell^2$ for all $N \in \mathbb{N}$.

13.3.2 The case of arbitrary dimension s

The general case in dimension $s \ge 1$ can be analysed using the same approach. Recall that the coordinates of a point are randomised independently from each other.

Let $f \in L_2([0,1]^s)$ have the following Walsh series expansion

$$f(\boldsymbol{x}) \sim \sum_{\boldsymbol{k} \in \mathbb{N}_0^s} \widehat{f}(\boldsymbol{k})\, {}_b\mathrm{wal}_{\boldsymbol{k}}(\boldsymbol{x}) =: S(\boldsymbol{x}, f). \tag{13.11}$$

Although we do not necessarily have equality in (13.11), the completeness of the Walsh function system $\{{}_b\mathrm{wal}_{\boldsymbol{k}} : \boldsymbol{k} \in \mathbb{N}_0^s\}$, see Theorem A.11, and Theorem A.19 imply that we do have

$$\mathrm{Var}[f] = \sum_{\boldsymbol{k}\in\mathbb{N}_0^s\setminus\{\boldsymbol{0}\}} |\widehat{f}(\boldsymbol{k})|^2 = \mathrm{Var}[S(\cdot, f)]. \tag{13.12}$$

Let $\boldsymbol{\ell} = (\ell_1, \ldots, \ell_s) \in \mathbb{N}_0^s$ and $L_{\boldsymbol{\ell}} = \{\boldsymbol{k} = (k_1, \ldots, k_s) \in \mathbb{N}_0^s : \lfloor b^{\ell_i - 1}\rfloor \le k_i < b^{\ell_i}$ for $1 \le i \le s\}$. Then let

$$\beta_{\boldsymbol{\ell}}(\boldsymbol{x}) = \sum_{\boldsymbol{k}\in L_{\boldsymbol{\ell}}} \widehat{f}(\boldsymbol{k})\, {}_b\mathrm{wal}_{\boldsymbol{k}}(\boldsymbol{x})$$

and

$$\sigma_{\boldsymbol{\ell}}^2(f) := \mathrm{Var}[\beta_{\boldsymbol{\ell}}] = \int_{[0,1]^s} |\beta_{\boldsymbol{\ell}}(\boldsymbol{x})|^2 \,\mathrm{d}\boldsymbol{x} = \sum_{\boldsymbol{k}\in L_{\boldsymbol{\ell}}} |\widehat{f}(\boldsymbol{k})|^2.$$

For $\boldsymbol{\ell} = (\ell_1, \ldots, \ell_s) \in \mathbb{N}_0^s \setminus \{\boldsymbol{0}\}$, let

$$G_{\boldsymbol{\ell}} = \frac{1}{N^2} \sum_{n,n'=0}^{N-1} \prod_{i=1}^{s} \left(\frac{b}{b-1} \chi_{\lfloor b^{\ell_i} x_{n,i}\rfloor = \lfloor b^{\ell_i} x_{n',i}\rfloor} - \frac{1}{b-1} \chi_{\lfloor b^{\ell_i - 1} x_{n,i}\rfloor = \lfloor b^{\ell_i - 1} x_{n',i}\rfloor} \right),$$

where $\boldsymbol{x}_n = (x_{n,1}, \ldots, x_{n,s})$ for $0 \le n \le N-1$.

If $\boldsymbol{k} \in L_{\boldsymbol{\ell}}$, then

$$\frac{1}{N^2} \sum_{n,n'=0}^{N-1} \mathbb{E}\left[{}_b\mathrm{wal}_{\boldsymbol{k}}(\boldsymbol{y}_n \ominus \boldsymbol{y}_{n'})\right] = G_{\boldsymbol{\ell}},$$

since the coordinates are randomised independently from each other. Owen [207] called the numbers $\Gamma_{\boldsymbol{\ell}} := N^2 G_{\boldsymbol{\ell}}$ *gain coefficients*, since, as we see below, they determine how much one gains compared to MC algorithms.

The following theorem is from Owen [207].

Theorem 13.6 *Let $f \in L_2([0,1]^s)$ and $\widehat{I}(f)$ be given by* (13.7). *Let the point set $\{\boldsymbol{y}_0, \ldots, \boldsymbol{y}_{N-1}\} \subseteq [0,1)^s$ be obtained by applying Owen's scrambling algorithm to the point set $\{\boldsymbol{x}_0, \ldots, \boldsymbol{x}_{N-1}\} \subseteq [0,1)^s$. Then the variance of the estimator $\widehat{I}(f)$ is given by*

$$\mathrm{Var}[\widehat{I}(f)] = \sum_{\boldsymbol{\ell}\in\mathbb{N}_0^s\setminus\{\boldsymbol{0}\}} G_{\boldsymbol{\ell}}\sigma_{\boldsymbol{\ell}}^2(f).$$

Proof From Proposition 13.1 and (13.12), it follows that the variance of the estimator $\widehat{I}(f)$ is given by

$$\mathrm{Var}[\widehat{I}(f)] = \mathbb{E}\Bigg[\sum_{\substack{\boldsymbol{k},\boldsymbol{k}'\in\mathbb{N}_0^s\\(\boldsymbol{k},\boldsymbol{k}')\neq(\boldsymbol{0},\boldsymbol{0})}} \widehat{f}(\boldsymbol{k})\overline{\widehat{f}(\boldsymbol{k}')}\frac{1}{N^2}\sum_{n,n'=0}^{N-1} {}_b\mathrm{wal}_{\boldsymbol{k}}(\boldsymbol{y}_n)\overline{{}_b\mathrm{wal}_{\boldsymbol{k}'}(\boldsymbol{y}_{n'})}\Bigg]$$

$$= \sum_{\substack{\boldsymbol{k},\boldsymbol{k}'\in\mathbb{N}_0^s\\(\boldsymbol{k},\boldsymbol{k}')\neq(\boldsymbol{0},\boldsymbol{0})}} \widehat{f}(\boldsymbol{k})\overline{\widehat{f}(\boldsymbol{k}')}\frac{1}{N^2}\sum_{n,n'=0}^{N-1} \mathbb{E}\left[{}_b\mathrm{wal}_{\boldsymbol{k}}(\boldsymbol{y}_n)\overline{{}_b\mathrm{wal}_{\boldsymbol{k}'}(\boldsymbol{y}_{n'})}\right].$$

The coordinates are randomised independently from each other, hence,

$$\mathbb{E}\left[{}_b\mathrm{wal}_{\boldsymbol{k}}(\boldsymbol{y}_n)\overline{{}_b\mathrm{wal}_{\boldsymbol{k}'}(\boldsymbol{y}_{n'})}\right] = \prod_{i=1}^{s}\mathbb{E}\left[{}_b\mathrm{wal}_{k_i}(y_{n,i})\overline{{}_b\mathrm{wal}_{k_i'}(y_{n',i})}\right].$$

Lemma 13.3 therefore implies that $\mathbb{E}\left[{}_b\mathrm{wal}_{\boldsymbol{k}}(\boldsymbol{y}_n)\overline{{}_b\mathrm{wal}_{\boldsymbol{k}'}(\boldsymbol{y}_{n'})}\right] = 0$ unless $\boldsymbol{k} = \boldsymbol{k}'$. Hence,

$$\mathrm{Var}[\widehat{I}(f)] = \sum_{\boldsymbol{k}\in\mathbb{N}_0^s\setminus\{\boldsymbol{0}\}} |\widehat{f}(\boldsymbol{k})|^2\frac{1}{N^2}\sum_{n,n'=0}^{N-1}\mathbb{E}\left[{}_b\mathrm{wal}_{\boldsymbol{k}}(\boldsymbol{y}_n\ominus\boldsymbol{y}_{n'})\right]$$

$$= \sum_{\boldsymbol{\ell}\in\mathbb{N}_0^s\setminus\{\boldsymbol{0}\}}\sum_{\boldsymbol{k}\in L_{\boldsymbol{\ell}}} |\widehat{f}(\boldsymbol{k})|^2\frac{1}{N^2}\sum_{n,n'=0}^{N-1}\mathbb{E}\left[{}_b\mathrm{wal}_{\boldsymbol{k}}(\boldsymbol{y}_n\ominus\boldsymbol{y}_{n'})\right]$$

$$= \sum_{\boldsymbol{\ell}\in\mathbb{N}_0^s\setminus\{\boldsymbol{0}\}} G_{\boldsymbol{\ell}}\sigma_{\boldsymbol{\ell}}^2(f).$$

□

In the previous result we did not make any assumption on the distribution properties of the point set $\{\boldsymbol{x}_0,\ldots,\boldsymbol{x}_{N-1}\}$. In the following, we consider the case when $\boldsymbol{x}_0,\ldots,\boldsymbol{x}_{N-1}$ form a digital (t,m,s)-net, see [270, 271]. The case where the points form a (t,m,s)-net (not necessarily digital) was considered in [207].

Corollary 13.7 *Let $f\in L_2([0,1]^s)$ and $\widehat{I}(f)$ be given by* (13.7). *Let the points $\{\boldsymbol{x}_0,\ldots,\boldsymbol{x}_{b^m-1}\}$ be a digital (t,m,s)-net over $\mathbb{Z}_b$ with generating matrices $C_1,\ldots,C_s$ over $\mathbb{Z}_b$. Then*

$$\mathrm{Var}[\widehat{I}(f)] = \sum_{\emptyset\neq\mathfrak{u}\subseteq\mathcal{I}_s}\frac{b^{|\mathfrak{u}|}}{(b-1)^{|\mathfrak{u}|}}\sum_{\boldsymbol{\ell}_{\mathfrak{u}}\in\mathbb{N}^{|\mathfrak{u}|}}\frac{\sigma^2_{(\boldsymbol{\ell}_{\mathfrak{u}},\boldsymbol{0})}(f)}{b^{|\boldsymbol{\ell}|_1}}|L_{(\boldsymbol{\ell}_{\mathfrak{u}},\boldsymbol{0})}\cap\mathcal{D}_\infty|,$$

where $\mathcal{D}_\infty = \mathcal{D}_\infty(C_1,\ldots,C_s)$ is the dual net as in Remark 4.77 and $L_{(\boldsymbol{\ell}_{\mathfrak{u}},\boldsymbol{0})} = \{\boldsymbol{k}\in\mathbb{N}_0^s : b^{\ell_i-1}\le k_i < b^{\ell_i}$ for $i\in\mathfrak{u}$ and $k_i = 0$ for $i\in\mathcal{I}_s\setminus\mathfrak{u}\}$ and where $|\boldsymbol{\ell}|_1 = \ell_1+\cdots+\ell_s$ for $\boldsymbol{\ell}=(\ell_1,\ldots,\ell_s)$.

Proof From Theorem 13.6, we have

$$\operatorname{Var}[\widehat{I}(f)] = \sum_{\boldsymbol{\ell}\in\mathbb{N}_0^s\setminus\{\boldsymbol{0}\}} G_{\boldsymbol{\ell}}\sigma_{\boldsymbol{\ell}}^2(f).$$

We rewrite this equation by separating out the cases where some components of $\boldsymbol{\ell}$ are zero, i.e.

$$\operatorname{Var}[\widehat{I}(f)] = \sum_{\emptyset\neq\mathfrak{u}\subseteq\mathcal{I}_s}\sum_{\boldsymbol{\ell}_{\mathfrak{u}}\in\mathbb{N}^{|\mathfrak{u}|}} G_{(\boldsymbol{\ell}_{\mathfrak{u}},\boldsymbol{0})}\sigma_{(\boldsymbol{\ell}_{\mathfrak{u}},\boldsymbol{0})}^2(f).$$

Many of the coefficients $G_{(\boldsymbol{\ell}_{\mathfrak{u}},\boldsymbol{0})}$ are zero, which we prove in the following. We can express $G_{(\boldsymbol{\ell}_{\mathfrak{u}},\boldsymbol{0})}$ as a Walsh series in the following way

$$\begin{aligned}
G_{(\boldsymbol{\ell}_{\mathfrak{u}},\boldsymbol{0})} &= \frac{1}{b^{2m}}\sum_{n,n'=0}^{b^m-1}\sum_{\mathfrak{v}\subseteq\mathfrak{u}}\frac{(-1)^{|\mathfrak{u}|-|\mathfrak{v}|}b^{|\mathfrak{v}|}}{(b-1)^{|\mathfrak{u}|}} \\
&\quad\times\prod_{i\in\mathfrak{v}}\chi_{\lfloor b^{\ell_i}x_{n,i}\rfloor=\lfloor b^{\ell_i}x_{n',i}\rfloor}\prod_{i\in\mathfrak{u}\setminus\mathfrak{v}}\chi_{\lfloor b^{\ell_i-1}x_{n,i}\rfloor=\lfloor b^{\ell_i-1}x_{n',i}\rfloor} \\
&= \frac{1}{b^{2m}}\sum_{n,n'=0}^{b^m-1}\sum_{\mathfrak{v}\subseteq\mathfrak{u}}\frac{(-1)^{|\mathfrak{u}|-|\mathfrak{v}|}b^{|\mathfrak{v}|}}{(b-1)^{|\mathfrak{u}|}}\frac{1}{|R_{\boldsymbol{\ell}_{\mathfrak{u}},\mathfrak{v}}|}\sum_{\boldsymbol{k}\in R_{\boldsymbol{\ell}_{\mathfrak{u}},\mathfrak{v}}} {}_b\mathrm{wal}_{\boldsymbol{k}}(\boldsymbol{x}_n\ominus\boldsymbol{x}_{n'}),
\end{aligned}$$

where $R_{\boldsymbol{\ell}_{\mathfrak{u}},\mathfrak{v}} = \{\boldsymbol{k}\in\mathbb{N}_0^s : 0\le k_i < b^{\ell_i} \text{ for } i\in\mathfrak{v} \text{ and } 0\le k_i < b^{\ell_i-1} \text{ for } i\in\mathfrak{u}\setminus\mathfrak{v}, \text{ and } k_i = 0 \text{ for } i\in\mathcal{I}_s\setminus\mathfrak{u}\}$ and hence, $|R_{\boldsymbol{\ell}_{\mathfrak{u}},\mathfrak{v}}| = b^{|\boldsymbol{\ell}_{\mathfrak{u}}|_1-|\mathfrak{u}|+|\mathfrak{v}|}$.

As $\{\boldsymbol{x}_0,\ldots,\boldsymbol{x}_{b^m-1}\}$ is a digital (t,m,s)-net in base b, we have

$$\begin{aligned}
G_{(\boldsymbol{\ell}_{\mathfrak{u}},\boldsymbol{0})} &= \sum_{\mathfrak{v}\subseteq\mathfrak{u}}\frac{(-1)^{|\mathfrak{u}|-|\mathfrak{v}|}b^{|\mathfrak{u}|-|\boldsymbol{\ell}|_1}}{(b-1)^{|\mathfrak{u}|}}\sum_{\boldsymbol{k}\in R_{\boldsymbol{\ell}_{\mathfrak{u}},\mathfrak{v}}}\frac{1}{b^{2m}}\sum_{n,n'=0}^{b^m-1} {}_b\mathrm{wal}_{\boldsymbol{k}}(\boldsymbol{x}_n\ominus\boldsymbol{x}_{n'}) \\
&= \frac{b^{|\mathfrak{u}|-|\boldsymbol{\ell}|_1}}{(b-1)^{|\mathfrak{u}|}}\sum_{\mathfrak{v}\subseteq\mathfrak{u}}(-1)^{|\mathfrak{u}|-|\mathfrak{v}|}\sum_{\boldsymbol{k}\in R_{\boldsymbol{\ell}_{\mathfrak{u}},\mathfrak{v}}}\frac{1}{b^m}\sum_{n=0}^{b^m-1} {}_b\mathrm{wal}_{\boldsymbol{k}}(\boldsymbol{x}_n) \\
&= \frac{b^{|\mathfrak{u}|-|\boldsymbol{\ell}|_1}}{(b-1)^{|\mathfrak{u}|}}\sum_{\mathfrak{v}\subseteq\mathfrak{u}}(-1)^{|\mathfrak{u}|-|\mathfrak{v}|}\sum_{\boldsymbol{k}\in R_{\boldsymbol{\ell}_{\mathfrak{u}},\mathfrak{v}}\cap\mathcal{D}_\infty} 1,
\end{aligned}$$

where $\mathcal{D}_\infty$ is the dual net as in Remark 4.77. Therefore,

$$\operatorname{Var}[\widehat{I}(f)] = \sum_{\emptyset\neq\mathfrak{u}\subseteq\mathcal{I}_s}\frac{b^{|\mathfrak{u}|}}{(b-1)^{|\mathfrak{u}|}}\sum_{\boldsymbol{\ell}_{\mathfrak{u}}\in\mathbb{N}^{|\mathfrak{u}|}}\frac{\sigma_{(\boldsymbol{\ell}_{\mathfrak{u}},\boldsymbol{0})}^2(f)}{b^{|\boldsymbol{\ell}|_1}}\sum_{\mathfrak{v}\subseteq\mathfrak{u}}(-1)^{|\mathfrak{u}|-|\mathfrak{v}|}\sum_{\boldsymbol{k}\in R_{\boldsymbol{\ell}_{\mathfrak{u}},\mathfrak{v}}\cap\mathcal{D}_\infty} 1.$$

For $\boldsymbol{k} \in R_{\boldsymbol{\ell}_{\mathfrak{u}},\mathfrak{u}}$, let $\mathfrak{w} = \mathfrak{w}(\boldsymbol{k}) \subseteq \mathfrak{u}$ be the smallest set $\mathfrak{w}$ such that $\boldsymbol{k} \in R_{\boldsymbol{\ell}_{\mathfrak{u}},\mathfrak{w}}$, i.e. $\boldsymbol{k} \in R_{\boldsymbol{\ell}_{\mathfrak{u}},\mathfrak{w}}$ and $\boldsymbol{k} \notin R_{\boldsymbol{\ell}_{\mathfrak{u}},\mathfrak{w}'}$ for $\mathfrak{w}' \subsetneq \mathfrak{w}$. Then

$$\sum_{\mathfrak{v}\subseteq\mathfrak{u}}(-1)^{|\mathfrak{u}|-|\mathfrak{v}|} \sum_{\boldsymbol{k}\in R_{\boldsymbol{\ell}_{\mathfrak{u}},\mathfrak{v}}\cap\mathcal{D}_\infty} 1 = \sum_{\boldsymbol{k}\in R_{\boldsymbol{\ell}_{\mathfrak{u}},\mathfrak{u}}\cap\mathcal{D}_\infty} \sum_{\mathfrak{w}(\boldsymbol{k})\subseteq\mathfrak{v}\subseteq\mathfrak{u}} (-1)^{|\mathfrak{u}|-|\mathfrak{v}|}.$$

The sum $\sum_{\mathfrak{w}(\boldsymbol{k})\subseteq\mathfrak{v}\subseteq\mathfrak{u}}(-1)^{|\mathfrak{u}|-|\mathfrak{v}|}$ is 0 unless $\mathfrak{w}(\boldsymbol{k}) = \mathfrak{u}$, in which case the sum is 1. As $\mathfrak{w}(\boldsymbol{k}) = \mathfrak{u}$ is equivalent to $\boldsymbol{k} \in L_{(\boldsymbol{\ell}_{\mathfrak{u}},\boldsymbol{0})}$, we obtain

$$\mathrm{Var}[\widehat{I}(f)] = \sum_{\emptyset\neq\mathfrak{u}\subseteq\mathcal{I}_s} \frac{b^{|\mathfrak{u}|}}{(b-1)^{|\mathfrak{u}|}} \sum_{\boldsymbol{\ell}_{\mathfrak{u}}\in\mathbb{N}^{|\mathfrak{u}|}} \frac{\sigma^2_{(\boldsymbol{\ell}_{\mathfrak{u}},\boldsymbol{0})}(f)}{b^{|\boldsymbol{\ell}|_1}} \sum_{\boldsymbol{k}\in L_{(\boldsymbol{\ell}_{\mathfrak{u}},\boldsymbol{0})}\cap\mathcal{D}_\infty} 1,$$

from which the result follows. □

Lemma 13.8 *Let $\mathcal{D}_\infty$ be the dual net of a digital (t, m, s)-net over $\mathbb{Z}_b$ with generating matrices $C_1, \ldots, C_s$ as used in Corollary 13.7. Then*

$$|L_{(\boldsymbol{\ell}_{\mathfrak{u}},\boldsymbol{0})} \cap \mathcal{D}_\infty| \le \begin{cases} 0 & \text{if } |\boldsymbol{\ell}_{\mathfrak{u}}|_1 \le m-t, \\ (b-1)^{|\mathfrak{u}|} & \text{if } m-t < |\boldsymbol{\ell}_{\mathfrak{u}}|_1 \le m-t+|\mathfrak{u}|, \\ (b-1)^{|\mathfrak{u}|} b^{|\boldsymbol{\ell}_{\mathfrak{u}}|_1-(m-t+|\mathfrak{u}|)} & \text{if } |\boldsymbol{\ell}_{\mathfrak{u}}|_1 > m-t+|\mathfrak{u}|. \end{cases}$$

Proof We have

$$L_{(\boldsymbol{\ell}_{\mathfrak{u}},\boldsymbol{0})} \cap \mathcal{D}_\infty = \{\boldsymbol{k} \in L_{(\boldsymbol{\ell}_{\mathfrak{u}},\boldsymbol{0})} : C_1^\top \mathrm{tr}_m(\mathbf{k}_1) + \cdots + C_s^\top \mathrm{tr}_m(\mathbf{k}_s) = \mathbf{0}\}.$$

As $k_i = 0$ for $i \in \mathcal{I}_s \setminus \mathfrak{u}$, we have

$$C_1^\top \mathrm{tr}_m(\mathbf{k}_1) + \cdots + C_s^\top \mathrm{tr}_m(\mathbf{k}_s) = \sum_{i\in\mathfrak{u}} C_i^\top \mathrm{tr}_m(\mathbf{k}_i).$$

We only consider the case $\mathfrak{u} = \mathcal{I}_s$; all the other cases can be shown exactly the same way.

As $b^{\ell_i-1} \le k_i < b^{\ell_i}$, we have $k_i = \kappa_{i,0} + \kappa_{i,1}b + \cdots + \kappa_{i,\ell_i-1}b^{\ell_i-1}$, where $\kappa_{i,\ell_i-1} \neq 0$.

For $1 \le i \le s$ let $\mathbf{c}_r^{(i)}$, denote the rth row of C_i for $1 \le r \le m$, and set $\mathbf{c}_r^{(i)} = \mathbf{0}$ for $r > m$. Then $C_1^\top \mathrm{tr}_m(\mathbf{k}_1) + \cdots + C_s^\top \mathrm{tr}_m(\mathbf{k}_s) = \mathbf{0}$ can be written as

$$\sum_{i=1}^{s}\sum_{r=1}^{\ell_i-1} \mathbf{c}_r^{(i)}\kappa_{i,r-1} = -\sum_{i=1}^{s} \mathbf{c}_{\ell_i}^{(i)}\kappa_{i,\ell_i-1}. \tag{13.13}$$

If $\sum_{i=1}^s \ell_i \le m-t$, then the vectors $\mathbf{c}_1^{(1)}, \ldots, \mathbf{c}_{\ell_1}^{(1)}, \ldots, \mathbf{c}_1^{(s)}, \ldots, \mathbf{c}_{\ell_s}^{(s)}$ are linearly independent by the digital (t, m, s)-net property of the generating matrices and therefore, (13.13) has only the trivial solution, for which $\boldsymbol{k} \notin L_{\boldsymbol{\ell}}$. Hence, $|L_{\boldsymbol{\ell}} \cap \mathcal{D}_\infty| = 0$ in this case.

If $\sum_{i=1}^s (\ell_i - 1) \le m-t$, then $\mathbf{c}_1^{(1)}, \ldots, \mathbf{c}_{\ell_1-1}^{(1)}, \ldots, \mathbf{c}_1^{(s)}, \ldots, \mathbf{c}_{\ell_s-1}^{(s)}$ are linearly independent by the digital (t, m, s)-net property of the generating matrices. Hence, for each right-hand side of (13.13), we have at most one solution and therefore $|L_{\boldsymbol{\ell}} \cap \mathcal{D}_\infty| \leq (b-1)^s$ in this case, since each $\kappa_{i,\ell_i - 1} \in \{1, \ldots, b-1\}$.

Now assume that $|\boldsymbol{\ell}|_1 > m - t + s$. Then $m - t$ of the vectors in (13.13) are linearly independent and the remaining digits can be chosen freely. Therefore, there are at most $(b-1)^s b^{|\boldsymbol{\ell}|_1 - (m-t+s)}$ solutions. □

Upon combining Corollary 13.7 and Lemma 13.8, we obtain the following theorem which extends the one-dimensional case as one would approximately expect; see [270, 271], and [207] for the analogous result for (t, m, s)-nets (not necessarily digital).

Theorem 13.9 *Let* $f \in L_2([0,1]^s)$ *and let* $\widehat{I}(f)$ *be given by* (13.7). *Let the points* $\{\boldsymbol{x}_0, \ldots, \boldsymbol{x}_{b^m-1}\}$ *be a digital* (t, m, s)*-net over* $\mathbb{Z}_b$. *Then*

$$\mathrm{Var}[\widehat{I}(f)] \leq b^{-m+t+s} \sum_{\substack{\boldsymbol{\ell} \in \mathbb{N}_0^s \\ |\boldsymbol{\ell}|_1 > m-t}} \sigma_{\boldsymbol{\ell}}^2(f).$$

For MC, one obtains a variance $\mathrm{Var}[\widehat{I}(f)] = \frac{1}{N} \sum_{\boldsymbol{\ell} \in \mathbb{N}_0^s \setminus \{\boldsymbol{0}\}} \sigma_{\boldsymbol{\ell}}^2(f)$. Hence, the gain of scrambled digital nets lies in the fact that we only sum over $\sigma_{\boldsymbol{\ell}}^2(f)$ for which $|\boldsymbol{\ell}|_1 > m - t$, although one incurs a penalty factor of b^t using scrambled digital (t, m, s)-nets. Notice that the gain coefficients $\Gamma_{\boldsymbol{\ell}}$ are 0 for $\boldsymbol{\ell} \in \mathbb{N}_0^s$ with $|\boldsymbol{\ell}|_1 \leq m - t$ and $\Gamma_{\boldsymbol{\ell}} = b^{t+s}$ for $\boldsymbol{\ell} \in \mathbb{N}_0^s$ with $|\boldsymbol{\ell}|_1 > m - t$.

Theorem 13.9 shows that $\mathrm{Var}[\widehat{I}(f)]$ for a scrambled $(0, m, s)$-net is always smaller than the variance for a MC algorithm. Further, for scrambled (t, m, s)-nets, we have

$$b^m \mathrm{Var}[\widehat{I}(f)] = b^{t+s} \sum_{\substack{\boldsymbol{\ell} \in \mathbb{N}_0^s \\ |\boldsymbol{\ell}|_1 > m-t}} \sigma_{\boldsymbol{\ell}}^2(f) \to 0 \quad \text{as } m \to \infty.$$

Therefore, scrambled (t, m, s)-nets outperform MC with respect to $\mathrm{Var}[\widehat{I}(f)]$ asymptotically, as, for MC, we have $N \mathrm{Var}[\widehat{I}(f)] = \sum_{\boldsymbol{\ell} \in \mathbb{N}_0^s \setminus \{\boldsymbol{0}\}} \sigma_{\boldsymbol{\ell}}^2(f)$ for all $N \in \mathbb{N}$.

Of particular interest in this context is also the result by Loh [158], who shows that a central limit theorem holds for the estimate $\widehat{I}(f)$ for which the quadrature points are based on a scrambled $(0, m, s)$-net. This allows one to obtain an approximate confidence interval from the variance estimates of $\widehat{I}(f)$.

13.4 Mean square worst-case error in the Sobolev spaces $\mathscr{H}_{\mathrm{sob},s,\boldsymbol{\gamma}}$

In this section we consider integrands from the unanchored weighted Sobolev space $\mathscr{H}_{\mathrm{sob},s,\boldsymbol{\gamma}}$ as introduced in Section 2.5 and considered in Section 12.2. Our approach is analogous to that in Chapter 12.

13.4.1 Scramble invariant kernels

Analogously to the digital shift invariant kernels of Section 12.1, we introduce 'scramble invariant kernels' associated with a given reproducing kernel K, an idea which goes back to [108] (and [103] for random shifts). Throughout this section, we assume that b is prime.

Let $\boldsymbol{y}, \boldsymbol{y}' \in [0,1)^s$ be obtained by applying Owen's scrambling algorithm to $\boldsymbol{x}, \boldsymbol{x}' \in [0,1)^s$. A reproducing kernel K with the property that $K(\boldsymbol{x}, \boldsymbol{x}') = K(\boldsymbol{y}, \boldsymbol{y}')$ for any points which can be obtained by applying Owen's scrambling algorithm to $\boldsymbol{x}, \boldsymbol{x}' \in [0,1)^s$ is called a *scramble invariant reproducing kernel* or, for short, a *scramble invariant kernel.*

For an arbitrary reproducing kernel, we associate a scramble invariant kernel with it; see [108].

Definition 13.10 For an arbitrary reproducing kernel K, we define the *associated scramble invariant kernel* K_{scr} by

$$K_{\text{scr}}(\boldsymbol{x}, \boldsymbol{x}') := \mathbb{E}\left[K(\boldsymbol{y}, \boldsymbol{y}')\right],$$

where the expectation is taken with respect to all Owen scrambled points $\boldsymbol{y}, \boldsymbol{y}'$ of $\boldsymbol{x}, \boldsymbol{x}'$.

The kernel K_{scr} is indeed scramble invariant as the relation $(\boldsymbol{x}, \boldsymbol{x}') \sim (\boldsymbol{z}, \boldsymbol{z}')$, where $\boldsymbol{z}, \boldsymbol{z}'$ are obtained by applying an Owen scrambling to $\boldsymbol{x}, \boldsymbol{x}'$, is an equivalence relation, i.e. it is reflexive $(\boldsymbol{x}, \boldsymbol{x}') \sim (\boldsymbol{x}, \boldsymbol{x}')$, symmetric $(\boldsymbol{z}, \boldsymbol{z}') \sim (\boldsymbol{x}, \boldsymbol{x}')$ and transitive $(\boldsymbol{x}, \boldsymbol{x}') \sim (\boldsymbol{y}, \boldsymbol{y}')$ and $(\boldsymbol{y}, \boldsymbol{y}') \sim (\boldsymbol{z}, \boldsymbol{z}')$ implies that $(\boldsymbol{x}, \boldsymbol{x}') \sim (\boldsymbol{z}, \boldsymbol{z}')$. Therefore, $K_{\text{scr}}(\boldsymbol{x}, \boldsymbol{x}') = K_{\text{scr}}(\boldsymbol{z}, \boldsymbol{z}')$.

We need several auxiliary results before we can prove the analogue to Lemma 12.2 for scrambling. We use the following observation.

Remark 13.11 Let Π be a given set of permutations. The mapping $x \mapsto x_\Pi$ is bijective when applied to all b-adic irrationals, i.e. all numbers in $[0,1)$ which cannot be written in a finite b-adic representation. Hence, there is an inverse to this mapping, which is again a scrambling. The set of permutations Π' such that for $y = x_\Pi$ we have $x = y_{\Pi'}$ for all b-adic irrationals x is denoted by Π^{-1}.

For a set $M \subseteq [0,1)$ and a given set of permutations Π, we write $M_\Pi = \{x_\Pi \in [0,1) : x \in M\}$.

Lemma 13.12 *Let $b \geq 2$ be an integer. Then the one-dimensional Lebesgue measure λ is invariant under Owen's scrambling. In other words, for a given set of permutations $\Pi = \{\pi_{x_1,\ldots,x_{k-1}} : k \in \mathbb{N}, x_1, \ldots, x_{k-1} \in \{0, \ldots, b-1\}\}$, where for $k = 1$ we set $\pi_{x_1,\ldots,x_{k-1}} = \pi$, and for all Lebesgue measurable sets $M \subseteq [0,1)$, we have $\lambda(M) = \lambda(M_\Pi)$.*

Proof Let a set of permutations Π be fixed. Let $x = \xi_1 b^{-1} + \xi_2 b^{-2} + \cdots \in [0, 1)$ and $y = x_\Pi = \eta_1 b^{-1} + \eta_2 b^{-2} + \cdots$. Then y is not defined if $\eta_j = b - 1$ for all indices $j \geq j_0$. Hence, the subset $\{y \in M_\Pi : y \text{ not defined}\}$ is countable.

Consider an elementary interval $J = [a/b^r, (a+1)/b^r)$ with $a = \alpha_0 + \alpha_1 b + \cdots + \alpha_{r-1} b^{r-1}$. Each $x \in J$ has the b-adic expansion $x = \alpha_{r-1} b^{-1} + \alpha_{r-2} b^{-2} + \cdots + \alpha_0 b^{-r} + \xi_{r+1} b^{-(r+1)} + \xi_{r+2} b^{-(r+2)} + \cdots$ with digits $\xi_j \in \{0, \ldots, b-1\}$ for all $j \geq r + 1$.

Now, for $x \in J$, we have

$$y = x_\Pi = \frac{\pi(\alpha_{r-1})}{b} + \frac{\pi_{\alpha_{r-1}}(\alpha_{r-2})}{b^2} + \cdots + \frac{\pi_{\alpha_{r-1},\ldots,\alpha_1}(\alpha_0)}{b^r} + \frac{\pi_{\alpha_{r-1},\ldots,\alpha_0}(\xi_{r+1})}{b^{r+1}} + \frac{\pi_{\alpha_{r-1},\ldots,\alpha_0,\xi_{r+1}}(\xi_{r+2})}{b^{r+2}} + \cdots.$$

Hence, for a given Π, $x \mapsto x_\Pi$ maps all but countably many points from J to the elementary interval

$$J_\Pi = \Big[\frac{\pi(\alpha_{r-1})}{b} + \frac{\pi_{\alpha_{r-1}}(\alpha_{r-2})}{b^2} + \cdots + \frac{\pi_{\alpha_{r-1},\ldots,\alpha_1}(\alpha_0)}{b^r}, \frac{\pi(\alpha_{r-1})}{b} + \frac{\pi_{\alpha_{r-1}(\alpha_{r-2})}}{b^2} + \cdots + \frac{\pi_{\alpha_{r-1},\ldots,\alpha_1}(\alpha_0)}{b^r} + \frac{1}{b^r}\Big).$$

Furthermore, for all but countably many points $y \in J_\Pi$, we can define the inverse mapping $y \mapsto y_{\Pi^{-1}}$. Hence, this mapping preserves the measure of elementary intervals.

Since every open subset from $[0, 1)$ can be written as a countable union of elementary intervals, it follows that $x \mapsto x_\Pi$ preserves the measure of every open subset of $[0, 1)$ and hence, the result follows for all Lebesgue measurable subsets from $[0, 1)$. □

Corollary 13.13 *Let* Π *be a given set of permutations. For all* $f \in L_2([0, 1]^s)$, *we have*

$$\int_{[0,1]^s} f(\boldsymbol{x}) \, \mathrm{d}\boldsymbol{x} = \int_{[0,1]^s} f(\boldsymbol{x}_\Pi) \, \mathrm{d}\boldsymbol{x}.$$

Proof It is enough to show the result for $s = 1$. Let Π be a given set of permutations and let $f \in L_2([0, 1])$. Define $g(x) = f(x_\Pi)$. For each $M \subseteq f([0, 1))$, we have

$$\begin{aligned} g^{-1}(M) &= \{x \in [0, 1) : f(x_\Pi) \in M\} \\ &= \{y_{\Pi^{-1}} \in [0, 1) : f(y) \in M\} \\ &= f^{-1}(M)_{\Pi^{-1}} \end{aligned}$$

and hence, by Lemma 13.12, we have $\lambda(g^{-1}(M)) = \lambda(f^{-1}(M))$. Now the result follows from the definition of the Lebesgue integral. □

For a given x, we denote by $\mathbb{E}_\Pi[f(y)]$ the expectation of $f(y) = f(x_\Pi)$, where $y = x_\Pi$ is the point obtained by applying Owen's scrambling to x, with respect to uniform choices of the permutations in Owen's scrambling.

Lemma 13.14 *Let a set of permutations Π be chosen uniformly and independent and identically distributed. Then, for any Riemann integrable function f, we have*

$$\mathbb{E}_\Pi\left[\int_0^1 f(x_\Pi)\,\mathrm{d}x\right] = \int_0^1 f(x)\,\mathrm{d}x = \mathbb{E}_\Pi\left[f(x_\Pi)\right] = \int_0^1 \mathbb{E}_\Pi[f(x_\Pi)]\,\mathrm{d}x.$$

Proof First note that

$$\int_0^1 f(x)\,\mathrm{d}x = \int_0^1 f(x_\Pi)\,\mathrm{d}x = \mathbb{E}_\Pi\left[\int_0^1 f(x_\Pi)\,\mathrm{d}x\right],$$

by Corollary 13.13, where the expectation is taken with respect to all random choices of sets of permutations Π. Further, we have

$$\mathbb{E}_\Pi[f(x_\Pi)] = \lim_{r\to\infty} U_r$$

with

$$U_r = \frac{1}{b}\sum_{y_1=0}^{b-1}\cdots\frac{1}{b}\sum_{y_r=0}^{b-1} f(y_1 b^{-1} + \cdots + y_r b^{-r}) = \frac{1}{b^r}\sum_{a=0}^{b^r-1} f(ab^{-r}).$$

This is a Riemann sum for the integral $\int_0^1 f(x)\,\mathrm{d}x$, hence

$$\int_0^1 f(x)\,\mathrm{d}x = \mathbb{E}_\Pi[f(x_\Pi)] = \int_0^1 \mathbb{E}_\Pi[f(x_\Pi)]\,\mathrm{d}x,$$

and hence, the result follows. □

Lemma 13.15 *Let a set of permutations Π be chosen uniformly and independent and identically distributed. Then for any integers $k, k' \geq 0$, we have*

$$\int_0^1\int_0^1 {}_b\mathrm{wal}_k(x)\overline{{}_b\mathrm{wal}_{k'}(y)}\,\mathrm{d}x\,\mathrm{d}y = \int_0^1\int_0^1 \mathbb{E}_\Pi\left[{}_b\mathrm{wal}_k(x_\Pi)\overline{{}_b\mathrm{wal}_{k'}(y_\Pi)}\right]\mathrm{d}x\,\mathrm{d}y$$

and for any $x \in [0, 1)$, we have

$$\mathbb{E}_\Pi\left[\int_0^1 {}_b\mathrm{wal}_k(x_\Pi)\overline{{}_b\mathrm{wal}_{k'}(y)}\,\mathrm{d}y\right] = \int_0^1 \mathbb{E}_\Pi\left[{}_b\mathrm{wal}_k(x_\Pi)\overline{{}_b\mathrm{wal}_{k'}(y_\Pi)}\right]\mathrm{d}y.$$

Proof We consider the first equation. If $(k, k') = (0, 0)$, then both sides are 1 and hence, the result follows in this case.

Now let $(k, k') \neq (0, 0)$. The left-hand side of the first equality is 0. Hence, consider now the right-hand side. Then we have

$$\begin{aligned}
&\int_0^1 \int_0^1 \mathbb{E}_\Pi \left[{}_b\mathrm{wal}_k(x_\Pi) \overline{{}_b\mathrm{wal}_{k'}(y_\Pi)} \right] \mathrm{d}x \, \mathrm{d}y \\
&= \sum_{r=0}^{\infty} \iint_{E_r} \mathbb{E}_\Pi \left[{}_b\mathrm{wal}_k(x_\Pi) \overline{{}_b\mathrm{wal}_{k'}(y_\Pi)} \right] \mathrm{d}x \, \mathrm{d}y \\
&\quad + \iint_{E_\infty} \mathbb{E}_\Pi \left[{}_b\mathrm{wal}_k(x_\Pi) \overline{{}_b\mathrm{wal}_{k'}(y_\Pi)} \right] \mathrm{d}x \, \mathrm{d}y,
\end{aligned}$$

where $E_r = \{(x, y) \in [0, 1]^2 : \lfloor x b^r \rfloor = \lfloor y b^r \rfloor, \lfloor x b^{r+1} \rfloor \neq \lfloor y b^{r+1} \rfloor\}$ and $E_\infty = \{(x, x) \in [0, 1]^2\}$. Note that $[0, 1]^2 = \bigcup_{r=0}^{\infty} E_r \cup E_\infty$ and by Lemma 13.3, we have for $(x, y) \in E_r$ that

$$\mathbb{E}_\Pi \left[{}_b\mathrm{wal}_k(x_\Pi) \overline{{}_b\mathrm{wal}_{k'}(y_\Pi)} \right] = \begin{cases} 0 & \text{if } k \neq k', \\ 1 & \text{if } 1 \leq k = k' < b^r, \\ -\frac{1}{b-1} & \text{if } b^r \leq k = k' < b^{r+1}, \\ 0 & \text{if } k = k' \geq b^{r+1}. \end{cases}$$

Hence, for $k \neq k'$ we have

$$\int_0^1 \int_0^1 \mathbb{E}_\Pi \left[{}_b\mathrm{wal}_k(x_\Pi) \overline{{}_b\mathrm{wal}_{k'}(y_\Pi)} \right] \mathrm{d}x \, \mathrm{d}y = 0$$

and the result follows for this case.

Assume that $k = k' > 0$ and let $k = \kappa_0 + \kappa_1 b + \cdots + \kappa_{a-1} b^{a-1}$ with $\kappa_{a-1} \neq 0$. Then we have

$$\begin{aligned}
&\int_0^1 \int_0^1 \mathbb{E}_\Pi \left[{}_b\mathrm{wal}_k(x_\Pi \ominus y_\Pi) \right] \mathrm{d}x \, \mathrm{d}y \\
&= \iint_{E_{a-1}} -\frac{1}{b-1} \, \mathrm{d}x \, \mathrm{d}y + \sum_{r=a}^{\infty} \iint_{E_r} 1 \, \mathrm{d}x \, \mathrm{d}y \\
&= -\frac{b^{-a+1}}{b-1} + \sum_{r=a}^{\infty} b^{-r} = 0.
\end{aligned}$$

The second equality can be shown in the same way as the first. □

As in Section 12.2, let

$$\widehat{K}(\boldsymbol{k}, \boldsymbol{k}') = \int_{[0,1]^s} \int_{[0,1]^s} K(\boldsymbol{x}, \boldsymbol{y}) \, \overline{{}_b\mathrm{wal}_{\boldsymbol{k}}(\boldsymbol{x})} \, {}_b\mathrm{wal}_{\boldsymbol{k}'}(\boldsymbol{y}) \, \mathrm{d}\boldsymbol{x} \, \mathrm{d}\boldsymbol{y},$$

for $\boldsymbol{k}, \boldsymbol{k}' \in \mathbb{N}_0^s$. Recall that $\widehat{K}(\boldsymbol{k}, \boldsymbol{k}') = \overline{\widehat{K}(\boldsymbol{k}, \boldsymbol{k}')}$ and therefore, $\widehat{K}(\boldsymbol{k}, \boldsymbol{k}') \in \mathbb{R}$. In the following lemma, we show how the scramble invariant kernel can be expressed in terms of $\widehat{K}(\boldsymbol{k}, \boldsymbol{k})$.

Lemma 13.16 *Let the reproducing kernel $K \in L_2([0,1]^{2s})$ be continuous and for $\boldsymbol{k} \in \mathbb{N}_0^s$, let*

$$\widehat{K}(\boldsymbol{k}, \boldsymbol{k}) = \int_{[0,1]^s} \int_{[0,1]^s} K(\boldsymbol{x}, \boldsymbol{y}) \overline{{}_b\mathrm{wal}_{\boldsymbol{k}}(\boldsymbol{x})}\, {}_b\mathrm{wal}_{\boldsymbol{k}}(\boldsymbol{y}) \,\mathrm{d}\boldsymbol{x} \,\mathrm{d}\boldsymbol{y}.$$

Assume that $\sum_{\boldsymbol{k} \in \mathbb{N}_0^s} |\widehat{K}(\boldsymbol{k}, \boldsymbol{k})| < \infty$. Then the scramble invariant kernel K_{scr} is given by

$$\begin{aligned} K_{\mathrm{scr}}(\boldsymbol{x}, \boldsymbol{x}') = {} & \sum_{\mathfrak{u} \subseteq \mathcal{I}_s} \sum_{\boldsymbol{\ell}_{\mathfrak{u}} \in \mathbb{N}^{|\mathfrak{u}|}} \sum_{\boldsymbol{k} \in L_{(\boldsymbol{\ell}_{\mathfrak{u}}, \boldsymbol{0})}} \widehat{K}(\boldsymbol{k}, \boldsymbol{k}) \\ & \times \frac{b^{|\mathfrak{u}|}}{b^{|\boldsymbol{\ell}|_1} (b-1)^{|\mathfrak{u}|}} \sum_{\mathfrak{v} \subseteq \mathfrak{u}} (-1)^{|\mathfrak{u}| - |\mathfrak{v}|} \sum_{\boldsymbol{h} \in R_{\boldsymbol{\ell}_{\mathfrak{u}}, \mathfrak{v}}} {}_b\mathrm{wal}_{\boldsymbol{h}}(\boldsymbol{x} \ominus \boldsymbol{x}'), \qquad (13.14) \end{aligned}$$

where $L_{\boldsymbol{\ell}} = \{\boldsymbol{k} = (k_1, \ldots, k_s) \in \mathbb{N}_0^s : \lfloor b^{\ell_i - 1} \rfloor \le k_i < b^{\ell_i} \text{ for } 1 < i < s\}$, $R_{\boldsymbol{\ell}_{\mathfrak{u}}, \mathfrak{v}} = \{\boldsymbol{h} \in \mathbb{N}_0^s : 0 \le h_i < b^{\ell_i} \text{ for } i \in \mathfrak{v} \text{ and } 0 \le h_i < b^{\ell_i - 1} \text{ for } i \in \mathfrak{u} \setminus \mathfrak{v}, \text{ and } h_i = 0 \text{ for } i \in \mathcal{I}_s \setminus \mathfrak{u}\}$.

Proof Using similar arguments as in the proof of Lemma 12.2, it can be shown that K_{scr} is continuous (this is Exercise 13.5). As $\sum_{\boldsymbol{k} \in \mathbb{N}_0^s} |\widehat{K}(\boldsymbol{k}, \boldsymbol{k})| < \infty$, it follows from the Walsh series expansion (13.14) of K_{scr} and from Section A.3 that K_{scr} coincides with its Walsh series at all points in $[0,1)^{2s}$. It remains to show that (13.14) is the Walsh series for K_{scr}.

Using the definition of the scramble invariant kernel, we have

$$\begin{aligned} \widehat{K}_{\mathrm{scr}}(\boldsymbol{k}, \boldsymbol{k}') &:= \int_{[0,1]^{2s}} K_{\mathrm{scr}}(\boldsymbol{x}, \boldsymbol{x}') \overline{{}_b\mathrm{wal}_{\boldsymbol{k}}(\boldsymbol{x})}\, {}_b\mathrm{wal}_{\boldsymbol{k}'}(\boldsymbol{x}') \,\mathrm{d}\boldsymbol{x} \,\mathrm{d}\boldsymbol{x}' \\ &= \int_{[0,1]^{2s}} \mathbb{E}_{\Pi} \left[K(\boldsymbol{x}_{\Pi}, \boldsymbol{x}'_{\Pi}) \right] \overline{{}_b\mathrm{wal}_{\boldsymbol{k}}(\boldsymbol{x})}\, {}_b\mathrm{wal}_{\boldsymbol{k}'}(\boldsymbol{x}') \,\mathrm{d}\boldsymbol{x} \,\mathrm{d}\boldsymbol{x}' \\ &= \mathbb{E}_{\Pi} \left[\int_{[0,1]^{2s}} K(\boldsymbol{x}_{\Pi}, \boldsymbol{x}'_{\Pi}) \overline{{}_b\mathrm{wal}_{\boldsymbol{k}}(\boldsymbol{x})}\, {}_b\mathrm{wal}_{\boldsymbol{k}'}(\boldsymbol{x}') \,\mathrm{d}\boldsymbol{x} \,\mathrm{d}\boldsymbol{x}' \right] \\ &= \mathbb{E}_{\Pi} \left[\int_{[0,1]^{2s}} K(\boldsymbol{x}, \boldsymbol{x}') \overline{{}_b\mathrm{wal}_{\boldsymbol{k}}(\boldsymbol{x}_{\Pi})}\, {}_b\mathrm{wal}_{\boldsymbol{k}'}(\boldsymbol{x}'_{\Pi}) \,\mathrm{d}\boldsymbol{x} \,\mathrm{d}\boldsymbol{x}' \right] \\ &= \int_{[0,1]^{2s}} K(\boldsymbol{x}, \boldsymbol{x}') \mathbb{E}_{\Pi} \left[\overline{{}_b\mathrm{wal}_{\boldsymbol{k}}(\boldsymbol{x}_{\Pi})}\, {}_b\mathrm{wal}_{\boldsymbol{k}'}(\boldsymbol{x}'_{\Pi}) \right] \mathrm{d}\boldsymbol{x} \,\mathrm{d}\boldsymbol{x}', \end{aligned}$$

where we used Corollary 13.13 and Remark 13.11. Lemma 13.3 implies that $\widehat{K}_{\mathrm{scr}}(\boldsymbol{k}, \boldsymbol{k}') = 0$ for $\boldsymbol{k} \neq \boldsymbol{k}'$.

Using Lemma 13.3, we obtain, as in the proof of Corollary 13.4, that for $\boldsymbol{k} = (\boldsymbol{k}_{\mathfrak{u}}, \boldsymbol{0}) \in L_{(\boldsymbol{\ell}, \boldsymbol{0})}$, where $\boldsymbol{\ell}_{\mathfrak{u}} \in \mathbb{N}^{|\mathfrak{u}|}$, we have

$$\begin{aligned}
&\mathbb{E}_{\Pi}\left[{}_b\mathrm{wal}_{\boldsymbol{k}}(\boldsymbol{x}_{\Pi})\, \overline{{}_b\mathrm{wal}_{\boldsymbol{k}}(\boldsymbol{x}'_{\Pi})}\right] \\
&= \prod_{i \in \mathfrak{u}} \left(\frac{b}{b-1} \chi_{\lfloor b^{\ell_i} x_i \rfloor = \lfloor b^{\ell_i} x'_i \rfloor} - \frac{1}{b-1} \chi_{\lfloor b^{\ell_i - 1} x_i \rfloor = \lfloor b^{\ell_i - 1} x'_i \rfloor} \right) \\
&= \sum_{\mathfrak{v} \subseteq \mathfrak{u}} \frac{(-1)^{|\mathfrak{u}|-|\mathfrak{v}|} b^{|\mathfrak{v}|}}{(b-1)^{|\mathfrak{u}|}} \prod_{i \in \mathfrak{v}} \chi_{\lfloor b^{\ell_i} x_i \rfloor = \lfloor b^{\ell_i} x'_i \rfloor} \prod_{i \in \mathfrak{u} \setminus \mathfrak{v}} \chi_{\lfloor b^{\ell_i - 1} x_i \rfloor = \lfloor b^{\ell_i - 1} x'_i \rfloor} \\
&= \sum_{\mathfrak{v} \subseteq \mathfrak{u}} \frac{(-1)^{|\mathfrak{u}|-|\mathfrak{v}|} b^{|\mathfrak{v}|}}{(b-1)^{|\mathfrak{u}|}} \frac{1}{|R_{\boldsymbol{\ell}_{\mathfrak{u}}, \mathfrak{v}}|} \sum_{\boldsymbol{h} \in R_{\boldsymbol{\ell}_{\mathfrak{u}}, \mathfrak{v}}} {}_b\mathrm{wal}_{\boldsymbol{h}}(\boldsymbol{x} \ominus \boldsymbol{x}') \\
&= \frac{b^{|\mathfrak{u}|}}{b^{|\boldsymbol{\ell}|_1}(b-1)^{|\mathfrak{u}|}} \sum_{\mathfrak{v} \subseteq \mathfrak{u}} (-1)^{|\mathfrak{u}|-|\mathfrak{v}|} \sum_{\boldsymbol{h} \in R_{\boldsymbol{\ell}_{\mathfrak{u}}, \mathfrak{v}}} {}_b\mathrm{wal}_{\boldsymbol{h}}(\boldsymbol{x} \ominus \boldsymbol{x}').
\end{aligned}$$

Therefore,

$$\begin{aligned}
K_{\mathrm{scr}}(\boldsymbol{x}, \boldsymbol{x}') = &\sum_{\mathfrak{u} \subseteq \mathcal{I}_s} \sum_{\boldsymbol{\ell}_{\mathfrak{u}} \in \mathbb{N}^{|\mathfrak{u}|}} \sum_{\boldsymbol{k} \in L_{(\boldsymbol{\ell}_{\mathfrak{u}}, \boldsymbol{0})}} \widehat{K}(\boldsymbol{k}, \boldsymbol{k}) \\
&\times \frac{b^{|\mathfrak{u}|}}{b^{|\boldsymbol{\ell}|_1}(b-1)^{|\mathfrak{u}|}} \sum_{\mathfrak{v} \subseteq \mathfrak{u}} (-1)^{|\mathfrak{u}|-|\mathfrak{v}|} \sum_{\boldsymbol{h} \in R_{\boldsymbol{\ell}_{\mathfrak{u}}, \mathfrak{v}}} {}_b\mathrm{wal}_{\boldsymbol{h}}(\boldsymbol{x} \ominus \boldsymbol{x}'),
\end{aligned}$$

which implies the result. □

For a point set $\mathcal{P} = \{\boldsymbol{x}_0, \ldots, \boldsymbol{x}_{N-1}\}$ in $[0, 1)^s$, let $\mathcal{P}_{\mathrm{scr}} = \{\boldsymbol{y}_0, \ldots, \boldsymbol{y}_{N-1}\}$ be an Owen scrambled version of $\mathcal{P}$.

The *mean square worst-case error* $\widehat{e}^2_{\mathrm{scr}}(\mathscr{H}, \mathcal{P})$ over all Owen scrambled versions of $\mathcal{P}$ is defined by

$$\widehat{e}^2_{\mathrm{scr}}(\mathscr{H}, \mathcal{P}) := \mathbb{E}[e^2(\mathscr{H}, \mathcal{P}_{\mathrm{scr}})],$$

where $e^2(\mathscr{H}, \mathcal{P}_{\mathrm{scr}})$ is the worst-case error (see Definition 2.10) in the reproducing kernel Hilbert space $\mathscr{H}$ for a QMC rule based on the quadrature points $\mathcal{P}_{\mathrm{scr}}$.

In the following theorem, we show that the mean square worst-case error for integration in a reproducing kernel Hilbert space with kernel K is the same as the worst-case error for integration in the reproducing kernel Hilbert space with kernel K_{scr}, the associated scramble invariant kernel. To stress the dependence on the reproducing kernel K, we write in the following $e(K, \mathcal{P})$ and $\widehat{e}^2_{\mathrm{scr}}(K, \mathcal{P})$ instead of $e(\mathscr{H}, \mathcal{P})$ and $\widehat{e}^2_{\mathrm{scr}}(\mathscr{H}, \mathcal{P})$.

Theorem 13.17 *For any reproducing kernel $K \in L_2([0,1]^{2s})$, which can be represented by a Walsh series, and point set $\mathcal{P}$, we have*

$$\widehat{e}^2_{\text{scr}}(K,\mathcal{P}) = \mathbb{E}_\Pi[e^2(K,\mathcal{P}_{\text{scr}})] = e^2(K_{\text{scr}},\mathcal{P}).$$

Proof According to Proposition 2.11, we have

$$e^2(K,\mathcal{P}) = \int_{[0,1]^{2s}} K(\boldsymbol{x},\boldsymbol{y})\,\mathrm{d}\boldsymbol{x}\,\mathrm{d}\boldsymbol{y} - \frac{2}{N}\sum_{n=0}^{N-1}\int_{[0,1]^s} K(\boldsymbol{x}_n,\boldsymbol{y})\,\mathrm{d}\boldsymbol{y} + \frac{1}{N^2}\sum_{n,m=0}^{N-1} K(\boldsymbol{x}_n,\boldsymbol{x}_m).$$

Therefore, we have

$$\begin{aligned}
&\mathbb{E}_\Pi\left[e^2(K,\mathcal{P}_{\text{scr}})\right]\\
&= \int_{[0,1]^{2s}} K(\boldsymbol{x},\boldsymbol{y})\,\mathrm{d}\boldsymbol{x}\,\mathrm{d}\boldsymbol{y} - \frac{2}{N}\sum_{n=0}^{N-1}\mathbb{E}_\Pi\left[\int_{[0,1]^s} K(\boldsymbol{x}_{n,\Pi},\boldsymbol{x})\,\mathrm{d}\boldsymbol{x}\right]\\
&\quad + \frac{1}{N^2}\sum_{n,m=0}^{N-1}\mathbb{E}_\Pi\left[K(\boldsymbol{x}_{n,\Pi},\boldsymbol{x}_{m,\Pi})\right].
\end{aligned}$$

Let the reproducing kernel K be represented by a Walsh series

$$K(\boldsymbol{x},\boldsymbol{y}) = \sum_{\boldsymbol{k},\boldsymbol{k}'\in\mathbb{N}_0^s} \widehat{K}(\boldsymbol{k},\boldsymbol{k}')\,{}_b\mathrm{wal}_{\boldsymbol{k}}(\boldsymbol{x})\,{}_b\mathrm{wal}_{\boldsymbol{k}'}(\boldsymbol{y}).$$

Note that Lemma 13.15 not only applies to the one-dimensional case but in any dimension, since the permutations in different coordinates are chosen independently from each other. Hence, by the first part of Lemma 13.15, we have

$$\begin{aligned}
&\int_{[0,1]^{2s}} K(\boldsymbol{x},\boldsymbol{y})\,\mathrm{d}\boldsymbol{x}\,\mathrm{d}\boldsymbol{y}\\
&= \sum_{\boldsymbol{k},\boldsymbol{k}'\in\mathbb{N}_0^s} \widehat{K}(\boldsymbol{k},\boldsymbol{k}')\int_{[0,1]^{2s}} {}_b\mathrm{wal}_{\boldsymbol{k}}(\boldsymbol{x})\,\overline{{}_b\mathrm{wal}_{\boldsymbol{k}'}(\boldsymbol{y})}\,\mathrm{d}\boldsymbol{x}\,\mathrm{d}\boldsymbol{y}\\
&= \sum_{\boldsymbol{k},\boldsymbol{k}'\in\mathbb{N}_0^s} \widehat{K}(\boldsymbol{k},\boldsymbol{k}')\int_{[0,1]^{2s}} \mathbb{E}_\Pi\left[{}_b\mathrm{wal}_{\boldsymbol{k}}(\boldsymbol{x}_\Pi)\,\overline{{}_b\mathrm{wal}_{\boldsymbol{k}'}(\boldsymbol{y}_\Pi)}\right]\mathrm{d}\boldsymbol{x}\,\mathrm{d}\boldsymbol{y}\\
&= \int_{[0,1]^{2s}} \mathbb{E}_\Pi\left[K(\boldsymbol{x}_\Pi,\boldsymbol{y}_\Pi)\right]\mathrm{d}\boldsymbol{x}\,\mathrm{d}\boldsymbol{y}.
\end{aligned}$$

By the second part of Lemma 13.15, we have

$$\begin{aligned}
&\mathbb{E}_\Pi\left[\int_{[0,1]^s} K(\boldsymbol{x}_{n,\Pi}, \boldsymbol{x})\,\mathrm{d}\boldsymbol{x}\right] \\
&= \sum_{\boldsymbol{k},\boldsymbol{k}'\in\mathbb{N}_0^s} \widehat{K}(\boldsymbol{k},\boldsymbol{k}')\,\mathbb{E}_\Pi\left[\int_{[0,1]^s} {}_b\mathrm{wal}_{\boldsymbol{k}}(\boldsymbol{x}_{n,\Pi})\,\overline{{}_b\mathrm{wal}_{\boldsymbol{k}'}(\boldsymbol{x})}\,\mathrm{d}\boldsymbol{x}\right] \\
&= \sum_{\boldsymbol{k},\boldsymbol{k}'\in\mathbb{N}_0^s} \widehat{K}(\boldsymbol{k},\boldsymbol{k}')\int_{[0,1]^s} \mathbb{E}_\Pi\left[{}_b\mathrm{wal}_{\boldsymbol{k}}(\boldsymbol{x}_{n,\Pi})\,\overline{{}_b\mathrm{wal}_{\boldsymbol{k}'}(\boldsymbol{x}_\Pi)}\right]\mathrm{d}\boldsymbol{x} \\
&= \int_{[0,1]^s} \mathbb{E}_\Pi\left[K(\boldsymbol{x}_{n,\Pi}, \boldsymbol{x}_\Pi)\right]\mathrm{d}\boldsymbol{x}.
\end{aligned}$$

Hence, we have

$$\begin{aligned}
&\mathbb{E}_\Pi\left[e^2(K, \mathcal{P}_{\mathrm{scr}})\right] \\
&= \int_{[0,1]^{2s}} \mathbb{E}_\Pi[K(\boldsymbol{x}_\Pi, \boldsymbol{y}_\Pi)]\,\mathrm{d}\boldsymbol{x}\,\mathrm{d}\boldsymbol{y} - \frac{2}{N}\sum_{n=0}^{N-1}\int_{[0,1]^s} \mathbb{E}_\Pi\left[K(\boldsymbol{x}_{n,\Pi}, \boldsymbol{x}_\Pi)\right]\mathrm{d}\boldsymbol{x} \\
&\quad + \frac{1}{N^2}\sum_{n,m=0}^{N-1} K_{\mathrm{scr}}(\boldsymbol{x}_n, \boldsymbol{x}_m) \\
&= \int_{[0,1]^{2s}} K_{\mathrm{scr}}(\boldsymbol{x}, \boldsymbol{y})\,\mathrm{d}\boldsymbol{x}\,\mathrm{d}\boldsymbol{y} - \frac{2}{N}\sum_{n=0}^{N-1}\int_{[0,1]^s} K_{\mathrm{scr}}(\boldsymbol{x}_n, \boldsymbol{x})\,\mathrm{d}\boldsymbol{x} \\
&\quad + \frac{1}{N^2}\sum_{n,m=0}^{N-1} K_{\mathrm{scr}}(\boldsymbol{x}_n, \boldsymbol{x}_m),
\end{aligned}$$

and the result follows. □

13.4.2 The scramble invariant kernel for $\mathscr{H}_{\mathrm{sob},s,\boldsymbol{\gamma}}$

In the following theorem, we determine the scramble invariant kernel in base $b \geq 2$ for the reproducing kernel K of the weighted Sobolev space $\mathscr{H}_{\mathrm{sob},s,\boldsymbol{\gamma}}$ (see Section 12.2). Notice that the reproducing kernel given by (12.1) is continuous, since B_2 is one-periodic. From Section A.3 (see also Exercise A.9) we therefore know that the kernel K and its Walsh series coincide at all points of the domain.

Proposition 13.18 *Let K be the reproducing kernel given by (12.1). Then, the corresponding scramble invariant kernel in prime base $b \geq 2$ is given by*

$$K_{\mathrm{scr}}(\boldsymbol{x}, \boldsymbol{y}) = \sum_{\mathfrak{u} \subseteq \mathcal{I}_s} \sum_{\boldsymbol{\ell}_{\mathfrak{u}} \in \mathbb{N}^{|\mathfrak{u}|}} \sum_{\boldsymbol{k} \in L_{(\boldsymbol{\ell}_{\mathfrak{u}}, \boldsymbol{0})}} r_{\mathrm{sob},b}(\boldsymbol{k}, \boldsymbol{\gamma})$$
$$\times \frac{b^{|\mathfrak{u}|}}{b^{|\boldsymbol{\ell}|_1}(b-1)^{|\mathfrak{u}|}} \sum_{\mathfrak{v} \subseteq \mathfrak{u}} (-1)^{|\mathfrak{u}|-|\mathfrak{v}|} \sum_{\boldsymbol{h} \in R_{\boldsymbol{\ell}_{\mathfrak{u}}, \mathfrak{v}}} {}_b\mathrm{wal}_{\boldsymbol{h}}(\boldsymbol{x} \ominus \boldsymbol{y}),$$

where $L_{\boldsymbol{\ell}} = \{\boldsymbol{k} = (k_1, \ldots, k_s) \in \mathbb{N}_0^s : \lfloor b^{\ell_i - 1} \rfloor \leq k_i < b^{\ell_i}$ for $1 \leq i \leq s\}$, $R_{\boldsymbol{\ell}_{\mathfrak{u}}, \mathfrak{v}} = \{\boldsymbol{h} \in \mathbb{N}_0^s : 0 \leq h_i < b^{\ell_i}$ for $i \in \mathfrak{v}$ and $0 \leq h_i < b^{\ell_i - 1}$ for $i \in \mathfrak{u} \setminus \mathfrak{v}$, and $h_i = 0$ for $i \in \mathcal{I}_s \setminus \mathfrak{u}\}$, and with $r_{\mathrm{sob},b}(\boldsymbol{k}, \boldsymbol{\gamma}) = \prod_{i=1}^s r_{\mathrm{sob},b}(k_i, \gamma_i)$, where, for $k = \kappa_0 + \kappa_1 b + \cdots + \kappa_{a-1} b^{a-1}$ with $\kappa_{a-1} \neq 0$, we define

$$r_{\mathrm{sob},b}(k, \gamma) = \begin{cases} 1 & \text{if } k = 0, \\ \frac{\gamma}{2b^{2a}} \left(\frac{1}{\sin^2(\kappa_{a-1}\pi/b)} - \frac{1}{3} \right) & \text{if } k > 0. \end{cases}$$

The proof follows from Lemma 13.16, Lemma 12.2 and Proposition 12.5.

In the next proposition, we show how the scramble invariant kernel can be simplified. For $x = \xi_1/b + \xi_2/b^2 + \cdots$ and $y = \eta_1/b + \eta_2/b^2 + \cdots$ we define

$$\phi_{\mathrm{scr}}(x, y) = \begin{cases} \frac{1}{6} & \text{if } x = y, \\ \frac{1}{6}\left(1 - (b+1)b^{-i_0}\right) & \text{if } \xi_{i_0} \neq \eta_{i_0} \\ & \text{and } \xi_i = \eta_i \text{ for } i = 1, \ldots, i_0 - 1. \end{cases} \tag{13.15}$$

Proposition 13.19 *Let K be the reproducing kernel given by (12.1). Then the corresponding scramble invariant kernel in prime base $b \geq 2$ is given by*

$$K_{\mathrm{scr}}(\boldsymbol{x}, \boldsymbol{y}) = \prod_{i=1}^{s} (1 + \gamma_i \phi_{\mathrm{scr}}(x_i, y_i))$$

for $\boldsymbol{x} = (x_1, \ldots, x_s)$ and $\boldsymbol{y} = (y_1, \ldots, y_s)$.

Proof From Proposition 13.18, we have

$$K_{\mathrm{scr}}(\boldsymbol{x}, \boldsymbol{y}) = \sum_{\mathfrak{u} \subseteq \mathcal{I}_s} \sum_{\boldsymbol{\ell}_{\mathfrak{u}} \in \mathbb{N}^{|\mathfrak{u}|}} \sum_{\boldsymbol{k} \in L_{(\boldsymbol{\ell}_{\mathfrak{u}}, \boldsymbol{0})}} r_{\mathrm{sob},b}(\boldsymbol{k}, \boldsymbol{\gamma})$$
$$\times \prod_{i \in \mathfrak{u}} \left(\frac{b}{b-1} \chi_{\lfloor b^{\ell_i} x_i \rfloor = \lfloor b^{\ell_i} y_i \rfloor} - \frac{1}{b-1} \chi_{\lfloor b^{\ell_i - 1} x_i \rfloor - \lfloor b^{\ell_i - 1} y_i \rfloor} \right).$$

Now

$$\sum_{\boldsymbol{k}\in L_{(\boldsymbol{\ell}_{\mathfrak{u}},0)}} r_{\mathrm{sob},b}(\boldsymbol{k},\boldsymbol{\gamma}) = \prod_{i\in\mathfrak{u}} \sum_{k_i=b^{\ell_i-1}}^{b^{\ell_i}-1} r_{\mathrm{sob},b}(k_i,\gamma_i).$$

Using the identity $\sum_{\kappa=1}^{b-1}\sin^{-2}(\kappa\pi/b) = (b^2-1)/3$, given in Corollary A.23, we obtain

$$\begin{aligned}
\sum_{k_i=b^{\ell_i-1}}^{b^{\ell_i}-1} r_{\mathrm{sob},b}(k_i,\gamma_i) &= \frac{\gamma_i}{2b^{2\ell_i}} \sum_{k_i=b^{\ell_i-1}}^{b^{\ell_i}-1}\left(\frac{1}{\sin^2(\kappa_{i,\ell_i-1}\pi/b)} - \frac{1}{3}\right)\\
&= \frac{\gamma_i}{2b^{\ell_i+1}}\left(\frac{b^2-1}{3} - \frac{b-1}{3}\right)\\
&= \frac{\gamma_i}{6b^{\ell_i}}(b-1).
\end{aligned}$$

Therefore,

$$\begin{aligned}
K_{\mathrm{scr}}(\boldsymbol{x},\boldsymbol{y}) &= \sum_{\mathfrak{u}\subseteq\mathcal{I}_s}\prod_{i\in\mathfrak{u}}\frac{\gamma_i}{6}\sum_{\boldsymbol{\ell}_{\mathfrak{u}}\in\mathbb{N}^{|\mathfrak{u}|}} b^{-|\boldsymbol{\ell}_{\mathfrak{u}}|_1}\prod_{i\in\mathfrak{u}}\left(b\chi_{\lfloor b^{\ell_i}x_i\rfloor=\lfloor b^{\ell_i}y_i\rfloor} - \chi_{\lfloor b^{\ell_i-1}x_i\rfloor=\lfloor b^{\ell_i-1}y_i\rfloor}\right)\\
&= \sum_{\mathfrak{u}\subseteq\mathcal{I}_s}\prod_{i\in\mathfrak{u}}\frac{\gamma_i}{6}\left[\sum_{\ell_i=1}^{\infty} b^{-\ell_i}\left(b\chi_{\lfloor b^{\ell_i}x_i\rfloor=\lfloor b^{\ell_i}y_i\rfloor} - \chi_{\lfloor b^{\ell_i-1}x_i\rfloor=\lfloor b^{\ell_i-1}y_i\rfloor}\right)\right]\\
&= \sum_{\mathfrak{u}\subseteq\mathcal{I}_s}\prod_{i\in\mathfrak{u}}\frac{\gamma_i}{6}\left[-\frac{1}{b} + \left(1-\frac{1}{b^2}\right)\sum_{\ell_i=1}^{\infty} b^{-\ell_i+1}\chi_{\lfloor b^{\ell_i}x_i\rfloor=\lfloor b^{\ell_i}y_i\rfloor}\right].
\end{aligned}$$

If $x_i = y_i$, then

$$\sum_{\ell_i=1}^{\infty} b^{-\ell_i+1}\chi_{\lfloor b^{\ell_i}x_i\rfloor=\lfloor b^{\ell_i}y_i\rfloor} = \sum_{\ell_i=1}^{\infty} b^{-\ell_i+1} = \frac{1}{1-b^{-1}}$$

and

$$\frac{\gamma_i}{6}\left[-\frac{1}{b} + \left(1-\frac{1}{b^2}\right)\sum_{\ell_i=1}^{\infty} b^{-\ell_i+1}\chi_{\lfloor b^{\ell_i}x_i\rfloor=\lfloor b^{\ell_i}y_i\rfloor}\right] = \frac{\gamma_i}{6} = \gamma_i\phi_{\mathrm{scr}}(x_i,y_i).$$

If $x_i \neq y_i$, then the sum $\sum_{\ell_i=1}^{\infty} b^{-\ell_i+1}\chi_{\lfloor b^{\ell_i}x_i\rfloor=\lfloor b^{\ell_i}y_i\rfloor}$ is finite as $\chi_{\lfloor b^{\ell_i}x_i\rfloor=\lfloor b^{\ell_i}y_i\rfloor} = 0$ for ℓ_i big enough. Let $j_0 = 0$ if $\chi_{\lfloor bx_i\rfloor=\lfloor by_i\rfloor} = 0$, otherwise let $j_0 \geq 1$ be the largest value of ℓ_i such that $\chi_{\lfloor b^{\ell_i} x_i \rfloor = \lfloor b^{\ell_i} y_i \rfloor} = 1$. Then

$$-\frac{1}{b} + \left(1 - \frac{1}{b^2}\right) \sum_{\ell_i=1}^{\infty} b^{-\ell_i+1} \chi_{\lfloor b^{\ell_i} x_i \rfloor = \lfloor b^{\ell_i} y_i \rfloor} = -\frac{1}{b} + \left(1 - \frac{1}{b^2}\right) \sum_{\ell_i=1}^{j_0} b^{-\ell_i+1}$$
$$= 1 - \frac{b+1}{b^{j_0+1}}.$$

If the first $i_0 - 1$ digits in the b-adic expansions of x_i and y_i coincide and the i_0th digits differ, then we have $j_0 = i_0 - 1$ and hence, we obtain

$$\frac{\gamma_i}{6}\left[-\frac{1}{b} + \left(1 - \frac{1}{b^2}\right) \sum_{\ell_i=1}^{\infty} b^{-\ell_i+1} \chi_{\lfloor b^{\ell_i} x_i \rfloor = \lfloor b^{\ell_i} y_i \rfloor}\right] = \frac{\gamma_i}{6}\left(1 - \frac{b+1}{b^{i_0}}\right)$$
$$= \gamma_i \phi_{\mathrm{scr}}(x_i, y_i).$$

Thus, it follows that

$$K_{\mathrm{scr}}(\boldsymbol{x}, \boldsymbol{y}) = \sum_{\mathfrak{u} \subseteq \mathcal{I}_s} \prod_{i \in \mathfrak{u}} \gamma_i \phi_{\mathrm{scr}}(x_i, y_i) = \prod_{i=1}^{s} (1 + \gamma_i \phi_{\mathrm{scr}}(x_i, y_i)). \qquad \square$$

13.4.3 A formula for the mean square worst-case error

Using Theorem 13.17 and the representation of the scramble invariant kernel, we can now give a formula for the mean square worst-case error for a QMC rule in the weighted Sobolev space $\mathscr{H}_{\mathrm{sob},s,\boldsymbol{\gamma}}$ by using a scrambled point set.

Theorem 13.20 *Let $\mathscr{H}_{\mathrm{sob},s,\boldsymbol{\gamma}}$ be the Sobolev space defined in Section 12.2. Let $b \geq 2$ be a prime number. The mean square worst-case error $\widehat{e}^2_{\mathrm{scr}}(\mathscr{H}_{\mathrm{sob},s,\boldsymbol{\gamma}}, \mathcal{P})$ in the weighted Sobolev space $\mathscr{H}_{\mathrm{sob},s,\boldsymbol{\gamma}}$ using a QMC rule based on the randomly scrambled point set $\mathcal{P} = \{\boldsymbol{x}_0, \ldots, \boldsymbol{x}_{N-1}\}$, with $\boldsymbol{x}_n = (x_{n,1}, \ldots, x_{n,s})$, is given by*

$$\widehat{e}^2_{\mathrm{scr}}(\mathscr{H}_{\mathrm{sob},s,\boldsymbol{\gamma}}, \mathcal{P}) = -1 + \frac{1}{N^2} \sum_{n,m=0}^{N-1} \sum_{\mathfrak{u} \subseteq \mathcal{I}_s} \sum_{\boldsymbol{\ell}_{\mathfrak{u}} \in \mathbb{N}^{|\mathfrak{u}|}} \sum_{\boldsymbol{k} \in L_{(\boldsymbol{\ell}_{\mathfrak{u}}, \boldsymbol{0})}} r_{\mathrm{sob},b}(\boldsymbol{k}, \boldsymbol{\gamma})$$
$$\times \frac{b^{|\mathfrak{u}|}}{b^{|\boldsymbol{\ell}|_1}(b-1)^{|\mathfrak{u}|}} \sum_{\mathfrak{v} \subseteq \mathfrak{u}} (-1)^{|\mathfrak{u}|-|\mathfrak{v}|} \sum_{\boldsymbol{h} \in R_{\boldsymbol{\ell}_{\mathfrak{u}}, \mathfrak{v}}} {}_b\mathrm{wal}_{\boldsymbol{h}}(\boldsymbol{x}_n \ominus \boldsymbol{x}_m)$$
$$= -1 + \frac{1}{N^2} \sum_{n,m=0}^{N-1} \prod_{i=1}^{s} (1 + \gamma_i \phi_{\mathrm{scr}}(x_{n,i}, x_{m,i})),$$

where the function ϕ_{scr} is given by (13.15).

Proof From Theorem 13.17 and from Proposition 2.11, we obtain that

$$\begin{aligned}\widehat{e}^2_{\mathrm{scr}}(\mathcal{H}_{\mathrm{sob},s,\boldsymbol{\gamma}}, \mathcal{P}) &= e^2(K_{\mathrm{scr}}, \mathcal{P}) \\ &= \int_{[0,1]^{2s}} K_{\mathrm{scr}}(\boldsymbol{x}, \boldsymbol{y}) \,\mathrm{d}\boldsymbol{x} \,\mathrm{d}\boldsymbol{y} - \frac{2}{N} \sum_{n=0}^{N-1} \int_{[0,1]^s} K_{\mathrm{scr}}(\boldsymbol{x}_n, \boldsymbol{y}) \,\mathrm{d}\boldsymbol{y} \\ &\quad + \frac{1}{N^2} \sum_{n,m=0}^{N-1} K_{\mathrm{scr}}(\boldsymbol{x}_n, \boldsymbol{x}_m) \\ &= -1 + \frac{1}{N^2} \sum_{n,m=0}^{N-1} K_{\mathrm{scr}}(\boldsymbol{x}_n, \boldsymbol{x}_m),\end{aligned}$$

as $\int_{[0,1]^s} K_{\mathrm{scr}}(\boldsymbol{x}, \boldsymbol{y}) \,\mathrm{d}\boldsymbol{x} = \int_{[0,1]^s} K_{\mathrm{scr}}(\boldsymbol{x}, \boldsymbol{y}) \,\mathrm{d}\boldsymbol{y} = 1$, which follows from Proposition 13.18 together with the orthogonality properties of the Walsh functions (see Proposition A.10). Now the desired result follows from Proposition 13.18 and Proposition 13.19. □

For all $x, y \in [0, 1)$ and all $w \in [0, 1]$, we have that

$$\phi_{\mathrm{scr}}(x, y) \leq \phi_{\mathrm{ds},w}(x, y),$$

where $\phi_{\mathrm{ds},w}(x, y)$ is defined as in Exercise 12.4 and which is related to the digital shift invariant kernel K'_{ds} of the weighted anchored Sobolev space $\mathcal{H}'_{\mathrm{sob},s,\boldsymbol{w},\boldsymbol{\gamma}}$ from Exercise 12.3 via (12.34). Comparing Theorem 13.20 to the result from Exercise 12.5, we therefore obtain that

$$\widehat{e}^2_{\mathrm{scr}}(\mathcal{H}_{\mathrm{sob},s,\boldsymbol{\gamma}}, \mathcal{P}) \leq \widehat{e}^2_{\mathrm{ds}}(\mathcal{H}'_{\mathrm{sob},s,\boldsymbol{w},\boldsymbol{\gamma}}, \mathcal{P}).$$

Hence, all results for $\widehat{e}^2_{\mathrm{ds}}(\mathcal{H}'_{\mathrm{sob},s,\boldsymbol{w},\boldsymbol{\gamma}}, \mathcal{P})$ from Exercises 12.8, 12.11 and 12.12 apply in the same way to $\widehat{e}^2_{\mathrm{scr}}(\mathcal{H}_{\mathrm{sob},s,\boldsymbol{\gamma}}, \mathcal{P})$.

13.5 Improved rate of convergence for smooth functions

The advantage of scrambling compared to a random digital shift lies in the fact that, for smooth integrands, one can obtain an improved rate of convergence. Owen [208] first showed that scrambling can yield a convergence of $O(N^{-3/2+\delta})$ for any $\delta > 0$ (here, N^δ stands for $\log N$ to some power). This was further improved in [211] to $O(N^{-3/2-1/s+\delta})$ for any $\delta > 0$. Rates of convergence of $O(N^{-2+\delta})$ for any $\delta > 0$ can be achieved by using a random shift together with the tent transformation; see [27, 104].

We prove the result for the one-dimensional case first. Let $f : [0, 1] \to \mathbb{R}$. In order to obtain an improved rate of convergence, we require that f has some smoothness. Owen [208] assumes that the first derivative satisfies a Hölder condition of some order $0 < \alpha \le 1$, whereas Yue and Hickernell [271] only assume that the mixed partial first derivatives up to order one in each variable are square integrable. Owen [211], on the other hand, assumes that the first derivative is continuous. The smoothness assumptions here are based on the integral modulus of continuity.

For a function $f : [0, 1] \to \mathbb{R}$, $f \in L_2([0, 1])$ and $0 < \delta < 1$, we define the *integral modulus of continuity* by

$$M_{f,2}(\delta) = \sup_{0 \le h \le \delta} \left(\int_0^{1-h} |f(x+h) - f(x)|^2 \, \mathrm{d}x \right)^{1/2}.$$

Assume, for instance, that f satisfies a Hölder condition; that is, there is some $0 < \alpha \le 1$ and a constant $C_f > 0$ which only depends on f, such that $|f(x + h) - f(x)| \le C_f h^\alpha$ for all $h > 0$ and x such that $x, x + h \in [0, 1]$. Then, the integral modulus of continuity satisfies

$$M_{f,2}(\delta) \le C_f \delta^\alpha.$$

The main property in obtaining an improved rate of convergence is an improved bound on $\sigma_\ell^2 = \sum_{k=b^{\ell-1}}^{b^\ell - 1} |\widehat{f}(k)|^2$. We show below that

$$\sigma_\ell^2(f) \le (b-1) M_{f,2}^2((b-1)b^{-\ell}) \quad \text{for all } \ell \in \mathbb{N},$$

from which we obtain the following corollary.

Corollary 13.21 *Let $f : [0, 1] \to \mathbb{R}$ satisfy a Hölder condition of order $0 < \alpha \le 1$. Then, for any $\ell \in \mathbb{N}$, we have*

$$\sigma_\ell^2(f) \le C_f^2 (b-1)^{1+2\alpha} b^{-2\alpha\ell},$$

where $C_f > 0$ does not depend on ℓ.

From Theorem 13.5 and Corollary 13.21, we now obtain the following result on the variance of the estimate $\widehat{I}(f)$.

Theorem 13.22 *Let $f : [0, 1] \to \mathbb{R}$ satisfy a Hölder condition of order $0 < \alpha \le 1$ with constant $C_f > 0$. Then, the variance of the estimate $\widehat{I}(f)$, which is based on a scrambled $(t, m, 1)$-net in base b, satisfies*

$$\mathrm{Var}[\widehat{I}(f)] \le b^{-(1+2\alpha)(m-t)} C_f^2 \frac{(b-1)^{1+2\alpha}}{b^{2\alpha} - 1}.$$

If $N = b^m$ denotes the number of points, then we can expect a convergence $\sqrt{\mathrm{Var}[\widehat{I}(f)]} \approx N^{-(1+2\alpha)/2}$ in probability. If $\alpha = 1$, then f satisfies a Lipschitz condition. In this case, we obtain $\sqrt{\mathrm{Var}[\widehat{I}(f)]} = O(N^{-3/2})$.

Consider now $s > 1$. The main property in obtaining an improved rate of convergence is again a bound on $\sigma_\ell^2(f)$.

A function $f : [0, 1] \to \mathbb{R}$ satisfies a Hölder condition with coefficient $0 < \lambda \leq 1$ if there is a constant $C_f > 0$ such that

$$|f(x) - f(y)| \leq C_f |x - y|^\alpha \quad \text{for all } x, y \in [0, 1].$$

The right-hand side of the above inequality forms a metric on $[0, 1]$. When one considers the higher dimensional domain $[0, 1]^s$ then $|x - y|$ is changed to some other metric on $[0, 1]^s$. Here we consider tensor product spaces and generalise the Hölder condition to higher dimensions in a way which is suitable for tensor product spaces in our context. Consider, for example, the function $f(\boldsymbol{x}) = \prod_{i=1}^s f_i(x_i)$, where $\boldsymbol{x} = (x_1, \ldots, x_s)$ and each $f_i : [0, 1] \to \mathbb{R}$ satisfies a Hölder condition with coefficient $0 < \alpha \leq 1$. Then it follows that for all $\emptyset \neq \mathfrak{u} \subseteq \mathcal{I}_s := \{1, \ldots, s\}$, we have

$$\prod_{i \in \mathfrak{u}} |f_i(x_i) - f_i(y_i)| \leq \prod_{i \in \mathfrak{u}} C_{f_i} \prod_{i \in \mathfrak{u}} |x_i - y_i|^\alpha \tag{13.16}$$

for all $x_i, y_i \in [0, 1]$ with $i \in \mathfrak{u}$. But here $\prod_{i=1}^s |x_i - y_i|$ is not a metric on $[0, 1]^s$.

Note that we have

$$\prod_{i \in \mathfrak{u}} |f_i(x_i) - f_i(y_i)| = \left| \sum_{v \subseteq \mathfrak{u}} (-1)^{|v| - |\mathfrak{u}|} \prod_{i \in v} f_i(x_i) \prod_{i \in \mathfrak{u} \setminus v} f_i(y_i) \right|, \tag{13.17}$$

which can be described in words in the following way: for given $\emptyset \neq \mathfrak{u} \subseteq \mathcal{I}_s$ let $x_i, y_i \in [0, 1]$ with $x_i \neq y_i$ for all $i \in \mathfrak{u}$; consider the box J with vertices $\{(a_i)_{i \in \mathfrak{u}} : a_i = x_i \text{ or } a_i = y_i \text{ for } i \in \mathfrak{u}\}$. Then (13.17) is the alternating sum of the function $\prod_{i \in \mathfrak{u}} f_i$ at the vertices of J where adjacent vertices have opposite signs. This sum can also be defined for functions on $[0, 1]^s$ which are not of product form.

Indeed, for a sub-interval $J = \prod_{i=1}^s [x_i, y_i)$ with $0 \leq x_i < y_i \leq 1$ and a function $f : [0, 1]^s \to \mathbb{R}$, let the function $\Delta(f, J)$ denote the alternating sum of f at the vertices of J where adjacent vertices have opposite signs. (Hence, for $f = \prod_{i=1}^s f_i$ we have $\Delta(f, J) = \prod_{i=1}^s (f_i(x_i) - f_i(y_i))$.)

We define the *generalised variation in the sense of Vitali of order* $0 < \alpha \leq 1$ by

$$V_\alpha^{(s)}(f) = \sup_{\mathcal{P}} \left(\sum_{J \in \mathcal{P}} \mathrm{Vol}(J) \left| \frac{\Delta(f, J)}{\mathrm{Vol}(J)^\alpha} \right|^2 \right)^{1/2},$$

where the supremum is extended over all partitions $\mathcal{P}$ of $[0, 1]^s$ into sub-intervals and $\mathrm{Vol}(J)$ denotes the volume of the sub-interval J.

For $\alpha = 1$ and if the partial derivatives of f are continuous on $[0,1]^s$, we also have the formula

$$V_1^{(s)}(f) = \left(\int_{[0,1]^s} \left| \frac{\partial^s f}{\partial x_1 \cdots \partial x_s}(\boldsymbol{x}) \right|^2 \mathrm{d}\boldsymbol{x} \right)^{1/2}.$$

Indeed, we have

$$|\Delta(f, J)| = \left| \int_J \frac{\partial^s f}{\partial x_1 \cdots \partial x_s}(\boldsymbol{x})\, \mathrm{d}\boldsymbol{x} \right| = \mathrm{Vol}(J) \left| \frac{\partial^s f}{\partial x_1 \cdots \partial x_s}(\boldsymbol{\zeta}_J) \right|$$

for some $\boldsymbol{\zeta}_J \in \overline{J}$, which follows by applying the mean value theorem to the inequality

$$\min_{\boldsymbol{x} \in \overline{J}} \left| \frac{\partial^s f}{\partial x_1 \cdots \partial x_s}(\boldsymbol{x}) \right| \le \mathrm{Vol}(J)^{-1} \left| \int_J \frac{\partial^s f}{\partial x_1 \cdots \partial x_s}(\boldsymbol{x})\, \mathrm{d}\boldsymbol{x} \right| \le \max_{\boldsymbol{x} \in \overline{J}} \left| \frac{\partial^s f}{\partial x_1 \cdots \partial x_s}(\boldsymbol{x}) \right|.$$

Therefore, we have

$$\sum_{J \in \mathcal{P}} \mathrm{Vol}(J) \left| \frac{\Delta(f, J)}{\mathrm{Vol}(J)} \right|^2 = \sum_{J \in \mathcal{P}} \mathrm{Vol}(J) \left| \frac{\partial^s f}{\partial x_1 \cdots \partial x_s}(\boldsymbol{\zeta}_J) \right|^2,$$

which is just a Riemann sum for the integral $\int_{[0,1]^s} \left| \frac{\partial^s f}{\partial x_1 \cdots \partial x_s} \right|^2 \mathrm{d}\boldsymbol{x}$, and thus the equality follows.

Until now we did not take projections to lower dimensional faces into account. For $\emptyset \ne \mathfrak{u} \subseteq \mathcal{I}_s$, let $V_\alpha^{(|\mathfrak{u}|)}(f_{\mathfrak{u}}; \mathfrak{u})$ be the generalised Vitali variation with coefficient $0 < \alpha \le 1$ of the $|\mathfrak{u}|$-dimensional function

$$f_{\mathfrak{u}}(\boldsymbol{x}_{\mathfrak{u}}) = \int_{[0,1]^{s-|\mathfrak{u}|}} f(\boldsymbol{x})\, \mathrm{d}\boldsymbol{x}_{\mathcal{I}_s \setminus \mathfrak{u}}.$$

For $\mathfrak{u} = \emptyset$ we have $f_\emptyset = \int_{[0,1]^s} f(\boldsymbol{x})\, \mathrm{d}\boldsymbol{x}_{\mathcal{I}_s}$ and we define $V_\alpha^{(|\emptyset|)}(f_\emptyset; \emptyset) = |f_\emptyset|$. Then

$$V_\alpha(f) = \left(\sum_{\mathfrak{u} \subseteq \mathcal{I}_s} \left(V_\alpha^{(|\mathfrak{u}|)}(f_{\mathfrak{u}}; \mathfrak{u}) \right)^2 \right)^{1/2} \tag{13.18}$$

is called the *generalised Hardy and Krause variation* of f on $[0,1]^s$.

A function f for which $V_\alpha(f) < \infty$ is said to be of *finite variation of order* α. We are now ready to show how the Walsh coefficients of functions with bounded variation decay.

Lemma 13.23 *Let $f : [0,1]^s \to \mathbb{R}$, $0 < \alpha \le 1$, and let $b \ge 2$. Then for any $\emptyset \ne \mathfrak{u} \subseteq \mathcal{I}_s$ and $\boldsymbol{\ell}_{\mathfrak{u}} = (\ell_i)_{i \in \mathfrak{u}} \in \mathbb{N}^{|\mathfrak{u}|}$ we have*

$$\sigma_{(\boldsymbol{\ell}_{\mathfrak{u}}, \boldsymbol{0})}(f) \le (b-1)^{(\alpha - 1/2)_+ |\mathfrak{u}|} b^{-\alpha |\boldsymbol{\ell}_{\mathfrak{u}}|} V_\alpha(f),$$

where $|\boldsymbol{\ell}_{\mathfrak{u}}|_1 = \sum_{i \in \mathfrak{u}} \ell_i$ and $(\alpha - 1/2)_+ = \max(\alpha - 1/2, 0)$.

Proof We show the result for $\mathfrak{u} = \mathcal{I}_s$ first. Let $\boldsymbol{\ell} = (\ell_1, \ldots, \ell_s) \in \mathbb{N}^s$ and $\boldsymbol{\ell} - \mathbf{1} = (\ell_1 - 1, \ldots, \ell_s - 1) \in \mathbb{N}_0^s$. Let $A_{\boldsymbol{\ell}} = \{\boldsymbol{a} = (a_1, \ldots, a_s) \in \mathbb{N}_0^s : 0 \le a_i < b^{\ell_i}$ for $1 \le i \le s\}$ and $[\boldsymbol{a}b^{-\boldsymbol{\ell}}, (\boldsymbol{a}+\mathbf{1})b^{-\boldsymbol{\ell}}) := \prod_{i=1}^s [a_i b^{-\ell_i}, (a_i+1)b^{-\ell_i})$.

Let $\boldsymbol{x} \in [\boldsymbol{a}b^{-\boldsymbol{\ell}}, (\boldsymbol{a}+\mathbf{1})b^{-\boldsymbol{\ell}})$, then

$$\begin{aligned}\sum_{\boldsymbol{k} \in A_{\boldsymbol{\ell}}} \widehat{f}(\boldsymbol{k})\, {}_b\mathrm{wal}_{\boldsymbol{k}}(\boldsymbol{x}) &= \int_{[0,1]^s} f(\boldsymbol{t}) \sum_{\boldsymbol{k} \in A_{\boldsymbol{\ell}}} {}_b\mathrm{wal}_{\boldsymbol{k}}(\boldsymbol{x} \ominus \boldsymbol{t})\,\mathrm{d}\boldsymbol{t} \\ &= b^{|\boldsymbol{\ell}|_1} \int_{[\boldsymbol{a}b^{-\boldsymbol{\ell}}, (\boldsymbol{a}+\mathbf{1})b^{-\boldsymbol{\ell}}]} f(\boldsymbol{t})\,\mathrm{d}\boldsymbol{t}.\end{aligned}$$

For $\boldsymbol{\ell} \in \mathbb{N}_0^s$ and $\boldsymbol{a} \in A_{\boldsymbol{\ell}}$ let

$$c_{\boldsymbol{\ell},\boldsymbol{a}} = \int_{[\boldsymbol{a}b^{-\boldsymbol{\ell}}, (\boldsymbol{a}+\mathbf{1})b^{-\boldsymbol{\ell}}]} f(\boldsymbol{t})\,\mathrm{d}\boldsymbol{t}.$$

For $\boldsymbol{x} \in [\boldsymbol{a}b^{-\boldsymbol{\ell}}, (\boldsymbol{a}+\mathbf{1})b^{-\boldsymbol{\ell}})$ let

$$\begin{aligned}g(\boldsymbol{x}) &:= \sum_{\mathfrak{u} \subseteq \mathcal{I}_s} (-1)^{|\mathfrak{u}|} \sum_{\boldsymbol{k} \in A_{\boldsymbol{\ell}-(\mathbf{1}_{\mathfrak{u}}, \mathbf{0}_{\mathcal{I}_s \setminus \mathfrak{u}})}} \widehat{f}(\boldsymbol{k})\, {}_b\mathrm{wal}_{\boldsymbol{k}}(\boldsymbol{x}) \\ &= \sum_{\mathfrak{u} \subseteq \mathcal{I}_s} (-1)^{|\mathfrak{u}|} b^{|\boldsymbol{\ell}-(\mathbf{1}_{\mathfrak{u}}, \mathbf{0}_{\mathcal{I}_s \setminus \mathfrak{u}})|_1} c_{\boldsymbol{\ell}-(\mathbf{1}_{\mathfrak{u}}, \mathbf{0}_{\mathcal{I}_s \setminus \mathfrak{u}}), (\lfloor \boldsymbol{a}_{\mathfrak{u}}/b \rfloor, \boldsymbol{a}_{\mathcal{I}_s \setminus \mathfrak{u}})},\end{aligned}$$

where $(\lfloor \boldsymbol{a}_{\mathfrak{u}}/b \rfloor, \boldsymbol{a}_{\mathcal{I}_s \setminus \mathfrak{u}})$ is the vector whose ith component is $\lfloor a_i/b \rfloor$ for $i \in \mathfrak{u}$ and a_i otherwise.

Using Plancherel's identity (see Theorem A.19) we obtain

$$\begin{aligned}\sigma_{\boldsymbol{\ell}}^2(f) &= \sum_{\mathfrak{u} \subseteq \mathcal{I}_s} (-1)^{|\mathfrak{u}|} \sum_{\boldsymbol{k} \in A_{\boldsymbol{\ell}-(\mathbf{1}_{\mathfrak{u}}, \mathbf{0}_{\mathcal{I}_s \setminus \mathfrak{u}})}} |\widehat{f}(\boldsymbol{k})|^2 = \int_0^1 |g(\boldsymbol{x})|^2\,\mathrm{d}\boldsymbol{x} \\ &= \sum_{\boldsymbol{a} \in A_{\boldsymbol{\ell}}} b^{-|\boldsymbol{\ell}|_1} \left| \sum_{\mathfrak{u} \subseteq \mathcal{I}_s} (-1)^{|\mathfrak{u}|} b^{|\boldsymbol{\ell}-(\mathbf{1}_{\mathfrak{u}}, \mathbf{0}_{\mathcal{I}_s \setminus \mathfrak{u}})|_1} c_{\boldsymbol{\ell}-(\mathbf{1}_{\mathfrak{u}}, \mathbf{0}), (\lfloor \boldsymbol{a}_{\mathfrak{u}}/b \rfloor, \boldsymbol{a}_{\mathcal{I}_s \setminus \mathfrak{u}})} \right|^2 \\ &= b^{|\boldsymbol{\ell}|_1} \sum_{\boldsymbol{a} \in A_{\boldsymbol{\ell}}} \left| \sum_{\mathfrak{u} \subseteq \mathcal{I}_s} (-1)^{|\mathfrak{u}|} b^{-|\mathfrak{u}|} c_{\boldsymbol{\ell}-(\mathbf{1}_{\mathfrak{u}}, \mathbf{0}), (\lfloor \boldsymbol{a}_{\mathfrak{u}}/b \rfloor, \boldsymbol{a}_{\mathcal{I}_s \setminus \mathfrak{u}})} \right|^2.\end{aligned}$$

We simplify the inner sum further. Let $\boldsymbol{e} = b\lfloor \boldsymbol{a}/b \rfloor$, i.e. the ith component of $\boldsymbol{e}$ is given by $e_i = b\lfloor a_i/b \rfloor$. Further let $\boldsymbol{d} = \boldsymbol{a} - \boldsymbol{e}$, i.e. the ith component of $\boldsymbol{d}$ is given by $d_i = a_i - e_i$. We have

$$\begin{aligned}
&\sum_{\mathfrak{u}\subseteq\mathcal{I}_s}(-1)^{|\mathfrak{u}|}b^{-|\mathfrak{u}|}c_{\boldsymbol{\ell}-(\mathbf{1}_{\mathfrak{u}},\mathbf{0}),(\lfloor \boldsymbol{a}_{\mathfrak{u}}/b\rfloor,\boldsymbol{a}_{\mathcal{I}_s\setminus\mathfrak{u}})}\\
&= \sum_{\mathfrak{u}\subseteq\mathcal{I}_s}(-1)^{|\mathfrak{u}|}b^{-|\mathfrak{u}|}\sum_{\boldsymbol{k}_{\mathfrak{u}}\in A_{\mathbf{1}_{\mathfrak{u}}}} c_{\boldsymbol{\ell},\boldsymbol{e}+(\boldsymbol{k}_{\mathfrak{u}},\boldsymbol{d}_{\mathcal{I}_s\setminus\mathfrak{u}})}\\
&= \sum_{\mathfrak{u}\subseteq\mathcal{I}_s}(-1)^{|\mathfrak{u}|}b^{-|\mathfrak{u}|}b^{-s+|\mathfrak{u}|}\sum_{\boldsymbol{k}\in A_1} c_{\boldsymbol{\ell},\boldsymbol{e}+(\boldsymbol{k}_{\mathfrak{u}},\boldsymbol{d}_{\mathcal{I}_s\setminus\mathfrak{u}})}\\
&= b^{-s}\sum_{\boldsymbol{k}\in A_1}\sum_{\mathfrak{u}\subseteq\mathcal{I}_s}(-1)^{|\mathfrak{u}|}c_{\boldsymbol{\ell},\boldsymbol{e}+(\boldsymbol{k}_{\mathfrak{u}},\boldsymbol{d}_{\mathcal{I}_s\setminus\mathfrak{u}})}\\
&= b^{-s}\sum_{\boldsymbol{k}\in A_1}\int_{[\boldsymbol{e}b^{-\boldsymbol{\ell}},(\boldsymbol{e}+\mathbf{1})b^{-\boldsymbol{\ell}}]}\sum_{\mathfrak{u}\subseteq\mathcal{I}_s}(-1)^{|\mathfrak{u}|}f(\boldsymbol{x}+b^{-\boldsymbol{\ell}}(\boldsymbol{k}_{\mathfrak{u}},\boldsymbol{d}_{\mathcal{I}_s\setminus\mathfrak{u}}))\,\mathrm{d}\boldsymbol{x}\\
&= b^{-s}\sum_{\boldsymbol{k}\in A_1}\int_{[\boldsymbol{a}b^{-\boldsymbol{\ell}},(\boldsymbol{a}+\mathbf{1})b^{-\boldsymbol{\ell}}]}\pm\Delta(f,J_{\boldsymbol{d},\boldsymbol{k},\boldsymbol{x}})\,\mathrm{d}\boldsymbol{x},
\end{aligned}$$

where $J_{\boldsymbol{d},\boldsymbol{k},\boldsymbol{x}} = \prod_{i=1}^{s}[(x_i+\min(k_i-d_i,0))b^{-\ell_i},(x_i+\max(k_i-d_i,0))b^{-\ell_i}]$ and where the sign in the integral depends on $J_{\boldsymbol{d},\boldsymbol{k},\boldsymbol{x}}$.

Therefore,

$$\begin{aligned}
\sigma_{\boldsymbol{\ell}}^2(f) &\le b^{|\boldsymbol{\ell}|_1-2s}\sum_{\boldsymbol{a}\in A_{\boldsymbol{\ell}}}\sum_{\boldsymbol{k}\in A_1}\int_{[\boldsymbol{a}b^{-\boldsymbol{\ell}},(\boldsymbol{a}+\mathbf{1})b^{-\boldsymbol{\ell}}]}|\Delta(f,J_{\boldsymbol{d},\boldsymbol{k},\boldsymbol{x}})|\,\mathrm{d}\boldsymbol{x}\\
&\qquad\times\sum_{\boldsymbol{k}'\in A_1}\int_{[\boldsymbol{a}b^{-\boldsymbol{\ell}},(\boldsymbol{a}+\mathbf{1})b^{-\boldsymbol{\ell}}]}|\Delta(f,J_{\boldsymbol{d},\boldsymbol{k}',\boldsymbol{x}})|\,\mathrm{d}\boldsymbol{x}\\
&= b^{|\boldsymbol{\ell}|_1-2s}\sum_{\boldsymbol{k},\boldsymbol{k}'\in A_1}\sum_{\boldsymbol{a}\in A_{\boldsymbol{\ell}}}\int_{[\boldsymbol{a}b^{-\boldsymbol{\ell}},(\boldsymbol{a}+\mathbf{1})b^{-\boldsymbol{\ell}}]}|\Delta(f,J_{\boldsymbol{d},\boldsymbol{k},\boldsymbol{x}})|\,\mathrm{d}\boldsymbol{x}\\
&\qquad\times\int_{[\boldsymbol{a}b^{-\boldsymbol{\ell}},(\boldsymbol{a}+\mathbf{1})b^{-\boldsymbol{\ell}}]}|\Delta(f,J_{\boldsymbol{d},\boldsymbol{k}',\boldsymbol{x}})|\,\mathrm{d}\boldsymbol{x}.
\end{aligned}$$

Using the Cauchy–Schwarz inequality, we have

$$\begin{aligned}
&\int_{[\boldsymbol{a}b^{-\boldsymbol{\ell}},(\boldsymbol{a}+\mathbf{1})b^{-\boldsymbol{\ell}}]}|\Delta(f,J_{\boldsymbol{d},\boldsymbol{k},\boldsymbol{x}})|\,\mathrm{d}\boldsymbol{x}\\
&\le\left(\int_{[\boldsymbol{a}b^{-\boldsymbol{\ell}},(\boldsymbol{a}+\mathbf{1})b^{-\boldsymbol{\ell}}]}1\,\mathrm{d}\boldsymbol{t}\right)^{1/2}\left(\int_{[\boldsymbol{a}b^{-\boldsymbol{\ell}},(\boldsymbol{a}+\mathbf{1})b^{-\boldsymbol{\ell}}]}|\Delta(f,J_{\boldsymbol{d},\boldsymbol{k},\boldsymbol{x}})|^2\,\mathrm{d}\boldsymbol{x}\right)^{1/2}\\
&= b^{-|\boldsymbol{\ell}|_1/2}\left(\int_{[\boldsymbol{a}b^{-\boldsymbol{\ell}},(\boldsymbol{a}+\mathbf{1})b^{-\boldsymbol{\ell}}]}|\Delta(f,J_{\boldsymbol{d},\boldsymbol{k},\boldsymbol{x}})|^2\,\mathrm{d}\boldsymbol{x}\right)^{1/2}.
\end{aligned}$$

Let $D_{\boldsymbol{a},\boldsymbol{k}} = \left(\int_{[\boldsymbol{a}b^{-\boldsymbol{\ell}},(\boldsymbol{a}+\boldsymbol{1})b^{-\boldsymbol{\ell}}]} |\Delta(f, J_{\boldsymbol{d},\boldsymbol{k},\boldsymbol{x}})|^2 \,\mathrm{d}\boldsymbol{x}\right)^{1/2}$. Then we have

$$\begin{aligned}\sigma_{\boldsymbol{\ell}}^2(f) &\le b^{-2s} \sum_{\boldsymbol{k},\boldsymbol{k}'\in A_1} \sum_{\boldsymbol{a}\in A_{\boldsymbol{\ell}}} D_{\boldsymbol{a},\boldsymbol{k}} D_{\boldsymbol{a},\boldsymbol{k}'} \\ &\le \max_{\boldsymbol{k},\boldsymbol{k}'\in A_1} \sum_{\boldsymbol{a}\in A_{\boldsymbol{\ell}}} D_{\boldsymbol{a},\boldsymbol{k}} D_{\boldsymbol{a},\boldsymbol{k}'} \\ &= \max_{\boldsymbol{k}\in A_1} \sum_{\boldsymbol{a}\in A_{\boldsymbol{\ell}}} D_{\boldsymbol{a},\boldsymbol{k}}^2,\end{aligned}$$

where the last equality follows as the Cauchy–Schwarz inequality is an equality for two vectors which are linearly dependent. Let $\boldsymbol{k}^*$ be the value of $\boldsymbol{k} \in A_1$ for which the sum $\sum_{\boldsymbol{a}\in A_{\boldsymbol{\ell}}} D_{\boldsymbol{a},\boldsymbol{k}}^2$ takes on its maximum. Then

$$\begin{aligned}\sigma_{\boldsymbol{\ell}}^2(f) &\le \sum_{\boldsymbol{a}\in A_{\boldsymbol{\ell}}} \int_{[\boldsymbol{a}b^{-\boldsymbol{\ell}},(\boldsymbol{a}+\boldsymbol{1})b^{-\boldsymbol{\ell}}]} |\Delta(f, J_{\boldsymbol{d},\boldsymbol{k}^*,\boldsymbol{x}})|^2 \,\mathrm{d}\boldsymbol{x} \\ &\le b^{-|\boldsymbol{\ell}|_1} \sum_{\boldsymbol{a}\in A_{\boldsymbol{\ell}}} \sup_{\boldsymbol{x}\in[\boldsymbol{a}b^{-\boldsymbol{\ell}},(\boldsymbol{a}+\boldsymbol{1})b^{-\boldsymbol{\ell}}]} |\Delta(f, J_{\boldsymbol{d},\boldsymbol{k}^*,\boldsymbol{x}})|^2 \\ &\le (b-1)^{(2\alpha-1)_+ s} b^{-2\alpha|\boldsymbol{\ell}|_1} \sum_{\boldsymbol{a}\in A_{\boldsymbol{\ell}}} \sup_{\boldsymbol{x}\in[\boldsymbol{a}b^{-\boldsymbol{\ell}},(\boldsymbol{a}+\boldsymbol{1})b^{-\boldsymbol{\ell}}]} \mathrm{Vol}(J_{\boldsymbol{d},\boldsymbol{k}^*,\boldsymbol{x}}) \left|\frac{\Delta(f, J_{\boldsymbol{d},\boldsymbol{k}^*,\boldsymbol{x}})}{\mathrm{Vol}(J_{\boldsymbol{d},\boldsymbol{k}^*,\boldsymbol{x}})^{\alpha}}\right|^2 \\ &\le (b-1)^{(2\alpha-1)_+ s} b^{-2\alpha|\boldsymbol{\ell}|_1} V_\alpha^s(f_{\mathcal{I}_s}; \mathcal{I}_s),\end{aligned}$$

where $(x)_+ = \max(x, 0)$.

For $\boldsymbol{\ell} = (\boldsymbol{\ell}_{\mathfrak{u}}, \boldsymbol{0})$ with $\boldsymbol{\ell}_{\mathfrak{u}} \in \mathbb{N}^{|\mathfrak{u}|}$ with $\emptyset \neq \mathfrak{u} \subset \mathcal{I}_s$ we just replace f with $\int_{[0,1]^{s-|\mathfrak{u}|}} f(\boldsymbol{x}) \,\mathrm{d}\boldsymbol{x}_{\mathcal{I}_s\setminus\mathfrak{u}}$ in the proof above to obtain the result. □

Assume that $f : [0, 1]^s \to \mathbb{R}$ has finite variation of order $0 < \alpha \le 1$. That is, $V_\alpha(f_{\mathfrak{u}}) < \infty$ for all $\emptyset \neq \mathfrak{u} \subseteq \mathcal{I}_s$. In this case Lemma 13.23 implies that

$$\sigma_{\boldsymbol{\ell}}^2(f) \le (b-1)^{(2\alpha-1)_+ s} b^{-2\alpha|\boldsymbol{\ell}|_1} V_\alpha^2(f),$$

for all $\boldsymbol{\ell} \in \mathbb{N}_0^s \setminus \{\boldsymbol{0}\}$.

Theorem 13.9 then yields for a digital (t, m, s)-net over $\mathbb{Z}_b$ that

$$\begin{aligned}\mathrm{Var}[\widehat{I}(f)] &\le b^{-m+t+s} \sum_{\substack{\boldsymbol{\ell}\in\mathbb{N}_0^s \\ |\boldsymbol{\ell}|_1 > m-t}} \sigma_{\boldsymbol{\ell}}^2(f) \\ &\le (b-1)^{(2\alpha-1)_+ s} b^{-m+t+s} V_\alpha^2(f) \sum_{\substack{\boldsymbol{\ell}\in\mathbb{N}_0^s \\ |\boldsymbol{\ell}|_1 > m-t}} b^{-2\alpha|\boldsymbol{\ell}|_1}\end{aligned}$$

$$= (b-1)^{(2\alpha-1)_+ s} b^{-m+t+s} V_\alpha^2(f) \sum_{\ell=m-t+1}^{\infty} b^{-2\alpha\ell} \sum_{\substack{\boldsymbol{\ell} \in \mathbb{N}_0^s \\ |\boldsymbol{\ell}|_1 = \ell}} 1$$

$$= (b-1)^{(2\alpha-1)_+ s} b^{-m+t+s} V_\alpha^2(f) \sum_{\ell=m-t+1}^{\infty} b^{-2\alpha\ell} \binom{\ell+s-1}{s-1}.$$

We need the following lemma.

Lemma 13.24 *For any real number $b > 1$ and any $k, t_0 \in \mathbb{N}$, we have*

$$\sum_{t=t_0}^{\infty} b^{-t} \binom{t+k-1}{k-1} \le b^{-t_0} \binom{t_0+k-1}{k-1} \left(1-\frac{1}{b}\right)^{-k}.$$

Proof By the binomial theorem we have

$$\sum_{t=t_0}^{\infty} b^{-t} \binom{t-t_0+k-1}{k-1} = b^{-t_0} \left(1-\frac{1}{b}\right)^{-k}.$$

Hence the result follows from the inequality

$$\binom{t+k-1}{k-1} \Big/ \binom{t-t_0+k-1}{k-1} = \frac{(t+k-1)(t+k-2)\cdots(t-t_0+k)}{t(t-1)\cdots(t-t_0+1)}$$
$$\le \binom{t_0+k-1}{k-1}.$$

□

Thus we obtain the following theorem which should be compared with [94, 211, 271].

Theorem 13.25 *Let $f : [0,1]^s \to \mathbb{R}$ have bounded variation $V_\alpha(f) < \infty$ of order $0 < \alpha \le 1$. Then the variance of the estimator $\mathrm{Var}[\widehat{I}(f)]$ using a randomly scrambled digital (t, m, s)-net over $\mathbb{Z}_b$ is bounded by*

$$\mathrm{Var}[\widehat{I}(f)] \le V_\alpha^2(f) b^{-(1+2\alpha)(m-t)} \frac{(b-1)^{(2\alpha-1)_+ s} b^{2s}}{b^{2\alpha}(b-1)^s} \binom{m-t+s}{s-1}.$$

Several remarks are in order.

Remark 13.26

1. If $N = b^m$ denotes the number of points, then we can expect a convergence $\sqrt{\mathrm{Var}[\widehat{I}(f)]} = O(N^{-\alpha-1/2}(\log N)^{(s-1)/2})$ in probability for integrands having bounded variation of order α.

2. If f has square integrable partial mixed derivatives up to order one in each variable, then we obtain a convergence of

$$\sqrt{\mathrm{Var}[\widehat{I}(f)]} = O(N^{-3/2}(\log N)^{(s-1)/2})$$

This is a significant improvement over a convergence of $O(N^{-1}(\log N)^{s-1})$ which one obtains for deterministic point sets.
3. If $f \in L_2([0,1]^s)$, but does not have bounded variation of some order $\alpha > 0$, then we still get a convergence of $\sqrt{\mathrm{Var}[\widehat{I}(f)]} = o(N^{-1/2})$ in probability. This convergence is still better than the MC rate.
4. The smoothness of the integrand does not have to be known a priori. QMC algorithms based on scrambled digital (t, m, s)-nets automatically take advantage of it.

On the other hand, scrambling does not seem to improve the convergence rate beyond $N^{-3/2}$ even if one assumes stronger smoothness assumptions on the integrand. A method which does take advantage of further smoothness is investigated in Chapter 15. Before we prove such results, we need to prove some bounds on the decay of the Walsh coefficients, which is done in the next chapter.

Exercises

13.1 Write down the permutations used in Figure 13.1 to scramble the picture.

13.2 Show that if one uses a randomly shifted digital net in a QMC rule, then one obtains an unbiased estimator of the integral.

13.3 Let $f(x) = x^2$. Calculate the nested ANOVA terms $\sigma_\ell^2(f)$ for $\ell \in \mathbb{N}_0$.

13.4 In analogy to a digital shift of depth m (see Definition 4.69), define Owen's scrambling of depth m. Here, one randomises the first m digits as in Owen's scrambling and the digits with index larger than m are randomised as in a digital shift of depth m. Define this scrambling method and prove an analogue to Lemma 13.3 for this randomisation.
Hint: See [161, p. 63] for the definition of the scrambling algorithm of depth m.

13.5 Show that if the reproducing kernel $K \in L_2([0,1]^s)$ is continuous, then the associated scramble invariant kernel K_{scr} is also continuous.
Hint: Use a similar method as in the proof of Lemma 12.2.

13.6 Show the second part of Lemma 13.15.

13.7 Use equation (13.15) to show that ϕ_{scr} is continuous and deduce that the scramble invariant kernel K_{scr} given in Proposition 13.19 is continuous.

13.8 Obtain a formula for the scramble invariant kernel associated with the reproducing kernel

$$K(\boldsymbol{x}, \boldsymbol{y}) = \prod_{i=1}^{s} K(x_i, y_i) = \prod_{i=1}^{s} \min(1 - x_j, 1 - y_j),$$

where $\boldsymbol{x} = (x_1, \ldots, x_s)$, $\boldsymbol{y} = (y_1, \ldots, y_s) \in [0,1]^s$.

13.9 Obtain a bound on $\widehat{e}^2_{\text{scr}}(\mathcal{H}_{\text{sob},s,\gamma}, \mathcal{P})$ in (13.4.3) by estimating the formula in Theorem 13.20 directly.

13.10 Prove Lemma 13.23 for the case $s = 1$.

13.11 Improve the constant in Theorem 13.25 by using a better bound on $\sigma_{\boldsymbol{\ell}}$ for $\boldsymbol{\ell} = (\boldsymbol{\ell}_{\mathfrak{u}}, \mathbf{0})$. *Hint:* Use $V_\alpha^{|\mathfrak{u}|}(f_{\mathfrak{u}}); \mathfrak{u})$ instead of $V_\alpha(f)$.

14

The decay of the Walsh coefficients of smooth functions

In the next chapter, we show that QMC rules can achieve improved rates of convergence for sufficiently smooth functions. The essential property which enables us to prove such results rests on the decay of the Walsh coefficients of smooth functions, which is the topic of this chapter. We follow [38] in our approach.

14.1 Motivation

The question we are going to answer in this section is the following: let $f : [0, 1) \to \mathbb{R}$ be a δ times continuously differentiable function. What can we say about the asymptotic behaviour of the Walsh coefficients $\widehat{f}(k)$ as $k \to \infty$?

First, let us compare this question with its analogue for Fourier series. Let $f : [0, 1) \to \mathbb{R}$ be a one-periodic, δ times continuously differentiable function. The Fourier coefficient $\widehat{f}_F(k) := \int_0^1 f(x) \mathrm{e}^{2\pi i k x} \, \mathrm{d}x$ then satisfies $\widehat{f}_F(k) = O(k^{-\delta})$; see, for example, [273, Theorem 13.14, p. 117]. In other words, the smoother the function f, the faster the Fourier coefficients decay.

Does the same hold for Walsh coefficients? The answer to this question has to be *No*. For one, consider the following: say $\widehat{f}(1) = 1$ and $\sum_{k=2}^{\infty} |\widehat{f}(k)| < 1$. Then, as $|{}_2\mathrm{wal}_k(x)| = 1$, it follows that the function $\sum_{k=1}^{\infty} \widehat{f}(k) \, {}_2\mathrm{wal}_k(x)$ must have a discontinuity at $1/2$. Hence, if the Walsh coefficients decay very quickly, then the function has a discontinuity.

An even more elaborate result in the same direction is known from Fine [79, Theorem VIII]. He proved the following theorem (note that he considered only base $b = 2$, so in the following we also restrict ourselves to $b = 2$, although the results are more generally true; see Exercise 14.8).

Theorem 14.1 *Let $b = 2$. The only absolutely continuous functions whose Walsh coefficients satisfy $\widehat{f}(k) = o(1/k)$ are the constants.*

This seems to provide an answer to the question posed earlier, but let us consider some examples to shed some more light on the result.

Example 14.2 Maybe the simplest example is to choose $F_1(x) = x$. In this case

$$\widehat{F_1}(k) = \begin{cases} 1/2 & \text{for } k = 0, \\ -1/(4k) & \text{for } k = 2^a \text{ with } a \geq 0, \\ 0 & \text{otherwise,} \end{cases}$$

as shown in Lemma A.22. Therefore, only for $k = 2^a$ do we have $\widehat{F_1}(k) = O(1/k)$; for all other $k > 0$, we have $\widehat{F_1}(k) = 0$.

Example 14.3 Now let us consider $F_2(x) = x^2$. We have

$$\widehat{F_2}(k) = \begin{cases} 1/3 & \text{for } k = 0, \\ -1/(4k) & \text{for } k = 2^a \text{ with } a \geq 0, \\ 2^{-a_1-a_2-3} & \text{for } k = 2^{a_1} + 2^{a_2} \text{ with } a_1 > a_2 \geq 0, \\ 0 & \text{otherwise.} \end{cases}$$

The case $k = 2^a$ is as in Example 14.2. The case $k = 2^{a_1} + 2^{a_2}$ is now more complicated. If we fix a_2 and let $a_1 \to \infty$, then $\widehat{F_2}(k) = O(1/k)$, but if, say $a_1 = a_2 + 1$ and $a_1 \to \infty$, then $\widehat{F_2}(k) = O(1/k^2)$. Again, if k has more than two non-zero digits in its base 2 expansion, then $\widehat{F_2}(k) = 0$.

For arbitrary polynomials, the result is as one would expect from the previous two examples.

Example 14.4 Let $F_3(x) = \mathrm{e}^{-2\pi \mathrm{i} x}$. We have $\widehat{F_3}(0) = 0$ and for $k = 2^{a_1} + \cdots + 2^{a_v}$ with $a_1 > \cdots > a_v \geq 0$, we have

$$\widehat{F_3}(k) = \frac{2\mathrm{i}^v}{\pi^v} \sum_{\substack{h_1,\ldots,h_v \in \mathbb{Z}, h_l \equiv 1 \pmod 2 \\ 1 = h_1 2^{a_1} + \cdots + h_v 2^{a_v}}} \prod_{l=1}^{v} \frac{1}{h_l}.$$

(A proof of this formula can be found in [35, Lemma 6.12]. As we use it only for illustration purposes, we do not include a proof here.) For $v = 1$, we have $\widehat{F_3}(1) = \frac{2i}{\pi}$ and $\widehat{F_3}(2^{a_1}) = 0$ for $a_1 > 0$. For $k = 2^{a_1} + 2^{a_2}$ with $a_2 > 0$, we have

$\widehat{F}_3(k) = 0$ and for $a_2 = 0$, we have

$$\begin{aligned}
\widehat{F}_3(k) &= -\frac{2}{\pi^2} \sum_{\substack{h_1,h_2 \in \mathbb{Z}, h_1,h_2 \equiv 1 \pmod 2 \\ 1 = h_1 2^{a_1} + h_2}} \frac{1}{h_1 h_2} \\
&= -\frac{2}{\pi^2} \sum_{h_1 \in \mathbb{Z}, h_1 \equiv 1 \pmod 2} \frac{1}{h_1(1 - h_1 2^{a_1})} \\
&= -\frac{2}{\pi^2} \sum_{h \in \mathbb{Z}} \frac{1}{(1+2h)(1-(1+2h)2^{a_1})} \\
&= \frac{2}{\pi^2} \sum_{h=0}^{\infty} \frac{1}{(1+2h)((1+2h)2^{a_1} - 1)} \\
&\quad + \frac{2}{\pi^2} \sum_{h=1}^{\infty} \frac{1}{(2h-1)(1+(2h-1)2^{a_1})} \\
&\le \frac{2}{\pi^2} \left(\frac{1}{2^{a_1} - 1} + \sum_{h=1}^{\infty} \frac{1}{2h(2h2^{a_1})} + \frac{1}{1+2^{a_1}} + \sum_{h=1}^{\infty} \frac{1}{2h(2h2^{a_1})} \right) \\
&\le \frac{2}{\pi^2} \left(\frac{1}{2^{a_1} - 1} + \frac{1}{1+2^{a_1}} + \frac{\pi^2}{12 \cdot 2^{a_1}} \right).
\end{aligned}$$

Hence, for $k = 2^{a_1} + 1$, we have $\widehat{F}_3(k) = O(1/k)$. The case for $v > 2$ could be analysed in a similar way, but gets very quickly involved.

In the following, we state another result due to Fine [79] that helps us to analyse the cases when $v > 2$.

Hence, we see that although Fine's result (Theorem 14.1) is of course true, it does not tell the whole story. Some of the Walsh coefficients of smooth functions do decay with order $1/k$, but others decay much more quickly (or are 0 altogether). In that context, the result which Fine uses to obtain Theorem 14.1 is of particular interest.

Theorem 14.5 *Let $b = 2$ and let the Walsh series associated with f be given by*

$$f(x) \sim \sum_{k=1}^{\infty} \widehat{f}(k)\, {}_2\mathrm{wal}_k(x)$$

and let

$$F(x) = \int_0^x f(t)\, \mathrm{d}t \sim \sum_{k=1}^{\infty} \widehat{F}(k)\, {}_2\mathrm{wal}_k(x).$$

Then, for fixed $k' \geq 0$, we have

$$\widehat{F}(2^a + k') = -2^{-a-2}\widehat{f}(k') + o(2^{-a}) \quad \text{as } a \to \infty.$$

Fine's argument for proving Theorem 14.1 based on Theorem 14.5 simply uses the observation that if there is one k' for which $\widehat{f}(k') \neq 0$, then

$$-2^a\widehat{F}(2^a + k') = \widehat{f}(k')/4 + o(1) \neq o(1).$$

But if all $\widehat{f}(k')$ vanish, then $f(x) = 0$ and $F(x) = c$.

We consider the above examples now in light of Theorem 14.5.

Example 14.6 First let us consider $F_1(x) = x$ again. Let $f_1(x) = \frac{\mathrm{d}}{\mathrm{d}x}F_1(x) = 1$. Then $\widehat{f_1}(k) = 1$ for $k = 0$ and 0 otherwise. Theorem 14.5 does now assert that $\widehat{F_1}(k) = O(1/k)$ for $k = 2^a$ and $\widehat{F_1}(k) = o(2^{-a})$ for $k = 2^a + k'$, with $k' > 0$, as $a \to \infty$. This is because $\widehat{f_1}(k') = 0$ for $k' > 0$. Note that this result is now stronger than just stating that the Walsh coefficients decay with order $1/k$. It says that if $k = 2^a + k'$, with $k' > 0$ fixed, then $\widehat{F_1}(k) = o(2^{-a})$ as $a \to \infty$.

Example 14.7 Let us now consider $F_3(x) = \mathrm{e}^{-2\pi\mathrm{i}x}$. Let $f_3(x) = \frac{\mathrm{d}}{\mathrm{d}x}F_3(x) = -2\pi\mathrm{i}\mathrm{e}^{-2\pi\mathrm{i}x}$. Now let $v = 3$ and $k = 2^{a_1} + 2^{a_2} + 2^{a_3}$. We have $f_3(x) = -2\pi\mathrm{i}F_3(x)$ and hence, we know how $\widehat{f_3}(k)$ behaves for $v \leq 2$ from Example 14.4. Let $k' = 2^{a_2} + 2^{a_3}$. Then, if $a_3 > 0$, we have $\widehat{f_3}(k') = 0$ and hence, $\widehat{F_3}(k) = o(2^{a_1})$. If $a_3 = 0$, then $\widehat{F_3}(k) = O(2^{-a_1-a_2}) + o(2^{-a_1})$.

Hence, Theorem 14.5 gives us more information than Theorem 14.1. Indeed, a generalisation of Theorem 14.5 can give us a complete picture on how the Walsh coefficients of smooth functions behave, as shown below.

14.2 A formula by Fine

We need the following lemma, which was first shown in [79] and appeared in many other papers (see, for example, [36] for a more general version). The following notation is used throughout this chapter: for $k \in \mathbb{N}$, we write $k = \kappa b^{a-1} + k'$ where $a \in \mathbb{N}$, $1 \leq \kappa < b$ and $0 \leq k' < b^{a-1}$.

Lemma 14.8 *For $k \in \mathbb{N}$ let $J_k(x) = \int_0^x \overline{{}_b\mathrm{wal}_k(t)}\,\mathrm{d}t$. Then*

$$J_k(x) = \frac{1}{b^a}\left(\frac{1}{1-\omega_b^{-\kappa}}\overline{{}_b\mathrm{wal}_{k'}(x)} + \left(\frac{1}{2} + \frac{1}{\omega_b^{-\kappa}-1}\right)\overline{{}_b\mathrm{wal}_k(x)}\right.$$
$$\left.+\sum_{c=1}^{\infty}\sum_{l=1}^{b-1}\frac{1}{b^c(\omega_b^l - 1)}\overline{{}_b\mathrm{wal}_{lb^{a+c-1}+k}(x)}\right).$$

For $k = 0$, i.e. $J_0(x) = \int_0^x 1 \,\mathrm{d}t = x$, we have

$$J_0(x) = \frac{1}{2} + \sum_{c=1}^{\infty} \sum_{l=1}^{b-1} \frac{1}{b^c(\omega_b^l - 1)} \overline{{}_b\mathrm{wal}_{lb^{c-1}}(x)}. \tag{14.1}$$

Proof Let $k = \kappa b^{a-1} + k'$ with $a \in \mathbb{N}$, $0 \le k' < b^{a-1}$ and $1 \le \kappa < b$. The function $\overline{{}_b\mathrm{wal}_{\kappa b^{a-1}}(y)}$ is constant on each interval $[rb^{-a}, (r+1)b^{-a})$ and $\overline{{}_b\mathrm{wal}_{k'}(y)}$ is constant on each interval $[cb^{-a+1}, (c+1)b^{-a+1})$. We have $\overline{{}_b\mathrm{wal}_k(y)} = \overline{{}_b\mathrm{wal}_{\kappa b^{a-1}}(y)}\ \overline{{}_b\mathrm{wal}_{k'}(y)}$. For any $0 \le c < b^{a-1}$, we have

$$\begin{aligned}\int_{cb^{-a+1}}^{(c+1)b^{-a+1}} \overline{{}_b\mathrm{wal}_k(t)} \,\mathrm{d}t &= \overline{{}_b\mathrm{wal}_{k'}(cb^{-a+1})} \int_{cb^{-a+1}}^{(c+1)b^{-a+1}} \overline{{}_b\mathrm{wal}_{\kappa b^{a-1}}(t)} \,\mathrm{d}t \\ &= \overline{{}_b\mathrm{wal}_{k'}(cb^{-a+1})} \frac{1}{b^a} \sum_{r=0}^{b-1} \overline{{}_b\mathrm{wal}_\kappa(r/b)} = 0.\end{aligned}$$

Thus, we have

$$J_k(x) = \overline{{}_b\mathrm{wal}_{k'}(x)} J_{\kappa b^{a-1}}(x).$$

Let $x = x_1 b^{-1} + x_2 b^{-2} + \cdots$ and $y = x_{a+1} b^{-1} + x_{a+2} b^{-2} + \cdots$, then we have

$$J_{\kappa b^{a-1}}(x) = b^{-a} \sum_{r=0}^{x_a - 1} \overline{{}_b\mathrm{wal}_\kappa(r/b)} + b^{-a}\, \overline{{}_b\mathrm{wal}_\kappa(x_a/b)} y.$$

We now investigate the Walsh series representation of the function $J_{\kappa b^{a-1}}(x)$. First note that $\overline{{}_b\mathrm{wal}_\kappa(x_a/b)} = \overline{{}_b\mathrm{wal}_{\kappa b^{a-1}}(x)}$. Further, by a slight adaption of formula (A.3), we obtain

$$y = \frac{1}{2} + \sum_{c=1}^{\infty} \sum_{l=1}^{b-1} \frac{1}{b^c(\omega_b^l - 1)} \overline{{}_b\mathrm{wal}_{lb^{c-1}}(y)}. \tag{14.2}$$

As $\overline{{}_b\mathrm{wal}_{lb^{c-1}}(y)} = \overline{{}_b\mathrm{wal}_{lb^{a+c-1}}(x)}$, we obtain

$$y = \frac{1}{2} + \sum_{c=1}^{\infty} \sum_{l=1}^{b-1} \frac{1}{b^c(\omega_b^l - 1)} \overline{{}_b\mathrm{wal}_{lb^{a+c-1}}(x)}.$$

Further, for $1 \le \kappa < b$, we define the function $\zeta_a(x) = \sum_{r=0}^{x_a - 1} \overline{{}_b\mathrm{wal}_\kappa(r/b)}$, where $a \in \mathbb{N}$ and $x = x_1 b^{-1} + x_2 b^{-2} + \cdots$ and where for $x_a = 0$ we set $\zeta_a(x) = 0$. The function ζ_a depends on x only through x_a; thus it is a step-function which is constant on the intervals $[cb^{-a}, (c+1)b^{-a})$ for $0 \le c \le b^a - 1$. The function ζ_a can be represented by a finite Walsh series. Indeed, $\zeta_a(x) = (1 - \overline{{}_b\mathrm{wal}_{\kappa b^{a-1}}(x)})$

$(1 - \overline{{}_b\mathrm{wal}_\kappa(1/b)})^{-1}$, which can be written as

$$\zeta_a(x) = \sum_{z=0}^{b-1} c_z \overline{{}_b\mathrm{wal}_{zb^{a-1}}(x)},$$

with $c_0 = (1 - \overline{{}_b\mathrm{wal}_\kappa(1/b)})^{-1} = (1 - \omega_b^{-\kappa})^{-1}$, $c_\kappa = -c_0$ and $c_z = 0$ for $z \notin \{0, \kappa\}$.

Altogether, we obtain

$$\begin{aligned} b^a J_{\kappa b^{a-1}}(x) &= \sum_{z=0}^{b-1} c_z \overline{{}_b\mathrm{wal}_{zb^{a-1}}(x)} + \frac{1}{2}\overline{{}_b\mathrm{wal}_{\kappa b^{a-1}}(x)} \\ &\quad + \sum_{c=1}^{\infty}\sum_{l=1}^{b-1} \frac{1}{b^c(\omega_b^l - 1)} \overline{{}_b\mathrm{wal}_{lb^{a+c-1}+\kappa b^{a-1}}(x)} \end{aligned}$$

and therefore,

$$\begin{aligned} b^a J_k(x) &= \sum_{z=0}^{b-1} c_z \overline{{}_b\mathrm{wal}_{zb^{a-1}+k'}(x)} + \frac{1}{2}\overline{{}_b\mathrm{wal}_k(x)} \\ &\quad + \sum_{c=1}^{\infty}\sum_{l=1}^{b-1} \frac{1}{b^c(\omega_b^l - 1)} \overline{{}_b\mathrm{wal}_{lb^{a+c-1}+k}(x)}. \end{aligned}$$

The result for $k = 0$ follows easily from (14.2). □

We also need the following elementary lemma.

Lemma 14.9 *For any* $1 \le \kappa < b$, *we have*

$$\left|\frac{1}{1-\omega_b^{-\kappa}}\right| \le \frac{1}{2\sin(\pi/b)} \quad \textit{and} \quad \left|\frac{1}{2} + \frac{1}{\omega_b^{-\kappa} - 1}\right| \le \frac{1}{2\sin(\pi/b)}.$$

We introduce some further notation which is used throughout this chapter.

We write $k \in \mathbb{N}$ in its b-adic expansion as $k = \kappa_1 b^{a_1-1} + \cdots + \kappa_v b^{a_v-1}$ with $v \in \mathbb{N}$, digits $1 \le \kappa_1, \ldots, \kappa_v < b$ and $a_1 > a_2 > \cdots > a_v \ge 1$. Hence, v is the number of non-zero b-adic digits of k. In this setting, we have $k' = k - \kappa_1 b^{a_1-1}$. Furthermore, for $v > 1$ let $k'' = k' - \kappa_2 b^{a_2-1}$ and hence, $0 \le k'' < b^{a_2-1}$. Similarly, for $l \in \mathbb{N}$ let $l = \lambda_1 b^{d_1-1} + \cdots + \lambda_w b^{d_w-1}$, where $w \in \mathbb{N}$, digits $1 \le \lambda_1, \ldots, \lambda_w < b$ and $d_1 > \cdots > d_w > 0$. Further, let $l' = l - \lambda_1 b^{d_1-1}$ and hence, $0 \le l' < b^{d_1-1}$. For $w > 1$, let $l'' = l' - \lambda_2 b^{d_2-1}$ and hence, $0 \le l'' < b^{d_2-1}$.

14.3 On the Walsh coefficients of polynomials and power series

In the following, we obtain bounds on the Walsh coefficients of monomials x^r. Let

$$\chi_{r,v}(a_1,\ldots,a_v;\kappa_1,\ldots,\kappa_v) = \int_0^1 x^r \overline{{}_b\mathrm{wal}_k(x)}\,\mathrm{d}x.$$

For $k = 0$, we define $\chi_{r,0}$, which is given by

$$\chi_{r,0} = \int_0^1 x^r\,\mathrm{d}x = \frac{1}{r+1}.$$

The Walsh coefficients of x^r are 0 if $v > r$; hence, we have $\chi_{r,v} = 0$ for $v > r$. This also follows from Lemma A.22, since by using the formula for x in Lemma A.22, one obtains only non-zero coefficients for $v \le r$ (see also [36, Lemma 3.7].)

The Walsh series for x is already known from Lemma 14.8, thus (note that we need to take the complex conjugate of (14.1) to obtain the Walsh series for x)

$$\chi_{1,1}(a_1;\kappa_1) = -b^{-a_1}(1-\omega_b^{-\kappa_1})^{-1}. \tag{14.3}$$

It can be checked that $|\chi_{1,1}| \le \frac{1}{2}$. Indeed, we always have

$$|\chi_{r,v}(a_1,\ldots,a_v;\kappa_1,\ldots,\kappa_v)| \le \int_0^1 x^r |\overline{{}_b\mathrm{wal}_k(x)}|\,\mathrm{d}x = \int_0^1 x^r\,\mathrm{d}x = \frac{1}{r+1}$$

for all $r, v \in \mathbb{N}_0$.

We obtain a recursive formula for the $\chi_{r,v}$ using integration by parts, namely

$$\int_0^1 x^r \overline{{}_b\mathrm{wal}_k(x)}\,\mathrm{d}x = J_k(x)x^r\Big|_0^1 - r\int_0^1 x^{r-1}J_k(x)\,\mathrm{d}x = -r\int_0^1 x^{r-1}J_k(x)\,\mathrm{d}x. \tag{14.4}$$

Using Lemma 14.8 and (14.4), we obtain for $1 \le v \le r$ and $r > 1$ that

$$\begin{aligned} &\chi_{r,v}(a_1,\ldots,a_v;\kappa_1,\ldots,\kappa_v) \\ &= -\frac{r}{b^{a_1}}\Bigg(\frac{1}{1-\omega_b^{-\kappa_1}}\chi_{r-1,v-1}(a_2,\ldots,a_v;\kappa_2,\ldots,\kappa_v) \\ &\quad + \left(\frac{1}{2}+\frac{1}{\omega_b^{-\kappa_1}-1}\right)\chi_{r-1,v}(a_1,\ldots,a_v;\kappa_1,\ldots,\kappa_v) \\ &\quad + \sum_{c=1}^{\infty}\sum_{\vartheta=1}^{b-1}\frac{1}{b^c(\omega_b^{\vartheta}-1)}\chi_{r-1,v+1}(a_1+c,a_1,\ldots,a_v;\vartheta,\kappa_1,\ldots,\kappa_v)\Bigg). \end{aligned} \tag{14.5}$$

From (14.5) and using induction, we can obtain

$$\chi_{r,r}(a_1,\ldots,a_r;\kappa_1,\ldots,\kappa_r) = \frac{-r}{b^{a_1}(1-\omega_b^{-\kappa_1})}\chi_{r-1,r-1}(a_2,\ldots,a_r;\kappa_2,\ldots,\kappa_r)$$
$$= \frac{(-1)^r r!}{b^{a_1+\cdots+a_r}}\prod_{w=1}^{r}\frac{1}{1-\omega_b^{-\kappa_w}}$$

and, with a bit more effort,

$$\chi_{r,r-1}(a_1,\ldots,a_{r-1};\kappa_1,\ldots,\kappa_{r-1})$$
$$= \frac{(-1)^r r!}{b^{a_1+\cdots+a_{r-1}}}\prod_{w=1}^{r-1}\frac{1}{1-\omega_b^{-\kappa_w}}\left(-\frac{1}{2}+\sum_{w=1}^{r-1}\left(\frac{1}{2}+\frac{1}{b^{a_w}(\omega_b^{-\kappa_w}-1)}\right)\right),$$

for all $r \in \mathbb{N}$.

In principle we can obtain all values of $\chi_{r,v}$ recursively using (14.5). We calculated already $\chi_{r,v}$ for $v = r, r-1$ and we could continue doing so for $v = r-2,\ldots,1$, but the formulae become increasingly complex, so we only prove a bound on them.

For any $r \in \mathbb{N}_0$ and a non-negative integer k with b-adic expansion given by $k = \kappa_1 b^{a_1-1} + \cdots + \kappa_v b^{a_v-1}$ with $v \in \mathbb{N}$, digits $1 \le \kappa_1,\ldots,\kappa_v < b$ and $a_1 > a_2 > \cdots > a_v \ge 1$ (if $k \neq 0$) we define

$$\mu_r(k) = \begin{cases} 0 & \text{for } r = 0, k \ge 0, \\ 0 & \text{for } k = 0, r \ge 0, \\ a_1 + \cdots + a_{\min(r,v)} & \text{otherwise.} \end{cases} \tag{14.6}$$

Lemma 14.10 *For $1 \le r < v$, we have $\chi_{r,v} = 0$ and for any $1 \le v \le r$, we have*

$$|\chi_{r,v}(a_1,\ldots,a_v;\kappa_1,\ldots,\kappa_v)|$$
$$\le \min_{0\le u\le v}\frac{1}{b^{\mu_u(k)}}\frac{r!}{(r-u+1)!}\frac{3^{\min(1,u)}}{(2\sin(\pi/b))^u}\left(1+\frac{1}{b}+\frac{1}{b(b+1)}\right)^{\max(0,u-1)}.$$

Proof The first result follows from Lemma A.22 (see also [36]).

For the second result, we use induction on r. We have already shown the result for $r = v = 1$.

Now assume that

$$|\chi_{r-1,v}(a_1,\ldots,a_v;\kappa_1,\ldots,\kappa_v)|$$
$$\le \min_{0\le u\le v}\frac{1}{b^{\mu_u(k)}}\frac{(r-1)!}{(r-u)!}\frac{3^{\min(1,u)}}{(2\sin(\pi/b))^u}\left(1+\frac{1}{b}+\frac{1}{b(b+1)}\right)^{\max(0,u-1)}.$$

We show that the result holds for r. We have already shown that $|\chi_{r,v}| \le \frac{1}{r+1}$, which proves the result for $u = 0$.

By taking the absolute value of (14.5) and using the triangular inequality, we obtain

$$\begin{aligned}
&|\chi_{r,v}(a_1,\ldots,a_v;\kappa_1,\ldots,\kappa_v)| \\
&\quad \le rb^{-a_1}\Bigg(|1-\omega_b^{-\kappa_1}|^{-1}|\chi_{r-1,v-1}(a_2,\ldots,a_v;\kappa_2,\ldots,\kappa_v)| \\
&\quad + |1/2+(\omega_b^{-\kappa_1}-1)^{-1}||\chi_{r-1,v}(a_1,\ldots,a_v;\kappa_1,\ldots,\kappa_v)| \\
&\quad + \sum_{c=1}^{\infty}\sum_{\vartheta=1}^{b-1} b^{-c}|\omega_b^{\vartheta}-1|^{-1}|\chi_{r-1,v+1}(a_1+c,a_1,\ldots,a_v;\vartheta,\kappa_1,\ldots,\kappa_v)|\Bigg).
\end{aligned} \tag{14.7}$$

Using Lemma 14.9, $|\chi_{r-1,v}| \le \frac{1}{r}$ and $\sum_{c=1}^{\infty} b^{-c} = \frac{1}{b-1}$, we obtain from (14.7) that

$$|\chi_{r,v}(a_1,\ldots,a_v;\kappa_1,\ldots,\kappa_v)| \le \frac{3b^{-a_1}}{2\sin(\pi/b)},$$

which proves the bound for $u=1$.

To prove the bound for $1 < u \le v$, we proceed in the same manner. Using Lemma 14.9 and

$$\begin{aligned}
&|\chi_{r-1,v}(a_1,\ldots,a_v;\kappa_1,\ldots,\kappa_v)| \\
&\quad \le \frac{1}{b^{\mu_{u-1}(k)}}\frac{(r-1)!}{(r-u+1)!}\frac{3^{\min(1,u-1)}}{(2\sin(\pi/b))^{u-1}}\left(1+\frac{1}{b}+\frac{1}{b(b+1)}\right)^{\max(0,u-2)},
\end{aligned}$$

we obtain

$$\begin{aligned}
&|\chi_{r,v}(a_1,\ldots,a_v;\kappa_1,\ldots,\kappa_v)| \\
&\quad \le \frac{rb^{-a_1}}{2\sin(\pi/b)}\Bigg(|\chi_{r-1,v-1}(a_2,\ldots,a_v;\kappa_2,\ldots,\kappa_v)| \\
&\qquad + |\chi_{r-1,v}(a_1,\ldots,a_v;\kappa_1,\ldots,\kappa_v)| \\
&\qquad + \sum_{c=1}^{\infty}\sum_{\vartheta=1}^{b-1} b^{-c}|\chi_{r-1,v+1}(a_1+c,a_1,\ldots,a_v;\vartheta,\kappa_1,\ldots,\kappa_v)|\Bigg) \\
&\quad \le \frac{1}{b^{\mu_u(k)}}\frac{r!}{(r-u+1)!}\frac{3^{\min(1,u)}}{(2\sin(\pi/b))^{u}}\left(1+\frac{1}{b}+\frac{1}{b(b+1)}\right)^{\max(0,u-2)} \\
&\qquad \times \left(1+b^{a_2-a_1}+\frac{b^{a_2-a_1}}{b+1}\right) \\
&\quad \le \frac{1}{b^{\mu_u(k)}}\frac{r!}{(r-u+1)!}\frac{3^{\min(1,u)}}{(2\sin(\pi/b))^{u}}\left(1+\frac{1}{b}+\frac{1}{b(b+1)}\right)^{\max(0,u-1)},
\end{aligned}$$

as $\sum_{c=1}^{\infty}\sum_{\vartheta=1}^{b-1} b^{-2c} = \frac{1}{b+1}$ and $a_1 > a_2$. Thus, the result follows. □

Now let $f(x) = f_0 + f_1 x + f_2 x^2 + \cdots$. The kth Walsh coefficient of f is given by

$$\widehat{f}(k) = \int_0^1 f(x)\overline{{}_b\mathrm{wal}_k(x)}\,\mathrm{d}x = \sum_{r=0}^{\infty} f_r \int_0^1 x^r\,\overline{{}_b\mathrm{wal}_k(x)}\,\mathrm{d}x$$

$$= \sum_{r=v}^{\infty} f_r \chi_{r,v}(a_1, \ldots, a_v; \kappa_1, \ldots, \kappa_v).$$

We can estimate the kth Walsh coefficient by

$$|\widehat{f}(k)| = \left|\sum_{r=v}^{\infty} \chi_{r,v}(a_1, \ldots, a_v; \kappa_1, \ldots, \kappa_v) f_r\right|$$

$$\leq \sum_{r=v}^{\infty} |\chi_{r,v}(a_1, \ldots, a_v; \kappa_1, \ldots, \kappa_v)||f_r|$$

$$\leq \sum_{r=v}^{\infty} |f_r| \min_{0 \leq u \leq v} \frac{1}{b^{\mu_u(k)}} \frac{r!}{(r-u+1)!} \frac{3^{\min(1,u)}}{(2\sin(\pi/b))^u} \times \left(1 + \frac{1}{b} + \frac{1}{b(b+1)}\right)^{\max(0,u-1)}$$

$$\leq \min_{0 \leq u \leq v} \frac{1}{b^{\mu_u(k)}} \frac{3^{\min(1,u)}}{(2\sin(\pi/b))^u} \left(1 + \frac{1}{b} + \frac{1}{b(b+1)}\right)^{\max(0,u-1)} \times \sum_{r=v}^{\infty} \frac{r!|f_r|}{(r-u+1)!}.$$

Hence, we have shown the following theorem.

Theorem 14.11 *Let $f(x) = f_0 + f_1 x + f_2 x^2 + \cdots$ and let $k \in \mathbb{N}$ with b-adic expansion $k = \kappa_1 b^{a_1 - 1} + \cdots + \kappa_v b^{a_v - 1}$ with $v \in \mathbb{N}$, digits $1 \leq \kappa_1, \ldots, \kappa_v < b$ and $a_1 > a_2 > \cdots > a_v \geq 1$. Then we have*

$$|\widehat{f}(k)| \leq \min_{0 \leq u \leq v} \frac{1}{b^{\mu_u(k)}} \frac{3^{\min(1,u)}}{(2\sin(\pi/b))^u} \left(1 + \frac{1}{b} + \frac{1}{b(b+1)}\right)^{\max(0,u-1)} \sum_{r=v}^{\infty} \frac{r!|f_r|}{(r-u+1)!}.$$

The bound in the theorem only makes sense, of course, for u for which $\sum_{r=v}^{\infty} \frac{r!|f_r|}{(r-u+1)!}$ is finite. We give some examples:

1. For $f \in C^{\infty}([0, 1])$, we have $f^{(r)}(0) = r! f_r$. If $|f^{(r)}(0)|$ grows exponentially (e.g. for $f(x) = \mathrm{e}^{ax}$ with $a > 1$), then $\sum_{r=v}^{\infty} \frac{|f^{(r)}(0)|}{(r-v+1)!}$ is finite for any $v \in \mathbb{N}$. The theorem implies that the Walsh coefficients decay with order $O(b^{-\mu_v(k)})$.

2. Using Sterling's formula, we obtain that $\frac{r!}{(r-v+1)!} \approx (r-v+1)^{v-1}$ as r tends to ∞. For $f(x) = \frac{1}{1-cx}$ with $0 < c < 1$, we have $f_r = c^r$. In this case we have

$$\sum_{r=v}^{\infty} \frac{r!|f_r|}{(r-v+1)!} \approx \sum_{r=v}^{\infty} (r-v+1)^{v-1} c^r = c^{v-1} \sum_{r=1}^{\infty} r^{v-1} c^r < \infty,$$

for all $v \in \mathbb{N}$. The theorem implies that the Walsh coefficients decay with order $O(b^{-\mu_v(k)})$.

For $f \in C^\infty([0,1])$ with $f(x) = \sum_{r=0}^{\infty} f_r x^r$, we define the semi-norm

$$\|f\| = \sum_{r=1}^{\infty} |f_r| = \sum_{r=1}^{\infty} \frac{|f^{(r)}(0)|}{r!}.$$

Then, the $(v-1)$th derivative of f is given by

$$f^{(v-1)}(x) = \sum_{r=0}^{\infty} \frac{(v-1+r)!}{r!} f_{v-1+r} x^r = \sum_{r=v-1}^{\infty} \frac{r!}{(r-v+1)!} f_r x^{r-v+1}$$

and

$$\|f^{(v-1)}\| = \sum_{r=v}^{\infty} \frac{r!|f_r|}{(r-v+1)!} = \sum_{r=v}^{\infty} \frac{|f^{(r)}(0)|}{(r-v+1)!}.$$

Hence, we obtain the following corollary from Theorem 14.11.

Corollary 14.12 *Let $f \in C^\infty([0,1])$ with $\|f^{(z)}\| < \infty$ for all $z \in \mathbb{N}_0$. Then, for every $k \in \mathbb{N}$ with b-adic expansion $k = \kappa_1 b^{a_1-1} + \cdots + \kappa_v b^{a_v-1}$ with $v \in \mathbb{N}$, digits $1 \le \kappa_1, \ldots, \kappa_v < b$ and $a_1 > a_2 > \cdots > a_v \ge 1$, we have*

$$|\widehat{f}(k)| \le \frac{1}{b^{\mu_v(k)}} \frac{3}{(2\sin(\pi/b))^v} \left(1 + \frac{1}{b} + \frac{1}{b(b+1)}\right)^{v-1} \|f^{(v-1)}\|.$$

Let us consider another example: let $f_r = r^{-\delta}$, with $\delta > 1$. For instance, we can choose $u = \min(v, \lceil \delta \rceil - 2)$ in the theorem above which guarantees that $\sum_{r=v}^{\infty} \frac{r!|f_r|}{(r-u+1)!} < \infty$. On the other hand, this sum is not finite for $\lceil \delta \rceil - 2 < u \le v$. The theorem implies that the Walsh coefficients decay with order $O(b^{-\mu_{\min(v,\lceil\delta\rceil-2)}(k)})$. Note that this function f is only $\lceil \delta \rceil - 2$ times continuously differentiable. We consider this case in the next section.

14.4 On the Walsh coefficients of functions in $C^\alpha([0,1])$

Before the next lemma, we recall the variation of fractional order introduced in Section 13.5: for $0 < \lambda \le 1$ and $f : [0,1] \to \mathbb{R}$, let

$$V_\lambda(f) = \sup_{\substack{N \in \mathbb{N} \\ 0=x_0<x_1<\cdots<x_N=1}} \sum_{n=1}^{N} |x_n - x_{n-1}| \frac{|f(x_n) - f(x_{n-1})|}{|x_n - x_{n-1}|^\lambda},$$

where the supremum is taken over all partitions of the interval $[0,1]$. For $\lambda = 1$, we obtain the total variation.

If f has a continuous first derivative on $[0,1]$, then

$$V_1(f) = \int_0^1 |f'(x)| \,\mathrm{d}x.$$

If f satisfies a Hölder condition of order $0 < \lambda \le 1$, i.e. $|f(x) - f(y)| \le C_f |x - y|^\lambda$ for all $x, y \in [0,1]$, then $V_\lambda(f) \le C_f$.

Lemma 14.13 *Let $f \in L_1([0,1])$ and let $k \in \mathbb{N}$ with $k = \kappa b^{a-1} + k'$ where $a \in \mathbb{N}$, $1 \le \kappa < b$, $0 \le k' < b^{a-1}$ and let $0 \le c < b^{a-1}$. Then*

$$\left| \int_{cb^{-a+1}}^{(c+1)b^{-a+1}} f(x) \overline{{}_b\mathrm{wal}_k(x)} \,\mathrm{d}x \right| \le b^{-a+1} \sup_{d,e} |f(e) - f(d)|,$$

where the supremum is taken over all $cb^{-a+1} \le d < e \le (c+1)b^{-a+1}$ with $b^a|e - d| \in \{1, \ldots, b-1\}$.

Proof We have $\overline{{}_b\mathrm{wal}_k(x)} = \overline{{}_b\mathrm{wal}_{\kappa b^{a-1}}(x)}\ \overline{{}_b\mathrm{wal}_{k'}(x)}$ and the function $\overline{{}_b\mathrm{wal}_{k'}(x)}$ is constant on the interval $[cb^{-a+1}, (c+1)b^{-a+1})$. Hence, we have

$$\left| \int_{cb^{-a+1}}^{(c+1)b^{-a+1}} f(x) \overline{{}_b\mathrm{wal}_k(x)} \,\mathrm{d}x \right| = \left| \int_{cb^{-a+1}}^{(c+1)b^{-a+1}} f(x) \overline{{}_b\mathrm{wal}_{\kappa b^{a-1}}(x)} \,\mathrm{d}x \right|.$$

Note that the function $\overline{{}_b\mathrm{wal}_{\kappa b^{a-1}}}$ is constant on each of the sub-intervals $[rb^{-a}, (r+1)b^{-a})$ for $0 \le r < b^a$. Without loss of generality we may assume that $c = 0$; for all other c the result follows by the same arguments. Thus, we have

$$\int_0^{b^{-a+1}} f(x) \overline{{}_b\mathrm{wal}_{\kappa b^{a-1}}(x)} \,\mathrm{d}x = \sum_{r=0}^{b-1} \overline{{}_b\mathrm{wal}_\kappa(r/b)} \int_{rb^{-a}}^{(r+1)b^{-a}} f(x) \,\mathrm{d}x.$$

Now let $a_r := \int_{rb^{-a}}^{(r+1)b^{-a}} f(x) \,\mathrm{d}x$ and $A := \frac{1}{b} \sum_{r=0}^{b-1} a_r$. Then we have

$$\sum_{r=0}^{b-1} \overline{{}_b\mathrm{wal}_\kappa(r/b)} a_r = \sum_{r=0}^{b-1} \overline{{}_b\mathrm{wal}_\kappa(r/b)} (a_r - A)$$

and

$$|a_r - A| \le \frac{1}{b}\sum_{t=0}^{b-1} |a_r - a_t| \le \max_{0\le t<b} |a_r - a_t|.$$

We have $a_t = \int_{rb^{-a}}^{(r+1)b^{-a}} f(x+(t-r)b^{-a})\,\mathrm{d}x$ and therefore,

$$\begin{aligned}
|a_r - a_t| &= \left| \int_{rb^{-a}}^{(r+1)b^{-a}} (f(x) - f(x+(t-r)b^{-a}))\,\mathrm{d}x \right| \\
&\le \int_{rb^{-a}}^{(r+1)b^{-a}} \left| f(x) - f(x+(t-r)b^{-a}) \right| \mathrm{d}x \\
&\le \frac{1}{b^a} \sup_{\max(0,r-t)\le xb^a \le \min(b,b+r-t)} \left| f(x) - f(x+(t-r)b^{-a}) \right|.
\end{aligned}$$

Therefore,

$$\begin{aligned}
\left| \sum_{r=0}^{b-1} \overline{{}_b\mathrm{wal}_\kappa(r/b) a_r} \right| &\le \sum_{r=0}^{b-1} |a_r - A| \\
&\le \sum_{r=0}^{b-1} \max_{0\le t<b} |a_r - a_t| \\
&\le b \max_{0\le r<t<b} |a_r - a_t| \\
&\le b^{-a+1} \max_{0\le \ell<b} \sup |f(x) - f(x+\ell b^{-a})|,
\end{aligned}$$

where the supremum is taken over all x for which $0 \le x \le b^{-a}(b-\ell)$. The result follows. □

In the following lemma, we now obtain a bound on the Walsh coefficients for functions of bounded variation. This lemma has already appeared in [79] (albeit in a slightly different form; see also [36, 217]).

Lemma 14.14 *Let $0 < \lambda \le 1$ and let $f \in L_2([0,1])$ satisfy $V_\lambda(f) < \infty$. Then, for any $k \in \mathbb{N}$, the kth Walsh coefficient of f satisfies*

$$|\widehat{f}(k)| \le b^{1-\lambda(a-1)} V_\lambda(f),$$

where $k = \kappa b^{a-1} + k'$, where $1 \le \kappa < b$, $a \in \mathbb{N}$ and $0 \le k' < b^{a-1}$.

Proof Let $f \in L_2([0,1])$ with kth Walsh coefficient $\widehat{f}(k)$. Let $k \in \mathbb{N}$ be given. Then we have

$$\left|\int_0^1 f(x)\,\overline{{}_b\mathrm{wal}_k(x)}\,\mathrm{d}x\right| \le \sum_{c=0}^{b^{a-1}-1}\left|\int_{cb^{-a+1}}^{(c+1)b^{-a+1}} f(x)\,\overline{{}_b\mathrm{wal}_k(x)}\,\mathrm{d}x\right|.$$

Now we use Lemma 14.13 and thereby obtain that the above sum is bounded by

$$\sum_{c=0}^{b^{a-1}-1} b^{-a+1}\sup_{d,e}|f(e)-f(d)|,$$

where the supremum is taken over all $cb^{-a+1} \le d < e \le (c+1)b^{-a+1}$ with $b^a|e-d| \in \{1,\ldots,b-1\}$. Now we have

$$\begin{aligned} &b^{-a+1}\sup_{d,e}|f(e)-f(d)| \\ &\le \sup\sum_{i=0}^{N-1}|y_{i+1}-y_i|^{1-\lambda}|f(y_{i+1})-f(y_i)|\frac{b^{-a+1}}{|y_{i+1}-y_i|^{1-\lambda}}, \end{aligned}$$

where the supremum on the right-hand side of the inequality is taken over all partitions of the interval $[cb^{-a+1},(c+1)b^{-a+1})$ of the form $N \in \mathbb{N}$ and $cb^{-a+1} = y_0 < y_1 < \cdots < y_N = (c+1)b^{-a+1}$ where $b^a|y_{i+1}-y_i| \in \{1,\ldots,b-1\}$ for $0 \le i \le N-1$.

For all $0 \le i \le N-1$, we have $b^{-a} \le |y_{i+1}-y_i| \le b^{-a+1}$ and therefore,

$$\frac{b^{-a+1}}{|y_{i+1}-y_i|^{1-\lambda}} \le b|y_{i+1}-y_i|^{\lambda} \le b^{1-\lambda(a-1)}$$

and hence,

$$b^{-a+1}\sup_{d,e}|f(e)-f(d)| \le b^{1-\lambda(a-1)}\sup\sum_{i=0}^{N-1}|y_{i+1}-y_i|^{1-\lambda}|f(y_{i+1})-f(y_i)|,$$

where the supremum is taken over all partitions of the interval $[cb^{-a+1},(c+1)b^{-a+1})$ of the above form.

Note that

$$\begin{aligned} &\sum_{c=0}^{b^{a-1}-1}\sup\sum_{i=0}^{N-1}|y_{i+1}-y_i|^{1-\lambda}|f(y_{i+1})-f(y_i)| \\ &\le \sup_{\substack{N\in\mathbb{N}\\ 0=x_0<x_1<\cdots<x_N=1}}\sum_{i=0}^{N-1}|x_{i+1}-x_i|\frac{|f(x_{i+1})-f(x_i)|}{|x_{i+1}-x_i|^{\lambda}} = V_\lambda(f), \end{aligned}$$

where the supremum on the left-hand side is taken over all partitions of the interval $[cb^{-a+1}, (c+1)b^{-a+1})$ of the above form and the supremum on the right-hand side is taken over all partitions of $[0, 1)$ into sub-intervals. Thus, the result follows. □

The decay of the Walsh coefficients of functions with smoothness $0 < \alpha \leq 1$ has already been considered and we deal with $\alpha > 1$ in the following.

Now let $f \in L_2([0, 1])$ with $V_\lambda(f) < \infty$ and let $F_1(x) := \int_0^x f(y)\,\mathrm{d}y$. Then, using integration by parts as in the previous section, we obtain for $k \in \mathbb{N}$

$$\widehat{F}_1(k) = \int_0^1 F_1(x)\overline{{}_b\mathrm{wal}_k(x)}\,\mathrm{d}x = -\int_0^1 f(x)J_k(x)\,\mathrm{d}x.$$

Substituting the Walsh series for J_k from Lemma 14.8, we obtain

$$\widehat{F}_1(k) = -\frac{1}{b^{a_1}}\left(\frac{1}{1-\omega_b^{-\kappa_1}}\widehat{f}(k') + \left(\frac{1}{2} + \frac{1}{\omega_b^{-\kappa_1}-1}\right)\widehat{f}(k)\right.$$
$$\left. + \sum_{c=1}^{\infty}\sum_{\vartheta=1}^{b-1}\frac{1}{b^c(\omega_b^{\vartheta}-1)}\widehat{f}(\vartheta b^{a_1+c-1}+k)\right).$$

Taking the absolute value on both sides and using the same estimations as in the previous section, we obtain

$$|\widehat{F}_1(k)| \leq \frac{b^{-a_1}}{2\sin(\pi/b)}\left(|\widehat{f}(k')| + |\widehat{f}(k)| + \sum_{c=1}^{\infty}\sum_{\vartheta=1}^{b-1}\frac{1}{b^c}|\widehat{f}(\vartheta b^{a_1+c-1}+k)|\right). \quad (14.8)$$

Thus, using Lemma 14.14, we obtain for $k \in \mathbb{N}$ with $v \geq 2$, that

$$|\widehat{F}_1(k)| \leq b^{-a_1-\lambda a_2}V_\lambda(f)\frac{b^{1+\lambda}}{2\sin(\pi/b)}(1+2b^{-\lambda}).$$

For $k = \kappa_1 b^{a_1-1}$, we obtain

$$|\widehat{F}_1(k)| \leq \frac{b^{-a_1}}{2\sin(\pi/b)}\left(|\widehat{f}(0)| + 2b^{1+\lambda}b^{-\lambda a_1}V_\lambda(f)\right).$$

Defining $F_\alpha(x) = \int_0^x F_{\alpha-1}(y)\,\mathrm{d}y$ for $\alpha \geq 1$, we can obtain bounds on the Walsh coefficients of F_α by using induction on α. Using similar arguments as in the proof of Lemma 14.10, we obtain for $v > \alpha$ that

$$|\widehat{F_\alpha}(k)| \leq b^{-\mu_\alpha(k)-\lambda a_{\alpha+1}}V_\lambda(f)\frac{b^{1+\lambda}(1+2b^{-\lambda})}{(2\sin(\pi/b))^\alpha}\left(1+\frac{1}{b}+\frac{1}{b(b+1)}\right)^{\alpha-1}, \quad (14.9)$$

and for $v = \alpha$ that

$$|\widehat{F_\alpha}(k)| \tag{14.10}$$
$$\leq \frac{b^{-\mu_\alpha(k)}}{(2\sin(\pi/b))^\alpha}\left(1+\frac{1}{b}+\frac{1}{b(b+1)}\right)^{\alpha-1}\left(|\widehat{f}(0)| + 2b^{1+\lambda}b^{-\lambda a_\alpha} V_\lambda(f)\right).$$

For $1 \leq v < \alpha$, we have

$$|\widehat{F_\alpha}(k)| \leq \frac{b^{-\mu_\alpha(k)}}{(2\sin(\pi/b))^v}\left(1+\frac{1}{b}+\frac{1}{b(b+1)}\right)^{v-1}$$
$$\times\left(|\widehat{F}_{\alpha-v}(0)| + 2b^{1+\lambda}b^{-\lambda a_v} V_\lambda(F_{\alpha-v})\right). \tag{14.11}$$

Note that we also have $F_\alpha(x) = \int_0^1 f(t)\frac{(x-t)_+^{\alpha-1}}{(\alpha-1)!}\,\mathrm{d}t$, where $(x-t)_+^{\alpha-1} = (x-t)^{\alpha-1}\chi_{[0,x)}(t)$ for $0 \leq x, t \leq 1$ and $\chi_{[0,x)}(t)$ is 1 for $t \in [0, x)$ and 0 otherwise.

A function $f \in C^\alpha([0,1])$, for which $V_\lambda(f^{(\alpha)}) < \infty$, can be represented by a Taylor series

$$f(x) = f(0) + \frac{f^{(1)}(0)}{1!}x + \cdots + \frac{f^{(\alpha-1)}(0)}{(\alpha-1)!}x^{\alpha-1} + \int_0^1 f^{(\alpha)}(t)\frac{(x-t)_+^{\alpha-1}}{(\alpha-1)!}\,\mathrm{d}t.$$

With this we can now obtain a bound on the Walsh coefficients of f. For $v \geq \alpha$, we know from above that

$$\int_0^1 \left(f(0) + \frac{f^{(1)}(0)}{1!}x + \cdots + \frac{f^{(\alpha-1)}(0)}{(\alpha-1)!}x^{\alpha-1}\right)\overline{{}_b\mathrm{wal}_k(x)}\,\mathrm{d}x = 0.$$

To bound the Walsh coefficient of $\int_0^1 f^{(\alpha)}(t)\frac{(x-t)_+^{\alpha-1}}{(\alpha-1)!}\,\mathrm{d}t$ for $v > \alpha$, we can use (14.9) to obtain

$$|\widehat{f}(k)| \leq b^{-\mu_\alpha(k)-\lambda a_{\alpha+1}} V_\lambda(f^{(\alpha)})\frac{b^{1+\lambda}(1+2b^{-\lambda})}{(2\sin(\pi/b))^\alpha}\left(1+\frac{1}{b}+\frac{1}{b(b+1)}\right)^{\alpha-1}.$$

For $v = \alpha$, we can use (14.10) to obtain

$$|\widehat{f}(k)| \leq \frac{b^{-\mu_\alpha(k)}}{(2\sin(\pi/b))^\alpha}\left(1+\frac{1}{b}+\frac{1}{b(b+1)}\right)^{\alpha-1}$$
$$\times\left(|\widehat{f^{(\alpha)}}(0)| + 2b^{1+\lambda}b^{-\lambda a_\alpha} V_\lambda(f^{(\alpha)})\right).$$

For $1 \leq v < \alpha$, we have

$$\left|\int_0^1 \left(f(0) + \frac{f^{(1)}(0)}{1!}x + \cdots + \frac{f^{(\alpha-1)}(0)}{(\alpha-1)!}x^{\alpha-1}\right)\overline{{}_b\mathrm{wal}_k(x)}\,\mathrm{d}x\right|$$
$$\leq b^{-\mu_\alpha(k)}\frac{3}{(2\sin(\pi/b))^v}\left(1+\frac{1}{b}+\frac{1}{b(b+1)}\right)^{v-1}\sum_{r=v}^{\alpha-1}\frac{|f^{(r)}(0)|}{(r-v+1)!}$$

and therefore, using (14.11), we obtain

$$|\widehat{f}(k)| \le \frac{b^{-\mu_\alpha(k)}}{(2\sin(\pi/b))^{v}}\left(1+\frac{1}{b}+\frac{1}{b(b+1)}\right)^{v-1}$$
$$\times\left[3\sum_{r=v}^{\alpha-1}\frac{|f^{(r)}(0)|}{(r-v+1)!}+\left(|\widehat{f^{(v)}}(0)|+2b^{1+\lambda}b^{-\lambda a_v}V_\lambda(f^{(v)})\right)\right],$$

where $\widehat{f^{(v)}}(0)$ denotes the 0th Walsh coefficient of $f^{(v)}$. We have shown the following theorem.

Theorem 14.15 *Let $f \in C^\alpha([0,1])$ with $V_\lambda(f^{(\alpha)}) < \infty$ and let $k \in \mathbb{N}$. Then, for $v > \alpha$, we have*

$$|\widehat{f}(k)| \le b^{-\mu_\alpha(k)-\lambda a_{\alpha+1}}V_\lambda(f^{(\alpha)})\frac{b^{1+\lambda}(1+2b^{-\lambda})}{(2\sin(\pi/b))^{\alpha}}\left(1+\frac{1}{b}+\frac{1}{b(b+1)}\right)^{\alpha-1},$$

for $\alpha = v$, we have

$$|\widehat{f}(k)| \le \frac{b^{-\mu_\alpha(k)}}{(2\sin(\pi/b))^{\alpha}}\left(1+\frac{1}{b}+\frac{1}{b(b+1)}\right)^{\alpha-1}$$
$$\times\left(\left|\int_0^1 f^{(\alpha)}(x)\,\mathrm{d}x\right|+2b^{1+\lambda}b^{-\lambda a_\alpha}V_\lambda(f^{(\alpha)})\right),$$

and for $v < \alpha$, we have

$$|\widehat{f}(k)| \le \frac{b^{-\mu_\alpha(k)}}{(2\sin(\pi/b))^{v}}\left(1+\frac{1}{b}+\frac{1}{b(b+1)}\right)^{v-1}$$
$$\times\left[3\sum_{r=v}^{\alpha-1}\frac{|f^{(r)}(0)|}{(r-v+1)!}+\left(\left|\int_0^1 f^{(v)}(x)\,\mathrm{d}x\right|+2b^{1+\lambda}b^{-\lambda a_v}V_\lambda(f^{(v)})\right)\right].$$

We also prove bounds on the decay of the Walsh coefficients of functions from Sobolev spaces. For this, we first need bounds on the Walsh coefficients of Bernoulli polynomials, which we consider in the next section.

14.5 On the Walsh coefficients of Bernoulli polynomials

For $r \in \mathbb{N}_0$, let $B_r(\cdot)$ denote the Bernoulli polynomial of degree r and $b_r(\cdot) = \frac{B_r(\cdot)}{r!}$. For example, we have $B_0(x) = 1$, $B_1(x) = x - 1/2$, $B_2(x) = x^2 - x + 1/6$ and so on. It is well known that $\int_0^1 B_r(x)\,\mathrm{d}x = 0$, for all $r \in \mathbb{N}$, see reference [1], and we note that $B_{2r}(|x-y|) = B_{2r}(\{x-y\})$.

Those polynomials have the properties

$$b_r'(x) = b_{r-1}(x) \quad \text{and} \quad \int_0^1 b_r(x) = 0 \quad \text{for all } r \in \mathbb{N}.$$

We obviously have $b_0'(x) = 0$ and $\int_0^1 b_0(x)\,\mathrm{d}x = 1$. Further, $B_r(1-x) = (-1)^r B_r(x)$ and also, $b_r(1-x) = (-1)^r b_r(x)$. The numbers $B_r = B_r(0)$ are the Bernoulli numbers and $B_r = 0$ for all odd $r \geq 3$. Further, for $r \in \mathbb{N}$, we have

$$b_r(x) = -\frac{1}{(2\pi \mathrm{i})^r} \sum_{h \in \mathbb{Z}\setminus\{0\}} h^{-r} \mathrm{e}^{2\pi \mathrm{i} h x}, \qquad \text{for } 0 \leq x \leq 1. \tag{14.12}$$

It is more convenient to deal with $b_r(\cdot)$ rather than the Bernoulli polynomials.

For $r, k \in \mathbb{N}$ with $k = \kappa_1 b^{a_1-1} + \cdots + \kappa_v b^{a_v-1}$ where $v \in \mathbb{N}$, $\kappa_1, \ldots, \kappa_v \in \{1, \ldots, b-1\}$ and $a_1 > a_2 > \cdots > a_v \geq 1$, let

$$\beta_r(k) = \beta_{r,v}(a_1, \ldots, a_v; \kappa_1, \ldots, \kappa_v) := \int_0^1 b_r(x) \overline{{}_b\mathrm{wal}_k(x)}\,\mathrm{d}x. \tag{14.13}$$

As for $\chi_{r,v}$, we also have $\beta_{r,v} = 0$ for $v > r$. Further, for $k = 0$, let $v = 0$ and we have $\beta_{r,0} = 0$ for all $r \in \mathbb{N}$.

The Walsh series for b_1 can be obtained from the Walsh series of J_0 from Lemma 14.8 and is given by (see also Appendix A)

$$b_1(x) = x - \frac{1}{2} = \sum_{c=1}^{\infty} \sum_{\vartheta=1}^{b-1} \frac{1}{b^c(\omega_b^{-\vartheta} - 1)} \, {}_b\mathrm{wal}_{\vartheta b^{c-1}}(x).$$

Thus,

$$\beta_{1,1}(a_1; \kappa_1) = -b^{-a_1}(1 - \omega_b^{-\kappa_1})^{-1}.$$

Using integration by parts and $J_k(0) = J_k(1) = 0$, we obtain for all $r > 1$ that

$$\int_0^1 b_r(x) \overline{{}_b\mathrm{wal}_k(x)}\,\mathrm{d}x = -\int_0^1 b_{r-1}(x) J_k(x)\,\mathrm{d}x. \tag{14.14}$$

Using Lemma 14.8 and (14.14), we obtain for $1 \leq v \leq r$ and $r > 1$ that

$$\begin{aligned} &\beta_{r,v}(a_1, \ldots, a_v; \kappa_1, \ldots, \kappa_v) \\ &= -\frac{1}{b^{a_1}} \Bigg(\frac{1}{1 - \omega_b^{-\kappa_1}} \beta_{r-1,v-1}(a_2, \ldots, a_v; \kappa_2, \ldots, \kappa_v) \\ &\quad + \left(\frac{1}{2} + \frac{1}{\omega_b^{-\kappa_1} - 1} \right) \beta_{r-1,v}(a_1, \ldots, a_v; \kappa_1, \ldots, \kappa_v) \\ &\quad + \sum_{c=1}^{\infty} \sum_{\vartheta=1}^{b-1} \frac{1}{b^c(\omega_b^{\vartheta} - 1)} \beta_{r-1,v+1}(a_1 + c, a_1, \ldots, a_v; \vartheta, \kappa_1, \ldots, \kappa_v) \Bigg). \end{aligned} \tag{14.15}$$

From (14.15), for all $r \in \mathbb{N}$, we can obtain

$$\beta_{r,r}(a_1,\ldots,a_r;\kappa_1,\ldots,\kappa_r) = \frac{(-1)^r}{b^{a_1+\cdots+a_r}} \prod_{w=1}^{r} \frac{1}{1-\omega_b^{-\kappa_w}}.$$

The first few values of $\beta_{r,v}$ are as follows:

- $r = 1$: $\beta_{1,0} = 0$, $\beta_{1,1}(a_1;\kappa_1) = -b^{-a_1}(1-\omega_b^{-\kappa_1})^{-1}$;
- $r = 2$: $\beta_{2,0} = 0$, $\beta_{2,1}(a_1;\kappa_1) = b^{-2a_1}(1-\omega_b^{-\kappa_1})^{-1}(1/2+(\omega_b^{-\kappa_1}-1)^{-1})$, $\beta_{2,2}(a_1,a_2;\kappa_1,\kappa_2) = b^{-a_1-a_2}(1-\omega_b^{-\kappa_1})^{-1}(1-\omega_b^{-\kappa_2})^{-1}$.

In principle we can obtain all values of $\beta_{r,v}$ recursively using (14.15). We have already calculated $\beta_{r,v}$ for $v = r$ and we could continue doing so for $v = r-1,\ldots,1$, but the formulae become increasingly complex, so we only prove a bound on them.

For any $r \geq 0$ and a non-negative integer k, we introduce the function

$$\mu_{r,\mathrm{per}}(k) = \begin{cases} 0 & \text{for } r = 0, k \geq 0, \\ 0 & \text{for } k = 0, r \geq 0, \\ a_1 + \cdots + a_v + (r-v)a_v & \text{for } 1 \leq v < r, \\ a_1 + \cdots + a_r & \text{for } v \geq r. \end{cases} \tag{14.16}$$

Lemma 14.16 *For any $r \geq 2$ and $1 \leq v \leq r$, we have*

$$|\beta_{r,v}(a_1,\ldots,a_v;\kappa_1,\ldots,\kappa_v)| \leq \frac{b^{-\mu_{r,\mathrm{per}}(k)}}{(2\sin(\pi/b))^r}\left(1+\frac{1}{b}+\frac{1}{b(b+1)}\right)^{r-2}.$$

Proof We prove the bound by induction on r. Using Lemma 14.9 it can easily be seen that the result holds for $r = 2$. Hence, assume now that $r > 2$ and the result holds for $r-1$. By taking the absolute value of (14.15) and using the triangular inequality together with Lemma 14.9, we obtain

$$\begin{aligned} |\beta_{r,v}(a_1,\ldots,a_v;\kappa_1,\ldots,\kappa_v)| &\leq \frac{b^{-a_1}}{2\sin(\pi/b)} \\ &\times \Bigg(|\beta_{r-1,v-1}(a_2,\ldots,a_v;\kappa_2,\ldots,\kappa_v)| + |\beta_{r-1,v}(a_1,\ldots,a_v;\kappa_1,\ldots,\kappa_v)| \\ &\quad + \sum_{c=1}^{\infty}\sum_{\vartheta=1}^{b-1}\frac{1}{b^c}|\beta_{r-1,v+1}(a_1+c,a_1,\ldots,a_v;\vartheta,\kappa_1,\ldots,\kappa_v)| \Bigg). \end{aligned}$$

We can now use the induction assumption for $|\beta_{r-1,v-1}|$, $|\beta_{r-1,v}|$, $|\beta_{r-1,v+1}|$. Hence, for $v > 1$, we obtain

$$|\beta_{r,v}(a_1,\ldots,a_v;\kappa_1,\ldots,\kappa_v)| \le \frac{b^{-\mu_{r,\mathrm{per}}(k)}}{(2\sin(\pi/b))^r}\left(1+\frac{1}{b}+\frac{1}{b(b+1)}\right)^{r-3} \times\left(1+b^{a_2-a_1}+\sum_{c=1}^{\infty}\sum_{\vartheta=1}^{b-1} b^{-2c}b^{a_2-a_1}\right).$$

By noting that $\sum_{c=1}^{\infty}\sum_{\vartheta=1}^{b-1} b^{-2c} = \frac{1}{b+1}$, and $a_1 > a_2$, we obtain the result.

For $v = 1$, note that $\beta_{r,0} = 0$. In this case we have

$$\begin{aligned}|\beta_{r,1}(a_1;\kappa_1)| &\le \frac{b^{-\mu_{r,\mathrm{per}}(k)}}{(2\sin(\pi/b))^r}\left(1+\frac{1}{b}+\frac{1}{b(b+1)}\right)^{r-3}\left(1+\sum_{c=1}^{\infty}\sum_{\vartheta=1}^{b-1} b^{-2c}\right)\\ &\le \frac{b^{-\mu_{r,\mathrm{per}}(k)}}{(2\sin(\pi/b))^r}\left(1+\frac{1}{b}+\frac{1}{b(b+1)}\right)^{r-2},\end{aligned}$$

which implies the result. □

The b_r are polynomials, but using (14.12) we can extend b_r periodically so that it is defined on $\mathbb{R}$. We denote those functions by $\widetilde{b}_r$. Then, for $r \in \mathbb{N}$, we have

$$\widetilde{b}_{2r}(x) = \frac{2(-1)^{r+1}}{(2\pi)^{2r}}\sum_{h=1}^{\infty} h^{-2r}\cos(2\pi hx) \qquad \text{for } x \in \mathbb{R},$$

and

$$\widetilde{b}_{2r+1}(x) = \frac{2(-1)^{r+1}}{(2\pi)^{2r+1}}\sum_{h=1}^{\infty} h^{-2r-1}\sin(2\pi hx) \qquad \text{for } x \in \mathbb{R}.$$

From this we can see that $\widetilde{b}_r(x) = (-1)^r\widetilde{b}_r(-x)$ for all $r \ge 2$. Note that for $x, y \in [0,1]$, we have $b_{2r}(|x-y|) = \widetilde{b}_{2r}(x-y)$ and $b_{2r+1}(|x-y|) = (-1)^{1_{x<y}}\widetilde{b}_{2r+1}(x-y)$, where $1_{x<y}$ is 1 for $x < y$ and 0 otherwise. We also extend $B_r(\cdot)$ periodically to $\mathbb{R}$, which we denote by $\widetilde{B}_r(\cdot)$.

In the next section, we also need a bound on the Walsh coefficients of $\widetilde{b}_r(x-y)$. For $k, l \in \mathbb{N}_0$, let

$$\begin{aligned}\gamma_r(k,l) &= \int_0^1\int_0^1 \widetilde{b}_r(x-y)\,\overline{{}_b\mathrm{wal}_k(x)}\,{}_b\mathrm{wal}_l(y)\,\mathrm{d}x\,\mathrm{d}y \qquad (14.17)\\ &= -\frac{1}{(2\pi\mathrm{i})^r}\sum_{h\in\mathbb{Z}\setminus\{0\}} h^{-r}\tau_{h,k}\overline{\tau_{h,l}},\end{aligned}$$

according to (14.12), where

$$\tau_{h,k} := \int_0^1 \mathrm{e}^{2\pi \mathrm{i} h x} \overline{{}_b\mathrm{wal}_k(x)}\,\mathrm{d}x.$$

We have $\gamma_r(k, 0) = \gamma_r(0, l) = 0$ for all $k, l \in \mathbb{N}_0$, as $\int_z^{1+z} \widetilde{b}_r(x)\,\mathrm{d}x = 0$ for any $z \in \mathbb{R}$. Further, we have $\gamma_r(l, k) = (-1)^r \overline{\gamma_r(k, l)}$ and therefore, also, $|\gamma_r(k, l)| = |\gamma_r(l, k)|$.

We obtain bounds on γ_r by induction. In the next lemma, we calculate the values of γ_2.

Lemma 14.17 *For all $k, l \in \mathbb{N}_0$, we have $\gamma_2(k, 0) = \gamma_2(0, l) = 0$. For $k, l \in \mathbb{N}$, we have*

$$\gamma_2(k,l) = \begin{cases} b^{-2a_1}\left(\frac{1}{2\sin^2(\kappa_1\pi/b)} - \frac{1}{3}\right) & \text{if } k = l, \\ b^{-a_1-d_1}(\omega_b^{-\kappa_1} - 1)^{-1}(\omega_b^{\lambda_1} - 1)^{-1} & \text{if } k' = l' > 0, \\ & \text{and } k \neq l, \\ b^{-a_1-d_1}(1/2 + (\omega_b^{-\lambda_1} - 1)^{-1})(\omega_b^{-\kappa_1} - 1)^{-1} & \\ +b^{-2a_1}(1/2 + (\omega_b^{\kappa_1} - 1)^{-1})(1 - \omega_b^{-\kappa_1})^{-1} & \text{if } k' = l, \\ b^{-a_1-d_1}(1/2 + (\omega_b^{\kappa_1} - 1)^{-1})(\omega_b^{\lambda_1} - 1)^{-1} & \\ +b^{-2d_1}(1/2 + (\omega_b^{-\lambda_1} - 1)^{-1})(1 - \omega_b^{\lambda_1})^{-1} & \text{if } k = l', \\ b^{-a_1-a_2}(1 - \omega_b^{-\kappa_2})^{-1}(\omega_b^{-\kappa_1} - 1)^{-1} & \text{if } k'' = l, \\ b^{-d_1-d_2}(1 - \omega_b^{\lambda_2})^{-1}(\omega_b^{\lambda_1} - 1)^{-1} & \text{if } k = l'', \\ 0 & \text{otherwise.} \end{cases}$$

Proof For all $k, l \in \mathbb{N}_0$, we have that $\gamma_2(k, 0) = \gamma_2(0, l) = 0$. Now assume that $k, l > 0$.

The Walsh series for $\widetilde{b}_2(x - y) = b_2(|x - y|) = \frac{(x-y)^2}{2} - \frac{|x-y|}{2} + \frac{1}{12}$ can be calculated in the following way: we have $x = \overline{J_0(x)}$ and $y = \overline{J_0(y)}$ and so

$$\frac{(x-y)^2}{2} = \frac{(\overline{J_0(x) - J_0(y)})^2}{2}.$$

Further,

$$|x - y| = x + y - 2\min(x, y) = x + y - 2\int_0^1 \chi_{[0,x)}(t)\chi_{[0,y)}(t)\,\mathrm{d}t,$$

where $\chi_{[0,x)}(t)$ is 1 for $t \in [0, x)$ and 0 otherwise. Note that $J_k(x) = \int_0^x \overline{{}_b\mathrm{wal}_k(t)}\,\mathrm{d}t = \int_0^1 \chi_{[0,x)}(t)\overline{{}_b\mathrm{wal}_k(t)}\,\mathrm{d}t$, which implies that

$$\chi_{[0,x)}(t) = \sum_{k=0}^{\infty} J_k(x)\, {}_b\mathrm{wal}_k(t).$$

Thus,

$$\int_0^1 \chi_{[0,x)}(t)\chi_{[0,y)}(t)\,\mathrm{d}t = \sum_{m,n=0}^{\infty} \overline{J_m(x)} J_n(y) \int_0^1 \overline{{}_b\mathrm{wal}_m(t)}\,{}_b\mathrm{wal}_n(t)\,\mathrm{d}t$$

$$= \sum_{m=0}^{\infty} \overline{J_m(x)} J_m(y).$$

The Walsh series for $\widetilde{b}_2(x-y)$ is therefore given by

$$\widetilde{b}_2(x-y) = \frac{(\overline{J_0(x)})^2 + (J_0(y))^2 - \overline{J_0(x)} - J_0(y)}{2} + \sum_{m=1}^{\infty} \overline{J_m(x)} J_m(y) + \frac{1}{12}.$$

We have

$$\begin{aligned}
&\gamma_2(k,l) \\
&= \int_0^1 \int_0^1 \widetilde{b}_2(x-y)\,\overline{{}_b\mathrm{wal}_k(x)}\,{}_b\mathrm{wal}_l(y)\,\mathrm{d}x\,\mathrm{d}y \\
&= \int_0^1 \int_0^1 \left[\frac{(\overline{J_0(x)})^2 + (J_0(y))^2 - \overline{J_0(x)} - J_0(y)}{2} + \sum_{m-1}^{\infty} \overline{J_m(x)} J_m(y) + \frac{1}{12} \right] \\
&\qquad \times \overline{{}_b\mathrm{wal}_k(x)}\,{}_b\mathrm{wal}_l(y)\,\mathrm{d}x\,\mathrm{d}y \\
&= \sum_{m=1}^{\infty} \int_0^1 \overline{J_m(x)\,{}_b\mathrm{wal}_k(x)}\,\mathrm{d}x \int_0^1 J_m(y)\,{}_b\mathrm{wal}_l(y)\,\mathrm{d}y.
\end{aligned}$$

It remains to consider the integral $\int_0^1 \overline{J_m(x)\,{}_b\mathrm{wal}_k(x)}\,\mathrm{d}x$. Let $m = \eta b^{e-1} + m'$, with $0 < \eta < b$, $e > 0$ and $0 \le m' < b^{e-1}$. Then, using Lemma 14.8, we have

$$\begin{aligned}
&\int_0^1 \overline{J_m(x)\,{}_b\mathrm{wal}_k(x)}\,\mathrm{d}x \\
&= b^{-e}\Bigg(\frac{1}{1-\omega_b^{\eta}} \int_0^1 {}_b\mathrm{wal}_{m'}(x)\,\overline{{}_b\mathrm{wal}_k(x)}\,\mathrm{d}x \\
&\qquad + \left(\frac{1}{2} + \frac{1}{\omega_b^{\eta} - 1}\right) \int_0^1 {}_b\mathrm{wal}_m(x)\,\overline{{}_b\mathrm{wal}_k(x)}\,\mathrm{d}x \\
&\qquad + \sum_{c=1}^{\infty} \sum_{\vartheta=1}^{b-1} \frac{1}{b^c(\omega_b^{-\vartheta} - 1)} \int_0^1 {}_b\mathrm{wal}_{\vartheta b^{e+c-1}+m}(x)\,\overline{{}_b\mathrm{wal}_k(x)}\,\mathrm{d}x \Bigg).
\end{aligned}$$

This integral is not 0 only if either $m' = k$, $m = k$ or $m + \vartheta b^{e+c-1} = k$ for some ϑ, c. Analogously, the same applies to the integral $\int_0^1 J_m(y)\,{}_b\mathrm{wal}_l(y)\,\mathrm{d}y$. Hence, we need only consider a few cases for which $\gamma_2(k,l)$ is non-zero, and by going through each of them, we obtain the result. □

Note that many values of $\gamma_2(k, l)$ are 0, in particular, if k and l are sufficiently 'different' from each other. This property is inherited by b_r for $r > 2$ via the recursion

$$\gamma_r(k,l) = -\frac{1}{b^{a_1}}\left(\frac{1}{1-\omega_b^{-\kappa_1}}\gamma_{r-1}(k',l) + \left(\frac{1}{2} + \frac{1}{\omega_b^{-\kappa}-1}\right)\gamma_{r-1}(k,l) + \sum_{c=1}^{\infty}\sum_{\vartheta=1}^{b-1}\frac{1}{b^c(\omega_b^{\vartheta}-1)}\gamma_{r-1}(\vartheta b^{c+a_1-1}+k,l)\right). \quad (14.18)$$

This recursion is obtained from

$$\gamma_r(k,l) = -\int_0^1\int_0^1 \widetilde{b}_{r-1}(x-y)J_k(x)\,{}_b\mathrm{wal}_l(y)\,\mathrm{d}x\,\mathrm{d}y, \quad (14.19)$$

which in turn can be obtained using integration by parts. In the following lemma, we show that $\gamma_r(k, l) = 0$ for many choices of k and l.

Lemma 14.18 *Let $k, l \in \mathbb{N}_0$. For $k \in \mathbb{N}$, we write $k = \kappa_1 b^{a_1-1} + \cdots + \kappa_v b^{a_v-1}$ with digits $1 \le \kappa_1, \ldots, \kappa_v < b$ and $a_1 > a_2 > \cdots > a_v \ge 1$ and for $l \in \mathbb{N}$ we write $l = \lambda_1 b^{d_1-1} + \cdots + \lambda_w b^{d_w-1}$ with digits $1 \le \lambda_1, \ldots, \lambda_w < b$ and $d_1 > d_2 > \cdots > d_v \ge 1$. Then we have:*

1. *For any $k, l \in \mathbb{N}_0$ and $r \in \mathbb{N}$, we have $\gamma_r(k, 0) = \gamma_r(0, l) = 0$.*
2. *For $k, l \in \mathbb{N}$ with $|v - w| > r \ge 2$, we have $\gamma_r(k, l) = 0$.*
3. *Let $k, l, r \in \mathbb{N}$, $r \ge 2$, such that $|v - w| \le r$.*
   (a) *If $v = 1$, but $(\kappa_1, a_1) \ne (\lambda_w, d_w)$, then $\gamma_r(k, l) = 0$.*
   (b) *If $w = 1$, but $(\lambda_1, d_1) \ne (\kappa_v, a_v)$, then $\gamma_r(k, l) = 0$.*
   (c) *If $r - 1 \le |v - w| \le r$, but*

$$(a_{v-\min(v,w)+1}, \ldots, a_v, \kappa_{v-\min(v,w)+1}, \ldots, \kappa_v) \ne (d_{w-\min(v,w)+1}, \ldots, d_w, \lambda_{w-\min(v,w)+1}, \ldots, \lambda_w),$$

   then $\gamma_r(k, l) = 0$.
   (d) *If $v, w > 1$ and $0 \le |v - w| \le r - 2$, but*

$$(a_{v-\min(v,w)+2}, \ldots, a_v, \kappa_{v-\min(v,w)+2}, \ldots, \kappa_v) \ne (d_{w-\min(v,w)+2}, \ldots, d_w, \lambda_{w-\min(v,w)+2}, \ldots, \lambda_w),$$

   then $\gamma_r(k, l) = 0$.

Proof

1. This has been shown already.
2. We have $\gamma_2(k, l) = 0$ for $|v - w| > 2$, which follows from Lemma 14.17. Let $r > 2$. Then, by repeatedly using (14.18), we can write $\gamma_r(k, l)$ as a sum of $\gamma_2(m_i, n_j)$

for some values m_i, n_j, i.e. $\gamma_r(k,l) = \sum_{i,j} a_{i,j}\gamma_2(m_i,n_j)$. But if $|v - w| > r$, then the difference between the number of non-zero digits of m_i and n_j is bigger than 2 and hence, $\gamma_r(k,l) = 0$ by Lemma 14.17.

3. For $r = 2$, the proof follows again from Lemma 14.17: if $v = 1$ ($w = 1$), then $k' = 0$ ($l' = 0$ respectively) and we only have the cases $k = l$, $k = l'$ ($l = k'$ respectively) and $k = l''$ ($l = k''$, respectively) for which the result follows. The case $1 \le |v - w| \le 2$ comprises the cases $k' = l, k = l', k'' = l$ and $k = l''$. The case $v = w$ can be obtained by considering $k = l$, and $k' = l'$ with $k \neq l$. For $r > 2$, we can again use (14.18) repeatedly to obtain a sum of $\gamma_2(m_i, n_j)$. The result then follows by using Lemma 14.17. □

In the following, we prove a bound on $|\gamma_r(k,l)|$ for arbitrary $r \ge 2$. We set

$$\mu_{r,\mathrm{per}}(k,l) := \max_{0 \le s \le r} \mu_{s,\mathrm{per}}(k) + \mu_{r-s,\mathrm{per}}(l). \tag{14.20}$$

Lemma 14.19 *For $r \ge 2$ and $k, l \in \mathbb{N}$, we have*

$$|\gamma_r(k,l)| \le \frac{2b^{-\mu_{r,\mathrm{per}}(k,l)}}{(2\sin(\pi/b))^r}\left(1 + \frac{1}{b} + \frac{1}{b(b+1)}\right)^{r-2}.$$

Proof For $r = 2$, we use Lemma 14.9 and Lemma 14.17 to obtain the result.

Now let $r > 2$. By taking the absolute value of (14.18) and using the triangular inequality together with Lemma 14.9, we obtain

$$|\gamma_r(k,l)| \le \frac{b^{-a_1}}{2\sin(\pi/b)}\Bigg(|\gamma_{r-1}(k',l)| + |\gamma_{r-1}(k,l)| + \sum_{c=1}^{\infty}\sum_{\vartheta=1}^{b-1}\frac{1}{b^c}|\gamma_{r-1}(\vartheta b^{a_1+c-1} + k, l)|\Bigg). \tag{14.21}$$

By using integration by parts with respect to the variable y in (14.17), we obtain a formula similar to (14.19). Hence, there is also an analogue to (14.21).

Without loss of generality, assume that $k \ge l$ (otherwise use the analogue to (14.21)) and assume that the result holds for $r - 1$. Then

$$\begin{aligned}|\gamma_r(k,l)| &\le \frac{2b^{-a_1}}{(2\sin(\pi/b))^r}\left(1 + \frac{1}{b} + \frac{1}{b(b+1)}\right)^{r-3} \\ &\quad\times\left(b^{-\mu_{r-1,\mathrm{per}}(k',l)} + b^{-\mu_{r-1,\mathrm{per}}(k,l)} + (b-1)\sum_{c=1}^{\infty} b^{-c-\mu_{r-1,\mathrm{per}}(b^{a_1+c-1}+k,l)}\right).\end{aligned}$$

We have $a_1 + \mu_{r-1,\mathrm{per}}(k',l) = \mu_{r,\mathrm{per}}(k,l)$, $a_1 + \mu_{r-1,\mathrm{per}}(k,l) > \mu_{r,\mathrm{per}}(k,l)$ and $a_1 + \mu_{r-1,\mathrm{per}}(b^{a_1+c-1} + k, l) = 2a_1 + c + \mu_{r-2,\mathrm{per}}(k,l) > c + \mu_{r,\mathrm{per}}(k,l)$.

Therefore, we obtain

$$|\gamma_r(k,l)| \le \frac{2b^{-\mu_{r,\mathrm{per}}(k,l)}}{(2\sin(\pi/b))^r}\left(1+\frac{1}{b}+\frac{1}{b(b+1)}\right)^{r-3}\left(1+\frac{1}{b}+\frac{b-1}{b}\sum_{c=1}^{\infty} b^{-2c}\right).$$

As $\sum_{c=1}^{\infty} b^{-2c} = (b^2-1)^{-1}$, the result follows. □

14.6 On the Walsh coefficients of functions in Sobolev spaces

In this section we consider functions in reproducing kernel Hilbert spaces. We consider the (unanchored) Sobolev space $\mathscr{H}_\alpha$ of real valued functions $f : [0,1] \to \mathbb{R}$, for which $\alpha \in \mathbb{N}$, and where the inner product is given by

$$\langle f, g\rangle_\alpha = \sum_{k=0}^{\alpha-1} \int_0^1 f^{(k)}(x)\,\mathrm{d}x \int_0^1 g^{(k)}(x)\,\mathrm{d}x + \int_0^1 f^{(\alpha)}(x) g^{(\alpha)}(x)\,\mathrm{d}x,$$

where $f^{(k)}$ denotes the kth derivative of f and where $f^{(0)} = f$. Let $\|f\|_\alpha = \sqrt{\langle f, f\rangle_\alpha}$. The reproducing kernel for this space is given by

$$\begin{aligned} K_\alpha(x,y) &= \sum_{k=0}^{\alpha} \frac{B_k(x)B_k(y)}{(k!)^2} - (-1)^\alpha \frac{\widetilde{B}_{2\alpha}(x-y)}{(2\alpha)!} \\ &= \sum_{k=0}^{\alpha} b_k(x) b_k(y) - (-1)^\alpha \widetilde{b}_{2\alpha}(x-y); \end{aligned}$$

see, for example, [259, Section 10.2]. For $\alpha = 1$, we have the Sobolev space from Section 2.5 and from Section 12.2 (in the unweighted form). It can be checked that

$$\begin{aligned} f(y) &= \langle f, K_\alpha(\cdot, y)\rangle_\alpha \\ &= \sum_{k=0}^{\alpha} \int_0^1 f^{(k)}(x)\,\mathrm{d}x\, b_k(y) - (-1)^\alpha \int_0^1 f^{(\alpha)}(x)\widetilde{b}_\alpha(x-y)\,\mathrm{d}x. \end{aligned}$$

Hence, the mth Walsh coefficient of f is given by

$$\begin{aligned} \widehat{f}(m) = &\sum_{k=0}^{\alpha} \int_0^1 f^{(k)}(x)\,\mathrm{d}x\, \widehat{b_k}(m) \\ &-(-1)^\alpha \int_0^1 \int_0^1 f^{(\alpha)}(x)\widetilde{b}_\alpha(x-y)\,\mathrm{d}x\, \overline{{}_b\mathrm{wal}_m(y)}\,\mathrm{d}y. \end{aligned} \tag{14.22}$$

A bound on the Walsh coefficients of $b_0(y), \ldots, b_\alpha(y)$ can be obtained from Lemma 14.16. For the remaining term, we use Lemma 14.19. We have

$$\widetilde{b}_\alpha(x-y) = \sum_{k,l=1}^{\infty} \gamma_\alpha(k,l)\, {}_b\mathrm{wal}_k(x)\, \overline{{}_b\mathrm{wal}_l(y)} = (-1)^\alpha \widetilde{b}_\alpha(y-x)$$

and therefore,

$$\begin{aligned}
&(-1)^\alpha \int_0^1 \int_0^1 f^{(\alpha)}(x) \widetilde{b}_\alpha(x-y)\,\mathrm{d}x\, \overline{{}_b\mathrm{wal}_m(y)}\,\mathrm{d}y \\
&= \int_0^1 \int_0^1 f^{(\alpha)}(x) \widetilde{b}_\alpha(y-x)\,\mathrm{d}x\, \overline{{}_b\mathrm{wal}_m(y)}\,\mathrm{d}y \\
&= \sum_{k,l=1}^{\infty} \gamma_\alpha(k,l) \int_0^1 f^{(\alpha)}(x) \overline{{}_b\mathrm{wal}_l(x)}\,\mathrm{d}x \int_0^1 {}_b\mathrm{wal}_k(y) \overline{{}_b\mathrm{wal}_m(y)}\,\mathrm{d}y \\
&= \sum_{l=1}^{\infty} \gamma_\alpha(m,l) \int_0^1 f^{(\alpha)}(x) \overline{{}_b\mathrm{wal}_l(x)}\,\mathrm{d}x.
\end{aligned}$$

Using Lemma 14.19, we can estimate the absolute value of the last expression by

$$\begin{aligned}
&\sum_{l=1}^{\infty} |\gamma_\alpha(m,l)| \int_0^1 |f^{(\alpha)}(x)|\,\mathrm{d}x \\
&\quad \le \int_0^1 |f^{(\alpha)}(x)|\,\mathrm{d}x \frac{2}{(2\sin(\pi/b))^\alpha} \left(1 + \frac{1}{b} + \frac{1}{b(b+1)}\right)^{\alpha-2} \sum_{\substack{l=1 \\ \gamma_\alpha(m,l)\neq 0}}^{\infty} b^{-\mu_{\alpha,\mathrm{per}}(m,l)}.
\end{aligned} \tag{14.23}$$

It remains to prove a bound on the rightmost sum, which we do in the following lemma.

Lemma 14.20 *For any $\alpha, m \in \mathbb{N}$, $\alpha \ge 2$, we have*

$$\sum_{\substack{k=1 \\ \gamma_\alpha(m,k)\neq 0}}^{\infty} b^{-\mu_{\alpha,\mathrm{per}}(m,k)} \le b^{-\mu_{\alpha,\mathrm{per}}(m)} \left(3 + \frac{2}{b} + \frac{2b+1}{b-1}\right).$$

Proof Let $m = \eta_1 b^{e_1-1} + \cdots + \eta_z b^{e_z-1}$, where $1 \le \eta_1, \ldots, \eta_z < b$ and $e_1 > \cdots > e_z > 0$. We consider now all natural numbers k for which $\gamma_\alpha(m,k) \neq 0$. From Lemma 14.18, we know that $\gamma_\alpha(m,k) = 0$ for $|v - z| > \alpha$. Hence, we only need to consider the cases where $|v - z| \le \alpha$:

- $v = \max(z-\alpha, 0)$: if $z - \alpha \le 0$, then this case does not occur; otherwise, there is only one k for which $\gamma_\alpha(m,k) \neq 0$, and we obtain the summand $b^{-\mu_{\alpha,\mathrm{per}}(m)}$.

- $v = \max(z - \alpha + 1, 0)$: again if $z - \alpha + 1 \le 0$, then this case does not occur; otherwise, we can bound this summand from above by $b^{-\mu_{\alpha,\mathrm{per}}(m)-1}$.
- $\max(z - \alpha + 1, 0) < v \le z$: first, let $v = 1$. Then $\kappa_1 = \eta_z$ and $a_1 = e_z$. Therefore, k is fixed, $\mu_{\alpha,\mathrm{per}}(m, k) = \mu_{\alpha,\mathrm{per}}(m)$, and $b^{-\mu_{\alpha,\mathrm{per}}(m,k)} = b^{-\mu_{\alpha,\mathrm{per}}(m)}$.

  Now let $v > 1$, which implies that $z > 1$ (as $z \ge v$) and $z - v + 2 \le \alpha$. In this case

$$(a_2, \ldots, a_v, \kappa_2, \ldots, \kappa_v) = (e_{z-v+2}, \ldots, e_z, \eta_{z-v+2}, \ldots, \eta_z).$$

  Thus,

$$\begin{aligned}\mu_{\alpha,\mathrm{per}}(m, k) &= \mu_{z-v+1,\mathrm{per}}(m) + a_1 + \mu_{\alpha-(z-v+2),\mathrm{per}}(k', k')\\ &\ge \mu_{\alpha,\mathrm{per}}(m) + a_1 - a_{v-z+\alpha}.\end{aligned}$$

  Note that $v - z + \alpha > 1$. Let $a'_v = a_1 - a_{v-z+\alpha} > v - z + \alpha - 2$. Then the sum over all k for which $1 < v \le z$ is bounded by

$$b^{-\mu_{\alpha,\mathrm{per}}(m)}(b-1)\sum_{v=2}^{z}\sum_{a'=v-1}^{\infty} b^{-a'} \le b^{-\mu_{\alpha,\mathrm{per}}(m)}\sum_{v=2}^{\infty} b^{-v+2} \le b^{-\mu_{\alpha,\mathrm{per}}(m)}\frac{b}{b-1}.$$

- $z + 1 \le v \le z + \alpha - 2$: if $z = 1$, then $2 \le v \le \alpha - 1$ and, by Lemma 14.18, we have $\eta_1 = \kappa_v$ and $e_1 = a_v$. In this case, $\mu_{\alpha,\mathrm{per}}(m, k) = \mu_{\alpha,\mathrm{per}}(k)$ and $\mu_{\alpha,\mathrm{per}}(k) - \mu_{\alpha,\mathrm{per}}(m) = (a_1 - a_v) + \cdots + (a_v - a_v) + (\alpha - v)(a_v - a_v) = a'_1 + \cdots + a'_{v-1}$, where $a'_i = a_i - a_v$ and $a'_1 > \cdots > a'_{v-1} > 0$. The sum over all k for which $2 \le v \le \alpha - 1$ and $\gamma_\alpha(m, k) \ne 0$ is then bounded by

$$\begin{aligned}&\sum_{v=2}^{\alpha-1}(b-1)^{v-1}\sum_{a_1>\cdots>a_{v-1}>a_v=e_1>0} b^{-\mu_{\alpha,\mathrm{per}}(k)}\\ &\quad\le b^{-\mu_{\alpha,\mathrm{per}}(m)}\sum_{v=2}^{\alpha-1}(b-1)^{v-1}\sum_{a'_1>\cdots>a'_{v-1}>0} b^{-a'_1-\cdots-a'_{v-1}}\\ &\quad\le b^{-\mu_{\alpha,\mathrm{per}}(m)}\sum_{v=2}^{\alpha-1} b^{-(v-2)}\\ &\quad\le b^{-\mu_{\alpha,\mathrm{per}}(m)}\frac{b}{b-1}.\end{aligned}$$

  For $z > 1$ and $z + 1 \le v \le z + \alpha - 2$, we have

$$(a_{v-z+2}, \ldots, a_v, \kappa_{v-z+2}, \ldots, \kappa_v) = (e_2, \ldots, e_z, \eta_2, \ldots, \eta_z)$$

  and $v - z + 2 \le \alpha$. Thus,

$$\begin{aligned}\mu_{\alpha,\mathrm{per}}(m, k) &= a_1 + \cdots + a_{v-z+1} + e_1 + \mu_{\alpha-(v-z+2),\mathrm{per}}(m', m')\\ &\ge \mu_{\alpha,\mathrm{per}}(m) - \mu_{\alpha-1,\mathrm{per}}(m') + a_1 + \cdots + a_{v-z+1}\\ &\quad + \mu_{\alpha-(v-z+2),\mathrm{per}}(m', m')\\ &\ge \mu_{\alpha,\mathrm{per}}(m) + a'_1 + \cdots + a'_{v-z+1},\end{aligned}$$

where $a_i' = a_i - e_2 = a_i - a_{v-z+2}$ and $a_1' > \cdots > a_{v-z+1}' > 0$. Thus, the sum over all k for which $z+1 \le v \le z+\alpha-2$ and $\gamma_\alpha(m,k) \neq 0$ is bounded by

$$b^{-\mu_{\alpha,\mathrm{per}}(m)} \sum_{v=z+1}^{z+\alpha-2} (b-1)^{v-z+1} \sum_{a_1'>\cdots>a_{v-z+1}'>0} b^{-a_1'-\cdots-a_{v-z+1}'}$$

$$\le b^{-\mu_{\alpha,\mathrm{per}}(m)} \sum_{v=z+1}^{z+\alpha-2} b^{-1-\cdots-(v-z)}$$

$$\le \frac{b^{-\mu_{\alpha,\mathrm{per}}(m)}}{b-1}.$$

- $v = z+\alpha$: in this case, $\mu_{\alpha,\mathrm{per}}(m,k) = a_1 + \cdots + a_\alpha - \mu_{\alpha,\mathrm{per}}(m) + \mu_{\alpha,\mathrm{per}}(m)$, where $\mu_{\alpha,\mathrm{per}}(m) \le \alpha a_{\alpha+1}$. Thus, $a_1 + \cdots + a_\alpha - \mu_{\alpha,\mathrm{per}}(m) \ge (a_1 - a_{\alpha+1}) + \cdots + (a_\alpha - a_{\alpha+1})$ and $a_1 > \cdots > a_\alpha > a_{\alpha+1}$. Hence, the sum over all k for which $v = z+\alpha$ is bounded by

$$(b-1)^\alpha b^{-\mu_{\alpha,\mathrm{per}}(m)} \sum_{a_1>\cdots>a_\alpha>0} b^{-a_1-\cdots-a_\alpha} \le b^{-\mu_{\alpha,\mathrm{per}}(m)} b^{-\alpha(\alpha-1)/2}.$$

- $v = z+\alpha-1$: in this case, $\mu_{\alpha,\mathrm{per}}(m,k) = a_1 + \cdots + a_\alpha - \mu_{\alpha,\mathrm{per}}(m) + \mu_{\alpha,\mathrm{per}}(m)$, where now $a_\alpha = e_1$ and $\kappa_\alpha = \eta_1$ are fixed. Hence, the sum over all k for which $v = z+\alpha-1$ is bounded by

$$(b-1)^{\alpha-1} b^{-\mu_{\alpha,\mathrm{per}}(m)} \sum_{a_1>\cdots>a_{\alpha-1}>0} b^{-a_1-\cdots-a_{\alpha-1}} \le b^{-\mu_{\alpha,\mathrm{per}}(m)} b^{-(\alpha-1)(\alpha-2)/2}.$$

By summing up the bounds obtained for each case, we obtain the result. □

From (14.22), Lemma 14.16, (14.23) and Lemma 14.20, we obtain the following theorem.

Theorem 14.21 *Let $\alpha \in \mathbb{N}$, $\alpha \ge 2$. Then, for any $k \in \mathbb{N}$, we have*

$$|\widehat{f}(k)| \le \sum_{w=v}^{\alpha} \left| \int_0^1 f^{(w)}(x)\,\mathrm{d}x \right| \frac{b^{-\mu_{w,\mathrm{per}}(k)}}{(2\sin(\pi/b))^w} \left(1 + \frac{1}{b} + \frac{1}{b(b+1)}\right)^{\max(0,w-2)}$$
$$+ \int_0^1 |f^{(\alpha)}(x)|\,\mathrm{d}x \frac{2b^{-\mu_{\alpha,\mathrm{per}}(k)}}{(2\sin(\pi/b))^\alpha} \left(1 + \frac{1}{b} + \frac{1}{b(b+1)}\right)^{\alpha-2}$$
$$\times \left(3 + \frac{2}{b} + \frac{2b+1}{b-1}\right),$$

for all $f \in \mathscr{H}_\alpha$, where for $v > \alpha$ the empty sum $\sum_{w=v}^{\alpha}$ is defined to be 0.

For $\alpha \in \mathbb{N}$ and a non-negative integer k, we use the function μ_α introduced in (14.6), for which we have $\mu_\alpha(0) = 0$ and $\mu_\alpha(k) = a_1 + \cdots + a_{\min(\alpha,v)}$

for $k \in \mathbb{N}$ with b-adic expansion $k = \kappa_1 b^{a_1-1} + \cdots + \kappa_v b^{a_v-1}$ with $v \in \mathbb{N}$, digits $1 \le \kappa_1, \ldots, \kappa_v < b$ and $a_1 > a_2 > \cdots > a_v \ge 1$.

Then, we have $\mu_{w,\mathrm{per}}(k) \ge \mu_\alpha(k)$ for $v \le w \le \alpha$ and $\mu_{\alpha,\mathrm{per}}(k) \ge \mu_\alpha(k)$ for all $\alpha \ge 2$ and $k \in \mathbb{N}$.

Using Hölder's inequality, we obtain the following corollary.

Corollary 14.22 *Let $\alpha \in \mathbb{N}$, $\alpha \ge 2$. Then, for any $k \in \mathbb{N}$, we have*

$$|\widehat{f}(k)| \le b^{-\mu_\alpha(k)} C_{\alpha,q} \|f\|_{p,\alpha},$$

where $\|f\|_{p,\alpha} = \left(\sum_{w=0}^{\alpha} \left| \int_0^1 f^{(w)}(x)\,\mathrm{d}x \right|^p + \int_0^1 |f^{(\alpha)}(x)|^p \,\mathrm{d}x\right)^{1/p}$, *where* $1/p + 1/q = 1$, *and*

$$C_{\alpha,q} := \left(\sum_{w=1}^{\alpha} \frac{1}{(2\sin(\pi/b))^{wq}} \left(1 + \frac{1}{b} + \frac{1}{b(b+1)}\right)^{q \max(0,w-2)} \right.$$

$$\left. + \frac{2^q}{(2\sin(\pi/b))^{\alpha q}} \left(1 + \frac{1}{b} + \frac{1}{b(b+1)}\right)^{q(\alpha-2)} \left(3 + \frac{2}{b} + \frac{2b+1}{b-1}\right)^q \right)^{1/q}.$$

The results can be extended to dimension $s \in \mathbb{N}$ by considering an s-dimensional Sobolev space $\mathscr{H}_{s,\alpha,\boldsymbol{\gamma}}$ with reproducing kernel

$$K_{s,\alpha,\boldsymbol{\gamma}}(\boldsymbol{x}, \boldsymbol{y}) = \sum_{\mathfrak{u} \subseteq \mathcal{I}_s} \gamma_{\mathfrak{u}} \prod_{i=1}^{s} \left(\sum_{k=1}^{\alpha} \frac{B_k(x_i) B_k(y_i)}{(k!)^2} - (-1)^\alpha \frac{B_{2\alpha}(|x_i - y_i|)}{(2\alpha)!} \right)$$

and with inner product

$$\langle f, g \rangle_{\mathscr{H}_{s,\alpha,\boldsymbol{\gamma}}} = \sum_{\mathfrak{u} \subseteq \mathcal{I}_s} \gamma_{\mathfrak{u}}^{-1} \sum_{\mathfrak{v} \subseteq \mathfrak{u}} \sum_{\boldsymbol{\tau}_{\mathfrak{u}\setminus\mathfrak{v}} \in \{1,\ldots,\alpha-1\}^{|\mathfrak{u}\setminus\mathfrak{v}|}} \int_{[0,1]^{|\mathfrak{v}|}}$$
$$\times \left(\int_{[0,1]^{s-|\mathfrak{v}|}} f^{(\boldsymbol{\tau}_{\mathfrak{u}\setminus\mathfrak{v}}, \boldsymbol{\alpha}_{\mathfrak{v}}, \boldsymbol{0})}(\boldsymbol{x}) \,\mathrm{d}\boldsymbol{x}_{\mathcal{I}_s\setminus\mathfrak{v}} \right)$$
$$\times \left(\int_{[0,1]^{s-|\mathfrak{v}|}} g^{(\boldsymbol{\tau}_{\mathfrak{u}\setminus\mathfrak{v}}, \boldsymbol{\alpha}_{\mathfrak{v}}, \boldsymbol{0})}(\boldsymbol{x}) \,\mathrm{d}\boldsymbol{x}_{\mathcal{I}_s\setminus\mathfrak{v}} \right) \mathrm{d}\boldsymbol{x}_{\mathfrak{v}},$$

where $\boldsymbol{\gamma} = (\gamma_i)_{i\ge1}$ is a sequence of positive weights, $\gamma_{\mathfrak{u}} = \prod_{i\in\mathfrak{u}} \gamma_i$, and where $(\boldsymbol{\tau}_{\mathfrak{u}\setminus\mathfrak{v}}, \boldsymbol{\alpha}_{\mathfrak{v}}, \boldsymbol{0})$ is the vector whose jth component is α if $j \in \mathfrak{v}$, 0 if $j \in \mathcal{I}_s \setminus \mathfrak{u}$ and τ_j if $j \in \mathfrak{u} \setminus \mathfrak{v}$ (where $\tau_{\mathfrak{u}\setminus\mathfrak{v}} = (\tau_j)_{j\in\mathfrak{u}\setminus\mathfrak{v}}$). For a vector $\boldsymbol{\eta} = (\eta_1, \ldots, \eta_s)$ we write $f^{(\boldsymbol{\eta})}(\boldsymbol{x}) := \frac{\partial^{\eta_1+\cdots+\eta_s}}{\partial x_1^{\eta_1} \ldots \partial x_s^{\eta_s}} f(\boldsymbol{x})$.

Note that for $\alpha = 1$, we obtain the weighted Sobolev space $\mathscr{H}_{\mathrm{sob},s,\boldsymbol{\gamma}}$ considered in Section 12.2, i.e. $\mathscr{H}_{s,1,\boldsymbol{\gamma}} = \mathscr{H}_{\mathrm{sob},s,\boldsymbol{\gamma}}$.

Then we have

$$f(\boldsymbol{y}) = \langle f, K_{s,\alpha,\boldsymbol{\gamma}}(\cdot, \boldsymbol{y})\rangle$$
$$= \sum_{\mathfrak{u}\subseteq\mathcal{I}_s} \gamma_{\mathfrak{u}}^{-1} \sum_{\mathfrak{v}\subseteq\mathfrak{u}} \sum_{\boldsymbol{\tau}_{\mathfrak{u}\setminus\mathfrak{v}}\in\{1,\ldots,\alpha-1\}^{|\mathfrak{u}\setminus\mathfrak{v}|}} \prod_{i\in\mathfrak{u}} b_{\tau_i}(y_i)$$
$$\times \int_{[0,1]^{|\mathfrak{v}|}} \int_{[0,1]^{s-|\mathfrak{v}|}} f^{(\boldsymbol{\tau}_{\mathfrak{u}\setminus\mathfrak{v}},\boldsymbol{\alpha}_{\mathfrak{v}},\boldsymbol{0})}(\boldsymbol{x})\,\mathrm{d}\boldsymbol{x}_{\mathcal{I}_s\setminus\mathfrak{v}} \prod_{j\in\mathcal{I}_s\setminus\mathfrak{u}} \widetilde{b}_\alpha(x_j - y_j)\,\mathrm{d}\boldsymbol{x}_{\mathfrak{v}}.$$

For $\boldsymbol{k} = (k_1, \ldots, k_s) \in \mathbb{N}_0^s$, we write $\mu_\alpha(\boldsymbol{k}) := \mu_\alpha(k_1) + \cdots + \mu_\alpha(k_s)$. Using the bounds on the Walsh coefficients of b_{τ_j} and $\widetilde{b}_\alpha(\cdot - y_j)$, we obtain the following theorem.

Theorem 14.23 *Let $\alpha \in \mathbb{N}$, $\alpha \geq 2$. Then, for any $\boldsymbol{k} \in \mathbb{N}^s$, we have*

$$|\widehat{f}(\boldsymbol{k})| \leq b^{-\mu_\alpha(\boldsymbol{k})} C_{\alpha,q,s} \|f\|_{p,\alpha},$$

where

$$\|f\|_{p,\alpha}^p := \sum_{\mathfrak{u}\subseteq\mathcal{I}_s} \gamma_{\mathfrak{u}}^{-1} \sum_{\mathfrak{v}\subseteq\mathfrak{u}} \sum_{\boldsymbol{\tau}_{\mathfrak{u}\setminus\mathfrak{v}}\in\{1,\ldots,\alpha-1\}^{|\mathfrak{u}\setminus\mathfrak{v}|}}$$
$$\times \int_{[0,1]^{|\mathfrak{v}|}} \left(\int_{[0,1]^{s-|\mathfrak{v}|}} f^{(\boldsymbol{\tau}_{\mathfrak{u}\setminus\mathfrak{v}},\boldsymbol{\alpha}_{\mathfrak{v}},\boldsymbol{0})}(\boldsymbol{x})\,\mathrm{d}\boldsymbol{x}_{\mathcal{I}_s\setminus\mathfrak{v}} \right)^p \mathrm{d}\boldsymbol{x}_{\mathfrak{v}},$$

where $1/p + 1/q = 1$, and $C_{\alpha,q,s} > 0$ is a constant independent of $\boldsymbol{k}$ and f.

In [38] it was also shown that the bounds on the Walsh coefficients shown above are essentially the best possible.

Notice that because the Walsh coefficients considered here converge fast, the Walsh series for functions f with smoothness $\alpha \geq 2$ converges absolutely. Indeed, we have

$$\sum_{k=0}^{\infty} |\widehat{f}(k)| \leq C_{\alpha,q} \|f\|_{p,\alpha} \sum_{k=0}^{\infty} b^{-\mu_\alpha(k)} < \infty.$$

Therefore, $\sum_{k=0}^{\infty} \widehat{f}(k)\, {}_b\mathrm{wal}_k(x)$ converges at every point $x \in [0, 1)$ and the result from Section A.3 applies.

Exercises

14.1 Calculate the Walsh coefficients of $F_1(x) = x$.
Hint: You can find the calculation for the general case in Appendix A.

14.2 Calculate the Walsh coefficients of $F_2(x) = x^2$.
Hint: Use Exercise 14.1.

14.3 Calculate the Walsh coefficients of x^3.
Hint: Use Exercise 14.1.

14.4 Calculate the Walsh coefficients of $F_3(x) = \mathrm{e}^{-2\pi \mathrm{i} x}$.
Hint: See [35, Lemma 6.12] for the general case.

14.5 Use Theorem 14.5 to elaborate more clearly on Example 14.3, as was done in Example 14.6.

14.6 Use Theorem 14.5 to consider arbitrary $v > 3$ in Example 14.7.

14.7 Let $f \in L_2([0,1])$ and let $F(x) = \int_0^x f(y)\,\mathrm{d}y$. Further, let $\widehat{F}(k)$ denote the kth Walsh coefficient of F. Let $k \in \mathbb{N}$ with $k = lb^{a-1} + k'$, $0 < l < b$ and $0 \le k' < b^{a-1}$. Show that we then have

$$\widehat{F}(k) = -b^{-a} \sum_{h=0}^{\infty} \widehat{f}(k'+h)\, \rho_k(h),$$

where

$$\rho_k(h) = \begin{cases} c_z + 2^{-1}\chi_{z=l} & \text{for } h = zb^{a-1}, \\ \upsilon_z b^{-i-1} & \text{for } h = zb^{a-1+i} + lb^{a-1}, i > 0, 0 < z < b, \\ 0 & \text{otherwise,} \end{cases}$$

and $\chi_{z=l} = 1$ for $z = l$ and 0 otherwise, $\upsilon_z = \sum_{r=0}^{b-1} {}_b\mathrm{wal}_z(r/b) = b/(\omega_b^z - 1)$ and c_z as in the proof of Lemma 14.8. Further, for $k = 0$, we have

$$\widehat{F}(0) = \widehat{f}(0) - \sum_{h=0}^{\infty} \widehat{f}(h)\, \phi(h),$$

where

$$\phi(h) = \begin{cases} 2^{-1} & \text{for } h = 0, \\ \upsilon_z b^{-i-1} & \text{for } h = zb^{a-1+i}, i > 0, 0 < z < b, \\ 0 & \text{otherwise.} \end{cases}$$

14.8 Prove Theorem 14.5 and Theorem 14.1 for Walsh functions in arbitrary base $b \ge 2$.
Hint: Use Exercise 14.7.

14.9 Now use Exercise 14.7 to elaborate more clearly on Example 14.3 as was done in Example 14.6.

14.10 Use Exercise 14.7 to consider arbitrary $v > 3$ in Example 14.7.

14.11 Show that if f has a continuous first derivative on $[0,1]$, then $V_1(f) = \int_0^1 |f'(x)|\,\mathrm{d}x$.

14.12 Find an explicit constant $C_{\alpha,q,s} > 0$ in Theorem 14.23.

14.13 Use Corollary 14.22 to obtain a bound on σ_ℓ defined in (13.5). Using this bound, obtain a bound on $\mathrm{Var}[\widehat{I}(f)]$, defined in (13.7), for functions f with $\|f\|_{p,\alpha} < \infty$.

15

Arbitrarily high order of convergence of the worst-case error

In this chapter we explain how digital nets and sequences can be modified to obtain the optimal rate of convergence for smooth functions. This theory was developed in [36] (and in [35] for periodic integrands).

15.1 Motivation for the definition of higher order digital nets and sequences

The definition of higher order digital nets can be explained in the following way. Assume that the integrand f can be represented by its Walsh series

$$f(\boldsymbol{x}) = \sum_{\boldsymbol{k} \in \mathbb{N}_0^s} \widehat{f}(\boldsymbol{k})\, {}_b\mathrm{wal}_{\boldsymbol{k}}(\boldsymbol{x}),$$

where $\widehat{f}(\boldsymbol{k}) = \int_{[0,1]^s} f(\boldsymbol{x}) \overline{{}_b\mathrm{wal}_{\boldsymbol{k}}(\boldsymbol{x})} \,\mathrm{d}\boldsymbol{x}$. Then, the integration error using a digital net $\{\boldsymbol{x}_0, \ldots, \boldsymbol{x}_{b^m-1}\}$ with generating matrices $C_1, \ldots, C_s$ is given by

$$\begin{aligned}
\left| \int_{[0,1]^s} f(\boldsymbol{x}) \,\mathrm{d}\boldsymbol{x} - \frac{1}{b^m} \sum_{n=0}^{b^m-1} f(\boldsymbol{x}_n) \right| &= \left| \widehat{f}(\boldsymbol{0}) - \frac{1}{b^m} \sum_{n=0}^{b^m-1} \sum_{\boldsymbol{k} \in \mathbb{N}_0^s} \widehat{f}(\boldsymbol{k})\, {}_b\mathrm{wal}_{\boldsymbol{k}}(\boldsymbol{x}) \right| \\
&= \left| \sum_{\boldsymbol{k} \in \mathbb{N}_0^s \setminus \{\boldsymbol{0}\}} \widehat{f}(\boldsymbol{k}) \frac{1}{b^m} \sum_{n=0}^{b^m-1} {}_b\mathrm{wal}_{\boldsymbol{k}}(\boldsymbol{x}_n) \right| \\
&\le \sum_{\boldsymbol{k} \in \mathcal{D}_\infty \setminus \{\boldsymbol{0}\}} |\widehat{f}(\boldsymbol{k})|,
\end{aligned}$$

where $\mathcal{D}_\infty = \mathcal{D}_\infty(C_1, \ldots, C_s)$ is defined in Remark 4.77, i.e.

$$\mathcal{D}_\infty = \{\boldsymbol{k} \in \mathbb{N}_0^s : C_1^\top \mathrm{tr}_m(\mathbf{k}_1) + \cdots + C_s^\top \mathrm{tr}_m(\mathbf{k}_s) = \boldsymbol{0}\},$$

where for $k \in \mathbb{N}_0$ with b-adic expansion $k = \sum_{j \ge 0} \kappa_j b^j$, we write $\mathrm{tr}_m(\mathbf{k}) := (\kappa_0, \ldots, \kappa_{m-1})^\top \in (\mathbb{Z}_b^m)^\top$. Let $\mathcal{D}_\infty' := \mathcal{D}_\infty \setminus \{\boldsymbol{0}\}$. Then, using the estimation from

Theorem 14.23, we obtain

$$\left|\int_{[0,1]^s} f(\boldsymbol{x})\,\mathrm{d}\boldsymbol{x} - \frac{1}{b^m}\sum_{n=0}^{b^m-1} f(\boldsymbol{x}_n)\right| \le C_{\alpha,q,s}\|f\|_{p,\alpha}\sum_{\boldsymbol{k}\in\mathcal{D}'_\infty} b^{-\mu_\alpha(\boldsymbol{k})}, \tag{15.1}$$

where $C_{\alpha,q,s} > 0$ is a constant independent of f and the quadrature points, $\|f\|_{p,\alpha}$ is a norm of f depending only on the integrand f, and $\sum_{\boldsymbol{k}\in\mathcal{D}'_\infty} b^{-\mu_\alpha}(\boldsymbol{k})$ only depends on the digital net. Here, as in Chapter 14, for any $\alpha \ge 0$ and a non-negative integer k with b-adic expansion $k = \kappa_1 b^{d_1-1} + \cdots + \kappa_v b^{d_v-1}$ with $v \in \mathbb{N}$, digits $1 \le \kappa_1, \ldots, \kappa_v < b$ and $a_1 > a_2 > \cdots > a_v \ge 1$ (if $k \neq 0$), the quantity $\mu_\alpha(k)$ is defined by

$$\mu_\alpha(k) = \begin{cases} 0 & \text{for } \alpha = 0, k \ge 0, \\ 0 & \text{for } k = 0, \alpha \ge 0, \\ d_1 + \cdots + d_{\min(\alpha,v)} & \text{otherwise.} \end{cases} \tag{15.2}$$

For $\boldsymbol{k} = (k_1, \ldots, k_s) \in \mathbb{N}_0^s$, we set $\mu_\alpha(\boldsymbol{k}) = \sum_{i=1}^s \mu_\alpha(k_i)$.

Assume that $\delta > 0$ is the largest integer such that $\|f\|_{p,\alpha} < \infty$ for all $\alpha \le \delta$. We call δ the smoothness of the integrand. Then, (15.1) applies for all $1 \le \alpha \le \delta$. In practice, the number δ might not be known for a given integrand; hence, we assume in the following that δ is an unknown number.

The aim is now to find digital nets, i.e. generating matrices $C_1, \ldots, C_s$ over $\mathbb{Z}_b$ such that $\sum_{\boldsymbol{k}\in\mathcal{D}'_\infty} b^{-\mu_\alpha(\boldsymbol{k})} = O(N^{-\alpha}(\log N)^{\alpha s})$ for all $1 \le \alpha \le \delta$, where the number of quadrature points $N = b^m$.

Roughly speaking, we show below that the sum $\sum_{\boldsymbol{k}\in\mathcal{D}'_\infty} b^{-\mu_\alpha(\boldsymbol{k})}$ is dominated by its largest term, which is given by $b^{-\mu^*_\alpha(C_1,\ldots,C_s)}$, where

$$\mu^*_\alpha(C_1, \ldots, C_s) := \min_{\boldsymbol{k}\in\mathcal{D}'_\infty} \mu_\alpha(\boldsymbol{k}).$$

In order to achieve a convergence of almost $N^{-\alpha} = b^{-\alpha m}$, we must also have that the largest term in $\sum_{\boldsymbol{k}\in\mathcal{D}'_\infty} b^{-\mu_\alpha(\boldsymbol{k})}$ is of this order; that is, we must have $\mu^*_\alpha(C_1, \ldots, C_s) \approx \alpha m$ (or say $\mu^*_\alpha(C_1, \ldots, C_s) > \alpha m - t$ for some constant t independent of m) for all $1 \le \alpha \le \delta$.

We can use the following analogy to find generating matrices $C_1, \ldots, C_s$ over $\mathbb{Z}_b$ which achieve $\mu^*_\alpha(C_1, \ldots, C_s) \approx \alpha m$: the definition of $\mu^*_\alpha(C_1, \ldots, C_s)$ is similar to the strength of a digital net as defined in Remark 4.53, that is, the quantity $m - t$. On the other hand, the classical case corresponds to $\alpha = 1$; hence, one can expect a relationship between $\mu^*_1(C_1, \ldots, C_s)$ and $m - t$.

Indeed, for matrices $C_1, \ldots, C_s$ over $\mathbb{Z}_b$, let $\mathbf{c}_j^{(i)} \in \mathbb{Z}_b^m$ be the jth row vector of C_i for $1 \le i \le s$ and $1 \le j \le m$. Then, the matrices $C_1, \ldots, C_s$ generate a digital (t, m, s)-net over $\mathbb{Z}_b$ if, for all $d_1, \ldots, d_s \in \mathbb{N}_0$ with $d_1 + \cdots + d_s \le m - t$, the vectors

$$\mathbf{c}_1^{(1)}, \ldots, \mathbf{c}_{d_1}^{(1)}, \ldots, \mathbf{c}_1^{(s)}, \ldots, \mathbf{c}_{d_s}^{(s)}$$

are linearly independent over $\mathbb{Z}_b$.

Now assume that the matrices $C_1, \ldots, C_s$ generate a digital (t, m, s)-net over $\mathbb{Z}_b$ and that we are given a $\boldsymbol{k} \in \mathbb{N}_0^s \setminus \{\mathbf{0}\}$ with $\mu_1(\boldsymbol{k}) \le m - t$. Let $d_i = \mu_1(k_i)$ for $1 \le i \le s$, then

$$C_1^\top \operatorname{tr}_m(\mathbf{k}_1) + \cdots + C_s^\top \operatorname{tr}_m(\mathbf{k}_s)$$

is a linear combination of the $\mu_1(\boldsymbol{k})$ vectors

$$(\mathbf{c}_1^{(1)})^\top, \ldots, (\mathbf{c}_{d_1}^{(1)})^\top, \ldots, (\mathbf{c}_1^{(s)})^\top, \ldots, (\mathbf{c}_{d_s}^{(s)})^\top.$$

As $\boldsymbol{k} \neq \mathbf{0}$ and $d_1 + \cdots + d_s = \mu_1(\boldsymbol{k}) \le m - t$, which implies that the vectors $\mathbf{c}_1^{(1)}, \ldots, \mathbf{c}_{d_1}^{(1)}, \ldots, \mathbf{c}_1^{(s)}, \ldots, \mathbf{c}_{d_s}^{(s)}$ are linearly independent, it follows that $C_1^\top \operatorname{tr}_m(\mathbf{k}_1) + \cdots + C_s^\top \operatorname{tr}_m(\mathbf{k}_s) \neq \mathbf{0} \in \mathbb{F}_b^m$. Thus, $\boldsymbol{k} \notin \mathcal{D}'_\infty$. This shows that if $C_1, \ldots, C_s$ generate a classical digital (t, m, s)-net and $\boldsymbol{k} \in \mathcal{D}'_\infty$, then $\mu_1(\boldsymbol{k}) > m - t$. This is precisely the type of result described above which we also want to have for $\alpha > 1$. Before we discuss this case, we have to make the following important remark:

Remark 15.1 In this chapter, we have to deal with generating matrices of size $n \times m$ with $n \ge m$ in place of $m \times m$ matrices. The construction principle for digital nets explained in Section 4.4 works along the same lines as for the classical case $n = m$. The only difference is that in the more general case the components of the points of the digital nets have n digits in their b-adic expansion (instead of m). We see below that this enlargement of the generating matrices is necessary in order to obtain the higher order convergence.

In the classical case $\alpha = 1$, we had some linear independence condition on the rows of the generating matrices which led to the desired result. We now want to generalise this linear independence condition to $1 \le \alpha \le \delta$ for some $\delta > 1$, i.e. we want that if $\boldsymbol{k} \in \mathbb{N}_0^s \setminus \{\mathbf{0}\}$ with $\mu_\alpha(\boldsymbol{k}) \le \alpha m - t$ (where t can depend on α), then the $n \times m$ matrices $C_1, \ldots, C_s$ should have linearly independent rows such that $C_1^\top \operatorname{tr}_n(\mathbf{k}_1) + \cdots + C_s^\top \operatorname{tr}_n(\mathbf{k}_s) \neq \mathbf{0} \in \mathbb{Z}_b^m$; that is we want to have that

$$\boldsymbol{k} \in \mathcal{D}'_{\infty,n} \text{ implies } \mu_\alpha(\boldsymbol{k}) > \alpha m - t \text{ for all } 1 \le \alpha \le \delta,$$

where the additional index n in $\mathcal{D}'_{\infty,n}$ indicates that the digit vectors are truncated after the first n digits (and not after m digits as for $m \times m$ matrices).

If we consider the first b^m points of a sequence, then we also want to have this property for all m larger than some m_0. Let $C_1, \ldots, C_s \in \mathbb{Z}_b^{\mathbb{N} \times \mathbb{N}}$ be the generating matrices of a digital sequence and let $C_1^{(n\times m)}, \ldots, C_s^{(n\times m)} \in \mathbb{Z}_b^{n\times m}$ be the corresponding left upper $n \times m$ matrices for $m, n \in \mathbb{N}$. Let $n = \sigma m$ for some $\sigma \in \mathbb{N}$. Then we want to have that

$$\boldsymbol{k} \in \mathcal{D}'_{\infty,\sigma m}(C_1^{(\sigma m\times m)}, \ldots, C_s^{(\sigma m\times m)})$$

implies that

$$\mu_\alpha(\boldsymbol{k}) > \alpha m - t \text{ for all } 1 \leq \alpha \leq \delta$$

for all $m \geq m_0$. A priori, it is not clear that such matrices can exist. In order to avoid proving results for an empty set, we can weaken the assumption by writing $\boldsymbol{k} \in \mathcal{D}'_{\infty,\sigma m}(C_1^{(\sigma m\times m)}, \ldots, C_s^{(\sigma m\times m)})$ implying that

$$\mu_\alpha(\boldsymbol{k}) > \beta\sigma m - t \quad \text{for all} \quad 1 \leq \alpha \leq \delta$$

for all $m \geq m_0$, for some β which depends on α and σ but not on m (if $\beta\sigma < \alpha$, then the assumption is obviously weaker). (For $\alpha = \delta = \beta = \sigma = 1$, we know from Chapter 8 that generating matrices exist which satisfy this property.) The largest term in $\sum_{\boldsymbol{k}\in\mathcal{D}'_\infty} b^{-\mu_\alpha(\boldsymbol{k})}$ is then of order $b^{-\beta\sigma m+t}$ and we show below that the sum $\sum_{\boldsymbol{k}\in\mathcal{D}'_\infty} b^{-\mu_\alpha(\boldsymbol{k})}$ is also of the same order. Hence, we obtain a convergence rate of order $\beta\sigma$. Thus, for $1 \leq \alpha \leq \delta$ and $\sigma \in \mathbb{N}$, we want to have generating matrices for which the above property is satisfied for $\beta = \beta(\alpha, \sigma)$ as large as possible.

In the following, we reconsider digital nets with generating matrices $C_1, \ldots, C_s \in \mathbb{Z}_b^{n\times m}$, rather than digital sequences. First, note that if $n < \alpha m - t$, then $\boldsymbol{k} = (b^n, 0, \ldots, 0) \in \mathcal{D}'_{\infty,n}$, but $\mu_\alpha(\boldsymbol{k}) = n + 1 \leq \alpha m - t$. Since, for a given digital net, the parameters m and n are fixed, $1 \leq \alpha \leq \delta$ and δ is unknown, i.e. δ can theoretically be arbitrarily large, this problem can in general not be avoided. A way out is to replace αm with n, or, to make it consistent with the requirements for digital sequences, with βn; that is, we want to have the property that $\boldsymbol{k} \in \mathcal{D}'_{\infty,n}$ implies that

$$\mu_\alpha(\boldsymbol{k}) > \beta n - t \text{ for all } 1 \leq \alpha \leq \delta,$$

where β and t depend on α and t is independent of m and n. In this case we obtain a convergence of order $b^{-\beta n}$. If we choose $\alpha = \delta$, then, from the lower bound by Sharygin [241], we know that the best possible convergence is $b^{-\alpha m}$. This implies that $\beta n \leq \alpha m$, since we want t to be independent of m and n. Further, the fact that $\boldsymbol{k} = (b^n, 0, \ldots, 0) \in \mathcal{D}'_{\infty,n}$ and $\mu_\alpha(\boldsymbol{k}) = n + 1$ also shows that $\min_{\boldsymbol{k}\in\mathcal{D}'_{\infty,n}} \mu_\alpha(\boldsymbol{k}) \leq n + 1$. Hence, we may without loss of generality also assume that $\beta \leq 1$.

Let $\boldsymbol{k} = (k_1, \ldots, k_s) \in \mathbb{N}_0^s \setminus \{\boldsymbol{0}\}$, where $k_i = \kappa_{i,1} b^{d_{i,1}-1} + \cdots + \kappa_{i,\nu_i} b^{d_{i,\nu_i}-1}$, with $n \geq d_{i,1} > \cdots > d_{i,\nu_j} > 0$ and digits $1 \leq \kappa_{i,1}, \ldots, \kappa_{i,\nu_i} < b$. Now

$C_1^\top \mathrm{tr}_n(\mathbf{k}_1) + \cdots + C_s^\top \mathrm{tr}_n(\mathbf{k}_s)$ is a linear combination of the rows

$$(\mathbf{c}_{d_{1,1}}^{(1)})^\top, \ldots, (\mathbf{c}_{d_{1,\nu_1}}^{(1)})^\top, \ldots, (\mathbf{c}_{d_{s,1}}^{(s)})^\top, \ldots, (\mathbf{c}_{d_{s,\nu_s}}^{(s)})^\top.$$

Thus, if the rows $\mathbf{c}_{d_{1,1}}^{(1)}, \ldots, \mathbf{c}_{d_{1,\nu_1}}^{(1)}, \ldots, \mathbf{c}_{d_{s,1}}^{(s)}, \ldots, \mathbf{c}_{d_{s,\nu_s}}^{(s)} \in \mathbb{Z}_b^m$ are linearly independent, then $C_1^\top \mathrm{tr}_n(\mathbf{k}_1) + \cdots + C_s^\top \mathrm{tr}_n(\mathbf{k}_s) \neq \mathbf{0}$ and therefore, $\boldsymbol{k} \notin \mathcal{D}'_{\infty,n}$.

If $C_1, \ldots, C_s \in \mathbb{Z}_b^{n \times m}$ are such that for all choices of $d_{i,1} > \cdots > d_{i,\nu_i} > 0$ for $1 \le i \le s$, with

$$d_{1,1} + \cdots + d_{1,\min(\alpha,\nu_1)} + \cdots + d_{s,1} + \cdots + d_{s,\min(\alpha,\nu_s)} \le \beta n - t,$$

the rows

$$\mathbf{c}_{d_{1,1}}^{(1)}, \ldots, \mathbf{c}_{d_{1,\nu_1}}^{(1)}, \ldots, \mathbf{c}_{d_{s,1}}^{(s)}, \ldots, \mathbf{c}_{d_{s,\nu_s}}^{(s)}$$

are linearly independent, then $\boldsymbol{k} \in \mathcal{D}'_{\infty,n}$ implies that $\mu_\alpha(\boldsymbol{k}) > \beta n - t$. (Note that we also include the case where some $\nu_i = 0$, in which case we just set $d_{i,1} + \cdots + d_{i,\min(\alpha,\nu_i)} = 0$.)

We can now formally define such digital nets for which the generating matrices satisfy such a property.

From now on let b be a prime and identify the finite field $\mathbb{F}_b$ with $\mathbb{Z}_b$.

Definition 15.2 Let $s, \alpha, n, m \in \mathbb{N}$, let $0 < \beta \le \min(1, \alpha m/n)$ be a real number and let $0 \le t \le \beta n$ be an integer. Let $\mathbb{Z}_b$ be the finite field of prime order b and let $C_1, \ldots, C_s \in \mathbb{Z}_b^{n \times m}$ where $\mathbf{c}_j^{(i)} \in \mathbb{Z}_b^m$ is the jth row vector of the matrix C_i for $1 \le j \le n$ and $1 \le i \le s$. If, for all $1 \le d_{i,\nu_i} < \cdots < d_{i,1} \le n$, where $0 \le \nu_i \le m$ for all $1 \le i \le s$, with

$$\sum_{i=1}^{s} \sum_{j=1}^{\min(\nu_i,\alpha)} d_{i,j} \le \beta n - t$$

the vectors

$$\mathbf{c}_{d_{1,\nu_1}}^{(1)}, \ldots, \mathbf{c}_{d_{1,1}}^{(1)}, \ldots, \mathbf{c}_{d_{s,\nu_s}}^{(s)}, \ldots, \mathbf{c}_{d_{s,1}}^{(s)}$$

are linearly independent over $\mathbb{Z}_b$, then the digital net with generating matrices $C_1, \ldots, C_s$ is called a *higher order digital* $(t, \alpha, \beta, n \times m, s)$*-net over* $\mathbb{Z}_b$ or, for short, a *digital* $(t, \alpha, \beta, n \times m, s)$*-net over* $\mathbb{Z}_b$.

Informally, we also refer to the nets defined above as higher order digital nets.

For $\alpha = \beta = 1$ and $n = m$, one obtains a digital (t, m, s)-net over $\mathbb{Z}_b$ as introduced in Section 4.4.

From duality theory (see Chapter 7) it follows that for a digital $(t, \alpha, \beta, n \times m, s)$-net, we have $\min_{\boldsymbol{k} \in \mathcal{D}'_{\infty,n}} \mu_{b,\alpha}(\boldsymbol{k}) > \beta n - t$. A proof of this fact is left as Exercise 15.1.

Remark 15.3 We can group the parameters in the following way:

- m, n, s are fixed parameters. Here, s denotes the number of generating matrices and m, n specify the size of the generating matrices, i.e. they are of size $n \times m$.
- α is a variable parameter, i.e. given (fixed) generating matrices can, for example, generate a $(t_1, 1, \beta_1, 10 \times 5, 5)$-net, a $(t_2, 2, \beta_2, 10 \times 5, 5)$-net and so on (note, the point set is always the same in each instance; the values $t_1, t_2, \ldots, \beta_1, \beta_2, \ldots$ may differ). This is necessary as, in the upper bounds, α is the smoothness of the integrand, which may not be known explicitly.
- t and β are dependent parameters, they depend on the generating matrices and on α. For given generating matrices, it is desirable to know the values of β and t for each value of $\alpha \in \mathbb{N}$.

In summary, the parameters $t, \alpha, \beta, n, m, s$ have the following meaning:

- The number s denotes the dimension of the point set.
- The point set has b^m points.
- The number n determines the maximum number of non-zero digits in the base b expansion of the coordinates of each point. By the arguments given above, it follows that the convergence of the integration error can, at best, only be of order b^{-n} (independently of how large one might choose the number of points b^m).
- t denotes the quality parameter of the point set; a low t means high quality.
- β is also a quality parameter. We see below that it is possible to achieve an integration error of order b^{-n}. Note that b^m is the number of points and that m and n can be chosen independently from each other. Hence, the order b^{-n} is only true for a range of n depending on m, which is the reason for the parameter β, i.e. the integration error is roughly $b^{-\beta n}$. Hence, β is a quality parameter related to the convergence rate.
- α is the smoothness parameter of the point set.
- $k := \lfloor \beta n \rfloor - t$ can be viewed as the strength of the higher order digital net; the convergence of the integration error is of the form b^{-k}.

We also define sequences of points for which the first b^m points form a digital $(t, \alpha, \beta, n \times m, s)$-net. In the classical case one can just consider the left upper $m \times m$ submatrices of the generating matrices of a digital sequence and determine the net properties of these for each $m \in \mathbb{N}$. Here, on the other hand, we are considering digital nets whose generating matrices are $n \times m$ matrices. Thus, we would have to consider the left upper $n_m \times m$ submatrices of the generating matrices of the digital sequence for each $m \in \mathbb{N}$ and where $(n_m)_{m \geq 1}$ is a sequence of natural numbers. For our purposes here, it is enough to consider only n_m of the form σm, for some given $\sigma \in \mathbb{N}$.

Definition 15.4 Let $s, \alpha, \sigma \in \mathbb{N}$ and $t \in \mathbb{N}_0$ and let $0 < \beta \leq \min(1, \alpha/\sigma)$ be a real number. Let $\mathbb{Z}_b$ be the finite field of prime order b and let $C_1, \ldots, C_s \in \mathbb{Z}_b^{\mathbb{N} \times \mathbb{N}}$

where $\mathbf{c}_j^{(i)} \in \mathbb{Z}_b^{\mathbb{N}}$ is the jth row vector of the matrix C_i for $j \in \mathbb{N}$ and $1 \le i \le s$. Further, let $C_i^{(\sigma m \times m)}$ denote the left upper $\sigma m \times m$ submatrix of C_i for $1 \le i \le s$. If, for all $m > t/(\beta\sigma)$, the matrices $C_1^{(\sigma m \times m)}, \ldots, C_s^{(\sigma m \times m)}$ generate a digital $(t, \alpha, \beta, \sigma m \times m, s)$-net over $\mathbb{Z}_b$, then the digital sequence with generating matrices $C_1, \ldots, C_s$ is called a *higher order digital* $(t, \alpha, \beta, \sigma, s)$*-sequence over* $\mathbb{Z}_b$ or, for short, a *digital* $(t, \alpha, \beta, \sigma, s)$*-sequence over* $\mathbb{Z}_b$.

Informally, we also refer to the sequences defined above as higher order digital sequences.

For $\alpha = \beta = \sigma = 1$, one obtains a digital (t, s)-sequence over $\mathbb{Z}_b$ as introduced in Section 4.4.

Note that, from above, we know that there is no digital $(t, \alpha, \beta, \sigma, s)$-sequence for which $\beta > \min(1, \alpha/\sigma)$. Hence, the assumption $\beta \le \min(1, \alpha/\sigma)$ only avoids cases for which digital $(t, \alpha, \beta, \sigma, s)$-sequences cannot exist.

The meaning of the parameters for higher order digital sequences is similar to the one for higher order nets. In particular, we now assume that $n = \sigma m$.

The question now is: do digital $(t, \alpha, \beta, n \times m, s)$-nets and $(t, \alpha, \beta, \sigma, s)$-sequences exist for all given $\alpha, \beta, \sigma, s \in \mathbb{N}$ and some t (which may depend on α and s but not on m) and all $m \in \mathbb{N}$? An affirmative answer to this question is given in the next section.

15.2 Construction of higher order digital nets and sequences

In this section, we present explicit constructions of digital $(t, \alpha, \beta, n \times m, s)$-nets and $(t, \alpha, \beta, \sigma, s)$-sequences over $\mathbb{Z}_b$. The basic construction principle appeared first in [35] and was slightly modified in [36]. The construction requires a parameter d, which, in case the smoothness of the integrand δ is known, should be chosen as $d = \delta$.

To construct a digital $(t, \alpha, \beta, dm \times m, s)$-net over $\mathbb{Z}_b$ (we only consider the case where $n = dm$), choose a usual digital (t', m, sd)-net over $\mathbb{Z}_b$. Let $C_1, \ldots, C_{sd} \in \mathbb{Z}_b^{m \times m}$ be the generating matrices of the digital (t', m, sd)-net. We recall that many explicit examples of such generating matrices are known; see Chapter 8. As we see below, the choice of the underlying (t', m, sd)-net has a direct impact on the bound on the quality parameter t of the digital $(t, \alpha, \beta, dm \times m, s)$-net. Let $\mathbf{c}_j^{(i)} \in \mathbb{Z}_b^m$ be the jth row vector of the $m \times m$ matrix C_i for $1 \le j \le m$ and $1 \le i \le sd$. Now, for $1 \le i \le s$, let the matrix D_i be made of the first rows of the matrices $C_{(i-1)d+1}, \ldots, C_{id}$, then the second rows of $C_{(i-1)d+1}, \ldots, C_{id}$ and so on. The matrix D_i is then a $dm \times m$ matrix over $\mathbb{Z}_b$ whose lth row vector $\boldsymbol{d}_l^{(i)} \in \mathbb{Z}_b^m$ is given by $\boldsymbol{d}_l^{(i)} = \mathbf{c}_u^{(v)}$ whenever $l = (u - i)d + v$ for $1 \le l \le dm$ with $(i-1)d + 1 \le v \le id$ and $1 \le u \le m$; that is, the row vectors of D_i from top to bottom are

$$\mathbf{c}_1^{((i-1)d+1)}, \ldots, \mathbf{c}_1^{(id)}, \mathbf{c}_2^{((i-1)d+1)}, \ldots, \mathbf{c}_2^{(id)}, \ldots, \mathbf{c}_m^{((i-1)d+1)}, \ldots, \mathbf{c}_m^{(id)}.$$

In the following, we prove that the above construction yields a $(t, \alpha, \beta, dm \times m, s)$-net over $\mathbb{Z}_b$. The proof of this result is simplified by using the following propagation rule which was first shown in [35, 36].

Proposition 15.5 *Let $\alpha' \in \mathbb{N}$ be given.*

1. *Let $\mathcal{P}$ be a digital $(t', \alpha', \beta', n \times m, s)$-net over $\mathbb{Z}_b$. Then, for any $\alpha \in \mathbb{N}$, $\mathcal{P}$ is also a digital $(t, \alpha, \beta, n \times m, s)$-net over $\mathbb{Z}_b$, where*
$$\beta = \beta' \min(1, \alpha/\alpha') \quad \text{and} \quad t = \lceil t' \min(1, \alpha/\alpha') \rceil .$$
2. *Let $\mathcal{S}$ be a digital $(t', \alpha', \beta', \sigma, s)$-sequence over $\mathbb{Z}_b$. Then, for any $\alpha \in \mathbb{N}$, $\mathcal{S}$ is also a digital $(t, \alpha, \beta, \sigma, s)$-sequence over $\mathbb{Z}_b$, where*
$$\beta = \beta' \min(1, \alpha/\alpha') \quad \text{and} \quad t = \lceil t' \min(1, \alpha/\alpha') \rceil .$$

Proof Let $C_1, \ldots, C_s \in \mathbb{Z}_b^{n \times m}$ be the generating matrices of $\mathcal{P}$. Let $\mathbf{c}_k^{(i)} \in \mathbb{Z}_b^m$ denote the kth row vector of C_i for $1 \le k \le n$ and $1 \le i \le s$.

Choose an $\alpha \in \mathbb{N}$. Then choose arbitrary $1 \le d_{i,\nu_i} < \cdots < d_{i,1} \le n$ such that
$$d_{1,1} + \cdots + d_{1,\min(\nu_1,\alpha)} + \cdots + d_{s,1} + \cdots + d_{s,\min(\nu_s,\alpha)} \le \beta n \min(1, \alpha/\alpha') - \lceil t \min(1, \alpha/\alpha') \rceil .$$

We need to show that the vectors
$$\mathbf{c}_{d_{1,\nu_1}}^{(1)}, \ldots, \mathbf{c}_{d_{1,1}}^{(1)}, \ldots, \mathbf{c}_{d_{s,\nu_s}}^{(s)}, \ldots, \mathbf{c}_{d_{s,1}}^{(s)}$$
are linearly independent over $\mathbb{Z}_b$. This is certainly the case as long as
$$d_{1,1} + \cdots + d_{1,\min(\nu_1,\alpha')} + \cdots + d_{s,1} + \cdots + d_{s,\min(\nu_s,\alpha')} \le \beta n - t,$$
since $\mathcal{P}$ is a digital $(t', \alpha', \beta', n \times m, s)$-net over $\mathbb{Z}_b$.

Now we have
$$\begin{aligned} & d_{1,1} + \cdots + d_{1,\min(\nu_1,\alpha')} + \cdots + d_{s,1} + \cdots + d_{s,\min(\nu_s,\alpha')} \\ & \le \frac{\alpha'}{\min(\alpha', \alpha)} \left(d_{1,1} + \cdots + d_{1,\min(\nu_1,\alpha)} + \cdots + d_{s,1} + \cdots + d_{s,\min(\nu_s,\alpha)} \right) \\ & \le \beta n - \frac{\alpha'}{\min(\alpha', \alpha)} \left\lceil t \frac{\min(\alpha', \alpha)}{\alpha'} \right\rceil \\ & \le \beta n - t, \end{aligned}$$
and hence, the result for higher order digital nets follows.

The result for higher order digital sequences follows from Definition 15.4 and the result for higher order digital nets. □

We note also that the propagation rules from Chapter 9 can be generalised to higher order digital nets; see [42].

Lemma 15.6 *Let $d \in \mathbb{N}$ and let $C_1, \ldots, C_{sd}$ be the generating matrices of a digital (t', m, sd)-net over $\mathbb{Z}_b$. Then, the matrices $D_1, \ldots, D_s$ defined above are generating matrices of a higher order digital $(t, d, 1, dm \times m, s)$-net over $\mathbb{Z}_b$ with*

$$t \le d\left(t' + \left\lfloor \frac{s(d-1)}{2} \right\rfloor\right).$$

Proof Let $\widetilde{t} := d\left(t' + \lfloor s(d-1)/2 \rfloor\right)$, let $\mathbf{d}_j^{(i)} \in \mathbb{Z}_b^m$ be the jth row vector of the matrix D_i for $1 \le j \le n$ and $1 \le i \le s$, and let the integers $d_{1,1}, \ldots, d_{1,\nu_1}, \ldots, d_{s,1}, \ldots, d_{s,\nu_s}$ be such that $1 \le d_{i,\nu_i} < \cdots < d_{i,1} \le dm$ for $1 \le i \le s$ and

$$d_{1,1} + \cdots + d_{1,\min(\nu_1,d)} + \cdots + d_{s,1} + \cdots + d_{s,\min(\nu_s,d)} \le dm - \widetilde{t}.$$

We need to show that the vectors

$$\mathbf{d}_{d_{1,1}}^{(1)}, \ldots, \mathbf{d}_{d_{1,\nu_1}}^{(1)}, \ldots, \mathbf{d}_{d_{s,1}}^{(s)}, \ldots, \mathbf{d}_{d_{s,\nu_s}}^{(s)}$$

are linearly independent over $\mathbb{Z}_b$.

For $1 \le i \le s$, the vectors $\{\mathbf{d}_{d_{i,\nu_i}}^{(i)}, \ldots, \mathbf{d}_{d_{i,1}}^{(i)}\}$ stem from the matrices $C_{(i-1)d+1}, \ldots, C_{id}$. For $(i-1)d + 1 \le f_i \le id$, let $e_{f_i} \in \mathbb{N}_0$ be the largest integer such that $(e_{f_i} - i)d + f_i \in \{d_{i,\nu_i}, \ldots, d_{i,1}\}$. If no such integer exists, we set $e_{f_i} = 0$.

For a real number x, let $(x)_+ = \max(0, x)$. For a given $1 \le i \le s$, we have

$$\begin{aligned} d_{i,1} + \cdots + d_{i,\min(\nu_i,d)} &\ge \sum_{f_i=(i-1)d+1}^{id} ((e_{f_i} - i)d + f_i)_+ \\ &\ge d \sum_{f_i=(i-1)d+1}^{id} e_{f_i} + \sum_{f_i=(i-1)d+1}^{id} (f_i - id) \\ &\ge d \sum_{f_i=(i-1)d+1}^{id} e_{f_i} - \frac{d(d-1)}{2}. \end{aligned}$$

Thus,

$$\begin{aligned} d \sum_{i=1}^{s} \sum_{f_i=(i-1)d+1}^{id} e_{f_i} &\le \sum_{i=1}^{s} (d_{i,1} + \cdots + d_{i,\min(\nu_i,d)}) + \frac{sd(d-1)}{2} \\ &\le dm - \widetilde{t} + \frac{sd(d-1)}{2} \end{aligned}$$

and therefore,

$$\begin{aligned}\sum_{i=1}^{s} \sum_{f_i=(i-1)d+1}^{id} e_{f_i} &\le m - \frac{\widetilde{t}}{d} + \frac{s(d-1)}{2} \\ &= m - t' - \left\lfloor \frac{s(d-1)}{2} \right\rfloor + \frac{s(d-1)}{2} \\ &\le m - t' + \frac{1}{2}.\end{aligned}$$

As e_{f_i}, m and t' are all integers, it follows that

$$\sum_{i=1}^{s} \sum_{f_i=(i-1)d+1}^{id} e_{f_i} \le m - t'.$$

Thus, it follows from the digital (t', m, sd)-net property of the digital net generated by $C_1, \ldots, C_{sd}$ that the vectors $\mathbf{d}_{d_{1,1}}^{(1)}, \ldots, \mathbf{d}_{d_{1,\nu_1}}^{(1)}, \ldots, \mathbf{d}_{d_{s,1}}^{(s)}, \ldots, \mathbf{d}_{d_{s,\nu_s}}^{(s)}$ are linearly independent and therefore it follows that

$$t \le \widetilde{t} = d\left(t' + \lfloor s(d-1)/2 \rfloor\right). \qquad \square$$

The quality of the digital nets obtained by the above construction was first investigated in [35, 36]. The following result for the above construction was shown in [42].

Theorem 15.7 *Let $d, \alpha \in \mathbb{N}$, let $C_1, \ldots, C_{sd}$ be the generating matrices of a digital (t', m, sd)-net over $\mathbb{Z}_b$. Then the matrices $D_1, \ldots, D_s$ defined as above are generating matrices of a higher order digital $(t, \alpha, \min(1, \alpha/d), dm \times m, s)$-net over $\mathbb{Z}_b$ with*

$$t \le \min(d, \alpha) \min\left(m, t' + \left\lfloor \frac{s(d-1)}{2} \right\rfloor\right).$$

Proof First note that if $m \le t' + \lfloor s(d-1)/2 \rfloor$, then $t = \min(d, \alpha)m$ and

$$\min(1, \alpha/d)dm - t = \min(d, \alpha)m - \min(d, \alpha)m = 0,$$

hence, in this case the bound is trivial.

If $m > t' + \lfloor s(d-1)/2 \rfloor$, then the result follows from Proposition 15.5 and Lemma 15.6. $\square$

Theorem 15.7 can be strengthened for $\alpha = 1$, in which case we obtain the following result shown in [37].

Proposition 15.8 *Let $d \in \mathbb{N}$ and let $C_1, \ldots, C_{sd}$ be the generating matrices of a digital (t, m, sd)-net over $\mathbb{Z}_b$. Then the matrices $D_1, \ldots, D_s$ defined above are the generating matrices of a digital (t, m, s)-net over $\mathbb{Z}_b$.*

Proof Let $d_1, \ldots, d_s \in \mathbb{N}_0$ such that $d_1 + \cdots + d_s \leq m - t$. Then the first d_i rows of D_i stem from the matrices $C_{(i-1)d+1}, \ldots, C_{id}$. Indeed, there are numbers $l_{(i-1)d+1}, \ldots, l_{id} \in \mathbb{N}_0$, such that $d_i = l_{(i-1)d+1} + \cdots + l_{id}$ with the property that the first d_i rows of D_i are exactly the union of the first $l_{(i-1)d+r}$ rows of $C_{(i-1)d+r}$ for $1 \leq r \leq d$. Hence, the fact that $\sum_{i=1}^{s} d_i = \sum_{i=1}^{s} \sum_{r=1}^{d} l_{(i-1)d+r} \leq m - t$ and the digital (t, m, sd)-net property of $C_1, \ldots, C_{sd}$ imply that the vectors from the union of the first d_i rows of D_i for all $1 \leq i \leq s$, are linearly independent. This implies that $D_1, \ldots, D_s$ generate a digital (t, m, s)-net. □

The above construction and Theorem 15.7 can easily be extended to digital $(t, \alpha, \beta, \sigma, s)$-sequences. Indeed, let $d \in \mathbb{N}$ and let $C_1, \ldots, C_{sd}$ be the generating matrices of a digital (t', sd)-sequence over $\mathbb{Z}_b$. Again, many explicit generating matrices are known; see Chapter 8. Let $\mathbf{c}_j^{(i)} \in \mathbb{Z}_b^{\mathbb{N}}$ be the jth row vector of C_i for $j \in \mathbb{N}$ and $1 \leq i \leq s$. Now let the matrix D_i be made of the first rows of the matrices $C_{(i-1)d+1}, \ldots, C_{id}$, then the second rows of $C_{(i-1)d+1}, \ldots, C_{id}$ and so on, i.e. the first few row vectors of D_i from the top are

$$\mathbf{c}_1^{((j-1)d+1)}, \ldots, \mathbf{c}_1^{(jd)}, \mathbf{c}_2^{((j-1)d+1)}, \ldots, \mathbf{c}_2^{(jd)}, \ldots.$$

The following theorem states that the matrices $D_1, \ldots, D_s$ are the generating matrices of a digital $(t, \alpha, \min(1, \alpha/d), d, s)$-sequence over $\mathbb{Z}_b$. This was first shown in [35, 36]; see also [39].

Theorem 15.9 *Let $d \in \mathbb{N}$ and let $C_1, \ldots, C_{sd}$ be the generating matrices of a digital (t', sd)-sequence over $\mathbb{Z}_b$. Then, for any $\alpha \in \mathbb{N}$, the matrices $D_1, \ldots, D_s$ defined above are generating matrices of a higher order digital $(t, \alpha, \min(1, \alpha/d), d, s)$-sequence over $\mathbb{Z}_b$ with*

$$t \leq \min(\alpha, d)\left(t' + \left\lfloor \frac{s(d-1)}{2} \right\rfloor\right).$$

The proof of this theorem is based on the result for higher order digital nets and is left to the reader as an exercise (see Exercise 15.3).

From the previous section, we know that we can expect a convergence rate of order $\beta\sigma$ for QMC rules based on higher order digital sequences. Theorem 15.9 implies that $\beta\sigma = \min(1, \alpha/d)d = \min(d, \alpha)$. Therefore, if $\delta \leq d$, where δ denotes the smoothness of the integrand, we obtain the optimal convergence rate of order α, whereas for $\delta \geq \alpha > d$, we obtain a convergence rate of order d. In other words, the construction yields the best possible result for all $\delta \leq d$.

Remark 15.10 Digital $(t, \alpha, \beta, \sigma, s)$-sequences over $\mathbb{Z}_b$ with $\beta\sigma = \alpha$ are optimal in terms of the convergence rate (note that $\beta\sigma > \alpha$ is not possible by Sharygin's result [241] and higher order sequences with $\beta\sigma < \alpha$ do not yield the optimal rate of convergence).

Assume that we are given a digital $(t', \alpha', \beta', \sigma, s)$-sequence $\mathcal{S}$ over $\mathbb{Z}_b$ for some fixed values of $t', \alpha', \beta', \sigma, s$ with $\alpha' = \beta'\sigma$. Then, Proposition 15.5 shows that for any $1 \le \alpha \le \alpha'$, the sequence $\mathcal{S}$ is a digital $(t, \alpha, \beta, \sigma, s)$-sequence over $\mathbb{Z}_b$ with

$$\beta\sigma = \beta' \min(1, \alpha/\alpha')\sigma = \alpha' \min(1, \alpha/\alpha') = \min(\alpha', \alpha) = \alpha.$$

Hence, if one shows that a digital sequence $\mathcal{S}$ is optimal for some value $\alpha' \in \mathbb{N}$, then it follows that the sequence $\mathcal{S}$ is also optimal for all $1 \le \alpha \le \alpha'$.

Analogous comments apply to higher order digital nets.

For $(t, \alpha, \beta, \sigma, s)$-sequences over $\mathbb{Z}_b$ with $\alpha = \beta\sigma$, there is also a lower bound on the quality parameter t from [39], which states that for all $\alpha \ge 2$, we have

$$t > s\frac{\alpha(\alpha - 1)}{2} - \alpha.$$

Assume now that $\delta \le d$, in which case Theorem 15.9 yields higher order digital sequences with $\beta\sigma = \min(1, \alpha/d)d = \min(d, \alpha) = \alpha$. As there are digital (t', sd)-sequences with $t' = O(sd)$, see [192, 193], Theorem 15.9 yields that there are higher order digital sequences with $\beta\sigma = \alpha$ and

$$t = O(\alpha s d).$$

In particular, this means that, asymptotically, the construction is optimal for $\alpha = d$, in which case we have $\beta\sigma = \alpha$ and

$$t = O(s\alpha^2).$$

See [39] for more information.

Again, Theorem 15.9 can be strengthened for $\alpha = 1$, in which case we obtain the following result.

Proposition 15.11 *Let $d \in \mathbb{N}$ and let $C_1, \ldots, C_{sd}$ be the generating matrices of a digital (t', sd)-sequence over $\mathbb{Z}_b$. Then the matrices $D_1, \ldots, D_s$ defined above are the generating matrices of a digital (t', s)-sequence over $\mathbb{Z}_b$.*

Again, the proof of this proposition is left to the reader as an exercise (see Exercise 15.4).

Geometrical properties of digital $(t, \alpha, \beta, n \times m, s)$-nets and their generalisation were shown in [39]. In the following section, we show pictures of those properties.

Figure 15.1 A digital $(3, 2, 1, 8 \times 4, 2)$-net over $\mathbb{Z}_2$ which is also a classical digital $(1, 4, 2)$-net over $\mathbb{Z}_2$.

15.3 Geometrical properties of higher order digital nets

In this section, we describe geometrical properties of higher order digital nets. For $d = 2$, the generating matrices $D_1 \in \mathbb{Z}_2^{2\cdot 4\times 4}$ and $D_2 \in \mathbb{Z}_2^{2\cdot 4\times 4}$ for the digital net over $\mathbb{Z}_2$ shown in Figure 15.1 are obtained from the classical digital $(1, 4, 4)$-net over $\mathbb{Z}_2$ with the following generating matrices:

$$C_1 = \begin{pmatrix} 1 & 0 & 0 & 0 \\ 0 & 1 & 0 & 0 \\ 0 & 0 & 1 & 0 \\ 0 & 0 & 0 & 1 \end{pmatrix}, \quad C_2 = \begin{pmatrix} 0 & 0 & 0 & 1 \\ 0 & 0 & 1 & 0 \\ 0 & 1 & 0 & 0 \\ 1 & 0 & 0 & 0 \end{pmatrix},$$

$$C_3 = \begin{pmatrix} 1 & 1 & 1 & 1 \\ 0 & 1 & 0 & 1 \\ 0 & 0 & 1 & 1 \\ 0 & 0 & 0 & 1 \end{pmatrix}, \quad C_4 = \begin{pmatrix} 0 & 1 & 1 & 0 \\ 1 & 1 & 0 & 1 \\ 0 & 0 & 0 & 1 \\ 0 & 0 & 1 & 0 \end{pmatrix}.$$

Using the construction principle from the previous section, we obtain

$$D_1 = \begin{pmatrix} 1 & 0 & 0 & 0 \\ 0 & 0 & 0 & 1 \\ 0 & 1 & 0 & 0 \\ 0 & 0 & 1 & 0 \\ 0 & 0 & 1 & 0 \\ 0 & 1 & 0 & 0 \\ 0 & 0 & 0 & 1 \\ 1 & 0 & 0 & 0 \end{pmatrix} \text{ and } D_2 = \begin{pmatrix} 1 & 1 & 1 & 1 \\ 0 & 1 & 1 & 0 \\ 0 & 1 & 0 & 1 \\ 1 & 1 & 0 & 1 \\ 0 & 0 & 1 & 1 \\ 0 & 0 & 0 & 1 \\ 0 & 0 & 0 & 1 \\ 0 & 0 & 1 & 0 \end{pmatrix}.$$

Theorem 15.7 implies that D_1 and D_2 generate a digital $(4, 2, 1, 8 \times 4, 2)$-net over $\mathbb{Z}_2$. Upon inspection, one can see that it is also a digital $(3, 2, 1, 8 \times 4, 2)$-net over

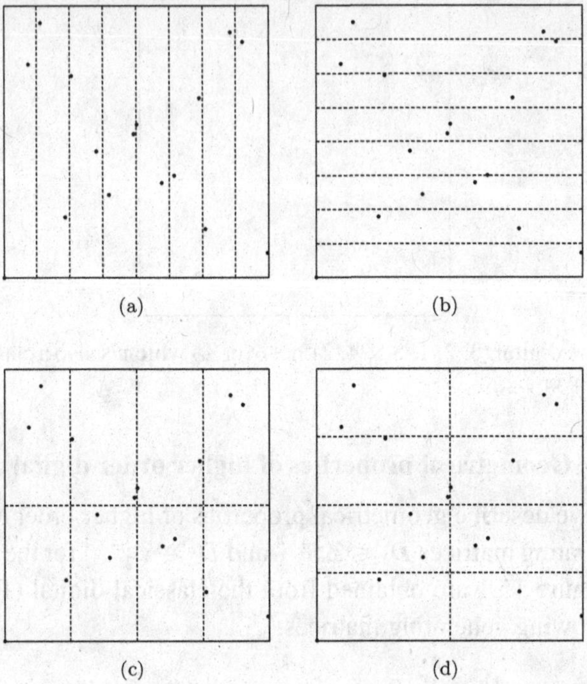

Figure 15.2 The digital $(3, 2, 1, 8 \times 4, 2)$-net is also a digital $(1, 4, 2)$-net, as each elementary interval of volume $1/8$ of every partition of the unit square contains exactly two points.

$\mathbb{Z}_2$, but not a digital $(2, 2, 1, 8 \times 4, 2)$-net over $\mathbb{Z}_2$ (the first two rows of D_1 and D_2 are linearly dependent).

Figure 15.2 shows that the point set is also a classical $(1, 4, 2)$-net over $\mathbb{Z}_2$.

Figure 15.3 shows a partition of the square for which each union of the shaded rectangles contains exactly two points. Figures 15.4 and 15.5 show that other partitions of the unit square are also possible where each union of shaded rectangles contains a fair number of points. Many other partitions of the square are possible where the point set always contains a fair number of points (see Definition 4.1) in each union of rectangles, see [39], but there are too many to show them all here. Even in the simple case considered here, there are 12 possible partitions, for each of which the point set is fair – this is quite remarkable since the point set itself has only 16 points (we exclude all those partitions for which the fairness would follow already from some other partition; otherwise there would be 34 of them). In the classical case, we have four such partitions, all of which are shown in Figure 15.2. (The partitions from the classical case are included in the generalised case; so, out of the 12 partitions, four are shown in Figure 15.2, one is shown in Figure 15.3, one is shown in Figure 15.5 and one is indicated in Figure 15.4.)

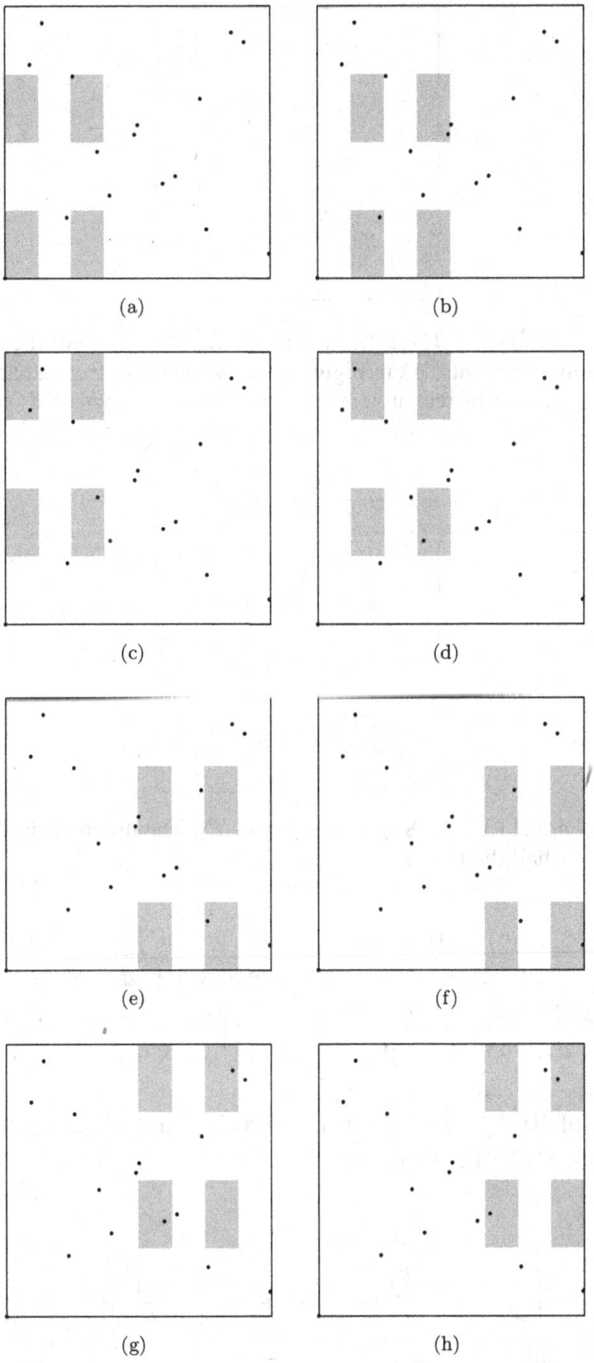

Figure 15.3 The digital (3, 2, 1, 8 × 4, 2)-net. The union of the shaded rectangles in each figure from (a) to (h) contains exactly two points.

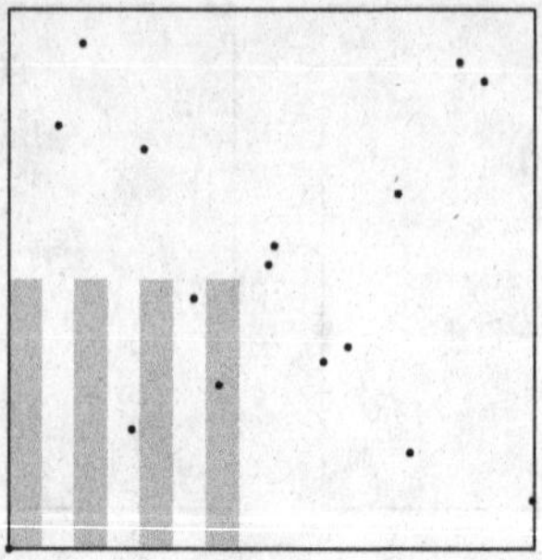

Figure 15.4 Digital $(3, 2, 1, 8 \times 4, 2)$-net over $\mathbb{Z}_2$. The union of the shaded rectangles contains two points. As in Figure 15.3 one can also form a partition of the square with this type of rectangle where each union of rectangles contains two points.

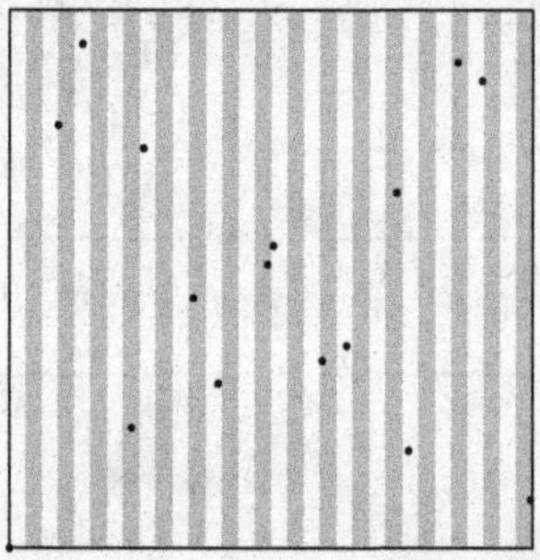

Figure 15.5 Digital $(3, 2, 1, 8 \times 4, 2)$-net over $\mathbb{Z}_2$. The union of the shaded rectangles contains half the points.

For $\boldsymbol{\nu} = (\nu_1, \ldots, \nu_s) \in \{0, \ldots, \alpha m\}^s$, let $|\boldsymbol{\nu}|_1 = \sum_{i=1}^s \nu_i$ and define $\boldsymbol{d}_{\boldsymbol{\nu}} = (d_{1,1}, \ldots, d_{1,\nu_1}, \ldots, d_{s,1}, \ldots, d_{s,\nu_s})$ with integers $1 \le d_{i,\nu_i} < \cdots < d_{i,1} \le \alpha m$ in case $\nu_i > 0$ and $\{d_{i,1}, \ldots, d_{i,\nu_i}\} = \emptyset$ in case $\nu_i = 0$, for $1 \le i \le s$. For given $\boldsymbol{\nu}$ and $\boldsymbol{d}_{\boldsymbol{\nu}}$, let $\boldsymbol{a}_{\boldsymbol{\nu}} \in \{0, \ldots, b-1\}^{|\boldsymbol{\nu}|_1}$, which we write as $\boldsymbol{a}_{\boldsymbol{\nu}} = (a_{1,d_{1,1}}, \ldots, a_{1,d_{1,\nu_1}}, \ldots, a_{s,d_{s,1}}, \ldots, a_{s,d_{s,\nu_s}})$.

The subsets of $[0, 1)^s$, which form a partition and which each have the fair number of points, are of the form

$$J(\boldsymbol{d}_{\boldsymbol{\nu}}, \boldsymbol{a}_{\boldsymbol{\nu}}) = \prod_{i=1}^{s} \bigcup_{\substack{a_{i,l}=0 \\ l \in \{1,\ldots,\alpha m\} \setminus \{d_{i,1},\ldots,d_{i,\nu_i}\}}}^{b-1} \left[\frac{a_{i,1}}{b} + \cdots + \frac{a_{i,\alpha m}}{b^{\alpha m}}, \frac{a_{i,1}}{b} + \cdots + \frac{a_{i,\alpha m}}{b^{\alpha m}} + \frac{1}{b^{\alpha m}} \right),$$

where $\sum_{i=1}^s \sum_{l=1}^{\nu_i} d_{i,l} \le \beta n - t$ and where $\boldsymbol{a}_{\boldsymbol{\nu}} \in \{0, \ldots, b-1\}^{|\boldsymbol{\nu}|_1}$.

Figures 15.2, 15.3, 15.4 and 15.5 give only a few examples of unions of intervals for which each subset of the partition contains the right number of points. As the $J(\boldsymbol{d}_\nu, \boldsymbol{a}_\nu)$, for fixed $\boldsymbol{\nu}$ and $\boldsymbol{d}_\nu$ (with $\boldsymbol{a}_\nu$ running through all possibilities) form a partition of $[0, 1)^s$, it is clear that the right number of points in $J(\boldsymbol{d}_\nu, \boldsymbol{a}_\nu)$ has to be $b^m \mathrm{Vol}(J(\boldsymbol{d}_\nu, \boldsymbol{a}_\nu))$. For example, the digital net in Figure 15.3 has 16 points and the partition consists of eight different subsets $J(\boldsymbol{d}_\nu, \boldsymbol{a}_\nu)$; hence, each $J(\boldsymbol{d}_\nu, \boldsymbol{a}_\nu)$ contains exactly $16/8 = 2$ points. (In general, the volume of $J(\boldsymbol{d}_\nu, \boldsymbol{a}_\nu)$ is given by $b^{-|\boldsymbol{\nu}|_1}$; see [39].)

15.4 Squared worst-case error in $\mathscr{H}_{s,\alpha,\gamma}$

In the following, we consider the worst-case error for multivariate integration in the Sobolev space $\mathscr{H}_{s,\alpha,\gamma}$ for $s, \alpha \in \mathbb{N}$, $\alpha \geq 2$ that was introduced in Section 14.6. A similar approach was used in [35] for periodic functions, whereas in [36], a reproducing kernel Hilbert space based on Walsh functions was introduced for which numerical integration was analysed. In our exposition we follow [7], where the Sobolev space $\mathscr{H}_{s,\alpha,\gamma}$ was considered.

The reproducing kernel for $\mathscr{H}_{s,\alpha,\gamma}$ is given by

$$K_{s,\alpha,\gamma}(\boldsymbol{x}, \boldsymbol{y}) = \sum_{\mathfrak{u} \subseteq \mathcal{I}_s} \gamma_{\mathfrak{u}} \prod_{i \in \mathfrak{u}} \left(\sum_{\tau=1}^{\alpha} \frac{B_\tau(x_i) B_\tau(y_i)}{(\tau!)^2} - (-1)^\alpha \frac{B_{2\alpha}(|x_i - y_i|)}{(2\alpha)!} \right) \tag{15.3}$$

and the inner product is

$$\langle f, g \rangle_{\mathscr{H}_{s,\alpha,\gamma}} = \sum_{\mathfrak{u} \subseteq \mathcal{I}_s} \gamma_{\mathfrak{u}}^{-1} \sum_{\mathfrak{v} \subseteq \mathfrak{u}} \sum_{\boldsymbol{\tau}_{\mathfrak{u} \setminus \mathfrak{v}} \in \{1,\ldots,\alpha-1\}^{|\mathfrak{u} \setminus \mathfrak{v}|}} \int_{[0,1]^{|\mathfrak{v}|}}$$
$$\left(\int_{[0,1]^{s-|\mathfrak{v}|}} f^{(\boldsymbol{\tau}_{\mathfrak{u} \setminus \mathfrak{v}}, \boldsymbol{\alpha}_{\mathfrak{v}}, \boldsymbol{0})}(\boldsymbol{x}) \,\mathrm{d}\boldsymbol{x}_{\mathcal{I}_s \setminus \mathfrak{v}} \right)$$
$$\times \left(\int_{[0,1]^{s-|\mathfrak{v}|}} g^{(\boldsymbol{\tau}_{\mathfrak{u} \setminus \mathfrak{v}}, \boldsymbol{\alpha}_{\mathfrak{v}}, \boldsymbol{0})}(\boldsymbol{x}) \,\mathrm{d}\boldsymbol{x}_{\mathcal{I}_s \setminus \mathfrak{v}} \right) \mathrm{d}\boldsymbol{x}_{\mathfrak{v}},$$

(where we used the same notation as in Section 14.6). We often represent $K_{s,\alpha,\gamma}$ by its Walsh series; in particular, we have

$$K_{s,\alpha,\gamma}(\boldsymbol{x}, \boldsymbol{y}) = \sum_{\boldsymbol{k}, \boldsymbol{l} \in \mathbb{N}_0^s} \widehat{K}_{s,\alpha,\gamma}(\boldsymbol{k}, \boldsymbol{l}) \, {}_b\mathrm{wal}_{\boldsymbol{k}}(\boldsymbol{x}) \overline{{}_b\mathrm{wal}_{\boldsymbol{l}}(\boldsymbol{y})}, \tag{15.4}$$

where

$$\widehat{K}_{s,\alpha,\gamma}(\boldsymbol{k}, \boldsymbol{l}) = \int_{[0,1]^{2s}} K_{s,\alpha,\gamma}(\boldsymbol{x}, \boldsymbol{y}) \overline{{}_b\mathrm{wal}_{\boldsymbol{k}}(\boldsymbol{x})} \, {}_b\mathrm{wal}_{\boldsymbol{l}}(\boldsymbol{y}) \,\mathrm{d}\boldsymbol{x} \,\mathrm{d}\boldsymbol{y}. \tag{15.5}$$

From Proposition 2.11, we know that the square worst-case error for QMC integration of functions from the Sobolev space $\mathscr{H}_{s,\alpha,\gamma}$ using a point set $\mathcal{P} = \{\boldsymbol{x}_0, \ldots, \boldsymbol{x}_{N-1}\}$ is given by

$$e^2(\mathscr{H}_{s,\alpha,\gamma}, \mathcal{P}) = \int_{[0,1]^{2s}} K_{s,\alpha,\gamma}(\boldsymbol{x}, \boldsymbol{y})\,\mathrm{d}\boldsymbol{x}\,\mathrm{d}\boldsymbol{y} - \frac{2}{N}\sum_{n=0}^{N-1}\int_{[0,1]^s} K_{s,\alpha,\gamma}(\boldsymbol{x}_n, \boldsymbol{x})d\boldsymbol{x}$$
$$+\frac{1}{N^2}\sum_{n,n'=0}^{N-1} K_{s,\alpha,\gamma}(\boldsymbol{x}_n, \boldsymbol{x}_{n'}).$$

The square initial error for QMC integration in $\mathscr{H}_{s,\alpha,\gamma}$ is given by

$$e^2(\mathscr{H}_{s,\alpha,\gamma}, 0) = \int_{[0,1]^{2s}} K_{s,\alpha,\gamma}(\boldsymbol{x}, \boldsymbol{y})\,\mathrm{d}\boldsymbol{x}\,\mathrm{d}\boldsymbol{y}.$$

Using (15.3) together with the fact that $\int_0^1 B_r(x)\,\mathrm{d}x = 0$ for all $r \in \mathbb{N}$ and $\int_0^1 B_{2\alpha}(|x-y|)\,\mathrm{d}x = 0$ for all $y \in [0,1)$, which follows from (14.12), we obtain the following result:

Theorem 15.12 *The square worst-case error for QMC integration in the Sobolev space $\mathscr{H}_{s,\alpha,\gamma}$ using the point set $\mathcal{P} = \{\boldsymbol{x}_0, \ldots, \boldsymbol{x}_{N-1}\}$ is given by*

$$e^2(\mathscr{H}_{s,\alpha,\gamma}, \mathcal{P}) = -1 + \frac{1}{N^2}\sum_{n,n'=0}^{N-1} K_{s,\alpha,\gamma}(\boldsymbol{x}_n, \boldsymbol{x}_{n'}). \tag{15.6}$$

Furthermore, the square initial error $e^2(\mathscr{H}_{s,\alpha,\gamma}, 0)$ for QMC integration in $\mathscr{H}_{s,\alpha,\gamma}$ is one.

We now consider the Walsh coefficients of the function

$$K_{1,\alpha,(1)}(x, y) := \sum_{\tau=1}^{\alpha} \frac{B_\tau(x)B_\tau(y)}{(\tau!)^2} - (-1)^\alpha \frac{B_{2\alpha}(|x-y|)}{(2\alpha)!},$$

which, for $k, l \in \mathbb{N}_0$, are defined by

$$\widehat{K}_{1,\alpha,(1)}(k,l) = \int_0^1\int_0^1 K_{1,\alpha,(1)}(x,y)\,\overline{{}_b\mathrm{wal}_k(x)}\,{}_b\mathrm{wal}_l(y)\,\mathrm{d}x\,\mathrm{d}y. \tag{15.7}$$

We note that for $l \in \mathbb{N}_0$, $\widehat{K}_{1,\alpha,(1)}(0,l) = 0$.

For $\boldsymbol{k} = (k_1, \ldots, k_s) \in \mathbb{N}_0^s$, we already used the notation $(\boldsymbol{k}_{\mathfrak{u}}, \boldsymbol{0})$ to denote the s-dimensional vector whose ith component is k_i for $i \in \mathfrak{u}$ and zero otherwise. On the other hand, for $\mathfrak{u} = \{v_1, \ldots, v_e\} \subseteq \mathcal{I}_s$ and $\boldsymbol{k}_{\mathfrak{u}} = (k_{v_1}, \ldots, k_{v_e}) \in \mathbb{N}^{|\mathfrak{u}|}$, we write

$(\boldsymbol{k}_{\mathfrak{u}}, \boldsymbol{0})$ for the s-dimensional vector whose ith component is k_i if $i \in \mathfrak{u}$ and zero otherwise.

The following lemma shows how to express the Walsh coefficients $\widehat{K}_{s,\alpha,\boldsymbol{\gamma}}$, given by (15.5), in terms of $\widehat{K}_{1,\alpha,(1)}$.

Lemma 15.13 *Let $\boldsymbol{k}, \boldsymbol{l} \in \mathbb{N}^s$, then for any $\mathfrak{u}, \mathfrak{v} \subseteq \mathcal{I}_s$ we have*

$$\widehat{K}_{s,\alpha,\boldsymbol{\gamma}}((\boldsymbol{k}_{\mathfrak{u}}, \boldsymbol{0}), (\boldsymbol{l}_{\mathfrak{v}}, \boldsymbol{0})) = \begin{cases} \gamma_{\mathfrak{u}} \prod_{i \in \mathfrak{u}} \widehat{K}_{1,\alpha,(1)}(k_i, l_i) & \text{for } \mathfrak{u} = \mathfrak{v}, \\ 0 & \text{for } \mathfrak{u} \neq \mathfrak{v}, \end{cases}$$

where the empty product $\prod_{i \in \emptyset}$ is set to one.

Proof Using equations (15.3) and (15.5), we obtain

$$\begin{aligned} &\widehat{K}_{s,\alpha,\boldsymbol{\gamma}}((\boldsymbol{k}_{\mathfrak{u}}, \boldsymbol{0}), (\boldsymbol{l}_{\mathfrak{v}}, \boldsymbol{0})) \\ &= \int_{[0,1]^{2s}} K_{s,\alpha,\boldsymbol{\gamma}}(\boldsymbol{x}, \boldsymbol{y}) \overline{{}_b\mathrm{wal}_{(\boldsymbol{k}_{\mathfrak{u}},\boldsymbol{0})}(\boldsymbol{x})}\, {}_b\mathrm{wal}_{(\boldsymbol{l}_{\mathfrak{v}},\boldsymbol{0})}(\boldsymbol{y}) \,\mathrm{d}\boldsymbol{x} \,\mathrm{d}\boldsymbol{y} \\ &= \int_{[0,1]^{2s}} \left[\sum_{\mathfrak{m} \subseteq \mathcal{I}_s} \prod_{i \in \mathfrak{m}} \gamma_i K_{1,\alpha,(1)}(x_i, y_i) \right] \overline{{}_b\mathrm{wal}_{(\boldsymbol{k}_{\mathfrak{u}},\boldsymbol{0})}(\boldsymbol{x})}\, {}_b\mathrm{wal}_{(\boldsymbol{l}_{\mathfrak{v}},\boldsymbol{0})}(\boldsymbol{y}) \,\mathrm{d}\boldsymbol{x} \,\mathrm{d}\boldsymbol{y} \\ &= \sum_{\mathfrak{w} \subseteq \mathcal{I}_s} \gamma_{\mathfrak{w}} \int_{[0,1]^{2s}} \prod_{i \in \mathfrak{w}} K_{1,\alpha,(1)}(x_i, y_i) \overline{{}_b\mathrm{wal}_{(\boldsymbol{k}_{\mathfrak{u}},\boldsymbol{0})}(\boldsymbol{x})}\, {}_b\mathrm{wal}_{(\boldsymbol{l}_{\mathfrak{v}},\boldsymbol{0})}(\boldsymbol{y}) \,\mathrm{d}\boldsymbol{x} \,\mathrm{d}\boldsymbol{y}. \end{aligned}$$

Note that $\int_0^1 K_{1,\alpha,(1)}(x, y) \,\mathrm{d}x = \int_0^1 K_{1,\alpha,(1)}(x, y) \,\mathrm{d}y = 0$ according to the properties of Bernoulli polynomials and that $\int_0^1 {}_b\mathrm{wal}_k(x) \,\mathrm{d}x = 0$ for $k \in \mathbb{N}$. Thus, if $\mathfrak{u} \neq \mathfrak{v}$, $\mathfrak{u} \neq \mathfrak{w}$ or $\mathfrak{v} \neq \mathfrak{w}$, the integral in the last line of the equation is zero. The remaining case $\mathfrak{u} = \mathfrak{v} = \mathfrak{w}$ yields $\gamma_{\mathfrak{u}} \prod_{i \in \mathfrak{u}} \widehat{K}_{1,\alpha,(1)}(k_i, l_i)$. □

The next theorem shows how to rewrite the worst-case error in terms of the Walsh coefficients of the reproducing kernel.

Theorem 15.14 *The square worst-case error for QMC integration in the Sobolev space $\mathscr{H}_{s,\alpha,\boldsymbol{\gamma}}$ using a higher order digital $(t, \alpha, \beta, n \times m, s)$-net $\mathcal{P}$ over $\mathbb{Z}_b$ with generating matrices $C_1, \ldots, C_s \in \mathbb{Z}_b^{n \times m}$ is given by*

$$e^2(\mathscr{H}_{s,\alpha,\boldsymbol{\gamma}}, \mathcal{P}) = \sum_{\emptyset \neq \mathfrak{u} \subseteq \mathcal{I}_s} \gamma_{\mathfrak{u}} \sum_{\substack{\boldsymbol{k}_{\mathfrak{u}}, \boldsymbol{l}_{\mathfrak{u}} \in \mathbb{N}^{|\mathfrak{u}|} \\ (\boldsymbol{k}_{\mathfrak{u}},\boldsymbol{0}),(\boldsymbol{l}_{\mathfrak{u}},\boldsymbol{0}) \in \mathcal{D}_{\infty,n}}} \prod_{i \in \mathfrak{u}} \widehat{K}_{1,\alpha,(1)}(k_i, l_i), \qquad (15.8)$$

where $\mathcal{D}_{\infty,n} = \{\boldsymbol{k} \in \mathbb{N}_0^s : C_1^\top \mathrm{tr}_n(\mathbf{k}_1) + \cdots + C_s^\top \mathrm{tr}_n(\mathbf{k}_s) = \mathbf{0}\}$.

Proof Let $\mathcal{P} = \{\boldsymbol{x}_0, \ldots, \boldsymbol{x}_{b^m-1}\}$. From equations (15.4) and (15.6), we obtain

$$\begin{aligned} e^2(\mathscr{H}_{s,\alpha,\boldsymbol{\gamma}}, \mathcal{P}) &= -1 + \frac{1}{b^{2m}} \sum_{j,j'=0}^{b^m-1} \left[\sum_{\boldsymbol{k},\boldsymbol{l} \in \mathbb{N}_0^s} \widehat{K}_{s,\alpha,\boldsymbol{\gamma}}(\boldsymbol{k}, \boldsymbol{l})\, {}_b\mathrm{wal}_{\boldsymbol{k}}(\boldsymbol{x}_j) \overline{{}_b\mathrm{wal}_{\boldsymbol{l}}(\boldsymbol{x}_{j'})} \right] \\ &= -1 + \frac{1}{b^{2m}} \sum_{\boldsymbol{k},\boldsymbol{l} \in \mathbb{N}_0^s} \widehat{K}_{s,\alpha,\boldsymbol{\gamma}}(\boldsymbol{k}, \boldsymbol{l}) \sum_{j,j'=0}^{b^m-1} {}_b\mathrm{wal}_{\boldsymbol{k}}(\boldsymbol{x}_j) \overline{{}_b\mathrm{wal}_{\boldsymbol{l}}(\boldsymbol{x}_{j'})} \\ &= \sum_{\boldsymbol{k},\boldsymbol{l} \in \mathcal{D}_{\infty,n} \setminus \{\boldsymbol{0}\}} \widehat{K}_{s,\alpha,\boldsymbol{\gamma}}(\boldsymbol{k}, \boldsymbol{l}). \end{aligned}$$

We now use Lemma 15.13 to obtain

$$\begin{aligned} e^2(\mathscr{H}_{s,\alpha,\boldsymbol{\gamma}}, \mathcal{P}) &= \sum_{\emptyset \neq \mathfrak{u} \subseteq \mathcal{I}_s} \sum_{\substack{\boldsymbol{k}_{\mathfrak{u}}, \boldsymbol{l}_{\mathfrak{u}} \in \mathbb{N}^{|\mathfrak{u}|} \\ (\boldsymbol{k}_{\mathfrak{u}}, \boldsymbol{0}), (\boldsymbol{l}_{\mathfrak{u}}, \boldsymbol{0}) \in \mathcal{D}_{\infty,n}}} \widehat{K}_{s,\alpha,\boldsymbol{\gamma}}((\boldsymbol{k}_{\mathfrak{u}}, \boldsymbol{0}), (\boldsymbol{l}_{\mathfrak{u}}, \boldsymbol{0})) \\ &= \sum_{\emptyset \neq \mathfrak{u} \subseteq \mathcal{I}_s} \gamma_{\mathfrak{u}} \sum_{\substack{\boldsymbol{k}_{\mathfrak{u}}, \boldsymbol{l}_{\mathfrak{u}} \in \mathbb{N}^{|\mathfrak{u}|} \\ (\boldsymbol{k}_{\mathfrak{u}}, \boldsymbol{0}), (\boldsymbol{l}_{\mathfrak{u}}, \boldsymbol{0}) \in \mathcal{D}_{\infty,n}}} \prod_{i \in \mathfrak{u}} \widehat{K}_{1,\alpha,(1)}(k_i, l_i). \end{aligned}$$

□

15.5 A bound on the Walsh coefficients

Our goal is to derive a bound on the square worst-case error which shows the optimal rate of convergence. As is shown in Section 15.6, a key ingredient for achieving this is a bound on the Walsh coefficients $\widehat{K}_{1,\alpha,(1)}$, as defined by (15.7). This was first considered in [7] and is the topic of this section (see [35] for the periodic case).

We note that for $k, l \in \mathbb{N}_0$

$$\begin{aligned} \left|\widehat{K}_{1,\alpha,(1)}(k,l)\right| &= \left| \int_0^1 \int_0^1 K_{1,\alpha,(1)}(x,y)\, \overline{{}_b\mathrm{wal}_k(x)}\, {}_b\mathrm{wal}_l(y) \,\mathrm{d}x \,\mathrm{d}y \right| \\ &= \left| \sum_{\tau=1}^{\alpha} \beta_\tau(k) \overline{\beta_\tau(l)} + (-1)^{\alpha+1} \gamma_{2\alpha}(k,l) \right| \\ &\le \sum_{\tau=1}^{\alpha} |\beta_\tau(k)||\beta_\tau(l)| + |\gamma_{2\alpha}(k,l)|, \end{aligned} \tag{15.9}$$

where β is defined by (14.13) and γ is defined by (14.17) in Section 14.5.

We now show that for $k, l \in \mathbb{N}$,

$$\sum_{\tau=1}^{\alpha} |\beta_\tau(k)||\beta_\tau(l)| + |\gamma_{2\alpha}(k,l)| \le C_{\alpha,b} b^{-\mu_\alpha(k)-\mu_\alpha(l)},$$

where $C_{\alpha,b} > 0$ only depends on α and b and where μ_α is defined by (15.2) (and (14.6)).

For $k, \alpha \in \mathbb{N}_0$, $\alpha \geq 2$, we have $\mu_{\alpha,\mathrm{per}}(k) \geq \mu_\alpha(k)$, where $\mu_{\alpha,\mathrm{per}}$ is defined by (14.16). We state the following lemma, which is comprised of results from Section 14.5 and Lemma 14.16.

Lemma 15.15 *Let $k \in \mathbb{N}$ be given by $k = \kappa_1 b^{a_1-1} + \cdots + \kappa_v b^{a_v-1}$, where $1 \leq \kappa_1, \ldots, \kappa_v < b$ and $a_1 > \cdots > a_v > 0$. Then, for any $\tau \in \mathbb{N}$, we have*

$$|\beta_\tau(k)| \leq \begin{cases} C_{\tau,b} b^{-\mu_{\tau,\mathrm{per}}(k)} & \text{if } 1 \leq v \leq \tau, \\ 0 & \text{if } v > \tau, \end{cases}$$

where, for $\tau = 1$, we have $C_{1,b} = (2\sin(\pi/b))^{-1}$ and for $\tau \geq 2$, we have $C_{\tau,b} = \left((1 + 1/b + 1/(b(b+1)))^{\tau-2}\right) / (2\sin(\pi/b))^\tau$.

Lemma 15.16 *For $k, l \in \mathbb{N}$ with b-adic expansions*

$$k = \kappa_1 b^{a_{k,1}-1} + \cdots + \kappa_{v_k} b^{a_{k,v_k}-1},$$
$$l = \iota_1 b^{a_{l,1}-1} + \cdots + \iota_{v_l} b^{a_{l,v_l}-1},$$

let $v := \max(v_k, v_l)$. Then, for all $\alpha \in \mathbb{N}$, we have

$$\sum_{\tau=1}^{\alpha} |\beta_\tau(k)||\beta_\tau(l)| \leq C'_{\alpha,b,v} b^{-\mu_\alpha(k)-\mu_\alpha(l)},$$

where $C'_{\alpha,b,v} = \sum_{\tau=v}^{\alpha} C_{\tau,b}^2 b^{-2(\tau-v)}$, $1 \leq v \leq \alpha$, with $C_{\tau,b}$ from Lemma 15.15 and $C'_{\alpha,b,v} = 0$, for $v > \alpha$.

Proof From Lemma 15.15, it follows that for $1 \leq \tau \leq \alpha$, $1 \leq v_k \leq \tau$, we get

$$\begin{aligned} |\beta_\tau(k)| &\leq C_{\tau,b} b^{-\mu_{\tau,\mathrm{per}}(k)} \\ &= C_{\tau,b} b^{-\mu_\tau(k)-(\tau-v_k)a_{k,v_k}} \\ &= C_{\tau,b} b^{-\mu_\alpha(k)-(\tau-v_k)a_{k,v_k}}, \end{aligned}$$

and for $1 \leq \tau \leq \alpha$, $v_k > \tau$, $\beta_\tau(k) = 0$. Therefore, we obtain for $v \geq 1$,

$$\begin{aligned} \sum_{\tau=1}^{\alpha} |\beta_\tau(k)||\beta_\tau(l)| &\leq \sum_{\tau=v}^{\alpha} C_{\tau,b} b^{-\mu_\tau(k)-(\tau-v_k)a_{k,v_k}} C_{\tau,b} b^{-\mu_\tau(l)-(\tau-v_l)a_{l,v_l}} \\ &\leq b^{-\mu_\alpha(k)-\mu_\alpha(l)} \sum_{\tau=v}^{\alpha} C_{\tau,b}^2 b^{-2(\tau-v)}. \end{aligned}$$

□

We now show how to find a bound for $|\gamma_{2\alpha}(k, l)|$.

Lemma 15.17 *Let $\gamma_{2\alpha}(k,l)$ be defined by (14.17), let $\alpha, k, l \in \mathbb{N}$ and $v = \max(v_l, v_k)$. Then it follows that*

$$|\gamma_{2\alpha}(k,l)| \le \widetilde{C}_{2\alpha,b} b^{-\mu_\alpha(k)-\mu_\alpha(l)-2(\alpha-v)_+},$$

where $\widetilde{C}_{2\alpha,b} = 2(1+1/b+1/(b(b+1)))^{2\alpha-2}/(2\sin(\pi/b))^{2\alpha}$.

Proof We first note that for $k, l \in \mathbb{N}$,

$$\mu_{2\alpha,\mathrm{per}}(k,l) \ge \mu_{\alpha,\mathrm{per}}(k) + \mu_{\alpha,\mathrm{per}}(l),$$

where $\mu_{2\alpha,\mathrm{per}}(k,l)$ is defined by (14.16). We now get

$$\begin{aligned}\mu_{\alpha,\mathrm{per}}(k) + \mu_{\alpha,\mathrm{per}}(l) &= \mu_\alpha(k) + (\alpha - v_k)_+ a_{v_k} + \mu_\alpha(l) + (\alpha - v_l)_+ a_{v_l} \\ &\ge \mu_\alpha(k) + \mu_\alpha(l) + 2(\alpha - v)_+\end{aligned}$$

and hence, the result follows from Lemma 14.19. □

The following proposition establishes the desired bound.

Proposition 15.18 *Let $\beta_\tau(k)$, $\beta_\tau(l)$ and $\gamma_{2\alpha}(k,l)$ be defined as above. Then, for $k, l, \alpha \in \mathbb{N}$, we have*

$$\sum_{\tau=1}^{\alpha} |\beta_\tau(k)||\beta_\tau(l)| + |\gamma_{2\alpha}(k,l)| \le D_{\alpha,b} b^{-\mu_\alpha(k)-\mu_\alpha(l)},$$

where $D_{\alpha,b} = \max_{1\le v\le\alpha}\left(C'_{\alpha,b,v} + \widetilde{C}_{2\alpha,b} b^{-2(\alpha-v)_+}\right)$ and where $C'_{\alpha,b,v}$ is defined in Lemma 15.16 and $\widetilde{C}_{2\alpha,b}$ is defined in Lemma 15.17.

Proof The proof follows immediately from Lemmas 15.16 and 15.17. □

For later reference, we show some values of $D_{\alpha,b}$ in Table 15.1 for different values of α and b. In brackets, we give the value of v for which the maximum was attained.

15.6 A bound on the worst-case error

In this section, we state a bound for the worst-case error for QMC integration in the Sobolev space $\mathscr{H}_{s,\alpha,\gamma}$, where $s, \alpha \in \mathbb{N}$, $\alpha \ge 2$.

Lemma 15.19 *The square worst-case error for QMC integration in the Sobolev space $\mathscr{H}_{s,\alpha,\gamma}$ using a higher order digital $(t, \alpha, \beta, n \times m, s)$-net $\mathcal{P}$ over $\mathbb{Z}_b$ with*

Table 15.1 Values of $D_{\alpha,b}$ for different values of α and b, and the values of v for which the maximum was attained is given in brackets.

α/b	2	3	5
2	0.4097(2)	0.5571(2)	2.1165(2)
3	0.2845(3)	0.3727(3)	2.3296(3)
4	0.2714(1)	0.3469(1)	2.5642(4)
5	0.2693(1)	0.3467(1)	2.8224(5)
6	0.2690(1)	0.3467(1)	3.1066(6)
7	0.2689(1)	0.3467(1)	3.4193(7)
8	0.2689(1)	0.3467(1)	3.7636(8)

generating matrices $C_1, \ldots, C_s \in \mathbb{Z}_b^{n\times m}$ can be bounded by

$$e^2(\mathscr{H}_{s,\alpha,\gamma}, \mathcal{P}) \le \sum_{\emptyset \neq \mathfrak{u} \subseteq \mathcal{I}_s} \gamma_{\mathfrak{u}} D_{\alpha,b}^{|\mathfrak{u}|} \Bigg(\sum_{\substack{\boldsymbol{k}_{\mathfrak{u}} \in \mathbb{N}^{|\mathfrak{u}|} \\ (\boldsymbol{k}_{\mathfrak{u}}, \boldsymbol{0}) \in \mathcal{D}_{\infty,n}}} b^{-\mu_\alpha(\boldsymbol{k}_{\mathfrak{u}})} \Bigg)^2,$$

where $D_{\alpha,b}$ is given in Proposition 15.18.

Proof From Lemma 15.13, Theorem 15.14, Equation (15.9) and Proposition 15.18, we get

$$\begin{aligned}
e^2(\mathscr{H}_{s,\alpha,\gamma}, \mathcal{P}) &\le \sum_{\emptyset \neq \mathfrak{u} \subseteq \mathcal{I}_s} \gamma_{\mathfrak{u}} \sum_{\substack{\boldsymbol{k}_{\mathfrak{u}}, \boldsymbol{l}_{\mathfrak{u}} \in \mathbb{N}^{|\mathfrak{u}|} \\ (\boldsymbol{k}_{\mathfrak{u}}, \boldsymbol{0}), (\boldsymbol{l}_{\mathfrak{u}}, \boldsymbol{0}) \in \mathcal{D}_{\infty,n}}} \prod_{i \in \mathfrak{u}} \left| \widehat{K}_{s,\alpha,(1)}(k_i, l_i) \right| \\
&\le \sum_{\emptyset \neq \mathfrak{u} \subseteq \mathcal{I}_s} \gamma_{\mathfrak{u}} \sum_{\substack{\boldsymbol{k}_{\mathfrak{u}}, \boldsymbol{l}_{\mathfrak{u}} \in \mathbb{N}^{|\mathfrak{u}|} \\ (\boldsymbol{k}_{\mathfrak{u}}, \boldsymbol{0}), (\boldsymbol{l}_{\mathfrak{u}}, \boldsymbol{0}) \in \mathcal{D}_{\infty,n}}} \prod_{i \in \mathfrak{u}} \left(\sum_{\tau=1}^{\alpha} |\beta_\tau(k_i)||\beta_\tau(l_i)| + |\gamma_{2\alpha}(k_i, l_i)| \right) \\
&\le \sum_{\emptyset \neq \mathfrak{u} \subseteq \mathcal{I}_s} \gamma_{\mathfrak{u}} \sum_{\substack{\boldsymbol{k}_{\mathfrak{u}}, \boldsymbol{l}_{\mathfrak{u}} \in \mathbb{N}^{|\mathfrak{u}|} \\ (\boldsymbol{k}_{\mathfrak{u}}, \boldsymbol{0}), (\boldsymbol{l}_{\mathfrak{u}}, \boldsymbol{0}) \in \mathcal{D}_{\infty,n}}} \prod_{i \in \mathfrak{u}} D_{\alpha,b} b^{-\mu_\alpha(k_i) - \mu_\alpha(l_i)} \\
&= \sum_{\emptyset \neq \mathfrak{u} \subseteq \mathcal{I}_s} \gamma_{\mathfrak{u}} D_{\alpha,b}^{|\mathfrak{u}|} \sum_{\substack{\boldsymbol{k}_{\mathfrak{u}}, \boldsymbol{l}_{\mathfrak{u}} \in \mathbb{N}^{|\mathfrak{u}|} \\ (\boldsymbol{k}_{\mathfrak{u}}, \boldsymbol{0}), (\boldsymbol{l}_{\mathfrak{u}}, \boldsymbol{0}) \in \mathcal{D}_{\infty,n}}} b^{-\mu_\alpha(\boldsymbol{k}_{\mathfrak{u}})} b^{-\mu_\alpha(\boldsymbol{l}_{\mathfrak{u}})},
\end{aligned}$$

and the result now follows. □

We see from Table 15.1 that $D_{\alpha,b} < 1$ for $b \in \{2, 3\}$ and $2 \le \alpha \le 8$; hence, in this case, $\left(D_{\alpha,b}\right)^{|\mathfrak{u}|}$ goes to zero exponentially fast for increasing values of $|\mathfrak{u}|$.

In Section 15.1 we derived a criterion for the generating matrices of a digital net based on the assumption that the sum $\sum_{\substack{\boldsymbol{k}_{\mathfrak{u}} \in \mathbb{N}^{|\mathfrak{u}|} \\ (\boldsymbol{k}_{\mathfrak{u}}, \boldsymbol{0}) \in \mathcal{D}_{\infty,n}}} b^{-\mu_\alpha(\boldsymbol{k}_{\mathfrak{u}})}$ for $\emptyset \neq \mathfrak{u} \subseteq \mathcal{I}_s$ is dominated by its largest term. The justification for this assumption is given in the following lemma, which was first shown in reference [36].

Lemma 15.20 *Let $s, \alpha \in \mathbb{N}$, $b \geq 2$ be a prime, $C_1, \ldots, C_s \in \mathbb{Z}_b^{n \times m}$ be the generating matrices of a higher order digital $(t, \alpha, \beta, n \times m, s)$-net over $\mathbb{Z}_b$ with $0 < \beta \leq 1$ such that βn is an integer. Then, for all $\emptyset \neq \mathfrak{u} \subseteq \mathcal{I}_s$, we have*

$$\sum_{\substack{\boldsymbol{k}_{\mathfrak{u}} \in \mathbb{N}^{|\mathfrak{u}|} \\ (\boldsymbol{k}_{\mathfrak{u}}, \boldsymbol{0}) \in \mathcal{D}_{\infty,n}}} b^{-\mu_\alpha(\boldsymbol{k}_{\mathfrak{u}})} \leq C_{|\mathfrak{u}|,b,\alpha} (\beta n - t + 2)^{|\mathfrak{u}|\alpha} b^{-(\beta n - t)},$$

where

$$C_{|\mathfrak{u}|,b,\alpha} = b^{|\mathfrak{u}|\alpha} \left(\frac{1}{b} + \left(\frac{b}{b-1} \right)^{|\mathfrak{u}|\alpha} \right).$$

Proof To simplify the notation, we prove the result only for $\mathfrak{u} = \mathcal{I}_s$. For all other subsets, the result follows by the same arguments.

We partition the set $\mathcal{D}'_{\infty,n}$ into parts where the highest digits of k_i are prescribed and we count the number of solutions of $C_1^\top \mathrm{tr}_n(\mathbf{k}_1) + \cdots + C_s^\top \mathrm{tr}_n(\mathbf{k}_s) = \mathbf{0}$. For $1 \leq i \leq s$, now let $d_{i,\alpha} < \cdots < d_{i,1}$ with $d_{i,1} \in \mathbb{N}$. Note that we now allow $d_{i,j} < 1$, in which case the contributions of those $d_{i,j}$ are to be ignored. This notation is adopted in order to avoid considering many special cases. Further, we write $\boldsymbol{d}_{s,\alpha} = (d_{1,1}, \ldots, d_{1,\alpha}, \ldots, d_{s,1}, \ldots, d_{s,\alpha})$ and define

$$\begin{aligned} \mathcal{D}'_{\infty,n}(\boldsymbol{d}_{s,\alpha}) = \{\boldsymbol{k} \in \mathcal{D}'_{\infty,n} \ : \ & k_i = \lfloor \kappa_{i,1} b^{d_{i,1}-1} + \cdots + \kappa_{i,\alpha} b^{d_{i,\alpha}-1} + l_i \rfloor \\ & \text{with } 0 \leq l_i < b^{d_{i,\alpha}-1} \text{ and } 1 \leq \kappa_{i,j} < b \text{ for } 1 \leq i \leq s\}, \end{aligned}$$

where $\lfloor \cdot \rfloor$ just means that the contributions of $d_{i,j} < 1$ are to be ignored.

Then we have

$$\begin{aligned} &\sum_{\boldsymbol{k} \in \mathcal{D}'_{\infty,n}} b^{-\mu_\alpha(\boldsymbol{k})} \\ &= \sum_{d_{1,1}=\alpha}^{\infty} \sum_{d_{1,2}=\alpha-1}^{d_{1,1}-1} \cdots \sum_{d_{1,\alpha}=1}^{d_{1,\alpha-1}-1} \cdots \sum_{d_{s,1}=\alpha}^{\infty} \sum_{d_{s,2}=\alpha-1}^{d_{s,1}-1} \cdots \sum_{d_{s,\alpha}=1}^{d_{s,\alpha-1}-1} \frac{|\mathcal{D}'_{\infty,n}(\boldsymbol{d}_{s,\alpha})|}{b^{|\boldsymbol{d}_{s,\alpha}|_1}}, \end{aligned} \tag{15.10}$$

where $|\boldsymbol{d}_{s,\alpha}|_1 = d_{1,1} + \cdots + d_{1,\alpha} + \cdots + d_{s,1} + \cdots + d_{s,\alpha}$. Some of the sums above can be empty, in which case we just set the corresponding summation index $d_{i,j} = 0$.

Note that by the digital $(t, \alpha, \beta, n \times m, s)$-net property, we have that $|\mathcal{D}'_{\infty,n}(\boldsymbol{d}_{s,\alpha})| = 0$ as long as $d_{1,1} + \cdots + d_{1,\alpha} + \cdots + d_{s,1} + \cdots + d_{s,\alpha} \le \beta n - t$. Hence, for $1 \le i \le s$ and $1 \le j \le \alpha$, let $d_{i,j} \ge 0$ be given such that $d_{1,1}, \ldots, d_{s,1} \in \mathbb{N}$, $d_{i,\alpha} < \cdots < d_{i,1}$ for $1 \le i \le s$ and where, if $d_{i,j} < 1$, we set $d_{i,j} = 0$ (in which case we also have $d_{i,j+1} = d_{i,j+2} = \cdots = 0$ and the inequalities $d_{i,j} > \cdots > d_{i,\alpha}$ are ignored) and $d_{1,1} + \cdots + d_{1,\alpha} + \cdots + d_{s,1} + \cdots + d_{s,\alpha} > \beta n - t$. We now need to estimate $|\mathcal{D}'_{\infty,n}(\boldsymbol{d}_{s,\alpha})|$; that is, we need to count the number of $\boldsymbol{k} \in \mathcal{D}'_{\infty,n}$ with $k_i = \lfloor \kappa_{i,1} b^{d_{i,1}-1} + \cdots + \kappa_{i,\alpha} b^{d_{i,\alpha}-1} + l_i \rfloor$.

There are, at most, $(b-1)^{\alpha s}$ choices for $\kappa_{1,1}, \ldots, \kappa_{s,\alpha}$ (we write 'at most' because if $d_{i,j} < 1$, then the corresponding $\kappa_{i,j}$ does not have any effect and therefore need not be included).

Now let $1 \le \kappa_{1,1}, \ldots, \kappa_{s,\alpha} < b$ be given and define

$$\mathbf{g} = \kappa_{1,1}(\mathbf{c}^{(1)}_{d_{1,1}})^\top + \cdots + \kappa_{1,\alpha}(\mathbf{c}^{(1)}_{d_{1,\alpha}})^\top + \cdots + \kappa_{s,1}(\mathbf{c}^{(s)}_{d_{s,1}})^\top + \cdots + \kappa_{s,\alpha}(\mathbf{c}^{(s)}_{d_{s,\alpha}})^\top,$$

where $\mathbf{c}^{(i)}_j \in \mathbb{Z}_b^m$ is the jth row vector of the matrix C_i for $1 \le j \le n$ and $1 \le i \le s$ and where we set $\mathbf{c}^{(i)}_j = \mathbf{0}$ if $j < 1$ or if $j > n$. Further, let

$$B = ((\mathbf{c}^{(1)}_1)^\top, \ldots, (\mathbf{c}^{(1)}_{d_{1,\alpha}-1})^\top, \ldots, (\mathbf{c}^{(s)}_1)^\top, \ldots, (\mathbf{c}^{(s)}_{d_{s,\alpha}-1})^\top).$$

Hence, $B \in \mathbb{Z}_b^{m \times (d_{1,\alpha} + \cdots + d_{s,\alpha} - s)}$. Now the task is to count the number of solutions $\mathbf{l} \in \mathbb{Z}_b^{d_{1,\alpha} + \cdots + d_{s,\alpha} - s}$ of $B\mathbf{l} = \mathbf{g}$.

As long as the columns of B are linearly independent, the number of solutions can at most be one. By the digital $(t, \alpha, \beta, n \times m, s)$-net property, this is certainly the case if (we write $(x)_+ = \max(x, 0)$)

$$\begin{aligned}(d_{1,\alpha} - 1)_+ + \cdots + (d_{1,\alpha} - \alpha)_+ + \cdots + (d_{s,\alpha} - 1)_+ + \cdots + (d_{s,\alpha} - \alpha)_+ \\ \le \alpha(d_{1,\alpha} + \cdots + d_{s,\alpha}) \\ \le \beta n - t,\end{aligned}$$

that is, as long as

$$d_{1,\alpha} + \cdots + d_{s,\alpha} \le \frac{\beta n - t}{\alpha}.$$

Now let $d_{1,\alpha} + \cdots + d_{s,\alpha} > \frac{\beta n - t}{\alpha}$. Then, by considering the rank of the matrix B and the dimension of the space of solutions of $B\mathbf{l} = \mathbf{0}$, it follows that the number of solutions of $B\mathbf{l} = \mathbf{g}$ is smaller than or equal to $b^{d_{1,\alpha} + \cdots + d_{s,\alpha} - \lfloor (\beta n - t)/\alpha \rfloor}$.

Thus, we have

$$|\mathcal{D}'_{\infty,n}(\boldsymbol{d}_{s,\alpha})| = 0$$

if $\sum_{i=1}^{s}\sum_{j=1}^{\alpha} d_{i,j} \le \beta n - t$, we have

$$|\mathcal{D}'_{\infty,n}(\boldsymbol{d}_{s,\alpha})| = (b-1)^{s\alpha}$$

if $\sum_{i=1}^{s}\sum_{j=1}^{\alpha} d_{i,j} > \beta n - t$ and $\sum_{i=1}^{s} d_{i,\alpha} \le \frac{\beta n - t}{\alpha}$, and finally we have

$$|\mathcal{D}'_{\infty,n}(\boldsymbol{d}_{s,\alpha})| \le (b-1)^{s\alpha} b^{d_{1,\alpha}+\cdots+d_{s,\alpha}-\lfloor(\beta n-t)/\alpha\rfloor}$$

if $\sum_{i=1}^{s}\sum_{j=1}^{\alpha} d_{i,j} > \beta n - t$ and $\sum_{i=1}^{s} d_{i,\alpha} > \frac{\beta n - t}{\alpha}$.

Now we are going to estimate the sum (15.10). Let S_1 be the sum in (15.10) where $\sum_{i=1}^{s}\sum_{j=1}^{\alpha} d_{i,j} > \beta n - t$ and $\sum_{i=1}^{s} d_{i,\alpha} \le \frac{\beta n - t}{\alpha}$. Let $l_1 = d_{1,1} + \cdots + d_{1,\alpha-1} + \cdots + d_{s,1} + \cdots + d_{s,\alpha-1}$ and let $l_2 = d_{1,\alpha} + \cdots + d_{s,\alpha}$. For given l_1, l_2, let $A(l_1 + l_2)$ denote the number of admissible choices of $d_{1,1}, \ldots, d_{s,\alpha}$ such that $l_1 + l_2 = \sum_{i=1}^{s}\sum_{j=1}^{\alpha} d_{i,j}$. Then we have

$$S_1 \le (b-1)^{s\alpha} \sum_{l_2=0}^{\lfloor\frac{\beta n - t}{\alpha}\rfloor} \frac{1}{b^{l_2}} \sum_{l_1=\beta n - t + 1 - l_2}^{\infty} \frac{A(l_1+l_2)}{b^{l_1}}.$$

We have $A(l_1 + l_2) \le \binom{l_1+l_2+s\alpha-1}{s\alpha-1}$ and hence, we obtain

$$S_1 \le (b-1)^{s\alpha} \sum_{l_2=0}^{\lfloor\frac{\beta n - t}{\alpha}\rfloor} \frac{1}{b^{l_2}} \sum_{l_1=\beta n - t + 1 - l_2}^{\infty} \frac{1}{b^{l_1}} \binom{l_1+l_2+s\alpha-1}{s\alpha-1}.$$

From Lemma 13.24, we have

$$\begin{aligned}(b-1)^{s\alpha} &\sum_{l_1=\beta n - t+1-l_2}^{\infty} \frac{1}{b^{l_1}} \binom{l_1+l_2+s\alpha-1}{s\alpha-1} \\ &\le b^{l_2-\beta n+t-1+s\alpha} \binom{\beta n - t + s\alpha}{s\alpha - 1}\end{aligned}$$

and further, we have

$$\sum_{l_2=0}^{\lfloor\frac{\beta n - t}{\alpha}\rfloor} \frac{b^{l_2}}{b^{l_2}} = \left\lfloor \frac{\beta n - t}{\alpha} \right\rfloor + 1.$$

Thus, we obtain

$$S_1 \le \left(\left\lfloor \frac{\beta n - t}{\alpha} \right\rfloor + 1 \right) b^{-\beta n + t - 1 + s\alpha} \binom{\beta n - t + s\alpha}{s\alpha - 1}.$$

Let S_2 be the part of (15.10) for which $\sum_{i=1}^{s}\sum_{j=1}^{\alpha} d_{i,j} > \beta n - t$ and $\sum_{i=1}^{s} d_{i,\alpha} > \frac{\beta n - t}{\alpha}$, i.e. we have

$$S_2 \le (b-1)^{s\alpha} \underbrace{\sum_{d_{1,1}=\alpha}^{\infty} \cdots \sum_{d_{1,\alpha}=1}^{d_{1,\alpha-1}-1} \sum_{d_{s,1}=\alpha}^{\infty} \cdots \sum_{d_{s,\alpha}=1}^{d_{s,\alpha-1}-1}}_{\text{+additional conditions}} \frac{b^{-\lfloor(\beta n - t)/\alpha\rfloor} b^{d_{1,\alpha}+\cdots+d_{s,\alpha}}}{b^{d_{1,1}+\cdots+d_{1,\alpha}+\cdots+d_{s,1}+\cdots+d_{s,\alpha}}},$$

where the 'additional conditions' are that $\sum_{i=1}^{s}\sum_{j=1}^{\alpha} d_{i,j} > \beta n - t$ and $\sum_{i=1}^{s} d_{i,\alpha} > \frac{\beta n - t}{\alpha}$. As above, let $l_1 = d_{1,1} + \cdots + d_{1,\alpha-1} + \cdots + d_{s,1} + \cdots + d_{s,\alpha-1}$ and let $l_2 = d_{1,\alpha} + \cdots + d_{s,\alpha}$. For given l_1, l_2, let $A(l_1 + l_2)$ denote the number of admissible choices of $d_{i,l}$ for $1 \le i \le s$ and $1 \le l \le \alpha$ such that $l_1 + l_2 = \sum_{i=1}^{s}\sum_{j=1}^{\alpha} d_{i,j}$. Note that $l_1 > (\alpha - 1)l_2$. Then we have $A(l_1 + l_2) \le \binom{l_1 + l_2 + s\alpha - 1}{s\alpha - 1}$ and hence, we obtain

$$S_2 \le (b-1)^{s\alpha} b^{-\lfloor(\beta n - t)/\alpha\rfloor} \sum_{l_2 = \lfloor \frac{\beta n - t}{\alpha} \rfloor + 1}^{\infty} \sum_{l_1 = (\alpha-1)l_2 + 1}^{\infty} \frac{1}{b^{l_1}} \binom{l_1 + l_2 + s\alpha - 1}{s\alpha - 1}.$$

By using Lemma 13.24 again, we have

$$(b-1)^{s\alpha} \sum_{l_1 = (\alpha-1)l_2 + 1}^{\infty} \frac{1}{b^{l_1}} \binom{l_1 + l_2 + s\alpha - 1}{s\alpha - 1} \le b^{s\alpha} b^{l_2(1-\alpha)-1} \binom{l_2\alpha + s\alpha}{s\alpha - 1}$$

and also

$$\begin{aligned}
& b^{s\alpha - 1 - \lfloor(\beta n - t)/\alpha\rfloor} \sum_{l_2 = \lfloor \frac{\beta n - t}{\alpha} \rfloor + 1}^{\infty} b^{l_2(1-\alpha)} \binom{l_2\alpha + s\alpha}{s\alpha - 1} \\
& \le b^{s\alpha - 1 - \lfloor(\beta n - t)/\alpha\rfloor} \sum_{l_2 = \beta n - t}^{\infty} b^{l_2(1-\alpha)/\alpha} \binom{l_2 + s\alpha}{s\alpha - 1} \\
& \le b^{s\alpha - 1 - \lfloor(\beta n - t)/\alpha\rfloor} (1 - b^{-1})^{-s\alpha} \binom{\beta n - t + s\alpha}{s\alpha - 1} b^{(\beta n - t)(1-\alpha)/\alpha}.
\end{aligned}$$

Hence, we have

$$S_2 \le \left(\frac{b^2}{b-1}\right)^{s\alpha} b^{-(\beta n - t)} \binom{\beta n - t + s\alpha}{s\alpha - 1}.$$

Note that we have $\sum_{k \in \mathcal{D}'_{\infty,n}} b^{-\mu_\alpha(k)} = S_1 + S_2$. Let $a \in \mathbb{N}$ and $b \in \mathbb{N}_0$, then we have

$$\binom{a+b}{b} = \prod_{i=1}^{b} \left(1 + \frac{a}{i}\right) \le (1+a)^b.$$

Therefore, we obtain

$$\begin{aligned} S_1 &\le \left(\left\lfloor \frac{\beta n - t}{\alpha} \right\rfloor + 1 \right) b^{-\beta n + t - 1 + s\alpha} (\beta n - t + 2)^{s\alpha - 1} \\ &\le (\beta n - t + 2)^{s\alpha} b^{-\beta n + t - 1 + s\alpha} \end{aligned}$$

and

$$S_2 \le \left(\frac{b^2}{b-1} \right)^{s\alpha} (\beta n - t + 2)^{s\alpha - 1} b^{-\beta n + t}.$$

Thus, we have

$$\sum_{\boldsymbol{k} \in \mathcal{D}'_{\infty,n}} b^{-\mu_\alpha(\boldsymbol{k})} \le C_{s,b,\alpha} (\beta n - t + 2)^{s\alpha} b^{-\beta n + t},$$

where

$$C_{s,b,\alpha} = b^{s\alpha} \left(\frac{1}{b} + \left(\frac{b}{b-1} \right)^{s\alpha} \right). \qquad \square$$

If βn is not an integer, then the same bound as in the above lemma applies where one replaces βn with $\lfloor \beta n \rfloor$.

The next result shows that by using digital $(t, \alpha, \beta, n \times m, s)$-nets over $\mathbb{Z}_b$, one can obtain optimal convergence rates for the worst-case error of QMC integration in the Sobolev space $\mathscr{H}_{s,\alpha,\boldsymbol{\gamma}}$; see [7].

Theorem 15.21 *Let $s, \alpha \in \mathbb{N}$ and let $b \ge 2$ be a prime number. Then, the worst-case error of QMC integration in the Sobolev space $\mathscr{H}_{s,\alpha,\boldsymbol{\gamma}}$ using a higher order digital $(t, \alpha, \beta, n \times m, s)$-net $\mathcal{P}$ over $\mathbb{Z}_b$ is bounded by*

$$e(\mathscr{H}_{s,\alpha,\boldsymbol{\gamma}}, \mathcal{P}) \le b^{-(\lfloor \beta n \rfloor - t)} \left(\sum_{\emptyset \ne \mathfrak{u} \subseteq \mathcal{I}_s} \gamma_{\mathfrak{u}} D''_{|\mathfrak{u}|,\alpha,b} (\lfloor \beta n \rfloor - t + 2)^{2|\mathfrak{u}|\alpha} \right)^{1/2},$$

where

$$D''_{|\mathfrak{u}|,\alpha,b} = D^{|\mathfrak{u}|}_{\alpha,b} b^{2|\mathfrak{u}|\alpha} \left(\frac{1}{b} + \left(\frac{b}{b-1} \right)^{|\mathfrak{u}|\alpha} \right)^2.$$

Proof The proof follows immediately from Lemmas 15.19 and 15.20. $\square$

Explicit constructions of higher order digital $(t, \alpha, \min(1, \alpha/d), dm \times m, s)$-nets over $\mathbb{Z}_b$ for all prime numbers b and $\alpha, d, m, s \in \mathbb{N}$ were given in Section 15.2. By choosing $d = \alpha$ in these constructions, Theorem 15.21 implies a convergence of the integration error of order $O(b^{-\alpha m} m^{s\alpha})$, which is optimal for the Sobolev space $\mathscr{H}_{s,\alpha,\boldsymbol{\gamma}}$ as it is optimal for the subspace of periodic functions; see [241].

Theorem 15.21 is also comparable to [35, Theorem 5.2], but with the important difference that here we do not assume that the integrand is periodic.

Theorem 15.21 also applies to digital $(t, \alpha, \beta, \sigma, s)$-sequences over $\mathbb{Z}_b$ which we state in the following corollary.

Corollary 15.22 *Let $s, \alpha \in \mathbb{N}$ and let $b \geq 2$ be a prime number. Then, the worst-case error of QMC integration in the Sobolev space $\mathscr{H}_{s,\alpha,\gamma}$ using the first b^m points of a higher order digital $(t, \alpha, \beta, \sigma, s)$-sequence $\mathcal{S}$ over $\mathbb{Z}_b$ as quadrature points, is bounded by*

$$e(\mathscr{H}_{s,\alpha,\gamma}, \mathcal{S}) \leq b^{-(\lfloor \beta\sigma m \rfloor - t)} \left(\sum_{\emptyset \neq \mathfrak{u} \subseteq \mathcal{I}_s} \gamma_{\mathfrak{u}} D''_{|\mathfrak{u}|,\alpha,b} (\lfloor \beta\sigma m \rfloor - t + 2)^{2|\mathfrak{u}|\alpha} \right)^{1/2},$$

for all $m > t/(\beta\sigma)$, where $D''_{|\mathfrak{u}|,\alpha,b}$ is as in Theorem 15.21.

Explicit constructions of higher order digital $(t, \alpha, \min(1, \alpha/d), d, s)$-sequences over $\mathbb{Z}_b$ for all prime numbers b and $\alpha, d, s \in \mathbb{N}$ were given in Section 15.2. For such a sequence, we obtain a convergence of

$$e(\mathscr{H}_{s,\alpha,\gamma}, \mathcal{S}) \leq b^{-(\min(\alpha,d)m - t)} \left(\sum_{\emptyset \neq \mathfrak{u} \subseteq \mathcal{I}_s} \gamma_{\mathfrak{u}} D''_{|\mathfrak{u}|,\alpha,b} (\min(\alpha, d)m - t + 2)^{2|\mathfrak{u}|\alpha} \right)^{1/2},$$

for all $m > t/\min(\alpha, d)$. By the result from Sharygin [241], this result is optimal (up to a power of m) for all $2 \leq \alpha \leq d$. (The case $\alpha = 1$ has been considered in Chapter 4, where the result is also optimal up to a power of m.) As d is a parameter of the construction which can be chosen freely, we can obtain arbitrarily high convergence rates for sufficiently smooth functions.

15.7 Higher order polynomial lattice point sets

In this section, we use the same approach as in Section 10.1 (see also [139]) to prove the existence of polynomial lattice point sets for which the figure of merit satisfies a certain condition. This allows us to prove existence results for the digital nets considered in this chapter.

We generalise the definition of polynomial lattice point sets from Definition 10.1 resp. Theorem 10.5 in Chapter 10 in a way which allows us to achieve higher order convergence by embedding it into the framework of the digital nets of the previous section. The following definition, stated first in [52], is a slight generalisation of polynomial lattices; see Definition 10.1.

Definition 15.23 Let b be a prime and let $s, m, n \in \mathbb{N}$, $1 \le m \le n$. Let υ_n be the map from $\mathbb{Z}_b((x^{-1}))$ to the interval $[0, 1)$ defined by

$$\upsilon_n\left(\sum_{l=w}^{\infty} t_l x^{-l}\right) = \sum_{l=\max(1,w)}^{n} t_l b^{-l}.$$

Choose $p \in \mathbb{Z}_b[x]$ with $\deg(p) = n$ and let $\boldsymbol{q} = (q_1, \ldots, q_s) \in \mathbb{Z}_b[x]^s$. Then $\mathcal{P}_{m,n}(\boldsymbol{q}, p)$ is the point set consisting of the b^m points

$$\boldsymbol{x}_h = \left(\upsilon_n\left(\frac{h(x)q_1(x)}{p(x)}\right), \ldots, \upsilon_n\left(\frac{h(x)q_s(x)}{p(x)}\right)\right) \in [0, 1)^s,$$

for $h \in \mathbb{Z}_b[x]$ with $\deg(h) < m$. The point set $\mathcal{P}_{m,n}(\boldsymbol{q}, p)$ is called a *higher order polynomial lattice point set* or, for short again, a *polynomial lattice point set* and a QMC rule using the point set $\mathcal{P}_{m,n}(\boldsymbol{q}, p)$ is called a *higher order polynomial lattice rule* or, for short again, a *polynomial lattice rule*.

Remark 15.24 The point set $\mathcal{P}_{m,n}(\boldsymbol{q}, p)$ consists of the first b^m points of $\mathcal{P}_{n,n}(\boldsymbol{q}, p) = \mathcal{P}(\boldsymbol{q}, p)$, i.e. the first b^m points of a classical polynomial lattice point set in the sense of Theorem 10.5. Hence, the definition of a polynomial lattice point set in Chapter 10 is covered by choosing $n = m$ in the definition above. Furthermore, it is important to note that for dimension $s = 1$ for $m < n$, the points of $\mathcal{P}_{m,n}(\boldsymbol{q}, p)$ are not equally spaced in general (in contrast to the case where $m = n$).

Using similar arguments as for the classical case $n = m$, it can be shown that the point set $\mathcal{P}_{m,n}(\boldsymbol{q}, p)$ is a digital net in the sense of Definition 4.47 (but with $n \times m$ generating matrices instead of $m \times m$ matrices). The generating matrices $C_1, \ldots, C_s$ of this digital net can be obtained in the following way: for $1 \le i \le s$, consider the expansions

$$\frac{q_i(x)}{p(x)} = \sum_{l=w_i}^{\infty} u_l^{(i)} x^{-l} \in \mathbb{Z}_b((x^{-1}))$$

where $w_i \in \mathbb{Z}$. Then the elements $c_{j,r}^{(i)}$ of the $n \times m$ matrix C_i over $\mathbb{Z}_b$ are given by

$$c_{j,r}^{(i)} = u_{r+j}^{(i)} \in \mathbb{Z}_b, \tag{15.11}$$

for $1 \le i \le s$, $1 \le j \le n$, $0 \le r \le m - 1$.

We recall some notation already introduced in Chapter 10. For a vector $\boldsymbol{k} = (k_1, \ldots, k_s) \in \mathbb{Z}_b[x]^s$ and $\boldsymbol{q} = (q_1, \ldots, q_s) \in \mathbb{Z}_b[x]^s$, we define the 'inner product'

$$\boldsymbol{k} \cdot \boldsymbol{q} = \sum_{i=1}^{s} k_i q_i \in \mathbb{Z}_b[x]$$

and we write $q \equiv 0 \pmod{p}$ if p divides q in $\mathbb{Z}_b[x]$. Further, for b prime we associate a non-negative integer $k = \kappa_0 + \kappa_1 b + \cdots + \kappa_a b^a$ with the polynomial $k(x) = \kappa_0 + \kappa_1 x + \cdots + \kappa_a x^a \in \mathbb{Z}_b[x]$ and vice versa. Let $G_{b,n} := \{q \in \mathbb{Z}_b[x] : \deg(q) < n\}$, where here and in the following, we use the convention $\deg(0) = -1$.

For polynomial lattice point sets with $n = m$, a connection between the figure of merit and the quality parameter, when one views $\mathcal{P}_{m,n}(\boldsymbol{q}, p)$ as a digital (t, m, s)-net over $\mathbb{Z}_b$, was established; see Section 10.1. In the following, we generalise these results.

A slight generalisation of Lemma 10.6 yields the following result whose proof is left as an exercise (see Exercise 15.6).

Lemma 15.25 *Let $p \in \mathbb{Z}_b[x]$ with $\deg(p) = n$ and let $\boldsymbol{q} \in \mathbb{Z}_b[x]^s$ be a generating vector for a higher order polynomial lattice point set $\mathcal{P}_{m,n}(\boldsymbol{q}, p)$ with generating matrices $C_1, \ldots, C_s \in \mathbb{Z}_b^{n \times m}$. Then for $\mathbf{k}_1, \ldots, \mathbf{k}_s \in (\mathbb{Z}_b^n)^\top$, we have*

$$C_1^\top \mathbf{k}_1 + \cdots + C_s^\top \mathbf{k}_s = \mathbf{0} \in (\mathbb{Z}_b^m)^\top$$

if and only if there is a polynomial $a \in \mathbb{Z}_b[x]$ with $a \equiv \boldsymbol{q} \cdot \boldsymbol{k} \pmod{p}$ and $\deg(a) < n - m$, where $\boldsymbol{k} = (k_1, \ldots, k_s) \in \mathbb{Z}_b[x]^s$, where $k_i(x) = \kappa_{i,0} + \kappa_{i,1} x + \cdots + \kappa_{i,n-1} x^{n-1}$, whenever $\mathbf{k}_i = (\kappa_{i,0}, \ldots, \kappa_{i,n-1})^\top \in (\mathbb{Z}_b^n)^\top$ for $1 \le i \le s$.

This result prompts the following definition.

Definition 15.26 The *dual net* for a higher order polynomial lattice point set $\mathcal{P}_{m,n}(\boldsymbol{q}, p)$ is given by

$$\mathcal{D}_{\boldsymbol{q},p} = \{\boldsymbol{k} \in G_{b,n}^s : \boldsymbol{q} \cdot \boldsymbol{k} \equiv a \pmod{p} \text{ with } \deg(a) < n - m\}.$$

Furthermore, let $\mathcal{D}'_{\boldsymbol{q},p} := \mathcal{D}_{\boldsymbol{q},p} \setminus \{\mathbf{0}\}$.

Hence, for $m = n$, we obtain the usual definition of the dual net of $\mathcal{P}(\boldsymbol{q}, p)$ from Definition 10.7, and for $m < n$, we obtain a superset.

Now let us generalise the figure of merit of a polynomial lattice point set. Let $k(x) = \kappa_0 + \kappa_1 x + \cdots + \kappa_a x^a \in \mathbb{Z}_b[x]$ with $\kappa_a \neq 0$. Then, the degree of the polynomial k is defined by $\deg(k) = a$ and for $k = 0$, we set $\deg(k) = -1$. For our purposes, we need to generalise this definition. Let $k(x) = \kappa_v x^{d_v - 1} + \cdots + \kappa_1 x^{d_1 - 1}$ with $\kappa_1, \ldots, \kappa_v \in \mathbb{Z}_b \setminus \{0\}$ and $0 < d_v < \cdots < d_1$. For $\alpha \in \mathbb{N}$, we now set $\deg_\alpha(k) = \sum_{r=1}^{\min(v,\alpha)} d_r$ and for $k = 0$, we set $\deg_\alpha(k) = 0$. Thus, we have, for example, $\deg_1(k) = \deg(k) + 1$. In what follows, we call $\deg_\alpha(k)$ the *α-degree* of the polynomial k. Using this notation, we can now generalise the classical definition of the figure of merit from Definition 10.8.

Definition 15.27 Let $p \in \mathbb{Z}_b[x]$ with $\deg(p) = n$ and let $\boldsymbol{q} \in \mathbb{Z}_b[x]^s$ be the generating vector of a polynomial lattice $\mathcal{P}_{m,n}(\boldsymbol{q}, p)$. For $\alpha \in \mathbb{N}$ the *figure of merit* $\rho_{\alpha,m,n}$

is given by

$$\rho_{\alpha,m,n}(\boldsymbol{q}, p) = -1 + \min_{\boldsymbol{k} \in \mathcal{D}'_{\boldsymbol{q},p}} \sum_{i=1}^{s} \deg_\alpha(k_i),$$

where $\boldsymbol{k} = (k_1, \ldots, k_s) \in \mathbb{Z}_b[x]^s$.

Note that for $n = m$ and $\alpha = 1$, we obtain the classical definition of the figure of merit $\rho(\boldsymbol{q}, p)$; see Definition 10.8.

Using Lemma 15.25, Theorem 10.9 can also be generalised to yield the following theorem.

Theorem 15.28 *Let $p \in \mathbb{Z}_b[x]$ with $\deg(p) = n$ and let $\boldsymbol{q} \in \mathbb{Z}_b[x]^s$ be the generating vector of a higher order polynomial lattice point set $\mathcal{P}_{m,n}(\boldsymbol{q}, p)$. Then, for any $\alpha \in \mathbb{N}$, the point set $\mathcal{P}_{m,n}(\boldsymbol{q}, p)$ is a higher order digital $(t, \alpha, \beta, n \times m, s)$-net over $\mathbb{Z}_b$ for any $0 < \beta \leq \min(1, \alpha m/n)$ and $0 \leq t \leq \beta n$ which satisfy*

$$t = \lfloor \beta n \rfloor - \rho_{\alpha,m,n}(\boldsymbol{q}, p).$$

We see that polynomial lattices of high quality have a large value of $\rho_{\alpha,m,n}$. In the following subsection, we show the existence of polynomial lattice point sets for which $\rho_{\alpha,m,n}$ satisfies a certain bound.

15.7.1 The existence of higher order polynomial lattice point sets based on the figure of merit

In this subsection, we prove the existence of good higher order polynomial lattice rules. The results here are based on [44].

First, note that we can restrict $\boldsymbol{q} \in \mathbb{Z}_b[x]^s$ to the set $G_{b,n}^s$ where $G_{b,n}$ denotes the set of all polynomials $q \in \mathbb{Z}_b[x]$ with $\deg(q) < n$.

The following lemma gives an upper bound on the number of polynomials in $G_{b,n}$ with a given α-degree. Note that we use the convention $\binom{n}{k} = 0$ for negative integers n.

Lemma 15.29 *Let $l, \alpha, n \in \mathbb{N}$, $\alpha \geq 2$, then the number of polynomials in $G_{b,n}$ with α-degree l is bounded by*

$$\#\{k \in G_{b,n} : \deg_\alpha(k) = l\} \leq C(\alpha, l),$$

where

$$C(\alpha, l) = \sum_{v=1}^{\alpha-1} (b-1)^v \binom{l - \frac{v(v-1)}{2} - 1}{v - 1}$$

$$+ \sum_{i=1}^{\lfloor l/\alpha \rfloor} (b-1)^\alpha b^{i-1} \binom{l - \alpha i - \frac{\alpha(\alpha-3)}{2} - 2}{\alpha - 2}.$$

Proof Let $k \in G_{b,n}$, $k = k_{d_v} x^{d_v - 1} + \cdots + k_{d_1} x^{d_1 - 1}$ with $0 < d_v < \cdots < d_1$ and $k_{d_r} \neq 0$ for $1 \leq r \leq v$. The α-degree of k is then given by $\deg_\alpha(k) = \sum_{r=1}^{\min(v,\alpha)} d_r$. We consider two cases:

1. $\alpha \leq v$: then we write

$$k = k_{d_1} x^{d_1 - 1} + \cdots + k_{d_\alpha} x^{d_\alpha - 1} + k_{d_\alpha - 1} x^{d_\alpha - 2} + \cdots + k_2 x + k_1.$$

As, in this case, only $d_1, \ldots, d_\alpha$ appear in the condition for the α-degree of k, we can choose the part $k_{d_\alpha - 1} x^{d_\alpha - 2} + \cdots + k_2 x + k_1$ arbitrarily and hence, we have at most $b^{d_\alpha - 1}$ possibilities for this part. Further, the k_{d_r} need to be non-zero which yields $(b-1)^\alpha$ possible choices. Now we have to count the number of $d_1, \ldots, d_\alpha$ with $0 < d_\alpha < \cdots < d_1$ and $d_1 + \cdots + d_\alpha = l$ or, equivalently, $(d_1 - d_\alpha) + \cdots + (d_{\alpha-1} - d_\alpha) = l - \alpha a_\alpha$. (Note that $l - \alpha d_\alpha$ must be at least non-negative.) This is the same as the number of $0 \leq b_{\alpha-1} \leq \cdots \leq b_1$ with $b_1 + \cdots + b_{\alpha-1} = l - \alpha d_\alpha - \frac{\alpha(\alpha-1)}{2}$; write $b_i = d_i - d_\alpha - (\alpha - i)$ for $1 \leq i \leq \alpha - 1$. However, this number is surely, at most, $\binom{l - \alpha d_\alpha - \frac{\alpha(\alpha-1)}{2} + \alpha - 2}{\alpha - 2}$.

Finally, d_α can run from 1 to, at most, $\lfloor l/\alpha \rfloor$ and hence, altogether there are, at most,

$$\sum_{d_\alpha = 1}^{\lfloor l/\alpha \rfloor} (b-1)^\alpha b^{d_\alpha - 1} \binom{l - \alpha d_\alpha - \frac{\alpha(\alpha-1)}{2} + \alpha - 2}{\alpha - 2}$$

polynomials $k = k_{d_v} x^{d_v - 1} + \cdots + k_{d_1} x^{d_1 - 1}$ with $0 < d_v < \cdots < d_1$ and $k_{d_r} \neq 0$ for $1 \leq r \leq v$, $\alpha \leq v$ and $\deg_\alpha(k) = l$.

2. $\alpha > v$: we count all $k = k_{d_v} x^{d_v - 1} + \cdots + k_{d_1} x^{d_1 - 1}$ with $0 < d_v < \cdots < d_1$, $k_{d_r} \neq 0$ for $1 \leq r \leq v$ and $d_1 + \cdots + d_v = l$.

For k_{d_r}, $1 \leq r \leq v$, we have exactly $(b-1)^v$ possible choices. The number of $0 < d_v < \cdots < d_1$ with $d_1 + \cdots + d_v = l$ is the same as the number of $0 \leq b_v \leq \cdots \leq b_1$ with $b_1 + \cdots + b_v = l - \frac{v(v+1)}{2}$; write $b_i = d_i - (v + 1 - i)$ for $1 \leq i \leq v$. This number can be bounded from above by $\binom{l - \frac{v(v+1)}{2} + v - 1}{v - 1}$. As v may be chosen from $\{1, \ldots, \alpha - 1\}$, we have, at most,

$$\sum_{v=1}^{\alpha - 1} (b-1)^v \binom{l - \frac{v(v+1)}{2} + v - 1}{v - 1}$$

polynomials $k = k_{d_v} x^{d_v - 1} + \cdots + k_{d_1} x^{d_1 - 1}$ with $0 < d_v < \cdots < d_1$ and $k_{d_r} \neq 0$ for $1 \leq r \leq v$, $\alpha > v$ and $\deg_\alpha(k) = l$.

The result follows by adding the two sums from the above two cases. □

Now we can prove a condition for the existence of a polynomial lattice with a certain figure of merit. The following theorem is the analogue to Theorem 10.13 for the case $\alpha = 1$.

Theorem 15.30 *Let $s, n, m, \alpha \in \mathbb{N}$, $s, \alpha \geq 2$, let b be a prime and let $p \in \mathbb{Z}_b[x]$ with $\deg(p) = n \geq m$ be irreducible. For $\rho \in \mathbb{N}_0$, define*

$$\Delta_b(s, \rho, \alpha) = \sum_{l=0}^{\rho} \sum_{i=1}^{s} \binom{s}{i} \sum_{\substack{l_1, \dots, l_i = 1 \\ l_1 + \dots + l_i = l}}^{\infty} \prod_{z=1}^{i} C(\alpha, l_z),$$

where $C(\alpha, l)$ is defined in Lemma 15.29.

1. *If $\Delta_b(s, \rho, \alpha) < b^m$, then there exists a $\boldsymbol{q} \in G_{b,n}^s$ with*
$$\rho_{\alpha,m,n}(\boldsymbol{q}, p) \geq \rho.$$
2. *If $\Delta_b(s, \rho, \alpha) < \frac{b^m}{s-1}$, then there exists a polynomial $q \in G_{b,n}$ such that $\boldsymbol{v}_s(q) \equiv (1, q, q^2, \dots, q^{s-1}) \pmod{p}$ satisfies*
$$\rho_{\alpha,m,n}(\boldsymbol{v}_s(q), p) \geq \rho.$$

Proof We show the first part of the theorem. There are $|G_{b,n}^s| = |G_{b,n}|^s = b^{ns}$ vectors $\boldsymbol{q}$ from which to choose. We estimate the number of vectors $\boldsymbol{q}$ for which $\rho_{\alpha,m,n}(\boldsymbol{q}, p) < \rho$ for some chosen $\rho \in \mathbb{N}_0$. If this number is smaller than the total number of possible choices, then it follows that there is at least one vector with $\rho_{\alpha,m,n}(\boldsymbol{q}, p) \geq \rho$.

For each non-zero vector $\boldsymbol{k} \in \mathbb{Z}_b[x]^s$, there are b^{ns-m} vectors $\boldsymbol{q} \in G_{b,n}^s$ such that $\boldsymbol{k} \cdot \boldsymbol{q} \equiv a \pmod{p}$ for some $a \in \mathbb{Z}_b[x]$ with $\deg(a) < n - m$.

Now let $A(l, s, \alpha)$ denote the number of non-zero vectors $\boldsymbol{k} \in \mathbb{Z}_b[x]^s$ with $\sum_{i=1}^{s} \deg_\alpha(k_i) = l$. The quantity $C(\alpha, l)$ defined in Lemma 15.29 is an upper bound on the number of non-zero polynomials $k \in \mathbb{Z}_b[x]$ with $\deg_\alpha(k) = l$. Thus, we have

$$A(l, s, \alpha) \leq \sum_{i=1}^{s} \binom{s}{i} \sum_{\substack{l_1, \dots, l_i = 1 \\ l_1 + \dots + l_i = l}}^{\infty} \prod_{z=1}^{i} C(\alpha, l_z).$$

Now $\sum_{l=0}^{\rho} A(l, s, \alpha)$ is a bound on the number of non-zero vectors $\boldsymbol{k} \in \mathbb{Z}_b[x]^s$ with $\sum_{i=1}^{s} \deg_\alpha(k_i) \leq \rho$. Hence, the number of vectors $\boldsymbol{q} \in G_{b,n}^s$ for which $\rho_{\alpha,m,n}(\boldsymbol{q}, p) < \rho$ is bounded by $b^{ns-m} \sum_{l=0}^{\rho} A(l, s, \alpha)$. Hence, if this number is smaller than b^{ns}, that is, if at least

$$b^{ns-m} \sum_{l=0}^{\rho} A(l, s, \alpha) < b^{ns},$$

then there exists a vector $\boldsymbol{q} \in G_{b,n}^s$ with $\rho_{\alpha,m,n}(\boldsymbol{q}, p) \geq \rho$. Hence, the result follows.

For the second part, we proceed as in the first, but note that there are $|G_{b,n}| = b^n$ polynomials $q \in G_{b,n}$ from which to choose and that for each non-zero vector $\boldsymbol{k} \in \mathbb{Z}_b[x]^s$, there are at least $(s-1)b^{n-m}$ of these polynomials q such that $\boldsymbol{k} \cdot \boldsymbol{v}_s(q) \equiv a \pmod{p}$ for some a with $\deg(a) < n - m$. If at least

$$(s-1)b^{n-m} \sum_{l=0}^{\rho} A(l, s, \alpha) < b^n,$$

then there exists a $q \in G_{b,n}$ such that $\boldsymbol{v}_s(q)$ satisfies $\rho_{\alpha,m,n}(\boldsymbol{v}_s(q), p) \ge \rho$. □

Above, we have shown the existence of higher order polynomial lattice point sets which are higher order digital $(t, \alpha, \beta, n \times m, s)$-nets over $\mathbb{Z}_b$ for which the quality parameter t satisfies a certain condition. This follows from Theorem 15.28 together with Theorem 15.30. Note that in the search for a polynomial lattice point set, we have to choose the value α up front. If we do not know the smoothness δ of the integrand, then it can happen that $\alpha \ne \delta$. Hence, in order for the bound in Theorem 15.21 to apply, we still need to know the figure of merit of some order α' of a polynomial lattice which was constructed using the parameter α (where possibly $\alpha \ne \alpha'$; the bound in Theorem 15.21 can then be used with $\lfloor \beta n \rfloor - t = \rho_{\alpha',m,n}$). Hence, in the following, we establish a propagation rule for polynomial lattices.

Theorem 15.31 *Let $\mathcal{P}_{m,n}(\boldsymbol{q}, p)$ be a higher order polynomial lattice point set with figure of merit $\rho_{\alpha,m,n}(\boldsymbol{q}, p)$. Then, for $\alpha' \ge \alpha$, we have*

$$\rho_{\alpha',m,n}(\boldsymbol{q}, p) \ge \rho_{\alpha,m,n}(\boldsymbol{q}, p)$$

and for $1 \le \alpha' \le \alpha$, we have

$$\rho_{\alpha',m,n}(\boldsymbol{q}, p) \ge \frac{\alpha'}{\alpha} \rho_{\alpha,m,n}(\boldsymbol{q}, p) - 2.$$

Proof First, let $\alpha' \ge \alpha$. Then, $\deg_{\alpha'}(k) \ge \deg_{\alpha}(k)$ for all $k \in \mathbb{Z}_b[x]$ and hence, the definition of the figure of merit implies the result. Now let $1 \le \alpha' \le \alpha$. Theorem 15.28 implies that the polynomial lattice point set $\mathcal{P}_{m,n}(\boldsymbol{q}, p)$ is a digital $(t, \alpha, \beta, n \times m, s)$-net over $\mathbb{Z}_b$ with $t = \lfloor \beta n \rfloor - \rho_{\alpha,m,n}(\boldsymbol{q}, p)$. From Proposition 15.5, it follows that $\mathcal{P}_{m,n}(\boldsymbol{q}, p)$ is also a digital $(t', \alpha', \beta', n \times m, s)$-net over $\mathbb{Z}_b$ with $\beta' = \beta\alpha'/\alpha$ and $t' = \lceil t\alpha'/\alpha \rceil$. Using Theorem 15.28 again, it follows that

$$\rho_{\alpha',m,n}(\boldsymbol{q}, p) = \lfloor \beta' n \rfloor - t' = \lfloor \beta n \alpha'/\alpha \rfloor - \lceil t\alpha'/\alpha \rceil \ge \frac{\alpha'}{\alpha} \rho_{\alpha,m,n}(\boldsymbol{q}, p) - 2.$$ □

15.7.2 The existence of higher order polynomial lattice rules based on the mean square worst-case error

We consider now the mean square worst-case error of randomly b-adic digitally shifted higher order polynomial lattice rules. The results here are based on [52].

Recall that the mean square worst-case error is defined by $\widehat{e}^2(\mathscr{H}_{s,\alpha,\boldsymbol{\gamma}}, \mathcal{P}) = \mathbb{E}[e^2(\mathscr{H}_{s,\alpha,\boldsymbol{\gamma}}, \mathcal{P}_{\boldsymbol{\sigma}})]$, where the expectation is with respect to all digital shifts $\boldsymbol{\sigma}$ which are applied in the same way as in Section 12.1.

Lemma 15.32 *Let b be a prime and let $s, \alpha \in \mathbb{N}$. Then, the mean square worst-case error of QMC integration in the Sobolev space $\mathscr{H}_{s,\alpha,\boldsymbol{\gamma}}$ using a polynomial lattice point set $\mathcal{P}$, which is randomised by a uniformly and independent and identically distributed chosen random shift $\boldsymbol{\sigma}$, is bounded by*

$$\widehat{e}^2(\mathscr{H}_{s,\alpha,\boldsymbol{\gamma}}, \mathcal{P}) \leq \sum_{\emptyset \neq \mathfrak{u} \subseteq \mathcal{I}_s} \gamma_{\mathfrak{u}} D_{\alpha,b}^{|\mathfrak{u}|} \sum_{\substack{\boldsymbol{k}_{\mathfrak{u}} \in \mathbb{N}^{|\mathfrak{u}|} \\ \mathrm{tr}_n((\boldsymbol{k}_{\mathfrak{u}}, \boldsymbol{0})) \in \mathcal{D}_{\boldsymbol{q},p}}} b^{-2\mu_\alpha(\boldsymbol{k}_{\mathfrak{u}})},$$

where the constant $D_{\alpha,b} > 0$ is defined in Proposition 15.18.

Proof According to Definition 15.26, for $\emptyset \neq \mathfrak{u} \subseteq \mathcal{I}_s$, we have

$$\sum_{\substack{\boldsymbol{k}_{\mathfrak{u}} \in \mathbb{N}^{|\mathfrak{u}|} \\ (\boldsymbol{k}_{\mathfrak{u}}, \boldsymbol{0}) \in \mathcal{D}_{\infty,n}}} b^{-\mu_\alpha(\boldsymbol{k}_{\mathfrak{u}})} = \sum_{\substack{\boldsymbol{k}_{\mathfrak{u}} \in \mathbb{N}^{|\mathfrak{u}|} \\ \mathrm{tr}_n((\boldsymbol{k}_{\mathfrak{u}}, \boldsymbol{0})) \in \mathcal{D}_{\boldsymbol{q},p}}} b^{-\mu_\alpha(\boldsymbol{k}_{\mathfrak{u}})},$$

where here we again identify integers $k = \kappa_0 + \kappa_1 b + \cdots + \kappa_a b^a$ with polynomials $k(x) = \kappa_0 + \kappa_1 x + \cdots + \kappa_a x^a \in \mathbb{Z}_b[x]$.

For a randomly digitally shifted digital net $\{\boldsymbol{x}_0 \oplus \boldsymbol{\sigma}, \ldots, \boldsymbol{x}_{b^m-1} \oplus \boldsymbol{\sigma}\}$, we have

$$\begin{aligned}
&\mathbb{E}\left[\left(\sum_{\substack{\boldsymbol{k}_{\mathfrak{u}} \in \mathbb{N}^{|\mathfrak{u}|} \\ \mathrm{tr}_n((\boldsymbol{k}_{\mathfrak{u}}, \boldsymbol{0})) \in \mathcal{D}_{\boldsymbol{q},p}}} b^{-\mu_\alpha(\boldsymbol{k}_{\mathfrak{u}})} \right)^2\right] \\
&= \mathbb{E}\left[\sum_{\boldsymbol{k}_{\mathfrak{u}}, \boldsymbol{l}_{\mathfrak{u}} \in \mathbb{N}^{|\mathfrak{u}|}} b^{-\mu_\alpha(\boldsymbol{k}_{\mathfrak{u}}) - \mu_\alpha(\boldsymbol{l}_{\mathfrak{u}})} \frac{1}{b^m} \sum_{h,j=0}^{b^m-1} {}_b\mathrm{wal}_{\boldsymbol{k}_{\mathfrak{u}}}(\boldsymbol{x}_{h,\mathfrak{u}} \oplus \boldsymbol{\sigma}) \overline{{}_b\mathrm{wal}_{\boldsymbol{l}_{\mathfrak{u}}}(\boldsymbol{x}_{j,\mathfrak{u}} \oplus \boldsymbol{\sigma})} \right] \\
&= \sum_{\substack{\boldsymbol{k}_{\mathfrak{u}} \in \mathbb{N}^{|\mathfrak{u}|} \\ \mathrm{tr}_n((\boldsymbol{k}_{\mathfrak{u}}, \boldsymbol{0})) \in \mathcal{D}_{\boldsymbol{q},p}}} b^{-2\mu_\alpha(\boldsymbol{k}_{\mathfrak{u}})},
\end{aligned}$$

where $\boldsymbol{x}_{h,\mathfrak{u}}$ is the projection of $\boldsymbol{x}_h$ to the components which belong to $\mathfrak{u}$. Now the result follows from Lemma 15.19. □

Further, we need the following lemma.

Lemma 15.33 *Let $\alpha \in \mathbb{N}$, then for every $1/(2\alpha) < \lambda \leq 1$, there exists a constant $0 < B_{b,\alpha,\lambda} < \infty$ such that*

$$\sum_{k=1}^{\infty} b^{-2\lambda\mu_\alpha(k)} \leq B_{b,\alpha,\lambda},$$

where

$$B_{b,\alpha,\lambda} := \widetilde{B}_{b,\alpha,\lambda} + \frac{(b-1)^{\alpha}}{b^{2\lambda\alpha}-b}\prod_{i=1}^{\alpha-1}\frac{1}{b^{2\lambda i}-1},$$

$$\widetilde{B}_{b,\alpha,\lambda} = \begin{cases} 0 & \text{if } \alpha = 1, \\ \alpha - 1 & \text{if } \alpha \geq 2 \text{ and } \lambda = 1/2, \\ \frac{(b-1)((b-1)^{\alpha-1}-(b^{2\lambda}-1)^{\alpha-1})}{(b-b^{2\lambda})(b^{2\lambda}-1)^{\alpha-1}} & \text{if } \alpha \geq 2 \text{ and } \lambda \neq 1/2. \end{cases}$$

Furthermore, the series $\sum_{k=1}^{\infty} b^{-2\lambda\mu_\alpha(k)}$ *diverges to* $+\infty$ *as* λ *tends to* $1/(2\alpha)$ *from the right.*

Proof Let $k = \kappa_1 b^{d_1-1} + \cdots + \kappa_v b^{d_v-1}$ where $v \in \mathbb{N}, 0 < d_v < \cdots < d_1$ and $1 \leq \kappa_i < b$. We divide the sum over all $k \in \mathbb{N}$ into two parts, namely first, where $1 \leq v \leq \alpha - 1$ and second, where $v > \alpha - 1$. For the first part, we have

$$\begin{aligned}
&\sum_{v=1}^{\alpha-1}(b-1)^{v}\sum_{0<d_v<\cdots<d_1}\frac{1}{b^{2\lambda(d_1+\cdots+d_v)}} \\
&= \sum_{v=1}^{\alpha-1}(b-1)^{v}\sum_{d_1=v}^{\infty}\frac{1}{b^{2\lambda d_1}}\sum_{d_2=v-1}^{d_1-1}\frac{1}{b^{2\lambda d_2}}\cdots\sum_{d_v=1}^{d_{v-1}-1}\frac{1}{b^{2\lambda d_v}} \\
&\leq \sum_{v=1}^{\alpha-1}\left(\frac{b-1}{b^{2\lambda}-1}\right)^{v} = \begin{cases} \alpha-1 & \text{if } \lambda = 1/2, \\ \frac{(b-1)((b-1)^{\alpha-1}-(b^{2\lambda}-1)^{\alpha-1})}{(b-b^{2\lambda})(b^{2\lambda}-1)^{\alpha-1}} & \text{if } \lambda \neq 1/2, \end{cases} \\
&=: \widetilde{B}_{b,\alpha,\lambda}.
\end{aligned}$$

For the second part, we have

$$\begin{aligned}
&(b-1)^{\alpha}\sum_{0<d_\alpha<\cdots<d_1}\frac{b^{d_\alpha-1}}{b^{2\lambda(d_1+\cdots+d_\alpha)}} \\
&= \frac{(b-1)^{\alpha}}{b}\sum_{d_1=\alpha}^{\infty}\frac{1}{b^{2\lambda d_1}}\sum_{d_2=\alpha-1}^{d_1-1}\frac{1}{b^{2\lambda d_2}}\cdots\sum_{d_\alpha=1}^{d_{\alpha-1}-1}\frac{b^{d_\alpha}}{b^{2\lambda d_\alpha}} \\
&= \frac{(b-1)^{\alpha}}{b}\sum_{d_\alpha=1}^{\infty}\frac{b^{d_\alpha}}{b^{2\lambda d_\alpha}}\sum_{d_{\alpha-1}=d_\alpha+1}^{\infty}\frac{1}{b^{2\lambda d_{\alpha-1}}}\cdots\sum_{d_2=d_3+1}^{\infty}\frac{1}{b^{2\lambda d_2}}\sum_{d_1=d_2+1}^{\infty}\frac{1}{b^{2\lambda d_1}} \\
&= \frac{(b-1)^{\alpha}}{b}\prod_{i=1}^{\alpha-1}\frac{1}{b^{2\lambda i}-1}\sum_{d_\alpha=1}^{\infty}\frac{b^{d_\alpha}}{b^{2\lambda d_\alpha}}\frac{1}{b^{2\lambda(\alpha-1)d_\alpha}} \\
&= \frac{(b-1)^{\alpha}}{b^{2\lambda\alpha}-b}\prod_{i=1}^{\alpha-1}\frac{1}{b^{2\lambda i}-1}.
\end{aligned}$$

Hence, we have shown that

$$\frac{(b-1)^{\alpha}}{b^{2\lambda\alpha}-b}\prod_{i=1}^{\alpha-1}\frac{1}{b^{2\lambda i}-1}\le\sum_{k=1}^{\infty}b^{-2\lambda\mu_{\alpha}(k)}$$

$$\le\left(\widetilde{B}_{b,\alpha,\lambda}+\frac{(b-1)^{\alpha}}{b^{2\lambda\alpha}-b}\prod_{i=1}^{\alpha-1}\frac{1}{b^{2\lambda i}-1}\right)=:B_{b,\alpha,\lambda}.$$

As $\frac{(b-1)^{\alpha}}{b^{2\lambda\alpha}-b}\prod_{i=1}^{\alpha-1}\frac{1}{b^{2\lambda i}-1}\to+\infty$ whenever $\lambda\to 1/(2\alpha)$ from the right we also obtain the second assertion. □

There is a crucial point made in the above lemma. In the averaging argument below, we use Jensen's inequality. This inequality basically works for all $0<\lambda\le 1$, but one needs to restrict the range of λ to ensure that the sum $\sum_{k=1}^{\infty}b^{-2\lambda\mu_{\alpha}(k)}$ is finite. In our case we only need $\lambda>1/(2\alpha)$, which is enough to show that the convergence can be arbitrarily close to α. This is possible because we know the essential structure of the Walsh coefficients. The details of the averaging argument are presented in the following.

For an irreducible polynomial p in $\mathbb{Z}_b[x]$, we denote the mean square worst-case error using polynomial lattice rules generated from the vector $\boldsymbol{q}$ by $\widehat{e}_p^2(\boldsymbol{q})$. We now define the average of $\widehat{e}_p^{2\lambda}(\boldsymbol{q})$ over all polynomials $\boldsymbol{q}\in G_{b,n}^s$ by

$$A_{m,n,s,\lambda}(p)=\frac{1}{b^{ns}}\sum_{\boldsymbol{q}\in G_{b,n}^s}\widehat{e}_p^{2\lambda}(\boldsymbol{q}),$$

where $n=\deg(p)$ and $1/(2\alpha)<\lambda\le 1$.

With Lemma 15.32, together with Jensen's inequality, we obtain

$$A_{m,n,s,\lambda}(p)\le\sum_{\emptyset\neq\mathfrak{u}\subseteq\mathcal{I}_s}\gamma_{\mathfrak{u}}^{\lambda}D_{\alpha,b}^{\lambda|\mathfrak{u}|}\frac{1}{b^{ns}}\sum_{\boldsymbol{q}\in G_{b,n}^s}\sum_{\substack{\boldsymbol{k}_{\mathfrak{u}}\in\mathbb{N}^{|\mathfrak{u}|}\\ \mathrm{tr}_n((\boldsymbol{k}_{\mathfrak{u}},\boldsymbol{0}))\in\mathcal{D}_{\boldsymbol{q},p}}}b^{-2\lambda\mu_{\alpha}(\boldsymbol{k}_{\mathfrak{u}})}.$$

In the following, we estimate the term

$$\frac{1}{b^{ns}}\sum_{\boldsymbol{q}\in G_{b,n}^s}\sum_{\substack{\boldsymbol{k}_{\mathfrak{u}}\in\mathbb{N}^{|\mathfrak{u}|}\\ \mathrm{tr}_n((\boldsymbol{k}_{\mathfrak{u}},\boldsymbol{0}))\in\mathcal{D}_{\boldsymbol{q},p}}}b^{-2\lambda\mu_{\alpha}(\boldsymbol{k}_{\mathfrak{u}})}$$

$$=\sum_{\boldsymbol{k}_{\mathfrak{u}}\in\mathbb{N}^{|\mathfrak{u}|}}b^{-2\lambda\mu_{\alpha}(\boldsymbol{k}_{\mathfrak{u}})}\frac{1}{b^{n|\mathfrak{u}|}}\sum_{\substack{\boldsymbol{q}_{\mathfrak{u}}\in G_{b,n}^{|\mathfrak{u}|}\\ \mathrm{tr}_n(\boldsymbol{k}_{\mathfrak{u}})\cdot\boldsymbol{q}_{\mathfrak{u}}\equiv a \pmod{p}\\ \deg(a)<n-m}}1. \tag{15.12}$$

The last sum is equal to the number of solutions $\boldsymbol{q}_{\mathfrak{u}}$ of the equation $\mathrm{tr}_n(\boldsymbol{k}_{\mathfrak{u}})\cdot\boldsymbol{q}_{\mathfrak{u}}\equiv a$ (mod p) for some polynomial a with $\deg(a)<n-m$. This number depends, of course, on $\boldsymbol{k}_{\mathfrak{u}}$.

First, consider the case where all components of $\mathrm{tr}_n(\boldsymbol{k}_{\mathfrak{u}})$ are multiples of p. Then every $\boldsymbol{q}_{\mathfrak{u}}$ trivially satisfies the equation $\mathrm{tr}_n(\boldsymbol{k}_{\mathfrak{u}}) \cdot \boldsymbol{q}_{\mathfrak{u}} \equiv 0 \pmod{p}$. Hence, in this case we have

$$\frac{1}{b^{n|\mathfrak{u}|}} \sum_{\substack{\boldsymbol{q}_{\mathfrak{u}} \in G_{b,n}^{|\mathfrak{u}|} \\ \mathrm{tr}_n(\boldsymbol{k}_{\mathfrak{u}}) \cdot \boldsymbol{q}_{\mathfrak{u}} \equiv a \pmod{p} \\ \deg(a) < n-m}} 1 = 1$$

and the sum over all $\boldsymbol{k}_{\mathfrak{u}}$ which satisfy this condition is therefore bounded by

$$\sum_{\substack{\boldsymbol{k}_{\mathfrak{u}} \in \mathbb{N}^{|\mathfrak{u}|} \\ \mathrm{tr}_n(k_j) \equiv 0 \pmod{p} \, \forall i \in \mathfrak{u}}} b^{-2\lambda \mu_\alpha(\boldsymbol{k}_{\mathfrak{u}})} = \left(\sum_{\substack{k=1 \\ p | \mathrm{tr}_n(k)}}^{\infty} b^{-2\lambda \mu_\alpha(k)} \right)^{|\mathfrak{u}|}.$$

Write $k \in \mathbb{N}$ as $k = b^n l + k'$ with $0 \le k' < b^n$. For $k' = 0$, we obtain $\mathrm{tr}_n(k) = 0$ and hence, $p | \mathrm{tr}_n(k)$. If $k' \neq 0$, then $\mathrm{tr}_n(k) = \mathrm{tr}_n(k')$. Therefore, we obtain

$$\sum_{\substack{k=1 \\ p | \mathrm{tr}_n(k)}}^{\infty} b^{-2\lambda \mu_\alpha(k)} = \sum_{l=1}^{\infty} b^{-2\lambda \mu_\alpha(l b^n)} + \sum_{l=0}^{\infty} \sum_{\substack{k=1 \\ p | k}}^{b^n - 1} b^{-2\lambda \mu_\alpha(k + b^n l)}.$$

For $1 \le k \le b^n - 1$, the corresponding polynomial can never be divided by the polynomial p, since $\deg(p) = n > \deg(k)$. Furthermore, for $l \neq 0$, it follows that $\mu_\alpha(b^n l) \ge n + \mu_\alpha(l)$. Hence, we obtain

$$\sum_{\substack{k=1 \\ p | \mathrm{tr}_n(k)}}^{\infty} b^{-2\lambda \mu_\alpha(k)} \le b^{-2\lambda n} \sum_{l=1}^{\infty} b^{-2\lambda \mu_\alpha(l)}.$$

It remains to consider the case where there is at least one component of $\boldsymbol{k}_{\mathfrak{u}}$ which is not a multiple of p. In this case, we have

$$\frac{1}{b^{n|\mathfrak{u}|}} \sum_{\substack{\boldsymbol{q}_{\mathfrak{u}} \in G_{b,n}^{|\mathfrak{u}|} \\ \boldsymbol{k}_{\mathfrak{u}} \cdot \boldsymbol{q}_{\mathfrak{u}} \equiv a \pmod{p} \\ \deg(a) < n-m}} 1 = \frac{1}{b^m}$$

and therefore, this part of (15.12) is bounded by

$$b^{-m} \left(\sum_{k=1}^{\infty} b^{-2\lambda \mu_\alpha(k)} \right)^{|\mathfrak{u}|}.$$

Altogether, we now obtain that

$$A_{m,n,s,\lambda}(p) \le \sum_{\emptyset \neq \mathfrak{u} \subseteq \mathcal{I}_s} \gamma_{\mathfrak{u}}^{\lambda} D_{\alpha,b}^{\lambda |\mathfrak{u}|} \left(\sum_{k=1}^{\infty} b^{-2\lambda \mu_\alpha(k)} \right)^{|\mathfrak{u}|} \left(b^{-m} + b^{-2\lambda n |\mathfrak{u}|} \right).$$

Using Lemma 15.33, we now obtain the following result.

Proposition 15.34 *Let $\alpha, s, m, n \in \mathbb{N}$, $1 \le m \le n$, let b be a prime, let $p \in \mathbb{Z}_b[x]$ be irreducible with $\deg(p) = n$ and let $1/(2\alpha) < \lambda \le 1$. Then*

$$A_{m,n,s,\lambda}(p) \le \sum_{\emptyset \ne \mathfrak{u} \subseteq \mathcal{I}_s} \gamma_{\mathfrak{u}}^{\lambda} D_{\alpha,b}^{\lambda|\mathfrak{u}|} B_{b,\alpha,\lambda}^{|\mathfrak{u}|} \left(b^{-m} + b^{-2\lambda n|\mathfrak{u}|}\right),$$

where the constant $D_{\alpha,b} > 0$ is defined in Proposition 15.18 and $B_{b,\alpha,\lambda}$ is defined in Lemma 15.33.

The following theorem now establishes the existence of good shifted polynomial lattice rules.

Theorem 15.35 *Let $\alpha, s, m, n \in \mathbb{N}$, $1 \le m \le n$, let b be a prime and let $p \in \mathbb{Z}_b[x]$ be irreducible with $\deg(p) = n$. Then there exists a digitally shifted higher order polynomial lattice point set $\mathcal{P}_{\sigma^*}(\boldsymbol{q}^*, p)$ with generating vector $\boldsymbol{q}^* \in G_{b,n}^s$ such that*

$$e(\mathscr{H}_{s,\alpha,\boldsymbol{\gamma}}, \mathcal{P}_{\sigma^*}(\boldsymbol{q}^*, p)) \le \frac{1}{b^{\min(\tau m, n)}} \left(2 \sum_{\emptyset \ne \mathfrak{u} \subseteq \mathcal{I}_s} \gamma_{\mathfrak{u}}^{1/(2\tau)} D_{\alpha,b}^{|\mathfrak{u}|/(2\tau)} B_{b,\alpha,1/(2\tau)}^{|\mathfrak{u}|}\right)^{\tau}$$

for all $1/2 \le \tau < \alpha$.

Proof For a given irreducible polynomial p with $\deg(p) = n$, let $\boldsymbol{q}^* \in G_{b,n}^s$ satisfy $\widehat{e}_p(\boldsymbol{q}^*) \le \widehat{e}_p(\boldsymbol{q})$ for all $\boldsymbol{q} \in G_{b,n}^s$. Then, it follows from Proposition 15.34 that for every $1/(2\alpha) < \lambda \le 1$, we have

$$\widehat{e}_p^{\,2\lambda}(\boldsymbol{q}^*) \le \frac{1}{b^{ns}} \sum_{\boldsymbol{q} \in G_{b,n}^s} \widehat{e}_p^{\,2\lambda}(\boldsymbol{q}) \le \sum_{\emptyset \ne \mathfrak{u} \subseteq \mathcal{I}_s} \gamma_{\mathfrak{u}}^{\lambda} D_{\alpha,b}^{\lambda|\mathfrak{u}|} B_{b,\alpha,\lambda}^{|\mathfrak{u}|} \left(b^{-m} + b^{-2\lambda n|\mathfrak{u}|}\right).$$

By using the estimation $b^{-m} + b^{-2\lambda n|\mathfrak{u}|} \le 2\max(b^{-m}, b^{-2\lambda n})$, we obtain

$$\widehat{e}_p(\boldsymbol{q}^*) \le 2^{1/(2\lambda)} \max(b^{-m/(2\lambda)}, b^{-n}) \left(\sum_{\emptyset \ne \mathfrak{u} \subseteq \mathcal{I}_s} \gamma_{\mathfrak{u}}^{\lambda} D_{b,\alpha}^{\lambda|\mathfrak{u}|} B_{b,\alpha,\lambda}^{|\mathfrak{u}|}\right)^{1/(2\lambda)}.$$

As the root mean square worst-case error $\widehat{e}_p(\boldsymbol{q}^*)$ taken over all digital shifts satisfies the above bound, it is clear that there must exist a shift $\boldsymbol{\sigma}^*$ such that the worst-case error using the $\boldsymbol{\sigma}^*$-shifted polynomial lattice rule generated from $\boldsymbol{q}^*$ satisfies this bound as well.

The result now follows by a change of variables together with the fact that $\max(b^{-\tau m}, b^{-n}) = b^{-\min(\tau m, n)}$. □

Remark 15.36 Again, it follows from Sharygin's result [241] that the upper bound in the above theorem is essentially the best possible.

The polynomial lattice rule considered in the above theorem is only shown to work for a fixed $\alpha \in \mathbb{N}$. In the following, we also show the existence of polynomial lattice rules which work well for a range of possible α's. Notice that we cannot use Theorem 15.31 since we do not know the figure of merit for the higher order polynomial lattices considered in Theorem 15.35.

Let ν be the equiprobable measure on the power set of $G_{b,n}^s$, i.e. $\nu(\boldsymbol{q}) = b^{-ns}$. For $c \geq 1$ and $1/2 \leq \tau < \alpha$, we define

$$\mathcal{C}_{b,\alpha}(c,\tau) = \left\{\boldsymbol{q} \in G_{b,n}^s : \widehat{e}_p(\boldsymbol{q}) \leq E_{b,\alpha,\boldsymbol{\gamma},s,m,n}(c,\tau)\right\},$$

where

$$E_{b,\alpha,\boldsymbol{\gamma},s,m,n}(c,\tau) := \frac{c^\tau}{b^{\min(\tau m,n)}}\left(2\sum_{\emptyset \neq \mathfrak{u} \subseteq \mathcal{I}_s} \gamma_{\mathfrak{u}}^{1/(2\tau)} D_{\alpha,b}^{|\mathfrak{u}|/(2\tau)} B_{b,\alpha,1/(2\tau)}^{|\mathfrak{u}|}\right)^\tau.$$

Furthermore, let

$$\begin{aligned}\mathcal{C}_{b,\alpha}(c) &= \bigcap_{1/2 \leq \tau < \alpha} \mathcal{C}_{b,\alpha}(c,\tau)\\ &= \left\{\boldsymbol{q} \in G_{b,n}^s : \widehat{e}_p(\boldsymbol{q}) \leq E_{b,\alpha,\boldsymbol{\gamma},s,m,n}(c,\tau) \text{ for all } 1/2 \leq \tau < \alpha\right\}.\end{aligned}$$

We obtain the following result.

Lemma 15.37 *Let $c \geq 1$ and $1/2 \leq \tau < \alpha$. Let $p \in \mathbb{Z}_b[x]$ be irreducible with $\deg(p) = n$. Then we have*

$$\nu(\mathcal{C}_{b,\alpha}(c,\tau)) > 1 - c^{-1}.$$

Proof We denote $\overline{\mathcal{C}}_{b,\alpha}(c,\tau) := G_{b,n}^s \setminus \mathcal{C}_{b,\alpha}(c,\tau)$. Then, for all $1/2 \leq \tau < \alpha$, we have

$$A_{m,n,s,1/(2\tau)}(p) > \frac{\nu(\overline{\mathcal{C}}_{b,\alpha}(c,\tau))2c}{b^{\min(m,n/\tau)}} \sum_{\emptyset \neq \mathfrak{u} \subseteq \mathcal{I}_s} \gamma_{\mathfrak{u}}^{1/(2\tau)} D_{\alpha,b}^{|\mathfrak{u}|/(2\tau)} B_{b,\alpha,1/(2\tau)}^{|\mathfrak{u}|}.$$

The result follows from Proposition 15.34 and ideas from the proof of Theorem 15.35. □

The above lemma shows that, for any given $\alpha \in \mathbb{N}$, there are many good polynomial lattice point sets. Hence, it is not surprising that there also exists a polynomial lattice rule which works well for a range of α's, say $1 \leq \alpha \leq \delta$. From now on we always assume that $n = \delta m$.

Lemma 15.38 *Let $c \geq 1$, then we have*

$$\nu(\mathcal{C}_{b,\alpha}(c)) > 1 - c^{-1}.$$

Proof Let $1/2 \leq \tau_* < \alpha$ be such that

$$E_{b,\alpha,\boldsymbol{\gamma},s,m,\delta m}(c,\tau_*) = \inf_{1/2 \leq \tau < \alpha} E_{b,\alpha,\boldsymbol{\gamma},s,m,\delta m}(c,\tau)$$

(note that by Lemma 15.33, we have $E_{b,\alpha,\gamma,s,m,\delta m}(c,\tau) \to +\infty$ whenever $\tau \to \alpha^-$ and hence, we can find τ_* with the demanded property). Then we have

$$\mathcal{C}_{b,\alpha}(c,\tau_*) \subseteq \bigcap_{1/2 \le \tau < \alpha} \mathcal{C}_{b,\alpha}(c,\tau) = \mathcal{C}_{b,\alpha}(c)$$

and hence, the result follows from Lemma 15.37. □

If we choose $c = \delta$ in Lemma 15.38, then we obtain $\nu(\mathcal{C}_{b,\alpha}(\delta)) > 1 - \delta^{-1}$ and consequently, we have

$$\nu\left(\bigcap_{\alpha=1}^{\delta} \mathcal{C}_{b,\alpha}(\delta)\right) = 1 - \nu\left(\bigcup_{\alpha=1}^{\delta} \overline{\mathcal{C}}_{b,\alpha}(\delta)\right) \ge 1 - \sum_{\alpha=1}^{\delta} \nu(\overline{\mathcal{C}}_{b,\alpha}(\delta)) > 0.$$

Hence, we obtain the following theorem which establishes the existence of a $\boldsymbol{q}^* \in G_{b,\delta m}^s$ which achieves the optimal convergence rate for a range of α's.

Theorem 15.39 *Let $s, \delta, m \in \mathbb{N}$ and let $p \in \mathbb{Z}_b[x]$ be irreducible with* $\deg(p) = \delta m$. *Then there exists a $\boldsymbol{q}^* \in G_{b,\delta m}^s$ such that*

$$\widehat{e}_{p,\alpha}(\boldsymbol{q}^*) \le \frac{\delta^{\tau_\alpha}}{b^{\tau_\alpha m}}\left(2 \sum_{\emptyset \ne \mathfrak{u} \subseteq \mathcal{I}_s} \gamma_{\mathfrak{u}}^{1/(2\tau_\alpha)} D_{\alpha,b}^{|\mathfrak{u}|/(2\tau_\alpha)} B_{b,\alpha,1/(2\tau_\alpha)}^{|\mathfrak{u}|}\right)^{\tau_\alpha}$$

for all $1 \le \alpha \le \delta$ and all $1/2 \le \tau_\alpha < \alpha$. Here, $\widehat{e}_{p,\alpha}(\boldsymbol{q}^*)$ means the root mean square worst-case error $\widehat{e}_p(\boldsymbol{q}^*)$ for integration in the space $\mathscr{H}_{s,\alpha,\boldsymbol{\gamma}}$.

In the following, we also show the existence of deterministic quadrature rules which work well for all spaces up to smoothness δ.

Let λ_s be the Lebesgue measure on the set $[0,1)^s$. Let $\boldsymbol{q}^*$ be taken from Theorem 15.35. For $\boldsymbol{\sigma} \in [0,1)^s$, let $e_p(\boldsymbol{q}^*, \boldsymbol{\sigma})$ denote the worst-case error of a polynomial lattice rule with generating vector $\boldsymbol{q}^*$ which is digitally shifted by $\boldsymbol{\sigma}$. For $c \ge 1$, we define

$$\mathcal{E}_{b,\alpha}(c) = \left\{\boldsymbol{\sigma}' \in [0,1)^s : e_p(\boldsymbol{q}^*, \boldsymbol{\sigma}') \le c \cdot \widehat{e}_p(\boldsymbol{q}^*)\right\}.$$

Further, let

$$\mathcal{F}_{b,\alpha}(c) = \Bigg\{\boldsymbol{\sigma}' \in [0,1)^s : e_p(\boldsymbol{q}^*, \boldsymbol{\sigma}') \le \frac{c}{b^{\min(\tau m, n)}} \times \left(2 \sum_{\emptyset \ne \mathfrak{u} \subseteq \mathcal{I}_s} \gamma_{\mathfrak{u}}^{1/(2\tau)} D_{\alpha,b}^{|\mathfrak{u}|/(2\tau)} B_{b,\alpha,1/(2\tau)}^{|\mathfrak{u}|}\right)^{\tau} \forall 1/2 \le \tau < \alpha\Bigg\}.$$

Then we have $\mathcal{E}_{b,\alpha}(c) \subseteq \mathcal{F}_{b,\alpha}(c)$. This follows from the proof of Theorem 15.35. Using Markov's inequality from probability theory, we obtain the following result.

Lemma 15.40 *Let $c \geq 1$ and $\alpha \in \mathbb{N}$. Then we have*

$$\lambda_s(\mathcal{F}_{b,\alpha}(c)) \geq \lambda_s(\mathcal{E}_{b,\alpha}(c)) > 1 - c^{-2}.$$

We can now also show that there exists a digital shift which can be used for a range of choices of α's. The proof of the following result is given as Exercise 15.9.

Theorem 15.41 *Let $s, \delta, m \in \mathbb{N}$ and let $p \in \mathbb{Z}_b[x]$ be irreducible with $\deg(p) = \delta m$. Then there exists a $\boldsymbol{q}^* \in G_{b,\delta m}^s$ and a $\boldsymbol{\sigma}^* \in [0,1)^s$ such that the worst-case error for the higher order polynomial lattice rule with generating vector $\boldsymbol{q}^*$ and shifted by $\boldsymbol{\sigma}^*$ is bounded by*

$$e_{p,\alpha}(\boldsymbol{q}^*, \boldsymbol{\sigma}^*) \leq b^{-\tau_\alpha m}\sqrt{\delta}\left(2 \sum_{\emptyset \neq \mathfrak{u} \subseteq \mathcal{I}_s} \gamma_{\mathfrak{u}}^{1/(2\tau_\alpha)} D_{\alpha,b}^{|\mathfrak{u}|/(2\tau_\alpha)} B_{b,\alpha,1/(2\tau_\alpha)}^{|\mathfrak{u}|}\right)^{\tau_\alpha}$$

for all $1 \leq \alpha \leq \delta$ and all $1/2 \leq \tau_\alpha < \alpha$.

Remark 15.42 Similar results can also be shown for higher order polynomial lattices with generating vectors of the form $(q, q^2, \ldots, q^s)$ with $q \in G_{b,m}$, with the difference that we have an additional factor of $s - 1$ in the upper bounds of the above results. Note that we need generating vectors of the form $(q, q^2, \ldots, q^s)$ rather than $(1, q, \ldots, q^{s-1})$ since the one-dimensional generating vector (1) does not necessarily yield a polynomial lattice which achieves the optimal rate of convergence. For more information, see [8].

Constructions of higher order polynomial lattice point sets using a CBC algorithm can be found in [8].

Exercises

15.1 Show that for a digital $(t, \alpha, \beta, n \times m, s)$-net over $\mathbb{Z}_b$, we have

$$\min_{\boldsymbol{k} \in \mathcal{D}'_{\infty,n}} \mu_{b,\alpha}(\boldsymbol{k}) > \beta n - t.$$

15.2 Let $f(x) = x$. Calculate the Walsh coefficients of f and construct a higher order digital net with b^m points such that $|\int_0^1 f(x)\,\mathrm{d}x - \sum_{n=0}^{b^m-1} f(x_n)|$ is as small as possible.

15.3 Prove Theorem 15.9.

15.4 Prove Proposition 15.11.

15.5 Show that the polynomial lattice given in Definition 15.23 is a digital net in the sense of Definition 4.47, but with $n \times m$ generating matrices which are given by (15.11).
Hint: Compare with the proof of Theorem 10.5.

15.6 Prove Lemma 15.25.

15.7 Prove Theorem 15.28.

15.8 Use Theorem 15.30 to calculate values of t and β for 'small' values of α, b, m, n, s. Compare the result to digital nets obtained using Theorem 15.7.
Hint: Parameters for classical digital nets can be found at *http://mint.sbg.ac.at/*.

15.9 Prove Theorem 15.41.
Hint: Use Lemma 15.40. The proof is very similar to the proof of Theorem 15.39.

15.10 Use Theorem 10.11 and the elaborations following it, to construct higher order polynomial lattice point sets for $s = 1$. What is the value of t and β when $\alpha = 2$?

16

Explicit constructions of point sets with the best possible order of L_2-discrepancy

Roth's lower bound on L_2-discrepancy (see Theorem 3.20) states that for any dimension $s \in \mathbb{N}$ there exists a $c_s > 0$ with the following property: for any cardinality $N \geq 2$ and any point set $\mathcal{P}$ consisting of N points in the s-dimensional unit-cube, we have

$$L_{2,N}(\mathcal{P}) \geq c_s \frac{(\log N)^{(s-1)/2}}{N}. \tag{16.1}$$

This lower bound is the best possible in the order of magnitude in N as shown first by Davenport [29] for $s = 2$ and then by Roth [229, 230] and Frolov [84] for arbitrary dimensions $s \in \mathbb{N}$. Davenport used point sets consisting of the $2N$ elements $(\{\pm n\alpha\}, n/N)$ for $1 \leq n \leq N$, where $N \in \mathbb{N}$ and α has a continued fraction expansion with bounded partial quotients. Further examples of two-dimensional point sets with the best possible order of L_2-discrepancy can be found in references [76, 77, 78, 128, 142, 223]. On the other hand, Roth's [230] proof for arbitrary dimension $s \geq 2$ is a pure existence result obtained by averaging arguments. Since then it has been a longstanding open problem to give a constructive version, i.e. to give, for any dimension s and cardinality $N \geq 2$, an explicit construction of a point set consisting of N points in the s-dimensional unit-cube whose L_2-discrepancy is bounded above by $C_s(\log N)^{(s-1)/2}/N$ with a positive C_s only depending on the dimension s. For $s = 3$, a construction based on a symmetrisation of the digital $(0, m, 3)$-net over $\mathbb{Z}_2$ from Example 4.57 has been given in [143] that leads to an upper bound of order of magnitude $\log N \sqrt{\log \log N}/N$ which is nearly the best possible, up to the $\sqrt{\log \log N}$ term. A breakthrough was achieved by Chen and Skriganov [22], who provided a complete solution to this problem. They constructed, for any dimension s and any cardinality $N \geq 2$, an s-dimensional point set of N points whose L_2-discrepancy satisfies an upper bound as given above. For $N = b^m$, these point sets are special digital (t, m, s)-nets over $\mathbb{Z}_b$. Later, Skriganov [244] showed that these point sets also have the best possible order of

L_q-discrepancy for each $1 < q < \infty$. Thereby, he simplified the proof method used in [22] dramatically (see also [23] for an overview). In this chapter, we present the construction due to Chen and Skriganov. In doing so, we mainly follow the approach used in [23], but we incorporate the simplifications of the proof method due to Skriganov [244].

The constant C_s in Chen and Skriganov's upper bound is rather large and not the best possible. We further show an upper bound of order of magnitude $(\log N)^{(s-1)/2}/N$, from which we deduce that the constant c_s in Theorem 16.1 is essentially the best possible. These constructions, first presented in [51] and [28] (see also [23]), are based on digitally shifted digital nets. As the result is obtained by averaging over all (but finitely many) digital shifts, the constructions are not fully constructive.

16.1 Point sets with the best possible order of L_2-discrepancy

The basic idea of Chen and Skriganov was to construct $\mathbb{Z}_b$-linear subspaces of $\mathbb{Z}_b^{sm}$ for which simultaneously the NRT weight (see Section 7.1) and the usual Hamming weight of their dual distributions are both large enough. Such $\mathbb{Z}_b$-linear subspaces give rise to digital nets over $\mathbb{Z}_b$ whose L_2-discrepancy is of the best possible order with respect to Roth's general lower bound. Starting from such nets, one can then give, for any integer $N \geq 2$, *explicit* constructions of point sets $\mathcal{P}_N$ consisting of N points in the s-dimensional unit-cube, whose L_2-discrepancy satisfies $L_{2,N}(\mathcal{P}_N) \leq C_{s,b}(\log N)^{(s-1)/2}/N$ for some $C_{s,b} > 0$ independent of N.

Chen and Skriganov's approach is based on duality theory as discussed in Chapter 7. Beside the already introduced NRT weight V_m, see Definition 7.1, and the corresponding minimal distance δ_m, see Definition 7.2, here the usual Hamming weight on $\mathbb{Z}_b^m$ also plays an important role. For the following, let b be a prime number.

Definition 16.1 For $\mathbf{a} = (a_1, \ldots, a_m)$ in $\mathbb{Z}_b^m$, the *Hamming weight* $\varkappa_m(\mathbf{a})$ is the number of indices $1 \leq i \leq m$ such that $a_i \neq 0$. For $\mathbf{A} = (\mathbf{a}_1, \ldots, \mathbf{a}_s) \in \mathbb{Z}_b^{sm}$, we define

$$\varkappa_m(\mathbf{A}) = \sum_{i=1}^{s} \varkappa_m(\mathbf{a}_i).$$

One can easily show that $\varkappa_m$ defines a metric on the vector space $\mathbb{Z}_b^{sm}$ (see Exercise 16.1).

Definition 16.2 For an arbitrary subset $\mathcal{C}$ of $\mathbb{Z}_b^{sm}$ containing at least two points, the *Hamming weight* of $\mathcal{C}$ is defined by

$$\varkappa_m(\mathcal{C}) = \min\{\varkappa_m(\mathbf{A} - \mathbf{B}) : \mathbf{A}, \mathbf{B} \in \mathcal{C} \text{ and } \mathbf{A} \neq \mathbf{B}\}.$$

If $\mathcal{C}$ is a $\mathbb{Z}_b$-linear subspace of $\mathbb{Z}_b^{sm}$, then this definition can be rewritten in the form

$$\varkappa_m(\mathcal{C}) = \min\{\varkappa_m(\mathbf{A}) : \mathbf{A} \in \mathcal{C} \setminus \{\mathbf{0}\}\}.$$

First, we are concerned with point sets whose cardinality is a power of a prime b. From this we then deduce a construction of point sets with arbitrary cardinalities $N \geq 2$.

We recall the definition of the mapping $\Phi_m : \mathbb{Z}_b^{sm} \to [0, 1)^s$ from Section 7.2. For $\mathbf{a} = (a_1, \ldots, a_m) \in \mathbb{Z}_b^m$, we set $\Phi_m(\mathbf{a}) = a_1 b^{-1} + \cdots + a_m b^{-m}$ and for $\mathbf{A} = (\mathbf{a}_1, \ldots, \mathbf{a}_s) \in \mathbb{Z}_b^{sm}$, we apply Φ_m to each component $\mathbf{a}_i$ of $\mathbf{A}$ for $1 \leq i \leq s$.

Theorem 16.3 *Let $b \geq 2s^2$ be a prime. Let $\mathcal{C} \subseteq \mathbb{Z}_b^{sm}$ be a $\mathbb{Z}_b$-linear subspace with $\dim(\mathcal{C}) = m$ such that its dual space $\mathcal{C}^\perp$ satisfies*

$$\varkappa_m(\mathcal{C}^\perp) \geq 2s + 1 \quad \textit{and} \quad \delta_m(\mathcal{C}^\perp) \geq m - t + 1.$$

Then, the L_2-discrepancy of the point set $\mathcal{P} = \Phi_m(\mathcal{C})$ can be bounded by

$$L_{2,b^m}(\mathcal{P}) < 2^{1-s} b^{s+t} \frac{(m+1)^{\frac{s-1}{2}}}{b^m}.$$

Remark 16.4 According to Theorem 7.14, the point set $\mathcal{P}$ from Theorem 16.3 is a digital (t, m, s)-net over $\mathbb{Z}_b$. Explicit constructions of $\mathbb{Z}_b$-linear subspaces satisfying the conditions from Theorem 16.3 are given in Section 16.4.

The proof of Theorem 16.3 is based on Walsh series analysis in conjunction with results from duality theory for digital nets. We postpone this proof until Section 16.3.

Let us turn now to point sets of arbitrary cardinality $N \geq 2$. Using Theorem 16.3, we show how to obtain point sets of arbitrary cardinality $N \geq 2$ of the best possible order of the L_2-discrepancy.

Theorem 16.5 *Let $b \geq 2s^2$ be a prime and let $g = 2s$. Assume that for every $w \in \mathbb{N}$, a $\mathbb{Z}_b$-linear subspace $\mathcal{C}_{g,w} \subseteq \mathbb{Z}_b^{sgw}$ with $\dim(\mathcal{C}_{g,w}) = gw$ can be constructed whose dual space $\mathcal{C}_{g,w}^\perp$ satisfies*

$$\varkappa_{gw}(\mathcal{C}_{g,w}^\perp) \geq g + 1 \quad \textit{and} \quad \delta_{gw}(\mathcal{C}_{g,w}^\perp) \geq gw + 1.$$

Then, for any integer $N \geq 2$, we can construct a point set $\mathcal{P}_N$ consisting of N points in $[0, 1)^s$ such that the L_2-discrepancy of $\mathcal{P}_N$ satisfies

$$L_{2,N}(\mathcal{P}_N) < 2^{1-s} b^{2s} \left(\frac{\log N}{\log b} + 2s + 1 \right)^{\frac{s-1}{2}} \frac{1}{N}.$$

Proof For an integer $N \geq 2$, we choose $w \in \mathbb{N}$ such that $b^{g(w-1)} < N \leq b^{gw}$. The $\mathbb{Z}_b$-linear subspace $\mathcal{C}_{g,w} \subseteq \mathbb{Z}_b^{sgw}$ with $\dim(\mathcal{C}_{g,w}) = gw$ satisfies the assumptions in Theorem 16.3 with $m = gw$ and $t = 0$ and hence, the L_2-discrepancy of the point set $\mathcal{P}_{g,w} = \Phi_{gw}(\mathcal{C}_{g,w})$ is bounded above by

$$L_{2,b^{gw}}(\mathcal{P}_{g,w}) < 2^{1-s} b^s \frac{(gw+1)^{\frac{s-1}{2}}}{b^{gw}}. \tag{16.2}$$

By Theorem 7.14, the point set $\mathcal{P}_{g,w}$ is a digital $(0, gw, s)$-net over $\mathbb{Z}_b$. Hence, the subset

$$\widetilde{\mathcal{P}}_N := \mathcal{P}_{g,w} \cap \left(\left[0, \frac{N}{b^{gw}}\right) \times [0,1)^{s-1} \right)$$

contains exactly N points. We define the point set

$$\mathcal{P}_N := \left\{ \left(\frac{b^{gw}}{N} x_1, x_2, \ldots, x_s \right) : (x_1, x_2, \ldots, x_s) \in \widetilde{\mathcal{P}}_N \right\}.$$

Then we have

$$\begin{aligned}
(N L_{2,N}(\mathcal{P}_N))^2 &= \int_{[0,1]^s} |A([\mathbf{0}, \mathbf{y}), N, \mathcal{P}_N) - N\lambda_s([\mathbf{0}, \mathbf{y}))|^2 \,\mathrm{d}\mathbf{y} \\
&= \int_0^1 \cdots \int_0^1 \Bigg| A\left(\left[0, \frac{N}{b^{gw}} y_1\right) \times \prod_{i=2}^{s} [0, y_i), N, \widetilde{\mathcal{P}}_N \right) \\
&\qquad - b^{gw} \frac{N}{b^{gw}} y_1 \cdots y_s \Bigg|^2 \,\mathrm{d}y_1 \cdots \mathrm{d}y_s \\
&= \frac{b^{gw}}{N} \int_0^{N/b^{gw}} \int_0^1 \cdots \int_0^1 \left| A([\mathbf{0}, \mathbf{y}), N, \widetilde{\mathcal{P}}_N) - b^{gw} \lambda_s([\mathbf{0}, \mathbf{y})) \right|^2 \,\mathrm{d}\mathbf{y} \\
&= \frac{b^{gw}}{N} \int_0^{N/b^{gw}} \int_0^1 \cdots \int_0^1 \left| A([\mathbf{0}, \mathbf{y}), b^{gw}, \mathcal{P}_{g,w}) - b^{gw} \lambda_s([\mathbf{0}, \mathbf{y})) \right|^2 \,\mathrm{d}\mathbf{y} \\
&\le \frac{b^{gw}}{N} \left(b^{gw} L_{2,b^{gw}}(\mathcal{P}_{g,w}) \right)^2.
\end{aligned}$$

With (16.2) we obtain

$$\begin{aligned}
(N L_{2,N}(\mathcal{P}_N))^2 &< \frac{b^{gw}}{N} 4^{1-s} b^{2s} (gw+1)^{s-1} \\
&\le b^g 4^{1-s} b^{2s} \left(\frac{\log N}{\log b} + g + 1 \right)^{s-1} \\
&= 4^{1-s} b^{4s} \left(\frac{\log N}{\log b} + 2s + 1 \right)^{s-1}.
\end{aligned}$$

Taking the square root and dividing by N, we finally obtain

$$L_{2,N}(\mathcal{P}_N) < 2^{1-s} b^{2s} \left(\frac{\log N}{\log b} + 2s + 1 \right)^{\frac{s-1}{2}} \frac{1}{N}. \qquad \square$$

Hence, if we have explicit constructions of $\mathbb{Z}_b$-linear subspaces $\mathcal{C}_{g,w}$ satisfying the assumptions in Theorem 16.5, then for every integer $N \geq 2$, we can explicitly construct a point set $\mathcal{P}_N$ consisting of N points in the s-dimensional unit-cube whose L_2-discrepancy is of the best possible order in the sense of Roth's theorem. Such constructions of $\mathcal{C}_{g,w}$ are provided in Section 16.4. The construction of $\mathcal{P}_N$ is then given by the proof of Theorem 16.5.

16.2 Further results from duality theory

As already mentioned, the proof of Theorem 16.3 is based on more detailed results from the duality theory for digital nets. These results are proven in this section.

In the following, we need a reflection map, which plays an important role in the geometrical interpretation of the map $\Phi_m : \mathbb{Z}_b^{sm} \to [0, 1)^s$, b a prime, that was introduced in (7.1).

Now for $\mathbf{a} = (a_1, \ldots, a_m) \in \mathbb{Z}_b^m$ the *reflection map* R is defined by $R\mathbf{a} := (a_m, \ldots, a_1)$ and for $\mathbf{A} = (\mathbf{a}_1, \ldots, \mathbf{a}_s) \in \mathbb{Z}_b^{sm}$, we define the reflection map R_s by $R_s\mathbf{A} := (R\mathbf{a}_1, \ldots, R\mathbf{a}_s)$. For a subset $\mathcal{C}$ of $\mathbb{Z}_b^{sm}$, let $R_s\mathcal{C} := \{R_s\mathbf{A} : \mathbf{A} \in \mathcal{C}\}$.

Remark 16.6 The NRT weight of the reflected element $R\mathbf{a} \in \mathbb{Z}_b^m$ gives information on the position of the point $\Phi_m(\mathbf{a})$ in the unit-interval. More precisely, for any non-zero $\mathbf{a} \in \mathbb{Z}_b^m$, we have

$$\frac{b^{v_m(R\mathbf{a})-1}}{b^m} \leq \Phi_m(\mathbf{a}) < \frac{b^{v_m(R\mathbf{a})}}{b^m},$$

where v_m is given in Definition 7.1. This can be seen as follows: assume that $v_m(R\mathbf{a}) = r \in \mathbb{N}$, i.e. $R\mathbf{a} = (a_m, \ldots, a_{m+1-r}, 0, \ldots, 0)$ and $a_{m+1-r} \neq 0$. Then $\mathbf{a} = (0, \ldots, 0, a_{m+1-r}, \ldots, a_m)$ and $\Phi_m(\mathbf{a}) = a_{m+1-r}b^{-m-1+r} + \cdots + a_m b^{-m}$ and hence, $b^{r-m-1} \leq \Phi_m(\mathbf{a}) < b^{r-m}$ as desired.

We define a subclass of the class of all s-dimensional, b-adic elementary intervals (see Definition 3.8).

Definition 16.7 For $m, b, s \in \mathbb{N}_0$, $b \geq 2$, $s \geq 1$, let $\mathcal{E}_{m,b,s}$ denote the class of all s-dimensional, b-adic elementary intervals of side length at least b^{-m}, i.e. $\mathcal{E}_{m,b,s}$ consist of all intervals of the form

$$\prod_{i=1}^{s} \left[\frac{\alpha_i}{b^{d_i}}, \frac{\alpha_i + 1}{b^{d_i}}\right)$$

with integers $0 \leq d_i \leq m$ and $0 \leq \alpha_i < b^{d_i}$ for all $1 \leq i \leq s$.

Lemma 16.8 *Let* **A** *and* **B** *be in* $\mathbb{Z}_b^{sm}$.

1. *We have* $V_m(R_s\mathbf{A}) \le (s-k)m$ *if and only if* $\Phi_m(\mathbf{A})$ *is contained in some elementary interval of the form* $\prod_{i=1}^{s}\left[0, \frac{1}{b^{d_i}}\right) \in \mathcal{E}_{m,b,s}$ *of order at least km.*
2. *We have* $V_m(R_s\mathbf{A} - R_s\mathbf{B}) \le (s-k)m$ *if and only if* $\Phi_m(\mathbf{A})$ *and* $\Phi_m(\mathbf{B})$ *are both contained in the same elementary interval* $J \in \mathcal{E}_{m,b,s}$ *of order at least km.*

Proof

1. Let $\mathbf{A} = (\mathbf{a}_1, \ldots, \mathbf{a}_s)$ and let us assume first that $V_m(R_s\mathbf{A}) \le (s-k)m$. It follows from Remark 16.6 that for any $1 \le i \le s$, we have $\Phi_m(\mathbf{a}_i) < b^{-d_i}$ where $d_i = m - v_m(R\mathbf{a}_i)$. Hence,

$$\Phi_m(\mathbf{A}) \in \prod_{i=1}^{s}\left[0, \frac{1}{b^{d_i}}\right).$$

Clearly we have $0 \le d_i \le m$ for every $1 \le i \le s$ and $d_1 + \cdots + d_s = sm - \sum_{i=1}^{s} v_m(R\mathbf{a}_i) = sm - V_m(R_s\mathbf{A}) \ge km$ such that the elementary interval is of order at least km.

On the other hand, assume that $V_m(R_s\mathbf{A}) > (s-k)m$. Again from Remark 16.6, we obtain $\Phi_m(\mathbf{a}_i) \ge b^{v_m(R\mathbf{a}_i)-m-1}$ if $\mathbf{a}_i \ne \mathbf{0}$. If $\Phi_m(\mathbf{A})$ is contained in $\prod_{i=1}^{s}\left[0, b^{-d_i}\right)$ with $0 \le d_i \le m$ for every $1 \le i \le s$ and of order at least km, then we have $b^{v_m(R\mathbf{a}_i)-m-1} \le \Phi_m(\mathbf{a}_i) < b^{-d_i}$ and hence, $d_i \le m - v_m(R\mathbf{a}_i)$ for all $1 \le i \le s$. It follows, then, that

$$d_1 + \cdots + d_s \le sm - V_m(R_s\mathbf{A}) < km,$$

which contradicts the assumption that the order of the interval is at least km.

2. Let $\mathbf{a} = (a_1, \ldots, a_m) \in \mathbb{Z}_b^m$ and $\mathbf{b} = (b_1, \ldots, b_m) \in \mathbb{Z}_b^m$. Then we have $\Phi_m(\mathbf{a} - \mathbf{b}) \in \left[0, b^{-d}\right)$ if and only if $a_i = b_i =: c_i$ for all $1 \le i \le d$. Hence,

$$\Phi_m(\mathbf{a}) = \frac{c_1}{b} + \cdots + \frac{c_d}{b^d} + \frac{a_{d+1}}{b^{d+1}} + \cdots + \frac{a_m}{b^m}$$

and

$$\Phi_m(\mathbf{b}) = \frac{c_1}{b} + \cdots + \frac{c_d}{b^d} + \frac{b_{d+1}}{b^{d+1}} + \cdots + \frac{b_m}{b^m}$$

or equivalently

$$\Phi_m(\mathbf{a}), \Phi_m(\mathbf{b}) \in \left[\frac{z}{b^d}, \frac{z+1}{b^d}\right),$$

where $z = c_d + c_{d-1}b + \cdots + c_1 b^{d-1}$.

Now the second assertion of the lemma follows from the first one in conjunction with these considerations. □

Lemma 16.9 *Let $\mathcal{C}$ and $\mathcal{C}^\perp$ be mutually dual $\mathbb{Z}_b$-linear subspaces of $\mathbb{Z}_b^{sm}$. Then, for any function $f : \mathbb{Z}_b^{sm} \to \mathbb{C}$, we have*

$$\sum_{\mathbf{A}\in\mathcal{C}} f(\mathbf{A}) = \frac{|\mathcal{C}|}{b^{sm}} \sum_{\mathbf{B}\in\mathcal{C}^\perp} \widehat{f}(\mathbf{B}),$$

where

$$\widehat{f}(\mathbf{B}) = \sum_{\mathbf{A}\in\mathbb{Z}_b^{sm}} \omega_b^{\mathbf{B}\cdot\mathbf{A}} f(\mathbf{A})$$

is the Walsh-transform of f and $\omega_b := \mathrm{e}^{2\pi \mathrm{i}/b}$

Proof If $\mathbf{B} \in \mathcal{C}^\perp$, then $\mathbf{A}\cdot\mathbf{B} = 0$ for all $\mathbf{A} \in \mathcal{C}$ and hence, $\sum_{\mathbf{A}\in\mathcal{C}} \omega_b^{\mathbf{A}\cdot\mathbf{B}} = \sum_{\mathbf{A}\in\mathcal{C}} 1 = |\mathcal{C}|$. If $\mathbf{B} \notin \mathcal{C}^\perp$, then there exists a $\mathbf{A}^* \in \mathcal{C}$ such that $\mathbf{A}^*\cdot\mathbf{B} \neq 0 \in \mathbb{Z}_b$ and hence, $\omega_b^{\mathbf{A}^*\cdot\mathbf{B}} \neq 1$. Then we have

$$\omega_b^{\mathbf{A}^*\cdot\mathbf{B}} \sum_{\mathbf{A}\in\mathcal{C}} \omega_b^{\mathbf{A}\cdot\mathbf{B}} = \sum_{\mathbf{A}\in\mathcal{C}} \omega_b^{(\mathbf{A}^*+\mathbf{A})\cdot\mathbf{B}} = \sum_{\mathbf{A}\in\mathcal{C}} \omega_b^{\mathbf{A}\cdot\mathbf{B}},$$

where the last equality holds true, since $\mathcal{C}$ is a $\mathbb{Z}_b$-linear subspace and $\mathbf{A}^* \in \mathcal{C}$. As $\omega_b^{\mathbf{A}^*\cdot\mathbf{B}} \neq 1$, we obtain $\sum_{\mathbf{A}\in\mathcal{C}} \omega_b^{\mathbf{A}\cdot\mathbf{B}} = 0$. Thus, we have shown that

$$\sum_{\mathbf{A}\in\mathcal{C}} \omega_b^{\mathbf{A}\cdot\mathbf{B}} = \begin{cases} |\mathcal{C}| & \text{if } \mathbf{B} \in \mathcal{C}^\perp, \\ 0 & \text{if } \mathbf{B} \notin \mathcal{C}^\perp. \end{cases} \tag{16.3}$$

(In fact, this identity already occurred in Lemma 4.75.) Therefore, we obtain

$$\begin{aligned}\sum_{\mathbf{B}\in\mathcal{C}^\perp} \widehat{f}(\mathbf{B}) &= \sum_{\mathbf{B}\in\mathcal{C}^\perp} \sum_{\mathbf{A}\in\mathbb{Z}_b^{sm}} \omega_b^{\mathbf{B}\cdot\mathbf{A}} f(\mathbf{A}) = \sum_{\mathbf{A}\in\mathbb{Z}_b^{sm}} f(\mathbf{A}) \sum_{\mathbf{B}\in\mathcal{C}^\perp} \omega_b^{\mathbf{B}\cdot\mathbf{A}} \\ &= |\mathcal{C}^\perp| \sum_{\mathbf{A}\in(\mathcal{C}^\perp)^\perp} f(\mathbf{A}) = \frac{b^{sm}}{|\mathcal{C}|} \sum_{\mathbf{A}\in\mathcal{C}} f(\mathbf{A}).\end{aligned}$$

□

For integers $0 \le d_1, \ldots, d_s \le m$ and $\alpha_1, \ldots, \alpha_s \in \mathbb{N}_0$ with $0 \le \alpha_i < b^{d_i}$ for all $1 \le i \le s$, we define $\mathcal{V}_{d_1,\ldots,d_s}^{\alpha_1,\ldots,\alpha_s}$ as the pre-image of the elementary interval $\prod_{i=1}^s \left[\frac{\alpha_i}{b^{d_i}}, \frac{\alpha_i+1}{b^{d_i}}\right)$ under the mapping Φ_m, i.e.

$$\mathcal{V}_{d_1,\ldots,d_s}^{\alpha_1,\ldots,\alpha_s} = \left\{\mathbf{A} \in \mathbb{Z}_b^{sm} : \Phi_m(\mathbf{A}) \in \prod_{i=1}^s \left[\frac{\alpha_i}{b^{d_i}}, \frac{\alpha_i+1}{b^{d_i}}\right)\right\}.$$

If $\alpha_1 = \cdots = \alpha_s = 0$, we write $\mathcal{V}_{d_1,\ldots,d_s}$ instead of $\mathcal{V}_{d_1,\ldots,d_s}^{0,\ldots,0}$. Notice that $|\mathcal{V}_{d_1,\ldots,d_s}^{\alpha_1,\ldots,\alpha_s}| = b^{sm-d_1-\cdots-d_s}$.

The proof of the subsequent lemma is left as an exercise (see Exercise 16.3).

Lemma 16.10 *Let $0 \le d_1, \ldots, d_s \le m$ be integers and let $\alpha_1, \ldots, \alpha_s \in \mathbb{N}_0$ with $0 \le \alpha_i < b^{d_i}$ for all $1 \le i \le s$. Then $\mathcal{V}_{d_1,\ldots,d_s}$ is a linear subspace of $\mathbb{Z}_b^{sm}$. Furthermore, we can write*

$$\mathcal{V}_{d_1,\ldots,d_s}^{\alpha_1,\ldots,\alpha_s} = \mathcal{V}_{d_1,\ldots,d_s} + \mathbf{B}_{d_1,\ldots,d_s}^{\alpha_1,\ldots,\alpha_s}$$

with a vector $\mathbf{B}_{d_1,\ldots,d_s}^{\alpha_1,\ldots,\alpha_s} \in \mathbb{Z}_b^{sm}$ which is uniquely defined up to translations in $\mathcal{V}_{d_1,\ldots,d_s}$ and hence, $\mathcal{V}_{d_1,\ldots,d_s}^{\alpha_1,\ldots,\alpha_s}$ is an affine subspace of $\mathbb{Z}_b^{sm}$.

Lemma 16.11 *Let $0 \le d_1, \ldots, d_s \le m$ be integers and let $d_i^* = m - d_i$ for all $1 \le i \le s$. Then we have $\mathcal{V}_{d_1,\ldots,d_s}^{\perp} = R_s \mathcal{V}_{d_1^*,\ldots,d_s^*}$.*

For the characteristic functions $\chi_{\mathcal{V}_{d_1,\ldots,d_s}}$ and $\chi_{R_s \mathcal{V}_{d_1^*,\ldots,d_s^*}}$ of the sets $\mathcal{V}_{d_1,\ldots,d_s}$ and $R_s \mathcal{V}_{d_1^*,\ldots,d_s^*}$, respectively, we have the relation

$$\widehat{\chi}_{\mathcal{V}_{d_1,\ldots,d_s}}(\mathbf{B}) = b^{sm-d_1-\cdots-d_s} \chi_{R_s \mathcal{V}_{d_1^*,\ldots,d_s^*}}(\mathbf{B}) \quad \text{for all } \mathbf{B} \in \mathbb{Z}_b^{sm}.$$

Proof For each point $\mathbf{A} = (\mathbf{a}_1, \ldots, \mathbf{a}_s) \in \mathcal{V}_{d_1,\ldots,d_s}$, we have

$$\mathbf{a}_i = (\underbrace{0, \ldots, 0}_{d_i \text{ components}}, a_{i,d_i+1}, \ldots, a_{i,m})$$

for all $1 \le i \le s$. Hence, $\mathcal{V}_{d_1^*,\ldots,d_s^*}$ consists of points $\mathbf{B} = (\mathbf{b}_1, \ldots, \mathbf{b}_s)$ of the form

$$\mathbf{b}_i = (\underbrace{0, \ldots, 0}_{m-d_i \text{ components}}, b_{i,m-d_i+1}, \ldots, b_{i,m})$$

for all $1 \le i \le s$. Since $m - d_i = d_i^*$, the first result follows.

We have, further,

$$\begin{aligned}\widehat{\chi}_{\mathcal{V}_{d_1,\ldots,d_s}}(\mathbf{B}) &= \sum_{\mathbf{A} \in \mathbb{Z}_b^{sm}} \omega_b^{\mathbf{B}\cdot\mathbf{A}} \chi_{\mathcal{V}_{d_1,\ldots,d_s}}(\mathbf{A}) \\ &= \sum_{\mathbf{A} \in \mathcal{V}_{d_1,\ldots,d_s}} \omega_b^{\mathbf{B}\cdot\mathbf{A}} = |\mathcal{V}_{d_1,\ldots,d_s}| \chi_{R_s \mathcal{V}_{d_1^*,\ldots,d_s^*}}(\mathbf{B}),\end{aligned}$$

where we have used (16.3). The result follows from the fact that $|\mathcal{V}_{d_1,\ldots,d_s}| = b^{sm-d_1-\cdots-d_s}$. □

Lemma 16.12 *Let $\mathcal{C}$ and $\mathcal{C}^{\perp}$ be mutually dual $\mathbb{Z}_b$-linear subspaces of $\mathbb{Z}_b^{sm}$. Then, for every set $\mathcal{V}_{d_1,\ldots,d_s}^{\alpha_1,\ldots,\alpha_s}$, we have*

$$|\mathcal{C} \cap \mathcal{V}_{d_1,\ldots,d_s}^{\alpha_1,\ldots,\alpha_s}| = \frac{|\mathcal{C}|}{b^{d_1+\cdots+d_s}} \sum_{\mathbf{B} \in \mathcal{C}^{\perp}} \omega_b^{\mathbf{B}\cdot\mathbf{B}_{d_1,\ldots,d_s}^{\alpha_1,\ldots,\alpha_s}} \chi_{R_s \mathcal{V}_{d_1^*,\ldots,d_s^*}}(\mathbf{B}).$$

Proof Using Lemma 16.9, we have

$$|\mathcal{C} \cap \mathcal{V}_{d_1,\ldots,d_s}^{\alpha_1,\ldots,\alpha_s}| = \sum_{\mathbf{A} \in \mathcal{C}} \chi_{\mathcal{V}_{d_1,\ldots,d_s}^{\alpha_1,\ldots,\alpha_s}}(\mathbf{A}) = \frac{|\mathcal{C}|}{b^{sm}} \sum_{\mathbf{B} \in \mathcal{C}^{\perp}} \widehat{\chi}_{\mathcal{V}_{d_1,\ldots,d_s}^{\alpha_1,\ldots,\alpha_s}}(\mathbf{B}). \tag{16.4}$$

From Lemma 16.10, it follows that $\chi_{\mathcal{V}^{\alpha_1,\ldots,\alpha_s}_{d_1,\ldots,d_s}}(\mathbf{A}) = \chi_{\mathcal{V}_{d_1,\ldots,d_s}}(\mathbf{A} - \mathbf{B}^{\alpha_1,\ldots,\alpha_s}_{d_1,\ldots,d_s})$ and hence, we have

$$\begin{aligned}
\widehat{\chi}_{\mathcal{V}^{\alpha_1,\ldots,\alpha_s}_{d_1,\ldots,d_s}}(\mathbf{B}) &= \sum_{\mathbf{A}\in\mathbb{Z}_b^{sm}} \omega_b^{\mathbf{B}\cdot\mathbf{A}} \chi_{\mathcal{V}_{d_1,\ldots,d_s}}(\mathbf{A} - \mathbf{B}^{\alpha_1,\ldots,\alpha_s}_{d_1,\ldots,d_s}) \\
&= \sum_{\mathbf{A}\in\mathbb{Z}_b^{sm}} \omega_b^{\mathbf{B}\cdot(\mathbf{A}+\mathbf{B}^{\alpha_1,\ldots,\alpha_s}_{d_1,\ldots,d_s})} \chi_{\mathcal{V}_{d_1,\ldots,d_s}}(\mathbf{A}) \\
&= \omega_b^{\mathbf{B}\cdot\mathbf{B}^{\alpha_1,\ldots,\alpha_s}_{d_1,\ldots,d_s}} \sum_{\mathbf{A}\in\mathbb{Z}_b^{sm}} \omega_b^{\mathbf{B}\cdot\mathbf{A}} \chi_{\mathcal{V}_{d_1,\ldots,d_s}}(\mathbf{A}) \\
&= \omega_b^{\mathbf{B}\cdot\mathbf{B}^{\alpha_1,\ldots,\alpha_s}_{d_1,\ldots,d_s}} \widehat{\chi}_{\mathcal{V}_{d_1,\ldots,d_s}}(\mathbf{B}) \\
&= \omega_b^{\mathbf{B}\cdot\mathbf{B}^{\alpha_1,\ldots,\alpha_s}_{d_1,\ldots,d_s}} b^{sm-d_1-\cdots-d_s} \chi_{R_s\mathcal{V}_{d_1^*,\ldots,d_s^*}}(\mathbf{B}),
\end{aligned}$$

where we used Lemma 16.11. The desired result follows by inserting this equality into (16.4). □

If $\alpha_1 = \cdots = \alpha_s = 0$, we can take $\mathbf{B}^{0,\ldots,0}_{d_1,\ldots,d_s} = \mathbf{0} \in \mathbb{Z}_b^{sm}$ and hence, we obtain the subsequent corollary.

Corollary 16.13 *Let $\mathcal{C}$ and $\mathcal{C}^\perp$ be mutually dual $\mathbb{Z}_b$-linear subspaces of $\mathbb{Z}_b^{sm}$. Then, for every integers $0 \le d_1, \ldots, d_s \le m$, we have*

$$|\mathcal{C} \cap \mathcal{V}_{d_1,\ldots,d_s}| = \frac{|\mathcal{C}|}{b^{d_1+\cdots+d_s}} |\mathcal{C}^\perp \cap R_s\mathcal{V}_{d_1^*,\ldots,d_s^*}|.$$

Lemma 16.14 *We have*

$$\{\mathbf{A} \in \mathbb{Z}_b^{sm} : V_m(\mathbf{A}) \le t\} = \bigcup_{\substack{d_1,\ldots,d_s=0 \\ d_1+\cdots+d_s\le t}}^{m} R_s\mathcal{V}_{d_1^*,\ldots,d_s^*},$$

where $d_i^* = m - d_i$ for all $1 \le i \le s$.

Proof We show the equivalent assertion

$$\{\mathbf{A} \in \mathbb{Z}_b^{sm} : V_m(R_s\mathbf{A}) \le t\} = \bigcup_{\substack{d_1,\ldots,d_s=0 \\ d_1+\cdots+d_s\le t}}^{m} \mathcal{V}_{d_1^*,\ldots,d_s^*},$$

where $d_i^* = m - d_i$ for all $1 \le i \le s$. Let $\mathbf{A} = (\mathbf{a}_1, \ldots, \mathbf{a}_s) \in \mathbb{Z}_b^{sm}$ with $V_m(R_s\mathbf{A}) \le t$. Then we find from Remark 16.6 that

$$\Phi_m(\mathbf{A}) \in \prod_{i=1}^{s} \left[0, \frac{1}{b^{d_i^*}}\right),$$

where $d_i^* = m - v_m(R\mathbf{a}_i) \le m$ for any $1 \le i \le s$. Hence, $d_1^* + \cdots + d_s^* = sm - V_m(R_s\mathbf{A}) \ge sm - t$ and further, $t \ge d_1 + \cdots + d_s$, where $d_i = m - d_i^*$ for $1 \le i \le s$. From this it follows that $\mathbf{A} \in \mathcal{V}_{d_1^*,\ldots,d_s^*}$ for some $d_1, \ldots, d_s \in \{0, \ldots, m\}$ with $d_1 + \cdots + d_s \le t$.

On the other hand, let $\mathbf{A} \in \mathcal{V}_{d_1^*,\ldots,d_s^*}$ with $d_1, \ldots, d_s \in \{0, \ldots, m\}$ and $d_1 + \cdots + d_s \le t$. Assume that $V_m(R_s\mathbf{A}) > t$. Using Remark 16.6, we obtain $d_i^* \le m - v_m(R\mathbf{a}_i)$ for all $1 \le i \le s$. Hence, $d_1^* + \cdots + d_s^* \le sm - V_m(R_s\mathbf{A}) < sm - t$ and further, $t < d_1 + \cdots + d_s \le t$, a contradiction. Thus, we must have $V_m(R_s\mathbf{A}) \le t$. □

The following lemma is a generalisation of Theorem 7.8 which can be obtained by choosing $d = m$.

Lemma 16.15 *Let $\mathcal{C}$ and $\mathcal{C}^\perp$ be mutually dual $\mathbb{Z}_b$-linear subspaces of $\mathbb{Z}_b^{sm}$ of dimensions d and $sm - d$, respectively and let $0 \le t \le d$ be an integer. Then each elementary interval in the class $\mathcal{E}_{m,b,s}$ of order $d - t$ contains exactly b^t points of $\Phi_m(\mathcal{C})$ if and only if we have $\delta_m(\mathcal{C}^\perp) \ge d - t + 1$.*

Proof Suppose that each elementary interval in the class $\mathcal{E}_{m,b,s}$ of order $d - t$ contains exactly b^t points of $\Phi_m(\mathcal{C})$. This means that for each $d_1, \ldots, d_s \in \{0, \ldots, m\}$ with $d_1 + \cdots + d_s \le d - t$ and any $\alpha_1, \ldots, \alpha_s$ with $0 \le \alpha_i < b^{d_i}$ for all $1 \le i \le s$, we have $|\mathcal{C} \cap \mathcal{V}_{d_1,\ldots,d_s}^{\alpha_1,\ldots,\alpha_s}| \le b^t$. Using Corollary 16.13, we obtain

$$b^t \ge |\mathcal{C} \cap \mathcal{V}_{d_1,\ldots,d_s}| = \frac{b^d}{b^{d_1+\cdots+d_s}} |\mathcal{C}^\perp \cap R_s\mathcal{V}_{d_1^*,\ldots,d_s^*}| \ge b^t |\mathcal{C}^\perp \cap R_s\mathcal{V}_{d_1^*,\ldots,d_s^*}|$$

with $d_1^* + \cdots + d_s^* \ge sm - d + t$. Therefore, we have $\mathcal{C}^\perp \cap R_s\mathcal{V}_{d_1^*,\ldots,d_s^*} = \{\mathbf{0}\}$ whenever $d_1 + \cdots + d_s \le d - t$. From Lemma 16.14, it follows then that the set

$$\{\mathbf{A} \in \mathbb{Z}_b^{sm} : V_m(\mathbf{A}) \le d - t\}$$

contains no point from $\mathcal{C}^\perp$ except the point $\mathbf{0}$. But this means that $\delta_m(\mathcal{C}^\perp) \ge d - t + 1$.

Now suppose that we have $\delta_m(\mathcal{C}^\perp) \ge d - t + 1$. Again from Lemma 16.14, we find that $\mathcal{C}^\perp \cap R_s\mathcal{V}_{d_1^*,\ldots,d_s^*}$ contains only the point $\mathbf{0}$ whenever $d_1^* + \cdots + d_s^* = sm - d + t$. For any $0 \le d_1, \ldots, d_s \le m$ with $d_1 + \cdots + d_s = d - t$ and any $0 \le \alpha_i < b^{d_i}$ for $1 \le i \le s$, we therefore obtain from Lemma 16.12,

$$\begin{aligned} |\mathcal{C} \cap \mathcal{V}_{d_1,\ldots,d_s}^{\alpha_1,\ldots,\alpha_s}| &= \frac{b^d}{b^{d-t}} \sum_{\mathbf{B} \in \mathcal{C}^\perp} \omega_b^{\mathbf{B}\cdot\mathbf{B}_{d_1,\ldots,d_s}^{\alpha_1,\ldots,\alpha_s}} \chi_{R_s\mathcal{V}_{d_1^*,\ldots,d_s^*}}(\mathbf{B}) \\ &= \frac{b^d}{b^{d-t}} \chi_{R_s\mathcal{V}_{d_1^*,\ldots,d_s^*}}(\mathbf{0}) = b^t. \end{aligned}$$

In other words, each elementary interval in the class $\mathcal{E}_{m,b,s}$ of order $d - t$ contains exactly b^t points of $\Phi_m(\mathcal{C})$. □

For later use we introduce a further notation, given in [22] as generalisation of [243, Definition 1.2], and we derive a consequence of Lemma 16.15.

Definition 16.16 Let $s \in \mathbb{N}$ and $m, k \in \mathbb{N}_0$ with $0 \le k \le s$. A set $\mathcal{P}$ consisting of b^{km} points in $[0,1)^s$ is called an *optimum* $[s,k,m]$*-distribution in base* b if every elementary interval in $\mathcal{E}_{m,b,s}$ of order km contains exactly one point of $\mathcal{P}$.

Every optimum $[s,k,m]$-distribution in base b is also a $((k-1)m, km, s)$-net in base b (see Exercise 16.2). In particular, for $k = 1$ we obtain that every optimum $[s,1,m]$-distribution in base b is a $(0,m,s)$-net in base b.

Lemma 16.17 *Let $\mathcal{C}$ be a subset of $\mathbb{Z}_b^{sm}$ consisting of b^{km} elements, where $1 \le k \le s$. Then $\Phi_m(R_s\mathcal{C})$ is an optimum $[s,k,m]$-distribution in base b if and only if $\delta_m(\mathcal{C}) = (s-k)m + 1$.*

Proof Suppose first that $\Phi_m(R_s\mathcal{C})$ is an optimum $[s,k,m]$-distribution in base b. Then, every elementary interval in $\mathcal{E}_{m,b,s}$ of order km contains exactly one point of $\Phi_m(R_s\mathcal{C})$. It follows from the second part of Lemma 16.8 that $\delta_m(\mathcal{C}) \ge (s-k)m + 1$. Since by Proposition 7.3 we must have $\delta_m(\mathcal{C}) \le (s-k)m + 1$, it follows that $\delta_m(\mathcal{C}) = (s-k)m + 1$.

On the other hand, assume that $\delta_m(\mathcal{C}) = (s-k)m + 1$. From the second part of Lemma 16.8, it follows that any elementary interval in $\mathcal{E}_{m,b,s}$ of order km contains, at most, one element of $\Phi_m(R_s\mathcal{C})$. For fixed $0 \le d_1, \ldots, d_s \le m$ with $d_1 + \cdots + d_s = km$, there are exactly b^{km} elementary intervals of the form $\prod_{i=1}^{s} \left[\frac{\alpha_i}{b^{d_i}}, \frac{\alpha_i+1}{b^{d_i}}\right)$ in $\mathcal{E}_{m,b,s}$ and these intervals form a partition of $[0,1)^s$. But $\mathcal{C}$ and hence, $\Phi_m(R_s\mathcal{C})$ also, contain exactly b^{km} elements and therefore, each of these elementary intervals contains exactly one point of $\Phi_m(R_s\mathcal{C})$. Thus, $\Phi_m(R_s\mathcal{C})$ is an optimum $[s,k,m]$-distribution in base b. □

Now we can prove the following corollary to Lemma 16.15. This result is used later in Section 16.4.

Corollary 16.18 *Let $\mathcal{C}$ and $\mathcal{C}^\perp$ be mutually dual $\mathbb{Z}_b$-linear subspaces of $\mathbb{Z}_b^{sm}$. Then $\Phi_m(\mathcal{C})$ is an optimum $[s,k,m]$-distribution in base b if and only if $\Phi_m(R_s\mathcal{C}^\perp)$ is an optimum $[s,s-k,m]$-distribution in base b.*

Proof From Lemma 16.15 with $d = km$ and $t = 0$, it follows that $\Phi_m(\mathcal{C})$ is an optimum $[s,k,m]$-distribution in base b if and only if $\delta_m(\mathcal{C}^\perp) \ge km + 1$. Invoking Proposition 7.3, we find that this is equivalent to $\delta_m(\mathcal{C}^\perp) = km + 1$.

By Lemma 16.17 this is equivalent to the fact that $\Phi_m(R_s\mathcal{C}^{\perp})$ is an optimum $[s, s-k, m]$ distribution in base b. □

Now we have collected all results from duality theory that are necessary for the proof of Theorem 16.3 and for the explicit construction of suitable $\mathbb{Z}_b$-linear subspaces of $\mathbb{Z}_b^{sm}$ in Section 16.4.

16.3 The proof of Theorem 16.3

We start with the consideration of the Walsh series expansion of the characteristic function of intervals and we approximate these Walsh series with truncated versions thereof. This leads to an approximation for the discrepancy function $\Delta_{\mathcal{P}}$. The error of this approximation is small whenever the NRT weight of the dual of the $\mathbb{Z}_b$-linear subspace $\mathcal{C}$ is large enough, or in view of Theorem 7.14, when the $\mathbb{Z}_b$-linear subspace $\mathcal{C}$ gives rise to a (t, m, s)-net over $\mathbb{Z}_b$ with small t.

In detail, we consider the Walsh series expansion of the characteristic function $\chi_{[0,y)}$ of the interval $[0, y)$ of the form

$$\chi_{[0,y)}(x) = \sum_{k=0}^{\infty} \widehat{\chi}_{[0,y)}(k)\, {}_b\mathrm{wal}_k(x),$$

where, for $k \in \mathbb{N}_0$, the kth Walsh coefficient is given by

$$\widehat{\chi}_{[0,y)}(k) = \int_0^1 \chi_{[0,y)}(x)\, \overline{{}_b\mathrm{wal}_k(x)}\, \mathrm{d}x = \int_0^y \overline{{}_b\mathrm{wal}_k(x)}\, \mathrm{d}x.$$

For given $m \in \mathbb{N}_0$, we approximate $\chi_{[0,y)}$ by the truncated series

$$\chi_{[0,y)}^{(m)}(x) = \sum_{k=0}^{b^m-1} \widehat{\chi}_{[0,y)}(k)\, {}_b\mathrm{wal}_k(x).$$

Note that $\chi_{[0,y)}^{(m)}$ is a Walsh polynomial and hence a piecewise constant function. The subsequent lemma gives the error of the approximation of $\chi_{[0,y)}$.

Lemma 16.19 *For any $m \in \mathbb{N}$, we have*

$$\chi_{[0,y)}(x) = \chi_{[0,y)}^{(m)}(x) + r_y^{(m)}(x),$$

where

$$0 \le \chi_{[0,y)}^{(m)}(x) \le 1 \quad \textit{and} \quad 0 \le |r_y^{(m)}(x)| \le \chi_{B_m(y)}(x).$$

Here, for $y \in [0, 1)$, we denote by $B_m(y) = \left[\frac{a}{b^m}, \frac{a+1}{b^m}\right)$ the unique elementary interval of order m containing y.

Proof Note first that we can write

$$\chi^{(m)}_{[0,y)}(x) = b^m \int_{B_m(x)} \chi_{[0,y)}(t)\,\mathrm{d}t. \tag{16.5}$$

The proof of this fact is left to the reader as an exercise (see Exercise 16.4). From (16.5), we obtain immediately that $0 \le \chi^{(m)}_{[0,y)}(x) \le 1$.

Write $r_y^{(m)}(x) = \chi_{[0,y)}(x) - \chi^{(m)}_{[0,y)}(x)$ and let $B_m(y) = \left[\frac{a}{b^m}, \frac{a+1}{b^m}\right)$. Then we consider three cases:

1. If $x < ab^{-m}$, then we have $\chi_{[0,y)}(x) = 1$ and $\chi^{(m)}_{[0,y)}(x) = 1$ and hence, $r_y^{(m)}(x) = 0 = \chi_{B_m(y)}(x)$.
2. If $x \ge (a+1)b^{-m}$, then we have $\chi_{[0,y)}(x) = 0$ and $\chi^{(m)}_{[0,y)}(x) = 0$ and hence, $r_y^{(m)}(x) = 0 = \chi_{B_m(y)}(x)$.
3. If $ab^{-m} \le x < (a+1)b^{-m}$. Then we have $B_m(y) = B_m(x)$ and

$$\chi^{(m)}_{[0,y)}(x) = b^m \int_{B_m(x)} \chi_{[0,y)}(t)\,\mathrm{d}t = b^m y - a.$$

If $x < y$, then we have $r_y^{(m)}(x) = 1 - b^m y + a$ and hence,

$$0 = 1 - b^m \frac{a+1}{b^m} + a < r_y^{(m)}(x) \le 1 - b^m \frac{a}{b^m} + a = 1 = \chi_{B_m(y)}(x).$$

If $x \ge y$, then we have $r_y^{(m)}(x) = a - b^m y$ and we get

$$0 = a - b^m \frac{a}{b^m} \ge r_y^{(m)}(x) > a - b^m \frac{a+1}{b^m} = -1 = -\chi_{B_m(y)}(x).$$

In any case we have $0 \le |r_y^{(m)}(x)| \le \chi_{B_m(y)}(x)$ and we are done. □

Next, we transfer these results to the higher dimensional case. For $\boldsymbol{y} = (y_1, \ldots, y_s)$, we approximate the characteristic function $\chi_{[\boldsymbol{0},\boldsymbol{y})} = \prod_{i=1}^s \chi_{[0,y_i)}$ of the s-dimensional interval $[\boldsymbol{0}, \boldsymbol{y})$ by the product

$$\chi^{(m)}_{[\boldsymbol{0},\boldsymbol{y})}(\boldsymbol{x}) = \prod_{i=1}^{s} \chi^{(m)}_{[0,y_i)}(x_i) \quad \text{where} \quad \boldsymbol{x} = (x_1, \ldots, x_s).$$

Lemma 16.20 *For any $\boldsymbol{y} = (y_1, \ldots, y_s)$ and $\boldsymbol{x} = (x_1, \ldots, x_s)$ in $[0,1)^s$ and any $m \in \mathbb{N}$, we have*

$$\chi_{[\boldsymbol{0},\boldsymbol{y})}(\boldsymbol{x}) = \chi^{(m)}_{[\boldsymbol{0},\boldsymbol{y})}(\boldsymbol{x}) + \sum_{i=1}^{s} r_{\boldsymbol{y}}^{(i,m)}(\boldsymbol{x}),$$

with

$$0 \le |r_{\boldsymbol{y}}^{(i,m)}(\boldsymbol{x})| \le \chi_{B_m(y_i)}(x_i).$$

Proof The lemma is shown by induction on the dimension s. The instance $s = 1$ is clear by Lemma 16.19. Now assume that the result holds true for a particular value of s. For $\boldsymbol{x} = (x_1, \ldots, x_s)$ and $\boldsymbol{y} = (y_1, \ldots, y_s)$ in $[0, 1)^s$, we write $(\boldsymbol{x}, x_{s+1}) = (x_1, \ldots, x_s, x_{s+1})$ and $(\boldsymbol{y}, y_{s+1}) = (y_1, \ldots, y_s, y_{s+1})$. Then $(\boldsymbol{x}, x_{s+1})$ and $(\boldsymbol{y}, y_{s+1})$ are contained in $[0, 1)^{s+1}$ and we have

$$\begin{aligned}
\chi_{[\mathbf{0},(\boldsymbol{y},y_{s+1}))}((\boldsymbol{x}, x_{s+1})) &= \chi_{[\mathbf{0},\boldsymbol{y})}(\boldsymbol{x})\chi_{[0,y_{s+1})}(x_{s+1}) \\
&= \left(\chi^{(m)}_{[\mathbf{0},\boldsymbol{y})}(\boldsymbol{x}) + \sum_{i=1}^{s} r^{(i,m)}_{\boldsymbol{y}}(\boldsymbol{x})\right)\chi_{[0,y_{s+1})}(x_{s+1}) \\
&= \chi^{(m)}_{[\mathbf{0},\boldsymbol{y})}(\boldsymbol{x})\chi_{[0,y_{s+1})}(x_{s+1}) + \sum_{i=1}^{s} r^{(i,m)}_{\boldsymbol{y}}(\boldsymbol{x})\chi_{[0,y_{s+1})}(x_{s+1}) \\
&= \chi^{(m)}_{[\mathbf{0},\boldsymbol{y})}(\boldsymbol{x})\chi^{(m)}_{[0,y_{s+1})}(x_{s+1}) + \chi^{(m)}_{[\mathbf{0},\boldsymbol{y})}(\boldsymbol{x})r^{(m)}_{y_{s+1}}(x_{s+1}) \\
&\quad + \sum_{i=1}^{s} r^{(i,m)}_{\boldsymbol{y}}(\boldsymbol{x})\chi_{[0,y_{s+1})}(x_{s+1}) \\
&= \chi^{(m)}_{[\mathbf{0},(\boldsymbol{y},y_{s+1}))}((\boldsymbol{x}, x_{s+1})) + \sum_{i=1}^{s+1} r^{(i,m)}_{(\boldsymbol{y},y_{s+1})}((\boldsymbol{x}, x_{s+1})),
\end{aligned}$$

where

$$r^{(s+1,m)}_{(\boldsymbol{y},y_{s+1})}((\boldsymbol{x}, x_{s+1})) = \chi^{(m)}_{[\mathbf{0},\boldsymbol{y})}(\boldsymbol{x})r^{(m)}_{y_{s+1}}(x_{s+1}),$$

and for $1 \le i \le s$,

$$r^{(i,m)}_{(\boldsymbol{y},y_{s+1})}((\boldsymbol{x}, x_{s+1})) = r^{(i,m)}_{\boldsymbol{y}}(\boldsymbol{x})\chi_{[0,y_{s+1})}(x_{s+1}).$$

From the induction hypothesis, we conclude that $0 \le |r^{(i,m)}_{(\boldsymbol{y},y_{s+1})}((\boldsymbol{x}, x_{s+1}))| \le \chi_{B_m(y_i)}(x_i)$ for any $1 \le i \le s$ and from Lemma 16.19, we obtain $0 \le |r^{(s+1,m)}_{(\boldsymbol{y},y_{s+1})}((\boldsymbol{x}, x_{s+1}))| \le \chi_{B_m(y_{s+1})}(x_{s+1})$. □

Now we use the approximation for the characteristic function as introduced above to define an approximation for the discrepancy function of a point set. For a point set $\mathcal{P} = \{\boldsymbol{x}_0, \ldots, \boldsymbol{x}_{N-1}\}$ in $[0, 1)^s$, define

$$\Theta_{\mathcal{P}}(\boldsymbol{y}) := \frac{1}{N}\sum_{n=0}^{N-1} \chi^{(m)}_{[\mathbf{0},\boldsymbol{y})}(\boldsymbol{x}_n) - \lambda_s([\mathbf{0}, \boldsymbol{y})).$$

The function $\Theta_{\mathcal{P}}$ is used as an approximation of the discrepancy function $\Delta_{\mathcal{P}}$ of the point set $\mathcal{P}$. In the following lemma, we give a bound on the approximation error when the point set $\mathcal{P}$ comes from a $\mathbb{Z}_b$-linear subspace such that the NRT weight of its dual space is large enough.

Lemma 16.21 *Let $\mathcal{C} \subseteq \mathbb{Z}_b^{sm}$ be a $\mathbb{Z}_b$-linear subspace of dimension m with dual space $\mathcal{C}^\perp$ satisfying $\delta_m(\mathcal{C}^\perp) \geq m - t + 1$. Let $\mathcal{P} = \Phi_m(\mathcal{C})$ be the corresponding digital (t, m, s)-net over $\mathbb{Z}_b$. Then, for every $\boldsymbol{y} \in [0, 1]^s$, we have*

$$|\Delta_{\mathcal{P}}(\boldsymbol{y}) - \Theta_{\mathcal{P}}(\boldsymbol{y})| \leq sb^{t-m}.$$

Proof For $\boldsymbol{y} \in [0, 1]^s$, we obtain from Lemma 16.20 that

$$\Delta_{\mathcal{P}}(\boldsymbol{y}) = \Theta_{\mathcal{P}}(\boldsymbol{y}) + \frac{1}{b^m} \sum_{i=1}^{s} \sum_{\boldsymbol{x} \in \mathcal{P}} r_{\boldsymbol{y}}^{(i,m)}(\boldsymbol{x})$$

with

$$0 \leq \sum_{\boldsymbol{x} \in \mathcal{P}} |r_{\boldsymbol{y}}^{(i,m)}(\boldsymbol{x})| \leq \sum_{\boldsymbol{x} \in \mathcal{P}} \chi_{B_m(y_i)}(x_i) = A(J_{\boldsymbol{y}}^{(i,m)}, b^m, \mathcal{P}),$$

where $J_{\boldsymbol{y}}^{(i,m)} = [0, 1)^{i-1} \times B_m(y_i) \times [0, 1)^{s-i}$. Clearly, $J_{\boldsymbol{y}}^{(i,m)}$ is an elementary interval of order m which in turn is contained in an elementary interval J of order $m - t$. By Theorem 7.14, the point set $\mathcal{P}$ is a digital (t, m, s)-net over $\mathbb{Z}_b$ and hence, J contains exactly b^t points from $\mathcal{P}$. Therefore, we have

$$A(J_{\boldsymbol{y}}^{(i,m)}, b^m, \mathcal{P}) \leq A(J, b^m, \mathcal{P}) = b^t$$

and the result follows. □

In the following, we investigate the approximation $\Theta_{\mathcal{P}}$ for the discrepancy function $\Delta_{\mathcal{P}}$ in more detail. If the dual space $\mathcal{C}^\perp$ of the $\mathbb{Z}_b$-linear subspace $\mathcal{C} = \Phi_m^{-1}(\mathcal{P})$ satisfies certain conditions, then we can show a representation of the mean square of $\Theta_{\mathcal{P}}$ in terms of the mean square of the Walsh coefficients of characteristic functions of intervals anchored in zero. This is the assertion of the subsequent Lemma 16.22. The key point, then, is that these conditions on the dual distribution $\mathcal{C}^\perp$ are satisfied whenever the Hamming weight $\varkappa_m$ of $\mathcal{C}^\perp$ is large enough. Good bounds on the mean square of the characteristic functions of intervals anchored in zero then lead to the assertion of Theorem 16.3.

Define the one-to-one mapping $\tau_m : \{0, \ldots, b^m - 1\} \to \mathbb{Z}_b^m$, $k = \kappa_0 + \kappa_1 b + \cdots + \kappa_{m-1} b^{m-1} \mapsto (\kappa_0, \ldots, \kappa_{m-1}) =: \mathbf{k}^\top$. For vectors $\boldsymbol{k} = (k_1, \ldots, k_s) \in \{0, \ldots, b^m - 1\}^s$, the mapping τ_m is defined componentwise.

Let $\mathcal{C}$ be a $\mathbb{Z}_b$-linear subspace of $\mathbb{Z}_b^{sm}$ of dimension m, let $\mathcal{C}^\perp$ denote its dual space and let $\mathcal{P} = \Phi_m(\mathcal{C})$ denote the corresponding digital (t, m, s)-net over $\mathbb{Z}_b$ with generating matrices $C_1, \ldots, C_s$. Using the above notation, we have

$$\begin{aligned} \mathcal{C}^\perp &= \{\mathbf{A} \in \mathbb{Z}_b^{sm} : C\mathbf{A}^\top = \mathbf{0}\} \\ &= \tau_m(\{\boldsymbol{k} \in \{0, \ldots, b^m - 1\}^s : C_1^\top \mathbf{k}_1 + \cdots + C_s^\top \mathbf{k}_s = \mathbf{0}\}) \\ &= \tau_m(\mathcal{D}(C_1, \ldots, C_s)), \end{aligned} \tag{16.6}$$

where $\mathcal{D}(C_1, \ldots, C_s)$ is the dual net as defined in Definition 4.76. Hence, $\tau_m^{-1}(\mathcal{C}^\perp) = \mathcal{D}(C_1, \ldots, C_s)$. Recall the definition $\mathcal{D}' = \mathcal{D} \setminus \{\mathbf{0}\}$.

Lemma 16.22 *Let $\mathcal{C}$ be a $\mathbb{Z}_b$-linear subspace of $\mathbb{Z}_b^{sm}$ of dimension m, let $\mathcal{C}^\perp$ denote its dual space and let $\mathcal{P} = \Phi_m(\mathcal{C})$ denote the corresponding digital (t, m, s)-net over $\mathbb{Z}_b$ with generating matrices $C_1, \ldots, C_s$. Assume that for any distinct $\boldsymbol{k}, \boldsymbol{k}' \in \mathcal{D}'(C_1, \ldots, C_s)$, the functions $\widehat{\chi}_{[\mathbf{0},\boldsymbol{y})}(\boldsymbol{k})$ and $\widehat{\chi}_{[\mathbf{0},\boldsymbol{y})}(\boldsymbol{k}')$ are mutually orthogonal. Then we have*

$$\int_{[0,1]^s} |\Theta_{\mathcal{P}}(\boldsymbol{y})|^2 \,\mathrm{d}\boldsymbol{y} = \sum_{\boldsymbol{k} \in \mathcal{D}'(C_1,\ldots,C_s)} \int_{[0,1]^s} \left|\widehat{\chi}_{[\mathbf{0},\boldsymbol{y})}(\boldsymbol{k})\right|^2 \mathrm{d}\boldsymbol{y}.$$

Proof For $\boldsymbol{k} = (k_1, \ldots, k_s) \in \mathbb{N}_0^s$ and $\boldsymbol{y} = (y_1, \ldots, y_s) \in [0, 1]^s$, we have

$$\widehat{\chi}_{[\mathbf{0},\boldsymbol{y})}(\boldsymbol{k}) = \widehat{\chi}_{[0,y_1)}(k_1) \cdots \widehat{\chi}_{[0,y_s)}(k_s).$$

Then we have

$$\begin{aligned}
\Theta_{\mathcal{P}}(\boldsymbol{y}) &= \frac{1}{b^m} \sum_{\boldsymbol{x} \in \mathcal{P}} \sum_{k_1,\ldots,k_s=0}^{b^m-1} \widehat{\chi}_{[\mathbf{0},\boldsymbol{y})}(\boldsymbol{k}) \,{}_b\mathrm{wal}_{\boldsymbol{k}}(\boldsymbol{x}) - \widehat{\chi}_{[\mathbf{0},\boldsymbol{y})}(\mathbf{0}) \\
&= \sum_{\substack{k_1,\ldots,k_s=0 \\ (k_1,\ldots,k_s)\neq 0}}^{b^m-1} \widehat{\chi}_{[\mathbf{0},\boldsymbol{y})}(\boldsymbol{k}) \frac{1}{b^m} \sum_{\boldsymbol{x} \in \mathcal{P}} {}_b\mathrm{wal}_{\boldsymbol{k}}(\boldsymbol{x}) \\
&= \sum_{\boldsymbol{k} \in \mathcal{D}'(C_1,\ldots,C_s)} \widehat{\chi}_{[\mathbf{0},\boldsymbol{y})}(\boldsymbol{k}),
\end{aligned}$$

where for the last identity, we used Lemma 4.75. Then we have

$$\begin{aligned}
\int_{[0,1]^s} |\Theta_{\mathcal{P}}(\boldsymbol{y})|^2 \,\mathrm{d}\boldsymbol{y} &= \int_{[0,1]^s} \sum_{\boldsymbol{k},\boldsymbol{k}' \in \mathcal{D}'(C_1,\ldots,C_s)} \overline{\widehat{\chi}_{[\mathbf{0},\boldsymbol{y})}(\boldsymbol{k})} \widehat{\chi}_{[\mathbf{0},\boldsymbol{y})}(\boldsymbol{k}') \,\mathrm{d}\boldsymbol{y} \\
&= \sum_{\boldsymbol{k},\boldsymbol{k}' \in \mathcal{D}'(C_1,\ldots,C_s)} \int_{[0,1]^s} \overline{\widehat{\chi}_{[\mathbf{0},\boldsymbol{y})}(\boldsymbol{k})} \widehat{\chi}_{[\mathbf{0},\boldsymbol{y})}(\boldsymbol{k}') \,\mathrm{d}\boldsymbol{y}.
\end{aligned}$$

Now the result follows from the orthogonality of $\widehat{\chi}_{[\mathbf{0},\boldsymbol{y})}(\boldsymbol{k})$ and $\widehat{\chi}_{[\mathbf{0},\boldsymbol{y})}(\boldsymbol{k}')$, i.e.

$$\int_{[0,1]^s} \overline{\widehat{\chi}_{[\mathbf{0},\boldsymbol{y})}(\boldsymbol{k})} \widehat{\chi}_{[\mathbf{0},\boldsymbol{y})}(\boldsymbol{k}') \,\mathrm{d}\boldsymbol{y} = 0$$

whenever $\boldsymbol{k} \neq \boldsymbol{k}'$. □

Now we are going to provide bounds on the mean square of the Walsh coefficients of the characteristic function of intervals anchored in zero. First, we prove exact formulae for the one-dimensional case that then lead to good estimates for the case of arbitrary dimensions.

Lemma 16.23 *We have*

$$\int_0^1 \left|\widehat{\chi}_{[0,y)}(0)\right|^2 \,\mathrm{d}y = \frac{1}{3}$$

and for any non-zero integer $k = \kappa_0 + \kappa_1 b + \cdots + \kappa_{a-1} b^{a-1}$ *with* $\kappa_i \in \mathbb{Z}_b$ *for all* $0 \le i < a$ *and* $\kappa_{a-1} \neq 0$, *we have*

$$\int_0^1 \left|\widehat{\chi}_{[0,y)}(k)\right|^2 \,\mathrm{d}y = \frac{1}{b^{2a}} \left(\frac{1}{2\sin^2(\pi \kappa_{a-1}/b)} - \frac{1}{6} \right).$$

Proof By Lemma A.22, we have

$$\widehat{\chi}_{[0,y)}(0) = y = \frac{1}{2} + \sum_{c=1}^{\infty} \sum_{\kappa=1}^{b-1} \frac{1}{b^c \left(\omega_b^{-\kappa} - 1\right)} \, {}_b\mathrm{wal}_{\kappa b^{c-1}}(y). \tag{16.7}$$

Hence,

$$\begin{aligned}
\left|\widehat{\chi}_{[0,y)}(0)\right|^2 &= \frac{1}{4} + \frac{1}{2} \sum_{c=1}^{\infty} \sum_{\kappa=1}^{b-1} \frac{1}{b^c \left(\omega_b^{-\kappa} - 1\right)} \, {}_b\mathrm{wal}_{\kappa b^{c-1}}(y) \\
&\quad + \frac{1}{2} \sum_{c=1}^{\infty} \sum_{\kappa=1}^{b-1} \frac{1}{b^c \left(\omega_b^{\kappa} - 1\right)} \, \overline{{}_b\mathrm{wal}_{\kappa b^{c-1}}(y)} \\
&\quad + \sum_{c=1}^{\infty} \sum_{\kappa=1}^{b-1} \sum_{c'=1}^{\infty} \sum_{\kappa'=1}^{b-1} \frac{1}{b^c \left(\omega_b^{-\kappa} - 1\right)} \, {}_b\mathrm{wal}_{\kappa b^{c-1}}(y) \frac{1}{b^{c'} \left(\omega_b^{\kappa} - 1\right)} \, \overline{{}_b\mathrm{wal}_{\kappa b^{c'-1}}(y)}.
\end{aligned}$$

Integration with respect to y and invoking Proposition A.9, Proposition A.10 and Corollary A.23, we obtain

$$\begin{aligned}
\int_0^1 \left|\widehat{\chi}_{[0,y)}(0)\right|^2 \,\mathrm{d}y &= \frac{1}{4} + \sum_{c=1}^{\infty} \sum_{\kappa=1}^{b-1} \frac{1}{b^{2c} \left|\omega_b^{\kappa} - 1\right|^2} \\
&= \frac{1}{4} + \frac{1}{4(b^2-1)} \sum_{\kappa=1}^{b-1} \frac{1}{\sin^2(\pi\kappa/b)} \\
&= \frac{1}{4} + \frac{1}{4(b^2-1)} \frac{b^2-1}{3} = \frac{1}{3}.
\end{aligned}$$

Now let $k = \kappa_0 + \kappa_1 b + \cdots + \kappa_{a-1} b^{a-1}$ with $\kappa_i \in \mathbb{Z}_b$ for all $0 \le i < a$ and $\kappa_{a-1} \neq 0$. Define $k' = k - \kappa_{a-1} b^{a-1}$. From Lemma 14.8, we know that

$$\widehat{\chi}_{[0,y)}(k) = \frac{1}{b^a}\Bigg(\sum_{z=0}^{b-1} c_z \overline{{}_b\mathrm{wal}_{zb^{a-1}+k'}(y)} + \frac{1}{2}\overline{{}_b\mathrm{wal}_k(y)}$$

$$+ \sum_{c=1}^{\infty}\sum_{\kappa=1}^{b-1} \frac{1}{b^c(\omega_b^{\kappa}-1)}\overline{{}_b\mathrm{wal}_{\kappa b^{a+c-1}+k}(y)}\Bigg), \tag{16.8}$$

where $c_0 = (1-\omega_b^{-\kappa_{a-1}})^{-1}$, $c_{\kappa_{a-1}} = (\omega_b^{-\kappa_{a-1}} - 1)^{-1}$ and $c_z = 0$ for $z \neq 0$ or $z \neq \kappa_{a-1}$. Using Proposition A.9 and Proposition A.10 again, we obtain

$$\int_0^1 \left|\widehat{\chi}_{[0,y)}(k)\right|^2 \,\mathrm{d}y = \int_0^1 \widehat{\chi}_{[0,y)}(k)\overline{\widehat{\chi}_{[0,y)}(k)}\,\mathrm{d}y$$

$$= \frac{1}{b^{2a}}\left(\sum_{z=0}^{b-1}|c_z|^2 + \frac{c_{\kappa_{a-1}} + \overline{c_{\kappa_{a-1}}}}{2} + \frac{1}{4} + \sum_{c=1}^{\infty}\sum_{\kappa=1}^{b-1}\frac{1}{b^{2c}|\omega_b^{\kappa}-1|^2}\right).$$

We have

$$\sum_{z=0}^{b-1}|c_z|^2 = \frac{1}{2\sin^2(\pi\kappa_{a-1}/b)} \quad \text{and} \quad \frac{c_{\kappa_{a-1}} + \overline{c_{\kappa_{a-1}}}}{2} = -\frac{1}{2}.$$

Hence, again with Corollary A.23,

$$\int_0^1 \left|\widehat{\chi}_{[0,y)}(k)\right|^2 \,\mathrm{d}y$$

$$= \frac{1}{b^{2a}}\left(\frac{1}{2\sin^2(\pi\kappa_{a-1}/b)} - \frac{1}{4} + \frac{1}{4(b^2-1)}\sum_{\kappa=1}^{b-1}\frac{1}{\sin^2(\pi\kappa/b)}\right)$$

$$= \frac{1}{b^{2a}}\left(\frac{1}{2\sin^2(\pi\kappa_{a-1}/b)} - \frac{1}{6}\right).$$

□

For convenience, we introduce the Hamming weight and the NRT weight also for non-negative integers.

Definition 16.24 For $k \in \mathbb{N}$ with b-adic expansion $k = \kappa_0 + \kappa_1 b + \cdots + \kappa_{a-1} b^{a-1}$ where $\kappa_{a-1} \neq 0$, we define the *NRT weight* by $\rho(k) = a$. Furthermore, we define $\rho(0) = 0$. The *Hamming weight* $\varkappa(k)$ of k is the number of non-zero digits κ_i. For $\boldsymbol{k} = (k_1, \ldots, k_s) \in \mathbb{N}_0^s$, let $\rho(\boldsymbol{k}) = \sum_{i=1}^{s} \rho(k_i)$ and $\varkappa(\boldsymbol{k}) = \sum_{i=1}^{s} \varkappa(k_i)$.

We clearly have $\rho(k) = 0$ if and only if $k = 0$ and also, the triangle inequality holds true. Hence, ρ defines a norm on $\mathbb{N}_0$. The same is true for the Hamming weight.

Note that the norms ρ and $\varkappa$ on $\mathbb{N}_0$ defined above are intimately related to the NRT weight and the Hamming weight defined in Definition 7.1 and Definition 16.1, respectively. In fact, if $k \in \{0, \ldots, b^m - 1\}$ with b-adic expansion $k = \kappa_0 + \kappa_1 b + \cdots + \kappa_{a-1} b^{a-1}$ where $\kappa_{a-1} \neq 0$, then we have

$$\rho(k) = v_m(\tau_m(k)) \quad \text{and} \quad \varkappa(k) = \varkappa_m(\tau_m(k)).$$

Lemma 16.25 *For every $\boldsymbol{k} \in \mathbb{N}_0^s$, we have*

$$\int_{[0,1]^s} \left|\widehat{\chi}_{[\boldsymbol{0},\boldsymbol{y})}(\boldsymbol{k})\right|^2 \, \mathrm{d}\boldsymbol{y} \leq \frac{b^{2s-2\rho(\boldsymbol{k})}}{8^s}.$$

Proof It suffices to show that the result holds in dimension $s = 1$, i.e. for every $k \in \mathbb{N}_0$, we have

$$\int_0^1 \left|\widehat{\chi}_{[0,y)}(k)\right|^2 \, \mathrm{d}y \leq \frac{b^{2-2\rho(k)}}{8}.$$

Assume that $k \neq 0$. For every $\kappa \in \{1, \ldots, b-1\}$, we have $\sin^{-2}(\pi\kappa/b) \leq b^2/4$ and from Lemma 16.23, we obtain

$$\int_0^1 \left|\widehat{\chi}_{[0,y)}(k)\right|^2 \, \mathrm{d}y \leq \frac{1}{b^{2\rho(k)}} \left(\frac{b^2}{8} - \frac{1}{6}\right) \leq \frac{b^{2-2\rho(k)}}{8}.$$

For $k = 0$ (note that $\rho(0) = 0$), we have from Lemma 16.23

$$\int_0^1 \left|\widehat{\chi}_{[0,y)}(0)\right|^2 \, \mathrm{d}y = \frac{1}{3} \leq \frac{b^2}{8}.$$

□

Lemma 16.26 *Let $\mathcal{C}$ be a $\mathbb{Z}_b$-linear subspace of $\mathbb{Z}_b^{sm}$ of dimension m. Suppose that its dual space $\mathcal{C}^\perp$ satisfies $\delta_m(\mathcal{C}^\perp) \geq m + 1 - t$. Let $C_1, \ldots, C_s$ be the generating matrices of the corresponding digital (t, m, s)-net $\mathcal{P} = \Phi_m(\mathcal{C})$ over $\mathbb{Z}_b$. Then we have*

$$\sum_{\boldsymbol{k} \in \mathcal{D}'(C_1,\ldots,C_s)} b^{2m-2\rho(\boldsymbol{k})} \leq b^{2t}(m+1)^{s-1}.$$

Proof Using (16.6), we have

$$\begin{aligned}
\sum_{\boldsymbol{k} \in \mathcal{D}'(C_1,\ldots,C_s)} b^{2m-2\rho(\boldsymbol{k})} &= \sum_{\mathbf{A} \in \mathcal{C}^\perp \setminus \{\mathbf{0}\}} b^{2m-2V_m(\mathbf{A})} \\
&= \sum_{\substack{d_1,\ldots,d_s=0 \\ d_1+\cdots+d_s \geq m+1-t}}^{m} b^{2(m-d_1-\cdots-d_s)} \mu_{d_1,\ldots,d_s},
\end{aligned}$$

where

$$\begin{aligned}\mu_{d_1,\ldots,d_s} &= \left|\left\{\mathbf{A} = (\mathbf{a}_1, \ldots, \mathbf{a}_s) \in \mathcal{C}^{\perp} : v_m(\mathbf{a}_i) = d_i \text{ for } 1 \le i \le s\right\}\right| \\ &\le \left|\left\{\mathbf{A} = (\mathbf{a}_1, \ldots, \mathbf{a}_s) \in \mathcal{C}^{\perp} : v_m(\mathbf{a}_i) \le d_i \text{ for } 1 \le i \le s\right\}\right|.\end{aligned}$$

Assume that $\mathbf{A} = (\mathbf{a}_1, \ldots, \mathbf{a}_s) \in \mathbb{Z}_b^{sm}$ and $v_m(\mathbf{a}_i) \le d_i$ for every $1 \le i \le s$. Then, by Remark 16.6, we have

$$\Phi_m(R\mathbf{a}_i) < \frac{b^{v_m(\mathbf{a}_i)}}{b^m} \le \frac{b^{d_i}}{b^m} = \frac{1}{b^{d_i^*}},$$

where we set $d_i^* = m - d_i$ for $1 \le i \le s$. Hence, $\Phi_m(R_s\mathbf{A}) \in \prod_{i=1}^s \left[0, b^{-d_i^*}\right)$ or equivalently, $R_s\mathbf{A} \in \mathcal{V}_{d_1^*,\ldots,d_s^*}$. This, however, is equivalent to $\mathbf{A} \in R_s\mathcal{V}_{d_1^*,\ldots,d_s^*}$ and hence, it follows that

$$\mu_{d_1,\ldots,d_s} \le \left|\mathcal{C}^{\perp} \cap R_s\mathcal{V}_{d_1^*,\ldots,d_s^*}\right| = b^{d_1+\cdots+d_s-m}\left|\mathcal{C} \cap \mathcal{V}_{d_1,\ldots,d_s}\right|,$$

where for the last equality, we used Corollary 16.13.

Now note that the elementary interval $J := \prod_{i=1}^s \left[0, b^{-d_i}\right)$ has volume $b^{-d_1-\cdots-d_s} \le b^{t-m-1} < b^{t-m}$. Hence, it is contained in an elementary interval of volume b^{t-m}. But since by Theorem 7.14 the point set $\Phi_m(\mathcal{C})$ is a digital (t, m, s)-net over $\mathbb{Z}_b$, it follows that J contains, at most, b^t points from $\Phi_m(\mathcal{C})$. Hence, $\left|\mathcal{C} \cap \mathcal{V}_{d_1,\ldots,d_s}\right| \le b^t$ and further,

$$\mu_{d_1,\ldots,d_s} \le b^{d_1+\cdots+d_s-m+t}.$$

Now we obtain

$$\begin{aligned}\sum_{\boldsymbol{k} \in \mathcal{D}'(C_1,\ldots,C_s)} b^{2m-2\rho(\boldsymbol{k})} &\le b^t \sum_{\substack{d_1,\ldots,d_s=0 \\ d_1+\cdots+d_s \ge m+1-t}}^{m} b^{m-d_1-\cdots-d_s} \\ &= b^t \sum_{r=m+1-t}^{sm} b^{m-r} \nu_{r,s},\end{aligned}$$

where

$$\nu_{r,s} := \left|\left\{(d_1, \ldots, d_s) \in \mathbb{N}_0^s : d_1 + \cdots + d_s = r \text{ and } d_i \le m \text{ for } 1 \le i \le s\right\}\right|.$$

We show that $\nu_{r,s} \le (m+1)^{s-1}$ for all $r, s \in \mathbb{N}$. Clearly, this holds true for $s = 1$ since $\nu_{r,1} = 1$. By induction we have

$$\nu_{r,s} = \sum_{i=0}^{m} \nu_{r-i,s-1} \le \sum_{i=0}^{m} (m+1)^{s-2} = (m+1)^{s-1}.$$

Now we obtain

$$\begin{aligned}\sum_{\boldsymbol{k}\in\mathcal{D}'(C_1,\ldots,C_s)} b^{2m-2\rho(\boldsymbol{k})} &\le b^t(m+1)^{s-1}\sum_{r=m+1-t}^{sm}\frac{b^m}{b^r}\\ &< b^{2t-1}(m+1)^{s-1}\sum_{r=0}^{\infty}\frac{1}{b^r}\\ &< b^{2t}(m+1)^{s-1}.\end{aligned}$$

□

It remains to show that the condition on $\mathcal{C}^\perp$ from Lemma 16.22 is satisfied whenever the Hamming weight of $\mathcal{C}^\perp$ is large enough.

Lemma 16.27 *Suppose that $\mathcal{C}$ is an m-dimensional $\mathbb{Z}_b$-linear subspace of $\mathbb{Z}_b^{sm}$ and let $\mathcal{C}^\perp$ denote its dual space satisfying $\varkappa_m(\mathcal{C}^\perp) \ge 2s+1$. Let $C_1,\ldots,C_s$ be the generating matrices of the corresponding digital net over $\mathbb{Z}_b$. Then, for any distinct $\boldsymbol{k},\boldsymbol{k}' \in \mathcal{D}'(C_1,\ldots,C_s)$, the functions $\widehat{\chi}_{[\boldsymbol{0},\boldsymbol{y})}(\boldsymbol{k})$ and $\widehat{\chi}_{[\boldsymbol{0},\boldsymbol{y})}(\boldsymbol{k}')$ are mutually orthogonal.*

Proof We have

$$\int_{[0,1]^s}\overline{\widehat{\chi}_{[\boldsymbol{0},\boldsymbol{y})}(\boldsymbol{k})}\widehat{\chi}_{[\boldsymbol{0},\boldsymbol{y})}(\boldsymbol{k}')\,\mathrm{d}\boldsymbol{y} = \prod_{i=1}^{s}\int_0^1\overline{\widehat{\chi}_{[0,y_i)}(k_i)}\widehat{\chi}_{[0,y_i)}(k_i')\,\mathrm{d}y_i, \tag{16.9}$$

where k_i, k_i' and y_i denote the ith component of $\boldsymbol{k}$, $\boldsymbol{k}'$ and $\boldsymbol{y}$, respectively. Since $\boldsymbol{k},\boldsymbol{k}' \in \mathcal{D}'(C_1,\ldots,C_s) = \tau_m^{-1}(\mathcal{C}^\perp)\setminus\{\boldsymbol{0}\}$ and since $\varkappa_m(\mathcal{C}^\perp)\ge 2s+1$, we obtain $\varkappa_m\left(\tau_m(\boldsymbol{k})-\tau_m(\boldsymbol{k}')\right)\ge 2s+1$ and hence, by the pigeon-hole principle, it follows that there exists an index $1\le i\le s$ such that

$$\varkappa_m(\tau_m(k_i)-\tau_m(k_i'))\ge 3.$$

In the following, we omit the index i for simplicity. We rewrite (16.7) and (16.8). For every $k\in\mathbb{N}_0$, we have

$$\overline{\widehat{\chi}_{[0,y)}(k)} = \frac{1}{b^{\rho(k)}}\,{}_b\mathrm{wal}_k(y)\upsilon_k(y),$$

where

$$\upsilon_0(y) := \frac{1}{2}\,{}_b\mathrm{wal}_0(y) + \sum_{c=1}^{\infty}\frac{1}{b^c}\sum_{\kappa=1}^{b-1}\frac{\omega_b^\kappa}{1-\omega_b^\kappa}\,{}_b\mathrm{wal}_{\kappa b^{c-1}}(y), \tag{16.10}$$

and where for $k \in \mathbb{N}$, with $k = \kappa_0 + \kappa_1 b + \cdots + \kappa_{a-1} b^{a-1}$ and hence, $\rho(k) = a$, we have

$$v_k(y) := \frac{1}{1-\omega_b^{\kappa_{a-1}}} \, {}_b\mathrm{wal}_{\ominus\kappa_{a-1}b^{a-1}}(y) + \left(\frac{1}{2} - \frac{1}{1-\omega_b^{\kappa_{a-1}}}\right) {}_b\mathrm{wal}_0(y)$$
$$+ \sum_{c=1}^{\infty} \frac{1}{b^c} \sum_{\kappa=1}^{b-1} \frac{\omega_b^{\kappa}}{1-\omega_b^{\kappa}} \, {}_b\mathrm{wal}_{\kappa b^{a+c-1}}(y). \tag{16.11}$$

From (16.10) and (16.11), we find that for every $k \in \mathbb{N}_0$, there exists a set $\mathcal{K}(k)$ of non-negative integers, depending only on k, such that

$$v_k(y) = \sum_{l \in \mathcal{K}(k)} u_l \, {}_b\mathrm{wal}_l(y),$$

where for every $l \in \mathcal{K}$, its b-adic expansion has, at most, one non-zero digit.

Suppose now that the non-negative integers k and k' are distinct. Let $k = \kappa_0 + \kappa_1 b + \cdots + \kappa_{a-1} b^{a-1}$ and $k' = \kappa'_0 + \kappa'_1 b + \cdots + \kappa'_{a'-1} b^{a'-1}$. Then there exist two sets of non-negative integers $\mathcal{K} = \mathcal{K}(k)$ and $\mathcal{K}' = \mathcal{K}(k')$ such that

$$v_k(y)\overline{v_{k'}(y)} = \sum_{l \in \mathcal{K}} \sum_{l' \in \mathcal{K}'} u_l \overline{u_{l'}} \, {}_b\mathrm{wal}_{l \ominus l'}(y).$$

For every $l \in \mathcal{K}$ and every $l' \in \mathcal{K}'$, the b-adic expansion of $l \ominus l'$ has, at most, two non-zero digits.

Now we obtain

$$\overline{\widehat{\chi}_{[0,y)}(k)}\widehat{\chi}_{[0,y)}(k') = \frac{1}{b^{a+a'}} \, {}_b\mathrm{wal}_{k \ominus k'}(y) \sum_{l \in \mathcal{K}} \sum_{l' \in \mathcal{K}'} u_l \overline{u_{l'}} \, {}_b\mathrm{wal}_{l \ominus l'}(y)$$
$$= \frac{1}{b^{a+a'}} \sum_{l \in \mathcal{K}} \sum_{l' \in \mathcal{K}'} u_l \overline{u_{l'}} \, {}_b\mathrm{wal}_{l \ominus l' \oplus k \ominus k'}(y).$$

The condition $\varkappa_m(\tau_m(k) - \tau_m(k')) \geq 3$ ensures that the b-adic expansion of $k \ominus k'$ has at least three non-zero digits. Therefore, the b-adic expansion of $l \ominus l' \oplus k \ominus k'$ has at least one non-zero digit and hence, $l \ominus l' \oplus k \ominus k' \neq 0$. Thus, it follows from Proposition A.9 that

$$\int_0^1 \overline{\widehat{\chi}_{[0,y)}(k)}\widehat{\chi}_{[0,y)}(k') \, \mathrm{d}y$$
$$= \frac{1}{b^{a+a'}} \sum_{l \in \mathcal{K}} \sum_{l' \in \mathcal{K}'} u_l \overline{u_{l'}} \int_0^1 {}_b\mathrm{wal}_{l \ominus l' \oplus k \ominus k'}(y) \, \mathrm{d}y = 0$$

and hence, the result follows from (16.9). □

Proof of Theorem 16.3 Let $b \geq 2s^2$ be a prime. Let $\mathcal{C}$ be an m-dimensional $\mathbb{Z}_b$-linear subspace of $\mathbb{Z}_b^{sm}$ such that its dual space $\mathcal{C}^\perp$ satisfies

$$\varkappa_m(\mathcal{C}^\perp) \geq 2s + 1 \quad \text{and} \quad \delta_m(\mathcal{C}^\perp) \geq m - t + 1.$$

Let $\mathcal{P} = \Phi_m(\mathcal{C})$ be the corresponding digital (t, m, s)-net over $\mathbb{Z}_b$ with generating matrices $C_1, \ldots, C_s$. From Lemma 16.27, we obtain that for any distinct $\boldsymbol{k}, \boldsymbol{k}' \in \mathcal{D}'(C_1, \ldots, C_s)$, the functions $\widehat{\chi}_{[\boldsymbol{0},\boldsymbol{y})}(\boldsymbol{k})$ and $\widehat{\chi}_{[\boldsymbol{0},\boldsymbol{y})}(\boldsymbol{k}')$ are mutually orthogonal. Hence, we may apply Lemmas 16.22, 16.25 and 16.26 to obtain

$$\begin{aligned}
\int_{[0,1]^s} |\Theta_{\mathcal{P}}(\boldsymbol{y})|^2 \,\mathrm{d}\boldsymbol{y} &= \sum_{\boldsymbol{k} \in \mathcal{D}'(C_1,\ldots,C_s)} \int_{[0,1]^s} \left|\widehat{\chi}_{[\boldsymbol{0},\boldsymbol{y})}(\boldsymbol{k})\right|^2 \mathrm{d}\boldsymbol{y} \\
&\leq \sum_{\boldsymbol{k} \in \mathcal{D}'(C_1,\ldots,C_s)} \frac{b^{2s-2\rho(\boldsymbol{k})}}{8^s} \\
&\leq \frac{b^{2(s+t)}}{8^s} \frac{(m+1)^{s-1}}{b^{2m}}. \qquad (16.12)
\end{aligned}$$

From Lemma 16.21, we obtain $|\Delta_{\mathcal{P}}(\boldsymbol{y})| \leq |\Theta_{\mathcal{P}}(\boldsymbol{y})| + sb^{t-m}$ and hence, together with (16.12), we get

$$\begin{aligned}
\int_{[0,1]^s} |\Delta_{\mathcal{P}}(\boldsymbol{y})|^2 \,\mathrm{d}\boldsymbol{y} &\leq 2 \int_{[0,1]^s} |\Theta_{\mathcal{P}}(\boldsymbol{y})|^2 \,\mathrm{d}\boldsymbol{y} + 2s^2 \frac{b^{2t}}{b^{2m}} \\
&\leq 2 \frac{b^{2(s+t)}}{8^s} \frac{(m+1)^{s-1}}{b^{2m}} + 2s^2 \frac{b^{2t}}{b^{2m}} \\
&\leq \frac{4b^{2s}}{4^s} b^{2t} \frac{(m+1)^{s-1}}{b^{2m}}.
\end{aligned}$$

The result of Theorem 16.3 follows on taking square roots. □

16.4 Explicit constructions

So far, we have shown that Theorem 16.3 holds and that this implies Theorem 16.5. It remains to give explicit constructions of $\mathbb{Z}_b$-linear subspaces $\mathcal{C}_{g,w}$ that satisfy the conditions of Theorem 16.5. This is done in this section.

The construction of these $\mathbb{Z}_b$-linear subspaces $\mathcal{C}_{g,w}$, first given by Chen and Skriganov [22], can be seen as a generalisation of the digital net construction due to Faure; see Section 8.1.

Let

$$f(z) = f_0 + f_1 z + \cdots + f_{r-1} z^{r-1}$$

be a polynomial in $\mathbb{Z}_b[x]$, where $r = \deg(f) + 1$. For every $j \in \mathbb{N}$, we consider the jth hyper-derivative

$$\partial^j f(z) = \sum_{i=0}^{r-1} \binom{i}{j} f_i z^{i-j},$$

where $\binom{i}{j}$ denotes a binomial coefficient modulo b and where we use the usual convention that $\binom{i}{j} = 0$ whenever $j > i$.

Let $b \geq gs$ be a prime, where g is a fixed positive integer. Then there exist gs distinct elements $\beta_{i,l} \in \mathbb{Z}_b$ for $1 \leq i \leq s$ and $1 \leq l \leq g$.

We define $\mathcal{C}_{g,w} \subseteq \mathbb{Z}_b^{sgw}$ as

$$\mathcal{C}_{g,w} := \{\mathbf{A}(f) = (\mathbf{a}_1(f), \ldots, \mathbf{a}_s(f)) \,:\, f \in \mathbb{Z}_b[z] \text{ and } \deg(f) < gw\},$$

where, for every $1 \leq i \leq s$, we have

$$\mathbf{a}_i(f) = \left(\left(\partial^{j-1} f(\beta_{i,l})\right)_{j=1}^{w}\right)_{l=1}^{g} \in \mathbb{Z}_b^{gw}.$$

(If we write $\mathbf{a}_i(f) = (\eta_{i,1}(f), \ldots, \eta_{i,gw}(f))$, then for $1 \leq l \leq g$ and $1 \leq j \leq w$, we have $\eta_{i,(l-1)w+j} = \partial^{j-1} f(\beta_{i,l})$.)

Clearly, $\mathcal{C}_{g,w}$ has exactly b^{gw} elements. Since the collection of polynomials in $\mathbb{Z}_b[z]$ with $\deg(f) < gw$ is closed under addition and scalar multiplication over $\mathbb{Z}_b$, it follows that $\mathcal{C}_{g,w}$ is a $\mathbb{Z}_b$-linear subspace of $\mathbb{Z}_b^{sgw}$.

The following theorem states that the set $\mathcal{C}_{g,w}$ satisfies all the conditions that are demanded in Theorem 16.5. Hence, for every $N \geq 2$, we can explicitly construct a point set $\mathcal{P}_N$ consisting of N points in the s-dimensional unit-cube whose L_2-discrepancy is the best possible with respect to the general lower bound due to Roth.

Theorem 16.28 *For every $g, w \in \mathbb{N}$ satisfying $b \geq gs$, the set $\mathcal{C}_{g,w} \in \mathbb{Z}_b^{sgw}$ is a $\mathbb{Z}_b$-linear subspace of $\mathbb{Z}_b^{sgw}$ of dimension gw. Its dual space $\mathcal{C}_{g,w}^{\perp}$ is of dimension $(s-1)gw$ and it satisfies*

$$\varkappa_{gw}(\mathcal{C}_{g,w}^{\perp}) \geq g + 1 \quad \text{and} \quad \delta_{gw}(\mathcal{C}_{g,w}^{\perp}) \geq gw + 1.$$

Corollary 16.29 *For every $g, w \in \mathbb{N}$ satisfying $b \geq gs$, the point set $\mathcal{P}_{g,w} = \Phi_{gw}(\mathcal{C}_{g,w})$ is a digital $(0, gw, s)$-net over $\mathbb{Z}_b$. The $gw \times gw$ generating matrices $C_1, \ldots, C_s$ over $\mathbb{Z}_b$ are given by*

$$C_i = (c_{u,v}^{(i)})_{u,v=1}^{gw}$$

with

$$c_{(l-1)w+j,k}^{(i)} = \binom{k-1}{j-1} \beta_{i,l}^{k-j}$$

for $1 \leq j \leq w$, $1 \leq l \leq g$, $1 \leq k \leq gw$ and $1 \leq i \leq s$.

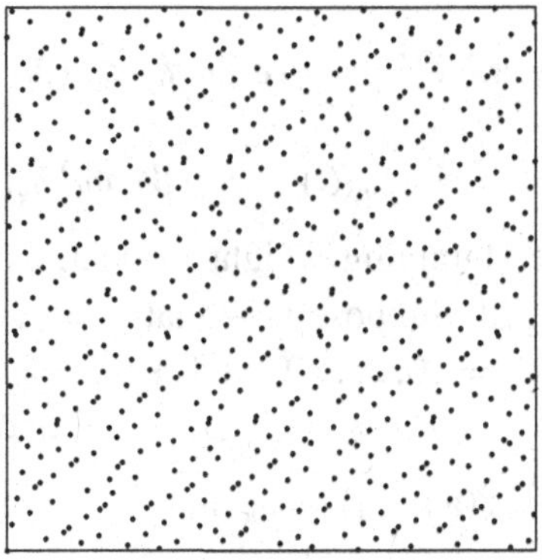

Figure 16.1 The digital (0, 4, 2)-net $\mathcal{P}_{2,2}$ over $\mathbb{Z}_5$ generated by C_1 and C_2.

Proof It follows from Theorem 16.28 in conjunction with Theorem 7.14 that $\mathcal{P}_{g,w}$ is a digital $(0, gw, s)$-net over $\mathbb{Z}_b$. The form of the generating matrices can be easily read from the definition of $\mathcal{C}_{g,w}$. □

For $g = 1$, the digital $(0, w, s)$-net $\mathcal{P}_{1,w}$ can also be obtained with the construction of Faure; see Section 8.1.

Example 16.30 For $s = g = w = 2$, we may choose $b = 5$, i.e. we obtain a $(0, 4, 2)$-net $\mathcal{P}_{2,2}$ over $\mathbb{Z}_5$. We choose different $\beta_{1,1}, \beta_{1,2}, \beta_{2,1}, \beta_{2,2} \in \mathbb{Z}_5$. Then the ith generating matrix, $i \in \{1, 2\}$ is given by

$$C_i = \begin{pmatrix} \binom{0}{0}\beta_{i,1}^0 & \binom{1}{0}\beta_{i,1}^1 & \binom{2}{0}\beta_{i,1}^2 & \binom{3}{0}\beta_{i,1}^3 \\ 0 & \binom{1}{1}\beta_{i,1}^0 & \binom{2}{1}\beta_{i,1}^1 & \binom{3}{1}\beta_{i,1}^2 \\ \binom{0}{0}\beta_{i,2}^0 & \binom{1}{0}\beta_{i,2}^1 & \binom{2}{0}\beta_{i,2}^2 & \binom{3}{0}\beta_{i,2}^3 \\ 0 & \binom{1}{1}\beta_{i,2}^0 & \binom{2}{1}\beta_{i,2}^1 & \binom{3}{1}\beta_{i,2}^2 \end{pmatrix}.$$

For example, when we choose $\beta_{1,1} = 0$, $\beta_{1,2} = 1$, $\beta_{2,1} = 2$ and $\beta_{2,2} = 3$, then

$$C_1 = \begin{pmatrix} 1 & 0 & 0 & 0 \\ 0 & 1 & 0 & 0 \\ 1 & 1 & 1 & 1 \\ 0 & 1 & 2 & 3 \end{pmatrix} \quad \text{and} \quad C_2 = \begin{pmatrix} 1 & 2 & 4 & 3 \\ 0 & 1 & 4 & 2 \\ 1 & 3 & 4 & 2 \\ 0 & 1 & 1 & 2 \end{pmatrix}.$$

The digital $(0, 4, 2)$-net $\mathcal{P}_{2,2}$ over $\mathbb{Z}_5$ generated by C_1 and C_2 is shown in Figure 16.1.

To prove Theorem 16.28, we follow Chen and Skriganov [22] again.

In the following, we study $\mathbb{Z}_b$-linear subspaces of $\mathbb{Z}_b^{sgw}$. For a vector $\mathbf{A} = (\mathbf{a}_1, \dots, \mathbf{a}_s) \in \mathbb{Z}_b^{sgw}$ with $\mathbf{a}_i = (\mathbf{a}_{i,1}, \dots, \mathbf{a}_{i,g})$ and with $\mathbf{a}_{i,j} \in \mathbb{Z}_b^w$ for $1 \leq i \leq s$ and $1 \leq j \leq g$, we define $\varkappa_w(\mathbf{A}) := \sum_{i=1}^s \sum_{j=1}^g \varkappa_w(\mathbf{a}_{i,j})$ and $V_w(\mathbf{A}) := \sum_{i=1}^s \sum_{j=1}^g v_w(\mathbf{a}_{i,j})$. Furthermore, $\varkappa_{gw}(\mathbf{A}) := \sum_{i=1}^s \varkappa_{gw}(\mathbf{a}_i)$ and $V_{gw}(\mathbf{A}) := \sum_{i=1}^s v_{gw}(\mathbf{a}_i)$.

Lemma 16.31

1. For every $\mathbf{A} = (\mathbf{a}_1, \ldots, \mathbf{a}_s) \in \mathbb{Z}_b^{sgw}$*, we have* $\varkappa_{gw}(\mathbf{A}) = \varkappa_w(\mathbf{A})$ *and* $V_{gw}(\mathbf{A}) \geq V_w(\mathbf{A})$.

2. For every $\mathcal{C} \subseteq \mathbb{Z}_b^{sgw}$*, we have* $\varkappa_{gw}(\mathcal{C}) = \varkappa_w(\mathcal{C})$ *and* $\delta_{gw}(\mathcal{C}) \geq \delta_w(\mathcal{C})$.

Proof The result for the Hamming weight is clear, as the number of non-zero elements remains unchanged. Suppose now that $\mathbf{a} = (\mathbf{a}_1, \ldots, \mathbf{a}_g) \in \mathbb{Z}_b^{gw}$ satisfies $\mathbf{a}_g = (0, \ldots, 0), \ldots, \mathbf{a}_{g-l+2} = (0, \ldots, 0)$ and $\mathbf{a}_{g-l+1} \neq (0, \ldots, 0)$ for some $1 \leq l \leq g$. Then we have $v_w(\mathbf{a}_g) = \cdots = v_w(\mathbf{a}_{g-l+2}) = 0$ and

$$v_{gw}(\mathbf{a}) = (g-l)w + v_w(\mathbf{a}_{g-l+1}) \geq v_w(\mathbf{a}_1) + \cdots + v_w(\mathbf{a}_{g-l+1}) = V_w(\mathbf{a}).$$

Hence, the results for the NRT weight follow as well. □

Now let $\Phi_w : \mathbb{Z}_b^{sgw} \to [0,1)^{sg}$, where for $\mathbf{A} = (\mathbf{a}_1, \ldots, \mathbf{a}_s) \in \mathbb{Z}_b^{sgw}$ with $\mathbf{a}_i = (\mathbf{a}_{i,1}, \ldots, \mathbf{a}_{i,g})$ and $\mathbf{a}_{i,l} = (\alpha_{i,l,1}, \ldots, \alpha_{i,l,w})$ for all $1 \leq i \leq s$ and $1 \leq l \leq g$, we define

$$\Phi_w(\mathbf{A}) = \left(\left(\frac{\alpha_{i,l,1}}{b} + \cdots + \frac{\alpha_{i,l,w}}{b^w} \right)_{l=1}^{g} \right)_{i=1}^{s}.$$

Lemma 16.32 *Let* $\mathcal{C}$ *and* $\mathcal{C}^\perp$ *be mutually dual* $\mathbb{Z}_b$*-linear subspaces of* $\mathbb{Z}_b^{sgw}$ *such that* $\Phi_w(\mathcal{C})$ *is an optimum* $[gs, gk, w]$*-distribution in base* b*. Then we have*

$$\delta_{gw}(\mathcal{C}^\perp) \geq kgw + 1 \quad \textit{and} \quad \varkappa_{gw}(\mathcal{C}^\perp) \geq kg + 1.$$

Proof Let $\mathcal{C} \subseteq \mathbb{Z}_b^{sgw}$ be such that $\Phi_w(\mathcal{C})$ is an optimum $[gs, gk, w]$-distribution in base b. Then it follows from Corollary 16.18 that $\Phi_w(R_{gs}\mathcal{C}^\perp)$ is an optimum $[gs, g(s-k), w]$-distribution in base b. Hence, we obtain from Lemma 16.31 and Lemma 16.17 that

$$\delta_{gw}(\mathcal{C}^\perp) \geq \delta_w(\mathcal{C}^\perp) = kgw + 1.$$

It remains to show the result for the Hamming weight. First, let $\mathbf{a} \in \mathbb{Z}_b^w$. If $\mathbf{a} \neq (0, \ldots, 0)$, then we have $w\varkappa_w(\mathbf{a}) \geq w \geq v_w(\mathbf{a})$. But for $\mathbf{a} = (0, \ldots, 0)$, we trivially have $w\varkappa_w(\mathbf{a}) = 0 = v_w(\mathbf{a})$. Hence, for all $\mathbf{a} \in \mathbb{Z}_b^w$, we have $w\varkappa_w(\mathbf{a}) \geq v_w(\mathbf{a})$ and hence, for all $\mathbf{A} \in \mathbb{Z}_b^{sgw}$, we have $\varkappa_w(\mathbf{A}) \geq \frac{1}{w}\delta_w(\mathbf{A})$. From this, Lemma 16.31 and Lemma 16.17, it follows that

$$\varkappa_{gw}(\mathcal{C}^\perp) = \varkappa_w(\mathcal{C}^\perp) \geq \frac{1}{w}\delta_w(\mathcal{C}^\perp) = kg + \frac{1}{w}.$$

But since $\varkappa_{gw}(\mathcal{C}^\perp)$ is an integer, we finally obtain $\varkappa_{gw}(\mathcal{C}^\perp) \geq kg + 1$. □

Now we show that $\Phi_w(\mathcal{C}_{g,w})$ is an optimum $[gs, g, w]$-distribution in base b. An application of Lemma 16.32 with $k = 1$ then gives the proof of Theorem 16.28.

Lemma 16.33 *The point set* $\Phi_w(\mathcal{C}_{g,w})$ *is an optimum* $[gs, g, w]$*-distribution in base* b*.*

Proof We have to show that every elementary interval in $\mathcal{E}_{w,b,gs}$ of order gw contains exactly one point of $\Phi_w(\mathcal{C}_{g,w})$. To this end, let J in $\mathcal{E}_{w,b,gs}$ be of order gw, i.e. of volume b^{-gw}. Hence, J is of the form

$$J = \prod_{i=1}^{s}\prod_{l=1}^{g}\left[\frac{\alpha_{i,l}}{b^{d_{i,l}}}, \frac{\alpha_{i,l}+1}{b^{d_{i,l}}}\right),$$

with integers $0 \le \alpha_{i,l} < b^{d_{i,l}}$, $0 \le d_{i,l} < w$ for all $1 \le i \le s$ and $1 \le l \le g$ and $\sum_{i=1}^{s}\sum_{l=1}^{g} d_{i,l} = gw$. We write $\alpha_{i,l} = \alpha_{i,l,d_{i,l}} + \alpha_{i,l,d_{i,l}-1}b + \cdots + \alpha_{i,l,1}b^{d_{i,l}-1}$.

For $\mathbf{A}(f) \in \mathcal{C}_{g,w}$, we have

$$\Phi_w(\mathbf{A}(f)) = \left(\left(\frac{f(\beta_{i,l})}{b} + \cdots + \frac{\partial^{w-1}f(\beta_{i,l})}{b^w}\right)_{l=1}^{g}\right)_{i=1}^{s}.$$

Hence, $\Phi_w(\mathbf{A}(f)) \in J$ if and only if for all $1 \le i \le s$ and $1 \le l \le g$, we have

$$\frac{f(\beta_{i,l})}{b} + \cdots + \frac{\partial^{w-1}f(\beta_{i,l})}{b^w} \in \left[\frac{\alpha_{i,l}}{b^{d_{i,l}}}, \frac{\alpha_{i,l}+1}{b^{d_{i,l}}}\right).$$

This is equivalent to the system

$$\partial^{j-1}f(\beta_{i,l}) = \alpha_{i,l,j} \tag{16.13}$$

for all $1 \le j \le d_{i,l}$ and all $1 \le i \le s$ and $1 \le l \le g$. It remains to show that this system has a unique solution $f \in \mathbb{Z}_b[z]$ with $\deg(f) < gw$.

To this end, we consider for all $1 \le i \le s$ and $1 \le l \le g$ the polynomials

$$r_{i,l}(z) := \sum_{j=1}^{d_{i,l}} \alpha_{i,l,j}(z-\beta_{i,l})^{j-1} \in \mathbb{Z}_b[z].$$

Assume that $f(z) = f_0 + f_1 z + \cdots + f_{gw-1}z^{gw-1}$ is a solution of the system (16.13). Then we have

$$\begin{aligned}
r_{i,l}(z) &= \sum_{j=1}^{d_{i,l}} \alpha_{i,l,j}(z-\beta_{i,l})^{j-1}\\
&= \sum_{j=1}^{d_{i,l}}\sum_{i=0}^{gw-1}\binom{i}{j-1} f_i \beta_{i,l}^{i-j+1}(z-\beta_{i,l})^{j-1}\\
&\equiv \sum_{i=0}^{gw-1} f_i \sum_{j=0}^{gw-1}\binom{i}{j}\beta_{i,l}^{i-j}(z-\beta_{i,l})^{j} \pmod{(z-\beta_{i,l})^{d_{i,l}}}\\
&\equiv \sum_{i=0}^{gw-1} f_i z^i \pmod{(z-\beta_{i,l})^{d_{i,l}}}\\
&= f(z).
\end{aligned}$$

Hence, for all $1 \leq i \leq s$ and $1 \leq l \leq g$, we have

$$f(z) \equiv r_{i,l}(z) \pmod{(z - \beta_{i,l})^{d_{i,l}}}. \tag{16.14}$$

On the other hand, if $f(z)$ is a solution of (16.14), then it is easy to see that it is also a solution of (16.13).

Thus, the system (16.13) is equivalent to the system of congruences (16.14).

Since the polynomials $(z - \beta_{i,l})^{d_{i,l}}$, for $1 \leq i \leq s$ and $1 \leq l \leq g$ are pairwise coprime, it follows from the Chinese remainder theorem in $\mathbb{Z}_b[x]$ that the system (16.14) has a unique solution $f \in \mathbb{Z}_b[x]$ with $\deg(f) < gw$. This completes the proof of Lemma 16.33. □

To summarise, Lemma 16.33 implies that $\mathcal{C}_{g,w}$, defined at the beginning of this section, satisfies the assumptions in Lemma 16.32. Choosing $k = 1$ in Lemma 16.32 in turn implies that $\mathcal{C}_{g,w}$ also satisfies the assumptions in Theorem 16.5. Then choose $\mathcal{P}_{g,w} = \Phi_{gw}(\mathcal{C}_{g,w})$, set

$$\widetilde{\mathcal{P}}_N := \mathcal{P}_{g,w} \cap \left(\left[0, \frac{N}{b^{gw}}\right) \times [0,1)^{s-1} \right)$$

and

$$\mathcal{P}_N := \left\{ \left(\frac{b^{gw}}{N} x_1, x_2, \ldots, x_s \right) : (x_1, x_2, \ldots, x_s) \in \widetilde{\mathcal{P}}_N \right\},$$

as in the proof of Theorem 16.5. Then the proof of Theorem 16.5 shows that $\mathcal{P}_N$ is the desired point set which achieves the optimal rate of convergence of the L_2-discrepancy. We have shown the following corollary.

Corollary 16.34 *Let $b \geq 2s^2$ be a prime, let $g = 2s$ and let $\mathcal{P}_N \subset [0,1)^s$ be defined as above. For any integer $N \geq 2$, the point set $\mathcal{P}_N$ consisting of N points satisfies*

$$L_{2,N}(\mathcal{P}_N) < 2^{1-s} b^{2s} \left(\frac{\log N}{\log b} + 2s + 1 \right)^{\frac{s-1}{2}} \frac{1}{N}.$$

16.5 Mean square weighted L_2-discrepancy of digitally shifted digital nets

In the following, we are concerned with the L_2-discrepancy of – in some sense – randomised digital nets. These considerations lead to further existence results for point sets with the best possible order of L_2-discrepancy in the sense of Roth's lower bound. The constructions presented here are based on digitally shifted digital nets where we average over all possible shifts. Hence, they contain a random element which means that they are not fully explicit as is the construction given by Chen and Skriganov. Nevertheless, it can be shown that a large portion from a finite class of digital shifts leads to the best possible order. As a by-product, these results show that the constant c_s in Roth's lower bound is essentially the best possible.

In more detail, we consider digital (t, m, s)-nets over $\mathbb{Z}_b$, b a prime, randomised by a digital shift of depth m as introduced in Definition 4.69 or by a simplified digital shift as introduced in Definition 4.70. Here, in dimension one, for a digital $(t, m, 1)$-net over $\mathbb{Z}_b$, say $\mathcal{P}_{b^m} = \{x_0, \ldots, x_{b^m-1}\}$ with $x_n = \frac{x_{n,1}}{b} + \cdots + \frac{x_{n,m}}{b^m}$, the randomised point set is given by $\widetilde{\mathcal{P}}_{b^m} = \{z_0, \ldots, z_{b^m-1}\}$, where $z_n = \frac{z_{n,1}}{b} + \cdots + \frac{z_{n,m}}{b^m} + \delta_n$ and $z_{n,i} = x_{n,i} + \varsigma_i \in \mathbb{Z}_b$ for $1 \le i \le m$. The digits $\varsigma_1, \ldots, \varsigma_m \in \mathbb{Z}_b$ are chosen uniformly, independent and identically distributed and for $0 \le n < b^m$ the $\delta_n \in [0, b^{-m})$ are chosen uniformly, independent and identically distributed in the case of a digital shift of depth m and $\delta_n = 1/(2b^m)$ for all $0 \le n < b^m$ in the case of the simplified digital shift. For higher dimensions, each coordinate is randomised independently and therefore, one just needs to apply the one-dimensional randomisation method to each coordinate independently.

The aim of this section is to prove a formula for the mean square L_2-discrepancy of randomised digital nets. This formula depends on the generating matrices of the digital net. The following result was first shown in [51, Theorem 1] for $b = 2$ and later generalised in [28, Theorem 1] to arbitrary prime bases b.

Theorem 16.35 *Let $\mathcal{P}_{b^m}$ be a digital (t, m, s)-net over $\mathbb{Z}_b$ with generating matrices $C_1, \ldots, C_s$.*

1. *Let $\widetilde{\mathcal{P}}_{b^m}$ be the point set obtained after applying a random digital shift of depth m independently to each coordinate of each point of $\mathcal{P}_{b^m}$. Then the mean square L_2-discrepancy of $\widetilde{\mathcal{P}}_{b^m}$ is given by*

$$\mathbb{E}\left[(L_{2,b^m}(\widetilde{\mathcal{P}}_{b^m}))^2\right] = \frac{1}{b^m 2^s}\left(1 - \left(1 - \frac{1}{3b^m}\right)^s\right) + \frac{1}{3^s} \sum_{\emptyset \ne \mathfrak{v} \subseteq \mathcal{I}_s} \left(\frac{3}{2}\right)^{|\mathfrak{v}|} \mathcal{B}(\mathfrak{v}),$$

where for $\mathfrak{v} = \{v_1, \ldots, v_e\} \subseteq \mathcal{I}_s$, we put

$$\mathcal{B}(\mathfrak{v}) = \sum_{\substack{k_1,\ldots,k_e=1 \\ C_{v_1}^\top \mathbf{k}_1 + \cdots + C_{v_e}^\top \mathbf{k}_e = \mathbf{0}}}^{b^m-1} \prod_{i=1}^{e} \psi(k_i),$$

with

$$\psi(k) = \frac{1}{b^{2\rho(k)}}\left(\frac{1}{\sin^2(\kappa_{a-1}\pi/b)} - \frac{1}{3}\right)$$

and $k = \kappa_0 + \kappa_1 b + \cdots + \kappa_{a-1} b^{a-1}$, $\kappa_{a-1} \ne 0$, and where $\rho(k) = a$ denotes the NRT weight of k.

2. *Let $\widehat{\mathcal{P}}_{b^m}$ be the point set obtained after applying a random simplified digital shift of depth m independently to each coordinate of each point of $\mathcal{P}_{b^m}$. Then the mean*

square L_2-discrepancy of $\widehat{\mathcal{P}}_{b^m}$ is given by

$$\mathbb{E}\left[(L_{2,b^m}(\widehat{\mathcal{P}}_{b^m}))^2\right] = 2\left(\frac{1}{3^s} - \left(\frac{1}{3} + \frac{1}{24b^{2m}}\right)^s\right) + \frac{1}{b^m 2^s}\left(1 - \left(1 - \frac{1}{3b^m}\right)^s\right) + \frac{1}{3^s}\sum_{\emptyset \neq \mathfrak{v} \subseteq \mathcal{I}_s} \left(\frac{3}{2}\right)^{|\mathfrak{v}|} \mathcal{B}(\mathfrak{v}),$$

where $\mathcal{B}(\mathfrak{v})$ is as above.

Note that for $1 \leq k < b^m$, we have $\psi(k) = r_{\mathrm{sob},b}(k, 1)$ with $r_{\mathrm{sob},b}$ defined as in Proposition 12.2.

From Theorem 16.35, we immediately obtain the following result.

Corollary 16.36 *Let $\mathcal{P}_{b^m}$ be a digital (t, m, s)-net over $\mathbb{Z}_b$. Let $\widetilde{\mathcal{P}}_{b^m}$ be the point set obtained after applying a random digital shift of depth m independently to each coordinate of each point of $\mathcal{P}_{b^m}$ and let $\widehat{\mathcal{P}}_{b^m}$ be the point set obtained after applying a random simplified digital shift of depth m independently to each coordinate of each point of $\mathcal{P}_{b^m}$. Then we have*

$$\mathbb{E}\left[(L_{2,b^m}(\widehat{\mathcal{P}}_{b^m}))^2\right] \leq \mathbb{E}\left[(L_{2,b^m}(\widetilde{\mathcal{P}}_{b^m}))^2\right].$$

The proof of Theorem 16.35 is based on the Walsh series representation of the formula for the weighted L_2-discrepancy given in Proposition 2.15. As we shall see later, the function ψ in the theorem above is related to Walsh coefficients of a certain function appearing in the formula for the L_2-discrepancy. We need two lemmas.

Lemma 16.37 *Let $x_1, x_2 \in [0, 1)$ and let $z_1, z_2 \in [0, 1)$ be the points obtained after applying a random digital shift of depth m to x_1 and x_2. Then we have*

$$\mathbb{E}\left[{}_b\mathrm{wal}_k(z_1)\overline{{}_b\mathrm{wal}_l(z_2)}\right] = \begin{cases} {}_b\mathrm{wal}_k(x_1 \ominus x_2) & \text{if } 0 \leq k = l < b^m, \\ 0 & \text{otherwise.} \end{cases}$$

Proof Let $x_n = \frac{x_{n,1}}{b} + \frac{x_{n,2}}{b^2} + \cdots$ for $n \in \{1, 2\}$. Further, let $\varsigma_1, \ldots, \varsigma_m \in \mathbb{Z}_b$ uniformly and independent and identically distributed and for $n \in \{1, 2\}$, let $\delta_n = \frac{\delta_{n,m+1}}{b^{m+1}} + \frac{\delta_{n,m+2}}{b^{m+2}} + \cdots \in [0, \frac{1}{b^m})$ be uniformly and independent and identically distributed. Then define $z_{n,j} = x_{n,j} + \varsigma_j \in \mathbb{Z}_b$ for $1 \leq j \leq m$ and $z_n = \frac{z_{n,1}}{b} + \cdots + \frac{z_{n,m}}{b^m} + \delta_n$ for $n \in \{1, 2\}$.

First, let $k, l \in \mathbb{N}$, more precisely, let $k = \kappa_0 + \kappa_1 b + \cdots + \kappa_{a-1}b^{a-1}$ and $l = \lambda_0 + \lambda_1 b + \cdots + \lambda_{c-1}b^{c-1}$ be the b-adic expansion of k and l with $\kappa_{a-1}, \lambda_{c-1} \neq 0$.

Further, we set $\kappa_a = \kappa_{a+1} = \cdots = 0$ and also $\lambda_c = \lambda_{c+1} = \cdots = 0$. Then

$$\begin{aligned}
&\mathbb{E}\left[{}_b\mathrm{wal}_k(z_1)\overline{{}_b\mathrm{wal}_l(z_2)}\right] \\
&= \omega_b^{\kappa_0 x_{1,1}+\cdots+\kappa_{m-1}x_{1,m}}\omega_b^{-\lambda_0 x_{2,1}-\cdots-\lambda_{m-1}x_{2,m}} \\
&\quad \times \frac{1}{b}\sum_{\varsigma_1=0}^{b-1}\omega_b^{(\kappa_0-\lambda_0)\varsigma_1}\cdots\frac{1}{b}\sum_{\varsigma_m=0}^{b-1}\omega_b^{(\kappa_{m-1}-\lambda_{m-1})\varsigma_m} \\
&\quad \times \frac{1}{b}\sum_{\delta_{1,m+1}=0}^{b-1}\omega_b^{\kappa_m\delta_{1,m+1}}\frac{1}{b}\sum_{\delta_{1,m+2}=0}^{b-1}\omega_b^{\kappa_{m+1}\delta_{1,m+2}}\cdots \\
&\quad \times \frac{1}{b}\sum_{\delta_{2,m+1}=0}^{b-1}\omega_b^{-\lambda_m\delta_{2,m+1}}\frac{1}{b}\sum_{\delta_{2,m+2}=0}^{b-1}\omega_b^{-\lambda_{m+1}\delta_{2,m+2}}\cdots. \qquad (16.15)
\end{aligned}$$

The product above consists only of finitely many factors as $\kappa_a = \kappa_{a+1} = \cdots = 0$ and for $j \geq \max(m, a)$, we have $\frac{1}{b}\sum_{\delta_{1,j+1}=0}^{b-1}\omega_b^{\kappa_j\delta_{1,j+1}} = 1$. The same argument holds for the last line in the equation above.

First, we consider the case where $a > m$. We have $\frac{1}{b}\sum_{\delta_{1,a}=0}^{b-1}\omega_b^{\kappa_{a-1}\delta_{1,a}} = 0$ and therefore, $\mathbb{E}[{}_b\mathrm{wal}_k(z_1)\overline{{}_b\mathrm{wal}_l(z_2)}] = 0$. The same holds if $c > m$. Now assume that there is an $1 \leq j \leq m$ such that $\kappa_{j-1} \neq \lambda_{j-1}$. Then we have $\kappa_{j-1} - \lambda_{j-1} \not\equiv 0 \pmod{b}$ and $\frac{1}{b}\sum_{\varsigma_j=0}^{b-1}\omega_b^{(\kappa_{j-1}-\lambda_{j-1})\varsigma_j} = 0$. Therefore, we obtain in this case $\mathbb{E}[{}_b\mathrm{wal}_k(z_1)\overline{{}_b\mathrm{wal}_l(z_2)}] = 0$. Now let $k = l$ and $0 \leq k < b^m$. It follows from (16.15) that

$$\begin{aligned}
\mathbb{E}\left[{}_b\mathrm{wal}_k(z_1)\overline{{}_b\mathrm{wal}_k(z_2)}\right] &= \omega_b^{\kappa_0(x_{1,1}-x_{2,1})+\cdots+\kappa_{m-1}(x_{1,m}-x_{2,m})} \\
&= {}_b\mathrm{wal}_k(x_1 \ominus x_2).
\end{aligned}$$

□

Lemma 16.38 *Let $x, x_1, x_2 \in [0, 1)$ and let $z, z_1, z_2 \in [0, 1)$ be the points obtained after applying a random digital shift of depth m to x, x_1 and x_2, respectively.*

1. *We have $\mathbb{E}[z] = 1/2$ and $\mathbb{E}[z^2] = 1/3$.*
2. *We have*

$$\mathbb{E}[|z_1 - z_2|] = \sum_{k=0}^{b^m-1}\tau_b(k)\,{}_b\mathrm{wal}_k(x_1 \ominus x_2),$$

where $\tau_b(0) = \frac{1}{3}$ and $\tau_b(k) = b^{-2\rho(k)}\left(\frac{1}{3} - \sin^{-2}(\kappa_{a-1}\pi/b)\right)$ for $k > 0$. Here, $k = \kappa_0 + \kappa_1 b + \cdots + \kappa_{a-1}b^{a-1}$, $\kappa_{a-1} \neq 0$ and $\rho(k) = a$ is the NRT weight of k.

3. We have

$$\mathbb{E}[\min(1-z_1, 1-z_2)] = \frac{1}{2}\left(1 - \sum_{k=0}^{b^m-1} \tau_b(k)\, {}_b\mathrm{wal}_k(x_1 \ominus x_2)\right).$$

Proof

1. We have $\mathbb{E}[z] = \int_0^1 z \, \mathrm{d}z = 1/2$ and $\mathbb{E}[z^2] = \int_0^1 z^2 \, \mathrm{d}z = 1/3$.
2. As $|z_1 - z_2| \in L_2([0,1]^2)$ and is continuous, it follows that the function $|z_1 - z_2|$ can be represented by its Walsh series (see Theorem A.11 in Section A.3). We have $|z_1 - z_2| = \sum_{k,l=0}^{\infty} \tau_b(k,l)\, {}_b\mathrm{wal}_k(z_1)\, \overline{{}_b\mathrm{wal}_l(z_2)}$, where

$$\tau_b(k,l) = \int_0^1 \int_0^1 |z_1 - z_2| \overline{{}_b\mathrm{wal}_k(z_1)}\, {}_b\mathrm{wal}_l(z_2) \, \mathrm{d}z_1 \, \mathrm{d}z_2.$$

In the proof of Proposition 12.5 (see (12.15)), it was shown that

$$\tau_b(k) := \tau_b(k,k) = \frac{1}{b^{2a}}\left(\frac{1}{3} - \frac{1}{\sin^2(\kappa_{a-1}\pi/b)}\right),$$

for $k > 0$ and $\tau_b(0,0) = \frac{1}{3}$. (We do not need to know $\tau_b(k,l)$ for $k \neq l$ for our purposes here.) From the linearity of the expectation value and from Lemma 16.37, we obtain

$$\begin{aligned} \mathbb{E}[|z_1 - z_2|] &= \sum_{k,l=0}^{\infty} \tau_b(k,l) \mathbb{E}\left[\, {}_b\mathrm{wal}_k(z_1)\, \overline{{}_b\mathrm{wal}_l(z_2)}\right] \\ &= \sum_{k=0}^{b^m-1} \tau_b(k)\, {}_b\mathrm{wal}_k(x_1 \ominus x_2). \end{aligned}$$

3. This result follows from the first two parts of the lemma, together with the formula $\min(z_1, z_2) = \frac{1}{2}(z_1 + z_2 - |z_1 - z_2|)$. □

Proof of Theorem 16.35 First, we prove the formula for a random digital shift of depth m. Let $\widetilde{\mathcal{P}}_{b^m} = \{\boldsymbol{z}_0, \ldots, \boldsymbol{z}_{b^m-1}\}$ and $\boldsymbol{z}_n = (z_{n,1}, \ldots, z_{n,s})$. From the formula for the weighted L_2-discrepancy given in Proposition 2.15, from Lemma 16.38 and from the linearity of expectation, we get

$$\begin{aligned} &\mathbb{E}\left[(L_{2,b^m}(\widetilde{\mathcal{P}}_{b^m}))^2\right] \\ &= \frac{1}{3^s} - \frac{2}{b^m}\sum_{n=0}^{b^m-1}\prod_{i=1}^{s}\frac{1-\mathbb{E}[z_{n,i}^2]}{2} + \frac{1}{b^{2m}}\sum_{n,h=0}^{b^m-1}\prod_{i=1}^{s}\mathbb{E}[\min(1-z_{n,i}, 1-z_{h,i})] \\ &= -\frac{1}{3^s} + \frac{1}{b^{2m}}\sum_{n=0}^{b^m-1}\prod_{i=1}^{s}\mathbb{E}[1-z_{n,i}] + \frac{1}{b^{2m}}\sum_{\substack{n,h=0 \\ n\neq h}}^{b^m-1}\prod_{i=1}^{s}\mathbb{E}[\min(1-z_{n,i}, 1-z_{h,i})]. \end{aligned}$$

Now we use Lemma 16.38 again to obtain

$$\mathbb{E}\left[(L_{2,b^m}(\widetilde{\mathcal{P}}_{b^m}))^2\right] = -\frac{1}{3^s} + \frac{1}{b^m}\frac{1}{2^s} + \frac{1}{b^{2m}} \sum_{\substack{n,h=0\\ n\neq h}}^{b^m-1} \prod_{i=1}^{s} \frac{1}{2}\left(1 - \sum_{k=0}^{b^m-1} \tau_b(k)\, {}_b\mathrm{wal}_k(x_{n,i} \ominus x_{h,i})\right).$$

We have

$$\prod_{i=1}^{s}\left(1 - \sum_{k=0}^{b^m-1} \tau_b(k)\, {}_b\mathrm{wal}_k(x_{n,i} \ominus x_{h,i})\right) = 1 + \sum_{\substack{\emptyset \neq \mathfrak{w} \subseteq \mathcal{I}_s\\ \mathfrak{w}=\{w_1,\ldots,w_d\}}} (-1)^{|\mathfrak{w}|} \sum_{k_1,\ldots,k_d=0}^{b^m-1} \prod_{i=1}^{d} \tau_b(k_i)\, {}_b\mathrm{wal}_{k_i}(x_{n,w_i} \ominus x_{h,w_i}).$$

Thus,

$$\mathbb{E}\left[(L_{2,b^m}(\widetilde{\mathcal{P}}_{b^m}))^2\right] = -\frac{1}{3^s} + \frac{1}{b^m}\frac{1}{2^s} + \frac{1}{b^{2m}} \sum_{\substack{n,h=0\\ n\neq h}}^{b^m-1} \frac{1}{2^s} + \frac{1}{2^s}\frac{1}{b^{2m}} \sum_{\substack{n,h=0\\ n\neq h}}^{b^m-1} \sum_{\substack{\emptyset \neq \mathfrak{w} \subseteq \mathcal{I}_s\\ \mathfrak{w}=\{w_1,\ldots,w_d\}}} (-1)^d \sum_{k_1,\ldots,k_d=0}^{b^m-1} \prod_{i=1}^{d} \tau_b(k_i)\, {}_b\mathrm{wal}_{k_i}(x_{n,w_i} \ominus x_{h,w_i}).$$

We have

$$\begin{aligned}\sum_{k=0}^{b^m-1} \tau_b(k) &= \frac{1}{3} + \sum_{a=1}^{m} \sum_{k=b^{a-1}}^{b^a-1} \frac{1}{b^{2a}}\left(\frac{1}{3} - \frac{1}{\sin^2(\kappa_{a-1}\pi/b)}\right)\\ &= \frac{1}{3} + \sum_{a=1}^{m} \frac{1}{b^{a+1}} \sum_{r=1}^{b-1}\left(\frac{1}{3} - \frac{1}{\sin^2(r\pi/b)}\right).\end{aligned}$$

From Corollary A.23, we know that $\sum_{r=1}^{b-1} \sin^{-2}(r\pi/b) = (b^2-1)/3$ and hence we get $\sum_{k=0}^{b^m-1} \tau_b(k) = 1/(3b^m)$. Therefore,

$$\sum_{\emptyset \neq \mathfrak{w} \subseteq \mathcal{I}_s} (-1)^{|\mathfrak{w}|} \sum_{k_1,\ldots,k_{|\mathfrak{w}|}=0}^{b^m-1} \prod_{i=1}^{|\mathfrak{w}|} \tau_b(k_i) = \sum_{\emptyset \neq \mathfrak{w} \subseteq \mathcal{I}_s} \left(-\frac{1}{3b^m}\right)^{|\mathfrak{w}|}$$
$$= \sum_{r=1}^{s} \binom{s}{r} \left(-\frac{1}{3b^m}\right)^r$$
$$= \left(1 - \frac{1}{3b^m}\right)^s - 1.$$

Now we add and substract $\frac{1}{2^s}\frac{1}{b^m}\left[\left(1 - \frac{1}{3b^m}\right)^s - 1\right]$ in the above expression in order to obtain

$$\mathbb{E}\left[(L_{2,b^m}(\widetilde{\mathcal{P}}_{b^m}))^2\right] = \frac{1}{2^s} - \frac{1}{3^s} + \left(1 - \left(1 - \frac{1}{3b^m}\right)^s\right) \frac{1}{b^m}\frac{1}{2^s}$$
$$+ \frac{1}{2^s}\frac{1}{b^{2m}} \sum_{n,h=0}^{b^m-1} \sum_{\substack{\emptyset \neq \mathfrak{w} \subseteq \mathcal{I}_s \\ \mathfrak{w}=\{w_1,\ldots,w_d\}}} (-1)^d \sum_{k_1,\ldots,k_d=0}^{b^m-1} \prod_{i=1}^{d} \tau_b(k_i)\, {}_b\mathrm{wal}_{k_i}(x_{n,w_i} \ominus x_{h,w_i}).$$

Since $\tau_b(0) = 1/3$, we have

$$\frac{1}{2^s}\frac{1}{b^{2m}} \sum_{n,h=0}^{b^m-1} \sum_{\emptyset \neq \mathfrak{w} \subseteq \mathcal{I}_s} (-1)^{|\mathfrak{w}|} \tau_b(0)^{|\mathfrak{w}|} = \frac{1}{3^s} - \frac{1}{2^s}.$$

Hence,

$$\mathbb{E}\left[(L_{2,b^m}(\widetilde{\mathcal{P}}_{b^m}))^2\right] = \frac{1}{2^s} - \frac{1}{3^s} + \left(1 - \left(1 - \frac{1}{3b^m}\right)^s\right) \frac{1}{b^m}\frac{1}{2^s} + \frac{1}{3^s} - \frac{1}{2^s}$$
$$+ \frac{1}{2^s}\frac{1}{b^{2m}} \sum_{\substack{\emptyset \neq \mathfrak{w} \subseteq \mathcal{I}_s \\ \mathfrak{w}=\{w_1,\ldots,w_d\}}} (-1)^d \sum_{\substack{k_1,\ldots,k_d=0 \\ (k_1,\ldots,k_d)\neq(0,\ldots,0)}}^{b^m-1} \sum_{n,h=0}^{b^m-1} \prod_{i=1}^{d} \tau_b(k_i)\, {}_b\mathrm{wal}_{k_i}(x_{n,w_i} \ominus x_{h,w_i}).$$

From the group structure of digital nets (see Lemma 4.72) and from Lemma 4.75, it follows that for any digital net generated by the $m \times m$ matrices $C_1, \ldots, C_s$, we have

$$\frac{1}{b^{2m}} \sum_{n,h=0}^{b^m-1} {}_b\mathrm{wal}_{k_1,\ldots,k_s}(\boldsymbol{x}_n \ominus \boldsymbol{x}_h) = \frac{1}{b^m} \sum_{n=0}^{b^m-1} {}_b\mathrm{wal}_{k_1,\ldots,k_s}(\boldsymbol{x}_n)$$
$$= \begin{cases} 1 & \text{if } C_1^\top \mathbf{k}_1 + \cdots + C_s^\top \mathbf{k}_s = \mathbf{0}, \\ 0 & \text{otherwise.} \end{cases}$$

Since we have that the d-dimensional projection of a digital (t, m, s)-net is again a digital (t, m, d)-net, we get (with $\mathfrak{w} = \{w_1, \ldots, w_d\}$)

$$\sum_{\substack{k_1,\ldots,k_d=0 \\ (k_1,\ldots,k_d)\neq(0,\ldots,0)}}^{b^m-1} \sum_{n,h=0}^{b^m-1} \prod_{i=1}^{d} \tau_b(k_i)\, {}_b\mathrm{wal}_{k_i}(x_{n,w_i} \ominus x_{h,w_i})$$

$$= b^{2m} \sum_{\substack{k_1,\ldots,k_d=0 \\ (k_1,\ldots,k_d)\neq(0,\ldots,0) \\ C_{w_1}^\top \mathbf{k}_1+\cdots+C_{w_d}^\top \mathbf{k}_d=\mathbf{0}}}^{b^m-1} \prod_{i=1}^{d} \tau_b(k_i)$$

$$= b^{2m} \sum_{\substack{\emptyset\neq\mathfrak{v}\subseteq\mathfrak{w} \\ \mathfrak{v}=\{v_1,\ldots,v_e\}}} \frac{1}{3^{|\mathfrak{w}|-|\mathfrak{v}|}} \sum_{\substack{k_1,\ldots,k_e=1 \\ C_{v_1}^\top \mathbf{k}_1+\cdots+C_{v_e}^\top \mathbf{k}_e=\mathbf{0}}}^{b^m-1} \prod_{i=1}^{e} \tau_b(k_i).$$

As $\prod_{i=1}^{e} \tau_b(k_i) = (-1)^e \prod_{i=1}^{e} \psi(k_i)$, we have

$$\sum_{\substack{k_1,\ldots,k_d=0 \\ (k_1,\ldots,k_d)\neq(0,\ldots,0)}}^{b^m-1} \sum_{n,h=0}^{b^m-1} \prod_{i=1}^{d} \tau_b(k_i)\, {}_b\mathrm{wal}_{k_i}(x_{n,w_i} \ominus x_{h,w_i}) = \frac{b^{2m}}{3^{|\mathfrak{w}|}} \sum_{\emptyset\neq\mathfrak{v}\subseteq\mathfrak{w}} (-3)^{|\mathfrak{v}|} \mathcal{B}(\mathfrak{v}).$$

Thus, we obtain

$$\mathbb{E}\left[(L_{2,b^m}(\widetilde{\mathcal{P}}_{b^m}))^2\right]$$
$$= \frac{1}{b^m 2^s}\left(1 - \left(1 - \frac{1}{3b^m}\right)^s\right) + \frac{1}{2^s} \sum_{\emptyset\neq\mathfrak{w}\subseteq\mathcal{I}_s} \left(-\frac{1}{3}\right)^{|\mathfrak{w}|} \sum_{\substack{\mathfrak{v}\subseteq\mathfrak{w} \\ \mathfrak{v}\neq\emptyset}} (-3)^{|\mathfrak{v}|} \mathcal{B}(\mathfrak{v}).$$

Now let $\mathfrak{v}$, with $\emptyset \neq \mathfrak{v} \subseteq \mathcal{I}_s$, be fixed. Then $\mathfrak{v} \subseteq \mathfrak{w} \subseteq \mathcal{I}_s$ is equivalent to $(\mathfrak{w} \setminus \mathfrak{v}) \subseteq (\mathcal{I}_s \setminus \mathfrak{v})$, provided that $\mathfrak{v} \subseteq \mathfrak{w}$. Therefore, for $|\mathfrak{v}| \leq w \leq s$, there are $\binom{s-|\mathfrak{v}|}{w-|\mathfrak{v}|}$ sets $\mathfrak{w}$ such that $|\mathfrak{w}| = w$ and $\mathfrak{v} \subseteq \mathfrak{w} \subseteq \mathcal{I}_s$. Hence,

$$\sum_{\emptyset\neq\mathfrak{w}\subseteq\mathcal{I}_s} \left(-\frac{1}{3}\right)^{|\mathfrak{w}|} \sum_{\emptyset\neq\mathfrak{v}\subseteq\mathfrak{w}} (-3)^{|\mathfrak{v}|} \mathcal{B}(\mathfrak{v})$$

$$= \sum_{\emptyset\neq\mathfrak{v}\subseteq\mathcal{I}_s} \sum_{w=|\mathfrak{v}|}^{s} \binom{s-|\mathfrak{v}|}{w-|\mathfrak{v}|} \left(-\frac{1}{3}\right)^{w} (-3)^{|\mathfrak{v}|} \mathcal{B}(\mathfrak{v})$$

$$= \sum_{\emptyset\neq\mathfrak{v}\subseteq\mathcal{I}_s} \sum_{w=0}^{s-|\mathfrak{v}|} \binom{s-|\mathfrak{v}|}{w} \left(-\frac{1}{3}\right)^{w} \mathcal{B}(\mathfrak{v})$$

$$= \sum_{\emptyset\neq\mathfrak{v}\subseteq\mathcal{I}_s} \left(\frac{2}{3}\right)^{s-|\mathfrak{v}|} \mathcal{B}(\mathfrak{v}),$$

and the first result follows.

It remains to prove the formula for the mean square weighted L_2-discrepancy for the case where the randomisation method is a simplified digital shift of depth m. Here, the starting point is again the formula for the weighted L_2-discrepancy given in Proposition 2.15.

Trivially, we have

$$b^m \int_0^{1/b^m} \left[1 - (x_{n,i} + \delta_n)\right] \mathrm{d}\delta_n = 1 - \left(x_{n,i} + \frac{1}{2b^m}\right).$$

For $1 \leq i \leq s$, the ith components of the points $\boldsymbol{x}_n \in \mathcal{P}_{b^m}$ are a one-dimensional digital net and hence, their base b representation has at most the first m digits unequal zero. Therefore, if $x_{n,i} > x_{h,i}$, then we have $x_{n,i} + \delta_n > x_{h,i} + \delta_h$ for arbitrary $\delta_n, \delta_h \in [0, 1/b^m)$. Hence, we obtain

$$\begin{aligned} b^{2m} \int_0^{1/b^m} \int_0^{1/b^m} & \min(1 - (x_{n,i} + \delta_n), 1 - (x_{h,i} + \delta_h))\, \mathrm{d}\delta_n\, \mathrm{d}\delta_h \\ &= \min\left(1 - \left(x_{n,i} + \frac{1}{2b^m}\right), 1 - \left(x_{h,i} + \frac{1}{2b^m}\right)\right). \end{aligned}$$

Further, we have

$$b^m \int_0^{1/b^m} \frac{1 - (x_{n,i} + \delta_n)^2}{2}\, \mathrm{d}\delta_n = \frac{1}{2}\left(1 - \left(x_{n,i} + \frac{1}{2b^m}\right)^2\right) - \frac{1}{24b^{2m}}.$$

From these considerations, together with Proposition 2.15 and Lemma 16.38, we find that

$$\mathbb{E}\left[(L_{2,b^m}(\widehat{\mathcal{P}}_{b^m}))^2\right] = 2\left(\frac{1}{3^s} - \left(\frac{1}{3} + \frac{1}{24b^{2m}}\right)^s\right) + \mathbb{E}\left[(L_{2,b^m}(\widetilde{\mathcal{P}}_{b^m}))^2\right],$$

and hence, the results follows from the first part of this proof. □

We derive an upper bound on the formulae shown in Theorem 16.35. Due to Corollary 16.36, it is enough to consider in the following only the case where the randomisation method is a digital shift of depth m. We have the following theorem.

Theorem 16.39 *Let $\mathcal{P}_{b^m}$ be a digital (t, m, s)-net over $\mathbb{Z}_b$ with $t < m$. Let $\widetilde{\mathcal{P}}_{b^m}$ be the point set obtained after applying a random digital shift of depth m independently to each coordinate of each point of $\mathcal{P}_{b^m}$. Then the mean square L_2-discrepancy of $\widetilde{\mathcal{P}}_{b^m}$ is bounded by*

$$\mathbb{E}\left[(L_{2,b^m}(\widetilde{\mathcal{P}}_{b^m}))^2\right] \leq \frac{1}{b^{2m}}\left(\frac{1}{6} + b^{2t}\left(\frac{b^2 - b + 3}{6}\right)^s (m - t)^{s-1}\right).$$

Note that using digital (t, s)-sequences over $\mathbb{Z}_b$, it follows that for fixed s and b there always exists a digital (t, m, s)-net over $\mathbb{Z}_b$, where $t \le T(s, b)$ is bounded for some natural number $T(s, b)$ independent of m and m can be chosen arbitrarily large. Hence, the above theorem shows that we can obtain a convergence rate of the root mean square L_2-discrepancy of order $O((\log b^m)^{(s-1)/2} b^{-m})$.

We need the following lemma for the proof of the above theorem.

Lemma 16.40 *Let $C_1, \ldots, C_s$ be the generating matrices of a digital (t, m, s)-net over $\mathbb{Z}_b$. Further, define $\mathcal{B}$ as in Theorem 16.35. Then, for any $\mathfrak{v} \subseteq \mathcal{I}_s$, we have*

$$\mathcal{B}(\mathfrak{v}) \le \frac{b^{2t}}{b^{2m}} \left(\frac{b^3}{3(b+1)} \right)^{|\mathfrak{v}|} \left(m - t + \frac{1}{b^3} \right)^{|\mathfrak{v}|-1}.$$

Proof To simplify the notation, we show the result only for $\mathfrak{v} = \mathcal{I}_s$. The other cases follow by the same arguments. For $k_i = \kappa_{i,0} + \kappa_{i,1} b + \cdots + \kappa_{i,a_i-1} b^{a_i-1}$ where $\kappa_{i,a_i-1} \ne 0$, for $1 \le i \le s$, we have

$$\begin{aligned} \mathcal{B}(\mathcal{I}_s) &= \sum_{\substack{k_1,\ldots,k_s=1 \\ C_1^\top \mathbf{k}_1 + \cdots + C_s^\top \mathbf{k}_s = \mathbf{0}}}^{b^m-1} \prod_{i-1}^{s} \frac{1}{b^{2a_i}} \left(\frac{1}{\sin^2(\kappa_{i,a_i-1}\pi/b)} - \frac{1}{3} \right) \\ &= \sum_{a_1,\ldots,a_s=1}^{m} \frac{1}{b^{2(a_1+\cdots+a_s)}} \underbrace{\sum_{k_1=b^{a_1-1}}^{b^{a_1}-1} \cdots \sum_{k_s=b^{a_s-1}}^{b^{a_s}-1}}_{C_1^\top \mathbf{k}_1 + \cdots + C_s^\top \mathbf{k}_s = \mathbf{0}} \prod_{i=1}^{s} \left(\frac{1}{\sin^2(\kappa_{i,a_i-1}\pi/b)} - \frac{1}{3} \right). \end{aligned} \tag{16.16}$$

For $1 \le i \le s$ and $1 \le j \le m$, let $\mathbf{c}_j^{(i)}$ denote the jth row vector of the matrix C_i. Hence, the condition in the sum from (16.16) can be written as

$$\begin{aligned} &\mathbf{c}_1^{(1)} \kappa_{1,0} + \cdots + \mathbf{c}_{a_1-1}^{(1)} \kappa_{1,a_1-2} + \mathbf{c}_{a_1}^{(1)} \kappa_{1,a_1-1} + \\ &\mathbf{c}_1^{(2)} \kappa_{2,0} + \cdots + \mathbf{c}_{a_2-1}^{(2)} \kappa_{2,a_2-2} + \mathbf{c}_{a_2}^{(2)} \kappa_{2,a_2-1} + \\ &\qquad \vdots \\ &\mathbf{c}_1^{(s)} \kappa_{s,0} + \cdots + \mathbf{c}_{a_s-1}^{(s)} \kappa_{s,a_s-2} + \mathbf{c}_{a_s}^{(s)} \kappa_{s,a_s-1} = \mathbf{0}. \end{aligned} \tag{16.17}$$

Since $C_1, \ldots, C_s$ generate a digital (t, m, s)-net over $\mathbb{Z}_b$, it follows from Lemma 4.52 that the vectors

$$\mathbf{c}_1^{(1)}, \ldots, \mathbf{c}_{a_1}^{(1)}, \ldots, \mathbf{c}_1^{(s)}, \ldots, \mathbf{c}_{a_s}^{(s)}$$

are linearly independent as long as $a_1 + \cdots + a_s \le m - t$, and hence we must have

$$a_1 + \cdots + a_s \ge m - t + 1. \tag{16.18}$$

Now let A denote the $m \times ((a_1 - 1) + \cdots + (a_s - 1))$ matrix with the column vectors given by $\left(\mathbf{c}_1^{(1)}\right)^\top, \ldots, \left(\mathbf{c}_{a_1-1}^{(1)}\right)^\top, \ldots, \left(\mathbf{c}_1^{(s)}\right)^\top, \ldots, \left(\mathbf{c}_{a_s-1}^{(s)}\right)^\top$, i.e.

$$A := \left(\left(\mathbf{c}_1^{(1)}\right)^\top, \ldots, \left(\mathbf{c}_{a_1-1}^{(1)}\right)^\top, \ldots, \left(\mathbf{c}_1^{(s)}\right)^\top, \ldots, \left(\mathbf{c}_{a_s-1}^{(s)}\right)^\top\right) \in \mathbb{Z}_b^{m\times((a_1-1)+\cdots+(a_s-1))}.$$

Further, let

$$\mathbf{f}_{\kappa_{1,a_1-1},\ldots,\kappa_{s,a_s-1}} := -\left(\mathbf{c}_{a_1}^{(1)\top}\kappa_{1,a_1-1} + \cdots + \mathbf{c}_{a_s}^{(s)\top}\kappa_{s,a_s-1}\right) \in (\mathbb{Z}_b^m)^\top$$

and

$$\mathbf{k} := (\kappa_{1,0}, \ldots, \kappa_{1,a_1-2}, \ldots, \kappa_{s,0}, \ldots, \kappa_{s,a_s-2})^\top \in (\mathbb{Z}_b^{(a_1-1)+\cdots+(a_s-1)})^\top.$$

Then, the linear equation system (16.17) can be written as

$$A\mathbf{k} = \mathbf{f}_{\kappa_{1,a_1-1},\ldots,\kappa_{s,a_s-1}} \tag{16.19}$$

and hence,

$$\begin{aligned}
&\underbrace{\sum_{k_1=b^{a_1-1}}^{b^{a_1}-1} \cdots \sum_{k_s=b^{a_s-1}}^{b^{a_s}-1}}_{C_1^\top \mathbf{k}_1+\cdots+C_s^\top \mathbf{k}_s=\mathbf{0}} \prod_{i=1}^{s}\left(\frac{1}{\sin^2(\kappa_{i,a_i-1}\pi/b)} - \frac{1}{3}\right) \\
&= \sum_{\kappa_{1,a_1-1},\ldots,\kappa_{s,a_s-1}=1}^{b-1} \prod_{i=1}^{s}\left(\frac{1}{\sin^2(\kappa_{i,a_i-1}\pi/b)} - \frac{1}{3}\right) \sum_{\substack{\mathbf{k}\in\mathbb{Z}_b^{(a_1-1)+\cdots+(a_s-1)} \\ A\mathbf{k}=\mathbf{f}_{\kappa_{1,a_1-1},\ldots,\kappa_{s,a_s-1}}}} 1 \\
&= \sum_{\kappa_{1,a_1-1},\ldots,\kappa_{s,a_s-1}=1}^{b-1} \prod_{i=1}^{s}\left(\frac{1}{\sin^2(\kappa_{i,a_i-1}\pi/b)} - \frac{1}{3}\right) \\
&\qquad \times \left|\left\{\mathbf{k} \in \mathbb{Z}_b^{(a_1-1)+\cdots+(a_s-1)} : A\mathbf{k} = \mathbf{f}_{\kappa_{1,a_1-1},\ldots,\kappa_{s,a_s-1}}\right\}\right|.
\end{aligned}$$

By the definition of the matrix A and since $C_1, \ldots, C_s$ are the generating matrices of a digital (t, m, s)-net over $\mathbb{Z}_b$, we have

$$\operatorname{rank}(A) = \begin{cases} (a_1 - 1) + \cdots + (a_s - 1) & \text{if } a_1 + \cdots + a_s \le m - t + s, \\ \ge m - t & \text{else.} \end{cases}$$

Let L denote the linear space of solutions of the homogeneous system $A\mathbf{k} = \mathbf{0}$ and let $\dim(L)$ denote the dimension of L. Then it follows that

$$\dim(L) = \begin{cases} 0 & \text{if } a_1 + \cdots + a_s \leq m - t + s, \\ \leq a_1 + \cdots + a_s - s - m + t & \text{else.} \end{cases}$$

Hence, if $a_1 + \cdots + a_s \leq m - t + s$, we find that the system (16.19) has, at most, one solution and if $a_1 + \cdots + a_s > m - t + s$, the system (16.19) has, at most, $b^{a_1+\cdots+a_s-s-m+t}$ solutions, i.e.

$$\underbrace{\sum_{k_1=b^{a_1-1}}^{b^{a_1}-1} \cdots \sum_{k_s=b^{a_s-1}}^{b^{a_s}-1}}_{C_1^\top \mathbf{k}_1+\cdots+C_s^\top \mathbf{k}_s=\mathbf{0}} \prod_{i=1}^{s} \left(\frac{1}{\sin^2(\kappa_{i,a_i-1}\pi/b)} - \frac{1}{3} \right)$$

$$\leq \sum_{\kappa_{1,a_1-1},\ldots,\kappa_{s,a_s-1}=1}^{b-1} \prod_{i=1}^{s} \left(\frac{1}{\sin^2(\kappa_{i,a_i-1}\pi/b)} - \frac{1}{3} \right)$$

$$\times \begin{cases} 1 & \text{if } a_1 + \cdots + a_s \leq m - t + s, \\ b^{a_1+\cdots+a_s-s-m+t} & \text{if } a_1 + \cdots + a_s > m - t + s. \end{cases}$$

Again we use $\sum_{k=1}^{b-1} \sin^{-2}(k\pi/b) = (b^2-1)/3$ from Corollary A.23. Therefore, together with condition (16.18), we obtain

$$\begin{aligned} \mathcal{B}(\mathcal{I}_s) \leq & \left(\frac{b^2-b}{3} \right)^s \sum_{\substack{a_1,\ldots,a_s=1 \\ m-t+1 \leq a_1+\cdots+a_s \leq m-t+s}}^{m} \frac{1}{b^{2(a_1+\cdots+a_s)}} + \\ & + \left(\frac{b^2-b}{3} \right)^s \sum_{\substack{a_1,\ldots,a_s=1 \\ a_1+\cdots+a_s > m-t+s}}^{m} \frac{1}{b^{2(a_1+\cdots+a_s)}} b^{a_1+\cdots+a_s-s-m+t} \\ =: & \Sigma_1 + \Sigma_2. \end{aligned} \tag{16.20}$$

Now we have to estimate the sums Σ_1 and Σ_2. First, we have

$$\begin{aligned} \Sigma_2 &= \left(\frac{b-1}{3} \right)^s \frac{b^t}{b^m} \sum_{l=m-t+s+1}^{sm} \frac{1}{b^l} \sum_{\substack{a_1,\ldots,a_s=1 \\ a_1+\cdots+a_s=l}}^{m} 1 \\ &\leq \left(\frac{b-1}{3} \right)^s \frac{b^t}{b^m} \sum_{l=m-t+s+1}^{\infty} \binom{l-1}{s-1} \frac{1}{b^l} \\ &= \left(\frac{b-1}{3b} \right)^s \frac{b^t}{b^m} \sum_{l=m-t+1}^{\infty} \binom{l+s-1}{s-1} \frac{1}{b^l}, \end{aligned}$$

where we used the fact that for fixed l, the number of positive integer solutions of $a_1 + \cdots + a_s = l$ is given by $\binom{l-1}{s-1}$. Now we apply Lemma 13.24 and obtain

$$\begin{aligned}\Sigma_2 &\leq \left(\frac{b-1}{3b}\right)^s \frac{b^t}{b^m} \frac{1}{b^{m-t+1}} \binom{m-t+s}{s-1} \left(\frac{b-1}{b}\right)^{-s} \\ &= \frac{1}{3^s} \frac{b^{2t}}{b^{2m}} \frac{1}{b} \binom{m-t+s}{s-1}. \end{aligned} \tag{16.21}$$

Finally, since

$$\binom{m-t+s}{s-1} = \frac{(m-t+2)(m-t+3)\cdots(m-t+s)}{1 \cdot 2 \cdots (s-1)} \leq (m-t+2)^{s-1},$$

we obtain

$$\Sigma_2 \leq \frac{1}{3^s} \frac{b^{2t}}{b^{2m}} \frac{1}{b} (m-t+2)^{s-1}.$$

Now we estimate Σ_1. If $m - t + 1 \geq s$, we proceed similarly to above and obtain

$$\begin{aligned}\Sigma_1 &= \left(\frac{b-1}{3b}\right)^s \sum_{l=m-t-s+1}^{m-t} \binom{l+s-1}{s-1} \frac{1}{b^{2l}} \\ &\leq \left(\frac{b-1}{3b}\right)^s \frac{1}{b^{2(m-t-s+1)}} \binom{m-t}{s-1} \left(1 - \frac{1}{b^2}\right)^{-s} \\ &= \frac{1}{3^s} \frac{b^{3s}}{(b+1)^s} \frac{b^{2t}}{b^{2m}} \frac{1}{b^2} \binom{m-t}{s-1} \qquad (16.22) \\ &\leq \frac{1}{3^s} \frac{b^{3s}}{(b+1)^s} \frac{b^{2t}}{b^{2m}} \frac{1}{b^2} \frac{(m-t)^{s-1}}{(s-1)!}. \end{aligned}$$

For this case, we obtain

$$\begin{aligned}\mathcal{B}(\mathcal{I}_s) &\leq \left(\frac{b^3}{3(b+1)}\right)^s \frac{b^{2t}}{b^{2m}} \left(\frac{1}{b^2} \frac{(m-t)^{s-1}}{(s-1)!} + \frac{1}{b} \frac{(b+1)^s}{b^{3s}} (m-t+2)^{s-1}\right) \\ &= \frac{b^{3s}}{3^s (b+1)^s} \frac{b^{2t}}{b^{2m}} \\ &\quad \times \left(\frac{1}{b^2} \frac{(m-t)^{s-1}}{(s-1)!} + \frac{b+1}{b^4} \left(\frac{b+1}{b^3}(m-t) + \frac{2(b+1)}{b^3}\right)^{s-1}\right). \end{aligned}$$

As $\frac{b+1}{b^3}(m-t) + \frac{2(b+1)}{b^3} \leq m - t + \frac{1}{b^3}$, provided that $m - t > 0$, we have

$$\mathcal{B}(\mathcal{I}_s) \leq \frac{b^{2t}}{b^{2m}} \frac{b^{3s}}{3^s (b+1)^s} \left(m - t + \frac{1}{b^3}\right)^{s-1},$$

which is the desired bound.

Now we consider the case where $m - t + 1 < s$. We have

$$\begin{aligned}\Sigma_1 &= \left(\frac{b-1}{3b}\right)^s \sum_{l=0}^{m-t} \binom{l+s-1}{s-1} \frac{1}{b^{2l}} \\ &\le \left(\frac{b-1}{3b}\right)^s \sum_{l=0}^{\infty} \binom{l+s-1}{s-1} \frac{1}{b^{2l}} \\ &= \frac{1}{3^s} \frac{b^s}{(b+1)^s} \le \frac{1}{b^4} \frac{b^{3s}}{3^s (b+1)^s} \frac{b^{2t}}{b^{2m}}. \end{aligned} \tag{16.23}$$

Thus, we obtain

$$\begin{aligned}\mathcal{B}(\mathcal{I}_s) &\le \frac{1}{b^4} \frac{b^{3s}}{3^s (b+1)^s} \frac{b^{2t}}{b^{2m}} + \frac{1}{3^s} \frac{b^{2t}}{b^{2m}} \frac{1}{b} (m-t+2)^{s-1} \\ &= \frac{b^{3s}}{3^s (b+1)^s} \frac{b^{2t}}{b^{2m}} \left(\frac{1}{b^4} + \frac{b+1}{b^4} \left(\frac{b+1}{b^3}(m-t) + \frac{2(b+1)}{b^3} \right)^{s-1} \right). \end{aligned}$$

Using the same arguments as above, we again obtain the desired result. □

Proof of Theorem 16.39 We use the formula of Theorem 16.35 together with Lemma 16.40 to obtain

$$\begin{aligned}\mathbb{E}\left[(L_{2,b^m}(\widetilde{\mathcal{P}}_{b^m}))^2\right] &\le \frac{1}{b^m 2^s} \left(1 - \left(1 - \frac{1}{3b^m}\right)^s\right) \\ &\quad + \frac{b^{2t}}{b^{2m}} \frac{1}{3^s} \sum_{\emptyset \ne \mathfrak{v} \subseteq \mathcal{I}_s} \left(\frac{b^3}{2(b+1)} \right)^{|\mathfrak{v}|} \left(m - t + \frac{1}{b^3} \right)^{|\mathfrak{v}|-1}. \end{aligned}$$

Since for $x < y$, we have $y^s - x^s = s\zeta^{s-1}(y-x)$, for a $x < \zeta < y$, we have $1 - \left(1 - (3b^m)^{-1}\right)^s \le s/(3b^m)$. As $s2^{-s} \le 1/2$ for $s \ge 1$, we obtain

$$\frac{1}{b^m 2^s} \left(1 - \left(1 - \frac{1}{3b^m}\right)^s\right) \le \frac{1}{6b^{2m}}.$$

Furthermore, we have

$$\begin{aligned}&\frac{1}{3^s} \sum_{\emptyset \ne \mathfrak{v} \subseteq \mathcal{I}_s} \left(\frac{b^3}{2(b+1)} \right)^{|\mathfrak{v}|} \left(m - t + \frac{1}{b^3} \right)^{|\mathfrak{v}|-1} \\ &\le (m-t)^{-1} \left(\frac{1}{3} + \frac{b^3}{6(b+1)} \left(m - t + \frac{1}{b^3} \right) \right)^s \\ &\le \left(\frac{b^2 - b + 3}{6} \right)^s (m-t)^{s-1}, \end{aligned}$$

provided that $m - t > 0$ and the result follows. □

We close this section with a result concerning the proportion of simplified digital shifts of depth m which yield a digitally shifted net with weighted L_2-discrepancy bounded above by a constant times the bound from Theorem 16.39.

Corollary 16.41 *Let $\mathcal{P}_{b^m}$ be a digital (t, m, s)-net over $\mathbb{Z}_b$ with $t < m$. Let $\widehat{\mathcal{P}}_{b^m,\boldsymbol{\sigma}_m}$ be the point set obtained after applying the simplified digital shift $\boldsymbol{\sigma}_m \in \mathbb{Z}_b^{sm}$ of depth m to each point of $\mathcal{P}_{b^m}$. For any $0 \le \alpha < 1$, there are more than $\alpha|\mathbb{Z}_b^{sm}|$ shifts $\boldsymbol{\sigma}_m \in \mathbb{Z}_b^{sm}$ such that*

$$L_{2,b^m}(\widehat{\mathcal{P}}_{b^m,\boldsymbol{\sigma}_m}) \le \frac{1}{b^m\sqrt{1-\alpha}}\left(\frac{1}{6} + b^{2t}\left(\frac{b^2-b+3}{6}\right)^s (m-t)^{s-1}\right)^{1/2}.$$

Proof Using Markov's inequality, Corollary 16.36, the upper bound from Theorem 16.39 and the notation $f_{t,m,s,b} := \frac{1}{b^{2m}}\left(\frac{1}{6} + b^{2t}\left(\frac{b^2-b+3}{6}\right)^s (m-t)^{s-1}\right)$, we have for $c \ge 1$ that

$$\begin{aligned} f_{t,m,s,b} &\ge \mathbb{E}\left[(L_{2,b^m}(\widehat{\mathcal{P}}_{b^m,\boldsymbol{\sigma}_m}))^2\right] \\ &> c^2 f_{t,m,s,b}\frac{\left|\left\{\boldsymbol{\sigma}_m \in \mathbb{Z}_b^{sm} : L_{2,b^m}(\widehat{\mathcal{P}}_{b^m,\boldsymbol{\sigma}_m}) > c\sqrt{f_{t,m,s,b}}\right\}\right|}{|\mathbb{Z}_b^{sm}|}. \end{aligned}$$

From this the result follows by substituting $\alpha = 1 - c^{-2}$. □

16.6 Asymptotics

In this section, we investigate the asymptotic behaviour of the L_2-discrepancy. In the following, let for $s, m \in \mathbb{N}$ the point set $\mathcal{P}_{t,s,2^m,\boldsymbol{\sigma}_{m,s}}$ be a digital (t, m, s)-net over $\mathbb{Z}_2$ shifted by the dyadic digital shift $\boldsymbol{\sigma}_{m,s}$ of depth m. We obtain the following theorem.

Theorem 16.42 *Let $s > 3$, $0 \le t < m$ and $m - t \ge s$ be such that a digital (t, m, s)-net over $\mathbb{Z}_2$ exists. Then there exists a dyadic digital shift $\boldsymbol{\sigma}_{m,s}$ of depth m such that for the shifted net $\mathcal{P}_{t,s,2^m,\boldsymbol{\sigma}_{m,s}}$, we have*

$$L_{2,2^m}(\mathcal{P}_{t,s,2^m,\boldsymbol{\sigma}_{m,s}}) \le \frac{2^t}{2^m}\sqrt{\binom{m-t+s}{s-1}\left(\frac{2}{3}\right)^s} + O\left(\frac{m^{(s-2)/2}}{2^m}\right).$$

Proof We obtain from Theorem 16.35 with $b = 2$,

$$\mathbb{E}\left[(L_{2,2^m}(\widetilde{\mathcal{P}}_{2^m}))^2\right] = \frac{1}{2^{m+s}}\left(1 - \left(1 - \frac{1}{3\cdot 2^m}\right)^s\right) + \frac{1}{3^s}\sum_{\emptyset\ne\mathfrak{v}\subseteq\mathcal{I}_s}\left(\frac{3}{2}\right)^{|\mathfrak{v}|}\mathcal{B}(\mathfrak{v}).$$

Lemma 16.40 shows that, in order to find the constant of the leading term, we only need to consider $\mathcal{B}(\mathcal{I}_s)$. From (16.20), (16.21) and (16.22), we obtain

$$\mathcal{B}(\mathcal{I}_s) \leq \frac{2^{2t}}{2^{2m}} \left(\frac{1}{2} \frac{1}{3^s} \binom{m-t+s}{s-1} + \frac{1}{4} \frac{8^s}{9^s} \binom{m-t}{s-1} \right).$$

As the bound in Theorem 16.35 was obtained by averaging over all shifts, it follows that there exists a shift which yields an L_2-discrepancy smaller than or equal to this bound. □

Observe that the bound in Theorem 16.42 is for large m, apart from the t, similar to Roth's general lower bound on L_2-discrepancy given in Theorem 3.20.

We now consider digital (t, s)-sequences over $\mathbb{Z}_2$. From [194, Theorem 4], it follows that for every dimension s, there exists a digital (t, s)-sequence over $\mathbb{Z}_2$ such that $t \leq 5s$. Thus, it follows that for all $s \in \mathbb{N}$ and $m > 5s$, there is a digital $(5s, m, s)$-net over $\mathbb{Z}_2$. (Note that if there is a digital (t, m, s)-net, then it follows that a digital $(t + 1, m, s)$-net also exists.) Let $\mathcal{P}_{s,5s,2^m,\boldsymbol{\sigma}_{m,s}}$ denote a digital $(5s, m, s)$-net over $\mathbb{Z}_2$ shifted by the digital shift $\boldsymbol{\sigma}_{m,s}$ of depth m. We are interested in the asymptotic behaviour of the L_2-discrepancy. Therefore, for m much larger than s and $t = 5s$, we have

$$\binom{m-t+s}{s-1} \leq \binom{m}{s-1} \leq \frac{m^{s-1}}{(s-1)!}.$$

Further, let $N = 2^m$, then $m = (\log N)/\log 2$. The following corollary follows now from Theorem 16.42.

Corollary 16.43 *For every $s \in \mathbb{N}$ and $m \geq 5s$, there exists a shifted digital $(5s, m, s)$-net $\mathcal{P}_{5s,s,2^m,\boldsymbol{\sigma}_{m,s}}$ over $\mathbb{Z}_2$ shifted by the dyadic digital shift $\boldsymbol{\sigma}_{m,s}$ of depth m such that*

$$L_{2,N}(\mathcal{P}_{5s,s,2^m,\boldsymbol{\sigma}_{m,s}}) \leq C_s \frac{(\log N)^{(s-1)/2}}{N} + O\left(\frac{(\log N)^{(s-2)/2}}{N} \right),$$

where $N = 2^m$ and where

$$C_s := \frac{2 2^s}{(\log 2)^{(s-1)/2} \sqrt{(s-1)!}}$$

depends only on the dimension s.

We note that the convergence of order $O((\log N)^{(s-1)/2} N^{-1})$ is the best possible with respect to Roth's lower bound and that the constant C_s tends faster than exponentially to zero as s approaches infinity.

Although C_s has until now been the smallest known constant of the leading term of an upper bound, compared to c_s from Theorem 3.20, C_s is not quite as good. Indeed, we have $C_s/c_s = 16 \cdot 88^s$. Nevertheless, we show later that the constant c_s from Theorem 3.20 cannot be improved by much.

It is known that for digital (t, s)-sequences over $\mathbb{Z}_2$, we always have $t > s \log_2 \frac{3}{2} - 4\log_2(s-2) - 23$ for all $s \geq 3$ by Schmid's result [234, Corollary 1]. Hence, for digital (t, m, s)-nets obtained from digital (t, s)-sequences over $\mathbb{Z}_2$, Theorem 16.42 cannot yield a constant of the form $a^{-s/2}((s-1)!)^{-1/2}$ for some $a > 1$. On the other hand, it is possible that for special choices of m and s, the quality parameter t of a digital (t, m, s)-net can be considerably lower than the quality parameter of the best (t, s)-sequence.

We derive an upper bound on the classical L_2-discrepancy of shifted Niederreiter–Xing nets [193] (see Section 8.3 and also [268] for a survey article). This enables us to show that Theorem 3.20 is also in the dimension s essentially the best possible.

Niederreiter and Xing [193, Corollary 3] showed that for every integer $d \geq 2$, there exists a sequence of digital $(t_k, t_k + d, s_k)$-nets over $\mathbb{Z}_2$ with $s_k \to \infty$ as $k \to \infty$ such that

$$\lim_{k\to\infty} \frac{t_k}{\log_2 s_k} = \left\lfloor \frac{d}{2} \right\rfloor, \tag{16.24}$$

and that this is also best possible. (We note that the sequence of digital nets from Niederreiter and Xing's result can be constructed explicitly.) Therefore, for any $d \in \mathbb{N}$, there exists a sequence of digital $(t_k, t_k + d, s_k)$-nets over $\mathbb{Z}_2$ and a k_d such that

$$\left\lceil \frac{t_k}{\log_2 s_k} \right\rceil = d \quad \text{and} \quad s_k \geq 2d + 2 \quad \text{for all } k \geq k_d. \tag{16.25}$$

(Note that if a digital $(t_k, t_k + d, s_k)$-net exists, then there also exists a digital $(t_k + 1, t_k + d + 1, s_k)$-net. Further, for $d = 1$, there exists a digital $(t, t+1, s)$-net for all $t, s \in \mathbb{N}$.) For a point set $\mathcal{P}$ in $[0, 1)^s$ with 2^m points, let

$$\mathcal{D}_{m,s}(\mathcal{P}) := \frac{2^m L_{2,2^m}(\mathcal{P})}{\sqrt{\binom{m+s+1}{s-1}}}. \tag{16.26}$$

The bound in Theorem 16.39 was obtained by averaging over all shifts. Hence, for any digital (t, m, s)-net, there is always a shift σ^* which yields an L_2-discrepancy smaller or equal to this bound. Let $\mathcal{P}_k(d)$ denote a shifted digital $(t_k, t_k + d, s_k)$-net over $\mathbb{Z}_2$ satisfying (16.25), which is shifted by such a shift σ^*. We prove an upper bound on $\mathcal{D}_{t_k+d,s_k}(\mathcal{P}_k(d))$ for fixed d.

In the following, let $k \geq k_d$. Let $\mathfrak{v} \subseteq \{1, \ldots, s_k\}$ and $l := |\mathfrak{v}|$. First, we consider the case where $l \geq d+2$. Note that $m - t = d$ for the nets considered here. Then (16.21) and (16.23) yield

$$\mathcal{B}(\mathfrak{v}) \leq \frac{1}{3^l}\frac{1}{4^d}\frac{1}{2}\binom{d+l}{d+1} + \frac{2^l}{9^l}.$$

For $0 < l \leq d+1$, we obtain from (16.21) and (16.22) that

$$\mathcal{B}(\mathfrak{v}) \leq \frac{1}{3^l}\frac{1}{4^d}\frac{1}{2}\binom{d+l}{d+1} + \frac{8^l}{9^l}\frac{1}{4^d}\frac{1}{4}\binom{d}{l-1}.$$

Therefore, we obtain

$$\begin{aligned}
&\frac{1}{3^{s_k}} \sum_{\emptyset \neq \mathfrak{v} \subseteq \mathcal{I}_s} \left(\frac{3}{2}\right)^{|\mathfrak{v}|} \mathcal{B}(\mathfrak{v}) \\
&\leq \frac{1}{3^{s_k}} \sum_{l=1}^{d+1} \left(\frac{3}{2}\right)^l \binom{s_k}{l} \left(\frac{1}{3^l}\frac{1}{4^d}\frac{1}{2}\binom{d+l}{d+1} + \frac{8^l}{9^l}\frac{1}{4^d}\frac{1}{4}\binom{d}{l-1}\right) \\
&\quad + \frac{1}{3^{s_k}} \sum_{l=d+2}^{s_k} \left(\frac{3}{2}\right)^l \binom{s_k}{l} \left(\frac{1}{3^l}\frac{1}{4^d}\frac{1}{2}\binom{d+l}{d+1} + \frac{2^l}{9^l}\right).
\end{aligned}$$

Now we have

$$\begin{aligned}
\frac{1}{3^{s_k}} \sum_{l=1}^{s_k} \left(\frac{3}{2}\right)^l \binom{s_k}{l} \frac{1}{3^l}\frac{1}{4^d}\frac{1}{2}\binom{d+l}{d+1} &\leq \frac{1}{2}\frac{1}{3^{s_k}}\frac{1}{4^d}\binom{d+s_k}{d+1} \sum_{l=0}^{s_k} \frac{1}{2^l}\binom{s_k}{l} \\
&= \frac{1}{2}\frac{1}{2^{s_k}}\frac{1}{4^d}\binom{d+s_k}{s_k-1}
\end{aligned}$$

and

$$\begin{aligned}
&\frac{1}{3^{s_k}} \sum_{l=1}^{d+1} \left(\frac{3}{2}\right)^l \binom{s_k}{l} \frac{8^l}{9^l}\frac{1}{4^d}\frac{1}{4}\binom{d}{l-1} + \frac{1}{3^{s_k}} \sum_{l=d+2}^{s_k} \left(\frac{3}{2}\right)^l \binom{s_k}{l} \frac{2^l}{9^l} \\
&= \frac{1}{3^{s_k}}\frac{1}{4^{d+1}} \sum_{l=1}^{d+1} \binom{s_k}{l} \left(\frac{4}{3}\right)^l \binom{d}{l-1} + \frac{1}{3^{s_k}} \sum_{l=d+2}^{s_k} \binom{s_k}{l} \frac{1}{3^l} \\
&\leq \frac{1}{3}\left(\frac{7}{12}\right)^d \frac{1}{3^{s_k}}\binom{s_k}{d+1} + \left(\frac{4}{9}\right)^{s_k},
\end{aligned}$$

as $\max_{1\le l\le d+1}\binom{s_k}{l}=\binom{s_k}{d+1}$ for $s_k\ge 2d+2$. Thus, we obtain

$$\frac{1}{3^{s_k}}\sum_{\emptyset\ne\mathfrak{v}\subseteq\mathcal{I}_s}\left(\frac{3}{2}\right)^{|\mathfrak{v}|}\mathcal{B}(\mathfrak{v})\le\frac{1}{2}\frac{1}{2^{s_k}}\frac{1}{4^d}\binom{d+s_k}{s_k-1}$$
$$+\frac{1}{3}\left(\frac{7}{12}\right)^d\frac{1}{3^{s_k}}\binom{s_k}{d+1}+\left(\frac{4}{9}\right)^{s_k}.$$

Further, we have $1-\left(1-(3\cdot 2^m)^{-1}\right)^s\le s/(3\cdot 2^m)$. Hence, it follows from the definition of $\mathcal{P}_k(d)$ and (16.24) that

$$L^2_{2,2^{t_k+d}}(\mathcal{P}_k(d))\le\frac{1}{2}\frac{1}{2^{s_k}}\frac{1}{4^d}\binom{d+s_k}{s_k-1}+\frac{1}{3}\left(\frac{7}{12}\right)^d\frac{1}{3^{s_k}}\binom{s_k}{d+1}$$
$$+\left(\frac{4}{9}\right)^{s_k}+\frac{s_k}{3\cdot 2^{2(t_k+d)+s_k}}. \tag{16.27}$$

In order to get a bound on $\mathcal{D}^2_{t_k+d,s_k}(\mathcal{P}_k(d))$, we need to multiply the inequality above by $4^{t_k+d}\left[\binom{t_k+d+s_k+1}{s_k-1}\right]^{-1}$. For the first term in the bound of (16.27), we get

$$\frac{1}{2}\frac{1}{2^{s_k}}\frac{1}{4^d}\binom{d+s_k}{s_k-1}4^{t_k+d}\left[\binom{t_k+d+s_k+1}{s_k-1}\right]^{-1}$$
$$=\frac{1}{2}\frac{1}{2^{s_k}}4^{t_k}\frac{(d+s_k)\cdots(d+2)}{(t_k+d+s_k+1)\cdots(t_k+d+3)}.$$

Let $r\ge 1$ be an integer which will be chosen later. From (16.24), it follows that for large enough k, we have $rt_k<s_k$. Further, we have $t_k>0$. We get

$$\frac{(t_k+d+s_k+1)\cdots(t_k+d+3)}{(d+s_k)\cdots(d+2)}=\left(1+\frac{t_k+1}{d+s_k}\right)\cdots\left(1+\frac{t_k+1}{d+2}\right)$$
$$\ge\prod_{j=1}^{r}\left(1+\frac{t_k+1}{jt_k+d+1}\right)^{t_k}.$$

Now we have

$$\prod_{j=1}^{r}\left(1+\frac{t_k+1}{jt_k+d+1}\right)\to\prod_{j=1}^{r}\left(1+\frac{1}{j}\right)=(r+1)\qquad\text{as } t_k\to\infty.$$

Therefore, for large enough k, we obtain

$$r^{t_k}\le\frac{(t_k+d+s_k+1)\cdots(t_k+d+3)}{(d+s_k)\cdots(d+2)}$$

and

$$\frac{1}{2}\frac{1}{2^{s_k}}\frac{1}{4^d}\binom{d+s_k}{s_k-1}4^{t_k+d}\left[\binom{t_k+d+s_k+1}{s_k-1}\right]^{-1} \leq \frac{1}{2}\frac{1}{2^{s_k}}\left(\frac{4}{r}\right)^{t_k}$$

for all $k \geq K_1(r,d)$, for some well chosen $K_1(r,d)$. Further, one can show that the other terms on the right-hand side of (16.27) decay faster than $\frac{1}{s_k}\frac{1}{4^d}\binom{d+s_k}{s_k-1}$ as $k \to \infty$. From (16.25) it follows that $t_k \geq (d-1)\log_2 s_k$ for all $k \geq K_2(d)$. Let $r = 8$, then we have $(4/r)^{t_k} \leq s_k^{1-d}$. Therefore, there exists a K_d such that for all $k \geq K_d$, we have

$$\mathcal{D}^2_{t_k+d,s_k}(\mathcal{P}_k(d)) \leq \frac{1}{2^{s_k}}\frac{1}{s_k^{d-1}}.$$

We summarise the result in the following theorem.

Theorem 16.44 *For any $d \in \mathbb{N}$, there exists an integer $K_d > 0$ and a sequence of shifted digital (t_k, t_k+d, s_k)-nets over $\mathbb{Z}_2$, $(\mathcal{P}_k(d))_{k\geq 1}$, with $s_k \to \infty$ as $k \to \infty$ and*

$$\left\lceil \frac{t_k}{\log_2 s_k} \right\rceil = d \qquad \textit{for all } k \geq K_d,$$

such that for all $k \geq K_d$, we have

$$L_{2,2^{t_k+d}}(\mathcal{P}_k(d)) \leq \frac{1}{2^{t_k+d}}\frac{1}{2^{s_k/2}}\frac{1}{s_k^{(d-1)/2}}\sqrt{\binom{t_k+d+s_k+1}{s_k-1}}.$$

We use (16.26) again. Then by using Theorem 3.20 and the result above, we obtain that for any $d \in \mathbb{N}$ and for all $k \geq K_d$, we have

$$\frac{1}{16}\frac{1}{2^{2s_k}} \leq \mathcal{D}_{t_k+d,s_k}(\mathcal{P}_k(d)) \leq \frac{1}{2^{s_k/2}}\frac{1}{s_k^{(d-1)/2}}. \tag{16.28}$$

This shows that the lower bound of Roth is also in s of the best possible form. The small remaining gap in the constant is not surprising as the result in Theorem 16.44 was obtained by averaging over well-distributed point sets. Some attempts have been made to improve Roth's lower bound, but no considerable progress has been made (see [160]). For small point sets, there exist other lower bounds which yield numerically better results than Roth's, but do not show the higher convergence rate (see [160]).

We note that the results in this section are, apart from the digital shift, constructive as they are based on Niederreiter–Xing constructions of digital nets and sequences.

Exercises

16.1 Show that the Hamming weight $\varkappa_m$ as given in Definition 16.1 defines a metric on the vector space $\mathbb{Z}_b^{sm}$.

16.2 Show that any optimum $[s, k, m]$-distribution in base b is also a $((k-1)m, km, s)$-net in base b.
Hint: See [243, Proposition 1.1].

16.3 Prove Lemma 16.10.

16.4 With the notation from Lemma 16.19, show that

$$\chi_{[0,y)}^{(m)}(x) = b^m \int_{B_m(x)} \chi_{[0,y)}(t)\, \mathrm{d}t.$$

16.5 Show that for $0 \leq k = \kappa_0 + \kappa_1 b + \cdots + \kappa_{a-1} b^{a-1} < b^m$, we have $a = v_m(\tau_m(k))$ and $\varkappa(k) = \varkappa_m(\tau_m(k))$.

16.6 Assume that for every $m \in \mathbb{N}$, we have a $(0, m, s)$-net $\mathcal{P}_m$ in base b such that

$$b^m L_{2,b^m}(\mathcal{P}_m) \leq f_{s,b}(m),$$

where $f_{s,b} : \mathbb{R}^+ \to \mathbb{R}^+$ is an increasing function. Construct for any cardinality $N \geq 2$ a point set $\mathcal{P}$ consisting of N points in the s-dimensional unit-cube whose L_2-discrepancy satisfies

$$N L_{2,N}(\mathcal{P}) \leq \sqrt{b} f_{s,b}\left(\lfloor \log_b N \rfloor + 1\right).$$

16.7 Assume that for every $m \in \mathbb{N}$, we have a $(0, m, s)$-net $\mathcal{P}_m$ in base b such that

$$b^m D_{b^m}^*(\mathcal{P}_m) \leq f_{s,b}(m),$$

where $f_{s,b} : \mathbb{R}^+ \to \mathbb{R}^+$ is an increasing function. Construct for any cardinality $N \geq 2$ a point set $\mathcal{P}$ consisting of N points in the s-dimensional unit-cube whose star discrepancy satisfies

$$N D_N^*(\mathcal{P}) \leq b f_{s,b}\left(\lfloor \log_b N \rfloor + 1\right).$$

16.8 Let $s = 2$, $g = 3$, $w = 2$ and choose $b = 7$. Find generating matrices of a digital $(0, 6, 2)$-net $\mathcal{P}_{3,2}$ over $\mathbb{Z}_7$ and write them down explicitly.

16.9 Generalise Theorem 16.35 to the case of weighted L_2-discrepancy. With the notation from Theorem 16.35, show that

$$\mathbb{E}\left[(L_{2,b^m,\boldsymbol{\gamma}}(\widetilde{\mathcal{P}}_{b^m}))^2\right]$$
$$= \sum_{\emptyset \neq \mathfrak{u} \subseteq \mathcal{I}_s} \gamma_{\mathfrak{u}} \left[\frac{1}{b^m 2^{|\mathfrak{u}|}}\left(1 - \left(1 - \frac{1}{3b^m}\right)^{|\mathfrak{u}|}\right) + \frac{1}{3^{|\mathfrak{u}|}} \sum_{\emptyset \neq \mathfrak{v} \subseteq \mathfrak{u}} \left(\frac{3}{2}\right)^{|\mathfrak{v}|} \mathcal{B}(\mathfrak{v})\right],$$

and

$$\mathbb{E}\left[(L_{2,b^m,\gamma}(\widehat{\mathcal{P}}_{b^m}))^2\right] = \sum_{\emptyset \neq \mathfrak{u} \subseteq \mathcal{I}_s} \gamma_{\mathfrak{u}} \left[2\left(\frac{1}{3^{|\mathfrak{u}|}} - \left(\frac{1}{3} + \frac{1}{24 b^{2m}}\right)^{|\mathfrak{u}|}\right) \right.$$
$$\left. + \frac{1}{b^m 2^{|\mathfrak{u}|}}\left(1 - \left(1 - \frac{1}{3b^m}\right)^{|\mathfrak{u}|}\right) + \frac{1}{3^{|\mathfrak{u}|}} \sum_{\emptyset \neq \mathfrak{v} \subseteq \mathfrak{u}} \left(\frac{3}{2}\right)^{|\mathfrak{v}|} \mathcal{B}(\mathfrak{v}) \right],$$

where $\mathcal{B}(\mathfrak{v})$ is as in Theorem 16.35.

Hint: Proceed as in the proof of Theorem 16.35, but use Proposition 3.60.

16.10 Let $\mathcal{P}_{b^m}$ be a digital (t, m, s)-net over $\mathbb{Z}_b$ with $t < m$. With the notation from Theorem 16.35, show that

$$\mathbb{E}[(L_{2,b^m,\gamma}(\widehat{\mathcal{P}}_{b^m}))^2] \le \mathbb{E}\left[(L_{2,b^m,\gamma}(\widetilde{\mathcal{P}}_{b^m}))^2\right]$$

and

$$\mathbb{E}\left[(L_{2,b^m,\gamma}(\widetilde{\mathcal{P}}_{b^m}))^2\right] \le \frac{1}{b^{2m}} \sum_{\emptyset \neq \mathfrak{u} \subseteq \mathcal{I}_s} \gamma_{\mathfrak{u}} \left[\frac{1}{6} + b^{2t}\left(\frac{b^2 - b + 3}{6}\right)^{|\mathfrak{u}|} (m - t)^{|\mathfrak{u}|-1}\right].$$

16.11 Let $\mathcal{P}_{b^m}$ be a digital $((t_{\mathfrak{u}})_{\emptyset \neq \mathfrak{u} \subseteq \mathcal{I}_s}, m, s)$-net over $\mathbb{Z}_b$, i.e. for $\emptyset \neq \mathfrak{u} \subseteq \mathcal{I}_s$ the projected point set $\mathcal{P}_{b^m,\mathfrak{u}}$ is a $(t_{\mathfrak{u}}, m, |\mathfrak{u}|)$-net over $\mathbb{Z}_b$; see Exercise 5.3. Assume that $\max_{\emptyset \neq \mathfrak{u} \subseteq \mathcal{I}_s} t_{\mathfrak{u}} < m$. Show that then

$$\mathbb{E}\left[(L_{2,b^m,\gamma}(\widetilde{\mathcal{P}}_{b^m}))^2\right] \le \frac{1}{b^{2m}} \sum_{\emptyset \neq \mathfrak{u} \subseteq \mathcal{I}_s} \gamma_{\mathfrak{u}} \left[\frac{1}{6} + b^{2t_{\mathfrak{u}}}\left(\frac{b^2 - b + 3}{6}\right)^{|\mathfrak{u}|} (m - t_{\mathfrak{u}})^{|\mathfrak{u}|-1}\right].$$

16.12 Let $b \ge 2$, $s > 3$, $0 \le t < m$ and $m - t \ge s$ be such that a digital (t, m, s)-net over $\mathbb{Z}_b$ exists. Show that there exists a digital shift $\boldsymbol{\sigma}_{m,s}$ of depth m such that for the shifted net $\mathcal{P}_{b,t,s,b^m,\boldsymbol{\sigma}_{m,s}}$, we have

$$L_{2,b^m}(\mathcal{P}_{b,t,s,b^m,\boldsymbol{\sigma}_{m,s}}) \le \frac{b^t}{b^m}\sqrt{\binom{m-t+s}{s-1}}\left(\frac{b^3}{6(b+1)}\right)^{s/2} \frac{\sqrt{2}}{b} + O\left(\frac{m^{(s-2)/2}}{2^m}\right).$$

16.13 For $s = 2$, let $\mathcal{P}_{2^m}$ be a digital $(0, m, 2)$-net over $\mathbb{Z}_2$. Let $\widetilde{\mathcal{P}}_{2^m}$ be the point set obtained after applying a random digital shift of depth m independently to each coordinate of each point of $\mathcal{P}_{2^m}$. Show that the mean square L_2-discrepancy of $\widetilde{\mathcal{P}}_{2^m}$ is given by

$$\mathbb{E}\left[(L_{2,2^m}(\widetilde{\mathcal{P}}_{2^m}))^2\right] = \frac{m}{24 \cdot 2^{2m}}.$$

Hint: Use Theorem 16.35. A proof can also be found in [51, Theorem 2].

16.14 The two-dimensional Hammersley net $\mathcal{H}_{b^m}$ over $\mathbb{Z}_b$ is the digital $(0, m, 2)$-net over $\mathbb{Z}_b$ generated by the matrices

$$C_1 = \begin{pmatrix} 1 & 0 & \dots & 0 & 0 \\ 0 & 1 & \ddots & & 0 \\ \vdots & \ddots & \ddots & \ddots & \vdots \\ 0 & & \ddots & 1 & 0 \\ 0 & 0 & \dots & 0 & 1 \end{pmatrix} \text{ and } C_2 = \begin{pmatrix} 0 & 0 & \dots & 0 & 1 \\ 0 & & \iddots & 1 & 0 \\ \vdots & \iddots & \iddots & \iddots & \vdots \\ 0 & 1 & \iddots & & 0 \\ 1 & 0 & \dots & 0 & 0 \end{pmatrix}.$$

Let $\widetilde{\mathcal{H}}_{b^m}$ be the point set obtained after applying a random digital shift of depth m independently to each coordinate of each point of $\mathcal{H}_{b^m}$. Show that the mean square L_2-discrepancy of $\widetilde{\mathcal{H}}_{b^m}$ is given by

$$\mathbb{E}\left[(L_{2,b^m}(\widetilde{\mathcal{H}}_{b^m}))^2\right] = \frac{b^4 + 5b^2 - 6}{180b^2}\frac{m}{b^{2m}}.$$

Hint: Use Theorem 16.35 and the formula $\sum_{\kappa=1}^{b-1} \sin^{-4}(\kappa\pi/b) = (b^4 + 10b^2 - 11)/45$. A proof can also be found in [28, Theorem 3].

16.15 Determine the mean square L_2-discrepancy of $\widehat{\mathcal{H}}_{b^m}$, where $\mathcal{H}_{b^m}$ is as in Exercise 16.14.

Appendix A

Walsh functions

Walsh functions play a very important role in the analysis of digital nets over $\mathbb{Z}_b$. In this Appendix we recall the definition of Walsh functions and we provide some important and useful results concerning these functions. Many of these results are used within this book without further comment. A standard reference for the theory of Walsh functions is Schipp *et al.* [232]. The overview here is mainly based on [216].

A.1 Definition of Walsh functions

In 1923, Walsh [260] introduced a system of functions which is in some way similar to the trigonometric function system $\{e^{2\pi i k x} : k \in \mathbb{Z}\}$ connected to the well-known Fourier theory. (However, the differences will become clear below.)

For $b \geq 2$, we denote by ω_b the primitive bth root of unity $e^{2\pi i/b}$.

Definition A.1 Let $k \in \mathbb{N}_0$ with b-adic expansion $k = \kappa_0 + \kappa_1 b + \kappa_2 b^2 + \cdots$ (this expansion is obviously finite). The *kth b-adic Walsh function* ${}_b\mathrm{wal}_k : \mathbb{R} \to \mathbb{C}$, periodic with period one, is defined as

$$ {}_b\mathrm{wal}_k(x) = \omega_b^{\kappa_0 \xi_1 + \kappa_1 \xi_2 + \kappa_2 \xi_3 + \cdots}, $$

for $x \in [0, 1)$ with b-adic expansion $x = \xi_1 b^{-1} + \xi_2 b^{-2} + \xi_3 b^{-3} + \cdots$ (unique in the sense that infinitely many of the digits ξ_i must be different from $b-1$).

We call the system $\{{}_b\mathrm{wal}_k : k \in \mathbb{N}_0\}$ the *b-adic Walsh function system.*

In the literature the function system defined above is often called the generalised Walsh function system. Only in the case where $b = 2$ does one speak of Walsh functions. However, within this book, we also speak of Walsh functions in the more general b-adic case.

One of the main differences between Walsh functions and the trigonometric functions is that Walsh functions are only piecewise continuous. This is clear, since Walsh functions are step functions as we now show.

Let $k \in \mathbb{N}_0$ with b-adic expansion $k = \kappa_0 + \kappa_1 b + \cdots + \kappa_{r-1} b^{r-1}$. Let $J = [a/b^r, (a+1)/b^r)$, with an integer $0 \leq a < b^r$, be a so-called *elementary b-adic interval of order r*. Let a have b-adic expansion of the form $a = \alpha_0 + \alpha_1 b + \cdots + \alpha_{r-1} b^{r-1}$. Then, any $x \in J$ has b-adic expansion $x = \alpha_{r-1} b^{-1} + \alpha_{r-2} b^{-2} + \cdots + \alpha_0 b^{-r} + \xi_{r+1} b^{-(r+1)} + \xi_{r+2} b^{-(r+2)} + \cdots$ with some digits $0 \leq \xi_i \leq b-1$ for $i \geq r+1$

and hence,

$$_b\mathrm{wal}_k(x) = \omega_b^{\kappa_0 \alpha_{r-1} + \cdots + \kappa_{r-1}\alpha_0} = {}_b\mathrm{wal}_k(a/b^r).$$

We summarise this result in the following proposition.

Proposition A.2 *Let $k \in \mathbb{N}$ with $b^{r-1} \leq k < b^r$. Then the kth Walsh function $_b\mathrm{wal}_k$ is constant on elementary b-adic intervals of order r of the form $[a/b^r, (a+1)/b^r)$ with value $_b\mathrm{wal}_k(a/b^r)$. Further, $_b\mathrm{wal}_0 = 1$ identical.*

Now we generalise the definition of Walsh functions to higher dimensions.

Definition A.3 For dimension $s \geq 2$ and $k_1, \ldots, k_s \in \mathbb{N}_0$, we define the *s-dimensional b-adic Walsh function* $_b\mathrm{wal}_{k_1,\ldots,k_s} : \mathbb{R}^s \to \mathbb{C}$ by

$$_b\mathrm{wal}_{k_1,\ldots,k_s}(x_1, \ldots, x_s) := \prod_{j=1}^{s} {}_b\mathrm{wal}_{k_j}(x_j).$$

For vectors $\boldsymbol{k} = (k_1, \ldots, k_s) \in \mathbb{N}_0^s$ and $\boldsymbol{x} = (x_1, \ldots, x_s) \in [0, 1)^s$, we write, with some abuse of notation,

$$_b\mathrm{wal}_{\boldsymbol{k}}(\boldsymbol{x}) := {}_b\mathrm{wal}_{k_1,\ldots,k_s}(x_1, \ldots, x_s).$$

The system $\{{}_b\mathrm{wal}_{\boldsymbol{k}} : \boldsymbol{k} \in \mathbb{N}_0^s\}$ is called the *s-dimensional b-adic Walsh function system.*

As any s-dimensional Walsh function is a product of one-dimensional Walsh functions, it is clear that s-dimensional Walsh functions are step functions too.

A.2 Basic properties of Walsh functions

We introduce some notation. By $\oplus$, we denote the *digitwise addition modulo b*, i.e. for $x = \sum_{i=w}^{\infty} \xi_i b^{-i}$ and $y = \sum_{i=w}^{\infty} \eta_i b^{-i}$, we define

$$x \oplus y := \sum_{i=w}^{\infty} \zeta_i b^{-i}, \quad \text{where} \quad \zeta_i \equiv \xi_i + \eta_i \pmod{b},$$

provided that infinitely many ζ_i are different from $b-1$. By $\ominus$, we denote the digitwise subtraction modulo b, i.e.

$$x \ominus y := \sum_{i=w}^{\infty} \zeta_i b^{-i}, \quad \text{where} \quad \zeta_i \equiv \xi_i - \eta_i \pmod{b},$$

provided that infinitely many ζ_i are different from $b-1$. Correspondingly, we define $\ominus x := 0 \ominus x$. For vectors $\boldsymbol{x}$ and $\boldsymbol{y}$, we define $\boldsymbol{x} \oplus \boldsymbol{y}$, $\boldsymbol{x} \ominus \boldsymbol{y}$ and $\ominus \boldsymbol{x}$ componentwise. Note that all these operations depend on the base b.

Proposition A.4 *For all $k, l \in \mathbb{N}_0$ we have*

$$_b\mathrm{wal}_k \cdot {}_b\mathrm{wal}_l = {}_b\mathrm{wal}_{k \oplus l} \quad \textit{and} \quad \frac{1}{_b\mathrm{wal}_k} = \overline{_b\mathrm{wal}_k} = {}_b\mathrm{wal}_{\ominus k}.$$

Proof Let $k = \kappa_0 + \kappa_1 b + \kappa_2 b^2 + \cdots$ and $l = \lambda_0 + \lambda_1 b + \lambda_2 b^2 + \cdots$. Then we have

$$\begin{aligned} _b\mathrm{wal}_k(x)\, {}_b\mathrm{wal}_l(x) &= \omega_b^{\sum_{i \geq 0} \kappa_i \xi_{i+1}} \omega_b^{\sum_{i \geq 0} \lambda_i \xi_{i+1}} = \omega_b^{\sum_{i \geq 0} (\kappa_i + \lambda_i) \xi_{i+1}} \\ &= \omega_b^{\sum_{i \geq 0} (\kappa_i \oplus \lambda_i) \xi_{i+1}} = {}_b\mathrm{wal}_{k \oplus l}(x), \end{aligned}$$

where we used the periodicity of $z \mapsto \omega_b^z$, and also

$$\frac{1}{{}_b\mathrm{wal}_k(x)} = \omega_b^{-\sum_{i\geq 0}\kappa_i\xi_{i+1}} = \omega_b^{\sum_{i\geq 0}(\ominus\kappa_i)\xi_{i+1}} = {}_b\mathrm{wal}_{\ominus k}(x). \qquad \square$$

As a corollary to Proposition A.4, we get its multi-dimensional analogue.

Corollary A.5 *For all $\boldsymbol{k}, \boldsymbol{l} \in \mathbb{N}_0^s$, we have*

$$_b\mathrm{wal}_{\boldsymbol{k}} \cdot {}_b\mathrm{wal}_{\boldsymbol{l}} = {}_b\mathrm{wal}_{\boldsymbol{k}\oplus\boldsymbol{l}} \quad \text{and} \quad \frac{1}{{}_b\mathrm{wal}_{\boldsymbol{k}}} = \overline{{}_b\mathrm{wal}_{\boldsymbol{k}}} = {}_b\mathrm{wal}_{\ominus\boldsymbol{k}}.$$

Proposition A.6 *Let $k \in \mathbb{N}_0$, then for all $x, y \in [0, 1)$ for which $x \oplus y$ and $x \ominus y$, respectively is defined, we have*

$$_b\mathrm{wal}_k(x)\, {}_b\mathrm{wal}_k(y) = {}_b\mathrm{wal}_k(x \oplus y) \text{ and } {}_b\mathrm{wal}_k(x)\, \overline{{}_b\mathrm{wal}_k(y)} = {}_b\mathrm{wal}_k(x \ominus y),$$

respectively.

Proof Let $k = \kappa_0 + \kappa_1 b + \kappa_2 b^2 + \cdots$ and assume that $x = \xi_1 b^{-1} + \xi_2 b^{-2} + \cdots$ and $y = \eta_1 b^{-1} + \eta_2 b^{-2} + \cdots$ satisfy the condition from the statement of the proposition. Then we have

$$\begin{aligned} {}_b\mathrm{wal}_k(x)\, {}_b\mathrm{wal}_k(y) &= \omega_b^{\sum_{i\geq 0}\kappa_i\xi_{i+1}} \omega_b^{\sum_{i\geq 0}\kappa_i\eta_{i+1}} \\ &= \omega_b^{\sum_{i\geq 0}\kappa_i(\xi_{i+1}+\eta_{i+1})} = {}_b\mathrm{wal}_k(x \oplus y), \end{aligned}$$

and

$$\begin{aligned} {}_b\mathrm{wal}_k(x)\, \overline{{}_b\mathrm{wal}_k(y)} &= \omega_b^{\sum_{i\geq 0}\kappa_i\xi_{i+1}} \omega_b^{-\sum_{i\geq 0}\kappa_i\eta_{i+1}} \\ &= \omega_b^{\sum_{i\geq 0}\kappa_i(\xi_{i+1}-\eta_{i+1})} = {}_b\mathrm{wal}_k(x \ominus y). \qquad \square \end{aligned}$$

Again, as corollary to Proposition A.6, we get its multi-dimensional analogue.

Corollary A.7 *Let $\boldsymbol{k} \in \mathbb{N}_0^s$, then for all $\boldsymbol{x}, \boldsymbol{y} \in [0, 1)^s$, for which $\boldsymbol{x} \oplus \boldsymbol{y}$ and $\boldsymbol{x} \ominus \boldsymbol{y}$, respectively is defined, we have*

$$_b\mathrm{wal}_{\boldsymbol{k}}(\boldsymbol{x}) \cdot {}_b\mathrm{wal}_{\boldsymbol{k}}(\boldsymbol{y}) = {}_b\mathrm{wal}_{\boldsymbol{k}}(\boldsymbol{x} \oplus \boldsymbol{y}) \text{ and } {}_b\mathrm{wal}_{\boldsymbol{k}}(\boldsymbol{x}) \cdot \overline{{}_b\mathrm{wal}_{\boldsymbol{k}}(\boldsymbol{y})} = {}_b\mathrm{wal}_{\boldsymbol{k}}(\boldsymbol{x} \ominus \boldsymbol{y}),$$

respectively.

Lemma A.8 *For $1 \leq k < b^r$, we have $\sum_{a=0}^{b^r-1} {}_b\mathrm{wal}_k(a/b^r) = 0$.*

Proof Let $k = \kappa_0 + \kappa_1 b + \cdots + \kappa_{r-1} b^{r-1}$. For $\kappa \in \{1, \ldots, b-1\}$, we have $\sum_{a=0}^{b-1} \omega_b^{\kappa a} = 0$ by the formula for a geometric sum and hence,

$$\sum_{a=0}^{b^r-1} {}_b\mathrm{wal}_k(a/b^r) = \sum_{a_0,\ldots,a_{r-1}=0}^{b-1} \omega_b^{\kappa_0 a_{r-1}+\cdots+\kappa_{r-1}a_0} = \prod_{i=0}^{r-1}\sum_{a=0}^{b-1} \omega_b^{\kappa_i a} = 0,$$

as there is an $i \in \{0, 1, \ldots, r-1\}$ such that $\kappa_i \neq 0$. $\square$

Proposition A.9 *We have*

$$\int_0^1 {}_b\mathrm{wal}_k(x)\,\mathrm{d}x = \begin{cases} 1 & \text{if } k = 0, \\ 0 & \text{if } k \neq 0. \end{cases}$$

Proof We have ${}_b\mathrm{wal}_0 \equiv 1$ and hence, the integral is 1 for $k = 0$. Now let $k = \kappa_0 + \kappa_1 b + \cdots + \kappa_{r-1} b^{r-1}$ with $\kappa_{r-1} \neq 0$. From Proposition A.2, we know that ${}_b\mathrm{wal}_k$ is constant on the elementary intervals of order r. Then we have

$$\int_0^1 {}_b\mathrm{wal}_k(x)\,\mathrm{d}x = \sum_{a=0}^{b^r-1} \int_{a/b^r}^{(a+1)/b^r} {}_b\mathrm{wal}_k(x)\,\mathrm{d}x = \frac{1}{b^r} \sum_{a=0}^{b^r-1} {}_b\mathrm{wal}_k(a/b^r)$$

and the result follows from Lemma A.8. □

The next result shows that the s-dimensional Walsh function system is orthonormal in $L_2([0, 1]^s)$.

Proposition A.10 *For all $\boldsymbol{k}, \boldsymbol{l} \in \mathbb{N}_0^s$, we have*

$$\int_{[0,1]^s} {}_b\mathrm{wal}_{\boldsymbol{k}}(\boldsymbol{x})\, \overline{{}_b\mathrm{wal}_{\boldsymbol{l}}(\boldsymbol{x})}\,\mathrm{d}\boldsymbol{x} = \begin{cases} 1 & \text{if } \boldsymbol{k} = \boldsymbol{l}, \\ 0 & \text{if } \boldsymbol{k} \neq \boldsymbol{l}. \end{cases}$$

Proof By Corollary A.5 we have ${}_b\mathrm{wal}_{\boldsymbol{k}} \cdot \overline{{}_b\mathrm{wal}_{\boldsymbol{l}}} = {}_b\mathrm{wal}_{\boldsymbol{k} \ominus \boldsymbol{l}}$. Hence,

$$\int_{[0,1]^s} {}_b\mathrm{wal}_{\boldsymbol{k}}(\boldsymbol{x})\, \overline{{}_b\mathrm{wal}_{\boldsymbol{l}}(\boldsymbol{x})}\,\mathrm{d}\boldsymbol{x} = \int_{[0,1]^s} {}_b\mathrm{wal}_{\boldsymbol{k} \ominus \boldsymbol{l}}(\boldsymbol{x})\,\mathrm{d}\boldsymbol{x}$$

and the result follows from Proposition A.9. □

Theorem A.11 *For fixed $b, s \in \mathbb{N}$, $b \geq 2$, the s-dimensional b-adic Walsh function system is a complete orthonormal basis in $L_2([0, 1]^s)$.*

For the proof of this fundamental result, we need some preparation.

Lemma A.12 *Let $b \geq 2$ be an integer. Then the one-dimensional Lebesgue measure λ is invariant under digitwise addition modulo b. In other words, for all $M \subseteq [0, 1)$ which are Lebesgue measurable and for all $x \in [0, 1)$, we have $\lambda(M) = \lambda(M \oplus x)$, where $M \oplus x := \{y \oplus x : y \in M\}$.*

Proof Let $x \in [0, 1)$ and $y \in M$ with $x = \xi_1 b^{-1} + \xi_2 b^{-2} + \cdots$ and $y = \eta_1 b^{-1} + \eta_2 b^{-2} + \cdots$. Then $x \oplus y$ is not defined, if $\xi_j + \eta_j \equiv b - 1 \pmod{b}$ or equivalently $\eta_j \equiv b - 1 - \xi_j \pmod{b}$ for all indices $j \geq j_0$. Hence, the subset $\{y \in M : y \oplus x$ not defined$\}$ is countable.

Consider an elementary interval $J = [a/b^r, (a+1)/b^r)$ with $a = \alpha_0 + \alpha_1 b + \cdots + \alpha_{r-1} b^{r-1}$. Each $y \in J$ has the b-adic expansion $y = \alpha_{r-1} b^{-1} + \alpha_{r-2} b^{-2} + \cdots + \alpha_0 b^{-r} + \eta_{r+1} b^{-(r+1)} + \eta_{r+2} b^{-(r+2)} + \cdots$ with digits $0 \leq \eta_j \leq b - 1$ for all $j \geq r + 1$.

Now, for $y \in J$, we have

$$y \oplus x = \frac{\alpha_{r-1} \oplus \xi_1}{b} + \cdots + \frac{\alpha_0 \oplus \xi_r}{b^r} + \frac{\eta_{r+1} \oplus \xi_{r+1}}{b^{r+1}} + \frac{\eta_{r+2} \oplus \xi_{r+2}}{b^{r+2}} + \cdots.$$

Hence, $y \mapsto y \oplus x$ maps all but countably many points from J to the elementary interval

$$J' = \left[\frac{\alpha_{r-1} \oplus x_1}{b} + \cdots + \frac{\alpha_0 \oplus x_r}{b^r}, \frac{\alpha_{r-1} \oplus x_1}{b} + \cdots + \frac{\alpha_0 \oplus x_r}{b^r} + \frac{1}{b^r}\right).$$

Furthermore, for all but countably many points $y \in J'$, we can define the inverse mapping $y \mapsto y \ominus x$. Hence, $\oplus x$ preserves the measure of elementary intervals.

Since every open subset from $[0, 1]$ can be written as a countable union of elementary intervals, it follows that $y \mapsto y \oplus x$ preserves the measure of every open subset of $[0, 1)$ and hence, the result follows for all Lebesgue measurable subsets from $[0, 1)$. □

Corollary A.13 *Let $\boldsymbol{c} \in [0, 1)^s$, then for all $f \in L_2([0, 1]^s)$, we have*

$$\int_{[0,1]^s} f(\boldsymbol{x}) \, \mathrm{d}\boldsymbol{x} = \int_{[0,1]^s} f(\boldsymbol{x} \oplus \boldsymbol{c}) \, \mathrm{d}\boldsymbol{x}.$$

Proof It is enough to show the result for $s = 1$. Let $c \in [0, 1)$ and let $f \in L_2([0, 1])$. Define $g(x) = f(x \oplus c)$. For each $M \subseteq f([0, 1])$, we have $g^{-1}(M) = f^{-1}(M) \ominus c$ and hence, by Lemma A.12, we have $\lambda(g^{-1}(M)) = \lambda(f^{-1}(M))$. Now the result follows from the definition of the Lebesgue-integral. □

Definition A.14 An *s-dimensional b-adic Walsh series* is a function $f : [0, 1]^s \to \mathbb{C}$ of the form

$$f = \sum_{\boldsymbol{k} \in \mathbb{N}_0^s} \widehat{f}(\boldsymbol{k}) \, {}_b\mathrm{wal}_{\boldsymbol{k}}$$

for certain $\widehat{f}(\boldsymbol{k}) \in \mathbb{C}$ which are called the *Walsh coefficients* or *Walsh–Fourier coefficients* of the function f. Furthermore, a *Walsh polynomial* is a finite Walsh series.

Remark A.15 For uniformly convergent Walsh series f, one can compute the $\boldsymbol{k}$th Walsh coefficient by

$$\widehat{f}(\boldsymbol{k}) = \int_{[0,1]^s} f(\boldsymbol{x}) \overline{{}_b\mathrm{wal}_{\boldsymbol{k}}(\boldsymbol{x})} \, \mathrm{d}\boldsymbol{x}.$$

We introduce very special Walsh polynomials, the so-called Walsh–Dirichlet kernels.

Definition A.16 For $\boldsymbol{k} = (k_1, \ldots, k_s) \in \mathbb{N}^s$, the *$\boldsymbol{k}$th Walsh–Dirichlet kernel* is defined as

$$D_{\boldsymbol{k}} = \sum_{l_1=0}^{k_1-1} \cdots \sum_{l_s=0}^{k_s-1} {}_b\mathrm{wal}_{l_1,\ldots,l_s}.$$

Lemma A.17 *For $n \in \mathbb{N}_0$, let $\boldsymbol{b}_n = (b^n, \ldots, b^n) \in \mathbb{N}^s$, then we have $D_{\boldsymbol{b}_n}(\boldsymbol{x}) = b^{ns} \chi_{[0,b^{-n})^s}(\boldsymbol{x})$ for $\boldsymbol{x} \in [0, 1)^s$.*

Proof For $s = 1$, we show the result by induction on $n \in \mathbb{N}_0$. Let $x \in [0, 1)$.

We have $D_1(x) = {}_b\mathrm{wal}_0(x) = 1 = b^{0 \cdot s} \chi_{[0,b^{-0})}(x)$ and hence, the result holds for $n = 0$. Assume that the formula holds for $D_{b^{n-1}}(x)$. Then we have

$$D_{b^n}(x) = \sum_{l=0}^{b^n-1} {}_b\mathrm{wal}_l(x) = \sum_{i=0}^{b-1} \sum_{l=0}^{b^{n-1}-1} {}_b\mathrm{wal}_{l \oplus i \cdot b^{n-1}}(x)$$

$$= \sum_{i=0}^{b-1} {}_b\mathrm{wal}_{i \cdot b^{n-1}}(x) \sum_{l=0}^{b^{n-1}-1} {}_b\mathrm{wal}_l(x)$$

$$= D_{b^{n-1}}(x) \sum_{i=0}^{b-1} {}_b\mathrm{wal}_{i \cdot b^{n-1}}(x) = D_{b^{n-1}}(x) \sum_{i=0}^{b-1} (\omega_b^{\xi_n})^i,$$

where ξ_n is the nth digit of x in its base b expansion. The last sum is equal to $b^{n-1}b = b^n$ if $x \in [0, b^{-n+1})$ and $\xi_n = 0$ which is equivalent to $x \in [0, b^{-n})$ and equal to 0 in all other cases. Hence, the result follows for $s = 1$.

For $s > 1$, the result follows immediately from the identity

$$D_{\boldsymbol{b}_n}(\boldsymbol{x}) = \sum_{l_1,\ldots,l_s=0}^{b^n-1} {}_b\mathrm{wal}_{l_1,\ldots,l_s}(\boldsymbol{x}) = \prod_{i=1}^{s} \sum_{l_i=0}^{b^n-1} {}_b\mathrm{wal}_{l_i}(x_i) = \prod_{i=1}^{s} D_{b^n}(x_i)$$

together with the result for the case $s = 1$. □

Proof of Theorem A.11 We know already from Proposition A.10 that Walsh functions are orthonormal in $L_2([0, 1]^s)$. Hence, it remains to show that the Walsh polynomials are dense in $L_2([0, 1]^s)$.

For $\boldsymbol{n} = (n_1, \ldots, n_s) \in \mathbb{N}^s$, denote by $S_{\boldsymbol{n}}(\boldsymbol{x}, f)$ the $\boldsymbol{n}$th partial sum of the form

$$S_{\boldsymbol{n}}(\boldsymbol{x}, f) = \sum_{l_1=0}^{n_1-1} \cdots \sum_{l_s=0}^{n_s-1} \widehat{f}(\boldsymbol{l})\, {}_b\mathrm{wal}_{l_1,\ldots,l_s}(\boldsymbol{x}),$$

with $\widehat{f}(\boldsymbol{l}) = \int_{[0,1]^s} f(\boldsymbol{t}) \overline{{}_b\mathrm{wal}_{\boldsymbol{l}}(\boldsymbol{t})}\, \mathrm{d}\boldsymbol{t}$. Then we have

$$S_{\boldsymbol{n}}(\boldsymbol{x}, f) = \sum_{l_1=0}^{n_1-1} \cdots \sum_{l_s=0}^{n_s-1} \left(\int_{[0,1]^s} f(\boldsymbol{t}) \overline{{}_b\mathrm{wal}_{l_1,\ldots,l_s}(\boldsymbol{t})\, \mathrm{d}\boldsymbol{t}} \right) {}_b\mathrm{wal}_{l_1,\ldots,l_s}(\boldsymbol{x})$$

$$= \int_{[0,1]^s} f(\boldsymbol{t}) \sum_{l_1=0}^{n_1-1} \cdots \sum_{l_s=0}^{n_s-1} {}_b\mathrm{wal}_{l_1,\ldots,l_s}(\boldsymbol{x} \ominus \boldsymbol{t})\, \mathrm{d}\boldsymbol{t}$$

$$= \int_{[0,1]^s} f(\boldsymbol{t}) D_{\boldsymbol{n}}(\boldsymbol{x} \ominus \boldsymbol{t})\, \mathrm{d}\boldsymbol{t} = \int_{[0,1]^s} f(\boldsymbol{x} \ominus \boldsymbol{t}) D_{\boldsymbol{n}}(\boldsymbol{t})\, \mathrm{d}\boldsymbol{t}.$$

With the help of this formula, we can now estimate the approximation error for certain partial sums. With Lemma A.17 we obtain

$$|S_{b_n}(\boldsymbol{x}, f) - f(\boldsymbol{x})| = \left| \int_{[0,1]^s} f(\boldsymbol{x} \ominus \boldsymbol{t}) D_{b_n}(\boldsymbol{t}) \, \mathrm{d}\boldsymbol{t} - b^{ns} \int_{[0,b^{-n})^s} f(\boldsymbol{x}) \, \mathrm{d}\boldsymbol{t} \right|$$
$$= b^{ns} \left| \int_{[0,b^{-n})^s} (f(\boldsymbol{x} \ominus \boldsymbol{t}) - f(\boldsymbol{x})) \, \mathrm{d}\boldsymbol{t} \right|$$
$$= b^{ns} \left| \int_{\boldsymbol{x} \ominus [0,b^{-n})^s} (f(\boldsymbol{t}) - f(\boldsymbol{x})) \, \mathrm{d}\boldsymbol{t} \right|$$
$$\leq \sup \left\{ |f(\boldsymbol{t}) - f(\boldsymbol{x})| \, : \, \boldsymbol{x}, \boldsymbol{t} \in \boldsymbol{x} \ominus [0, b^{-n})^s \right\} b^{ns} \lambda_s(\boldsymbol{x} \ominus [0, b^{-n})^s).$$

Assume now that $f \in C([0,1]^s)$. Hence, f is also uniformly continuous on $[0,1]^s$ and thus, for every $\varepsilon > 0$, there exists an $N_0 = N_0(\varepsilon)$ such that for all $n > N_0$ and for all $\boldsymbol{x}, \boldsymbol{y} \in [0,1]^s$ with $|\boldsymbol{x} - \boldsymbol{y}|_\infty < b^{-n}$, we have $|f(\boldsymbol{x}) - f(\boldsymbol{y})| < \varepsilon$.

Obviously, $\lambda_s\left(\boldsymbol{x} \ominus [0, b^{-n})^s\right) = b^{-ns}$ and hence, we obtain

$$|S_{b_n}(\boldsymbol{x}, f) - f(\boldsymbol{x})| < \varepsilon$$

for all $n > N_0(\varepsilon)$ and this holds independently from $\boldsymbol{x}$ as f is uniformly continuous. Hence,

$$\|S_{b_n}(\boldsymbol{x}, \cdot) - f\|_\infty < \varepsilon$$

for all $n > N_0(\varepsilon)$. This means that the Walsh polynomials are dense in $C([0,1]^s)$ with respect to the sup-norm $\|\cdot\|_\infty$ which in turn is dense in $L_2([0,1]^s)$ with respect to the L_2-norm $\|\cdot\|_2$. Hence, the Walsh polynomials are also dense in $L_2([0,1]^s)$.

Since $L_2([0,1]^s)$ is a Hilbert space, we now have that the Walsh functions are a complete orthonormal system in $L_2([0,1]^s)$. □

Note that Bessel's inequality

$$\sum_{\boldsymbol{k} \in \mathbb{N}_0^s} |\widehat{f}(\boldsymbol{k})|^2 \leq \int_{[0,1]^s} |f(\boldsymbol{x})|^2 \, \mathrm{d}\boldsymbol{x} \tag{A.1}$$

holds for functions $f \in L_2([0,1]^s)$. Since

$$0 \leq \int_{[0,1]^s} |f(\boldsymbol{x}) - S_{\boldsymbol{n}}(\boldsymbol{x}, f)|^2 \, \mathrm{d}\boldsymbol{x}$$
$$= \int_{[0,1]^s} |f(\boldsymbol{x})|^2 \, \mathrm{d}\boldsymbol{x} - \int_{[0,1]^s} f(\boldsymbol{x}) \overline{S_{\boldsymbol{n}}(\boldsymbol{x}, f)} \, \mathrm{d}\boldsymbol{x}$$
$$- \int_{[0,1]^s} \overline{f(\boldsymbol{x})} S_{\boldsymbol{n}}(\boldsymbol{x}, f) \, \mathrm{d}\boldsymbol{x} + \int_{[0,1]^s} |S_{\boldsymbol{n}}(\boldsymbol{x}, f)|^2 \, \mathrm{d}\boldsymbol{x}$$
$$= \int_{[0,1]^s} |f(\boldsymbol{x})|^2 \, \mathrm{d}\boldsymbol{x} - \sum_{l_1=0}^{n_1-1} \cdots \sum_{l_s=0}^{n_s-1} |\widehat{f}(l_1, \ldots, l_s)|^2, \tag{A.2}$$

we have $\sum_{l_1=0}^{n_1-1} \cdots \sum_{l_s=0}^{n_s-1} |\widehat{f}(l_1, \ldots, l_s)|^2 \leq \int_{[0,1]^s} |f(\boldsymbol{x})|^2 \, \mathrm{d}\boldsymbol{x}$, and by considering $n_1, \ldots, n_s \to \infty$, the result follows. We also have the following lemma.

Lemma A.18 *Let $\{a_{\boldsymbol{k}} \in \mathbb{C} : \boldsymbol{k} \in \mathbb{N}_0^s\}$ be a set of complex numbers such that $\sum_{\boldsymbol{k}\in\mathbb{N}_0^s} |a_{\boldsymbol{k}}|^2 < \infty$. Then the Walsh series $\sum_{\boldsymbol{k}\in\mathbb{N}_0^s} a_{\boldsymbol{k}}\, {}_b\mathrm{wal}_{\boldsymbol{k}}$ converges in $L_2([0,1]^s)$.*

Proof Since $L_2([0,1]^s)$ is complete, we only need to show that the partial sums $S_{\boldsymbol{n}} = \sum_{l_1=0}^{n_1-1} \cdots \sum_{l_s=0}^{n_s-1} a_{l_1,\ldots,l_s}\, {}_b\mathrm{wal}_{l_1,\ldots,l_s}$, where $\boldsymbol{n} = (n_1, \ldots, n_s) \in \mathbb{N}^s$, form a Cauchy sequence in $L_2([0,1]^s)$.

Indeed, for any $\boldsymbol{n}, \boldsymbol{n}' \in \mathbb{N}_0^s$ with $\boldsymbol{n} = (n_1, \ldots, n_s)$ and $\boldsymbol{n}' = (n_1', \ldots, n_s')$, where we assume that $n_1 > n_1', \ldots, n_s > n_s'$, we have

$$\int_{[0,1]^s} |S_{\boldsymbol{n}}(\boldsymbol{x}, f) - S_{\boldsymbol{n}'}(\boldsymbol{x}, f)|^2 \,\mathrm{d}\boldsymbol{x} = \sum_{l_1=n_1'}^{n_1-1} \cdots \sum_{l_s=n_s'}^{n_s-1} |a_{l_1,\ldots,l_s}|^2 \to 0$$

as $n_1', \ldots, n_s' \to \infty$. Thus, the partial sums $S_{\boldsymbol{n}}$ form a Cauchy sequence and hence the result follows as $L_2([0,1]^s)$ is complete. □

The completeness of the Walsh function system shown in Theorem A.11 is equivalent to the statement that Plancherel's identity

$$\int_{[0,1]^s} |f(\boldsymbol{x})|^2 \,\mathrm{d}\boldsymbol{x} = \sum_{\boldsymbol{k}\in\mathbb{N}_0^s} |\widehat{f}(\boldsymbol{k})|^2$$

holds. This is shown in the following theorem (see, for example, reference [119, Section I.5] for a more general statement).

Theorem A.19 *The following statements are equivalent:*

1. The Walsh function system is complete in $L_2([0,1]^s)$.
2. For every $f \in L_2([0,1]^s)$, we have

$$\int_{[0,1]^s} |f(\boldsymbol{x})|^2 \,\mathrm{d}\boldsymbol{x} = \sum_{\boldsymbol{k}\in\mathbb{N}_0^s} |\widehat{f}(\boldsymbol{k})|^2.$$

3. For every $f \in L_2([0,1]^s)$, we have

$$\lim_{n_1,\ldots,n_s\to\infty} \int_{[0,1]^s} |f(\boldsymbol{x}) - S_{n_1,\ldots,n_s}(\boldsymbol{x}, f)|^2 \,\mathrm{d}\boldsymbol{x} = 0.$$

Proof The equivalence of (2) and (3) follows from (A.2).

Assume now that (2) holds. Let $\langle g, h\rangle_{L_2} = \int_{[0,1]^s} g(\boldsymbol{x})\overline{h(\boldsymbol{x})} \,\mathrm{d}\boldsymbol{x}$ denote the inner product in $L_2([0,1]^s)$. If a function $f \in L_2([0,1]^s)$ is orthogonal to ${}_b\mathrm{wal}_{\boldsymbol{k}}$ for all $\boldsymbol{k} \in \mathbb{N}_0^s$, it follows that $\widehat{f}(\boldsymbol{k}) = \langle f, {}_b\mathrm{wal}_{\boldsymbol{k}}\rangle_{L_2} = 0$ for all $\boldsymbol{k} \in \mathbb{N}_0^s$ and (2) implies that $\int_{[0,1]^s} |f(\boldsymbol{x})|^2 \,\mathrm{d}\boldsymbol{x} = 0$. Thus, the Walsh function system is complete in $L_2([0,1]^s)$ and hence, (2) implies (1).

Assume now that (1) holds. We complete the proof by showing that (3) follows. From Bessel's inequality and Lemma A.18, it follows that for every $f \in L_2([0,1]^s)$, we have $S(\cdot, f) := \sum_{\boldsymbol{k}\in\mathbb{N}_0^s} \widehat{f}(\boldsymbol{k})\, {}_b\mathrm{wal}_{\boldsymbol{k}} \in L_2([0,1]^s)$. Hence, $\langle f - S(\cdot, f), {}_b\mathrm{wal}_{\boldsymbol{k}}\rangle = 0$ for all $\boldsymbol{k} \in \mathbb{N}_0^s$. Thus, if the Walsh function system $\{{}_b\mathrm{wal}_{\boldsymbol{k}} : \boldsymbol{k} \in \mathbb{N}_0^s\}$ is complete, it follows that $\int_{[0,1]^s} |f(\boldsymbol{x}) - S(\boldsymbol{x}, f)|^2 \,\mathrm{d}\boldsymbol{x} = 0$. □

A.3 Convergence of the Walsh series

For our purposes here, we need strong assumptions on the convergence of the Walsh series $\sum_{k=0}^{\infty} \widehat{f}(k)\, {}_b\mathrm{wal}_k(x)$ to the function f, i.e. we require that the partial series $\sum_{k=0}^{L} \widehat{f}(k)\, {}_b\mathrm{wal}_k(x)$ converges to $f(x)$ at every point $x \in [0, 1)$ as $L \to \infty$.

For continuous functions $f : [0, 1) \to \mathbb{R}$, we can use the argument in [79, p. 373] to show that certain partial sums of the Walsh series converge at every point $x \in [0, 1)$ to the function value $f(x)$. Indeed, for a given $x \in [0, 1)$, we have

$$\begin{aligned}\sum_{k=0}^{b^\ell-1} \widehat{f}(k)\, {}_b\mathrm{wal}_k(x) &= \int_0^1 f(y) \sum_{k=0}^{b^\ell-1} {}_b\mathrm{wal}_k(x) \overline{{}_b\mathrm{wal}_k(y)}\, \mathrm{d}y \\ &= b^\ell \int_{b^{-\ell}\lfloor b^\ell x\rfloor}^{b^{-\ell}\lfloor b^\ell x\rfloor + b^{-\ell}} f(y)\, \mathrm{d}y.\end{aligned}$$

As the function f is continuous, it follows that $\sum_{k=0}^{b^\ell-1} \widehat{f}(k)\, {}_b\mathrm{wal}_k(x)$ converges to $f(x)$ as $\ell \to \infty$. Hence, if the partial sums $\sum_{k=0}^{L} \widehat{f}(k)\, {}_b\mathrm{wal}_k(x)$ are a Cauchy sequence, then we also have $\sum_{k=0}^{L} \widehat{f}(k)\, {}_b\mathrm{wal}_k(x)$ converging to $f(x)$ as $L \to \infty$.

For instance, if $\sum_{k=0}^{\infty} |\widehat{f}(k)| < \infty$, then the partial sums $\sum_{k=0}^{L} \widehat{f}(k)\, {}_b\mathrm{wal}_k(x)$ are a Cauchy sequence and hence, $\sum_{k=0}^{b^\ell-1} \widehat{f}(k)\, {}_b\mathrm{wal}_k(x)$ converges to $f(x)$ as $\ell \to \infty$. In this case the convergence is even uniformly in x.

We have shown the following result which is sufficient for our purposes. For more elaborate results in this direction, see [232].

Theorem A.20 *Let $f : [0, 1] \to \mathbb{R}$ be a continuous function and assume that $\sum_{k=0}^{\infty} |\widehat{f}(k)| < \infty$. Then $\sum_{k=0}^{L} \widehat{f}(k)\, {}_b\mathrm{wal}_k(x)$ converges uniformly to $f(x)$ as $L \to \infty$ and we have*

$$f(x) = \sum_{k=0}^{\infty} \widehat{f}(k)\, {}_b\mathrm{wal}_k(x) \quad \textit{for all } x \in [0, 1).$$

Remark A.21 We remark that in [260] it was shown that there are continuous functions f for which $\sum_{k=0}^{L} \widehat{f}(k)\, {}_b\mathrm{wal}_k(x)$ does not converge at some given point x as $L \to \infty$. Therefore, continuity is not a sufficient condition to ensure that $\sum_{k=0}^{L} \widehat{f}(k)\, {}_b\mathrm{wal}_k(x)$ is a Cauchy sequence.

However, Walsh [260] already proved the following result. If the function f is not merely continuous but has bounded variation (for instance, if f has a derivative which is square integrable, i.e. $\int_0^1 |f'(y)|^2\, \mathrm{d}y < \infty$, then f has bounded variation), then it follows that $\sum_{k=0}^{L} \widehat{f}(k)\, {}_b\mathrm{wal}_k(x)$ is a Cauchy sequence for every x. Hence, in this case we have $\sum_{k=0}^{L} {}_b\mathrm{wal}_k(x) \to f(x)$ as $L \to \infty$ for all x.

The argument above can also be extended to continuous functions $f : [0, 1)^s \to \mathbb{R}$; see Exercise A.9.

A.4 Walsh series expansions of a certain function

In this section, we provide the b-adic Walsh series representations of a function which is used throughout this book.

Lemma A.22 *For $b \geq 2$ an integer and $x \in [0, 1)$, we have*

$$x - \frac{1}{2} = \sum_{a=1}^{\infty} \sum_{\kappa=1}^{b-1} \frac{1}{b^a(\omega_b^{-\kappa} - 1)} {}_b\mathrm{wal}_{\kappa b^{a-1}}(x). \tag{A.3}$$

Proof Let $x = \xi_1 b^{-1} + \xi_2 b^{-2} + \cdots$ and $k = \kappa_{a-1} b^{a-1} + \cdots + \kappa_1 b + \kappa_0$, where $\kappa_{a-1} \neq 0$. Then we have

$$\begin{aligned}
&\int_0^1 \left(x - \tfrac{1}{2}\right) \overline{{}_b\mathrm{wal}_k(x)} \,\mathrm{d}x \\
&= \sum_{\xi_1=0}^{b-1} \cdots \sum_{\xi_a=0}^{b-1} \omega_b^{-(\xi_1\kappa_0 + \cdots + \xi_a\kappa_{a-1})} \int_{\frac{\xi_1}{b} + \cdots + \frac{\xi_a}{b^a}}^{\frac{\xi_1}{b} + \cdots + \frac{\xi_a}{b^a} + \frac{1}{b^a}} \left(x - \tfrac{1}{2}\right) \mathrm{d}x \\
&= \frac{1}{b^a} \sum_{\xi_1=0}^{b-1} \omega_b^{-\xi_1\kappa_0} \cdots \sum_{\xi_a=0}^{b-1} \omega_b^{-\xi_a\kappa_{a-1}} \left(\frac{\xi_1}{b} + \cdots + \frac{\xi_a}{b^a}\right),
\end{aligned} \tag{A.4}$$

where we used the facts that

$$\int_{\frac{\xi_1}{b} + \cdots + \frac{\xi_a}{b^a}}^{\frac{\xi_1}{b} + \cdots + \frac{\xi_a}{b^a} + \frac{1}{b^a}} \left(x - \tfrac{1}{2}\right) \mathrm{d}x = \frac{1}{b^a}\left(\frac{\xi_1}{b} + \cdots + \frac{\xi_a}{b^a}\right) + \frac{1}{2b^a}\left(\frac{1}{b^a} - 1\right)$$

and $\sum_{\xi_a=0}^{b-1} \omega_b^{-\xi_a\kappa_{a-1}} = 0$ for $\kappa_{a-1} \neq 0$. For any digits $0 \leq \xi_1, \ldots, \xi_{a-1} \leq b-1$, we have

$$\begin{aligned}
\sum_{\xi_a=0}^{b-1} \left(\frac{\xi_1}{b} + \cdots + \frac{\xi_{a-1}}{b^{a-1}} + \frac{\xi_a}{b^a}\right) \omega_b^{-\xi_a\kappa_{a-1}} &= \sum_{\xi_a=0}^{b-1} \frac{\xi_a}{b^a} \omega_b^{-\xi_a\kappa_{a-1}} \\
&= \frac{b}{b^a(\omega_b^{-\kappa_{a-1}} - 1)},
\end{aligned}$$

as for $\kappa_{a-1} \neq 0$, we have

$$\sum_{\xi_a=0}^{b-1} \omega_b^{-\xi_a\kappa_{a-1}} = 0 \text{ and } \sum_{\xi_a=0}^{b-1} \xi_a \omega_b^{-\xi_a\kappa_{a-1}} = \frac{b}{\omega_b^{-\kappa_{a-1}} - 1}. \tag{A.5}$$

Therefore, we obtain from (A.4)

$$\int_0^1 \left(x - \tfrac{1}{2}\right) \overline{{}_b\mathrm{wal}_k(x)} \,\mathrm{d}x = \frac{b}{b^{2a}(\omega_b^{-\kappa_{a-1}} - 1)} \sum_{\xi_1=0}^{b-1} \omega_b^{-\xi_1\kappa_0} \cdots \sum_{\xi_{a-1}=0}^{b-1} \omega_b^{-\xi_{a-1}\kappa_{a-2}}.$$

For an integer $0 \leq \kappa \leq b-1$, we use

$$\sum_{\xi=0}^{b-1} \omega_b^{-\xi\kappa} = \begin{cases} b & \text{if } \kappa = 0, \\ 0 & \text{if } \kappa \neq 0, \end{cases}$$

and obtain

$$\int_0^1 \left(x - \tfrac{1}{2}\right) \overline{{}_b\mathrm{wal}_k(x)}\,\mathrm{d}x = \begin{cases} \frac{1}{b^a(\omega_b^{-\kappa_{a-1}}-1)} & \text{if } \kappa_0 = \cdots = \kappa_{a-2} = 0, \\ 0 & \text{otherwise.} \end{cases}$$

Thus, for $x \in [0, 1)$, we have

$$x - \frac{1}{2} = \sum_{a=1}^{\infty} \sum_{\kappa=1}^{b-1} \frac{1}{b^a(\omega_b^{-\kappa} - 1)} \, {}_b\mathrm{wal}_{\kappa b^{a-1}}(x).$$ □

With Lemma A.22 we can prove a formula for a trigonometric sum which is often used throughout this book.

Corollary A.23 *For $b \geq 2$ and for $l \in \{-(b-1), \ldots, b-1\}$, we have*

$$\sum_{\kappa=1}^{b-1} \frac{\omega_b^{\kappa l}}{\sin^2(\kappa\pi/b)} = 2(|l|(|l| - b) + \frac{b^2 - 1}{3}.$$

In particular, $\sum_{\kappa=1}^{b-1} \sin^{-2}(\kappa\pi/b) = (b^2 - 1)/3$.

Proof Using Lemma A.22 and the orthogonality properties of the Walsh functions (see Proposition A.10), we obtain (see also (12.8))

$$2\sum_{a=1}^{\infty} \sum_{\kappa=1}^{b-1} \frac{1}{b^{2a}|\omega_b^{\kappa} - 1|^2} = \int_0^1 \int_0^1 |x - y|^2 \,\mathrm{d}x\,\mathrm{d}y = \frac{1}{6}$$

and hence,

$$\sum_{\kappa=1}^{b-1} \frac{1}{|\omega_b^{\kappa} - 1|^2} = \frac{b^2 - 1}{12}.$$

For $1 \leq l \leq b - 1$, we use (12.7), which states that for any $x, y \in [0, 1)$, we have

$$\begin{aligned} &\int_0^1 |(x \oplus \sigma) - (y \oplus \sigma)|^2 \,\mathrm{d}\sigma \\ &= \frac{1}{6} - 2\sum_{a=1}^{\infty} \sum_{\kappa=1}^{b-1} \frac{1}{b^{2a}|\omega_b^{\kappa} - 1|^2} \, {}_b\mathrm{wal}_{\kappa b^{a-1}}(x) \overline{{}_b\mathrm{wal}_{\kappa b^{a-1}}(y)}. \end{aligned}$$

Take $x = l/b$ and $y = 0$, then the left-hand side of the equation yields

$$\begin{aligned}\int_0^1 |(x \oplus \sigma) - (y \oplus \sigma)|^2 \,\mathrm{d}\sigma &= \int_0^1 \left|\left(\frac{l}{b} \oplus \sigma\right) - \sigma\right|^2 \mathrm{d}\sigma \\ &= \int_0^{\frac{b-l}{b}} \left|\left(\frac{l}{b} + \sigma\right) - \sigma\right|^2 \mathrm{d}\sigma + \int_{\frac{b-l}{b}}^1 \left|\left(\frac{l-b}{b} + \sigma\right) - \sigma\right|^2 \mathrm{d}\sigma \\ &= \int_0^{\frac{b-l}{b}} \frac{l^2}{b^2}\,\mathrm{d}\sigma + \int_{\frac{b-l}{b}}^1 \frac{(l-b)^2}{b^2}\,\mathrm{d}\sigma \\ &= \frac{b-l}{b}\frac{l^2}{b^2} + \left(1 - \frac{b-l}{b}\right)\frac{(l-b)^2}{b^2} \\ &= \frac{l(b-l)}{b^2},\end{aligned}$$

and for the right-hand side, we obtain

$$\begin{aligned}&\frac{1}{6} - 2\sum_{a=1}^{\infty}\sum_{\kappa=1}^{b-1} \frac{1}{b^{2a}|\omega_b^{\kappa} - 1|^2}\, {}_b\mathrm{wal}_{\kappa b^{a-1}}(x)\,\overline{{}_b\mathrm{wal}_{\kappa b^{a-1}}(y)} \\ &= \frac{1}{6} - 2\sum_{\kappa=1}^{b-1} \frac{\omega_b^{l\kappa}}{b^2|\omega_b^{\kappa} - 1|^2} - 2\sum_{a=2}^{\infty}\frac{1}{b^{2a}}\sum_{\kappa=1}^{b-1}\frac{1}{|\omega_b^{\kappa} - 1|^2} \\ &= \frac{b^2-1}{6b^2} - \frac{2}{b^2}\sum_{\kappa=1}^{b-1}\frac{\omega_b^{l\kappa}}{|\omega_b^{\kappa} - 1|^2}.\end{aligned}$$

Thus, for $0 \le l \le b-1$, we have

$$\sum_{\kappa=1}^{b-1} \frac{\omega_b^{\kappa l}}{|\omega_b^{\kappa} - 1|^2} = \frac{|l|(|l| - b)}{2} + \frac{b^2-1}{12}. \tag{A.6}$$

To show that (A.6) holds for $-(b-1) \le l \le -1$, use $x = 0$ and $y = -l/b$ in the argument above. The details are omitted.

Further, observe that $|\omega_b^{\kappa} - 1|^2 = |\mathrm{e}^{\pi \mathrm{i}\kappa/b}|^2|\mathrm{e}^{\pi \mathrm{i}\kappa/b} - \mathrm{e}^{-\pi \mathrm{i}\kappa/b}|^2 = 4\sin^2(\kappa\pi/b)$ and therefore we have the desired result for $-(b-1) \le l \le b-1$. □

Exercises

A.1 Show that a Walsh function can only take finitely many function values, namely the bth roots of unity.

A.2 For $k \in \mathbb{N}_0$, the *kth Rademacher function* $r_k : \mathbb{R} \to \mathbb{R}$, periodic with period one, is defined by $r_0(x) = 1$ for all $x \in [0, 1)$ and for $k \in \mathbb{N}$, $r_k(x) = (-1)^j$ if $x \in [j/2^k, (j+1)/2^k)$ for some integer $0 \le j \le 2^k - 1$.

1. Show that the system of Rademacher functions is a subclass of the dyadic (i.e. $b = 2$) Walsh function system.
2. For $b = 2$, give a definition of Walsh functions in terms of Rademacher functions.

A.3 Let $\boldsymbol{k} = (k_1, \ldots, k_s) \in \mathbb{N}_0^s$ with $b^{r_i} \le k_i < b^{r_i+1}$ for all $1 \le i \le s$. Show that ${}_b\mathrm{wal}_{\boldsymbol{k}}$ is constant on an elementary interval of the form

$$\prod_{i=1}^{s} \left[\frac{a_i}{b^{r_i}}, \frac{a_i + 1}{b^{r_i}} \right)$$

where $0 \le a_i < b^{r_i}$ are integers for all $1 \le i \le s$.

A.4 Show that we have

$$\frac{1}{{}_b\mathrm{wal}_k(x)} = \overline{{}_b\mathrm{wal}_k(x)} = {}_b\mathrm{wal}_k(\ominus x)$$

whenever $\ominus x$ is defined.

A.5 Let $f : [0, 1]^s \to \mathbb{R}$ be a function which is constant on any interval of the form $\prod_{i=1}^{s} [a_i b^{-n}, (a_i + 1) b^{-n})$ with integers $0 \le a_i < b^n$. Show that f is a Walsh polynomial.

A.6 Show that for all $\boldsymbol{k} \in \mathbb{N}^s$, we have $\int_{[0,1]^s} D_{\boldsymbol{k}}(\boldsymbol{x}) \, \mathrm{d}\boldsymbol{x} = 1$.

A.7 Verify Bessel's inequality (A.1) for the function $f(x) = x^2$.

A.8 Show that the Rademacher functions, defined in Exercise A.2, are not complete.

A.9 Show that the result on the convergence of Walsh series in Section A.3 also holds for s-dimensional continuous functions $f : [0, 1]^s \to \mathbb{R}$ for which $\sum_{\boldsymbol{k} \in \mathbb{N}_0^s} |\widehat{f}(\boldsymbol{k})| < \infty$.
Hint: See [36, Section 3.3] for the result.

A.10 Define a function $f : [0, 1) \to \mathbb{R}$ for which $\sum_{k=0}^{\infty} |\widehat{f}(k)| = \infty$.

A.11 Let $b = 2$ and $f(x) = x$. Draw the graphs of f and of $\sum_{k=0}^{2^l - 1} \widehat{f}(k) \, {}_b\mathrm{wal}_k(x)$ for $l = 0, 1, 2, 3$.

Appendix B
Algebraic function fields

Many important digital constructions such as, for example, Niederreiter–Xing nets and sequences are based on the theory of algebraic function fields. In this appendix we give a brief summary of the basic definitions and facts of this field that are necessary for the construction of digital nets and sequences. The following survey is based on Niederreiter's overview article [180] and on the first chapter of Stichtenoth's book [254]. A recent introduction to the subject can also be found in [197]. Further information can also be found in Weiss [264] or Niederreiter and Xing [195]. For the proofs of the results, we refer to these references.

B.1 Valued fields

Definition B.1 Let K be an arbitrary field. A (non-Archimedean) *valuation* of K is a map $\nu : K \to \mathbb{R} \cup \{+\infty\}$ which satisfies the properties

1. $\nu(x) = \infty$ if and only if $x = 0$, the zero element of K;
2. for all $x, y \in K$ we have $\nu(xy) = \nu(x) + \nu(y)$;
3. for all $x, y \in K$ we have $\nu(x + y) \geq \min(\nu(x), \nu(y))$; and
4. $\nu(K^*) \neq \{0\}$.

If, furthermore, $\nu(K^*)$ is a discrete set, then ν is called a *discrete valuation*. In particular, when $\nu(K^*) = \mathbb{Z}$, then we call ν a *normalised valuation*. A pair (K, ν) is called a normalised field.

Throughout this overview we only consider discrete valuations.

Example B.2 Let $K = \mathbb{Q}$ and let p be an arbitrary prime number. For each $x \in \mathbb{Q} \setminus \{0\} =: \mathbb{Q}^*$, there exists a unique integer $m \in \mathbb{Z}$ such that $x = p^m \frac{a}{b}$ where p is neither a divisor of a nor of b. Then define $|x|_p := p^{-m}$ and further, set $|0|_p := 0$. The map $|\cdot|_p : \mathbb{Q} \to \mathbb{R}_0^+$, called the (normalised) p-adic absolute value on $\mathbb{Q}$, satisfies

1. $|x|_p = 0$ if and only if $x = 0$;
2. for all $x, y \in \mathbb{Q}$, we have $|xy|_p = |x|_p |y|_p$; and
3. for all $x, y \in \mathbb{Q}$, we have $|x + y|_p \leq \max(|x|_p, |y|_p) \leq |x|_p + |y|_p$.

Any map defined in $\mathbb{Q}$ that satisfies the properties 1.,2. and 3. in the wider sense and that has at least one value different from 1 on $\mathbb{Q}^*$ is called an *absolute value* on $\mathbb{Q}$. A further example is the ordinary absolute value $|\cdot|$.

It follows from the unique prime factorisation of integers that for any $x \in \mathbb{Q}^*$, we have the identity

$$|x| \cdot \prod_p |x|_p = 1,$$

where $\prod_p$ denotes the product over all prime numbers p. Now for $x \in \mathbb{Q}^*$, $x = p^m \frac{a}{b}$ such that $p \nmid a$ and $p \nmid b$, we set

$$\nu_p(x) := -\log_p |x|_p = m$$

where $\log_p$ is the logarithm to the base p. Furthermore, we set $\nu_p(0) := +\infty$. Then it is easy to check that for any prime number p, the map $\nu_p : \mathbb{Q} \to \mathbb{Z} \cup \{+\infty\}$ is a normalised valuation of $\mathbb{Q}$, the so-called *p-adic valuation of* $\mathbb{Q}$.

The proof of the following proposition is an easy exercise, or can alternatively be found in reference [180].

Proposition B.3 *Let (K, ν) be a valued field. Then we have*

1. $\nu(1) = \nu(-1) = 0$;
2. *for all $x \in K$, we have $\nu(-x) = \nu(x)$;*
3. *for all $x, y \in K$, $y \neq 0$, we have $\nu(xy^{-1}) = \nu(x) - \nu(y)$;*
4. *for all $x, y \in K$ with $\nu(x) \neq \nu(y)$, we have $\nu(x + y) = \min(\nu(x), \nu(y))$; and*
5. *$\nu(K^*)$ is a non-zero discrete subgroup of $(\mathbb{R}, +)$.*

We illustrate item 4 of the above proposition with an example.

Example B.4 Let $K = \mathbb{Q}$ and $\nu = \nu_p$, the p-adic valuation of $\mathbb{Q}$ for a given prime p. Let $x, y \in \mathbb{Z} \setminus \{0\}$ and write them in the form $x = p^m a$, $y = p^n b$ with $a, b \in \mathbb{Z}$, $p \nmid a$, $p \nmid b$ and $m, n \in \mathbb{N}_0$. If we suppose that $m < n$, then we have $x + y = p^m(a + p^{n-m}b)$ with $a + p^{n-m}b \equiv a \not\equiv 0 \pmod{p}$. Hence,

$$\nu(x + y) = m = \min(\nu(x), \nu(y)).$$

B.2 Places and valuation rings

Two valuations, ν and μ, of a field K are called *equivalent* if there exists a constant $c > 0$ such that $\nu(x) = c\mu(x)$ for all $x \in K$. This definition yields an equivalence relation between valuations of a field.

Definition B.5 An equivalence class P of valuations of a field K is called a *place* of K.

Since $\nu(K^*)$ is a non-zero discrete subgroup of $(\mathbb{R}, +)$, we have $\nu(K^*) = \alpha\mathbb{Z}$ for some positive $\alpha \in \mathbb{R}$. Thus, there exists a uniquely determined normalised valuation of K that is equivalent to ν. This means that every place P of K contains a uniquely determined normalised valuation of K that is denoted by ν_P. Hence, places of K can be identified by normalised valuations of K.

Definition B.6 Let P be a place of K. Then

$$O_P := \{x \in K : \nu_P(x) \geq 0\}$$

is called the *valuation ring* of P.

It follows easily from Definition B.1 and Proposition B.3 that O_P is an integral domain with $1 \in O_P$.

Proposition B.7 *Let P be a place of K. The valuation ring O_P of P has a unique maximal ideal which is given by*

$$M_P := \{x \in K : \nu_P(x) > 0\}.$$

In particular, O_P/M_P is a field.

A proof of this result can be found in [180]. The ideal M_P is even a principal ideal which can be seen as follows. Take any $t \in O_P$ with $\nu_P(t) = 1$. For $x \in O_P$, we have $\nu_P(tx) = \nu_P(t) + \nu_P(x) = 1 + \nu_P(x) > 0$ and hence, $tO_P \subseteq M_P$. On the other hand, let $x \in M_P$. Since $\nu_P(t) = 1$, it follows that $t \neq 0$. Hence, $x = tt^{-1}x$ and $\nu_P(t^{-1}x) = \nu_P(x) - 1 \geq 0$. Thus, $M_P \subseteq tO_P$. Together, we have $M_P = tO_P$. Such a t is called a *local parameter* at P.

Definition B.8 The field O_P/M_P is called the *residue class field* of P. The ring homomorphism $O_P \to O_P/M_P$, $x \mapsto x + M_P$, is called the *residue class map* of P.

Example B.9 For a given prime p, let ν_p be the p-adic valuation of $\mathbb{Q}$ (which is obviously normalised). Write all rationals $\frac{a}{b}$ in reduced form, i.e. $\gcd(a, b) = 1$. Then we have

$$O_p = \left\{\frac{a}{b} \in \mathbb{Q} : \gcd(b, p) = 1\right\} \quad \text{and} \quad M_p = \left\{\frac{a}{b} \in \mathbb{Q} : p|a\right\}.$$

For any $b \in \mathbb{Z}$, write $\overline{b}$ for the residue class of b modulo p. If $\gcd(b, p) = 1$, then $\overline{b} \in \mathbb{Z}_p := \mathbb{Z}/p\mathbb{Z}$ has a multiplicative inverse $\overline{b}^{-1} \in \mathbb{Z}_p$. The map $\psi : O_p \to \mathbb{Z}_p$ given by $\psi\left(\frac{a}{b}\right) = \overline{a}\overline{b}^{-1}$ is a well-defined ring homomorphism with kernel M_p and so, by the homomorphism theorem, we find that O_p/M_p is isomorphic to the field $\mathbb{Z}_p$.

B.3 Rational function fields

Let k be an arbitrary field and let $k(x)$ be the rational function field over k in the variable x. In this context, k is called the *constant field* of $k(x)$. We always assume that the constant field k is a finite field. The elements of $k(x)$ can be represented in the form $\frac{f(x)}{g(x)}$ with $f(x), g(x) \in k[x]$, $g(x) \neq 0$ and $\gcd(f(x), g(x)) = 1$.

Valuations of $k(x)$ can be constructed in the same way as for $\mathbb{Q}$ with primes p replaced by irreducible polynomials. Fix a monic irreducible polynomial $p(x) \in k[x]$. Using unique factorisation in $k[x]$, every non-zero rational function $r(x) \in k(x)$ can be written in the form

$$r(x) = p(x)^m \frac{f(x)}{g(x)}$$

with a unique $m \in \mathbb{Z}$, where $p(x) \nmid f(x)$ and $p(x) \nmid g(x)$. Then we put

$$\nu_{p(x)}(r(x)) = m$$

and furthermore, we define $\nu_{p(x)}(0) = \infty$. One can easily check that $\nu_{p(x)}$ is a normalised valuation of $k(x)$.

Another normalised valuation of $k(x)$ can be obtained from the degree map. If $r(x) = \frac{f(x)}{g(x)} \neq 0$, then we set

$$\nu_\infty(r(x)) := \deg(g(x)) - \deg(f(x))$$

and furthermore, $\nu_\infty(0) = \infty$. Again it is easy to check that ν_∞ is a normalised valuation of $k(x)$.

The valuations $\nu_{p(x)}$, with monic and irreducible $p(x) \in k[x]$ and ν_∞ are pairwise non-equivalent, since $\nu_{p(x)}(p(x)) = 1$, whereas $\nu_{q(x)}(p(x)) = 0$ for monic irreducible polynomials $q(x) \neq p(x)$, and $\nu_\infty(p(x)) < 0$. Thus, we get a set of places of $k(x)$ by

$$\{p(x) \in k[x] \,:\, p(x) \in k[x] \text{ monic and irreducible}\} \cup \{\infty\}.$$

where the constant field k is finite (we always assume this within this overview), then the above-defined set of places already gives all places of the rational function field $k(x)$. The proof of the following result can be found in [180].

Theorem B.10 *If the constant field k is finite, then the set of all places of $k(x)$ is given by*

$$\{p(x) \in k[x] \,:\, p(x) \in k[x] \text{ monic and irreducible}\} \cup \{\infty\}.$$

The places $p(x)$ are called the *finite* places of $k(x)$ and the place ∞ is called the *infinite* place of $k(x)$.

Remark B.11 If the field k is algebraically closed, which means that every polynomial $f(x) \in k[x]$ of positive degree has a root in k, then the monic irreducible polynomials over k are exactly the monomials $x - a$ with $a \in k$. Thus, the set of places can be identified with $k \cup \{\infty\}$.

Example B.12 As for $\mathbb{Q}$ (see Example B.9) one can show that the residue class field of the place $p(x)$ is isomorphic to $k[x]/(p(x))$ where $(p(x))$ denotes the principal ideal defined by $p(x)$; that is, $O_{p(x)}/M_{p(x)} \cong k[x]/(p(x))$ and $[O_{p(x)}/M_{p(x)} : k] = \deg(p(x))$.

For the place ∞, we have

$$O_\infty = \left\{ \frac{f(x)}{g(x)} \in k(x) \,:\, \deg(f(x)) \leq \deg(g(x)) \right\}$$

and

$$M_\infty = \left\{ \frac{f(x)}{g(x)} \in k(x) \,:\, \deg(f(x)) < \deg(g(x)) \right\}.$$

Every $r(x) \in O_\infty$ can be written in the form

$$r(x) = \frac{a_d x^d + a_{d-1}x^{d-1} + \cdots + a_0}{x^d + b_{d-1}x^{d-1} + \cdots + b_0}$$

with $a_i, b_j \in k$. Hence, the map $\psi : O_\infty \to k$, $\psi(r(x)) = a_d$, is a well-defined surjective ring homomorphism with kernel M_∞. Hence, the residue class field of the place ∞ is isomorphic to k, i.e. $O_\infty/M_\infty \cong k$ and $[O_\infty/M_\infty : k] = 1$.

Remark B.13 For every non-zero $r(x) \in k(x)$, we have

$$\nu_\infty(r(x)) + \sum_{p(x)} \nu_{p(x)}(r(x)) \deg(p(x)) = 0,$$

where the sum is extended over all monic irreducible polynomials $p(x) \in k[x]$. Note that the sum makes sense, since $\nu_{p(x)}(r(x)) = 0$ for all but finitely many polynomials $p(x)$. Because of the properties of valuations, it suffices to show the formula for non-zero monic polynomials $f(x) \in k[x]$. Assume that $f(x) = \prod_{i=1}^{n} p_i(x)^{m_i}$ is the canonical factorisation of $f(x)$ into powers of irreducible polynomials. Then we have

$$\sum_{p(x)} \nu_{p(x)}(f(x)) \deg(p(x)) = \sum_{i=1}^{n} m_i \deg(p_i(x)) = \deg(f(x)) = -\nu_\infty(f(x)).$$

For the next assertion, see [180, Remark 5.4].

Proposition B.14 *Every valuation of a rational function field $k(x)$ with finite constant field k is discrete.*

B.4 Algebraic function fields and their valuations

An algebraic function field (in one variable) is a finite extension of a field of rational functions (in one variable). More rigorously:

Definition B.15 A field F is an *algebraic function field* over the finite field k if there exists a transcendental element $z \in F$ over k such that F is a finite extension of the rational function field $k(z)$.

An example of an algebraic function field is, of course, a rational function field over a finite field.

Now we consider valuations of algebraic function fields. The proof of the subsequent proposition is given implicitly in [180, Proof of Proposition 6.2].

Proposition B.16 *The restriction μ of a valuation ν of an algebraic function field F to $k(z)$ yields a valuation of $k(z)$.*

By the above proposition, μ is a valuation of $k(z)$ and hence, by Proposition B.14, discrete. Since $[F : k(z)] < \infty$, we obtain the following result.

Corollary B.17 *Every valuation of an algebraic function field is discrete.*

Obviously, for equivalent valuations of F, the restrictions to $k(z)$ are equivalent as well. Thus, a place Q of F corresponds by restriction to a unique place P of $k(z)$. In this context one says that *Q lies over P* or *P lies under Q*. Hence, by Theorem B.10, every place of F lies either over a place of $k(z)$ that corresponds to a monic irreducible polynomial from $k[z]$ or over the infinite place of $k(z)$.

Proposition B.18 *Let F be an algebraic function field over the finite field k. Then the residue class field O_P/M_P of every place P of F is a finite extension of an isomorphic copy of k.*

In a sense the converse of Proposition B.16 is also true. Every valuation of a rational function field can be extended to a valuation of an algebraic function field. For a proof of the following result, see [254, Section III.1] or [264, Sections 2–4].

Theorem B.19 *Let F be a finite extension of the rational function field $k(z)$. Then every place of $k(z)$ lies under at least one and at most $[F : k(z)]$ places of F.*

Let $\widetilde{k}$ be the algebraic closure of k in F, i.e.

$$\widetilde{k} = \{x \in F \ : \ x \text{ is algebraic over } k\}.$$

Then $\widetilde{k}$ is a field with $k \subseteq \widetilde{k} \subseteq F$, called the *full constant field* of F. It can be shown (see [180, Proposition 6.5]) that $\widetilde{k}$ is a finite extension of the finite field k and hence, $\widetilde{k}$ is a finite field too. Note also that $k(z) \subseteq \widetilde{k}(z) \subseteq F$ and so F is a finite extension of $\widetilde{k}(z)$. Furthermore, z is also transcendental over $\widetilde{k}$. Therefore, F is also an algebraic function field over $\widetilde{k}$.

In the following, we usually assume that k is already the full constant field of F. We stress this by using the notation F/k for an algebraic function field with full constant field k.

Definition B.20 The *degree* $\deg(P)$ of a place P of F/k is defined as the degree of the residue class field O_P/M_P of P over k, i.e. $\deg(P) = [O_P/M_P : k]$. A place of F/k of degree 1 is called a *rational place* of F/k.

Example B.21 Let $F = k(x)$ be a rational function field over k. For any non-constant rational function $r(x) \in F$, there exists a place P of F such that $\nu_P(r(x)) \neq 0$. Let $r(x) \in F$ be algebraic over k, hence $r(x) \in \widetilde{k}$. By means of the minimal polynomial, we get

$$r(x)^d + c_{d-1}r(x)^{d-1} + \cdots + c_0 = 0$$

with $c_0, \ldots, c_{d-1} \in k$ and $c_0 \neq 0$. Assume that $r(x)$ is non-constant. Then there is a place P such that $\nu_P(r(x)) \neq 0$ and we have $\nu_P(r(x)^d + c_{d-1}r(x)^{d-1} + \cdots + c_0) = \nu_P(0) = \infty$. If $\nu_P(r(x)) < 0$, then

$$\nu_P(r(x)^d + c_{d-1}r(x)^{d-1} + \cdots + c_0) = \nu_P(r(x)^d) = d\nu_P(r(x)) < 0,$$

a contradiction. If, on the other hand, $\nu_P(r(x)) > 0$, then

$$\nu_P(r(x)^d + c_{d-1}r(x)^{d-1} + \cdots + c_0) = \nu_P(c_0) = 0$$

since $c_0 \neq 0$ (see Exercise B.6), again a contradiction. Hence, $r(x)$ must be constant and so $\widetilde{k} = k$ or, in other words, the full constant field of F is k. By Example B.12, the degree of a finite place $p(x)$ of F is $\deg(p(x))$ and the degree of the place ∞ of F is 1. If $k = \mathbb{F}_b$, then F has exactly $b + 1$ rational places.

For an algebraic function field F/k, we denote by $\mathbb{P}_F$ the set of all places of F. We note that $\mathbb{P}_F$ is a denumerable set.

Remark B.22 If $k = \mathbb{F}_b$, then for all $a \in k^*$, we have $a^{b-1} = 1$ and so for any place $P \in \mathbb{P}_F$, we have

$$0 = \nu_P(1) = \nu_P(a^{b-1}) = (b-1)\nu_P(a)$$

and hence, $\nu_P(a) = 0$ for all $P \in \mathbb{P}_F$.

For a place $P \in \mathbb{P}_F$ and a function $f \in F/k$ with $\nu_P(f) \geq 0$, we denote by $f(P)$ the residue class of $f + M_P$ of f in O_P/M_P. Thus, by Proposition B.18, $f(P) \in O_P/M_P$ can be viewed as an element of a finite extension of k.

Now choose a sequence $(t_r)_{r\in\mathbb{Z}}$ of elements in F such that $\nu_P(t_r) = r$ for all $r \in \mathbb{Z}$.

For a given function $f \in F/k$, we can find an integer v such that $\nu_P(f) \geq v$ and hence, we have

$$\nu_P\left(\frac{f}{t_v}\right) = \nu_P(f) - v \geq 0.$$

Put

$$a_v := \left(\frac{f}{t_v}\right)(P),$$

i.e. a_v is the value of the function f/t_v at the place P and hence, $a_v \in O_P/M_P$. Since ν_P is a normalised valuation, it follows that

$$\nu_P\left(\frac{f}{t_v} - a_v\right) \geq 1,$$

or equivalently, $\nu_P(f - a_v t_v) \geq v + 1$ and from this we obtain that

$$\nu_P\left(\frac{f - a_v t_v}{t_{v+1}}\right) \geq 0.$$

Now put

$$a_{v+1} := \left(\frac{f - a_v t_v}{t_{v+1}}\right)(P).$$

Again, $a_{v+1} \in O_P/M_P$ and $\nu_P(f - a_v t_v - a_{v+1} t_{v+1}) \geq v + 2$.

We can proceed by induction. Assume that we have obtained a sequence $(a_r)_{r=v}^m$, $m > v$, of elements of O_P/M_P such that

$$\nu_P\left(f - \sum_{r=v}^{k} a_r t_r\right) \geq k + 1$$

for all $v \leq k \leq m$. Put

$$a_{m+1} := \left(\frac{f - \sum_{r=v}^{m} a_r t_r}{t_{m+1}}\right)(P).$$

Again, $a_{m+1} \in O_P/M_P$ and $\nu_P\left(f - \sum_{r=v}^{m+1} a_r t_r\right) \geq m + 2$.

In this way we obtain an infinite sequence $(a_r)_{r=v}^{\infty}$ of elements of O_P/M_P such that

$$\nu_P\left(f - \sum_{r=v}^{m} a_r t_r\right) \geq m + 1$$

for all $m \geq v$.

The above construction can be summarised in the formal expansion

$$f = \sum_{r=v}^{\infty} a_r t_r.$$

This expansion is called the *local expansion* of the function f at P. A typical choice for the t_r is $t_r = t^r$ with t being a local parameter at P (and hence, $\nu_P(t_r) = \nu_P(t^r) = r$ by Proposition B.3).

The local expansion shows that for a given $f \in F/k$ and a place P of F, there exists a sequence $(f_n)_{n=v}^{\infty}$ of special elements $f_n := \sum_{r=v}^{n} a_r t_r$ of F/k such that f_n tends to f at P, i.e. $\nu_P(f - f_n) \to \infty$ as $n \to \infty$.

B.5 Divisors

Definition B.23 A *divisor* D of F is a formal sum

$$D = \sum_{P \in \mathbb{P}_F} m_P P$$

with all $m_P \in \mathbb{Z}$ and $m_P \neq 0$ for at most finitely many $P \in \mathbb{P}_F$.

A place $P \in \mathbb{P}_F$ is also a divisor (put $m_P = 1$ and $m_Q = 0$ for all $Q \in \mathbb{P}_F$, $Q \neq P$). In this context, a place P is called a *prime divisor.*

The divisors of F form a group under the addition law

$$D + E = \sum_{P \in \mathbb{P}_F} m_P P + \sum_{P \in \mathbb{P}_F} n_P P = \sum_{P \in \mathbb{P}_F} (m_P + n_P) P.$$

The zero element is the zero divisor

$$0 := \sum_{P \in \mathbb{P}_F} m_P P \quad \text{with all } m_P = 0.$$

The additive inverse of $D = \sum_{P \in \mathbb{P}_F} m_P P$ is

$$-D = \sum_{P \in \mathbb{P}_F} (-m_P) P.$$

The abelian group of all divisors of F is called the *divisor group* $\mathrm{Div}(F)$ of F.

Definition B.24 The *support* $\mathrm{supp}(D)$ of a divisor $D = \sum_{P \in \mathbb{P}_F} m_P P$ is given by

$$\mathrm{supp}(D) = \{P \in \mathbb{P}_F \ : \ m_P \neq 0\}.$$

By the definition of a divisor, $\mathrm{supp}(D)$ is a finite subset of $\mathbb{P}_F$.

If $D = \sum_{P \in \mathbb{P}_F} m_P P$, then it is often convenient to write $m_P = \nu_P(D)$. Thus, a divisor D can also be represented in the form

$$D = \sum_{P \in \mathrm{supp}(D)} \nu_P(D) P.$$

Definition B.25 If $D \in \mathrm{Div}(F)$ is as above, then the *degree* $\deg(D)$ is defined by

$$\deg(D) = \sum_{P \in \mathrm{supp}(D)} \nu_P(D) \deg(P).$$

It is not difficult to show that the *degree map* $\deg : \mathrm{Div}(F) \to \mathbb{Z}$ is a group homomorphism. Consequently, the divisors of F of degree 0 (i.e. the kernel of the group homomorphism deg) form a subgroup $\mathrm{Div}^0(F)$ of $\mathrm{Div}(F)$.

One can introduce a partial order on $\mathrm{Div}(F)$ by saying that $D_1 \leq D_2$, if

$$\nu_P(D_1) \leq \nu_P(D_2) \quad \text{for all} \quad P \in \mathbb{P}_F.$$

A divisor $D \geq 0$ is called *positive* (or *effective*).

If F is the rational function field and if $f \in F^*$, then, obviously, $\nu_P(f) \neq 0$ for at most finitely many $P \in \mathbb{P}_F$. The same is true for an arbitrary algebraic function field F/k. Thus, the following definition makes sense.

Definition B.26 Let F be an algebraic function field and $f \in F^*$. Then the *principal divisor* $\mathrm{div}(f)$ of f is defined by

$$\mathrm{div}(f) = \sum_{P \in \mathbb{P}_F} \nu_P(f)P.$$

The set of all principal divisors of F is denoted by $\mathrm{Princ}(F)$.

If F is the rational function field and $f \in F^*$, then by Remark B.13 and Example B.21, we have

$$\deg(\mathrm{div}(f)) = \sum_{P \in \mathbb{P}_F} \nu_P(f) \deg(P) = 0.$$

The same formula holds for an arbitrary function field F/k. For a proof of the subsequent result, see [254, Section I.4].

Proposition B.27 The degree of every principal divisor is 0.

The set $\mathrm{Princ}(F)$ of all principal divisors of F forms a subgroup of $\mathrm{Div}^0(F)$. The factor group $\mathrm{Cl}(F) := \mathrm{Div}^0(F)/\mathrm{Princ}(F)$ is finite and its cardinality $h(F) := |\mathrm{Cl}(F)|$ is called the *divisor class number* of F.

B.6 The Riemann–Roch theorem

For any divisor D of F/k, we form the *Riemann–Roch space*

$$\mathcal{L}(D) := \{f \in F^* \,:\, \mathrm{div}(f) + D \geq 0\} \cup \{0\}.$$

This means that $\mathcal{L}(D)$ consists of all $f \in F$ with

$$\nu_P(f) \geq -\nu_P(D) \quad \text{for all } P \in \mathbb{P}_F.$$

It is easy to show that $\mathcal{L}(D)$ is a vector space over k.

Example B.28 For $f \in F^*$, we have that $f \in \mathcal{L}(0)$ if and only if $\nu_P(f) \geq 0$ for all $P \in \mathbb{P}_F$. But as $\deg(\mathrm{div}(f)) = \sum_{P \in \mathbb{P}_F} \nu_P(f) \deg(P) = 0$ by Proposition B.27, it follows that $f \in \mathcal{L}(0)$ if and only if $\nu_P(f) = 0$ for all $P \in \mathbb{P}_F$. This in turn can be shown to be equivalent to the fact that $f \in k^*$. Hence, for the zero divisor, we have $\mathcal{L}(0) = k$.

Remark B.29 If $\deg(D) < 0$, then necessarily $\mathcal{L}(D) = \{0\}$, for if we had a non-zero $f \in \mathcal{L}(D)$, then by applying the degree map to $\mathrm{div}(f) + D \geq 0$, we get $0 + \deg(D) \geq 0$, which is a contradiction.

The vector space $\mathcal{L}(D)$ has a finite dimension over k which is denoted by $\ell(D)$. By Example B.28, we have $\ell(0) = 1$ and by Remark B.29, we have $\ell(D) = 0$ whenever $\deg(D) < 0$.

Theorem B.30 (Riemann–Roch theorem) *Let F/k be an algebraic function field with finite full constant field k. Then there exists a constant c such that for any divisor D of F, we have*

$$\ell(D) \geq \deg(D) + 1 - c.$$

For a proof, see [254, Sections I.4 and I.5]. As a consequence of the Riemann–Roch theorem, we can define the number

$$g = \max_{D \in \mathrm{Div}(F)} (\deg(D) - \ell(D) + 1).$$

This integer $g = g(F/k)$ is called the *genus* of F/k, a very important invariant of an algebraic function field. By putting $D = 0$ in its definition, we see that $g \geq 0$ always. Note that by definition of g, we have

$$\ell(D) \geq \deg(D) + 1 - g \quad \text{for all } D \in \mathrm{Div}(F).$$

Theorem B.31 (Supplement to the Riemann–Roch Theorem) *If $\deg(D) \geq 2g - 1$, then*

$$\ell(D) = \deg(D) + 1 - g.$$

Example B.32 If F is a rational function field, then it is easy to verify that

$$\ell(D) \geq \deg(D) + 1 \quad \text{for all } D \in \mathrm{Div}(F).$$

Therefore, $g(F) = 0$. In fact, rational function fields over finite fields can be characterised by the property of having genus 0.

An algebraic function field of genus 1 is also called an elliptic function field. Elliptic function fields F/k with $k = \mathbb{F}_b$ can be characterised. In all cases, F is a quadratic extension of $k(x)$. If b is odd, then $F = k(x)(y)$ for some $y \in F$ with $y^2 = f(x)$ where $f(x) \in k[x]$ is square-free of degree 3. If b is even, then $F = k(x)(y)$ for some $y \in F$ with either $y^2 + y = f(x)$ with $f \in k[x]$ of degree 3 or $y^2 + y = x + 1/(ax + c)$ with $a, c \in k$ and $a \neq 0$.

There is no general explicit formula for the genus of an algebraic function field except for some special families.

Example B.33 Let $k = \mathbb{F}_b$ with b odd and let $k(x)$ be the rational function field. Let $F = k(x)(y)$ be the quadratic extension defined by $y^2 = f(x)$ where $f \in k[x]$ is square-free of degree $d \geq 1$. Then $g(F/k) = \lfloor d - 1/2 \rfloor$. For a proof, see [254, Section III.7].

Exercises

B.1 Give a proof of Proposition B.3.

B.2 Show that the valuation Ring O_P of a place P is an integral domain.

B.3 Show that the multiplicative group of units of O_P is given by $U_P := \{x \in K : \nu_P(x) = 0\}$.
Hint: A proof can be found in [180].

B.4 For a given prime p, let ν_p be the p-adic valuation of $\mathbb{Q}$. Determine U_p.

B.5 Let $k(x)$ be the rational function field over a field k and let $p(x) \in k[x]$ be a monic irreducible polynomial. Show that $\nu_{p(x)}$ and ν_∞, as defined in Section B.3, are both normalised valuations of $k(x)$.
Hint: A proof for ν_∞ can be found in [180].

B.6 Show that if the constant field is finite, then for any valuation ν of $k(x)$, we have $\nu(a) = 0$ for all $a \in k^*$.
Hint: A proof can be found in [180].

B.7 Determine U_∞, the multiplicative group of units of O_∞ from Example B.12.

B.8 Show that the degree map deg : $\mathrm{Div}(F) \to \mathbb{Z}$ is a group homomorphism.

B.9 Let F be an algebraic function field with full constant field k. Show that for $f \in k^*$, we have $\mathrm{div}(f) = 0$.

B.10 Show that the set $\mathrm{Princ}(F)$ of principal divisors of F forms a subgroup of $\mathrm{Div}^0(F)$.
Hint: Note that $\mathrm{div}(fg) = \mathrm{div}(f) + \mathrm{div}(g)$ for all $f, g \in F^*$.

B.11 Let D be a divisor of F/k. Show that the Riemann–Roch space $\mathcal{L}(D)$ is a vector space over k.

References

[1] M. Abramowitz and I. A. Stegun. *Handbook of Mathematical Functions*. Dover, New York, 1971. (450)

[2] M. J. Adams and B. L. Shader. A construction for (t, m, s)-nets in base q. *SIAM J. Discrete Math.*, 10:460–468, 1997. (256)

[3] I. A. Antonov and V. M. Saleev. An effective method for the computation of λP_τ-sequences. *Zh. Vychisl. Mat. i Mat. Fiz.*, 19:243–245, 1979. (In Russian.) (267)

[4] N. Aronszajn. Theory of reproducing kernels. *Trans. Amer. Math. Soc.*, 68:337–404, 1950. (21, 22, 29, 36, 38)

[5] E. I. Atanassov. Efficient CPU-specific algorithm for generating the generalized Faure sequences. In *Large-scale scientific computing, Lect. Notes Comput. Sci. 2907*, pp. 121–127. Springer, Berlin, 2004. (267)

[6] E. I. Atanassov. On the discrepancy of the Halton sequences. *Math. Balkanica (N.S.)*, 18:15–32, 2004. (74, 75)

[7] J. Baldeaux and J. Dick. QMC rules of arbitrary high order: Reproducing kernel Hilbert space approach. *Constr. Approx.*, 30:495–527, 2009. (481, 484, 492)

[8] J. Baldeaux, J. Dick, G. Greslehner and F. Pillichshammer. Construction algorithms for generalized polynomial lattice rules. Submitted, 2009. (507)

[9] J. Baldeaux, J. Dick and F. Pillichshammer. Duality theory and propagation rules for generalized nets. Submitted, 2009. (286)

[10] J. Beck. A two-dimensional van Aardenne Ehrenfest theorem in irregularities of distribution. *Compos. Math.*, 72:269–339, 1989. (66)

[11] J. Beck and W. W. L. Chen. *Irregularities of distribution*. Cambridge University Press, Cambridge, 1987. (61)

[12] R. Béjian. Minoration de la discrépance d'une suite quelconque sur T. *Acta Arith.*, 41:185–202, 1982. (66)

[13] R. Béjian and H. Faure. Discrépance de la suite de van der Corput. *C. R. Acad. Sci. Paris Sér. A-B*, 285:313–316, 1977. (82)

[14] J. Bierbrauer, Y. Edel and W. Ch. Schmid. Coding-theoretic constructions for (t, m, s)-nets and ordered orthogonal arrays. *J. Combin. Des.*, 10:403–418, 2002. (242, 256, 286, 344)

[15] D. Bilyk and M. T. Lacey. On the small ball inequality in three dimensions. *Duke Math. J.*, 143:81–115, 2008. (67)

[16] D. Bilyk, M. T. Lacey and A. Vagharshakyan. On the small ball inequality in all dimensions. *J. Funct. Anal.*, 254:2470–2502, 2008. (67)

[17] T. Blackmore and G. H. Norton. Matrix-product codes over $\mathbb{F}_q$. *Appl. Algebra Eng. Comm. Comput.*, 12:477–500, 2001. (288, 289)

[18] P. Bratley and B. L. Fox. Algorithm 659: Implementing Sobol's quasirandom sequence generator. *ACM Trans. Math. Softw.*, 14:88–100, 1988. (267)

[19] P. Bratley, B. L. Fox and H. Niederreiter. Implementation and tests of low-discrepancy sequences. *ACM Trans. Model. Comput. Simul.*, 2:195–213, 1992. (268)

[20] H. Chaix and H. Faure. Discrépance et diaphonie en dimension un. *Acta Arith.*, 63:103–141, 1993. (In French.) (180)

[21] W. W. L. Chen. On irregularities of point distribution. *Mathematika*, 27:153–170, 1980. (66)

[22] W. W. L. Chen and M. M. Skriganov. Explicit constructions in the classical mean squares problem in irregularities of point distribution. *J. Reine Angew. Math.*, 545:67–95, 2002. (xii, 66, 167, 180, 509, 510, 519, 531, 533)

[23] W. W. L. Chen and M. M. Skriganov. Orthogonality and digit shifts in the classical mean squares problem in irregularities of point distribution. In *Diophantine Approximation: Festschrift for Wolfgang Schmidt*, pp. 141–159. Springer, Berlin, 2008. (510)

[24] K. L. Chung. *A course in probability theory*. Academic Press (a subsidiary of Harcourt Brace Jovanovich, Publishers), New York, London, second edition, 1974, vol. 21 of *Probability and Mathematical Statistics*. (398)

[25] J. W. Cooley and J. W. Tukey. An algorithm for the machine calculation of complex Fourier series. *Math. Comp.*, 19:297–301, 1965. (327, 328)

[26] R. Cools, F. Y. Kuo and D. Nuyens. Constructing embedded lattice rules for multivariable integration. *SIAM J. Sci. Comput.*, 28:2162–2188, 2006. (337)

[27] L. L. Cristea, J. Dick, G. Leobacher and F. Pillichshammer. The tent transformation can improve the convergence rate of quasi-Monte Carlo algorithms using digital nets. *Numer. Math.*, 105:413–455, 2007. (xii, 424)

[28] L. L. Cristea, J. Dick and F. Pillichshammer. On the mean square weighted $\mathcal{L}_2$ discrepancy of randomized digital nets in prime base. *J. Complexity*, 22:605–629, 2006. (510, 537, 558)

[29] H. Davenport. Note on irregularities of distribution. *Mathematika*, 3:131–135, 1956. (66, 509)

[30] P. J. Davis. *Circulant matrices*. John Wiley & Sons, New York, Chichester, Brisbane, 1979. (326)

[31] N. G. de Bruijn and K. A. Post. A remark on uniformly distributed sequences and Riemann integrability. *Nederl. Akad. Wetensch. Proc. Ser. A 71=Indag. Math.*, 30:149–150, 1968. (48)

[32] L. de Clerck. A method for exact calculation of the star discrepancy of plane sets applied to the sequences of Hammersley. *Monatsh. Math.*, 101:261–278, 1986. (83)

[33] J. Dick. On the convergence rate of the component-by-component construction of good lattice rules. *J. Complexity*, 20:493–522, 2004. (390)

[34] J. Dick. The construction of extensible polynomial lattice rules with small weighted star discrepancy. *Math. Comp.*, 76:2077–2085, 2007. (335)

[35] J. Dick. Explicit constructions of quasi-Monte Carlo rules for the numerical integration of high dimensional periodic functions. *SIAM J. Numer. Anal.*, 45:2141–2176, 2007. (xii, 435, 464, 465, 471, 472, 474, 475, 481, 484, 493)

[36] J. Dick. Walsh spaces containing smooth functions and quasi-Monte Carlo rules of arbitrary high order. *SIAM J. Numer. Anal.*, 46:1519–1553, 2008. (xii, 17, 34, 437, 440, 441, 446, 465, 471, 472, 474, 475, 481, 488, 571)

[37] J. Dick. On quasi-Monte Carlo rules achieving higher order convergence. In *Monte Carlo and quasi-Monte Carlo methods 2008*, pp. 73–96. Springer, Berlin, 2009. (474)

[38] J. Dick. The decay of the walsh coefficients of smooth functions. *Bull. Austral. Math. Soc.*, 80:430–453, 2009. (434, 463)

[39] J. Dick and J. Baldeaux. Equidistribution properties of generalized nets and sequences. In *Monte Carlo and quasi-Monte Carlo methods 2008*, pp. 305–322. Springer, Berlin, 2009. (475, 476, 478, 481)

[40] J. Dick and P. Kritzer. Star discrepancy estimates for digital $(t, m, 2)$-nets and digital $(t, 2)$-sequences over $\mathbb{Z}_2$. *Acta Math. Hungar.*, 109:239–254, 2005. (180)

[41] J. Dick and P. Kritzer. A best possible upper bound on the star discrepancy of $(t, m, 2)$-nets. *Monte Carlo Methods Appl.*, 12:1–17, 2006. (181, 184)

[42] J. Dick and P. Kritzer. Duality theory and propagation rules for generalized digital nets. *Math. Comp.*, 79:993–1017, 2010. (473, 474)

[43] J. Dick, P. Kritzer, G. Leobacher and F. Pillichshammer. Constructions of general polynomial lattice rules based on the weighted star discrepancy. *Finite Fields Appl.*, 13:1045–1070, 2007. (315, 316, 317, 320, 331, 336)

[44] J. Dick, P. Kritzer, F. Pillichshammer and W. Ch. Schmid. On the existence of higher order polynomial lattices based on a generalized figure of merit. *J. Complexity*, 23:581–593, 2007. (496)

[45] J. Dick, F. Y. Kuo, F. Pillichshammer and I. H. Sloan. Construction algorithms for polynomial lattice rules for multivariate integration. *Math. Comp.*, 74:1895–1921, 2005. (xii, 317)

[46] J. Dick, G. Leobacher and F. Pillichshammer. Construction algorithms for digital nets with low weighted star discrepancy. *SIAM J. Numer. Anal.*, 43:76–95, 2005. (313, 324)

[47] J. Dick and H. Niederreiter. On the exact t-value of Niederreiter and Sobol′ sequences. *J. Complexity*, 24:572–581, 2008. (265)

[48] J. Dick and H. Niederreiter. Duality for digital sequences. *J. Complexity*, 25:406–414, 2009. (244, 256)

[49] J. Dick, H. Niederreiter and F. Pillichshammer. Weighted star discrepancy of digital nets in prime bases. In *Monte Carlo and quasi-Monte Carlo methods 2004*, pp. 77–96. Springer, Berlin, 2006. (180, 219, 232, 233)

[50] J. Dick and F. Pillichshammer. Multivariate integration in weighted Hilbert spaces based on Walsh functions and weighted Sobolev spaces. *J. Complexity*, 21:149–195, 2005. (23, 43, 44, 364, 392, 393)

[51] J. Dick and F. Pillichshammer. On the mean square weighted $\mathcal{L}_2$ discrepancy of randomized digital (t, m, s)-nets over $\mathbb{Z}_2$. *Acta Arith.*, 117:371–403, 2005. (510, 537, 557)

[52] J. Dick and F. Pillichshammer. Strong tractability of multivariate integration of arbitrary high order using digitally shifted polynomial lattice rules. *J. Complexity*, 23:436–453, 2007. (493, 499)

[53] J. Dick, F. Pillichshammer and B. J. Waterhouse. The construction of good extensible rank-1 lattices. *Math. Comp.*, 77:2345–2373, 2008. (335, 337)

[54] J. Dick, I. H. Sloan, X. Wang and H. Woźniakowski. Liberating the weights. *J. Complexity*, 20:593–623, 2004. (39, 368)

[55] B. Doerr and M. Gnewuch. Construction of low-discrepancy point sets of small size by bracketing covers and dependent randomized rounding. In *Monte Carlo and quasi-Monte Carlo methods 2006*, pp. 299–312. Springer, Berlin, 2007. (92)

[56] B. Doerr, M. Gnewuch, P. Kritzer and F. Pillichshammer. Component-by-component construction of low-discrepancy point sets of small size. *Monte Carlo Meth. Appl.*, 14:129–149, 2008. (92)

[57] B. Doerr, M. Gnewuch and A. Srivastav. Bounds and constructions for the star discrepancy via δ-covers. *J. Complexity*, 21:691–709, 2005. (90, 92, 106)

[58] B. Doerr, M. Gnewuch and M. Wahlström. Implementation of a component-by-component algorithm to generate small low-discrepancy samples. In *Monte Carlo and quasi-Monte Carlo methods 2008*, pp. 323–338. Springer, Berlin, 2009. (92)

[59] B. Doerr, M. Gnewuch and M. Wahlström. Algorithmic construction of low-discrepancy point sets via dependent randomized rounding. *J. Complexity*, to appear, 2010. (92)

[60] M. Drmota, G. Larcher and F. Pillichshammer. Precise distribution properties of the van der Corput sequence and related sequences. *Manuscripta Math.*, 118:11–41, 2005. (82)

[61] M. Drmota and R. F. Tichy. *Sequences, Discrepancies and Applications*. Springer, Berlin, 1997. (xi, 46, 50, 60, 68, 90)

[62] Y. Edel and J. Bierbrauer. Construction of digital nets from BCH-codes. In *Monte Carlo and quasi-Monte Carlo methods 1996 (Salzburg)*, vol. 127 of *Lecture notes in statistics*, pp. 221–231. Springer, New York, 1998. (256)

[63] Y. Edel and J. Bierbrauer. Families of ternary (t, m, s)-nets related to BCH-codes. *Monatsh. Math.*, 132:99–103, 2001. (256)

[64] P. Erdős and P. Turán. On a problem in the theory of uniform distribution. I. *Indagationes Math.*, 10:370–378, 1948. (68)

[65] P. Erdős and P. Turán. On a problem in the theory of uniform distribution. II. *Indagationes Math.*, 10:406–413, 1948. (68)

[66] H. Faure. Improvement of a result of H. G. Meijer on Halton sequences. *Publ. du Dép. de Math. de Limoges.* (In French.) 1980. (74)

[67] H. Faure. Discrépances de suites associées à un système de numération (en dimension un). *Bull. Soc. Math. France*, 109:143–182, 1981. (In French.) (82)

[68] H. Faure. Discrépance de suites associées à un système de numération (en dimension s). *Acta Arith.*, 41:337–351, 1982. (In French.) (xi, xii, 108, 132, 180, 263, 267)

[69] H. Faure. On the star-discrepancy of generalized Hammersley sequences in two dimensions. *Monatsh. Math.*, 101:291–300, 1986. (83)

[70] H. Faure. Good permutations for extreme discrepancy. *J. Number Theory*, 42:47–56, 1992. (82)

[71] H. Faure. Discrepancy and diaphony of digital (0, 1)-sequences in prime base. *Acta Arith.*, 117:125–148, 2005. (82, 180)

[72] H. Faure. Irregularities of distribution of digital (0, 1)-sequences in prime base. *Integers*, 5:A7, 12 pp. (electronic), 2005. (82, 180)

[73] H. Faure. Van der Corput sequences towards general (0, 1)-sequences in base b. *J. Théor. Nombres Bordeaux*, 19:125–140, 2007. (82)

[74] H. Faure. Star extreme discrepancy of generalized two-dimensional Hammersley point sets. *Unif. Distrib. Theory*, 3:45–65, 2008. (83, 180)

[75] H. Faure and H. Chaix. Minoration de discrépance en dimension deux. *Acta Arith.*, 76:149–164, 1996. (In French.) (180)

[76] H. Faure and F. Pillichshammer. L_2 discrepancy of two-dimensional digitally shifted Hammersley point sets in base b. In *Monte Carlo and quasi-Monte Carlo methods 2008*, pp. 355–368. Springer, Berlin, 2009. (509)

[77] H. Faure and F. Pillichshammer. L_p discrepancy of generalized two-dimensional Hammersley point sets. *Monatsh. Math.*, 158:31–61, 2009. (509)

[78] H. Faure, F. Pillichshammer, G. Pirsic and W. Ch. Schmid. L_2 discrepancy of generalized two-dimensional Hammersley point sets scrambled with arbitrary permutations. *Acta Arith.*, 141:395–418, 2010. (509)

[79] N. J. Fine. On the Walsh functions. *Trans. Amer. Math. Soc.*, 65:372–414, 1949. (434, 436, 437, 446, 567)

[80] B. L. Fox. Algorithm 647: Implementation and relative efficiency of quasirandom sequence generators. *ACM Trans. Math. Softw.*, 12:362–376, 1986. (267)

[81] B. L. Fox. *Strategies for quasi-Monte Carlo*. Kluwer Academic, Boston, MA, 1999. (1)

[82] K. Frank and S. Heinrich. Computing discrepancies of Smolyak quadrature rules. *J. Complexity*, 12:287–314, 1996. (32)

[83] M. Frigo and S. G. Johnson. FFTW: An adaptive software architecture for the FFT. *Proc. 1998 IEEE Intl. Conf. Acoustic Speech and Signal Processing*, 3:1381–1384, 1998. (327)

[84] K. K. Frolov. Upper bound of the discrepancy in metric L_p, $2 \leq p < \infty$. *Dokl. Akad. Nauk SSSR*, 252:805–807, 1980. (66, 509)

[85] P. Glasserman. *Monte Carlo methods in financial engineering*, vol. 53 of *Applications of Mathematics (New York)*. Springer-Verlag, New York, 2004. (1, 13)

[86] M. Gnewuch. Bracketing numbers for axis-parallel boxes and applications to geometric discrepancy. *J. Complexity*, 24:154–172, 2008. (90, 106)

[87] M. Gnewuch, A. Srivastav and C. Winzen. Finding optimal volume subintervals with k points and calculating the star discrepancy are NP-hard problems. *J. Complexity*, 25:115–127, 2009. (32)

[88] V. S. Grozdanov and S. S. Stoilova. On the theory of b-adic diaphony. *C. R. Acad. Bulgare Sci.*, 54:31–34, 2001. (103)

[89] J. H. Halton. On the efficiency of certain quasi-random sequences of points in evaluating multi-dimensional integrals. *Numer. Math.*, 2:84–90, 1960. (74)

[90] J. H. Halton and S. K. Zaremba. The extreme and the L^2 discrepancies of some plane sets. *Monatsh. Math.*, 73:316–328, 1969. (83)

[91] J. Hartinger and V. Ziegler. On corner avoidance properties of random-start Halton sequences. *SIAM J. Numer. Anal.*, 45:1109–1121, 2007. (401)

[92] S. Heinrich. Efficient algorithms for computing the L_2 discrepancy. *Math. Comp.*, 65:1621–1633, 1996. (32)

[93] S. Heinrich. Some open problems concerning the star-discrepancy. *J. Complexity*, 19:416–419, 2003. (92)

[94] S. Heinrich, F. J. Hickernell and R. X. Yue. Optimal quadrature for Haar wavelet spaces. *Math. Comp.*, 73:259–277, 2004. (431)

[95] S. Heinrich, E. Novak, G. Wasilkowski and H. Woźniakowski. The inverse of the star-discrepancy depends linearly on the dimension. *Acta Arith.*, 96:279–302, 2001. (90)

[96] P. Hellekalek. General discrepancy estimates: the Walsh function system. *Acta Arith.*, 67:209–218, 1994. (68, 105)

[97] P. Hellekalek. On the assessment of random and quasi-random point sets. In *Random and quasi-random point sets*, vol. 138 of *Lecture Notes in Statistics*, pp. 49–108. Springer, New York, 1998. (104)

[98] P. Hellekalek. Digital (t, m, s)-nets and the spectral test. *Acta Arith.*, 105:197–204, 2002. (178, 179)

[99] P. Hellekalek and H. Leeb. Dyadic diaphony. *Acta Arith.*, 80:187–196, 1997. (103, 104)

[100] P. Hellekalek and P. Liardet. The dynamic associated with certain digital sequences. In *Probability and number theory – Kanazawa 2005, Advanced studies in pure mathematics,* pp. 105–131. Mathematical Society of Japan, Tokyo, 2007. (136)

[101] F. J. Hickernell. Quadrature error bounds with applications to lattice rules. *SIAM J. Numer. Anal.*, 33:1995–2016, 1996. (xi)

[102] F. J. Hickernell. A generalized discrepancy and quadrature error bound. *Math. Comp.*, 67:299–322, 1998. (25)

[103] F. J. Hickernell. Lattice rules: how well do they measure up? In *Random and quasi-random point sets*, vol. 138 of *Lecture Notes in Statistics*, pp. 109–166. Springer, New York, 1998. (44, 413)

[104] F. J. Hickernell. Obtaining $O(N^{-2+\epsilon})$ convergence for lattice quadrature rules. In *Monte Carlo and quasi-Monte Carlo methods, 2000 (Hong Kong)*, pp. 274–289. Springer, Berlin, 2002. (xii, 424)

[105] F. J. Hickernell and H. S. Hong. Computing multivariate normal probabilities using rank-1 lattice sequences. In *Scientific computing (Hong Kong, 1997)*, pp. 209–215. Springer, Singapore, 1997. (329)

[106] F. J. Hickernell, P. Kritzer, F. Y. Kuo and D. Nuyens. Weighted compound integration rules with higher order convergence for all n. Submitted, 2010. (28)

[107] F. J. Hickernell and H. Niederreiter. The existence of good extensible rank-1 lattices. *J. Complexity*, 19:286–300, 2003. (217, 222, 330)

[108] F. J. Hickernell and R.-X. Yue. The mean square discrepancy of scrambled (t, s)-sequences. *SIAM J. Numer. Anal.*, 38:1089–1112, 2000. (396, 413)

[109] A. Hinrichs. Covering numbers, Vapnik–Červonenkis classes and bounds for the star-discrepancy. *J. Complexity*, 20:477–483, 2004. (90)

[110] A. Hinrichs, F. Pillichshammer and W. Ch. Schmid. Tractability properties of the weighted star discrepancy. *J. Complexity*, 24:134–143, 2008. (99, 102)

[111] E. Hlawka. Funktionen von beschränkter Variation in der Theorie der Gleichverteilung. *Ann. Mat. Pura Appl.*, 54:325–333, 1961. (In German.) (xi, 33)

[112] E. Hlawka. Über die Diskrepanz mehrdimensionaler Folgen mod 1. *Math. Z.*, 77:273–284, 1961. (In German.) (18, 33)

[113] E. Hlawka. Zur angenäherten Berechnung mehrfacher Integrale. *Monatsh. Math.*, 66:140–151, 1962. (In German.) (84)

[114] L. K. Hua and Y. Wang. *Applications of number theory to numerical analysis*. Springer, Berlin, 1981. (xi, 74)

[115] S. Joe. Component by component construction of rank-1 lattice rules having $O(n^{-1}(\ln(n))^d)$ star discrepancy. In *Monte Carlo and quasi-Monte Carlo methods 2002*, pp. 293–298. Springer, Berlin, 2004. (85)

[116] S. Joe. Construction of good rank-1 lattice rules based on the weighted star discrepancy. In *Monte Carlo and quasi-Monte Carlo methods 2004*, pp. 181–196. Springer, Berlin, 2006. (217)

[117] S. Joe and F. Y. Kuo. Constructing Sobol′ sequences with better two-dimensional projections. *SIAM J. Sci. Comput.*, 30:2635–2654, 2008. (267)

[118] S. Joe and I. H. Sloan. On computing the lattice rule criterion *R*. *Math. Comp.*, 59:557–568, 1992. (85)

[119] Y. Katznelson. *An introduction to harmonic analysis*. Cambridge Mathematical Library. Cambridge University Press, Cambridge, third edition, 2004. (566)

[120] A. Keller. Myths of computer graphics. In *Monte Carlo and quasi-Monte Carlo methods 2004*, pp. 217–243. Springer, Berlin, 2006. (1)

[121] J. F. Koksma. Een algemeene stelling uit de theorie der gelijkmatige verdeeling modulo 1. *Mathematica B (Zutphen)*, 11:7–11, 1942/43. (xi, 19, 33)

[122] J. F. Koksma. Some theorems on Diophantine inequalities. *Scriptum no. 5*, Math. Centrum Amsterdam, 1950. (68)

[123] N. M. Korobov. Approximate evaluation of repeated integrals. *Dokl. Akad. Nauk SSSR*, 124:1207–1210, 1959. (84)

[124] N. M. Korobov. Properties and calculation of optimal coefficients. *Dokl. Akad. Nauk SSSR*, 132:1009–1012, 1960. (In Russian.) (106, 306)

[125] P. Kritzer. Improved upper bounds on the star discrepancy of (t, m, s)-nets and (t, s)-sequences. *J. Complexity*, 22:336–347, 2006. (180, 183, 196)

[126] P. Kritzer. On the star discrepancy of digital nets and sequences in three dimensions. In *Monte Carlo and quasi-Monte Carlo methods 2004*, pp. 273–287. Springer, Berlin, 2006. (180)

[127] P. Kritzer, G. Larcher and F. Pillichshammer. A thorough analysis of the discrepancy of shifted Hammersley and van der Corput point sets. *Ann. Mat. Pura Appl. (4)*, 186:229–250, 2007. (82)

[128] P. Kritzer and F. Pillichshammer. An exact formula for the L_2 discrepancy of the shifted Hammersley point set. *Unif. Distrib. Theory*, 1:1–13, 2006. (509)

[129] P. Kritzer and F. Pillichshammer. Constructions of general polynomial lattices for multivariate integration. *Bull. Austral. Math. Soc.*, 76:93–110, 2007. (384)

[130] L. Kuipers and H. Niederreiter. *Uniform distribution of sequences*. John Wiley, New York, 1974. Reprint, Dover Publications, Mineola, NY, 2006. (xi, xii, 19, 32, 43, 46, 48, 50, 58, 61, 66, 67, 68, 73, 103, 104)

[131] F. Y. Kuo. Component-by-component constructions achieve the optimal rate of convergence for multivariate integration in weighted Korobov and Sobolev spaces. *J. Complexity*, 19:301–320, 2003. (390)

[132] G. Larcher. A best lower bound for good lattice points. *Monatsh. Math.*, 104:45–51, 1987. (87)

[133] G. Larcher. A class of low-discrepancy point-sets and its application to numerical integration by number-theoretical methods. In *Österreichisch-Ungarisch-Slowakisches Kolloquium über Zahlentheorie (Maria Trost, 1992)*, vol. 318 of *Grazer Math. Ber.*, pp. 69–80. Karl-Franzens-Univ. Graz, 1993. (xii, 363)

[134] G. Larcher. Nets obtained from rational functions over finite fields. *Acta Arith.*, 63:1–13, 1993. (180, 316)

[135] G. Larcher. On the distribution of an analog to classical Kronecker-sequences. *J. Number Theory*, 52:198–215, 1995. (134, 180)

[136] G. Larcher. A bound for the discrepancy of digital nets and its application to the analysis of certain pseudo-random number generators. *Acta Arith.*, 83:1–15, 1998. (180, 199)

[137] G. Larcher. Digital point sets: analysis and application. In *Random and quasi-random point sets*, vol. 138 of *Lecture Notes in Statistics*, pp. 167–222. Springer, New York, 1998. (146, 167, 213)

[138] G. Larcher. On the distribution of digital sequences. In *Monte Carlo and quasi-Monte Carlo methods 1996 (Salzburg)*, vol. 127 of *Lecture notes in statistics*, pp. 109–123. Springer, New York, 1998. (180, 199, 206, 227, 228)

[139] G. Larcher, A. Lauss, H. Niederreiter and W. Ch. Schmid. Optimal polynomials for (t, m, s)-nets and numerical integration of multivariate Walsh series. *SIAM J. Numer. Anal.*, 33:2239–2253, 1996. (306, 309, 493)

[140] G. Larcher and H. Niederreiter. Generalized (t, s)-sequences, Kronecker-type sequences, and diophantine approximations of formal Laurent series. *Trans. Amer. Math. Soc.*, 347:2051–2073, 1995. (132, 180, 191, 196, 225)

[141] G. Larcher, H. Niederreiter and W. Ch. Schmid. Digital nets and sequences constructed over finite rings and their application to quasi-Monte Carlo integration. *Monatsh. Math.*, 121:231–253, 1996. (125, 146, 163, 167, 211)

[142] G. Larcher and F. Pillichshammer. Walsh series analysis of the L_2-discrepancy of symmetrisized point sets. *Monatsh. Math.*, 132:1–18, 2001. (180, 509)

[143] G. Larcher and F. Pillichshammer. On the L_2-discrepancy of the Sobol–Hammersley net in dimension 3. *J. Complexity*, 18:415–448, 2002. (180, 509)

[144] G. Larcher and F. Pillichshammer. Sums of distances to the nearest integer and the discrepancy of digital nets. *Acta Arith.*, 106:379–408, 2003. (83, 180, 181)

[145] G. Larcher and F. Pillichshammer. Walsh series analysis of the star discrepancy of digital nets and sequences. In *Monte Carlo and quasi-Monte Carlo methods 2002*, pp. 315–327. Springer, Berlin, 2004. (180)

[146] G. Larcher, F. Pillichshammer and K. Scheicher. Weighted discrepancy and high-dimensional numerical integration. *BIT*, 43:123–137, 2003. (180)

[147] G. Larcher and W. Ch. Schmid. On the numerical integration of high-dimensional Walsh-series by quasi-Monte Carlo methods. *Math. Comput. Simulation*, 38:127–134, 1995. (234, 363)

[148] G. Larcher and C. Traunfellner. On the numerical integration of Walsh series by number-theoretic methods. *Math. Comp.*, 63:277–291, 1994. (xii, 363)

[149] K. M. Lawrence. A combinatorial characterization of (t, m, s)-nets in base b. *J. Combin. Des.*, 4:275–293, 1996. (240, 242)

[150] K. M. Lawrence, A. Mahalanabis, G. L. Mullen and W. Ch. Schmid. Construction of digital (t, m, s)-nets from linear codes. In *Finite fields and applications (Glasgow, 1995)*, vol. 233 of *London Mathematical Society Lecture Notes Series*, pp. 189–208. Cambridge University Press, Cambridge, 1996. (253)

[151] P. L'Ecuyer. Quasi-Monte Carlo methods with applications in finance. *Finance and Stochastics*, 13:307–349, 2009. (1)

[152] P. L'Ecuyer and P. Hellekalek. Random number generators: selection criteria and testing. In *Random and quasi-random point sets*, vol. 138 of *Lecture Notes in Statistics*, pp. 223–265. Springer, New York, 1998. (13)

[153] P. L'Ecuyer and Ch. Lemieux. Recent advances in randomized quasi-Monte Carlo methods. In *Modeling uncertainty*, vol. 46 of *International Series in Operation. Research Management Science*, pp. 419–474. Kluwer Acaderic Publishers, Boston, MA, 2002. (330, 401)

[154] Ch. Lemieux. *Monte Carlo and quasi-Monte Carlo sampling*. Springer Series in Statistics. Springer, New York, 2008. (1, 13, 401)

[155] Ch. Lemieux and P. L'Ecuyer. Randomized polynomial lattice rules for multivariate integration and simulation. *SIAM J. Sci. Comput.*, 24:1768–1789, 2003. (299)

[156] G. Leobacher and F. Pillichshammer. Bounds for the weighted L^p discrepancy and tractability of integration. *J. Complexity*, 19:529–547, 2003. (107)

[157] R. Lidl and H. Niederreiter. *Introduction to finite fields and their applications*. Cambridge University Press, Cambridge, first edition, 1994. (254, 255, 299)

[158] W.-L. Loh. On the asymptotic distribution of scrambled net quadrature. *Ann. Statist.*, 31:1282–1324, 2003. (412)

[159] W. J. Martin and D. R. Stinson. Association schemes for ordered orthogonal arrays and (T, M, S)-nets. *Canad. J. Math.*, 51:326–346, 1999. (242, 256)

[160] J. Matoušek. On the L_2-discrepancy for anchored boxes. *J. Complexity*, 14:527–556, 1998. (400, 555)
[161] J. Matoušek. *Geometric discrepancy*. Springer, Berlin, 1999. (400, 432)
[162] J. Matoušek and J. Nešetřil. *Invitation to discrete mathematics*. Oxford University Press, Oxford, second edition, 2009. (238)
[163] H. G. Meijer. The discrepancy of a g-adic sequence. *Nederl. Akad. Wetensch. Proc. Ser. A 71=Indag. Math.*, 30:54–66, 1968. (74, 234)
[164] G. L. Mullen. Orthogonal hypercubes and related designs. *J. Statist. Plann. Inference*, 73:177–188, 1998. (239)
[165] G. L. Mullen and W. Ch. Schmid. An equivalence between (t, m, s)-nets and strongly orthogonal hypercubes. *J. Combin. Theory Ser. A*, 76:164–174, 1996. (239, 240, 243)
[166] G. L. Mullen and G. Whittle. Point sets with uniformity properties and orthogonal hypercubes. *Monatsh. Math.*, 113:265–273, 1992. (239)
[167] H. Niederreiter. On the distribution of pseudo-random numbers generated by the linear congruential method. III. *Math. Comp.*, 30:571–597, 1976. (221)
[168] H. Niederreiter. Existence of good lattice points in the sense of Hlawka. *Monatsh. Math.*, 86:203–219, 1978. (87, 180)
[169] H. Niederreiter. Low-discrepancy point sets. *Monatsh. Math.*, 102:155–167, 1986. (245)
[170] H. Niederreiter. Pseudozufallszahlen und die Theorie der Gleichverteilung. *Österreich. Akad. Wiss. Math.-Natur. Kl. Sitzungsber. II*, 195:109–138, 1986. (In German.) (xii, 68, 234)
[171] H. Niederreiter. Quasi-Monte Carlo methods and pseudo-random numbers. *Bull. Amer. Math. Soc.*, 84:957–1041, 1986. (xi)
[172] H. Niederreiter. Point sets and sequences with small discrepancy. *Monatsh. Math.*, 104:273–337, 1987. (xi, 108, 117, 132, 153, 180, 234, 235)
[173] H. Niederreiter. Low-discrepancy and low-dispersion sequences. *J. Number Theory*, 30:51–70, 1988. (xi, xii, 263, 264, 268)
[174] H. Niederreiter. A combinatorial problem for vector spaces over finite fields. *Discrete Math.*, 96:221–228, 1991. (246)
[175] H. Niederreiter. Low-discrepancy point sets obtained by digital constructions over finite fields. *Czechoslovak Math. J.*, 42:143–166, 1992. (68, 298, 302, 303)
[176] H. Niederreiter. Orthogonal arrays and other combinatorial aspects in the theory of uniform point distributions in unit cubes. *Discrete Math.*, 106/107:361–367, 1992. (238, 239, 242)
[177] H. Niederreiter. *Random number generation and quasi-Monte Carlo methods*. Number 63 in CBMS–NSF Series in Applied Mathematics. SIAM, Philadelphia, 1992. (xi, 12, 13, 15, 17, 32, 34, 59, 68, 73, 74, 82, 85, 87, 88, 108, 123, 141, 146, 150, 167, 180, 181, 182, 184, 191, 192, 193, 194, 195, 197, 219, 232, 234, 264, 266, 298, 299, 302, 303, 305, 313, 315, 342)
[178] H. Niederreiter. Finite fields, pseudorandom numbers, and quasirandom points. In *Finite fields, coding theory, and advances in communications and computing (Las Vegas, NV, 1991)*, vol. 141 of *Lecture Notes in Pure and Applied Mathematics*, pp. 375–394. Dekker, New York, 1993. (300)
[179] H. Niederreiter. Constructions of (t, m, s)-nets. In *Monte Carlo and quasi-Monte Carlo methods 1998*, pp. 70–85. Springer, Berlin, 2000. (285)
[180] H. Niederreiter. Algebraic function fields over finite fields. In *Coding theory and cryptology (Singapore, 2001)*, vol. 1 of *Lecture Notes Series, Institute for Mathematical. Science National University Singapore*, pp. 259–282. World

Scientific Publishers, River Edge, NJ, 2002. (572, 573, 574, 575, 576, 577, 581, 582)

[181] H. Niederreiter. Error bounds for quasi-Monte Carlo integration with uniform point sets. *J. Comput. Appl. Math.*, 150:283–292, 2003. (15)

[182] H. Niederreiter. The existence of good extensible polynomial lattice rules. *Monatsh. Math.*, 139:295–307, 2003. (330, 331)

[183] H. Niederreiter. Digital nets and coding theory. In *Coding, cryptography and combinatorics*, vol. 23 of *Progr. Comput. Sci. Appl. Logic*, pp. 247–257. Birkhäuser, Basel, 2004. (244, 256, 344)

[184] H. Niederreiter. Constructions of (t, m, s)-nets and (t, s)-sequences. *Finite Fields Appl.*, 11:578–600, 2005. (244, 253, 286, 347)

[185] H. Niederreiter. Nets, (t, s)-sequences and codes. In *Monte Carlo and quasi-Monte Carlo methods 2006*, pp. 83–100. Springer, Berlin, 2008. (256)

[186] H. Niederreiter and F. Özbudak. Constructions of digital nets using global function fields. *Acta Arith.*, 105:279–302, 2002. (268)

[187] H. Niederreiter and F. Özbudak. Matrix-product constructions of digital nets. *Finite Fields Appl.*, 10:464–479, 2004. (288, 289)

[188] H. Niederreiter and F. Pillichshammer. Construction algorithms for good extensible lattice rules. *Constr. Approx.*, 30:361–393, 2009. (337)

[189] H. Niederreiter and G. Pirsic. Duality for digital nets and its applications. *Acta Arith.*, 97:173–182, 2001. (xii, 166, 167, 244, 246, 256, 290)

[190] H. Niederreiter and G. Pirsic. A Kronecker product construction for digital nets. In *Monte Carlo and quasi-Monte Carlo methods, 2000 (Hong Kong)*, pp. 396–405. Springer, Berlin, 2002. (344)

[191] H. Niederreiter and C. P. Xing. Low-discrepancy sequences obtained from algebraic function fields over finite fields. *Acta Arith.*, 72:281–298, 1995. (xii)

[192] H. Niederreiter and C. P. Xing. Low-discrepancy sequences and global function fields with many rational places. *Finite Fields Appl.*, 2:241–273, 1996. (120, 127, 143, 144, 275, 277, 476)

[193] H. Niederreiter and C. P. Xing. Quasirandom points and global function fields. In S. Cohen and H. Niederreiter, eds, *Finite fields and applications*, vol. 233 of *London Mathematical Society Lecture Note Series*, pp. 269–296, Cambridge University Press, Cambridge, 1996. (476, 552)

[194] H. Niederreiter and C. P. Xing. Nets, (t, s)-sequences, and algebraic geometry. In *Random and quasi-random point sets*, vol. 138 of *Lecture Notes in Statistics*, pp. 267–302. Springer, New York, 1998. (198, 251, 292, 551)

[195] H. Niederreiter and C. P. Xing. *Rational points on curves over finite fields: theory and applications*, vol. 285 of *London Mathematical Society Lecture Notes Series*. Cambridge University Press, Cambridge, 2001. (572)

[196] H. Niederreiter and C. P. Xing. Constructions of digital nets. *Acta Arith.*, 102:189–197, 2002. (294)

[197] H. Niederreiter and C. P. Xing. *Algebraic geometry in coding theory and cryptography*. Princeton University Press, Princeton and Oxford, 2009. (268, 572)

[198] E. Novak. Numerische Verfahren für hochdimensionale Probleme und der Fluch der Dimension. *Jahresber. Deutsch. Math.-Verein.*, 101:151–177, 1999. (In German.) (89)

[199] E. Novak and H. Woźniakowski. When are integration and discrepancy tractable? In *Foundations of computational mathematics (Oxford, 1999)*, vol. 284 of *London Mathematical Society Lecture Notes Series*, pp. 211–266. Cambridge University Press, Cambridge, 2001. (94, 103)

[200] E. Novak and H. Woźniakowski. *Tractability of Multivariate Problems. Volume I: Linear Information.* European Mathematical Society Publishing House, Zurich, 2008. (34, 94, 103, 368)

[201] E. Novak and H. Woźniakowski. L_2 discrepancy and multivariate integration. In *Analytic number theory*, pp. 359–388. Cambridge University Press, Cambridge, 2009. (94, 103)

[202] E. Novak and H. Woźniakowski. *Tractability of multivariate problems. Volume II: standard information for functionals*. European Mathematical Society Publishing House, Zurich, 2010. (34, 92, 94, 103)

[203] D. Nuyens. *Fast construction of good lattice rules*. PhD thesis, Departement Computerwetenschappen, Katholieke Universiteit Leuven, 2007. (323)

[204] D. Nuyens and R. Cools. Fast algorithms for component-by-component construction of rank-1 lattice rules in shift-invariant reproducing kernel Hilbert spaces. *Math. Comp.*, 75:903–920, 2006. (322, 325)

[205] D. Nuyens and R. Cools. Fast component-by-component construction, a reprise for different kernels. In *Monte Carlo and quasi-Monte Carlo methods 2004*, pp. 373–387. Springer, Berlin, 2006. (322, 323, 325)

[206] A. B. Owen. Randomly permuted (t, m, s)-nets and (t, s)-sequences. In *Monte Carlo and quasi-Monte Carlo Methods in scientific computing (Las Vegas, NV, 1994)*, vol. 106 of *Lecture Notes in Statistics*, pp. 299–317. Springer, New York, 1995. (xii, 243, 396, 397, 400)

[207] A. B. Owen. Monte Carlo variance of scrambled net quadrature. *SIAM J. Numer. Anal.*, 34:1884–1910, 1997. (xii, xiii, 396, 401, 402, 408, 409, 412)

[208] A. B. Owen. Scrambled net variance for integrals of smooth functions. *Ann. Statist.*, 25:1541–1562, 1997. (396, 424, 425)

[209] A. B. Owen. Monte Carlo, quasi-Monte Carlo, and randomized quasi-Monte Carlo. In *Monte Carlo and quasi-Monte Carlo methods 1998*, pp. 86–97, Springer, Berlin, 2000. (xii, 396)

[210] A. B. Owen. Quasi-Monte Carlo for integrands with point singularities at unknown locations. In *Monte Carlo and quasi-Monte Carlo methods 2004*, pp. 403–417. Springer, Berlin, 2006. (401)

[211] A. B. Owen. Local antithetic sampling with scrambled nets. *Ann. Statist.*, 36:2319–2343, 2008. (401, 424, 425, 431)

[212] F. Pillichshammer. On the L_p-discrepancy of the Hammersley point set. *Monatsh. Math.*, 136:67–79, 2002. (180)

[213] F. Pillichshammer. Improved upper bounds for the star discrepancy of digital nets in dimension 3. *Acta Arith.*, 108:167–189, 2003. (180, 182)

[214] F. Pillichshammer and G. Pirsic. Discrepancy of hyperplane nets and cyclic nets. In *Monte Carlo and quasi-Monte Carlo methods 2008*, Berlin, 2009. Springer. (355)

[215] F. Pillichshammer and G. Pirsic. The quality parameter of cyclic nets and hyperplane nets. *Unif. Distrib. Theory*, 4:69–79, 2009. (352, 353)

[216] G. Pirsic. Schnell konvergierende Walshreihen über Gruppen. Master's thesis, Institute for Mathematics, University of Salzburg, (In German.) 1995. (559)

[217] G. Pirsic. *Embedding theorems and numerical integration of Walsh series over groups*. PhD thesis, Institute for Mathematics, University of Salzburg, 1997. (127, 446)

[218] G. Pirsic. Base changes for (t, m, s)-nets and related sequences. *Österreich. Akad. Wiss. Math.-Natur. Kl. Sitzungsber. II*, 208:115–122 (2000), 1999. (127)

[219] G. Pirsic. A software implementation of Niederreiter–Xing sequences. In *Monte Carlo and quasi-Monte Carlo methods, 2000 (Hong Kong)*, pp. 434–445. Springer, Berlin, 2002. (279)

[220] G. Pirsic. A small taxonomy of integration node sets. *Österreich. Akad. Wiss. Math.-Natur. Kl. Sitzungsber. II*, 214:133–140 (2006), 2005. (349)

[221] G. Pirsic, J. Dick and F. Pillichshammer. Cyclic digital nets, hyperplane nets and multivariate integration in Sobolev spaces. *SIAM J. Numer. Anal.*, 44:385–411, 2006. (166, 344, 346, 347)

[222] G. Pirsic and W. Ch. Schmid. Calculation of the quality parameter of digital nets and application to their construction. *J. Complexity*, 17:827–839, 2001. (299)

[223] P. D. Proĭnov. Symmetrization of the van der Corput generalized sequences. *Proc. Jap. Acad. Ser. A Math. Sci.*, 64:159–162, 1988. (509)

[224] C. M. Rader. Discrete Fourier transforms when the number of data samples is prime. *Proc. IEEE*, 5:1107–1108, 1968. (325)

[225] I. Radović, I. M. Sobol′ and R. F. Tichy. Quasi-Monte Carlo methods for numerical integration: comparison of different low discrepancy sequences. *Monte Carlo Meth. Appl.*, 2:1–14, 1996. (136)

[226] D. Raghavarao. *Constructions and combinatorial problems in design of experiments*. Wiley Series in Probability and Mathematical Statistics. John Wiley & Sons Inc., New York, 1971. (242)

[227] M. Yu. Rosenbloom and M. A. Tsfasman. Codes in the m-metric. *Problemi Peredachi Inf.*, 33:45–52, 1997. (245)

[228] K. F. Roth. On irregularities of distribution. *Mathematika*, 1:73–79, 1954. (xii, 60, 61, 82)

[229] K. F. Roth. On irregularities of distribution III. *Acta Arith.*, 35:373–384, 1979. (66, 509)

[230] K. F. Roth. On irregularities of distribution IV. *Acta Arith.*, 37:67–75, 1980. (66, 509)

[231] J. Sándor, D. S. Mitrinović and B. Crstici. *Handbook of number theory. I*. Springer, Dordrecht, 2006. Second printing of the 1996 original. (81)

[232] F. Schipp, W. R. Wade and P. Simon. *Walsh series. An introduction to dyadic harmonic analysis*. Adam Hilger Ltd., Bristol, 1990. (559, 567)

[233] W. Ch. Schmid. *(t, m, s)-nets: digital construction and combinatorial aspects*. PhD thesis, Institute for Mathematics, University of Salzburg, 1995. (240, 253, 286)

[234] W. Ch. Schmid. Shift-nets: a new class of binary digital (t, m, s)-nets. In *Monte Carlo and quasi-Monte Carlo methods 1996 (Salzburg)*, vol. 127 of *Lecture Notes in Statistics*, pp. 369–381. Springer, New York, 1998. (552)

[235] W. Ch. Schmid. Improvements and extensions of the 'Salzburg tables' by using irreducible polynomials. In *Monte Carlo and quasi-Monte Carlo methods 1998 (Claremont, CA)*, pp. 436–447. Springer, Berlin, 2000. (299, 306)

[236] W. Ch. Schmid and R. Wolf. Bounds for digital nets and sequences. *Acta Arith.*, 78:377–399, 1997. (155)

[237] W. M. Schmidt. Irregularities of distribution VII. *Acta Arith.*, 21:45–50, 1972. (66)

[238] W. M. Schmidt. Irregularities of distribution. X. In *Number theory and algebra*, pp. 311–329. Academic Press, New York, 1977. (66)

[239] R. Schürer and W. Ch. Schmid. MinT: a database for optimal net parameters. In *Monte Carlo and quasi-Monte Carlo methods 2004*, pp. 457–469. Springer, Berlin, 2006. (275)

[240] R. Schürer and W. Ch. Schmid. MinT- New features and new results. In *Monte Carlo and quasi-Monte Carlo methods 2008*, pp. 171–189. Springer, Berlin, 2009. (242, 256)

[241] I. F. Sharygin. A lower estimate for the error of quadrature formulas for certain classes of functions. *Zh. Vychisl. Mat. i Mat. Fiz.*, 3:370–376, 1963. (In Russian.) (468, 476, 492, 493, 504)

[242] V. Sinescu and S. Joe. Good lattice rules with a composite number of points based on the product weighted star discrepancy. In *Monte Carlo and quasi-Monte Carlo methods 2006*, pp. 645–658. Springer, Berlin, 2008. (86)

[243] M. M. Skriganov. Coding theory and uniform distributions. *Algebra i Analiz*, 13:191–239, 2001. Translation in St. Petersburg *Math. J.* 13:2, 2002, 301–337. (166, 244, 256, 519, 556)

[244] M. M. Skriganov. Harmonic analysis on totally disconnected groups and irregularities of point distributions. *J. Reine Angew. Math.*, 600:25–49, 2006. (66, 180, 509, 510)

[245] I. H. Sloan and S. Joe. *Lattice methods for multiple integration*. Oxford University Press, New York and Oxford, 1994. (88, 298)

[246] I. H. Sloan, F. Y. Kuo and S. Joe. Constructing randomly shifted lattice rules in weighted Sobolev spaces. *SIAM J. Numer. Anal.*, 40:1650–1665, 2002. (xii, 390)

[247] I. H. Sloan, F. Y. Kuo and S. Joe. On the step-by-step construction of quasi-Monte Carlo integration rules that achieve strong tractability error bounds in weighted Sobolev spaces. *Math. Comp.*, 71:1609–1640, 2002. (xii, 390)

[248] I. H. Sloan and A. V. Reztsov. Component-by-component construction of good lattice rules. *Math. Comp.*, 71:263–273, 2002. (85)

[249] I. H. Sloan and H. Woźniakowski. When are quasi-Monte Carlo algorithms efficient for high-dimensional integrals? *J. Complexity*, 14:1–33, 1998. (xi, 25, 34, 35, 45, 93, 94)

[250] I. H. Sloan and H. Woźniakowski. Tractability of multivariate integration for weighted Korobov classes. *J. Complexity*, 17:697–721, 2001. (44)

[251] I. H. Sloan and H. Woźniakowski. Tractability of integration in non-periodic and periodic weighted tensor product Hilbert spaces. *J. Complexity*, 18:479–499, 2002. (43, 368)

[252] I. M. Sobol′. Functions of many variables with rapidly convergent Haar series. *Soviet Math. Dokl.*, 1:655–658, 1960. (xiii)

[253] I. M. Sobol′. Distribution of points in a cube and approximate evaluation of integrals. *Ž. Vyčisl. Mat. i Mat. Fiz.*, 7:784–802, 1967. (xi, xii, xiii, 108, 114, 123, 132, 153, 180, 263, 266)

[254] H. Stichtenoth. *Algebraic function fields and codes*. Universitext. Springer, Berlin, 1993. (572, 577, 580, 581)

[255] S. Tezuka. Polynomial arithmetic analogue of Halton sequences. *ACM Trans. Model. Comput. Simul.*, 3:99–107, 1993. (266)

[256] S. Tezuka. *Uniform random numbers: theory and practice*. Kluwer International Series in Engineering and Computer Science. Kluwer, Boston, 1995. (1, 266)

[257] S. Tezuka and H. Faure. I-binomial scrambling of digital nets and sequences. *J. Complexity*, 19:744–757, 2003. (400)

[258] H. Triebel. Bases in function spaces, sampling, discrepancy, numerical integration. To appear, 2009. (34)

[259] G. Wahba. *Spline models for observational data*, Vol. 59 of *CBMS-NSF Regional Conference Series in Applied Mathematics*. Society for Industrial and Applied Mathematics (SIAM), Philadelphia, PA, 1990. (458)

[260] J. L. Walsh. A closed set of normal orthogonal functions. *Amer. J. Math.*, 45:5–24, 1923. (559, 567)

[261] X. Wang. A constructive approach to strong tractability using quasi-Monte Carlo algorithms. *J. Complexity*, 18:683–701, 2002. (223)

[262] X. Wang. Strong tractability of multivariate integration using quasi-Monte Carlo algorithms. *Math. Comp.*, 72:823–838, 2003. (223)

[263] T. T. Warnock. Computational investigations of low discrepancy point sets. In *Applications of number theory to numerical analysis*, pp. 319–343. Academic Press, New York 1972. (31)

[264] E. Weiss. *Algebraic number theory*. McGraw-Hill Book Co., Inc., New York, 1963. (572, 577)

[265] H. Weyl. Über die Gleichverteilung von Zahlen mod. Eins. *Math. Ann.*, 77:313–352, 1916. (In German.) (xi, 47)

[266] H. Woźniakowski. Efficiency of quasi-Monte Carlo algorithms for high dimensional integrals. In *Monte Carlo and quasi-Monte Carlo methods 1998 (Claremont, CA)*, pp. 114–136. Springer, Berlin, 2000. (93)

[267] C. P. Xing and H. Niederreiter. A construction of low-discrepancy sequences using global function fields. *Acta Arith.*, 73:87–102, 1995. (xii, 278, 280, 281)

[268] C. P. Xing and H. Niederreiter. Digital nets, duality, and algebraic curves. In *Monte Carlo and quasi-Monte Carlo methods 2002*, pp. 155–166. Springer, Berlin, 2004. (552)

[269] R.-X. Yue and F. J. Hickernell. Integration and approximation based on scramble sampling in arbitrary dimensions. *J. Complexity*, 17:881–897, 2001. (396)

[270] R.-X. Yue and F. J. Hickernell. The discrepancy and gain coefficients of scrambled digital nets. *J. Complexity*, 18:135–151, 2002. (396, 409, 412)

[271] R.-X. Yue and F J. Hickernell. Strong tractability of integration using scrambled Niederreiter points. *Math. Comp.*, 74:1871–1893, 2005. (396, 409, 412, 425, 431)

[272] S. K. Zaremba. Some applications of multidimensional integration by parts. *Ann. Poln. Math.*, 21:85–96, 1968. (18, 33)

[273] A. Zygmund. *Trigonometric series*. Cambridge University Press, Cambridge, 1959. (434)

Index

admissible
(tuple), 200
interval, 200
algebraic function field, 576
α-degree, 495
ANOVA decomposition, 40
crossed, 401
nested, 401, 402

b-adic diaphony, 103
b-adic spectral test, 104, 179
base change propagation rule, 292
Bernoulli polynomial, 450
Bessel's inequality, 565

circulant matrix, 326
component-by-component (CBC) construction, 85, 317, 335, 358, 384
CBC sieve algorithm, 335, 337
constant field, 574
construction
component-by-component (CBC), 85, 317, 335, 358, 384
direct product, 251, 285
double m, 290
fast CBC, 322
matrix-product, 288, 289
$(u, u + v)$-, 286, 290
curse of dimensionality, 10, 93
cyclic net over $\mathbb{F}_b$, 345, 346
star discrepancy, 360
weighted star discrepancy, 360

degree
(of a divisor), 579
(of a place), 577
map, 579
δ-cover, 104
digital net, 147
character property, 165
group structure, 163, 378
overall generating matrix, 166, 248
row space, 248
scrambling, 396
star discrepancy, 200, 209, 213, 221
strength, 152
subgroup, 164
weighted star discrepancy, 210
digital sequence, 168
group structure, 176
star discrepancy, 206, 208, 227, 228
subgroup, 176
uniformly distributed modulo one, 172, 174
well-distributed modulo one, 174
digital shift, 159, 162, 175
digital shift invariant kernel, 363, 364, 368, 374
digital shift of depth m, 161, 537
digital $(t, \alpha, \beta, n \times m, s)$-net over $\mathbb{Z}_b$, 469
digital $(t, \alpha, \beta, \sigma, s)$-sequence over $\mathbb{Z}_b$, 471
digital (t, m, s)-net over $\mathbb{F}_b$, 147
quality parameter, 149, 211, 249, 301
star discrepancy, 200, 209, 213, 221
digital $(\mathbf{T}, s)$-sequence over $\mathbb{F}_b$, 169
quality function, 170, 224
star discrepancy, 206, 208, 227, 228
digitally shifted
point set, 159
sequence, 175
digitwise addition modulo b, 560
direct product construction, 251, 285
direction numbers, 267
discrepancy
extreme, 56
L_2-, 19, 31, 60
L_q-, 60, 95
minimal L_2-, 93
minimal star, 89, 198
minimal weighted L_2-, 97
minimal weighted star, 97
star, 19, 31, 56, 95
weighted L_q-, 95
weighted star, 95

discrepancy function
one-dimensional, 18
s-dimensional, 31
discrete exponential valuation, 224, 264
discrete valuation, 572
divisibility chain, 330
divisor, 579
class number, 580
group, 579
(d, k, m, s)-system over $\mathbb{F}_b$, 246, 253
(d, m, s)-system over $\mathbb{F}_b$, 246, 247
double m construction, 290
dual code, 255
dual net, 166, 208, 303, 351, 352
dual space chain, 257

elementary interval, 52
Erdős-Turán-Koksma inequality, 68
extensible polynomial lattice point set, 330
star discrepancy, 338
weighted star discrepancy, 334
extensible polynomial lattice rule, 330
extreme discrepancy, 56

fair
point set, 14, 109
subset, 109
fast CBC construction, 322
fast Fourier transform, 328
Faure sequence, 267
figure of merit, 303, 352, 495
formal Laurent series, 224, 264
full constant field, 577

gain coefficients, 408, 412
generalised Niederreiter sequence, 266
generating
matrices, 147, 168, 299, 345, 346, 348
vector, 301
genus, 581
good lattice point, 85

Hölder condition, 13, 425, 445
Hammersley point set, 82, 119, 142, 152, 182
Hamming weight, 254, 510, 526
Hankel matrix, 299
higher order digital $(t, \alpha, \beta, n \times m, s)$-net over $\mathbb{Z}_b$, 469
quality parameter, 470
smoothness parameter, 470
strength, 470
higher order digital $(t, \alpha, \beta, \sigma, s)$-sequence over $\mathbb{Z}_b$, 471
higher order polynomial lattice point set, 494
dual net, 495
figure of merit, 495
higher order polynomial lattice rule, 494
Hlawka's identity, 18, 33
hyperplane net over $\mathbb{F}_b$, 348
dual net, 352
figure of merit, 352
quality parameter, 352
star discrepancy, 355, 357, 359
weighted star discrepancy, 356, 357, 359

inequality
Bessel's, 565
Erdős-Turán-Koksma, 68
Jensen's, 380
Koksma, 19
Koksma–Hlawka, 33
initial error, 27, 366
intractability, 93
inverse
L_2-discrepancy, 93
star discrepancy, 89
weighted L_2-discrepancy, 97
weighted star discrepancy, 97

Jensen's inequality, 380

Koksma's inequality, 19
Koksma–Hlawka inequality, 33
Korobov lattice point set, 106
Korobov space, 42, 43, 106
Korobov vector, 106, 306, 320, 387

L_2-discrepancy, 19, 31, 60
Latin square, 234
lattice point set, 84
lattice rule, 84
linear code, 254
linear independence parameter, 150, 170, 304
local expansion, 579
local parameter, 574
low discrepancy point set, 83
low discrepancy sequence, 74, 196
L_q-discrepancy, 60, 95

matrix, circulant, 326
matrix-product construction, 288, 289
mean square worst-case error, 366, 376, 377, 391, 418
minimal
L_2-discrepancy, 93
star discrepancy, 89, 198
weighted L_2-discrepancy, 97
weighted star discrepancy, 97
minimum distance, 245
modulus of continuity, 5
integral, 425
Monte Carlo algorithm, 395
Monte Carlo method, 12

net
cyclic, 345, 346
digital, 147
digital (t, m, s)-, 147
dual, 166, 208
hyperplane, 348
Niederreiter–Özbudak, 268

strict (t, m, s)-, 118
(t, m, s)-, 117
Niederreiter sequence, 264, 268
Niederreiter–Özbudak net, 268
Niederreiter–Xing sequence, 275
normalised
field, 572
valuation, 572
NRT weight, 245, 510, 526
NSC matrix, 289

optimum $[s, k, m]$-distribution, 519
ordered orthogonal array, 240
orthogonal array, 239
orthogonal squares, 234
overall generating matrix, 166, 248
Owen's lemma, 403
Owen's scrambling algorithm, 396, 400
of depth m, 432

parity-check matrix, 255
Pascal matrix, 267
place, 573
Plancherel's identity, 566
polynomial lattice point set, 298, 300, 350, 494
dual net, 303
extensible, 330
figure of merit, 303
quality parameter, 303, 342
star discrepancy, 309, 315, 319, 322
weighted star discrepancy, 310, 316, 319, 320, 322
polynomial lattice rule, 299, 494
prime divisor, 579
principal divisor, 580
projective plane of order b, 238
propagation rule, 119–121, 125, 143, 155, 175, 251, 285, 472

QMC rule, 16
quality function, 133, 170, 224
quality parameter, 118, 132, 149, 211, 249, 301, 303, 342, 352, 470
quasi–Monte Carlo algorithm, 16
quasi–Monte Carlo method, 13

Rader transform, 325
radical inverse function, 55, 119
rational place, 577
regular lattice, 72, 111, 116, 118
centred, 4, 10, 73
centred quasi-, 14
representer of the integration error, 28
reproducing kernel, 21
reproducing kernel Hilbert space, 21
reproducing property, 22
residue class
field, 574
map, 574
Riemann-Roch space, 580
Riemann-Roch Theorem, 581
Roth's lower bound on L_2-discrepancy, 60, 509

scramble invariant kernel, 413, 420
sequence
digital, 168
digital $(\mathbf{T}, s)$-, 169
Faure, 267
generalised Niederreiter, 266
Niederreiter, 264
Niederreiter–Xing, 275
Sobol′, 266
strict $(\mathbf{T}, s)$-, 133
strict (t, s)-, 132
$(\mathbf{T}, s)$-, 133
(t, s)-, 132
uniformly distributed modulo one, 47, 135, 172, 174
van der Corput, 55, 138, 139, 142, 143, 177
van der Corput-Halton, 73
well-distributed modulo one, 48, 136, 174
Xing-Niederreiter, 278
sieve algorithm, 335
signed b-adic digit expansion, 78
simplified digital shift, 162, 537
Sobol′ sequence, 266
Sobolev space
anchored, 36
unanchored, 36, 458
unanchored (weighted), 368
square of order b, 234
star discrepancy, 19, 31, 56, 95
strength, 152, 239, 240, 470
superposition of digital nets, 223
support (of a divisor), 579

(t, m, s)-net in base b, 117
quality parameter, 118
star discrepancy, 181–183, 191, 198
weighted star discrepancy, 197, 231
trace code for digital nets, 292
tractability
polynomial, 90, 97
strong, 97, 223, 320, 359, 383
triangle inequality
for the discrepancy, 58
for the worst-case error, 28
$(\mathbf{T}, s)$-sequence in base b, 133
quality function, 133
star discrepancy, 191–194, 196
strict, 133
uniformly distributed modulo one, 135
well-distributed modulo one, 136
(t, s)-sequence in base b, 132
quality parameter, 132
star discrepancy, 194, 195
strict, 132
uniformly distributed modulo one, 135
well-distributed modulo one, 136
$((t_{\mathfrak{u}})_{\emptyset \neq \mathfrak{u} \subseteq \mathcal{I}_s}, m, s)$-net in base b, 231
quality parameter, 231
weighted star discrepancy, 231

unbiased estimator, 398
uniform distribution modulo one, 47
$(u, u + v)$-construction, 286, 290

valuation, 572
  discrete, 572
  equivalent, 573
  normalised, 572
valuation ring, 574
van der Corput sequence, 55, 138, 139, 142, 143, 177
van der Corput–Halton sequence, 73
variation
  fractional order, 445
  in the sense of Hardy and Krause, 34, 427
  in the sense of Vitaly, 426
  total, 13, 33, 445

Walsh
  coefficients, 434, 440, 445, 446, 450, 458, 563
  function, 559, 560
  function system, 559, 560
  polynomial, 563
  series, 436, 463, 563
  space, 23
  space (weighted), 44
Walsh-Dirichlet kernel, 401, 563
Walsh-transform, 515
weighted
  L_q-discrepancy, 95
  star discrepancy, 95
weights, 94
  finite order, 95
  product, 95, 368
well-distribution modulo one, 47
Weyl criterion
  (for the Walsh function system), 52
  (for the trigonometric function system), 49
worst-case error, 21, 27, 28, 366

Xing-Niederreiter sequence, 278

Zaremba's identity, 18, 33

Printed in the United States
By Bookmasters